MODERN AND CONTEMPORARY DRAMA

MIRIAM GILBERT
University of Iowa

CARL H. KLAUS
University of Iowa

BRADFORD S. FIELD, JR.
Wayne State University

Theatrical Illustrations by A. G. Smith
University of Windsor

D1507234

www. rate my professors. com

BEDFORD/ST. MARTIN'S
Boston ◆ New York

Senior editor: Karen Allanson
Associate editor: Melissa Cook Candela
Manager, publishing services: Emily Berleth
Project management: Denise Quirk
Cover design: Tom McKeveny
Cover photo: Martha Swope

Library of Congress Catalog Card Number: 92-62771

Manufactured in the United States of America.

43210
f e

For information, write: Bedford/St. Martin's, 75 Arlington Street, Boston, MA 02116   (617-399-4000)

ISBN: 0-312-09077-3

CREDITS

Credits and copyrights are continued at the back of the book on pages 887–88, which constitute an extension of the copyright page.

PREFACE

Modern and Contemporary Drama offers the first and only collection of plays devoted exclusively to representing the broad cultural, historical, and theatrical range of *both* modern *and* contemporary drama. The range of this collection may be seen in the fact that it contains the work of twenty-eight different playwrights from twelve different countries, writing over a span of more than 150 years. Given this scope, our collection contains one of the earliest manifestations of modern drama in Georg Büchner's *Woyzeck* (1836). By the same token, it contains one of the most recent and important examples of contemporary drama in David Henry Hwang's *M. Butterfly* (1988), the striking and unsettling quality of which is reflected in the cover shot from the premiere of Hwang's play. Between these two historical, cultural, and theatrical extremes, our collection provides the work of such widely varied and significant playwrights as Henrik Ibsen, August Strindberg, Anton Chekhov, George Bernard Shaw, Luigi Pirandello, Sean O'Casey, Federico Garcia Lorca, Bertolt Brecht, Eugene O'Neill, Arthur Miller, Tennessee Williams, Eugène Ionesco, Samuel Beckett, Edward Albee, Imamu Amiri Baraka, Harold Pinter, Tom Stoppard, Maria Irene Fornes, Ntozake Shange, Athol Fugard, Caryl Churchill, Sam Shepard, Marsha Norman, August Wilson, Václav Havel, and Timberlake Wertenbaker. The five women playwrights and five writers of color who figure in that list, as well as the numerous plays in our collection that focus on issues of gender and race, provide a rich set of opportunities to explore the various ways that such urgent matters have been confronted by modern and contemporary dramatists.

Drama, of course, reflects not only the interests of dramatists and the influence of their cultural situation, but also the complex artistic circumstances created by the design of theaters and the creative contributions of producers, directors, set designers, and actors, all of which come together in the performance of plays. Given such a rich array of important considerations, we have provided five different kinds of apparatus that we hope will contribute to understanding and enjoying the plays in this collection:

1. General introductions to each period of drama, illustrated with detailed line drawings of theaters typical of the period, so that each play can be seen in the context of the stage for which it was originally performed;

2. Introductions to each dramatist, surveying their theatrical careers and their major works, as well as discussing issues related not only to understanding but also to staging their plays;

3. Production shots following each play from a challenging twentieth-century production of that play; these production shots illustrate important dramatic moments in each play as performed by major actors or repertory groups from the United States, Canada, England, and Europe;

4. Provocative reviews of each illustrated production which collectively exemplify a wide range of approaches to understanding dramatic performance; and

5. An appendix list of film and video productions of the plays in this collection, including a list of film and video distributors from whom copies may be obtained.

Thus from dramatist, to play, to performance, *Modern and Contemporary Drama* constitutes an invitation to experience the richly varied world of theater.

ACKNOWLEDGMENTS

For their suggestions of plays to be included in this collection and for their reactions to draft versions of the table of contents, we are grateful to: Gilbert L. Bloom, Ball State University; Michael Friedman, University of Scranton; Gary Harrington, Salisbury State University; Amy Koritz, Tulane University; Stan Kozikowski, Bryant College; John Mock, Chemekta Community College; Janet Reed, University of Cincinnati; James Reynolds, Ashland University; Tramble T. Turner, Pennsylvania State University—Ogontz; David Walker, Oberlin College; Charles S. Watson, University of Alabama—Tuscaloosa.

For their excellent research assistance in preparing the apparatus, we are grateful to Julie Schmid and Kate Moncrief (both of the University of Iowa). For their expert work in bringing this book into print, we are grateful to the staff of St. Martin's Press, especially Denise Quirk, project manager, and Emily Berleth, manager, publishing services. We owe special thanks to Melissa Cook Candela, our former associate editor, for her outstanding work in gathering reactions to the table of contents and in securing permissions for plays, production shots, and reviews. Above all, we are indebted to Cathy Pusateri, our former senior editor, for launching this ambitious project and for her support throughout the complex process of creating the collection and bringing the book into print.

MIRIAM GILBERT
CARL H. KLAUS
BRADFORD S. FIELD, JR.

CONTENTS

MODERN THEATER

Modern drama, like modern painting and other forms of modern art, developed not in the twentieth century, as might be casually assumed, but during the nineteenth century. It was born out of a widespread reaction against the subject matters, forms, and methods of staging that had prevailed in many eighteenth- and early nineteenth-century plays—against aristocratic or exotic heroes and heroines, against the rigorous unities of a neoclassical tragedy or the flamboyant events of a romantic melodrama, against declamatory styles of acting or spectacular forms of setting, against theatrical conventions that were regarded as being too far from the truth of ordinary existence. "Reality," in turn, became a watchword among early modern dramatists, actors, directors, and set designers. Indeed, the realistic impulse in one form or another so heavily influenced theater through the first half of the twentieth century that the history of modern drama may well be understood in terms of the movements that grew out of realism, either as a refinement of it or as a reaction against it.

Realism in its most literal sense developed out of a desire to bring the stage into greater conformity with the surface details of ordinary human experience. This impulse first manifested itself in the efforts of set designers to create a full-scale visual illusion in the theater, to make the stage setting look like an interior place where ordinary people actually lived and worked—or, as one recent director has put it, to show "a real chair in a real setting." This concept of staging clearly required a set more visually plausible than the sliding wings and canvas backdrops of the neoclassical stage, which usually depicted doors and windows, sometimes even chairs, by means of perspective painting on the backdrop, instead of incorporating movable doors, windows, and furniture.

To create the illusion of a three-dimensional interior, nineteenth-century set designers devised a set composed of flats arranged to form connected walls enclosing three sides of the stage, with the fourth wall removed so that the audience could look into a stage room that spatially seemed just like a real one. The realistic illusion of this stage design, known as the box set, was enhanced by movable windows and doors built into the walls of the back or side flats, as well as by false thickness pieces built into the window and door openings, which gave them an air of solidity. When the interior walls of the set were decorated and hung with fixtures, and when the floor space enclosed by the walls was equipped with rugs, furniture, and other props, the stage resembled a real room in every respect (see Figure 1). By the middle of the nineteenth century, the box set had been used in theaters throughout Europe, and its subsequent importance to the history of drama may be seen in the fact that detailed interiors figure prominently in almost all the plays written in the modern realistic tradition, such as Ibsen's *A Doll's House,* Strindberg's *Miss Julie,* Chekhov's *The Cherry Orchard,* Shaw's *Major Barbara,* O'Casey's *Juno and the Paycock,* and Williams' *Cat on a Hot Tin Roof.*

The development of the box set took place during the same period as major technological advances in lighting. Gaslights, as well as lime or calcium light, superseded oil lamps during the first half of the nineteenth century, making

Figure 1. The box set decorated with wall and window hangings, as well as with furniture and props, to create the illusion of an actual room.

possible not only a greater degree of power and control in stage lighting, but also a variety of realistic effects, such as the illusion of sunlight, moonlight, or lamplight coming through doors and windows. During the second half of the nineteenth century, the invention of the carbon arc lamp and finally the incandescent lamp not only freed theaters from the terrible fire hazards of gaslights, but also encouraged directors and designers to invent elaborately realistic lighting effects.

Acting styles were slower to approximate the natural gestures, movements, and tones of voices appropriate to realistic staging, in part because the declamatory style of romantic acting was highly popular with audiences, but also because anything less pronounced would have been inadequate to make a clearly audible and visual impression in the cavernous theaters common during the late eighteenth century and much of the nineteenth. The auditoriums in these theaters were typically based on a design that was calculated to accommodate as large an audience as possible—sometimes as many as four thousand—with little concern for the needs of the actors or of the spectators. That design can readily be understood by first imagining a large cylinder at whose base is seated the majority of the audience, looking at a large opening that has been pierced in the cylinder to form the proscenium arch of the stage (see Figure 2). Then imagine that the builders or remodelers of such theaters, in order to fit in more paying spectators, hung balconies at four or five levels around the inside walls of the cylinder above the base (see Figure 3). Clearly, an actor or actress performing in these theaters had to develop an exaggerated style of movement, gesture, and intonation to make an impact on the audience sitting in those balconies.

But during the late nineteenth and early twentieth centuries, theater architecture began to undergo significant modifications, which were intended to create better acoustical, visual, and spatial arrangements for actors and spectators. Cylindrical designs were gradually abandoned in favor of fan-shaped auditoriums with rising tiers of seats, all facing the stage (see Figure 4). In auditoriums based on this design—a design that now prevails in many commercial, community, and college theaters—the clear sightlines and favorable acoustics made it possible for performers to develop and use a more natural style of acting. And where theaters of this design were not available, directors

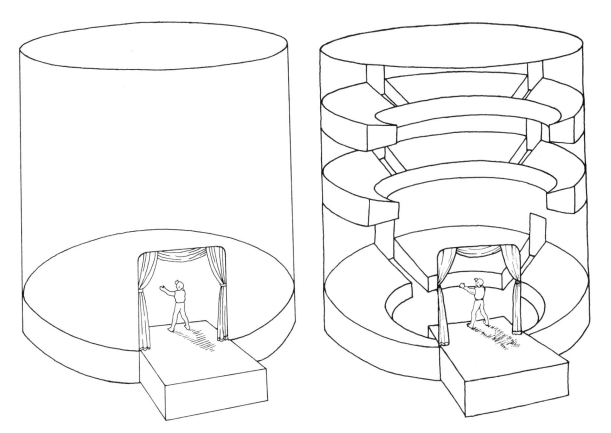

Figure 2. The cylindrical design of late eighteenth- and early nineteenth-century theaters.

Figure 3. The cylindrically designed theater, showing multiple balconies remote from the actor on stage.

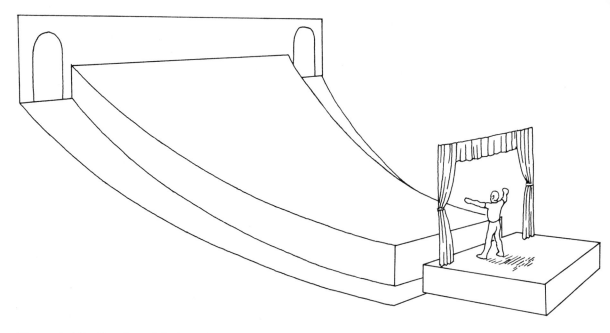

Figure 4. The fan-shaped design of modern theaters with rising tiers of seats, which provide clear sightlines for spectators and facilitate naturalistic styles of acting for performers.

and performers who were committed to naturalistic styles of acting and production deliberately searched for small, intimate halls where they could set up a stage and perform in conditions suitable to their artistic beliefs.

The emergence during the late nineteenth century of repertory groups committed to naturalistic theater constitutes one of the most important contributions to the development of modern drama. One of the earliest and most influential figures in this repertory movement was André Antoine, an amateur actor, who in 1887 quit his job at the Paris Gas Company and founded the Théàtre Libre, a group dedicated to staging the plays of Ibsen, Strindberg, and their followers in meticulously naturalistic productions. Antoine's company was based on a principle, which nowadays is taken for granted but was then highly unusual, of integrating every aspect of production—costuming, setting, blocking, and acting—to create a totally unified illusion. Instead of seeking star performers, he worked to develop an ensemble of actors and actresses, painstakingly rehearsing them so that each performer was responsive not only to the demands of his or her individual role, but also to the needs of every other role at every moment in a production. Antoine's example quickly inspired similar companies to be formed throughout Europe and America.

The most well-known and influential organization to develop during the early repertory movement was the Moscow Art Theater, founded in 1898 by Konstantin Stanislavsky, an amateur actor and director, and by Vladimir Nemirovich-Danchenko, a successful playwright. The Moscow Art Theater achieved its early fame by producing the plays of Chekhov in a style that accentuated their emotional and psychological subtlety. This style entailed not only a detailed attention to elements of staging—including even the use of music to underline important emotional moments—but also a carefully defined method of acting, propounded by Stanislavsky, whose fundamental purpose was to create "the inner life of a human spirit." Stanislavsky's method, which he subsequently expounded in several highly influential books—among them *My Life in Art* (1924) and *An Actor Prepares* (1926)—required actors to think "about the inner side of a role, and how to create its spiritual life through the help of the internal process of living the part. You must live it by actually experiencing feelings that are analogous to it, each and every time you repeat the process of creating it." The illusion of reality, as Stanislavsky defined it, depended on using the theater to dramatize not simply the external but, more important, the internal condition of human experience.

Stanislavsky's emphasis on the "inner side of a role," on "living the part," would have been impossible without dramatic roles that called for such an approach, without plays that offer probing studies of psychologically complex characters in complex social, domestic, and personal situations. In this profound sense, realistic and naturalistic drama originated not from an interest in representing the surface details, the literal image, of human activity, but out of a concern with reflecting the environmental and psychological conditions that account for the problematic quality of ordinary human experience. In this sense Ibsen is often considered the "father" of modern drama. Beginning in 1877, for example, Ibsen wrote a series of realistic "problem" plays, in which he systematically shattered popular illusions about such then sacred institutions as marriage and religion—plays in which he showed the inner life of his characters as they come to recognize the painful realities of their personal situations. Chekhov dramatized a similar kind of experience in his turn-of-the-century plays, though he presented his characters as being at once comic, pitiable, and admirably human in their futile efforts to overcome both the romantic illusions and the banal necessities of their existence. Strindberg exposed even harsher realities in his naturalistic dramatizations of the sexual antagonism between men and women.

In portraying characters, the early modern dramatists relied not only on the psychological nuances of dialogue and action, but also on the emblematic significances of the box set itself, for its detailed interiors may be seen as tangibly revealing not only a particular place in which the characters exist, but also exposing the quality of their existence. In *A Doll's House*, for example, the setting called for in Ibsen's stage directions—a room cluttered with bric-a-brac and overstuffed chairs—is as stifling and deceiving as the marriage of Nora and Helmer. In Chekhov's *The Cherry Orchard*, the cozy nursery where the play begins and ends is an emblem of the childish and irrepressibly romantic illusions that govern the thoughts of Ranevskaya and Gayev and that make them incapable of coming to terms with the changing society around them. And in *Miss Julie*, the kitchen, which constitutes the setting for the entire play, is a continual reminder of the cultural and psychological servitude that Jean, the valet, is bent on overthrowing.

Though the realism of box sets and the naturalism of psychologically motivated characters was dramatically compelling, modern drama also developed along nonrealistic and even anti-realistic lines. As early as 1835, a young medical researcher named Georg Büchner began writing plays that challenged the romantic historical dramas of Germany's Friedrich Schiller, plays whose protagonists (Mary Stuart, William Tell, Joan of Arc) are clearly heroic figures. Though Büchner's first play, *Danton's Death*, dealt with the major political event of the eighteenth century, the French Revolution, his treatment of it was decidedly nonromantic, both in characterization and in style. Instead of blank verse and classical dramatic structure, Büchner turned to prose and an almost cinematic juxtaposition of scenes. Büchner, in fact, was so far ahead of his time that editions of his work did not even appear until the second half of the century. Indeed, the first performance of *Woyzeck*, Büchner's major work, did not take place until 1913, one hundred years after his birth.

By the late nineteenth century, various anti-realistic tendencies—known as symbolism, expressionism, and surrealism—had already taken form in the critical statements and plays of *avant-garde* dramatists. Proponents of these counter-realistic movements argued that dramatic truth was not to be found in the tangible surfaces of a box set nor even in the intangible life of a psychologically complex character, but in symbols, images, legends, myths, fantasies, dreams, and other mysterious manifestations of spirituality, subjectivity, or the unconscious. Symbolists, for example, claimed the existence of a higher truth than was evident in external reality, and they aimed to create in the theater a mysterious and quasi-religious experience. Expressionists believed that truth existed not in the external appearance of reality but in the subjective perception of reality, no matter how psychologically distorted that perception might be, and they often sought to dramatize how the world appears to a disturbed and convulsive mind. Surrealists claimed that truth was to be found not in the logic of everyday events but in the irrational processes of the unconscious mind, and they tried to re-create the strange combinations of the familiar and the mysterious that often take place in dreams.

From a late twentieth-century perspective, these various anti-realistic tendencies now seem commonplace, but in their own day they were revolutionary, and they attracted not only experimental writers, but major dramatists who had already established themselves as masters of realistic and naturalistic drama. Ibsen's late plays, especially *The Lady from the Sea* (1888) and *When We Dead Awaken* (1899) are manifestly symbolic not only in their titles but also in their settings and in their action. Although Strindberg began by writing such naturalistic plays as *The Father* (1887) and *Miss Julie* (1888), he later turned to the fantasy world of *A Dream Play* (1901) and the haunting, personal symbolism of *The Ghost Sonata* (1907). Even Shaw, so thoroughly committed to a theater of intellectual and social realism, wrote a five-play parable set in the Garden of Eden, Mesopotamia, as well as England both in his own time and the future in *Back to Methuselah* (1920). For the American playwright O'Neill, symbolic and expressionistic drama came early in his career rather than at the end, in the psychologically distorted perceptions of *The Emperor Jones* (1920), the symbolic events of *The Hairy Ape* (1922), and the expressionistic symbols of *The Great God Brown* (1926). In Italy, Luigi Pirandello dramatized the enduring struggle between appearance and reality by bringing on stage both "actors" and "characters," the latter group dizzying in their simultaneous reality and nonreality. And though the Spanish playwright Garcia Lorca called his last play, *The House of Bernarda Alba* (1936), "a photographic document," the text begins with symbolic insistence on the "very white room" in Bernarda's house, and ends with Bernarda insisting on the spiritual whiteness of her youngest daughter: "My daughter died a virgin."

Symbolic drama of the early modern period was mirrored in a variety of staging techniques that were often intentionally designed to obliterate any hint of a realistic environment. In France, the main exponent of symbolist staging was Aurelien-Marie Lugné-Poe, who established an avant-garde repertory group, known as the Théàtre de l'Oeuvre, which was dedicated to the production of symbolist plays. In Lugné-Poe's productions, scenery was often reduced to painted, abstract backdrops; props and furniture were often minimal or nonexistent; lighting was often minimal and dispersed instead of focussed; and actors strived to evoke a mood rather than to reveal psychological motivation. Expressionistic stagings, which were largely developed in German theater during the 1920s, replaced representational settings with expressively stylized backdrops, showing exterior or interior locations that had been distorted and exaggerated in color and shape; lighting was often harshly focussed or nervously scattered; and actors strived through disjointed movements and telegraphic speech patterns to evoke human behavior as it might be perceived by a psychologically convulsive personality. Surrealistic stagings, which were launched by Antonin Artaud and André Breton in Parisian theaters of the 1920s, pushed productions even further toward expressive abstraction in backdrops, costumes, lighting, and acting styles.

By the end of the twenties, these counterrealistic movements, though polemically extreme in their practices, had worked substantial changes in the style of drama and of theatrical production—changes that resulted in a synthesis of realistic and naturalistic methods with symbolic, expressionistic, or surrealistic techniques. The power of such a synthesis was convincingly displayed in the work of Bertolt Brecht, the major German playwright and director of the twentieth century. From the 1920s through the early 1950s, Brecht wrote an extensive series of plays that were simultaneously realistic in their depiction of human motives and values, expressionistic in their episodic structure, and politically explicit in their ideology. And he created stagings for his plays with the Berliner Ensemble that used realistic costumes and set pieces combined with an abstract backdrop, visible lighting instruments, visible scene changing, and scene titles or other messages projected onto the backdrop. By means of this synthesis, Brecht aimed both to engage an audience in the situation of his characters and to distance them sufficiently so that they would be provoked to think about its social and political implications. Once Brecht had established the theatrical power of such a synthesis, it gradually came to be a dominant approach in serious theater of the twentieth century. Tennessee Williams, for example, blended realism and expressionism in all of his plays, beginning with his notes on music, lighting, and pantomime for *The Glass Menagerie* (1944) and continuing with his emphasis on the bedroom and the bed in *Cat on a Hot Tin Roof* (1955). So, when Arthur Miller's *Death of a Salesman* (1949) opened on Broadway with a striking combination of naturalistic and expressionistic effects, both in the physical set and in the play's structure, his mixture of styles evoked almost no surprise at all.

GEORG BÜCHNER

1813–1837

Though he died quite young, in his brief life Georg Büchner led three distinctly different lives. His first and most successful was as a medical researcher and lecturer, a profession that came naturally to the son of a doctor. Büchner was educated at Darmstadt in his native Germany and then in 1831 went to Strasbourg to study medicine but after two years returned to Germany, conforming to a state law that insisted that students from Hesse (the region in which Büchner lived) had to study at the state university. Here he began his second life as a student revolutionary, involved in an underground society aimed at attacking the regime of Ludwig II, grand duke of Hesse. As coauthor of *The Hessian Courier* (1834), a manifesto against the extortionist tactics of the grand duke, Büchner attempted to arouse his readers by reminding them of the French Revolution and its disappointing political aftermath: France, only temporarily a republic, became again a monarchy, and Germany, frightened by the violence in France, gave its people constitutions that served to quiet revolt rather than establish true freedom. To escape possible arrest, Büchner left Germany for Strasbourg in 1835, finished his medical studies, wrote a treatise on the nervous system of the barbel (a large fish), and then on the strength of that treatise moved to Zurich in late 1836, where he was offered a lectureship. A promising career as a teacher and researcher, if not as a revolutionary, seemed to open before him, only to close on February 19, 1837, when he died of typhoid fever.

In the last few years before his death, Büchner had also begun to lead a third life, that of a dramatist. At first, playwriting may have seemed merely a way to make money, since he composed his first work, *Danton's Death*, in 1835 and sent it to a well-known editor, together with a letter indicating that he was financially strapped. But after his return to Strasbourg, Büchner translated two plays by Victor Hugo and wrote a second play, *Leonce and Lena* (1836), in response to a competition for the best German comedy; his manuscript arrived after the deadline and so was not eligible. His third play, *Woyzeck*, must also date from 1836, but it remained in manuscript form, in several incomplete drafts. A fourth play, *Pietro Aretino*, survives only in its title.

Büchner's choice to write about the French Revolution at a time when he was desperate for money and planning to leave Germany to avoid arrest may have contributed to his distinctly unheroic portrayal of major figures from the Revolution. Set in 1794, near the end of the Reign of Terror, *Danton's Death* focuses on internal power struggles rather than the larger social context. In this play, Robespierre and Saint-Just are portrayed as coldly calculating individuals who use abstractions such as "freedom" and "humanity" to hide their manipulative search for power. But Georges Danton, rather than heroically opposing these men, seems strangely passive, refusing to leave Paris even though his friends warn him, preferring to spend his time not only with his wife, Julie, but with numerous prostitutes. Though he rouses himself during his trial to remind his accusers of his actions in the early days of the Revolution, he sinks at the play's end to a fatalistic aphorism: "The world is chaos. Nothingness is the world-god yet to be born." Büchner's historical play never glorifies the Revolution. In keeping with this unglorified view of the Revolution, *Danton's Death* is written in prose rather than blank verse, and it presents the voices not only of Danton and Robespierre but of nameless citizens and of powerless women. "What are we but puppets, manipulated on wires by unknown powers?" asks Danton as he muses to Julie about the rightness of his actions, a metaphor used as stage setting in Jonathan Miller's 1971 production, which featured side boxes with headless mannequins, as well as projections of Roman statues.

Büchner's vision of human beings as puppets emerges again in *Leonce and Lena*, a play that superficially seems completely different from *Danton's Death* and its specific historical context. Büchner sets up a fairy-tale world in which Prince Leonce, unwilling to accept an arranged marriage, and Princess Lena, equally unwilling to sacrifice herself, both disguise themselves and run away. Of course, they meet and fall in love, but the names of their countries, Popo and Pipi, with their echoes of excrement and urination, should alert us to the darker side of the fairy-tale world. In the final scene, disguised as "two world-famous automatons," Leonce and Lena are married. When they remove their masks, they find that instead of "escaping into Paradise" they "have been deceived." Though the tone of the play is light, the storyline clearly argues the inability of human beings to control their destinies.

Though *Danton's Death* and *Leonce and Lena* are strikingly different in setting and tone, though one play deals with actual figures of the French Revolution and the other with imaginary and comic royal personages, both plays are "costume dramas," requiring the creation of a world noticeably unlike the one in which Büchner actually lived. In contrast, *Woyzeck* is based on a real murder that took place in Leipzig in 1821, when Johann Christian Woyzeck stabbed his ex-mistress seven times. Woyzeck's execution did not take place until three years after the murder because of several appeals; but two investigations by a court-appointed physician, Johann Clarus, concluded that Woyzeck was legally responsible for his actions. While these reports, available to Büchner through his father, aimed at justifying Woyzeck's execution, they also included many of the details that might well have been used to argue for extenuating circumstances, particularly Woyzeck's claims that he had visions and heard voices.

Yet *Woyzeck*'s peculiar force comes not from its basis in real life but from Büchner's extraordinarily stripped-down style. Gone are the long speeches of argument that punctuate *Danton's Death*; gone are the long pseudo-meditations of *Leonce and Lena*. Instead, the characters in *Woyzeck* speak in short, choppy phrases, in allusions rather than explanations, in snatches of songs or of biblical quotations. Such a style fits the central character who finds it difficult to express his feelings, and who finally seeks refuge in violent action rather than in language. Significantly, the characters in this play who *can* speak freely are the ones we most mistrust: the Captain who preaches a meaningless morality while driving Woyzeck mad with his insinuations about Marie, Woyzeck's common-law wife, and the Doctor, who preaches human freedom to the man he is using for his bizarre scientific experiments. Gone too is any attempt at linear development or an intrigue plot. In its place is a series of short scenes, some involving just four or six speeches. The language, the action, the motivation, the scene structure—all are fragmentary.

Fragmentary is more than a metaphor for the form and content of *Woyzeck*; it is an accurate description of the playtext itself. For unlike any other work in this volume, *Woyzeck* is incomplete. It exists only in a manuscript that contains four different versions or groupings of scenes: one contains twenty-one scenes, a second has nine scenes, a third has two scenes, and the fourth has seventeen scenes. Some scenes seem to be revisions of others, while others appear only once. These different versions raise a host of questions about Büchner's unresolved intentions. Does the play begin with Woyzeck and Andres in the field (as in two sequences of the manuscript) or with the fair (Scene 3 in our text), thereby immediately introducing Woyzeck, Marie, and the Sergeant who will become her new lover? How many times does Woyzeck tell Andres he hears a voice telling him to stab only to be met with the prosaic remedy of "brandy with a painkiller in it" (Scene 13)? The scene appears in two different forms, and one might reasonably argue that Büchner meant it to appear just once, or that he wanted the scene in twice, to emphasize Woyzeck's "voices" and Andres's lack of sympathy. Scenes 18 and 27 appear on a separate page of the manuscript and nowhere else, with no indication of where Büchner meant to put them. The choice to use Scene 27 as the final scene is also an interpretation of one of the play's unresolved questions. Does Woyzeck drown himself after throwing away the knife he used to kill Marie, perhaps because of guilt (the last lines of Scene 24 echo Lady Macbeth's famous lines), or does he merely wash himself off and return to town where his child seems to reject him (Scene 27)?

Thus, every reader of the play is, to some extent, acting as its editor, just as Henry J. Schmidt has titled his translation in this volume a "reconstruction of the text." Schmidt has worked from the most complete modern edition of the play available and has considered all the variant scenes, as well as the order that the manuscript does suggest for certain scenes. But, as Mel Gussow suggests in his review of the New York Shakespeare Festival production, "the play is open to free-handed interpretation" and to various production styles. In this production, JoAnne Akalaitis draws on images from the twentieth century, such as the antiseptically white mechanic chair in which the Captain sits while Woyzeck shaves him (see Figure 1). The townspeople who surround Woyzeck after the murder wear clothes evoking the 1930s and 1940s (see Figure 2). Images of the concentration camps dominate the production: Gussow explicitly links Woyzeck to a prisoner at Dachau, while the murder of Marie (see Figure 3) takes place in what seems to be an empty shower room, evoking memories of the "shower rooms" that were really gas chambers in which thousands of prisoners died. These visual reminders of the prejudice and hatred of the twentieth century testify to the play's enduring power. Though the fragmentary nature of the play on the page may at times frustrate editors and readers, the play onstage shows us pieces of a life that coalesce into an emblem of contemporary pain and despair.

WOYZECK

BY GEORG BÜCHNER / A RECONSTRUCTION OF THE ORIGINAL TEXT TRANSLATED BY HENRY J. SCHMIDT

CHARACTERS

FRANZ WOYZECK	FIRST APPRENTICE
MARIE	SECOND APPRENTICE
CAPTAIN	KARL, *an idiot*
DOCTOR	KATEY
DRUM MAJOR	GRANDMOTHER
SERGEANT	FIRST CHILD
ANDRES	SECOND CHILD
MARGRET	THIRD CHILD
BARKER	FIRST PERSON
ANNOUNCER	SECOND PERSON
OLD MAN	COURT CLERK
CHILD	JUDGE
JEW	SOLDIERS, STUDENTS, YOUNG MEN, GIRLS,
INNKEEPER	CHILDREN

BARKER / ANNOUNCER } *can be played by one actor*

1

(*Open field. The town in the distance.*)

(WOYZECK *and* ANDRES *are cutting branches in the bushes.*)

WOYZECK: Hey, Andres! That streak across the grass— that's where heads roll at night. Once somebody picked one up, thought it was a hedgehog. Three days and three nights, and he was lying in a coffin. (*Softly.*) Andres, it was the Freemasons.° That's it— the Freemasons! Shh!

ANDRES: (*Sings.*)

I saw two big rabbits
Chewing up the green, green grass . . .

WOYZECK: Shh! Something's moving!

ANDRES:

Chewing up the green, green grass
Till it all was gone.

WOYZECK: Something's moving behind me—under me. (*Stamps on the ground.*) Hollow! You hear that? It's all hollow down there. The Freemasons!

ANDRES: I'm scared.

WOYZECK: It's so quiet—that's strange. You feel like holding your breath. Andres!

Freemasons, an international secret society.

ANDRES: What?

WOYZECK: Say something! (*Stares off into the distance.*) Andres! Look how bright it is! There's fire raging around the sky, and a noise is coming down like trumpets. It's coming closer! Let's go! Don't look back! (*Drags him into the bushes.*)

ANDRES: (*After a pause.*) Woyzeck! Do you still hear it?

WOYZECK: Quiet, everything's quiet, like the world was dead.

ANDRES: Listen! They're drumming. We've got to get back.

2

(*The town.*)

(MARIE *with her* CHILD *at the window.* MARGRET. *A parade goes by, the* DRUM MAJOR *leading.*)

MARIE: (*Rocking the* CHILD *in her arms.*) Hey, boy! Ta-ra-ra-ra! You hear it? They're coming.

MARGRET: What a man, like a tree!

MARIE: He stands on his feet like a lion. (*The* DRUM MAJOR *greets them.*)

MARGRET: Say, what a friendly look you gave him, neighbor. We're not used to that from you.

MARIE: (*Sings.*)

A soldier is a handsome fellow . . .

MARGRET: Your eyes are still shining.

MARIE: So what? Why don't you take *your* eyes to the Jew and have them polished—maybe they'll shine enough to sell as two buttons.

MARGRET: What? Why, Mrs. Virgin! I'm a decent woman, but you—you can stare through seven pairs of leather pants!

MARIE: Bitch! *(Slams the window shut.)* Come on, boy. What do they want from us, anyway? You're only the son of a whore, and you make your mother happy with your bastard face. Ta-ta! *(Sings.)*

Maiden, how sorrow can sting,
You've got a son but no ring!
Oh, who cares what is right,
I'll sing to you all night:
Rockabye baby, my baby are you,
Nobody cares what we do.

Johnny, hitch up your six horses fleet,
Go bring them something to eat.
From oats they will turn,
From water they'll turn,
Only cool wine will be fine, hooray!
Only cool wine will be fine.

(A knock at the window.)

MARIE: Who's that? Is that you, Franz? Come on in!

WOYZECK: I can't. Have to go to roll call.

MARIE: What's the matter with you, Franz?

WOYZECK: *(Mysteriously.)* Marie, there was something out there again—a lot. Isn't it written: "And lo, the smoke of the country went up as the smoke of a furnace"?°

MARIE: Franz . . .

WOYZECK: It followed me until I reached town. What's going to happen?

MARIE: Franz!

WOYZECK: I've got to go. *(He leaves.)*

MARIE: That man! He's seeing things. He didn't even look at his own child. He'll go crazy with those thoughts of his. Why are you so quiet, son? Are you scared? It's getting so dark, you'd think you were blind. Usually there's a light shining in. I can't stand it. It frightens me. *(Goes off.)*

3

(Fair booths. Lights. People.)

(An OLD MAN sings to a barrel organ, a CHILD dances.)

OLD MAN:

How long we live, just time will tell,
We all have got to die,
We know that very well!

MARIE: Hey! Wow!

WOYZECK: Poor man, old man! Poor child! Little child! Cares and fairs! Hey, Marie, should I . . . ?

MARIE: Even a fool must have some sense to be able to say: Foolish world! Beautiful world!

BARKER: *(In front of a booth, with a WOMAN wearing pants. He presents a costumed monkey. The BARKER speaks with a French accent.)* Gentlemen! Gentlemen! Look at this creature, as God made it—he's nothing, nothing at all. Now see the effect of art: he walks upright, wears coat and pants, carries a sword! Ho! Take a bow! Presto—you're a baron. Give me a kiss! *(The monkey trumpets.)* The little fellow is musical. Ladies and gentlemen, here is to be seen the astronomical horse and the little cannery-birds°—they're favorites of all potentates of Europe—they're members of all learned societies. They'll tell you everything: how old you are, how many children you have, what kind of illnesses. *(Points to the monkey.)* He shoots a pistol, stands on one leg. It's all education; he has merely a beastly reason, or rather a very reasonable beastliness—he's no dumb individual like a lot of people, present company excepted. Observe the progress of civilization. Everything progresses—a horse, a monkey, a cannery-bird! The monkey is already a soldier. That's not much—it's the lowest level of the human race. Enter! The presentation will begin. The commencement of the beginning will start immediately.

WOYZECK: Want to?

MARIE: All right. It ought to be good. Look at his tassels—and the woman's got pants on!

(SERGEANT. DRUM MAJOR.)

SERGEANT: Hold it! Over there. Look at her! What a piece!

DRUM MAJOR: Goddamn! Good enough for the propagation of cavalry regiments and the breeding of drum majors!

SERGEANT: Look how she holds her head—you'd think that black hair would pull her down like a weight. And those eyes, black . . .

DRUM MAJOR: It's like looking down a well or a chimney. Come on, after her!

MARIE: *(Entering the booth.)* Those lights! My eyes!

WOYZECK: Yeah, like a barrel of black cats with fiery eyes. Hey, what a night!

(Inside the booth.)

ANNOUNCER: *(Presenting a horse.)* Show your talent! Show your beastly wisdom. Put human society to shame. Gentlemen, this animal that you see here, with a tail on his body, with his four hoofs, is a

---

"And lo, . . . furnace," Gen. 19:28, the destruction of Sodom and Gomorrah.

---

cannery-birds, the Barker says *Canaillevogel* instead of *Kanarienvogel,* meaning "canaries."

member of all learned societies, is a professor at our university with whom the students learn to ride and fight. That was simple comprehension. Now think with double *raison*.° What do you do when you think with double *raison?* Is there in the learned *société*° an ass? *(The horse shakes its head.)* Now you understand double *raison?* That is beastiognomy.° Yes, that is no dumb animal, that's a person! A human being, a beastly human being, but still an animal, *une bête. (The horse behaves improperly.)* That's right, put *société* to shame. You see, the beast is still nature, unideal nature. Take a lesson from him. Go ask the doctor, it's very unhealthy.° All this means: Man, be natural. You were created from dust, sand, dirt. Do you want to be more than dust, sand, dirt? Observe his reason: he can add, but he can't count on his fingers. How come? He simply can't express himself, explain himself. He's a transformed person! Tell the gentlemen what time it is. Does anyone have a watch—a watch?

SERGEANT: A watch! *(Slowly and grandly he pulls a watch out of his pocket.)* There you are.

MARIE: This I've got to see. *(She climbs into the first row. The SERGEANT helps her.)*

4

(Room.)

(MARIE sits with her CHILD on her lap, a piece of mirror in her hand.)

MARIE: *(Looks at herself in the mirror.)* These stones really sparkle! What kind are they? What did he call them? Go to sleep, son! Shut your eyes tight. *(The CHILD covers his eyes with his hands.)* Tighter—stay quiet or he'll come get you. *(Sings.)*

> Close up your shop, fair maid,
> A gypsy boy's in the glade.
> He'll lead you by the hand
> Off into gypsyland.

(Looks in the mirror again.) It must be gold. The likes of us only have a little corner in the world and a little piece of mirror, but my mouth is just as red as the great ladies with their mirrors from top to toe, and handsome lords who kiss their hands. I'm just a poor woman. *(The CHILD sits up.)* Shh, son, eyes shut! Look, the sandman! He's running along the wall. *(She flashes with the mirror.)* Eyes shut, or he'll look into them, and you'll go blind.

(WOYZECK enters behind her. She jumps up with her hands over her ears.)

---

raison, reason. *société,* company. **beastiognomy,** *viehsionomik:* a pun on "beast" and "physiognomy." **unhealthy,** meaning "to hold it in."

WOYZECK: What's that you got there?

MARIE: Nothing.

WOYZECK: Something's shining under your fingers.

MARIE: An earring. I found it.

WOYZECK: I've never found anything like that. Two at once.

MARIE: What am I—a whore?

WOYZECK: It's all right, Marie. Look, the boy's asleep. Lift him up under his arms, the chair's hurting him. Those shiny drops on his forehead; everything under the sun is work. Sweat, even in our sleep. Us poor people! Here's some more money, Marie, my pay and some from my captain.

MARIE: Bless you, Franz.

WOYZECK: I have to go. See you tonight, Marie. Bye.

MARIE: *(Alone, after a pause.)* What a bitch I am. I could stab myself. Oh, what a world! Everything goes to hell anyhow, man and woman alike.

5

(The CAPTAIN. WOYZECK.)

(The CAPTAIN in a chair, WOYZECK shaves him.)

CAPTAIN: Take it easy, Woyzeck, take it easy. One thing at a time. You're making me dizzy. You're going to finish early today—what am I supposed to do with the extra ten minutes? Woyzeck, just think, you've still got a good thirty years to live, thirty years! That's 360 months, and days, hours, minutes! What are you going to do with that ungodly amount of time? Get organized, Woyzeck.

WOYZECK: Yes, Cap'n.

CAPTAIN: I fear for the world when I think about eternity. Activity, Woyzeck, activity! Eternal—that's eternal—that is—eternal—you realize that, of course. But then again it's not eternal, it's only a moment, yes, a moment. Woyzeck, it frightens me to think that the earth rotates in one day. What a waste of time! What will come of that? Woyzeck, I can't look at a mill wheel anymore or I get melancholy.

WOYZECK: Yes, Cap'n.

CAPTAIN: Woyzeck, you always look so upset. A good man doesn't act like that, a good man with a good conscience. Say something, Woyzeck. What's the weather like?

WOYZECK: It's bad, Cap'n, bad—wind.

CAPTAIN: I can feel it, there's something rapid out there. A wind like that reminds me of a mouse. *(Cunningly.)* I believe it's coming from the south-north.

WOYZECK: Yes, Cap'n.

CAPTAIN: Ha-ha-ha! South-north! Ha-ha-ha! Oh, are you stupid, terribly stupid! *(Sentimentally.)* Woyzeck, you're a good man, a good man—*(With dignity.)* but Woyzeck, you've got no morality. Morality—that's when you are moral, you understand. It's a good word. You have a child without the blessing of the church, as our Reverend Chaplain says, without the blessing of the church. *I* didn't make that up.

WOYZECK: Cap'n, the good Lord isn't going to look at a poor worm only because amen was said over it before it was created. The Lord said: "Suffer little children to come unto me."

CAPTAIN: What's that you're saying? What kind of a crazy answer is that? You're getting me all confused. When I say *you,* I mean you—you!

WOYZECK: Us poor people. You see, Cap'n—money, money. If you don't have money . . . Just try to raise your own kind on morality in this world. After all, we're flesh and blood. The likes of us are unhappy in this world and in the next. I guess if we ever got to Heaven, we'd have to help with the thunder.

CAPTAIN: Woyzeck, you have no virtue. You're not a virtuous person. Flesh and blood? When I'm lying at the window after it has rained, and I watch the white stockings as they go tripping down the street—damn it, Woyzeck, then love comes all over me. I've got flesh and blood, too. But Woyzeck, virtue, virtue! How else could I make time go by? I always say to myself: you're a virtuous man, *(Sentimentally.)* a good man, a good man.

WOYZECK: Yes, Cap'n, virtue! I haven't figured it out yet. You see, us common people, we don't have virtue. We act like nature tells us. But if I was a gentleman, and had a hat and a watch and a topcoat and could talk refined, then I'd be virtuous, too. Virtue must be nice, Cap'n. But I'm just a poor guy.

CAPTAIN: That's fine, Woyzeck. You're a good man, a good man. But you think too much, that's unhealthy. You always look so upset. This discussion has really worn me out. You can go now—and don't run like that! Slowly, nice and slow down the street.

6

(MARIE. DRUM MAJOR.)

DRUM MAJOR: Marie!

MARIE: *(Looking at him expressively.)* Go march up and down for me. A chest like a bull and a beard like a lion. Nobody else is like that. No woman is prouder than me.

DRUM MAJOR: Sundays when I have my plumed helmet and my white gloves—goddamn, Marie! The prince always says: man, you're quite a guy!

MARIE: *(Mockingly.)* Aw, go on! *(Goes up to him.)* What a man!

DRUM MAJOR: What a woman! Hell, let's breed a race of drum majors, hey? *(He embraces her.)*

MARIE: *(Moody.)* Leave me alone!

DRUM MAJOR: You wildcat!

MARIE: *(Violently.)* Just try to touch me!

DRUM MAJOR: You've got the devil in your eyes.

MARIE: For all I care. What does it matter?

7

(On the street.)

(MARIE. WOYZECK.)

WOYZECK: *(Stares at her, shakes his head.)* Hm! I don't see anything, I don't see anything. Oh, I should be able to see it; I should be able to grab it with my fists.

MARIE: *(Intimidated.)* What's the matter, Franz? You're out of your mind, Franz.

WOYZECK: A sin so fat and so wide—it stinks enough to smoke the angels out of Heaven. You've got a red mouth, Marie. No blister on it? Good-bye, Marie. You're as beautiful as sin. Can mortal sin be so beautiful?

MARIE: Franz, you're delirious.

WOYZECK: Damn it! Was he standing here like this, like this?

MARIE: As the day is long and the world is old, lots of people can stand on one spot, one after another.

WOYZECK: I saw him.

MARIE: You can see all sorts of things if you've got two eyes and aren't blind, and the sun is shining.

WOYZECK: With my own eyes!

MARIE: *(Fresh.)* So what!

8

(At the DOCTOR's.*)*

(WOYZECK. *The* DOCTOR.)

DOCTOR: What is this I hear, Woyzeck? A man of honor!

WOYZECK: What is it, Doctor?

DOCTOR: I saw it, Woyzeck. You pissed on the street, you pissed on the wall like a dog. And you get two cents a day. Woyzeck, that's bad. The world's getting bad, very bad.

WOYZECK: But Doctor, the call of nature . . .

DOCTOR: The call of nature, the call of nature! Nature! Haven't I proved that the *musculus constrictor vesicae°* is subject to the will? Nature! Woyzeck, man is free. In man alone is individuality exalted to freedom. Couldn't hold it in! *(Shakes his head, puts his hands behind his back, and paces back and forth.)* Did you eat your peas already, Woyzeck? I'm revolutionizing science, I'll blow it sky-high. Urea ten per cent, ammonium chloride, hyperoxidic. Woyzeck, try pissing again. Go in there and try.

WOYZECK: I can't, Doctor.

---

musculus constrictor vesicae, muscle controlling the bladder.

DOCTOR: *(With emotion.)* But pissing on the wall! I have it in writing. Here's the contract. I saw it all—saw it with my own eyes. I was just holding my nose out the window, letting the sun's rays hit it, so as to examine the process of sneezing. *(Goes up to him.)* No, Woyzeck, I'm not getting angry. Anger is unhealthy, unscientific. I am calm, perfectly calm. My pulse is beating at its usual sixty, and I tell you this in all cold-bloodedness. Now, who would get excited about a human being, a human being? If it were a Proteus that were dying—! But you shouldn't have pissed on the wall . . .

WOYZECK: You see, Doctor, sometimes you've got a certain character, a certain structure. But with nature, that's something else, you see, with nature. *(He cracks his knuckles.)* That's like—how should I put it—for example . . .

DOCTOR: Woyzeck, you're philosophizing again.

WOYZECK: *(Confidingly.)* Doctor, have you ever seen anything of double nature? When the sun's standing high at noon and the world seems to be going up in flames, I've heard a terrible voice talking to me!

DOCTOR: Woyzeck, you've got an *aberratio!*°

WOYZECK: *(Puts his finger to his nose.)* The toadstools, Doctor. There—that's where it is. Have you seen how they grow in patterns? If only someone could read that.

DOCTOR: Woyzeck, you've got a marvelous *aberratio mentalis partialis,*° second species, beautifully developed. Woyzeck, you're getting a raise. Second species: fixed idea with a generally rational condition. You're doing everything as usual? Shaving your captain?

WOYZECK: Yes, sir.

DOCTOR: Eating your peas?

WOYZECK: Same as ever, Doctor. My wife gets the money for the household.

DOCTOR: Going on duty?

WOYZECK: Yes, sir.

DOCTOR: You're an interesting case. Subject Woyzeck, you're getting a raise. Now behave yourself. Show me your pulse! Yes.

9

(Street.)

(CAPTAIN. DOCTOR. *The* CAPTAIN *comes panting down the street, stops, pants, looks around.)*

CAPTAIN: Doctor, I feel sorry for horses when I think that the poor beasts have to go everywhere on foot. Don't run like that! Don't wave your cane around in the air like that! You'll run yourself to death that way. A good man with a good conscience doesn't go so fast. A good man . . . *(He catches the* DOCTOR *by the coat.)* Doctor, allow me to save a human life. You're racing . . . Doctor, I'm so melancholy. I get so emotional. I always start crying when I see my coat hanging on the wall—there it is.

DOCTOR: Hm! Bloated, fat, thick neck, apoplectic constitution. Yes, Captain, you might be stricken by an *apoplexia cerebralis.*° But you might get it just on one side and be half paralyzed, or—best of all—you might become mentally affected and just vegetate from then on. Those are approximately your prospects for the next four weeks. Moreover, I can assure you that you will be a most interesting case, and if, God willing, your tongue is partially paralyzed, we'll make immortal experiments.

CAPTAIN: Doctor, don't frighten me! People have been known to die of fright, of pure, sheer fright. I can see them now, with flowers in their hands—but they'll say, he was a good man, a good man. You damn coffin nail!

DOCTOR: *(Holds out his hat.)* What's this, Captain? That's brain-less!

CAPTAIN: *(Makes a crease.)* What's this, Doctor? That's increase!

DOCTOR: I take my leave, most honorable Mr. Drill-prick.

CAPTAIN: Likewise, dearest Mr. Coffin Nail.

*(*WOYZECK *comes running down the street.)*

CAPTAIN: Hey, Woyzeck, why are you running past us like that? Stay here, Woyzeck. You're running around like an open razor blade. You might cut someone! You're running like you had to shave a regiment of castrates and would be hanged while the last hair was disappearing. But about those long beards—what was I going to say? Woyzeck—those long beards . . .

DOCTOR: A long beard on the chin. Pliny° speaks of it. Soldiers should be made to give them up.

CAPTAIN: *(Continues.)* Hey? What about those long beards? Say, Woyzeck, haven't you found a hair from a beard in your soup bowl yet? Hey? You understand, of course, a human hair, from the beard of an engineer, a sergeant, a—drum major? Hey, Woyzeck? But you've got a decent wife. Not like others.

WOYZECK: Yes, sir! What are you trying to say, Cap'n?

CAPTAIN: Look at the face he's making! Now, it doesn't necessarily have to be in the soup, but if you hurry around the corner, you might find one on a pair of

---

aberratio, aberration.   *aberratio mentalis partialis,* partial aberration.

apoplexia cerebralis, brain tumor.   *Pliny,* Roman scholar (A.D. 23–79), although the story that Alexander the Great ordered his soldiers to shave their beards to prevent the enemy from grabbing them actually derives from the Greek historian Plutarch (A.D. 46–119).

lips—a pair of lips, Woyzeck. I know what love is, too, Woyzeck. Say! You're as white as chalk!

WOYZECK: Cap'n, I'm just a poor devil—and that's all I have in the world. Cap'n, if you're joking . . .

CAPTAIN: Joking? Me? Who do you think you are?

DOCTOR: Your pulse, Woyzeck, your pulse—short, hard, skipping, irregular.

WOYZECK: Cap'n, the earth is hot as hell—for me it's ice cold! Ice cold—hell is cold, I'll bet. It can't be! God! God! It can't be!

CAPTAIN: Listen, fellow, how'd you like to be shot, how'd you like to have a couple of bullets in your head? You're looking daggers at me; but I only mean well, because you're a good man, Woyzeck, a good man.

DOCTOR: Facial muscles rigid, tense, occasionally twitching. Posture erect, tense.

WOYZECK: I'm going. A lot is possible. A man! A lot is possible. The weather's nice, Cap'n. Look: such a beautiful, hard, rough sky—you'd almost feel like pounding a block of wood into it and hanging yourself on it, only because of the hyphen between yes, and yes again—and no. Cap'n, yes and no? Is no to blame for yes, or yes for no? I'll have to think about that. *(Goes off with long strides, first slowly, then ever faster.)*

DOCTOR: *(Races after him.)* A phenomenon! Woyzeck! Another raise!

CAPTAIN: These people make me dizzy. Look at them go—that tall rascal takes off like the shadow before a spider, and the short one—he's trotting along. The tall one is lightning and the short one is thunder. Ha-ha! After them. Grotesque! Grotesque!

10

(The guardroom.)

(WOYZECK. ANDRES.)

ANDRES: *(Sings.)*

> *Our hostess has a pretty maid,*
> *She's in her garden night and day,*
> *She sits inside her garden . . .*

WOYZECK: Andres!

ANDRES: Huh?

WOYZECK: Nice weather.

ANDRES: Sunday weather. There's music outside town. All the broads are out there already, everybody's sweating—it's really moving along.

WOYZECK: *(Restlessly.)* A dance, Andres. They're dancing.

ANDRES: Yeah, at the Horse and at the Star.

WOYZECK: Dancing, dancing.

ANDRES: Big deal. *(Sings.)*

> *She sits inside her garden,*
> *Until the bells have all struck twelve,*
> *And stares at all the soldiers.*

WOYZECK: Andres, I can't keep still.

ANDRES: Stupid!

WOYZECK: I've got to get out of here. I can't see straight. Dancing. Dancing. With their hot hands. Damn it, Andres!

ANDRES: What do you want?

WOYZECK: I've got to go.

ANDRES: With that broad?

WOYZECK: I've got to get out. It's so hot in here.

11

(Inn.)

(The windows are open, a dance. Benches in front of the house. APPRENTICES.)

FIRST APPRENTICE:

> *This shirt I've got, I don't know whose,*
> *My soul it stinks like booze . . .*

SECOND APPRENTICE: Brother, shall I in friendship bore a hole in your nature? Onward! I want to bore a hole in your nature. I'm quite a guy, too, you know. I'm going to kill all the fleas on his body.

FIRST APPRENTICE: My soul, my soul it stinks like booze. Even money must eventually decay. Forget-me-not! Oh, is this world beautiful! Brother, I could cry a rain barrel full of tears. I wish our noses were two bottles and we could pour them down each other's throats.

OTHERS: *(In chorus.)*

> *A hunter from the west*
> *Once went riding through the woods.*
> *Hip-hip, hooray! A hunter's life is always gay,*
> *O'er meadow and o'er stream,*
> *Oh, hunting is my dream!*

(WOYZECK stands at the window. MARIE and the DRUM MAJOR dance past without seeing him.)

MARIE: *(Dancing by.)* On! and on, on and on!

WOYZECK: *(Chokes.)* On and on! On and on! *(Jumps up violently and sinks back on the bench.)* On and on, on and on. *(Beats his hands together.)* Spin around, roll around. Why doesn't God blow out the sun so that everything can roll around in lust, man and woman, man and beast. They'll do it in broad daylight, they'll do it on our hands, like flies. Woman! That woman is hot, hot! On and on, on and on. *(Jumps up.)* The bastard! Look how he's grabbing her, grabbing her body! He—he's got her now, like I used to have her!

FIRST APPRENTICE: *(Preaches on the table.)* Yet when a wanderer stands leaning against the stream of time and/or gives answer in the wisdom of God, asking himself: Why does Man exist? Why does Man exist? But verily I say unto you: how could the farmer, the cooper, the shoemaker, the doctor exist if God hadn't created man? How could the tailor exist if God hadn't given man a feeling of shame? How could the soldier exist, if men didn't feel the necessity of killing one another? Therefore, do not ye despair, yes, yes, life is lovely and fine, yet all that is earthly is passing, even money must eventually decay. In conclusion, my dear friends, let us piss crosswise so that a Jew will die.

12

(Open field.)

WOYZECK: On and on! On and on! Shh! Music! *(Stretches out on the ground.)* Ha—what—what are you saying? Louder, louder . . . stab—stab the bitch to death? Stab—stab the bitch to death. Should I? Must I? Do I hear it over there, is the wind saying it too? It goes on and on—stab her to death . . . to death.

13

(Night.)

(ANDRES *and* WOYZECK *in a bed.)*

WOYZECK: *(Shakes* ANDRES.*)* Andres! Andres! I can't sleep. When I close my eyes, everything starts turning, and I hear the fiddles, on and on, on and on, and then there's a voice from the wall. Don't you hear anything?
ANDRES: Oh, yeah. Let them dance! God bless us, amen. *(Falls asleep again.)*
WOYZECK: It keeps saying: stab, stab! And it floats between my eyes like a knife.
ANDRES: Drink some brandy with a painkiller in it. That'll cut your fever.

14

(Inn.)

(DRUM MAJOR. WOYZECK. ONLOOKERS.)

DRUM MAJOR: I'm a man! *(Pounds his chest.)* A man, you hear? Who wants to start something? If you're not drunk as a lord, stay away from me. I'll shove your nose up your ass. I'll . . . *(To* WOYZECK.*)* Man, have a drink. A man gotta drink. I wish the world was booze, booze.
WOYZECK: *(Whistles.)*
DRUM MAJOR: You bastard, you want me to pull your tongue out of your throat and wrap it around you?

(They wrestle, WOYZECK *loses.)* You want me to leave you enough breath to fart with?

*(*WOYZECK *sits on the bench, exhausted and trembling.)*

DRUM MAJOR: He thinks he's so great. Ha!

Oh, brandy, that's my life,
Oh, brandy gives me courage!

AN ONLOOKER: He sure got his.
ANOTHER: He's bleeding.
WOYZECK: One thing after another.

15

(Shop.)

(WOYZECK. *The* JEW.)

WOYZECK: The pistol costs too much.
JEW: Well, do you want it or don't you?
WOYZECK: How much is the knife?
JEW: It's good and straight. You want to cut your throat with it? Well, how about it? I'll give it to you as cheap as anybody else. Your death'll be cheap—but not for nothing. How about it? You'll have an economical death.
WOYZECK: That can cut more than just bread.
JEW: Two cents.
WOYZECK: There! *(Goes off.)*
JEW: There! Like it was nothing. But it's money! The dog.

16

(Room.)

(MARIE. KARL, *the idiot.* CHILD.)

MARIE: *(Leafs through the Bible.)* "And no guile is found in his mouth"° . . . My God! my God! Don't look at me. *(Pages further.)* "And the scribes and Pharisees brought unto him a woman taken in adultery, and set her in the midst . . . And Jesus said unto her, 'Neither do I condemn thee: go, and sin no more'"° *(Clasps her hands together.)* My God! My God, I can't. God, just give me enough strength to pray. *(The* CHILD *snuggles up to her.)* The boy is like a knife in my heart. Karl! He's sunning himself.
KARL: *(Lies on the ground and tells himself fairy tales on his fingers.)* This one has a golden crown—he's a king. Tomorrow I'll go get the queen's child. Blood sausage says, come on, liver sausage! *(He takes the* CHILD *and is quiet.)*
MARIE: Franz hasn't come, not yesterday, not today. It's getting hot in here. *(She opens the window.)* "And

---

"And no guile . . . mouth," 1 Peter 2:22. ***"And the scribes . . . more,"*** John 8:3–11.

stood at his feet weeping, and began to wash his feet with tears, and did wipe them with the hairs of her head, and kissed his feet, and anointed them with ointment."° (Beats her breast.) It's all dead! Savior, Savior, I wish I could anoint your feet!

17

(Barracks.)

(ANDRES. WOYZECK rummages through his things.)

WOYZECK: This jacket isn't part of the uniform, Andres. You can use it, Andres. The crucifix is my sister's— so's the little ring. I've got an icon, too—two hearts in beautiful gold. It was in my mother's Bible, and it says:

May pain be my reward,
Through pain I love my Lord.

Lord, like Thy body, red and sore,
So be my heart forevermore.

My mother can only feel the sun shining on her hands now. That doesn't matter.
ANDRES: (Blankly, answers to everything.) Yeah.
WOYZECK: (Pulls out a piece of paper.) Friedrich Johann Franz Woyzeck, soldier, rifleman in the second regiment, second battalion, fourth company, born on the Feast of the Annunciation. Today I'm thirty years, seven months, and twelve days old.
ANDRES: Franz, you better go to the hospital. You poor guy—drink brandy with a painkiller in it. That'll kill the fever.
WOYZECK: You know, Andres, when the carpenter nails those boards together, nobody knows who's going to be lying between them.

18

(The DOCTOR's courtyard.)

(STUDENTS below, the DOCTOR at the attic window.)

DOCTOR: Gentlemen, I am on the roof like David when he saw Bathsheba,° but all I see are panties hanging in the garden of the girls' boarding house. Gentlemen, we are dealing with the important question of the relationship of subject to object. If we take only one of the things in which the organic self-affirmation of the Divine manifests itself to such a high degree, and examine its relationship to space,

to the earth, to the planetary system . . . gentlemen, if I throw this cat out of the window, how will it relate to the centrum gravitationis° and to its own instinct? Hey, Woyzeck. (Shouts.) Woyzeck! (DOCTOR comes down.)
WOYZECK: Doctor, it bites!
DOCTOR: The fellow holds the beast so tenderly, like it was his own grandmother!
WOYZECK: Doctor, I've got the shivers.
DOCTOR: (Elated.) Say, that's wonderful, Woyzeck! (Rubs his hands. He takes the cat.) What's this, gentlemen— a new species of rabbit louse, a beautiful species. (He pulls out a magnifying glass.) Gentlemen—(The cat runs off.) gentlemen, that animal has no scientific instinct. Gentlemen, instead of that you can see something else. Take note of this man—for a quarter of a year he hasn't eaten anything but peas. Notice the result. Feel how uneven his pulse is. There—and the eyes.
WOYZECK: Doctor, everything's getting black. (He sits down.)
DOCTOR: Courage! Just a few more days, Woyzeck, and then it'll be all over. Feel him, gentlemen, feel him. (STUDENTS feel his temples, pulse, and chest.) Apropos, Woyzeck, wiggle your ears for the gentlemen. I meant to show it to you before. He uses two muscles. Come on, hop to it!
WOYZECK: Oh, Doctor!
DOCTOR: You dog, do I have to wiggle them for you? Are you going to act like the cat? This, gentlemen, represents a transition to the donkey, frequently resulting from being brought up by women and from the use of the mother tongue. How much hair has your mother pulled out for a tender memory? It's gotten very thin in the last few days. Yes, the peas, gentlemen.

19

(Street.)

(MARIE with little girls in front of the house door. GRANDMOTHER. Then WOYZECK.)

GIRLS:

How bright the sun on Candlemas Day,
On fields of golden grain.
As two by two they marched along
Down the country lane.
The pipers up in front,
The fiddlers in a chain.
Their red socks . . .

"And stood at his feet . . . ointment," Luke 7:37–38.
David when he saw Bathsheba, cf. 2 Sam. 11:2ff.

centrum gravitationis, center of gravity.

FIRST CHILD: I don't like it!
SECOND CHILD: What do you want, anyway?
THIRD CHILD: Why'd you start it?
SECOND CHILD: Yeah, why?
FIRST CHILD: Because!
SECOND CHILD: Why because?
THIRD CHILD: Who's going to sing—? *(Looks questioningly around the circle and points to the* FIRST CHILD.)
FIRST CHILD: I can't.
ALL THE CHILDREN: Marie, you sing to us.
MARIE: Come, you little crabs.

(Children's games: "Ring-around-a-rosy" and "King Herod."°)

Grandmother, tell a story.
GRANDMOTHER: Once upon a time, there was a poor little child with no father and no mother. Everything was dead, and no one was left in the whole world. Everything was dead, and the child went and cried day and night. And since nobody was left on the earth, he wanted to go up to the heavens, 'cause the moon was looking at him so friendly, and when he finally got to the moon, the moon was a piece of rotten wood, and then he went to the sun, and when he got there, the sun was a wilted sunflower, and when he got to the stars, they were little golden flies stuck up there like the shrike° sticks them on the blackthorn; and when he wanted to go back down to the earth, the earth was an upset pot, and the child was all alone, and he sat down and cried, and there he sits to this day, all alone.
WOYZECK: Marie!
MARIE: *(Startled.)* What is it?
WOYZECK: Marie, we have to go. It's time.
MARIE: Where to?
WOYZECK: How do I know?

20

(Evening. The town in the distance.)

(MARIE. WOYZECK.)

MARIE: That must be the town back there. It's dark.
WOYZECK: Stay here. Come on, sit down.
MARIE: But I have to get back.
WOYZECK: You won't get sore feet.
MARIE: What's gotten into you!
WOYZECK: Do you know how long it's been, Marie?
MARIE: Two years since Pentecost.°

"*King Herod,*" the name of the children's game or rhyme derives from the biblical figure who ordered the massacre of children (Matt. 2). **shrike,** also known as the "butcher bird" because it impales its prey on thorns. **Pentecost,** Christian festival commemorating the revelation of the Holy Spirit to the apostles.

WOYZECK: Do you know how long it's going to be?
MARIE: I've got to go make supper.
WOYZECK: Are you freezing, Marie? But you're warm. How hot your lips are! Hot—the hot breath of a whore—but I'd give heaven and earth to kiss them once more. Once you're cold, you don't freeze anymore. The morning dew won't make you freeze.
MARIE: What are you talking about?
WOYZECK: Nothing. *(Silence.)*
MARIE: Look how red the moon is.
WOYZECK: Like a bloody blade.
MARIE: What are you up to? Franz, you're so pale. *(He pulls out the knife.)* Franz—wait! For God's sake—help!
WOYZECK: Take that and that! Can't you die? There! There! Ah—she's still twitching. Not yet? Not yet? Still alive? *(Keeps on stabbing.)* Are you dead? Dead! Dead! *(People approach, he runs off.)*

21

(Two people.)

FIRST PERSON: Wait!
SECOND PERSON: You hear it? Shh! Over there!
FIRST PERSON: Ooh! There! What a sound!
SECOND PERSON: That's the water, it's calling. Nobody has drowned for a long time. Let's go. It's bad to hear things like that.
FIRST PERSON: Ooh! There it is again. Like someone dying.
SECOND PERSON: It's weird. It's so foggy—gray mist everywhere and the beetles humming like broken bells. Let's get out of here!
FIRST PERSON: No—it's too clear, too loud. Up this way. Come on.

22

(Inn.)

(WOYZECK. KATEY. KARL. INNKEEPER. *People.)*

WOYZECK: Dance, all of you, on and on. Sweat and stink. He'll get you all in the end. *(Sings.)*

Our hostess has a pretty maid,
She's in her garden night and day,
She sits inside her garden,
Until the bells have all struck twelve,
And stares at all the soldiers.

(He dances.) Come on, Katey! Sit down! I'm hot, hot. *(He takes off his jacket.)* That's the way it is: the devil takes one and lets the other go. Katey, you're hot! Why? Katey, you'll be cold someday, too. Be reasonable. Can't you sing something?
KATEY: *(Sings.)*

For Swabian hills I do not yearn,
And flowing gowns I always spurn,
For flowing gowns and pointed shoes
A servant girl should never choose.

WOYZECK: No, no shoes. You can go to hell without shoes, too.
KATEY: *(Dances.)*

For shame, my love, I'm not your own,
Just keep your money and sleep alone.

WOYZECK: Yes, you're right! I don't want to make myself bloody.
KATEY: But what's that on your hand?
WOYZECK: Who? Me?
KATEY: Red . . . blood! *(People gather around.)*
WOYZECK: Blood? Blood.
INNKEEPER: Ooh. Blood.
WOYZECK: I guess I must have cut myself on my right hand.
INNKEEPER: But how'd it get on your elbow?
WOYZECK: I wiped it off.
INNKEEPER: What! With your right hand on your right elbow? You're talented.
KARL: And then the giant said: I smell, I smell, I smell human flesh. Phew! That stinks already.
WOYZECK: Damn it, what do you want? What do you care? Get away, or the first one who . . . God damn it! You think I killed someone? Am I a murderer? What are you staring at? Look at yourselves! Out of my way! *(He runs out.)*

23

(Night. The town in the distance.)

(WOYZECK alone.)

WOYZECK: The knife? Where's the knife? Here's where I left it. It'll give me away! Closer, still closer! What kind of a place is this? What's that I hear? Something's moving. Shh! Over there. Marie? Ah— Marie! Quiet. Everything's quiet! You're so pale, Marie. Why is that red thread around your neck? Who helped you earn that for your sins? They made you black, black! Now I've made you white. Your black hair looks so wild. Didn't you do your braids today? Something's lying over there! Cold, wet, still. Got to get away from here. The knife, the knife—is that it? There! People—over there. *(He runs off.)*

24

(WOYZECK at a pond.)

WOYZECK: Down it goes! *(He throws the knife in.)* It sinks like a stone in the dark water. The moon is like a bloody blade. Is the whole world going to give me away? No—it's too far in front—when people go swimming—*(He goes into the pond and throws it far out.)* All right, now—but in the summer, when they go diving for shells . . . Oh, it'll rust. Who'll recognize it? I wish I'd smashed it! Am I still bloody? I better wash myself. There's a spot—and there's another.°

25

(Street.)

(Children.)

FIRST CHILD: Come on! Marie!
SECOND CHILD: What's wrong?
FIRST CHILD: Don't you know? Everybody's gone out there already. Someone's lying there!
SECOND CHILD: Where?
FIRST CHILD: To the left through the forest, near that red cross.
SECOND CHILD: Let's go, so we can still see something. Otherwise they'll carry her away.

26

(COURT CLERK, DOCTOR, JUDGE.)

CLERK: A good murder, a real murder, a beautiful murder. As good a murder as you'd ever want to see. We haven't had one like this for a long time.

27

(KARL. The CHILD. WOYZECK.)

KARL: *(Holds the CHILD on his lap.)* He fell in the water, he fell in the water, he fell in the water.
WOYZECK: Son—Christian!
KARL: *(Stares at him.)* He fell in the water.
WOYZECK: *(Wants to caress the CHILD, who turns away and screams.)* My God!
KARL: He fell in the water.
WOYZECK: Christian, you'll get a horsey. Da-da! *(The CHILD resists. To KARL.)* Here, go buy the boy a horsey.
KARL: *(Stares at him.)*
WOYZECK: Hop-hop! Horsey!
KARL: *(Cheers.)* Hop-hop! Horsey! Horsey! *(Runs off with the CHILD.)*

(WOYZECK remains, alone.)

There's a spot . . . another, cf. *Macbeth* 5.1.

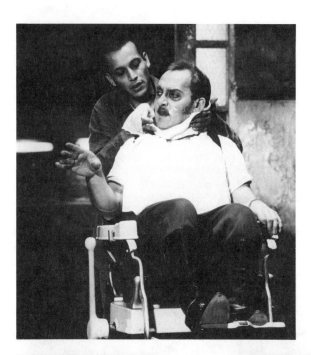

Figure 1. Woyzeck (Jesse Borrego) shaves the Captain (Zach Grenier) in the 1992 New York Shakespeare Festival production, directed by JoAnne Akalaitis. (Photograph: Martha Swope.)

Figure 2. The townspeople stare at Woyzeck (Jesse Borrego) after the murder of Marie in the 1992 New York Shakespeare Festival production, directed by JoAnne Akalaitis. (Photograph: Martha Swope.)

Figure 3. The murder of Marie (Sheila Tousey) takes place in slow motion, focusing attention on Woyzeck's (Jesse Borrego) upraised hand and Marie's attempt to stop the knife's descent in the 1992 New York Shakespeare Festival production, directed by JoAnne Akalaitis. (Photograph: Martha Swope).

Staging of *Woyzeck*

REVIEW OF THE NEW YORK SHAKESPEARE FESTIVAL PRODUCTION, 1992, BY MEL GUSSOW

The title character in "Woyzeck" is, we are told, "running around like an open razor blade." The image, in common with the play itself, is as precise as it is terrifying. Woyzeck, a military barber and the most ordinary of common men, is overcome by dementia. He hears strange sounds, sees visions and is driven to a desperate act of murder. Along with "Danton's Death," the play certified Georg Büchner's reputation as the first modern playwright. Written in the 1830's and discovered as fragments after the author's death, the work foreshadowed explorations by Kafka, Brecht and Beckett. The modernism of Büchner is basic to JoAnne Akalaitis's compelling production of the Joseph Papp Public Theater in New York.

Because of the nonlinear style and the focus on an irrational antihero, the play is open to free-handed interpretation. In search of "Woyzeck," Ms. Akalaitis uses alternate scenes and extracts from early drafts of the play, filtering Henry J. Schmidt's translation through her fervid theatrical imagination. The difficulty this director has had in dealing with Shakespeare is not in evidence in her treatment of Büchner.

In the reordering of scenes the play gains in momentum, accruing intensity and psychological awareness as Woyzeck moves through the last stages of his calamitous life. The director has given greater centricity to the role of Marie, Woyzeck's common-law wife and the object of his homicidal impulse. But of course this is still Woyzeck's tragedy, as he is crushed by people and events beyond his control.

Ms. Akalaitis has accentuated the folk elements within the play, crucial to Büchner, for whom this was a ballad-like dramatization of an actual occurrence. Philip Glass's sizzling music is often paired with folk-style lyrics by Paul Schmidt, and martial clog dancing adds to the ritualistic background.

In contrast to the stark simplicity of Richard Foreman's version of the play several seasons ago at Hartford Stage, Ms. Akalaitis's approach has a visual richness. The productions are equally valid but they are so dissimilar in concept that they could be staged together in repertory. Naturally they share the same themes, characters and impact.

Ms. Akalaitis takes a cue from her own early work as a director and playwright with Mabou Mines, in terms of using imagery to enhance a text, as she did in "Dressed Like an Egg," her lush collage of the life of Colette. With "Woyzeck," she seems to be influenced by German Expressionist art. In scene after scene there are striking stage pictures of people caught in a frenzy or in a moment of aggrieved anticipation.

The military barracks that is the central environment of the play would need no conversion to become a concentration camp. As designed by Marina Draghici, who did the impressive settings for Caryl Churchill's "Mad Forest," the scenery simulates all the coldness and malevolence of a life in confinement. The bare plastered walls and streaked windows, evocatively lighted by Mimi Jordan Sherin, are like conjurations of the paintings of Anselm Kiefer.

Woyzeck (Jesse Borrego) tears across the stage in a fever. In his rag uniform and with a haunted look in his deep-set eyes, Mr. Borrego resembles a prisoner of Dachau suddenly released and brought into a blinding light. Repeatedly he is transfixed like an apparition in a nightmare.

Shaving his captain (Zach Grenier), Woyzeck strops his razor for so long that it seems as if he is sharpening his blade for slaughter. The autocratic officer flinches as the barber approaches his chair; still he never stops badgering his subordinate. Wherever Woyzeck turns, he is besieged, even, as it turns out, in his home, up to then his single sanctuary. In response, he tries to outrun his demons.

In those moments when things stand still, velocity is replaced by what could be called frieze frames. Townspeople sit in a line as in a pew and a grandmother tells the bleakest and most Büchnerian of fairy tales: "Once upon a time there was a poor child with no father and no mother; everything was dead, and no one was left in the whole world."

Ms. Akalaitis uses her painterly eye to illuminate motifs, but along the way there are a few questionable directorial choices. The production begins awkwardly with a film clip of Mr. Borrego climbing rocks. This is apparently a scene from Ms. Akalaitis's adaptation of other Büchner works, which she entitled "Leon and Lena (Lenz)," and presented at the Guthrie Theater. The film has no direct bearing on the play we are seeing. The carnival sequence is surprisingly mundane and a scene of soldiers showering detracts from a later, symbolic moment when Woyzeck tries to wash away his bloody deed.

Furthermore, some of the acting lacks resilience, even allowing for the fact that those characters who have no names, like the drum major, are intended to be emblematic. But the production is anchored by the actors in the three most important roles: the commandingly imperious Mr. Grenier as the captain, Sheila Tousey as Marie and Mr. Borrego, who grasps the tortured essence of Woyzeck.

When he turns against Marie, who has been his only source of stability, he attacks her as if she were the incarnation of everything that had been bedeviling him. The scene is staged with ferocity: the victim is helpless, the murderer uncontrollable. Around the time he was creating "Woyzeck," Büchner wrote a letter to his parents in which he commented on German militarism and what he considered to be the brute force of the law. He asked, "Aren't we in an eternal state of violence?" That question and its accompanying cry for help are searingly captured by the playwright and by Ms. Akalaitis as his contemporary interpreter.

HENRIK IBSEN

1828–1906

When Ibsen was born, his father was a prosperous merchant in Skien, a small town in the southeastern part of Norway, but by the time Ibsen was eight his father had gone bankrupt and the family was compelled to leave its spacious home for quarters in an attic apartment filled with the abandoned possessions of a previous tenant. Ibsen never forgot that painful reversal of fortune. In fact, he recorded its details in an unfinished autobiography that he began in 1881. That early exposure to human suffering was to leave its mark on many of his plays, not in any specific autobiographical sense, but in a general concern with the economic, social, and psychological conditions that afflict the lives of ordinary men and women.

During his early dramatic career, from 1851 to 1867, when he was still influenced by the style and subject matter of romantic theater, Ibsen wrote a series of plays in blank verse, most of them based on Norwegian myth and history. Yet even in these works, particularly *Brand* (1866) and *Peer Gynt* (1867), Ibsen revealed a concern with moral and social issues that was to characterize his later plays. In Brand he created a protagonist so single-mindedly committed to his religious ministry that he sacrifices first his child, then his wife, and ultimately himself to the fulfillment of his mission; then in the character of Peer Gynt, the demonic antithesis of Brand, he created a protagonist so committed to his own selfish desires that he devotes his life to a series of fanatically deceitful adventures with which he deceives even himself, until at the moment of his death he discovers his irredeemable hollowness. Although *Brand* and *Peer Gynt* made Ibsen famous and financially secure, they were the last works he was to write in the tradition of romantic drama.

Beginning with *The League of Youth* (1869), a play that attacked the hypocrisy of provincial politics and politicians, Ibsen turned from history, myth, and folklore to contemporary social problems, from romantic idealism to realistic drama, from verse to prose. In *The Pillars of Society* (1877), he continued his iconoclastic aims by exposing the disreputable behavior of a socially respectable businessman and by reforming him through the agency of a socially liberated woman. Having attacked business and politics, he then went after the most sacred of all social institutions—marriage—by making the heroine of this next play, *A Doll's House* (1879), a young wife who gradually becomes aware that she has been turned into a helpless child by her husband, whom she abandons after discovering that he is an emotional hypocrite. Ibsen's audience was shocked by the ending of *A Doll's House,* but he was unrelenting in his attack and answered their outrage with *Ghosts* (1881), whose heroine heeds the advice of her minister to remain with her husband and, therefore, must spend the rest of her life concealing her own feelings and the truth about her husband's dissolute behavior. Ibsen's frank treatment of syphilis in *Ghosts,* and his implicit attack on Norwegian social and religious values, roused even stronger criticism than *A Doll's House.* It is not surprising that Ibsen's next play, *An Enemy of the People*

(1882), dealt with the difficulty of being the outsider who brings unpleasant truths to the attention of the community. Then, in a startling reversal, Ibsen made the truth bringer in *The Wild Duck* (1884) a morally ambiguous figure, so intent on forcing long-hid secrets into the open that he destroys an entire family. In his late, symbolic plays, particularly *Rosmersholm* (1886), *Hedda Gabler* (1890), and *The Master Builder* (1892), Ibsen moved away from his concern with social problems into a psychological exploration of emotionally and sexually driven individuals who become entangled in self-destructive personal relationships.

This body of plays quickly earned Ibsen the reputation of a fighting social realist—a description applied to him by his Anglo-Irish contemporary, George Bernard Shaw, in *The Quintessence of Ibsenism* (1891). And from his own time to this day, many of Ibsen's prose plays have been interpreted primarily as pieces of social criticism. *A Doll's House,* for example, is frequently celebrated nowadays as an attack on male chauvinism and an affirmation of womens' rights. And there is much about the relationship of Torvald and Nora that supports this interpretation, not the least of which is his nearly total subjugation and humiliation of her—his conception of her as his "little songbird" and "doll"—as well as her final rejection of his belief that "First and foremost, you're a wife and a mother," and her consequent decision "to think things out for myself and try to find my own answer." Yet it is also important to recognize that *A Doll's House,* like Ibsen's other prose plays, is first and foremost a psychologically realistic work about a human being in an ordinary world who slowly and painfully comes to an extraordinary understanding about the importance of personal integrity in human affairs. That special understanding leads Nora to assert that "I am first and foremost a human being." And that belief leads her at last to leave Torvald not because he has subjugated her, but because he has profoundly disappointed her by valuing his material welfare and social status more highly than her human love. So it is that she is moved to tell Torvald "you neither think nor talk like the man I could share my life with." The implication of these remarks seems to be that she could have forgiven him everything had he finally been true to her hopeful vision of him. Her departure, then, might well be seen as the logical consequence of her shattered illusions about Torvald, rather than an assertion of her woman's rights.

Ibsen himself may well have meant to show both Nora and Torvald as being imprisoned in their relationship, even though for years the play has been read as his plea for female emancipation. Ibsen explicitly disclaimed a feminist interpretation of the play several years after its production, when speaking to a meeting of the Norwegian Association for Women's Rights: "I must decline the honor of being said to have worked for the Women's Rights movement. I am not even very sure what Women's Rights are. To me it has been a question of human rights." Given Ibsen's disclaimer, the play might well be interpreted as a skillfully constructed piece that begins as a suspense story (Will Nora be able to keep Torvald from learning her guilty secret?), but develops into a painfully probing exposure of a human relationship based on misunderstanding and lack of communication, a relationship that denies both individuals their human rights. As Nora accurately observes near the end, "In eight whole years—longer even—ever since we first met, we've never exchanged a serious word on any serious thing." The problem of the play, in this sense, appears to be less an issue of Nora's rights than the issue of what a marriage must be if it is to achieve the "miracle of miracles"—a true and lasting relationship that allows both partners their human rights.

Just the same, readers and spectators may find themselves troubled by the plausibility of Nora's transformation from a naive young wife into a resolutely independent human being—from someone who at the beginning of the play is given over to relishing her macaroons, begging money from Torvald, and flirting with Dr. Rank into someone who at the end is able to abandon all of these comfortable pleasures, as well as her children, without having any "idea what will happen to me." This transformation provides a major problem for any actress who plays the role of Nora, as Walter Kerr noted in his review of the 1971 production starring Claire Bloom: "How does one turn an enchanting child into a dominating adult, especially when the transition is missing?" To do so, as Kerr makes clear in his review, evidently requires an actress to convey more than mere childishness in the beginning, even as it requires her to convey something other than mere domination at the end. And photographs of Claire Bloom performing the role of Nora show that in the beginning of the play she did suggest a degree of thoughtful reservation far exceeding that of a child (see Figure 1), much as at the end of the play she expressed a sense of painful awareness and resoluteness not to be expected of a merely dominating adult (see Figures 2 and 3). In her facial expression, as in the austere clothing she wears during the final scene, Claire Bloom portrays Nora as someone who is clearly aware that in slamming the door on Torvald she has relinquished a set of emotional ties that still tug at her without any clear sense of what will become of her.

A DOLL'S HOUSE

BY HENRIK IBSEN / TRANSLATED BY MICHAEL MEYER

CHARACTERS

TORVALD HELMER, *a lawyer*
NORA, *his wife*
DR. RANK
MRS. LINDE
NILS KROGSTAD, *also a lawyer*
The HELMERS' *three small children*

ANNE-MARIE, *their nurse*
HELEN, *the maid*
A PORTER

SCENE

The action takes place in the Helmers' apartment.

ACT 1

(A comfortably and tastefully, but not expensively furnished room. Backstage right a door leads out to the hall; backstage left, another door to HELMER's study. Between these two doors stands a piano. In the middle of the left-hand wall is a door, with a window downstage of it. Near the window, a round table with armchairs and a small sofa. In the right-hand wall, slightly upstage, is a door; downstage of this, against the same wall, a stove lined with porcelain tiles, with a couple of armchairs and a rocking-chair in front of it. Between the stove and the side door is a small table. Engravings on the wall. A what-not with china and other bric-a-brac; a small bookcase with leather-bound books. A carpet on the floor; a fire in the stove. A winter day.

A bell rings in the hall outside. After a moment, we hear the front door being opened. NORA *enters the room, humming contentedly to herself. She is wearing outdoor clothes and carrying a lot of parcels, which she puts down on the table right. She leaves the door to the hall open; through it, we can see a* PORTER *carrying a Christmas tree and a basket. He gives these to the* MAID, *who has opened the door for them.)*

NORA: Hide that Christmas tree away, Helen. The children mustn't see it before I've decorated it this evening. *(to the* PORTER, *taking out her purse)* How much—?

PORTER: A shilling.

NORA: Here's half a crown. No, keep it.

(The PORTER *touches his cap and goes.* NORA *closes the door. She continues to laugh happily to herself as she removes her coat, etc. She takes from her pocket a bag containing macaroons and eats a couple. Then she tiptoes across and listens at her husband's door.)*

NORA: Yes, he's here. *(Starts humming again as she goes over to the table, right.)*

HELMER *(from his room)*: Is that my skylark twittering out there?

NORA *(opening some of the parcels)*: It is!

HELMER: Is that my squirrel rustling?

NORA: Yes!

HELMER: When did my squirrel come home?

NORA: Just now. *(Pops the bag of macaroons in her pocket and wipes her mouth.)* Come out here, Torvald, and see what I've bought.

HELMER: You mustn't disturb me! *(Short pause, then he opens the door and looks in, his pen in his hand.)* Bought, did you say? All that? Has my little squanderbird been overspending again?

NORA: Oh, Torvald, surely we can let ourselves go a little this year! It's the first Christmas we don't have to scrape.

HELMER: Well, you know, we can't afford to be extravagant.

NORA: Oh yes, Torvald, we can be a little extravagant now. Can't we? Just a tiny bit? You've got a big salary now, and you're going to make lots and lots of money.

HELMER: Next year, yes. But my new salary doesn't start till April.

NORA: Pooh; we can borrow till then.

HELMER: Nora! *(Goes over to her and takes her playfully by the ear.)* What a little spendthrift you are! Suppose I were to borrow fifty pounds today, and you spent it all over Christmas, and then on New Year's Eve a tile fell off a roof on to my head—

NORA *(puts her hand over his mouth)*: Oh, Torvald! Don't say such dreadful things!

HELMER: Yes, but suppose something like that did happen? What then?

NORA: If anything as frightful as that happened, it wouldn't make much difference whether I was in debt or not.

HELMER: But what about the people I'd borrowed from?

NORA: Them? Who cares about them? They're strangers.

HELMER: Oh, Nora, Nora, how like a woman! No, but seriously, Nora, you know how I feel about this. No debts! Never borrow! A home that is founded on debts can never be a place of freedom and beauty. We two have stuck it out bravely up to now; and we shall continue to do so for the short time we still have to.

NORA *(goes over toward the stove)*: Very well, Torvald. As you say.

HELMER *(follows her)*: Now, now! My little songbird mustn't droop her wings. What's this? Is little squirrel sulking? *(Takes out his purse.)* Nora; guess what I've got here!

NORA *(turns quickly)*: Money!

HELMER: Look. *(Hands her some banknotes.)* I know how these small expenses crop up at Christmas.

NORA *(counts them)*: One—two—three—four. Oh, thank you, Torvald, thank you! I should be able to manage with this.

HELMER: You'll have to.

NORA: Yes, yes, of course I will. But come over here, I want to show you everything I've bought. And so cheaply! Look, here are new clothes for Ivar—and a sword. And a horse and a trumpet for Bob. And a doll and a cradle for Emmy—they're nothing much, but she'll pull them apart in a few days. And some bits of material and handkerchiefs for the maids. Old Anne-Marie ought to have had something better, really.

HELMER: And what's in that parcel?

NORA *(cries)*: No, Torvald, you mustn't see that before this evening!

HELMER: Very well. But now, tell me, you little spendthrift, what do you want for Christmas?

NORA: Me? Oh, pooh, I don't want anything.

HELMER: Oh, yes, you do. Now tell me, what, within reason, would you most like?

NORA: No, I really don't know. Oh, yes—Torvald—!

HELMER: Well?

NORA *(plays with his coat-buttons, not looking at him)*: If you really want to give me something, you could—you could—

HELMER: Come on, out with it.

NORA *(quickly)*: You could give me money, Torvald. Only as much as you feel you can afford; then later I'll buy something with it.

HELMER: But, Nora—

NORA: Oh yes, Torvald dear, please! Please! Then I'll wrap up the notes in pretty gold paper and hang them on the Christmas tree. Wouldn't that be fun?

HELMER: What's the name of that little bird that can never keep any money?

NORA: Yes, yes, squanderbird; I know. But let's do as I say, Torvald; then I'll have time to think about what I need most. Isn't that the best way? Mm?

HELMER *(smiles)*: To be sure it would be, if you could keep what I gave you and really buy yourself something with it. But you'll spend it on all sorts of useless things for the house, and then I'll have to put my hand in my pocket again.

NORA: Oh, but Torvald—

HELMER: You can't deny it, Nora dear. *(Puts his arm round her waist.)* The squanderbird's a pretty little creature, but she gets through an awful lot of money. It's incredible what an expensive pet she is for a man to keep.

NORA: For shame! How can you say such a thing? I save every penny I can.

HELMER *(laughs)*: That's quite true. Every penny you can. But you can't.

NORA *(hums and smiles, quietly gleeful)*: Hm. If you only knew how many expenses we larks and squirrels have, Torvald.

HELMER: You're a funny little creature. Just like your father used to be. Always on the look-out for some way to get money, but as soon as you have any it just runs through your fingers, and you never know where it's gone. Well, I suppose I must take you as you are. It's in your blood. Yes, yes, yes, these things are hereditary, Nora.

NORA: Oh, I wish I'd inherited more of Papa's qualities.

HELMER: And I wouldn't wish my darling little songbird to be any different from what she is. By the way, that reminds me. You look awfully—how shall I put it?—awfully guilty today.

NORA: Do I—

HELMER: Yes, you do. Look me in the eyes.

NORA *(looks at him)*: Well?

HELMER *(wags his finger)*: Has my little sweet-tooth been indulging herself in town today, by any chance?

NORA: No, how can you think of such a thing?

HELMER: Not a tiny little digression into a pastry shop?

NORA: No, Torvald, I promise—

HELMER: Not just a wee jam tart?

NORA: Certainly not.

HELMER: Not a little nibble at a macaroon?

NORA: No, Torvald—I promise you, honestly—

HELMER: There, there. I was only joking.

NORA *(goes over to the table, right)*: You know I could never act against your wishes.

HELMER: Of course not. And you've given me your word—*(Goes over to her.)* Well, my beloved Nora, you keep your little Christmas secrets to yourself. They'll be revealed this evening, I've no doubt, once the Christmas tree has been lit.

NORA: Have you remembered to invite Dr. Rank?

HELMER: No. But there's no need; he knows he'll be dining with us. Anyway, I'll ask him when he comes this morning. I've ordered some good wine. Oh, Nora, you can't imagine how I'm looking forward to this evening.

NORA: So am I. And, Torvald, how the children will love it!

HELMER: Yes, it's a wonderful thing to know that one's position is assured and that one has an

ample income. Don't you agree? It's good to
know that, isn't it?

NORA: Yes, it's almost like a miracle.

HELMER: Do you remember last Christmas? For three
whole weeks you shut yourself away every evening to make flowers for the Christmas tree, and
all those other things you were going to surprise
us with. Ugh, it was the most boring time I've
ever had in my life.

NORA: I didn't find it boring.

HELMER *(smiles)*: But it all came to nothing in the end,
didn't it?

NORA: Oh, are you going to bring that up again? How
could I help the cat getting in and tearing
everything to bits?

HELMER: No, my poor little Nora, of course you
couldn't. You simply wanted to make us happy,
and that's all that matters. But it's good that
those hard times are past.

NORA: Yes, it's wonderful.

HELMER: I don't have to sit by myself and be bored.
And you don't have to tire your pretty eyes and
your delicate little hands—

NORA *(claps her hands)*: No, Torvald, that's true, isn't
it—I don't have to any longer? Oh, it's really all
just like a miracle. *(Takes his arm.)* Now, I'm going
to tell you what I thought we might do, Torvald.
As soon as Christmas is over—*(A bell rings in the
hall.)* Oh, there's the doorbell. *(Tidies up one or two
things in the room.)* Someone's coming. What a
bore.

HELMER: I'm not at home to any visitors. Remember!

MAID *(in the doorway)*: A lady's called, madam. A
stranger.

NORA: Well, ask her to come in.

MAID: And the doctor's here too, sir.

HELMER: Has he gone to my room?

MAID: Yes, sir.

*(HELMER goes into his room. The MAID shows in MRS.
LINDE, who is dressed in travelling clothes, and closes the
door.)*

MRS. LINDE *(shyly and a little hesitantly)*: Good evening,
Nora.

NORA *(uncertainly)*: Good evening—

MRS. LINDE: I don't suppose you recognize me.

NORA: No, I'm afraid I— Yes, wait a minute—
surely—*(Exclaims.)* Why, Christine! Is it really
you?

MRS. LINDE: Yes, it's me.

NORA: Christine! And I didn't recognize you! But
how could I—? *(More quietly.)* How you've
changed, Christine!

MRS. LINDE: Yes, I know. It's been nine years—nearly
ten—

NORA: Is it so long? Yes, it must be. Oh, these last
eight years have been such a happy time for me!

So you've come to town? All that way in winter!
How brave of you!

MRS. LINDE: I arrived by the steamer this morning.

NORA: Yes, of course—to enjoy yourself over Christmas. Oh, how splendid! We'll have to celebrate!
But take off your coat. You're not cold, are you?
(Helps her off with it.) There! Now let's sit down
here by the stove and be comfortable. No, you
take the armchair. I'll sit here in the rocking-
chair. *(Clasps MRS. LINDE's hands.)* Yes, now you
look like your old self. It was just at first that—
you've got a little paler, though, Christine. And
perhaps a bit thinner.

MRS. LINDE: And older, Nora. Much, much older.

NORA: Yes, perhaps a little older. Just a tiny bit. Not
much. *(Checks herself suddenly and says earnestly.)*
Oh, but how thoughtless of me to sit here and
chatter away like this! Dear, sweet Christine, can
you forgive me?

MRS. LINDE: What do you mean, Nora?

NORA *(quietly)*: Poor Christine, you've become a
widow.

MRS. LINDE: Yes. Three years ago.

NORA: I know, I know—I read it in the papers. Oh,
Christine, I meant to write to you so often,
honestly. But I always put it off, and something
else always cropped up.

MRS. LINDE: I understand, Nora dear.

NORA: No, Christine, it was beastly of me. Oh, my
poor darling, what you've gone through! And he
didn't leave you anything?

MRS. LINDE: No.

NORA: No children, either?

MRS. LINDE: No.

NORA: Nothing at all, then?

MRS. LINDE: Not even a feeling of loss or sorrow.

NORA *(looks incredulously at her)*: But, Christine, how is
that possible?

MRS. LINDE *(smiles sadly and strokes NORA's hair)*: Oh,
these things happen, Nora.

NORA: All alone. How dreadful that must be for you.
I've three lovely children. I'm afraid you can't
see them now, because they're out with nanny.
But you must tell me everything—

MRS. LINDE: No, no, no. I want to hear about you.

NORA: No, you start. I'm not going to be selfish today.
I'm just going to think about you. Oh, but there's
one thing I *must* tell you. Have you heard of the
wonderful luck we've just had?

MRS. LINDE: No. What?

NORA: Would you believe it—my husband's just been
made manager of the bank!

MRS. LINDE: Your husband? Oh, how lucky—!

NORA: Yes, isn't it? Being a lawyer is so uncertain, you
know, especially if one isn't prepared to touch
any case that isn't—well—quite nice. And of
course Torvald's been very firm about that—and

I'm absolutely with him. Oh, you can imagine how happy we are! He's joining the bank in the New Year, and he'll be getting a big salary, and lots of percentages too. From now on we'll be able to live quite differently—we'll be able to do whatever we want. Oh, Christine, it's such a relief! I feel so happy! Well, I mean, it's lovely to have heaps of money and not to have to worry about anything. Don't you think?

MRS. LINDE: It must be lovely to have enough to cover one's needs, anyway.

NORA: Not just our needs! We're going to have heaps and heaps of money!

MRS. LINDE (smiles): Nora, Nora, haven't you grown up yet? When we were at school you were a terrible little spendthrift.

NORA (laughs quietly): Yes, Torvald still says that. (Wags her finger.) But "Nora, Nora" isn't as silly as you think. Oh, we've been in no position for me to waste money. We've both had to work.

MRS. LINDE: You too?

NORA: Yes, little things—fancy work, crocheting, embroidery and so forth. (Casually.) And other things too. I suppose you know Torvald left the Ministry when we got married? There were no prospects for promotion in his department, and of course he needed more money. But the first year he overworked himself quite dreadfully. He had to take on all sorts of extra jobs, and worked day and night. But it was too much for him, and he became frightfully ill. The doctors said he'd have to go to a warmer climate.

MRS. LINDE: Yes, you spent a whole year in Italy, didn't you?

NORA: Yes. It wasn't easy for me to get away, you know. I'd just had Ivar. But of course we had to do it. Oh, it was a marvelous trip! And it saved Torvald's life. But it cost an awful lot of money, Christine.

MRS. LINDE: I can imagine.

NORA: Two hundred and fifty pounds. That's a lot of money, you know.

MRS. LINDE: How lucky you had it.

NORA: Well, actually, we got it from my father.

MRS. LINDE: Oh, I see. Didn't he die just about that time?

NORA: Yes, Christine, just about then. Wasn't it dreadful, I couldn't go and look after him. I was expecting little Ivar any day. And then I had my poor Torvald to care for—we really didn't think he'd live. Dear, kind Papa! I never saw him again, Christine. Oh, it's the saddest thing that's happened to me since I got married.

MRS. LINDE: I know you were very fond of him. But you went to Italy—?

NORA: Yes. Well, we had the money, you see, and the doctors said we mustn't delay. So we went the month after Papa died.

MRS. LINDE: And your husband came back completely cured?

NORA: Fit as a fiddle!

MRS. LINDE: But—the doctor?

NORA: How do you mean?

MRS. LINDE: I thought the maid said that the gentleman who arrived with me was the doctor.

NORA: Oh yes, that's Doctor Rank, but he doesn't come because anyone's ill. He's our best friend, and he looks us up at least once every day. No, Torvald hasn't had a moment's illness since we went away. And the children are fit and healthy and so am I. (Jumps up and claps her hands.) Oh God, oh God, Christine, isn't it a wonderful thing to be alive and happy! Oh, but how beastly of me! I'm only talking about myself. (Sits on a footstool and rests her arms on MRS. LINDE's knee.) Oh, please don't be angry with me! Tell me, is it really true you didn't love your husband? Why did you marry him, then?

MRS. LINDE: Well, my mother was still alive; and she was helpless and bedridden. And I had my two little brothers to take care of. I didn't feel I could say no.

NORA: Yes, well, perhaps you're right. He was rich then, was he?

MRS. LINDE: Quite comfortably off, I believe. But his business was unsound, you see, Nora. When he died it went bankrupt, and there was nothing left.

NORA: What did you do?

MRS. LINDE: Well, I had to try to make ends meet somehow, so I started a little shop, and a little school, and anything else I could turn my hand to. These last three years have been just one endless slog for me, without a moment's rest. But now it's over, Nora. My poor dear mother doesn't need me any more; she's passed away. And the boys don't need me either; they've got jobs now and can look after themselves.

NORA: How relieved you must feel—

MRS. LINDE: No, Nora. Just unspeakably empty. No one to live for any more. (Gets up restlessly.) That's why I couldn't bear to stay out there any longer, cut off from the world. I thought it'd be easier to find some work here that will exercise and occupy my mind. If only I could get a regular job—office work of some kind—

NORA: Oh but, Christine, that's dreadfully exhausting; and you look practically finished already. It'd be much better for you if you could go away somewhere.

MRS. LINDE (goes over to the window): I have no Papa to pay for my holidays, Nora.

NORA (gets up): Oh, please don't be angry with me.

MRS. LINDE: My dear Nora, it's I who should ask you

not to be angry. That's the worst thing about this kind of situation—it makes one so bitter. One has no one to work for; and yet one has to be continually sponging for jobs. One has to live; and so one becomes completely egocentric. When you told me about this luck you've just had with Torvald's new job—can you imagine?—I was happy not so much on your account, as on my own.

NORA: How do you mean? Oh, I understand. You mean Torvald might be able to do something for you?

MRS. LINDE: Yes, I was thinking that.

NORA: He will too, Christine. Just you leave it to me. I'll lead up to it so delicately, so delicately; I'll get him in the right mood. Oh, Christine, I do so want to help you.

MRS. LINDE: It's sweet of you to bother so much about me, Nora. Especially since you know so little of the worries and hardships of life.

NORA: You say *I* know little of—?

MRS. LINDE (*smiles*): Well, good heavens—those bits of fancy work of yours—well, really—! You're a child, Nora.

NORA (*tosses her head and walks across the room*): You shouldn't say that so patronizingly.

MRS. LINDE: Oh?

NORA: You're like the rest. You all think I'm incapable of getting down to anything serious—

MRS. LINDE: My dear—

NORA: You think I've never had any worries like the rest of you.

MRS. LINDE: Nora dear, you've just told me about all your difficulties—

NORA: Pooh—that! (*Quietly.*) I haven't told you about the big thing.

MRS. LINDE: What big thing? What do you mean?

NORA: You patronize me, Christine; but you shouldn't. You're proud that you've worked so long and so hard for your mother.

MRS. LINDE: I don't patronize anyone, Nora. But you're right—I am both proud and happy that I was able to make my mother's last months on earth comparatively easy.

NORA: And you're also proud at what you've done for your brothers.

MRS. LINDE: I think I have a right to be.

NORA: I think so too. But let me tell you something, Christine. I too have done something to be proud and happy about.

MRS. LINDE: I don't doubt it. But—how do you mean?

NORA: Speak quietly! Suppose Torvald should hear! He mustn't, at any price—no one must know, Christine—no one but you.

MRS. LINDE: But what is this?

NORA: Come over here. (*Pulls her down on to the sofa beside her.*) Yes, Christine—I too have done something to be happy and proud about. It was I who saved Torvald's life.

MRS. LINDE: Saved his—? How did you save it?

NORA: I told you about our trip to Italy. Torvald couldn't have lived if he hadn't managed to get down there—

MRS. LINDE: Yes, well—your father provided the money—

NORA (*smiles*): So Torvald and everyone else thinks. But—

MRS. LINDE: Yes?

NORA: Papa didn't give us a penny. It was I who found the money.

MRS. LINDE: You? All of it?

NORA: Two hundred and fifty pounds. What do you say to that?

MRS. LINDE: But Nora, how could you? Did you win a lottery or something?

NORA (*scornfully*): Lottery? (*Sniffs.*) What would there be to be proud of in that?

MRS. LINDE: But where did you get it from, then?

NORA (*hums and smiles secretively*): Hm; tra-la-la-la!

MRS. LINDE: You couldn't have borrowed it.

NORA: Oh? Why not?

MRS. LINDE: Well, a wife can't borrow money without her husband's consent.

NORA (*tosses her head*): Ah, but when a wife has a little business sense, and knows how to be clever—

MRS. LINDE: But Nora, I simply don't understand—

NORA: You don't have to. No one has said I borrowed the money. I could have got it in some other way. (*Throws herself back on the sofa.*) I could have got it from an admirer. When a girl's as pretty as I am—

MRS. LINDE: Nora, you're crazy!

NORA: You're dying of curiosity now, aren't you, Christine?

MRS. LINDE: Nora, dear, you haven't done anything foolish?

NORA (*sits up again*): Is it foolish to save one's husband's life?

MRS. LINDE: I think it's foolish if without his knowledge you—

NORA: But the whole point was that he mustn't know! Great heavens, don't you see? He hadn't to know how dangerously ill he was. I was the one they told that his life was in danger and that only going to a warm climate could save him. Do you suppose I didn't try to think of other ways of getting him down there? I told him how wonderful it would be for me to go abroad like other young wives: I cried and prayed; I asked him to remember my condition, and said he ought to be nice and tender to me; and then I suggested he might quite easily borrow the money. But then he got almost angry with me, Christine. He said I was frivolous, and that it was his duty as a husband not to pander to my moods and caprices—I think that's what he called them. Well, well, I thought, you've got to be saved somehow. And then I thought of a way—

MRS. LINDE: But didn't your husband find out from your father that the money hadn't come from him?

NORA: No, never. Papa died just then. I'd thought of letting him into the plot and asking him not to tell. But since he was so ill—! And as things turned out, it didn't become necessary.

MRS. LINDE: And you've never told your husband about this?

NORA: For heaven's sake, no! What an idea! He's frightfully strict about such matters. And besides—he's so proud of being a *man*—it'd be so painful and humiliating for him to know that he owed anything to me. It'd completely wreck our relationship. This life we have built together would no longer exist.

MRS. LINDE: Will you never tell him?

NORA (*thoughtfully, half-smiling*): Yes—some time, perhaps. Years from now, when I'm no longer pretty. You mustn't laugh! I mean of course, when Torvald no longer loves me as he does now; when it no longer amuses him to see me dance and dress up and play the fool for him. Then it might be useful to have something up my sleeve. (*Breaks off.*) Stupid, stupid, stupid! That time will never come. Well, what do you think of my big secret, Christine? I'm not completely useless, am I? Mind you, all this has caused me a frightful lot of worry. It hasn't been easy for me to meet my obligations punctually. In case you don't know, in the world of business there are things called quarterly instalments and interest, and they're a terrible problem to cope with. So I've had to scrape a little here and save a little there as best I can. I haven't been able to save much on the housekeeping money, because Torvald likes to live well, and I couldn't let the children go short of clothes—I couldn't take anything out of what he gives me for them. The poor little angels!

MRS. LINDE: So you've had to stint yourself, my poor Nora?

NORA: Of course. Well, after all, it was my problem. Whenever Torvald gave me money to buy myself new clothes, I never used more than half of it; and I always bought what was cheapest and plainest. Thank heaven anything suits me, so that Torvald's never noticed. But it made me a bit sad sometimes, because it's lovely to wear pretty clothes. Don't you think?

MRS. LINDE: Indeed it is.

NORA: And then I've found one or two other sources of income. Last winter I managed to get a lot of copying to do. So I shut myself away and wrote every evening, late into the night. Oh, I often got so tired. But it was great fun, though, sitting there working and earning money. It was almost like being a man.

MRS. LINDE: But how much have you managed to pay off like this?

NORA: Well, I can't say exactly. It's awfully difficult to keep an exact check on these kind of transactions. I only know I've paid everything I've managed to scrape together. Sometimes I really didn't know where to turn. (*Smiles.*) Then I'd sit here and imagine some rich old gentleman had fallen in love with me—

MRS. LINDE: What! What gentleman?

NORA: Silly! And that now he'd died and when they opened his will it said in big letters: "Everything I possess is to be paid forthwith to my beloved Mrs. Nora Helmer in cash."

MRS. LINDE: But, Nora dear, who was this gentleman?

NORA: Great heavens, don't you understand? There wasn't any old gentleman; he was just something I used to dream up as I sat here evening after evening wondering how on earth I could raise the money. But what does it matter? The old bore can stay imaginary as far as I'm concerned, because now I don't have to worry any longer! (*Jumps up.*) Oh, Christine, isn't it wonderful! I don't have to worry any more! No more troubles! I can play all day with the children, I can fill the house with pretty things, just the way Torvald likes. And, Christine, it'll soon be spring, and the air'll be fresh and the skies blue,—and then perhaps we'll be able to take a little trip somewhere. I shall be able to see the sun again. Oh, yes, yes, it's a wonderful thing to be alive and happy!

(*The bell rings in the hall.*)

MRS. LINDE (*gets up*): You've a visitor. Perhaps I'd better go.

NORA: No, stay. It won't be for me. It's someone for Torvald—

MAID (*in the doorway*): Excuse me, madam, a gentleman's called who says he wants to speak to the master. But I didn't know—seeing as the doctor's with him—

NORA: Who is this gentleman?

KROGSTAD (*in the doorway*): It's me, Mrs. Helmer.

(MRS. LINDE *starts, composes herself and turns away to the window.*)

NORA (*takes a step towards him and whispers tensely*): You? What is it? What do you want to talk to my husband about?

KROGSTAD: Business—you might call it. I hold a minor post in the bank, and I hear your husband is to become our new chief—

NORA: Oh—then it isn't—?

KROGSTAD: Pure business, Mrs. Helmer. Nothing more.

NORA: Well, you'll find him in his study.

(Nods indifferently as she closes the hall door behind him. Then she walks across the room and sees to the stove.)

MRS. LINDE: Nora, who was that man?

NORA: A lawyer called Krogstad.

MRS. LINDE: It was him, then.

NORA: Do you know that man?

MRS. LINDE: I used to know him—some years ago. He was a solicitor's clerk in our town, for a while.

NORA: Yes, of course, so he was.

MRS. LINDE: How he's changed!

NORA: He was very unhappily married, I believe.

MRS. LINDE: Is he a widower now?

NORA: Yes, with a lot of children. Ah, now it's alight.

(She closes the door of the stove and moves the rocking-chair a little to one side.)

MRS. LINDE: He does—various things now, I hear?

NORA: Does he? It's quite possible—I really don't know. But don't let's talk about business. It's so boring.

(DR. RANK enters from HELMER's study.)

RANK *(still in the doorway)*: No, no, my dear chap, don't see me out. I'll go and have a word with your wife. *(Closes the door and notices MRS. LINDE.)* Oh, I beg your pardon. I seem to be *de trop* here too.

NORA: Not in the least. *(Introduces them.)* Dr. Rank. Mrs. Linde.

RANK: Ah! A name I have often heard in this house. I believe I passed you on the stairs as I came up.

MRS. LINDE: Yes. Stairs tire me; I have to take them slowly.

RANK: Oh, have you hurt yourself?

MRS. LINDE: No, I'm just a little run down.

RANK: Ah, is that all? Then I take it you've come to town to cure yourself by a round of parties?

MRS. LINDE: I have come here to find work.

RANK: Is that an approved remedy for being run down?

MRS. LINDE: One has to live, Doctor.

RANK: Yes, people do seem to regard it as a necessity.

NORA: Oh, really, Dr. Rank. I bet you want to stay alive.

RANK: You bet I do. However miserable I sometimes feel, I still want to go on being tortured for as long as possible. It's the same with all my patients; and with people who are morally sick, too. There's a moral cripple in with Helmer at this very moment—

MRS. LINDE *(softly)*: Oh!

NORA: Whom do you mean?

RANK: Oh, a lawyer fellow called Krogstad—you wouldn't know him. He's crippled all right; morally twisted. But even he started off by announcing, as though it were a matter of enormous importance, that he had to live.

NORA: Oh? What did he want to talk to Torvald about?

RANK: I haven't the faintest idea. All I heard was something about the bank.

NORA: I didn't know that Krog—that this man Krogstad had any connection with the bank.

RANK: Yes, he's got some kind of job down there. *(to MRS. LINDE)* I wonder if in your part of the world you too have a species of human being that spends its time fussing around trying to smell out moral corruption? And when they find a case they give him some nice, comfortable position so that they can keep a good watch on him. The healthy ones just have to lump it.

MRS. LINDE: But surely it's the sick who need care most?

RANK *(shrugs his shoulders)*: Well, there we have it. It's that attitude that's turning human society into a hospital.

(NORA, lost in her own thoughts, laughs half to herself and claps her hands.)

RANK: Why are you laughing? Do you really know what society is?

NORA: What do I care about society? I think it's a bore. I was laughing at something else—something frightfully funny. Tell me, Dr. Rank—will everyone who works at the bank come under Torvald now?

RANK: Do you find that particularly funny?

NORA *(smiles and hums)*: Never mind! Never you mind! *(Walks around the room.)* Yes, I find it very amusing to think that we—I mean, Torvald—has obtained so much influence over so many people. *(Takes the paper bag from her pocket.)* Dr. Rank, would you like a small macaroon?

RANK: Macaroons! I say! I thought they were forbidden here.

NORA: Yes, well, these are some Christine gave me.

MRS. LINDE: What? I—?

NORA: All right, all right, don't get frightened. You weren't to know Torvald had forbidden them. He's afraid they'll ruin my teeth. But, dash it—for once—! Don't you agree, Dr. Rank? Here! *(Pops a macaroon into his mouth.)* You too, Christine. And I'll have one too. Just a little one. Two at the most. *(Begins to walk round again.)* Yes, now I feel really, really happy. Now there's just one thing in the world I'd really love to do.

RANK: Oh? And what is that?

NORA: Just something I'd love to say to Torvald.

RANK: Well, why don't you say it?

NORA: No, I daren't. It's too dreadful.

MRS. LINDE: Dreadful?

RANK: Well, then, you'd better not. But you can say it to us. What is it you'd so love to say to Torvald?

NORA: I've the most extraordinary longing to say: "Bloody hell!"

RANK: Are you mad?

MRS. LINDE: My dear Nora—!

RANK: Say it. Here he is.

NORA (hiding the bag of macaroons): Ssh! Ssh!

(HELMER, with his overcoat on his arm and his hat in his hand, enters from his study.)

NORA (goes to meet him): Well, Torvald dear, did you get rid of him?

HELMER: Yes, he's just gone.

NORA: May I introduce you—? This is Christine. She's just arrived in town.

HELMER: Christine—? Forgive me, but I don't think—

NORA: Mrs. Linde, Torvald dear. Christine Linde.

HELMER: Ah. A childhood friend of my wife's, I presume?

MRS. LINDE: Yes, we knew each other in earlier days.

NORA: And imagine, now she's traveled all this way to talk to you.

HELMER: Oh?

MRS. LINDE: Well, I didn't really—

NORA: You see, Christine's frightfully good at office work, and she's mad to come under some really clever man who can teach her even more than she knows already—

HELMER: Very sensible, madam.

NORA: So when she heard you'd become head of the bank—it was in her local paper—she came here as quickly as she could and—Torvald, you will, won't you? Do a little something to help Christine? For my sake?

HELMER: Well, that shouldn't be impossible. You are a widow, I take it, Mrs. Linde?

MRS. LINDE: Yes.

HELMER: And you have experience of office work?

MRS. LINDE: Yes, quite a bit.

HELMER: Well then, it's quite likely I may be able to find some job for you—

NORA (claps her hands): You see, you see!

HELMER: You've come at a lucky moment, Mrs. Linde.

MRS. LINDE: Oh, how can I ever thank you—?

HELMER: There's absolutely no need. (Puts on his overcoat.) But now I'm afraid I must ask you to excuse me—

RANK: Wait. I'll come with you.

(He gets his fur coat from the hall and warms it at the stove.)

NORA: Don't be long, Torvald dear.

HELMER: I'll only be an hour.

NORA: Are you going too, Christine?

MRS. LINDE (puts on her outdoor clothes): Yes, I must start to look round for a room.

HELMER: Then perhaps we can walk part of the way together.

NORA (helps her): It's such a nuisance we're so cramped here—I'm afraid we can't offer to—

MRS. LINDE: Oh, I wouldn't dream of it. Goodbye, Nora dear, and thanks for everything.

NORA: Au revoir. You'll be coming back this evening, of course. And you too, Dr. Rank. What? If you're well enough? Of course you'll be well enough. Wrap up warmly, though.

(They go out, talking, into the hall. Children's voices are heard from the stairs.)

NORA: Here they are! Here they are!

(She runs out and opens the door. ANNE-MARIE, the nurse, enters with the children.)

NORA: Come in, come in! (Stoops down and kisses them.) Oh, my sweet darlings—! Look at them, Christine! Aren't they beautiful?

RANK: Don't stand here chattering in this draught!

HELMER: Come, Mrs. Linde. This is for mothers only.

(DR. RANK, HELMER, and MRS. LINDE go down the stairs. The NURSE brings the children into the room. NORA follows, and closes the door to the hall.)

NORA: How well you look! What red cheeks you've got! Like apples and roses! (The children answer her inaudibly as she talks to them.) Have you had fun? That's splendid. You gave Emmy and Bob a ride on the sledge? What, both together? I say! What a clever boy you are, Ivar! Oh, let me hold her for a moment, Anne-Marie! My sweet little baby doll! (Takes the smallest child from the NURSE and dances with her.) Yes, yes, Mummy will dance with Bob too. What? Have you been throwing snowballs? Oh, I wish I'd been there! No, don't—I'll undress them myself, Anne-Marie. No, please let me; it's such fun. Go inside and warm yourself; you look frozen. There's some hot coffee on the stove. (The NURSE goes into the room on the left. NORA takes off the children's outdoor clothes and throws them anywhere while they all chatter simultaneously.) What? A big dog ran after you? But he didn't bite you? No, dogs don't bite lovely little baby dolls. Leave those parcels alone, Ivar. What's in them? Ah, wouldn't you like to know! No, no; it's nothing nice. Come on, let's play a game. What shall we play? Hide and seek. Yes, let's play hide and seek. Bob shall hide first. You want me to? All right, let me hide first.

(NORA and the children play around the room, and in the adjacent room to the left, laughing and shouting. At *length* NORA *hides under the table. The children rush in, look, but cannot find her. Then they hear her half-stifled laughter, run to the table, lift up the cloth and see her. Great excitement. She crawls out as though to frighten them. Further excitement. Meanwhile, there has been a knock on the door leading from the hall, but no one has noticed it. Now the door is half-opened and* KROGSTAD *enters. He waits for a moment; the game continues.)*

KROGSTAD: Excuse me, Mrs. Helmer—

NORA *(turns with a stifled cry and half jumps up)*: Oh! What do you want?

KROGSTAD: I beg your pardon; the front door was ajar. Someone must have forgotten to close it.

NORA *(gets up)*: My husband is not at home, Mr. Krogstad.

KROGSTAD: I know.

NORA: Well, what do you want here, then?

KROGSTAD: A word with you.

NORA: With—? *(to the children, quietly)* Go inside to Anne-Marie. What? No, the strange gentleman won't do anything to hurt Mummy. When he's gone we'll start playing again.

(She takes the children into the room on the left and closes the door behind them.)

NORA *(uneasy, tense)*: You want to speak to me?

KROGSTAD: Yes.

NORA: Today? But it's not the first of the month yet.

KROGSTAD: No, it is Christmas Eve. Whether or not you have a merry Christmas depends on you.

NORA: What do you want? I can't give you anything today—

KROGSTAD: We won't talk about that for the present. There's something else. You have a moment to spare?

NORA: Oh, yes. Yes, I suppose so; though—

KROGSTAD: Good. I was sitting in the café down below and I saw your husband cross the street—

NORA: Yes.

KROGSTAD: With a lady.

NORA: Well?

KROGSTAD: Might I be so bold as to ask: was not that lady a Mrs. Linde?

NORA: Yes.

KROGSTAD: Recently arrived in town?

NORA: Yes, today.

KROGSTAD: She is a good friend of yours, is she not?

NORA: Yes, she is. But I don't see—

KROGSTAD: I used to know her too once.

NORA: I know.

KROGSTAD: Oh? You've discovered that. Yes, I thought you would. Well then, may I ask you a straight question: is Mrs. Linde to be employed at the bank?

NORA: How dare you presume to cross-examine me, Mr. Krogstad? You, one of my husband's em-

ployees? But since you ask, you shall have an answer. Yes, Mrs. Linde is to be employed by the bank. And I arranged it, Mr. Krogstad. Now you know.

KROGSTAD: I guessed right, then.

NORA *(walks up and down the room)*: Oh, one has a little influence, you know. Just because one's a woman it doesn't necessarily mean that—When one is in a humble position, Mr. Krogstad, one should think twice before offending someone who—hm—

KROGSTAD: —who has influence?

NORA: Precisely.

KROGSTAD *(changes his tone)*: Mrs. Helmer, will you have the kindness to use your influence on my behalf?

NORA: What? What do you mean?

KROGSTAD: Will you be so good as to see that I keep my humble position at the bank?

NORA: What do you mean? Who is thinking of removing you from your position?

KROGSTAD: Oh, you don't need to play the innocent with me. I realize it can't be very pleasant for your friend to risk bumping into me; and now I also realize whom I have to thank for being hounded out like this.

NORA: But I assure you—

KROGSTAD: Look, let's not beat about the bush. There's still time, and I'd advise you to use your influence to stop it.

NORA: But, Mr. Krogstad, I have no influence!

KROGSTAD: Oh? I thought you just said—

NORA: But I didn't mean it like that! I? How on earth could you imagine that I would have any influence over my husband?

KROGSTAD: Oh, I've known your husband since we were students together. I imagine he has his weaknesses like other married men.

NORA: If you speak impertinently of my husband, I shall show you the door.

KROGSTAD: You're a bold woman, Mrs. Helmer.

NORA: I'm not afraid of you any longer. Once the New Year is in, I'll soon be rid of you.

KROGSTAD *(more controlled)*: Now listen to me, Mrs. Helmer. If I'm forced to, I shall fight for my little job at the bank as I would fight for my life.

NORA: So it sounds.

KROGSTAD: It isn't just the money; that's the last thing I care about. There's something else—well, you might as well know. It's like this, you see. You know of course, as everyone else does, that some years ago I committed an indiscretion.

NORA: I think I did hear something—

KROGSTAD: It never came into court; but from that day, every opening was barred to me. So I turned my hand to the kind of business you know about. I had to do something; and I don't think I was one of the worst. But now I want to give up all that. My sons are growing up; for their sake, I must try to regain what respectability I can. This job in the bank was the first step on the ladder. And now your husband wants to kick me off that ladder back into the dirt.

NORA: But my dear Mr. Krogstad, it simply isn't in my power to help you.

KROGSTAD: You say that because you don't want to help me. But I have the means to make you.

NORA: You don't mean you'd tell my husband that I owe you money?

KROGSTAD: And if I did?

NORA: That'd be a filthy trick! *(Almost in tears.)* This secret that is my pride and my joy—that he should hear about it in such a filthy, beastly way—hear about it from you! It'd involve me in the most dreadful unpleasantness—

KROGSTAD: Only—unpleasantness?

NORA *(vehemently)*: All right, do it! You'll be the one who'll suffer. It'll show my husband the kind of man you are, and then you'll never keep your job.

KROGSTAD: I asked you whether it was merely domestic unpleasantness you were afraid of.

NORA: If my husband hears about it, he will of course immediately pay you whatever is owing. And then we shall have nothing more to do with you.

KROGSTAD *(Takes a step closer)*: Listen, Mrs. Helmer. Either you've a bad memory or else you know very little about financial transactions. I had better enlighten you.

NORA: What do you mean?

KROGSTAD: When your husband was ill, you came to me to borrow two hundred and fifty pounds.

NORA: I didn't know anyone else.

KROGSTAD: I promised to find that sum for you—

NORA: And you did find it.

KROGSTAD: I promised to find that sum for you on certain conditions. You were so worried about your husband's illness and so keen to get the money to take him abroad that I don't think you bothered much about the details. So it won't be out of place if I refresh your memory. Well—I promised to get you the money in exchange for an I.O.U., which I drew up.

NORA: Yes, and which I signed.

KROGSTAD: Exactly. But then I added a few lines naming your father as security for the debt. This paragraph was to be signed by your father.

NORA: Was to be? He did sign it.

KROGSTAD: I left the date blank for your father to fill in when he signed this paper. You remember, Mrs. Helmer?

NORA: Yes, I think so—

KROGSTAD: Then I gave you back this I.O.U. for you to post to your father. Is that not correct?

NORA: Yes.

KROGSTAD: And of course you posted it at once; for within five or six days you brought it along to me with your father's signature on it. Whereupon I handed you the money.

NORA: Yes, well. Haven't I repaid the instalments as agreed?

KROGSTAD: Mm—yes, more or less. But to return to what we were speaking about—that was a difficult time for you just then, wasn't it, Mrs. Helmer?

NORA: Yes, it was.

KROGSTAD: Your father was very ill, if I am not mistaken.

NORA: He was dying.

KROGSTAD: He did in fact die shortly afterwards?

NORA: Yes.

KROGSTAD: Tell me, Mrs. Helmer, do you by any chance remember the date of your father's death? The day of the month, I mean.

NORA: Papa died on the twenty-ninth of September.

KROGSTAD: Quite correct; I took the trouble to confirm it. And that leaves me with a curious little problem—*(Takes out a paper.)*—which I simply cannot solve.

NORA: Problem? I don't see—

KROGSTAD: The problem, Mrs. Helmer, is that your father signed this paper three days after his death.

NORA: What? I don't understand—

KROGSTAD: Your father died on the twenty-ninth of September. But look at this. Here your father has dated his signature the second of October. Isn't that a curious little problem, Mrs. Helmer? *(Nora is silent.)* Can you suggest any explanation? *(She remains silent.)* And there's another curious thing. The words "second of October" and the year are written in a hand which is not your father's, but which I seem to know. Well, there's a simple explanation to that. Your father could have forgotten to write in the date when he signed, and someone else could have added it before the news came of his death. There's nothing criminal about that. It's the signature itself I'm wondering about. It *is* genuine, I suppose, Mrs. Helmer? It was your father who wrote his name here?

NORA *(after a short silence, throws back her head and looks defiantly at him)*: No, it was not. It was I who wrote Papa's name there.

KROGSTAD: Look, Mrs. Helmer, do you realize this is a dangerous admission?

NORA: Why? You'll get your money.

KROGSTAD: May I ask you a question? Why didn't you send this paper to your father?

NORA: I couldn't. Papa was very ill. If I'd asked him to sign this, I'd have had to tell him what the money was for. But I couldn't have told him in his condition that my husband's life was in danger. I couldn't have done that!

KROGSTAD: Then you would have been wiser to have given up your idea of a holiday.

NORA: But I couldn't! It was to save my husband's life. I couldn't put it off.

KROGSTAD: But didn't it occur to you that you were being dishonest towards me?

NORA: I couldn't bother about that. I didn't care about you. I hated you because of all the beastly difficulties you'd put in my way when you knew how dangerously ill my husband was.

KROGSTAD: Mrs. Helmer, you evidently don't appreciate exactly what you have done. But I can assure you that it is no bigger nor worse a crime then the one I once committed, and thereby ruined my whole social position.

NORA: You? Do you expect me to believe that you would have taken a risk like that to save your wife's life?

KROGSTAD: The law does not concern itself with motives.

NORA: Then the law must be very stupid.

KROGSTAD: Stupid or not, if I show this paper to the police, you will be judged according to it.

NORA: I don't believe that. Hasn't a daughter the right to shield her father from worry and anxiety when he's old and dying? Hasn't a wife the right to save her husband's life? I don't know much about the law, but there must be something somewhere that says that such things are allowed. You ought to know about that, you're meant to be a lawyer, aren't you? You can't be a very good lawyer, Mr. Krogstad.

KROGSTAD: Possibly not. But business, the kind of business we two have been transacting—I think you'll admit I understand something about that? Good. Do as you please. But I tell you this. If I get thrown into the gutter for a second time, I shall take you with me.

(He bows and goes out through the hall.)

NORA *(stands for a moment in thought, then tosses her head)*: What nonsense! He's trying to frighten me! I'm not that stupid. *(Busies herself gathering together the children's clothes; then she suddenly stops.)* But—? No, it's impossible. I did it for love, didn't I?

THE CHILDREN *(in the doorway, left)*: Mummy, the strange gentleman's gone out into the street.

NORA: Yes, yes, I know. But don't talk to anyone about the strange gentleman. You hear? Not even to Daddy.

CHILDREN: No, Mummy, Will you play with us again now?

NORA: No, no. Not now.

CHILDREN: Oh but, Mummy, you promised!

NORA: I know, but I can't just now. Go back to the nursery. I've got a lot to do. Go away, my darlings, go away. *(She pushes them gently into the other room, and closes the door behind them. She sits on the sofa, takes up her embroidery, stitches for a few moments, but soon stops.)* No! *(Throws the embroidery aside, gets up, goes to the door leading to the hall and calls.)* Helen! Bring in the Christmas tree! *(She goes to the table on the left and opens the drawer in it; then pauses again.)* No, but it's utterly impossible!

MAID *(enters with the tree)*: Where shall I put it, madam?

NORA: There, in the middle of the room.

MAID: Will you be wanting anything else?

NORA: No, thank you. I have everything I need.

(The MAID puts down the tree and goes out.)

NORA *(busy decorating the tree)*: Now—candles here—and flowers here. That loathsome man! Nonsense, nonsense, there's nothing to be frightened about. The Christmas tree must be beautiful. I'll do everything that you like, Torvald. I'll sing for you, dance for you—

(HELMER, with a bundle of papers under his arm, enters.)

NORA: Oh—are you back already?

HELMER: Yes. Has anyone been here?

NORA: Here? No.

HELMER: That's strange. I saw Krogstad come out of the front door.

NORA: Did you? Oh yes, that's quite right—Krogstad was here for a few minutes.

HELMER: Nora, I can tell from your face, he's been here and asked you to put in a good word for him.

NORA: Yes.

HELMER: And you were to pretend you were doing it of your own accord? You weren't going to tell me he'd been here? He asked you to do that too, didn't he?

NORA: Yes, Torvald. But—

HELMER: Nora, Nora! And you were ready to enter into such a conspiracy? Talking to a man like that, and making him promises—and then, on top of it all, to tell me an untruth!

NORA: An untruth?

HELMER: Didn't you say no one had been here? *(Wags his finger.)* My little songbird must never do that again. A songbird must have a clean beak to sing with; otherwise she'll starting twittering out of tune. *(Puts his arm around her waist.)* Isn't that the way we want things? Yes, of course it is. *(Lets go of her.)* So let's hear no more about that. *(Sits down in front of the stove.)* Ah, how cosy and peaceful it is here. *(Glances for a few moments at his papers.)*

NORA *(busy with the tree, after a short silence)*: Torvald.

HELMER: Yes.

NORA: I'm terribly looking forward to that fancy

dress ball at the Stenborgs on Boxing Day.

HELMER: And I'm terribly curious to see what you're going to surprise me with.

NORA: Oh, it's so maddening.

HELMER: What is?

NORA: I can't think of anything to wear. It all seems so stupid and meaningless.

HELMER: So my little Nora's come to that conclusion, has she?

NORA (behind his chair, resting her arms on its back): Are you very busy, Torvald?

HELMER: Oh—

NORA: What are those papers?

HELMER: Just something to do with the bank.

NORA: Already?

HELMER: I persuaded the trustees to give me authority to make certain immediate changes in the staff and organization. I want to have everything straight by the New Year.

NORA: Then that's why this poor man Krogstad—

HELMER: Hm.

NORA (still leaning over his chair, slowly strokes the back of his head): If you hadn't been so busy, I was going to ask you an enormous favour, Torvald.

HELMER: Well, tell me. What was it to be?

NORA: You know I trust your taste more than anyone's. I'm so anxious to look really beautiful at the fancy dress ball. Torvald, couldn't you help me to decide what I shall go as, and what kind of costume I ought to wear?

HELMER: Aha! So little Miss Independent's in trouble and needs a man to rescue her, does she?

NORA: Yes, Torvald. I can't get anywhere without your help.

HELMER: Well, well, I'll give the matter thought. We'll find something.

NORA: Oh, how kind of you! (Goes back to the tree. Pause.) How pretty these red flowers look! But, tell me is it so dreadful, this thing that Krogstad's done?

HELMER: He forged someone else's name. Have you any idea what that means?

NORA: Mightn't he have been forced to do it by some emergency?

HELMER: He probably just didn't think—that's what usually happens. I'm not so heartless as to condemn a man for an isolated action.

NORA: No, Torvald, of course not!

HELMER: Men often succeed in re-establishing themselves if they admit their crime and take their punishment.

NORA: Punishment?

HELMER: But Krogstad didn't do that. He chose to try and trick his way out of it; and that's what has morally destroyed him.

NORA: You think that would—?

HELMER: Just think how a man with that load on his conscience must always be lying and cheating and dissembling; how he must wear a mask even in the presence of those who are dearest to him, even his own wife and children! Yes, the children. That's the worst danger, Nora.

NORA: Why?

HELMER: Because an atmosphere of lies contaminates and poisons every corner of the home. Every breath that the children draw in such a house contains the germs of evil.

NORA (comes closer behind him): Do you really believe that?

HELMER: Oh, my dear, I've come across it so often in my work at the bar. Nearly all young criminals are the children of mothers who are constitutional liars.

NORA: Why do you say mothers?

HELMER: It's usually the mother; though of course the father can have the same influence. Every lawyer knows that only too well. And yet this fellow Krogstad has been sitting at home all these years poisoning his children with his lies and pretences. That's why I say that, morally speaking, he is dead. (Stretches out his hands toward her.) So my pretty little Nora must promise me not to plead his case. Your hand on it. Come, come, what's this? Give me your hand. There. That's settled, now. I assure you it'd be quite impossible for me to work in the same building as him. I literally feel physically ill in the presence of a man like that.

NORA (draws her hand from his and goes over to the other side of the Christmas tree) How hot it is in here! And I've so much to do.

HELMER (gets up and gathers his papers): Yes, and I must try to get some of this read before dinner. I'll think about your costume too. And I may even have something up my sleeve to hang in gold paper on the Christmas tree. (Lays his hand on her head.) My precious little songbird!

(He goes into his study and closes the door.)

NORA (softly, after a pause): It's nonsense. It must be. It's impossible. It must be impossible!

NURSE (in the doorway, left): The children are asking if they can come in to Mummy.

NORA: No, no, no; don't let them in! You stay with them, Anne-Marie.

NURSE: Very good, madam. (Closes the door.)

NORA (pale with fear): Corrupt my little children—! Poison my home! (Short pause. She throws back her head.) It isn't true! It couldn't be true!

ACT 2

(The same room. In the corner by the piano the Christmas tree stands, stripped and disheveled, its candles burned to their sockets. NORA's outdoor clothes lie on the sofa. She is *alone in the room, walking restlessly to and fro. At length she stops by the sofa and picks up her coat.)*

NORA *(drops the coat again)*: There's someone coming! *(Goes to the door and listens.)* No, it's no one. Of course—no one'll come today, it's Christmas Day. Nor tomorrow. But perhaps—! *(Opens the door and looks out.)* No. Nothing in the letter-box. Quite empty. *(Walks across the room.)* Silly, silly. Of course he won't do anything. It couldn't happen. It isn't possible. Why, I've three small children.

(The NURSE, carrying a large cardboard box, enters from the room on the left.)

NURSE: I found those fancy dress clothes at last, madam.

NORA: Thank you. Put them on the table.

NURSE *(does so)*: They're all rumpled up.

NORA: Oh, I wish I could tear them into a million pieces!

NURSE: Why, madam! They'll be all right. Just a little patience.

NORA: Yes, of course. I'll go and get Mrs. Linde to help me.

NURSE: What, out again? In this dreadful weather? You'll catch a chill, madam.

NORA: Well, that wouldn't be the worst. How are the children?

NURSE: Playing with their Christmas presents, poor little dears. But—

NORA: Are they still asking to see me?

NURSE: They're so used to having their Mummy with them.

NORA: Yes, but, Anne-Marie, from now on I shan't be able to spend so much time with them.

NURSE: Well, children get used to anything in time.

NORA: Do you think so? Do you think they'd forget their mother if she went away from them—for ever?

NURSE: Mercy's sake, madam! For ever!

NORA: Tell me, Anne-Marie—I've so often wondered. How could you bear to give your child away—to strangers?

NURSE: But I had to when I came to nurse my little Miss Nora.

NORA: Do you mean you wanted to?

NURSE: When I had the chance of such a good job? A poor girl what's got into trouble can't afford to pick and choose. That good-for-nothing didn't lift a finger.

NORA: But your daughter must have completely forgotten you.

NURSE: Oh no, indeed she hasn't. She's written to me twice, once when she got confirmed and then again when she got married.

NORA *(hugs her)*: Dear old Anne-Marie, you were a good mother to me.

NURSE: Poor little Miss Nora, you never had any mother but me.

NORA: And if my little ones had no one else, I know you would—no, silly, silly, silly! *(Opens the cardboard box.)* Go back to them, Anne-Marie. Now I must—Tomorrow you'll see how pretty I shall look.

NURSE: Why, there'll be no one at the ball as beautiful as my Miss Nora.

(She goes into the room, left.)

NORA *(begins to unpack the clothes from the box, but soon throws them down again)* Oh, if only I dared go out! If I could be sure no one would come and nothing would happen while I was away! Stupid, stupid! No one will come. I just musn't think about it. Brush this muff. Pretty gloves, pretty gloves! Don't think about it, don't think about it! One, two, three, four, five, six—*(Cries.)* Ah—they're coming—!

(She begins to run towards the door, but stops uncertainly. MRS. LINDE enters from the hall, where she has been taking off her outdoor clothes.)

NORA: Oh, it's you, Christine. There's no one else out there, is there? Oh, I'm so glad you've come.

MRS. LINDE: I hear you were at my room asking for me.

NORA: Yes, I just happened to be passing. I want to ask you to help me with something. Let's sit down here on the sofa. Look at this. There's going to be a fancy dress ball tomorrow night upstairs at Consul Stenborg's, and Torvald wants me to go as a Neapolitan fisher-girl and dance the tarantella. I learned it on Capri.

MRS. LINDE: I say, are you going to give a performance?

NORA: Yes, Torvald says I should. Look, here's the dress. Torvald had it made for me in Italy; but now it's all so torn, I don't know—

MRS. LINDE: Oh, we'll soon put that right; the stitching's just come away. Needle and thread? Ah, here we are.

NORA: You're being awfully sweet.

MRS. LINDE *(sews)*: So you're going to dress up tomorrow, Nora? I must pop over for a moment to see how you look. Oh, but I've completely forgotten to thank you for that nice evening yesterday.

NORA *(gets up and walks across the room)*: Oh, I didn't think it was as nice as usual. You ought to have come to town a little earlier, Christine. . . . Yes, Torvald understands how to make a home look attractive.

MRS. LINDE: I'm sure you do, too. You're not your father's daughter for nothing. But tell me. Is Dr. Rank always in such low spirits as he was yesterday?

NORA: No, last night it was very noticeable. But he's got a terrible disease; he's got spinal tuberculosis, poor man. His father was a frightful creature who kept mistresses and so on. As a result Dr. Rank has been sickly ever since he was a child—you understand—

MRS. LINDE (puts down her sewing): But, my dear Nora, how on earth did you get to know about such things?

NORA (walks about the room): Oh, don't be silly, Christine—when one has three children, one comes into contact with women who—well, who know about medical matters, and they tell one a thing or two.

MRS. LINDE (sews again; a short silence): Does Dr. Rank visit you every day?

NORA: Yes, every day. He's Torvald's oldest friend, and a good friend to me too. Dr. Rank's almost one of the family.

MRS. LINDE: But, tell me—is he quite sincere? I mean, doesn't he rather say the sort of thing he thinks people want to hear?

NORA: No, quite the contrary. What gave you that idea?

MRS. LINDE: When you introduced me to him yesterday, he said he'd often heard my name mentioned here. But later I noticed your husband had no idea who I was. So how could Dr. Rank—?

NORA: Yes, that's quite right, Christine. You see, Torvald's so hopelessly in love with me that he wants to have me all to himself—those were his very words. When we were first married, he got quite jealous if I as much as mentioned any of my old friends back home. So naturally, I stopped talking about them. But I often chat with Dr. Rank about that kind of thing. He enjoys it, you see.

MRS. LINDE: Now listen, Nora. In many ways you're still a child; I'm a bit older than you and have a little more experience of the world. There's something I want to say to you. You ought to give up this business with Dr. Rank.

NORA: What business?

MRS. LINDE: Well, everything. Last night you were speaking about this rich admirer of yours who was going to give you money—

NORA: Yes, and who doesn't exist—unfortunately. But what's that got to do with—?

MRS. LINDE: Is Dr. Rank rich?

NORA: Yes.

MRS. LINDE: And he has no dependents?

NORA: No, no one. But—

MRS. LINDE: And he comes here to see you every day?

NORA: Yes, I've told you.

MRS. LINDE: But how dare a man of his education be so forward?

NORA: What on earth are you talking about?

MRS. LINDE: Oh, stop pretending, Nora. Do you think I haven't guessed who it was who lent you that two hundred pounds?

NORA: Are you out of your mind? How could you imagine such a thing? A friend, someone who comes here every day! Why, that'd be an impossible situation!

MRS. LINDE: Then it really wasn't him?

NORA: No, of course not. I've never for a moment dreamed of—anyway, he hadn't any money to lend then. He didn't come into that till later.

MRS. LINDE: Well, I think that was a lucky thing for you, Nora dear.

NORA: No, I could never have dreamed of asking Dr. Rank—though I'm sure that if I ever did ask him—

MRS. LINDE: But of course you won't.

NORA: Of course not. I can't imagine that it should ever become necessary. But I'm perfectly sure that if I did speak to Dr. Rank—

MRS. LINDE: Behind your husband's back?

NORA: I've got to get out of this other business; and that's been going on behind his back. I've got to get out of it.

MRS. LINDE: Yes, well, that's what I told you yesterday. But—

NORA (walking up and down): It's much easier for a man to arrange these things than a woman—

MRS. LINDE: One's own husband, yes.

NORA: Oh, bosh. (Stops walking.) When you've completely repaid a debt, you get your I.O.U. back, don't you?

MRS. LINDE: Yes, of course.

NORA: And you can tear it into a thousand pieces and burn the filthy, beastly thing!

MRS. LINDE (looks hard at her, puts down her sewing and gets up slowly): Nora, you're hiding something from me.

NORA: Can you see that?

MRS. LINDE: Something has happened since yesterday morning. Nora, what is it?

NORA (goes toward her): Christine! (Listens.) Ssh! There's Torvald. Would you mind going into the nursery for a few minutes? Torvald can't bear to see sewing around. Anne-Marie'll help you.

MRS. LINDE (gathers some of her things together): Very well. But I shan't leave this house until we've talked this matter out.

(She goes into the nursery, left. As she does so, HELMER enters from the hall.)

NORA (runs to meet him): Oh, Torvald dear, I've been so longing for you to come back!

HELMER: Was that the dressmaker?

NORA: No, it was Christine. She's helping me mend

my costume. I'm going to look rather splendid in that.

HELMER: Yes, that was quite a bright idea of mine, wasn't it?

NORA: Wonderful! But wasn't it nice of me to give in to you?

HELMER (*takes her chin in his hand*): Nice—to give in to your husband? All right, little silly, I know you didn't mean it like that. But I won't disturb you. I expect you'll be wanting to try it on.

NORA: Are you going to work now?

HELMER: Yes. (*Shows her a bundle of papers.*) Look at these. I've been down to the bank—(*Turns to go into his study.*)

NOVA: Torvald.

HELMER (*stops*): Yes.

NORA: If little squirrel asked you really prettily to grant her a wish—

HELMER: Well?

NORA: Would you grant it to her?

HELMER: First I should naturally have to know what it was.

NORA: Squirrel would do lots of pretty tricks for you if you granted her wish.

HELMER: Out with it, then.

NORA: Your little skylark would sing in every room—

HELMER: My little skylark does that already.

NORA: I'd turn myself into a little fairy and dance for you in the moonlight, Torvald.

HELMER: Nora, it isn't that business you were talking about this morning?

NORA (*comes closer*): Yes, Torvald—oh, please! I beg of you!

HELMER: Have you really the nerve to bring that up again?

NORA: Yes, Torvald, yes, you must do as I ask! You must let Krogstad keep his place at the bank!

HELMER: My dear Nora, his is the job I'm giving to Mrs. Linde.

NORA: Yes, that's terribly sweet of you. But you can get rid of one of the other clerks instead of Krogstad.

HELMER: Really, you're being incredibly obstinate. Just because you thoughtlessly promised to put in a word for him, you expect me to—

NORA: No, it isn't that, Helmer. It's for your own sake. That man writes for the most beastly newspapers—you said so yourself. He could do you tremendous harm. I'm so dreadfully frightened of him—

HELMER: Oh, I understand. Memories of the past. That's what's frightening you.

NORA: What do you mean?

HELMER: You're thinking of your father, aren't you?

NORA: Yes, yes. Of course. Just think what those dreadful men wrote in the papers about Papa! The most frightful slanders. I really believe it

would have lost him his job if the Ministry hadn't sent you down to investigate, and you hadn't been so kind and helpful to him.

HELMER: But my dear little Nora, there's a considerable difference between your father and me. Your father was not a man of unassailable reputation. But I am; and I hope to remain so all my life.

NORA: But no one knows what spiteful people may not dig up. We could be so peaceful and happy now, Torvald—we could be free from every worry—you and I and the children. Oh, please Torvald, please—!

HELMER: The very fact of your pleading his cause makes it impossible for me to keep him. Everyone at the bank already knows that I intend to dismiss Krogstad. If the rumor got about that the new manager had allowed his wife to persuade him to change his mind—

NORA: Well, what then?

HELMER: Oh, nothing, nothing. As long as my little Miss Obstinate gets her way—! Do you expect me to make a laughing-stock of myself before my entire staff—give people the idea that I am open to outside influence? Believe me, I'd soon feel the consequences! Besides—there's something else that makes it impossible for Krogstad to remain in the bank while I am its manager.

NORA: What is that?

HELMER: I might conceivably have allowed myself to ignore his moral obloquies—

NORA: Yes, Torvald, surely?

HELMER: And I hear he's quite efficient at his job. But we—well, we were schoolfriends. It was one of those friendships that one enters into over-hastily and so often comes to regret later in life. I might as well confess the truth. We—well, we're on Christian name terms. And the tactless idiot makes no attempt to conceal it when other people are present. On the contrary, he thinks it gives him the right to be familiar with me. He shows off the whole time, with "Torvald this," and "Torvald that." I can tell you, I find it damned annoying. If he stayed, he'd make my position intolerable.

NORA: Torvald, you can't mean this seriously.

HELMER: Oh? And why not?

NORA: But it's so petty.

HELMER: What did you say? Petty? You think *I* am petty?

NORA: No, Torvald dear, of course you're not. That's just why—

HELMER: Don't quibble! You call my motives petty. Then I must be petty too. Petty! I see. Well, I've had enough of this. (*Goes to the door and calls into the hall.*) Helen!

NORA: What are you going to do?

HELMER (*searching among his papers*): I'm going to settle this matter once and for all. (*The* MAID *enters.*) Take this letter downstairs at once. Find a messenger and see that he delivers it. Immediately! The address is on the envelope. Here's the money.

MAID: Very good, sir. (*Goes out with the letter.*)

HELMER (*putting his papers in order*): There now, little Miss Obstinate.

NORA (*tensely*): Torvald—what was in that letter?

HELMER: Krogstad's dismissal.

NORA: Call her back, Torvald! There's still time. Oh, Torvald, call her back! Do it for my sake—for your own sake—for the children! Do you hear me, Torvald? Please do it! You don't realize what this may do to us all!

HELMER: Too late.

NORA: Yes. Too late.

HELMER: My dear Nora, I forgive you this anxiety. Though it is a bit of an insult to me. Oh, but it is! Isn't it an insult to imply that I should be frightened by the vindictiveness of a depraved hack journalist? But I forgive you, because it so charmingly testifies to the love you bear me. (*Takes her in his arms.*) Which is as it should be, my own dearest Nora. Let what will happen, happen. When the real crisis comes, you will not find me lacking in strength or courage. I am man enough to bear the burden for us both.

NORA (*fearfully*): What do you mean?

HELMER: The whole burden, I say—

NORA (*calmly*): I shall never let you do that.

HELMER: Very well. We shall share it, Nora—as man and wife. And that is as it should be. (*Caresses her.*) Are you happy now? There, there, there; don't look at me with those frightened little eyes. You're simply imagining things. You go ahead now and do your tarantella, and get some practice on that tambourine. I'll sit in my study and close the door. Then I won't hear anything, and you can make all the noise you want. (*Turns in the doorway.*) When Dr. Rank comes, tell him where to find me. (*He nods to her, goes into his room with his papers and closes the door.*)

NORA (*desperate with anxiety, stands as though transfixed, and whispers*): He said he'd do it. He will do it. He will do it, and nothing'll stop him. No, never that. I'd rather anything. There must be some escape—! Some way out—! (*The bell rings in the hall.*) Dr. Rank—! Anything but that! Anything, I don't care—!

(*She passes her hand across her face, composes herself, walks across and opens the door to the hall.* DR. RANK *is standing there, hanging up his fur coat. During the following scene it begins to grow dark.*)

NORA: Good evening, Dr. Rank. I recognized your ring. But you mustn't go in to Torvald yet. I think he's busy.

RANK: And—you?

NORA (*as he enters the room and she closes the door behind him*): Oh, you know very well I've always time to talk to you.

RANK: Thank you. I shall avail myself of that privilege as long as I can.

NORA: What do you mean by that? As long as you *can*?

RANK: Yes. Does that frighten you?

NORA: Well, it's rather a curious expression. Is something going to happen?

RANK: Something I've been expecting to happen for a long time. But I didn't think it would happen quite so soon.

NORA (*seizes his arm*): What is it? Dr. Rank, you must tell me!

RANK (*sits down by the stove*): I'm on the way out. And there's nothing to be done about it.

NORA (*sighs with relief*): Oh, it's you—?

RANK: Who else? No, it's no good lying to oneself. I am the most wretched of all my patients, Mrs. Helmer. These last few days I've been going through the books of this poor body of mine, and I find I am bankrupt. Within a month I may be rotting up there in the churchyard.

NORA: Ugh, what a nasty way to talk!

RANK: The facts aren't exactly nice. But the worst is that there's so much else that's nasty to come first. I've only one more test to make. When that's done I'll have a pretty accurate idea of when the final disintegration is likely to begin. I want to ask you a favor. Helmer's a sensitive chap, and I know how he hates anything ugly. I don't want him to visit me when I'm in hospital—

NORA: Oh but, Dr. Rank—

RANK: I don't want him there. On any pretext. I shan't have him allowed in. As soon as I know the worst, I'll send you my visiting card with a black cross on it, and then you'll know that the final filthy process has begun.

NORA: Really, you're being quite impossible this evening. And I did hope you'd be in a good mood.

RANK: With death on my hands? And all this to atone for someone else's sin? Is there justice in that? And in every single family, in one way or another, the same merciless law of retribution is at work—

NORA (*holds her hands to her ears*): Nonsense! Cheer up! Laugh!

RANK: Yes, you're right. Laughter's all the damned thing's fit for. My poor innocent spine must pay for the fun my father had as a gay young lieutenant.

NORA (*at the table, left*): You mean he was too fond of asparagus and *foie gras*?

RANK: Yes; and truffles too.

NORA: Yes, of course, truffles, yes. And oysters too, I suppose?

RANK: Yes, oysters, oysters. Of course.

NORA: And all that port and champagne to wash them down. It's too sad that all those lovely things should affect one's spine.

RANK: Especially a poor spine that never got any pleasure out of them.

NORA: Oh yes, that's the saddest thing of all.

RANK (*looks searchingly at her*): Hm—

NORA (*after a moment*): Why did you smile?

RANK: No, it was you who laughed.

NORA: No, it was you who smiled, Dr. Rank!

RANK (*gets up*): You're a worse little rogue than I thought.

NORA: Oh, I'm full of stupid tricks today.

RANK: So it seems.

NORA (*puts both her hands on his shoulders*): Dear, dear Dr. Rank, you mustn't die and leave Torvald and me.

RANK: Oh, you'll soon get over it. Once one is gone, one is soon forgotten.

NORA (*looks at him anxiously*): Do you believe that?

RANK: One finds replacements, and then—

NORA: Who will find a replacement?

RANK: You and Helmer both will, when I am gone. You seem to have made a start already, haven't you? What was this Mrs. Linde doing here yesterday evening?

NORA: Aha! But surely you can't be jealous of poor Christine?

RANK: Indeed I am. She will be my successor in this house. When I have moved on, this lady will—

NORA: Ssh—don't speak so loud! She's in there!

RANK: Today again? You see!

NORA: She's only come to mend my dress. Good heavens, how unreasonable you are! (*Sits on the sofa.*) Be nice now, Dr. Rank. Tomorrow you'll see how beautifully I shall dance; and you must imagine that I'm doing it just for you. And for Torvald, of course; obviously. (*Takes some things out of the box.*) Dr. Rank, sit down here and I'll show you something.

RANK (*sits*): What's this?

NORA: Look here! Look!

RANK: Silk stockings!

NORA: Flesh-coloured. Aren't they beautiful? It's very dark in here now, of course, but tomorrow—! No, no, no; only the soles. Oh well, I suppose you can look a bit higher if you want to.

RANK: Hm—

NORA: Why are you looking so critical? Don't you think they'll fit me?

RANK: I can't really give you a qualified opinion on that.

NORA (*looks at him for a moment*): Shame on you! (*Flicks him on the ear with the stockings.*) Take that. (*Puts them back in the box.*)

RANK: What other wonders are to be revealed to me?

NORA: I shan't show you anything else. You're being naughty.

(*She hums a little and looks among the things in the box.*)

RANK (*after a short silence*): When I sit here like this being so intimate with you, I can't think—I cannot imagine what would have become of me if I had never entered this house.

NORA (*smiles*): Yes, I think you enjoy being with us, don't you?

RANK (*more quietly, looking into the middle distance*): And now to have to leave it all—

NORA: Nonsense. You're not leaving us.

RANK (*as before*): And not to be able to leave even the most wretched token of gratitude behind; hardly even a passing sense of loss; only an empty place, to be filled by the next comer.

NORA: Suppose I were to ask you to—? No—

RANK: To do what?

NORA: To give me proof of your friendship—

RANK: Yes, yes?

NORA: No, I mean—to do me a very great service—

RANK: Would you really for once grant me that happiness?

NORA: But you've no idea what it is.

RANK: Very well, tell me, then.

NORA: No, but, Dr. Rank, I can't. It's far too much—I want your help and advice, and I want you to do something for me.

RANK: The more the better. I've no idea what it can be. But tell me. You do trust me, don't you?

NORA: Oh, yes, more than anyone. You're my best and truest friend. Otherwise I couldn't tell you. Well then, Dr. Rank—there's something you must help me to prevent. You know how much Torvald loves me—he'd never hesitate for an instant to lay down his life for me—

RANK (*leans over toward her*): Nora—do you think he is the only one—?

NORA (*with a slight start*): What do you mean?

RANK: Who would gladly lay down his life for you?

NORA (*sadly*): Oh, I see.

RANK: I swore to myself I would let you know that before I go. I shall never have a better opportunity. . . . Well, Nora, now you know that. And now you also know that you can trust me as you can trust nobody else.

NORA (*rises; calmly and quietly*): Let me pass, please.

RANK (*makes room for her but remains seated*): Nora—

NORA (*in the doorway to the hall*): Helen, bring the lamp. (*Goes over to the stove.*) Oh, dear Dr. Rank, this was really horrid of you.

RANK (*gets up*): That I have loved you as deeply as anyone else has? Was that horrid of me?

NORA: No—but that you should go and tell me. That was quite unnecessary—

RANK: What do you mean? Did you know, then—?

(The MAID enters with the lamp, puts it on the table and goes out.)

RANK: Nora—Mrs. Helmer—I am asking you, did you know this?

NORA: Oh, what do I know, what did I know, what didn't I know—I really can't say. How could you be so stupid, Dr. Rank? Everything was so nice.

RANK: Well, at any rate now you know that I am ready to serve you, body and soul. So—please continue.

NORA *(looks at him)*: After this?

RANK: Please tell me what it is.

NORA: I can't possibly tell you now.

RANK: Yes, yes! You mustn't punish me like this. Let me be allowed to do what I can for you.

NORA: You can't do anything for me now. Anyway, I don't need any help. It was only my imagination—you'll see. Yes, really. Honestly. *(Sits in the rocking chair, looks at him and smiles.)* Well, upon my word you *are* a fine gentleman, Dr. Rank. Aren't you ashamed of yourself, now that the lamp's been lit?

RANK: Frankly, no. But perhaps I ought to say— *adieu?*

NORA: Of course not. You will naturally continue to visit us as before. You know quite well how Torvald depends on your company.

RANK: Yes, but you?

NORA: Oh, I always think it's enormous fun having you here.

RANK: That was what misled me. You're a riddle to me, you know. I'd often felt you'd just as soon be with me as with Helmer.

NORA: Well, you see, there are some people whom one loves, and others whom it's almost more fun to be with.

RANK: Oh yes, there's some truth in that.

NORA: When I was at home, of course I loved Papa best. But I always used to think it was terribly amusing to go down and talk to the servants; because they never told me what I ought to do; and they were such fun to listen to.

RANK: I see. So I've taken their place?

NORA *(jumps up and runs over to him)*: Oh, dear sweet Dr. Rank, I didn't mean that at all. But I'm sure you understand—I feel the same about Torvald as I did about Papa.

MAID *(enters from the hall)*: Excuse me, madam. *(Whispers to her and hands her a visiting card.)*

NORA *(glances at the card)*: Oh! *(Puts it quickly in her pocket.)*

RANK: Anything wrong?

NORA: No, no, nothing at all. It's just something that—it's my new dress.

RANK: What? But your costume is lying over there.

NORA: Oh—that, yes—but there's another—I ordered it specially—Torvald mustn't know—

RANK: Ah, so that's your big secret?

NORA: Yes, yes. Go in and talk to him—he's in his study—keep him talking for a bit—

RANK: Don't worry. He won't get away from me. *(Goes into HELMER's study.)*

NORA *(to the MAID)*: Is he waiting in the kitchen?

MAID: Yes, madam, he came up the back way—

NORA: But didn't you tell him I had a visitor?

MAID: Yes, but he wouldn't go.

NORA: Wouldn't go?

MAID: No, madam, not until he'd spoken with you.

NORA: Very well, show him in; but quietly. Helen, you mustn't tell anyone about this. It's a surprise for my husband.

MAID: Very good, madam. I understand. *(Goes.)*

NORA: It's happening. It's happening after all. No, no, no, it can't happen, it mustn't happen.

(She walks across and bolts the door of HELMER's study. The MAID opens the door from the hall to admit KROGSTAD, and closes it behind him. He is wearing an overcoat, heavy boots and a fur cap.)

NORA *(goes toward him)*: Speak quietly. My husband's at home.

KROGSTAD: Let him hear.

NORA: What do you want from me?

KROGSTAD: Information.

NORA: Hurry up, then. What is it?

KROGSTAD: I suppose you know I've been given the sack.

NORA: I couldn't stop it, Mr. Krogstad. I did my best for you, but it didn't help.

KROGSTAD: Does your husband love you so little? He knows what I can do to you, and yet he dares to—

NORA: Surely you don't imagine I told him?

KROGSTAD: No, I didn't really think you had. It wouldn't have been like my old friend Torvald Helmer to show that much courage—

NORA: Mr. Krogstad, I'll trouble you to speak respectfully of my husband.

KROGSTAD: Don't worry, I'll show him all the respect he deserves. But since you're so anxious to keep this matter hushed up, I presume you're better informed than you were yesterday of the gravity of what you've done?

NORA: I've learned more than you could ever teach me.

KROGSTAD: Yes, a bad lawyer like me—

NORA: What do you want from me?

KROGSTAD: I just wanted to see how things were with you, Mrs. Helmer. I've been thinking about you all day. Even duns and hack journalists have hearts, you know.

NORA: Show some heart, then. Think of my little children.

KROGSTAD: Have you and your husband thought of mine? Well, let's forget that. I just wanted to tell you, you don't need to take this business too seriously. I'm not going to take any action for the present.

NORA: Oh, no—you won't, will you? I knew it.

KROGSTAD: It can all be settled quite amicably. There's no need for it to become public. We'll keep it among the three of us.

NORA: My husband must never know about this.

KROGSTAD: How can you stop him? Can you pay the balance of what you owe me?

NORA: Not immediately.

KROGSTAD: Have you any means of raising the money during the next few days?

NORA: None that I would care to use.

KROGSTAD: Well, it wouldn't have helped anyway. However much money you offered me now I wouldn't give you back that paper.

NORA: What are you going to do with it?

KROGSTAD: Just keep it. No one else need ever hear about it. So in case you were thinking of doing anything desperate—

NORA: I am.

KROGSTAD: Such as running away—

NORA: I am.

KORGSTAD: Or anything more desperate—

NORA: How did you know?

KROGSTAD: —just give up the idea.

NORA: How did you know?

ⱪROGSTAD: Most of us think of that at first. I did. But I hadn't the courage—

NORA (dully): Neither have I.

KROGSTAD (relieved): It's true, isn't it? You haven't the courage either?

NORA: No. I haven't. I haven't.

KROGSTAD: It'd be a stupid thing to do anyway. Once the first little domestic explosion is over. . . . I've got a letter in my pocket here addressed to your husband—

NORA: Telling him everything?

KROGSTAD: As delicately as possibly.

NORA (quickly): He must never see that letter. Tear it up. I'll find the money somehow—

KROGSTAD: I'm sorry, Mrs. Helmer, I thought I'd explained—

NORA: Oh, I don't mean the money I owe you. Let me know how much you want from my husband, and I'll find it for you.

KROGSTAD: I'm not asking your husband for money.

NORA: What do you want, then?

KROGSTAD: I'll tell you. I want to get on my feet again, Mrs. Helmer. I want to get to the top. And your husband's going to help me. For eighteen months now my record's been clean. I've been in hard straits all that time; I was content to fight my way back inch by inch. Now I've been chucked back into the mud, and I'm not going to be satisfied with just getting back my job. I'm going to get to the top, I tell you. I'm going to get back into the bank, and it's going to be higher up. Your husband's going to create a new job for me—

NORA: He'll never do that!

KROGSTAD: Oh, yes he will. I know him. He won't dare to risk a scandal. And once I'm in there with him, you'll see! Within a year I'll be his right-hand man. It'll be Nils Krogstad who'll be running that bank, not Torvald Helmer!

NORA: That will never happen.

KROGSTAD: Are you thinking of—?

NORA: Now I have the courage.

KROGSTAD: Oh, you can't frighten me. A pampered little pretty like you—

NORA: You'll see! You'll see!

KROGSTAD: Under the ice? Down in the cold, black water? And then, in the spring to float up again, ugly, unrecognizable, hairless—?

NORA: You can't frighten me.

KROGSTAD: And you can't frighten me. People don't do such things, Mrs. Helmer. And anyway, what'd be the use? I've got him in my pocket.

NORA: But afterwards? When I'm no longer—?

KROGSTAD: Have you forgotten that then your reputation will be in my hands? (She looks at him speechlessly.) Well, I've warned you. Don't do anything silly. When Helmer's read my letter, he'll get in touch with me. And remember, it's your husband who's forced me to act like this. And for that I'll never forgive him. Goodbye, Mrs. Helmer. (He goes out through the hall.)

NORA (runs to the hall door, opens it a few inches and listens): He's going. He's not going to give him the letter. Oh, no, no, it couldn't possibly happen. (Opens the door a little wider). What's he doing? Standing outside the front door. He's not going downstairs. Is he changing his mind? Yes, he—!

(A letter falls into the letter-box. KROGSTAD's footsteps die away down the stairs.)

NORA (with a stifled cry, runs across the room toward the table by the sofa. A pause): In the letter-box. (Steals timidly over toward the hall door.) There it is! Oh, Torvald, Torvald! Now we're lost!

MRS. LINDE (enters from the nursery with NORA's costume): Well, I've done the best I can. Shall we see how it looks—-?

NORA (whispers hoarsely): Christine, come here.

MRS. LINDE (throws the dress on the sofa): What's wrong

with you? You look as though you'd seen a ghost!

NORA: Come here. Do you see that letter? There—look—through the glass of the letter-box.

MRS. LINDE: Yes, yes, I see it.

NORA: That letter's from Krogstad—

MRS. LINDE: Nora! It was Krogstad who lent you the money!

NORA: Yes. And now Torvald's going to discover everything.

MRS. LINDE: Oh, believe me, Nora, it'll be best for you both.

NORA: You don't know what's happened. I've committed a forgery—

MRS. LINDE: But, for heaven's sake—!

NORA: Christine, all I want is for you to be my witness.

MRS. LINDE: What do you mean? Witness what?

NORA: If I should go out of my mind—and it might easily happen—

MRS. LINDE: Nora!

NORA: Or if anything else should happen to me—so that I wasn't here any longer—

MRS. LINDE: Nora, Nora, you don't know what you're saying!

NORA: If anyone should try to take the blame, and say it was all his fault—you understand—?

MRS. LINDE: Yes, yes—but how can you think—?

NORA: Then you must testify that it isn't true, Christine. I'm not mad—I know exactly what I'm saying—and I'm telling you, no one else knows anything about this. I did it entirely on my own. Remember that.

MRS. LINDE: All right. But I simply don't understand—

NORA: Oh, how could you understand? A miracle—is—about to happen.

MRS. LINDE: Miracle?

NORA: Yes. A miracle. But it's so frightening, Christine. It *mustn't* happen, not for anything in the world.

MRS. LINDE: I'll go over and talk to Krogstad.

NORA: Don't go near him. He'll only do something to hurt you.

MRS. LINDE: Once upon a time he'd have done anything for my sake.

NORA: He?

MRS. LINDE: Where does he live?

NORA: Oh, how should I know—? Oh yes, wait a moment—! *(Feels in her pocket.)* Here's his card. But the letter, the letter—!

HELMER *(from his study, knocks on the door)*: Nora!

NORA *(cries in alarm)*: What is it?

HELMER: Now, now, don't get alarmed. We're not coming in, you've closed the door. Are you trying on your costume?

NORA: Yes, yes—I'm trying on my costume. I'm going to look so pretty for you, Torvald.

MRS. LINDE *(who has been reading the card)*: Why, he lives just round the corner.

NORA: Yes; but it's no use. There's nothing to be done now. The letter's lying there in the box.

MRS. LINDE: And your husband has the key?

NORA: Yes, he always keeps it.

MRS. LINDE: Krogstad must ask him to send the letter back unread. He must find some excuse—

NORA: But Torvald always opens the box at just about this time—

MRS. LINDE: You must stop him. Go in and keep him talking. I'll be back as quickly as I can.

(She hurries out through the hall.)

NORA *(goes over to* HELMER's *door, opens it and peeps in)*: Torvald!

HELMER *(offstage)*: Well, may a man enter his own drawing room again? Come on, Rank, now we'll see what—*(In the doorway.)* But what's this?

NORA: What, Torvald dear?

HELMER: Rank's been preparing me for some great transformation scene.

RANK *(in the doorway)*: So I understood. But I seem to have been mistaken.

NORA: Yes, no one's to be allowed to see me before tomorrow night.

HELMER: But, my dear Nora, you look quite worn out. Have you been practising too hard?

NORA: No, I haven't practised at all yet.

HELMER: Well, you must.

NORA: Yes, Torvald, I must, I know. But I can't get anywhere without your help. I've completely forgotten everything.

HELMER: Oh, we'll soon put that to rights.

NORA: Yes, help me, Torvald. Promise me you will? Oh, I'm so nervous. All those people—! You must forget everything except me this evening. You mustn't think of business—I won't even let you touch a pen. Promise me, Torvald?

HELMER: I promise. This evening I shall think of nothing but you—my poor, helpless little darling. Oh, there's just one thing I must see to—*(Goes toward the hall door.)*

NORA: What do you want out there?

HELMER: I'm only going to see if any letters have come.

NORA: No, Torvald, no!

HELMER: Why, what's the matter?

NORA: Torvald, I beg you. There's nothing there.

HELMER: Well, I'll just make sure.

(He moves toward the door. NORA *runs to the piano and plays the first bars of the tarantella.)*

HELMER *(at the door, turns)*: Aha!

NORA: I can't dance tomorrow if I don't practise with you now.

HELMER (*goes over to her*): Are you really so frightened, Nora dear?

NORA: Yes, terribly frightened. Let me start practising now, at once—we've still time before dinner. Oh, do sit down and play for me, Torvald dear. Correct me, lead me, the way you always do.

HELMER: Very well, my dear, if you wish it.

(*He sits down at the piano.* NORA *seizes the tambourine and a long multi-coloured shawl from the cardboard box, wraps the latter hastily around her, then takes a quick leap into the center of the room.*)

NORA: Play for me! I want to dance!

(HELMER *plays and* NORA *dances.* DR. RANK *stands behind* HELMER *at the piano and watches her.*)

HELMER (*as he plays*): Slower, slower!

NORA: I can't!

HELMER: Not so violently, Nora.

NORA: I must!

HELMER (*stops playing*): No, no, this won't do at all.

NORA (*laughs and swings her tambourine*): Isn't that what I told you?

RANK: Let me play for her.

HELMER (*gets up*): Yes, would you? Then it'll be easier for me to show her.

(RANK *sits down at the piano and plays.* NORA *dances more and more wildly.* HELMER *has stationed himself by the stove and tries repeatedly to correct her, but she seems not to hear him. Her hair works loose and falls over her shoulders; she ignores it and continues to dance.* MRS. LINDE *enters.*)

MRS. LINDE (*stands in the doorway as though tongue-tied*): Ah—!

NORA (*as she dances*): Christine, we're having such fun!

HELMER: But, Nora darling, you're dancing as if your life depended on it.

NORA: It does.

HELMER: Rank, stop it! This is sheer lunacy. Stop it, I say!

(RANK *ceases playing.* NORA *suddenly stops dancing.*)

HELMER (*goes over to her*): I'd never have believed it. You've forgotten everything I taught you.

NORA (*throws away the tambourine*): You see!

HELMER: I'll have to show you every step.

NORA: You see how much I need you! You must show me every step of the way. Right to the end of the dance. Promise me you will, Torvald?

HELMER: Never fear. I will.

NORA: You mustn't think about anything but me—today or tomorrow. Don't open any letters—don't even open the letter-box—

HELMER: Aha, you're still worried about that fellow—

NORA: Oh, yes, yes, him too.

HELMER: Nora, I can tell from the way you're behaving, there's a letter from him already there.

NORA: I don't know. I think so. But you mustn't read it now. I don't want anything ugly to come between us till it's all over.

RANK (*quietly, to* HELMER): Better give her her way.

HELMER (*puts his arm around her*): My child shall have her way. But tomorrow night, when your dance is over—

NORA: Then you will be free.

MAID (*appears in the doorway, right*): Dinner is served, madam.

NORA: Put out some champagne, Helen.

MAID: Very good, madam. (*Goes.*)

HELMER: I say! What's this, a banquet?

NORA: We'll drink champagne until dawn! (*Calls.*) And, Helen! Put out some macaroons! Lots of macaroons—for once!

HELMER (*takes her hands in his*): Now, now, now. Don't get so excited. Where's my little songbird, the one I know?

NORA: All right. Go and sit down—and you too, Dr. Rank. I'll be with you in a minute. Christine, you must help me put my hair up.

RANK (*quietly, as they go*): There's nothing wrong, is there? I mean, she isn't—er—expecting—?

HELMER: Good heavens no, my dear chap. She just gets scared like a child sometimes—I told you before—

(*They go out right.*)

NORA: Well?

MRS. LINDE: He's left town.

NORA: I saw it from your face.

MRS. LINDE: He'll be back tomorrow evening. I left a note for him.

NORA: You needn't have bothered. You can't stop anything now. Anyway, it's wonderful really, in a way—sitting here and waiting for the miracle to happen.

MRS. LINDE: Waiting for what?

NORA: Oh, you wouldn't understand. Go in and join them. I'll be with you in a moment.

(MRS. LINDE *goes into the dining-room.*)

NORA (*stands for a moment as though collecting herself. Then she looks at her watch*): Five o'clock. Seven hours till midnight. Then another twenty-four hours till midnight tomorrow. And then the tarantella will be finished. Twenty-four and seven? Thirty-one hours to live.

HELMER (*appears in the doorway, right*): What's happened to my little songbird?

NORA (*runs to him with here arms wide*): Your songbird is here!

ACT 3

(*The same room. The table which was formerly by the sofa has been moved into the centre of the room; the chairs surround it as before. The door to the hall stands open. Dance music can be heard from the floor above.* MRS. LINDE *is seated at the table, absent-mindedly glancing through a book. She is trying to read, but seems unable to keep her mind on it. More than once she turns and listens anxiously toward the front door.*)

MRS. LINDE (*looks at her watch*): Not here yet. There's not much time left. Please God he hasn't—! (*Listens again.*) Ah, here he is. (*Goes out into the hall and cautiously opens the front door. Footsteps can be heard softly ascending the stairs. She whispers.*) Come in. There's no one here.

KROGSTAD (*in the doorway*): I found a note from you at my lodgings. What does this mean?

MRS. LINDE: I must speak with you.

KROGSTAD: Oh? And must our conversation take place in this house?

MRS. LINDE: We couldn't meet at my place; my room has no separate entrance. Come in. We're quite alone. The maid's asleep, and the Helmers are at the dance upstairs.

KROGSTAD (*comes into the room*): Well, well! So the Helmers are dancing this evening? Are they indeed?

MRS. LINDE: Yes, why not?

KROGSTAD: True enough. Why not?

MRS. LINDE: Well, Krogstad. You and I must have a talk together.

KROGSTAD: Have we two anything further to discuss?

MRS. LINDE: We have a great deal to discuss.

KROGSTAD: I wasn't aware of it.

MRS. LINDE: That's because you've never really understood me.

KROGSTAD: Was there anything to understand? It's the old story, isn't it—a woman chucking a man because something better turns up?

MRS. LINDE: Do you really think I'm so utterly heartless? You think it was easy for me to give you up?

KROGSTAD: Wasn't it?

MRS. LINDE: Oh, Nils, did you really believe that?

KROGSTAD: Then why did you write to me the way you did?

MRS. LINDE: I had to. Since I had to break with you, I thought it my duty to destroy all the feelings you had for me.

KROGSTAD (*clenches his fists*): So that was it. And you did this for money!

MRS. LINDE: You mustn't forget I had a helpless mother to take care of, and two little brothers. We couldn't wait for you, Nils. It would have been so long before you'd had enough to support us.

KROGSTAD: Maybe. But you had no right to cast me off for someone else.

MRS. LINDE: Perhaps not. I've often asked myself that.

KROGSTAD (*more quietly*): When I lost you, it was just as though all solid ground had been swept from under my feet. Look at me. Now I am a shipwrecked man, clinging to a spar.

MRS. LINDE: Help may be near at hand.

KROGSTAD: It was near. But then you came, and stood between it and me.

MRS. LINDE: I didn't know, Nils. No one told me till today that this job I'd found was yours.

KROGSTAD: I believe you, since you say so. But now you know, won't you give it up?

MRS. LINDE: No—because it wouldn't help you even if I did.

KROGSTAD: Wouldn't it? I'd do it all the same.

MRS. LINDE: I've learned to look at things practically. Life and poverty have taught me that.

KROGSTAD: And life has taught me to distrust fine words.

MRS. LINDE: Then it's taught you a useful lesson. But surely you still believe in actions?

KROGSTAD: What do you mean?

MRS. LINDE: You said you were like a shipwrecked man clinging to a spar.

KROGSTAD: I have good reason to say it.

MRS. LINDE: I'm in the same position as you. No one to care about, no one to care for.

KROGSTAD: You made your own choice.

MRS. LINDE: I had no choice—then.

KROGSTAD: Well?

MRS. LINDE: Nils, suppose we two shipwrecked souls could join hands?

KROGSTAD: What are you saying?

MRS. LINDE: Castaways have a better chance of survival together than on their own.

KROGSTAD: Christine!

MRS. LINDE: Why do you suppose I came to this town?

KROGSTAD: You mean—you came because of me?

MRS. LINDE: I must work if I'm to find life worth living. I've always worked, for as long as I can remember; it's been the greatest joy of my life—my only joy. But now I'm alone in the world, and I feel so dreadfully lost and empty. There's no joy in working just for oneself. Oh, Nils, give me something—someone—to work for.

KROGSTAD: I don't believe all that. You're just being hysterical and romantic. You want to find an excuse for self-sacrifice.

MRS. LINDE: Have you ever known me to be hysterical?

KROGSTAD: You mean you really—? Is it possible? Tell me—you know all about my past?

MRS. LINDE: Yes.

KROGSTAD: And you know what people think of me here?

MRS. LINDE: You said just now that with me you might have become a different person.

KROGSTAD: I know I could have.

MRS. LINDE: Could it still happen?

KROGSTAD: Christine—do you really mean this?

Yes—you do—I see it in your face. Have you really the courage—?

MRS. LINDE: I need someone to be a mother to; and your children need a mother. And you and I need each other. I believe in you, Nils. I am afraid of nothing—with you.

KROGSTAD (clasps her hands): Thank you, Christine—thank you! Now I shall make the world believe in me as you do! Oh—but I'd forgotten—

MRS. LINDE (listens): Ssh! The tarantella! Go quickly, go!

KROGSTAD: Why? What is it?

MRS. LINDE: You hear that dance? As soon as it's finished, they'll be coming down.

KROGSTAD: All right, I'll go. It's no good, Christine. I'd forgotten—you don't know what I've just done to the Helmers.

MRS. LINDE: Yes, Nils. I know.

KROGSTAD: And yet you'd still have the courage to—?

MRS. LINDE: I know what despair can drive a man like you to.

KROGSTAD: Oh, if only I could undo this!

MRS. LINDE: You can. Your letter is still lying in the box.

KROGSTAD: Are you sure?

MRS. LINDE: Quite sure. But—

KROGSTAD (looks searchingly): Is that why you're doing this? You want to save your friend at any price? Tell me the truth. Is that the reason?

MRS. LINDE: Nils, a woman who has sold herself once for the sake of others doesn't make the same mistake again.

KROGSTAD: I shall demand my letter back.

MRS. LINDE: No, no.

KROGSTAD: Of course I shall. I shall stay here till Helmer comes down. I'll tell him he must give me back my letter—I'll say it was only to do with my dismissal, and that I don't want him to read it—

MRS. LINDE: No, Nils, you mustn't ask for that letter back.

KROGSTAD: But—tell me—wasn't that the real reason you asked me to come here?

MRS. LINDE: Yes—at first, when I was frightened. But a day has passed since then, and in that time I've seen incredible things happen in this house. Helmer must know the truth. This unhappy secret of Nora's must be revealed. They must come to a full understanding; there must be an end of all these shiftings and evasions.

KROGSTAD: Very well. If you're prepared to risk it. But one thing I can do—and at once—

MRS. LINDE (listens): Hurry! Go, go! The dance is over. We aren't safe here another moment.

KROGSTAD: I'll wait for you downstairs.

MRS. LINDE: Yes, do. You can see me home.

KROGSTAD: I've never been so happy in my life before!

(He goes through the front door. The door leading from the room into the hall remains open.)

MRS. LINDE (tidies the room a little and gets her hat and coat): What a change! Oh, what a change! Someone to work for—to live for! A home to bring joy into! I won't let this chance of happiness slip through my fingers. Oh, why don't they come? (Listens.) Ah, here they are. I must get my coat on.

(She takes her hat and coat. HELMER's and NORA's voices become audible outside. A key is turned in the lock and HELMER leads NORA almost forcibly into the hall. She is dressed in an Italian costume with a large black shawl. He is in evening dress, with a black cloak.)

NORA (still in the doorway, resisting him): No, no, no—not in here! I want to go back upstairs. I don't want to leave so early.

HELMER: But my dearest Nora—

NORA: Oh, please, Torvald, please! Just another hour!

HELMER: Not another minute, Nora, my sweet. You know what we agreed. Come along, now. Into the drawing-room. You'll catch cold if you stay out here.

(He leads her, despite her efforts to resist him, gently into the room.)

MRS. LINDE: Good evening.

NORA: Christine!

HELMER: Oh, hullo, Mrs. Linde. You still here?

MRS. LINDE: Please forgive me. I did so want to see Nora in her costume.

NORA: Have you been sitting here waiting for me?

MRS. LINDE: Yes, I got here too late, I'm afraid. You'd already gone up. And I felt I really couldn't go back home without seeing you.

HELMER (takes off NORA's shawl): Well, take a good look at her. She's worth looking at, don't you think? Isn't she beautiful, Mrs. Linde?

MRS. LINDE: Oh, yes, indeed—

HELMER: Isn't she unbelievably beautiful? Everyone at the party said so. But dreadfully stubborn she is, bless her pretty little heart. What's to be done about that? Would you believe it, I practically had to use force to get her away!

NORA: Oh, Torvald, you're going to regret not letting me stay—just half an hour longer.

HELMER: Hear that, Mrs. Linde? She dances her tarantella—makes a roaring success—and very well deserved—though possibly a trifle too realistic—more so than was aesthetically necessary, strictly speaking. But never mind that. Main thing is—she had a success—roaring success. Was I going to let her stay on after that and spoil the impression? No, thank you. I took my beautiful little Capri signorina—my capricious little Capricienne, what?—under my arm—a swift round of the ballroom, a curtsey to the company, and, as they say in novels, the beautiful apparition disappeared! An exit should always be dramatic, Mrs. Linde. But unfortunately that's just what I can't get Nora to realize. I say, it's hot in here. *(Throws his cloak on a chair and opens the door to his study.)* What's this? It's dark in here. Ah, yes, of course—excuse me. *(Goes in and lights a couple of candles.)*

NORA *(whispers swiftly, breathlessly)*: Well?

MRS. LINDE *(quietly)*: I've spoken to him.

NORA: Yes?

MRS. LINDE: Nora—you must tell your husband everything.

NORA *(dully)*: I knew it.

MRS. LINDE: You've nothing to fear from Krogstad. But you must tell him.

NORA: I shan't tell him anything.

MRS. LINDE: Then the letter will.

NORA: Thank you, Christine. Now I know what I must do. Ssh!

HELMER *(returns)*: Well, Mrs. Linde, finished admiring her?

MRS. LINDE: Yes. Now I must say good night.

HELMER: Oh, already? Does this knitting belong to you?

MRS. LINDE *(takes it)*: Thank you, yes. I nearly forgot it.

HELMER: You knit, then?

MRS. LINDE: Why, yes.

HELMER: Know what? You ought to take up embroidery.

MRS. LINDE: Oh? Why?

HELMER: It's much prettier. Watch me, now. You hold the embroidery in your left hand, like this, and then you take the needle in your right hand and go in and out in a slow, easy movement—like this. I am right, aren't I?

MRS. LINDE: Yes, I'm sure—

HELMER: But knitting, now—that's an ugly business—can't help it. Look—arms all huddled up—great clumsy needles going up and down—makes you look like a damned Chinaman. I say, that really was a magnificent champagne they served us.

MRS. LINDE: Well, good night, Nora. And stop being stubborn. Remember!

HELMER: Quite right, Mrs. Linde!

MRS. LINDE: Good night, Mr. Helmer.

HELMER *(accompanies her to the door)*: Good night, good night! I hope you'll manage to get home all right? I'd gladly—but you haven't far to go, have you? Good night, good night. *(She goes. He closes the door behind her and returns.)* Well, we've got rid of her at last. Dreadful bore that woman is!

NORA: Aren't you very tired, Torvald?

HELMER: No, not in the least.

NORA: Aren't you sleepy?

HELMER: Not a bit. On the contrary, I feel extraordinarily exhilarated. But what about you? Yes, you look very sleepy and tired.

NORA: Yes, I am very tired. Soon I shall sleep.

HELMER: You see, you see! How right I was not to let you stay longer!

NORA: Oh, you're always right, whatever you do.

HELMER *(kisses her on the forehead)*: Now my little songbird's talking just like a real big human being. I say, did you notice how cheerful Rank was this evening?

NORA: Oh? Was he? I didn't have a chance to speak with him.

HELMER: I hardly did. But I haven't seen him in such a jolly mood for ages. *(Look at her for a moment, then comes closer.)* I say, it's nice to get back to one's home again, and be all alone with you. Upon my word, you're a distractingly beautiful young woman.

NORA: Don't look at me like that, Torvald!

HELMER: What, not look at my most treasured possession? At all this wonderful beauty that's mine, mine alone, all mine.

NORA *(goes round to the other side of the table)*: You mustn't talk to me like that tonight.

HELMER *(follows her)*: You've still the tarantella in your blood, I see. And that makes you even more desirable. Listen! Now the other guests are beginning to go. *(More quietly.)* Nora—soon the whole house will be absolutely quiet.

NORA: Yes, I hope so.

HELMER: Yes, my beloved Nora, of course you do! Do you know—when I'm out with you among other people like we were tonight, do you know why I say so little to you, why I keep so aloof from you, and just throw you an occasional glance? Do you know why I do that? It's because I pretend to myself that you're my secret mistress, my clandestine little sweetheart, and that nobody knows there's anything at all between us.

NORA: Oh, yes, yes, yes—I know you never think of anything but me.

HELMER: And then when we're about to go, and I wrap the shawl round your lovely young shoulders, over this wonderful curve of your neck—Then I pretend to myself that you are my young bride, that we've just come from the wedding, that I'm taking you to my house for the first time—that, for the first time, I am alone with you—quite alone with you, as you stand there young and trembling and beautiful. All evening I've had no eyes for anyone but you. When I saw you dance the tarantella, like a huntress, a temptress, my blood grew hot, I couldn't stand it any longer! That was why I seized you and dragged you down here with me—

NORA: Leave me, Torvald! Get away from me! I don't want all this.

HELMER: What? Now, Nora, you're joking with me. Don't want, don't want—? Aren't I your husband—?

(There is a knock on the front door.)

NORA *(starts)*: What was that?

HELMER *(goes toward the hall)*: Who is it?

RANK *(outside)*: It's me. May I come in for a moment?

HELMER *(quietly, annoyed)*: Oh, what does he want now? *(Calls.)* Wait a moment. *(Walks over and opens the door.)* Well! Nice of you not to go by without looking in.

RANK: I thought I heard your voice, so I felt I had to say goodbye. *(His eyes travel swiftly around the room.)* Ah, yes—these dear rooms, how well I know them. What a happy, peaceful home you two have.

HELMER: You seemed to be having a pretty happy time yourself upstairs.

RANK: Indeed I did. Why not? Why shouldn't one make the most of this world? As much as one can, and for as long as one can. The wine was excellent—

HELMER: Especially the champagne.

RANK: You noticed that too? It's almost incredible how much I managed to get down.

NORA: Torvald drank a lot of champagne too, this evening.

RANK: Oh?

NORA: Yes. It always makes him merry afterwards.

RANK: Well, why shouldn't a man have a merry evening after a well-spent day?

HELMER: Well-spent? Oh, I don't know that I can claim that.

RANK *(slaps him across the back)*: I can, though, my dear fellow!

NORA: Yes, of course, Dr. Rank—you've been carrying out a scientific experiment today, haven't you?

RANK: Exactly.

HELMER: Scientific experiment! Those are big words for my little Nora to use!

NORA: And may I congratulate you on the finding?

RANK: You may indeed.

NORA: It was good, then?

RANK: The best possible finding—both for the doctor and the patient. Certainty.

NORA *(quickly)*: Certainty?

RANK: Absolute certainty. So aren't I entitled to have a merry evening after that?

NORA: Yes, Dr. Rank. You were quite right to.

HELMER: I agree. Provided you don't have to regret it tomorrow.

RANK: Well, you never get anything in this life without paying for it.

NORA: Dr. Rank—you like masquerades, don't you?

RANK: Yes, if the disguises are sufficiently amusing.

NORA: Tell me. What shall we two wear at the next masquerade?

HELMER: You little gadabout! Are you thinking about the next one already?

RANK: We two? Yes, I'll tell you. You must go as the Spirit of Happiness—

HELMER: You try to think of a costume that'll convey that.

RANK: Your wife need only appear as her normal, everyday self—

HELMER: Quite right! Well said! But what are you going to be? Have you decided that?

RANK: Yes, my dear friend. I have decided that.

HELMER: Well?

RANK: At the next masquerade, I shall be invisible.

HELMER: Well, that's a funny idea.

RANK: There's a big, black hat—haven't you heard of the invisible hat? Once it's over your head, no one can see you any more.

HELMER *(represses a smile)*: Ah yes, of course.

RANK: But I'm forgetting what I came for. Helmer, give me a cigar. One of your black Havanas.

HELMER: With the greatest pleasure. *(Offers him the box.)*

RANK *(takes one and cuts off the tip)*: Thank you.

NORA *(strikes a match)*: Let me give you a light.

RANK: Thank you. *(She holds out the match for him. He lights his cigar.)* And now—goodbye.

HELMER: Goodbye, my dear chap, goodbye.

NORA: Sleep well, Dr. Rank.

RANK: Thank you for that kind wish.

NORA: Wish me the same.

RANK: You? Very well—since you ask. Sleep well. And thank you for the light. *(He nods to them both and goes.)*

HELMER *(quietly)*: He's been drinking too much.

NORA *(abstractedly)*: Perhaps.

(HELMER takes his bunch of keys from his pocket and goes out into the hall.)

NORA: Torvald, what do you want out there?

HELMER: I must empty the letter-box. It's absolutely full. There'll be no room for the newspapers in the morning.

NORA: Are you going to work tonight?

HELMER: You know very well I'm not. Hullo, what's this? Someone's been at the lock.

NORA: At the lock—?

HELMER: Yes, I'm sure of it. Who on earth—? Surely not one of the maids? Here's a broken hairpin. Nora, it's yours—

NORA *(quickly)*: Then it must have been the children.

HELMER: Well, you'll have to break them of that habit. Hm, hm. Ah, that's done it. *(Takes out the contents of the box and calls into the kitchen.)* Helen! Helen!

Put out the light on the staircase. *(Comes back into the drawing room with the letters in his hand and closes the door to the hall.)* Look at this! You see how they've piled up? *(Glances through them.)* What on earth's this?

NORA *(at the window)*: The letter! Oh, no, Torvald, no!

HELMER: Two visiting cards—from Rank.

NORA: From Dr. Rank?

HELMER *(looks at them)*: Peter Rank, M.D. They were on top. He must have dropped them in as he left.

NORA: Has he written anything on them?

HELMER: There's a black cross above his name. Look. Rather gruesome, isn't it? It looks just as though he was announcing his death.

NORA: He is.

HELMER: What? Do you know something? Has he told you anything?

NORA: Yes. When these cards come, it means he's said goodbye to us. He wants to shut himself up in his house and die.

HELMER: Ah, poor fellow. I knew I wouldn't be seeing him for much longer. But so soon—! And now he's going to slink away and hide like a wounded beast.

NORA: When the time comes, it's best to go silently. Don't you think so, Torvald?

HELMER *(walks up and down)*: He was so much a part of our life. I can't realize that he's gone. His suffering and loneliness seemed to provide a kind of dark background to the happy sunlight of our marriage. Well, perhaps it's best this way. For him, anyway. *(Stops walking.)* And perhaps for us too, Nora. Now we have only each other. *(Embraces her.)* Oh, my beloved wife—I feel as though I could never hold you close enough. Do you know, Nora, often I wish some terrible danger might threaten you, so that I could offer my life and my blood, everything, for your sake.

NORA *(tears herself loose and says in a clear, firm voice)*: Read your letters now, Torvald.

HELMER: No, no. Not tonight. Tonight I want to be with you, my darling wife—

NORA: When your friend is about to die—?

HELMER: You're right. This news has upset us both. An ugliness has come between us; thoughts of death and dissolution. We must try to forget them. Until then—you go to your room; I shall go to mine.

NORA *(throws her arms round his neck)*: Good night, Torvald! Good night!

HELMER *(kisses her on the forehead)*: Good night, my darling little songbird. Sleep well, Nora. I'll go and read my letters.

(He goes into the study with the letters in his hand, and closes the door.)

NORA *(wild-eyed, fumbles around, seizes* HELMER's *cloak,* throws it round herself and whispers quickly, hoarsely)*: Never see him again. Never. Never. Never. *(Throws the shawl over her head.)* Never see the children again. Them too. Never. Never. Oh—the icy black water! Oh—that bottomless—that—! Oh, if only it were all over! Now he's got it—he's reading it. Oh, no, no! Goodbye, Torvald! Goodbye, my darlings!

(She turns to run into the hall. As she does so, HELMER *throws open his door and stands there with an open letter in his hand.)*

HELMER: Nora!

NORA *(shrieks)*: Ah—!

HELMER: What is this? Do you know what is in this letter?

NORA: Yes, I know. Let me go! Let me go!

HELMER *(holds her back)*: Go? Where?

NORA *(tries to tear herself loose)*: You mustn't try to save me, Torvald!

HELMER *(staggers back)*: Is it true? Is it true, what he writes? Oh, my God! No, no—it's impossible, it can't be true!

NORA: It *is* true. I've loved you more than anything else in the world.

HELMER: Oh, don't try to make silly excuses.

NORA *(takes a step toward him)*: Torvald—

HELMER: Wretched woman! What have you done?

NORA: Let me go! You're not going to suffer for my sake. I won't let you!

HELMER: Stop being theatrical. *(Locks the front door.)* You're going to stay here and explain yourself. Do you understand what you've done? Answer me! Do you understand?

NORA *(looks unflinchingly at him and, her expression growing colder, says)*: Yes. Now I am beginning to understand.

HELMER *(walking round the room)*: Oh, what a dreadful awakening! For eight whole years—she who was my joy and my pride—a hypocrite, a liar—worse, worse—a criminal! Oh, the hideousness of it! Shame on you, shame!

*(*NORA *is silent and stares unblinkingly at him.)*

HELMER *(stops in front of her)*: I ought to have guessed that something of this sort would happen. I should have foreseen it. All your father's recklessness and instability—be quiet!—I repeat, all your father's recklessness and instability he has handed on to you. No religion, no morals, no sense of duty! Oh, how I have been punished for closing my eyes to his faults! I did it for your sake. And now you reward me like this.

NORA: Yes. Like this.

HELMER: Now you have destroyed all my happiness. You have ruined my whole future. Oh, it's too dreadful to contemplate! I am in the power of a man who is completely without scruples. He can do what he likes with me, demand what he pleases, order me to do anything—I dare not disobey him. I am condemned to humiliation and ruin simply for the weakness of a woman.

NORA: When I am gone from this world, you will be free.

HELMER: Oh, don't be melodramatic. Your father was always ready with that kind of remark. How would it help me if you were "gone from this world," as you put it? It wouldn't assist me in the slightest. He can still make all the facts public; and if he does, I may quite easily be suspected of having been an accomplice in your crime. People may think that I was behind it—that it was I who encouraged you! And for all this I have to thank you, you whom I have carried on my hands through all the years of our marriage! Now do you realize what you've done to me?

NORA (coldly calm): Yes.

HELMER: It's so unbelievable I can hardly credit it. But we must try to find some way out. Take off that shawl. Take it off, I say! I must try to buy him off somehow. This thing must be hushed up at any price. As regards our relationship—we must appear to be living together just as before. Only *appear*, of course. You will therefore continue to reside here. That is understood. But the children shall be taken out of your hands. I dare no longer entrust them to you. Oh, to have to say this to the woman I once loved so dearly—and whom I still—! Well, all that must be finished. Henceforth there can be no question of happiness; we must merely strive to save what shreds and tatters—(*The front door bell rings.* HELMER *starts.*) What can that be? At this hour? Surely not—? He wouldn't—? Hide yourself, Nora. Say you're ill.

(NORA *does not move.* HELMER *goes to the door of the room and opens it. The* MAID *is standing half-dressed in the hall.*)

MAID: A letter for madam.

HELMER: Give it me. (*Seizes the letter and shuts the door.*) Yes, it's from him. You're not having it. I'll read this myself.

NORA: Read it.

HELMER (*by the lamp*): I hardly dare to. This may mean the end for us both. No. I must know. (*Tears open the letter hastily; reads a few lines; looks at a piece of paper which is enclosed with it; utters a cry of joy.*) Nora! (*She looks at him questioningly.*) Nora! No—I must read it once more. Yes, yes, it's true! I am saved! Nora, I am saved!

NORA: What about me?

HELMER: You too, of course. We're both saved, you and I. Look! He's returning your I.O.U. He writes that he is sorry for what has happened—a happy accident has changed his life—oh, what does it matter what he writes? We are saved, Nora! No one can harm you now. Oh, Nora, Nora—no, first let me destroy this filthy thing. Let me see—! (*Glances at the I.O.U.*) No, I don't want to look at it. I shall merely regard the whole business as a dream. (*He tears the I.O.U. and both letters into pieces, throws them into the stove and watches them burn.*) There. Now they're destroyed. He wrote that ever since Christmas Eve you've been—oh, these must have been three dreadful days for you, Nora.

NORA: Yes. It's been a hard fight.

HELMER: It must have been terrible—seeing no way out except—no, we'll forget the whole sordid business. We'll just be happy and go on telling ourselves over and over again: "It's over! It's over!" Listen to me, Nora. You don't seem to realize. It's over! Why are you looking so pale? Ah, my poor little Nora, I understand. You can't believe that I have forgiven you. But I have, Nora. I swear it to you. I have forgiven you everything. I know that what you did you did for your love of me.

NORA: That is true.

HELMER: You have loved me as a wife should love her husband. It was simply that in your inexperience you chose the wrong means. But do you think I love you any the less because you don't know how to act on your own initiative? No, no. Just lean on me. I shall counsel you. I shall guide you. I would not be a true man if your feminine helplessness did not make you doubly attractive in my eyes. You mustn't mind the hard words I said to you in those first dreadful moments when my whole world seemed to be tumbling about my ears. I have forgiven you, Nora. I swear it to you; I have forgiven you.

NORA: Thank you for your forgiveness.

(*She goes out through the door, right.*)

HELMER: No, don't go—(*Looks in.*) What are you doing there?

NORA (*offstage*): Taking off my fancy dress.

HELMER (*by the open door*): Yes, do that. Try to calm yourself and get your balance again, my frightened little songbird. Don't be afraid. I have broad wings to shield you. (*Begins to walk around near the door.*) How lovely and peaceful this little home of ours is, Nora. You are safe here; I shall watch over you like a hunted dove which I have snatched unharmed from the claws of the falcon. Your wildly beating little heart shall find peace with me. It will happen, Nora; it will take time, but it will happen, believe me. Tomorrow all this will seem quite different. Soon everything will be as it was before. I shall no longer need to remind you that I have forgiven you; your own heart will tell you that it is true. Do you really think I could ever bring myself to disown you, or even to reproach you? Ah, Nora, you don't understand what goes on in a husband's heart. There is something indescribably wonderful and satisfying for a husband in knowing that he has forgiven his wife—forgiven her unreservedly, from the bottom of his heart. It means that she has become his property in a double sense; he has, as it were, brought her into the world anew; she is now not only his wife but also his child. From now on that is what you shall be to me, my poor, helpless, bewildered little creature. Never be frightened of anything again, Nora. Just open your heart to me. I shall be both your will and your conscience. What's this? Not in bed? Have you changed?

NORA (*in her everyday dress*): Yes, Torvald. I've changed.

HELMER: But why now—so late—?

NORA: I shall not sleep tonight.

HELMER: But, my dear Nora—

NORA (*looks at her watch*): It isn't that late. Sit down here, Torvald. You and I have a lot to talk about.

(*She sits down on one side of the table.*)

HELMER: Nora, what does this mean? You look quite drawn—

NORA: Sit down. It's going to take a long time. I've a lot to say to you.

HELMER (*sits down on the other side of the table*): You alarm me, Nora. I don't understand you.

NORA: No, that's just it. You don't understand me. And I've never understood you—until this evening. No, don't interrupt me. Just listen to what I have to say. You and I have got to face facts, Torvald.

HELMER: What do you mean by that?

NORA (*after a short silence*): Doesn't anything strike you about the way we're sitting here?

HELMER: What?

NORA: We've been married for eight years. Does it occur to you that this is the first time that we two, you and I, man and wife, have ever had a serious talk together?

HELMER: Serious? What do you mean, serious?

NORA: In eight whole years—no, longer—ever since we first met—we have never exchanged a serious word on a serious subject.

HELMER: Did you expect me to drag you into all my worries—worries you couldn't possibly have helped me with?

NORA: I'm not talking about worries. I'm simply saying that we have never sat down seriously to try to get to the bottom of anything.

HELMER: But, my dear Nora, what on earth has that got to do with you?

NORA: That's just the point. You have never understood me. A great wrong has been done to me, Torvald. First by Papa, and then by you.

HELMER: What? But we two have loved you more than anyone in the world!

NORA (*shakes her head*): You have never loved me. You just thought it was fun to be in love with me.

HELMER: Nora, what kind of a way is this to talk?

NORA: It's the truth, Torvald. When I lived with Papa, he used to tell me what he thought about everything, so that I never had any opinions but his. And if I did have any of my own, I kept them quiet, because he wouldn't have liked them. He called me his little doll, and he played with me just the way I played with my dolls. Then I came here to live in your house—

HELMER: What kind of a way is that to describe our marriage?

NORA (*undisturbed*): I mean, then I passed from Papa's hands into yours. You arranged everything the way you wanted it, so that I simply took over your taste in everything—or pretended I did—I don't really know—I think it was a little of both—first one and then the other. Now I look back on it, it's as if I've been living here like a pauper, from hand to mouth. I performed tricks for you, and you gave me food and drink. But that was how you wanted it. You and Papa have done me a great wrong. It's your fault that I have done nothing with my life.

HELMER: Nora, how can you be so unreasonable and ungrateful? Haven't you been happy here?

NORA: No; never. I used to think I was; but I haven't ever been happy.

HELMER: Not—not happy?

NORA: No. I've just had fun. You've always been very kind to me. But our home has never been anything but a playroom. I've been your doll-wife, just as I used to be Papa's doll-child. And the children have been my dolls. I used to think it was fun when you came in and played with me, just as they think it's fun when I go in and play games with them. That's all our marriage has been, Torvald.

HELMER: There may be a little truth in what you say, though you exaggerate and romanticize. But from now on it'll be different. Playtime is over. Now the time has come for education.

NORA: Whose education? Mine or the children's?

HELMER: Both yours and the children's, my dearest Nora.

NORA: Oh, Torvald, you're not the man to educate me into being the right wife for you.

HELMER: How can you say that?

NORA: And what about me? Am I fit to educate the children?

HELMER: Nora!

NORA: Didn't you say yourself a few minutes ago that you dare not leave them in my charge?

HELMER: In a moment of excitement. Surely you don't think I meant it seriously?

NORA: Yes. You were perfectly right. I'm not fitted to educate them. There's something else I must do first. I must educate myself. And you can't help me with that. It's something I must do by myself. That's why I'm leaving you.

HELMER (jumps up): What did you say?

NORA: I must stand on my own feet if I am to find out the truth about myself and about life. So I can't go on living here with you any longer.

HELMER: Nora, Nora!

NORA: I'm leaving you now, at once. Christine will put me up for tonight—

HELMER: You're out of your mind! You can't do this! I forbid you!

NORA: It's no use your trying to forbid me any more. I shall take with me nothing but what is mine. I don't want anything from you, now or ever.

HELMER: What kind of madness is this?

NORA: Tomorrow I shall go home—I mean, to where I was born. It'll be easiest for me to find some kind of a job there.

HELMER: But you're blind! You've no experience of the world—

NORA: I must try to get some, Torvald.

HELMER: But to leave your home, your husband, your children! Have you thought what people will say?

NORA: I can't help that. I only know that I must do this.

HELMER: But this is monstrous! Can you neglect your most sacred duties?

NORA: What do you call my most sacred duties?

HELMER: Do I have to tell you? Your duties towards your husband, and your children.

NORA: I have another duty which is equally sacred.

HELMER: You have not. What on earth could that be?

NORA: My duty towards myself.

HELMER: First and foremost you are a wife and a mother.

NORA: I don't believe that any longer. I believe that I am first and foremost a human being, like you—or anyway, that I must try to become one. I know most people think as you do, Torvald, and I know there's something of the sort to be found in books. But I'm no longer prepared to accept what people say and what's written in books. I

must think things out for myself, and try to find my own answer.

HELMER: Do you need to ask where your duty lies in your own home? Haven't you an infallible guide in such matters—your religion?

NORA: Oh, Torvald, I don't really know what religion means.

HELMER: What are you saying?

NORA: I only know what Pastor Hansen told me when I went to confirmation. He explained that religion meant this and that. When I get away from all this and can think things out on my own, that's one of the questions I want to look into. I want to find out whether what Pastor Hansen said was right—or anyway, whether it is right for me.

HELMER: But it's unheard of for so young a woman to behave like this! If religion cannot guide you, let me at least appeal to your conscience. I presume you have some moral feelings left? Or—perhaps you haven't? Well, answer me.

NORA: Oh, Torvald, that isn't an easy question to answer. I simply don't know. I don't know where I am in these matters. I only know that these things mean something quite different to me from what they do to you. I've learned now that certain laws are different from what I'd imagined them to be; but I can't accept that such laws can be right. Has a woman really not the right to spare her dying father pain, or save her husband's life? I can't believe that.

HELMER: You're talking like a child. You don't understand how society works.

NORA: No, I don't. But now I intend to learn. I must try to satisfy myself which is right, society or I.

HELMER: Nora, you're ill; you're feverish. I almost believe you're out of your mind.

NORA: I've never felt so sane and sure in my life.

HELMER: You feel sure that it is right to leave your husband and your children?

NORA: Yes. I do.

HELMER: Then there is only one possible explanation.

NORA: What?

HELMER: That you don't love me any longer.

NORA: No, that's exactly it.

HELMER: Nora! How can you say this to me?

NORA: Oh, Torvald, it hurts me terribly to have to say it, because you've always been so kind to me. But I can't help it. I don't love you any longer.

HELMER (controlling his emotions with difficulty): And you feel quite sure about this too?

NORA: Yes, absolutely sure. That's why I can't go on living here any longer.

HELMER: Can you also explain why I have lost your love?

NORA: Yes, I can. It happened this evening, when the

miracle failed to happen. It was then that I realized you weren't the man I'd thought you to be.

HELMER: Explain more clearly. I don't understand you.

NORA: I've waited so patiently, for eight whole years—well, good heavens, I'm not such a fool as to suppose that miracles occur every day. Then this dreadful thing happened to me, and then I *knew*: "Now the miracle will take place!" When Krogstad's letter was lying out there, it never occurred to me for a moment that you would let that man trample over you. I *knew* that you would say to him: "Publish the facts to the world." And when he had done this—

HELMER: Yes, what then? When I'd exposed my wife's name to shame and scandal—

NORA: Then I was certain that you would step forward and take all the blame on yourself, and say: "I am the one who is guilty!"

HELMER: Nora!

NORA: You're thinking I wouldn't have accepted such a sacrifice from you? No, of course I wouldn't! But what would my word have counted for against yours? That was the miracle I was hoping for, and dreading. And it was to prevent it happening that I wanted to end my life.

HELMER: Nora, I would gladly work for you night and day, and endure sorrow and hardship for your sake. But no man can be expected to sacrifice his honor, even for the person he loves.

NORA: Millions of women have done it.

HELMER: Oh, you think and talk like a stupid child.

NORA: That may be. But you neither think nor talk like the man I could share my life with. Once you'd got over your fright—and you weren't frightened of what might threaten me, but only of what threatened you—once the danger was past, then as far as you were concerned it was exactly as though nothing had happened. I was your little songbird just as before—your doll whom henceforth you would take particular care to protect from the world because she was so weak and fragile. *(Gets up.)* Torvald, in that moment I realized that for eight years I had been living here with a complete stranger, and had borne him three children—! Oh, I can't bear to think of it! I could tear myself to pieces!

HELMER *(sadly)*: I see it, I see it. A gulf has indeed opened between us. Oh, but Nora—couldn't it be bridged?

NORA: As I am now, I am no wife for you.

HELMER: I have the strength to change.

NORA: Perhaps—if your doll is taken from you.

HELMER: But to be parted—to be parted from you! No, no, Nora, I can't conceive of it happening!

NORA *(goes into the room, right)*: All the more necessary that it should happen.

(She comes back with her outdoor things and a small traveling-bag, which she puts down on a chair by the table.)

HELMER: Nora, Nora, not now! Wait till tomorrow!

NORA *(puts on her coat)*: I can't spend the night in a strange man's house.

HELMER: But can't we live here as brother and sister, then—?

NORA *(fastens her hat)*: You know quite well it wouldn't last. *(Puts on her shawl.)* Goodbye, Torvald. I don't want to see the children. I know they're in better hands than mine. As I am now, I can be nothing to them.

HELMER: But some time, Nora—some time—?

NORA: How can I tell? I've no idea what will happen to me.

HELMER: But you are my wife, both as you are and as you will be.

NORA: Listen, Torvald. When a wife leaves her husband's house, as I'm doing now, I'm told that according to the law he is freed of any obligations towards her. In any case, I release you from any such obligations. You mustn't feel bound to me in any way, however small, just as I shall not feel bound to you. We must both be quite free. Here is your ring back. Give me mine.

HELMER: That too?

NORA: That too.

HELMER: Here it is.

NORA: Good. Well, now it's over. I'll leave the keys here. The servants know about everything to do with the house—much better than I do. Tomorrow, when I have left town, Christine will come to pack the things I brought here from home. I'll have them sent on after me.

HELMER: This is the end then! Nora, will you never think of me any more?

NORA: Yes, of course. I shall often think of you and the children and this house.

HELMER: May I write to you, Nora?

NORA: No. Never. You mustn't do that.

HELMER: But at least you must let me send you—

NORA: Nothing. Nothing.

HELMER: But if you should need help—?

NORA: I tell you, no. I don't accept things from strangers.

HELMER: Nora—can I never be anything but a stranger to you?

NORA *(picks up her bag)*: Oh, Torvald! Then the miracle of miracles would have to happen.

HELMER: The miracle of miracles?

NORA: You and I would both have to change so much

that—oh, Torvald, I don't believe in miracles any longer.

HELMER: But I want to believe in them. Tell me. We should have to change so much that—?

NORA: That life together between us two could become a marriage. Goodbye.

(She goes out through the hall.)

HELMER *(sinks down on a chair by the door and buries his face in his hands)*: Nora! Nora! *(Looks round and gets up.)* Empty! She's gone! *(A hope strikes him.)* The miracle of miracles—?

(The street door is slammed shut downstairs.)

Figure 1. Nora (Claire Bloom) shows Torvald (Donald Madden) a doll that she has bought as a Christmas present for one of their children in the Playhouse production of *A Doll's House,* directed by Patrick Garland, New York, 1971. (Photograph: Henry Grossman.)

Figure 3. Nora (Claire Bloom) prepares to leave Torvald (Donald Madden) in the final scene of the Playhouse production of *A Doll's House,* directed by Patrick Garland, New York, 1971. The transformation of Nora that Claire Bloom sought to project through her performance of the role may be seen by comparing her facial expression and costume in this photograph with those shown in Figures 1 and 2. (Photograph: Henry Grossman.)

Figure 2. Torvald (Donald Madden) berates Nora (Claire Bloom) after reading the blackmail letter from Krogstad in the Playhouse production of *A Doll's House,* directed by Patrick Garland, New York, 1971. (Photograph: Henry Grossman.)

Staging of *A Doll's House*

REVIEW OF THE PLAYHOUSE PRODUCTION, NEW YORK, 1971, BY WALTER KERR

The difficulty with Ibsen today is that we must try to take two separate things seriously, the playwright's ideas and the playwright's playwriting. The ideas, of course, present no particular problem. One has only to listen to Claire Bloom's last long speech in the current—and very sleek—revival of "A Doll's House," which will soon be alternating with "Hedda Gabler" at the Playhouse, or to glance at the brief excerpts from Ibsen's "Notes for a Modern Tragedy" that have been included in the program to know that the ideas were sound, advanced, on target. "A woman cannot be herself in modern society," the notes read, "It is an exclusively male society, with laws made by men and with prosecutors and judges who assess female conduct from a male standpoint." Kate Millett sounds old-fashioned beside that.

But how, how, how do you take the playwriting seriously? From what vantage point, what perch or roost or perspective in time, can you attend, without doubling up, to the spectacle of a woman so determined to keep a secret from her husband that she promptly spills it, virtually within his hearing, to the very first acquaintance who walks in the door? Add to that the fact that she hasn't seen the acquaintance in years, and doesn't even recognize her when they do meet, and you've got a rather peculiar secret-keeper on your hands.

Peculiar things are going to keep happening, peculiar and predictable. Ibsen did work by notebook, which means that he jotted down most logically all the little twists and turns of motivation he was going to need and then clipped them together to make a scene whether they precisely flowed or not. If they didn't flow, he forced them ("Tell me, is it true you didn't love your husband?").

The terrible danger in this shuffled-note method is that you are going to hear the papers rustling, the clips slipping on. You can't *help* hearing them. And so you know, infallibly, that the moment the child-wife Nora exclaims "Oh, God, it's good to be alive and happy!," a doorbell will ring and a furtive fellow will slip in who's going to bring down her doll's house in ruins. Just as you know, with a certainty close to hilarity, that when Nora's fatuous lord and master, Torvald, exclaims "I often wish you were threatened with some impending disaster so that I could risk everything!," disaster is not only impending but here. Torvald has only to go to the mailbox ("I'm going to see if there's any mail"), slit open the first letter to hand, and the fat is in the fire. (In the current

production, the fat is not only in the fire, Nora is on the floor, having been hurled there by a vigorous spouse who, it turns out, is willing to risk nothing.)

The underpinnings are all transparent, line by line and blow by blow, and we must struggle to induce in ourselves a state of mind that holds humor at bay in honor of the social proposition being so implausibly stated. It's a real battle, one that is often lost; Ibsen believed in his mechanics as well as in his creed, and we cannot. The effort isn't exacerbating, especially; we needn't come away exhausted from it. It is possible to look at the foolishness and feel fond, if not doting, as we wait for the message that is going to come of it all. But it's nip and tuck the whole way, and the thin ice of the situation poses extremely thorny problems for actors.

It's not only a matter of how the good lady doing Nora is going to try to stitch together the two parts of the role, the giddy, fawning creature who is willing to leap up and down like a puppy dog snatching at proffered bones for two acts and the serene, stern woman who lays down the new law in Act 3, having matured wonderfully during intermission. It's a matter of how everyone onstage, pompous husband, long-lost confidante, sniveling blackmailer, dying Dr. Rank who is willing to offer Nora his love with his next-to-last breath, is going to get us past the preposterous and into the ringing preachment. Do they try to steal home, eliding all that is awkward as quietly as possible? Do they rush it, pouncing upon line two before we have quite noticed line one? Do they stylize it, lifting themselves into daguerreotype postures that plainly have little to do with reality?

The present company, under Patrick Garland's direction, has tried taking it by storm, with a bit of the daguerreotype thrown in. Donald Madden, a Torvald who might well see Dr. Rank about hypertension, glides across the highly lacquered floor (this Nora has such difficulty getting money out of her husband that you feel he won't even allow the lady carpeting) to exchange his wife's swift kisses for quickly palmed coins as though the two were Harlequins giving a summer-park performance in a high wind. Robert Gerringer, the forger who has come to accuse Nora of forgery (motives do get piggy-backed in this odd way), keeps his mouth open and working so that no matter who is talking his teeth will show.

All work at a high pitch and in some fever, as though a Racinian *tirade* might spin off into space at any moment. (If you have never seen "A Doll's

House," and I was stunned to discover how many first-nighters never had, this is a crystal-clear reading of it, laid out like silverware.) And there are some genuine successes within the near-stylization. Roy Shuman's Dr. Rank, for instance, is highly mannered: head thrown back, hands always on the point of clapping, eyes darting this way and that as he bluntly, briskly mocks himself and his approaching death. The effect is perfect, that of a man already halfway to the horizon waving farewell with his thumb to his nose. I have never seen the part more robustly or more persuasively played. Patricia Elliott's Kristine, so quickly privy to Nora's secrets, speaks vast amounts of exposition exquisitely, then zeroes in fiercely upon the play's point as she grips her shawl severely and remembers that her only happiness has lain in work.

But what of Nora? Claire Bloom has made, I think, an admirable choice, though a choice with a canker to it. Most Noras won't sacrifice the opportunity to charm, to be bird-like and winsome and if possible adorable, during the first two acts. And you can't entirely blame *them*. Nora is, as written in these acts, a ninny underneath, a girl who really can't feel any sympathy for creditors because, after all, they're "strangers," a girl who, though her secret debt is much on her mind, hasn't the faintest notion of how much of it she's paid off. She subsists, it would seem, on macaroons. But actresses who go for charm and a pretty mindlessness are stuck with the last act. How does one turn an enchanting child into a dominating adult, especially when the transition is missing?

Miss Bloom tries to create the transition from the beginning, which is surely an intelligent thing to do. Even as her Nora is nestling her pretty head against her husband's waistcoat while she seduces him with quick flattery into giving her old friend a job, there is a strain about the eyes, an indication of an intelligence withheld, that adds initial dimension to the role. Where most Noras seem to have an instinct for being playful, fluttering as to the cocoon born, Miss Bloom's playfulness is plainly put on, a trick she has learned, a device that does not wholly engage her.

She is constantly listening to herself make the sounds a pompous husband expects, aware of their insincerity and worried about the gulf between what she is doing and what she might be feeling. Faintly alienated from the outset, she has given us a base for the play's ending. The reserve that we felt in her was the conscience that might have been awakened at any time but is not in fact awakened until it is time to make that speech and slam that door.

The catch to doing it this way, because the part is split in the writing, is a curious sense of heartlessness that overtakes Nora en route. Being to a degree disengaged, she seems not only indifferent to her children and extremely obtuse about her friend Kristine's personal problems but horrendously cold-blooded about the devoted Dr. Rank. He announces his impending death and she scarcely looks up from her sewing. He makes a gesture of love toward her, a gesture that has to be disinterested because he will never see her again, and she recoils as though he had proposed, perhaps, another forgery. Clipping the butterfly's wings leaves us with something of a dragonfly. Or are we merely being given a bit of "Hedda" ahead of time?

Miss Bloom works honorably, looks well, arrives at her last scene logically, and doesn't seem anyone you'd care to trust your heart with (I'm not thinking of Torvald, who is an oaf, but, say, of Dr. Rank, who is not). Miss Bloom has cooled Nora to make the way for the ultimate avalanche; the move does take away anything that was ever very appealing about her.

Good try. The problem, which persists, lies in the play. Ibsen simply could not, or did not, get his meaning and his method to match up. When he speaks of "laws made by men" and "judges who assess female conduct from a male standpoint," we know exactly what he is talking about. We also know that he is right. But the technical illustration in the play proper runs like this. Nora has forged her father's signature to get money to help her ailing husband, who must not know he is being helped. Why didn't she have her father sign the document? Because he, too, was ailing; she didn't want to trouble him. Thus there are two kinds of law: male law (don't forge) and female law (don't bother father). Serious as the point is, the illustration can only make us smile.

The actors must try to make us contain the smile, which, in this revival, they occasionally do.

AUGUST STRINDBERG

1849–1912

Throughout his life Strindberg suffered from a variety of psychological anxieties and compulsions, and throughout his career he exploited his personal and psychic life in his novels, short stories, poetry, essays, and plays. He was raised in Stockholm, Sweden, the fourth of twelve children and the first born in wedlock. His mother died when he was thirteen, and his father immediately married the housekeeper. Strindberg himself was married three times and divorced three times, and each of his marriages was a tormenting experience both for him and the woman, particularly his first marriage to Siri von Essen, an aspiring actress of little talent who divorced her husband, a baron, in order to marry Strindberg. Before the marriage, Strindberg had worked briefly in various jobs, as a tutor, a telegraph clerk, an actor, and a librarian, but once he became involved with Siri he devoted himself almost exclusively to his writing. They remained married from 1877 to 1891, but long before they were divorced their affection for one another had given way to sexual quarrels, mutual jealousies, and bitter recriminations. During the disintegration of the marriage, Strindberg turned out a series of autobiographical novels, among them *A Fool's Defence* (1886), based on his involvement with Siri and her former husband, as well as a series of powerful naturalistic plays, all dealing with forms of psychological and sexual strife between men and women, including *The Father* (1887), *Miss Julie* (1888), *The Creditors* (1889), and *The Stronger* (1890).

Strindberg was married once again in 1893, this time to a young Austrian journalist, but their relationship quickly disintegrated into many of the same patterns that had characterized his first marriage. And by 1894 Strindberg himself was beginning to experience a psychological disintegration that was to extend over the next two years, a period during which he suffered from a profound sense of guilt and spiritual torment, as well as from a variety of paranoic hallucinations, focussing both on supernatural powers and on the doctor to whom he eventually committed himself for treatment. During this period he immersed himself in the mystical works of Emanuel Swedenborg and other religious writers, as well as turning his hand to painting and experiments in alchemy. By 1897, he had already chronicled his psychological and spiritual crisis in a thinly veiled novel, *Inferno*, and by 1898 he had begun another immensely productive period of writing that was to continue until the end of his life. Overall, he produced more than seventy plays and dramatic fragments.

During the period following his psychological inferno, Strindberg turned out a series of twenty-one chronicle plays, many of them in the manner of Shakespeare's, dealing with figures and periods in Swedish history from the thirteenth to the eighteenth century. But the most important plays of his later period reflect the preoccupations that flowed from his spiritual crisis, and they are concerned with the exposure of evil, as in *The Dance of Death* (1901), *A Dream Play* (1902), and *The Ghost Sonata* (1907), or with guilt and expiation, as in *Crime and Crime* (1899) and *Easter* (1901), or with spiritual pilgrimage, as in *To Damascus*

(1898–1904) and *The Great Highway* (1909). In these plays, Strindberg turned away from the purely naturalistic methods of his earlier plays, using expressionistic and symbolic techniques to dramatize his troubled vision of human experience. In *A Dream Play,* for example, the world is seen entirely through the experience and perception of the Daughter of Indra, the child of a deity, whose descent to earth and subsequent encounters with various human beings reflect and reproduce, as Strindberg explained in his note on the play, "the disconnected but apparently logical form of a dream." Because it is a dream, "Anything can happen; everything is possible and probable . . . The characters are split, double and multiply; they evaporate, crystallise, scatter and converge. But a single consciousness holds sway over them all—that of the dreamer." The dreamer, of course, was Strindberg himself, and the disconnected events of the play vividly project his melancholy vision of the human landscape. *The Ghost Sonata* is another expressionistic and symbolic fantasy, this time displaying the macabre spectacle of a demonic household as it is progressively unveiled to the eyes of a young student—clearly Strindberg's alter ego—who ends the play by proclaiming the world to be "this madhouse, this prison, this charnelhouse." In their expressionistic techniques, these later plays prefigure a major aspect of modern and contemporary drama. In their preoccupation with dreams and the disconnected logic of psychic experience, they are arresting parallels to the work of Freud, whose first important study of the unconscious, *The Interpretation of Dreams,* did not appear until 1900.

But even in his naturalistic plays of the eighties, such as *Miss Julie*, Strindberg was advanced for his time, both in his dramatic techniques and in his psychological insight. He took great pains to identify his innovations in a lengthy "Foreword" to *Miss Julie* that he wrote after the play was accepted for publication. He called attention, for example, to the improvisational miming of Kristin early in the play, to the improvisational miming and dancing of the peasants, and to the improvisational monologue of Kristin mumbling in her sleep. He was aware of the classical precedents for mime, dancing, and monologue in drama, much as he was aware of the Italian Renaissance precedents for improvisational performance, but he also recognized that realistic conventions of his time had excluded these dramatic possibilities from the stage, whereas he considered them not only consistent with, but essential to a naturalistic illusion. In the same context, he also called attention to the fact that the play is designed to be staged without intermission, and that the set is to be diagonally arranged, "so that the actors may play full-face and in half-profile when they are sitting opposite one another at the table." He might also have pointed out that the action is set in a kitchen that really functions, for the play begins with Kristin frying a piece of kidney on the stove, and it reaches a climax with Jean beheading Julie's greenfinch on the kitchen chopping block. In all these respects, Strindberg carried naturalistic theater further than any of his contemporaries—extending it to its logical and psychological limits.

In the psychological conception of Jean and Julie, as well as in the unfolding of their relationship, Strindberg also challenged his contemporaries, particularly Emile Zola, the first major proponent of naturalistic drama, who in 1874 had written a manifesto proclaiming that heredity and environment are the sole determinants of human nature and behavior, and that dramatists are, therefore, obliged to reflect these circumstances in their plays. Strindberg, however, was clearly not content to limit himself to so narrow a conception of human behavior as he makes clear in the "Foreword" to *Miss Julie:*

> I see Miss Julie's tragic fate to be the result of many circumstances: the mother's character, the father's mistaken upbringing of the girl, her own weak nature, and the influence of her fiancé on a weak, degenerate mind. Also, more directly, the festive mood of Midsummer Eve, her father's absence, her monthly indisposition, her pre-occupation with animals, the excitement of dancing, the magic of dusk, the strongly aphrodisiac influence of flowers, and finally the chance that drives the couple into a room alone—to which must be added the urgency of the excited man.
>
> My treatment of the theme, morever, is neither exclusively physiological nor psychological. I have not put the blame wholly on the inheritance from her mother, nor on her physical condition at the time, nor on immorality. I have not even preached a moral sermon; in the absence of a priest I leave this to the cook.
>
> I congratulate myself on this multiplicity of motives as being up-to-date, and if others have done the same thing before me, then I congratulate myself on not being alone in my "paradoxes," as all innovations are called.

Strindberg's comments here and elsewhere in the "Foreword" may well serve as a warning against trying to interpret the play within any kind of simplistic framework. It is an enactment of a class struggle, as Strindberg notes, and as is repeatedly evident in the play from the dialogue and action of Julie, Jean, and Kristin. It is also, in part, an enactment of sexual warfare, as Strindberg and the play make painfully clear. But these two aspects of the conflict are inextricably woven together and complicated further by the subtle aspects of personality that mark both Jean and Julie as individuals rather than social or sexual types. The unfolding of their conflict is thus continually surprising and revealing, and until the very end of the play when Julie walks out of the kitchen with the razor in her hand the resolution of their conflict is never predictable, though it is thoroughly plausible.

Because of the complexity and the intensity of their struggle, *Miss Julie* is an extremely difficult play to produce, as noted in one of the reviews of the National Theatre production reprinted following the text. Photographs of that production show Albert Finney as Jean and Maggie Smith as Julie at various moments during their conflict—from their initial confrontation in the kitchen (see Figure 1) to their long conversation following the departure of the peasants (see Figure 2), to the final moments of the play (see Figure 3). Although their facial expressions clearly betray a lack of ferocity that one of the reviewers criticized in the production, they do show Jean's unnerving callousness, and they also suggest the subtle unfolding of Julie's tragic demise.

MISS JULIE
A Naturalistic Tragedy

BY AUGUST STRINDBERG / TRANSLATED BY ELIZABETH SPRIGGE

CHARACTERS

MISS JULIE, *aged 25*
JEAN, *the valet, aged 30*
KRISTIN, *the cook, aged 35*

SCENE:

The large kitchen of a Swedish manor house in a country district in the 1880s.

(Midsummer Eve.

The kitchen has three doors, two small ones into JEAN'S and KRISTIN'S bedrooms, and a large, glass-fronted double one, opening on to a courtyard. This is the only way to the rest of the house.

Through these glass doors can be seen part of a fountain with a cupid, lilac bushes in flower and the tops of some Lombardy poplars. On one wall are shelves edged with scalloped paper on which are kitchen utensils of copper, iron and tin.

To the left is the corner of a large tiled range and part of its chimney-hood, to the right the end of the servants' dinner table with chairs beside it.

The stove is decorated with birch boughs, the floor strewn with twigs of juniper. On the end of the table is a large Japanese spice jar full of lilac.

There are also an ice-box, a scullery table and a sink.

Above the double door hangs a big old-fashioned bell; near it is a speaking-tube.

A fiddle can be heard from the dance in the barn near-by.

KRISTIN *is standing at the stove, frying something in a pan. She wears a light-colored cotton dress and a big apron.*

JEAN *enters, wearing livery and carrying a pair of large riding-boots with spurs, which he puts in a conspicuous place.)*

JEAN: Miss Julie's crazy again to-night, absolutely crazy.

KRISTIN: Oh, so you're back, are you?

JEAN: When I'd taken the Count to the station, I came back and dropped in at the Barn for a dance. And who did I see there but our young lady leading off with the gamekeeper. But the moment she sets eyes on me, up she rushes and invites me to waltz with her. And how she waltzed—I've never seen anything like it! She's crazy.

KRISTIN: Always has been, but never so bad as this last fortnight since the engagement was broken off.

JEAN: Yes, that was a pretty business, to be sure. He's a decent enough chap, too, even if he isn't rich.

Oh, but they're choosy! *(Sits down at the end of the table.)* In any case, it's a bit odd that our young—er—lady would rather stay at home with yokels than go with her father to visit her relations.

KRISTIN: Perhaps she feels a bit awkward, after that bust-up with her fiancé.

JEAN: Maybe. That chap had some guts, though. Do you know the sort of thing that was going on, Kristin? I saw it with my own eyes, though I didn't let on I had.

KRISTIN: You saw them . . . ?

JEAN: Didn't I just! Came across the pair of them one evening in the stable-yard. Miss Julie was doing what she called "training" him. Know what that was? Making him jump over her riding-whip—the way you teach a dog. He did it twice and got a cut each time for his pains, but when it came to the third go, he snatched the whip out of her hand and broke it into smithereens. And then he cleared off.

KRISTIN: What goings on! I never did!

JEAN: Well, that's how it was with that little affair . . . Now, what have you got for me, Kristin? Something tasty?

KRISTIN *(serving from the pan to his plate)*: Well, it's just a little bit of kidney I cut off their joint.

JEAN *(smelling it)*: Fine! That's my special delice. *(Feels the plate.)* But you might have warmed the plate.

KRISTIN: When you choose to be finicky you're worse than the Count himself. *(Pulls his hair affectionately.)*

JEAN *(crossly)*: Stop pulling my hair. You know how sensitive I am.

KRISTIN: There, there! It's only love, you know.

(JEAN eats. KRISTIN brings a bottle of beer.)

JEAN: Beer on Midsummer Eve? No thanks! I've got something better than that. *(From a drawer in the table brings out a bottle of red wine with a yellow seal.)*

68

Yellow seal, see! Now get me a glass. You use a glass with a stem of course when you're drinking it straight.

KRISTIN (*giving him a wine-glass*): Lord help the woman who gets you for a husband, you old fusser! (*She puts the beer in the ice-box and sets a small saucepan on the stove.*)

JEAN: Nonsense! You'll be glad enough to get a fellow as smart as me. And I don't think it's done you any harm, people calling me your fiancé. (*Tastes the wine.*) Good, Very good indeed. But not quite warmed enough. (*Warms the glass in his hand.*) We bought this in Dijon. Four francs the liter without the bottle, and duty on top of that. What are you cooking now? It stinks.

KRISTIN: Some bloody muck Miss Julie wants for Diana.

JEAN: You should be more refined in your speech, Kristin. But why should you spend a holiday cooking for that bitch? Is she sick or what?

KRISTIN: Yes, she's sick. She sneaked out with the pug at the lodge and got in the usual mess. And that, you know, Miss Julie won't have.

JEAN: Miss Julie's too high-and-mighty in some respects, and not enough in others, just like her mother before her. The Countess was more at home in the kitchen and cowsheds than anywhere else, but would she ever go driving with only one horse? She went round with her cuffs filthy, but she had to have the coronet on the cuff-links. Our young lady—to come back to her—hasn't any proper respect for herself or her position. I mean she isn't refined. In the Barn just now she dragged the gamekeeper away from Anna and made him dance with her—no waiting to be asked. We wouldn't do a think like that. But that's what happens when the gentry try to behave like the common people—they become common . . . Still she's a fine girl. Smashing! What shoulders! And what—er—etcetera!

KRISTIN: Oh come off it! I know what Clara says, and she dresses her.

JEAN: Clara? Pooh, you're all jealous! But I've been out riding with her . . . and as for her dancing!

KRISTIN: Listen, Jean. You will dance with me, won't you, as soon as I'm through.

JEAN: Of course I will.

KRISTIN: Promise?

JEAN: Promise? When I say I'll do a thing I do it. Well thanks for the supper. It was a real treat. (*Corks the bottle.*)

(JULIE *appears in the doorway, speaking to someone outside.*)

JULIE: I'll be back in a moment. Don't wait.

(JEAN *slips the bottle into the drawer and rises respectfully.*

JULIE *enters and joins* KRISTIN *at the stove.*)

Well, have you made it? (KRISTIN *signs that* JEAN *is near them.*)

JEAN (*gallantly*): Have you ladies got some secret?

JULIE (*flipping his face with her handkerchief*): You're very inquisitive.

JEAN: What a delicious smell! Violets.

JULIE (*coquettishly*): Impertinence! Are you an expert of scent too? I must say you know how to dance. Now don't look. Go away. (*The music of a schottische begins.*)

JEAN (*with impudent politeness*): Is it some witches' brew you're cooking on Midsummer Eve? Something to tell your stars by, so you can see your future?

JULIE (*sharply*): If you could see that you'd have good eyes. (*to* KRISTIN) Put it in a bottle and cork it tight. Come and dance this schottische with me, Jean.

JEAN (*hesitating*): I don't want to be rude, but I've promised to dance this one with Kristin.

JULIE: Well, she can have another, can't you, Kristin? You'll lend me Jean, won't you?

KRISTIN (*bottling*): It's nothing to do with me. When you're so condescending, Miss, it's not his place to say no. Go on, Jean, and thank Miss Julie for the honor.

JEAN: Frankly speaking, Miss, and no offense meant, I wonder if it's wise for you to dance twice running with the same partner, specially as those people are so ready to jump to conclusions.

JULIE (*flaring up*): What did you say? What sort of conclusions? What do you mean?

JEAN (*meekly*): As you choose not to understand, Miss Julie, I'll have to speak more plainly. It looks bad to show a preference for one of your retainers when they're all hoping for the same unusual favor.

JULIE: Show a preference! The very idea! I'm surprised at you. I'm doing the people an honor by attending their ball when I'm mistress of the house, but if I'm really going to dance, I mean to have a partner who can lead and doesn't make me look ridiculous.

JEAN: If those are your orders, Miss, I'm at your service.

JULIE (*gently*): Don't take it as an order. Tonight we're all just people enjoying a party. There's no question of class. So now give me your arm. Don't worry, Kristin, I shan't steal your sweetheart.

(JEAN *gives* JULIE *his arm and leads her out. Left alone,* KRISTIN *plays her scene in an unhurried, natural way, humming to the tune of the schottische, played on a distant violin. She clears* JEAN's *place, washes up and puts things away, then takes off her apron, brings out a small mirror from a drawer, props it against the jar of lilac, lights a candle, warms a small pair of tongs and curls her fringe. She goes to the door and listens, then turning back to the table finds* MISS JULIE'S *handkerchief. She smells it, then meditatively smooths it out and folds it. Enter* JEAN.)

JEAN: She really *is* crazy. What a way to dance! With people standing grinning at her too from behind the doors. What's got into her, Kristin?

KRISTIN: Oh, it's just her time coming on. She's always queer then. Are you going to dance with me now?

JEAN: Then you're not wild with me for cutting that one.

KRISTIN: You know I'm not—for a little thing like that. Besides, I know my place.

JEAN *(putting his arm round her waist)*: You're a sensible girl, Kristin, and you'll make a very good wife . . .

(Enter JULIE, *unpleasantly surprised.)*

JULIE *(with forced gaiety)*: You're a fine beau—running away from your partner.

JEAN: Not away, Miss Julie, but as you see back to the one I deserted.

JULIE *(changing her tone)*: You really can dance, you know. But why are you wearing your livery on a holiday. Take it off at once.

JEAN: Then I must ask you to go away for a moment, Miss. My black coat's here. *(Indicates it hanging on the door to his room.)*

JULIE: Are you so shy of me—just over changing a coat? Go into your room then—or stay here and I'll turn my back.

JEAN: Excuse me then, Miss. *(He goes to his room and is partly visible as he changes his coat.)*

JULIE: Tell me, Kristin, is Jean your fiancé? You seem very intimate.

KRISTIN: My fiancé? Yes, if you like. We call it that.

JULIE: Call it?

KRISTIN: Well, you've had a fiancé yourself, Miss, and . . .

JULIE: But we really were engaged.

KRISTIN: All the same it didn't come to anything.

*(*JEAN *returns in his black coat.)*

JULIE: *Très gentil, Monsieur Jean. Très gentil.*

JEAN: *Vous voulez plaisanter, Madame.*

JULIE: *Et vous voulez parler français.*° Where did you learn it?

JEAN: In Switzerland, when I was steward at one of the biggest hotels in Lucerne.

JULIE: You look quite the gentleman in that get-up. Charming. *(Sits at the table.)*

Très . . . gentil, Very nice, Monsieur Jean, very nice. *Vous . . . Madame,* You like to joke, Madame. *Et . . . français,* And you want to speak French.

JEAN: Oh, you're just flattering me!

JULIE *(annoyed)*: Flattering you?

JEAN: I'm too modest to believe you would pay real compliments to a man like me, so I must take it you are exaggerating—that this is what's known as flattery.

JULIE: Where on earth did you learn to make speeches like that? Perhaps you've been to the theater a lot.

JEAN: That's right. And traveled a lot too.

JULIE: But you come from this neighborhood, don't you?

JEAN: Yes, my father was a laborer on the next estate—the District Attorney's place. I often used to see you, Miss Julie, when you were little, though you never noticed me.

JULIE: Did you really?

JEAN: Yes. One time specially I remember . . . but I can't tell you about that.

JULIE: Oh do! Why not? This is just the time.

JEAN: No, I really can't now. Another time perhaps.

JULIE: Another time means never. What harm in now?

JEAN: No harm, but I'd rather not. *(Points to* KRISTIN, *now fast asleep.)* Look at her.

JULIE: She'll make a charming wife, won't she? I wonder if she snores.

JEAN: No, she doesn't, but she talks in her sleep.

JULIE *(cynically)*: How do you know she talks in her sleep?

JEAN *(brazenly)*: I've heard her. *(Pause. They look at one another.)*

JULIE: Why don't you sit down?

JEAN: I can't take such a liberty in your presence.

JULIE: Supposing I order you to.

JEAN: I'll obey.

JULIE: Then sit down. No, wait a minute. Will you get me a drink first?

JEAN: I don't know what's in the ice-box. Only beer, I expect.

JULIE: There's no only about it. My taste is so simple I prefer it to wine.

*(*JEAN *takes a bottle from the ice-box, fetches a glass and plate and serves the beer.)*

JEAN: At your service.

JULIE: Thank you. Won't you have some yourself?

JEAN: I'm not really a beer-drinker, but if it's an order. . . .

JULIE: Order? I should have thought it was ordinary manners to keep your partner company.

JEAN: That's a good way of putting it. *(He opens another bottle and fetches a glass.)*

JULIE: Now drink my health. *(He hesitates.)* I believe the man really is shy.

*(*JEAN *kneels and raises his glass with mock ceremony.)*

JEAN: To the health of my lady!

JULIE: Bravo! Now kiss my shoe and everything will be perfect. (*He hesitates, then boldly takes hold of her foot and lightly kisses it.*) Splendid. You ought to have been an actor.

JEAN (*rising*): We can't go on like this, Miss Julie. Someone might come in and see us.

JULIE: Why would that matter?

JEAN: For the simple reason that they'd talk. And if you knew the way their tongues were wagging out there just now, you . . .

JULIE: What were they saying? Tell me. Sit down.

JEAN (*sitting*): No offense meant, Miss, but . . . well, their language wasn't nice, and they were hinting . . . oh, you know quite well what. You're not a child, and if a lady's seen drinking alone at night with a man—and a servant at that—then . . .

JULIE: Then what? Besides, we're not alone. Kristin's here.

JEAN: Yes, asleep.

JULIE: I'll wake her up. (*Rises.*) Kristin, are you asleep? (KRISTIN *mumbles in her sleep.*) Kristin! Goodness, how she sleeps!

KRISTIN (*in her sleep*): The Count's boots are cleaned—put the coffee on—yes, yes, at once . . . (*Mumbles incoherently.*)

JULIE (*tweaking her nose*): Wake up, can't you!

JEAN (*sharply*): Let her sleep.

JULIE: What?

JEAN: When you've been standing at the stove all day you're likely to be tired at night. And sleep should be respected.

JULIE (*changing her tone*): What a nice idea. It does you credit. Thank you for it. (*Holds out her hand to him.*) Now come out and pick some lilac for me. (*During the following* KRISTIN *goes sleepily in to her bedroom.*)

JEAN: Out with you, Miss Julie?

JULIE: Yes.

JEAN: It wouldn't do. It really wouldn't.

JULIE: I don't know what you mean. You can't possibly imagine that . . .

JEAN: I don't, but others do.

JULIE: What? That I'm in love with the valet?

JEAN: I'm not a conceited man, but such a thing's been known to happen, and to these rustics nothing's sacred.

JULIE: You, I take it, are an aristocrat.

JEAN: Yes, I am.

JULIE: And I am coming down in the world.

JEAN: Don't come down, Miss Julie. Take my advice. No one will believe you came down of your own accord. They'll all say you fell.

JULIE: I have a higher opinion of our people than you. Come and put it to the test. Come on. (*Gazes into his eyes.*)

JEAN: You're very strange, you know.

JULIE: Perhaps I am, but so are you. For that matter everything is strange. Life, human beings, everything, just scum drifting about on the water until it sinks—down and down. That reminds me of a dream I sometimes have, in which I'm on top of a pillar and can't see any way of getting down. When I look down I'm dizzy; I have to get down but I haven't the courage to jump. I can't stay there and I long to fall, but I don't fall. There's no respite. There can't be any peace at all for me until I'm down, right down on the ground. And if I did get to the ground I'd want to be under the ground . . . Have you ever felt like that?

JEAN: No. In my dream I'm lying under a great tree in a dark wood. I want to get up, up to the top of it, and look out over the bright landscape where the sun is shining and rob that high nest of its golden eggs. And I climb and climb, but the trunk is so thick and smooth and it's so far to the first branch. But I know if I can once reach that first branch I'll go to the top just as if I'm on a ladder. I haven't reached it yet, but I shall get there, even if only in my dreams.

JULIE: Here I am chattering about dreams with you. Come on. Only into the park. (*She takes his arm and they go toward the door.*)

JEAN: We must sleep on nine midsummer flowers tonight; then our dreams will come true, Miss Julie. (*They turn at the door. He has a hand to his eye.*)

JULIE: Have you got something in your eye? Let me see.

JEAN: Oh, it's nothing. Just a speck of dust. It'll be gone in a minute.

JULIE: My sleeve must have rubbed against you. Sit down and let me see to it. (*Takes him by the arm and makes him sit down, bends his head back and tries to get the speck out with the corner of her handkerchief.*) Keep still now, quite still. (*Slaps his hand.*) Do as I tell you. Why, I believe you're trembling, big, strong man though you are! (*Feels his biceps.*) What muscles!

JEAN (*warning*): Miss Julie!

JULIE: Yes, Monsieur Jean?

JEAN: *Attention. Je ne suis qu'un homme.*°

JULIE: Will you stay still! There now. It's out. Kiss my hand and say thank you.

JEAN (*rising*): Miss Julie, listen, Kristin's gone to bed now. Will you listen?

JULIE: Kiss my hand first.

JEAN: Very well, but you'll have only yourself to blame.

JULIE: For what?

JEAN: For what! Are you still a child at twenty-five? Don't you know it's dangerous to play with fire?

Attention . . . homme, Careful, I'm only a man.

JULIE: Not for me. I'm insured.

JEAN (*bluntly*): No, you're not. And even if you are, there's still stuff here to kindle a flame.

JULIE: Meaning yourself?

JEAN: Yes. Not because I'm me, but because I'm a man and young and . . .

JULIE: And good looking? What incredible conceit! A Don Juan perhaps? Or a Joseph? Good Lord, I do believe you are a Joseph!

JEAN: Do you?

JULIE: I'm rather afraid so.

(JEAN *goes boldly up and tries to put his arms round her and kiss her. She boxes his ears.*)

How dare you!

JEAN: Was that in earnest or a joke?

JULIE: In earnest.

JEAN: Then what went before was in earnest too. You take your games too seriously and that's dangerous. Anyhow I'm tired of playing now and beg leave to return to my work. The Count will want his boots first thing and it's past midnight now.

JULIE: Put those boots down.

JEAN: No. This is my work, which it's my duty to do. But I never undertook to be your playfellow and I never will be. I consider myself too good for that.

JULIE: You're proud.

JEAN: In some ways—not all.

JULIE: Have you ever been in love?

JEAN: We don't put it that way, but I've been gone on quite a few girls. And once I went sick because I couldn't have the one I wanted. Sick, I mean, like those princes in the Arabian Nights who couldn't eat or drink for love.

JULIE: Who was she? (*No answer.*) Who was she?

JEAN: You can't force me to tell you that.

JULIE: If I ask as an equal, ask as a—friend? Who was she?

JEAN: You.

JULIE (*sitting*): How absurd!

JEAN: Yes, ludicrous if you like. That's the story I wouldn't tell you before, see, but now I will . . . Do you know what the world looks like from below? No, you don't. No more than the hawks and falcons do whose backs one hardly ever sees because they're always soaring up aloft. I lived in a laborer's hovel with seven other children and a pig, out in the gray fields where there isn't a single tree. But from the window I could see the wall round the Count's park with apple-trees above it. That was the Garden of Eden, guarded by many terrible angels with flaming swords. All the same I and the other boys managed to get to the tree of life. Does all this make you despise me?

JULIE: Goodness, all boys steal apples!

JEAN: You say that now, but all the same you do despise me. However, one time I went into the Garden of Eden with my mother to weed the onion beds. Close to the kitchen garden there was a Turkish pavilion hung all over with jasmine and honeysuckle. I hadn't any idea what it was used for, but I'd never seen such a beautiful building. People used to go in and then come out again, and one day the door was left open. I crept up and saw the walls covered with pictures of kings and emperors, and the windows had red curtains with fringes—you know now what the place was, don't you? I . . . (*Breaks off a piece of lilac and holds it for* JULIE *to smell. As he talks, she takes it from him.*) I had never been inside the manor, never seen anything but the church, and this was more beautiful. No matter where my thoughts went, they always came back—to that place. The longing went on growing in me to enjoy it fully, just once. *Enfin,*° I sneaked in, gazed and admired. Then I heard someone coming. There was only one way out for the gentry, but for me there was another and I had no choice but to take it. (JULIE *drops the lilac on the table.*) Then I took to my heels, plunged through the raspberry canes, dashed across the strawberry beds and found myself on the rose terrace. There I saw a pink dress and a pair of white stockings—it was you. I crawled into a weed pile and lay there right under it among prickly thistles and damp rank earth. I watched you walking among the roses and said to myself: "If it's true that a thief can get to heaven and be with the angels, it's pretty strange that a laborer's child here on God's earth mayn't come in the park and play with the Count's daughter."

JULIE (*sentimentally*): Do you think all poor children feel the way you did?

JEAN (*taken aback, then rallying*): *All* poor children? . . . Yes, of course they do. Of course.

JULIE: It must be terrible to be poor.

JEAN (*with exaggerated distress*): Oh yes, Miss Julie, yes. A dog may lie on the Countess's sofa, a horse may have his nose stroked by a young lady, but a servant . . . (*Change of tone.*) well, yes, now and then you meet one with guts enough to rise in the world, but how often? Anyhow, do you know what I did? Jumped into the millstream with my clothes on, was pulled out and got a hiding. But the next Sunday, when Father and all the rest went to Granny's, I managed to get left behind. Then I washed with soap and hot water, put my

---

Enfin, Well.

best clothes on and went to church so as to see you. I did see you and went home determined to die. But I wanted to die beautifully and peacefully, without any pain. Then I remembered it was dangerous to sleep under an elder bush. We had a big one in full bloom, so I stripped it and climbed into the oats-bin with the flowers. Have you ever noticed how smooth oats are? Soft to touch as human skin . . . Well, I closed the lid and shut my eyes, fell asleep, and when they woke me I was very ill. But I didn't die, as you see. What I meant by all that I don't know. There was no hope of winning you—you were simply a symbol of the hopelessness of ever getting out of the class I was born in.

JULIE: You put things very well, you know. Did you go to school?

JEAN: For a while. But I've read a lot of novels and been to the theater. Besides, I've heard educated folk talking—that's what's taught me most.

JULIE: Do you stand round listening to what we're saying?

JEAN: Yes, of course. And I've heard quite a bit too! On the carriage box or rowing the boat. Once I heard you, Miss Julie, and one of your young lady friends . . .

JULIE: Oh! Whatever did you hear?

JEAN: Well, it wouldn't be nice to repeat it. And I must say I was pretty startled. I couldn't think where you had learnt such words. Perhaps, at bottom, there isn't as much difference between people as one's led to believe.

JULIE: How dare you! We don't behave as you do when we're engaged.

JEAN (looking hard at her): Are you sure? It's no use making out so innocent to me.

JULIE: The man I gave my love to was a scoundrel.

JEAN: That's what you always say—afterward.

JULIE: Always?

JEAN: I think it must be always. I've heard the expression several times in similar circumstances.

JULIE: What circumstances?

JEAN: Like those in question. The last time . . .

JULIE (rising): Stop. I don't want to hear any more.

JEAN: Nor did she—curiously enough. May I go to bed now please?

JULIE (gently): Go to bed on Midsummer Eve?

JEAN: Yes. Dancing with that crowd doesn't really amuse me.

JULIE: Get the key of the boathouse and row me out on the lake. I want to see the sun rise.

JEAN: Would that be wise?

JULIE: You sound as though you're frightened for your reputation.

JEAN: Why not? I don't want to be made a fool of, nor to be sent packing without references when I'm trying to better myself. Besides, I have Kristin to consider.

JULIE: So now it's Kristin.

JEAN: Yes, but it's you I'm thinking about too. Take my advice and go to bed.

JULIE: Am I to take orders from you?

JEAN: Just this once, for your own sake. Please. It's very late and sleepiness goes to one's head and makes one rash. Go to bed. What's more, if my ears don't deceive me, I hear people coming this way. They'll be looking for me, and if they find us here, you're done for.

(The CHORUS approaches, singing. During the following dialogue the song is heard in snatches, and in full when the peasants enter.)

Out of the wood two women came,
Tridiri-ralla, tridiri-ra.
The feet of one were bare and cold,
Tridiri-ralla-la.

The other talked of bags of gold,
Tridiri-ralla, tridiri-ra.
But neither had a sou to her name,
Tridiri-ralla-la.

The bridal wreath I give to you,
Tridiri-ralla, tridiri-ra.
But to another I'll be true,
Tridiri-ralla-la.

JULIE: I know our people and I love them, just as they do me. Let them come. You'll see.

JEAN: No, Miss Julie, they don't love you. They take your food, then spit at it. You must believe me. Listen to them, just listen to what they're singing . . . No, don't listen.

JULIE (listening): What are they singing?

JEAN: They're mocking—you and me.

JULIE: Oh no! How horrible! What cowards!

JEAN: A pack like that's always cowardly. But against such odds there's nothing we can do but run away.

JULIE: Run away? Where to? We can't get out and we can't go into Kristin's room.

JEAN: Into mine then. Necessity knows no rules. And you can trust me. I really am your true and devoted friend.

JULIE: But supposing . . . supposing they were to look for you in there?

JEAN: I'll bolt the door, and if they try to break in I'll shoot. Come on. (Pleading.) Please come.

JULIE (tensely): Do you promise . . . ?

JEAN: I swear!

(JULIE goes quickly into his room and he excitedly follows her. Led by the fiddler, the peasants enter in festive attire *with flowers in their hats. They put a barrel of beer and a keg of spirits, garlanded with leaves, on the table, fetch glasses and begin to carouse. The scene becomes a ballet. They form a ring and dance and sing and mime. "Out of the wood two women came." Finally they go out, still singing.* JULIE *comes in alone. She looks at the havoc in the kitchen, wrings her hands, then takes out her powder puff and powders her face.* JEAN *enters in high spirits.*)

JEAN: Now you see! And you heard, didn't you? Do you still think it's possible for us to stay here?

JULIE: No, I don't. But what can we do?

JEAN: Run away. Far away. Take a journey.

JULIE: Journey? But where to?

JEAN: Switzerland. The Italian lakes. Ever been there?

JULIE: No. Is it nice?

JEAN: Ah! Eternal summer, oranges, evergreens . . . ah!

JULIE: But what would we do there?

JEAN: I'll start a hotel. First-class accommodation and first-class customers.

JULIE: Hotel?

JEAN: There's life for you. New faces all the time, new languages—no time for nerves or worries, no need to look for something to do—work rolling up of its own accord. Bells ringing night and day, trains whistling, buses coming and going, and all the time gold pieces rolling on to the counter. There's life for you!

JULIE: For *you*. And I?

JEAN: Mistress of the house, ornament of the firm. With your looks, and your style . . . oh, it's bound to be a success! Terrific! You'll sit like a queen in the office and set your slaves in motion by pressing an electric button. The guests will file past your throne and nervously lay their treasure on your table. You've no idea the way people tremble when they get their bills. I'll salt the bills and you'll sugar them with your sweetest smiles. Ah, let's get away from here! (*Produces a time-table.*) At once, by the next train. We shall be at Malmö at six-thirty, Hamburg eight-forty next morning, Frankfort-Basle the following day, and Como by the St. Gotthard Pass in—let's see— three days. Three days!

JULIE: That's all very well. But Jean, you must give me courage. Tell me you love me. Come and take me in your arms.

JEAN (*reluctantly*): I'd like to, but I daren't. Not again in this house. I love you—that goes without saying. You can't doubt that, Miss Julie, can you?

JULIE (*shyly, very feminine*): Miss? Call me Julie. There aren't any barriers between us now. Call me Julie.

JEAN (*uneasily*): I can't. As long as we're in this house, there *are* barriers between us. There's the past

and there's the Count. I've never been so servile to anyone as I am to him. I've only to hear his bell and I shy like a horse. Even now, when I look at his boots, standing there so proud and stiff, I feel my back beginning to bend. (*Kicks the boots.*) It's those old, narrow-minded notions drummed into us as children . . . but they can soon be forgotten. You've only got to get to another country, a republic, and people will bend themselves double before my porter's livery. Yes, double they'll bend themselves, but I shan't. I wasn't born to bend. I've got guts. I've got character, and once I reach that first branch, you'll watch me climb. Today I'm valet, next year I'll be proprietor, in ten years I'll have made a fortune, and then I'll go to Rumania, get myself decorated and I may, I only say *may*, mind you, end up as a Count.

JULIE (*sadly*): That would be very nice.

JEAN: You see in Rumania one can buy a title, and then you'll be a Countess after all. My Countess.

JULIE: What do I care about all that? I'm putting those things behind me. Tell me you love me, because if you don't . . . if you don't, what am I?

JEAN: I'll tell you a thousand times over—later. But not here. No sentimentality now or everything will be lost. We must consider this thing calmly like reasonable people. (*Takes a cigar, cuts and lights it.*) You sit down there and I'll sit here and we'll talk as if nothing happened.

JULIE: My God, have you no feelings at all?

JEAN: Nobody has more. But I know how to control them.

JULIE: A short time ago you were kissing my shoe. And now . . .

JEAN (*harshly*): Yes, that was then. Now we have something else to think about.

JULIE: Don't speak to me so brutally.

JEAN: I'm not. Just sensibly. One folly's been committed, don't let's have more. The Count will be back at any moment and we've got to settle our future before that. Now, what do you think of my plans? Do you approve?

JULIE: It seems a very good idea—but just one thing. Such a big undertaking would need a lot of capital. Have you got any?

JEAN (*chewing his cigar*): I certainly have. I've got my professional skill, my wide experience, and my knowledge of foreign languages. That's capital worth having, it seems to me.

JULIE: But it won't buy even one railway ticket.

JEAN: Quite true. That's why I need a backer to advance some ready cash.

JULIE: How could you get that at a moment's notice?

JEAN: You must get it, if you want to be my partner.

JULIE: I can't. I haven't any money of my own. (*Pause.*)

JEAN: Then the whole thing's off.

JULIE: And . . . ?

JEAN: We go on as we are.

JULIE: Do you think I'm going to stay under this roof as your mistress? With everyone pointing at me. Do you think I can face my father after this? No. Take me away from here, away from this shame, this humiliation. Oh my God, what have I done? My God, my God! *(Weeps.)*

JEAN: So that's the tune now, is it? What have you done? Same as many before you.

JULIE *(hysterically)*: And now you despise me. I'm falling, I'm falling.

JEAN: Fall as far as me and I'll lift you up again.

JULIE: Why was I so terribly attracted to you? The weak to the strong, the falling to the rising? Or was it love? Is that love? Do you know what love is?

JEAN: Do I? You bet I do. Do you think I never had a girl before?

JULIE: The things you say, the things you think!

JEAN: That's what life's taught me, and that's what I am. It's no good getting hysterical or giving yourself airs. We're both in the same boat now. Here, my dear girl, let me give you a glass of something special. *(Opens the drawer, takes out the bottle of wine and fills two used glasses.)*

JULIE: Where did you get that wine?

JEAN: From the cellar.

JULIE: My father's burgundy.

JEAN: Why not, for his son-in-law?

JULIE: And I drink beer.

JEAN: That only shows your taste's not so good as mine.

JULIE: Thief!

JEAN: Are you going to tell on me?

JULIE: Oh God! The accomplice of a petty thief! Was I blind drunk? Have I dreamt this whole night? Midsummer Eve, the night for innocent merrymaking.

JEAN: Innocent, eh?

JULIE: Is anyone on earth as wretched as I am now?

JEAN: Why should *you* be? After such a conquest. What about Kristin in there? Don't you think she has any feelings?

JULIE: I did think so, but I don't any longer. No. A menial is a menial . . .

JEAN: And a whore is a whore.

JULIE *(falling to her knees, her hands clasped)*: O God in heaven, put an end to my miserable life! Lift me out of this filth in which I'm sinking. Save me! Save me!

JEAN: I must admit I'm sorry for you. When I was in the onion bed and saw you up there among the roses, I . . . yes, I'll tell you now . . . I had the same dirty thoughts as all boys.

JULIE: You, who wanted to die because of me?

JEAN: In the oats-bin? That was just talk.

JULIE: Lies, you mean.

JEAN *(getting sleepy)*: More or less. I think I read a story in some paper about a chimney-sweep who shut himself up in a chest full of lilac because he'd been summonsed for not supporting some brat . . .

JULIE: So this is what you're like.

JEAN: I had to think up something. It's always the fancy stuff that catches the women.

JULIE: Beast!

JEAN: *Merde!*

JULIE: Now you have seen the falcon's back.

JEAN: Not exactly its *back*.

JULIE: I was to be the first branch.

JEAN: But the branch was rotten.

JULIE: I was to be a hotel sign.

JEAN: And I the hotel.

JULIE: Sit at your counter, attract your clients and cook their accounts.

JEAN: I'd have done that myself.

JULIE: That any human being can be so steeped in filth!

JEAN: Clean it up then.

JULIE: Menial! Lackey! Stand up when I speak to you.

JEAN: Menial's whore, lackey's harlot, shut your mouth and get out of here! Are you the one to lecture me for being coarse? Nobody of my kind would ever be as coarse as you were tonight. Do you think any servant girl would throw herself at a man that way? Have you ever seen a girl of my class asking for it like that? I haven't. Only animals and prostitutes.

JULIE *(broken)*: Go on. Hit me, trample on me—it's all I deserve. I'm rotten. But help me! If there's any way out at all, help me.

JEAN *(more gently)*: I'm not denying myself a share in the honor of seducing you, but do you think anybody in my place would have dared look in your direction if you yourself hadn't asked for it? I'm still amazed . . .

JULIE: And proud.

JEAN: Why not? Though I must admit the victory was too easy to make me lose my head.

JULIE: Go on hitting me.

JEAN *(rising)*: No. On the contrary I apologize for what I've said. I don't hit a person who's down—least of all a woman. I can't deny there's a certain satisfaction in finding that what dazzled one below was just moonshine, that the falcon's back is gray after all, that there's powder on the lovely cheek, that polished nails can have black tips, that the handkerchief is dirty although it smells of scent. On the other hand it hurts to find that what I was struggling to reach wasn't high and isn't real. It hurts to see you fallen so low you're far lower than your own cook. Hurts like when you see the last flowers of summer lashed to pieces by rain and turned to mud.

JULIE: You're talking as if you're already my superior.

JEAN: I am. I might make you a Countess, but you could never make me a Count, you know.

JULIE: But I am the child of a Count, and you could never be that.

JEAN: True, but I might be the father of Counts if . . .

JULIE: You're a thief. I'm not.

JEAN: There are worse things than being a thief—much lower. Besides, when I'm in a place I regard myself as a member of the family to some extent, as one of the children. You don't call it stealing when children pinch a berry from over-laden bushes. *(His passion is roused again.)* Miss Julie, you're a glorious woman, far too good for a man like me. You were carried away by some kind of madness, and now you're trying to cover up your mistake by persuading yourself you're in love with me. You're not, although you may find me physically attractive, which means your love's no better than mine. But I wouldn't be satisfied with being nothing but an animal for you, and I could never make you love me.

JULIE: Are you sure?

JEAN: You think there's a chance? Of my loving you, yes, of course. You're beautiful, refined *(Takes her hand.)* educated, and you can be nice when you want to be. The fire you kindle in a man isn't likely to go out. *(Puts his arm round her.)* You're like mulled wine, full of spices, and your kisses . . . *(He tries to pull her to him, but she breaks away.)*

JULIE: Let go of me! You won't win me that way.

JEAN: Not that way, how then? Not by kisses and fine speeches, not by planning the future and saving you from shame? How then?

JULIE: How? How? I don't know. There isn't any way. I loathe you—loathe you as I loathe rats, but I can't escape from you.

JEAN: Escape with me.

JULIE *(pulling herself together)*: Escape? Yes, we must escape. But I'm so tired. Give me a glass of wine. *(He pours it out. She looks at her watch.)* First we must talk. We still have a little time. *(Empties the glass and holds it out for more.)*

JEAN: Don't drink like that. You'll get tipsy.

JULIE: What's that matter?

JEAN: What's it matter? It's vulgar to get drunk. Well, what have you got to say?

JULIE: We've got to run away, but we must talk first—or rather, I must, for so far you've done all the talking. You've told me about your life, now I want to tell you about mine, so that we really know each other before we begin this journey together.

JEAN: Wait. Excuse my saying so, but don't you think

you may be sorry afterward if you give away your secrets to me?

JULIE: Aren't you my friend?

JEAN: On the whole. But don't rely on me.

JULIE: You can't mean that. But anyway everyone knows my secrets. Listen. My mother wasn't well-born; she came of quite humble people, and was brought up with all those new ideas of sex-equality and women's rights and so on. She thought marriage was quite wrong. So when my father proposed to her, she said she would never become his *wife* . . . but in the end she did. I came into the world, as far as I can make out, against my mother's will, and I was left to run wild, but I had to do all the things a boy does—to prove women are as good as men. I had to wear boys' clothes; I was taught to handle horses—and I wasn't allowed in the dairy. She made me groom and harness and go out hunting; I even had to try to plough. All the men on the estate were given the women's jobs, and the women the men's, until the whole place went to rack and ruin and we were the laughing-stock of the neighborhood. At last my father seemed to have come to his senses and rebelled. He changed everything and ran the place his own way. My mother got ill—I don't know what was the matter with her, but she used to have strange attacks and hide herself in the attic or the garden. Sometimes she stayed out all night. Then came the great fire which you have heard people talking about. The house and the stables and the barns—the whole place burnt to the ground. In very suspicious circumstances. Because the accident happened the very day the insurance had to be renewed, and my father had sent the new premium, but through some carelessness of the messenger it arrived too late. *(Refills her glass and drinks.)*

JEAN: Don't drink any more.

JULIE: Oh, what does it matter? We were destitute and had to sleep in the carriages. My father didn't know how to get money to rebuild, and then my mother suggested he should borrow from an old friend of hers, a local brick man-ufacturer. My father got the loan and, to his surprise, without having to pay interest. So the place was rebuilt. *(Drinks.)* Do you know who set fire to it?

JEAN: Your lady mother.

JULIE: Do you know who the brick manufacturer was?

JEAN: Your mother's lover?

JULIE: Do you know whose the money was?

JEAN: Wait . . . no, I don't know that.

JULIE: It was my mother's.

JEAN: In other words the Count's, unless there was a

settlement.

JULIE: There wasn't any settlement. My mother had a little money of her own which she didn't want my father to control, so she invested it with her—friend.

JEAN: Who grabbed it.

JULIE: Exactly. He appropriated it. My father came to know all this. He couldn't bring an action, couldn't pay his wife's lover, nor prove it was his wife's money. That was my mother's revenge because he made himself master in his own house. He nearly shot himself then—at least there's a rumor he tried and didn't bring it off. So he went on living, and my mother had to pay dearly for what she'd done. Imagine what those five years were like for me. My natural sympathies were with my father, yet I took my mother's side, because I didn't know the facts. I'd learnt from her to hate and distrust men—you know how she loathed the whole male sex. And I swore to her I'd never become the slave of any man.

JEAN: And so you got engaged to that attorney.

JULIE: So that he should be my slave.

JEAN: But he wouldn't be.

JULIE: Oh yes, he wanted to be, but he didn't have the chance. I got bored with him.

JEAN: Is that what I saw—in the stable-yard?

JULIE: What did you see?

JEAN: What I saw was him breaking off the engagement.

JULIE: That's a lie. It was I who broke it off. Did he say it was him? The cad.

JEAN: He's not a cad. Do you hate men, Miss Julie?

JULIE: Yes . . . most of the time. But when that weakness comes, oh . . . the shame!

JEAN: Then do you hate me?

JULIE: Beyond words. I'd gladly have you killed like an animal.

JEAN: Quick as you'd shoot a mad dog, eh?

JULIE: Yes.

JEAN: But there's nothing here to shoot with—and there isn't a dog. So what do we do now?

JULIE: Go abroad.

JEAN: To make each other miserable for the rest of our lives?

JULIE: No, to enjoy ourselves for a day or two, for a week, for as long as enjoyment lasts, and then—to die . . .

JEAN: Die? How silly! I think it would be far better to start a hotel.

JULIE (without listening): . . . die on the shores of Lake Como, where the sun always shines and at Christmas time there are green trees and glowing oranges.

JEAN: Lake Como's a rainy hole and I didn't see any oranges outside the shops. But it's a good place for tourists. Plenty of villas to be rented by—er—honeymoon couples. Profitable business that. Know why? Because they all sign a lease for six months and all leave after three weeks.

JULIE (naïvely): After three weeks? Why?

JEAN: They quarrel, of course. But the rent has to be paid just the same. And then it's let again. So it goes on and on, for there's plenty of love although it doesn't last long.

JULIE: You don't want to die with me?

JEAN: I don't want to die at all. For one thing I like living and for another I consider suicide's a sin against the Creator who gave us life.

JULIE: You believe in God—you?

JEAN: Yes, of course. And I go to church every Sunday. Look here. I'm tired of all this. I'm going to bed.

JULIE: Indeed! And do you think I'm going to leave things like this? Don't you know what you owe the woman you've ruined?

JEAN (taking out his purse and throwing a silver coin on the table): There you are. I don't want to be in anybody's debt.

JULIE (pretending not to notice the insult): Don't you know what the law is?

JEAN: There's no law unfortunately that punishes a woman for seducing a man.

JULIE: But can you see anything for it but to go abroad, get married and then divorce?

JEAN: What if I refuse this mésalliance?

JULIE: Mésalliance?

JEAN: Yes for me. I'm better bred than you, see! Nobody in my family committed arson.

JULIE: How do you know?

JEAN: Well, you can't prove otherwise, because we haven't any family records outside the Registrar's office. But I've seen your family tree in that book on the drawing-room table. Do you know who the founder of your family was? A miller who let his wife sleep with the King one night during the Danish war. I haven't any ancestors like that. I haven't any ancestors at all, but I might become one.

JULIE: This is what I get for confiding in someone so low, for sacrificing my family honor . . .

JEAN: Dishonor! Well, I told you so. One shouldn't drink because then one talks. And one shouldn't talk.

JULIE: Oh, how ashamed I am, how bitterly ashamed! If at least you loved me!

JEAN: Look here—for the last time—what do you want? Am I to burst into tears? Am I to jump over your riding whip? Shall I kiss you and carry you off to Lake Como for three weeks, after which . . . What am I to do? What do you want? This is getting unbearable, but that's what comes of playing around with women. Miss Julie, I can see how miserable you are; I know you're going through hell, but I don't understand you. We don't have scenes like this; we don't go in for hating each other. We make love for fun in our spare time, but we haven't all day and all night for it like you. I think you must be ill. I'm sure you're ill.

JULIE: Then you must be kind to me. You sound almost human now.

JEAN: Well, be human yourself. You spit at me, then won't let me wipe it off—on you.

JULIE: Help me, help me! Tell me what to do, where to go.

JEAN: Jesus, as if I knew!

JULIE: I've been mad, raving mad, but there must be a way out.

JEAN: Stay here and keep quiet. Nobody knows anything.

JULIE: I can't. People do know. Kristin knows.

JEAN: They don't know and they wouldn't believe such a thing.

JULIE (hesitating): But—it might happen again.

JEAN: That's true.

JULIE: And there might be—consequences.

JEAN (in panic): Consequences! Fool that I am I never thought of that. Yes, there's nothing for it but to go. At once. I can't come with you. That would be a complete give-away. You must go alone—abroad—anywhere.

JULIE: Alone! Where to? I can't.

JEAN: You must. And before the Count gets back. If you stay, we know what will happen. Once you've sinned you feel you might as well go on, as the harm's done. Then you get more and more reckless and in the end you're found out. No. You must go abroad. Then write to the Count and tell him everything, except that it was me. He'll never guess that—and I don't think he'll want to.

JULIE: I'll go if you come with me.

JEAN: Are you crazy, woman? "Miss Julie elopes with valet." Next day it would be in the headlines, and the Count would never live it down.

JULIE: I can't go. I can't stay. I'm so tired, so completely worn out. Give me orders. Set me going. I can't think any more, can't act . . .

JEAN: You see what weaklings you are. Why do you give yourselves airs and turn up your noses as if you're the lords of creation? Very well, I'll give you your orders. Go upstairs and dress. Get money for the journey and come down here again.

JULIE (softly): Come up with me.

JEAN: To your room? Now you've gone crazy again. (Hesitates a moment.) No! Go along at once. (Takes her hand and pulls her to the door.)

JULIE (as she goes): Speak kindly to me, Jean.

JEAN: Orders always sound unkind. Now you know. Now you know.

(Left alone, JEAN sighs with relief, sits down at the table, takes out a note-book and pencil and adds up figures, now and then aloud. Dawn begins to break. KRISTIN enters dressed for church, carrying his white dickey and tie.)

KRISTIN: Lord Jesus, look at the state the place is in! What have you been up to? (Turns out the lamp.)

JEAN: Oh, Miss Julie invited the crowd in. Did you sleep through it? Didn't you hear anything?

KRISTIN: I slept like a log.

JEAN: And dressed for church already.

KRISTIN: Yes, you promised to come to Communion with me today.

JEAN: Why, so I did. And you've got my bib and tucker. I see. Come on then. (Sits. KRISTIN begins to put his things on. Pause. Sleepily.) What's the lesson today?

KRISTIN: It's about the beheading of John the Baptist, I think.

JEAN: That's sure to be horribly long. Hi, you're choking me! Oh Lord, I'm so sleepy, so sleepy!

KRISTIN: Yes, what have you been doing up all night? You look absolutely green.

JEAN: Just sitting here talking with Miss Julie.

KRISTIN: She doesn't know what's proper, that one. (Pause.)

JEAN: I say, Kristin.

KRISTIN: What?

JEAN: It's queer really, isn't it, when you come to think of it? Her.

KRISTIN: What's queer?

JEAN: The whole thing. (Pause.)

KRISTIN (looking at the half-filled glasses on the table): Have you been drinking together too?

JEAN: Yes.

KRISTIN: More shame you. Look me straight in the face.

JEAN: Yes.

KRISTIN: Is it possible? Is it possible?

JEAN (after a moment): Yes, it is.

KRISTIN: Oh! This I would never have believed. How low!

JEAN: You're not jealous of her, surely?

KRISTIN: No, I'm not. If it had been Clara or Sophie I'd have scratched your eyes out. But not of her. I don't know why; that's how it is though. But it's disgusting.

JEAN: You're angry with her then.

KRISTIN: No. With you. It was wicked of you, very very wicked. Poor girl. And, mark my words, I won't stay here any longer now—in a place where one can't respect one's employers.

JEAN: Why should one respect them?

KRISTIN: You should know since you're so smart. But you don't want to stay in the service of people who aren't respectable, do you? I wouldn't demean myself.

JEAN: But it's rather a comfort to find out they're no better than us.

KRISTIN: I don't think so. If they're no better there's nothing for us to live up to. Oh and think of the Count! Think of him. He's been through so much already. No I won't stay in the place any longer. A fellow like you too! If it had been that attorney now or somebody of her own class . . .

JEAN: Why, what's wrong with . . .

KRISTIN: Oh, you're all right in your own way, but when all's said and done there is a difference between one class and another. No, this is something I'll never be able to stomach. That our young lady who was so proud and so down on men you'd never believe she'd let one come near her should go and give herself to one like you. She who wanted to have poor Diana shot for running after the lodge-keeper's pug. No. I must say . . .! Well, I won't stay here any longer. On the twenty-fourth of October, I quit.

JEAN: And then?

KRISTIN: Well, since you mention it, it's about time you began to look around, if we're ever going to get married.

JEAN: But what am I to look for? I shan't get a place like this when I'm married.

KRISTIN: I know you won't. But you might get a job as porter or caretaker in some public institution. Government rations are small but sure, and there's a pension for the widow and children.

JEAN: That's all very fine, but it's not in my line to start thinking at once about dying for my wife and children. I must say I had rather bigger ideas.

KRISTIN: You and your ideas! You've got obligations too, and you'd better start thinking about them.

JEAN: Don't *you* start pestering me about obligations. I've had enough of that. (*Listens to a sound upstairs.*) Anyway we've got plenty of time to work things out. Go and get ready now and we'll be off to church.

KRISTIN: Who's that walking about upstairs?

JEAN: Don't know—unless it's Clara.

KRISTIN (*going*): You don't think the Count could have come back without our hearing him?

JEAN (*scared*): The Count? No, he can't have. He'd have rung for me.

KRISTIN: God help us! I've never known such goings on. (*Exit.*)

(*The sun has now risen and is shining on the treetops. The light gradually changes until it slants in through the windows.* JEAN *goes to the door and beckons.* JULIE *enters in traveling clothes, carrying a small bird-cage covered with a cloth which she puts on a chair.*)

JULIE: I'm ready.

JEAN: Hush! Kristin's up.

JULIE (*in a very nervous state*): Does she suspect anything?

JEAN: Not a thing. But, my God, what a sight you are!

JULIE: Sight! What do you mean?

JEAN: You're white as a corpse and—pardon me—your face is dirty.

JULIE: Let me wash then. (*Goes to the sink and washes her face and hands.*) There. Give me a towel. Oh! The sun is rising!

JEAN: And that breaks the spell.

JULIE: Yes. The spell of Midsummer Eve . . . But listen, Jean. Come with me. I've got the money.

JEAN (*skeptically*): Enough?

JULIE: Enough to start with. Come with me. I can't travel alone today. It's Midsummer Day, remember. I'd be packed into a suffocating train among crowds of people who'd all stare at me. And it would stop at every station while I yearned for wings. No, I can't do that. I simply can't. There will be memories too; memories of Midsummer Days when I was little. The leafy church—birch and lilac—the gaily spread dinner table, relatives, friends—everything in the park—dancing and music and flowers and fun. Oh, however far you run away—there'll always be memories in the baggage car—and remorse and guilt.

JEAN: I will come with you, but quickly now then, before it's too late. At once.

JULIE: Put on your things. (*Picks up the cage.*)

JEAN: No luggage, mind. That would give us away.

JULIE: No, only what we can take with us in the carriage.

JEAN (*fetching his hat*): What on earth have you got there? What is it?

JULIE: Only my greenfinch. I don't want to leave it behind.

JEAN: Well, I'll be damned! We're to take a bird-cage along, are we? You're crazy. Put that cage down.

JULIE: It's the only thing I'm taking from my home. The only living creature who cares for me since Diana went off like that. Don't be cruel. Let me take it.

JEAN: Put that cage down, I tell you—and don't talk so loud. Kristin will hear.

JULIE: No, I won't leave it in strange hands. I'd rather you killed it.

JEAN: Give the little beast here then and I'll wring its neck.

JULIE: But don't hurt it, don't . . . no, I can't.

JEAN: Give it here, I *can*.

JULIE (*taking the bird out of the cage and kissing it*): Dear little Serena, must you die and leave your mistress?

JEAN: Please don't make a scene. It's *your* life and

future we're worrying about. Come on, quick now!

(*He snatches the bird from her, puts it on a board and picks up a chopper.* JULIE *turns away.*)

You should have learnt how to kill chickens instead of target-shooting. Then you wouldn't faint at a drop of blood.

JULIE (*screaming*): Kill me too! Kill me! You who can butcher an innocent creature without a quiver. Oh, how I hate you, how I loathe you! There is blood between us now. I curse the hour I first saw you. I curse the hour I was conceived in my mother's womb.

JEAN: What's the use of cursing. Let's go.

JULIE (*going to the chopping-block as if drawn against her will*): No, I won't go yet. I can't . . . I must look. Listen! There's a carriage. (*Listens without taking her eyes off the board and chopper.*) You don't think I can bear the sight of blood. You think I'm so weak. Oh, how I should like to see your blood and your brains on a chopping-block! I'd like to see the whole of your sex swimming like that in a sea of blood. I think I could drink out of your skull, bathe my feet in your broken breast and eat your heart roasted whole. You think I'm weak. You think I love you, that my womb yearned for your seed and I want to carry your offspring under my heart and nourish it with my blood. You think I want to bear your child and take your name. By the way, what is your name? I've never heard your surname. I don't suppose you've got one. I should be "Mrs. Hovel" or "Madam Dunghill." You dog wearing my collar, you lackey with my crest on your buttons! I share you with my cook; I'm my own servant's rival! Oh! Oh! Oh! . . . You think I'm a coward and will run away. No, now I'm going to stay—and let the storm break. My father will come back . . . find his desk broken open . . . his money gone. Then he'll ring the bell—twice for the valet—and then he'll send for the police . . . and I shall tell everything. Everything. Oh how wonderful to make an end of it all—a real end! He has a stroke and dies and that's the end of all of us. Just peace and quietness . . . eternal rest. The coat of arms broken on the coffin and the Count's line extinct . . . But the valet's line goes on in an orphanage, wins laurels in the gutter and ends in jail.

JEAN: There speaks the noble blood! Bravo, Miss Julie. But now, don't let the cat out of the bag.

(KRISTIN *enters dressed for church, carrying a prayer-book.* JULIE *rushes to her and flings herself into her arms for protection.*)

JULIE: Help me, Kristin! Protect me from this man!

KRISTIN (*unmoved and cold*): What goings-on for a feast day morning! (*Sees the board.*) And what a filthy mess. What's it all about? Why are you screaming and carrying on so?

JULIE: Kristin, you're a woman and my friend. Beware of that scoundrel!

JEAN (*embarrassed*): While you ladies are talking things over, I'll go and shave. (*Slips into his room.*)

JULIE: You must understand. You must listen to me.

KRISTIN: I certainly don't understand such loose ways. Where are you off to in those traveling clothes? And he had his hat on, didn't he, eh?

JULIE: Listen, Kristin. Listen, I'll tell you everything.

KRISTIN: I don't want to know anything.

JULIE: You must listen.

KRISTIN: What to? Your nonsense with Jean? I don't care a rap about that; it's nothing to do with me. But if you're thinking of getting him to run off with you, we'll soon put a stop to that.

JULIE (*very nervously*): Please try to be calm, Kristin, and listen. I can't stay here, nor can Jean—so we must go abroad.

KRISTIN: Hm, hm!

JULIE (*brightening*): But you see, I've had an idea. Supposing we all three go—abroad—to Switzerland and start a hotel together . . . I've got some money, you see . . . and Jean and I could run the whole thing—and I thought you would take charge of the kitchen. Wouldn't that be splendid? Say yes, do. If you come with us everything will be fine. Oh do say yes! (*Puts her arms round* KRISTIN.)

KRISTIN (*coolly thinking*): Hm, hm.

JULIE (*presto tempo*): You've never traveled, Kristin. You should go abroad and see the world. You've no idea how nice it is traveling by train—new faces all the time and new countries. On our way through Hamburg we'll go to the zoo—you'll love that—and we'll go to the theater and the opera too . . . and when we get to Munich there'll be the museums, dear, and pictures by Rubens and Raphael—the great painters, you know . . . You've heard of Munich, haven't you? Where King Ludwig lived—you know, the king who went mad, . . . We'll see his castles—some of his castles are still just like in fairy-tales . . . and from there it's not far to Switzerland—and the Alps. Think of the Alps, Kristin dear, covered with snow in the middle of summer . . . and there are oranges there and trees that are green the whole year round . . .

(JEAN *is seen in the door of his room, sharpening his razor on a strop which he holds with his teeth and his left hand. He listens to the talk with satisfaction and now and then nods approval.* JULIE *continues, tempo prestissimo.*)

And then we'll get a hotel . . . and I'll sit at the desk, while Jean receives the guests and goes out marketing and writes letters . . . There's life for you! Trains whistling, buses driving up, bells ringing upstairs and downstairs . . . and I shall make out the bills—and I shall cook them too . . . you've no idea how nervous travelers are when it comes to paying their bills. And you—you'll sit like a queen in the kitchen . . . of course there won't be any standing at the stove for you. You'll always have to be nicely dressed and ready to be seen, and with your looks—no, I'm not flattering you—one fine day you'll catch yourself a husband . . . some rich Englishman, I shouldn't wonder—they're the ones who are easy *(Slowing down.)* to catch . . . and then we'll get rich and build ourselves a villa on Lake Como . . . of course it rains there a little now and then—but *(Dully.)* the sun must shine there too sometimes—even though it seems gloomy—and if not—then we can come home again—come back—*(Pause.)*—here—or somewhere else . . .

KRISTIN: Look here, Miss Julie, do you believe all that yourself?

JULIE *(exhausted)*: Do I believe it?

KRISTIN: Yes.

JULIE *(wearily)*: I don't know. I don't believe anything any more. *(Sinks down on the bench; her head in her arms on the table.)* Nothing. Nothing at all.

KRISTIN *(turning to JEAN)*: So you meant to beat it, did you?

JEAN *(disconcerted, putting the razor on the table)*: Beat it? What are you talking about? You've heard Miss Julie's plan, and though she's tired now with being up all night, it's a perfectly sound plan.

KRISTIN: Oh, is it? If you thought I'd work for that . . .

JEAN *(interrupting)*: Kindly use decent language in front of your mistress. Do you hear?

KRISTIN: Mistress?

JEAN: Yes.

KRISTIN: Well, well, just listen to that!

JEAN: Yes, it would be a good thing if you did listen and talked less. Miss Julie is your mistress and what's made you lose your respect for her now ought to make you feel the same about yourself.

KRISTIN: I've always had enough self-respect—

JEAN: To despise other people.

KRISTIN: —not to go below my own station. Has the Count's cook ever gone with the groom or the swineherd? Tell me that.

JEAN: No, you were lucky enough to have a high-class chap for your beau.

KRISTIN: High-class all right—selling the oats out of the Count's stable.

JEAN: You're a fine one to talk—taking a commission on the groceries and bribes from the butcher.

KRISTIN: What the devil . . . ?

JEAN: And now you can't feel any respect for your employers. You, you!

KRISTIN: Are you coming to church with me? I should think you need a good sermon after your fine deeds.

JEAN: No, I'm not going to church today. You can go alone and confess your own sins.

KRISTIN: Yes, I'll do that and bring back enough forgiveness to cover yours too. The Saviour suffered and died on the cross for all our sins, and if we go to Him with faith and a penitent heart, He takes all our sins upon Himself.

JEAN: Even grocery thefts?

JULIE: Do you believe that, Kristin?

KRISTIN: That is my living faith, as sure as I stand here. The faith I learnt as a child and have kept ever since, Miss Julie. "But where sin abounded, grace did much more abound."

JULIE: Oh, if I had your faith! Oh, if . . .

KRISTIN: But you see you can't have it without God's special grace, and it's not given to all to have that.

JULIE: Who is it given to then?

KRISTIN: That's the great secret of the workings of grace, Miss Julie. God is no respecter of persons, and with Him the last shall be first . . .

JULIE: Then I suppose He does respect the last.

KRISTIN *(continuing)*: . . . and it is easier for a camel to go through the eye of a needle than for a rich man to enter into the kingdom of God. That's how it is, Miss Julie. Now I'm going—alone, and on my way I shall tell the groom not to let any of the horses out, in case anyone should want to leave before the Count gets back. Good-by. *(Exit.)*

JEAN: What a devil! And all on account of a greenfinch.

JULIE *(wearily)*: Never mind the greenfinch. Do you see any way out of this, any end to it?

JEAN *(pondering)*: No.

JULIE: If you were in my place, what would you do?

JEAN: In your place? Wait a bit. If I was a woman—a lady of rank who had—fallen. I don't know. Yes, I do know now.

JULIE *(picking up the razor and making a gesture)*: This?

JEAN: Yes. But *I* wouldn't do it, you know. There's a difference between us.

JULIE: Because you're a man and I'm a woman? What is the difference?

JEAN: The usual difference—between man and woman.

JULIE *(holding the razor)*: I'd like to. But I can't. My father couldn't either, that time he wanted to.

JEAN: No, he didn't want to. He had to be revenged first.

JULIE: And now my mother is revenged again, through me.

JEAN: Didn't you ever love your father, Miss Julie?

JULIE: Deeply, but I must have hated him too—unconsciously. And he let me be brought up to despise my own sex, to be half woman, half man.

Whose fault is what's happened? My father's, my mother's, or my own? My own? I haven't anything that's my own. I haven't one single thought that I didn't get from my father, one emotion that didn't come from my mother, and as for this last idea—about all people being equal—I got that from him, my fiancé—that's why I call him a cad. How can it be my fault? Push the responsibility on to Jesus, like Kristin does? No, I'm too proud and—thanks to my father's teaching—too intelligent. As for all that about a rich person not being able to get into heaven, it's just a lie, but Kristin, who has money in the savings-bank, will certainly not get in. Whose fault is it? What does it matter whose fault it is? In any case I must take the blame and bear the consequences.

JEAN: Yes, but . . . *(There are two sharp rings on the bell.* JULIE *jumps to her feet.* JEAN *changes into his livery.)* The Count is back. Supposing Kristin . . . *(Goes to the speaking-tube, presses it and listens.)*

JULIE: Has he been to his desk yet?

JEAN: This is Jean, sir. *(Listens.)* Yes, sir. *(Listens.)* Yes, sir, very good, sir. *(Listens.)* At once, sir? *(Listens.)* Very good, sir. In half an hour.

JULIE *(in panic)*: What did he say? My God, what did he say?

JEAN: He ordered his boots and his coffee in half an hour.

JULIE: Then there's half an hour . . . Oh, I'm so tired! I can't do anything. Can't be sorry, can't run away, can't stay, can't live—can't die. Help me. Order me, and I'll obey like a dog. Do me this last service—save my honor, save his name. You know what I ought to do, but haven't the strength to do. Use your strength and order me to do it.

JEAN: I don't know why—I can't now—I don't understand . . . It's just as if this coat made me—I can't give you orders—and now that the Count has spoken to me—I can't quite explain, but . . . well, that devil of a lackey is bending my back again. I believe if the Count came down now and ordered me to cut my throat, I'd do it on the spot.

JULIE: Then pretend you're him and I'm you. You did some fine acting before, when you knelt to

me and played the aristocrat. Or . . . Have you ever seen a hypnotist at the theater? *(He nods.)* He says to the person "Take the broom," and he takes it. He says "Sweep," and he sweeps . . .

JEAN: But the person has to be asleep.

JULIE *(as if in a trance)*: I am asleep already . . . the whole room has turned to smoke—and you look like a stove—a stove like a man in black with a tall hat—your eyes are glowing like coals when the fire is low—and your face is a white patch like ashes. *(The sunlight has now reached the floor and lights up* JEAN.*)* How nice and warm it is! *(She holds out her hands as though warming them at a fire.)* And so light— and so peaceful.

JEAN *(putting the razor in her hand)*: Here is the broom. Go now while it's light—out to the barn—and . . . *(Whispers in her ear.)*

JULIE *(waking)*: Thank you. I am going now—to rest. But just tell me that even the first can receive the gift of grace.

JEAN: The first? No, I can't tell you that. But wait . . . Miss Julie, I've got it! You aren't one of the first any longer. You're one of the last.

JULIE: That's true, I'm one of the very last. I *am* the last. Oh! . . . But now I can't go. Tell me again to go.

JEAN: No, I can't now either. I can't.

JULIE: And the first shall be last.

JEAN: Don't think, don't think. You're taking my strength away too and making me a coward. What's that? I thought I saw the bell move . . . To be so frightened of a bell! Yes, but it's not just a bell. There's somebody behind it—a hand moving it—and something else moving the hand— and if you stop your ears—if you stop your ears—yes, then it rings louder than ever. Rings and rings until you answer—and then it's too late. Then the police come and . . . and . . . *(The bell rings twice loudly.* JEAN *flinches, then straightens himself up.)* It's horrible. But there's no other way to end it . . . Go!

*(*JULIE *walks firmly out through the door.)*

CURTAIN

Figure 1. Julie (Maggie Smith) waves her scented handkerchief at Jean (Albert Finney) in the National Theatre production of *Miss Julie,* directed by Michael Elliott, London, 1966. (Photograph: Angus McBean.)

Figure 2. Jean (Albert Finney) and Julie (Maggie Smith) during a pause in their long conversation, after the peasants have departed, in the National Theatre production of *Miss Julie,* directed by Michael Elliott, London, 1966. (Photograph: Dominic.)

Figure 3. Julie (Maggie Smith) holds her greenfinch in her hands while Jean (Albert Finney) waits ready to behead it on the chopping board in the National Theatre production of *Miss Julie*, directed by Michael Elliott, London, 1966. (Photograph: Angus McBean, Harvard Theatre Collection.)

Staging of *Miss Julie*

REVIEW OF THE NATIONAL THEATRE PRODUCTION, 1966, BY THE LONDON *TIMES* DRAMA CRITIC

Miss Julie brings Mr. Finney and Miss Smith together in Strindberg's sexual dual between servant and mistress. The duel itself comes over with less than its usual ferocity as the production gives as much emphasis to the private fantasies of the antagonists as to their actual encounter. Jean's dream of social advancement and Julie's dream of falling to destruction are the real things: each to the other is only the accidental means of embodying them. Not that Michael Elliott's production is lacking in aggressiveness: Miss Smith's erotic arrogance in the first scene is matched by the casual brutality with which Mr. Finney at the end chops off the tame bird's head.

But it is rather that the partners (Julie in particular) are acting under a somnambulistic spell. The production does not stretch Miss Smith far enough away from comedy; and her voice is still obstinately without pathos. But Mr. Finney's Jean is a subtle compound of materialism and social pretension; and there is a fine icy Christine by Jeanne Watts, who gives the claustrophobic drama a link with the outer world. The pantomine interlude, alas, has defeated Mr. Elliott like other directors before him.

REVIEW OF THE NATIONAL THEATRE PRODUCTION, 1966, BY HUGH LEONARD

Second nights can be dangerous. Actors loosen their collars, tuck in their frayed nerve-ends and uncross their fingers. A happy tiredness descends on the company like fall-out; and the first casualty is timing. Then a drawer sticks, a line is fluffed and a laugh comes at the wrong place. Panic sets in, and last night's champagne goes incurably flat. Perhaps this was what happened to *Miss Julie* at the National Theatre, but Michael Elliott's direction wasn't quite up to the task to begin with. This is a veritable bitch of a play, in which a miss is as bad as a mile. Big guns are needed; and although Mr. Elliott had them, they were trained in the wrong direction. For great stretches of time we were obliged to look at the back of Albert Finney's head and at Maggie Smith in half-profile. Savagely emotional scenes were played at a murmur in dingy lighting and a set which reduced Strindberg's 'large kitchen' to a pokey room with swaying roof-beams. The callous beheading of the chaffinch generated hardly an 'ugh!', and the play's ending was so indeterminately staged that the audience sat in puzzled silence waiting for more.

Not that the production was a disaster. But it wasn't Strindberg either. Mr. Finney's valet was good, but muted; and, as Miss Julie, Miss Smith wasn't nearly patrician enough. To fall spectacularly, one needs height first and foremost; and it is Julie's pretensions which dictate her suicide. With no discernible social gap existing between Julie and her father's valet, half the play's values were lost. Miss Smith is always delightful to watch and listen to; but this isn't her part any more than Strindberg is suited to Mr. Elliott.

ANTON CHEKHOV

1860–1904

Anton Chekhov was born in Taganrog, a Crimean resort not far from Yalta, where he wrote his last play, *The Cherry Orchard,* when he was dying of tuberculosis. Although his grandfather had been a serf who amassed enough money not only to buy his freedom but also an estate, his father, plagued by the debts of an unsuccessful grocery, was forced to leave Taganrog and move the family to Moscow. Chekhov himself remained in Taganrog to finish his schooling, but his years there could hardly have been pleasant ones, for his poverty compelled him to earn money by doing homework for his fellow students, and Taganrog itself, like most seaside resorts of that era, was filled with the sick and aged. So it is not surprising that the resorts that appear repeatedly in Chekhov's works, such as the "villas" that Lopahin proposes to build along the river bank, are always associated with tedium and futility. By 1880, Chekhov, too, had left Taganrog and moved to Moscow, where he entered medical school and started to write short stories to help support himself and his family. He became a physician and practiced medicine for a time, yet he gradually came to spend more and more effort on his writing, less and less on medicine. By 1888, he was practicing only during epidemics, when there was a shortage of doctors, whereas he was writing so much that he had already published 300 stories. During the 1880s, Chekhov had also started writing for the stage—first one-act plays, which he began doing in 1884, the year of his graduation from medical school, then full-length works, the earliest of which appeared in 1887. Most of his one-act plays are farcical studies of middle-class aspirations to sophisticated society, such as *The Boor* and *The Marriage Proposal,* which were well received and still continue to be performed. His early full-length works, such as *Ivanov* (1887), and *The Wood Demon* (1889), an early version of *Uncle Vanya,* were bitter failures, so much so that he did not write another serious full-length play until *The Seagull* (1896), which was first produced in St. Petersburg.

The Seagull, a psychologically realistic play, which bears witness to the drama of human loneliness and frustration, failed dismally in its opening production, for it was a radical departure from Russian theatrical tastes of the time. Chekhov's audience was unaccustomed to his low-key realism, to his subtle revelations of character, to his apparently plotless drama of Russian life, for this kind of drama was completely at odds with the melodramatic thrillers then being imported from Paris. The Russian actors were also unprepared for it, since they had never tried, nor seen, any style of performance other than the bombastic acting of the period that had been popularized by the English actor Edmund Kean. And the management of the theater where it was produced did not give the actors much of a chance to develop an appropriately low-key style, allowing them only nine days for rehearsals. *The Seagull* was literally laughed off the stage in St. Petersburg. Although Chekhov vowed never to write another play, he did permit *The Seagull* to be printed in a literary magazine, where it caught the interest of two wealthy young men, Constantin Stanislavski and Vladimir Nemirovich-

Danchenko, whose theatrical ambitions brought them together in 1898 to form the Moscow Art Theater. This group was based on the new principles of ensemble acting then being attempted throughout Europe, where acting companies were following the model established by the German troupe of the Duke of Saxe-Meinegen. But Stanislavski and Nemirovich-Danchenko were not content simply to develop an ensemble. They aimed to develop an acting company with a distinctively new style of performance, a style that was understated rather than overstated, realistic instead of melodramatic. That style was perfectly attuned to the psychological nuances of *The Seagull,* and thus they chose to conclude their first season with a revival of the play. That revival turned out to be the making of both Chekhov and the Moscow Art Theater, for though the rest of their season had been a series of failures, *The Seagull* was met with thunderous applause by the audience.

Chekhov's plays do not actually try to elicit dynamic roars of approval. Indeed, they are all wry, sometimes wearied, sometimes satirical displays of futility in human behavior—of the inability to act decisively, even when such action would seem to be easily within the range of human capacity. In *Uncle Vanya* (1899), for example, the central character learns that the professor for whom he has slaved without reward is not the personification of wisdom, as he had thought, but is instead a mediocre academic windbag. Consequently, he is moved to shoot the professor at point-blank range, but misses him. And he is seen at the end of the play repressing the knowledge he has of his own wasted life, unlearning what he has learned by a titanic effort in futility. Chekhov's next play, *The Three Sisters* (1901), is a study of shared futility, enacted by the title characters, who though left with an ample inheritance never fulfill any of their personal hopes, professional ambitions, or mundane desires, not even the simple desire that moves them throughout the play: to go to Moscow. *The Three Sisters* was followed three years later by the production of *The Cherry Orchard* in January 1904, six months before Chekhov died of tuberculosis.

The Cherry Orchard may be seen as a full-scale version of cultural futility—of the inability of an old aristocratic social order to preserve itself, of the inability of a new bourgeois order to find meaning in anything beyond the acquisition of money and land. Everyone in the play owns, wants to own, or wants to maintain ownership of someone or something, and the play witnesses everyone gaining or losing the things they wish to own. Whether the audience is to laugh at this spectacle, or to weep, or simply to be bemused, is a difficult question. Chekhov called the play a comedy, and he apparently intended it to be comic, judging from correspondence with Stanislavski and Nemirovich-Danchenko. Yet Stanislavski's letters just as clearly show that he did not consider it a comedy at all—that he viewed it as a tragic expression of Russian life:

> It is not a comedy, not a farce, as you wrote—it is a tragedy no matter if you do indicate a way out into a better world in the last act . . . when I read it for the second time . . . I wept like a woman, I tried to control myself, but could not. I can hear you say: "But please, this is a farce . . ." No, for the ordinary person this is a tragedy.

Stanislavski's decision to produce the play as a tragedy moved Chekhov to complain that he was turning it into a piece of sniveling sentimentality, and Stanislavski did modify his interpretation somewhat during the next thirty years that he produced it, but he never came around to seeing the characters as laughable.

The conflict between Chekhov and Stanislavski is, of course, irreconcilable, because the play repeatedly hovers between the comic and the tragic. Yet Peter Brook's production, first staged in Paris in 1981, then performed in New York in 1988, seems to have achieved the delicate combination of moods which the play evokes. One has only to look at the contrasting shots of Mrs. Ranevsky, Lopakhin, and Gayev (see Figures 1 and 2) to see what Brook and his actors achieved. As seen in Figure 1, Mrs. Ranevsky dances with delight to be back in her old home, while Gayev looks on and Lopakhin, still the outsider, the peasant, sits on the floor; later (see Figure 2), Lopakhin tells Mrs. Ranevsky that she must sell the cherry orchard, and the set look on her face reveals both sadness and defiance. Again Gayev looks on, as he does throughout the play, never really accomplishing anything in spite of his many speeches, but this time his expression reflects his sister's melancholy. The characters and their feelings stand out with particular force because, as Frank Rich notes in his review following the text, Brook has avoided any kind of elaborate scenery, restricting himself just to Oriental rugs and a few other suggestive furnishings. This choice, seemingly a strange one for a play set in an ample country house in nineteenth-century Russia, nonetheless reflects the play's constant evocation of places, people, and ways of life which are out of sight, and often out of reach, such as Paris, or Mrs. Ranevsky's lover, or Pishchik's daughter Dashenka, or the cherry orchard, though each has an almost-palpable reality. Without detailed sets and furnishings, the actors must conjure up both the onstage and the offstage realities—and in so doing, demonstrate that all of those realities are equally unstable and, at last, equally unreachable.

THE CHERRY ORCHARD

BY ANTON CHEKHOV / TRANSLATED BY DAVID MAGARSHACK

CHARACTERS

LYUBOV (LYUBA) ANDREYEVNA RANEVSKY, *a landowner*
ANYA, *her daughter, aged seventeen*
VARYA, *her adopted daughter, aged twenty-four*
LEONID ANDREYEVICH GAYEV, *Mrs. Ranevsky's brother*
YERMOLAY ALEXEYEVICH LOPAKHIN, *a businessman*
PETER (PYOTR) SERGEYEVICH TROFIMOV, *a student*
BORIS BORISOVICH SIMEONOV-PISHCHIK, *a landowner*
CHARLOTTE IVANOVNA, *a governess*
SIMON PANTELEYEVICH YEPIKHODOV, *a clerk*

DUNYASHA, *a maid*
FIRS, *a manservant, aged eighty-seven*
YASHA, *a young manservant*
A HIKER
A STATIONMASTER
A POST OFFICE CLERK
GUESTS *and* SERVANTS

SCENE

The action takes place on MRS. RANEVSKY'S *estate.*

ACT 1

(A room which is still known as the nursery. One of the doors leads to ANYA'S *room. Daybreak; the sun will be rising soon. It is May. The cherry trees are in blossom, but it is cold in the orchard. Morning frost. The windows of the room are shut. Enter* DUNYASHA, *carrying a candle, and* LOPAKHIN *with a book in his hand.)*

LOPAKHIN: The train's arrived, thank goodness. What's the time?

DUNYASHA: Nearly two o'clock, sir. *(Blows out the candle.)* It's light already.

LOPAKHIN: How late was the train? Two hours at least. *(Yawns and stretches.)* What a damn fool I am! Came here specially to meet them at the station and fell asleep. . . . Sat down in a chair and dropped off. What a nuisance! Why didn't you wake me?

DUNYASHA: I thought you'd gone, sir. *(Listens.)* I think they're coming.

LOPAKHIN *(listening)*: No. . . . I should have been there to help them with the luggage and so on. *(Pause.)* Mrs. Ranevsky's been abroad for five years. I wonder what she's like now. . . . She's such a nice person. Simple, easy-going. I remember when I was a lad of fifteen, my late father—he used to keep a shop in the village—punched me in the face and made my nose bleed. We'd gone into the yard to fetch something, and he was drunk. Mrs. Ranevsky—I remember it as if it happened yesterday, she was such a young girl then and so slim—took me to the washstand in this very room, the nursery. "Don't cry, little peasant," she said, "it won't matter by the time you're wed." *(Pause.)* Little peasant . . . It's quite true my father was a peasant, but here I am wearing a white waistcoat and brown shoes. A dirty peasant in a fashionable shop. . . . Except, of course, that I'm a rich man now, rolling in money. But, come to think of it, I'm a plain peasant still. . . . *(Turns the pages of his book.)* Been

reading this book and haven't understood a word. Fell asleep reading it.

(Pause.)

DUNYASHA: The dogs have been awake all night; they know their masters are coming.

LOPAKHIN: What's the matter, Dunyasha? Why are you in such a state?

DUNYASHA: My hands are shaking. I think I'm going to faint.

LOPAKHIN: A little too refined, aren't you, Dunyasha? Quite the young lady. Dress, hair. It won't do, you know. Remember your place!

(Enter YEPIKHODOV *with a bunch of flowers; he wears a jacket and brightly polished high-boots which squeak loudly; on coming in, he drops the flowers.)*

YEPIKHODOV *(picking up the flowers)*: The gardener sent these. Said to put them in the dining room. *(Hands the flowers to* DUNYASHA.)

LOPAKHIN: Bring me some kvass while you're about it.

DUNYASHA: Yes, sir. *(Goes out.)*

YEPIKHODOV: Thirty degrees, morning frost, and the cherry trees in full bloom. Can't say I think much of our climate, sir. *(Sighs.)* Our climate isn't particularly accommodating, is it, sir? Not when you want it to be, anyway. And another thing. The other day I bought myself this pair of boots, and believe me, sir, they squeak so terribly that it's more than a man can endure. Do you happen to know of something I could grease them with?

LOPAKHIN: Go away. You make me tired.

YEPIKHODOV: Every day, sir, I'm overtaken by some calamity. Not that I mind. I'm used to it. I just smile. *(*DUNYASHA *comes in and hands* LOPAKHIN *the kvass.)* I'll be off. *(Bumps into a chair and knocks it over.)* There you are, sir. *(Triumphantly.)* You see, sir, pardon the expression, this sort of circumstance . . . I mean to say . . . Remarkable! Quite remarkable! *(Goes out.)*

DUNYASHA: I simply must tell you, sir: Yepikhodov has proposed to me.

LOPAKHIN: Oh?

DUNYASHA: I really don't know what to do, sir. He's ever such a quiet fellow, except that sometimes he starts talking and you can't understand a word he says. It sounds all right and it's ever so moving, only you can't make head or tail of it. I like him a little, I think. I'm not sure though. He's madly in love with me. He's such an unlucky fellow, sir. Every day something happens to him. Everyone teases him about it. They've nicknamed him Twenty-two Calamities.

LOPAKHIN *(listens)*: I think I can hear them coming.

DUNYASHA: They're coming! Goodness, I don't know what's the matter with me. I've gone cold all over.

LOPAKHIN: Yes, they are coming all right. Let's go and meet them. Will she recognize me? We haven't seen each other for five years.

DUNYASHA *(agitated)*: I'm going to faint. Oh dear, I'm going to faint!

(Two carriages can be heard driving up to the house. LOPAKHIN *and* DUNYASHA *go out quickly. The stage is empty. People can be heard making a noise in the adjoining rooms.* FIRS, *who has been to meet* MRS. RANEVSKY *at the station, walks across the stage hurriedly, leaning on a stick. He wears an old-fashioned livery coat and a top hat; he keeps muttering to himself, but it is impossible to make out a single word. The noise offstage becomes louder. A voice is heard: "Let's go through here."* MRS. RANEVSKY, ANYA, *and* CHARLOTTE, *with a lap dog on a little chain, all wearing traveling clothes,* VARYA, *wearing an overcoat and a head scarf,* GAYEV, SIMEONOV-PISHCHIK, LOPAKHIN, DUNYASHA, *carrying a bundle and an umbrella, and other* SERVANTS *with luggage walk across the stage.)*

ANYA: Let's go through here. Remember this room, Mother?

MRS. RANEVSKY *(joyfully, through tears)*: The nursery!

VARYA: It's so cold. My hands are quite numb. *(to* MRS. RANEVSKY*)* Your rooms, the white one and the mauve one, are just as you left them, Mother dear.

MRS. RANEVSKY: The nursery! My dear, my beautiful room! I used to sleep here when I was a little girl. *(Cries.)* I feel like a little girl again now. *(Kisses her brother and* VARYA, *and then her brother again.)* Varya is the same as ever. Looks like a nun. And I also recognized Dunyasha. *(Kisses* DUNYASHA.*)*

GAYEV: The train was two hours late. How do you like that? What a way to run a railway!

CHARLOTTE *(to* PISHCHIK*)*: My dog also eats nuts.

PISHCHIK *(surprised)*: Good Lord!

(All, except ANYA *and* DUNYASHA, *go out.)*

DUNYASHA: We thought you'd never come. *(Helps* ANYA *off with her coat and hat.)*

ANYA: I haven't slept for four nights on our journey. Now I'm chilled right through.

DUNYASHA: You left before Easter. It was snowing and freezing then. It's different now, isn't it? Darling Anya! *(Laughs and kisses her.)* I've missed you so much, my darling, my precious! Oh, I must tell you at once! I can't keep it to myself a minute longer. . . .

ANYA *(apathetically)*: What is it this time?

DUNYASHA: Our clerk, Yepikhodov, proposed to me after Easter.

ANYA: Always the same. *(Tidying her hair.)* I've lost all my hairpins. *(She is so tired, she can hardly stand.)*

DUNYASHA: I don't know what to think. He loves me so much, so much!

ANYA *(tenderly, looking through the door into her room)*: My own room, my own windows, just as if I'd never been away! I'm home again! As soon as I get up in the morning, I'll run out into the orchard. . . . Oh, if only I could sleep. I didn't sleep all the way back, I was so worried.

DUNYASHA: Mr. Trofimov arrived the day before yesterday.

ANYA *(joyfully)*: Peter!

DUNYASHA: He's asleep in the bathhouse. He's been living there. Afraid of being a nuisance, he says. *(Glancing at her watch.)* I really ought to wake him, except that Miss Varya told me not to. "Don't you dare wake him!" she said.

*(*VARYA *comes in with a bunch of keys at her waist.)*

VARYA: Dunyasha, coffee quick! Mother's asking for some.

DUNYASHA: I won't be a minute! *(Goes out.)*

VARYA: Well, thank goodness you're all back. You're home again, my darling. *(Caressing her.)* My darling is home again! My sweet child is home again.

ANYA: I've had such an awful time!

VARYA: I can imagine it.

ANYA: I left before Easter. It was terribly cold then. All the way Charlotte kept talking and doing her conjuring tricks. Why did you force Charlotte on me?

VARYA: But you couldn't have gone alone, darling, could you? You're only seventeen!

ANYA: In Paris it was also cold and snowing. My French is awful. I found Mother living on the fourth floor. When I got there, she had some French visitors, a few ladies and an old Catholic priest with a book. The place was full of tobacco smoke and terribly uncomfortable. Suddenly I felt sorry for Mother, so sorry that I took her head in my arms, held it tightly, and couldn't let go. Afterwards Mother was very sweet to me. She was crying all the time.

VARYA (*through tears*): Don't go on, Anya. Please don't.

ANYA: She'd already sold her villa near Mentone. She had nothing left. Nothing! I hadn't any money, either. There was hardly enough for the journey. Mother just won't understand! We had dinner at the station and she would order the most expensive things and tip the waiters a ruble each. Charlotte was just the same. Yasha, too, demanded to be given the same kind of food. It was simply awful! You see, Yasha is Mother's manservant. We've brought him back with us.

VARYA: Yes, I've seen the scoundrel.

ANYA: Well, what's been happening? Have you paid the interest on the mortgage?

VARYA: Heavens, no!

ANYA: Dear, oh dear . . .

VARYA: The estate will be up for sale in August.

ANYA: Oh dear!

LOPAKHIN (*puts his head through the door and bleats*): Bah-h-h! (*Goes out.*)

VARYA (*through tears*): Oh, I'd like to hit him! (*Shakes her fist.*)

ANYA (*gently embracing* VARYA): Varya, has he proposed to you? (VARYA *shakes her head.*) But he loves you. Why don't you two come to an understanding? What are you waiting for?

VARYA: I don't think anything will come of it. He's so busy. He can't be bothered with me. Why, he doesn't even notice me. I wish I'd never known him. I can't stand the sight of him. Everyone's talking about our wedding, everyone's congratulating me, while there's really nothing in it. It's all so unreal. Like a dream. (*In a different tone of voice.*) You've got a new brooch. Like a bee, isn't it?

ANYA (*sadly*): Yes, Mother bought it. (*Goes to her room, talking quite happily, like a child.*) You know, I went up in a balloon in Paris!

VARYA: My darling's home again! My dearest one's home again! (DUNYASHA *has come back with a coffeepot and is making coffee;* VARYA *is standing at the door of* ANYA's *room.*) All day long, darling, I'm busy about the house, and all the time I'm dreaming, dreaming. If only we could find a rich husband for you! My mind would be at rest then. I'd go into a convent and later on a pilgrimage to Kiev . . . to Moscow. Just keep going from one holy place to another. On and on. . . . Wonderful!

ANYA: The birds are singing in the orchard. What's the time?

VARYA: It's past two. It's time you were asleep, darling. (*Goes into* ANYA's *room.*) Wonderful!

(*Enter* YASHA *with a traveling rug and a small bag.*)

YASHA (*crossing the stage, in an affected genteel voice*): May I be permitted to go through here?

DUNYASHA: I can hardly recognize you, Yasha. You've changed so much abroad.

YASHA: Hmmm . . . And who are you, may I ask?

DUNYASHA: When you left, I was no bigger than this. (*Shows her height from the floor with her hand.*) I'm Dunyasha, Fyodor Kozoedov's daughter. Don't you remember me?

YASHA: Mmmm . . . Juicy little cucumber! (*Looks round, then puts his arms around her; she utters a little scream and drops a saucer.* YASHA *goes out hurriedly.*)

VARYA (*in the doorway, crossly*): What's going on there?

DUNYASHA (*in tears*): I've broken a saucer.

VARYA: That's lucky.

ANYA (*coming out of her room*): Mother must be told Peter's here.

VARYA: I gave orders not to wake him.

ANYA (*pensively*): Father died six years ago. A month after our brother, Grisha, was drowned in the river. Such a pretty little boy. He was only seven. Mother took it badly. She went away, went away never to come back. (*Shudders.*) Peter Trofimov was Grisha's tutor. He might remind her . . .

(FIRS *comes in, wearing a jacket and a white waistcoat.*)

FIRS (*walks up to the coffeepot anxiously*): Madam will have her coffee here. (*Puts on white gloves.*) Is the coffee ready? (*Sternly, to* DUNYASHA.) You there! Where's the cream?

DUNYASHA: Oh dear! (*Goes out quickly.*)

FIRS (*fussing round the coffeepot*): The nincompoop! (*Muttering to himself.*) She's come from Paris. . . . Master used to go to Paris. . . . Aye, by coach. . . . (*Laughs.*)

VARYA: What are you talking about, Firs?

FIRS: Sorry, what did you say? (*Joyfully.*) Madam is home again! Home at last! I can die happy now. (*Weeps with joy.*)

(*Enter* MRS. RANEVSKY, GAYEV, [LOPAKHIN], *and* SIMEONOV-PISHCHIK, *the last one wearing a Russian long-waisted coat of expensive cloth and wide trousers. As he enters,* GAYEV *moves his arms and body as if he were playing billiards.*)

MRS. RANEVSKY: How does it go now? Let me think. Pot the red in the corner. Double into the middle pocket.

GAYEV: And straight into the corner! A long time ago, Lyuba, you and I slept in this room. Now I'm fifty-one. . . . Funny, isn't it!

LOPAKHIN: Aye, time flies.

GAYEV: I beg your pardon?

LOPAKHIN: "Time flies," I said.

GAYEV: The place reeks of patchouli.

ANYA: I'm off to bed. Good night, Mother. (*Kisses her mother.*)

MRS. RANEVSKY: My sweet little darling! (*Kisses her hands.*) You're glad to be home, aren't you? I still can't believe it.

ANYA: Good night, Uncle.

GAYEV (*kissing her face and hands*): God bless you. You're so like your mother! (*to his sister*) You were just like her at that age, Lyuba.

(ANYA *shakes hands with* LOPAKHIN *and* PISHCHIK. *Goes out and shuts the door behind her.*)

MRS. RANEVSKY: She's terribly tired.

PISHCHIK: It was a long journey.

VARYA (*to* LOPAKHIN *and* PISHCHIK): Well, gentlemen, it's past two o'clock. You mustn't outstay your welcome, must you?

MRS. RANEVSKY (*laughs*): You're just the same, Varya. (*Draws* VARYA *to her and kisses her.*) Let me have my coffee first and then we'll all go. (FIRS *puts a little cushion under her feet.*) Thank you, Firs dear. I've got used to having coffee. I drink it day and night. Thank you, Firs, thank you, my dear old man. (*Kisses* FIRS.)

VARYA: I'd better make sure they've brought all the things in. (*Goes out.*)

MRS. RANEVSKY: Is it really me sitting here? (*Laughs.*) I feel like jumping about, waving my arms. (*Covers her face with her hands.*) And what if it's all a dream? God knows, I love my country. I love it dearly. I couldn't look out of the train for crying. (*Through tears.*) But, I suppose I'd better have my coffee. Thank you, Firs, thank you, dear old man. I'm so glad you're still alive.

FIRS: The day before yesterday . . .

GAYEV: He's a little deaf.

LOPAKHIN: At five o'clock I've got to leave for Kharkov. What a nuisance! I wish I could have had a good look at you, a good talk with you. You're still as magnificent as ever. . . .

PISHCHIK (*breathing heavily*): Lovelier, I'd say. Dressed in the latest Paris fashion. If only I were twenty years younger—ho-ho-ho!

LOPAKHIN: This brother of yours says that I'm an ignorant oaf, a tightfisted peasant, but I don't mind. Let him talk. All I want is that you should believe in me as you used to, that you should look at me as you used to with those wonderful eyes of yours. Merciful heavens! My father was a serf of your father and your grandfather, but you, you alone, did so much for me in the past that I forgot everything, and I love you just as if you were my own flesh and blood, more than my own flesh and blood.

MRS. RANEVSKY: I can't sit still, I can't. . . . (*Jumps up and walks about the room in great agitation.*) This happiness is more than I can bear. Laugh at me if you like. I'm making such a fool of myself. Oh, my darling little bookcase . . . (*Kisses the bookcase.*) My sweet little table . . .

GAYEV: You know, of course, that Nanny died here while you were away.

MRS. RANEVSKY (*sits down and drinks her coffee*): Yes, God rest her soul. They wrote to tell me about it.

GAYEV: Anastasy, too, is dead. Boss-eyed Peter left me for another job. He's with the Police Superintendent in town now. (*Takes a box of fruit drops out of his pocket and sucks one.*)

PISHCHIK: My daughter Dashenka—er—wishes to be remembered to you.

LOPAKHIN: I'd like to say something very nice and cheerful to you. (*Glances at his watch.*) I shall have to be going in a moment and there isn't much time to talk. As you know, your cherry orchard's being sold to pay your debts. The auction is on the twenty-second of August. But there's no need to worry, my dear. You can sleep soundly. There's a way out. Here's my plan. Listen carefully, please. Your estate is only about twelve miles from town, and the railway is not very far away. Now, all you have to do is break up your cherry orchard and the land along the river into building plots and lease them out for country cottages. You'll then have an income of at least twenty-five thousand a year.

GAYEV: I'm sorry, but what utter nonsense!

MRS. RANEVSKY: I don't quite follow you, Lopakhin.

LOPAKHIN: You'll be able to charge your tenants at least twenty-five rubles a year for a plot of about three acres. I bet you anything that if you advertise now, there won't be a single plot left by the autumn. They will all be snapped up. In fact, I congratulate you. You are saved. The site is magnificent and the river is deep enough for bathing. Of course, the place will have to be cleared, tidied up. . . . I mean, all the old buildings will have to be pulled down, including, I'm sorry to say, this house, but it isn't any use to anybody any more, is it? The old cherry orchard will have to be cut down.

MRS. RANEVSKY: Cut down? My dear man, I'm very sorry but I don't think you know what you're talking about. If there's anything of interest, anything quite remarkable, in fact, in the whole county, it's our cherry orchard.

LOPAKHIN: The only remarkable thing about this orchard is that it's very large. It only produces a crop every other year, and even then you don't know what to do with the cherries. Nobody wants to buy them.

GAYEV: Why, you'll find our orchard mentioned in the encyclopedia.

LOPAKHIN (*glancing at his watch*): If we can't think of anything and if we can't come to any decision, it won't be only your cherry orchard but your whole estate that will be sold at auction on the twenty-second of August. Make up your mind. I tell you, there is no other way. Take my word for it. There isn't.

FIRS: In the old days, forty or fifty years ago, the cherries used to be dried, preserved, made into jam, and sometimes—

GAYEV: Do shut up, Firs.

FIRS: —and sometimes cartloads of dried cherries were sent to Moscow and Kharkov. Fetched a lot of money, they did. Soft and juicy, those cherries were. Sweet and such a lovely smell . . . They knew the recipe then. . . .

MRS. RANEVSKY: And where's the recipe now?

FIRS: Forgotten. No one remembers it.

PISHCHIK (to MRS. RANEVSKY): What was it like in Paris? Eh? Eat any frogs?

MRS. RANEVSKY: I ate crocodiles.

PISHCHIK: Good Lord!

LOPAKHIN: Till recently there were only the gentry and the peasants in the country. Now we have holiday-makers. All our towns, even the smallest, are surrounded by country cottages. I shouldn't be surprised if in twenty years the holiday-maker multiplies enormously. All your holiday-maker does now is drink tea on the veranda, but it's quite in the cards that if he becomes the owner of three acres of land, he'll do a bit of farming on the side, and then your cherry orchard will become a happy, prosperous, thriving place.

GAYEV (indignantly): What nonsense!

(Enter VARYA and YASHA.)

VARYA: I've got two telegrams in here for you, Mother dear. (Picks out a key and unlocks the old-fashioned bookcase with a jingling noise.) Here they are.

MRS. RANEVSKY: They're from Paris. (Tears the telegrams up without reading them.) I've finished with Paris.

GAYEV: Do you know how old this bookcase is, Lyuba? Last week I pulled out the bottom drawer and saw some figures burned into it. This bookcase was made exactly a hundred years ago. What do you think of that? Eh? We ought really to celebrate its centenary. An inanimate object, but say what you like, it's a bookcase after all.

PISHCHIK (amazed): A hundred years! Good Lord!

GAYEV: Yes, indeed. It's quite something. (Feeling round the bookcase with his hands.) Dear, highly esteemed bookcase, I salute you. For over a hundred years you have devoted yourself to the glorious ideals of goodness and justice. Throughout the hundred years your silent appeal to fruitful work has never faltered. It sus-tained (through tears) in several generations of our family, their courage and faith in a better future and fostered in us the ideals of goodness and social consciousness.

(Pause.)

LOPAKHIN: Aye. . . .

MRS. RANEVSKY: You haven't changed a bit, have you, darling Leonid?

GAYEV (slightly embarrassed): Off the right into a corner! Pot into the middle pocket!

LOPAKHIN (glancing at his watch): Well, afraid it's time I was off.

YASHA (handing MRS. RANEVSKY her medicine): Your pills, ma'am.

PISHCHIK: Never take any medicines, dear lady. I don't suppose they'll do you much harm. but they won't do you any good either. Here, let me have 'em, my dear lady. (Takes the box of pills from her, pours the pills into the palm of his hand, blows on them, puts them all into his mouth, and washes them down with kvass.) There!

MRS. RANEVSKY (alarmed): You're mad!

PISHCHIK: Swallowed the lot.

LOPAKHIN: The glutton!

(All laugh.)

FIRS: He was here at Easter, the gentleman was. Ate half a bucketful of pickled cucumbers, he did. . . . (Mutters.)

MRS. RANEVSKY: What is he saying?

VARYA: He's been muttering like that for the last three years. We've got used to it.

YASHA: Old age!

(CHARLOTTE, in a white dress, very thin and tightly laced, a lorgnette dangling from her belt, crosses the stage.)

LOPAKHIN: I'm sorry, Miss Charlotte, I haven't had the chance of saying how-do-you-do to you. (Tries to kiss her hand.)

CHARLOTTE (snatching her hand away): If I let you kiss my hand, you'll want to kiss my elbow, then my shoulder . . .

LOPAKHIN: It's not my lucky day. (They all laugh.) My dear Charlotte, show us a trick, please.

MRS. RANEVSKY: Yes, do show us a trick, Charlotte.

CHARLOTTE: I won't. I'm off to bed. (Goes out.)

LOPAKHIN: We'll meet again in three weeks. (Kisses MRS. RANEVSKY's hand.) Good-bye for now. I must go. (to GAYEV) So long. (Embraces PISHCHIK.) So long. (Shakes hands with VARYA and then with FIRS and YASHA.) I wish I didn't have to go. (to MRS. RANEVSKY) Let me know if you make up your mind about the country cottages. If you decide to go ahead, I'll get you a loan of fifty thousand or more. Think it over seriously.

VARYA (*angrily*): For goodness' sake, go!

LOPAKHIN: I'm going, I'm going. . . .(*Goes out.*)

GAYEV: The oaf! However, I'm sorry. Varya's going to marry him, isn't she? He's Varya's intended.

VARYA: Don't say things you'll be sorry for, Uncle.

MRS. RANEVSKY: But why not, Varya? I should be only too glad. He's a good man.

PISHCHIK: A most admirable fellow, to tell the truth. My Dashenka—er—also says that—er—says all sorts of things. (*Drops off and snores, but wakes up immediately.*) By the way, my dear lady, you will lend me two hundred and forty rubles, won't you? Must pay the interest on the mortgage tomorrow.

VARYA(*terrified*): We have no money; we haven't!

MRS. RANEVSKY: We really haven't any, you know.

PISHCHIK: Have a good look around—you're sure to find it. (*Laughs.*) I never lose hope. Sometimes I think it's all over with me, I'm done for, then— hey presto—they build a railway over my land and pay me for it. Something's bound to turn up, if not today, then tomorrow. I'm certain of it. Dashenka might win two hundred thousand. She's got a ticket in the lottery, you know.

MRS. RANEVSKY: Well, I've finished my coffee. Now to bed.

FIRS (*brushing* GAYEV's *clothes admonishingly*): Put the wrong trousers on again, sir. What am I to do with you?

VARYA (*in a low voice*): Anya's asleep. (*Opens a window quietly.*) The sun has risen. It's no longer cold. Look, Mother dear. What lovely trees! Heavens, what wonderful air! The starlings are singing.

GAYEV (*opens another window.*): The orchard's all white. Lyuba, you haven't forgotten, have you? The long avenue there—it runs on and on, straight as an arrow. It gleams on moonlit nights. Remember? You haven't forgotten, have you?

MRS. RANEVSKY (*looking through the window at the orchard*): Oh, my childhood, oh, my innocence! I slept in this nursery. I used to look out at the orchard from here. Every morning happiness used to wake with me. The orchard was just the same in those days. Nothing has changed. (*Laughs happily.*) White, all white! Oh, my orchard! After the dark, rainy autumn and the cold winter, you're young again, full of happiness; the heavenly angels haven't forsaken you. If only this heavy load could be lifted from my heart; if only I could forget my past!

GAYEV: Well, and now they're going to sell the orchard to pay our debts. Funny, isn't it?

MRS. RANEVSKY: Look! Mother's walking in the orchard in . . . a white dress! (*Laughs happily.*) It *is* Mother!

GAYEV: Where?

VARYA: Really, Mother dear, what are you saying?

MRS. RANEVSKY: There's no one there. I just imagined it. Over there, on the right, near the turning to the summer house, a little white tree's leaning over. It looks like a woman. (*Enter* TROFIMOV. *He is dressed in a shabby student's uniform and wears glasses.*) What an amazing orchard! Masses of white blossom. A blue sky . . .

TROFIMOV: I say, Mrs. Ranevsky . . .(*She looks round at him.*) I've just come to say hello. I'll go at once. (*Kisses her hand warmly.*) I was told to wait till morning, but I—I couldn't, I couldn't.

(MRS. RANEVSKY *gazes at him in bewilderment.*)

VARYA(*through tears*): This is Peter Trofimov.

TROFIMOV: Peter Trofimov. Your son Grisha's old tutor. I haven't changed so much, have I?

(MRS. RANEVSKY *embraces him and weeps quietly.*)

GAYEV(*embarrassed*): There, there, Lyuba.

VARYA (*cries*): I did tell you to wait till tomorrow, didn't I, Peter?

MRS. RANEVSKY: Grisha, my . . . little boy. Grisha . . . my son.

VARYA: It can't be helped, Mother. It was God's will.

TROFIMOV (*gently, through tears*): Now, now . . .

MRS. RANEVSKY (*weeping quietly*): My little boy died, drowned. Why? Why, my friend? (*More quietly.*) Anya's asleep in there and here I am shouting, making a noise. . . . Well, Peter? You're not as good-looking as you were, are you? Why not? Why have you aged so much?

TROFIMOV: A peasant woman in a railway carriage called me "a moth-eaten gentleman."

MRS. RANEVSKY: You were only a boy then. A charming young student. Now you're growing thin on top, you wear glasses. . . . You're not still a student, are you? (*Walks toward the door.*)

TROFIMOV: I expect I shall be an eternal student.

MRS. RANEVSKY (*kisses her brother and then* VARYA): Well, go to bed now. You, Leonid, have aged too.

PISHCHIK (*following her*): So, we're off to bed now, are we? Oh dear, my gout! I think I'd better stay the night here. Now, what about letting me have the—er—two hundred and forty rubles tomorrow morning, dear lady? Early tomorrow morning. . . .

GAYEV: He does keep on, doesn't he?

PISHCHIK: Two hundred and forty rubles—to pay the interest on the mortgage.

MRS. RANEVSKY: But I haven't any money, my dear man.

PISHCHIK: I'll pay you back, dear lady. Such a trifling sum.

MRS. RANEVSKY: Oh, all right. Leonid will let you have it. Let him have it, Leonid.

GAYEV: Let him have it? The hell I will.

MRS. RANEVSKY: What else can we do? Let him have it,

please. He needs it. He'll pay it back.

(MRS. RANEVSKY, TROFIMOV, PISHCHIK, *and* FIRS *go out.* GAYEV, VARYA, *and* YASHA *remain.*)

GAYEV: My sister hasn't got out of the habit of throwing money about. (*to* YASHA) Out of my way, fellow. You reek of the hen house.

YASHA (*grins*): And you, sir, are the same as ever.

GAYEV: I beg your pardon? (*to* VARYA) What did he say?

VARYA (*to* YASHA): Your mother's come from the village. She's been sitting in the servants' quarters since yesterday. She wants to see you.

YASHA: Oh, bother her!

VARYA: You shameless bounder!

YASHA: I don't care. She could have come tomorrow, couldn't she? (*Goes out.*)

VARYA: Dear Mother is just the same as ever. Hasn't changed a bit. If you let her, she'd give away everything.

GAYEV: I suppose so. (*Pause.*) When a lot of remedies are suggested for an illness, it means that the illness is incurable. I've been thinking, racking my brains; I've got all sorts of remedies, lots of them, which, of course, means that I haven't got one. It would be marvelous if somebody left us some money. It would be marvelous if we found a very rich husband for Anya. It would be marvelous if one of us went to Yaroslavl to try our luck with our great-aunt, the Countess. She's very rich, you know. Very rich.

VARYA (*crying*): If only God would help us.

GAYEV: Don't howl! Our aunt is very rich, but she doesn't like us. First, because my sister married a lawyer and not a nobleman. . . . (ANYA *appears in the doorway.*) She did not marry a nobleman, and she has not been leading an exactly blameless life, has she? She's a good, kind, nice person. I love her very much. But, however much you try to make allowances for her, you have to admit that she is an immoral woman. You can sense it in every movement she makes.

VARYA (*in a whisper*): Anya's standing in the doorway.

GAYEV: I beg your pardon? (*Pause.*) Funny thing, there's something in my right eye. Can't see properly. On Thursday, too, in the district court . . .

(ANYA *comes in.*)

VARYA: Why aren't you asleep, Anya?

ANYA: I can't sleep, I can't.

GAYEV: My little darling! (*Kisses* ANYA's *face and hands.*) My dear child! (*Through tears.*) You're not my niece, you're my angel. You're everything to me. Believe me. Do believe me.

ANYA: I believe you, Uncle. Everyone loves you, everyone respects you, but, dear Uncle, you shouldn't talk so much. What were you saying just now about Mother, about your own sister? What did you say it for?

GAYEV: Well, yes, yes. (*He takes her hand and covers his face with it.*) You're quite right. It was dreadful. Dear God, dear God, help me! That speech I made to the bookcase today—it was so silly. The moment I finished it, I realized how silly it was.

VARYA: It's quite true, Uncle dear. You oughtn't to talk so much. Just don't talk, that's all.

ANYA: If you stopped talking, you'd feel much happier yourself.

GAYEV: Not another word. (*Kisses* ANYA's *and* VARYA's *hands.*) Not another word. Now to business. Last Thursday I was at the county court, and, well—er—I met a lot of people there, and we started talking about this and that, and—er—it would seem that we might manage to raise some money on a promissory note and pay the interest to the bank.

VARYA: Oh, if only God would help us!

GAYEV: I shall be there again on Tuesday, and I'll have another talk. (*to* VARYA) For goodness' sake, don't howl! (*to* ANYA) Your mother will have a talk with Lopakhin. I'm sure he won't refuse her. After you've had your rest, you'll go to Yaroslavl to see your great-aunt, the Countess. That's how we shall tackle the problem from three different sides, and I'm sure we'll get it settled. The interest we shall pay. Of that I'm quite sure. (*Puts a fruit drop in his mouth.*) I give you my word of honor, I swear by anything you like, the estate will not be sold! (*Excitedly.*) Why, I'll stake my life on it! Here's my hand; call me a rotten scoundrel if I allow the auction to take place. I stake my life on it!

ANYA (*has regained her composure; she looks happy*): You're so good, Uncle dear! So clever! (*Embraces him.*) I'm no longer worried now. Not a bit worried. I'm happy.

(*Enter* FIRS.)

FIRS (*reproachfully*): Have you no fear of God, sir? When are you going to bed?

GAYEV: Presently, presently. Go away, Firs. Never mind, I'll undress this time. Well, children, bye-bye now. More about it tomorrow. Now you must go to bed. (*Kisses* ANYA *and* VARYA.) I'm a man of the eighties. People don't think much of that time, but let me tell you, I've suffered a great deal for my convictions during my life. It's not for nothing that the peasants love me. You have to know your peasant, you have to know how to—

ANYA: There you go again, Uncle.

VARYA: Please, Uncle dear, don't talk so much.

FIRS (*angrily*): Sir!

GAYEV: I'm coming, I'm coming. You two go to bed. Off two cushions into the middle. Pot the white!

(GAYEV goes out, FIRS shuffling off after him.)

ANYA: I'm not worried any longer now. I don't feel like going to Yaroslavl. I don't like my great-aunt, but I'm no longer worried. I ought to thank Uncle for that. *(Sits down.)*

VARYA: I ought to go to bed, and I shall be going in a moment, I must tell you first that something unpleasant happened here while you were away. You know, of course, that only a few old servants live in the old servants' quarters: Yefimushka, Polia, Evstigney, and, well, also Karp. They had been letting some tramps sleep there, but I didn't say anything about it. Then I heard that they were telling everybody that I'd given orders for them to be fed on nothing but dried peas. I'm supposed to be a miser, you see. It was all that Evstigney's doing. Well, I said to myself, if that's how it is, you just wait! So I sent for Evstigney. *(Yawns.)* He comes. "What do you mean," I said, "Evstigney, you silly old fool?" *(Looks at ANYA)* Darling! *(Pause.)* Asleep . . . *(Takes ANYA by the arm.)* Come to bed, dear. . . . Come on! *(Leads her by the arm.)* My darling's fallen asleep. Come along. *(They go out. A shepherd's pipe is heard playing from far away on the other side of the orchard.* TROFIMOV *walks across the stage and, catching sight of* VARYA *and* ANYA, *stops.)* Shh! She's asleep, asleep. Come along, my sweet.

ANYA *(softly, half asleep)*: I'm so tired. . . . I keep hearing harness bells. Uncle . . . dear . . . Mother and Uncle . . .

VARYA: Come on, my sweet, come on. . . .

(They go into ANYA's room.)

TROFIMOV *(deeply moved)*: My sun! My spring!

CURTAIN

ACT 2

(Open country. A small tumbledown wayside chapel. Near it, a well, some large stones, which look like old grave-stones, and an old bench. A road can be seen leading to GAYEV's *estate. On one side, a row of tall dark poplars; it is there that the cherry orchard begins. In the distance, some telegraph poles, and far, far away on the horizon, the outlines of a large town that is visible only in very fine, clear weather. The sun is about to set.* CHARLOTTE, YASHA, *and* DUNYASHA *are sitting on the bench;* YEPIKHODOV *is standing nearby and is playing a guitar; they all sit sunk in thought.* CHARLOTTE *wears a man's old peaked hat; she has taken a shotgun from her shoulder and is adjusting the buckle on the strap.)*

CHARLOTTE *(pensively)*: I haven't a proper passport, I don't know how old I am, and I can't help thinking that I'm still a young girl. When I was a little girl, my father and mother used to travel the fairs and give performances—very good ones. I used to do the *salto mortale* and all sorts of other tricks. When Father and Mother died, a German lady adopted me and began educating me. Very well. I grew up and became a governess, but where I came from and who I am, I do not know. Who my parents were, I do not know either. They may not even have been married. I don't know. *(Takes a cucumber out of her pocket and starts eating it.)* I don't know anything. *(Pause.)* I'm longing to talk to someone, but there is no one to talk to. I haven't anyone. . . .

YEPIKHODOV *(plays his guitar and sings)*: "What care I for the world and its bustle? What care I for my friends and my foes?" . . . Nice to play a mandolin.

DUNYASHA: It's a guitar, not a mandolin. *(She looks at herself in a hand mirror and powders her face.)*

YEPIKHODOV: To a madman in love, it's a mandolin. *(Sings softly.)* "If only my heart was warmed by the fire of love requited."

(YASHA joins in.)

CHARLOTTE: How terribly these people sing! Ugh! Like hyenas.

DUNYASHA *(to YASHA)*: All the same, you're ever so lucky to have been abroad.

YASHA: Why, of course. Can't help agreeing with you there. *(Yawns, then lights a cigar.)*

YEPIKHODOV: Stands to reason. Abroad, everything's in excellent complexion. Been like that for ages.

YASHA: Naturally.

YEPIKHODOV: I'm a man of some education, I read all sorts of remarkable books, but what I simply can't understand is where it's all leading to. I mean, what do I really want—to live or to shoot myself? In any case, I always carry a revolver. Here it is. *(Shows them his revolver.)*

CHARLOTTE: That's done. Now I can go. *(Puts the shotgun over her shoulder.)* You're a very clever man, Yepikhodov. You frighten me to death. Women must be madly in love with you. Brrr! *(Walking away.)* These clever people are all so stupid. I've no one to talk to. Always alone, alone, I've no one, and who I am and what I am for is a mystery. *(Walks off slowly.)*

YEPIKHODOV: Strictly speaking, and apart from all other considerations, what I ought to say about myself, among other things, is that Fate treats me without mercy, like a storm a small boat. Even supposing I'm mistaken, why in that case should I wake up this morning and suddenly find a spider of quite enormous dimensions on my chest? As big as that. (*Uses both hands to show the spider's size.*) Or again, I pick up a jug of kvass and there's something quite outrageously indecent in it, like a cockroach. (*Pause.*) Have you ever read Buckle's *History of Civilization?* (*Pause.*) May I have a word or two with you, Dunyasha?

DUNYASHA: Oh, all right. What is it?

YEPIKHODOV: I'd be very much obliged if you'd let me speak to you in private. (*Sighs.*)

DUNYASHA (*embarrassed*): All right, only first bring me my cape, please. It's hanging near the wardrobe. It's so damp here.

YEPIKHODOV: Very well, I'll fetch it. . . . Now I know what to do with my revolver. (*Picks up his guitar and goes out strumming it.*)

YASHA: Twenty-two Calamities! A stupid fellow, between you and me. (*Yawns.*)

DUNYASHA: I hope to goodness he won't shoot himself. (*Pause.*) I'm ever so nervous. I can't help being worried all the time. I was taken into service when I was a little girl, and now I can't live like a peasant any more. See my hands? They're ever so white, as white as a young lady's. I've become so nervous, so sensitive, so like a lady. I'm afraid of everything. I'm simply terrified. So if you deceived me, Yasha, I don't know what would happen to my nerves.

YASHA (*kisses her*): Little cucumber! Mind you, I expect every girl to be respectable. What I dislike most is for a girl to misbehave herself.

DUNYASHA: I've fallen passionately in love with you, Yasha. You're so educated. You can talk about anything.

(*Pause.*)

YASHA (*yawning*): You see, in my opinion, if a girl is in love with somebody, it means she's immoral. (*Pause.*) It is so pleasant to smoke a cigar in the open air. (*Listens.*) Someone's coming. It's them. . . . (DUNYASHA *embraces him impulsively.*) Please go home and look as if you've been down to the river for a swim. Take that path or they'll think I had arranged to meet you here. Can't stand that sort of thing.

DUNYASHA (*coughing quietly*): Your cigar has given me an awful headache. (*Goes out.*)

(YASHA *remains sitting near the chapel. Enter* MRS. RANEVSKY, GAYEV, *and* LOPAKHIN.)

LOPAKHIN: You must make up your minds once and for all. There's not much time left. After all, it's quite a simple matter. Do you agree to lease your land for country cottages or don't you? Answer me in one word: yes or no. Just one word.

MRS. RANEVSKY: Who's been smoking such horrible cigars here? (*Sits down.*)

GAYEV: Now that they've built the railway, things are

much more convenient. (*Sits down*). We've been to town for lunch—pot the red in the middle! I really should have gone in to have a game first.

MRS. RANEVSKY: There's plenty of time.

LOPAKHIN: Just one word. (*Imploringly.*) Please give me your answer!

GAYEV (*yawns*): I beg your pardon?

MRS. RANEVSKY (*looking in her purse*): Yesterday I had a lot of money, but I've hardly any left today. My poor Varya! Tries to economize by feeding everybody on milk soup and the old servants in the kitchen on peas, and I'm just throwing money about stupidly. (*Drops her purse, scattering some gold coins.*) Goodness gracious, all over the place! (*She looks annoyed.*)

YASHA: Allow me to pick 'em up, madam. It won't take a minute. (*Starts picking up the coins.*)

MRS. RANEVSKY: Thank you, Yasha. Why on earth did I go out to lunch? That disgusting restaurant of yours with its stupid band, and those tablecloths smelling of soap. Why did you have to drink so much, Leonid? Or eat so much? Or talk so much? You did talk a lot again in the restaurant today and all to no purpose. About the seventies and the decadents . . . And who to? Talking about the decadents to waiters!

LOPAKHIN: Aye. . . .

GAYEV (*waving his arm*): I'm incorrigible, that's clear. (*Irritably to* YASHA.) What are you hanging around here for?

YASHA (*laughs*): I can't hear your voice without laughing, sir.

GAYEV (*to his sister*): Either he or I.

MRS. RANEVSKY: Go away, Yasha. Run along.

YASHA (*returning the purse to* MRS. RANEVSKY): At once, madam. (*Is hardly able to suppress his laughter.*) This very minute. (*Goes out.*)

LOPAKHIN: The rich merchant Deriganov is thinking of buying your estate. I'm told he's coming to the auction himself.

MRS. RANEVSKY: Where did you hear that?

LOPAKHIN: That's what they're saying in town.

GAYEV: Our Yaroslavl great-aunt has promised to send us money, but when and how much we do not know.

LOPAKHIN: How much will she send? A hundred thousand? Two hundred?

MRS. RANEVSKY: Well, I hardly think so. Ten or fifteen thousand at most. We must be thankful for that.

LOPAKHIN: I'm sorry, but such improvident people as you, such peculiar, unbusinesslike people, I've never met in my life! You're told in plain language that your estate's going to be sold, and you don't seem to understand.

MRS. RANEVSKY: But what are we to do? Tell us, please.

LOPAKHIN: I tell you every day. Every day I go on repeating the same thing over and over again. You must let out the cherry orchard and the land for country cottages, and you must do it now, as quickly as possible. The auction is on top of you! Try to understand! The moment you decide to let your land, you'll be able to raise as much money as you like, and you'll be saved.

MRS. RANEVSKY: Country cottages, holiday-makers— I'm sorry, but it's so vulgar.

GAYEV: I'm of your opinion entirely.

LOPAKHIN: I shall burst into tears or scream or have a fit. I can't stand it. You've worn me out! (to GAYEV) You're a silly old woman!

GAYEV: I beg your pardon?

LOPAKHIN: A silly old woman! (He gets up to go.)

MRS. RANEVSKY (in dismay): No, don't go. Please stay. I beg you. Perhaps we'll think of something.

LOPAKHIN: What is there to think of?

MRS. RANEVSKY: Please don't go. I beg you. Somehow I feel so much more cheerful with you here. (Pause.) I keep expecting something to happen, as though the house was going to collapse on top of us.

GAYEV (deep in thought): Cannon off the cushion. Pot into the middle pocket. . . .

MRS. RANEVSKY: I'm afraid we've sinned too much—

LOPAKHIN: You sinned!

GAYEV (putting a fruit drop into his mouth): They say I squandered my entire fortune on fruit drops. (Laughs.)

MRS. RANEVSKY: Oh, my sins! . . . I've always thrown money about aimlessly, like a madwoman. Why, I even married a man who did nothing but pile up debts. My husband died of champagne. He drank like a fish. Then, worse luck, I fell in love with someone, had an affair with him, and it was just at that time—it was my first punishment, a blow that nearly killed me—that my boy was drowned in the river here. I went abroad, never to come back, never to see that river again. I shut my eyes and ran, beside myself, and he followed me—pitilessly, brutally. I bought a villa near Mentone because he had fallen ill. For the next three years I knew no rest, nursing him day and night. He wore me out. Everything inside me went dead. Then, last year, I had to sell the villa to pay my debts. I left for Paris, where he robbed me, deserted me, and went to live with another woman. I tried to poison myself. Oh, it was all so stupid, so shaming. . . . It was then that I suddenly felt an urge to go back to Russia, to my homeland, to my daughter. (Dries her eyes.) Lord, O Lord, be merciful! Forgive me my sins! Don't punish me any more! (Takes a telegram from her pocket.) I received this telegram from Paris today. He asks me to forgive him. He implores me to go back. (Tears up the telegram.) What's that? Music? (Listens intently.)

GAYEV: That's our famous Jewish band. Remember? Four fiddles, a flute, and a double bass.

MRS. RANEVSKY: Does it still exist? We ought to arrange a party and have them over to the house.

LOPAKHIN (listening): I don't hear anything. (Sings quietly.) "And the Germans, if you pay 'em, will turn a Russian into a Frenchman." (Laughs.) I saw an excellent play at the theatre last night. It was very amusing.

MRS. RANEVSKY: I don't suppose it was amusing at all. You shouldn't be watching plays, but should be watching yourselves more often. What dull lives you live. What nonsense you talk.

LOPAKHIN: Perfectly true. Let's admit quite frankly that the life we lead is utterly stupid. (Pause.) My father was a peasant, an idiot. He understood nothing. He taught me nothing. He just beat me when he was drunk and always with a stick. As a matter of fact, I'm just as big a blockhead and an idiot myself. I never learnt anything, and my handwriting is so abominable that I'm ashamed to let people see it.

MRS. RANEVSKY: You ought to get married, my friend.

LOPAKHIN: Yes. That's true.

MRS. RANEVSKY: Married to our Varya. She's a nice girl.

LOPAKHIN: Aye. . . .

MRS. RANEVSKY: Her father was a peasant too. She's a hard-working girl, and she loves you. That's the important thing. Why, you've been fond of her for a long time yourself.

LOPAKHIN: Very well. I've no objection. She's a good girl.

(Pause.)

GAYEV: I've been offered a job in a bank. Six thousand a year. Have you heard, Lyuba?

MRS. RANEVSKY: You in a bank! You'd better stay where you are.

(FIRS comes in carrying an overcoat.)

FIRS (to GAYEV): Please put it on, sir. It's damp out here.

GAYEV (putting on the overcoat): You're a damned nuisance, my dear fellow.

FIRS: Come along, sir. Don't be difficult. . . . This morning, too, you went off without saying a word. (Looks him over.)

MRS. RANEVSKY: How you've aged, Firs!

FIRS: What's that, ma'am?

LOPAKHIN: Your mistress says you've aged a lot.

FIRS: I've been alive a long time. They were trying to marry me off before your dad was born. . . . (Laughs.) When freedom came, I was already chief valet. I refused to accept freedom and stayed on with my master. (*Pause.*) I well remember how glad everyone was, but what they were glad about, they did not know themselves.

LOPAKHIN: It wasn't such a bad life before, was it? At least, they flogged you.

FIRS (*not hearing him*): I should say so. The peasants stuck to their masters and the masters to their peasants. Now everybody does what he likes. You can't understand nothing.

GAYEV: Shut up, Firs. I have to go to town tomorrow. I've been promised an introduction to a general who might lend us some money on a promissory note.

LOPAKHIN: Nothing will come of it. You won't pay the interest, either. You may be sure of that.

MRS. RANEVSKY: Oh, he's just imagining things. There aren't any generals.

(*Enter* TROFIMOV, ANYA, *and* VARYA.)

GAYEV: Here they are at last.

ANYA: There's Mother.

MRS. RANEVSKY (*affectionately*): Come here, come here, my dears. (*Embracing* ANYA *and* VARYA.) If you only knew how much I love you both. Sit down beside me. That's right.

(*All sit down.*)

LOPAKHIN: Our eternal student is always walking about with the young ladies.

TROFIMOV: Mind your own business.

LOPAKHIN: He's nearly fifty and he's still a student.

TROFIMOV: Do drop your idiotic jokes.

LOPAKHIN: Why are you so angry, you funny fellow?

TROFIMOV: Well, stop pestering me.

LOPAKHIN (*laughs*): Tell me, what do you think of me?

TROFIMOV: Simply this: You're a rich man and you'll soon be a millionaire. Now, just as a beast of prey devours everything in its path and so helps to preserve the balance of nature, so you, too, perform a similar function.

(*They all laugh.*)

VARYA: You'd better tell us about the planets, Peter.

MRS. RANEVSKY: No, let's carry on with what we were talking about yesterday.

TROFIMOV: What was that?

GAYEV: Pride.

TROFIMOV: We talked a lot yesterday, but we didn't arrive at any conclusion. As you see it, there's something mystical about the proud man. You may be right for all I know. But try to look at it simply, without being too clever. What sort of pride is it, is there any sense in it. if, physiologically, man is far from perfect? If, in fact, he is, in the vast majority of cases, coarse, stupid, and

profoundly unhappy? It's time we stopped admiring ourselves. All we must do is—work!

GAYEV: We're going to die all the same.

TROFIMOV: Who knows? And what do you mean by "we're going to die"? A man may possess a hundred senses. When he dies, he loses only the five we know. The other ninety-five live on.

MRS. RANEVSKY: How clever you are, Peter!

LOPAKHIN (*ironically*): Oh, frightfully!

TROFIMOV: Mankind marches on, perfecting its powers. Everything that is incomprehensible to us now, will one day become familiar and comprehensible. All we have to do is to work and do our best to assist those who are looking for truth. Here in Russia only a few people are working so far. The vast majority of the educated people I know, do nothing. They aren't looking for anything. They are quite incapable of doing any work. They call themselves intellectuals, but speak to their servants as inferiors and treat the peasants like animals. They're not particularly keen on their studies, they don't do any serious reading, they are bone idle, they merely talk about science, and they understand very little about art. They are all so solemn, they look so very grave, they talk only of important matters, they philosophize. Yet anyone can see that our workers are abominably fed, sleep on bare boards, thirty and forty to a room—bedbugs everywhere, stench, damp, moral turpitude. It's therefore obvious that all our fine phrases are merely a way of deluding ourselves and others. Tell me, where are all those children's crèches people are talking so much about? Where are the reading rooms? You find them only in novels. Actually, we haven't any. All we have is dirt, vulgarity, brutality. I dislike and I'm frightened of all these solemn countenances, just as I'm frightened of all serious conversations. Why not shut up for once?

LOPAKHIN: Well, I get up at five o'clock in the morning. I work from morning till night, and I've always lots of money on me—mine and other people's—and I can see what the people around me are like. One has only to start doing something to realize how few honest, decent people there are about. Sometimes when I lie awake, I keep thinking; Lord, you've given us vast forests, boundless plains, immense horizons, and living here, we ourselves ought really to be giants—

MRS. RANEVSKY: You want giants, do you? They're all right only in fairy tales. Elsewhere they frighten me. (YEPIKHODOV *crosses the stage in the background, playing his guitar. Pensively.*) There goes Yepikhodov.

ANYA (*pensively*): There goes Yepikhodov.

GAYEV: The sun's set, ladies and gentlemen.

TROFIMOV: Yes.

GAYEV (softly, as though declaiming): Oh, nature, glorious nature! Glowing with eternal radiance, beautiful and indifferent, you, whom we call Mother, uniting in yourself both life and death, you—life-giver and destroyer . . .

VARYA (imploringly): Darling Uncle!

ANYA: Uncle, again!

TROFIMOV: You'd far better pot the red in the middle.

GAYEV: Not another word! Not another word!

(They all sit deep in thought. Everything is still. The silence is broken only by the subdued muttering of FIRS. Suddenly a distant sound is heard. It seems to come from the sky, the sound of a breaking string, slowly dying away, melancholy.)

MRS. RANEVSKY: What's that?

LOPAKHIN: I don't know. I expect a bucket must have broken somewhere far away in a coal mine, but somewhere a very long distance away.

GAYEV: Perhaps it was a bird, a heron or something.

TROFIMOV: Or an eagle-owl.

MRS. RANEVSKY (shudders): It makes me feel dreadful for some reason.

(Pause.)

FIRS: Same thing happened before the misfortune: the owl hooted and the samovar kept hissing.

GAYEV: Before what misfortune?

FIRS: Before they gave us our freedom.

(Pause.)

MRS. RANEVSKY: Come, let's go in, my friends. It's getting dark. (to ANYA) There are tears in your eyes. What's the matter, darling. (Embraces her.)

ANYA: It's nothing, Mother. Nothing.

TROFIMOV: Someone's coming.

(A HIKER appears. He wears a shabby white peaked cap and an overcoat; he is slightly drunk.)

HIKER: Excuse me, is this the way to the station?

GAYEV: Yes, follow that road.

HIKER: I'm greatly obliged to you sir. (Coughs.) Glorious weather . . . (Declaiming.) Brother, my suffering brother, come to the Volga, you whose groans . . . (to VARYA) Mademoiselle, won't you give thirty kopecks to a starving Russian citizen?

(VARYA, frightened, utters a little scream.)

LOPAKHIN (angrily): There's a limit to the most disgraceful behavior.

MRS. RANEVSKY (at a loss): Here, take this. (Looks for some money in her purse.) No silver. Never mind, have this gold one.

HIKER: Profoundly grateful to you, ma'am. (Goes out.)

(Laughter.)

VARYA (frightened): I'm going away. I'm going away. Good heavens, Mother dear, there's no food for the servants in the house, and you gave him a gold sovereign!

MRS. RANEVSKY: What's to be done with a fool like me? I'll give you all I have when we get home. You'll lend me some more money, Lopakhin, won't you?

LOPAKHIN: With pleasure.

MRS. RANEVSKY: Let's go in. It's time. By the way, Varya, we've found you a husband here. Congratulations.

VARYA (through tears): This isn't a joking matter, Mother.

LOPAKHIN: Okhmelia, go to a nunnery!

GAYEV: Look at my hands. They're shaking. It's a long time since I had a game of billiards.

LOPAKHIN: Okhmelia, O nymph, remember me in your prayers!

MRS. RANEVSKY: Come along, come along, it's almost supper time.

VARYA: That man frightened me. My heart's still pounding.

LOPAKHIN: Let me remind you, ladies and gentlemen: The cherry orchard is up for sale on the twenty-second of August. Think about it! Think!

(They all go out except TROFIMOV and ANYA.)

ANYA (laughing): I'm so glad the hiker frightened Varya. Now we are alone.

TROFIMOV: Varya's afraid we might fall in love. That's why she follows us around for days on end. With her narrow mind she cannot grasp that we are above love. The whole aim and meaning of our life is to bypass everything that is petty and illusory, that prevents us from being free and happy. Forward! Let us march on irresistibly toward the bright star shining there in the distance! Forward! Don't lag behind, friends!

ANYA (clapping her hands excitedly): You talk so splendidly! (Pause.) It's so heavenly here today!

TROFIMOV: Yes, the weather is wonderful.

ANYA: What have you done to me, Peter? Why am I no longer as fond of the cherry orchard as before? I loved it so dearly. I used to think there was no lovelier place on earth than our orchard.

TROFIMOV: The whole of Russia is our orchard. The earth is great and beautiful. There are lots of lovely places on it. (Pause.) Think, Anya: your grandfather, your great-grandfather, and all your ancestors owned serfs. They owned living souls. Can't you see human beings looking at you from every cherry tree in your orchard, from every leaf and every tree trunk? Don't you hear their voices? To own living souls—that's what has changed you all so much, you who are living now and those who lived before you. That's why your mother, you yourself, and your uncle no longer realize that you are living on borrowed capital, at other people's expense, at the expense of those whom you don't admit farther than your entrance hall. We are at least two hundred years behind the times. We haven't got anything at all. We have no definite attitude toward our past. We just philosophize, complain of depression, or drink vodka. Isn't it abundantly clear that before we start living in the present, we must atone for our past, make an end of it? And atone for it we can only by suffering, by extraordinary, unceasing labor. Understand that, Anya.

ANYA: The house we live in hasn't really been ours for a long time. I'm going to leave it. I give you my word.

TROFIMOV: If you have the keys of the house, throw them into the well and go away. Be free as the wind.

ANYA (*rapturously*): How well you said it!

TROFIMOV: Believe me, Anya, believe me! I'm not yet thirty, I'm young, I'm still a student, but I've been through hell more than once. I'm driven from pillar to post. In winter I'm half-starved, I'm ill, worried, poor as a beggar. You can't imagine the terrible places I've been to! And yet, always, every moment of the day and night, my heart was full of ineffable visions of the future. I feel, I'm quite sure, that happiness is coming, Anya. I can see it coming already.

ANYA (*pensively*): The moon is rising.

(YEPIKHODOV *can be heard playing the same sad tune as before on his guitar. The moon rises. Somewhere near the poplars* VARYA *is looking for* ANYA *and calling,* "Anya, where are you?")

TROFIMOV: Yes, the moon is rising. (*Pause.*) There it is—happiness! It's coming nearer and nearer. Already I can hear its footsteps, and if we never see it, if we never know it, what does that matter? Others will see it.

VARYA (*offstage*): Anya, where are you?

TROFIMOV: That Varya again! (*Angrily.*) Disgusting!

ANYA: Never mind, let's go to the river. It's lovely there.

TROFIMOV: Yes, let's.

(*They go out.*)

VARYA (*offstage*): Anya! Anya!

CURTAIN

ACT 3

(*The drawing room, separated by an archway from the ballroom. A candelabra is alight. The Jewish band can be heard playing in the entrance hall. It is the same band that is mentioned in Act Two. Evening. In the ballroom people are dancing the Grande Ronde.* SIMEONOV-PISHCHIK's *voice can be heard crying out,* "Promenade à une paire!" *They all come out into the drawing room:* PISHCHIK *and* CHARLOTTE *the first couple,* TROFIMOV *and* MRS. RANEVSKY *the second,* ANYA *and a* POST OFFICE CLERK *the third,* VARYA *and the* STATIONMASTER *the fourth, and so on.* VARYA *is quietly crying and dries her eyes as she dances. The last couple consists of* DUNYASHA *and a partner. They walk across the drawing room.* PISHCHIK *shouts,* "Grande Ronde balancez!" *and* "Les cavaliers à genoux et remerciez vos dames!")

(FIRS, *wearing a tailcoat, brings in soda water on a tray.* PISHCHIK *and* TROFIMOV *come into the drawing room.*)

PISHCHIK: I've got high blood-pressure. I've had two strokes already, and I find dancing hard work. But, as the saying goes, if you're one of a pack, wag your tail, whether you bark or not. As a matter of fact, I'm as strong as a horse. My father, may he rest in peace, liked his little joke, and speaking about our family pedigree, he used to say that the ancient Simeonov-Pishchiks came from the horse that Caligula had made a senator. (*Sits down.*) But you see, the trouble is that I have no money. A hungry dog believes only in meat. (*Snores, but wakes up again at once.*) I'm just the same. All I can think of is money.

TROFIMOV: There really is something horsy about you.

PISHCHIK: Well, a horse is a good beast. You can sell a horse.

(*From an adjoining room comes the sound of people playing billiards.* VARYA *appears in the ballroom under the archway.*)

TROFIMOV (*teasing her*): Mrs. Lopakhin! Mrs. Lopakhin!

VARYA (*angrily*): Moth-eaten gentleman!

TROFIMOV: Well, I am a moth-eaten gentleman and proud of it.

VARYA (*brooding bitterly*): We've hired a band, but how we are going to pay for it, I don't know. (*Goes out.*)

TROFIMOV (*to* PISHCHIK): If the energy you have wasted throughout your life looking for money to pay the interest on your debts had been spent on something else, you'd most probably have succeeded in turning the world upside down.

PISHCHIK: Nietzsche, the famous philosopher—a great man, a man of great intellect—says in his works that there's nothing wrong about forging bank notes.

TROFIMOV: Have you read Nietzsche?

PISHCHIK: Well, actually, Dashenka told me about it. I don't mind telling you, though, that in my present position I might even forge bank notes. The day after tomorrow I've got to pay three hundred and ten rubles. I've already got one hundred and thirty. *(Feels his pockets in alarm.)* My money's gone, I've lost my money! *(Through tears.)* Where is it? *(Happily.)* Ah, here it is, in the lining. Lord the shock brought me out in a cold sweat!

(Enter MRS. RANEVSKY *and* CHARLOTTE.*)*

MRS. RANEVSKY *(hums a popular Georgian dance tune)*: Why is Leonid so late? What's he doing in town? *(to* DUNYASHA*)* Offer the band tea, please.

TROFIMOV: I don't suppose the auction has taken place.

MRS. RANEVSKY: What a time to have a band! What a time to give a party! Oh, well, never mind. *(Sits down and hums quietly.)*

CHARLOTTE *(hands* PISHCHIK *a pack of cards)*: Here's a pack of cards. Think of a card.

PISHCHIK: All right.

CHARLOTTE: Now shuffle the pack. That's right. Now give it to me. Now, then, my dear Mr. Pishchik, *eins, zwei, drei!* Look in your breast pocket. Is it there?

PISHCHIK *(takes the card out of his breast pocket)*: The eight of spades! Absolutely right! *(Surprised.)* Good Lord!

CHARLOTTE *(holding a pack of cards on the palm of her hand, to* TROFIMOV*)*: Tell me, quick, what's the top card?

TROFIMOV: Well, let's say the queen of spades.

CHARLOTTE: Here it is. *(to* PISCHIK*)*: What's the top card now?

PISHCHIK: The ace of hearts.

CHARLOTTE: Here you are! *(Claps her hands and the pack of cards disappears.)* What lovely weather we've having today. *(A mysterious female voice, which seems to come from under the floor, answers: "Oh yes, glorious weather, madam!")* You're my ideal, you're so nice! *(The voice: "I like you very much too, madam.")*

STATIONMASTER *(clapping his hands)*: Bravo, Madam Ventriloquist!

PISHCHIK *(looking surprised)*: Good Lord! Enchanting, Miss Charlotte, I'm simply in love with you.

CHARLOTTE: In love! Are you sure you can love? *Guter Mensch, aber schlecter Musikant.* [A good man, but a poor musician.]

TROFIMOV *(claps* PISHCHIK *on the shoulder)*: Good old horse!

CHARLOTTE: Attention, please. One more trick. *(She takes a rug from a chair.)* Here's a very good rug. I'd like to sell it. *(Shaking it.)* Who wants to buy it?

PISHCHIK *(surprised)*: Good Lord!

CHARLOTTE: *Eins, zwei, drei!* *(Quickly snatching up the rug, which she had let fall, she reveals* ANYA *standing behind it.* ANYA *curtseys, runs to her mother, embraces her, and runs back to the ballroom, amid general enthusiasm.)*

MRS. RANEVSKY *(applauding)*: Bravo, bravo!

CHARLOTTE: Now, once more. *Eins, zwei, drei!* *(Lifts the rug; behind it stands* VARYA, *who bows.)*

PISHCHIK *(surprised)*: Good Lord!

CHARLOTTE: The end! *(Throws the rug over* PISHCHIK, *curtseys, and runs off to the ballroom.)*

PISHCHIK *(running after her)*: The hussy! What a woman, eh? What a woman! *(Goes out.)*

MRS. RANEVSKY: Still no Leonid. I can't understand what he can be doing in town all this time. It must be over now. Either the estate has been sold or the auction didn't take place. Why keep us in suspense so long?

VARYA *(trying to comfort her)*: I'm certain Uncle must have bought it.

TROFIMOV *(sarcastically)*: Oh, to be sure!

VARYA: Our great-aunt sent him power of attorney to buy the estate in her name and transfer the mortgage to her. She's done it for Anya's sake. God will help us and Uncle will buy it. I'm sure of it.

MRS. RANEVSKY: Your great-aunt sent fifteen thousand to buy the estate in her name. She doesn't trust us—but the money wouldn't even pay the interest. *(She covers her face with her hands.)* My whole future is being decided today, my future. . . .

TROFIMOV *(teasing* VARYA*)*: Mrs. Lopakhin!

VARYA *(crossly)*: Eternal student! Expelled twice from the university, weren't you?

MRS. RANEVSKY: Why are you so cross, Varya? He's teasing you about Lopakhin. Well, what of it? Marry Lopakhin if you want to. He is a nice, interesting man. If you don't want to, don't marry him. Nobody's forcing you, darling.

VARYA: I regard such a step seriously, Mother dear. I don't mind being frank about it: He is a nice man, and I like him.

MRS. RANEVSKY: Well, marry him. What are you waiting for? That's what I can't understand.

VARYA: But, Mother dear, I can't very well propose to him myself, can I? Everyone's been talking to me about him for the last two years. Everyone! But he either says nothing or makes jokes. I quite understand. He's making money. He has his business to think of, and he hasn't time for me. If I had any money, just a little, a hundred rubles, I'd give up everything and go right away as far as possible. I'd have gone into a convent.

TROFIMOV: Wonderful!

VARYA *(to* TROFIMOV*)*: A student ought to be intelligent! *(In a gentle voice, through tears.)* How plain you've grown, Peter! How you've aged! (to MRS. RANEVSKY, no longer crying) I can't live without having something to do, Mother! I must be doing something all the time.

(Enter YASHA.)

YASHA (hardly able to restrain his laughter): Yepikhodov's broken a billiard cue! (Goes out.)

VARYA: What's Yepikhodov doing here? Who gave him permission to play billiards? Can't understand these people! (Goes out.)

MRS. RANEVSKY: Don't tease her, Peter. Don't you see she is unhappy enough already?

TROFIMOV: She's a bit too conscientious. Pokes her nose into other people's affairs. Wouldn't leave me and Anya alone all summer. Afraid we might have an affair. What business is it of hers? Besides, the idea never entered my head. Such vulgarity is beneath me. We are above love.

MRS. RANEVSKY: So, I suppose I must be beneath love. (In great agitation.) Why isn't Leonid back? All I want to know is: Has the estate been sold or not? Such a calamity seems so incredible to me that I don't know what to think. I'm completely at a loss. I feel like screaming, like doing something silly. Help me, Peter. Say something. For God's sake, say something!

TROFIMOV: What does it matter whether the estate's been sold today or not? The estate's been finished and done with long ago. There's no turning back. The road to it is closed. Stop worrying, my dear. You mustn't deceive yourself. Look the truth straight in the face for once in your life.

MRS. RANEVSKY: What truth? You can see where truth is and where it isn't, but I seem to have gone blind. I see nothing. You boldly solve all important problems, but tell me, dear boy, isn't it because you're young, isn't it because you haven't had the time to live through the consequences of any of your problems? You look ahead boldly, but isn't it because you neither see nor expect anything terrible to happen to you, because life is still hidden from your young eyes? You're bolder, more honest, you see much deeper than any of us, but think carefully, try to understand our position, be generous even a little, spare me. I was born here, you know. My father and mother lived here, and my grandfather also. I love this house. Life has no meaning for me without the cherry orchard, and if it has to be sold, then let me be sold with it. (Embraces TROFIMOV and kisses him on the forehead.) Don't you see, my son was drowned here. (Weeps.) Have pity on me, my good, kind friend.

TROFIMOV: You know I sympathize with you with all my heart.

MRS. RANEVSKY: You should have put it differently. (Takes out her handkerchief. A telegram falls on the floor.) My heart is so heavy today. You can't imagine how heavy. I can't bear this noise. The slightest sound makes me shudder. I'm trembling all over. I'm afraid to go to my room. I'm terrified to be alone. . . . Don't condemn me, Peter. I love you as my own son. I'd gladly let Anya marry you, I swear I would. Only, my dear boy, you must study, you must finish your course at the university. You never do anything. You just drift from one place to another. That's what's so strange. Isn't that so? Isn't it? And you should do something about your beard. Make it grow, somehow. (Laughs.) You are funny!

TROFIMOV (picking up the telegram): I have no wish to be handsome.

MRS. RANEVSKY: That telegram's from Paris. I get one every day. Yesterday and today. That wild man is ill again, in trouble again. He asks me to forgive him. He begs me to come back to him, and I really think I ought to be going back to Paris to be near him for a bit. You're looking very stern, Peter. But what's to be done, my dear boy? What am I to do? He's ill. He's lonely. He's unhappy. Who'll look after him there? Who'll stop him from doing something silly? Who'll give him his medicine at the right time? And, why hide it? Why be silent about it? I love him. That's obvious. I love him. I love him. He's a millstone round my neck and he's dragging me down to the bottom with him, but I love the millstone, and I can't live without it. (Presses TROFIMOV's hand.) Don't think badly of me, Peter. Don't say anything. Don't speak.

TROFIMOV (through tears): For God's sake—forgive my being so frank, but he left you penniless!

MRS. RANEVSKY: No, no, no! You mustn't say that. (Puts her hands over her ears.)

TROFIMOV: Why, he's a scoundrel, and you're the only one who doesn't seem to know it. He's a petty scoundrel, a nonentity.

MRS. RANEVSKY (angry but restraining herself): You're twenty-six or twenty-seven, but you're still a schoolboy—a sixth-grade schoolboy!

TROFIMOV: What does that matter?

MRS. RANEVSKY: You ought to be a man. A person of your age ought to understand people who are in love. You ought to be in love yourself. You ought to fall in love. (Angrily.) Yes! Yes! And you're not so pure either. You're just a prude, a ridiculous crank, a freak!

TROFIMOV (horrified): What is she saying?

MRS. RANEVSKY: "I'm above love!" You're not above

love, you're simply what Firs calls a nincompoop. Not have a mistress at your age!

TROFIMOV (*horrified*): This is terrible! What is she saying? (*Walks quickly into the ballroom, clutching his head.*) It's dreadful! I can't! I'll go away! (*Goes out but immediately comes back.*) All is at an end between us! (*Goes out into the hall.*)

MRS. RANEVSKY (*shouting after him*): Peter, wait! You funny boy, I was only joking. Peter!

(*Someone can be heard running rapidly up the stairs and then suddenly falling downstairs with a crash.* ANYA *and* VARYA *scream, followed immediately by laughter.*)

MRS. RANEVSKY: What's happened?

ANYA (*laughing, runs in*): Peter's fallen down the stairs! (*Runs out.*)

MRS. RANEVSKY: What an eccentric! (*The* STATIONMASTER *stands in the middle of the ballroom and recites "The Fallen Woman" by Alexey Tolstoy. The others listen. But he has hardly time to recite a few lines when the sound of a waltz comes from the entrance hall, and the recitation breaks off. Everyone dances.* TROFIMOV, ANYA, VARYA, *and* MRS. RANEVSKY *enter from the hall.*) Well, Peter dear, you pure soul, I'm sorry. . . . Come, let's dance. (*Dances with* TROFIMOV.)

(ANYA *and* VARYA *dance together.* FIRS *comes in and stands his walking stick near the side door.* YASHA *has also come in from the drawing room and is watching the dancing.*)

YASHA: Well, Grandpa!

FIRS: I'm not feeling too well. We used to have generals, barons, and admirals at our dances before, but now we send for the post office clerk and the stationmaster. Even they are not too keen to come. Afraid I'm getting weak. The old master, the mistress's grandfather that is, used to give us powdered sealing wax for medicine. It was his prescription for all illnesses. I've been taking sealing wax every day for the last twenty years or more. That's perhaps why I'm still alive.

YASHA: You make me sick, Grandpa. (*Yawns*). I wish you was dead.

FIRS: Ugh, you nincompoop! (*Mutters.*)

(TROFIMOV *and* MRS. RANEVSKY *dance in the ballroom and then in the drawing room.*)

MRS. RANEVSKY: Merci. I think I'll sit down a bit. (*Sits down.*) I'm tired.

(*Enter* ANYA.)

ANYA (*agitated*): A man in the kitchen said just now that the cherry orchard has been sold today.

MRS. RANEVSKY: Sold? Who to?

ANYA: He didn't say. He's gone away now.

(ANYA *dances with* TROFIMOV; *both go off to the ballroom.*)

YASHA: Some old man gossiping, madam. A stranger.

FIRS: Master Leonid isn't here yet. Hasn't returned. Wearing his light autumn overcoat. He might catch cold. Oh, these youngsters!

MRS. RANEVSKY: I shall die! Yasha, go and find out who bought it.

YASHA: But he's gone, the old man has. (*Laughs.*)

MRS. RANEVSKY (*a little annoyed*): Well, what are you laughing at? What are you so pleased about?

YASHA: Yepikhodov's a real scream. Such a fool. Twenty-two Calamities!

MRS. RANEVSKY: Firs, where will you go if the estate's sold?

FIRS: I'll go wherever you tell me, ma'am.

MRS. RANEVSKY: You look awful! Are you ill? You'd better go to bed.

FIRS: Me to bed, ma'am? (*Ironically.*) If I goes to bed, who's going to do the waiting? Who's going to look after everything? I'm the only one in the whole house.

YASHA (*to* MRS. RANEVSKY): I'd like to ask you a favor, madam. If you go back to Paris, will you take me with you? It's quite impossible for me to stay here. (*Looking round, in an undertone.*) You know perfectly well yourself what an uncivilized country this is—the common people are so immoral—and besides, it's so boring here, the food in the kitchen is disgusting, and on top of it, there's that old Firs wandering about, muttering all sorts of inappropriate words. Take me with you, madam, please!

(*Enter* PISHCHIK.)

PISHCHIK: May I have the pleasure of a little dance, fair lady? (MRS. RANEVSKY *goes with him.*) I'll have one hundred and eighty rubles off you all the same, my dear, charming lady. . . . I will, indeed. (*They dance.*) One hundred and eighty rubles. . . .

(*They go into the ballroom.*)

YASHA (*singing softly*): "Could you but feel the agitated beating of my heart."

(*In the ballroom a woman in a gray top hat and check trousers can be seen jumping about and waving her arms. Shouts of "Bravo, Charlotte! Bravo!"*)

DUNYASHA (*stops to powder her face*): Miss Anya told me to join the dancers because there are lots of gentlemen and very few ladies. But dancing makes me dizzy and my heart begins beating so fast. I say, Firs, the post office clerk said something to me just now that quite took my breath away.

(*The music becomes quieter.*)

FIRS: What did he say to you?

DUNYASHA: "You're like a flower," he said.

YASHA (*yawning*): What ignorance! (*Goes out.*)

DUNYASHA: Like a flower! I'm ever so delicate, and I love people saying nice things to me!

FIRS: You'll come to a bad end, my girl. Mark my words.

(*Enter* YEPIKHODOV.)

YEPIKHODOV: You seem to avoid me, Dunyasha. Just as if I was some insect. (*Sighs.*) Oh, life!

DUNYASHA: What do you want?

YEPIKHODOV: No doubt you may be right. (*Sighs.*) But, of course, if one looks at things from a certain point of view, then, if I may say so and if you'll forgive my frankness, you have reduced me absolutely to a state of mind. I know what Fate has in store for me. Every day some calamity overtakes me, but I got used to it so long ago that I just look at my Fate and smile. You gave me your word, and though I—

DUNYASHA: Let's talk about it some other time. Leave me alone now. Now, I am dreaming. (*Plays with her fan.*)

YEPIKHODOV: Every day some calamity overtakes me, and I—let me say it quite frankly—why, I just smile, laugh even.

(*Enter* VARYA *from the ballroom.*)

VARYA: Are you still here, Simon! What an ill-mannered fellow you are, to be sure! (*to* DUNYASHA) Be off with you, Dunyasha. (*to* YEPIKHODOV) First you go and play billiards and break a cue, and now you wander about the drawing room as if you were a guest.

YEPIKHODOV: It's not your place to reprimand me, if you don't mind my saying so.

VARYA: I'm not reprimanding you. I'm telling you. All you do is drift about from one place to another without ever doing a stroke of work. We're employing an office clerk, but goodness knows why.

YEPIKHODOV (*offended*): Whether I work or drift about, whether I eat or play billards, is something which only people older than you, people who know what they're talking about, should decide.

VARYA: How dare you talk to me like that? (*Flaring up.*) How dare you? I don't know what I'm talking about, don't I? Get out of here! This instant!

YEPIKHODOV (*cowed*): Express yourself with more delicacy, please.

VARYA (*beside herself*): Get out of here this minute! Out! (*He goes toward the door, and she follows him.*) Twenty-two Calamities! Don't let me see you here again! Never set foot here again! (*YEPIKHODOV goes out. He can be heard saying behind the door: "I'll lodge a complaint."*) Oh, so you're coming back, are you? (*Picks up the stick which* FIRS *has left near the door.*) Come on, come on, I'll show you! Coming are you? Well, take that! (*Swings the stick as* LOPAKHIN *comes in.*)

LOPAKHIN: Thank you very much!

VARYA (*angrily and derisively*): I'm so sorry!

LOPAKHIN: It's quite all right. Greatly obliged to you for the kind reception.

VARYA: Don't mention it. (*Walks away, then looks round and inquires gently.*) I didn't hurt you, did I?

LOPAKHIN: Oh no, not at all. There's going to be an enormous bump on my head for all that.

(*Voices in the ballroom: "Lopakhin's arrived. Lopakhin!"*)

PISHCHIK: Haven't heard from you or seen you for ages, my dear fellow! (*Embraces* LOPAKHIN.) Do I detect a smell of brandy, dear boy? We're doing very well here, too.

(*Enter* MRS. RANEVSKY.)

MRS. RANEVSKY: Is it you, Lopakhin? Why have you been so long? Where's Leonid?

LOPAKHIN: He came back with me. He'll be here in a moment.

MRS. RANEVSKY (*agitated*): Well, what happened? Did the auction take place? Speak, for heaven's sake!

LOPAKHIN (*embarrassed, fearing to betray his joy*): The auction was over by four o'clock. We missed our train and had to wait till half past nine. (*With a deep sigh.*) Oh dear, I'm afraid I feel a little dizzy.

(*Enter* GAYEV. *He carries some parcels in his right hand and wipes away his tears with his left.*)

MRS. RANEVSKY: What's the matter, Leonid? Well! (*Impatiently, with tears.*) Quick, tell me for heaven's sake!

GAYEV (*doesn't answer, only waves his hands resignedly; to* FIRS, *weeping*): Here, take these—anchovies, Kerch herrings . . . I've had nothing to eat all day. I've had a terrible time. (*The door of the billiard room is open; the click of billiard balls can be heard and* YASHA's *voice: "Seven and eighteen!"* GAYEV's *expression changes. He is no longer crying.*) I'm awfully tired. Come and help me change, Firs.

(*GAYEV goes off through the ballroom to his own room, followed by* FIRS.)

PISHCHIK: Well, what happened at the auction? Come, tell us!

MRS. RANEVSKY: Has the cherry orchard been sold?

LOPAKHIN: It has.

MRS. RANEVSKY: Who bought it?

LOPAKHIN: I bought it. (*Pause.* MRS. RANEVSKY *is crushed; she would have collapsed on the floor if she had not been standing near an armchair.* VARYA *takes the keys from her belt, throws them on the floor in the center of the drawing room, and goes out.*) I bought it! One moment, please, ladies and gentlemen. I feel dazed. I can't talk. . . . (*Laughs.*) Deriganov was already there when we got to the auction. Gayev had only fifteen thousand, and Deriganov began his bidding at once with thirty thousand over and above the mortgage. I realized the position at once and took up his challenge. I bid forty. He bid forty-five. He kept raising his bid by five thousand and I by adding another ten thousand. Well, it was soon over. I bid ninety thousand on top of the arrears, and the cherry orchard was knocked down to me. Now the cherry orchard is mine! Mine! (*Laughs loudly.*) Merciful heavens, the cherry orchard's mine! Come on, tell me, tell me I'm drunk. Tell me I'm out of my mind. Tell me I'm imagining it all. (*Stamps his feet.*) Don't laugh at me! If my father and my grandfather were to rise from their graves and see what's happened, see how their Yermolay, their beaten and half-literate Yermolay, Yermolay who used to run around barefoot in winter, see how that same Yermolay bought this estate, the most beautiful estate in the world! I've bought the estate where my father and grandfather were slaves, where they weren't even allowed inside the kitchen. I must be dreaming. I must be imagining it all. It can't be true. It's all a figment of your imagination, shrouded in mystery. (*Picks up the keys, smiling affectionately.*) She's thrown down the keys. Wants to show she's no longer the mistress here. (*Jingles the keys.*) Oh well, never mind. (*The band is heard tuning up.*) Hey you, musicians, play something! I want to hear you. Come, all of you! Come and watch Yermolay Lopakhin take an axe to the cherry orchard. Watch the trees come crashing down. We'll cover the place with country cottages, and our grandchildren and great-grandchildren will see a new life springing up here. Strike up the music! (*The band plays.* MRS. RANEVSKY *has sunk into a chair and is weeping bitterly. Reproachfully.*) Why did you not listen to me? You poor dear, you will never get it back now. (*With tears.*) Oh, if only all this could be over soon, if only our unhappy, disjointed life could somehow be changed soon.

PISHCHIK (*takes his arm, in an undertone*): She's crying. Let's go into the ballroom. Let's leave her alone. Come on. (*Takes his arm and leads him away to the ballroom.*)

LOPAKHIN: What's the matter? You there in the band, play up, play up! Let's hear you properly. Let's have everything as I want it now. (*Ironically.*) Here comes the new landowner, the owner of the cherry orchard! (*Knocks against a small table*

accidentally and nearly knocks over the candelabra.) I can pay for everything!

(LOPAKHIN *goes out with* PISHCHIK. *There is no one left in the ballroom except* MRS. RANEVSKY, *who remains sitting in a chair, hunched up and crying bitterly. The band plays quietly.* ANYA *and* TROFIMOV *come in quickly.* ANYA *goes up to her mother and kneels in front of her.* TROFIMOV *remains standing by the entrance to the ballroom.*)

ANYA: Mother, Mother, why are you crying? My dear, good, kind Mother, my darling Mother, I love you; God bless you, Mother. The cherry orchard is sold. It's gone. That's true, quite true, but don't cry, Mother. You still have your life ahead of you, and you've still got your kind and pure heart. . . . Come with me, darling. Come. Let's go away from here. We shall plant a new orchard, an orchard more splendid than this one. You will see it, you will understand, and joy, deep, serene joy, will steal into your heart, sink into it like the sun in the evening, and you will smile, Mother! Come, darling! Come!

CURTAIN

ACT 4

(*The scene is the same as in the first act. There are no curtains at the windows or pictures on the walls. Only a few pieces of furniture are left. They have been stacked in one corner as if for sale. There is a feeling of emptiness. Near the front door and at the back of the stage, suitcases, traveling bags, etc., are piled up. The door on the left is open and the voices of* VARYA *and* ANYA *can be heard.* LOPAKHIN *stands waiting.* YASHA *is holding a tray with glasses of champagne. In the entrance hall* YEPIKHODOV *is tying up a box. There is a constant murmur of voices offstage, the voices of peasants who have come to say good-bye.* GAYEV's *voice is heard: "Thank you, my dear people, thank you."*)

YASHA: The peasants have come to say good-bye. In my opinion, sir, the peasants are decent enough fellows, but they don't understand a lot.

(*The murmur of voices dies away.* MRS. RANEVSKY *and* GAYEV *come in through the entrance hall; she is not crying, but she is pale. Her face is quivering. She cannot speak.*)

GAYEV: You gave them your purse, Lyuba. You shouldn't. You really shouldn't!

MRS. RANEVSKY: I—I couldn't help it. I just couldn't help it.

(*Both go out.*)

LOPAKHIN (*calling through the door after them*): Please take a glass of champagne. I beg you. One glass each before we leave. I forgot to bring any from town, and I could find only one bottle at the station. Please! (*Pause.*) Why, don't you want any? (*Walks away from the door.*) If I'd known, I wouldn't have bought it. Oh well, I don't think I'll have any, either. (YASHA *puts the tray down carefully on a chair.*) You'd better have some, Yasha.

YASHA: Thank you, sir. To those who're going away! And here's to you, sir, who're staying behind! (*Drinks.*) This isn't real champagne. Take it from me, sir.

LOPAKHIN: Paid eight rubles a bottle. (*Pause.*) Damn cold here.

YASHA: The stoves haven't been lit today. We're leaving, anyway. (*Laughs.*)

LOPAKHIN: What's so funny?

YASHA: Oh, nothing. Just feeling happy.

LOPAKHIN: It's October, but it might just as well be summer: it's so sunny and calm. Good building weather. (*Glances at his watch and calls through the door.*) I say, don't forget the train leaves in forty-seven minutes. In twenty minutes we must start for the station. Hurry up!

(TROFIMOV *comes in from outside, wearing an overcoat.*)

TROFIMOV: I think it's about time we were leaving. The carriages are at the door. Where the blazes could my galoshes have got to? Disappeared without a trace. (*Through the door.*) Anya, I can't find my galoshes! Can't find them!

LOPAKHIN: I've got to go to Kharkov. I'll leave with you on the same train. I'm spending the winter in Kharkov. I've been hanging about here too long. I'm worn out with having nothing to do. I can't live without work. Don't know what to do with my hands. They just flop about as if they belonged to someone else.

TROFIMOV: Well, we'll soon be gone and then you can resume your useful labors.

LOPAKHIN: Come on, have a glass of champagne.

TROFIMOV: No, thank you.

LOPAKHIN: So you're off to Moscow, are you?

TROFIMOV: Yes. I'll see them off to town, and I'm off to Moscow tomorrow.

LOPAKHIN: I see. I suppose the professors have stopped lecturing while you've been away. They're all waiting for you to come back.

TROFIMOV: Mind your own business.

LOPAKHIN: How many years have you been studying at the university?

TROFIMOV: Why don't you think of something new for a change? This is rather old, don't you think?—and stale. (*Looking for his galoshes.*) I don't suppose we shall ever meet again, so let me give you a word of advice as a farewell gift: Don't wave your arms about. Get rid of the habit of throwing your arms about. And another thing: To build country cottages in the hope that in the fullness of time vacationers will become landowners is the same as waving your arms about. Still, I like you in spite of everything. You've got fine sensitive fingers, like an artist's, and you have a fine sensitive soul.

LOPAKHIN (*embraces him*): My dear fellow, thanks for everything. Won't you let me lend you some money for your journey? You may need it.

TROFIMOV: Need it? Whatever for?

LOPAKHIN: But you haven't any, have you?

TROFIMOV: Oh, but I have. I've just got some money for a translation. Got it here in my pocket. (*Anxiously.*) Where could those galoshes of mine have got to?

VARYA (*from another room*): Oh, take your filthy things! (*Throws a pair of galoshes onto the stage.*)

TROFIMOV: Why are you so cross, Varya? Good heavens, these are not my galoshes!

LOPAKHIN: I had about three thousand acres of poppy sown last spring. Made a clear profit of forty thousand. When my poppies were in bloom, what a beautiful sight they were! Well, so you see, I made forty thousand and I'd be glad to lend you some of it because I can afford to. So why be so high and mighty? I'm a peasant. . . . I'm offering it to you without ceremony.

TROFIMOV: Your father was a peasant, my father was a pharmacist, all of which proves exactly nothing. (LOPAKHIN *takes out his wallet.*) Put it back! Put it back! If you offered me two hundred thousand, I wouldn't accept it. I'm a free man. Everything you prize so highly, everything that means so much to all of you, rich or poor, has no more power over me than a bit of fluff blown about in the air. I can manage without you. I can pass you by. I'm strong and proud. Mankind is marching toward a higher truth, toward the greatest happiness possible on earth, and I'm in the front ranks!

LOPAKHIN: Will you get there?

TROFIMOV: I will. (*Pause.*) I will get there or show others the way to get there.

(*The sound of an axe striking a tree can be heard in the distance.*)

LOPAKHIN: Well, good-bye, my dear fellow. Time to go. You and I are trying to impress one another, but life goes on regardless. When I work hard for hours on end, I can think more clearly, and then I can't help feeling that I, too, know what I live for. Have you any idea how many people in Russia exist goodness only knows why? However, no matter. It isn't they who make the world go round. I'm told Gayev has taken a job at the bank at six thousand a year. He'll never stick to it. Too damn lazy.

ANYA (*in the doorway*): Mother asks you not to begin

cutting the orchard down till she's gone.

TROFIMOV: Really, haven't you any tact at all? (*Goes out through the hall.*)

LOPAKHIN: Sorry, I'll see to it at once, at once! The damned idiots! (*Goes out after* TROFIMOV.)

ANYA: Has Firs been taken to the hospital?

YASHA: I told them to this morning. They must have taken him, I should think.

ANYA (*to* YEPIKHODOV, *who is crossing the ball-room*): Please find out if Firs has been taken to the hospital.

YASHA (*offended*): I told Yegor this morning. I haven't got to tell him a dozen times, have I?

YEPIKHODOV: Old man Firs, if you want my final opinion, is beyond repair, and it's high time he was gathered to his fathers. So far as I'm concerned, I can only envy him. (*Puts a suitcase on a hatbox and squashes it.*) There, you see! I knew it. (*Goes out.*)

YASHA (*sneeringly*): Twenty-two Calamities!

VARYA (*from behind the door*): Has Firs been taken to the hospital?

ANYA: He has.

VARYA: Why didn't they take the letter for the doctor?

ANYA: We'd better send it on after him. (*Goes out.*)

VARYA (*from the next room*): Where's Yasha? Tell him his mother's here. She wants to say good-bye to him.

YASHA (*waves his hand impatiently*): Oh, that's too much!

(*All this time* DUNYASHA *has been busy with the luggage. Now that* YASHA *is alone, she goes up to him.*)

DUNYASHA: You haven't even looked at me once, Yasha. You're going away, leaving me behind. (*Bursts out crying and throws her arms around his neck.*)

YASHA: Must you cry? (*Drinks champagne.*) I'll be back in Paris in a week. Tomorrow we catch the express and off we go! That's the last you'll see of us. I can hardly believe it, somehow. *Vive la France!* I hate it here. It doesn't suit me at all. It's not the kind of life I like. I'm afraid it can't be helped. I've had enough of all this ignorance. More than enough. (*Drinks champagne.*) So what's the use of crying? Behave yourself and you won't end up crying.

DUNYASHA (*powdering her face, looking in a hand mirror*): Write to me from Paris, please. I did love you, Yasha, after all. I loved you so much. I'm such an affectionate creature, Yasha.

YASHA: They're coming here. (*Busies himself around the suitcases, humming quietly.*)

(*Enter* MRS. RANEVSKY, GAYEV, ANYA, *and* CHARLOTTE.)

GAYEV: We ought to be going. There isn't much time

left. (*Looking at* YASHA.) Who's smelling of pickled herrings here?

MRS. RANEVSKY: In another ten minutes we ought to be getting into the carriages. (*Looks round the room.*) Good-bye, dear house, good-bye, old grandfather house! Winter will pass, spring will come, and you won't be here any more. They'll have pulled you down. The things these walls have seen! (*Kisses her daughter affectionately.*) My precious one, you look radiant. Your eyes are sparkling like diamonds. Happy? Very happy?

ANYA: Oh yes, very! A new life is beginning, Mother!

GAYEV (*gaily*): It is, indeed. Everything's all right now. We were all so worried and upset before the cherry orchard was sold, but now, when everything has been finally and irrevocably settled, we have all calmed down and even cheered up. I'm a bank official now, a financier. Pot the red in the middle. As for you, Lyuba, say what you like, but you too are looking a lot better. There's no doubt about it.

MRS. RANEVSKY: Yes, my nerves are better, that's true. (*Someone helps her on with her hat and coat.*) I sleep well. Take my things out, Yasha. It's time. (*to* ANYA) We'll soon be seeing each other again, darling. I'm going to Paris. I'll live there on the money your great-aunt sent from Yaroslavl to buy the estate—three cheers for Auntie!—but the money won't last long, I'm afraid.

ANYA: You'll come home soon, Mother, very soon. I'm going to study, pass my school exams, and then I'll work and help you. We shall read all sorts of books together, won't we, Mother? (*Kisses her mother's hands.*) We shall read during the autumn evenings. We'll read lots and lots of books, and a new, wonderful world will open up to us. (*Dreamily.*) Oh, do come back, Mother!

MRS. RANEVSKY: I'll come back, my precious. (*Embraces her daughter.*)

(*Enter* LOPAKHIN. CHARLOTTE *quietly hums a tune.*)

GAYEV: Happy Charlotte! She's singing!

CHARLOTTE (*picks up a bundle that looks like a baby in swaddling clothes*): My darling baby, go to sleep, my baby. (*A sound of a baby crying is heard.*) Hush, my sweet, my darling boy. (*The cry is heard again.*) Poor little darling, I'm so sorry for you! (*Throws the bundle down.*) So you will find me another job, won't you? I can't go on like this.

LOPAKHIN: We'll find you one, don't you worry.

GAYEV: Everybody's leaving us. Varya's going away. All of a sudden, we're no longer wanted.

CHARLOTTE: I haven't anywhere to live in town. I must go away. (*Sings quietly.*) It's all the same to me. . . .

(*Enter* PISHCHIK.)

LOPAKHIN: The nine days' wonder!

PISHCHIK (*out of breath*): Oh dear, let me get my breath back! I'm all in. Dear friends . . . a drink of water, please.

GAYEV: Came to borrow some money, I'll be bound. Not from me this time. Better make myself scarce. (*Goes out.*)

PISHCHIK: Haven't seen you for ages, dearest lady. (*to* LOPAKHIN) You here too? Glad to see you . . . man of immense intellect. . . . Here, that's for you, take it. (*Gives* LOPAKHIN *money.*) Four hundred rubles. That leaves eight hundred and forty I still owe you.

LOPAKHIN (*puzzled, shrugging his shoulders*): I must be dreaming. Where did you get it?

PISHCHIK: One moment . . . Terribly hot . . . Most extraordinary thing happened. Some Englishmen came to see me. They found some kind of white clay on my land. (*to* MRS. RANEVSKY) Here's four hundred for you too, beautiful ravishing lady. (*Gives her the money.*) The rest later. (*Drinks some water.*) Young fellow in the train just now was telling me that some—er—great philosopher advises people to jump off roofs. "Jump!" he says, and that'll solve all your problems. (*With surprise.*) Good Lord! More water, please.

LOPAKHIN: Who were these Englishmen?

PISHCHIK: I let them a plot of land with the clay on a twenty-four years' lease. And now you must excuse me, my friends. I'm in a hurry. Must be rushing off somewhere else. To Znoykov's, to Kardamonov's . . . Owe them all money. (*Drinks.*) Good-bye. I'll look in on Thursday.

MRS. RANEVSKY: We're just leaving for town. I'm going abroad tomorrow.

PISHCHIK: What? (*In a worried voice.*) Why are you going to town? Oh! I see! The furniture, the suitcases . . . Well, no matter. (*Through tears.*) No matter. Men of immense intellect, these Englishmen. . . . No matter. . . . No matter. I wish you all the best. May God help you. . . . No matter. Everything in this world comes to an end. (*Kisses* MRS. RANEVSKY'S *hand.*) When you hear that my end has come, remember the—er—old horse and say: Once there lived a man called Simeonov-Pishchik; may he rest in peace. Remarkable weather we've been having. . . . Yes. (*Goes out in great embarrassment, but immediately comes back and says, standing in the doorway.*) My Dashenka sends her regards. (*Goes out.*)

MRS. RANEVSKY: Well, we can go now. I'm leaving with two worries on my mind. One concerns Firs. He's ill. (*With a glance at her watch.*) We still have about five minutes.

ANYA: Firs has been taken to the hospital, Mother. Yasha sent him off this morning.

MRS. RANEVSKY: My other worry concerns Varya. She's used to getting up early and working. Now that she has nothing to do, she's like a fish out of water. She's grown thin and pale, and she's always crying, poor thing. (*Pause.*) You must have noticed it, Lopakhin. As you very well know, I'd always hoped to see her married to you. Indeed, everything seemed to indicate that you two would get married. (*She whispers to* ANYA, *who nods to* CHARLOTTE, *and they both go out.*) She loves you, you like her, and I simply don't know why you two always seem to avoid each other. I don't understand it.

LOPAKHIN: To tell you the truth, neither do I. The whole thing's odd somehow. If there's still time, I'm ready even now. . . . Let's settle it at once and get it over. I don't feel I'll ever propose to her without you here.

MRS. RANEVSKY: Excellent! Why, it shouldn't take more than a minute. I'll call her at once.

LOPAKHIN: And there's champagne here too. Appropriate to the occasion. (*Looks at the glasses.*) They're empty. Someone must have drunk it. (*YASHA coughs.*) Lapped it up, I call it.

MRS. RANEVSKY (*excitedly*): Fine! We'll go out. Yasha, *allez!* I'll call her. (*Through the door.*) Varya, leave what you're doing and come here for a moment. Come on.

(MRS. RANEVSKY *goes out with* YASHA.)

LOPAKHIN (*glancing at his watch*): Aye. . . .

(*Pause. Behind the door suppressed laughter and whispering can be heard. Enter* VARYA.)

VARYA (*spends a long time examining the luggage*): Funny, can't find it.

LOPAKHIN: What are you looking for?

VARYA: Packed it myself, and can't remember.

(*Pause.*)

LOPAKHIN: Where are you going now, Varya?

VARYA: Me? To the Ragulins'. I've agreed to look after their house—to be their housekeeper, I suppose.

LOPAKHIN: In Yashnevo, isn't it? About fifty miles from here. (*Pause.*) Aye. . . . So life's come to an end in this house.

VARYA (*examining the luggage*): Where can it be? Must have put it in the trunk. Yes, life's come to an end in this house. It will never come back.

LOPAKHIN: I'm off to Kharkov by the same train. Lots to see to there. I'm leaving Yepikhodov here to keep an eye on things. I've given him the job.

VARYA: Have you?

LOPAKHIN: This time last year it was already snowing, you remember. Now it's calm and sunny. A bit cold, though. Three degrees of frost.

VARYA: I haven't looked. (*Pause.*) Anyway, our thermometer's broken.

(*Pause. A voice from outside, through the door: "Mr. Lopakhin!"*)

LOPAKHIN (*as though he had long been expecting this call*): Coming! (*Goes out quickly.*)

(VARYA *sits down on the floor, lays her head on a bundle of clothes, and sobs quietly. The door opens and* MRS. RANEVSKY *comes in cautiously.*)

MRS. RANEVSKY: Well? (*Pause.*) We must go.

VARYA (*no longer crying, dries her eyes*): Yes, it's time, Mother dear. I'd like to get to the Ragulins' today, I only hope we don't miss the train.

MRS. RANEVSKY (*calling through the door.*): Anya, put your things on.

(*Enter* ANYA, *followed by* GAYEV *and* CHARLOTTE. GAYEV *wears a warm overcoat with a hood.* SERVANTS *and* COACHMEN *come in.* YEPIKHODOV *is busy with the luggage.*)

MRS. RANEVSKY: Now we can be on our way.

ANYA (*joyfully*): On our way. Oh, yes!

GAYEV: My friends, my dear, dear friends, leaving this house for good, how can I remain silent, how can I, before parting from you, refrain from expressing the feelings which now pervade my whole being—

ANYA (*imploringly*): Uncle!

VARYA: Uncle dear, please don't.

GAYEV (*dejectedly*): Double the red into the middle. . . . Not another word!

(*Enter* TROFIMOV, *followed by* LOPAKHIN.)

TROFIMOV: Well, ladies and gentlemen, it's time to go.

LOPAKHIN: Yepikhodov, my coat!

MRS. RANEVSKY: Let me sit down a minute. I feel as though I've never seen the walls and ceilings of this house before. I look at them now with such eagerness, with such tender emotion. . . .

GAYEV: I remember when I was six years old sitting on this window sill on Trinity Sunday and watching Father going to church.

MRS. RANEVSKY: Have all the things been taken out?

LOPAKHIN: I think so. (*To* YEPIKHODOV *as he puts on his coat.*) Mind, everything's all right here, Yepikhodov.

YEPIKHODOV (*in a hoarse voice*): Don't you worry, sir.

LOPAKHIN: What's the matter with your voice?

YEPIKHODOV: I've just had a drink of water and I must have swallowed something.

YASHA (*contemptuously*): What ignorance!

MRS. RANEVSKY: There won't be a soul left in this place when we've gone.

LOPAKHIN: Not till next spring.

(VARYA *pulls an umbrella out of a bundle of clothes with such force that it looks as if she were going to hit someone with it;* LOPAKHIN *pretends to be frightened.*)

VARYA: Good heavens, you didn't really think that—

TROFIMOV: Come on, let's get into the carriages! It's time. The train will be in soon.

VARYA: There are your galoshes, Peter. By that suitcase. (*Tearfully.*) Oh, how dirty they are, how old. . . .

TROFIMOV (*putting on his galoshes*): Come along, ladies and gentlemen.

(*Pause.*)

GAYEV (*greatly put out, afraid of bursting into tears*): Train . . . station . . . in off into the middle pocket . . . double the white into the corner.

MRS. RANEVSKY: Come along!

LOPAKHIN: Is everyone here? No one left behind? (*Locks the side door on the left.*) There are some things in there. I'd better keep it locked. Come on!

ANYA: Good-bye, old house! Good-bye, old life!

TROFIMOV: Welcome new life!

(TROFIMOV *goes out with* ANYA. VARYA *casts a last look round the room and goes out unhurriedly.* YASHA *and* CHARLOTTE, *carrying her lap dog, go out.*)

LOPAKHIN: So, it's till next spring. Come along, ladies and gentlemen. Till we meet again. (*Goes out.*)

(MRS. RANEVSKY *and* GAYEV *are left alone. They seem to have been waiting for this moment. They fling their arms around each other, sobbing quietly, restraining themselves, as though afraid of being overheard.*)

GAYEV (*in despair*): My sister! My sister!

MRS. RANEVSKY: Oh, my dear, my sweet, my beautiful orchard! My life, my youth, my happiness, good-bye! . . .

ANYA (*offstage, happily, appealingly*): Mo-ther!

TROFIMOV (*offstage, happily, excited*): Where are you?

MRS. RANEVSKY: One last look at the walls and the windows. Mother loved to walk in this room.

GAYEV: My sister, my sister!

ANYA (*offstage*): Mo-ther!

TROFIMOV (*offstage*): Where are you?

MRS. RANEVSKY: We're coming.

(*They go out. The stage is empty. The sound of all the doors being locked is heard, then of carriages driving off. It grows quiet. The silence is broken by the muffled noise of an axe striking a tree, sounding forlorn and sad. Footsteps can be heard.* FIRS *appears from the door on the right. He is dressed, as always, in a jacket and white waistcoat. He is wearing slippers. He looks ill.*)

FIRS (*walks up to the door and tries the handle*): Locked! They've gone. (*Sits down on the sofa.*) Forgot all about me. Never mind. Let me sit down here for a bit. Forgotten to put on his fur coat, the young master has. Sure of it. Gone off in his light overcoat. *(Sighs anxiously.)* I should have seen to it. . . . Oh, these youngsters! *(Mutters something which cannot be understood.)* My life's gone just as if I'd never lived. . . . *(Lies down.)* I'll lie down a bit. No strength left, Nothing's left. Nothing. Ugh, you—nincompoop! *(Lies motionless.)*

(A distant sound is heard, which seems to come from the sky, the sound of a breaking string, slowly dying away, melancholy. It is followed by silence, broken only by the sound of an axe striking a tree far away in the orchard.)

CURTAIN

Figure 1. Mrs. Ranevsky (Natasha Parry) dances with delight to be back in her old home, while Gayev (Erland Josephson) looks on and Lopakhin (Brian Dennehy) sits on the floor in the Peter Brook production of *The Cherry Orchard,* directed by Peter Brook, 1988. (Photograph: Martha Swope.)

Figure 2. Lopakhin (Brian Dennehy) tells Mrs. Ranevsky (Natasha Parry) that she must sell the cherry orchard, while Gayev (Erland Josephson) looks on, the melancholy expression on his face echoing that of his sister, in the Peter Brook production of *The Cherry Orchard,* directed by Peter Brook, 1988. (Photograph: Martha Swope.)

Staging of *The Cherry Orchard*

REVIEW OF THE PETER BROOK PRODUCTION, 1988, BY FRANK RICH

It is not until the final act of *The Cherry Orchard* that the malevolent thud of an ax signals the destruction of a family's ancestral estate and, with it, the traumatic uprooting of a dozen late-nineteenth-century Russian lives. But in Peter Brook's production of Chekhov's play, the landscape seems to have been cleared before Act I begins. Mr. Brook has stripped *The Cherry Orchard* of its scenery, its front curtain, its intermissions. Even the house in which the play unfolds—the Brooklyn Academy of Music's semirestored Majestic Theater—looks half-demolished, a once-genteel palace of gilt and plush now a naked, faded shell of crumbling brick, chipped paint and forgotten hopes.

What little decorative elegance remains can be found on the vast stage floor, which Mr. Brook has covered, as is his wont, with dark Oriental rugs. And that—plus an extraordinary international cast, using a crystalline new translation by Elisaveta Lavrova—proves to be all that's needed. On this director's magic carpets, *The Cherry Orchard* flies. By banishing all forms of theatrical realism except the only one that really matters—emotional truth—Mr. Brook has found the pulse of a play that its author called "not a drama but a comedy, in places almost a farce." That pulse isn't to be confused with the somber metronomic beat of the Act IV ax—the Stanislavskian gloom that Chekhov so despised—and it isn't the kinetic, too frequently farcical gait of Andrei Serban's fascinating 1977 production at Lincoln Center. The real tone of *The Cherry Orchard* is that of a breaking string—that mysterious unidentifiable offstage sound that twice interrupts the action, unnerving the characters and audience alike with the sensation that unfathomable life is inexorably rushing by.

We feel that strange tingle, an exquisite pang of joy and suffering, again and again. When the beautiful Natasha Parry, as the bankrupt landowner Lyubov, returns to her estate from Paris, her brimming eyes take in the vast reaches of the auditorium in a single sweeping glance of nostalgic longing. But when she says, "I feel like a little girl again," the husky darkness of her voice fills in the scarred decades since childhood, relinquishing the girlishness even as it is reclaimed. Later, Miss Parry will simply sit in a chair, quietly crying, as Brian Dennehy, in the role of the merchant Lopakhin, announces that he has purchased her estate at auction. Lopakhin, whose ancestors were serfs on the land he now owns, can't help celebrating his purchase, but his half-jig of victory is slowly tempered by the realization that he has forfeited any chance of affection from the aristocratic woman he has just bought out. A bear of a man, Mr. Dennehy ends up prostrate on the floor be-

hind Miss Parry's chair, tugging ineffectually at her hem. We're left with an indelible portrait of not one but two well-meaning souls who have lost what they most loved by recognizing their own desires too late.

That Lopakhin is as sympathetic and complex a figure as Lyubov, rather than a malicious arriviste, is a tribute not just to Mr. Dennehy's performance but also to Mr. Brook's entire approach to the play. When Trofimov (Zeljko Ivanek), the eternal student, angrily tells Miss Parry to "face the truth" for once in her life, she responds rhetorically, "What truth?" The director, like Chekhov, recognizes that there is no one truth. Each character must be allowed his own truth—a mixture of attributes and convictions that can't easily be typed or judged. Mr. Dennehy gives us both sides (and more) of the man whom Trofimov variously calls a "beast of prey" and "a fine, sensitive soul." Mr. Ivanek does the same with Trofimov, providing a rounded view of the sometimes foolish but fundamentally idealistic young man whose opinions swing so wildly. Though the student may look immature telling off Lyubov or Lopakhin, his vision of a happier future is so stirring that Mr. Ivanek quite rightly prompts the moon to rise while proclaiming it ("I can feel my happiness coming—I can see it!") at the end of Act II.

Miss Parry, Mr. Dennehy and Mr. Ivanek are all brilliant under Mr. Brook's guidance, and they're not alone. As Lyubov's brother, Gaev—a forlorn representative of Czarist Russia's obsolete, decaying nobility—the Swedish actor Erland Josephson embodies the fossilized remains of a civilization. Elegant of bearing yet fuzzy of expression, his voice mellifluous yet childlike, he snaps into focus only when drifting into imaginary billiard games. One of the evening's comic high points is his absurdly gratuitous tribute to a century-old family bookcase, but the hilarity of his futility is matched by the poignance of his Act III entrance, in which his exhausted posture and sad, dangling bundle of anchovy and herring tins announce the estate's sale to his sister well before Lopakhin does.

As Firs, the octogenarian family retainer, Roberts Blossom is a tall, impish, bearded figure in formal black, stooping over his cane—a spindly, timeless ghost from the past, as rooted to the soil as the trees we never see. Stephanie Roth is a revelation as Varya, whose fruitless religious piety is balanced by a bravery that saves her from despair when her last prayer for happiness, a marriage proposal from Lopakhin, flickers and then dies in Mr. Dennehy's eyes. Linda Hunt (Charlotta), Jan Triska (Yepikhodov) and Mike Nussbaum (Pishchik) find the melancholy humor of true Old World clowns in their subsidiary, more broadly conceived roles. If the play's younger generation—Rebecca Miller (Anya), Kate Mailer (Dunyasha) and David Pierce (Yasha)—is not of the same class, holding one's own with a company of this stature is no small achievement in itself.

In keeping with his work with the actors, Mr. Brook's staging has a supple, airy flow that avoids cheap laughs or sentimentality yet is always strikingly theatrical. In Act III, the reveling dancers twirl around velvet screens in choreographic emulation of the ricocheting rumors of the estate's sale. Throughout the evening, the transitions of mood are lightning fast. In an instant, Miss Parry's reminiscence of her son's drowning can be dispelled by the jaunty strains of a nearby band. Neither Lyubov nor anyone else is allowed the self-pity that would plunge *The Cherry Orchard* from the flickering tearfulness of regret into the maudlin sobs of phony high drama.

The mood that is achieved instead, though not tragic, recalls Mr. Brook's *Endgame*-inspired *King Lear* of the 1960s. Beckett is definitely on the director's mind, as is evident not just from the void in which he sets the play but also by his explicit evocation of the Beckett humor in several scenes. When Miss Hunt's governess gives her monologue describing her utter lack of identity—she doesn't know who she is or where she came from—it's a cheeky, center-stage effusion of existential verbal slapstick, with a vegetable for a prop, right out of *Waiting for Godot* or *Happy Days*. When, at evening's end, old Firs is locked by accident in the mansion, we're keenly aware of the repetition of the word "nothing" in his final speech. As Mr. Blossom falls asleep in his easy chair, illuminated by a bare shaft of light and accompanied by the far-off sound of the ax, one can't be blamed for thinking of Krapp reviewing his last tape.

But the delicate connections Mr. Brook draws between Beckett and Chekhov are inevitable and to the point, not arch and pretentious, and they help explain why this *Cherry Orchard* is so right. Though Chekhov was dying when he wrote this play, he didn't lose his perspective on existence and the people who endure it. Horrible, inexplicable things happen to the characters in *The Cherry Orchard*—the shadow of death is always cloaking their shoulders, as it does Beckett's lost souls— but, as Mr. Brook writes in the program, "they have not given up." They simply trudge on, sometimes with their senses of humor intact, sometimes with a dogged faith in the prospects for happiness.

That's the human comedy, and, if it isn't riotously funny, one feels less alone in the solitary plight, indeed exhilarated, watching it unfold on stage as honestly and buoyantly and poetically as a dream. This is a *Cherry Orchard* that pauses for breath only when life does, for people to recoup after dying a little. I think Mr. Brook has given us the Chekhov production that every theatergoer fantasizes about but, in my experience, almost never finds.

GEORGE BERNARD SHAW

1856–1950

Shaw did not write his first play until he was thirty-six, but by the time of his death he had written forty-seven full-length plays, as well as a number of playlets, and thus had become one of the most prolific dramatists in the history of the English theater. He was born and raised in Dublin, in the midst of an unhappy marriage, his father an unsuccessful merchant who turned to drink, his mother a talented singer who scorned the domestic chores of tending a household. By the time he was fifteen, he had dropped out of school, where according to his own account he learned only that schools are a form of imprisonment, and by the time he was twenty he had abandoned an office job in Dublin and gone to live in London with his mother, who had previously moved there and set herself up as a professional teacher of music. He had vowed never to do another "honest day's work," but to make his way in the world as a writer, and from 1876 to 1885 he leaned on his mother for financial support while he turned out five novels, none of which he was able to get published.

Although the early 1880s were a period of literary frustration for Shaw, they did prove to be a time in which he made intellectual discoveries that were to influence most of his thinking and writing. In 1882 he first heard about Karl Marx and subsequently became a lifelong convert to socialism, confessing later that "The importance of the economic basis of society dawned on me," and that "Marx made a man of me." Then in 1884, having studied *Das Kapital* in a Marxist reading circle, he joined the Fabians, a socialist group that, though influenced by Marx, did not regard the state as a class structure to be overthrown but as a social mechanism to be gradually altered and used for the promotion of public welfare. To achieve this goal, Shaw and his Fabian colleagues publicized their positions on every economic, political, and social issue of the day, from local government reform to poor law reform, from trade unionism to women's rights, making their views known in leaflets, newspapers, pamphlets, and books, in lecture halls and on street corners. By the late 1880s Shaw was also writing art criticism, book reviews, and music criticism for several London newspapers. And in 1891, he also made his views known on the state of drama by coming out with *The Quintessence of Ibsenism,* a fiery little book in which he sought to awaken English theater to the social consciousness embodied in Ibsen's plays.

Having sharpened his prose on so wide a variety of cultural and social issues, Shaw himself was uniquely prepared to become the English counterpart of Ibsen, and in 1892 he launched his theatrical career with *Widowers' Houses,* a dramatic attack on the evils of slum landlordism, which he showed to be an emblem of the capitalist system. But even in this first play, as in nearly all of the others he was to write, Shaw's dramatic technique was vastly different from that of Ibsen. Whereas Ibsen had probed the inner lives and problems of his characters in plays suffused with a Scandinavian air of gloom, Shaw turned his characters into witty spokesmen (and spokeswomen) for his social and political views. Shaw's experience in politics and critical reviewing had clearly taught him

117

that comic wit is often the most powerful means of awakening an audience and winning its support. His plays are thus populated with witty characters who take part in equally witty plots.

In the years that followed his first play, Shaw used his comic techniques to expose and satirize an astonishing array of follies or evils in economics, politics, society, theology, morality, science, and literature. In *The Philanderer* (1893), he exposed the hypocritical morality of prevailing marriage laws and celebrated the advanced morality of Ibsen's "new woman." In *Mrs. Warren's Profession* (1893), a play about prostitution, he showed that "Rich men without conviction are more dangerous in modern society than poor women without chastity." In *Arms and the Man* (1894), he mocked romantic notions about love and war by making his hero a blunt realist who throws away his cartridges and replaces them with chocolates, because he knows enough to realize that cartridges will be useless during a cavalry charge, but that chocolates will be invaluable after the charge is over. In *Candida* (1895), he had another go at the conventional morality of marriage by creating as his heroine a very superior woman whose strength is revealed to lie in the way she conceals her strength. In *The Devil's Disciple* (1897), a play about the American revolution, he portrayed all of the English, with the exception of the suave General Burgoyne, as being stuffed shirts and fools, while the hero of the play is a plucky American, whose heroism is shown to be the result not of idealistic motives but of fortuitous circumstances. In *Caesar and Cleopatra* (1899), he mocked Shakespeare's view of Roman history, as it had been presented in *Julius Caesar* and *Antony and Cleopatra*, by turning Cleopatra into a naive and fearful sixteen year old, who is schooled in political wisdom by the hero of the play, namely Caesar, whom Shaw portrayed as a "naturally great" man, whose greatness derives from his ability "to estimate the value of truth, money, or success in any particular instance quite independently of convention and moral generalization." Caesar was to be the first in a series of Shavian supermen and superwomen, whose power Shaw perceived as flowing from their "free vitality," a quality Shaw regarded as fundamental in liberating human beings and social institutions from imprisoning attitudes, habits, and beliefs.

Shaw propounded his views not only in his plays, but also in prefaces that he wrote for the published versions of the plays. By means of these prefaces, which were often as long as the plays themselves, Shaw used his incisive prose style to explicate his characters, plots, and themes, as well as to gain a wider audience for his ideas than was possible in the theater alone. *Man and Superman* (1903), for example, which brilliantly dramatizes Shaw's ideas of the "life force" and "creative evolution," appeared in published form with a lengthy essay on modern society and the need for the superman, as well as a tract called "The Revolutionists Handbook and Pocket Companion," which had been mentioned in the first act of the play, and a collection of Shaw's aphorisms on related subjects. In the preface to *Back to Methuselah* (1921), a thirty-thousand word essay on a ninety-thousand word play, Shaw gave the fullest explication he was ever to offer for his optimistic faith in the "life force" as a means of redeeming civilization. But by that time World War I had already taken place, and Shaw had recognized the destructive social and political bankruptcy of his generation in the apocalyptic vision of *Heartbreak House* (1919), much as he was later to dramatize the tragic conflict between political institutions and genius in *St. Joan* (1923).

In 1905, however, when *Major Barbara* first appeared, Shaw was still so confident in the future of creative evolution, so convinced that the vitality of liberated thought could work a progressive improvement in the human condition, that he sought to provoke a similar awareness in his audience by embodying the life force in Undershaft, the munitions maker—the merchant of destruction. By endowing Undershaft with the vision of a superman, Shaw did not, of course, intend to make a case for warfare, just as he did not mean to defend education or classical scholarship by turning Adolphus Cusins, the professor of Greek, into Undershaft's chosen successor. Here, as in virtually all his other plays, Shaw created his hero out of a highly implausible figure because he wanted to shock his audience out of their conventional attitudes about morality, society, and politics. And, like a typical Shavian hero, Undershaft does possess the free vitality of mind—and the dazzling verbal wit—that will shock almost any audience, much as they shock virtually everyone in Undershaft's family.

Undershaft's moral, social, and political views—his assertions, for example, that "poverty is a sin" and the English parliament "a gabble shop"—are ultimately far more shocking than his armament business, but these two aspects of Undershaft are in the end inseparable. The nature of his business, after all, gives him a unique power, as well as a unique understanding of power, which neither the parliament nor the Salvation Army possesses. In his debates with Lady Britomart, Stephen, Barbara, and Cusins, the aim of Undershaft is to provoke them into recognizing that politics, morality, and intelligence are helpless to improve the human condition; only with power can progress be achieved. Yet Undershaft also recognizes that progress requires the moral and intelligent exercise of power—a synthesis whose ideal outcome is envisioned in Undershaft's model working community at the end of Act III. And it is this special awareness of Undershaft that moves him to vie for the allegiance of Barbara and Cusins, since they embody the morality and intelligence needed to perpetuate and extend his vision of progress.

Major Barbara, like all of Shaw's plays, is built around a contest between very powerfully willed individuals—a contest that in this case Shaw intended to portray as a modern counterpart to the struggle represented in Euripides' *The Bacchae* between Dionysus and Pentheus, between the mystical forces in nature and the efforts of the human mind to repress them. Undershaft is clearly a Dionysian figure in the energy, even the religious ecstasy, that he brings to his debates first with Lady Britomart, then with Barbara, and finally with Cusins. Thus, any staging of *Major Barbara* requires a very powerful and resourceful actor to play the role of Undershaft, and in its 1970 production of the play, the Royal Shakespeare Company evidently found just such an actor in the person of Brewster Mason, judging from the review of that production. Photographs of the production show the authority that Mason projected in the role during his first act confrontation with Lady Britomart (see Figure 1), as well as the lively wit that he conveyed during his argument with Barbara at the end of the play (see Figure 3). The photograph from Act 1 also shows the image of Marx leering ironically over the household of Lady Britomart, much as the photograph from

Act 2 (see Figure 2) presents the image of the British lion hovering ironically over Barbara's Salvation Army shelter, much as the photograph from Act 3 (Figure 3) shows the cannon projecting powerfully out of Undershaft's munitions factory. By using these set pieces, the designer clearly intended to remind the audience of the social and political struggles embodied in the play, as well as of Shaw's optimistic faith in the power of liberated thought and Fabian socialism. And in 1905, of course, it was still possible for enlightened human beings to believe in the possibility of uniting power with intelligence and morality.

MAJOR BARBARA

BY GEORGE BERNARD SHAW

CHARACTERS

SIR ANDREW UNDERSHAFT

LADY BRITOMART UNDERSHAFT, *his wife*

BARBARA, *his elder daugher, a Major in the Salvation Army*

SARAH, *his younger daughter*

STEPHEN, *his son*

ADOLPHUS CUSINS, *a professor of Greek in love with Barbara*

CHARLES LOMAX, *young-man-about-town, engaged to Sarah*

MORRISON, *Lady Britomart's butler*

BRONTERRE O'BRIEN ("SNOBBY") PRICE, *a cobbler-carpenter down on his luck*

MRS ROMOLA ("RUMMY") MITCHENS, *a worn-out lady who relies on the Salvation Army*

JENNY HILL, *a young Salvation Army worker*

PETER SHIRLEY, *an unemployed coal-broker*

BILL WALKER, *a bully*

MRS BAINES, *Commissioner in the Salvation Army*

BILTON, *a foreman at Perivale St. Andrews*

SCENE

The action of the play occurs within several days in January, 1906. ACT 1: *The library of* LADY BRITOMART'S *house in Wilton Crescent, a fashionable London suburb.* ACT 2: *The yard of the Salvation Army shelter in West Ham, an industrial suburb in London's East End.* ACT 3: *The library in* LADY BRITOMART'S *house; a parapet overlooking Perivale St Andrews, a region in Middlesex northwest of London.*

ACT 1

(It is after dinner in January 1906, in the library in LADY BRITOMART UNDERSHAFT'S *house in Wilton Crescent. A large and comfortable settee is in the middle of the room, upholstered in dark leather. A person sitting on it (it is vacant at present) would have, on his right,* LADY BRITOMART'S *writing table, with the lady herself busy at it; a smaller writing-table behind him on his left; the door behind him on* LADY BRITOMART'S *side; and a window with a window-seat directly on his left. Near the window is an armchair.*

LADY BRITOMART *is a woman of fifty or thereabouts, well dressed and yet careless of her dress, well bred and quite reckless of her breeding, well mannered and yet appallingly outspoken and indifferent to the opinion of her interlocutors, amiable and yet peremptory, arbitrary, and high-tempered to the last bearable degree, and withal a very typical managing matron of the upper class, treated as a naughty child until she grew into a scolding mother, and finally settling down with plenty of practical ability and worldly experience, limited in the oddest way with domestic and class limitations, conceiving the universe exactly as if it were a large house in Wilton Crescent, though handling her corner of it very effectively on that assumption, and being quite enlightened and liberal as to the books in the library, the pictures on the walls, the music in the portfolios, and the articles in the papers.*

Her son, STEPHEN, *comes in. He is a gravely correct young man under 25, taking himself very seriously, but still in some awe of his mother, from childish habit and bachelor shyness rather than from any weakness of character.)*

STEPHEN: What's the matter?

LADY BRITOMART: Presently, Stephen.

(STEPHEN *submissively walks to the settee and sits down. He takes up a liberal weekly called* The Speaker)

LADY BRITOMART: Don't begin to read, Stephen. I shall require all your attention.

STEPHEN: It was only while I was waiting—

LADY BRITOMART: Don't make excuses, Stephen. *(He puts down* The Speaker.) *Now! (She finishes her writing; rises; and comes to the settee.)* I have not kept you waiting very long, I think.

STEPHEN: Not at all, mother.

LADY BRITOMART: Bring me my cushion. *(He takes the cushion from the chair at the desk and arranges it for her as she sits down on the settee.)* Sit down. *(He sits down and fingers his tie nervously.)* Don't fiddle with your tie, Stephen: there is nothing the matter with it.

STEPHEN: I beg your pardon. *(He fiddles with his watch chain instead.)*

LADY BRITOMART: Now are you attending to me, Stephen?

STEPHEN: Of course, mother.

LADY BRITOMART: No: it's not of course. I want something much more than your everyday matter-of-course attention. I am going to speak to you very seriously, Stephen. I wish you would let that chain alone.

STEPHEN *(hastily relinquishing the chain)*: Have I done anything to annoy you, mother? If so, it was quite unintentional.

LADY BRITOMART *(astonished)*: Nonsense! *(With some*

121

remorse.) My poor boy, did you think I was angry with you?

STEPHEN: What is it, then, mother? You are making me very uneasy.

LADY BRITOMART (*squaring herself at him rather aggressively*): Stephen: may I ask how soon you intend to realize that you are a grown-up man, and that I am only a woman?

STEPHEN (*amazed*): Only a—

LADY BRITOMART: Don't repeat my words, please: it is a most aggravating habit. You must learn to face life seriously, Stephen. I really cannot bear the whole burden of our family affairs any longer. You must advise me: you must assume the responsibility.

STEPHEN: I!

LADY BRITOMART: Yes, you, of course. You were twenty-four last June. You've been at Harrow and Cambridge. You've been to India and Japan. You must know a lot of things, now; unless you have wasted your time most scandalously. Well, advise me.

STEPHEN (*much perplexed*): You know I have never interfered in the household—

LADY BRITOMART: No: I should think not. I don't want you to order the dinner.

STEPHEN: I mean in our family affairs.

LADY BRITOMART: Well, you must interfere now; for they are getting quite beyond me.

STEPHEN (*troubled*): I have thought sometimes that perhaps I ought; but really, mother, I know so little about them; and what I do know is so painful—it is so impossible to mention some things to you—(*He stops, ashamed.*)

LADY BRITOMART: I suppose you mean your father.

STEPHEN (*almost inaudibly*): Yes.

LADY BRITOMART: My dear: we can't go on all our lives not mentioning him. Of course you were quite right not to open the subject until I asked you to; but you are old enough now to be taken into my confidence, and to help me to deal with him about the girls.

STEPHEN: But the girls are all right. They are engaged.

LADY BRITOMART (*complacently*): Yes; I have made a very good match for Sarah. Charles Lomax will be a millionaire at thirty-five. But that is ten years ahead; and in the meantime his trustees cannot under the terms of his father's will allow him more than £800 a year.

STEPHEN: But the will says also that if he increases his income by his own exertions, they may double the increase.

LADY BRITOMART: Charles Lomax's exertions are much more likely to decrease his income than to increase it. Sarah will have to find at least another £800 a year for the next ten years; and

even then they will be as poor as church mice. And what about Barbara? I thought Barbara was going to make the most brilliant career of all of you. And what does she do? Joins the Salvation Army; discharges her maid; lives on a pound a week; and walks in one evening with a professor of Greek whom she has picked up in the street, and who pretends to be a Salvationist, and actually plays the big drum for her in public because he has fallen head over ears in love with her.

STEPHEN: I was certainly rather taken aback when I heard they were engaged. Cusins is a very nice fellow certainly; nobody would ever guess that he was born in Australia; but—

LADY BRITOMART: Oh, Adolphus Cusins will make a very good husband. After all, nobody can say a word against Greek: it stamps a man at once as an educated gentleman. And my family, thank Heaven, is not a pigheaded Tory one. We are Whigs, and believe in liberty. Let snobbish people say what they please: Barbara shall marry, not the man they like, but the man *I* like.

STEPHEN: Of course I was thinking only of his income. However, he is not likely to be extravagant.

LADY BRITOMART: Don't be too sure of that, Stephen. I know your quiet, simple, refined, poetic people like Adolphus—quite content with the best of everything! They cost more than your extravagant people, who are always as mean as they are second rate. No; Barbara will need at least £2000 a year. You see it means two additional households. Besides, my dear, you must marry soon. I don't approve of the present fashion of philandering bachelors and late marriages; and I am trying to arrange something for you.

STEPHEN: It's very good of you, mother; but perhaps I had better arrange that for myself.

LADY BRITOMART: Nonsense! you are much too young to begin matchmaking: you would be taken in by some pretty little nobody. Of course I don't mean that you are not to be consulted: you know that as well as I do. (STEPHEN *closes his lips and is silent.*) Now don't sulk, Stephen.

STEPHEN: I am not sulking, mother. What has all this got to do with—with—with my father?

LADY BRITOMART: My dear Stephen: where is the money to come from? It is easy enough for you and the other children to live on my income as long as we are in the same house; but I can't keep four families in four separate houses. You know how poor my father is: he has barely seven thousand a year now; and really, if he were not the Earl of Stevenage, he would have to give up society. He can do nothing for us. He says, naturally enough, that it is absurd that he should be asked to provide for the children of a man who is rolling in money. You see, Stephen, your father must be fabulously wealthy, because there is always a war going on somewhere.

STEPHEN: You need not remind me of that, mother. I have hardly ever opened a newspaper in my life without seeing our name in it. The Undershaft torpedo! The Undershaft quick firers! The Undershaft ten inch! The Undershaft disappearing rampart gun! The Undershaft submarine! and now the Undershaft aerial battleship! At Harrow they called me the Woolwich Infant.° At Cambridge it was the same. A little brute at King's who was always trying to get up revivals, spoilt my Bible—your first birthday present to me—by writing under my name, "Son and heir to Undershaft and Lazarus, Death and Destruction Dealers: address, Christendom and Judea." But that was not so bad as the way I was kowtowed to everywhere because my father was making millions by selling cannons.

LADY BRITOMART: It is not only the cannons, but the war loans that Lazarus arranges under cover of giving credit for the cannons. You know, Stephen, it's perfectly scandalous. Those two men, Andrew Undershaft and Lazarus, positively have Europe under their thumbs. That is why your father is able to behave as he does. He is above the law. Do you think Bismarck or Gladstone or Disraeli could have openly defied every social and moral obligation all their lives as your father has? They simply wouldn't have dared. I asked Gladstone to take it up. I asked *The Times* to take it up. I asked the Lord Chamberlain to take it up. But it was just like asking them to declare war on the Sultan. They wouldn't. They said they couldn't touch him. I believe they were afraid.

STEPHEN: What could they do? He does not actually break the law.

LADY BRITOMART: Not break the law! He is always breaking the law. He broke the law when he was born; his parents were not married.

STEPHEN: Mother! Is that true?

LADY BRITOMART: Of course it's true: that was why we separated.

STEPHEN: He married without letting you know this!

LADY BRITOMART (*rather taken aback by this inference*): Oh, no. To do Andrew justice, that was not the sort of thing he did. Besides, you know the Undershaft motto: Unashamed. Everybody knew.

STEPHEN: But you said that was why you separated.

LADY BRITOMART: Yes, because he was not content

with being a foundling himself; he wanted to disinherit you for another foundling. That was what I couldn't stand.

STEPHEN (*ashamed*): Do you mean for—for—for—

LADY BRITOMART: Don't stammer, Stephen. Speak distinctly.

STEPHEN: But this is so frightful to me, mother. To have to speak to you about such things!

LADY BRITOMART: It's not pleasant for me, either, especially if you are still so childish that you must make it worse by a display of embarrassment. It is only in the middle classes, Stephen, that people get into a state of dumb helpless horror when they find that there are wicked people in the world. In our class, we have to decide what is to be done with wicked people; and nothing should disturb our self-possession. Now ask your questions properly.

STEPHEN: Mother: you have no consideration for me. For Heaven's sake either treat me as a child, as you always do, and tell me nothing at all; or tell me everything and let me take it as best I can.

LADY BRITOMART: Treat you as a child! What do you mean? It is most unkind and ungrateful of you to say such a thing. You know I have never treated any of you as children. I have always made you my companions and friends, and allowed you perfect freedom to do and say whatever you liked, so long as you liked what I could approve of.

STEPHEN (*desperately*): I daresay we have been the very imperfect children of a very perfect mother; but I do beg of you to let me alone for once, and tell me about this horrible business of my father wanting to set me aside for another son.

LADY BRITOMART (*amazed*): Another son! I never said anything of the kind. I never dreamt of such a thing. This is what comes of interrupting me.

STEPHEN: But you said—

LADY BRITOMART (*cutting him short*): Now be a good boy, Stephen, and listen to me patiently. The Undershafts are descended from a foundling in the parish of St Andrew Undershaft in the city. That was long ago, in the reign of James the First. Well, this foundling was adopted by an armorer and gunmaker. In the course of time the foundling succeeded to the business; and from some notion of gratitiude, or some vow or something, he adopted another foundling, and left the business to him. And that foundling did the same. Ever since that, the cannon business has always been left to an adopted foundling named Andrew Undershaft.

STEPHEN: But did they never marry? Were there no legitimate sons?

LADY BRITOMART: Oh yes: they married just as your father did; and they were rich enough to buy

---

Woolwich Infant, Woolwich was a well-known arsenal; Stephen's nickname puns on his father's cannon business.

land for their own children and leave them well provided for. But they always adopted and trained some foundling to succeed them in the business; and of course they always quarreled with their wives furiously over it. Your father was adopted in that way; and he pretends to consider himself bound to keep up the tradition and adopt somebody to leave the business to. Of course I was not going to stand that. There may have been some reason for it when the Undershafts could only marry women in their own class, whose sons were not fit to govern great estates. But there could be no excuse for passing over my son.

STEPHEN (*dubiously*): I am afraid I should make a poor hand of managing a cannon foundry.

LADY BRITOMART: Nonsense! you could easily get a manager and pay him a salary.

STEPHEN: My father evidently had no great opinion of my capacity.

LADY BRITOMART: Stuff, child! you were only a baby; it had nothing to do with your capacity. Andrew did it on principle, just as he did every perverse and wicked thing on principle. When my father remonstrated, Andrew actually told him to his face that history tells us of only two successful institutions: one the Undershaft firm, and the other the Roman Empire under the Antonines. That was because the Antonine emperors all adopted their successors. Such rubbish! The Stevenages are as good as the Antonines, I hope; and you are a Stevenage. But that was Andrew all over. There you have the man! Always clever and unanswerable when he was defending nonsense and wickedness; always awkward and sullen when he had to behave sensibly and decently.

STEPHEN: Then it was on my account that your home life was broken up, mother. I am sorry.

LADY BRITOMART: Well dear, there were other differences. I really cannot bear an immoral man. I am not a Pharisee, I hope; and I should not have minded his merely doing wrong things: we are none of us perfect. But your father didn't exactly do wrong things: he said them and thought them: that was what was so dreadful. He really had a sort of religion of wrongness. Just as one doesn't mind men practicing immorality so long as they own that they are in the wrong by preaching morality; so I couldn't forgive Andrew for preaching immorality while he practiced morality. You would all have grown up without principles, without any knowledge of right and wrong, if he had been in the house. You know, my dear, your father was a very attractive man in some ways. Children did not dislike him; and he took advantage of it to put the wickedest ideas into their heads, and make

them quite unmanageable. I did not dislike him myself: very far from it; but nothing can bridge over moral disagreement.

STEPHEN: All this simply bewilders me, mother. People may differ about matters of opinion, or even about religion; but how can they differ about right and wrong? Right is right; and wrong is wrong; and if a man cannot distinguish them properly, he is either a fool or a rascal: that's all.

LADY BRITOMART (*touched*): That's my own boy! (*She pats his cheek.*) Your father never could answer that: he used to laugh and get out of it under cover of some affectionate nonsense. And now that you understand the situation, what do you advise me to do?

STEPHEN: Well, what can you do?

LADY BRITOMART: I must get the money somehow.

STEPHEN: We cannot take money from him. I had rather go and live in some cheap place like Bedford Square or even Hampstead than take a farthing of his money.

LADY BRITOMART: But after all, Stephen, our present income comes from Andrew.

STEPHEN (*shocked*): I never knew that.

LADY BRITOMART: Well, you surely didn't suppose your grandfather had anything to give me. The Stevenages could not do everything for you. We gave you social position. Andrew had to contribute something. He had a very good bargain, I think.

STEPHEN (*bitterly*): We are utterly dependent on him and his cannons, then?

LADY BRITOMART: Certainly not: the money is settled. But he provided it. So you see it is not a question of taking money from him or not: it is simply a question of how much. I don't want any more for myself.

STEPHEN: Nor do I.

LADY BRITOMART: But Sarah does; and Barbara does. That is, Charlex Lomax and Adolphus Cusins will cost them more. So I must put my pride in my pocket and ask for it, I suppose. That is your advice, Stephen, is it not?

STEPHEN: No.

LADY BRITOMART (*sharply*): Stephen!

STEPHEN: Of course if you are determined—

LADY BRITOMART: I am not determined: I ask your advice; and I am waiting for it. I will not have all the responsibility thrown on my shoulders.

STEPHEN (*obstinately*): I would die sooner than ask him for another penny.

LADY BRITOMART (*resignedly*): You mean that *I* must ask him. Very well, Stephen: it shall be as you wish. You will be glad to know that your grandfather concurs. But he thinks I ought to ask Andrew to come here and see the girls. After all he must have some natural affection for them.

STEPHEN: Ask him here!!

LADY BRITOMART: Do not repeat my words, Stephen. Where else can I ask him?

STEPHEN: I never expected you to ask him at all.

LADY BRITOMART: Now don't tease, Stephen. Come! you see that it is necessary that he should pay us a visit, don't you?

STEPHEN (reluctantly): I suppose so, if the girls cannot do without his money.

LADY BRITOMART: Thank you, Stephen; I knew you would give me the right advice when it was properly explained to you. I have asked your father to come this evening. (STEPHEN bounds from his seat.) Don't jump, Stephen: it fidgets me.

STEPHEN (in utter consternation): Do you mean to say that my father is coming here to-night—that he may be here at any moment?

LADY BRITOMART (looking at her watch): I said nine. (He gasps, she rises.) Ring the bell, please. (STEPHEN goes to the smaller writing table; presses a button on it; and sits at it with his elbows on the table and his head in his hands, outwitted and overwhelmed.) It is ten minutes to nine yet; and I have to prepare the girls. I asked Charles Lomax and Adolphus to dinner on purpose that they might be here. Andrew had better see them in case he should cherish any delusions as to their being capable of supporting their wives. (The butler enters: LADY BRITOMART goes behind the settee to speak to him.) Morrison: go up to the drawing-room and tell everybody to come down here at once. (MORRISON withdraws. LADY BRITOMART turns to STEPHEN.) Now remember, Stephen: I shall need all your countenance and authority. (He rises and tries to recover some vestige of these attributes.) Give me a chair, dear. (He pushes a chair forward from the wall to where she stands, near the smaller writing table. She sits down; and he goes to the armchair, into which he throws himself.) I don't know how Barbara will take it. Ever since they made her a major in the Salvation Army she has developed a propensity to have her own way and order people about which quite cows me sometimes. It's not lady-like: I'm sure I don't know where she picked it up. Anyhow, Barbara shan't bully me; but still it's just as well that your father should be here before he has time to refuse to meet him or make a fuss. Don't look nervous, Stephen: it will only encourage Barbara to make difficulties. I am nervous enough, goodness knows; but I don't shew it.

(SARAH and BARBARA come in with their respective young men, CHARLES LOMAX and ADOLPHUS CUSINS. SARAH is slender, bored, and mundane. BARBARA is robuster, jollier, much more energetic. SARAH is fashionably dressed: BARBARA is in Salvation Army uniform. LOMAX, a young man about town, is like many other young men about town. He is afflicted with a frivolous sense of humor which plunges him at the most inopportune moments into paroxysms of imperfectly suppressed laughter. CUSINS is a spectacled student, slight, thin haired, and sweet voiced, with a more complex form of LOMAX's complaint. His sense of humor is intellectual and subtle, and is complicated by an appalling temper. The life-long struggle of a benevolent temperament and a high conscience against impulses of inhuman ridicule and fierce impatience has set up a chronic strain which has visibly wrecked his constitution. He is a most implacable, determined, tenacious, intolerant person who by mere force of character presents himself as—and indeed actually is—considerate, gentle, explanatory, even mild and apologetic, capable possibly of murder, but not of cruelty or coarseness. By the operation of some instinct which is not merciful enough to blind him with the illusions of love, he is obstinately bent on marrying BARBARA. LOMAX likes SARAH and thinks it will be rather a lark to marry her. Consequently he has not attempted to resist LADY BRITOMART's arrangements to that end.

All four look as if they had been having a good deal of fun in the drawing room. The girls enter first, leaving the swains outside. SARAH comes to the settee. BARBARA comes in after her and stops at the door.)

BARBARA: Are Cholly and Dolly to come in?

LADY BRITOMART (forcibly): Barbara: I will not have Charles called Cholly: the vulgarity of it positively makes me ill.

BARBARA: It's all right, mother: Cholly is quite correct nowadays. Are they to come in?

LADY BRITOMART: Yes, if they will behave themselves.

BARBARA (through the door): Come in, Dolly; and behave yourself.

(BARBARA comes to her mother's writing table. CUSINS enters smiling, and wanders toward LADY BRITOMART.)

SARAH (calling): Come in, Cholly. (LOMAX enters, controlling his features very imperfectly, and places himself vaguely between SARAH and BARBARA.)

LADY BRITOMART (peremptorily): Sit down all of you. (They sit. CUSINS crosses to the window and seats himself there. LOMAX takes a chair. BARBARA sits at the writing table and SARAH on the settee.) I don't in the least know what you are laughing at, Adolphus. I am surprised at you, though I expected nothing less from Charles Lomax.

CUSINS (in a remarkably gentle voice): Barbara has been trying to teach me the West Ham Salvation March.

LADY BRITOMART: I see nothing to laugh at in that; nor should you if you are really converted.

CUSINS (sweetly): You were not present. It was really funny, I believe.

LOMAX: Ripping.

LADY BRITOMART: Be quiet, Charles. Now listen to me, children. Your father is coming here this evening.

(*General stupefaction.* LOMAX, SARAH, *and* BARBARA *rise;* SARAH *scared, and* BARBARA *amused and expectant.*)

LOMAX (*remonstrating*): Oh I say!

LADY BRITOMART: You are not called on to say anything, Charles.

SARAH: Are you serious, mother?

LADY BRITOMART: Of course I am serious. It is on your account, Sarah, and also on Charles's. (*Silence.* SARAH *sits, with a shrug,* CHARLES *looks painfully unworthy.*) I hope you are not going to object, Barbara.

BARBARA: I! why should I? My father has a soul to be saved like anybody else. He's quite welcome as far as I am concerned. (*She sits on the table, and softly whistles, "Onward, Christian Soldiers."*)

LOMAX (*still remonstrant*): But really, don't you know! Oh I say!

LADY BRITOMART (*frigidly*): What do you wish to convey, Charles?

LOMAX: Well, you must admit that this is a bit thick.

LADY BRITOMART (*turning with ominous suavity to* CUSINS): Adolphus: you are a professor of Greek. Can you translate Charles Lomax's remarks into reputable English for us?

CUSINS (*cautiously*): If I may say so, Lady Brit, I think Charles has rather happily expressed what we all feel. Homer, speaking of Autolycus, uses the same phrase. πυκινὸν δόμον ελθεῖν means a bit thick.°

LOMAX (*handsomely*): Not that I mind, you know, if Sarah don't. (*He sits.*)

LADY BRITOMART (*crushingly*): Thank you. Have I your permission, Adolphus, to invite my own husband to my own house?

CUSINS (*gallantly*): You have my unhesitating support in everything you do.

LADY BRITOMART: Tush! Sarah: have you nothing to say?

SARAH: Do you mean that he is coming regularly to live here?

LADY BRITOMART: Certainly not. The spare room is ready for him if he likes to stay for a day or two and see a little more of you; but there are limits.

The Greek *pykinon domon elthein* (*Iliad*, Book X, line 267) translates as "to come to a thick [*i.e.*, well-built] house." Cusins is punning on Undershaft's homecoming and a more literal sense of *thick*. Autolycus, in Greek legend, was a thief with the power of making himself and his stolen goods invisible.

SARAH: Well, he can't eat us, I suppose. *I* don't mind.

LOMAX (*chuckling*): I wonder how the old man will take it.

LADY BRITOMART: Much as the old woman will, no doubt, Charles.

LOMAX (*abashed*): I didn't mean—at least—

LADY BRITOMART: You didn't think, Charles. You never do; and the result is, you never mean anything. And now please attend to me, children. Your father will be quite a stranger to us.

LOMAX: I suppose he hasn't seen Sarah since she was a little kid.

LADY BRITOMART: Not since she was a little kid, Charles, as you express it with that elegance of diction and refinement of thought that never seem to desert you. Accordingly—er— (*Impatiently.*) Now I have forgotten what I was going to say. That comes of your provoking me to be sarcastic, Charles. Adolphus: will you kindly tell me where I was.

CUSINS (*sweetly*): You were saying that as Mr. Undershaft has not seen his children since they were babies, he will form his opinon of the way you have brought them up from their behavior to-night, and that therefore you wish us all to be particularly careful to conduct ourselves well, especially Charles.

LADY BRITOMART (*with emphatic approval*): Precisely.

LOMAX: Look here, Dolly: Lady Brit didn't say that.

LADY BRITOMART (*vehemently*): I did, Charles. Adolphus's recollection is perfectly correct. It is most important that you should be good; and I do beg you for once not to pair off into opposite corners and giggle and whisper while I am speaking to your father.

BARBARA: All right, mother. We'll do you credit. (*She comes off the table, and sits in her chair with ladylike elegance.*)

LADY BRITOMART: Remember, Charles, that Sarah will want to feel proud of you instead of ashamed of you.

LOMAX: Oh I say! there's nothing to be exactly proud of, don't you know.

LADY BRITOMART: Well, try and look as if there was. (MORRISON, *pale and dismayed, breaks into the room in unconcealed disorder.*)

MORRISON: Might I speak a word to you, my lady?

LADY BRITOMART: Nonsense! Shew him up.

MORRISON: Yes, my lady. (*He goes.*)

LOMAX: Does Morrison know who it is?

LADY BRITOMART: Of course. Morrison has always been with us.

LOMAX: It must be a regular corker for him, don't you know.

LADY BRITOMART: Is this a moment to get on my nerves, Charles, with your outrageous expressions?

LOMAX: But this is something out of the ordinary, really—

MORRISON (*at the door*): The—er—Mr. Undershaft. (*He retreats in confusion.*)

(ANDREW UNDERSHAFT *comes in. All rise.* LADY BRITOMART *meets him in the middle of the room behind the settee.*

ANDREW *is, on the surface, a stoutish, easygoing elderly man, with kindly patient manners, and an engaging simplicity of character. But he has a watchful, deliberate, waiting, listening face, and formidable reserves of power, both bodily and mental in his capacious chest and long head. His gentleness is partly that of a strong man who has learnt by experience that his natural grip hurts ordinary people unless he handles them very carefully, and partly the mellowness of age and success. He is also a little shy in his present very delicate situation.*)

LADY BRITOMART: Good evening, Andrew.

UNDERSHAFT: How d'ye do, my dear.

LADY BRITOMART: You look a good deal older.

UNDERSHAFT (*apologetically*): I am somewhat older. (*Taking her hand with a touch of courtship.*) Time has stood still with you.

LADY BRITOMART (*throwing away his hand*): Rubbish! This is your family.

UNDERSHAFT (*surprised*): Is it so large? I am sorry to say my memory is failing very badly in some things.

(*He offers his hand with paternal kindness to* LOMAX).

LOMAX (*jerkily shaking his hand*): Ahdedoo.

UNDERSHAFT: I can see you are my eldest. I am very glad to meet you again, my boy.

LOMAX (*remonstrating*): No, but look here don't you know—(*Overcome.*) Oh I say!

LADY BRITOMART (*recovering from momentary speechlessness*): Andrew: do you mean to say that you don't remember how many children you have?

UNDERSHAFT: Well, I am afraid I— They have grown so much—er. Am I making any ridiculous mistake? I may as well confess: I recollect only one son. But so many things have happened since, of course—er—

LADY BRITOMART (*decisively*): Andrew: you are talking nonsense. Of course you have only one son.

UNDERSHAFT: Perhaps you will be good enough to introduce me, my dear.

LADY BRITOMART: This is Charles Lomax, who is engaged to Sarah.

UNDERSHAFT: My dear sir, I beg your pardon.

LOMAX: Notatall. Delighted, I assure you.

LADY BRITOMART: This is Stephen.

UNDERSHAFT (*bowing*): Happy to make your acquaintance, Mr. Stephen. Then (*Going to* CUSINS.) you must be my son. (*Taking* CUSINS' *hands in his.*)

How are you, my young friend? (*to* LADY BRITOMART) He is very like you, my love.

CUSINS: You flatter me, Mr. Undershaft. My name is Cusins: engaged to Barbara. (*Very explicitly.*) That is Major Barbara Undershaft, of the Salvation Army. That is Sarah, your second daughter. This is Stephen Undershaft, your son.

UNDERSHAFT: My dear Stephen, I beg your pardon.

STEPHEN: Not at all.

UNDERSHAFT: Mr. Cusins: I am indebted to you for explaining so precisely. (*Turning to* SARAH.) Barbara, my dear—

SARAH (*prompting him*): Sarah.

UNDERSHAFT: Sarah, of course. (*They shake hands. He goes over to* BARBARA.) Barbara—I am right this time, I hope.

BARBARA: Quite right. (*They shake hands.*)

LADY BRITOMART (*resuming command*): Sit down, all of you. Sit down, Andrew. (*She comes forward and sits on the settee.* CUSINS *also brings his chair forward on her left.* BARBARA *and* STEPHEN *resume their seats.* LOMAX *gives his chair to* SARAH *and goes for another.*)

UNDERSHAFT: Thank you, my love.

LOMAX (*conversationally, as he brings a chair forward between the writing table and the settee, and offers it to* UNDERSHAFT): Takes you some time to find out exactly where you are, don't it?

UNDERSHAFT (*accepting the chair, but remaining standing*): That is not what embarrasses me, Mr. Lomax. My difficulty is that if I play the part of a father, I shall produce the effect of an intrusive stranger; and if I play the part of a discreet stranger, I may appear a callous father.

LADY BRITOMART: There is no need for you to play any part at all, Andrew. You had much better be sincere and natural.

UNDERSHAFT (*submissively*): Yes, my dear: I daresay that will be best. (*He sits down comfortably.*) Well, here I am. Now what can I do for you all?

LADY BRITOMART: You need not do anything, Andrew. You are one of the family. You can sit with us and enjoy yourself. (*A painfully conscious pause.* BARBARA *makes a face at* LOMAX, *whose too long suppressed mirth immediately explodes in agonized neighings.*)

LADY BRITOMART (*outraged*): Charles Lomax: if you can behave yourself, behave yourself. If not, leave the room.

LOMAX: I'm awfully sorry, Lady Brit; but really, you know, upon my soul! (*He sits on the settee between* LADY BRITOMART *and* UNDERSHAFT, *quite overcome.*)

BARBARA: Why don't you laugh if you want to, Cholly? It's good for your inside.

LADY BRITOMART: Barbara: you have had the education of a lady. Please let your father see that; and don't talk like a street girl.

UNDERSHAFT: Never mind me, my dear. As you know, I am not a gentleman; and I was never educated.

LOMAX (*encouragingly*): Nobody'd know it, I assure you. You look all right, you know.

CUSINS: Let me advise you to study Greek, Mr. Undershaft. Greek scholars are privileged men. Few of them know Greek; and none of them know anything else; but their position is unchallengeable. Other languages are the qualifications of waiters and commercial travellers: Greek is to a man of position what the hallmark is to silver.

BARBARA: Dolly: don't be insincere. Cholly: fetch your concertina and play something for us.

LOMAX (*jumps up eagerly, but checks himself to remark doubtfully to* UNDERSHAFT): Perhaps that sort of thing isn't in your line, eh?

UNDERSHAFT: I am particularly fond of music.

LOMAX (*delighted*): Are you? Then I'll get it. (*He goes upstairs for the instrument.*)

UNDERSHAFT: Do you play, Barbara?

BARBARA: Only the tambourine. But Cholly's teaching me the concertina.

UNDERSHAFT: Is Cholly also a member of the Salvation Army?

BARBARA: No: he says it's bad form to be a dissenter. But I don't despair of Cholly. I made him come yesterday to a meeting at the dock gates, and take the collection in his hat.

UNDERSHAFT (*looks whimsically at his wife*)!!

LADY BRITOMART: It is not my doing, Andrew. Barbara is old enough to take her own way. She has no father to advise her—

BARBARA: Oh yes she has. There are no orphans in the Salvation Army.

UNDERSHAFT: Your father there has a great many children and plenty of experience, eh?

BARBARA (*looking at him with quick interest and nodding*): Just so. How did you come to understand that? (LOMAX *is heard at the door trying the concertina.*)

LADY BRITOMART: Come in, Charles. Play us something at once.

LOMAX: Righto! (*He sits down in his former place, and preludes.*)

UNDERSHAFT: One moment, Mr. Lomax. I am rather interested in the Salvation Army. Its motto might be my own: Blood and Fire.

LOMAX (*shocked*): But not your sort of blood and fire, you know.

UNDERSHAFT: My sort of blood cleanses: my sort of fire purifies.

BARBARA: So do ours. Come down tomorrow to my shelter—the West Ham shelter—and see what we're doing. We're going to march to a great meeting in the Assembly Hall at Mile End.° Come and see the shelter and then march with us: it will do you a lot of good. Can you play anything?

UNDERSHAFT: In my youth I earned pennies, and even shillings occasionally, in the streets and in public house parlors by my natural talent for stepdancing. Later on, I became a member of the Undershaft orchestral society, and performed passably on the tenor trombone.

LOMAX (*scandalized–putting down the concertina*): Oh I say!

BARBARA: Many a sinner has played himself into heaven on the trombone, thanks to the Army.

LOMAX (*to* BARBARA, *still rather shocked*): Yes; but what about the cannon business, don't you know? (*to* UNDERSHAFT) Getting into heaven is not exactly in your line, is it?

LADY BRITOMART: Charles!!!

LOMAX: Well; but it stands to reason, don't it? The cannon business may be necessary and all that: we can't get on without cannons; but it isn't right, you know. On the other hand, there may be a certain amount of tosh about the Salvation Army—I belong to the Established Church myself—but still you can't deny that it's religion; and you can't go against religion, can you? At least unless you're downright immoral, don't you know.

UNDERSHAFT: You hardly appreciate my position, Mr. Lomax—

LOMAX (*hastily*): I'm not saying anything against you personally—

UNDERSHAFT: Quite so, quite so. But consider for a moment. Here I am, a profiteer in mutilation and murder. I find myself in a specially amiable humor just now because, this morning, down at the foundry, we blew twenty-seven dummy soldiers into fragments with a gun which formerly destroyed only thirteen.

LOMAX (*leniently*): Well, the more destructive war becomes, the sooner it will be abolished, eh?

UNDERSHAFT: Not at all. The more destructive war becomes, the more fascinating we find it. No, Mr. Lomax: I am obliged to you for making the usual excuse for my trade; but I am not ashamed of it. I am not one of those men who keep their morals and their business in watertight compartments. All the spare money my trade rivals spend on hospitals, cathedrals, and other recep-

---

Mile End, One of London's oldest districts, where William Booth held a religious meeting that launched the Salvation Army.

tacles for conscience money, I devote to experiments and researches in improved methods of destroying life and property. I have always done so; and I always shall. Therefore your Christmas card moralities of peace on earth and goodwill among men are of no use to me. Your Christianity, which enjoins you to resist not evil, and to turn the other cheek, would make me a bankrupt. My morality—my religion—must have a place for cannons and torpedoes in it.

STEPHEN (coldly–almost sullenly): You speak as if there were half a dozen moralities and religions to choose from, instead of one true morality and one true religion.

UNDERSHAFT: For me there is only one true morality; but it might not fit you, as you do not manufacture aerial battleships. There is only one true morality for every man; but every man has not the same true morality.

LOMAX (overtaxed): Would you mind saying that again? I didn't quite follow it.

CUSINS: It's quite simple. As Euripides says, one man's meat is another man's poison morally as well as physically.

UNDERSHAFT: Precisely.

LOMAX: Oh, that. Yes, yes, yes. True. True.

STEPHEN: In other words, some men are honest and some are scoundrels.

BARBARA: Bosh. There are no scoundrels.

UNDERSHAFT: Indeed? Are there any good men?

BARBARA: No. Not one. There are neither good men nor scoundrels: there are just children of one Father; and the sooner they stop calling one another names the better. You needn't talk to me: I know them. I've had scores of them through my hands: scoundrels, criminals, infidels, philanthropists, missionaries, city councillors, all sorts. They're all just the same sort of sinner; and there's the same salvation ready for them all.

UNDERSHAFT: May I ask have you ever saved a maker of cannons?

BARBARA: No. Will you let me try?

UNDERSHAFT: Well, I will make a bargain with you. If I go to see you tomorrow in your Salvation Shelter, will you come the day after to see me in my cannon works?

BARBARA: Take care. It may end in your giving up the cannons for the sake of the Salvation Army.

UNDERSHAFT: Are you sure it will not end in your giving up the Salvation Army for the sake of cannons?

BARBARA: I will take my chance of that.

UNDERSHAFT: And I will take my chance of the other. (They shake hands on it.) Where is your shelter?

BARBARA: In West Ham. At the sign of the cross. Ask anybody in Canning Town. Where are your works?

UNDERSHAFT: In Perivale St Andrews. At the sign of the sword. Ask anybody in Europe.

LOMAX: Hadn't I better play something?

BARBARA: Yes. Give us "Onward, Christian Soldiers."

LOMAX: Well, that's rather a strong order to begin with, don't you know. Suppose I sing "Thou'rt passing hence, my brother." It's much the same tune.

BARBARA: It's too melancholy. You get saved, Cholly; and you'll pass hence, my brother, without making such a fuss about it.

LADY BRITOMART: Really, Barbara, you go on as if religion were a pleasant subject. Do have some sense of propriety.

UNDERSHAFT: I do not find it an unpleasant subject, my dear. It is the only one that capable people really care for.

LADY BRITOMART (looking at her watch): Well, if you are determined to have it, I insist on having it in a proper and respectable way. Charles: ring for prayers. (General amazement. STEPHEN rises in dismay.)

LOMAX (rising): Oh I say!

UNDERSHAFT (rising): I am afraid I must be going.

LADY BRITOMART: You cannot go now, Andrew: it would be most improper. Sit down. What will the servants think?

UNDERSHAFT: My dear: I have conscientious scruples. May I suggest a compromise? If Barbara will conduct a little service in the drawing room, with only Mr. Lomax as organist, I will attend it willingly. I will even take part, if a trombone can be procured.

LADY BRITOMART: Don't mock, Andrew.

UNDERSHAFT (shocked–to BARBARA): You don't think I am mocking, my love, I hope.

BARBARA: No, of course not; and it wouldn't matter if you were: half the Army came to their first meeting for a lark. (Rising.) Come along. (She throws her arm round her father and sweeps him out, calling to the others from the threshold.) Come, Dolly. Come, Cholly.

(CUSINS rises.)

LADY BRITOMART: I will not be disobeyed by everybody. Adolphus: sit down. (He does not.) Charles: you may go. You are not fit for prayers: you cannot keep your countenance.

LOMAX: Oh I say! (He goes out.)

LADY BRITOMART (continuing): But you, Adolphus, can behave yourself if you choose to. I insist on your staying.

CUSINS: My dear Lady Brit: there are things in the family prayer book that I couldn't bear to hear you say.

LADY BRITOMART: What things, pray?

CUSINS: Well, you would have to say before all the servants that we have done things we ought not to have done, and left undone things we ought to have done, and there is no health in us. I cannot bear to hear you doing yourself such an injustice, and Barbara such an injustice. As for myself, I flatly deny it: I have done my best. I shouldn't dare to marry Barbara—I couldn't look you in the face—if it were true. So I must go to the drawing room.

LADY BRITOMART (offended): Well, go. (He starts for the door.) And remember this, Adolphus (He turns to listen.) I have a strong suspicion that you went to the Salvation Army to worship Barbara and nothing else. And I quite appreciate the clever way in which you systematically humbug me. I have found you out. Take care Barbara doesn't. That's all.

CUSINS (with unruffled sweetness): Don't tell on me. (He steals out.)

LADY BRITOMART: Sarah: if you want to go, go. Anything's better than to sit there as if you wished you were a thousand miles away.

SARAH (languidly): Very well, mamma. (She goes.)

(LADY BRITOMART, with a sudden flounce, gives way to a little gust of tears.)

STEPHEN (going to her): Mother: what's the matter?

LADY BRITOMART (swishing away her tears with her handkerchief): Nothing. Foolishness. You can go with him, too, if you like, and leave me with the servants.

STEPHEN: Oh, you mustn't think that, mother. I—I don't like him.

LADY BRITOMART: The others do. That is the injustice of a woman's lot. A woman has to bring up her children; and that means to restrain them, to deny them things they want, to set them tasks, to punish them when they do wrong, to do all the unpleasant things. And then the father, who has nothing to do but pet them and spoil them, comes in when all her work is done and steals their affection from her.

STEPHEN: He has not stolen our affection from you. It is only curiosity.

LADY BRITOMART (violently): I won't be consoled, Stephen. There is nothing the matter with me. (She rises and goes toward the door.)

STEPHEN: Where are you going, mother?

LADY BRITOMART: To the drawing room, of course. (She goes out. "Onward, Christian Soldiers," on the concertina, with tambourine accompaniment, is heard when the door opens.) Are you coming, Stephen?

STEPHEN: No. Certainly not. (She goes. He sits down on the settee, with compressed lips and an expression of strong dislike.)

ACT 2

(The yard of the West Ham shelter of the Salvation Army is a cold place on a January morning. The building itself, an old warehouse, is newly whitewashed. Its gabled end projects into the yard in the middle, with a door on the ground floor, and another in the loft above it without any balcony or ladder, but with a pulley rigged over it for hoisting sacks. Those who come from this central gable end into the yard have the gateway leading to the street on their left, with a stone horse-trough just beyond it, and, on the right, a penthouse shielding a table from the weather. There are forms at the table; and on them are seated a man and a woman, both much down on their luck, finishing a meal of bread (one thick slice each, with margarine and golden syrup) and diluted milk.

The man, a workman out of employment, is young, agile, a talker, a poser, sharp enough to be capable of anything in reason except honest or altruistic considerations of any kind. The woman is a commonplace old bundle of poverty and hardworn humanity. She looks sixty and probably is forty-five. If they were rich people, gloved and muffed and well wrapped up in furs and overcoats, they would be numbed and miserable; for it is a grindingly cold, raw, January day; and a glance at the background of grimy warehouses and leaden sky visible over the whitewashed walls of the yard would drive any idle rich person straight to the Mediterranean. But these two, being no more troubled with visions of the Mediterranean than of the moon, and being compelled to keep more of their clothes in the pawnshop, and less on their persons, in winter than in summer, are not depressed by the cold: rather are they stung into vivacity, to which their meal has just now given an almost jolly turn. The man takes a pull at his mug, and then gets up and moves about the yard with his hands deep in his pockets, occasionally breaking into a stepdance.)

THE WOMAN: Feel better arter your meal, sir?

THE MAN: No. Call that a meal! Good enough for you, p'raps; but wot is it to me, an intelligent workin' man?

THE WOMAN: Workin' man! Wot are you?

THE MAN: Painter.

THE WOMAN (skeptically): Yus, I dessay.

THE MAN: Yus, you dessay! I know. Every loafer that can't do nothink calls 'isself a painter. Well, I'm a real painter: grainer, finisher, thirty-eight bob a week when I can get it.

THE WOMAN: Then why don't you go and get it?

THE MAN: I'll tell you why. Fust: I'm intelligent—fffff! it's rotten cold here (He dances a step or two.)—yes; intelligent beyond the station o' life into which it has pleased the capitalists to call me;

and they don't like a man that sees through 'em. Second, an intelligent bein' needs a doo share of 'appiness; so I drink somethink cruel when I get the chawnce. Third, I stand by my class and do as little as I can so's to leave 'arf the job for me fellow workers. Fourth, I'm fly° enough to know wot's inside the law and wot's outside it; and inside it I do as the capitalists do: pinch wot I can lay me 'ands on. In a proper state of society I am sober, industrious, and honest: in Rome, so to speak, I do as the Romans do. Wot's the consequence? When trade is bad—and it's rotten bad just now—and the employers 'az to sack 'arf their men, they generally start on me.

THE WOMAN: What's your name?

THE MAN: Price. Bronterre O'Brien Price. Usually called Snobby Price, for short.

THE WOMAN: Snobby's a carpenter, ain't it? You said you was a painter.

PRICE: Not that kind of snob, but the genteel sort. I'm too uppish, owing to my intelligence, and my father being a Chartist and a reading, thinking man: a stationer, too. I'm none of your common hewers of wood and drawers of water; and don't you forget it. (*He returns to his seat at the table, and takes up his mug.*) Wot's your name?

THE WOMAN: Rummy Mitchens, sir.

PRICE (*quaffing the remains of his milk to her*): Your 'elth, Miss Mitchens.

RUMMY (*correcting him*): Missis Mitchens.

PRICE: Wot! Oh Rummy, Rummy! Respectable married woman, Rummy, gittin' rescued by the Salvation Army by pretendin' to be a bad un. Same old game!

RUMMY: What am I to do? I can't starve. Them Salvation lasses is dear good girls; but the better you are, the worse they likes to think you were before they rescued you. Why shouldn't they 'av a bit o' credit, poor loves? they're worn to rags by their work. And where would they get the money to rescue us if we was to let on we're no worse than other people? You know what ladies and gentlemen are.

PRICE: Thievin' swine! Wish I 'ad their job, Rummy, all the same. Wot does Rummy stand for? Pet name p'raps?

RUMMY: Short for Romola.

PRICE: For wot!?

RUMMY: Romola. It was out of a new book.° Somebody me mother wanted me to grow up like.

PRICE: We're companions in misfortune, Rummy. Both of us got names that nobody cawn't pronounce. Consequently I'm Snobby and you're Rummy because Bill and Sally wasn't good enough for our parents. Such is life!

RUMMY: Who saved you, Mr. Price? Was it Major Barbara?

PRICE: No: I come here on my own. I'm goin' to be Bronterre O'Brien Price, the converted painter. I know wot they like. I'll tell 'em how I blasphemed and gambled and wopped my poor old mother—

RUMMY (*shocked*): Used you to beat your mother?

PRICE: Not likely. She used to beat me. No matter: you come and listen to the converted painter, and you'll hear how she was a pious woman that taught me my prayers at 'er knee, and how I used to come home drunk and drag her out o' the bed be 'er snow-white 'airs, an' lam into 'er with the poker.

RUMMY: That's what's so unfair to us women. Your confessions is just as big lies as ours: you don't tell what you really done no more than us; but you men can tell your lies right out at the meetin's and be made much of for it; while the sort o' confessions we 'az to make 'az to be whispered to one lady at a time. It ain't right, spite of all their piety.

PRICE: Right! Do you s'pose the Army 'd be allowed if it went and did right? Not much. It combs our 'air and makes us good little blokes to be robbed and put upon. But I'll play the game as good as any of 'em. I'll see somebody struck by lightnin', or hear a voice sayin' "Snobby Price: where will you spend eternity?" I'll 'ave a time of it, I tell you.

RUMMY: You won't be let drink, though.

PRICE: I'll take it out in gorspellin', then. I don't want to drink if I can get fun enough any other way.

(JENNY HILL, *a pale, overwrought, pretty Salvation lass of eighteen, comes in through the yard gate, leading* PETER SHIRLEY, *a half hardened, half worn-out elderly man, weak with hunger.*)

JENNY (*supporting him*): Come! pluck up. I'll get you something to eat. You'll be all right then.

PRICE (*rising and hurrying officiously to take the old man off* JENNY's *hands*): Poor old man! Cheer up, brother: you'll find rest and peace and 'appiness 'ere. Hurry up with the food, miss: 'e's fair done. (JENNY *hurries into the shelter.*) 'Ere, buck up, daddy! she's fetchin y'a thick slice o' bread'n treacle, an' a mug o' skyblue.° (*He seats him at the corner of the table.*)

RUMMY (*gaily*): Keep up your old 'art! Never say die!

SHIRLEY: I'm not an old man. I'm only forty-six. I'm

---

fly, sharp, shrewd. ***new book,*** probably George Eliot's historical novel, *Romola,* first published in the early 1860s.

skyblue, diluted, watery milk.

as good as ever I was. The grey patch come in my hair before I was thirty. All it wants is three pennorth o' hair dye: am I to be turned on the streets to starve for it? Holy God! I've worked ten to twelve hours a day since I was thirteen, and paid my way all through; and now am I to be thrown into the gutter and my job given to a young man that can do it no better than me because I've black hair that goes white at the first change?

PRICE (*cheerfully*): No good jawrin' about it. You're only a jumped-up, jerked-off, 'orspittle-turned-out incurable of an ole workin' man: who cares about you? Eh? Make the thievin' swine give you a meal: they've stole many a one from you. Get a bit o' your own back. (JENNY *returns with the usual meal.*) There you are, brother. Awsk a blessin' an' tuck that into you.

SHIRLEY (*looking at it ravenously but not touching it, and crying like a child*): I never took anything before.

JENNY (*petting him*): Come, come! the Lord sends it to you: he wasn't above taking bread from his friends; and why should you be? Besides, when we find you a job you can pay us for it if you like.

SHIRLEY (*eagerly*): Yes, yes: that's true. I can pay you back: it's only a loan. (*Shivering.*) Oh Lord! oh Lord! (*He turns to the table and attacks the meal ravenously.*)

JENNY: Well, Rummy, are you more comfortable now?

RUMMY: God bless you, lovey! you've fed my body and saved my soul, haven't you? (JENNY, *touched, kisses her.*) Sit down and rest a bit: you must be ready to drop.

JENNY: I've been going hard since morning. But there's more work than we can do. I mustn't stop.

RUMMY: Try a prayer for just two minutes. You'll work all the better after.

JENNY (*her eyes lighting up*): Oh isn't it wonderful how a few minutes prayer revives you! I was quite lightheaded at twelve o'clock, I was so tired; but Major Barbara just sent me to pray for five minutes; and I was able to go on as if I had only just begun. (*to* PRICE) Did you have a piece of bread?

PRICE (*with unction*): Yes, miss; but I've got the piece that I value more; and that's the peace that passeth hall hannerstennin.

RUMMY (*fervently*): Glory Hallelujah!

(BILL WALKER, *a rough customer of about twenty-five, appears at the yard gate and looks malevolently at* JENNY.)

JENNY: That makes me so happy. When you say that, I feel wicked for loitering here. I must get to work again.

(*She is hurrying to the shelter, when the newcomer moves quickly up to the door and intercepts her. His manner is so threatening that she retreats as he comes at her truculently, driving her down the yard.*)

BILL: Aw knaow you. You're the one that took aw'y maw girl. You're the one that set 'er agen me. Well, I'm gowin' to 'ev 'er aht. Not that Aw care a carse for 'er or you: see? But Aw'll let 'er knaow; and Aw'll let you knaow. Aw'm goin' to give her a doin' that'll teach 'er to cat aw'y from me. Nah in wiv you and tell 'er to cam aht afore Aw cam in and kick 'er aht. Tell 'er Bill Walker wants 'er. She'll knaow wot thet means; and if she keeps me witin' it'll be worse. You stop to jawr beck at me; and Aw'll stawt on you: d'ye 'eah? There's your w'y. In you gow. (*He takes her by the arm and slings her towards the door of the shelter. She falls on her hand and knee.* RUMMY *helps her up again.*)

PRICE (*rising and venturing irresolutely toward* BILL): Easy there, mate. She ain't doin' you no 'arm.

BILL: 'Oo are you callin' mite? (*Standing over him threateningly.*) You're gowin' to stend up for 'er, aw yer? Put ap your 'ends.

RUMMY (*running indignantly to him to scold him*): Oh, you great brute— (*He instantly swings his left hand back against her face. She screams and reels back to the trough, where she sits down, covering her bruised face with her hands and rocking herself and moaning with pain.*)

JENNY (*going to her*): Oh, God forgive you! How could you strike an old woman like that?

BILL (*seizing her by the hair so violently that she also screams, and tearing her away from the old woman*): You Gawd forgimme again and Aw'll Gawd forgive you one on the jawr thet'll stop you pryin' for a week. (*Holding her and turning fiercely on* PRICE.) 'Ev you ennything to s'y agen it?

PRICE (*intimidated*): No, matey, she ain't anything to do with me.

BILL: Good job for you! Aw'd pat two meals into you and fawt you with one finger arter, you stawved cur. (*to* JENNY) Nah are you gown' to fetch aht Mog Ebbijem: or em Aw to knock your fice off you and fetch her meself?

JENNY (*writhing in his grasp*): Oh, please, someone go in and tell Major Barbara—(*She screams again as he wrenches her head down; and* PRICE *and* RUMMY *flee into the shelter.*)

BILL: You want to gow in and tell your Mijor of me, do you?

JENNY: Oh, please, don't drag my hair. Let me go.

BILL: Do you or down't you? (*She stifles a scream.*) Yus or nao?

JENNY: God give me strength—

BILL (*striking her with his fist in the face*): Gow an' shaow her thet, and tell her if she wants one lawk it to cam and interfere with me. (JENNY, *crying with pain, goes into the shed. He goes to the form and addresses the old man.*) 'Eah: finish your mess; and git aht o' maw w'y.

SHIRLEY (*springing up and facing him fiercely, with the mug in his hand*): You take a liberty with me, and I'll smash you over the face with the mug and cut your eye out. Ain't you satisfied—young whelps like you—with takin' the bread out o' the mouths of your elders that have brought you up and slaved for you, but you must come shovin and cheekin' and bullyin' in here, where the bread o' charity is sickenin' in our stummicks?

BILL (*contemptuously, but backing a little*): Wot good are you, you aold palsy mag? Wot good are you?

SHIRLEY: As good as you and better. I'll do a day's work agen you or any fat young soaker of your age. Go and take my job at Horrockses, where I worked for ten year. They want young men there: they can't afford to keep men over forty-five. They're very sorry—give you a character and happy to help you to get anything suited to your years—sure a steady man won't be long out of a job. Well, let 'em try you. They'll find the differ. What do you know? Not as much as how to beeyave yourself—layin' your dirty fist across the mouth of a respectable woman!

BILL: Downt provowk me to l'y it acrost yours: d'ye 'eah?

SHIRLEY (*with blighting contempt*): Yes: you like an old man to hit, don't you, when you've finished with the women. I ain't seen you hit a young one yet.

BILL (*stung*): You loy, you aold soupkitchener, you. There was a yang menn 'eah. Did Aw offer to 'itt him or did Aw not?

SHIRLEY: Was he starvin' or was he not? Was he a man or only a crosseyed thief an' a loafer? Would you hit my son-in-law's brother?

BILL: 'Oo's 'ee?

SHIRLEY: Todger Fairmile o' Balls Pond. Him that won £20 off the Japanese wrastler at the music hall by standin' out 17 minutes 4 seconds agen him.

BILL (*sullenly*): Aw'm nao music 'awl wrastler. Ken he box?

SHIRLEY: Yes: an' you can't.

BILL: Wot! Aw cawn't, cawn't Aw? Wot's thet you s'y? (*Threatening him.*)

SHIRLEY (*not budging an inch*): Will you box Todger Fairmile if I put him on to you? Say the word.

BILL (*subsiding with a slouch*): Aw'll stend ap to enny menn alawv, if he was ten Todger Fairmawls. But Aw don't set ap to be a perfeshnal.

SHIRLEY (*looking down on him with unfathomable disdain*): You box! Slap an old woman with the back o' your hand! You hadn't even the sense to

hit her where a magistrate couldn't see the mark of it you silly young lump of conceit and ignorance. Hit a girl in the jaw and on'y make her cry! If Todger Fairmile'd done it, she wouldn't 'a got up inside o' ten minutes, no more than you would if he got on to you. Yah! I'd set about you myself if I had a week's feedin' in me instead o' two months' starvation. (*He turns his back on him and sits down moodily at the table.*)

BILL (*following him and stooping over him to drive the taunt in*): You loy! you've the bread and treacle in you that you cam 'eah to beg.

SHIRLEY (*bursting into tears*): Oh God! it's true: I'm only an old pauper on the scrap heap. (*Furiously.*) But you'll come to it yourself; and then you'll know. You'll come to it sooner than a teetotaller like me, fillin' yourself with gin at this hour o' the mornin!

BILL: Aw'm nao gin drinker, you oald lawr; bat wen Aw want to give my girl a bloomin' good 'awdin' Aw lawk to 'ev a bit o' devil in me: see? An 'eah Aw emm, talking to a rotten aold blawter like you stead o' given' 'er wot for. (*Working himself into a rage.*) Aw'm goin' in there to fetch her aht. (*He makes vengefully for the shelter door.*)

SHIRLEY: You're goin' to the station on a stretcher, more likely; and they'll take the gin and the devil out of you there when they get you inside. You mind what you're about: the major here is the Earl o' Stevenage's granddaughter.

BILL (*checked*): Garn!

SHIRLEY: You'll see.

BILL (*his resolution oozing*): Well, Aw ain't dan nathin' to 'er.

SHIRLEY: S'pose she said you did! who'd believe you?

BILL (*very uneasy, skulking back to the corner of the penthouse*): Gawd! there's no jastice in this cantry. To think wot them people can do! Aw'm as good as 'er.

SHIRLEY: Tell her so. It's just what a fool like you would do.

(BARBARA, *brisk and businesslike, comes from the shelter with a note book, and addresses herself to* SHIRLEY. BILL, *cowed, sits down in the corner on a form, and turns his back on them.*)

BARBARA: Good morning.

SHIRLEY (*standing up and taking off his hat*): Good morning, miss.

BARBARA: Sit down: make yourself at home. (*He hesitates; but she puts a friendly hand on his shoulder and makes him obey.*) Now then! since you've made friends with us, we want to know all about you. Names and addresses and trades.

SHIRLEY: Peter Shirley. Fitter. Chucked out two months ago because I was too old.

BARBARA (*not at all surprised*): You'd pass still. Why didn't you dye your hair?

SHIRLEY: I did. Me age come out at a coroner's inquest on me daughter.

BARBARA: Steady?

SHIRLEY: Teetotaller. Never out of a job before. Good worker. And sent to the knackers like an old horse!

BARBARA: No matter: if you did your part God will do his.

SHIRLEY (*suddenly stubborn*): My religion's no concern of anybody but myself.

BARBARA (*guessing*): I know. Secularist?

SHIRLEY (*hotly*): Did I offer to deny it?

BARBARA: Why should you? My own father's a Secularist, I think. Our Father—yours and mine—fulfills himself in many ways; and I daresay he knew what he was about when he made a Secularist of you. So buck up, Peter! we can always find a job for a steady man like you. (SHIRLEY, *disarmed and a little bewildered, touches his hat. She turns from him to* BILL.) What's your name?

BILL (*insolently*): Wot's thet to you?

BARBARA (*calmly making a note*): Afraid to give his name. Any trade?

BILL: 'Oo's afride to give 'is nime? (*Doggedly, with a sense of heroically defying the House of Lords in the person of Lord Stevenage.*) If you want to bring a chawge agen me, bring it. (*She waits, unruffled.*) Moy nime's Bill Walker.

BARBARA (*as if the name were familiar: trying to remember how*): Bill Walker? (*Recollecting.*) Oh, I know: you're the man that Jenny Hill was praying for inside just now. (*She enters his name in her note book.*)

BILL: 'Oo's Jenny 'Ill? And wot call 'as she to pr'y for me?

BARBARA: I don't know. Perhaps it was you that cut her lip.

BILL (*defiantly*): Yus, it was me that cat her lip. Aw ain't afride o' you.

BARBARA: How could you be, since you're not afraid of God? You're a brave man, Mr. Walker. It takes some pluck to do our work here; but none of us dare lift our hand against a girl like that, for fear of her father in heaven.

BILL (*sullenly*): I want nan o' your kentin' jawr.° I spowse you think Aw cam 'eah to beg from you, like this demmiged lot 'eah. Not me. Aw down't want your bread and scripe° and ketlep.° Aw don't b'lieve in your Gawd, no more than you do yourself.

BARBARA (*sunnily apologetic and ladylike, as on a new footing with him*): Oh, I beg your pardon for putting your name down, Mr. Walker. I didn't understand. I'll strike it out.

BILL (*taking this as a slight, and deeply wounded by it*): 'Eah! you let maw nime alown. Ain't it good enaff to be in your book?

BARBARA (*considering*): Well, you see, there's no use putting down your name unless I can do something for you, is there? What's your trade?

BILL (*still smarting*): Thets nao concern o' yours.

BARBARA: Just so. (*Very businesslike.*) I'll put you down as (*Writing.*) the man who—struck—poor little Jenny Hill—in the mouth.

BILL (*rising threateningly*): See 'eah. Awve 'ed enaff o' this.

BARBARA (*quite sunny and fearless*): What did you come to us for?

BILL: Aw cam for maw gel, see? Aw cam to tike her aht o' this and to brike 'er jawr for 'er.

BARBARA (*complacently*): You see I was right about your trade. (BILL, *on the point of retorting furiously, finds himself, to his great shame and terror, in danger of crying instead. He sits down again suddenly.*) What's her name?

BILL (*dogged*): 'Er nime's Mog Ebbijem: thet's wot her nime is.

BARBARA: Mog Habbijam! Oh, she's gone to Canning Town, to our barracks there.

BILL (*fortified by his resentment of* MOG's *perfidy*): Is she? (*Vindictively.*) Then Aw'm gowin' to Kennintahn arter her. (*He crosses to the gate; hesitates; finally comes back at* BARBARA.) Are you loyin' to me to git shat o' me?

BARBARA: I don't want to get shut of you. I want to keep you here and save your soul. You'd better stay: you're going to have a bad time today, Bill.

BILL: 'Oo's gowin' to give it to me? You, p'reps?

BARBARA: Someone you don't believe in. But you'll be glad afterwards.

BILL (*slinking off*): Aw'll gow to Kennintahn to be aht o' reach o' your tangue. (*Suddenly turning on her with intense malice.*) And if Aw down't fawnd Mog there, Aw'll cam beck and do two years for you, s'elp me Gawd if Aw downt!

BARBARA (*a shade kindlier, if possible*): It's no use, Bill. She's got another bloke.

BILL: Wot!

BARBARA: One of her own converts. He fell in love with her when he saw her with her soul saved, and her face clean, and her hair washed.

BILL (*surprised*): Wottud she wash it for, the carroty slat? It's red.

BARBARA: It's quite lovely now, because she wears a new look in her eyes with it. It's a pity you're too late. The new bloke has put your nose out of joint, Bill.

---

kentin' jawr, canting jaw; i.e. Salvation Army talk. **scripe,** thinly spread butter.   **ketlep,** thin drink, usually tea and milk.

BILL: Aw'll put his nowse aht o' joint for him. Not that Aw care a carse for 'er, mawnd thet. But Aw'll teach her to drop me as if Aw was dirt. And Aw'll teach him to meddle with maw judy. Wots 'iz bleedin nime?

BARBARA: Sergeant Todger Fairmile.

SHIRLEY (*rising with grim joy*): I'll go with him, miss. I want to see them two meet. I'll take him to the infirmary when it's over.

BILL (*to* SHIRLEY, *with undissembled misgiving*): Is thet 'im you was speakin' on?

SHIRLEY: That's him.

BILL: 'Im that wrastled in the music 'awl?

SHIRLEY: The competitions at the National Sportin' Club was worth nigh a hundred a year to him. He's gev 'em up now for religion; so he's a bit fresh for want of the exercise he was accustomed to. He'll be glad to see you. Come along.

BILL: Wot's 'is wight?

SHIRLEY: Thirteen four. (BILL's *last hope expires.*)

BARBARA: Go and talk to him, Bill. He'll convert you.

SHIRLEY: He'll convert your head into a mashed potato.

BILL (*sullenly*): Aw ain't afride of 'im. Aw ain't afride of ennybody. Bat 'e can lick me. She's dan me. (*He sits down moodily on the edge of the horse trough.*)

SHIRLEY: You ain't goin'. I thought not. (*He resumes his seat.*)

BARBARA (*calling*): Jenny!

JENNY (*appearing at the shelter door with a plaster on the corner of her mouth*): Yes, Major.

BARBARA: Send Rummy Mitchens out to clear away here.

JENNY: I think she's afraid.

BARBARA (*her resemblance to her mother flashing out for a moment*): Nonsense! She must do as she's told.

JENNY (*calling into the shelter*): Rummy: the Major says you must come.

(JENNY *comes to* BARBARA, *purposely keeping on the side next* BILL, *lest he should suppose that she shrank from him or bore malice.*)

BARBARA: Poor little Jenny! Are you tired? (*Looking at the wounded cheek.*) Does it hurt?

JENNY: No: it's all right now. It was nothing.

BARBARA (*critically*): It was as hard as he could hit, I expect. Poor Bill! You don't feel angry with him, do you?

JENNY: Oh, no, no, no: indeed I don't, Major, bless his poor heart! (BARBARA *kisses her; and she runs away merrily into the shelter.* BILL *writhes with an agonizing return of his new and alarming symptoms, but says nothing.* RUMMY MITCHENS *comes from the shelter.*)

BARBARA (*going to meet* RUMMY): Now Rummy, bustle. Take in those mugs and plates to be washed; and throw the crumbs about for the birds.

(RUMMY *takes the three plates and mugs; but* SHIRLEY *takes back his mug from her, as there is still some milk left in it.*)

RUMMY: There ain't any crumbs. This ain't a time to waste good bread on birds.

PRICE (*appearing at the shelter door*): Gentleman come to see the shelter, Major. Says he's your father.

BARBARA: All right. Coming. (SNOBBY *goes back into the shelter, followed by* BARBARA.)

RUMMY (*stealing across to Bill and addressing him in a subdued voice, but with intense conviction*): I'd 'av the lor of you, you flat eared pignosed potwalloper, if she'd let me. You're no gentleman, to hit a lady in the face. (BILL, *with greater things moving in him, takes no notice.*)

SHIRLEY (*following her*): Here! in with you and don't get yourself into more trouble by talking.

RUMMY (*with hauteur*): I ain't 'ad the pleasure o' being hintroduced to you, as I can remember. (*She goes into the shelter with the plates.*)

SHIRLEY: That's the—

BILL (*savagely*): Downt you talk to me, d'ye 'eah? You lea' me alown, or Aw'll do you a mischief. Aw'm not dirt under your feet, ennywy.

SHIRLEY (*calmly*): Don't you be afeerd. You ain't such prime company that you need expect to be sought after. (*He is about to go into the shelter when* BARBARA *comes out, with* UNDERSHAFT *on her right.*)

BARBARA: Oh, there you are, Mr. Shirley! (*Between them.*) This is my father: I told you he was a Secularist, didn't I? Perhaps you'll be able to comfort one another.

UNDERSHAFT (*startled*): A Secularist! Not the least in the world: on the contrary, a confirmed mystic.

BARBARA: Sorry, I'm sure. By the way, papa, what is your religion? In case I have to introduce you again.

UNDERSHAFT: My religion? Well, my dear, I am a Millionaire. That is my religion.

BARBARA: Then I'm afraid you and Mr. Shirley won't be able to comfort one another after all. You're not a Millionaire, are you, Peter?

SHIRLEY: No; and proud of it.

UNDERSHAFT (*gravely*): Poverty, my friend, is not a thing to be proud of.

SHIRLEY (*angrily*): Who made your millions for you? Me and my like. What's kep' us poor? Keepin' you rich. I wouldn't have your conscience, not for all your income.

UNDERSHAFT: I wouldn't have your income, not for all your conscience, Mr. Shirley. (*He goes to the penthouse and sits down on a form.*)

BARBARA (*stopping* SHIRLEY *adroitly as he is about to retort*): You wouldn't think he was my father, would you, Peter? Will you go into the shelter and lend the lasses a hand for a while: we're worked off our feet.

SHIRLEY (*bitterly*): Yes, I'm in their debt for a meal, ain't I?

BARBARA: Oh, not because you're in their debt, but for love of them, Peter, for love of them. (*He cannot understand, and is rather scandalized.*) There! don't stare at me. In with you; and give that conscience of yours a holiday. (*Bustling him into the shelter.*)

SHIRLEY (*as he goes in*): Ah! it's a pity you never was trained to use your reason, miss. You'd have been a very taking lecturer on Secularism.

(BARBARA *turns to her father.*)

UNDERSHAFT: Never mind me, my dear. Go about your work; and let me watch it for a while.

BARBARA: All right.

UNDERSHAFT: For instance, what's the matter with that outpatient over there?

BARBARA (*looking at* BILL, *whose attitude has never changed, and whose expression of brooding wrath has deepened*): Oh, we shall cure him in no time. Just watch. (*She goes over to* BILL *and waits. He glances up at her and casts his eyes down again, uneasy, but grimmer than ever.*) It would be nice to just stamp on Mog Habbijam's face, wouldn't it, Bill?

BILL (*starting up from the trough in consternation*): It's a loy: Aw never said so. (*She shakes her head.*) 'Oo taold you wot was in moy mawnd?

BARBARA: Only your new friend.

BILL: Wot new friend?

BARBARA: The devil, Bill. When he gets round people they get miserable, just like you.

BILL (*with a heartbreaking attempt at devil-may-care cheerfulness*): Aw ain't miserable. (*He sits down again, and stretches his legs in an attempt to seem indifferent.*)

BARBARA: Well, if you're happy, why don't you look happy, as we do?

BILL (*his legs curling back in spite of him*): Aw'm 'eppy enaff. Aw tell you. Woy cawn't you lea' me alown? Wot 'ev I dan to you? Aw ain't smashed your fice, 'ev Aw?

BARBARA (*softly: wooing his soul*): It's not me that's getting at you, Bill.

BILL: 'Oo else is it?

BARBARA: Somebody that doesn't intend you to smash women's faces, I suppose. Somebody or something that wants to make a man of you.

BILL (*blustering*): Mike a menn o' me! Ain't Aw a menn? eh? 'Oo sez Aw'n not a menn?

BARBARA: There's a man in you somewhere, I suppose. But why did he let you hit poor little Jenny Hill? That wasn't very manly of him, was it?

BILL (*tormented*): 'Ev dan wiv it, Aw tell you. Chack it. Aw'm sick o' your Jenny 'Ill and 'er silly little fice.

BARBARA: Then why do you keep thinking about it? Why does it keep coming up against you in your mind? You're not getting converted, are you?

BILL (*with conviction*): Not ME. Not lawkly.

BARBARA: That's right, Bill. Hold out against it. Put out your strength. Don't let's get you cheap. Todger Fairmile said he wrestled for three nights against his salvation harder than he ever wrestled with the Jap at the music hall. He gave in to the Jap when his arm was going to break. But he didn't give in to his salvation until his heart was going to break. Perhaps you'll escape that. You havn't any heart, have you?

BILL: Wot d'ye mean? Woy ain't Aw got a 'awt the sime as ennybody else?

BARBARA: A man with a heart wouldn't have bashed poor little Jenny's face, would he?

BILL (*almost crying*): Ow, will you lea' me alown? 'Ev Aw ever offered to meddle with you, that you cam neggin' and provowkin' me lawk this? (*He writhes convulsively from his eyes to his toes.*)

BARBARA (*with a steady soothing hand on his arm and a gentle voice that never lets go*): It's your soul that's hurting you, Bill, and not me. We've been through it all ourselves. Come with us. Bill. (*He looks wildly round.*) To brave manhood on earth and eternal glory in heaven. (*He is on the point of breaking down.*) Come. (*A drum is heard in the shelter; and* BILL, *with a gasp, escapes from the spell as* BARBARA *turns quickly.* ADOLPHUS *enters from the shelter with a big drum.*) Oh! there you are, Dolly. Let me introduce a new friend of mine, Mr. Bill Walker. This is my bloke, Bill: Mr Cusins. (CUSINS *salutes with his drumstick.*)

BILL: Gowin to merry 'im?

BARBARA: Yes.

BILL (*fervently*): Gawd 'elp 'im! Gaw-aw-aw-awd 'elp 'im!

BARBARA: Why? Do you think he won't be happy with me?

BILL: Awve aony 'ed to stend it for a mawnin': 'e'll 'ev to stend it for a lawftawm.

CUSINS: That is a frightful reflection, Mr. Walker. But I can't tear myself away from her.

BILL: Well, Aw ken. (*to* BARBARA) 'Eah! do you knaow where Aw'm gowin to, and wot Aw'm gowin' to do?

BARBARA: Yes: you're going to heaven; and you're coming back here before the week's out to tell me so.

BILL: You loy. Aw'm gowin to Kennintahn, to spit in Todger Fairmawl's eye. Aw bashed Jenny 'Ill's fice; an nar Aw'll git me aown fice beshed and cam beck and shaow it to 'er. 'Ee'll 'itt me 'ardern Aw 'itt er. That'll mike us square. (*to* ADOLPHUS) Is that fair or it is not? You're a genlm'n: you aughter knaow.

BARBARA: Two black eyes won't make one white one, Bill.

BILL: Aw didn't awst you. Cawnt you never keep your mahth shat? Oy awst the genlm'n.

CUSINS (*reflectively*): Yes: I think you're right, Mr. Walker. Yes: I should do it. It's curious: it's exactly what an ancient Greek would have done.

BARBARA: But what good will it do?

CUSINS: Well, it will give Mr Fairmile some exercise; and it will satisfy Mr. Walker's soul.

BILL: Rot! there ain't nao such a thing as a saoul. Ah kin you tell wevver Aw've a saoul or not? You never seen it.

BARBARA: I've seen it hurting you when you went against it.

BILL (*with compressed aggravation*): If you was maw gel and took the word aht o' me mahth lawk thet, Aw'd give you sathink you'd feel 'urtin, Aw would. (*to* ADOLPHUS) You tike maw tip, mite. Stop 'er jawr; or you'll doy afoah your tawn. (*With intense expression.*) Wore aht: thet's you'll be: wore aht. (*He goes away through the gate.*)

CUSINS (*looking after him*): I wonder!

BARBARA: Dolly! (*Indignant, in her mother's manner.*)

CUSINS: Yes, my dear, it's very wearing to be in love with you. If it lasts, I quite think I shall die young.

BARBARA: Should you mind?

CUSINS: Not at all. (*He is suddenly softened, and kisses her over the drum, evidently not for the first time, as people cannot kiss over a big drum without practice.* UNDERSHAFT *coughs.*)

BARBARA: It's all right, papa, we've not forgotten you. Dolly: explain the place to papa: I havn't time. (*She goes busily into the shelter.*)

(UNDERSHAFT *and* ADOLPHUS *now have the yard to themselves.* UNDERSHAFT, *seated on a form, and still keenly attentive, looks hard at* ADOLPHUS. ADOLPHUS *looks hard at him.*)

UNDERSHAFT: I fancy you guess something of what is in my mind, Mr Cusins. (CUSINS *flourishes his drumsticks as if in the act of beating a lively rataplan, but makes no sound.*) Exactly so. But suppose Barbara finds you out!

CUSINS: You know, I do not admit that I am imposing on Barbara. I am quite genuinely interested in the views of the Salvation Army. The fact is, I am a sort of collector of religions; and the curious thing is that I find I can believe them all. By the way, have you any religion?

UNDERSHAFT: Yes.

CUSINS: Anything out of the common?

UNDERSHAFT: Only that there are two things necessary to Salvation.

CUSINS (*disappointed, but polite*): Ah, the Church Cate-chism. Charles Lomax also belongs to the Established Church.

UNDERSHAFT: The two things are—

CUSINS: Baptism and—

UNDERSHAFT: No. Money and gunpowder.

CUSINS (*surprised, but interested*): That is the general opinion of our governing classes. The novelty is in hearing any man confess it.

UNDERSHAFT: Just so.

CUSINS: Excuse me: is there any place in your religion for honor, justice, truth, love, mercy and so forth?

UNDERSHAFT: Yes: they are the graces and luxuries of a rich, strong, and safe life.

CUSINS: Suppose one is forced to choose between them and money or gunpowder?

UNDERSHAFT: Choose money and gunpowder; for without enough of both you cannot afford the others.

CUSINS: That is your religion?

UNDERSHAFT: Yes.

(*The cadence of this reply makes a full close in the conversation.* CUSINS *twists his face dubiously and contemplates* UNDERSHAFT. UNDERSHAFT *contemplates him.*)

CUSINS: Barbara won't stand that. You will have to choose between your religion and Barbara.

UNDERSHAFT: So will you, my friend. She will find out that that drum of yours is hollow.

CUSINS: Father Undershaft: you are mistaken: I am a sincere Salvationist. You do not understand the Salvation Army. It is the army of joy, of love, of courage: it has banished the fear and remorse and despair of the old hell-ridden evangelical sects: it marches to fight the devil with trumpet and drum, with music and dancing, with banner and palm, as becomes a sally from heaven by its happy garrison. It picks the waster out of the public house and makes a man of him: it finds a worm wriggling in a back kitchen, and lo! a woman! Men and women of rank too, sons and daughters of the Highest. It takes the poor professor of Greek, the most artificial and self-suppressed of human creatures, from his meal of roots, and lets loose the rhapsodist in him; reveals the true worship of Dionysos to him; sends him down the public street drumming dithyrambs. (*He plays a thundering flourish on the drum.*)

UNDERSHAFT: You will alarm the shelter.

CUSINS: Oh, they are accustomed to these sudden ecstasies of piety. However, if the drum worries you— (*He pockets the drumsticks; unhooks the drum; and stands it on the ground opposite the gateway.*)

UNDERSHAFT: Thank you.

CUSINS: You remember what Euripides says about your money and gunpowder?

UNDERSHAFT: No.

CUSINS (declaiming):

> One and another
> In money and guns may outpass his brother;
> And men in their millions float and flow
> And seethe with a million hopes as leaven;
> And they win their will; or they miss their will;
> And their hopes are dead or are pined for still;
> But whoe'er can know
> As the long days go
> That to live is happy, has found his heaven.

My translation: what do you think of it?

UNDERSHAFT: I think, my friend, that if you wish to know, as the long days go, that to live is happy, you must first acquire money enough for a decent life, and power enough to be your own master.

CUSINS: You are damnably discouraging. (He resumes his declamation.)

> Is it so hard a thing to see
> That the spirit of God—whate'er it be—
> The law that abides and changes not, ages long,
> The Eternal and Nature-born: these things be strong?
> What else is Wisdom? What of Man's endeavor,
> Or God's high grace so lovely and so great?
> To stand from fear set free? to breathe and wait?
> To hold a hand uplifted over Fate?
> And shall not Barbara be loved for ever?

UNDERSHAFT: Euripides mentions Barbara, does he?

CUSINS: It is a fair translation. The word means Loveliness.

UNDERSHAFT: May I ask—as Barbara's father—how much a year she is to be loved for ever on?

CUSINS: As Barbara's father, that is more your affair than mine. I can feed her by teaching Greek: that is about all.

UNDERSHAFT: Do you consider it a good match for her?

CUSINS (with polite obstinacy): Mr Undershaft: I am in many ways a weak, timid, ineffectual person; and my health is far from satisfactory. But whenever I feel that I must have anything, I get it sooner or later. I feel that way about Barbara. I don't like marriage: I feel intensely afraid of it; and I don't know what I shall do with Barbara or what she will do with me. But I feel that I and nobody else must marry her. Please regard that as settled— Not that I wish to be arbitrary; but why should I waste your time in discussing what is inevitable?

UNDERSHAFT: You mean that you will stick at nothing: not even the conversion of the Salvation Army to the worship of Dionysos.

CUSINS: The business of the Salvation Army is to save, not to wrangle about the name of the pathfinder. Dionysos or another: what does it matter?

UNDERSHAFT (rising and approaching him): Professor Cusins: you are a young man after my own heart.

CUSINS: Mr Undershaft: you are, as far as I am able to gather, a most infernal old rascal; but you appeal very strongly to my sense of ironic humor.

(UNDERSHAFT mutely offers his hand. They shake.)

UNDERSHAFT (suddenly concentrating himself): And now to business.

CUSINS: Pardon me. We were discussing religion. Why go back to such an uninteresting and unimportant subject as business?

UNDERSHAFT: Religion is our business at present, because it is through religion alone that we can win Barbara.

CUSINS: Have you, too, fallen in love with Barbara?

UNDERSHAFT: Yes, with a father's love.

CUSINS: A father's love for a grown-up daughter is the most dangerous of all infatuations. I apologize for mentioning my own pale, coy, mistrustful fancy in the same breath with it.

UNDERSHAFT: Keep to the point. We have to win her; and we are neither of us Methodists.

CUSINS: That doesn't matter. The power Barbara wields here—the power that wields Barbara herself—is not Calvinism, not Presbyterianism, not Methodism—

UNDERSHAFT: Not Greek Paganism either, eh?

CUSINS: I admit that. Barbara is quite original in her religion.

UNDERSHAFT (triumphantly): Aha! Barbara Undershaft would be. Her inspiration comes from within herself.

CUSINS: How do you suppose it got there?

UNDERSHAFT (in towering excitement): It is the Undershaft inheritance. I shall hand on my torch to my daughter. She shall make my converts and preach my gospel!—

CUSINS: What! Money and gunpowder!

UNDERSHAFT: Yes, money and gunpowder; freedom and power; command of life and command of death.

CUSINS (urbanely: trying to bring hin down to earth): This is extremely interesting, Mr. Undershaft. Of course you know that you are mad.

UNDERSHAFT (with redoubled force): And you?

CUSINS: Oh, mad as a hatter. You are welcome to my secret since I have discovered yours. But I am astonished. Can a madman make cannons?

UNDERSHAFT: Would anyone else than a madman make them? And now (With surging energy.) question for question. Can a sane man translate Euripides?

CUSINS: No.

UNDERSHAFT (*seizing him by the shoulder*): Can a sane woman make a man of a waster or a woman of a worm?

CUSINS (*reeling before the storm*): Father Colossus—Mammoth Millionaire—

UNDERSHAFT (*pressing him*): Are there two mad people or three in this Salvation shelter to-day?

CUSINS: You mean Barbara is as mad as we are?

UNDERSHAFT (*pushing him lightly off and resuming his equanimity suddenly and completely*): Pooh, Professor! Let us call things by their proper names. I am a millionaire; you are a poet; Barbara is a savior of souls. What have we three to do with the common mob of slaves and idolaters? (*He sits down again with a shrug of contempt for the mob.*)

CUSINS: Take care! Barbara is in love with the common people. So am I. Have you never felt the romance of that love?

UNDERSHAFT (*cold and sardonic*): Have you ever been in love with Poverty, like St. Francis? Have you ever been in love with Dirt, like St. Simeon? Have you ever been in love with disease and suffering, like our nurses and philanthropists? Such passions are not virtues, but the most unnatural of all the vices. This love of the common people may please an earl's granddaugher and a university professor; but I have been a common man and a poor man; and it has no romance for me. Leave it to the poor to pretend that poverty is a blessing: leave it to the coward to make a religion of his cowardice by preaching humility: we know better than that. We three must stand together above the common people: how else can we help their children to climb up beside us? Barbara must belong to us, not to the Salvation Army.

CUSINS: Well, I can only say that if you think you will get her away from the Salvation Army by talking to her as you have been talking to me, you don't know Barbara.

UNDERSHAFT: My friend: I never ask for what I can buy.

CUSINS (*in a white fury*): Do I understand you to imply that you can buy Barbara?

UNDERSHAFT: No; but I can buy the Salvation Army.

CUSINS: Quite impossible.

UNDERSHAFT: You shall see. All religious organizations exist by selling themselves to the rich.

CUSINS: Not the Army. That is the Church of the poor.

UNDERSHAFT: All the more reason for buying it.

CUSINS: I don't think you quite know what the Army does for the poor.

UNDERSHAFT: Oh, yes, I do. It draws their teeth: that

is enough for me—as a man of business—

CUSINS: Nonsense! It makes them sober—

UNDERSHAFT: I prefer sober workmen. The profits are larger.

CUSINS: —honest—

UNDERSHAFT: Honest workmen are the most economical.

CUSINS: —attached to their homes—

UNDERSHAFT: So much the better: they will put up with anything sooner than change their shop.

CUSINS: —happy—

UNDERSHAFT: An invaluable safeguard against revolution.

CUSINS: —unselfish—

UNDERSHAFT: Indifferent to their own interests, which suits me exactly.

CUSINS: —with their thoughts on heavenly things—

UNDERSHAFT (*rising*): And not on Trade Unionism nor Socialism. Excellent.

CUSINS (*revolted*): You really are an infernal old rascal.

UNDERSHAFT (*indicating* PETER SHIRLEY, *who has just come from the shelter and strolled dejectedly down the yard between them*): And this is an honest man?

SHIRLEY: Yes; and what 'av I got by it? (*He passes on bitterly and sits on the form, in the corner of the penthouse.*)

(SNOBBY PRICE, *beaming sanctimoniously, and* JENNY HILL, *with a tambourine full of coppers, come from the shelter and go to the drum, on which* JENNY *begins to count the money.*)

UNDERSHAFT (*replying to* SHIRLEY): Oh, your employers must have got a good deal by it from first to last.

(*He sits on the table, with one foot on the side form.* CUSINS, *overwhelmed, sits down on the same form nearer the shelter.* BARBARA *comes from the shelter to the middle of the yard. She is excited and a little overwrought.*)

BARBARA: We've just had a splendid experience meeting at the other gate in Cripps's Lane. I've hardly ever seen them so much moved as they were by your confession, Mr. Price.

PRICE: I could almost be glad of my past wickedness if I could believe that it would 'elp to keep hathers stright.

BARBARA: So it will, Snobby. How much, Jenny?

JENNY: Four and tenpence, Major.

BARBARA: Oh, Snobby, if you had given your poor mother just one more kick, we should have got the whole five shillings!

PRICE: If she heard you say that, miss, she'd be sorry I didn't. But I'm glad. Oh what a joy it will be to her when she hears I'm saved!

UNDERSHAFT: Shall I contribute the odd twopence,

Barbara? The millionaire's mite, eh? (*He takes a couple of pennies from his pocket.*)

BARBARA: How did you make that twopence?

UNDERSHAFT: As usual. By selling cannons, torpedoes, submarines, and my new patent Grand Duke hand grenade.

BARBARA: Put it back in your pocket. You can't buy your Salvation here for twopence: you must work it out.

UNDERSHAFT: Is twopence not enough? I can afford a little more, if you press me.

BARBARA: Two million millions would not be enough. There is bad blood on your hands; and nothing but good blood can cleanse them. Money is no use. Take it away. (*She turns to* CUSINS.) Dolly: you must write another letter for me to the papers. (*He makes a wry face.*) Yes: I know you don't like it; but it must be done. The starvation this winter is beating us: everybody is unemployed. The General says we must close this shelter if we can't get more money. I force the collections at the meetings until I am ashamed: don't I, Snobby?

PRICE: It's a fair treat to see you work it, Miss. The way you get them up from three-and-six to four-and-ten with that hymn, penny by penny and verse by verse was a caution. Not a Cheap Jack° on Mile End Waste could touch you at it.

BARBARA: Yes; but I wish we could do without it. I am getting at last to think more of the collection than of the people's souls. And what are those hatfuls of pence and halfpence? We want thousands! tens of thousands! hundreds of thousands! I want to convert people, not to be always begging for the Army in a way I'd die sooner than beg for myself.

UNDERSHAFT (*in profound irony*): Genuine unselfishness is capable of anything, my dear.

BARBARA (*unsuspectingly, as she turns away to take the money from the drum and put it in a cash bag she carries*): Yes, isn't it? (UNDERSHAFT *looks sardonically at* CUSINS.)

CUSINS (*aside to* UNDERSHAFT): Mephistopheles! Machiavelli!

BARBARA (*tears coming into her eyes as she ties the bag and pockets it*): How are we to feed them? I can't talk religion to a man with bodily hunger in his eyes. (*Almost breaking down.*) It's frightful.

JENNY (*running to her*): Major, dear—

BARBARA (*rebounding*): No: don't comfort me. It will be all right. We shall get the money.

UNDERSHAFT: How?

JENNY: By praying for it, of course. Mrs. Baines says she prayed for it last night; and she has never

prayed for it in vain: never once. (*She goes to the gate and looks out into the street.*)

BARBARA (*who has dried her eyes and regained her composure*): By the way, dad, Mrs. Baines has come to march with us to our big meeting this afternoon; and she is very anxious to meet you, for some reason or other. Perhaps she'll convert you.

UNDERSHAFT: I shall be delighted, my dear.

JENNY (*at the gate: excitedly*): Major! Major! here's that man back again.

BARBARA: What man?

JENNY: The man that hit me. Oh, I hope he's coming back to join us.

(BILL WALKER, *with frost on his jacket, comes through the gate, his hands deep in his pockets and his chin sunk between his shoulders, like a cleaned-out gambler. He halts between* BARBARA *and the drum.*)

BARBARA: Hullo, Bill! Back already!

BILL (*nagging at her*): Bin talkin' ever sence, 'ev you?

BARBARA: Pretty nearly. Well, has Todger paid you out for poor Jenny's jaw?

BILL: Nao 'e ain't.

BARBARA: I thought your jacket looked a bit snowy.

BILL: Sao it is snaowy. You want to knaow where the snaow cam from, down't you?

BARBARA: Yes.

BILL: Well, it cam from orf the grahnd in Pawkinses Corner in Kennintahn. It got rabbed orf be maw shaoulders: see?

BARBARA: Pity you didn't rub some off with your knees, Bill! that would have done you a lot of good.

BILL (*with sour mirthless humor*): Aw was sivin' anather menn's knees at the tawm. 'E was kneelin' on moy 'ed, 'e was.

JENNY: Who was kneeling on your head?

BILL: Todger was. 'E was pryin' for me: pryin' comfortable wiv me as a cawpet. Sow was Mog. Sao was the aol bloomin' meetin'. Mog she sez "Ow Lawd brike is stabborn sperrit; bat down't 'urt is dear 'art." Thet was wot she said. "Downt 'urt is dear 'art"! An 'er blowk—thirteen stun four!—kneelin' wiv all is wight on me. Fanny, aint it?

JENNY: Oh no. We're so sorry, Mr. Walker.

BARBARA (*enjoying it frankly*): Nonsense! of course it's funny. Served you right, Bill! You must have done something to him first.

BILL (*doggedly*): Aw did wot Aw said Aw'd do. Aw spit in 'is eye. 'E looks ap at the sky and sez. "Ow that Aw should be fahnd worthy to be spit upon for the gospel's sike!" 'e sez; an Mog sez "Glaory 'Allelloolier!"; an' then 'e called me Braddher, and dahned me as if Aw was a kid and 'e was me mather worshin' me a Setterda nawt. Aw 'ednt jast nao shaow wiv 'im at all. 'Arf the street

---

Cheap Jack, a salesman, usually hawking his ware on sidewalks.

pr'yed; and the tather 'arf larfed fit to split theirselves. *(to* BARBARA*)* There! are you settisfawd nah?

BARBARA *(her eyes dancing)*: Wish I'd been there, Bill.

BILL: Yus: you'd 'a got in a hextra bit o' talk on me, wouldn't you?

JENNY: I'm so sorry, Mr. Walker.

BILL *(fiercely)*: Down't you gow bein' sorry for me: you've no call. Listen 'eah. Aw browk your jawr.

JENNY: No, it didn't hurt me: indeed it didn't, except for a moment. It was only that I was frightened.

BILL: Aw down't want to be forgive be you, or be ennybody. Wot Aw did Aw'll p'y for. Aw trawd to gat me aown jawr browk to settisfaw you—

JENNY *(distressed)*: Oh no—

BILL *(impatiently)*: Tell y' Aw did: cawnt you listen to wot's bein' taold you? All Aw got be it was being mide a sawt of in the public street for me pines. Well, if Aw cawnt settisfaw you one wy, Aw ken another. Listen 'eah! Aw 'ed two quid sived agen the frost; an Aw've a pahnd of it left. A mite o'mawn last week 'ed words with the judy 'e's gowin to merry. 'E give 'er wotfor; an' 'e's bin fawned fifteen bob. 'E 'ed a rawt to 'itt 'er cause they was gowin to be merrid; but Aw 'ednt nao rawt to 'itt you; sao put anather fawv bob on an cal it a pahnd's worth. *(He produces a sovereign.)* 'Eahs the manney. Tike it; and lets 'ev no more o' your forgivin' an' pryin' and your Mijor jawrin' me. Let wot Aw dan be dan an' pide for; and let there be a end of it.

JENNY: Oh, I couldn't take it, Mr. Walker. But if you would give a shilling or two to poor Rummy Mitchens! you really did hurt her; and she's old.

BILL *(contemptuously)*: Not lawkly. Aw'd give her anather as soon as look at 'er. Let her 'ev the lawr o' me as she threatened! She ain't forgiven me: not mach. Wot Aw dan to 'er is not on me mawnd—wot she *(Indicating* BARBARA.*)* mawt call on me conscience—no more than stickin' a pig. It's this Christian gime o' yours that Aw wown't 'ev pl'yed agen me: this bloomin' forgivin' an neggin' an jawrin' that mikes a menn thet sore that 'iz lawf's a burden to 'im. Aw wown't 'ev it. Aw tell you; sao tike your manney and stop thraowin' your silly beshed fice hap agen me.

JENNY: Major: may I take a little of it for the Army?

BARBARA: No: the Army is not to be bought. We want your soul, Bill; and we'll take nothing less.

BILL *(bitterly)*: Aw knaow. Me an' maw few shillin's is not good enaff for you. You're a earl's grendorter, you are. Nathink less than a 'anderd pahnd for you.

UNDERSHAFT: Come, Barbara! you could do a great deal of good with a hundred pounds. If you will set this gentleman's mind at ease by taking his pound, I will give the other ninety-nine.

*(*BILL, *dazed by such opulence, instinctively touches his cap.)*

BARBARA: Oh, you're too extravagant, papa. Bill offers twenty pieces of silver. All you need offer is the other ten. That will make the standard price to buy anybody who's for sale. I'm not; and the Army's not. *(to* BILL*)* You'll never have another quiet moment, Bill, until you come round to us. You can't stand out against your salvation.

BILL *(sullenly)*: Aw cawnt stend aht agen music 'awl wrastlers and awtful tangued women. Aw've offered to p'y. Aw can do no more. Tike it or leave it. There it is. *(He throws the sovereign on the drum, and sits down on the horse trough. The coin fascinates* SNOBBY PRICE, *who takes an early opportunity of dropping his cap on it.)*

*(*MRS BAINES *comes from the shelter. She is dressed as a Salvation Army Commissioner. She is an earnest looking woman of about forty, with a caressing urgent voice, and an appealing manner.)*

BARBARA: This is my father, Mrs Baines *(*UNDERSHAFT *comes from the table taking his hat off with marked civility.)* Try what you can do with him. He won't listen to me, because he remembers what a fool I was when I was a baby. *(She leaves them together and chats with* JENNY.*)*

MRS BAINES: Have you been shewn over the shelter, Mr Undershaft? You know the work we're doing, of course.

UNDERSHAFT *(very civilly)*: The whole nation knows it, Mrs. Baines.

MRS BAINES: No sir: the whole nation does not know it, or we should not be crippled as we are for want of money to carry our work through the length and breadth of the land. Let me tell you that there would have been rioting this winter in London but for us.

UNDERSHAFT: You really think so?

MRS BAINES: I know it, I remember 1886, when you rich gentlemen hardened your hearts against the cry of the poor. They broke the windows of your clubs in Pall Mall.

UNDERSHAFT *(gleaming with approval of their method)*: And the Mansion House Fund went up next day from thirty thousand pounds to seventy-nine thousand! I remember quite well.

MRS BAINES: Well, won't you help me to get at the people? They won't break windows then. Come here, Price. Let me shew you to this gentleman. *(*PRICE *comes to be inspected.)* Do you remember the window breaking?

PRICE: My ole father thought it was the revolution, ma'am.

MRS BAINES: Would you break windows now?

PRICE: Oh no ma'am. The windows of 'eaven 'av bin

opened to me. I know now that the rich man is a sinner like myself.

RUMMY (*appearing above at the loft door*): Snobby Price!

SNOBBY: Wot is it?

RUMMY: Your mother's askin' for you at the other gate in Crippses Lane. She's heard about your confession. (PRICE *turns pale.*)

MRS BAINES: Go, Mr Price; and pray with her.

JENNY: You can go through the shelter, Snobby.

PRICE (*to* MRS BAINES): I couldn't face her now, ma'am, with all the weight of my sins fresh on me. Tell her she'll find her son at 'ome, waitin' for her in prayer. (*He skulks off through the gate, incidentally stealing the sovereign on his way out by picking up his cap from the drum.*)

MRS BAINES (*with swimming eyes*): You see how we take the anger and the bitterness against you out of their hearts, Mr. Undershaft.

UNDERSHAFT: It is certainly most convenient and gratifying to all large employers of labor, Mrs Baines.

MRS BAINES: Barbara: Jenny: I have good news: most wonderful news. (JENNY *runs to her.*) My prayers have been answered. I told you they would, Jenny, didn't I?

JENNY: Yes, yes.

BARBARA (*moving nearer to the drum*): Have we got money enough to keep the shelter open?

MRS BAINES: I hope we shall have enough to keep all the shelters open. Lord Saxmundham has promised us five thousand pounds—

BARBARA: Hooray!

JENNY: Glory!

MRS BAINES: —if—

BARBARA: "If!" If what?

MRS BAINES: —if five other gentlemen will give a thousand each to make it up to ten thousand.

BARBARA: Who is Lord Saxmundham? I never heard of him.

UNDERSHAFT (*who has pricked up his ears at the peer's name, and is now watching* BARBARA *curiously*): A new creation, my dear. You have heard of Sir Horace Bodger?

BARBARA: Bodger! Do you mean the distiller? Bodger's whisky!

UNDERSHAFT: That is the man. He is one of the greatest of our public benefactors. He restored the cathedral at Hakington. They made him a baronet for that. He gave half a million to the funds of his party: they made him a baron for that.

SHIRLEY: What will they give him for the five thousand?

UNDERSHAFT: There is nothing left to give him. So the five thousand, I should think, is to save his soul.

MRS BAINES: Heaven grant it may! Oh Mr Un-

dershaft, you have some very rich friends. Can't you help us towards the other five thousand? We are going to hold a great meeting this afternoon at the Assembly Hall in the Mile End Road. If I could only announce that one gentleman had come forward to support Lord Saxmundham, others would follow. Don't you know somebody? couldn't you? wouldn't you? (*Her eyes fill with tears.*) Oh, think of those poor people, Mr. Undershaft: think of how much it means to them, and how little to a great man like you.

UNDERSHAFT (*sardonically gallant*): Mrs Baines: you are irresistible. I can't disappoint you; and I can't deny myself the satisfaction of making Bodger pay up. You shall have your five thousand pounds.

MRS BAINES: Thank God!

UNDERSHAFT: You don't thank me?

MRS BAINES: Oh sir, don't try to be cynical: don't be ashamed of being a good man. The Lord will bless you abundantly; and our prayers will be like a strong fortification round you all the days of your life. (*With a touch of caution.*) You will let me have the cheque to shew at the meeting, won't you? Jenny: go in and fetch a pen and ink. (JENNY *runs to the shelter door.*)

UNDERSHAFT: Do not disturb Miss Hill: I have a fountain pen. (JENNY *halts. He sits at the table and writes the cheque.* CUSINS *rises to make room for him. They all watch him silently.*)

BILL (*cynically, aside to* BARBARA, *his voice and accent horribly debased*): Wot prawce Selvytion nah?

BARBARA: Stop. (UNDERSHAFT *stops writing: they all turn to her in surprise.*) Mrs Baines: are you really going to take his money?

MRS BAINES (*astonished*): Why not, dear?

BARBARA: Why not! Do you know what my father is? Have you forgotten that Lord Saxmundham is Bodger the whisky man? Do you remember how we implored the County Council to stop him from writing Bodger's Whisky in letters of fire against the sky; so that the poor drink-ruined creatures on the Embankment could not wake up from their snatches of sleep without being reminded of their deadly thirst by that wicked sky sign? Do you know that the worst thing I have had to fight here is not the devil, but Bodger, Bodger, Bodger, with his whisky, his distilleries, and his tied houses?° Are you going to make our shelter another tied house for him, and ask me to keep it?

BILL: Rotten dranken whisky it is too.

MRS BAINES: Dear Barbara: Lord Saxmundham has a

---

tied houses, taverns owned directly or indirectly by a brewer who expects the bars to serve only his own products.

soul to be saved like any of us. If heaven has found the way to make a good use of his money, are we to set outselves up against the answer to our prayers?

BARBARA: I know he has a soul to be saved. Let him come down here; and I'll do my best to help him to his salvation. But he wants to send his cheque down to buy us, and go on being as wicked as ever.

UNDERSHAFT (*with a reasonableness which* CUSINS *alone perceives to be ironical*): My dear Barbara: alcohol is a very necessary article. It heals the sick—

BARBARA: It does nothing of the sort.

UNDERSHAFT: Well, it assists the doctor: that is perhaps a less questionable way of putting it. It makes life bearable to millions of people who could not endure their existence if they were quite sober. It enables Parliament to do things at eleven at night that no sane person would do at eleven in the morning. Is it Bodger's fault that this inestimable gift is deplorably abused by less than one percent of the poor? (*He turns again to the table; signs the cheque; and crosses it.*)

MRS BAINES: Barbara: will there be less drinking or more if all those poor souls we are saving come tomorrow and find the doors of our shelters shut in their faces? Lord Saxmundham gives us the money to stop drinking—to take his own business from him.

CUSINS (*impishly*): Pure self-sacrifice on Bodger's part, clearly! Bless dear Bodger! (BARBARA *almost breaks down as* ADOLPHUS, *too, fails her.*)

UNDERSHAFT (*tearing out the cheque and pocketing the book as he rises and goes past* CUSINS *to* MRS BAINES): I also, Mrs Baines, may claim a little disinterestedness. Think of my business! think of the widows and orphans! the men and lads torn to pieces with shrapnel and poisoned with lyddite! (MRS BAINES *shrinks; but he goes on remorselessly.*) The oceans of blood, not one drop of which is shed in a really just cause! the ravaged crops! the peaceful peasants forced, women and men, to till their fields under the fire of opposing armies on pain of starvation! the bad blood of the fierce little cowards at home who egg on others to fight for the gratification of their national vanity! All this makes money for me: I am never richer, never busier than when the papers are full of it. Well, it is your work to preach peace on earth and good-will to men. (MRS BAINES'S *face lights up again.*) Every convert you make is a vote against war. (*Her lips move in prayer.*) Yet I give you this money to help you to hasten my own commercial ruin. (*He gives her the cheque.*)

CUSINS (*mounting the form in an ecstasy of mischief*): The millennium will be inaugurated by the unselfishness of Undershaft and Bodger. Oh be joyful!

(*He takes the drum-sticks from his pocket and flourishes them.*)

MRS BAINES (*taking the cheque*): The longer I live the more proof I see that there is an Infinite Goodness that turns everything to the work of salvation sooner or later. Who would have thought that any good could have come out of war and drink? And yet their profits are brought today to the feet of salvation to do its blessed work. (*She is affected to tears.*)

JENNY (*running to* MRS BAINES *and throwing her arms round her*): Oh dear! how blessed, how glorious it all is!

CUSINS (*in a convulsion of irony*): Let us seize this unspeakable moment. Let us march to the great meeting at once. Excuse me just an instant. (*He rushes into the shelter.* JENNY *takes her tambourine from the drum head.*)

MRS BAINES: Mr Undershaft: have you ever seen a thousand people fall on their knees with one impulse and pray? Come with us to the meeting. Barbara shall tell them that the Army is saved, and saved through you.

CUSINS (*returning impetuously from the shelter with a flag and a trombone, and coming between* MRS BAINES *and* UNDERSHAFT): You will carry the flag down the first street, Mrs. Baines. (*He gives her the flag.*) Mr Undershaft is a gifted trombonist: he shall intone an Olympian diapason to the West Ham Salvation March. (*Aside to* UNDERSHAFT, *as he forces the trombone on him.*) Blow, Machiavelli, blow.

UNDERSHAFT (*aside to him, as he takes the trombone*): The trumpet in Zion! (CUSINS *rushes to the drum, which he takes up and puts on.* UNDERSHAFT *continues, aloud.*) I will do my best. I could vamp a bass if I knew the tune.

CUSINS: It is a wedding chorus from one of Donizetti's operas,° but we have converted it. We convert everything to good here, including Bodger. You remember the chorus. "For thee immense rejoicing—*immenso giubilo—immenso giubilo.*" (*With drum obbligato.*) Rum tum ti tum tum tum tum ti ta—

BARBARA: Dolly: you are breaking my heart.

CUSINS: What is a broken heart more or less here? Dionysos Undershaft has descended. I am possessed.

MRS BAINES: Come, Barbara: I must have my dear Major to carry the flag with me.

JENNY: Yes, yes, Major darling.

(CUSINS *snatches the tambourine out of* JENNY'S *hand and mutely offers it to* BARBARA.)

---

one . . . operas, Lucia di Lammermoor.

BARBARA (*coming forward a little as she puts the offer behind her with a shudder, whilst* CUSINS *recklessly tosses the tambourine back to* JENNY *and goes to the gate*): I can't come.

JENNY: Not come!

MRS BAINES (*with tears in her eyes*): Barbara: do you think I am wrong to take the money?

BARBARA (*impulsively going to her and kissing her*): No, no: God help you dear, you must: you are saving the Army. Go; and may you have a great meeting!

JENNY: But aren't you coming?

BARBARA: No. (*She begins taking off the silver S brooch from her collar.*)

MRS BAINES: Barbara: what are you doing?

JENNY: Why are you taking your badge off? You can't be going to leave us, Major.

BARBARA (*quietly*): Father: come here.

UNDERSHAFT (*coming to her*): My dear! (*Seeing that she is going to pin the badge on his collar, he retreats to the penthouse in some alarm.*)

BARBARA (*following him*): Don't be frightened. (*She pins the badge on and steps back toward the table, shewing him to the others.*) There! It's not much for £5000, is it?

MRS BAINES: Barbara: if you won't come and pray with us, promise me you will pray for us.

BARBARA: I can't pray now. Perhaps I shall never pray again.

MRS BAINES: Barbara!

JENNY: Major!

BARBARA (*almost delirious*): I can't bear any more. Quick march!

CUSINS (*calling to the procession in the street outside*): Off we go. Play up, there! *Immenso giubilo.* (*He gives the time with his drum; and the band strikes up the march, which rapidly becomes more distant as the procession moves briskly away.*)

MRS BAINES: I must go, dear. You're overworked: you will be all right tomorrow. We'll never lose you. Now Jenny: step out with the old flag. Blood and Fire! (*She marches out through the gate with her flag.*)

JENNY: Glory Hallelujah! (*Flourishing her tambourine and marching.*)

UNDERSHAFT (*to* CUSINS, *as he marches out past him easing the slide of his trombone*): "My ducats and my daughter"!°

CUSINS (*following him out*): Money and gunpowder!

BARBARA: Drunkenness and Murder! My God: why hast thou forsaken me?

My ... daughter, Undershaft here echoes Shylock's reaction to his daughter Jessica's elopement with Lorenzo (*The Merchant of Venice,* II, viii, 17).

(*She sinks on the form with her face buried in her hands. The march passes away into silence.* BILL WALKER *steals across to her.*)

BILL (*taunting*): Wot prawce selvytion nah?

SHIRLEY: Don't you hit her when she's down.

BILL: She 'itt me wen aw wiz dahn. Waw shouldn't Aw git a bit o' me aown beck?

BARBARA (*raising her head*): I didn't take your money, Bill. (*She crosses the yard to the gate and turns her back on the two men to hide her face from them.*)

BILL (*sneering after her*): Naow, it warn't enaff for you. (*Turning to the drum, he misses the money.*) 'Ellow! If you ain't took it sammun else 'ez. Were's it gorn? Bly me if Jenny 'Ill didn't tike it arter all!

RUMMY (*screaming at him from the loft*): You lie, you dirty blackguard! Snobby Price pinched it off the drum when he took up his cap. I was up here all the time an see 'im do it.

BILL: Wot! Stowl maw manney! Waw didn't you call thief on him, you silly aold macker you?

RUMMY: To serve you aht for 'ittin me acrost the face. It's cost y'pahnd, that 'az. (*Raising a paean of squalid triumph.*) I done you. I'm even with you. I've 'ad it aht o' y—(BILL *snatches up* SHIRLEY'S *mug and hurls it at her. She slams the loft door and vanishes. The mug smashes against the door and falls in fragments.*)

BILL (*beginning to chuckle*): Tell us, aol menn, wot o'clock this mawnin' was it wen 'im as they call Snobby Prawce was sived?

BARBARA (*turning to him more composedly, and with unspoiled sweetness*): About half past twelve, Bill. And he pinched your pound at a quarter to two. *I* know. Well, you can't afford to lose it. I'll send it to you.

BILL (*his voice and accent suddenly improving*): Not if Aw wiz to stawve for it. Aw ain't to be bought.

SHIRLEY: Ain't you? You'd sell yourself to the devil for a pint o' beer; only there ain't no devil to make the offer.

BILL (*unshamed*): Sao Aw would, mite, and often 'ev, cheerful. But she cawn't baw me. (*Approaching* BARBARA.) You wanted maw saoul, did you? Well, you ain't got it.

BARBARA: I nearly got it, Bill. But we've sold it back to you for ten thousand pounds.

SHIRLEY: And dear at the money!

BARBARA: No, Peter: it was worth more than money.

BILL (*salvationproof*): It's nao good: you cawn't get rahnd me, nah. Aw down't b'lieve in it; and Aw've seen tod'y that Aw was rawt. (*Going.*) Sao long, aol soupkitchener! Ta, ta, Mijor Earl's Grendorter! (*Turning at the gate.*) Wot prawce selvytion nah? Snobby Prawce! Ha! ha!

BARBARA (*offering her hand*): Goodbye, Bill.

BILL (*taken aback, half plucks his cap off; then shoves it on again defiantly)*: Git aht. (BARBARA *drops her hand, discouraged. He has a twinge of remorse.)* But thet's aw rawt, you knaow. Nathink pasn'l. Naow mellice. Sao long, Judy. (He goes.)

BARBARA: No malice. So long, Bill.

SHIRLEY *(shaking his head)*: You make too much of him, Miss, in your innocence.

BARBARA *(going to him)*: Peter: I'm like you now. Cleaned out, and lost my job.

SHIRLEY: You've youth and hope. That's two better than me.

BARBARA: I'll get you a job, Peter. That's hope for you: the youth will have to be enough for me. *(She counts her money.)* I have just enough left for two teas at Lockharts,° a Rowton doss° for you, and my tram and bus home. *(He frowns and rises with offended pride. She takes his arm.)* Don't be proud, Peter: it's sharing between friends. And promise me you'll talk to me and not let me cry. *(She draws him toward the gate.)*

SHIRLEY: Well, I'm not accustomed to talk to the like of you—

BARBARA *(urgently)*: Yes, yes: you must talk to me. Tell me about Tom Paine's books and Bradlaugh's lectures.° Come along.

SHIRLEY: Ah, if you would only read Tom Paine in the proper spirit, Miss! *(They go out through the gate together.)*

ACT 3

(Next day after lunch LADY BRITOMART *is writing in the library in Wilton Crescent.* SARAH *is reading in the armchair near the window.* BARBARA, *in ordinary fashionable dress, pale and brooding, is on the settee.* CHARLES LOMAX *enters. He starts on seeing* BARBARA *fashionably attired and in low spirits.)*

LOMAX: You've left off your uniform!

(BARBARA says nothing; but an expression of pain passes over her face.)

LADY BRITOMART *(warning him in low tones to be careful)*: Charles!

LOMAX *(much concerned, coming behind the settee and bending sympathetically over* BARBARA*)*: I'm awfully sorry, Barbara. You know I helped you all I could with the concertina and so forth. *(Momentously.)* Still, I have never shut my eyes to the fact that there is a certain amount of tosh about the

---

Salvation Army. Now the claims of the Church of England—

LADY BRITOMART: That's enough, Charles. Speak of something suited to your mental capacity.

LOMAX: But surely the Church of England is suited to all our capacities.

BARBARA *(pressing his hand)*: Thank you for your sympathy, Cholly. Now go and spoon with Sarah.

LOMAX *(dragging a chair from the writing table and seating himself affectionately by* SARAH'S *side)*: How is my ownest today?

SARAH: I wish you wouldn't tell Cholly to do things, Barbara. He always comes straight and does them. Cholly: we're going to the works this afternoon.

LOMAX: What works?

SARAH: The cannon works.

LOMAX: What? Your governor's shop!

SARAH: Yes.

LOMAX: Oh I say!

(CUSINS enters in poor condition. He also starts visibly when he sees BARBARA *without her uniform.)*

BARBARA: I expected you this morning, Dolly. Didn't you guess that?

CUSINS *(sitting down beside her)*: I'm sorry. I have only just breakfasted.

SARAH: But we've just finished lunch.

BARBARA: Have you had one of your bad nights?

CUSINS: No: I had rather a good night: in fact, one of the most remarkable nights I have ever passed.

BARBARA: The meeting?

CUSINS: No: after the meeting.

LADY BRITOMART: You should have gone to bed after the meeting. What were you doing?

CUSINS: Drinking.

LADY BRITOMART: Adolphus!
SARAH: Dolly!
BARBARA: Dolly!
LOMAX: Oh I say!

LADY BRITOMART: What were you drinking, may I ask?

CUSINS: A most devilish kind of Spanish burgundy, warranted free from added alcohol: a Temperance burgundy in fact. Its richness in natural alcohol made any addition superfluous.

BARBARA: Are you joking, Dolly?

CUSINS *(patiently)*: No. I have been making a night of it with the nominal head of this household: that is all.

LADY BRITOMART: Andrew made you drunk!

CUSINS: No: he only provided the wine. I think it was Dionyosos who made me drunk. *(to* BARBARA*)* I told you I was possessed.

LADY BRITOMART: You're not sober yet. Go home to bed at once.

Lockharts, a fashionable tearoom in London. **Rowton doss,** Mr. Rowton owned a string of inexpensive lodging-houses (doss). **Bradlaugh's lectures,** Charles Bradlaugh (1833–1891), like Paine, advocated free-thought in religion and republicanism in politics.

CUSINS: I have never before ventured to reproach you, Lady Brit; but how could you marry the Prince of Darkness?

LADY BRITOMART: It was much more excusable to marry him than to get drunk with him. That is a new accomplishment of Andrew's, by the way. He usen't to drink.

CUSINS: He doesn't now. He only sat there and completed the wreck of my moral basis, the rout of my convictions, the purchase of my soul. He cares for you, Barbara. That is what makes him so dangerous to me.

BARBARA: That has nothing to do with it, Dolly. There are larger loves and diviner dreams than the fireside ones. You know that, don't you?

CUSINS: Yes: that is our understanding. I know it. I hold to it. Unless he can win me on that holier ground he may amuse me for a while; but he can get no deeper hold, strong as he is.

BARBARA: Keep to that; and the end will be right. Now tell me what happened at the meeting?

CUSINS: It was an amazing meeting. Mrs Baines almost died of emotion. Jenny Hill simply gibbered with hysteria. The Prince of Darkness played his trombone like a madman; its brazen roarings were like the laughter of the damned. 117 conversions took place then and there. They prayed with the most touching sincerity and gratitude for Bodger, and for the anonymous donor of the £5000. Your father would not let his name be given.

LOMAX: That was rather fine of the old man, you know. Most chaps would have wanted the advertisement.

CUSINS: He said all the charitable instituitons would be down on him like kites on a battle field if he gave his name.

LADY BRITOMART: That's Andrew all over. He never does a proper thing without giving an improper reason for it.

CUSINS: He convinced me that I have all my life been doing improper things for proper reasons.

LADY BRITOMART: Adolphus: now that Barbara has left the Salvation Army, you had better leave it too. I will not have you playing that drum in the streets.

CUSINS: Your orders are already obeyed, Lady Brit.

BARBARA: Dolly: were you ever really in earnest about it? Would you have joined if you had never seen me?

CUSINS (disingenuously): Well—er—well, possibly, as a collector of religions—

LOMAX (cunningly): Not as a drummer, though, you know. You are a very clearheaded brainy chap, Dolly; and it must have been apparent to you that there is a certain amount of tosh about—

LADY BRITOMART: Charles: if you must drivel, drivel like a grown-up man and not like a schoolboy.

LOMAX (out of countenance): Well, drivel is drivel, don't you know, whatever a man's age.

LADY BRITOMART: In good society in England, Charles, men drivel at all ages by repeating silly formulas with an air of wisdom. Schoolboys make their own formulas out of slang, like you. When they reach your age, and get political private secretaryships and things of that sort, they drop slang and get their formulas out of *The Spectator* or *The Times*. You will find that there is a certain amount of tosh about *The Times*; but at least its language is reputable.

LOMAX (overwhelmed): You are so awfully strong-minded, Lady Brit—

LADY BRITOMART: Rubbish! (MORRISON comes in.) What is it?

MORRISON: If you please, my lady, Mr Undershaft has just drove up to the door.

LADY BRITOMART: Well, let him in. (MORRISON hesistates.) What's the matter with you?

MORRISON: Shall I announce him, my lady; or is he at home here, so to speak, my lady?

LADY BRITOMART: Announce him.

MORRISON: Thank you, my lady. You won't mind my asking, I hope. The occasion is in a manner of speaking new to me.

LADY BRITOMART: Quite right. Go and let him in.

MORRISON: Thank you, my lady. (He withdraws.)

LADY BRITOMART: Children: go and get ready. (SARAH and BARBARA go upstairs for their out-of-door wraps.) Charles: go and tell Stephen to come down here in five minutes: you will find him in the drawing room. (CHARLES goes.) Adolphus: tell them to send round the carriage in about fifteen minutes. (ADOLPHUS goes.)

MORRISON (at the door): Mr Undershaft.

(UNDERSHAFT comes in. MORRISON goes out.)

UNDERSHAFT: Alone! How fortunate!

LADY BRITOMART (rising): Don't be sentimental, Andrew. Sit down. (She sits on the settee: he sits beside her, on her left. She comes to the point before he has time to breathe.) Sarah must have £800 a year until Charles Lomax comes into his property. Barbara will need more, and need it permanently, because Adolphus hasn't any property.

UNDERSHAFT (resignedly): Yes, my dear: I will see to it. Anything else? for yourself, for instance?

LADY BRITOMART: I want to talk to you about Stephen.

UNDERSHAFT (rather wearily): Don't my dear. Stephen doesn't interest me.

LADY BRITOMART: He does interest me. He is our son.

UNDERSHAFT: Do you really think so? He has induced us to bring him into the world; but he chose his parents very incongruously, I think. I see nothing of myself in him, and less of you.

LADY BRITOMART: Andrew: Stephen is an excellent son, and a most steady, capable, highminded young man. You are simply trying to find an excuse for disinheriting him.

UNDERSHAFT: My dear Biddy: the Undershaft tradition disinherits him. It would be dishonest of me to leave the cannon foundry to my son.

LADY BRITOMART: It would be most unnatural and improper of you to leave it to anyone else, Andrew. Do you suppose this wicked and immoral tradition can be kept up for ever? Do you pretend that Stephen could not carry on the foundry just as well as all the other sons of the big business houses?

UNDERSHAFT: Yes: he could learn the office routine without understanding the business, like all the other sons; and the firm would go on by its own momentum until the real Undershaft—probably an Italian or a German—would invent a new method and cut him out.

LADY BRITOMART: There is nothing that any Italian or German could do that Stephen could not do. And Stephen at least has breeding.

UNDERSHAFT: The son of a foundling! Nonsense!

LADY BRITOMART: My son, Andrew! And even you may have good blood in your veins for all you know.

UNDERSHAFT: True. Probably I have. That is another argument in favor of a foundling.

LADY BRITOMART: Andrew: don't be aggravating. And don't be wicked. At present you are both.

UNDERSHAFT: This conversation is part of the Undershaft tradition, Biddy. Every Undershaft's wife has treated him to it ever since the house was founded. It is mere waste of breath. If the tradition be ever broken it will be for an abler man than Stephen.

LADY BRITOMART *(pouting)*: Then go away.

UNDERSHAFT *(deprecatory)*: Go away!

LADY BRITOMART: Yes: go away: If you will do nothing for Stephen, you are not wanted here. Go to your foundling, whoever he is; and look after him.

UNDERSHAFT: The fact is, Biddy—

LADY BRITOMART: Don't call me Biddy. I don't call you Andy.

UNDERSHAFT: I will not call my wife Britomart: it is not good sense. Seriously, my love, the Undershaft tradition has landed me in a difficulty. I am getting on in years; and my partner Lazarus has at last made a stand and inisisted that the succession must be settled one way or the other; and of course he is quite right. You see, I haven't found a fit successor yet.

LADY BRITOMART *(obstinately)*: There is Stephen.

UNDERSHAFT: That's just it: all the foundlings I can find are exactly like Stephen.

LADY BRITOMART: Andrew!!

UNDERSHAFT: I want a man with no relations and no schooling: that is, a man who would be out of the running altogether if he were not a strong man. And I can't find him. Every blessed foundling nowadays is snapped up in his infancy by Barnardo homes° or School Board officers, or Boards of Guardians; and if he shews the least ability, he is fastened on by schoolmasters: trained to win scholarships like a racehorse; crammed with secondhand ideas; drilled and disciplined in docility and what they call good taste; and lamed for life so that he is fit for nothing but teaching. If you want to keep the foundry in the family you had better find an eligible foundling and marry him to Barbara.

LADY BRITOMART: Oh! Barbara! Your pet! You would sacrifice Stephen to Barbara.

UNDERSHAFT: Cheerfully. And you, my dear, would boil Barbara to make soup for Stephen.

LADY BRITOMART: Andrew: this is not a question of our likings and dislikings: it is a question of duty. It is your duty to make Stephen your successor.

UNDERSHAFT: Just as much as it is your duty to submit to your husband. Come, Biddy! these tricks of the governing class are no use with me. I am one of the governing class myself; and it is a waste of time giving tracts to a missionary. I have the power in this matter; and I am not to be humbugged into using it for your purposes.

LADY BRITOMART: Andrew: you can talk my head off; but you can't change wrong into right. And your tie is all on one side. Put it straight.

UNDERSHAFT *(disconcerted)*: It won't stay unless it's pinned—*(He fumbles at it with childish grimaces.)*

(STEPHEN comes in.)

STEPHEN *(at the door)*: I beg your pardon. *(About to retire.)*

LADY BRITOMART: No: come in, Stephen. *(STEPHEN comes forward to his mother's writing table.)*

UNDERSHAFT *(not very cordially)*: Good afternoon.

STEPHEN *(coldly)*: Good afternoon.

UNDERSHAFT *(to LADY BRITOMART)*: He knows all about the tradition, I suppose?

LADY BRITOMART: Yes. *(to STEPHEN)* It is what I told you last night, Stephen.

UNDERSHAFT *(sulkily)*: I understand you want to come into the cannon business.

STEPHEN: *I* go into trade. Certainly not.

UNDERSHAFT *(opening his eyes, greatly eased in mind and manner)*: Oh! in that case—

Barnado homes, Thomas J. Barnardo founded homes in which destitute children could be given industrial training.

LADY BRITOMART: Cannons are not trade, Stephen. They are enterprise.

STEPHEN: I have no intention of becoming a man of business in any sense. I have no capacity for business and no taste for it. I intend to devote myself to politics.

UNDERSHAFT (*rising*): My dear boy: this is an immense relief to me. And I trust it may prove an equally good thing for the country. I was afraid you would consider yourself disparaged and slighted. (*He moves toward* STEPHEN *as if to shake hands with him.*)

LADY BRITOMART (*rising and interposing*): Stephen: I cannot allow you to throw away an enormous property like this.

STEPHEN (*stiffly*): Mother: there must be an end of treating me as a child, if you please. (*LADY BRITOMART recoils, deeply wounded by his tone.*) Until last night I did not take your attitude seriously, because I did not think you meant it seriously. But I find now that you left me in the dark as to matters which you should have explained to me years ago. I am extremely hurt and offended. Any further discussion of my intentions had better take place with my father, as between one man and another.

LADY BRITOMART: Stephen! (*She sits down again, her eyes filling with tears.*)

UNDERSHAFT (*with grave compassion*): You see, my dear, it is only the big men who can be treated as children.

STEPHEN: I am sorry, mother, that you have forced me—

UNDERSHAFT (*stopping him*): Yes, yes, yes, yes: that's all right, Stephen. She won't interfere with you any more: your independence is achieved: you have won your latchkey. Don't rub it in; and above all, don't apologize. (*He resumes his seat.*) Now what about your future, as between one man and another—I beg your pardon, Biddy: as between two men and a woman.

LADY BRITOMART (*who has pulled herself together strongly*): I quite understand, Stephen. By all means go your own way if you feel strong enough. (*STEPHEN sits down magisterially in the chair at the writing table with an air of affirming his majority.*)

UNDERSHAFT: It is settled that you do not ask for the succession to the cannon business.

STEPHEN: I hope it is settled that I repudiate the cannon business.

UNDERSHAFT: Come, come! don't be so devilishly sulky: it's boyish. Freedom should be generous. Besides, I owe you a fair start in life in exchange for disinheriting you. You can't become prime minister all at once. Haven't you a turn for something? What about literature, art, and so forth?

STEPHEN: I have nothing of the artist about me, either in faculty or character, thank Heaven!

UNDERSHAFT: A philosopher, perhaps, Eh?

STEPHEN: I make no such ridiculous pretension.

UNDERSHAFT: Just so. Well, there is the army, the navy, the Church, the Bar. The Bar requires some ability. What about the Bar?

STEPHEN: I have not studied law. And I am afraid I have not the necessary push—I believe that is the name barristers give to their vulgarity—for success in pleading.

UNDERSHAFT: Rather a difficult case, Stephen. Hardly anything left but the stage, is there? (*STEPHEN makes an impatient movement.*) Well, come! is there anything you know or care for?

STEPHEN (*rising and looking at him steadily*): I know the difference between right and wrong.

UNDERSHAFT (*hugely tickled*): You don't say so! What! no capacity for business, no knowledge of law, no sympathy with art, no pretension to philosophy; only a simple knowledge of the secret that has puzzled all the philosophers, baffled all the lawyers, muddled all the men of business, and ruined most of the artists: the secret of right and wrong. Why, man, you're a genius, a master of masters, a god! At twenty-four, too!

STEPHEN (*keeping his temper with difficulty*): You are pleased to be facetious. I pretend to nothing more than any honorable English gentleman claims as his birthright. (*He sits down angrily.*)

UNDERSHAFT: Oh, that's everybody's birthright. Look at poor little Jenny Hill, the Salvation lassie! She would think you were laughing at her if you asked her to stand up in the street and teach grammar or geography or mathematics or even drawing room dancing; but it never occurs to her to doubt that she can teach morals and religion. You are all alike, you respectable people. You can't tell me the bursting strain of a ten-inch gun, which is a very simple matter; but you all think you can tell me the bursting strain of a man under temptation. You daren't handle high explosives; but you're all ready to handle honesty and truth and justice and the whole duty of man, and kill one another at that game. What a country! What a world!

LADY BRITOMART (*uneasily*): What do you think he had better do, Andrew?

UNDERSHAFT: Oh, just what he wants to do. He knows nothing and he thinks he knows everything. That points clearly to a political career. Get him a private secretaryship to someone who can get him an Under Secretaryship; and then leave him alone. He will find his natural and proper place in the end on the Treasury Bench.

STEPHEN (*springing up again*): I am sorry, sir, that you force me to forget the respect due to you as my father. I am an Englishman and I will not hear the Government of my country insulted. (*He thrusts his hands in his pockets and walks angrily across to the window.*)

UNDERSHAFT (*with a touch of brutality*): The government of your country! *I* am the government of your country: I, and Lazarus. Do you suppose that you and half a dozen amateurs like you, sitting in a row in that foolish gabble shop, can govern Undershaft and Lazarus? No, my friend: you will do what pays us. You will make war when it suits us, and keep peace when it doesn't. You will find out that trade requires certain measures when we have decided on those measures. When I want anything to keep my dividends up, you will discover that my want is a national need. When other people want something to keep my dividends down, you will call out the police and military. And in return you shall have the support and applause of my newspapers, and the delight of imagining that you are a great statesman. Government of your country! Be off with you, my boy, and play with your caucuses and leading articles and historic parties and great leaders and burning questions and the rest of your toys. *I* am going back to my counting house to pay the piper and call the tune.

STEPHEN (*actually smiling, and putting his hand on his father's shoulder with indulgent patronage*): Really, my dear father, it is impossible to be angry with you. You don't know how absurd all this sounds to me. You are very properly proud of having been industrious enough to make money; and it is greatly to your credit that you have made so much of it. But it has kept you in circles where you are valued for your money and deferred to for it, instead of in the doubtless very old-fashioned and behind-the-times public school and university where I formed my habits of mind. It is natural for you to think that money governs England; but you must allow me to think I know better.

UNDERSHAFT: And what does govern England, pray?

STEPHEN: Character, father, character.

UNDERSHAFT: Whose character? Yours or mine?

STEPHEN: Neither yours nor mine, father, but the best elements in the English national character.

UNDERSHAFT: Stephen: I've found your profession for you. You're a born journalist. I'll start you with a high-toned weekly review. There!

(*Before* STEPHEN *can reply* SARAH, BARBARA, LOMAX, *and* CUSINS *come in ready for walking.* BARBARA *crosses the room to the window and looks out.* CUSINS *drifts amiably to the armchair.* LOMAX *remains near the door, whilst* SARAH *comes to her mother.*

STEPHEN *goes to the smaller writing table and busies himself with his letters.*)

SARAH: Go and get ready, mamma: the carriage is waiting. (LADY BRITOMART *leaves the room.*)

UNDERSHAFT (*to* SARAH): Good day, my dear. Good afternoon, Mr Lomax.

LOMAX (*vaguely*): Ahdedoo.

UNDERSHAFT (*to* CUSINS): Quite well after last night, Euripides, eh?

CUSINS: As well as can be expected.

UNDERSHAFT: That's right. (*to* BARBARA) So you are coming to see my death and devastation factory, Barbara?

BARBARA (*at the window*): You came yesterday to see my salvation factory. I promised you a return visit.

LOMAX (*coming forward between* SARAH *and* UNDERSHAFT): You'll find it awfully interesting. I've been through the Woolwich Arsenal; and it gives you a ripping feeling of security, you know, to think of the lot of beggars we could kill if it came to fighting. (*to* UNDERSHAFT, *with sudden solemnity*) Still, it must be rather an awful reflection for you, from the religious point of view as it were. You're getting on, you know, and all that.

SARAH: You don't mind Cholly's imbecility, papa, do you?

LOMAX (*much taken aback*): Oh I say!

UNDERSHAFT: Mr. Lomax looks at the matter in a very proper spirit, my dear.

LOMAX: Just so. That's all I meant, I assure you.

SARAH: Are you coming, Stephen?

STEPHEN: Well, I am rather busy—er— (*magnanimously.*) Oh well, yes: I'll come. That is, if there is room for me.

UNDERSHAFT: I can take two with me in a little motor I am experimenting with for field use. You won't mind its being rather unfashionable. It's not painted yet; but it's bullet proof.

LOMAX (*appalled at the prospect of confronting Wilton Crescent in an unpainted motor*): Oh I say!

SARAH: The carriage for me, thank you. Barbara doesn't mind what she's seen in.

LOMAX: I say, Dolly old chap: do you really mind the car being a guy?° Because of course if you do I'll go in it. Still—

CUSINS: I prefer it.

LOMAX: Thanks awfully, old man. Come, my ownest. (*He hurries out to secure his seat in the carriage.* SARAH *follows him.*)

---

guy, conspicuously grotesque object which invites ridicule.

CUSINS (*moodily walking across to* LADY BRITOMART'*s writing table.*): Why are we two coming to this Works Department of Hell? that is what I ask myself.

BARBARA: I have always thought of it as a sort of pit where lost creatures with blackened faces stirred up smoky fires and were driven and tormented by my father. Is it like that, dad?

UNDERSHAFT (*scandalized*): My dear! It is a spotlessly clean and beautiful hillside town.

CUSINS: With a Methodist chapel? Oh do say there's a Methodist chapel.

UNDERSHAFT: There are two: a Primitive one and a sophisticated one. There is even an Ethical Society; but it is not much patronized, as my men are all strongly religious. In the High Explosives Sheds they object to the presence of Agnostics as unsafe.

CUSINS: And yet they don't object to you!

BARBARA: Do they obey all your orders?

UNDERSHAFT: I never give them any orders. When I speak to one of them it's "Well, Jones, is the baby doing well? and has Mrs Jones made a good recovery?" "Nicely, thank you, sir." And that's all.

CUSINS: But Jones has to be kept in order. How do you maintain discipline among your men?

UNDERSHAFT: I don't. They do. You see, the one thing Jones won't stand is any rebellion from the man under him, or any assertion of social equality between the wife of the man with 4 shillings a week less than himself, and Mrs Jones! Of course they all rebel against me, theoretically. Practically, every man of them keeps the man just below him in his place. I never meddle with them. I never bully them. I don't even bully Lazarus. I say that certain things are to be done; but I don't order anybody to do them. I don't say, mind you, that there is no ordering about and snubbing and even bullying. The men snub the boys and order them about; the carmen snub the sweepers; the artisans snub the unskilled laborers; the foremen drive and bully both the laborers and artisans; the assistant engineers find fault with the foremen; the chief engineers drop on the assistants; the departmental managers worry the chiefs; and the clerks have tall hats and hymnbooks and keep up the social tone by refusing to associate on equal terms with anybody. The result is a colossal profit, which comes to me.

CUSINS (*revolted*): You really are a—well, what I was saying yesterday.

BARBARA: What was he saying yesterday?

UNDERSHAFT: Never mind, my dear. He thinks I have made you unhappy. Have I?

BARBARA: Do you think I can be happy in this vulgar silly dress? I! who have worn the uniform. Do you understand what you have done to me? Yesterday I had a man's soul in my hand. I set him in the way of life with his face to salvation. But when we took your money he turned back to drunkenness and derision. (*With intense conviction.*) I will never forgive you that. If I had a child, and you destroyed its body with your explosives—if you murdered Dolly with your horrible guns—I could forgive you if my forgiveness would open the gates of heaven to you. But to take a human soul from me, and turn it into the soul of a wolf! that is worse than any murder.

UNDERSHAFT: Does my daughter despair so easily? Can you strike a man in the heart and leave no mark on him?

BARBARA (*her face lighting up*): Oh, you are right: he can never be lost now: where was my faith?

CUSINS: Oh, clever, clever devil!

BARBARA: You may be a devil; but God speaks through you sometimes. (*She takes her father's hands and kisses them.*) You have given me back my happiness: I feel it deep down now, though my spirit is troubled.

UNDERSHAFT: You have learnt something. That always feels at first as if you had lost something.

BARBARA: Well, take me to the factory of death; and let me learn something more. There must be some truth or other behind all this frightful irony. Come, Dolly. (*She goes out.*)

CUSINS: My guardian angel! (*to* UNDERSHAFT) Avaunt! (*He follows* BARBARA.)

STEPHEN (*quietly, at the writing table*): You must not mind Cusins, father. He is a very amiable good fellow; but he is a Greek scholar and naturally a little eccentric.

UNDERSHAFT: Ah, quite so. Thank you, Stephen. Thank you. (*He goes out.*)

(STEPHEN *smiles patronizingly; buttons his coat responsibly; and crosses the room to the door.* LADY BRITOMART, *dressed for out-of-doors, opens it before he reaches it. She looks round for the others; looks at* STEPHEN; *and turns to go without a word.*)

STEPHEN (*embarrassed*): Mother—

LADY BRITOMART: Don't be apologetic, Stephen. And don't forget that you have outgrown your mother. (*She goes out.*)

(*Perivale St Andrews lies between two Middlesex hills, half climbing the northern one. It is an almost smokeless town of white walls, roofs of narrow green slates or red tiles, tall trees, domes, campaniles, and slender chimney shafts, beautifully situated and beautiful in itself. The best view of it is obtained from the crest of a slope about half a mile to the east, where the high explosives are dealt with. The foundry lies hidden in the depths between, the tops of*) *its chimneys sprouting like huge skittles into the middle distance. Across the crest runs an emplacement of concrete, with a firestep, and a parapet which suggests a fortification, because there is a huge cannon of the obsolete Woolwich Infant pattern peering across it at the town. The cannon is mounted on an experimental gun carriage: possibly the original model of the Undershaft disappearing rampart gun alluded to by Stephen. The firestep, being a convenient place to sit, is furnished here and there with straw disc cushions; and at one place there is the additional luxury of a fur rug.*

BARBARA *is standing on the firestep, looking over the parapet towards the town. On her right is the cannon; on her left the end of a shed raised on piles, with a ladder of three or four steps up to the door, which opens outwards and has a little wooden landing at the threshold, with a fire bucket in the corner of the landing. Several dummy soldiers more or less mutilated, with straw protruding from their gashes, have been shoved out of the way under the landing. A few others are nearly upright against the shed; and one has fallen forward and lies, like a grotesque corpse, on the emplacement. The parapet stops short of the shed, leaving a gap which is the beginning of the path down the hill through the foundry to the town. The rug is on the firestep near this gap. Down on the emplacement behind the cannon is a trolley carrying a huge conical bombshell with a red band painted on it. Further to the right is the door of an office, which, like the sheds, is of the lightest possible construction.*

CUSINS *arrives by the path from the town.)*

BARBARA: Well?

CUSINS: Not a ray of hope. Everything perfect! wonderful! real! It only needs a cathedral to be a heavenly city instead of a hellish one.

BARBARA: Have you found out whether they have done anything for old Peter Shirley?

CUSINS: They have found him a job as gatekeeper and timekeeper. He's frightfully miserable. He calls the timekeeping brainwork, and says he isn't used to it; and his gate lodge is so splendid that he's ashamed to use the rooms, and skulks in the scullery.

BARBARA: Poor Peter!

(STEPHEN arrives from the town. He carries a fieldglass.)

STEPHEN *(enthusiastically):* Have you two seen the place? Why did you leave us?

CUSINS: I wanted to see everything I was not intended to see; and Barbara wanted to make the men talk.

STEPHEN: Have you found anything discreditable?

CUSINS: No. They call him Dandy Andy and are proud of his being a cunning old rascal; but it's all horribly, frightfully, immorally, unanswerably perfect.

(SARAH arrives.)

SARAH: Heavens! what a place! *(She crosses to the trolley)* Did you see the nursing home? *(She sits down on the shell.)*

STEPHEN: Did you see the libraries and schools?

SARAH: Did you see the ball room and the banqueting chamber in the Town Hall!?

STEPHEN: Have you gone into the insurance fund, the pension fund, the building society, the various applications of cooperation!?

(UNDERSHAFT comes from the office, with a sheaf of telegrams in his hand.)

UNDERSHAFT: Well, have you seen everything? I'm sorry I was called away. *(Indicating the telegrams.)* Good news from Manchuria.

STEPHEN: Another Japanese victory?

UNDERSHAFT: Oh, I don't know. Which side wins does not concern us here. No: the good news is that the aerial battleship is a tremendous success. At the first trial it has wiped out a fort with three hundred soldiers in it.

CUSINS *(from the platform):* Dummy soldiers?

UNDERSHAFT *(striding across to STEPHEN and kicking the prostrate dummy brutally out of his way):* No: the real thing.

(CUSINS and BARBARA exchange glances. Then CUSINS sits on the step and buries his face in his hands. BARBARA gravely lays her hand on his shoulder. He looks up at her in whimsical desperation.)

UNDERSHAFT: Well, Stephen, what do you think of the place?

STEPHEN: Oh, magnificent. A perfect triumph of modern industry. Frankly, my dear father, I have been a fool: I had no idea of what it all meant: of the wonderful forethought, the power of organization, the administrative capacity, the financial genius, the colossal capital it represents. I have been repeating to myself as I came through your streets "Peace hath her victories no less renowned than War." I have only one misgiving about it all.

UNDERSHAFT: Out with it.

STEPHEN: Well, I cannot help thinking that all this provision for every want of your workmen may sap their independence and weaken their sense of responsibility. And greatly as we enjoyed our tea at that splendid restaurant—how they gave us all that luxury and cake and jam and cream for threepence I really cannot imagine!—still you must remember that restaurants break up home life. Look at the continent, for instance! Are you sure so much pampering is really good for the men's characters?

UNDERSHAFT: Well you see, my dear boy, when you

are organizing civilization you have to make up your mind whether trouble and anxiety are good things or not. If you decide that they are, then I take it, you simply don't organize civilization; and there you are, with trouble and anxiety enough to make us all angels! But if you decide the other way, you may as well go through with it. However, Stephen. our characters are safe here. A sufficient dose of anxiety is always provided by the fact that we may be blown to smithereens at any moment.

SARAH: By the way, papa, where do you make the explosives?

UNDERSHAFT: In separate little sheds, like that one. When one of them blows up, it costs very little; and only the people quite close to it are killed.

(STEPHEN, *who is quite close to it, looks at it rather scaredly, and moves away quickly to the cannon. At the same moment the door of the shed is thrown abruptly open; and a foreman in overalls and list slippers° comes out on the little landing and holds the door for* LOMAX, *who appears in the doorway.*)

LOMAX (*with studied coolness*): My good fellow: you needn't get into a state of nerves. Nothing's going to happen to you; and I suppose it wouldn't be the end of the world if anything did. A little bit of British pluck is what you want, old chap. (*He descends and strolls across to* SARAH.)

UNDERSHAFT (*to the foreman*): Anything wrong, Bilton?

BILTON (*with ironic calm*): Gentleman walked into the high explosives shed and lit a cigaret, sir: that's all.

UNDERSHAFT: Ah, quite so. (*Going over to* LOMAX.) Do you happen to remember what you did with the match?

LOMAX: Oh come! I'm not a fool. I took jolly good care to blow it out before I chucked it away.

BILTON: The top of it was red hot inside, sir.

LOMAX: Well, suppose it was! I didn't chuck it into any of your messes.

UNDERSHAFT: Think no more of it, Mr. Lomax. By the way, would you mind lending me your matches?

LOMAX (*offering his box*): Certainly.

UNDERSHAFT: Thanks. (*He pockets the matches.*)

LOMAX (*lecturing to the company generally*): You know, these high explosives don't go off like gunpowder, except when they're in a gun. When they're spread loose, you can put a match to them without the least risk: they just burn quietly like a bit

---

list slippers, soft cloth slippers used here to minimize friction.

of paper. (*Warming to the scientific interest of the subject.*) Did you know that, Undershaft? Have you ever tried?

UNDERSHAFT: Not on a large scale, Mr. Lomax. Bilton will give you a sample of gun cotton when you are leaving if you ask him. You can experiment with it at home. (BILTON *looks puzzled.*)

SARAH: Bilton will do nothing of the sort, papa. I suppose it's your business to blow up the Russians and Japs; but you might really stop short of blowing up poor Cholly. (BILTON *gives it up and retires into the shed.*)

LOMAX: My ownest, there is no danger. (*He sits beside her on the shell.*)

(LADY BRITOMART *arrives from the town with a bouquet.*)

LADY BRITOMART (*impetuously*): Andrew: you shouldn't have let me see this place.

UNDERSHAFT: Why, my dear?

LADY BRITOMART: Never mind why: you shouldn't have: that's all. To think of all that (*Indicating the town.*) being yours! and that you have kept it to yourself all these years!

UNDERSHAFT: It does not belong to me. I belong to it. It is the Undershaft inheritance.

LADY BRITOMART: It is not. Your ridiculous cannons and that noisy banging foundry may be the Undershaft inheritance; but all that plate and linen, all that furniture and those houses and orchards and gardens belong to us. They belong to me: they are not a man's business. I won't give them up. You must be out of your senses to throw them all away; and if you persist in such folly, I will call in a doctor.

UNDERSHAFT (*stooping to smell the bouquet*): Where did you get the flowers, my dear?

LADY BRITOMART: Your men presented them to me in your William Morris Labor Church.

CUSINS: Oh! It needed only that. A Labor Church! (*He mounts the firestep distractedly, and leans with his elbows on the parapet, turning his back to them.*)

LADY BRITOMART: Yes, with Morris's words in mosaic letters ten feet high round the dome. NO MAN IS GOOD ENOUGH TO BE ANOTHER MAN'S MASTER. The cynicism of it!

UNDERSHAFT: It shocked the men at first, I am afraid. But now they take no more notice of it than of the ten commandments in church.

LADY BRITOMART: Andrew: you are trying to put me off the subject of the inheritance by profane jokes. Well, you shan't. I don't ask it any longer for Stephen: he has inherited far too much of your perversity to be fit for it. But Barbara has rights as well as Stephen. Why should not Adolphus succeed to the inheritance? I could manage the town for him; and he can look after the cannons, if they are really necessary.

UNDERSHAFT: I should ask nothing better if Adolphus were a foundling. He is exactly the sort of new blood that is wanted in English business. But he's not a foundling; and there's an end of it. *(He makes for the office door.)*

CUSINS *(turning to them)*: Not quite. *(They all turn and stare at him.)* I think—Mind! I am not committing myself in any way as to my future course—but I think the foundling difficulty can be got over. *(He jumps down to the emplacement.)*

UNDERSHAFT *(coming back to him)*: What do you mean?

CUSINS : Well, I have something to say which is in the nature of a confession.

SARAH:
LADY BRITOMART: } Confession!
BARBARA:
STEPHEN:

LOMAX: Oh I say!

CUSINS: Yes, a confession. Listen, all. Until I met Barbara I thought myself in the main an honorable, truthful man, because I wanted the approval of my conscience more than I wanted anything else. But the moment I saw Barbara, I wanted her far more than the approval of my conscience.

LADY BRITOMART: Adolphus!

CUSINS: It is true. You accused me yourself, Lady Brit, of joining the Army to worship Barbara; and so I did. She bought my soul like a flower at a street corner; but she bought it for herself.

UNDERSHAFT: What! Not for Dionysos or another?

CUSINS: Dionysos and all the others are in herself. I adored what was divine in her, and was therefore a true worshipper. But I was romantic about her too. I thought she was a woman of the people, and that a marriage with a professor of Greek would be far beyond the wildest social ambitions of her rank.

LADY BRITOMART: Adolphus!!

LOMAX: Oh I say!!!

CUSINS: When I learnt the horrible truth—

LADY BRITOMART: What do you mean by the horrible truth, pray?

CUSINS: That she was enormously rich; that her grandfather was an earl; that her father was the Prince of Darkness—

UNDERSHAFT: Chut!

CUSINS: —and that I was only an adventurer trying to catch a rich wife, then I stooped to deceive her about my birth.

BARBARA *(rising)*: Dolly!

LADY BRITOMART: Your birth! Now Adolphus, don't dare to make up a wicked story for the sake of these wretched cannons. Remember: I have seen photographs of your parents; and the Agent General for South Western Australia knows

them personally and has assured me that they are most respectable married people.

CUSINS: So they are in Australia; but here they are outcasts. Their marriage is legal in Australia, but not in England. My mother is my father's deceased wife's sister; and in this island I am consequently a foundling. *(Sensation.)*

BARBARA: Silly! *(She climbs to the cannon, and leans, listening, in the angle it makes with the parapet.)*

CUSINS: Is the subterfuge good enough, Machiavelli?

UNDERSHAFT *(thoughtfully)*: Biddy: this may be a way out of the difficulty.

LADY BRITOMART: Stuff! A man can't make cannons any the better for being his own cousin instead of his proper self. *(She sits down on the rug with a bounce that expresses her downright contempt for their casuistry.)*

UNDERSHAFT *(to CUSINS)*: You are an educated man. That is against the tradition.

CUSINS: One in ten thousand times it happens that the schoolboy is a born master of what they try to teach him. Greek has not destroyed my mind: it has nourished it. Besides, I did not learn it at an English public school.

UNDERSHAFT: Hm! Well, I cannot afford to be too particular: you have cornered the foundling market. Let it pass. You are eligible, Euripides: you are eligible.

BARBARA: Dolly: yesterday morning, when Stephen told us all about the tradition, you became very silent; and you have been strange and excited ever since. Were you thinking of your birth then?

CUSINS: When the finger of Destiny suddenly points at a man in the middle of his breakfast, it makes him thoughtful.

UNDERSHAFT: Aha! You have had your eye on the business, my young friend, have you?

CUSINS: Take care! There is an abyss of moral horror between me and your accursed aerial battleships.

UNDERSHAFT: Never mind the abyss for the present. Let us settle the practical details and leave your final decision open. You know that you will have to change your name. Do you object to that?

CUSINS: Would any man named Adolphus—any man called Dolly!—object to be called something else?

UNDERSHAFT: Good. Now, as to money! I propose to treat you handsomely from the beginning. You shall start at a thousand a year.

CUSINS *(with sudden heat, his spectacles twinkling with mischief)*: A thousand! You dare offer a miserable thousand to the son-in-law of a millionaire! No, by Heavens, Machiavelli! you shall not cheat me. You cannot do without me; and I can do without you. I must have two thousand five hundred a year for two years. At the end of that time, if I am a failure, I go. But if I am a success, and stay on, you must give me the other five thousand.

UNDERSHAFT: What other five thousand?

CUSINS: To make the two years up to five thousand a year. The two thousand five hundred is only half pay in case I should turn out a failure. The third year I must have ten per cent on the profits.

UNDERSHAFT (*taken aback*): Ten per cent! Why, man, do you know what my profits are?

CUSINS: Enormous, I hope; otherwise I shall require twenty-five per cent.

UNDERSHAFT: But, Mr Cusins, this is a serious matter of business. You are not bringing any capital into the concern.

CUSINS: What! no capital! Is my mastery of Greek no capital? Is my access to the subtlest thought, the loftiest poetry yet attained by humanity, no capital? My character! my intellect! my life! my career! what Barbara calls my soul! are these no capital? Say another word; and I double my salary.

UNDERSHAFT: Be reasonable—

CUSINS (*peremptorily*): Mr Undershaft: you have my terms. Take them or leave them.

UNDERSHAFT (*recovering himself*): Very well. I note your terms; and I offer you half.

CUSINS (*disgusted*): Half!

UNDERSHAFT (*firmly*): Half.

CUSINS: You call yourself a gentleman; and you offer me half!!

UNDERSHAFT: I do not call myself a gentleman; but I offer you half.

CUSINS: This to your future partner! your successor! your son-in-law!

BARBARA: You are selling your own soul, Dolly, not mine. Leave me out of the bargain, please.

UNDERSHAFT: Come! I will go a step further for Barbara's sake. I will give you three fifths; but that is my last word.

CUSINS: Done!

LOMAX: Done in the eye! Why *I* get only eight hundred, you know.

CUSINS: By the way, Mac, I am a classical scholar, not an arithmetical one. Is three fifths more than half or less?

UNDERSHAFT: More, of course.

CUSINS: I would have taken two hundred and fifty. How you can succeed in business when you are willing to pay all that money to a University don who is obviously not worth a junior clerk's wages!—well! What will Lazarus say?

UNDERSHAFT: Lazarus is a gentle romantic Jew who cares for nothing but string quartets and stalls at fashionable theatres. He will be blamed for your rapacity in money matters, poor fellow! as he has hitherto been blamed for mine. You are a shark of the first order, Euripides. So much the better for the firm!

BARBARA: Is the bargain closed, Dolly? Does your soul belong to him now?

CUSINS: No: the price is settled: that is all. The real tug of war is still to come. What about the moral question?

LADY BRITOMART: There is no moral question in the matter at all, Adolphus. You must simply sell cannons and weapons to people whose cause is right and just, and refuse them to foreigners and criminals.

UNDERSHAFT (*determinedly*): No: none of that. You must keep the true faith of an Armorer, or you don't come in here.

CUSINS: What on earth is the true faith of an Armorer?

UNDERSHAFT: To give arms to all men who offer an honest price for them, without respect of persons or principles: to aristocrat and republican, to Nihilist and Tsar, to Capitalist and Socialist, to Protestant and Catholic, to burglar and policeman, to black man, white man and yellow man, to all sorts and conditions, all nationalities, all faiths, all follies, all causes and all crimes. The first Undershaft wrote up in his shop IF GOD GAVE THE HAND, LET NOT MAN WITHHOLD THE SWORD. The second wrote up ALL HAVE THE RIGHT TO FIGHT: NONE HAVE THE RIGHT TO JUDGE. The third wrote up TO MAN THE WEAPON: TO HEAVEN THE VICTORY. The fourth had no literary turn; so he did not write up anything; but he sold cannons to Napoleon under the nose of George the Third. The fifth wrote up PEACE SHALL NOT PREVAIL SAVE WITH A SWORD IN HER HAND. The sixth, my master, was the best of all. He wrote up NOTHING IS EVER DONE IN THIS WORLD UNTIL MEN ARE PREPARED TO KILL ONE ANOTHER IF IT IS NOT DONE. After that, there was nothing left for the seventh to say. So he wrote up, simply, UNASHAMED.

CUSINS: My good Machiavelli, I shall certainly write something up on the wall; only as I shall write it in Greek, you won't be able to read it. But as to your Armorer's faith, if I take my neck out of the noose of my own morality I am not going to put it into the noose of yours. I shall sell cannons to whom I please and refuse them to whom I please. So there!

UNDERSHAFT: From the moment when you become Andrew Undershaft, you will never do as you please again. Don't come here lusting for power, young man.

CUSINS: If power were my aim I should not come here for it. You have no power.

UNDERSHAFT: None of my own, certainly.

CUSINS: I have more power than you, more will. You do not drive this place: it drives you. And what drives the place?

UNDERSHAFT (*enigmatically*): A will of which I am a part.

BARBARA (*startled*): Father! Do you know what you are saying; or are you laying a snare for my soul?

CUSINS: Don't listen to his metaphysics, Barbara. The place is driven by the most rascally part of society, the money hunters, the pleasure hunters, the military promotion hunters; and he is their slave.

UNDERSHAFT: Not necessarily. Remember the Armorer's Faith. I will take an order from a good man as cheerfully as from a bad one. If you good people prefer preaching and shirking to buying my weapons and fighting the rascals, don't blame me. I cannot make courage and conviction. Bah! you tire me, Euripides, with your morality mongering. Ask Barbara: she understands. (*He suddenly reaches up and takes* BARBARA's *hands, looking powerfully into her eyes.*) Tell him, my love, what power really means.

BARBARA (*hypnotized*): Before I joined the Salvation Army, I was in my own power; and the consequence was that I never knew what to do with myself. When I joined it, I had not time enough for all the things I had to do.

UNDERSHAFT (*approvingly*): Just so. And why was that, do you suppose?

BARBARA: Yesterday I should have said, because I was in the power of God. (*She resumes her self-possession, withdrawing her hands from his with a power equal to his own.*) But you came and shewed me that I was in the power of Bodger and Undershaft. Today I feel—oh! how can I put it into words? Sarah: do you remember the earthquake at Cannes, when we were little children?—how little the surprise of the first shock mattered compared to the dread and horror of waiting for the second? That is how I feel in this place today. I stood on the rock I thought eternal; and without a word of warning it reeled and crumbled under me. I was safe with an infinite wisdom watching me, an army marching to Salvation with me; and in a moment, at a stroke of your pen in a cheque book, I stood alone; and the heavens were empty. That was the first shock of the earthquake: I am waiting for the second.

UNDERSHAFT: Come, come, my daughter! don't make too much of your little tinpot tragedy. What do we do here when we spend years of work and thought and thousands of pounds of solid cash on a new gun or an aerial battleship that turns out just a hairsbreadth wrong after all? Scrap it.

Scrap it without wasting another hour or another pound on it. Well, you have made for yourself something that you call a morality or a religion or what not. It doesn't fit the facts. Well, scrap it. Scrap it and get one that does fit. That is what is wrong with the world at present. It scraps its obsolete steam engines and dynamos; but it won't scrap its old prejudices and its old moralities and its old religions and its old political constitutions. What's the result? In machinery it does very well; but in morals and religion and politics it is working at a loss that brings it nearer bankruptcy every year. Don't persist in that folly. If your old religion broke down yesterday, get a newer and a better one for tomorrow.

BARBARA: Oh how gladly I would take a better one to my soul! But you offer me a worse one. (*Turning on him with sudden vehemence.*) Justify yourself: shew me some light through the darkness of this dreadful place, with its beautifully clean workshops, and respectable workmen and model homes.

UNDERSHAFT: Cleanliness and respectability do not need justification, Barbara: they justify themselves. I see no darkness here, no dreadfulness. In your Salvation shelter I saw poverty, misery, cold and hunger. You gave them bread and treacle and dreams of heaven. I give from thirty shillings a week to twelve thousand a year. They find their own dreams; but I look after the drainage.

BARBARA: And their souls?

UNDERSHAFT: I save their souls just as I saved yours.

BARBARA (*revolted*): You saved my soul! What do you mean?

UNDERSHAFT: I fed you and clothed you and housed you. I took care that you should have money enough to live handsomely—more than enough; so that you could be wasteful, careless, generous. That saved your soul from the seven deadly sins.

BARBARA (*bewildered*): The seven deadly sins!

UNDERSHAFT: Yes, the deadly seven. (*Counting on his fingers.*) Food, clothing, firing, rent, taxes, respectability and children. Nothing can lift those seven millstones from Man's neck but money; and the spirit cannot soar until the millstones are lifted. I lifted them from your spirit. I enabled Barbara to become Major Barbara; and I saved her from the crime of poverty.

CUSINS: Do you call poverty a crime?

UNDERSHAFT: The worst of crimes. All the other crimes are virtues beside it: all the other dishonors are chivalry itself by comparison. Poverty blights whole cities; spreads horrible pestilences; strikes dead the very souls of all who come within sight, sound or smell of it. What you call crime is nothing: a murder here and a theft there, a blow now and a curse then: what do they matter? they are only the accidents and illnesses of life: there are not fifty genuine professional criminals in London. But there are millions of poor people, abject people, dirty people, ill fed, ill clothed people. They poison us morally and physically: they kill the happiness of society: they force us to do away with our own liberties and to organize unnatural cruelties for fear they should rise against us and drag us down into their abyss. Only fools fear crime: we all fear poverty. Pah! (*Turning on* BARBARA.) you talk of your half-saved ruffian in West Ham: you accuse me of dragging his soul back to perdition. Well, bring him to me here; and I will drag his soul back again to salvation for you. Not by words and dreams; but by thirty-eight shillings a week, a sound house in a handsome street, and a permanent job. In three weeks he will have a fancy waistcoat; in three months a tall hat and a chapel sitting; before the end of the year he will shake hands with a duchess at a Primrose League° meeting, and join the Conservative Party.

BARBARA: And will he be the better for that?

UNDERSHAFT: You know he will. Don't be a hypocrite, Barbara. He will be better fed, better housed, better clothed, better behaved; and his children will be pounds heavier and bigger. That will be better than an American cloth° mattress in a shelter, chopping firewood, eating bread and treacle, and being forced to kneel down from time to time to thank heaven for it: knee drill, I think you call it. It is cheap work converting starving men with a Bible in one hand and a slice of bread in the other. I will undertake to covert West Ham to Mahometanism on the same terms. Try your hand on my men: their souls are hungry because their bodies are full.

BARBARA: And leave the east end to starve?

UNDERSHAFT (*his energetic tone dropping into one of bitter and brooding remembrance*): I was an east ender. I moralized and starved until one day I swore that I would be a full-fed free man at all costs—that nothing should stop me except a bullet, neither reason nor morals nor the lives of other men. I said "Thou shalt starve ere I starve"; and with that word I became free and great. I was a dangerous man until I had my will: now I am a useful, beneficent, kindly person. That is the

history of most self-made millionaires, I fancy. When it is the history of every Englishman we shall have an England worth living in.

LADY BRITOMART: Stop making speeches, Andrew. This is not the place for them.

UNDERSHAFT (*punctured*): My dear: I have no other means of conveying my ideas.

LADY BRITOMART: Your ideas are nonsense. You got on because you were selfish and unscrupulous.

UNDERSHAFT: Not at all. I had the strongest scruples about poverty and starvation. Your moralists are quite unscrupulous about both: they make virtues of them. I had rather be a thief than a pauper. I had rather be a murderer than a slave. I don't want to be either; but if you force the alternative on me, then, by Heaven, I'll choose the braver and more moral one. I hate poverty and slavery worse than any other crimes whatsoever. And let me tell you this. Poverty and slavery have stood up for centuries to your sermons and leading articles: they will not stand up to my machine guns. Don't preach at them: don't reason with them. Kill them.

BARBARA: Killing. Is that your remedy for everything?

UNDERSHAFT: It is the final test of conviction, the only lever strong enough to overturn a social system, the only way of saying Must. Let six hundred and seventy fools loose in the street; and three policemen can scatter them. But huddle them together in a certain house in Westminster; and let them go through certain ceremonies and call themselves certain names until at last they get the courage to kill; and your six hundred and seventy fools become a government. Your pious mob fills up ballot papers and imagines it is governing its masters; but the ballot paper that really governs is the paper that has a bullet wrapped up in it.

CUSINS: That is perhaps why, like most intelligent people, I never vote.

UNDERSHAFT: Vote! Bah! When you vote, you only change the names of the cabinet. When you shoot, you pull down governments, inaugurate new epochs, abolish old orders and set up new. Is that historically true, Mr. Learned Man, or is it not?

CUSINS: It is historically true. I loathe having to admit it. I repudiate your sentiments. I abhor your nature. I defy you in every possible way. Still, it is true. But it ought not to be true.

UNDERSHAFT: Ought! ought! ought! ought! ought! Are you going to spend your life saying ought, like the rest of our moralists? Turn your oughts into shalls, man. Come and make explosives with me. Whatever can blow men up can blow society up. The history of the world is the history of

---

Primrose League, Primrose League, named after Disraeli's favorite flower. Founded in 1883, the League followed Lord Beaconsfield's Conservative politics. ***American cloth,*** long used in England for oilcloth.

those who had courage enough to embrace this truth. Have you the courage to embrace it, Barbara?

LADY BRITOMART: Barbara, I positively forbid you to listen to your father's abominable wickedness. And you, Adolphus, ought to know better than to go about saying that wrong things are true. What does it matter whether they are true if they are wrong?

UNDERSHAFT: What does it matter whether they are wrong if they are true?

LADY BRITOMART (rising): Children: come home instantly. Andrew: I am exceedingly sorry I allowed you to call on us. You are wickeder than ever. Come at once.

BARBARA (shaking her head): It's no use running away from wicked people, mamma.

LADY BRITOMART: It is every use. It shews your disapprobation of them.

BARBARA: It does not save them.

LADY BRITOMART: I can see that you are going to disobey me. Sarah: are you coming home or are you not?

SARAH: I daresay it's very wicked of papa to make cannons; but I don't think I shall cut him on that account.

LOMAX (pouring oil on the troubled waters): The fact is, you know, there is a certain amount of tosh about this notion of wickedness. It doesn't work. You must look at facts. Not that I would say a word in favor of anything wrong; but then, you see, all sorts of chaps are always doing all sorts of things; and we have to fit them in somehow, don't you know. What I mean is, that you can't go cutting everybody; and that's about what it comes to. (Their rapt attention to his eloquence makes him nervous.) Perhaps I don't make myself clear.

LADY BRITOMART: You are lucidity itself, Charles. Because Andrew is successful and has plenty of money to give to Sarah, you will flatter him and encourage him in his wickedness.

LOMAX (unruffled): Well, where the carcase is, there will the eagles be gathered, don't you know. (to UNDERSHAFT) Eh? What?

UNDERSHAFT: Precisely. By the way, may I call you Charles?

LOMAX: Delighted. Cholly is the usual ticket.

UNDERSHAFT (to LADY BRITOMART): Biddy—

LADY BRITOMART (violently): Don't dare call me Biddy. Charles Lomax: you are a fool. Adolphus Cusins: you are a Jesuit. Stephen: you are a prig. Barbara: you are a lunatic. Andrew: you are a vulgar tradesman. Now you all know my opinion; and my conscience is clear, at all events. (She sits down with a vehemence that the rug fortunately softens.)

UNDERSHAFT: My dear: you are the incarnation of morality. (She snorts.) Your conscience is clear and your duty done when you have called everybody names. Come, Euripides! it is getting late; and we all want to go home. Make up your mind.

CUSINS: Understand this, you old demon—

LADY BRITOMART: Adolphus!

UNDERSHAFT: Let him alone, Biddy. Proceed, Euripides.

CUSINS: You have me in a horrible dilemma. I want Barbara.

UNDERSHAFT: Like all young men, you greatly exaggerate the difference between one young woman and another.

BARBARA: Quite true, Dolly.

CUSINS: I also want to avoid being a rascal.

UNDERSHAFT (with biting contempt): You lust for personal righteousness, for self-approval, for what you call a good conscience, for what Barbara calls salvation, for what I call patronizing people who are not so lucky as yourself.

CUSINS: I do not: all the poet in me recoils from being a good man. But there are things in me that I must reckon with. Pity—

UNDERSHAFT: Pity! The scavenger of misery.

CUSINS: Well, love.

UNDERSHAFT: I know. You love the needy and the outcast: you love the oppressed races, the negro, the Indian ryot, the underdog everywhere. Do you love the Japanese? Do you love the French? Do you love the English?

CUSINS: No. Every true Englishman detests the English. We are the wickedest nation on earth; and our success is a moral horror.

UNDERSHAFT: That is what comes of your gospel of love, is it?

CUSINS: May I not love even my father-in-law?

UNDERSHAFT: Who wants your love, man? By what right do you take the liberty of offering it to me? I will have your due heed and respect, or I will kill you. But your love! Damn your impertinence!

CUSINS (grinning): I may not be able to control my affections, Mac.

UNDERSHAFT: You are fencing, Euripides. You are weakening: your grip is slipping. Come! try your last weapon. Pity and love have broken in your hand: forgiveness is still left.

CUSINS: No: forgiveness is a beggar's refuge. I am with you there: we must pay our debts.

UNDERSHAFT: Well said. Come! you will suit me. Remember the words of Plato.

CUSINS (starting): Plato! You dare quote Plato to me!

UNDERSHAFT: Plato says, my friend, that society cannot be saved until either the Professors of Greek take to making gunpowder, or else the makers of gunpowder become Professors of Greek.

CUSINS: Oh, tempter, cunning tempter!

UNDERSHAFT: Come! choose, man, choose.

CUSINS: But perhaps Barbara will not marry me if I make the wrong choice.

BARBARA: Perhaps not.

CUSINS (desperately perplexed): You hear!

BARBARA: Father: do you love nobody?

UNDERSHAFT: I love my best friend.

LADY BRITOMART: And who is that, pray?

UNDERSHAFT: My bravest enemy. That is the man who keeps me up to the mark.

CUSINS: You know, the creature is really a sort of poet in his way. Suppose he is a great man, after all!

UNDERSHAFT: Suppose you stop talking and make up your mind, my young friend.

CUSINS: But you are driving me against my nature. I hate war.

UNDERSHAFT: Hatred is the coward's revenge for being intimidated. Dare you make war on war? Here are the means: my friend Mr Lomax is sitting on them.

LOMAX (springing up): Oh I say! You don't mean that this thing is loaded, do you? My ownest: come off it.

SARAH (sitting placidly on the shell): If I am to be blown up, the more thoroughly it is done the better. Don't fuss, Cholly.

LOMAX (to UNDERSHAFT, strongly remonstrant): Your own daughter, you know.

UNDERSHAFT: So I see. (to CUSINS) Well, my friend, may we expect you here at six tomorrow morning?

CUSINS (firmly): Not on any account. I will see the whole establishment blown up with its own dynamite before I will get up at five. My hours are healthy, rational hours: eleven to five.

UNDERSHAFT: Come when you please: before a week you will come at six and stay until I turn you out for the sake of your health. (Calling.) Bilton! (He turns to LADY BRITOMART, who rises.) My dear: let us leave these two young people to themselves for a moment. (BILTON comes from the shed.) I am going to take you through the gun cotton shed.

BILTON (barring the way): You can't take anything explosive in here, sir.

LADY BRITOMART: What do you mean? Are you alluding to me?

BILTON (unmoved): No, ma'am. Mr. Undershaft has the other gentleman's matches in his pocket.

LADY BRITOMART (abruptly): Oh! I beg your pardon. (She goes into the shed.)

UNDERSHAFT: Quite right, Bilton, quite right: here you are. (He gives BILTON the box of matches.) Come, Stephen. Come, Charles. Bring Sarah. (He passes into the shed.)

(BILTON opens the box and deliberately drops the matches into the fire-bucket.)

LOMAX: Oh I say! (BILTON stolidly hands him the empty box.) Infernal nonsense! Pure scientific ignorance! (He goes in.)

SARAH: Am I all right, Bilton?

BILTON: You'll have to put on list slippers, miss: that's all. We've got 'em inside. (She goes in.)

STEPHEN (very seriously to CUSINS): Dolly, old fellow, think. Think before you decide. Do you feel that you are a sufficiently practical man? It is a huge undertaking, an enormous responsibility. All this mass of business will be Greek to you.

CUSINS: Oh, I think it will be much less difficult than Greek.

STEPHEN: Well, I just want to say this before I leave you to yourselves. Don't let anything I have said about right and wrong prejudice you against this great chance in life. I have satisfied myself that the business is one of the highest character and a credit to our country. (Emotionally.) I am very proud of my father. I— (Unable to proceed, he presses CUSINS' hand and goes hastily into the shed, followed by BILTON.)

(BARBARA and CUSINS, left alone together, look at one another silently.)

CUSINS: Barbara: I am going to accept this offer.

BARBARA: I thought you would.

CUSINS: You understand, don't you, that I had to decide without consulting you. If I had thrown the burden of the choice on you, you would sooner or later have despised me for it.

BARBARA: Yes: I did not want you to sell your soul for me any more than for this inheritance.

CUSINS: It is not the sale of my soul that troubles me: I have sold it too often to care about that. I have sold it for a professorship. I have sold it for an income. I have sold it to escape being imprisoned for refusing to pay taxes for hangmen's ropes and unjust wars and things that I abhor. What is all human conduct but the daily and hourly sale of our souls for trifles? What I am now selling it for is neither money nor position nor comfort, but for reality and for power.

BARBARA: You know that you will have no power, and that he has none.

CUSINS: I know. It is not for myself alone. I want to make power for the world.

BARBARA: I want to make power for the world too; but it must be spiritual power.

CUSINS: I think all power is spiritual: these cannons will not go off by themselves. I have tried to make spiritual power by teaching Greek. But the world can never be really touched by a dead language and a dead civilization. The people must have power; and the people cannot have Greek. Now the power that is made here can be wielded by all men.

BARBARA: Power to burn women's houses down and kill their sons and tear their husbands to pieces.

CUSINS: You cannot have power for good without having power for evil too. Even mother's milk nourishes murderers as well as heroes. This power which only tears men's bodies to pieces has never been so horribly abused as the intellectual power, the imaginative power, the poetic, religious power that can enslave men's souls. As a teacher of Greek I gave the intellectual man weapons against the common man. I now want to give the common man weapons against the intellectual man. I love the common people. I want to arm them against the lawyers, the doctors, the priests, the literary men, the professors, the artists, and the politicians, who, once in authority, are more disastrous and tyrannical than all the fools, rascals, and imposters. I want a power simple enough for common men to use, yet strong enough to force the intellectual oligarchy to use its genius for the general good.

BARBARA: Is there no higher power than that? *(Pointing to the shell.)*

CUSINS: Yes; but that power can destroy the higher powers just as a tiger can destroy a man: therefore Man must master that power first. I admitted this when the Turks and Greeks were last at war. My best pupil went out to fight for Hellas. My parting gift to him was not a copy of Plato's *Republic,* but a revolver and a hundred Undershaft cartridges. The blood of every Turk he shot—if he shot any—is on my head as well as on Undershaft's. That act committed me to this place for ever. Your father's challenge has beaten me. Dare I make war on war? I dare. I must. I will. And now, is it all over between us?

BARBARA *(touched by his evident dread of her answer)*: Silly baby Dolly! How could it be!

CUSINS *(overjoyed)*: Then you—you—you—Oh for my drum! *(He flourishes imaginary drumsticks.)*

BARBARA *(angered by his levity)*: Take care, Dolly, take care. Oh, if only I could get away from you and from father and from it all! if I could have the wings of a dove and fly away to heaven!

CUSINS: And leave me!

BARBARA: Yes, you, and all the other naughty mischievous children of men. But I can't. I was happy in the Salvation Army for a moment. I escaped from the world into a paradise of enthusiasm and prayer and soul saving; but the moment our money ran short, it all came back to Bodger: it was he who saved our people: he, and the Prince of Darkness, my papa. Undershaft and Bodger: their hands stretch everywhere: when we feed a starving fellow creature, it is with their bread, because there is no other bread; when we tend the sick, it is in the hospitals they

endow; if we turn from the churches they build, we must kneel on the stones of the streets they pave. As long as that lasts, there is no getting away from them. Turning our backs on Bodger and Undershaft is turning our backs on life.

CUSINS: I thought you were determined to turn your back on the wicked side of life.

BARBARA: There is no wicked side: life is all one. And I never wanted to shirk my share in whatever evil must be endured, whether it be sin or suffering. I wish I could cure you of middle-class ideas, Dolly.

CUSINS *(gasping)*: Middle cl—! A snub! A social snub to me! from the daughter of a foundling!

BARBARA: That is why I have no class, Dolly: I come straight out of the heart of the whole people. If I were middle-class I should turn my back on my father's business; and we should both live in an artistic drawing room, with you reading the reviews in one corner, and I in the other at the piano, playing Schumann: both very superior persons, and neither of us a bit of use. Sooner than that, I would sweep out the guncotton shed, or be one of Bodger's barmaids. Do you know what would have happened if you had refused papa's offer?

CUSINS: I wonder!

BARBARA: I should have given you up and married the man who accepted it. After all, my dear old mother has more sense than any of you. I felt like her when I saw this place—felt that I must have it—that never, never, never, could I let it go; only she thought it was the houses and the kitchen ranges and the linen and china, when it was really all the human souls to be saved: not weak souls in starved bodies, sobbing with gratitude for a scrap of bread and treacle, but fullfed, quarrelsome, snobbish, uppish creatures, all standing on their little rights and dignities, and thinking that my father ought to be greatly obliged to them for making so much money for him—and so he ought. That is where salvation is really wanted. My father shall never throw it in my teeth again that my converts were bribed with bread. *(She is transfigured.)* I have got rid of the bribe of bread. I have got rid of the bribe of heaven. Let God's work be done for its own sake: the work he had to create us to do because it cannot be done except by living men and women. When I die, let him be in my debt, not I in his; and let me forgive him as becomes a woman of my rank.

CUSINS: Then the way of life lies through the factory of death?

BARBARA: Yes, through the raising of hell to heaven and of man to God, through the unveiling of an eternal light in the Valley of The Shadow. *(Seiz-*

ing him with both hands.) Oh, did you think my courage would never come back? did you believe that I was a deserter? that I, who have stood in the streets, and taken my people to my heart, and talked of the holiest and greatest things with them, could ever turn back and chatter foolishly to fashionable people about nothing in a drawing room? Never, never, never, never: Major Barbara will die with the colors. Oh! and I have my dear little Dolly boy still; and he has found me my place and my work. Glory Hallelujah! *(She kisses him.)*

CUSINS: My dearest: consider my delicate health. I cannot stand as much happiness as you can.

BARBARA: Yes: it is not easy work being in love with me, is it? But it's good for you. *(She runs to the shed, and calls, childlike.)* Mamma! Mamma! *(BIL-TON comes out of the shed, followed by* UNDERSHAFT.*)* I want mamma.

UNDERSHAFT: She is taking off her list slippers, dear. *(He passes on to* CUSINS.*)* Well? What does she say?

CUSINS: She has gone right up into the skies.

LADY BRITOMART *(coming from the shed and stopping on the steps, obstructing* SARAH, *who follows with* LOMAX. BARBARA *clutches like a baby at her mother's skirt)*: Barbara: when will you learn to be independent and to act and think for yourself? I know as well as possible what that cry of "Mamma, Mamma," means. Always running to me!

SARAH *(touching* LADY BRITOMART'S *ribs with her finger tips and imitating a bicycle horn)*: Pip! pip!

LADY BRITOMART *(highly indignant)*: How dare you say Pip! pip! to me, Sarah? You are both very naughty children. What do you want, Barbara?

BARBARA: I want a house in the village to live in with Dolly. *(Dragging at the skirt.)* Come and tell me which one to take.

UNDERSHAFT *(to* CUSINS*)*: Six o'clock tomorrow morning, Euripides.

CURTAIN

Figure 1. Undershaft (Brewster Mason) and Lady Britomart (Elizabeth Spriggs) greet one another at the beginning of his visit to meet Sarah (Lisa Harrow) and Barbara (Judi Dench), while Lomax (Michael Gambon, *left*) and Cusins (Richard Pasco, *right*) look on in the Royal Shakespeare Company production of *Major Barbara*, directed by Clifford Williams, London, 1970. (Photograph: Patrick Eagar.)

Figure 2. Cusins (Richard Pasco) offers the tambourine to Barbara (Judi Dench) while Mrs. Baines (Janet Henfrey, *far left*) and Jenny (Juliet Ackroyd) look on in the Royal Shakespeare Company production of *Major Barbara,* directed by Clifford Williams, London, 1970. (Photograph: Patrick Eagar.)

Figure 3. Undershaft (Brewster Mason) lectures Barbara (Judi Dench) about the faith of the armorer, while Sarah (Lisa Harrow) and Lomax (Michael Gambon) look on in the Royal Shakespeare Company production of *Major Barbara,* directed by Clifford Williams, London, 1970. (Photograph: Patrick Eagar.)

Staging of *Major Barbara*

REVIEW OF THE ROYAL SHAKESPEARE
COMPANY PRODUCTION, 1970, BY STANLEY
PRICE

"Through universal education and cheap printing poor boys became rich and powerful. Dickens, rich. Shaw, also. He boasted that reading Karl Marx made a man of him. I don't know about that, but Marxism for the great public made him a millionaire. If you wrote for an élite, like Proust, you did not become rich, but if your theme was social injustice and your ideas radical you were rewarded by wealth, fame and influence."

Thus old Mr Sammler in Saul Bellow's fine recent novel *Mr Sammler's Planet*. Shaw himself would scarcely have taken umbrage. In his preface to *Major Barbara* he quotes with approval Samuel Butler's insistence on the necessity of 'an earnest and constant sense of the importance of money'.

Major Barbara hymns the necessary virtue of money, and castigates the unnecessary vice of poverty. Undershaft, the devil's advocate of benevolent capitalism, who builds the new Jerusalem around an armaments empire in a garden city, lists the seven deadly sins as "food, clothing, firing, rent, taxes, respectability and children. Nothing can lift those seven millstones from man's neck but money, and the spirit cannot soar until the millstones are lifted." Thus, ultimately, Undershaft, destroyer of lives, triumphs over the savers of souls. With the loaded dice of Shavian paradox this is accomplished because Undershaft is a creator and beneficent distributor of wealth, whilst the Salvationists merely exploit the helplessness of poverty: bread and scrape today to gain eternal jam tomorrow.

First produced in 1905, *Major Barbara* remains a remarkably relevant battle-cry to contemporary barricades. The Undershaft motto is "Nothing is ever done in this world until men are prepared to kill one another if it is not done." This is the jingoism of revolution; that we must make war in order to make love. It is a far cry from the gradualism of Shaw's Fabian contemporaries, or the ineffectuality of much current youthful protest. In the Preface, Shaw further comments on the deserved powerlessness of society's prisons, punishments and bayonets against the dedicated self-sacrifice of one anarchist acting out of outraged conscience. Shaw's remedy is "simply not to outrage their consciences." The play's contemporary aptness leaves one, 65 years on, speculating on Shaw's probable attitudes to student militancy, hijacking, and the sale of arms to South Africa. Would Shaw have been another Russell, lifted deferentially from a squat in Whitehall? Or merely another Boss/Brecht manufacturing bon-mots while hippy Plebeians rehearsed their uprising, and his idealised Undershafts showed their feet of clay in the face of Russian naval menace in the Indian Ocean.

As possibly befits both this contemporary relevance and the Royal Shakespeare Company's first Shaw play, Clifford Williams' production gives priority to the words and arguments. He has not been lured into reducing the full-scale of the big Aldwych stage to drawing-room proportions, the normal procedure for productions trying to imply that there is more action going on in a Shaw play than there really is. This principle seems based on the theory that actors doing nothing in a confined space appear busier than actors doing nothing in a large space. And it is interesting to note that Ralph Koltai's set is conceived vertically—actors ascend and descend rather than exit left and right.

The play begins on the large, empty stage beneath a huge banner of Karl Marx—fair warning about the production's prime concern. Stage hands in Edwardian disguise move on the f & f of Lady Britomart's library, mere token furnishings in the large unoccupied areas. The Salvation Army hostel scene is played out in an area vast as an aeroplane hangar. The effect initially seems to dwarf the characters, yet ultimately manages to focus maximum attention on what they are saying. The cast copes magnificently with the wide-open spaces by the uniform excellence of their diction, intelligence and movement.

Brewster Mason's Undershaft is a model of intelligent concise playing. Every seemingly cynical word seems mined and minted from years of hard experience, at the same time advancing heavyweight argument with the agility of a featherweight. Elizabeth Spriggs makes Lady Britomart a sharp-tongued Elizabethan battleaxe without ever descending into caricature. Lady Britomart's barbed intelligence enables her to ask all the questions, while her secure upper-class poise allows her to ignore anybody else's answers. These are two splendidly matching performances at the core of the play, ably abetted by a delightfully spry tour-de-force from Richard Pasco as the intellectually chameleon Adolphus Cusins. Peering quizzically over rimless spectacles, he keeps one constantly guessing whether he is driven from Academia through Salvationism into tycoonery by his search for love, truth or plain intellectual survival.

The excellence of these leads is matched by some fine supporting playing from Roger Rees, Michael Gambon, Don Henderson, Milton Johns and Miles Anderson.

Always I come to Shaw's heroines with acute misgivings. Major Barbara herself seems perched uneasily between that awful pertness that Shaw offered as feminism in *Man and Superman* and the lighter comedies, and the almost hockey-playing saintliness that reached its apotheosis in *Saint Joan.* Judi Dench may have seemed the perfect answer to the problem. There has always been an openness and wholesomeness about her playing that is made dramatic by a quality of vulnerability. As Barbara, however, she tends to emphasize the more embarrassingly self-conscious moments of the Major's missionary zeal. Shaw was fascinated by people who were motivated by passion, especially religious passion. Judi Dench plays Barbara as a tomboy who chose the Church rather than the Hunt, and somewhere the passion and fascination are lost. I would suggest it was more Shaw's fault than Miss Dench's if I did not still have a glowing memory of Wendy Hiller in the old film to make me eat my words.

Mr Sammler's critique of rich, radical Mr Shaw ends with "I have an objection to extended explanations. There are too many. This makes the mental life of mankind ungovernable. . . . It is not as if I were certain that human beings can be controlled at any level of complexity. I would not swear that mankind was governable." Sammler is an old-world survivalist who has seen and despaired of the New World. Shaw, for all his anti-religious protest, was a salvationist at heart. He wanted salvation now rather than later—"Let God's work be done for its own sake." The Aldwych's excellent production gives full measure to Shaw's plea for benevolence and salvation as the worthy end, whatever the means of the revolution that has to come.

LUIGI PIRANDELLO

1867–1936

Pirandello's life was in many respects as problematic as the existence of the characters in his plays, and he playfully acknowledged its confusion by declaring himself to be "the son of Chaos." His father was actually the owner of a lucrative sulfur mine, and Pirandello was born on his father's country estate in a southern Sicilian locale, whose name was derived from the Greek word, chaos. Although his father had intended him to have a career in business, Pirandello was already writing poetry by the time he was sixteen, and when he was eighteen, having failed in a brief business venture, his father sent him off to the University of Rome. He subsequently attended the University of Bonn, where in 1891 he earned a doctorate in philology, but instead of pursuing a career in teaching and research he returned to Rome and immersed himself in writing poetry and fiction. By 1894, he had already published two volumes of poetry and a collection of short stories. Also in 1894, he was married off in an arrangement negotiated by his father and another sulfur-mine owner who wanted to unite their business interests. For its first ten years, the marriage was evidently a happy one, supported by the substantial wealth of both sets of parents, but in 1904 both sulfur mines were destroyed by a flood. The news of this disaster was so shocking to Pirandello's wife that she fainted on hearing it, was subsequently completely paralyzed for six months, and then gradually went insane. Pirandello was forced to take a position teaching literature at a girl's school, an arrangement that provoked his wife to have hysterical fits of jealousy. Her derangement repeatedly caused her to become physically violent, yet Pirandello persisted in taking care of her himself for fifteen years, until in 1919 his friends finally convinced him to have her committed to a mental institution.

Pirandello continued to write during all the years of living through his wife's insanity and through the insanity of World War I, which divided his allegiances between Germany, a country he admired for its learning and scholarship, and Italy, his own country, which entered the conflict in 1916 on the side of the English and French. By 1916, he had published several volumes of short stories, several novels, several collections of poetry, and three one-act plays, and in virtually all these works he expressed a relativistic view of existence that he appears to have been driven to by the chaotic nature of his own personal experience. In his most well-known novel, *The Late Mattia Pascal* (1905), for example, he told the story of a man who discovers that because he left some belongings on a bridge everyone thinks he has committed suicide. Having made this discovery, the man decides to capitalize on the misunderstanding by trying to start a new life, free of the deceptions and role-playing that had characterized his old one. But he at once realizes that he must take a new role, in order to prevent his earlier identity from being discovered, and thus gradually recognizes that his personality is not his own creation, but an appearance forced on him by what is expected in his own society.

The predicament of Mattia Pascal epitomizes Pirandello's persistent concerns: the inescapable compulsion of human beings to play roles, to assume so many guises, in fact, that they can never be certain even of their own personal character, much less that of anyone else they encounter in the world. Pirandello explicitly defined his concern with these problems in 1920, shortly before the appearance of *Six Characters in Search of an Author* (1922):

> I think that life is a very sad piece of buffoonery: because we have in ourselves, without being able to know why, wherefore or whence, the need to deceive ourselves constantly by creating a reality (one for each and never the same for all), which from time to time is discovered to be vain and illusory.

The vanity and the illusoriness of this "buffoonery" provided Pirandello with the grounds for all of his writing:

> My art is full of bitter compassion for all those who deceive themselves; but this compassion cannot fail to be followed by the ferocious derision of destiny which condemns man to deception.

His "bitter compassion," fed by the irrationality of the war, evidently moved him to turn to playwriting, for between 1916 and 1921 in a fury of productivity he produced a total of fifteen plays.

Pirandello dramatized his relativistic vision most explicitly in a play appropriately titled *Right You Are, If You Think You Are* (1917), which depicts the futile attempts of an Italian community to unravel the truth about a husband, his wife, and his mother-in-law who have come to live in their city. The mother-in-law, for example, tells one story about their situation, which is subsequently contradicted by that of the husband, who appears to demonstrate that his mother-in-law is insane, but his version of their situation is, in turn, discredited by another story from his mother-in-law that appears to prove that he is a madman, and the action of the play repeatedly complicates the problem of determining the truth about the family without ever resolving it. As the wife (who appears only at the end of the play) says, "I am the one that each of you thinks I am." Truth is thus presented to be as unstable, as variable, as the differing perceptions of every member in the community. The maddening implications of this vision were dramatized by Pirandello in *Enrico IV* (1922), a play that portrays the schizophrenic experience of a man who recovers from a long psychotic delusion about himself only to perpetuate his madness as a deliberate pose. But at the end of the play, his deliberate choice turns into an eternal necessity, when he kills a man who has accused him of being sane and finds that in order to escape a charge of murder he must retreat forever into the role of being a madman.

By the end of his life, Pirandello had dramatized his haunting view of existence in nearly forty plays, but none of them achieved the enduring fame of *Six Characters in Search of an Author* (1922). Its unique dramatic power is in large part the result of Pirandello's reclaiming of a traditional dramatic form—the play within the play—and a traditional dramatic metaphor for the vanity of existence—"Life's but . . . a poor player that struts and frets his hour upon the stage and then is heard no more." Pirandello has used these traditional elements to present his relativistic vision in its most disturbingly complicated form. From the moment the six characters appear on stage seeking an author to tell their story and a producer to dramatize their experience, Pirandello gradually unfolds the dizzying ramifications of his relativistic view: in the Father's repeated explanations of it that the Producer repeatedly denies even in the face of the hopeless confusion unfolding before him, in the repeated attempts of the Stepdaughter to have the story played from her perspective that the Father repeatedly claims to be a distortion of his true character, in the almost inarticulate desire of the Mother to have her older son express the affection and forgiveness that she feels is warranted from her point of view, in the Son's attempt to proclaim his lack of complicity in the gruesome tragedy despite being one of the villains of the piece, and, of course, in the inability of any of the characters or actors to understand each other at all. The play moves inexorably to its final frenzy of yelling, one side shouting "Reality!" the other "Make-believe!" And Pirandello's symbolic comment on this confusion is to plunge the theater into darkness, so that even the Producer, so staunchly sure of the truth, cannot see where he is going. Although the play is clearly an enactment of Pirandello's relativistic philosophy, it may also be seen as dramatizing the problematic relationship between art and life, between performance and exis-tence. The characters' search for an author may also be viewed as a compelling psychological study of the anxiety—even the schizophrenia—that results from the felt absence of a stable authority figure. Even the Father, the traditional image of authority, is seeking a reliable source of authority, but the only authority figure in the play, the Producer, is equally unreliable.

When *Six Characters* was first produced in Rome, the audience turned into a madhouse of excitement at the end of the play. When it was produced in Paris in 1923, it stunned the French theatrical world and led to a torrent of dramatic imitations. Wherever and whenever it is produced, in fact, it provokes the ex-citement of audiences and critics, as evidenced by the review of the American Conservatory Theater production, reprinted following the text. Photographs of that production clearly show the haunting expressions and gestures the per-formers displayed in acting the roles of the six characters (see Figures 1 and 2) as well as the outrage of the Stepdaughter at the moment the Father is attempt-ing to seduce her (Figure 3), a moment epitomizing Pirandello's disturbing view of experience.

SIX CHARACTERS IN SEARCH OF AN AUTHOR

BY LUIGI PIRANDELLO / TRANSLATED BY FREDERICK MAY

CHARACTERS OF THE PLAY IN THE MAKING

THE FATHER
THE MOTHER
THE STEPDAUGHTER
THE SON
THE BOY (nonspeaking)
THE LITTLE GIRL (nonspeaking)
MADAME PACE (who is called into being)

THE ACTORS IN THE COMPANY

THE PRODUCER (Director)
THE LEADING LADY
THE LEADING MAN
THE SECOND FEMALE LEAD (referred to as THE SECOND
ACTRESS in the text.)
THE INGENUE
THE JUVENILE LEAD
OTHER ACTORS AND ACTRESSES

THE STAGE MANAGER
THE PROMPTER
THE PROPERTY MAN
THE FOREMAN OF THE STAGE CREW
THE PRODUCER'S SECRETARY
THE COMMISSIONAIRE
STAGE HANDS AND OTHER THEATRE PERSONNEL

SCENE

Daytime: The Stage of a Theatre

N.B. The play has neither acts nor scenes. Its performance will be interrupted twice: once—though the curtain will not be lowered—when the PRODUCER and the principal CHARACTERS go away to write the script and the ACTORS leave the stage, and a second time when the Man on the Curtain lets it fall by mistake.

ACT 1

(When the audience enters the auditorium the curtain is up and the stage is just as it would be during the daytime. There is no set and there are no wings; it is empty and in almost total darkness. This is in order that right from the very beginning the audience shall receive the impression of being present, not at a performance of a carefully rehearsed play, but at a performance of a play that suddenly happens.

Two small flights of steps, one right and one left, give access to the stage from the auditorium.

On the stage itself, the prompter's dome has been removed, and is standing just to one side of the prompt box.

Downstage, on the other side, a small table and an armchair with its back turned to the audience have been set for the Producer.

Two more small tables, one rather larger than the other, together with several chairs, have been set downstage so that they are ready if needed for the rehearsal. There are other chairs scattered about to the left and to the right for the actors, and, in the background, to one side and almost hidden, there is a pianoforte.

When the house lights go down the FOREMAN comes on to the stage through the back door. He is dressed in blue dungarees and carries his tools in a bag slung at his belt. From a corner at the back of the stage he takes one or two

slats of wood, brings them down front, kneels down and starts nailing them together. At the sound of his hammer the STAGE MANAGER rushes in from the direction of the dressing-rooms.)

STAGE MANAGER: Hey! What are you doing?

FOREMAN: What am I doing? Hammering . . . nails.

STAGE MANAGER: At this time of day? *(He looks at his watch.)* It's gone half-past ten! The Producer'll be here any minute now and he'll want to get on with his rehearsal.

FOREMAN: And let me tell *you* something . . . I've got to have time to do *my* work, too.

STAGE MANAGER: You'll get it, you'll get it. . . . But you can't do that *now*.

FOREMAN: When can I do it then?

STAGE MANAGER: After the rehearsal. Now, come on. . . . Clear up all this mess, and let me get on with setting the second act of *The Game As He Played It*.

(The FOREMAN gathers his pieces of wood together, muttering and grumbling all the while, and goes off. Meanwhile, the ACTORS OF THE COMPANY have begun to come on to the stage through the door back. First one comes in, then another, then two together . . . just as they please. There are nine or ten of them in all–as many as you would suppose you would need for the rehearsal of Pirandello's play, The Game As He Played It, which

has been called for today. As they come in they greet one another and the STAGE MANAGER *with a cheery 'Good morning'. Some of them go off to their dressing-rooms; others, and among them the* PROMPTER, *who is carrying the prompt copy rolled up under his arm, remain on the stage, waiting for the* PRODUCER *to come and start the rehearsal. While they are waiting—some of them standing, some seated about in small groups—they exchange a few words among themselves. One lights a cigarette, another complains about the part that he's been given and a third reads out an item of news from a theatrical journal for the benefit of the other actors. It would be best if all the* ACTORS *and* ACTRESSES *could be dressed in rather bright and gay clothes. This first improvised scene should be played very naturally and with great vivacity. After a while, one of the comedy men can sit down at the piano and start playing a dance-tune. The younger* ACTORS *and* ACTRESSES *start dancing.)*

STAGE MANAGER *(clapping his hands to restore order)*: Come on, now, come on! That's enough of that! Here's the producer!

(The music and dancing come to a sudden stop. The ACTORS *turn and look out into the auditorium and see the* PRODUCER, *who is coming in through the door. He comes up the gangway between the stalls, bowler hat on head, stick under arm, and a large cigar in his mouth, to the accompaniment of a chorus of 'Good-mornings' from the* ACTORS *and climbs up one of the flights of steps on to the stage. His* SECRETARY *offers him his post—a newspaper or so, a script.)*

PRODUCER: Any letters?

SECRETARY: None at all. This is all the post there is.

PRODUCER *(handing him back the script)*: Put it in my office. *(Then, looking around and turning to the* STAGE MANAGER.*)* Oh, you can't see a thing here! Ask them to give us a spot of light, please.

STAGE MANAGER: Right you are!

(He goes off to give the order and a short while after the whole of the right side of the stage, where the ACTORS *are standing, is lit up by a bright white light. In the meantime the* PROMPTER *has taken his place in his box, switched on his light and spread his script out in front of him.)*

PRODUCER *(clapping his hands)*: Come on, let's get started! *(to the* STAGE MANAGER*)* Anyone missing?

STAGE MANAGER: The Leading Lady.

PRODUCER: As usual! *(Looks at his watch.)* We're ten minutes late already. Make a note, will you, please, to remind me to give her a good talking-to about being so late! It might teach her to get to rehearsals on time in the future.

(He has scarcely finished his rebuke when the voice of the LEADING LADY *is heard at the back of the auditorium.)*

LEADING LADY: No, please don't! Here I am! Here I am! *(She is dressed completely in white, with a large and rather dashing and provocative hat, and is carrying a dainty little lap-dog. She runs down the aisle and hastily climbs up the steps on to the stage.)*

PRODUCER: You've set your heart on always keeping us waiting, haven't you?

LEADING LADY: Forgive me! I hunted everywhere for a taxi so that I should get here on time! But you haven't started yet, anyway. And I don't come on immediately. *(Then, calling the* STAGE MANAGER *by name, she gives him the lap-dog.)* Please put him in my dressing-room . . . and mind you shut the door!

PRODUCER *(grumblingly)*: And she has to bring a dog along too! As if there weren't enough dogs around here! *(He claps his hands again and turns to the* PROMPTER.*)* Come on now, let's get on with Act II of *The Game As He Played It.* *(He sits down in the armchair.)* Now, ladies and gentlemen, who's on?

(The ACTORS *and* ACTRESSES *clear away from the front of the stage and go and sit to one side, except for the three who start the scene, and the* LEADING LADY. *She has paid no attention to the* PRODUCER'S *question and has seated herself at one of the little tables.)*

PRODUCER *(to the* LEADING LADY*)*: Ah! So you're in this scene, are you?

LEADING LADY: Me? Oh, no!

PRODUCER *(annoyed)*: Then for God's sake get off!

(And the LEADING LADY *gets up and goes and sits with the others.)*

PRODUCER *(to the* PROMPTER*)*: Now, let's get started!

PROMPTER *(reading from his script)*: "The house of Leone Gala. A strange room, half dining-room, half study."

PRODUCER *(turning to the* STAGE MANAGER*)*: We'll use the red set.

STAGE MANAGER *(making a note on a sheet of paper)*: The red set. Right!

PROMPTER *(continuing to read from his script)*: "A table laid for a meal and a desk with books and papers. Bookshelves with books on them. Glass-fronted cupboards containing valuable china. A door back leading into Leone's bedroom. A side door left, leading into the kitchen. The main entrance is right."

PRODUCER *(getting up and pointing)*: Right! Now listen carefully—over there, the main entrance. And over here, the kitchen. *(Turning to the* ACTOR *who is to play the part of Socrates.)* You'll make your entrances and exits this side. *(to the* STAGE MANAGER*)* We'll have that green-baize door at the back there . . . and some curtains. *(He goes and sits down again.)*

STAGE MANAGER *(making a note)*: Right you are!

PROMPTER (reading): "Scene I. Leone Gala, Guido Venanzi, Filippo, who is called Socrates." (to the PRODUCER) Do I have to read the stage directions as well?

PRODUCER: Yes, yes, of course! I've told you that a hundred times!

PROMPTER (reading): "When the curtain rises. Leone Gala, wearing a cook's hat and apron, is busy beating an egg in a basin, with a wooden spoon. Filippo, also dressed as a cook, is beating another egg. Guido Venanzi is sitting listening to them."

LEADING MAN (to the PRODUCER): Excuse me, but do I really have to wear a cook's hat?

PRODUCER (irritated by this observation): So it seems! That's certainly what's written there! (He points to the script.)

LEADING MAN: Forgive me for saying so, but it's ridiculous.

PRODUCER (bounding to feet in fury): Ridiculous! Ridiculous! What do you expect me to do if the French haven't got any more good comedies to send us, and we're reduced to putting on plays by Pirandello? And if you can understand his plays . . . you're a better man than I am! He deliberately goes out of his way to annoy people, so that by the time the play's through everybody's fed up . . . actors, critics, audience, everybody! (The ACTORS laugh. Then getting up and going over to the LEADING MAN, the PRODUCER cries.) Yes, my dear fellow, a cook's hat! And you beat eggs! And do you think that, having these eggs to beat, you then have nothing more on your hands? Oh, no, not a bit of it. . . . You have to represent the shell of the eggs that you're beating! (The ACTORS start laughing again and begin to make ironical comments among themselves.) Shut up! And listen when I'm explaining things! (Turning again to the LEADING MAN.) Yes, my dear fellow, the shell . . . or, as you might say, the empty form of reason, without that content of instinct which is blind! You are reason and your wife is instinct, in a game where you play the parts which have been given you. And all the time you're playing your part, you are the self-willed puppet of yourself. Understand?

LEADING MAN (spreading out his hands): Me? No!

PRODUCER (returning to his seat): Neither do I! However, let's get on with it! It's going to be a wonderful flop, anyway! (In a confidential tone.) I suggest you turn to the audience a bit more . . . about three-quarters face. Otherwise, what with the abstruseness of the dialogue, and the audience's not being able to hear you, the whole thing'll go to hell. (Clapping his hands again.) Now, come along! Come along! Let's get started!

PROMPTER: Excuse me, sir, do you mind if I put the top back on my box? There's a bit of a draught.

PRODUCER: Of course! Go ahead! Go ahead!

(Meanwhile the COMMISSIONAIRE has entered the auditorium. He is wearing a braided cap and, having covered the length of the aisle, he comes up to the edge of the stage to announce the arrival of the SIX CHARACTERS to the PRODUCER. They have followed the COMMISSIONAIRE into the auditorium and have walked behind him as he has come up to the stage. They look about them, a little perplexed and a little dismayed.

In any production of this play it is imperative that the producer should use every means possible to avoid any confusion between the SIX CHARACTERS and the ACTORS. The placing of the two groups, as they will be indicated in the stage-directions once the CHARACTERS are on the stage, will no doubt help. So, too, will their being lit in different colors. But the most effective and most suitable method of distinguishing them that suggests itself, is the use of special masks for the CHARACTERS, masks specially made from some material which will not grow limp with perspiration and will at the same time be light enough to be worn by the actors playing these parts. They should be cut so as to leave the eyes, the nose and the mouth free. In this way the deep significance of the play can be brought out. The CHARACTERS should not, in fact, appear as phantasms, but as created realities, unchangeable creations of the imagination and, therefore, more real and more consistent than the ever-changing naturalness of the ACTORS.

The masks will assist in giving the impression of figures constructed by art, each one fixed immutably in the expression of that sentiment which is fundamental to it. That is to say in REMORSE for the FATHER, REVENGE for the STEPDAUGHTER, CONTEMPT for the SON and SORROW for the MOTHER. Her mask should have wax tears fixed in the corners of the eyes and coursing down the cheeks, just like those which are carved and painted in the representations of the Mater Dolorosa that are to be seen in churches.

Her dress, too, should be of a special material and cut. It should be severely plain, its folds stiff, giving in fact the appearance of having been carved, and not of being made of any material that you can just go out and buy or have cut-out and made up into a dress by any ordinary dressmaker.

The FATHER is a man of about fifty. He is not bald but his reddish hair is thin at the temples. His moustache is thick and coils over his still rather youthful-looking mouth, which all too often falls open in a purposeless, uncertain smile. His complexion is pale and this is especially noticeable when one has occasion to look at his forehead, which is particularly broad. His blue, oval-shaped eyes are very clear and piercing. He is wearing a dark jacket and light-coloured trousers. At times his manner is all sweetness and light, at others it is hard and harsh.

The MOTHER appears as a woman crushed and ter-

rified by an intolerable weight of shame and abasement. She is dressed in a modest black and wears a thick crepe widow's veil. When she lifts her veil she reveals a wax-like face; it is not, however at all sickly looking. She keeps her eyes downcast all the time. The STEPDAUGHTER, *who is eighteen, is defiant, bold, arrogant—almost shamelessly so. She is very beautiful. She, too, is dressed in mourning but carries it with a decided air of showy elegance. She shows contempt for the very timid, dejected, half-frightened manner of her younger brother, a rather grubby and unprepossessing* BOY *of fourteen, who is also dressed in black. On the other hand she displays a very lively tenderness for her small sister, a* LITTLE GIRL *of about four, who is wearing a white frock with a black silk sash round her waist.*

The SON *is a tall young man of twenty-two. He is wearing a mauve-coloured overcoat and has a long green scarf twisted round his neck. He appears as if he has stiffened into an attitude of contempt for the* FATHER *and of supercilious indifference toward the* MOTHER.)

COMMISSIONAIRE (*cap in hand*): Excuse me, sir.

PRODUCER (*snapping at him rudely*): Now what's the matter?

COMMISSIONAIRE: There are some people here, sir, asking for you.

(*The* PRODUCER *and the* ACTORS *turn in astonishment and look out into the auditorium.*)

PRODUCER (*furiously*): But I've got a rehearsal on at the moment! And you know quite well that no one's allowed in here while a rehearsal's going on. (*Then addressing the* CHARACTERS.) Who are you? What do you want?

FATHER (*he steps forward, followed by the others, and comes to the foot of one of the flights of steps*): We are here in search of an author.

PRODUCER (*caught between anger and utter astonishment*): In search of an author? Which author?

FATHER: Any author, sir.

PRODUCER: But there's no author here. . . . We're rehearsing a new play.

STEPDAUGHTER (*vivaciously, as she rushes up the steps*): So much the better! Then so much the better, sir! We can be your new play.

ONE OF THE ACTORS (*amidst the lively comments and laughter of the others*): Oh, just listen to her! *Listen* to her!

FATHER (*following the* STEPDAUGHTER *on to the stage*): Yes, but if there isn't any author. . . . (*to the* PRODUCER) Unless you'd like to be the author. . . .

(*Holding the* LITTLE GIRL *by the hand, the* MOTHER, *followed by the* BOY, *climbs up the first steps leading to the stage and stands there expectantly. The* SON *remains morosely below.*)

PRODUCER: Are you people trying to be funny?

FATHER: No. . . . How can you suggest such a thing? On the contrary, we are bringing you a terrible and grievous drama.

STEPDAUGHTER: And we might make your fortune for you.

PRODUCER: Perhaps you'll do me the kindness of getting out of this theatre! We've got no time to waste on lunatics!

FATHER (*he is wounded by this, but replies in a gentle tone*): Oh . . . But you know very well, don't you, that life is full of things that are infinitely absurd, things that, for all their impudent absurdity, have no need to masquerade as truth, because they are true.

PRODUCER: What the devil are you talking about?

FATHER: What I'm saying is that reversing the usual order of things, forcing oneself to a contrary way of action, may well be construed as madness. As, for instance, when we create things which have all the appearance of reality in order that they shall look like the realities themselves. But allow me to observe that if this indeed be madness, it is, nonetheless, the sole *raison d'etre* of your profession.

(*The* ACTORS *stir indignantly at this.*)

PRODUCER (*getting up and looking him up and down*): Oh, yes? do you think ours is a profession of lunatics, do you?

FATHER: Yes, making what isn't true *seem* true . . . without having to . . . for fun. . . . Isn't it your function to give life on the stage to imaginary characters?

PRODUCER (*immediately, making himself spokesman for the growing anger of his actors*): I should like you to know, my dear sir, that the actor's profession is a most noble one. and although nowadays, with things in the state they are, our playwrights give us stupid comedies to act, and puppets to represent instead of men, I'd have you know that it is our boast that we have given life, here on these very boards, to immortal works!

(*The* ACTORS *satisfiedly murmur their approval and applaud the* PRODUCER.)

FATHER (*breaking in and following hard on his argument*): There you are! Oh, that's it exactly! To living beings . . . to beings who are more alive than those who breathe and wear clothes! Less real, perhaps, but truer! We're in complete agreement!

(*The* ACTORS *look at each other in utter astonishment.*)

PRODUCER: But . . . What on earth! . . . But you said just now . . .

FATHER: No, I said that because of your . . . because

you shouted at us that you had no time to waste on lunatics . . . while nobody can know better than you that nature makes use of the instrument of human fantasy to pursue her work of creation on a higher level.

PRODUCER: True enough! True enough! But where does all this get us?

FATHER: Nowhere. I only wish to show you that one is born into life in so many ways, in so many forms. . . . As a tree, or as a stone; as water or as a butterfly. . . . Or as a woman. And that one can be born a character.

PRODUCER (ironically, feigning amazement): And you together with these other people, were born a character?

FATHER: Exactly. And alive, as you see. (The PRODUCER and the ACTORS burst out laughing as if at some huge joke.) (Hurt.) I'm sorry that you laugh like that because, I repeat, we carry within ourselves a terrible and grievous drama, as you can deduce for yourselves from this woman veiled in black.

(And so saying, he holds out his hand to the MOTHER and helps her up the last few steps and, continuing to hold her hand, leads her with a certain tragic solemnity to the other side of the stage, which immediately lights up with a fantastic kind of light. The LITTLE GIRL and the BOY follow their MOTHER. Next the SON comes up and goes and stands to one side, in the background. Then the STEPDAUGHTER follows him on to the stage; she stands downstage, leaning against the proscenium arch. The ACTORS are at first completely taken-aback and then, caught in admiration at this development, they burst into applause—just as if they had had a show put on for their benefit.)

PRODUCER (at first utterly astonished and then indignant): Shut up! what the . . . ! (Then turning to the CHARACTERS.) And you get out of here! Clear out of here! (to the STAGE MANAGER) For God's sake, clear them out!

STAGE MANAGER (coming forward, but then stopping as if held back by some strange dismay): Go away! Go away!

FATHER (to the PRODUCER): No, no! Listen. . . . We. . . .

PRODUCER (shouting): I tell you, we've got work to do!

LEADING MAN: You can't go about playing practical jokes like this. . . .

FATHER (resolutely coming forward): I wonder at your incredulity. Is it perhaps that you're not accustomed to seeing the characters created by an author leaping to life up here on the stage, when they come face to face with each other? Or is it, perhaps, that there's no script there (He points to the prompt box.) that contains us?

STEPDAUGHTER (smiling, she steps toward the PRODUCER; then, in a wheedling voice): Believe me, sir, we really are six characters . . . and very, very interesting! But we've been cut adrift.

FATHER (brushing her aside): Yes, that's it, we've been cut adrift. (And then immediately to the PRODUCER.) In the sense, you understand, that the author who created us as living beings, either couldn't or wouldn't put us materially into the world of art. And it was truly a crime . . . because he who has the good fortune to be born a living character may snap his fingers at Death even. He will never die! Man . . . The writer . . . The instrument of creation . . . Will die. . . . But what is created by him will never die. And in order to live eternally he has not the slightest need of extraordinary gifts or of accomplishing prodigies. Who was Sancho Panza? Who was Don Abbondio? And yet they live eternally because—living seeds—they had the good fortune to find a fruitful womb—a fantasy which knew how to raise and nourish them, and to make them live through all eternity.

PRODUCER: All this is very, very fine indeed. . . . But what do you want here?

FATHER: We wish to live, sir!

PRODUCER (ironically): Through all eternity?

FATHER: No sir; just a moment . . . in you.

AN ACTOR: Listen to him! . . . listen to him!

LEADING LADY: They want to live in us!

JUVENILE LEAD (pointing to the STEPDAUGHTER): I've no objection . . . so long as I get her.

FATHER: Listen! Listen! The play is in the making. (to the PRODUCER) But if you and your actors are willing, we can settle it all between us without further delay.

PRODUCER (annoyed): But what do you want to settle? We don't go in for that sort of concoction here! We put on comedies and dramas here.

FATHER: Exactly! That's the very reason why we came to you.

PRODUCER: And where's the script?

FATHER: It is in us, sir. (The ACTORS laugh.) The drama is in us. We are the drama and we are impatient to act it—so fiercely does our inner passion urge us on.

STEPDAUGHTER (scornful, treacherous, alluring, with deliberate shamelessness): My passion. . . . If you only knew! My passion . . . for him! (She points to the FATHER and makes as if to embrace him, but then bursts into strident laughter.)

FATHER (at once, angrily): You keep out of this for the moment! And please don't laugh like that!

STEPDAUGHTER: Oh . . . mayn't I? Then perhaps you'll allow me, ladies and gentlemen. . . . Although it's scarcely two months since my father died . . . just you watch how I can dance and sing! (Mischievously she starts to sing Dave Stamper's

"Prends garde à Tchou-Tchin-Tchou" in the fox-trot or slow one-step version by Francois Salabert. She sings the first verse, accompanying it with a dance.)

Les chinois sont un peuple malin,
De Shangai à Pékin,
Ils ont mis des écriteaux partout:
Prenez garde à Tchou-Tchin-Tchou!

(While she is singing and dancing, the ACTORS, *and especially the younger ones, as if attracted by some strange fascination, move toward her and half raise their hands as though to catch hold of her. She runs away, and when the* ACTORS *burst into applause, and the* PRODUCER *rebukes her, she stands where she is, quietly, abstractedly, and as if her thoughts were far away.)*

ACTORS *and* ACTRESSES *(laughing and clapping)*: Well done! Jolly good!

PRODUCER *(irately)*: Shut up! What do you think this is . . . a cabaret? *(Then taking the* FATHER *a little to one side, he says with a certain amount of consternation.)* Tell me something. . . . Is she mad?

FATHER: What do you mean, mad? It's worse than that!

STEPDAUGHTER *(immediately rushing up to the* PRODUCER*)*: Worse! Worse! Oh it's something very much worse than that! Listen! Let's put this drama on at once . . . Please! Then you'll see that at a certain moment I . . . when this little darling here. . . . *(Takes the* LITTLE GIRL *by the hand and brings her over to the* PRODUCER.*)* . . . Isn't she a dear? *(Takes her in her arms and kisses her.)* You little darling! . . . You dear little darling! *(Puts her down again, adding in a moved tone, almost without wishing to.)* Well, when God suddenly takes this child away from her poor mother, and that little imbecile there *(Roughly grabbing hold of the* BOY *by the sleeve and thrusting him forward.)* does the stupidest of all stupid things, like the idiot he is *(Pushing him back toward the* MOTHER.*)* . . . Then you will see me run away. Yes, I shall run away! And, oh, how I'm longing for that moment to come! Because after all the very intimate things that have happened between him and me *(With a horrible wink in the direction of the* FATHER.*)* I can't remain any longer with these people . . . having to witness my mother's anguish because of that queer fish there *(Pointing to the* SON.*)* Look at him! Look at him! See how indifferent, how frigid he is . . . because he's the legitimate son . . . *he* is! He despises me, he despises him *(Pointing to the* BOY.*)*, he despises that dear little creature. . . . Because we're bastards! Do you understand? . . . Because we're *bastards!* *(She goes up to the* MOTHER *and embraces her.)* And he doesn't want to recog-

nize this poor woman as his mother. . . . This poor woman . . . who is the mother of us all! He looks down at her as if she were only the mother of us three bastards! The wretch! *(She says all this very quickly and very excitedly. She raises her voice at the word 'bastards' and the final "wretch" is delivered in a low voice and almost spat out.)*

MOTHER *(to the* PRODUCER, *an infinity of anguish in her voice)*: Please, in the name of these two little children . . . I beg you. . . . *(She grows faint and sways on her feet.)* Oh, my God! *(Consternation and bewilderment among the* ACTORS.*)*

FATHER *(rushing over to support her, accompanied by most of the* ACTORS*)*: Quick . . . a chair. . . . A chair for this poor widow!

ACTORS *(rushing over)*: Has she fainted? Has she fainted?

PRODUCER: Quick, get a chair . . . get a chair!

(One of the ACTORS *brings a chair, the others stand around, anxious to help in any way they can. The* MOTHER *sits on the chair; she attempts to prevent the* FATHER *from lifting the veil which hides her face.)*

FATHER: Look at her. . . . Look at her. . . .

MOTHER: No, no! My God! Stop it, please!

FATHER: Let them see you. *(He lifts her veil.)*

MOTHER *(rising and covering her face with her hands in desperation)*: I beg you, sir, . . . Don't let this man carry out his plan! You must prevent him. . . . It's horrible!

PRODUCER *(utterly dumbfounded)*: I don't get this at all. . . . I haven't got the slightest idea what you're talking about. *(to the* FATHER*)* Is this lady your wife?

FATHER *(immediately)*: Yes, sir, my wife.

PRODUCER: Then how does it come about that she's a widow if you're still alive?

(The ACTORS *find relief for their bewilderment and astonishment in a noisy burst of laughter.)*

FATHER *(wounded, speaking with sharp resentment)*: Don't laugh! Don't laugh like that, for pity's sake! It is in this fact that her drama lies. She had another man. Another man who ought to be here.

MOTHER *(with a cry)*: No! No!

STEPDAUGHTER: He's got the good luck to be dead. . . . He died two months ago, as I just told you. We're still wearing mourning for him, as you can see.

FATHER: But it's not because he's dead that he's not here. No, he's not here because . . . Look at her! Look at her, please, and you'll understand immediately! Her drama does not lie in the love of two men for whom she, being incapable of love, could feel nothing. . . . Unless, perhaps, it be a little gratitude . . . to him, not to me. She is not a woman. . . . She is a mother. And her drama. . . . And how powerful it is! How powerful it is! . . . Her drama lies entirely, in fact, in these four children . . . The children of the two men that she had.

MOTHER: Did you say that I had them? Do you dare to say that I *had* these two men . . . to suggest that I wanted them? *(to the* PRODUCER*)* It was his doing. He gave him to me! He forced him on me! He forced me. . . . He forced me to go away with that other man!

STEPDAUGHTER *(at once, indignantly)*: It's not true!

MOTHER *(startled)*: Not true?

STEPDAUGHTER: It's not true! It's not true, I say.

MOTHER: And what can you possibly know about it?

STEPDAUGHTER: It's not true! *(to the* PRODUCER*)* Don't believe her! Do you know why she said that? Because of him. *(Pointing to the* SON.*)* That's why she said it! Because she tortures herself, wears herself out with anguish, because of the indifference of that son of hers. She wants him to believe that if she abandoned him when he was two years old it was because he *(Pointing to the* FATHER.*)* forced her to do it.

MOTHER *(forcefully)*: He forced me to do it! He forced me, as God is my witness! *(to the* PRODUCER*)* Ask him *(Pointing to her* HUSBAND.*)* if it's not true! Make him tell my son! She *(Pointing to her* DAUGHTER.*)* knows nothing at all about the matter.

STEPDAUGHTER: I know that while my father lived you were always happy. . . . You had a peaceful and contented life together. Deny it if you can!

MOTHER: I don't deny it! No. . . .

STEPDAUGHTER: He was always most loving, always kindness itself towards you. *(to the* BOY, *angrily)* Isn't it true? Go on. . . . Say it's true! Why don't you speak, you stupid little idiot?

MOTHER: Leave the poor boy alone! Why do you want to make me appear an ungrateful woman? I don't want to say anything against your father. . . . I only said that it wasn't my fault, and that it wasn't just to satisfy my own desires that I left his house and abandoned my son.

FATHER: What she says is true. It was my doing.

(There is a pause.)

LEADING MAN *(to the other* ACTORS*)*: My God! What a show!

LEADING LADY: And we're the audience this time!

JUVENILE LEAD: For once in a while.

PRODUCER *(who is beginning to show a lively interest)*: Let's listen to this! Let's hear what they've got to say! *(And saying this he goes down the steps into the auditorium and stands in front of the stage, as if to get an impression of the scene from the audience's point of view.)*

SON *(without moving from where he is, speaking coldly, softly, ironically)*: Yes! Listen to the chunk of philosophy you're going to get now. He will tell you all about the Demon of Experiment.

FATHER: You're a cynical idiot, as I've told you a hundred times. *(Down to the* PRODUCER.*)* He mocks me because of this expression that I've discovered in my own defence.

SON *(contemptuously)*: Words! Words!

FATHER: Yes! Words! Words! They can always bring consolation to us. . . . To everyone of us. . . . When we're confronted by something for which there's no explanation. . . . When we're face to face with an evil that consumes us. . . . The consolation of finding a word that tells us nothing, but that brings us peace.

STEPDAUGHTER: And dulls our sense of remorse, too. Yes! That above all!

FATHER: Dulls our sense of remorse? No, that's not true. It wasn't with words alone that I quietened remorse within me.

STEPDAUGHTER: No, you did it with a little money as well. Yes! Oh, yes! with a little money as well! With the hundred lire that he was going to offer me . . . as payment, ladies and gentlemen!

(A movement of horror on the part of the ACTORS.*)*

SON *(contemptuously to his* STEPSISTER*)*: That was vile!

STEPDAUGHTER: Vile? There they were, in a pale blue envelope, on the little mahogany table in the room behind Madame Pace's shop. Madame Pace. . . . One of those *Madames* who pretend to sell *Robes et Manteaux* so that they can attract us poor girls from decent families into their workrooms.

SON: And she's bought the right to tyrannise over the whole lot of us with those hundred lire that he was going to pay her. . . . But by good fortune. . . . And let me emphasise this. . . . He had no reason to pay her anything.

STEPDAUGHTER: Yes, but it was a very near thing! Oh, yes, it was, you know! *(She bursts out laughing.)*

MOTHER *(rising to protest)*: For shame! For shame!

STEPDAUGHTER *(immediately)*: Shame? No! This is my revenge! I'm trembling with desire. . . . Simply trembling with desire to live that scene! That room. . . . Over there the divan, the long mirror and a screen. . . . And in front of the window that little mahogany table. . . . And the pale blue envelope with the hundred lire inside. Yes, I can see it quite clearly! I'd only have to stretch out my hand and I could pick it up! But you gentlemen really ought to turn your backs now, because I'm almost naked. I no longer blush, because he's the one who does the blushing now.

(Pointing to FATHER.*)* But, let me tell you, he was very pale then. . . . Very pale indeed! *(to the* PRODUCER*)* You can believe *me!*

PRODUCER: I haven't the vaguest idea what you're talking about!

FATHER: I can well believe it! When you get things hurled at you like that. Put your foot down. . . . And let me speak before you believe all these horrible slanders she's so viciously heaping upon me. . . . Without letting me get a word of explanation in.

STEPDAUGHTER: Ah, but this isn't the place for your long-winded fairy-stories, you know!

FATHER: But I'm not going to. . . . I want to explain things to him!

STEPDAUGHTER: Oh yes . . . I bet you do! You'll explain everything so that it suits you, won't you?

(At this point the PRODUCER *comes back on stage to restore order.)*

FATHER: But can't you see that here we have the cause of all the trouble! In the use of words! Each one of us has a whole world of things inside him. . . . And each one of us has his own particular world. How can we understand each other if into the words which I speak I put the sense and the value of things as I understand them within myself. . . . While at the same time whoever is listening to them inevitably assumes them to have the sense and value that they have for him. . . . The sense and value that they have in the world that he has within him? We think we understand one another. . . . But we never really do understand! Look at this situation, for example! All my pity, all the pity that I feel for this woman *(Pointing to the* MOTHER*)* she sees as the most ferocious cruelty.

MOTHER: But you turned me out of the house!

FATHER: There! Do you hear? I turned her out! She really believed that I was turning her out!

MOTHER: You know how to talk . . . I don't. . . . But believe me *(Turning to the* PRODUCER.*)* after he had married me. . . . Goodness knows why! For I was a poor, humble woman. . . .

FATHER: But it was just because of that. . . . It was your humility that I loved in you. I married you for your humility, believing . . . *(He breaks off, for she is making gestures of contradiction. Then, seeing how utterly impossible it is to make her understand him, he opens his arms wide in a gesture of despair and turns to the* PRODUCER.*)* No! . . . You see? She says no! It's terrifying, believe me! It's really terrifying, this deafness *(He taps his forehead.)*. . . . This mental deafness of hers! Affection. . . . Yes! . . . For her children! But deaf . . . Mentally deaf. . . . Deaf to the point of desperation.

STEPDAUGHTER: True enough! But now you make

him tell us what good all his cleverness has ever done us.

FATHER: If we could only foresee all the ill that can result from the good that we believe we are doing.

(Meanwhile the LEADING LADY, *with ever-increasing fury, has been watching the* LEADING MAN, *who is busy carrying on a flirtation with the* STEPDAUGHTER. *Unable to stand it any longer she now steps forward and says to the* PRODUCER.*)*

LEADING LADY: Excuse me, but are you going on with the rehearsal?

PRODUCER: Why, of course! Of course! But just at the moment I want to hear what these people have to say!

JUVENILE LEAD: This is really something quite new!

INGENUE: It's most interesting!

LEADING LADY: For those that are interested! *(And she looks meaningly in the direction of the* LEADING MAN.*)*

PRODUCER *(to the* FATHER*)*: But you'll have to explain everything clearly. *(He goes and sits down.)*

FATHER: Yes. . . . Well. . . . You see . . . I had a poor man working under me. . . . He was my secretary, and devoted to me. . . . Who understood her in every way . . . In everything *(Pointing to the* MOTHER.*)* Oh, there wasn't the slightest suspicion of anything wrong. He was a good man. A humble man. . . . Just like her. . . . They were incapable . . . both of them . . . not only of doing evil . . . but even of thinking it!

STEPDAUGHTER: So, instead, he thought about it for them! And then got on with it.

FATHER: It's not true! I thought that what I should be doing would be for their good. . . . And for mine, too . . . I confess it! Yes, things had come to such a pass that I couldn't say a single word to either of them without their immediately exchanging an understanding look. . . . Without the one's immediately trying to catch the other's eye. . . . For advice as to how to take what I had said. . . . So that I shouldn't get into a bad temper. As you'll readily appreciate it was enough to keep me in a state of continual fury. . . . Of intolerable exasperation!

PRODUCER: But. . . . Forgive my asking. . . . Why didn't you give this secretary of yours the sack?

FATHER: That's exactly what I did do, as a matter of fact. But then I had to watch that poor woman wandering forlornly about the house like some poor lost creature . . . Like one of those stray animals you take in out of charity.

MOTHER: But . . .

FATHER *(immediately turning on her, as if to forestall what she is about to say)*: Your son! You were going to tell him about your son, weren't you?

MOTHER: But first of all he tore my son away from me!

FATHER: Not out of any desire to be cruel though! I took him away so that, by living in the country, in contact with Nature, he might grow up strong and healthy.

STEPDAUGHTER (*pointing to him, ironically*): And just look at him!

FATHER (*immediately*): And is it my fault, too, that he's grown up the way he has? I sent him to a wet-nurse in the country . . . a peasant's wife . . . because my wife didn't seem strong enough to me. . . . Although she came of a humble family, and it was for that reason that I'd married her! Just a whim maybe. . . . But then . . . what was I to do? I've always had this cursed longing for a certain solid moral healthiness.

(*At this the* STEPDAUGHTER *breaks out afresh into noisy laughter.*)

Make her stop that noise! I can't stand it!

PRODUCER: Be quiet! Let me hear what he has to say, for God's sake!

(*At the* PRODUCER'S *rebuke she immediately returns to her former attitude. . . . Absorbed and distant, a half-smile on her lips. The* PRODUCER *comes down off the stage again to see how it looks from the auditorium.*)

FATHER: I could no longer stand the sight of that woman near me (*Pointing to the* MOTHER.) Not so much because of the irritation she caused me . . . the nausea . . . the very real nausea with which she inspired me. . . . But rather because of the pain . . . the pain and the anguish that I was suffering on her account.

MOTHER: And he sent me away!

FATHER: Well provided with everything. . . . To that other man. . . . So that she might be free of me.

MOTHER: And so that he might be free as well!

FATHER: Yes, I admit it. And a great deal of harm came as a result of it. . . . But I meant well. . . . And I did it more for her sake than for my own. I swear it! (*He folds his arms. Then immediately turning to the* MOTHER.) Did I ever lose sight of you? Tell me, did I ever lose sight of you until that fellow took you away suddenly to some other town . . . all unknown to me. . . . Just because he'd got some queer notion into his head about the interest I was showing in you. . . . An interest which was pure, I assure you, sir. . . . Without the slightest suspicion of any ulterior motive about it! I watched the new little family that grew up around her with incredible tenderness. She can testify to that. (*He points to the* STEPDAUGHTER.)

STEPDAUGHTER: Oh, I most certainly can! I was such a sweet little girl. . . . Such a sweet little girl, you see. . . . With plaits down to my shoulders . . . and my knickers a little bit longer than my frock. I used to see him standing there by the door of the school as I came out. He came to see how I was growing up. . . .

FATHER: Oh, this is vile! Treacherous! Infamous!

STEPDAUGHTER: Oh, no! What makes you say it's infamous?

FATHER: It's infamous! Infamous! (*Then turning excitedly to the* PRODUCER *he goes on in an explanatory tone.*) After she'd gone away (*Pointing to the* MOTHER.), my house suddenly seemed empty. She had been a burden on my spirit, but she had filled my house with her presence! Left alone I wandered through the rooms like some lost soul. This boy here (*Pointing to the* SON), having been brought up away from home. . . . I don't know . . . But . . . but when he returned home he no longer seemed to be my son. With no mother to link him to me, he grew up entirely on his own. . . . A creature apart . . . absorbed in himself . . . with no tie of intellect or affection to bind him to me. And then. . . . And, strange as it may seem, it's the simple truth . . . I became curious about her little family. . . . Gradually I was attracted to this family which had come into being as a result of what I had done. And the thought of it began to fill the emptiness that I felt all around me. I felt a real need . . . a very real need . . . to believe that she was happy, at peace, absorbed in the simple everyday duties of life. I wanted to look on her as being fortunate because she was far removed from the complicated torments of my spirit. And so, to have some proof of this, I used to go and watch that little girl come out of school.

STEPDAUGHTER: I should just say he did! He used to follow me along the street. He would smile at me and when I reached home he'd wave to me . . . like this. I would look at him rather provocatively, opening my eyes wide. I didn't know who he might be. I told my mother about him and she knew at once who it must be. (*The* MOTHER *nods agreement.*) At first she didn't want to let me go to school again. . . . And she kept me away for several days. And when I did go back, I saw him waiting for me at the door again . . . looking ridiculous . . . with a brown paper bag in his hand. He came up to me and patted me. . . . And then he took a lovely large straw hat out of the bag . . . with lots of lovely roses on it . . . And all for me.

PRODUCER: This is a bit off the point, you know.

SON (*contemptuously*): Yes. . . . Literature! Literature!

FATHER: Literature indeed! This is life! Passion!

PRODUCER: It may be. But you certainly can't act this sort of stuff!

FATHER: I agree with you. Because all this is only

leading up to the main action. I'm not suggesting that this part should be acted. And as a matter of fact, as you can quite well see, she *(Pointing to the* STEPDAUGHTER.*)* is no longer that little girl with plaits down to her shoulders. . . .

STEPDAUGHTER: . . . and her knickers a little bit longer than her frock!

FATHER: It is now that the drama comes! Something new, something complex. . . .

STEPDAUGHTER *(coming forward, her voice gloomy, fierce)*: As soon as my father died. . . .

FATHER *(at once, not giving her a chance to continue)*: . . . they fell into the most wretched poverty! They came back here. . . . And because of her stupidity *(Pointing to the* MOTHER.*)* I didn't know a thing about it. It's true enough that she can hardly write her own name. . . . But she might have got her daughter or that boy to write and tell me that they were in need!

MOTHER: Now tell me, sir, how was I to know that this was how he'd feel?

FATHER: That's exactly where you went wrong, in never having got to know how I felt about something.

MOTHER: After so many years away from him. . . . And after all that had happened. . . .

FATHER: And is it my fault that that fellow took you away from here as he did? *(Turning to the* PRODUCER.*)* I tell you, they disappeared overnight. . . . He'd found some sort of a job away from here . . . I couldn't trace them at all. . . . So, of necessity, my interest in them dwindled. And this was how it was for quite a number of years. The drama broke out, unforeseen, and violent in its intensity, when they returned. . . . When I was impelled by the demands of my miserable flesh, which is still alive with desire. . . . Oh, the wretchedness, the unutterable wretchedness of the man who's alone and who detests the vileness of casual affairs! When he's not old enough to do without a woman, and not really young enough to be able to go and look for one without feeling a sense of shame. Wretchedness, did I say? It's horrible! It's horrible! Because no woman is any longer capable of giving him love. And when he realises this, he ought to do without. . . . Yes, yes, I know! . . . Each one of us, when he appears before his fellow men, is clothed with a certain dignity. But deep down inside himself he knows what unconfessable things go on in the secrecy of his own heart. We give way . . . we give way to temptation. . . . Only to rise up again immediately, filled with a great eagerness to re-establish our dignity in all its solid entirety. . . . Just as if it were a tombstone on some grave in which we had buried, in which we had hidden from our eyes, every sign, and the very memory

itself of our shame. And everyone is just like that! Only there are some of us who lack the courage to talk about certain things.

STEPDAUGHTER: They've got the courage to do them, though. . . . All of them!

FATHER: Yes, all of them! But only in secret! And that's why it needs so much more courage to talk about them! A man's only got to mention these things, and the words have hardly left his lips before he's been labelled a cynic. And all the time it's not true. He's just like everybody else. . . . In fact he's better than they are, because he's not afraid to reveal with the light of his intelligence that red blush of shame which is inherent in human bestiality. . . . That shame to which bestial man closes his eyes, in order not to see it. And woman. . . . Yes, woman. . . . What kind of a being is she? She looks at you, tantalisingly, invitingly. You take her in your arms. And no sooner is she clasped firmly in your arms than she shuts her eyes. It is the sign of her mission, the sign by which she says to man. "Blind yourself, for I am blind."

STEPDAUGHTER: And what about when she no longer shuts her eyes? When she no longer feels the need to hide her blushing shame from herself by closing her eyes? When she sees instead . . . dry-eyed and dispassionate . . . the blushing shame of man, who has blinded himself without love? Oh, what disgust, what unutterable disgust, does she feel then for all these intellectual complications, for all this philosophy which reveals the beast in man and then tries to save him, tries to excuse him . . . I just can't stand here and listen to him! Because when a man is obliged to 'simplify' life bestially like that—when he throws overboard every vestige of 'humanity', every chaste desire, every pure feeling. . . . All sense of idealism, of duty, or modesty and of shame. . . . Then nothing is more contemptible, infuriating and revoltingly nauseating than their maudlin remorse. . . . Those crocodile tears!

PRODUCER: Now let's get back to the point! Let's get to the point! This is just a lot of beating about the bush!

FATHER: Very well. But a fact is like a sack. . . . When it's empty it won't stand up. And in order to make it stand up you must first of all pour into it all the reasons and all the feelings which have caused it to exist. I couldn't possibly be expected to know that when that man died and they returned here in such utter poverty, she *(Pointing to the* MOTHER.*)* would go out to work as a dress-maker in order to support the children. . . . Nor that, of all people, she'd gone to work for that . . . for Madame Pace.

STEPDAUGHTER: Who's a high-class dress-maker, if

you ladies and gentlemen would really like to know. On the surface she does work for only the best sort of people. But she arranges things so that these fine ladies act as a screen . . . without prejudice to the others . . . who are only so-so.

MOTHER: Believe me, it never entered my head for one moment that that old hag gave me work because she had her eye on my daughter. . . .

STEPDAUGHTER: Poor Mummy! Do you know what that woman used to do when I took her back the work that my mother had done? She would point out to me how the material had been ruined by giving it to my mother to sew. . . . Oh, she'd grumble about this! And she'd grumble about that! And so, you understand, I had to pay for it. . . . And all the time this poor creature thought she was sacrificing herself for me and for those two children, as she sat up all night sewing away at work for Madame Pace. *(Gestures and exclamations of indignation from the* ACTORS.*)*

PRODUCER *(immediately)*: And it was there, one day, that you met . . .

STEPDAUGHTER *(pointing to the* FATHER*)*: . . . him! Yes, him! An old client! Now there's a scene for you to put on! Absolutely superb!

FATHER: With her . . . the Mother . . . arriving. . . .

STEPDAUGHTER *(immediately, treacherously)*: . . . almost in time!

FATHER *(a cry)*: No! In time! In time! Fortunately I recognized her in time! And I took them all back home with me! Now you can imagine what the situation is like for both of us. She, just as you see her. . . . And I no longer able to look her in the face.

STEPDAUGHTER: It's utterly ridiculous! How can I possibly be expected, after all that, to be a modest young miss . . . well-bred and virtuous . . . in accordance with his confounded aspirations for a "solid moral healthiness"?

FATHER: My drama lies entirely in this one thing. . . . In my being conscious that each one of us believes himself to be a single person. But it's not true. . . . Each one of us is many persons. . . . Many persons . . . according to all the possibilities of being that there are within us. . . . With some people we are one person. . . . With others we are somebody quite different. . . . And all the time we are under the illusion of always being one and the same person for everybody. . . . We believe that we are always this one person in whatever it is we may be doing. But it's not true! It's not true! And we see this very clearly when by some tragic chance we are, as it were, caught up whilst in the middle of doing something and find ourselves suspended in midair. And then we perceive that all of us was not in what we were doing, and that it would, there-fore, be an atrocious injustice to us to judge us by that action alone . . . to keep us suspended like that. . . . To keep us in a pillory . . . throughout all existence . . . as if our whole life were completely summed up in that one deed. Now do you understand the treachery of this girl? She surprised me somewhere where I shouldn't have been . . . and doing something that I shouldn't have been doing with her. . . . She surprised an aspect of me that should never have existed for her. And now she is trying to attach to me a reality such as I could never have expected I should have to assume for her. . . . The reality that lies in one fleeting, shameful moment of my life. And this, this above all, is what I feel most strongly about. And as you can see, the drama acquires a tremendous value from this concept. Then there's the position of the others. . . . His . . .*(Pointing to the* SON.*)*

SON *(shrugging his shoulders scornfully)*: Leave me alone! I've got nothing to do with all this!

FATHER: What do you mean . . . you've got nothing to do with all this?

SON: I've got nothing to do with it. . . . And I don't want to have anything to do with it, because, as you quite well know, I wasn't meant to be mixed up in all this with the rest of you!

STEPDAUGHTER: Common, that's what we are! And he's a fine gentleman! But, as you may have noticed, every now and again I fix him with a contemptuous look, and he lowers his eyes. . . . Because he knows the harm he's done me!

SON *(scarcely looking at her)*: I?

STEPDAUGHTER: Yes, you! You! It's all your fault that I became a prostitute! *(A movement of horror from the* ACTORS.*)* Did you or did you not deny us, by the attitude you adopted—I won't say the intimacy of your home—but even that mere hospitality which makes guests feel at their ease? We were invaders who had come to disturb the kingdom of your legitimacy. I should just like you *(This to the* PRODUCER.*)* to be present at certain little scenes that took place between him and me. He says that I tyrannised over everybody. . . . But it was just because of the way that he behaved that I took advantage of the thing that he calls 'vile.' . . . Why I exploited the reason for my coming into his house with my mother . . . Who is his mother as well! And I went into that house as mistress of it!

SON *(slowly coming forward)*: It's all very easy for them. . . . It's fine sport. . . . All of them ganging up against me. But just imagine the position of a son whose fate it is one fine day, while he's sitting quietly at home, to see arriving an impudent and brazen young woman who asks for his father—and heaven knows what her business is with him!

Later he sees her come back, as brazen as ever, bringing that little girl with her. And finally he sees her treating her father—without knowing in the least why—in a very equivocal and very much to-the-point manner . . . asking him for money, in a tone of voice which leads you to suppose that he must give it to her. . . . Must give it to her, because he has every obligation to do so. . . .

FATHER: As indeed I have! It's an obligation I owe your mother!

SON: How should I know that? When had I never seen or even heard of her? Then one day I see her arrive with *her* (*Pointing to the* STEPDAUGH-TER.) together with that boy and the little girl. And they say to me, "This is *your* mother, too, you know." Little by little I begin to understand. . . . Largely as a result of the way she goes on (*Pointing to the* STEPDAUGHTER *again.*). . . . Why is it that they've come to live with us. . . . So suddenly . . . So unexpectedly. . . . What I feel, what I experience, I neither wish, nor am able, to express. I wouldn't even wish to confess it to myself. No action, therefore, can be hoped for from me in this affair. Believe me, I am a dramatically unrealised character . . . and I do not feel the least bit at ease in their company. So please leave me out of it!

FATHER: What! But it's just because you're like that. . . .

SON (*in violent exasperation*): And what do you know about it? How do you know what I'm like? When have you ever bothered yourself about me?

FATHER: I admit it! I admit it! But isn't that a dramatic situation in itself? This aloofness of yours, which is so cruel to me and to your mother. . . . Your mother who returns home and sees you almost for the first time . . . You're so grown up that she doesn't recognise you, but she knows that you're her son. (*Pointing to the* MOTHER *and addressing the* PRODUCER.) There, look! She's crying!

STEPDAUGHTER (*angrily, stamping her foot*): Like the fool she is!

FATHER (*pointing to the* STEPDAUGHTER): She can't stand him! (*Then returning to the subject of the* SON.) He says he's got nothing to do with all this, when, as a matter of fact, almost the whole action hinges on him. Look at that little boy. . . . See how he clings to his mother all the time, frightened and humiliated. . . . And it's *his* fault that he's like that! Perhaps his position is the most painful of all. . . . More than any of them he feels himself to be an outsider. And so the poor little chap feels mortified, humiliated at being taken into my home . . . out of charity, as it were. (*Confidentially.*) He's just like his father. Humble. . . . Doesn't say a word. . . .

PRODUCER: I don't think it's a good idea to have him in. You've no idea what a nuisance boys are on the stage.

FATHER: Oh, . . . but he won't be a nuisance for long . . . He disappears almost immediately. And the little girl, too. . . . In fact, she's the first to go.

PRODUCER: This is excellent! I assure you I find this all very interesting. . . . Very interesting indeed! I can see we've got the makings of a pretty good play here.

STEPDAUGHTER (*trying to butt in*): When you've got a character like me!

FATHER (*pushing her to one side in his anxiety to hear what decision the* PRODUCER *has come to*): You be quiet!

PRODUCER (*continuing, heedless of the interruption*): And it's certainly something new. . . . Ye-es! . . .

FATHER: Absolutely brand new!

PRODUCER: You had a nerve, though. I must say. . . . Coming here and chucking the idea at me like that. . . .

FATHER: Well, you understand, born as we are for the stage. . . .

PRODUCER: Are you amateur actors?

FATHER: No . . . I say that we're born for the stage because . . .

PRODUCER: Oh, don't try and con me with that one! You're an old hand at this game.

FATHER: No. I only act as much as anyone acts the part that he sets himself to perform, or the part that he is given in life. And in me it is passion itself, as you can see, that always becomes a little theatrical of its own accord . . . as it does in everyone . . . once it becomes exalted.

PRODUCER: Oh well, that as may be! That as may be! . . . But you do understand, without an author . . . I could give you the address of somebody who'd . . .

FATHER: No! . . . Look here. . . . You be the author!

PRODUCER: Me? What the devil are you talking about?

FATHER: Yes, you! You! Why not?

PRODUCER: Because I've never written anything in my life! That's why not!

FATHER: Then why not try your hand at it now? There's nothing to it. Everybody's doing it! And your job's made all the easier for you because we are here, all of us, alive before you. . . .

PRODUCER: That's not enough!

FATHER: Not enough? When you see us live our drama . . .

PRODUCER: Yes! Yes! But we'll still need somebody to write the play.

FATHER: No. . . . Someone to take it down possibly, while we act it out, scene by scene. It'll be quite sufficient if we make a rough sketch of it first and then have a run through.

PRODUCER (*climbing back on to the stage, tempted by*

this): H'm! . . . You almost succeed in tempting me. . . . H'm! It would be rather fun! We could certainly have a shot at it.

FATHER: Of course! Oh, you'll see what wonderful scenes'll emerge! I can tell you what they are here and now.

PRODUCER: You tempt me. . . . You tempt me. . . . Let's have a go at it! . . . Come with me into my office. *(Turning to the* ACTORS.) You can have a few minutes' break. . . . But don't go too far away. I want you all back again in about a quarter of an hour or twenty minutes. *(To the* FATHER.) Well, let's see what we can make of it! We might get something really extraordinary out of it. . . .

FATHER: There's no *might* about it! They'd better come along too, don't you think? *(Pointing to the other* CHARACTERS.)

PRODUCER: Yes, bring 'em along! Bring 'em along! *(Starts going off and then turns back to the* ACTORS.) Now remember, don't be late back! You've got a quarter of an hour!

(The PRODUCER *and the* SIX CHARACTERS *cross the stage and disappear. The* ACTORS *remain looking at one another in astonishment.)*

LEADING MAN: Is he serious? What's he going to do?

JUVENILE LEAD: This is utter madness!

A THIRD ACTOR: Does he expect us to knock up a play in five minutes?

JUVENILE LEAD: Yes . . . like the actors in the old Comedia dell'Arte.

LEADING LADY: Well, if he thinks that I'm going to have anything to do with fun and games of that sort. . . .

INGENUE: And you certainly don't catch me joining in!

A FOURTH ACTOR: I should like to know who those people are. *(He is alluding to the* CHARACTERS.)

THIRD ACTOR: Who do you think they're likely to be? They're probably escaped lunatics. . . . Or crooks!

JUVENILE LEAD: And does he really take what they say seriously?

INGENUE: Vanity! That's what it is. . . . The vanity of appearing as an author!

LEADING MAN: It's absolutely unheard of! If the stage has come to this. . . .

A FIFTH ACTOR: I'm rather enjoying it!

THIRD ACTOR: Oh, well! After all, we shall have the pleasure of seeing what comes of it all!

(And talking among themselves in this way the ACTORS *leave the stage. Some go out through the door back, some go in the direction of the dressing-rooms. The curtain remains up.)*

(The performance is suspended for twenty minutes.)

ACT 2

(The call-bells ring, warning the audience that the performance is about to be resumed. The ACTORS, *the* STAGE MANAGER, *the* FOREMAN *of the stage crew, the* PROMPTER *and the* PROPERTY MAN *reassemble on stage. Some come from the dressing-rooms, some through the door back, some even from the auditorium. The* PRODUCER *enters from his office accompanied by the* SIX CHARACTERS. *The houselights are extinguished and the stage lighting is as before.)*

PRODUCER: Now come on, ladies and gentlemen! Are we all here? Let me have your attention please! Now let's make a start! *(Then calls the* FOREMAN.)

FOREMAN: Yes, sir?

PRODUCER: Set the stage for the parlour scene. A couple of flats and a door will do. As quickly as you can!

(The FOREMAN *runs off at once to carry out this order and is setting the stage as directed whilst the* PRODUCER *is making his arrangements with the* STAGE MANAGER, *the* PROPERTY MAN, *the* PROMPTER *and the* ACTORS. *The flats he has set up are painted in pink and gold stripes.)*

PRODUCER *(to* PROPERTY MAN): Just have a look, please, and see if we've got some sort of sofa or divan in the props room.

PROPERTY MAN: There's the green one, sir.

STEPDAUGHTER: No, no, green won't do! It was yellow . . . yellow flowered plush. . . . A huge thing . . . and most comfortable.

PROPERTY MAN: Well, we haven't got anything like that.

PRODUCER: It doesn't matter! Give me what there is!

STEPDAUGHTER: What do you mean, it doesn't matter? Madame Pace's famous sofa!

PRODUCER: We only want it for this run-through. Please don't interfere. *(to the* STAGE MANAGER) Oh, and see if we've got a shop-window . . . something rather long and narrowish is what we want.

STEPDAUGHTER: And a little table . . . the little mahogany table for the pale blue envelope.!

STAGE MANAGER *(to* PRODUCER): There's that little one. . . . You know, the gold-painted one.

PRODUCER: That'll do fine! Shove it on!

FATHER: You need a long mirror.

STEPDAUGHTER: And the screen! I must have a screen, please. . . . Else how can I manage?

STAGE MANAGER: Don't you worry, Miss! We've got masses of them!

PRODUCER *(to the* STEPDAUGHTER): And some clotheshangers and so on, h'm?

STEPDAUGHTERS: Oh, yes, lots!

PRODUCER *(to the* STAGE MANAGER): See how many we've got and get somebody to bring them up.

STAGE MANAGER: Right you are, sir, I'll see to it!

(The STAGE MANAGER *goes off about his business and while the* PRODUCER *is talking to the* PROMPTER *and later to the* CHARACTERS *and* ACTORS, *he gets the stage hands to bring up the furniture and properties and proceeds to arrange them in what he thinks is the best sort of order.)*

PRODUCER *(to the* PROMPTER*)*: Now if you'll get into position while they're setting the stage. . . . Look, here's an outline of the thing. . . . Act I . . . Act II . . . *(he holds out some sheets of paper to him).* But you'll really have to excel yourself this time.

PROMPTER: You mean, take it down in shorthand?

PRODUCER *(pleasantly surprised)*: Oh, good man! Can you do shorthand?

PROMPTER: I mayn't know much about prompting, but shorthand. . . .

PRODUCER: Better and better. *(Turning to a* STAGE-HAND*.)* Go and get some paper out of my room. . . . A large wadge. . . . As much as you can find!

(The STAGE-HAND *hurries off and returns shortly with a thick wad of paper which he gives to the* PROMPTER.*)*

PRODUCER *(to the* PROMPTER*)*: Follow the scenes closely as we play them and try to fix the lines . . . or at least the most important ones. *(Then, turning to the* ACTORS.*)* Right, ladies and gentlemen, clear the stage, please! No, come over this side *(He waves them over to his left.)* . . . and pay careful attention to what goes on.

LEADING LADY: Excuse me, but we . . .

PRODUCER *(forestalling what she is going to say)*: There won't be any improvising to do, don't you worry!

LEADING MAN: What do we have to do, then?

PRODUCER: Nothing. For the moment all you've got to do is to stay over there and watch what happens. You'll get your parts later. Just now we're going to have a rehearsal . . . or as much of one as we can in the circumstances! And they'll be doing the rehearsing. *(He points to the* CHARACTERS.*)*

FATHER *(in consternation, as if he had tumbled from the clouds into the midst of all the confusion on stage).* We are? But, excuse me, in what way will it be a rehearsal?

PRODUCER: Well . . . a rehearsal . . . a rehearsal for their benefit. *(He points to the* ACTORS.*)*

FATHER: But if we're the characters . . .

PRODUCER: Just so, "the characters." But it's not characters that act here. It's actors who do the acting here. The characters remain there, in the script. *(He points to the prompt-box.)* . . . When there is a script!

FATHER: Precisely! And since there is no script and you have the good fortune to have the characters here alive before your very eyes. . . .

PRODUCER: Oh, this is wonderful! Do you want to do everything on your own? Act . . . present yourselves to the public!

FATHER: Yes, just as we are.

PRODUCER: And let me tell you you'd make a wonderful sight!

LEADING MAN: And what use should we be then?

PRODUCER: You're not going to pretend that you can act, are you? Why, it's enough to make a cat laugh. . . . *(And as a matter of fact, the* ACTORS *burst out laughing.)* There you are, you see, they're laughing at the idea! *(Then, remembering.)* But, to the point! I must tell you what your parts are. That's not so very difficult. They pretty well cast themselves. *(to the* SECOND ACTRESS*)* You, the MOTHER. *(to the* FATHER*)* We'll have to find a name for her.

FATHER: Amalia.

PRODUCER: But that's your wife's name. We can hardly call her by her real name.

FATHER: And why not, when that's her name? But, perhaps, it is has to be that lady . . . *(A slight gesture to indicate the* SECOND ACTRESS.*)* I see *her* *(Pointing to the* MOTHER.*)* as Amalia. But do as you like. . . . *(His confusion grows.)* I don't know what to say to you. . . . I'm already beginning. . . . I don't know how to express it . . . to hear my own words ringing false . . . as if they had another sound from the one I had meant to give them. . . .

PRODUCER: Now don't you worry about that! Don't you worry about it at all! We'll think about how to get the right tone of voice. And as for the name. . . . If you want it to be Amalia, Amalia it shall be. Or we'll find some other name. Just for the present we'll refer to the characters in this way. *(to the* JUVENILE LEAD*)* You, the Son . . . *(to the* LEADING LADY*)* And you'll play the Stepdaughter, of course. . . .

STEPDAUGHTER *(excitedly)*: What! What did you say? That woman there. . . . Me! *(She bursts out laughing.)*

PRODUCER *(angrily)*: And what's making you laugh?

LEADING LADY *(indignantly)*: Nobody has ever dared to laugh at me before! Either you treat me with respect or I'm walking out!

STEPDAUGHTER: Oh, no, forgive me! I wasn't laughing at you.

PRODUCER *(to* STEPDAUGHTER*)*: You should feel yourself honoured to be played by . . .

LEADING LADY *(immediately, disdainfully)*: . . . "that woman there."

STEPDAUGHTER: But my remark wasn't meant as a criticism of you . . . I was thinking about myself. . . . Because I can't see myself in you at all. I don't know how to . . . you're not a bit like me!

FATHER: Yes, that's the point I wanted to make! Look . . . all that we express. . . .

PRODUCER: What do you mean . . . *all that you express?* Do you think that this whatever-it-is that you express is something you've got inside you? Not a bit of it.

FATHER: Why . . . aren't even the things we express our own?

PRODUCER: Of course they aren't! The things that you express become material here for the actors, who give it body and form, voice and gesture. And, let me tell you, my actors have given expression to much loftier material than this. This stuff of yours is so trivial that, believe me, if it comes off on the stage, the credit will all be due to my actors.

FATHER: I don't dare to contradict you! But please believe me when I tell you that we . . . who have these bodies . . . these features. . . . Who are as you see us now . . . We are suffering horribly. . . .

PRODUCER (*cutting in impatiently*): . . . But the make-up will remedy all that. . . . At least as far as your faces are concerned!

FATHER: Perhaps. . . . But what about our voices? . . . What about our gestures? . . .

PRODUCER: Now, look here! You, as yourself, just cannot exist here! Here there's an actor who'll play you. And let that be an end to all this argument!

FATHER: I understand. . . . And now I think I see why our author didn't wish to put us on the stage after all. . . . He saw us as we are. . . . Alive. . . . He saw us as living beings. . . . I don't want to offend your actors. . . . Heaven forbid that I should! . . . But I think that seeing myself acted now . . . by I don't know whom . . .

LEADING MAN (*rising with some dignity and coming over, followed by a laughing group of young actresses*): By me, if you have no objection.

FATHER (*humbly, mellifluously*): I am deeply honoured, sir. (*He bows.*) But. . . . Well. . . . I think that however much of his art this gentleman puts into absorbing me into himself. . . . However much he wills it. . . . (*He becomes confused.*)

LEADING MAN: Go on! Go on! (*The actresses laugh.*)

FATHER: Well, I should say that the performance he'll give. . . . Even if he makes himself up to look as much like me as he can. . . . I should say that with his figure . . . (*All the ACTORS laugh.*) . . . it will be difficult for it to be a performance of me . . . of me as I really am. It will rather be . . . leaving aside the question of his appearance. . . . It will be how he interprets what I am . . . how he sees me. . . . If he sees me as anything at all. . . . And not as I, deep down within myself, feel myself to be. And it certainly seems to me that whoever is called upon to criticise us will have to take this into account.

PRODUCER: So you're already thinking about what the critics will say, are you? And here I am, still trying to get the play straight! The critics can say what they like. We'd be much better occupied in thinking about getting the play on. . . . If we can. (*Stepping out of the group and looking around him.*) Now, come on, let's make a start! Is everything ready? (*to the ACTORS and CHARACTERS*) Come on, don't clutter up the place! Let me see how it looks! (*He comes down from the stage.*) And now, don't let's lose any more time! (*to the STEP-DAUGHTER*) Do you think the set looks all right?

STEPDAUGHTER: To be perfectly honest, I just don't recognise it at all!

PRODUCER: Good Lord, you surely didn't hope that we were going to reconstruct that room behind Madame Pace's shop here on the stage, did you? (*to the FATHER*) You did tell me it had flowered wallpaper, didn't you?

FATHER: Yes, white.

PRODUCER: Well, it's not white—and it's got stripes on it—but it'll have to do! As for the furniture, I think we've more or less got everything we need. Bring that little table down here a bit! (*The STAGE-HANDS do so. Then he says to the PROPERTY MAN.*) Now, will you go and get an envelope. . . . A pale blue one if you can. . . . And give it to that gentleman. (*He points to the FATHER.*)

PROPERTY MAN: The kind you put letters in?

PRODUCER and FATHER: Yes, the kind you put letters in!

PROPERTY MAN: Yes, sir! At once, sir! (*Exit.*)

PRODUCER: Now, come on! First scene—the young lady. (*The LEADING LADY comes forward.*) No! No! Wait a moment! I said the young lady! (*Pointing to the STEPDAUGHTER.*) You stay there and watch. . . .

STEPDAUGHTER (*immediately adding*): . . . how I make it live!

LEADING LADY (*resentfully*): I'll know how to make it live, don't you worry, once I get started!

PRODUCER (*with his hands to his head*): Ladies and gentlemen, don't let's have any arguing! Please! Right! Now . . . The first scene is between the young lady and Madame Pace. Oh! (*He looks around rather helplessly and then comes back on stage.*) What about this Madame Pace?

FATHER: She's not with us, sir.

PRODUCER: And what do we do about her?

FATHER: But she's alive! She's alive too!

PRODUCER: Yes, yes! But where is she?

FATHER: If you'll just allow me to have a word with your people. . . . (*Turning to the ACTRESSES.*) I wonder if you ladies would do me the kindness of lending me your hats for a moment.

THE ACTRESSES (*a chorus . . . half-laughing, half-surprised*): What? Our hats?

What did he say?
Why?
Listen to the man!

PRODUCER: What are you going to do with the women's hats?

(The ACTORS *laugh.)*

FATHER: Oh, nothing . . . I just want to put them on these pegs for a moment. And perhaps one of you ladies would be so kind as to take off your coat, too.

THE ACTORS *(laughter and surprise in their voices)*: Their coats as well? And after that? The man must be mad!

ONE OR TWO OF THE ACTRESSES *(surprise and laughter in their voices)*: But why?
Only our coats?

FATHER: So that I can hang them here. . . . Just for a moment or so. . . . Please do me this favour. Will you?

THE ACTRESSES *(they take off their hats. One or two take off their coats as well, all laughing the while. They go over and hang the coats here and there on the pegs and hangers)*:
And why not?
Here you are!
This really is funny!
Do we have to put them on show?

FATHER: Precisely. . . . You have to put them on show . . . Like this!

PRODUCER: Is one allowed to know what you're up to?

FATHER: Why yes. If we set the stage better, who knows whether she may not be attracted by the objects of her trade and perhaps appear among us. . . . *(He invites them to look toward the door at the back of the stage.)* Look! Look!

(The door opens and MADAME PACE *comes in and takes a few steps forward. She is an enormously fat old harridan of a woman, wearing a pompous carrot-coloured tow wig with a red rose stuck into one side of it, in the Spanish manner. She is heavily made up and dressed with clumsy elegance in a stylish red silk dress. In one hand she carries an ostrich feather fan; the other hand is raised and a lighted cigarette is poised between two fingers. Immediately they see this apparition, the* ACTORS *and the* PRODUCER *bound off the stage with howls of fear, hurling themselves down the steps into the auditorium and making as if to dash up the aisle. The* STEPDAUGHTER, *however, rushes humbly up to* MADAME PACE, *as if greeting her mistress.)*

STEPDAUGHTER *(rushing up to her)*: Here she is! Here she is!

FATHER *(beaming)*: It's Madame Pace! What did I tell you? Here she is!

PRODUCER *(his first surprise overcome, he is now indignant)*: What sort of a game do you call this?

LEADING MAN:	*almost at the*	Hang it all, what's going on?
JUVENILE LEAD:	*same moment and all*	Where did *she* spring from?
INGENUE:	*speaking at*	They were keeping her in reserve!
LEADING LADY:	*once.*	So it's back to the music hall and conjuring tricks, is it?

FATHER *(dominating the protesting voices)*: One moment, please! Why should you wish to destroy this prodigy of reality, which was born, which was evoked, attracted and formed by this scene itself? . . . A reality which has more right to live here than you have. . . . Because it is so very much more alive than you are. . . . Why do you want to spoil it all, just because of some niggling, vulgar convention of truth? . . . Which of you actresses will be playing the part of Madame Pace? Well, *that* woman *is* Madame Pace! Grant me at least that the actress who plays her will be less true than she is. . . . For *she* is Madame Pace in person! Look! My daughter recognised her and went up to her at once. Now, watch the scene! Just watch it! *(Hesitantly the* PRODUCER *and the* ACTORS *climb back on to the stage. But while the* ACTORS *have been protesting and the* FATHER *has been replying to them, the scene between the* STEPDAUGHTER *and* MADAME PACE *has begun. It is carried on in an undertone, very quietly—naturally in fact—in a manner that would be quite impossible on the stage. When the* ACTORS *obey the* FATHER'S *demand that they shall watch what is happening, they see that* MADAME PACE *has already put her hand under the* STEPDAUGHTER'S *chin to raise her head and is talking to her. Hearing her speak in a completely unintelligible manner they are held for a moment. But almost immediately their attention flags.)*

PRODUCER: Well?

LEADING MAN: But what's she saying?

LEADING LADY: We can't hear a thing!

JUVENILE LEAD: Speak up! Louder!

STEPDAUGHTER *(she leaves* MADAME PACE *and comes down to the group of* ACTORS. MADAME PACE *smiles—a priceless smile)*: Did you say, 'Louder?' What do you mean, 'Louder?' What we're talking about is scarcely the sort of thing to be shouted from the roof-tops. I was able to yell it out just now so that I could shame *him* (Pointing to the FATHER.) . . . so that I could have my revenge! But it's quite another matter for Madame Pace. . . . It would mean prison for her.

PRODUCER: Indeed? So that's how it is, is it? But let me tell you something, my dear young lady. . . . Here in the theatre you've got to make yourself heard! The way you're doing this bit at the moment even those of us who're on stage can't hear you! Just imagine what it'll be like with an audience out front. This scene's got to be got over. And anyway there's nothing to prevent you from speaking up when you're on together. . . . We shan't be here to listen to you. . . . We're only here now because it's a rehearsal. Pretend you're alone in the room behind the shop, where nobody can hear you.

(The STEPDAUGHTER *elegantly, charmingly—and with a mischievous smile—wags her finger two or three times in disagreement.)*

PRODUCER: What do you mean, 'No?'

STEPDAUGHTER *(in a mysterious whisper)*: There's someone who'll hear us if she *(Pointing to* MADAME PACE.*)* speaks up.

PRODUCER *(in utter consternation)*: Do you mean to say that there's somebody else who's going to burst in on us? *(The* ACTORS *make as if to dive off the stage again.)*

FATHER: No! No! They're alluding to me. I have to be there, waiting behind the door. . . . And Madame Pace knows it. So, if you'll excuse me, I'll go. . . . So that I'm all ready to make my entrance. *(He starts off toward the back of the stage.)*

PRODUCER *(stopping him)*: No! No! Wait a moment! When you're here you have to respect the conventions of the theatre! Before you get ready to go on to that bit. . . .

STEPDAUGHTER: No! Let's get on with it at once! At once! I'm dying with desire, I tell you . . . to live this scene. . . . To live it! If he wants to get on with it right away, I'm more than ready!

PRODUCER *(shouting)*: But first of all, the scene between you and her *(Pointing to* MADAME PACE.*)* has got to be over! Do you understand?

STEPDAUGHTER: Oh, my God! She's just been telling me what you already know. . . . That once again my mother's work has been badly done. . . . That the dress is spoilt . . . And that I must be patient if she is to go on helping us in our misfortune.

MADAME PACE *(stepping forward, a grand air of importance about her)*: But, yes, señor, porque I not want to make profit . . . to take advantage. . . .

PRODUCER *(more than a touch of terror in his voice)*: What? Does she speak like that?

(The ACTORS *burst into noisy laughter.)*

STEPDAUGHTER *(laughing too)*: Yes, she speaks like that, half in English, half in Spanish. . . . It's most comical.

MADAME PACE: Ah, no, it does not to me seem good manners that you laugh of me when I . . . force myself to . . . hablar, as I can, English, señor!

PRODUCER: Indeed, no! It's very wrong of us! You speak like that! Yes, speak like that, Madame!

It'll bring the house down! We couldn't ask for anything better. It'll bring a little comic relief into the crudity of the situation. Yes, you talk like that! It's absolutely wonderful!

STEPDAUGHTER: Wonderful! And why not? When you hear a certain sort of suggestion made to you in a lingo like that. . . . There's not much doubt about what your answer's going to be. . . . Because it almost seems like a joke. You feel inclined to laugh when you hear there's an 'old señor', who wants to 'amuse himself with me'. An 'old señor', eh, Madame?

MADAME PACE: Not so very old. . . . Not quite so young, yes? And if he does not please to you. . . . Well, he has . . . *prudencia.*

MOTHER *(absorbed as they are in the scene, the* ACTORS *have been paying no attention to her. Now, to their amazement and consternation, she leaps up and attacks* MADAME PACE. *At her cry they jump, then hasten smilingly to restrain her, for she, meanwhile, has snatched off* MADAME PACE'S *wig and has thrown it to the ground)*: You old devil! You old witch! You murderess! Oh, my daughter!

STEPDAUGHTER *(rushing over to restrain her* MOTHER*)*: No, Mummy, no! Please!

FATHER *(rushing over at the same time)*: Calm yourself, my dear! Just be calm! Now . . . come and sit down again!

MOTHER: Take that woman out of my sight, then!

(In the general excitement the PRODUCER, *too, has rushed over and the* STEPDAUGHTER *now turns to him.)*

STEPDAUGHTER: It's impossible for my mother to remain here!

FATHER *(to the* PRODUCER*)*: They can't be here together. That's why, when we first came, that woman wasn't with us. If they're on at the same time the whole thing is inevitably given away in advance.

PRODUCER: It doesn't matter! It doesn't matter a bit! This is only a first run-through. . . . Just to give us a rough idea how it goes. Everything'll come in useful . . . I can sort out the bits and pieces later. . . . I'll make something out of it, even if it is all jumbled up. *(Turning to the* MOTHER *and leading her back to her chair.)* Now, please be calm, and sit down here, nice and quietly.

(Meanwhile the STEPDAUGHTER *has gone down centre stage again. She turns to* MADAME PACE.*)*

STEPDAUGHTER: Go on, Madame, go on!

MADAME PACE *(offended)*: Ah, no thank you! Here I do not do nothing more with your mother present!

STEPDAUGHTER: Now, come on! Show in the 'old señor' who wants to 'amuse himself with me'. *(Turning imperiously on the rest.)* Yes, this scene has got to be played. So let's get on with it! *(to*

MADAME PACE) You can go!

MADAME PACE: Ah, I am going . . . I am going. . . . Most assuredly I am going! *(Exit furiously, ramming her wig back on and glowering at the* ACTORS, *who mockingly applaud her.)*

STEPDAUGHTER *(to the* FATHER*)*: And now you make your entrance! There's no need for you to go out and come in again! Come over here! Pretend that you've already entered! Now, I'm standing here modestly, my eyes on the ground. Come on! Speak up! Say, 'Good afternoon, Miss,' in that special tone of voice . . . you know. . . . Like somebody who's just come in from the street.

PRODUCER *(by this time he is down off the stage)*: Listen to her! Are you running this rehearsal, or am I? *(To the* FATHER, *who is looking perplexed and undecided)* Go on, do as she tells you! Go to the back of the stage. . . . Don't exit! . . . And then come forward again.

(The FATHER *does as he is told. He is troubled and very pale. But as he approaches from the back of the stage he smiles, already absorbed in the reality of his created life. He smiles as if the drama which is about to break upon him is as yet unknown to him. The* ACTORS *become intent on the scene which is beginning.)*

PRODUCER *(whispering quickly to the* PROMPTER, *who has taken up his position)*: Get ready to write now!

THE SCENE

FATHER *(coming forward, a new note in his voice)*: Good afternoon, Miss.

STEPDAUGHTER *(her head bowed, speaking with restrained disgust)*: Good afternoon!

FATHER *(studying her a little, looking up into her face from under the brim of her hat [which almost hides it], and perceiving that she is very young, exclaims, almost to himself, a little out of complacency, a little, too, from the fear of compromising himself in a risky adventure)*: H'm! But. . . . M'm. . . . This won't be the first time, will it? The first time that you've been here?

STEPDAUGHTER *(as before)*: No, sir.

FATHER: You've been in here before? *(And since the* STEPDAUGHTER *nods in affirmation.)* More than once? *(He waits a little while for her reply, resumes his study of her, again looking up into her face from under the brim of her hat, smiles and then says.)* Then . . . well . . . it shouldn't any longer be so. . . . May I take off your hat?

STEPDAUGHTER *(immediately forestalling him, unable to restrain her disgust)*: No, sir, I'll take it off myself! *(Convulsed, she hurriedly takes it off.)*

(The MOTHER *is on tenterhooks throughout. The* TWO CHILDREN *cling to their* MOTHER *and they, she and the* SON *form a group on the side opposite the* ACTORS, *watching the scene. The* MOTHER *follows the words and the actions of the* STEPDAUGHTER *and the* FATHER *with varying expressions of sorrow, of indignation, of anxiety and of horror; from time to time she hides her face in her hands and sobs.)*

MOTHER: Oh, my God! My God!

FATHER *(he remains for a moment as if turned to stone by this sob. Then he resumes in the same tone of voice as before)*: Here, let me take it. I'll hang it up for you. *(He takes the hat from her hands.)* But such a charming, such a dear little head really ought to have a much smarter hat than this! Would you like to come and help me choose one from among these hats of Madame's? Will you?

INGENUE *(breaking in)*: Oh, I say! Those are *our* hats!

PRODUCER *(at once, furiously)*: For God's sake, shut up! Don't try to be funny! We're doing our best to rehearse this scene, in case you weren't aware of the fact! *(Turning to* STEPDAUGHTER.*)* Go on from where you left off, please.

STEPDAUGHTER *(continuing)*: No thank you, sir.

FATHER: Come now, don't say no. Do say you'll accept it. . . . Just to please me. I shall be most upset if you won't. . . . Look, here are some rather nice ones. And then it would please Madame. She puts them out on show on purpose, you know.

STEPDAUGHTER: No . . . listen! I couldn't wear it.

FATHER: You're thinking perhaps about what they'll say when you come home wearing a new hat? Well now, shall I tell you what to do? Shall I tell you what to say when you get home?

STEPDAUGHTER *(quickly—she is at the end of her tether)*: No, it's not that! I couldn't wear it because I'm . . . As you see. . . . You should have noticed already . . . *(indicating her black dress.)*

FATHER: That you're in mourning! Of course. . . . Oh, forgive me! Of course! Oh, I beg your pardon! Believe me. . . . I'm most profoundly sorry. . . .

STEPDAUGHTER *(summoning all her strength and forcing herself to conquer her contempt, her indignation and her nausea)*: Stop! Please don't say any more! I really ought to be thanking you. There's no need for you to feel so very sorry or upset! Please don't give another thought to what I said! I, too, you understand. . . . *(Tries hard to smile and adds.)* I really must forget that I'm dressed like this!

PRODUCER *(interrupting them; he climbs back on the stage and turns to the* PROMPTER*)*: Hold it! Stop a minute! Don't write that down. Leave out that last bit. *(Turning to the* FATHER *and the* STEPDAUGHTER.*)* It's going very well! Very well indeed! *(Then to the* FATHER.*)* And then you go on as we arranged. *(to the* ACTORS*)* Rather delightful, that bit where he offers her the hat, don't you think?

STEPDAUGHTER: Ah, but the best bit's coming now! Why aren't we going on?

PRODUCER: Now be patient, please! Just for a little while! *(Turning to the* ACTORS.) Of course it'll have to be treated rather lightly. . . .

LEADING MAN: . . . M'm . . . and put over slickly. . . .

LEADING LADY: Of course! There's nothing difficult about it at all. *(to the* LEADING MAN) Shall we try it now?

LEADING MAN: As far as I'm . . . I'll go and get ready for my entrance. *(Exits to take up his position outside the door back.)*

PRODUCER *(to the* LEADING LADY): Now, look. . . . The scene between you and Madame Pace is finished. I'll get down to writing it up properly afterwards. You're standing. . . . Where are you going?

LEADING LADY: Just a moment! I want to put my hat back on. . . . *(Goes over, takes her hat down and puts it on.)*

PRODUCER: Good! Now you stand here. With your head bowed down a bit.

STEPDAUGHTER *(amused)*: But she's not dressed in black!

LEADING LADY: I *shall* be dressed in black. . . . And much more becomingly than you are!

PRODUCER *(to the* STEPDAUGHTER): Shut up . . . please! And watch! You'll learn something. *(Claps his hands.)* Now come on! Let's get going! Entrance! *(He goes down from the stage again to see how it looks from out front. The door back opens and the* LEADING MAN *steps forward. He has the lively, raffish, self-possessed air of an elderly gallant. The playing of this scene by the* ACTORS *will appear from the very first words as something completely different from what was played before, without its having, even in the slightest degree, the air of a parody. It should appear rather as if the scene has been touched up. Quite naturally the* FATHER *and the* STEPDAUGHTER, *not being able to recognise themselves at all in the* LEADING LADY *and* LEADING MAN, *yet hearing them deliver the very words they used, react in a variety of ways, now with a gesture, now with a smile, with open protest even, to the impression they receive. They are surprised, lost in wonder, in suffering . . . as we shall see. The* PROMPTER's *voice is clearly heard throughout the scene.)*

LEADING MAN: Good afternoon, Miss!

FATHER *(immediately, unable to restrain himself)*: No! No! *(And the* STEPDAUGHTER, *seeing the* LEADING MAN *enter in this way, bursts out laughing.)*

PRODUCER *(infuriated)*: Shut up! And once and for all . . . Stop that laughing! We shan't get anywhere if we go on like this!

STEPDAUGHTER *(moving away from the proscenium)*: Forgive me . . . but I couldn't help laughing! This lady *(Pointing to the* LEADING LADY.) stands just where you put her, without budging an inch . . . But if she's meant to be me.

. . . I can assure you that if I heard anybody saying 'Good afternoon' to me in that way and in that tone of voice I'd burst out laughing. . . . So I had to, you see.

FATHER *(coming forward a little, too)*: Yes, that's it exactly. . . . His manner. . . . The tone of voice. . . .

PRODUCER: To hell with your manner and your tone of voice! Just stand to one side, if you don't mind, and let me get a look at this rehearsal.

LEADING MAN *(coming forward)*: Now if I've got to play an old fellow who's coming into a house of rather doubtful character. . . .

PRODUCER: Oh, don't take any notice of him! Now, *please!* Start again, please! It was going very nicely. *(There is a pause—he is clearly waiting for the* LEADING MAN *to begin again.)* Well?

LEADING MAN: Good afternoon, Miss.

LEADING LADY: Good afternoon!

LEADING MAN *(repeating the* FATHER's *move—that is, looking up into the* LEADING LADY's *face from under the brim of her hat; but then expressing very clearly first his satisfaction and then his fear)*: M'm . . . this won't be the first time, I hope. . . .

FATHER *(unable to resist the temptation to correct him)*: Not 'hope'—'will it?', 'will it?'

PRODUCER: You say 'will it?' . . . It's a question.

LEADING MAN *(pointing to the* PROMPTER): I'm sure he said, 'hope.'

PRODUCER: Well, it's all one! 'Hope' or whatever it was! Go on, please! Go on. . . . Oh, there was one thing . . . I think perhaps it ought not to be quite so heavy. . . . Hold on, I'll show you what I mean. Watch me. . . . *(Comes back on to the stage. Then, making his entrance, he proceeds to play the part.)* Good afternoon, Miss.

LEADING LADY: Good afternoon. . . .

PRODUCER: M'm. . . . *(Turning to the* LEADING MAN *to impress on him the way he has looked up at the* LEADING LADY *from under the brim of her hat.)* Surprise, fear and satisfaction. *(Then turning back to the* LEADING LADY.) It won't be the first time, will it, that you've been here? *(Turning again to the* LEADING MAN *enquiringly.)* Is that clear? *(to the* LEADING LADY) And then you say, 'No, sir.' *(to the* LEADING MAN) There you are. . . . It wants to be a little more . . . what shall I say? . . . A little more flexible. A little more *souple!* *(He goes down from the stage again.)*

LEADING LADY: No, sir. . . .

LEADING MAN: You've been here before? More than once?

PRODUCER: Wait a minute! You must let her *(pointing to the* LEADING LADY.) get her nod in first. You've been here before? *(The* LEADING LADY *lifts her head a little, closing her eyes painfully as if in disgust and then when the* PRODUCER *says* DOWN, *nods twice.)*

STEPDAUGHTER (*unable to restrain herself*): Oh, my God! (*And immediately she puts her hand over her mouth to stifle her laughter.*)

PRODUCER (*turning*): What's the matter?

STEPDAUGHTER (*immediately*): Nothing! Nothing!

PRODUCER (*to the* LEADING MAN): It's your cue. . . . Carry straight on.

LEADING MAN: More than once? Well then . . . Come along . . . May I take off your hat? (*The* LEADING MAN *says this last line in such a tone of voice and accompanies it with such a gesture that the* STEPDAUGHTER, *who has remained with her hands over her mouth, can no longer restrain herself. She tries desperately to prevent herself from laughing but a noisy burst of laughter comes irresistibly through her fingers.*)

LEADING LADY (*turning indignantly*): I'm not going to stand here and be made a fool of by that woman!

LEADING MAN: And neither am I. Let's pack the whole thing in.

PRODUCER (*shouting at the* STEPDAUGHTER): Once and for all, will you shut up!

STEPDAUGHTER: Yes. . . . Forgive me, please! . . . Forgive me!

PRODUCER: The trouble with you is that you've got no manners! You go too far!

FATHER (*trying to intervene*): Yes, sir, you're quite right! Quite right! But you must forgive her. . . .

PRODUCER (*climbing back on to the stage*): What do you want me to forgive? It's absolutely disgusting the way she's behaving!

FATHER: Yes. . . . But . . . Oh, believe me . . . Believe me, it has such a strange effect. . . .

PRODUCER: Strange? How do you mean, 'Strange'? What's so strange about it?

FATHER: You see, sir, I admire . . . I admire your actors . . . That gentleman there (*Pointing to the* LEADING MAN.) and that lady (*Pointing to the* LEADING LADY.) . . . But . . . Well . . . The truth is . . . They're certainly not us!

PRODUCER: I should hope not! How do you expect them to be you if they're actors?

FATHER: Just so, actors. And they play our parts well, both of them. But when they act . . . To us they seem to be doing something quite different. They want to be the same . . . And all the time they just aren't.

PRODUCER: But how aren't they the same? What are they then?

FATHER: Something that becomes theirs . . . And no longer ours.

PRODUCER: But that's inevitable! I've told you that already.

FATHER: Yes. I understand . . . I understand that. . . .

PRODUCER: Well then, let's hear no more on the subject! (*Turning to the* ACTORS.) We'll run through it later by ourselves in the usual way. I've always had a strong aversion to holding rehearsals with the author present. He's never satisfied! (*Turning to the* FATHER *and the* STEPDAUGHTER.) Now, come on, Let's get on with it! And let's see if we can have no more laughing! (*to the* STEPDAUGHTER.)

STEPDAUGHTER: Oh, I shan't laugh any more! I promise you! My big bit's coming now. . . . Just you wait and see!

PRODUCER: Well, then. . . . When you say, 'Please don't give another thought to what I said! I, too, you understand. . . .' (*Turning to the* FATHER.) You come in at once with, 'I understand! I understand! and immediately ask . . .

STEPDAUGHTER (*interrupting him*): What? What does he ask?

PRODUCER: . . . why you're in mourning.

STEPDAUGHTER: Oh, no! That's not it at all! Listen! When I told him that I mustn't think about my being in mourning, do you know what his answer was? 'Well, then, let's take this little frock off at once, shall we!'

PRODUCER: That would be wonderful! Wonderful! That *would* bring the house down!

STEPDAUGHTER: But it's the truth!

PRODUCER: But what's the truth got to do with it? Acting's what we're here for! Truth's all very fine. . . . But only up to a point.

STEPDAUGHTER: And what do you want then?

PRODUCER: You'll see! You'll see. Leave everything to me.

STEPDAUGHTER: No, I won't! What you'd like to do, no doubt, is to concoct a romantic, sentimental little affair out of my disgust, out of all the reasons, each more cruel, each viler than the other, why I am this sort of woman, why I am what I am! An affair with him! He asks me why I'm in mourning and I reply with tears in my eyes that my father died only two months ago. No! No! He must say what he said then, 'Well, then, let's take this little frock off at once, shall we? And I . . . my heart still grieving for my father's death. . . . I went behind there. . . . Do you understand? . . . There, behind that screen! And then, my fingers trembling with shame and disgust, I took off my frock, undid my brassiere. . . .

PRODUCER (*running his hands through his hair*): For God's sake! What on earth are you saying, girl?

STEPDAUGHTER (*crying out excitedly*): The truth! The truth!

PRODUCER: Yes, it probably is the truth! I'm not denying it! And I understand . . . I fully appreciate all your horror: But you must realise that we simply can't put this kind of thing on the stage.

STEPDAUGHTER: Oh, you can't, can't you? If that's how things are, thanks very much! I'm going!

PRODUCER: No! No! Look here! . . .

STEPDAUGHTER: I'm going! I'm not stopping here! You worked it all out together, didn't you? . . . The pair of you. . . . You and him. . . . When you were in there. . . . You worked out what was going to be possible on the stage. Oh, thanks very much! I understand! He wants to jump to the bit where he presents his spiritual torments! *(This is said harshly.)* But I want to present my own drama! *Mine! Mine!*

PRODUCER *(his shoulders shaking with annoyance)*: Ah! There we have it! *Your* drama! Look here . . . you'll have to forgive me for telling you this . . . but there isn't only your part to be considered! Each of the others has his drama, too. *(He points to the* FATHER.*)* He has his and your Mother has hers. You can't have one character coming along like this, becoming too prominent, invading the stage in and out of season and overshadowing all the rest. All the characters must be contained within one harmonious picture, and presenting only what it is proper to present. I'm very well aware that everyone carries a complete life within himself and that he wants to put it before the whole world. But it's here that we run into difficulties: how are we to bring out only just so much as is absolutely necessary? . . . And at the same time, of course, to take into account all the other characters. . . . And yet in that small fragment we have to be able to hint at all the rest of the secret life of that character. Ah, it would be all very pleasant if each character could have a nice little monologue. . . . Or without making any bones about it, give a lecture, in which he could tell his audience what's bubbling and boiling away inside him. *(His tone is good-humoured, conciliatory.)* You must restrain yourself. And believe me, it's in your own interest, too. Because all this fury . . . this exasperation and this disgust . . . They make a bad impression. Especially when . . . And pardon me for mentioning this. . . . You yourself have confessed that you'd had other men there at Madame Pace's before him. . . . And more than once!

STEPDAUGHTER *(bowing her head. She pauses a moment in recollection and then, a deeper note in her voice)*: That is true! But you must remember that those other men mean *him* for me, just as much as he himself does!

PRODUCER *(uncomprehending)*: What? The other men mean *him*? What do you mean?

STEPDAUGHTER: Isn't it true that in the case of someone who's gone wrong, the person who was responsible for the first fault is responsible for all the faults which follow? And in my case, he is responsible. . . . Has been ever since before I was born. Look at him, and see if it isn't true!

PRODUCER: Very well, then! And does this terrible weight of remorse that is resting on his spirit seem so slight a thing to you? Give him the chance of acting it!

STEPDAUGHTER: How? How can he act all his 'noble' remorse, all his 'moral' torments, if you want to spare him all the horror of one day finding in his arms. . . . After he had asked her to take off her frock . . . her grief still undulled by time. . . . The horror of finding in his arms that child. . . . A woman now, and a fallen woman already. . . . That child whom he used to go and watch as she came out of school? *(She says these last words in a voice trembling with emotion. The* MOTHER, *hearing her talk like this, is overcome by distress which expresses itself at first in stifled sobs. Finally she breaks out into a fit of bitter crying. Everyone is deeply moved. There is a long pause.)*

STEPDAUGHTER *(gravely and resolutely, as soon as the* MOTHER *shows signs of becoming a little quieter)*: At the moment we are here, unknown as yet by the public. Tomorrow you will present us as you wish. . . . Making up your play in your own way. But would you really like to see our drama? To see it flash into life as it did in reality?

PRODUCER: Why, of course! I couldn't ask for anything better, so that from now on I can use as much as possible of it.

STEPDAUGHTER: Well, then, ask my Mother to leave us.

MOTHER *(rising, her quiet weeping changed to a sharp cry)*: No! No! Don't you allow them to do it! Don't allow them to do it!

PRODUCER: But it's only so that I can see how it goes.

MOTHER: I can't bear it! I can't bear it!

PRODUCER: But since it's already happened, I don't understand!

MOTHER: No, it's happening now! It happens all the time! My torment is no pretence, sir. I am alive and I am present always. . . . At every moment of my torment . . . A torment which is for ever renewing itself. Always alive and always present. But those two children there . . . Have you heard them say a single word? They can no longer speak! They cling to me still. . . . In order to keep my torment living and present! But for themselves they no longer exist! They no longer exist! And she *(Pointing to the* STEPDAUGHTER.*)* . . . She has run away. . . . Run away from me and is lost. . . . Lost! . . . And if I see her here before me it is for this reason and for this reason alone. . . . To renew at all times. . . . Forever. . . . To bring before me again, present and living, the anguish that I have suffered on her account too.

FATHER *(solemnly)*: The eternal moment, as I told you, sir. She *(He points to the* STEPDAUGHTER.*)* . . . She is here in order to fix me. . . . To hold me suspended throughout all eternity. . . . In the pillory of that one fleeting shameful moment in my life. She cannot renounce her role . . . And you, sir, cannot really spare me my agony.

PRODUCER: Quite so, but I didn't say that I wouldn't present it. As a matter of fact it'll form the basis of the first act. . . . Up to the point where she surprises you *(Pointing to the* MOTHER.*)*

FATHER: That is right. Because it is my sentence. All our passion. . . . All our suffering. . . . Which must culminate in *her* cry. *(Pointing to the* MOTHER.*)*

STEPDAUGHTER: I can still hear it ringing in my ears! That cry sent me mad! You can play me just as you like . . . It doesn't matter. Dressed, if you like, provided that I can have my arms bare at least. . . . Just my arms bare. . . . Because, you see, standing there. . . . *(She goes up to the* FATHER *and rests her head on his chest.)* With my head resting on his chest like this . . . and with my arms round his neck . . . I could see a vein throbbing away in my arm. And then . . . Just as if that pulsing vein alone gave me a sense of horror . . . I shut my eyes tight and buried my head in his chest. *(Turning towards the* MOTHER.*)* Scream, Mummy! Scream! *(She buries her head in the* FATHER'S *chest and, raising her shoulders as if in order not to hear the cry, adds in a voice stifled with torment.)* Scream, as you screamed then!

MOTHER *(rushing upon them to separate them)*: No! No! She's my daughter! *(And having torn her daughter away.)* You brute! You brute! She's my daughter! Can't you see that she's my daughter?

PRODUCER *(retreating at the cry right up to the footlights, amid the general dismay of the* ACTORS*)*: Excellent! Excellent! And then . . . Curtain! Curtain!

FATHER *(rushing over to him convulsively)*: Yes, because that's how it really happened!

PRODUCER *(quite convinced, admiration in his voice)*: Oh, yes, we must have the curtain there. . . . That cry and then . . . Curtain! Curtain!

(At the repeated shouts of the PRODUCER *the* STAGE-HAND *on the curtain lets it down, leaving the* PRODUCER *and the* FATHER *between it and the footlights.)*

PRODUCER *(looking up, his arms raised)*: Oh, the damned fool! I say, 'Curtain' . . . Meaning that I want the act to end there. . . . And he really does go and bring the curtain down. *(to the* FATHER, *lifting up a corner of the curtain.)* Oh, yes! That's absolutely wonderful! Very good indeed! That'll get them! There's no *if* or *but* about it. . . . That line and then . . . *Curtain!* We've got something in that first act . . . or I'm a Dutchman! *(Disappears through the curtain with the* FATHER.*)*

ACT 3

(When the curtain goes up again the audience sees that the STAGE-HANDS *have dismantled the previous set and put on in its place a small garden fountain. On one side of the stage the* ACTORS *are sitting in a row, and on the other side, the* CHARACTERS. *The* PRODUCER *is standing in a meditative attitude in the middle of the stage with his hand clenched over his mouth. There is a brief pause.)*

PRODUCER *(with a shrug of his shoulders)*: Oh, well! . . . Let's get on with Act II! Now if you'll only leave it all to me, as we agreed, everything'll sort itself out.

STEPDAUGHTER: This is where we make our entry into his house . . . *(Pointing to the* FATHER.*)* In spite of him! *(Pointing to the* SON.*)*

PRODUCER *(out of patience)*: Yes, yes! But leave it to me, I tell you!

STEPDAUGHTER: Well. . . . So long as it's made quite clear that it was against his wishes.

MOTHER *(from the corner, shaking her head)*: For all the good that's come of it. . . .

STEPDAUGHTER *(turning to her quickly)*: That doesn't matter! The more harm that it's done us, the more remorse for him!

PRODUCER *(impatiently)*: I understand all that! I'll take it all into account! don't you worry about it!

MOTHER *(a supplicant note in her voice)*: But I do beg you, sir . . . To set my conscience at rest. . . . To make it quite plain that I tried in every way I could to . . .

STEPDAUGHTER *(interrupting contemptuously and continuing her* MOTHER'S *speech)*: . . . to pacify me, to persuade me not to get my own back. . . . *(to the* PRODUCER*)* Go on . . . do what she asks you! Give her that satisfaction. . . . Because she's quite right, you know! I'm enjoying myself no end, because . . . Well, just look . . . The meeker she is, the more she tries to wriggle her way into his heart, the more he holds himself aloof, the more distant he becomes. I can't think why she bothers!

PRODUCER: Are we going to get started on the second act or are we not?

STEPDAUGHTER: I won't say another word! But, you know, it won't be possible to play it all in the garden, as you suggested.

PRODUCER: Why not?

STEPDAUGHTER: Because he *(Pointing to the* SON *again.)* shuts himself up in his room all the time. . . . Holding himself aloof. . . . And, what's more, there's all the boy's part. . . . Poor bewildered little devil. . . . As I told you, all that takes place indoors.

PRODUCER: I know all about that! On the other hand you do understand that we can hardly stick up notices telling the audience what the scene is. . . . Or change the set three or four times in one act.

LEADING MAN: They used to in the good old days.

PRODUCER: Oh, yes. . . . When the intelligence of the audience was about up to the level of that little girl's there. . . .

LEADING LADY: And it does make it easier to get the sense of illusion.

FATHER (immediately, rising): Illusion, did you say? For Heaven's sake, please don't use the word illusion! Please don't use that word. . . . It's a particularly cruel one for us!

PRODUCER (astounded): And why's that?

FATHER: It's cruel! Cruel! You should have known that!

PRODUCER: What ought we to say then? We were referring to the illusion that we have to create on this stage . . . for the audience. . . .

LEADING MAN: . . . with our acting. . . .

PRODUCER: . . . the illusion of a reality!

FATHER: I understand, sir. But you . . . Perhaps you can't understand us. Forgive me! Because . . . you see . . . for you and for your actors, all this is only . . . and quite rightly so. . . . All this is only a game.

LEADING LADY (indignantly interrupting him): What do you mean, a game? We're not children! We're serious actors!

FATHER: I don't deny it! And in fact, in using the term, I was referring to your art which must, as this gentleman has said, create a perfect illusion of reality.

PRODUCER: Precisely!

FATHER: Now just consider the fact that we (Pointing quickly to himself and to the other FIVE CHARACTERS.) as ourselves, have no other reality outside this illusion!

PRODUCER (in utter astonishment, looking round at his actors who show the same bewildered amazement): And what does all that mean?

FATHER (the ghost of a smile on his face. There is a brief pause while he looks at them all): As I said. . . . What other reality should we have? What for you is an illusion that you have to create, for us, on the other hand, is our sole reality. The only reality we know. (There he takes a step or two toward the PRODUCER and adds.) But it's not only true in our case, you know. Just think it over. (He looks into his eyes.) Can you tell me who you are? (And he stands there pointing his index finger at him.)

PRODUCER (disturbed, a half-smile on his lips): What? Who am I? I'm myself!

FATHER: And suppose I were to tell you that that wasn't true? Suppose I told you that you were me? . . .

PRODUCER: I should say that you were mad! (The ACTORS laugh.)

FATHER: You're quite right to laugh, because here everything's a game. (to the PRODUCER) And you can object, therefore, that it's only in fun that that gentleman (Pointing to the LEADING MAN.) who is himself must be me who, on the contrary, am myself. . . . That is, the person you see here. There, you see. I've caught you in a trap! (The ACTORS laugh again.)

PRODUCER (annoyed): But you said all this not ten minutes ago! Do we have to go over all that again?

FATHER: No. As a matter of fact that wasn't what I intended. I should like to invite you to abandon this game . . . (Looking at the LEADING LADY as if to forestall what she will say.) Your art! Your art! . . . The game that it is customary for you and your actors to play here in this theatre. And once again I ask you in all seriousness. . . . Who are you?

PRODUCER (turning to the ACTORS in utter amazement, an amazement not unmixed with irritation): What a cheek the fellow has! A man who calls himself a character comes here and asks me who I am!

FATHER (with dignity, but in no way haughtily): A character, sir, may always ask a man who he is. Because a character has a life which is truly his, marked with his own special characteristics. . . . And as a result he is always somebody! Whilst a man. . . . And I'm not speaking of you personally at the moment. . . . Man in general . . . Can quite well be nobody.

PRODUCER: That as may be! But you're asking me these questions. Me, do you understand? The Producer! The boss!

FATHER (softly, with gentle humility): But only in order to know if you, you as you really are now, are seeing yourself as, for instance, after all the time that has gone by, you see yourself as you were at some point in the past. . . . With all the illusions that you had then . . . with everything . . . all the things you had deep down inside you . . . everything that made up your external world . . . everything as it appeared to you then . . . and as it was, as it was in reality for you then! Well . . . thinking back on those illusions which you no longer have . . . on all those things that no longer seem to be what they were once upon a time . . . don't you feel that . . . I won't say these boards. . . . No! . . . That the very earth itself is slipping away from under your feet, when you reflect that in the same way this you that you now feel yourself to be . . . all your reality as it is today . . . is destined to seem an illusion tomorrow?

PRODUCER (not having understood much of all this, and somewhat taken aback by this argument): Well? And where does all this get us, anyway?

FATHER: Nowhere. I only want to make you see that if

we (*Again pointing to himself and to the other* CHARACTERS.) have no reality outside the world of illusion, it would be as well if you mistrusted your own reality. . . . The reality that you breathe and touch today . . . Because like the reality of yesterday, it is fated to reveal itself as a mere illusion tomorrow.

PRODUCER (*deciding to make fun of him*): Oh, excellent! And so you'd say that you and this play of yours that you've been putting on for my benefit are more real than I am?

FATHER (*with the utmost seriousness*): Oh, without a doubt.

PRODUCER: Really?

FATHER: I thought that you'd understood that right from the very beginning.

PRODUCER: More real than I am?

FATHER: If your reality can change from one day to the next. . . .

PRODUCER: But everybody knows that it can change like that! It's always changing. . . . Just like everybody else's.

FATHER (*with a cry*): No, ours doesn't change! You see. . . . That's the difference between us! Our reality doesn't change. . . . It can't change. . . . It can never be in any way different from what it is. . . . Because it is already fixed. . . . Just as it is. . . . For ever! For ever it is *this* reality. . . . It's terrible! . . . This immutable reality. . . . It should make you shudder to come near us!

PRODUCER (*quickly, suddenly struck by an idea. He moves over and stands squarely in front of him*): I should like to know, however, when anyone ever saw a character step out of his part and begin a long dissertation on it like the one you've just been making. . . . Expounding it. . . . Explaining it. . . . Can you tell me? . . . I've never seen it happen before!

FATHER: You have never seen it happen before because authors usually hide the details of their work of creation. Once the characters are alive. . . . Once they are standing truly alive before their author. . . . He does nothing but follow the words and gestures that they suggest to him. . . . And he must want them to be what they themselves want to be. For woe betide him if he doesn't do what they wish him to do! When a character is born he immediately acquires such an independence . . . Even of his own author. . . . That everyone can imagine him in a whole host of situations in which his author never thought of placing him. . . . They can even imagine his acquiring, sometimes, a significance that the author never dreamt of giving him.

PRODUCER: Yes. . . . I know all that!

FATHER: Well, then, why are you so astonished at seeing us? Just imagine what a misfortune it is for a character to be born alive. . . . Created by the imagination of an author who afterwards sought to deny him life. . . . Now tell me whether a character who has been left unrealised in this way. . . . Living, yet without a life. . . . Whether this character hasn't the right to do what we are doing now. . . . Here and now. . . . For your benefit? . . . After we had spent . . . Oh, such ages, believe me! . . . Doing it for his benefit . . . Trying to persuade him, trying to urge him to realise us. . . . First of all I would present myself to him. . . . Then she would . . . (*Pointing to the* STEPDAUGHTER.) . . . And then her poor Mother. . . .

STEPDAUGHTER (*coming forward as if in a trance*): Yes, what he says is true. . . . I would go and tempt him. . . . There, in his gloomy study. . . . Just at twilight. . . . He would be sitting there, sunk in an armchair. . . . Not bothering to stir himself and switch on the light. . . . Content to let the room get darker and darker. . . . Until the whole room was filled with a darkness that was alive with our presence. . . . We were there to tempt him. . . . (*And then, as if she saw herself as still in that study and irritated by the presence of all those actors.*) Oh, go away. . . . All of you! Leave us alone! Mummy . . . and her son. . . . I and the little girl. . . . The boy by himself. . . . Always by himself. . . . Then he and I together. (*A faint gesture in the direction of the* FATHER) And then. . . . By myself. . . . By myself . . . alone in that darkness. (*A sudden turn round as if she wished to seize and fix the vision that she has of herself, the living vision of herself that she sees shining in the darkness.*) Yes, my life! Ah, what scenes, what wonderful scenes we suggested to him! And I . . . I tempted him more than any of them. . . .

FATHER: Indeed you did! And it may well be that it's all your fault that he wouldn't give us the life we asked for. . . . You were too persistent. . . . Too impudent. . . . You exaggerated too much. . . .

STEPDAUGHTER: What? When it was he who wanted me to be what I am? (*She goes up to the* PRODUCER *and says confidentially.*) I think it's much more likely that he refused because he felt depressed . . . or because of his contempt for the theatre. . . . Or at least, for the present-day theatre with all its pandering to the box-office. . . .

PRODUCER: Let's get on! Let's get on, for God's sake! Let's have some action!

STEPDAUGHTER: It looks to me as if we've got too much action for you already. . . . Just staging our entry into his house. (*Pointing to the* FATHER.) You yourself said that you couldn't stick up notices or be changing the set every five minutes.

PRODUCER: And neither can we! Of course we can't! What we've got to do is to combine and group all the action into one continuous well-knit scene. . . . Not the sort of thing that you want. . . . With, first of all, your younger brother coming home from school and wandering about the house like some lost soul. . . . Hiding behind doors and brooding on a plan that . . . What did you say it does to him?

STEPDAUGHTER: Dries him up. . . . Shrivels him up completely.

PRODUCER: M'm! Well, as you said. . . . And all the time you can see it more and more clearly in his eyes. . . . Wasn't that what you said?

STEPDAUGHTER: Yes. . . . just look at him! (*Pointing to where he is standing by his* MOTHER.)

PRODUCER: And then, at the same time, you want the child to be playing in the garden, blissfully unaware of everything. The boy in the house, the little girl in the garden. . . . I ask you!

STEPDAUGHTER: Yes . . . happily playing in the sun! That is the only pleasure that I have. . . . Her happiness. . . . All the joy that she gets from playing in the garden. . . . After the wretchedness and the squalor of that horrible room where we all four slept together. . . . And she had to sleep with me. . . . Just think of it. . . . My vile contaminated body next to hers! . . . With her holding me tight in her loving, innocent, little arms! She only had to get a glimpse of me in the garden and she'd run up to me and take me by the hand. She wasn't interested in the big flowers . . . she'd run about looking for the . . . 'weeny' ones. . . . So that she could point them out to me. . . . And she'd be so happy. . . . So excited. . . . (*As she says this she is torn by the memory of it all and gives a long, despairing cry, dropping her head on to her hands which are lying loosely on the little table in front of her. At the sight of her emotion everyone is deeply moved. The* PRODUCER *goes up to her almost paternally and says comfortingly.*)

PRODUCER: We'll have the garden in . . . don't you worry. . . . We'll have the garden scene in. . . . Just you wait and see. . . . You'll be quite satisfied with how I arrange it. . . . We'll play everything in the garden. (*Calling a* STAGE-HAND.) Hey (*his name*)! Let me have something in the shape of a tree or two. . . . A couple of not-too-large cypresses in front of this fountain! (*Two small cypresses descend from the flies. The* FOREMAN *dashes up and fixes them with struts and nails.*)

PRODUCER (*to the* STEPDAUGHTER): That'll do. . . . For the moment anyway. . . . It'll give us a rough idea. (*Calls to the* STAGE-HAND *again.*) Oh (*his name*), let me have something for a sky, will you?

STAGE HAND (*up aloft*): Eh?

PRODUCER: Something for a sky! A flat to go behind the fountain! (*And a white backcloth descends from the flies.*)

PRODUCER: Not white! I said I wanted a sky! Oh, well, it doesn't matter. . . . Leave it! Leave it! . . . I'll fix it myself. . . . (*Calls.*) Hey! . . . You there on the lights! . . . Everything off. . . . And let me have the moonlight blues on! . . . Blues in the batten! . . . A couple of blue spots on the backcloth! . . . Yes, that's it! That's just right!

(*There is now a mysterious moonlit effect about the scene, and the* ACTORS *are prompted to move about and to speak as they would if they were indeed walking in a moonlit garden.*)

PRODUCER (*to the* STEPDAUGHTER): There, do you see? Now the Boy, instead of hiding behind doors inside the house, can move about the garden and hide behind these trees. But, you know, it'll be rather difficult to find a little girl to play that scene with you. . . . The one where she shows you the flowers. (*Turning to the* BOY.) Now come down here a bit! Let's see how it works out! (*Then, since the* BOY *doesn't move.*) Come on! Come on! (*He drags him forward and tries to make him hold his head up. But after every attempt down it falls again.*) Good God, here's a fine how d'ye do. . . . There's something queer about this boy. . . . What's the matter with him? . . . My God, he'll have to say *something.* . . . (*He goes up to him, puts a hand on his shoulder and places him behind one of the trees.*) Now. . . . Forward a little! . . . Let me see you! . . . M'm! . . . Now hide yourself. . . . That's it! Now try popping your head out a bit. . . . Take a look round. . . . (*He goes to one side to study the effect and the* BOY *does what he has been told to do. The* ACTORS *look on, deeply affected and quite dismayed.*) That's excellent! . . . Yes, excellent! (*Turning again to the* STEPDAUGHTER.) Suppose the little girl were to catch sight of him there as he was looking out, and run over to him. . . . Wouldn't that drag a word or two out of him? . . .

STEPDAUGHTER (*rising*): It's no use your hoping that he'll speak. . . . At least not so long as *he's* here. (*Pointing to the* SON.) If you want him to speak, you'll have to send *him* away first.

SON (*going resolutely toward the steps down into the auditorium*): Willingly! I'm only too happy to oblige. Nothing could possibly suit me better!

PRODUCER (*immediately catching hold of him*): Hey! Oh no you don't! Where are you going? You hang on a minute!

(*The* MOTHER *rises in dismay, filled with anguish at the thought that he really is going away. She instinctively raises her arms to prevent him from going, without, however, moving from where she is standing.*)

SON (*he has reached the footlights*): I tell you . . . There's absolutely nothing for me to do here! Let me go, please! Let me go! (*This to the* PRODUCER.)

PRODUCER: What do you mean . . . There's nothing for you to do?

STEPDAUGHTER (*placidly, ironically*): Don't bother to hold him back! He won't go away!

FATHER: He has to play that terrible scene with his Mother in the garden.

SON (*immediately, fiercely, resolutely*): I'm not playing anything! I've said that all along! (*To the* PRODUCER) Let me go!

STEPDAUGHTER (*running over, then addressing the* PRODUCER) Do you mind? (*She gets him to lower the hand with which he has been restraining the* SON.) Let him go! (*Then turning to the* SON, *as soon as the* PRODUCER *has dropped his arm.*) Well, go on. . . . Leave us!

(*The* SON *stands where he is, still straining in the direction of the steps, but, as if held back by some mysterious force, he cannot go down them. Then, amidst the utter dismay and anxious bewilderment of the* ACTORS, *he wanders slowly along the length of the footlights in the direction of the other flight of steps. Once there, he again finds himself unable to descend, much as he would wish to. The* STEPDAUGHTER *has watched his progress intently, her eyes challenging, defiant. Now she bursts out laughing.*)

STEPDAUGHTER: He can't, you see! He can't leave us! He must remain here. . . . He has no choice but to remain with us! He's chained to us. . . . Irrevocably! But if I . . . Who really do run away when what is inevitable happens. . . . And I run away because of my hatred for him. . . . I run away just because I can no longer bear the sight of him. . . . Well, if I can still stay here. . . . If I can still put up with his company and with having to have him here before my eyes. . . . Do you think it's likely that he can run away? Why, he was to stay here with that precious father of his. . . . With his mother. . . . Because now she has no other children but him. . . . (*Turning to her* MOTHER.) Come on, Mummy! Come on. . . . (*Turning to the* PRODUCER *and pointing to the* MOTHER.) There. . . . you see. . . . She'd got up to prevent him from going. . . . (*to her* MOTHER, *as if willing her actions by some magic power*) Come on! Come on! (*Then to the* PRODUCER.) You can imagine just how reluctant she is to give this proof of her affection in front of your actors. But so great is her desire to be with him that . . . There! . . . You see? . . . She's willing to live out again her scene with him! (*And as a matter of fact the* MOTHER *has gone up to her* SON, *and scarcely has the* STEPDAUGHTER *finished speaking before she makes a gesture to indicate her agreement.*)

SON (*immediately*): No! No! You're not going to drag me into this! If I can't get away, I shall stay here! But I repeat that I'm not going to do any acting at all!

FATHER (*trembling with excitement, to the* PRODUCER): You can force him to act!

SON: Nobody can force me!

FATHER: I can and I will!

STEPDAUGHTER: Wait! Wait! First of all the little girl has to go to the fountain. . . . (*Goes over to the* LITTLE GIRL. *She drops on to her knees in front of her and takes her face in her hands.*) Poor little darling. . . . You're looking so bewildered. . . . With those beautiful eyes. . . . You must be wondering just where you are. We're on a stage, dear! What's a stage? Well . . . It's a place where you play at being serious. They put on plays here. And now we're putting a play on. Really and truly! Even you. . . . (*Embracing her, clasping her to her breast and rocking her for a moment or so*) Oh, you little darling. . . . My dear little darling, what a terrible play for you. . . . What a horrible end they've thought out for you! The garden, the fountain. . . . Yes, it's a make-believe fountain . . . The pity is, darling, that everything's make-believe here . . . But perhaps you like a make-believe fountain better than a real one. . . . So that you can play in it. . . . M'm? No. . . . It'll be a game for the others. . . . Not for you unfortunately . . . Because you're real. . . . And you really play by a real fountain. . . . A lovely big green one, with masses of bamboo palms casting shadows. . . . Looking at your reflection in the water. . . . And lots and lots of little baby ducklings swimming about in it, breaking the shadow into a thousand little ripples. You try to take hold of one of the ducklings. . . . (*With a shriek which fills everybody with dismay.*) No, Rosetta, no! Your Mummy's not looking after you. . . . And all because of that swine there. . . . Her son! I feel as if all the devils in hell were loose inside me. . . . And he . . . (*Leaves the* LITTLE GIRL *and turns with her usual scorn to the* BOY.) What are you doing . . . drooping there like that? . . . Always the little beggar-boy! It'll be your fault too if that baby drowns. . . . Because of the way you go on. . . . As if I didn't pay for everybody when I got you into this house. (*Seizing his arm to make him take his hand out of his pocket.*) What have you got there? What are you trying to hide? Out with it! Take that hand out of your pocket! (*She snatches his hand out of his pocket and to everybody's horror reveals that it is clenched round a revolver. She looks at him for a little while, as if satisfied. Then she says somberly.*) M'm! Where did you get that gun from? . . . And how did you manage to lay your hands on it? (*And since the* BOY, *in his utter dismay—his eyes are staring and vacant—does not reply.*) You idiot! If I'd been you I shouldn't have killed myself. . . . I'd have killed one of *them*. . . . Or the pair of them! Father and son together! (*She hides them behind the cypress tree where he was lurking before. Then she takes the* LITTLE GIRL *by the hand and leads her towards the fountain. She puts her into the basin of the fountain, and makes her lie down so that she is completely hidden. Finally she goes down on her knees and buries her head in her hands on the rim of the basin of the fountain.*)

PRODUCER: That's it! Good! (*Turning to the* SON.) And at the same time. . . .

SON (*angrily*): What do you mean . . . 'And at the same time'? Oh, no! . . . Nothing of the sort! There never was any scene between her and me! (*Pointing to the* MOTHER.) You make her tell you what really happened! (*Meanwhile the* SECOND ACTRESS *and the* JUVENILE LEAD *have detached themselves from the group of* ACTORS *and are standing gazing intently at the* MOTHER *and the* SON *so that later thay can act these parts.*)

MOTHER: Yes, it's true, sir! I'd gone to his room at the time.

SON: There! Did you hear? To my room! Not into the garden!

PRODUCER: That doesn't matter at all! As I said we'll have to run all the action together into one composite scene!

SON (*becoming aware that the* JUVENILE LEAD *is studying him*): What do you want?

JUVENILE LEAD: Nothing! I was just looking at you.

SON (*turning to the* SECOND ACTRESS): Oh! . . . And *you're* here too, are you? All ready to play *her* part, I suppose? (*Pointing to the* MOTHER.)

PRODUCER: That's the idea! And if you want my opinion you ought to be damned grateful for all the attention they're paying you.

SON: Indeed? Thank you! But hasn't it dawned on you yet that you aren't going to be able to stage this play? Not even the tiniest vestige of us is to be found in you. . . . And all the time your actors are studying us from the outside. Do you think it's possible for us to live confronted by a mirror which, not merely content with freezing us in that particular picture which is the fixing of our expression, has to throw an image back at us which we can no longer recognise? . . . Our own features, yes. . . . But twisted into a horrible grimace.

FATHER: He's quite right! He's quite right, you know!

PRODUCER (*to the* JUVENILE LEAD *and* SECOND ACTRESS): Right you are! Get back with the others!

SON: It's no use your bothering! I'm not having anything to do with this!

PRODUCER: You be quiet for the moment, and let me listen to what your mother has to say. (*to the* MOTHER) You were saying? . . . You'd gone to his room? . . .

MOTHER: Yes, I'd gone to his room. . . . I couldn't bear the strain any longer! I wanted to pour out my heart to him. . . . I wanted to tell him of all the anguish that was tormenting me. . . . But as soon as he saw me come in . . .

SON: There was no scene between us! I rushed out of the room. . . . I didn't want to get involved in any scenes! Because I never have been involved in any! Do you understand?

MOTHER: Yes! That *is* what happened! That is what happened!

PRODUCER: But for the purposes of this play we've simply *got* to have a scene between you and him! Why . . . it's absolutely *essential!*

MOTHER: I'm quite ready to take part in one! Oh, if you could only find some way to give me an opportunity of speaking to him . . . if only for a moment. . . . So that I can pour out my heart to him!

FATHER (*going up to the* SON, *in a great rage*): You'll do what she asks, do you understand? You'll do what your Mother asks!

SON (*more stubbornly than ever*): I'm doing nothing!

FATHER (*taking hold of him by the lapels of his coat and shaking him*): My God, you'll do what I tell you! Or else . . . Can't you hear how she's pleading with you? Haven't you a spark of feeling in you for your Mother?

SON (*grappling with the* FATHER): No, I haven't! For God's sake, let's have done with all this. . . . Once and for all, let's have done with it!

(*General agitation. The* MOTHER *is terrified and tries to get between them in order to separate them.*)

MOTHER: Please! Please!

FATHER (*without relinquishing his hold*): You must obey me! You *must!*

SON (*struggling with him and finally hurling him to the ground. He falls near the steps amidst general horror*): What's come over you? Why are you in this terrible state of frenzy? Haven't you any sense of decency? . . . Going about parading your shame. . . . And ours, too. I'm having nothing to do with this affair! Nothing, do you hear? And by making this stand I am interpreting the wishes of our author, who didn't wish to put us on the stage!

PRODUCER: Oh, God! You come along here and . . .

SON (*pointing to the* FATHER): *He* did! I didn't.

PRODUCER: Aren't you here now?

SON: It was he who wanted to come. . . . And he dragged us all along with him. Then the pair of them went in there with you and agreed on what was to go into the play. But he didn't only stick to what really did occur. . . . No, as if that wasn't enough for any man, he had to put in things that never even happened!

PRODUCER: Well, then, you tell me what really happened! You can at least do that! You rushed out of your room without saying a word?

SON (*he hesitates for a moment*): Without saying a word!

I didn't want to get involved in a scene!

PRODUCER (*pressing him*): And then? What did you do then?

SON (*everybody's attention is on him; amidst the anguished silence he takes a step or two across the front of the stage*): Nothing. . . . As I was crossing the garden . . . (*He breaks off and becomes gloomy and absorbed.*)

PRODUCER (*urging him to speak, very much moved by this extraordinary reserve*): Well? As you were crossing the garden?

SON (*in exasperation, shielding his face with his arm*): Why do you want to force me to tell you? It's horrible!

(*The* MOTHER *is trembling all over and stifled sobs come from her as she looks toward the fountain.*)

PRODUCER (*slowly, quietly . . . he has seen where the* MOTHER *is looking and he now turns to the* SON *with growing apprehension*): The little girl?

SON (*staring straight in front of him, out into the auditorium*): There . . . In the fountain. . . .

FATHER (*from where he is on the floor, pointing with tender pity to the* MOTHER): She was following him. . . .

PRODUCER (*anxiously to the* SON): And what did you do?

SON (*slowly, continuing to stare in front of him*): I rushed up to the fountain. . . . I was about to dive in and fish her out. . . . Then all of a sudden I pulled up short. . . . Behind that tree I saw something that made my blood run cold. . . . The boy. . . . The boy was standing there. . . . Stock still. . . . With madness in his eyes. . . . Staring like some insane creature at his little sister, who was lying drowned in the fountain! (*The* STEPDAUGHTER, *who has all this while been bent over the fountain in order to hide the* LITTLE GIRL, *is sobbing desperately—her sobs coming like an echo from the background. There is a pause.*) I moved towards him. . . . And then . . . (*And from behind the trees where the* BOY *is hidden a revolver shot rings out.*)

MOTHER (*with a heartrending cry she rushes behind the trees accompanied by the* SON *and all the* ACTORS. *There is general confusion*): Oh, my son! My son! (*And then amidst the general hubbub and shouting.*) Help! Oh, help!

PRODUCER (*amidst all the shouting, he tries to clear a space while the* BOY *is carried off behind the skycloth*): Is he wounded? Is he badly hurt?

(*By now everybody, except for the* PRODUCER *and the* FATHER, *who is still on the ground by the steps, has disappeared behind the skycloth. They can be heard muttering and exclaiming in great consternation. Then first from one side, then from the other, the* ACTORS *re-enter.*)

LEADING LADY (*re-entering right, very much moved*): He's dead, poor boy! He's dead! Oh what a terrible thing to happen!

LEADING MAN (*re-entering left, laughing*): What do you mean, dead? It's all make-believe! It's all just a pretence! Don't get taken in by it!

OTHER ACTORS (*entering from the right*): Make-believe? Pretence? Reality! Reality! He's dead!

OTHERS (*from the left*): No! Make-believe! It's all a pretence!

FATHER (*rising and crying out to them*): What do you mean, pretence? Reality, ladies and gentlemen, reality! Reality! (*And desperation in his face, he too disappears behind the backcloth.*)

PRODUCER (*at the end of his tether*): Pretence! Reality! Go to hell, the whole lot of you! Lights! Lights! Lights!

(*The stage and the auditorium are suddenly flooded with very bright light. The* PRODUCER *breathes again as if freed from a tremendous burden. They all stand there looking into one another's eyes, in an agony of suspense and dismay.*)

PRODUCER: My God! Nothing like this has ever happened to me before! I've lost a whole day on their account! (*He looks at his watch.*) You can go home now. . . . All of you! There's nothing we can do now! It's too late to start rehearsing again! I'll see you all this evening. (*And as soon as the* ACTORS *have said 'Goodbye!' and gone he calls out to the* ELECTRICIAN.) Hey (*his name*) Everything off! (*He has hardly got the words out before the theatre is plunged for a moment into utter darkness.*) Hell! You might at least leave me one light on, so that I can see where I'm going!

(*And immediately behind the backcloth, a green flood lights up. It projects the silhouettes of the* CHARACTERS [*minus the* BOY *and the* LITTLE GIRL], *clear-cut and huge, on to the backcloth. The* PRODUCER *is terrified and leaps off the stage. As he does so the green flood is switched off—rather as if its having come on in the first instance had been due to the* ELECTRICIAN'S *having pulled the wrong switch—and the stage is again lit in blue. Slowly the* CHARACTERS *come in and advance to the front of the stage. The* SON *comes in first, from the right, followed by the* MOTHER, *who has her arms outstretched toward him. Then the* FATHER *comes in from the left. They stop halfway down the stage and stand there like people in a trance. Last of all the* STEPDAUGHTER *comes in from the left and runs toward the steps which lead down into the auditorium. With her foot on the top step she stops for a moment to look at the other three and bursts into strident laughter. Then she hurls herself down the steps and runs up the aisle. She stops at the back of the auditorium and turns to look at the three figures standing on the stage. She bursts out laughing again. And when she has disappeared from the auditorium you can still hear her terrible laughter coming from the foyer beyond. A short pause and then,* CURTAIN.)

Figure 1. The Little Girl, the Boy, the Stepdaughter (Barbara Colby), the Son (Paul Shenar), the Mother (Josephine Nichols), and the Father (Richard Dysart) in the American Conservatory Theater production of *Six Characters in Search of an Author,* directed by William Ball and Byron Ringland, San Francisco, 1967. (Photograph: Hank Kranzler.)

Figure 2. The six characters *(standing right)* explain their situation to the producer and actors *(seated left)* in the American Conservatory Theater production of *Six Characters in Search of an Author,* directed by William Ball and Byron Ringland, San Francisco, 1967. (Photograph: Hank Kranzler.)

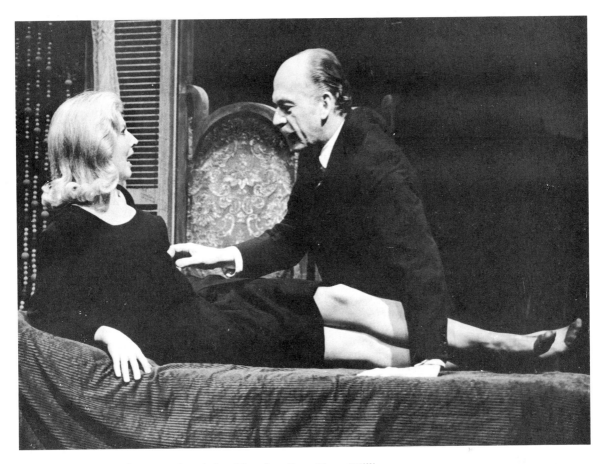

Figure 3. The Father as played by The Leading Man (William Patterson) attempts to seduce the Stepdaughter as played by The Leading Lady (Michael Learned) in the American Conservatory Theater production of *Six Characters in Search of an Author*, directed by William Ball and Byron Ringland, San Francisco, 1967. (Photograph: Hank Kranzler.)

Staging of *Six Characters in Search of an Author*

**REVIEW OF THE AMERICAN CONSERVATORY
THEATER PRODUCTION, 1967, BY JEANNE
MILLER**

The American Conservatory Theater's production of Luigi Pirandello's "Six Characters in Search of an Author" combines all the elements of a suspense melodrama, a philosophical riddle and a black comedy.

It opened last night at Marines' Theater, directed by William Ball and Byron Ringland who have freed the play of many of its enigmas. The tragi-comedy begins quite hilariously with a theatrical company in rehearsal—ACT itself, as a matter of fact, preparing a scene from Brandon Thomas' "Charley's Aunt."

The performers are bouncy and energetic, dressed in brightly colored hippie clothing. Therefore, the appearance of the six characters, starkly garbed in black and undulating in a silent and choreographed lament, strikes an instant and eerie note of fascinating menace.

This same level of paradox is admirably sustained throughout the evening, as the drama veers from the tortured self-analysis of the characters to the shallow interpretation of their passionate history by the actors.

The characters who break into the rehearsal have been abandoned by the author who created them and doomed to wander endlessly unless someone records their story.

The director of the acting company, after futilely attempting to evict them from the theater, finally agrees to have their grim tale portrayed by his troupe. Pandemonium ensues when the actors make a superficial travesty out of the characters' tragic plight.

Richard A. Dysart, who plays the father, is the principal spokesman for Pirandello's cerebrations about reality and illusion. In the hands of a less talented actor, this exposition could easily descend to the level of a windy intellectual exercise. But Dysart infuses his role with such tormented and guilt-ridden emotion that he is enormously moving, especially when he lucidly projects the playwright's thesis about the permanence and value of art in contrast to the absurdity and transiency of life.

Josephine Nichols, too, is excellent as the hapless mother whose frozen, hollow-eyed despair is especially poignant. As the step-daughter, Barbara Colby approaches her role with a steely erotic abandon that is exceedingly effective.

Paul Shenar is properly arrogant and disdainful as the embittered son. And Scott Hylands is engaging as the befuddled director who becomes fascinated and finally distraught by the behavior of the characters. Dion Chesse is also outstanding as the actor who portrays the father.

A note of mordant humor as well as high camp is introduced by the appearance of an actor, Jay Doyle, who plays the role of Madame Pace, the brothel-keeper.

Ball and Ringland have wittily and intelligently kept the production rippling and singing with tremendous theatrical vitality.

SEAN O'CASEY

1880–1964

Although the Abbey Theatre of Dublin did not produce any of his plays until he was forty-three, and though he permanently left Ireland three years later— angered by the tempestuous reception of his work and saddened by the political self-destructiveness of his countrymen—Sean O'Casey remains the most distinguished dramatist of Irish experience to have emerged in the twentieth century or in any other period. The youngest of thirteen children, of whom only five survived, O'Casey (christened John Casey by his Protestant parents) was born and raised amid the poverty and squalor of Dublin's overpopulated tenements, in a painful world that he evocatively detailed in his monumental six-volume autobiography. As a child, he suffered not only from a miserable diet consisting all too often of nothing more than bread and tea, but also from an eye disease that left him nearly blind as an adult. After his father's death when O'Casey was only six, he was raised by his mother, whose heroic struggle to support her surviving children clearly inspired his conception of the brave and devoted women who figure prominently in his best-known dramas of Irish experience, *The Shadow of a Gunman* (1923), *Juno and the Paycock* (1924), and *The Plough and the Stars* (1926).

Young O'Casey also suffered from the tyranny of incompetent schoolmasters, whose brutality moved him to quit school before he was thirteen and to take on a series of unskilled jobs as a candlemaker, dockhand, hod carrier, and roadworker—jobs that brought him into touch with the life and language of the common laborers and the down-and-outers, who also figure in his early dramas of urban Irish experience. Having quit school, he taught himself, with the help of his older sister, to read and write. And, with the encouragement of an older brother, he took part in amateur theatrical performances that exposed him to the works of Shakespeare and of Dion Boucicault, an Irish melodramatic playwright who dominated the popular Irish, English, and American stages throughout much of the late nineteenth century. Thus, by the age of eighteen, he had already tried his hand at playwriting, though he was never able to get these early plays published or produced.

By his early twenties, O'Casey had also become involved with various nationalistic groups that aimed at gaining Irish independence from Britain. Inspired by the nationalistic movement, he not only learned to play the bagpipes and founded a pipers band, but he also learned the Irish language, taught it to fellow workers in the Gaelic League, and even went so far as to Gaelicize his name to Sean O'Cathasaigh. By his late-thirties, however, O'Casey had become disillusioned with the impractical and often self-serving behavior of the Irish nationalistic leaders as well as with the factionalism that developed among such competing groups as the "Free Staters," who were willing to accept partial independence for Ireland within the British Empire, and the "Diehards," who believed only in complete independence for Ireland. Such factionalism gave rise to the bitterly divisive civil war of 1922. Thus, during his early-forties, he Anglicized his surname to O'Casey.

O'Casey's impatience with the impractical idealism of his countrymen is reflected, in *Juno and the Paycock,* by Johnny Boyle's assertion that "a principle's a principle," which his mother counters with her assertion that "you lost your best principle, me boy, when you lost your arm; them's the only sort o' principles that's any good to a workin' man." In speaking for the principles of "a workin' man," Juno Boyle voices O'Casey's enduring interest in the plight of the impoverished Irish laborer, reflected in his affiliation with the Irish labor unions during the bitter general strike of 1913 and in the Socialist thinking he clearly espouses in such proletarian "morality" plays as *Within the Gates* (1934) and *The Star Turns Red* (1940). Ultimately, in his later visionary plays, such as *Red Roses for Me* (1942) and *Cock-a-doodle Dandy* (1949), O'Casey moves beyond any kind of doctrinaire thinking to an affirmation of the life force itself.

Though the visionary fantasies of his later plays are often seen as diverging radically from the naturalistic mode of his earlier work, O'Casey's writing is almost always characterized by a complex and quite daring mixture of theatrical elements and situations, which finally make it difficult, if not misleading, to attempt a clear-cut categorization of any of his plays. In *The Shadow of a Gunman,* for example, the first of his plays to be staged by the Abbey Theatre, O'Casey sets the action in a Dublin tenement house during the 1920 guerilla warfare between the Irish Republican Army and the British Black and Tans. But within this harshly naturalistic setting, he portrays both the comic and the tragic consequences of his characters' various masquerades, illusions, and self-delusions, by contrasting the vanity of a self-styled poet, with the cowardice of a mock-heroic clown, with the courage of an impressionable young working girl. So, too, in one of his best-known later plays, *Red Roses for Me,* O'Casey sets the action in the impoverished world of working-class Dublin during the general strike of 1913. Yet, over the course of the play, he depicts not only the comic squabbles and the pathetic sufferings of his characters, but also the miraculous, though temporary, transformation of their world through the dream vision of an idealized Ireland.

The technique of juxtaposing the heroic and the mock-heroic is central to both *Juno and the Paycock* and *The Plough and the Stars.* The plot of *Juno,* for example, blends melodrama (the ambiguously-stated will, as well as the pregnant and abandoned girl) with real tragedy (the betrayal of Robbie Tancred, the abduction of Johnny Boyle, and the self-destruction of Ireland). Similarly, *The Plough and the Stars* dramatizes the events of a major moment in Irish history— the Easter Rising of 1916—from the viewpoint of the ordinary people who are both part of history and trapped by it. Even more controversially, O'Casey repeatedly questions the validity of the bloody struggle for Irish independence by associating it with braggart and cowardly characters, as well as by emphasizing its toll upon the women, who are shown losing their families or their lives as a result of events related to the Irish struggle.

O'Casey's exploration of his culture is nowhere more complexly dramatized than in *Juno and the Paycock,* which swirls around a number of strikingly different characters and moods: the comic posturings of Jack Boyle and the slapstick pratfalls of his companion Joxer (see Figure 1); the increasingly pathetic situation of Johnny Boyle and Mary Boyle, brother and sister each trapped by their own misguided choices; the effusive jollity of Maisie Madigan; the visionary prayer of the bereaved Mrs. Tancred (see Figure 2); and always the compassionate yet practical generosity of Juno. This rich tapestry of characters is further complicated by O'Casey's ambiguous depiction of them. Mary Boyle, for example, is both the victimized girl and the slogan-spouting young woman who frets about the color of her hair ribbon; Juno is the only practical and stabilizing element in her family, yet she never really tries to restrain Boyle from spending the inheritance they have not yet received; and Boyle, though selfish and pompous, is also an enduringly comic figure derived from both the braggadocio of Roman comedy and the vainly blustering stage Irishman, whose language and posture are laughably far above his station in life. Johnny Boyle epitomizes O'Casey's ambiguous conception of his characters, and a powerful actor in the role can easily make us share his torment (see Figure 3) even while we recognize his political treachery.

The difficulty of balancing these widely varying characters, moods, and situations is reflected in the two reviews of the 1980 Royal Shakespeare Company production that are reprinted following the text of the play. Though responding to the same production, these reviewers perceive it and judge it quite differently. Derek Mahon, for example, laments its lack of "star turns," its failure to display "the vividness of personality" that animates the strikingly different characters, whereas John Elsom applauds the carefully orchestrated "naturalism" that unifies all the scenes and thus overcomes "the combination of tragedy and farce" that has often troubled audiences and critics. The disagreement of these reviewers reflects the quarrel about the play's serio-comic ending, which juxtaposes the poignant spectacle of Juno, echoing Mrs. Tancred's prayer to "Take away this murdherin' hate, an' give us Thine own eternal love!" with the return of Joxer and Boyle, both drunk. Their concluding slapstick appearance has so often troubled readers, directors, and spectators that it was cut from a professional recording made in the 1950s, which led O'Casey to defend it as "the comic highlight (and the tragic highlight too) of the play."

JUNO AND THE PAYCOCK

BY SEAN O'CASEY

CHARACTERS IN THE PLAY

'CAPTAIN' JACK BOYLE
JUNO BOYLE, *his wife*
JOHNNY BOYLE ⎫ *their children*
MARY BOYLE ⎬
'JOXER' DALY ⎭ *Residents in*
MRS. MAISIE MADIGAN *the Tenement*
'NEEDLE' NUGENT, *a tailor*
MRS. TANCRED
JERRY DEVINE
CHARLES BENTHAM, *a school teacher*
AN IRREGULAR MOBILIZER
TWO IRREGULARS
A COAL-BLOCK VENDOR

A SEWING MACHINE MAN
TWO FURNITURE REMOVAL MEN
TWO NEIGHBOURS

SCENE

ACT 1—*The living apartment of a two-roomed tenancy of the Boyle family, in a tenement house in Dublin.*
ACT 2—*The same.*
ACT 3—*The same.*
A few days elapse between Acts 1 and 2, and two months between Acts 2 and 3.
During Act 3 the curtain is lowered for a few minutes to denote the lapse of one hour.
Period of the play, 1922.

ACT 1

The living-room of a two-room tenancy occupied by the Boyle family in a tenement house in Dublin. Left, a door leading to another part of the house; left of door a window looking into the street; at back a dresser; farther to right at back, a window looking into the back of the house. Between the window and the dresser is a picture of the Virgin; below the picture, on a bracket, is a crimson bowl in which a floating votive light is burning. Farther to the right is a small bed partly concealed by cretonne hangings strung on a twine. To the right is the fireplace; near the fireplace is a door leading to the other room. Beside the fireplace is a box containing coal. On the mantelshelf is an alarm clock lying on its face. In a corner near the window looking into the back is a galvanized bath. A table and some chairs. On the table are breakfast things for one. A teapot is on the hob and a frying-pan stands inside the fender. There are a few books on the dresser and one on the table. Leaning against the dresser is a long-handled shovel—the kind invariably used by labourers when turning concrete or mixing mortar. Johnny Boyle is sitting crouched beside the fire. Mary with her jumper off—it is lying on the back of a chair—is arranging her hair before a tiny mirror perched on the table. Beside the mirror is stretched out the morning paper, which she looks at when she isn't gazing into the mirror. She is a well-made and good-looking girl of twenty-two. Two forces are working in her mind—one, through the circumstances of her life, pulling her back; the other, through the influence of books she has read, pushing her forward. The opposing forces are apparent in her speech and her manners, both of which are degraded by her environment, and improved by her acquaintance—slight though it be—with literature. The time is early forenoon.

MARY: *(Looking at the paper)* On a little by-road, out beyant Finglas, he was found.

(MRS. BOYLE enters by door on right; she has been shopping and carries a small parcel in her hand. She is forty-five years of age, and twenty years ago she must have been a pretty woman; but her face has now assumed that look which ultimately settles down upon the faces of the women of the working-class; a look of listless monotony and harassed anxiety, blending with an expression of mechanical resistance. Were circumstances favourable, she would probably be a handsome, active and clever woman.)

MRS. BOYLE: Isn't he come in yet?

MARY: No, mother.

MRS. BOYLE: Oh, he'll come in when he likes; struttin' about the town like a paycock with Joxer, I suppose. I hear all about Mrs. Tancred's son is in this mornin's paper.

MARY: The full details are in it this mornin'; seven wounds he had—one entherin' the neck, with an exit wound beneath the left shoulder-blade; another in the left breast penethratin' the heart, an' . . .

JOHNNY: *(Springing up from the fire)* Oh, quit that readin' for God's sake! Are yous losin' all your feelin's? It'll soon be that none of you'll read anythin' that's not about butcherin'!

(He goes quickly into the room on left.)

MARY: He's gettin' very sensitive, all of a sudden!

MRS. BOYLE: I'll read it myself, Mary, by an' by, when I come home. Everybody's sayin' that he was a Die-hard—thanks be to God that Johnny had nothin' to do with him this long time. . . . (*Opening the parcel and taking out some sausages, which she places on a plate*) Ah, then, if that father o' yours doesn't come in soon for his breakfast, he may go without any; I'll not wait much longer for him.

MARY: Can't you let him get it himself when he comes in?

MRS. BOYLE: Yes, an' let him bring in Joxer Daly along with him? Ay, that's what he'd like an' that's what he's waitin' for—till he thinks I'm gone to work, an' then sail in with the boul' Joxer, to burn all the coal an' dhrink all the tea in the place, to show them what a good Samaritan he is! But I'll stop here till he comes in, if I have to wait till to-morrow mornin'.

Voice of JOHNNY *inside*: Mother!

MRS. BOYLE: Yis?

Voice of JOHNNY: Bring us in a dhrink o' wather.

MRS. BOYLE: Bring in that fella a dhrink o' wather, for God's sake, Mary.

MARY: Isn't he big an' able enough to come out an' get it himself?

MRS. BOYLE: If you weren't well yourself you'd like somebody to bring you in a dhrink o' wather.

(She brings in drink and returns.)

MRS. BOYLE: Isn't it terrible to have to be waitin' this way! You'd think he was bringin' twenty poun's a week into the house the way he's going on. He wore out the Health Insurance long ago, he's afther wearin' out the unemployment dole, an', now, he's thryin' to wear out me! An' constantly singin', no less, when he ought always to be on his knees offerin' up a Novena for a job!

MARY: (*Trying a ribbon fillet-wise around her head*) I don't like this ribbon, ma; I think I'll wear the green—it looks betther than the blue.

MRS. BOYLE: Ah, wear whatever ribbon you like, girl, only don't be botherin' me. I don't know what a girl on strike wants to be wearin' a ribbon round her head for, or silk stockin's on her legs either; it's wearin' them things that make the employers think they're givin' yous too much money.

MARY: The hour is past now when we'll ask the employers' permission to wear what we like.

MRS. BOYLE: I don't know why you wanted to walk out for Jennie Claffey; up to this you never had a good word for her.

MARY: What's the use of belongin' to a Trades Union if you won't stand up for your principles? Why did they sack her? It was a clear case of victimization. We couldn't let her walk the streets, could we?

MRS. BOYLE: No, of course yous couldn't—yous wanted to keep her company. Wan victim wasn't enough. When the employers sacrifice wan victim, the Trades Unions go wan betther be sacrificin' a hundred.

MARY: It doesn't matther what you say, ma—a principle's a principle.

MRS. BOYLE: Yis; an' when I go into oul' Murphy's to-morrow, an' he gets to know that, instead o' payin' all, I'm goin' to borry more, what'll he say when I tell him a principle's a principle? What'll we do if he refuses to give us any more on tick?

MARY: He daren't refuse—if he does, can't you tell him he's paid?

MRS. BOYLE: It's lookin' as if he was paid, whether he refuses or no.

(JOHNNY *appears at the door on left. He can be plainly seen now; he is a thin, delicate fellow, something younger than* MARY. *He has evidently gone through a rough time. His face is pale and drawn; there is a tremulous look of indefinite fear in his eyes. The left sleeve of his coat is empty, and he walks with a slight halt.*)

JOHNNY: I was lyin' down; I thought yous were gone. Oul' Simon Mackay is thrampin' about like a horse over me head, an' I can't sleep with him—they're like thunder-claps in me brain! The curse o'—God forgive me for goin' to curse!

MRS. BOYLE: There, now; go back an' lie down again an' I'll bring you in a nice cup o' tay.

JOHNNY: Tay, tay, tay! You're always thinkin' o' tay. If a man was dyin', you'd thry to make him swally a cup o' tay!

(He goes back.)

MRS. BOYLE: I don't know what's goin' to be done with him. The bullet he got in the hip in Easter Week was bad enough; but the bomb that shatthered his arm in the fight in O'Connell Street put the finishin' touch on him. I knew he was makin' a fool of himself. God knows I went down on me bended knees to him not to go agen the Free State.

MARY: He stuck to his principles, an', no matther how you may argue, ma, a principle's a principle.

Voice of JOHNNY: Is Mary goin' to stay here?

MARY: No, I'm not goin' to stay here; you can't expect me to be always at your beck an' call, can you?

Voice of JOHNNY: I won't stop here be meself!

MRS. BOYLE: Amn't I nicely handicapped with the whole o' yous! I don't know what any o' yous ud do without your ma. (*To* JOHNNY) Your father'll be here in a minute, an' if you want anythin', he'll get it for you.

JOHNNY: I hate assin' him for anythin'. . . . He hates to be assed to stir. . . . Is the light lightin' before the picture o' the Virgin?

MRS. BOYLE: Yis, yis! The wan inside to St. Anthony isn't enough, but he must have another wan to the Virgin here!

(JERRY DEVINE *enters hastily. He is about twenty-five, well set, active and earnest. He is a type, becoming very common now in the Labour Movement, of a mind knowing enough to make the mass of his associates, who know less, a power, and too little to broaden that power for the benefit of all.* MARY *seizes her jumper and runs hastily into room left.)*

JERRY: (*Breathless*) Where's the Captain, Mrs. Boyle, where's the Captain?

MRS. BOYLE: You may well ass a body that: he's wherever Joxer Daly is—dhrinkin' in some snug or another.

JERRY: Father Farrell is just afther stoppin' to tell me to run up an' get him to go to the new job that's goin' on in Rathmines; his cousin is foreman o' the job, an' Father Farrell was speakin' to him about poor Johnny an' his father bein' idle so long, an' the foreman told Father Farrell to send the Captain up an' he'd give him a start—I wondher where I'd find him?

MRS. BOYLE: You'll find he's ayther in Ryan's or Foley's.

JERRY: I'll run round to Ryan's—I know it's a great house o' Joxer's.

(He rushes out.)

MRS. BOYLE: (*Piteously*) There now, he'll miss that job, or I know for what! If he gets win' o' the word, he'll not come back till evenin', so that it'll be too late. There'll never be any good got out o' him so long as he goes with that shouldher-shruggin' Joxer. I killin' meself workin', an' he sthruttin' about from mornin' till night like a paycock!

(The steps of two persons are heard coming up a flight of stairs. They are the footsteps of CAPTAIN BOYLE *and* JOXER. CAPTAIN BOYLE *is singing in a deep, sonorous, self-honoring voice.)*

THE CAPTAIN: Sweet Spirit, hear me prayer! Hear . . . oh . . . hear . . . me prayer . . . hear, oh, hear . . . Oh, he . . . ar . . . oh, he . . . ar . . . me . . . pray . . . er!

JOXER: (*Outside*) Ah, that's a darlin' song, a daaarlin' song!

MRS. BOYLE: (*Viciously*) Sweet spirit hear his prayer! Ah, then, I'll take me solemn affeydavey, it's not for a job he's prayin'!

(She sits down on the bed so that the cretonne hangings hide her from the view of those entering.

THE CAPTAIN *comes in. He is a man of about sixty; stout, grey-haired and stocky. His neck is short, and his head looks like a stone ball that one sometimes sees on top of a gate-post. His cheeks, reddish-purple, are puffed out, as if he were always repressing an almost irrepressible ejaculation. On his upper lip is a crisp, tightly cropped moustache; he carries himself with the upper part of his body slightly thrown back, and his stomach slightly thrust forward. His walk is a slow, consequential strut. His clothes are dingy, and he wears a faded seaman's-cap with a glazed peak.)*

BOYLE: (*To* JOXER, *who is still outside*) Come on, come on in, Joxer; she's gone out long ago, man. If there's nothing else to be got, we'll furrage out a cup o' tay, anyway. It's the only bit I get in comfort when she's away. 'Tisn't Juno should be her pet name at all, but Deirdre of the Sorras, for she's always grousin'.

(JOXER steps cautiously into the room. He may be younger than the CAPTAIN *but he looks a lot older. His face is like a bundle of crinkled paper; his eyes have a cunning twinkle; he is spare and loosely built; he has a habit of constantly shrugging his shoulders with a peculiar twitching movement, meant to be ingratiating. His face is invariably ornamented with a grin.)*

JOXER: It's a terrible thing to be tied to a woman that's always grousin'. I don't know how you stick it—it ud put years on me. It's a good job she has to be so ofen away, for (*with a shrug*) when the cat's away, the mice can play!

BOYLE: (*With a commanding and complacent gesture*) Pull over to the fire, Joxer, an' we'll have a cup o' tay in a minute.

JOXER: Ah, a cup o' tay's a darlin' thing, a daaarlin' thing—the cup that cheers but doesn't . . .

(JOXER's rhapsody is cut short by the sight of JUNO *coming forward and confronting the two cronies. Both are stupefied.)*

MRS. BOYLE: (*With sweet irony—poking the fire, and turning her head to glare at* JOXER) Pull over to the fire, Joxer Daly, an' we'll have a cup o' tay in a minute! Are you sure, now, you wouldn't like an egg?

JOXER: I can't stop, Mrs. Boyle; I'm in a desperate hurry, a desperate hurry.

MRS. BOYLE: Pull over to the fire, Joxer Daly; people is always far more comfortabler here than they are in their own place.

(JOXER makes hastily for the door. BOYLE *stirs to follow him; thinks of something to relieve the situation—stops, and says suddenly:)*

Joxer!

JOXER: (*At door ready to bolt*) Yis?

BOYLE: You know the foreman o' that job that's goin' on down in Killesther, don't you, Joxer?

JOXER: (*Puzzled*) Foreman—Killesther?

BOYLE: (*With a meaning look*) He's a butty o' yours, isn't he?

JOXER: (*The truth dawning on him*) The foreman at Killesther—oh yis, yis. He's an oul' butty o' mine—oh, he's a darlin' man, a daarlin' man.

BOYLE: Oh, then, it's a sure thing. It's a pity we didn't go down at breakfast first thing this mornin'—we might ha' been working now; but you didn't know it then.

JOXER: (*With a shrug*) It's betther late than never.

BOYLE: It's nearly time we got a start, anyhow; I'm fed up knockin' round, doin' nothin'. He promised you—gave you the straight tip?

JOXER: Yis. 'Come down on the blow o' dinner,' says he, 'an' I'll start you, an' any friend you like to brin' with you.' 'Ah,' says I, 'you're a darlin' man, a daaarlin' man.'

BOYLE: Well, it couldn't come at a betther time—we're a long time waitin' for it.

JOXER: Indeed we were; but it's a long lane that has no turnin'.

BOYLE: The blow up for dinner is at one—wait till I see what time it 'tis.

(He goes over to the mantelpiece, and gingerly lifts the clock.)

MRS. BOYLE: Min' now, how you go on fiddlin' with that clock—you know the least little thing sets it asthray.

BOYLE: The job couldn't come at a betther time; I'm feelin' in great fettle, Joxer. I'd hardly believe I ever had a pain in me legs, an' last week I was nearly crippled with them.

JOXER: That's betther an' betther; ah, God never shut wan door but He opened another!

BOYLE: It's only eleven o'clock; we've lashin's o' time. I'll slip on me oul' moleskins afther breakfast, an' we can saunther down at our ayse. *(Putting his hand on the shovel)* I think, Joxer, we'd betther bring our shovels?

JOXER: Yis, Captain, yis; it's betther to go fully prepared an' ready for all eventualities. You bring your long-tailed shovel, an' I'll bring me navvy. We mighten' want them, an', then agen, we might: for want of a nail the shoe was lost, for want of a shoe the horse was lost, an' for want of a horse the man was lost—aw, that's a darlin' proverb, a daarlin' . . .

(As JOXER is finishing his sentence, MRS. BOYLE approaches the door and JOXER retreats hurriedly. She shuts the door with a bang.)

BOYLE: *(Suggestively)* We won't be long pullin' ourselves together agen when I'm working for a few weeks.

(MRS. BOYLE takes no notice.)

BOYLE: The foreman on the job is an oul' butty o' Joxer's; I have an idea that I know him meself. *(Silence)* . . . There's a button off the back o' me moleskin trousers. . . . If you leave out a needle an' thread I'll sew it on meself. . . . Thanks be to God, the pains in me legs is gone, anyhow!

MRS. BOYLE: *(With a burst)* Look here, Mr. Jacky Boyle, them yarns won't go down with Juno. I know you an' Joxer Daly of an oul' date, an' if you think you're able to come it over me with them fairy tales, you're in the wrong shop.

BOYLE: *(Coughing subduedly to relieve the tenseness of the situation)* U-u-u-ugh!

MRS. BOYLE: Butty o' Joxer's! Oh, you'll do a lot o' good as long as you continue to be a butty o' Joxer's!

BOYLE: U-u-u-ugh!

MRS. BOYLE: Shovel! Ah, then, me boyo, you'd do far more work with a knife an' fork than ever you'll do with a shovel! If there was e'er a genuine job goin' you'd be dh'other way about—not able to lift your arms with the pains in your legs! Your poor wife slavin' to keep the bit in your mouth, an' you galli-vantin' about all the day like a paycock!

BOYLE: It ud be betther for a man to be dead, betther for a man to be dead.

MRS. BOYLE: *(Ignoring the interruption)* Everybody callin' you 'Captain', an' you only wanst on the wather, in an oul' collier from here to Liverpool, when any-body, to listen or look at you, ud take you for a second Christo For Columbus!

BOYLE: Are you never goin' to give us a rest?

MRS. BOYLE: Oh, you're never tired o' lookin' for a rest.

BOYLE: D'ye want to dhrive me out o' the house?

MRS. BOYLE: It ud be easier to dhrive you out o' the house than to dhrive you into a job. Here, sit down an' take your breakfast—it may be the last you'll get, for I don't know where the next is goin' to come from.

BOYLE: If I get this job we'll be all right.

MRS. BOYLE: Did ye see Jerry Devine?

BOYLE: *(Testily)* No, I didn't see him.

MRS. BOYLE: No, but you seen Joxer. Well, he was here lookin' for you.

BOYLE: Well, let him look!

MRS. BOYLE: Oh, indeed, he may well look, for it ud be hard for him to see you, an' you stuck in Ryan's snug.

BOYLE: I wasn't in Ryan's snug—I don't go into Ryan's.

MRS. BOYLE: Oh, is there a mad dog there? Well, if you weren't in Ryan's you were in Foley's.

BOYLE: I'm telling you for the last three weeks I haven't tasted a dhrop of intoxicatin' liquor. I wasn't in ayther wan snug or dh'other—I could swear that on a prayer-book—I'm as innocent as the child un-born!

MRS. BOYLE: Well, if you'd been in for your breakfast you'd ha' seen him.

BOYLE: *(Suspiciously)* What does he want me for?

MRS. BOYLE: He'll be back any minute an' then you'll soon know.

BOYLE: I'll dhrop out an' see if I can meet him.

MRS. BOYLE: You'll sit down an' take your breakfast, an' let me go to me work, for I'm an hour late already waitin' for you.

BOYLE: You needn't ha' waited, for I'll take no break- fast—I've a little spirit left in me still!

MRS. BOYLE: Are you goin' to have your breakfast—yes or no?

BOYLE: *(Too proud to yield)* I'll have no breakfast—yous can keep your breakfast. *(Plaintively)* I'll knock out a bit somewhere, never fear.

MRS. BOYLE: Nobody's goin' to coax you—don't think that.

(She vigorously replaces the pan and the sausages in the press.)

BOYLE: I've a little spirit left in me still.

(JERRY DEVINE enters hastily.)

JERRY: Oh, here you are at last! I've been searchin' for you everywhere. The foreman in Foley's told me you hadn't left the snug with Joxer ten minutes before I went in.

MRS. BOYLE: An' he swearin' on the holy prayer-book that he wasn't in no snug!

BOYLE: *(To JERRY)* What business is it o' yours whether I was in a snug or no? What do you want to be gallopin' about afther me for? Is a man not to be allowed to leave his house for a minute without havin' a pack o' spies, pimps an' informers cantherin' at his heels?

JERRY: Oh, you're takin' a wrong view of it, Mr. Boyle; I simply was anxious to do you a good turn. I have a message for you from Father Farrell: He says that if you go to the job that's on in Rathmines, an' ask for Foreman Managan, you'll get a start.

BOYLE: That's all right, but I don't want the motions of me body to be watched the way an asthronomer ud watch a star. If you're folleyin' Mary aself, you've no pereeogative to be folleyin' me. *(Suddenly catching his thigh)* U-ugh, I'm afther gettin' a terrible twinge in me right leg!

MRS. BOYLE: Oh, it won't be very long now till it travels into your left wan. It's miraculous that whenever he scents a job in front of him, his legs begin to fail him! Then, me bucko, if you lose this chance, you may go an' furrage for yourself!

JERRY: This job'll last for some time too, Captain, an' as soon as the foundations are in, it'll be cushy enough.

BOYLE: Won't it be a climbin' job? How d'ye expect me to be able to go up a ladder with these legs? An', if I get up aself, how am I goin' to get down agen?

MRS. BOYLE: *(Viciously)* Get wan o' the labourers to carry you down in a hod! You can't climb a laddher, but you can skip like a goat into a snug!

JERRY: I wouldn't let myself be let down that easy, Mr. Boyle; a little exercise, now, might do you all the good in the world.

BOYLE: It's a docthor you should have been, Devine—maybe you know more about the pains in me legs than meself that has them?

JERRY: *(Irritated)* Oh, I know nothin' about the pains in your legs; I've brought the message that Father Farrell gave me, an' that's all I can do.

MRS. BOYLE: Here, sit down an' take your breakfast, an' go an' get ready; an' don't be actin' as if you couldn't pull a wing out of a dead bee.

BOYLE: I want no breakfast, I tell you; it ud choke me afther all that's been said. I've a little spirit left in me still.

MRS. BOYLE: Well, let's see your spirit, then, an' go in at wanst an' put on your moleskin trousers!

BOYLE: *(Moving towards the door on left)* It ud be betther for a man to be dead! U-ugh! There's another twinge in me other leg! Nobody but meself knows the sufferin' I'm goin' through with the pains in these legs o' mine!

(He goes into the room on left as MARY comes out with her hat in her hand.)

MRS. BOYLE: I'll have to push off now, for I'm terrible late already, but I was determined to stay an' hunt that Joxer this time.

(She goes off.)

JERRY: Are you going out, Mary?

MARY: It looks like it when I'm putting on my hat, doesn't it?

JERRY: The bitther word agen, Mary.

MARY: You won't allow me to be friendly with you; if I thry, you deliberately misundherstand it.

JERRY: I didn't always misundherstand it; you were often delighted to have the arms of Jerry around you.

MARY: If you go on talkin' like this, Jerry Devine, you'll make me hate you!

JERRY: Well, let it be either a weddin' or a wake! Listen, Mary, I'm standin' for the Secretaryship of our Union. There's only one opposin' me; I'm popular with all the men, an' a good speaker—all are sayin' that I'll get elected.

MARY: Well?

JERRY: The job's worth three hundred an' fifty pounds a year, Mary. You an' I could live nice an' cosily on that; it would lift you out o' this place an' . . .

MARY: I haven't time to listen to you now—I have to go.

(She is going out, when JERRY bars the way.)

JERRY: *(Appealingly)* Mary, what's come over you with me for the last few weeks? You hardly speak to me, an' then only a word with a face o' bitterness on it. Have you forgotten, Mary, all the happy evenin's that were as sweet as the scented hawthorn that sheltered the sides o' the road as we sauntered through the country?

MARY: That's all over now. When you get your new job, Jerry, you won't be long findin' a girl far better than I am for your sweetheart.

JERRY: Never, never, Mary! No matther what happens, you'll always be the same to me.

MARY: I must be off; please let me go, Jerry.

JERRY: I'll go a bit o' the way with you.

MARY: You needn't, thanks; I want to be by meself.

JERRY: *(Catching her arm)* You're goin' to meet another fella; you've clicked with someone else, me lady!

MARY: That's no concern o' yours, Jerry Devine; let me go!

JERRY: I saw yous comin' out o' the Cornflower Dance Class, an' you hangin' on his arm—a thin, lanky strip of a Micky Dazzler, with a walkin'-stick an' gloves!

Voice of JOHNNY: (*Loudly*) What are you doin' there—pullin' about everything!

Voice of BOYLE: (*Loudly and viciously*) I'm puttin' on me moleskin trousers!

MARY: You're hurtin' me arm! Let me go, or I'll scream, an' then you'll have the oul' fella out on top of us!

JERRY: Don't be so hard on a fella, Mary, don't be so hard.

BOYLE: (*Appearing at the door*) What's the meanin' of all this hillabaloo?

MARY: Let me go, let me go!

BOYLE: D'ye hear me—what's all this hillabaloo about?

JERRY: (*Plaintively*) Will you not give us one kind word, one kind word, Mary?

BOYLE: D'ye hear me talkin' to yous? What's all this hillabaloo for?

JERRY: Let me kiss your hand, your little, tiny, white hand!

BOYLE: Your little, tiny, white hand—are you takin' leave o' your senses, man?

(MARY *breaks away and rushes out.*)

BOYLE: This is nice goin's on in front of her father!

JERRY: Ah, dhry up, for God's sake!

(*He follows* MARY.)

BOYLE: Chiselurs don't care a damn now about their parents, they're bringin' their fathers' grey hairs down with sorra to the grave, an' laughin' at it, laughin' at it. Ah, I suppose it's just the same everywhere—the whole worl's in a state o' chassis! (*He sits by the fire*) Breakfast! Well, they can keep their breakfast for me. Not if they went down on their bended knees would I take it—I'll show them I've a little spirit left in me still! (*He goes over to the press, takes out a plate and looks at it*) Sassige! Well, let her keep her sassige. (*He returns to the fire, takes up the teapot and gives it a gentle shake*) The tea's wet right enough.

(*A pause; he rises, goes to the press, takes out the sausage, puts it on the pan, and puts both on the fire. He attends the sausage with a fork.*)

BOYLE: (*Singing*)

When the robins nest agen,
And the flowers are in bloom,
When the Springtime's sunny smile seems to banish all
   sorrow an' gloom;
Then me bonny blue-ey'd lad, if me heart be true till
   then—
He's promised he'll come back to me,
When the robins nest agen!

(*He lifts his head at the high note, and then drops his eyes to the pan.*)

BOYLE: (*Singing*)

When the . . .

(*Steps are heard approaching; he whips the pan off the fire and puts it under the bed, then sits down at the fire. The door opens and a bearded man looking in says:*)

You don't happen to want a sewin' machine?

BOYLE: (*Furiously*) No, I don't want e'er a sewin' machine!

(*He returns the pan to the fire, and commences to sing again.*)

BOYLE: (*Singing*)

When the robins nest agen,
And the flowers they are in bloom,
He's . . .

(*A thundering knock is heard at the street door.*)

BOYLE: There's a terrible tatheraraa—that's a stranger—that's nobody belongin' to the house.

(*Another loud knock.*)

JOXER: (*Sticking his head in at the door*) Did ye hear them tatherarahs?

BOYLE: Well, Joxer, I'm not deaf.

JOHNNY: (*Appearing in his shirt and trousers at the door on left; his face is anxious and his voice is tremulous*) Who's that at the door; who's that at the door? Who gave that knock—d'ye yous hear me—are yous deaf or dhrunk or what?

BOYLE: (*To* JOHNNY) How the hell do I know who 'tis? Joxer, stick your head out o' the window an' see.

JOXER: An' mebbe get a bullet in the kisser? Ah, none o' them thricks for Joxer! It's betther to be a coward than a corpse!

BOYLE: (*Looking cautiously out of the window*) It's a fella in a thrench coat.

JOHNNY: Holy Mary, Mother o' God, I . . .

BOYLE: He's goin' away—he must ha' got tired knockin'.

(JOHNNY *returns to the room on left.*)

BOYLE: Sit down an' have a cup o' tay, Joxer.

JOXER: I'm afraid the missus ud pop in on us agen before we'd know where we are. Somethin's tellin' me to go at wanst.

BOYLE: Don't be superstitious, man; we're Dublin men, an' not boyos that's only afther comin' up from the bog o' Allen—though if she did come in, right enough, we'd be caught like rats in a thrap.

JOXER: An' you know the sort she is—she wouldn't listen to reason—an' wanse bitten twice shy.

BOYLE: (*Going over to the window at back*) If the worst

came to the worst, you could dart out here, Joxer; it's only a dhrop of a few feet to the roof of the return room, an' the first minute she goes into dh'other room I'll give you the bend, an' you can slip in an' away.

JOXER: (*Yielding to the temptation*) Ah, I won't stop very long anyhow. (*Picking up a book from the table*) Whose is the buk?

BOYLE: Aw, one o' Mary's; she's always readin' lately—nothin' but thrash, too. There's one I was lookin' at dh'other day: three stories, *The Doll's House, Ghosts,* an' *The Wild Duck*—buks only fit for chiselurs!

JOXER: Didja ever rade *Elizabeth, or Th' Exile o' Sibayria?* . . . Ah, it's a darlin' story, a daarlin' story!

BOYLE: You eat your sassige, an' never min' *Th' Exile o' Sibayria.*

(*Both sit down;* BOYLE *fills out tea, pours gravy on* JOXER's *plate, and keeps the sausage for himself.*)

JOXER: What are you wearin' your moleskin trousers for?

BOYLE: I have to go to a job, Joxer. Just afther you'd gone, Devine kem runnin' in to tell us that Father Farrell said if I went down to the job that's goin' on in Rathmines I'd get a start.

JOXER: Be the holy, that's good news!

BOYLE: How is it good news? I wondher if you were in my condition, would you call it good news?

JOXER: I thought . . .

BOYLE: You thought! You think too sudden sometimes, Joxer. D'ye know, I'm hardly able to crawl with the pains in me legs!

JOXER: Yis, yis; I forgot the pains in your legs. I know you can do nothin' while they're at you.

BOYLE: You forgot; I don't think any of yous realize the state I'm in with the pains in my legs. What ud happen if I had to carry a bag o' cement?

JOXER: Ah, any man havin' the like of them pains id be down an' out, down an' out.

BOYLE: I wouldn't mind if he had said it to meself; but, no, oh no, he rushes in an' shouts it out in front o' Juno, an' you know what Juno is, Joxer. We all know Devine knows a little more than the rest of us, but he doesn't act as if he did; he's a good boy, sober, able to talk an' all that, but still . . .

JOXER: Oh ay; able to argufy, but still . . .

BOYLE: If he's runnin' afther Mary, aself, he's not goin' to be runnin' afther me. Captain Boyle's able to take care of himself. After all, I'm not gettin' brought up on Virol. I never heard him usin' a curse; I don't believe he was ever dhrunk in his life—sure he's not like a Christian at all!

JOXER: You're afther takin' the word out o' me mouth—after all, a Christian's natural, but he's unnatural.

BOYLE: His oul' fella was just the same—a Wicklow man.

JOXER: A Wicklow man! That explains the whole thing. I've met many a Wicklow man in me time, but I never met wan that was any good.

BOYLE: 'Father Farrell,' says he, 'sent me down to tell you.' Father Farrell! . . . D'ye know, Joxer, I never like to be beholden to any o' the clergy.

JOXER: It's dangerous, right enough.

BOYLE: If they do anything for you, they'd want you to be livin' in the Chapel. . . . I'm goin' to tell you somethin', Joxer, that I wouldn't tell to anybody else—the clergy always had too much power over the people in this unfortunate country.

JOXER: You could sing that if you had an air to it!

BOYLE: (*Becoming enthusiastic*) Didn't they prevent the people in '47 from seizin' the corn, an' they starvin'; didn't they down Parnell; didn't they say that hell wasn't hot enough nor eternity long enough to punish the Fenians? We don't forget, we don't forget them things, Joxer. If they've taken everything else from us, Joxer, they've left us our memory.

JOXER: (*Emotionally*) For mem'ry's the only friend that grief can call its own, that grief . . . can . . . call . . . its own!

BOYLE: Father Farrell's beginnin' to take a great intherest in Captain Boyle; because of what Johnny did for his country, says he to me wan day. It's a curious way to reward Johnny be makin' his poor oul' father work. But that's what the clergy want, Joxer—work, work, work for me an' you; havin' us mulin' from mornin' till night, so that they may be in b180 fettle when they come hoppin' round for their dues! Job! Well, let him give his job to wan of his hymn-singin', prayer-spoutin', craw-thumpin' Confraternity men!

(*The voice of a coal-block vendor is heard chanting in the street.*)

Voice of COAL VENDOR: Blocks . . . coal-blocks! Blocks . . . coal-blocks!

JOXER: God be with the young days when you were steppin' the deck of a manly ship, with the win' blowin' a hurricane through the masts, an' the only sound you'd hear was, 'Port your helm!' an' the only answer, 'Port it is, sir!'

BOYLE: Them was days, Joxer, them was days. Nothin' was too hot or too heavy for me then. Sailin' from the Gulf o' Mexico to the Antarctic Ocean. I seen things, I seen things, Joxer, that no mortal man should speak about that knows his Catechism. Ofen, an' ofen, when I was fixed to the wheel with a marlin-spike, an' the win's blowin' fierce an' the waves lashin' an' lashin', till you'd think every minute was goin' to be your last, an' it blowed, an' blowed—blew is the right word, Joxer, but blowed is what the sailors use. . . .

JOXER: Aw, it's a darlin' word, a daarlin' word.

BOYLE: An', as it blowed an' blowed, I ofen looked up

at the sky an' assed meself the question—what is
the stars, what is the stars?

Voice of COAL VENDOR: Any blocks, coal-blocks; blocks,
coal-blocks!

JOXER: Ah, that's the question, that's the question—
what is the stars?

BOYLE: An' then, I'd have another look, an' I'd ass meself—what is the moon?

JOXER: Ah, that's the question—what is the moon, what
is the moon?

(Rapid steps are heard coming towards the door. BOYLE
makes desperate efforts to hide everything; JOXER *rushes
to the window in a frantic effort to get out;* BOYLE *begins
to innocently lilt 'Oh, me darlin' Jennie, I will be thrue
to thee', when the door is opened, and the black face of
the* COAL VENDOR *appears.)*

COAL VENDOR: D'yez want any blocks?

BOYLE: *(With a roar)* No, we don't want any blocks!

JOXER: *(Coming back with a sigh of relief)* That's afther
puttin' the heart across me—I could ha' sworn it
was Juno. I'd betther be goin', Captain; you couldn't
tell the minute Juno'd hop in on us.

BOYLE: Let her hop in; we may as well have it out first
as at last. I've made up me mind—I'm not goin' to
do only what she damn well likes.

JOXER: Them sentiments does you credit, Captain; I
don't like to say anything as between man an' wife,
but I say as a butty, as a butty, Captain, that you've
stuck it too long, an' that it's about time you showed
a little spunk.

How can a man die betther than facin' fearful odds,
For th' ashes of his fathers an' the temples of his gods?

BOYLE: She has her rights—there's no one denyin' it,
but haven't I me rights too?

JOXER: Of course you have—the sacred rights o' man!

BOYLE: Today, Joxer, there's goin' to be issued a proclamation be me, establishin' an independent Republic, an' Juno'll have to take an oath of allegiance.

JOXER: Be firm, be firm, Captain; the first few minutes'll
be the worst: if you gently touch a nettle it'll sting
you for your pains; grasp it like a lad of mettle, an'
as soft as silk remains!

Voice of JUNO *outside:* Can't stop, Mrs. Madigan—I
haven't a minute!

JOXER: *(Flying out of the window)* Holy God, here she is!

BOYLE: *(Packing the things away with a rush in the press)* I
knew that fella ud stop till she was in on top of us!

(He sits down by the fire.)

JUNO *enters hastily; she is flurried and excited.)*

JUNO: Oh, you're in—you must have been only afther
comin' in?

BOYLE: No, I never went out.

JUNO: It's curious, then, you never heard the knockin'.

(She puts her coat and hat on bed.)

BOYLE: Knockin'? Of course I heard the knockin'.

JUNO: An' why didn't you open the door, then? I suppose you were so busy with Joxer that you hadn't
time.

BOYLE: I haven't seen Joxer since I seen him before.
Joxer! What ud bring Joxer here?

JUNO: D'ye mean to tell me that the pair of yous wasn't
collogin' together here when me back was turned?

BOYLE: What ud we be collogin' together about? I have
somethin' else to think of besides collogin' with
Joxer. I can swear on all the holy prayer-books . . .

MRS. BOYLE: That you weren't in no snug! Go on in at
wanst now, an' take off that moleskin trousers o'
yours, an' put on a collar an' tie to smarten yourself
up a bit. There's a visitor comin' with Mary in a
minute, an' he has great news for you.

BOYLE: A job, I suppose; let us get wan first before we
start lookin' for another.

MRS. BOYLE: That's the thing that's able to put the win'
up you. Well, it's no job, but news that'll give you
the chance o' your life.

BOYLE: What's all the mystery about?

MRS. BOYLE: G'win an' take off the moleskin trousers
when you're told!

*(*BOYLE *goes into room on left.*
MRS. BOYLE *tidies up the room, puts the shovel under the
bed, and goes to the press.)*

MRS. BOYLE: Oh, God bless us, looka the way everything's thrun about! Oh, Joxer was here, Joxer was
here!

*(*MARY *enters with* CHARLIE BENTHAM; *he is a young
man of twenty-five, tall, good-looking, with a very high
opinion of himself generally. He is dressed in a brown
coat, brown knee-breeches, grey stockings, a brown
sweater, with a deep blue tie; he carries gloves and a
walking-stick.)*

MRS. BOYLE: *(Fussing round)* Come in, Mr. Bentham; sit
down, Mr. Bentham, in this chair; it's more comfortabler than that, Mr. Bentham. Himself'll be
here in a minute; he's just takin' off his trousers.

MARY: Mother!

BENTHAM: Please don't put yourself to any trouble, Mrs.
Boyle—I'm quite all right here, thank you.

MRS. BOYLE: An' to think of you knowin' Mary, an' she
knowin' the news you had for us, an' wouldn't let
on; but it's all the more welcomer now, for we were
on our last lap!

Voice of JOHNNY *inside:* What are you kickin' up all the
racket for?

BOYLE: *(Roughly)* I'm takin' off me moleskin trousers!

JOHNNY: Can't you do it, then, without lettin' th' whole
house know you're takin' off your trousers? What
d'ye want puttin' them on an' takin' them off again?

BOYLE: Will you let me alone, will you let me alone? Am

I never goin' to be done thryin' to please th' whole o' yous?

MRS. BOYLE: (*To* BENTHAM) You must excuse th' state o' th' place, Mr. Bentham; th' minute I turn me back that man o' mine always makes a litther o' th' place, a litther o' th' place.

BENTHAM: Don't worry, Mrs. Boyle; it's all right, I assure . . .

BOYLE: (*Inside*) Where's me braces; where in th' name o' God did I leave me braces? . . . Ay, did you see where I put me braces?

JOHNNY: (*Inside, calling out*) Ma, will you come in here an' take da away ou' o' this or he'll dhrive me mad.

MRS. BOYLE: (*Going towards the door*) Dear, dear, dear, that man'll be lookin' for somethin' on th' day o' Judgement. (*Looking into room and calling to* BOYLE) Look at your braces, man, hangin' round your neck!

BOYLE: (*Inside*) Aw, Holy God!

MRS. BOYLE: (*Calling*) Johnny, Johnny, come out here for a minute.

JOHNNY: Ah, leave Johnny alone, an' don't be annoyin' him!

MRS. BOYLE: Come on, Johnny, till I inthroduce you to Mr. Bentham. (*To* BENTHAM) My son, Mr. Bentham; he's afther goin' through the mill. He was only a chiselur of a Boy Scout in Easter Week, when he got hit in the hip; and his arm was blew off in the fight in O'Connell Street. (JOHNNY *comes in.*) Here he is, Mr. Bentham; Mr. Bentham, Johnny. None can deny he done his bit for Irelan', if that's goin' to do him any good.

JOHNNY: (*Boastfully*) I'd do it agen, ma, I'd do it agen; for a principle's a principle.

MRS. BOYLE: Ah, you lost your best principle, me boy, when you lost your arm; them's the only sort o' principles that's any good to a workin' man.

JOHNNY: Ireland only half free'll never be at peace while she has a son left to pull a trigger.

MRS. BOYLE: To be sure, to be sure—no bread's a lot betther than half a loaf. (*Calling loudly in to* BOYLE) Will you hurry up there?

(BOYLE *enters in his best trousers, which aren't too good, and looks very uncomfortable in his collar and tie.*)

MRS. BOYLE: This is my husband; Mr. Boyle, Mr. Bentham.

BENTHAM: Ah, very glad to know you, Mr. Boyle. How are you?

BOYLE: Ah, I'm not too well at all; I suffer terrible with pains in me legs. Juno can tell you there what . . .

MRS. BOYLE: You won't have many pains in your legs when you hear what Mr. Bentham has to tell you.

BENTHAM: Juno! What an interesting name! It reminds one of Homer's glorious story of ancient gods and heroes.

BOYLE: Yis, doesn't it? You see, Juno was born an' chris-

tened in June; I met her in June; we were married in June, an' Johnny was born in June, so wan day I says to her, 'You should ha' been called Juno,' an' the name stuck to her ever since.

MRS. BOYLE: Here, we can talk o' them things agen; let Mr. Bentham say what he has to say now.

BENTHAM: Well, Mr. Boyle, I suppose you'll remember a Mr. Ellison of Santry—he's a relative of yours, I think.

BOYLE: (*Viciously*) Is it that prognosticator an' procrastinator? Of course I remember him.

BENTHAM: Well, he's dead, Mr. Boyle . . .

BOYLE: Sorra many'll go into mournin' for him.

MRS. BOYLE: Wait till you hear what Mr. Bentham has to say, an' then, maybe, you'll change your opinion.

BENTHAM: A week before he died he sent for me to write his will for him. He told me that there were two only that he wished to leave his property to: his second cousin, Michael Finnegan of Santry, and John Boyle, his first cousin, of Dublin.

BOYLE: (*Excitedly*) Me, is it me, me?

BENTHAM: You, Mr. Boyle; I'll read a copy of the will that I have here with me, which has been duly filed in the Court of Probate.

(*He takes a paper from his pocket and reads:*)

6th February 1922
This is the last Will and Testament of William Ellison, of Santry, in the County of Dublin. I hereby order and wish my property to be sold and divided as follows:—

£20 to the St. Vincent de Paul Society.

£60 for Masses for the repose of my soul (5s. for each Mass).

The rest of my property to be divided between my first and second cousins.

I hereby appoint Timothy Buckly, of Santry, and Hugh Brierly, of Coolock, to be my Executors.

(*Signed*) WILLIAM ELLISON.
HUGH BRIERLY.
TIMOTHY BUCKLY.
CHARLES BENTHAM, N.T.

BOYLE: (*Eagerly*) An' how much'll be comin' out of it, Mr. Bentham?

BENTHAM: The Executors told me that half of the property would be anything between £1500 and £2000.

MARY: A fortune, father, a fortune!

JOHNNY: We'll be able to get out o' this place now, an' go somewhere we're not known.

MRS. BOYLE: You won't have to trouble about a job for awhile, Jack.

BOYLE: (*Fervently*) I'll never doubt the goodness o' God agen.

BENTHAM: I congratulate you, Mr. Boyle.

(*They shake hands.*)

BOYLE: An' now, Mr. Bentham, you'll have to have a wet.

BENTHAM: A wet?

BOYLE: A wet—a jar—a boul!

MRS. BOYLE: Jack, you're speakin' to Mr. Bentham, an' not to Joxer.

BOYLE: (*Solemnly*) Juno . . . Mary . . . Johnny . . . we'll have to go into mournin' at wanst. . . . I never expected that poor Bill ud die so sudden. . . . Well, we all have to die some day . . . you, Juno, to-day . . . an' me, maybe, to-morrow. . . . It's sad, but it can't be helped. . . . Requiescat in pace . . . or, usin' our oul' tongue like St. Patrick or St. Bridget, Guh sayeree jeea ayera!

MARY: Oh, father, that's not Rest in Peace; that's God save Ireland.

BOYLE: U-u-ugh, it's all the same—isn't it a prayer? . . . Juno, I'm done with Joxer; he's nothin' but a prognosticator an' a . . .

JOXER: (*Climbing angrily through the window and bounding into the room*) You're done with Joxer, are you? Maybe you thought I'd stop on the roof all the night for you! Joxer out on the roof with the win' blowin' through him was nothin' to you an' your friend with the collar an' tie!

MRS. BOYLE: What in the name o' God brought you out on the roof; what were you doin' there?

JOXER: (*Ironically*) I was dhreamin' I was standin' on the bridge of a ship, an' she sailin' the Antartic Ocean, an' it blowed, an' blowed, an' I lookin' up at the sky an' sayin', what is the stars, what is the stars?

MRS. BOYLE: (*Opening the door and standing at it*) Here, get ou' o' this, Joxer Daly; I was always thinkin' you had a slate off.

JOXER: (*Moving to the door*) I have to laugh every time I look at the deep-sea sailor; an' a row on a river ud make him seasick!

BOYLE: Get ou' o' this before I take the law into me own hands!

JOXER: (*Going out*) Say aw rewaeawr, but not good-bye. Lookin' for work, an' prayin' to God he won't get it!

(*He goes.*)

MRS. BOYLE: I'm tired tellin' you what Joxer was; maybe now you see yourself the kind he is.

BOYLE: He'll never blow the froth off a pint o' mine agen, that's a sure thing. Johnny . . . Mary . . . you're to keep yourselves to yourselves for the future. Juno, I'm done with Joxer. . . . I'm a new man from this out. . . .

(*Clasping* JUNO's *hand, and singing emotionally:*)

O, me darlin' Juno, I will be thrue to thee;
Me own, me darlin' Juno, you're all the world to me.

CURTAIN

ACT 2

The same, but the furniture is more plentiful, and of a vulgar nature. A glaringly upholstered armchair and lounge; cheap pictures and photos everywhere. Every available spot is ornamented with huge vases filled with artificial flowers. Crossed festoons of colored paper chains stretch from end to end of ceiling. On the table is an old attaché case. It is about six in the evening, and two days after the First Act. BOYLE, *in his shirt-sleeves, is voluptuously stretched on the sofa; he is smoking a clay pipe. He is half asleep. A lamp is lighting on the table. After a few moments' pause the voice of* JOXER *is heard singing softly outside at the door—'Me pipe I'll smoke, as I dhrive me moke—are you there, Mor . . . ee . . . ar . . . i . . . teee!'*

BOYLE: (*Leaping up, takes a pen in his hand and busies himself with papers*) Come along, Joxer, me son, come along.

JOXER: (*Putting his head in*) Are you be yourself?

BOYLE: Come on, come on; that doesn't matther; I'm masther now, an' I'm goin' to remain masther.

(JOXER *comes in.*)

JOXER: How d'ye feel now, as a man o' money?

BOYLE: (*Solemnly*) It's a responsibility, Joxer, a great responsibility.

JOXER: I suppose 'tis now, though you wouldn't think it.

BOYLE: Joxer, han' me over that attackey case on the table there. (JOXER *hands the case.*) Ever since the Will was passed I've run hundreds o' dockyments through me han's—I tell you, you have to keep your wits about you.

(*He busies himself with papers.*)

JOXER: Well, I won't disturb you; I'll dhrop in when . . .

BOYLE: (*Hastily*) It's all right, Joxer, this is the last one to be signed to-day.

(*He signs a paper, puts in into the case, which he shuts with a snap, and sits back pompously in the chair.*)

Now, Joxer, you want to see me; I'm at your service—what can I do for you, me man?

JOXER: I've just dhropped in with the £3:5s. that Mrs. Madigan riz on the blankets an' table for you, an' she says you're to be in no hurry payin' it back.

BOYLE: She won't be long without it; I expect the first cheque for a couple o' hundhred any day. There's the five bob for yourself—go on, take it, man; it'll not be the last you'll get from the Captain. Now an' agen we have our differ, but we're there together all the time.

JOXER: Me for you, an' you for me, like the two Musketeers.

BOYLE: Father Farrell stopped me to-day an' tole me how glad he was I fell in for the money.

JOXER: He'll be stoppin' you ofen enough now; I suppose it was 'Mr.' Boyle with him?

BOYLE: He shuk me be the han' . . .

JOXER: (*Ironically*) I met with Napper Tandy, an' he
shuk me be the han'!

BOYLE: You're seldom asthray, Joxer, but you're wrong
shipped this time. What you're sayin' of Father Farrell is very near to blasfeemey. I don't like any one
to talk disrespectful of Father Farrell.

JOXER: You're takin' me up wrong, Captain; I wouldn't
let a word be said agen Father Farrell—the heart o'
the rowl, that's what he is; I always said he was a
darlin' man, a daarlin' man.

BOYLE: Comin' up the stairs who did I meet but that
bummer, Nugent. 'I seen you talkin' to Father Farrell,' says he, with a grin on him. 'He'll be folleyin'
you,' says he, 'like a Guardian Angel from this
out'—all the time the oul' grin on him, Joxer.

JOXER: I never seen him yet but he had that oul' grin
on him!

BOYLE: 'Mr. Nugent,' says I, 'Father Farrell is a man o'
the people, an', as far as I know the History o' me
country, the priests was always in the van of the
fight for Irelan's freedom.'

JOXER: (*Fervently*)

Who was it led the van, Soggart Aroon?
Since the fight first began, Soggart Aroon?

BOYLE: 'Who are you tellin'?' says he. 'Didn't they let
down the Fenians, an' didn't they do in Parnell?
An' now . . .' 'You ought to be ashamed o' yourself,'
says I, interruptin' him, 'not to know the History o'
your country.' An' I left him gawkin' where he was.

JOXER: Where ignorance 's bliss 'tis folly to be wise; I
wondher did he ever read the Story o' Irelan'.

BOYLE: Be J. L. Sullivan? Don't you know he didn't.

JOXER: Ah, it's a darlin' buk, a daarlin' buk!

BOYLE: You'd betther be goin', now, Joxer; his Majesty,
Bentham, 'll be here any minute, now.

JOXER: Be the way things is lookin', it'll be a match
between him an' Mary. She's thrun over Jerry altogether. Well, I hope it will, for he's a darlin' man.

BOYLE: I'm glad you think so—I don't. (*Irritably*) What's
darlin' about him?

JOXER: (*Nonplussed*) I only seen him twiced; if you want
to know me, come an' live with me.

BOYLE: He's too dignified for me—to hear him talk
you'd think he knew as much as a Boney's Oracu-
lum. He's given up his job as teacher, an' is goin' to
become a solicitor in Dublin—he's been studyin'
law. I suppose he thinks I'll set him up, but he's
wrong shipped. An' th' other fella—Jerry's as bad.
The two o' them ud give you a pain in your face,
listenin' to them; Jerry believin' in nothin', an' Bentham believin' in everythin'. One that says all is God
an' no man; an' th' other that says all is man an' no
God!

JOXER: Well, I'll be off now.

BOYLE: Don't forget to dhrop down afther awhile; we'll
have a quiet jar, an' a song or two.

JOXER: Never fear.

BOYLE: An' tell Mrs. Madigan that I hope we'll have the
pleasure of her organization at our little enther-
tainment.

JOXER: Righto; we'll come down together.

(*He goes out.*
JOHNNY *comes from room on left, and sits down moodily
at the fire.* BOYLE *looks at him for a few moments, and
shakes his head. He fills his pipe.*)

Voice of JUNO *at the door*: Open the door, Jack; this thing
has me nearly kilt with the weight.

(BOYLE *opens the door.* JUNO *enters carrying the box of
a gramophone, followed by* MARY *carrying the horn and
some parcels.* JUNO *leaves the box on the table and flops
into a chair.*)

JUNO: Carryin' that from Henry Street was no joke.

BOYLE: U-u-ugh, that's a grand-lookin' insthrument—
how much was it?

JUNO: Pound down, an' five to be paid at two shillin's a
week.

BOYLE: That's reasonable enough.

JUNO: I'm afraid we're runnin' into too much debt; first
the furniture, an' now this.

BOYLE: The whole lot won't be much out of £2000.

MARY: I don't know what you wanted a gramophone
for—I know Charlie hates them; he says they're
destructive of real music.

BOYLE: Desthructive of music—that fella ud give you a
pain in your face. All a gramophone wants is to be
properly played; its thrue wondher is only felt when
everythin's quiet—what a gramophone wants is
dead silence!

MARY: But, father, Jerry says the same; afther all, you
can only appreciate music when your ear is
properly trained.

BOYLE: That's another fella ud give you a pain in your
face. Properly thrained! I suppose you couldn't appreciate football unless your fut was properly
thrained.

MRS. BOYLE: (*To* MARY) Go on in ower that an' dress, or
Charlie'll be in on you, an' tea nor nothin'll be ready.

(MARY *goes into room left.*)

MRS. BOYLE: (*Arranging table for tea*) You didn't look at
our new gramophone, Johnny?

JOHNNY: 'Tisn't gramophones I'm thinking of.

MRS. BOYLE: An' what is it you're thinkin' of, allanna?

JOHNNY: Nothin', nothin', nothin'.

MRS. BOYLE: Sure, you must be thinkin' of somethin';
it's yourself that has yourself the way y'are; sleepin'

wan night in me sisther's, an' the nex' in your father's brother's—you'll get no rest goin' on that way.

JOHNNY: I can rest nowhere, nowhere, nowhere.

MRS. BOYLE: Sure, you're not thryin' to rest anywhere.

JOHNNY: Let me alone, let me alone, let me alone, for
God's sake.

(A knock at street door.)

MRS. BOYLE: (In a flutter) Here he is; here's Mr. Bentham!

BOYLE: Well, there's room for him; it's a pity there's not
a brass band to play him in.

MRS. BOYLE: We'll han' the tea round, an' not be clus-
thered round the table, as if we never seen nothin'.

(Steps are heard approaching, and JUNO opening the
door, allows BENTHAM to enter.)

JUNO: Give your hat an' stick to Jack, there . . . sit down,
Mr. Bentham . . . no, not there . . . in th' easy chair
be the fire . . . there, that's betther. Mary'll be out
to you in a minute.

BOYLE: (Solemnly) I seen be the paper this mornin' that
Consols was down half per cent. That's serious, min'
you, an' shows the whole counthry's in a state o'
chassis.

MRS. BOYLE: What's Consols, Jack?

BOYLE: Consols? Oh, Consols is—oh, there's no use
tellin' women what Consols is—th' wouldn't un-
dherstand.

BENTHAM: It's just as you were saying, Mr. Boyle . . .

(MARY enters, charmingly dressed.)

BENTHAM: Oh, good evening, Mary; how pretty you're
looking!

MARY: (Archly) Am I?

BOYLE: We were just talkin' when you kem in, Mary; I
was tellin' Mr. Bentham that the whole counthry's
in a state o' chassis.

MARY: (To BENTHAM) Would you prefer the green or
the blue ribbon round me hair, Charlie?

MRS. BOYLE: Mary, your father's speakin'.

BOYLE: (Rapidly) I was jus' tellin' Mr. Bentham that the
whole counthry's in a state o' chassis.

MARY: I'm sure you're frettin', da, whether it is or no.

MRS. BOYLE: With all our churches an' religions, the
worl's not a bit the betther.

BOYLE: (With a commanding gesture) Tay!

(MARY and MRS. BOYLE dispense the tea.)

MRS. BOYLE: An' Irelan's takin' a leaf out o' the worl's
buk; when we got the makin' of our own laws I
thought we'd never stop to look behind us, but
instead of that we never stopped to look before us!
If the people ud folley up their religion betther
there'd be a better chance for us—what do you
think, Mr. Bentham?

BENTHAM: I'm afraid I can't venture to express an opinion on that point, Mrs. Boyle; dogma has no attraction for me.

MRS. BOYLE: I forgot you didn't hold with us: what's
this you said you were?

BENTHAM: A Theosophist, Mrs. Boyle.

MRS. BOYLE: An' what in the name o' God's a Theosophist?

BOYLE: A Theosophist, Juno, 's a—tell her, Mr. Bentham, tell her.

BENTHAM: It's hard to explain in a few words: The-
osophy's founded on The Vedas, the religious
books of the East. Its central theme is the existence
of an all-pervading Spirit—the Life-Breath. Nothing really exists but this one Universal Life-Breath.
And whatever even seems to exist separately from
this Life-Breath, doesn't really exist at all. It is all
vital force in man, in all animals, and in all vegeta-
tion. This Life-Breath is called the Prawna.

MRS. BOYLE: The Prawna! What a comical name!

BOYLE: Prawna; yis, the Prawna. (Blowing gently through
his lips) That's the Prawna!

MRS. BOYLE: Whisht, whisht, Jack.

BENTHAM: The happiness of man depends upon his
sympathy with this Spirit. Men who have reached
a high state of excellence are called Yogi. Some men
become Yogi in a short time, it may take others
millions of years.

BOYLE: Yogi! I seen hundreds of them in the streets
o' San Francisco.

BENTHAM: It is said by these Yogi that if we practise
certain mental exercises we would have powers denied to others—for instance, the faculty of seeing
things that happen miles and miles away.

MRS. BOYLE: I wouldn't care to meddle with that sort o'
belief; it's a very curious religion, altogether.

BOYLE: What's curious about it? Isn't all religions curious?—if they weren't, you wouldn't get any one to
believe them. But religions is passin' away—they've
had their day like everything else. Take the real
Dublin people, f'rinstance: they know more about
Charlie Chaplin an' Tommy Mix than they do about
SS. Peter an' Paul!

MRS. BOYLE: You don't believe in ghosts, Mr. Bentham?

MARY: Don't you know he doesn't, mother?

BENTHAM: I don't know that, Mary. Scientists are beginning to think that what we call ghosts are sometimes
seen by persons of a certain nature. They say that
sensational actions, such as the killing of a person,
demand great energy, and that energy lingers in
the place where the action occurred. People may
live in the place and see nothing, when someone
may come along whose personality has some peculiar connection with the energy of the place, and,
in a flash, the person sees the whole affair.

JOHNNY: (Rising swiftly, pale and affected) What sort o'
talk is this to be goin' on with? Is there nothin'
better to be talkin' about but the killin' o' people?

My God, isn't it bad enough for these things to happen without talkin' about them!

(*He hurriedly goes into the room on left.*)

BENTHAM: Oh, I'm very sorry, Mrs. Boyle; I never thought . . .

MRS. BOYLE: (*Apologetically*) Never mind, Mr. Bentham, he's very touchy.

(*A frightened scream is heard from* JOHNNY *inside.*)

MRS. BOYLE: Mother of God, what's that?

(*He rushes out again, his face pale, his lips twitching, his limbs trembling.*)

JOHNNY: Shut the door, shut the door, quick, for God's sake! Great God, have mercy on me! Blessed Mother o' God, shelter me, shelther your son!

MRS. BOYLE: (*Catching him in her arms*) What's wrong with you? What ails you? Sit down, sit down, here, on the bed . . . there now . . . there now.

MARY: Johnny, Johnny, what ails you?

JOHNNY: I seen him, I seen him . . . kneelin' in front o' the statue . . . merciful Jesus, have pity on me!

MRS. BOYLE: (*To* BOYLE) Get him a glass o' whisky . . . quick, man, an' don't stand gawkin'.

(BOYLE *gets the whisky.*)

JOHNNY: Sit here, sit here, mother . . . between me an' the door.

MRS. BOYLE: I'll sit beside you as long as you like, only tell me what was it came across you at all?

JOHNNY: (*After taking some drink*) I seen him. . . . I seen Robbie Tancred kneelin' down before the statue . . . an' the red light shinin' on him . . . an' when I went in . . . he turned an' looked at me . . . an' I seen the woun's bleedin' in his breast. . . . Oh, why did he look at me like that? . . . it wasn't my fault that he was done in. . . . Mother o' God, keep him away from me!

MRS. BOYLE: There, there, child, you've imagined it all. There was nothin' there at all—it was the red light you seen, an' the talk we had put all the rest into your head. Here, dhrink more o' this—it'll do you good. . . . An', now, stretch yourself down on the bed for a little. (*To* BOYLE) Go in, Jack, an' show him it was only in his own head it was.

BOYLE: (*Making no move*) E-e-e-eh; it's all nonsense; it was only a shadda he saw.

MARY: Mother o' God, he made me heart lep!

BENTHAM: It was simply due to an overwrought imagination—we all get that way at times.

MRS. BOYLE: There, dear, lie down in the bed, an' I'll put the quilt across you . . . e-e-e-eh, that's it . . . you'll be as right as the mail in a few minutes.

JOHNNY: Mother, go into the room an' see if the light's lightin' before the statue.

MRS. BOYLE: (*To* BOYLE) Jack, run in an' see if the light's lightin' before the statue.

BOYLE: (*To* MARY) Mary, slip in an' see if the light's lightin' before the statue.

(MARY *hesitates to go in.*)

BENTHAM: It's all right; Mary, I'll go.

(*He goes into the room; remains for a few moments, and returns.*)

BENTHAM: Everything's just as it was—the light burning bravely before the statue.

BOYLE: Of course; I knew it was all nonsense.

(*A knock at the door.*)

BOYLE: (*Going to open the door*) E-e-e-eh.

(*He opens it, and* JOXER, *followed by* MRS. MADIGAN, *enters.* MRS. MADIGAN *is a strong, dapper little woman of about forty-five; her face is almost always a widespread smile of complacency. She is a woman who, in manner at least, can mourn with them that mourn, and rejoice with them that do rejoice. When she is feeling comfortable, she is inclined to be reminiscent; when others say anything, or following a statement made by herself, she has a habit of putting her head a little to one side, and nodding it rapidly several times in succession, like a bird pecking at a hard berry. Indeed, she has a good deal of the bird in her, but the bird instinct is by no means a melodious one. She is ignorant, vulgar and forward, but her heart is generous withal. For instance, she would help a neighbor's sick child; she would probably kill the child, but her intention would be to cure it; she would be more at home helping a drayman to lift a fallen horse. She is dressed in a rather soiled grey dress and a vivid purple blouse; in her hair is a huge comb, ornamented with huge colored beads. She enters with a gliding step, beaming smile and nodding head.* BOYLE *receives them effusively.*)

BOYLE: Come on in, Mrs. Madigan; come on in; I was afraid you weren't comin'. . . . (*Slyly*) There's some people able to dhress, ay, Joxer?

JOXER: Fair as the blossoms that bloom in the May, an' sweet as the scent of the new-mown hay. . . . Ah, well she may wear them.

MRS. MADIGAN: (*Looking at* MARY) I know some as are as sweet as the blossoms that bloom in the May—oh, no names, no pack dhrill!

BOYLE: An' now I'll inthroduce the pair o' yous to Mary's intended: Mr. Bentham, this is Mrs. Madigan, an oul' back-parlour neighbour, that, if she could help it at all, ud never see a body shuk!

BENTHAM: (*Rising, and tentatively shaking the hand of* MRS. MADIGAN) I'm sure, it's a great pleasure to know you, Mrs. Madigan.

MRS. MADIGAN: An' I'm goin' to tell you, Mr. Bentham, you're goin' to get as nice a bit o' skirt in Mary, there, as ever you seen in your puff. Not like some of the dhressed-up dolls that's knockin' about lookin' for men when it's a skelpin' they want. I remember, as well as I remember yestherday, the day she was born—of a Tuesday, the 25th o' June, in the year 1901, at thirty-three minutes past wan in the day be Foley's clock, the pub at the corner o' the street. A cowld day it was too, for the season o' the year, an' I remember sayin' to Joxer, there, who I met comin' up th' stairs, that the new arrival in Boyle's ud grow up a hardy chiselur if it lived, an' that she'd be somethin' one o' these days that nobody suspected, an' so signs on it, here she is to-day, goin' to be married to a young man lookin' as if he'd be fit to commensurate in any position in life it ud please God to call him!

BOYLE: (*Effusively*) Sit down, Mrs. Madigan, sit down, me oul' sport. (*To* BENTHAM) This is Joxer Daly, Past Chief Ranger of the Dear Little Shamrock Branch of the Irish National Foresters, an oul' front-top neighbour, that never despaired, even in the darkest days of Ireland's sorra.

JOXER: Nil desperandum, Captain, nil desperandum.

BOYLE: Sit down, Joxer, sit down. The two of us was ofen in a tight corner.

MRS. BOYLE: Ay, in Foley's snug!

JOXER: An' we kem out of it flyin', we kem out of it flyin', Captain.

BOYLE: An' now for a dhrink—I know yous won't refuse an oul' friend.

MRS. MADIGAN: (*To* JUNO) Is Johnny not well, Mrs. . . .

MRS. BOYLE: (*Warningly*) S-s-s-sh.

MRS. MADIGAN: Oh, the poor darlin'.

BOYLE: Well, Mrs. Madigan, is it tea or what?

MRS. MADIGAN: Well, speakin' for meself, I jus' had me tea a minute ago, an' I'm afraid to dhrink any more—I never the same when I dhrink too much tay. Thanks, all the same, Mr. Boyle.

BOYLE: Well, what about a bottle o' stout or a dhrop o' whisky?

MRS. MADIGAN: A bottle o' stout ud be a little too heavy for me stummock afther me tay. . . . A-a-ah, I'll thry the ball o' malt.

(BOYLE *prepares the whisky.*)

MRS. MADIGAN: There's nothin' like a ball o' malt occasional like—too much of it isn't good. (*To* BOYLE, *who is adding water*) Ah, God, Johnny, don't put too much wather on it! (*She drinks.*) I suppose yous'll be lavin' this place.

BOYLE: I'm looking for a place near the sea; I'd like the place that you might say was me cradle, to be me grave as well. The sea is always callin' me.

JOXER: She is callin', callin', callin', in the win' an' on the sea.

BOYLE: Another dhrop o' whisky, Mrs. Madigan?

MRS. MADIGAN: Well, now, it ud be hard to refuse seein' the suspicious times that's in it.

BOYLE: (*With a commanding gesture*) Song! . . . Juno . . . Mary . . . 'Home to Our Mountains'!

MRS. MADIGAN: (*Enthusiastically*) Hear, hear!

JOXER: Oh, tha's a darlin' song, a daarlin' song!

MARY: (*Bashfully*) Ah no, da; I'm not in a singin' humour.

MRS. MADIGAN: Gawn with you, child, an' you only goin' to be marrid; I remember as well as I remember yestherday,—it was on a lovely August evenin', exactly, accordin' to date, fifteen years ago, come the Tuesday folleyin' the nex' that's comin' on, when me own man—*the Lord be good to him*—an' me was sittin' shy together in a doty little nook on a counthry road, adjacent to The Stiles. 'That'll scratch your lovely, little white neck,' says he, ketchin' hould of a danglin' bramble branch, holdin' clusters of the loveliest flowers you ever seen, an' breakin' it off, so that his arm fell, accidental like, roun' me waist, an' as I felt it tightenin', an' tightenin', an' tightenin', I thought me buzzom was every minute goin' to burst out into a roystherin' song about

'The little green leaves that were shakin' on the threes,
The gallivantin' buttherflies, an' buzzin' o' the bees!'

BOYLE: Ordher for the song!

JUNO: Come on, Mary—we'll do our best.

(JUNO *and* MARY *stand up, and choosing a suitable position, sing simply 'Home to Our Mountains'. They bow to the company, and return to their places.*)

BOYLE: (*Emotionally, at the end of song*) Lull . . . me . . . to . . . rest!

JOXER: (*Clapping his hands*) Bravo, bravo! Darlin' girulls, darlin' girulls!

MRS. MADIGAN: Juno, I never seen you in bether form.

BENTHAM: Very nicely rendered indeed.

MRS. MADIGAN: A noble call, a noble call!

MRS. BOYLE: What about yourself, Mrs. Madigan?

(*After some coaxing,* MRS. MADIGAN *rises, and in a quavering voice sings the following verse:*)

If I were a blackbird I'd whistle and sing;
I'd follow the ship that my thrue love was in;
An' on the top riggin', I'd there build me nest,
An' at night I would sleep on me Willie's white breast!

(*Becoming husky, amid applause, she sits down.*)

MRS. MADIGAN: Ah, me voice is too husky now, Juno; though I remember the time when Maisie Madigan could sing like a nightingale at matin' time. I remember as well as I remember yestherday, at a party given to celebrate the comin' of the first chiselur to Annie an' Benny Jimeson—who was the barber, yous may remember, in Henrietta Street, that, after Easter Week, hung out a green, white an' orange pole, an' then, when the Tans started their Jazz dancin', whipped it in agen, an' stuck out a red, white an' blue wan instead, givin' as an excuse that a barber's pole was strictly non-political—singin' 'An' You'll Remember Me' with the top notes quiverin' in a dead hush of pethrified attention, folleyed be a clappin' o' han's that shuk the tumblers on the table, an' capped by Jimeson, the barber, sayin' that it was the best rendherin' of 'You'll Remember Me' he ever heard in his natural!

BOYLE: (*Peremptorily*) Ordher for Joxer's song!

JOXER: Ah no, I couldn't; don't ass me, Captain.

BOYLE: Joxer's song, Joxer's song—give us wan of your shut-eyed wans.

(JOXER *settles himself in his chair; takes a drink; clears his throat; solemnly closes his eyes, and begins to sing in a very querulous voice:*)

She is far from the lan' where her young hero sleeps,
An' lovers around her are sighing   (*He hesitates.*)
An' lovers around her are sighin' . . . sighin' . . .
sighin' . . .   (*A pause*)

BOYLE: (*Imitating* JOXER)

And lovers around her are sighing!

What's the use of you thryin' to sing the song if you don't know it?

MARY: Thry another one, Mr. Daly—maybe you'd be more fortunate.

MRS. MADIGAN: Gawn, Joxer; thry another wan.

JOXER: (*Starting again*)

I have heard the mavis singin' his love song to the
*   morn;*
I have seen the dew-dhrop clingin' to the rose jus' newly
*   born; but . . . but . . . (frantically) To the rose jus'*
*   newly born . . . newly born . . . born.*

JOHNNY: Mother, put on the gramophone, for God's sake, an' stop Joxer's bawlin'.

BOYLE: (*Commandingly*) Gramophone! . . . I hate to see fellas thryin' to do what they're not able to do.

(BOYLE *arranges the gramophone, and is about to start it, when voices are heard of persons descending the stairs.*)

MRS. BOYLE: (*Warningly*) Whisht, Jack, don't put it on, don't put it on yet; this must be poor Mrs. Tancred comin' down to go to the hospital—I forgot all about them bringin' the body to the church to-night. Open the door, Mary, an' give them a bit o' light.

(MARY *opens the door, and* MRS. TANCRED—*a very old women, obviously shaken by the death of her son—appears, accompanied by several neighbors. The first few phrases are spoken before they appear.*)

FIRST NEIGHBOUR: It's a sad journey we're goin' on, but God's good, an' the Republicans won't be always down.

MRS. TANCRED: Ah, what good is that to me now? Whether they're up or down—it won't bring me darlin' boy from the grave.

MRS. BOYLE: Come in an' have a hot cup o' tay, Mrs. Tancred, before you go.

MRS. TANCRED: Ah, I can take nothin' now, Mrs. Boyle—I won't be long afther him.

FIRST NEIGHBOUR: Still an' all, he died a noble death, an' we'll bury him like a king.

MRS. TANCRED: An' I'll go on livin' like a pauper. Ah, what's the pains I suffered bringin' him into the world to carry him to his cradle, to the pains I'm sufferin' now, carryin' him out o' the world to bring him to his grave!

MARY: It would be better for you not to go at all, Mrs. Tancred, but to stay at home beside the fire with some o' the neighbours.

MRS. TANCRED: I seen the first of him, an' I'll see the last of him.

MRS. BOYLE: You'd want a shawl, Mrs. Tancred; it's a cowld night, an' the win's blowin' sharp.

MRS. MADIGAN: (*Rushing out*) I've a shawl above.

MRS. TANCRED: Me home is gone now; he was me only child, an' to think that he was lyin' for a whole night stretched out on the side of a lonely counthry lane, with his head, his darlin' head, that I ofen kissed an' fondled, half hidden in the wather of a runnin' brook. An' I'm told he was the leadher of the ambush where me nex' door neighbour, Mrs. Mannin', lost her Free State soldier son. An' now here's the two of us oul' women, standin' one on each side of a scales o' sorra, balanced be the bodies of our two dead darlin' sons. (MRS. MADIGAN *returns, and wraps a shawl around her.*) God bless you, Mrs. Madigan. . . . (*She moves slowly towards the door*) Mother o' God, Mother o' God, have pity on the pair of us! . . . O Blessed Virgin, where were you when me darlin' son was riddled with bullets, when me darlin' son was riddled with bullets! . . . Sacred Heart of the Crucified Jesus, take away our hearts o' stone . . . an' give us hearts o' flesh! . . . Take away this murdherin' hate . . . an' give us Thine own eternal love!

(*They pass out of the room.*)

MRS. BOYLE: (*Explanatorily to* BENTHAM) That was Mrs. Tancred of the two-pair back; her son was found, e'er yesterday, lyin' out beyant Finglas riddled with bullets. A Die-hard he was, be all accounts. He was a nice quiet boy, but latherly he went to hell, with his Republic first, an' Republic last an' Republic over all. He often took tea with us here, in the oul' days, an' Johnny, there, an' him used to be always together.

JOHNNY: Am I always to be havin' to tell you that he was no friend o' mine? I never cared for him, an' he could never stick me. It's not because he was Commandant of the Battalion that I was Quarther-Masther of, that we were friends.

MRS. BOYLE: He's gone now—the Lord be good to him! God help his poor oul' creature of a mother, for no matther whose friend or enemy he was, he was her poor son.

BENTHAM: The whole thing is terrible, Mrs. Boyle; but the only way to deal with a mad dog is to destroy him.

MRS. BOYLE: An' to think of me forgettin' about him bein' brought to the church to-night, an' we singin' an' all, but it was well we hadn't the gramophone goin', anyhow.

BOYLE: Even if we had aself. We've nothin' to do with these things, one way or t'other. That's the Government's business, an' let them do what we're payin' them for doin'.

MRS. BOYLE: I'd like to know how a body's not to mind these things; look at the way they're afther leavin' the people in this very house. Hasn't the whole house, nearly, been massacreed? There's young Dougherty's husband with his leg off; Mrs. Travers that had her son blew up be a mine in Inchegeela, in Co. Cork; Mrs. Mannin' that lost wan of her sons in an ambush a few weeks ago, an' now, poor Mrs. Tancred's only child gone west with his body made a collandher of. Sure, if it's not our business, I don't know whose business it is.

BOYLE: Here, there, that's enough about them things; they don't affect us, an' we needn't give a damn. If they want a wake, well, let them have a wake. When I was a sailor, I was always resigned to meet with a wathery grave; an' if they want to be soldiers, well, there's no use o' them squealin' when they meet a soldier's fate.

JOXER: Let me like a soldier fall—me breast expandin' to th' ball!

MRS. BOYLE: In wan way, she deserves all she got; for lately, she let th' Die-hards make an open house of th' place; an' for th' last couple of months, either when th' sun was risin' or when th' sun was settin', you had C.I.D. men burstin' into your room, assin' you where were you born, where were you christened, where were you married, an' where would you be buried!

JOHNNY: For God's sake, let us have no more o' this talk.

MRS. MADIGAN: What about Mr. Boyle's song before we start th' gramophone?

MARY: (Getting her hat, and putting it on) Mother, Charlie and I are goin' out for a little sthroll.

MRS. BOYLE: All right, darlin'.

BENTHAM: (Going out with MARY) We won't be long away, Mrs. Boyle.

MRS. MADIGAN: Gwan, Captain, gwan.

BOYLE: E-e-e-e-eh, I'd want to have a few more jars in me, before I'd be in fettle for singin'.

JOXER: Give us that poem you writ t'other day. (To the rest) Aw, it's a darlin' poem, a daarlin' poem.

MRS. BOYLE: God bless us, is he startin' to write poetry!

BOYLE: (Rising to his feet) E-e-e-e-eh.

(He recites in an emotional, consequential manner the following verses:)

Shawn an' I were friends, sir, to me he was all in all.
His work was very heavy and his wages were very small.
None betther on th' beach as Docker, I'll go bail,
'Tis now I'm feelin' lonely, for to-day he lies in jail.
He was not what some call pious—seldom at church or prayer;
For the greatest scoundrels I know, sir, goes every Sunday there.
Fond of his pint—well, rather, but hated the Boss by creed
But never refused a copper to comfort a pal in need.

E-e-e-e-eh.

(He sits down.)

MRS. MADIGAN: Grand, grand; you should folly that up, you should folly that up.

JOXER: It's a daarlin' poem!

BOYLE: (Delightedly) E-e-e-e-eh.

JOHNNY: Are yous goin' to put on th' gramophone to-night, or are yous not?

MRS. BOYLE: Gwan, Jack, put on a record.

MRS. MADIGAN: Gwan, Captain, gwan.

BOYLE: Well, yous'll want to keep a dead silence.

(He sets a record, starts the machine, and it begins to play 'If you're Irish, come into the Parlour'. As the tune is in full blare, the door is suddenly opened by a brisk, little bald-headed man, dressed circumspectly in a black suit; he glares fiercely at all in the room; he is 'NEEDLE' NUGENT, a tailor. He carries his hat in his hand.)

NUGENT: (Loudly, above the noise of the gramophone) Are yous goin' to have that thing bawlin' an' the funeral of Mrs. Tancred's son passin' the house? Have none of yous any respect for the Irish people's National regard for the dead?

(BOYLE stops the gramophone.)

MRS. BOYLE: Maybe, Needle Nugent, it's nearly time we had a little less respect for the dead, an' a little more regard for the livin'.

MRS. MADIGAN: We don't want you, Mr. Nugent, to teach us what we learned at our mother's knee. You don't look yourself as if you were dyin' of grief; if y'ass Maisie Madigan anything, I'd call you a real thrue Die-hard an' live-soft Republican, attendin' Republican funerals in the day, an' stoppin' up half the night makin' suits for the Civic Guards!

(Persons are heard running down to the street, some saying, 'Here it is, here it is.' NUGENT *withdraws, and the rest, except* JOHNNY, *go to the window looking into the street, and look out. Sounds of a crowd coming nearer are heard; portion are singing:)*

To Jesus' Heart all burning
With fervent love for men,
My heart with fondest yearning
Shall raise its joyful strain.
While ages course along,
Blest be with loudest song
The Sacred Heart of Jesus
By every heart and tongue.

MRS. BOYLE: Here's the hearse, here's the hearse!

BOYLE: There's t'oul' mother walkin' behin' the coffin.

MRS. MADIGAN: You can hardly see the coffin with the wreaths.

JOXER: Oh, it's a darlin' funeral, a daarlin' funeral!

MRS. MADIGAN: W'd have a betther view from the street.

BOYLE: Yes—this place ud give you a crick in your neck.

(They leave the room, and go down. JOHNNY *sits moodily by the fire.*
A young man enters; he looks at JOHNNY *for a moment.)*

THE YOUNG MAN: Quarther-Masther Boyle.

JOHNNY: *(With a start)* The Mobilizer!

THE YOUNG MAN: You're not at the funeral?

JOHNNY: I'm not well.

THE YOUNG MAN: I'm glad I've found you; you were stoppin' at your aunt's; I called there but you'd gone. I've to give you an ordher to attend a Battalion Staff meetin' the night afther to-morrow.

JOHNNY: Where?

THE YOUNG MAN: I don't know; you're to meet me at the Pillar at eight o'clock; then we're to go to a place I'll be told of to-night; there we'll meet a mothor that'll bring us to the meeting. They think you might be able to know somethin' about them that gave the bend where Commandant Tancred was shelterin'.

JOHNNY: I'm not goin', then. I know nothing about Tancred.

THE YOUNG MAN: *(At the door)* You'd betther come for your own sake—remember your oath.

JOHNNY: *(Passionately)* I won't go! Haven't I done enough for Ireland! I've lost me arm, an' me hip's desthroyed so that I'll never be able to walk right agen! Good God, haven't I done enough for Ireland?

THE YOUNG MAN: Boyle, no man can do enough for Ireland!

(He goes.)

(Faintly in the distance the crowd is heard saying:)

Hail, Mary, full of grace, the Lord is with Thee;
Blessed art Thou amongst women, and blessed, etc.

CURTAIN

ACT 3

The same as Act 2. It is about half-past six on a November evening; a bright fire burns in the grate; MARY, *dressed to go out, is sitting on a chair by the fire, leaning forward, her hands under her chin, her elbows on her knees. A look of dejection, mingled with uncertain anxiety, is on her face. A lamp, turned low, is lighting on the table. The votive light under the picture of the Virgin gleams more redly than ever.* MRS. BOYLE *is putting on her hat and coat. It is two months later.*

MRS. BOYLE: An' has Bentham never even written to you since—not one line for the past month?

MARY: *(Tonelessly)* Not even a line, mother.

MRS. BOYLE: That's very curious. . . . What came between the two of yous at all? To leave you so sudden, an' yous so great together. . . . To go away t' England, an' not to even leave you his address. . . . The way he was always bringin' you to dances, I thought he was mad afther you. Are you sure you said nothin' to him?

MARY: No, mother—at least nothing that could possibly explain his givin' me up.

MRS. BOYLE: You know you're a bit hasty at times, Mary, an' say things you shouldn't say.

MARY: I never said to him what I shouldn't say, I'm sure of that.

MRS. BOYLE: How are you sure of it?

MARY: Because I love him with all my heart and soul, mother. Why, I don't know; I often thought to myself that he wasn't the man poor Jerry was, but I couldn't help loving him, all the same.

MRS. BOYLE: But you shouldn't be frettin' the way you are; when a woman loses a man, she never knows what she's afther losin', to be sure, but, then, she never knows what she's afther gainin', either. You're not the one girl of a month ago—you look like one pinin' away. It's long ago I had a right to bring you to the doctor, instead of waitin' till to-night.

MARY: There's no necessity, really, mother, to go to the doctor; nothing serious is wrong with me—I'm run down and disappointed, that's all.

MRS. BOYLE: I'll not wait another minute; I don't like the look of you at all. . . . I'm afraid we made a mistake in throwin' over poor Jerry. . . . He'd have been betther for you than that Bentham.

MARY: Mother, the best man for a woman is the one for whom she has the most love, and Charlie had it all.

MRS. BOYLE: Well, there's one thing to be said for him— he couldn't have been thinkin' of the money, or he wouldn't ha' left you . . . it must ha' been somethin' else.

MARY: (*Wearily*) I don't know . . . I don't know, mother . . . only I think . . .

MRS. BOYLE: What d'ye think?

MARY: I imagine . . . he thought . . . we weren't . . . good enough for him.

MRS. BOYLE: An' what was he himself, only a school teacher? Though I don't blame him for fightin' shy of people like that Joxer fella an' that oul' Madigan wan—nice sort o' people for your father to introduce to a man like Mr. Bentham. You might have told me all about this before now, Mary; I don't know why you like to hide everything from your mother; you knew Bentham, an' I'd ha' known nothin' about it if it hadn't bin for the Will; an' it was only to-day, afther long coaxin', that you let out that he's left you.

MARY: It would have been useless to tell you—you wouldn't understand.

MRS. BOYLE: (*Hurt*) Maybe not. . . . Maybe I wouldn't understand. . . . Well, we'll be off now.

(*She goes over to door left, and speaks to* BOYLE *inside.*)

MRS. BOYLE: We're goin' now to the doctor's. Are you goin' to get up this evenin'?

BOYLE: (*From inside*) The pains in me legs is terrible! It's me should be poppin' off to the doctor instead o' Mary, the way I feel.

MRS. BOYLE: Sorra mend you! A nice way you were in last night—carried in in a frog's march, dead to the world. If that's the way you'll go on when you get the money it'll be the grave for you, an asylum for me and the Poorhouse for Johnny.

BOYLE: I thought you were goin'?

MRS. BOYLE: That's what has you as you are—you can't bear to be spoken to. Knowin' the way we are, up to our ears in debt, it's a wondher you wouldn't ha' got up to go to th' solicitor's an' see if we could ha' gotten a little o' the money even.

BOYLE: (*Shouting*) I can't be goin' up there night, noon an' mornin', can I? He can't give the money till he gets it, can he? I can't get blood out of a turnip, can I?

MRS. BOYLE: It's nearly two months since we heard of the Will, an' the money seems as far off as ever. . . . I suppose you know we owe twenty pouns to oul' Murphy?

BOYLE: I've a faint recollection of you tellin' me that before.

MRS. BOYLE: Well, you'll go over to the shop yourself for the things in future—I'll face him no more.

BOYLE: I thought you said you were goin'?

MRS. BOYLE: I'm goin' now; come on, Mary.

BOYLE: Ey, Juno, ey!

MRS. BOYLE: Well, what d'ye want now?

BOYLE: Is there e'er a bottle o' stout left?

MRS. BOYLE: There's two o' them here still.

BOYLE: Show us in one o' them an' leave t'other there till I get up. An' throw us in the paper that's on the table, an' the bottle o' Sloan's Liniment that's in th' drawer.

MRS. BOYLE: (*Getting the liniment and the stout*) What paper is it you want—the *Messenger*?

BOYLE: *Messenger*! The *News o' the World*!

(MRS. BOYLE *brings in the things asked for, and comes out again.*)

MRS. BOYLE: (*At door*) Mind the candle, now, an' don't burn the house over our heads. I left t'other bottle o' stout on the table.

(*She puts bottle of stout on table. She goes out with* MARY. *A cork is heard popping inside.*
A pause; then outside the door is heard the voice of JOXER *lilting softly:* 'Me pipe I'll smoke, as I dhrive me moke . . . are you . . . there . . . Mor . . . ee . . . ar . . . i . . . teee!' *A gentle knock is heard, and after a pause the door opens, and* JOXER, *followed by* NUGENT, *enters.*)

JOXER: Be God, they must be all out; I was thinkin' there was somethin' up when he didn't answer the signal. We seen Juno an' Mary goin', but I didn't see him, an' it's very seldom he escapes me.

NUGENT: He's not goin' to escape me—he's not goin' to be let go to the fair altogether.

JOXER: Sure, the house couldn't hould them lately; an' he goin' about like a mastherpiece of the Free State counthry; forgettin' their friends; forgettin' God— wouldn't even lift his hat passin' a chapel! Sure they were bound to get a dhrop! An' you really think there's no money comin' to him afther all?

NUGENT: Not as much as a red rex, man; I've been a bit anxious this long time over me money, an' I went up to the solicitor's to find out all I could—ah, man, they were goin' to throw me down the stairs. They toul' me that the oul' cock himself had the stairs worn away comin' up afther it, an' they black in the face tellin' him he'd get nothin'. Some way or another that the Will is writ he won't be entitled to get as much as a make!

JOXER: Ah, I thought there was somethin' curious about the whole thing; I've bin havin' sthrange dhreams for the last couple o' weeks. An' I notice that that Bentham fella doesn't be comin' here now—there must be somethin' on the mat there too. Anyhow, who, in the name o' God, ud leave anythin' to that oul' bummer? Sure it ud be unnatural. An' the way Juno an' him's been throwin' their weight about for the last few months! Ah, him that goes a borrowin' goes a sorrowin'!

NUGENT: Well, he's not goin' to throw his weight about in the suit I made for him much longer. I'm tellin' you seven pouns aren't to be found growin' on the bushes these days.

JOXER: An' there isn't hardly a neighbour in the whole street that hasn't lent him money on the strength of what he was goin' to get, but they're after backing the wrong horse. Wasn't it a mercy o' God that I'd nothin' to give him! The softy I am, you know, I'd ha' lent him me last juice! I must have had somebody's good prayers. Ah, afther all, an honest man's the noblest work o' God!

(BOYLE *coughs inside.*)

JOXER: Whisht, damn it, he must be inside in bed.

NUGENT: Inside o' bed or outside of it, he's goin' to pay me for that suit, or give it back—he'll not climb up my back as easily as he thinks.

JOXER: Gwan in at wanst, man, an' get it off him, an' don't be a fool.

NUGENT: (*Going to door left, opening it and looking in*) Ah, don't disturb yourself, Mr. Boyle; I hope you're not sick?

BOYLE: Th' oul' legs, Mr. Nugent, the oul' legs.

NUGENT: I just called over to see if you could let me have anything off the suit?

BOYLE: E-e-e-eh, how much is this it is?

NUGENT: It's the same as it was at the start—seven pouns.

BOYLE: I'm glad you kem, Mr. Nugent; I want a good heavy top-coat—Irish frieze, if you have it. How much would a top-coat like that be, now?

NUGENT: About six pouns.

BOYLE: Six pouns—six an' seven, six an' seven is thirteen—that'll be thirteen pouns I'll owe you.

(JOXER *slips the bottle of stout that is on the table into his pocket.* NUGENT *rushes into the room, and returns with suit on his arm; he pauses at the door.*)

NUGENT: You'll owe me no thirteen pouns. Maybe you think you're betther able to owe it than pay it!

BOYLE: (*Frantically*) Here, come back to hell ower that—where're you goin' with them clothes o' mine?

NUGENT: Where am I goin' with them clothes o' yours? Well, I like your damn cheek!

BOYLE: Here, what am I goin' to dhress meself in when I'm goin' out?

NUGENT: What do I care what you dhress yourself in! You can put yourself in a bolsther cover, if you like.

(*He goes towards the other door, followed by* JOXER.)

JOXER: What'll he dhress himself in! Gentleman Jack an' his frieze coat!

(*They go out.*)

BOYLE: (*Inside*) Ey, Nugent; ey, Mr. Nugent, Mr. Nugent!

(*After a pause* BOYLE *enters hastily, buttoning the braces of his moleskin trousers; his coat and vest are on his arm;*

he throws these on a chair and hurries to the door on right.)

BOYLE: Ey, Mr. Nugent, Mr. Nugent!

JOXER: (*Meeting him at the door*) What's up, what's wrong, Captain?

BOYLE: Nugent's been here an' took away me suit—the only things I had to go out in!

JOXER: Tuk your suit—for God's sake! An' what were you doin' while he was takin' them?

BOYLE: I was in bed when he stole in like a thief in the night, an' before I knew even what he was thinkin' of, he whipped them from the chair an' was off like a redshank!

JOXER: An' what, in the name o' God, did he do that for?

BOYLE: What did he do it for? How the hell do I know what he done it for?—jealousy an' spite, I suppose.

JOXER: Did he not say what he done it for?

BOYLE: Amn't I afther tellin' you that he had them whipped up an' was gone before I could open me mouth?

JOXER: That was a very sudden thing to do; there mus' be somethin' behin' it. Did he hear anythin', I wondher?

BOYLE: Did he hear anythin'?—you talk very queer, Joxer—what could he hear?

JOXER: About you not gettin' the money, in some way or t'other?

BOYLE: An' what ud prevent me from gettin' th' money?

JOXER: That's jus' what I was thinkin'—what ud prevent you from gettin' the money—nothin', as far as I can see.

BOYLE: (*Looking round for bottle of stout, with an exclamation*) Aw, holy God!

JOXER: What's up, Jack?

BOYLE: He must have afther lifted the bottle o' stout that Juno left on the table!

JOXER: (*Horrified*) Ah no, ah no; he wouldn't be afther doin' that now.

BOYLE: An' who done it then? Juno left a bottle o' stout here, an' it's gone—it didn't walk, did it?

JOXER: Oh, that's shockin'; ah, man's inhumanity to man makes countless thousands mourn!

MRS. MADIGAN: (*Appearing at the door*) I hope I'm not disturbin' you in any discussion on your forthcomin' legacy—if I may use the word—an' that you'll let me have a barny for a minute or two with you, Mr. Boyle.

BOYLE: (*Uneasily*) To be sure, Mrs. Madigan—an oul' friend's always welcome.

JOXER: Come in the evenin', come in th' mornin'; come when you're assed, or come without warnin', Mrs. Madigan.

BOYLE: Sit down, Mrs. Madigan.

MRS. MADIGAN: (*Ominously*) Th' few words I have to say can be said standin'. Puttin' aside all formularies, I suppose you remember me lendin' you some time ago three pouns that I raised on blankets an' furniture in me uncle's?

BOYLE: I remember it well. I have it recorded in me book—three pouns five shillings from Maisie Madigan, raised on articles pawned; an', item: fourpence, given to make up the price of a pint, on th' principle that no bird ever flew on wan wing; all to be repaid at par, when the ship comes home.

MRS. MADIGAN: Well, ever since I shoved in the blankets I've been perishing with th' cowld, an' I've decided, if I'll be too hot in th' next' world aself, I'm not goin' to be too cowld in this wan; an' consequently, I want me three pouns, if you please.

BOYLE: This is a very sudden demand, Mrs. Madigan, an' can't be met; but I'm willin' to give you a receipt in full, in full.

MRS. MADIGAN: Come on, out with th' money, an' don't be jack-actin'.

BOYLE: You can't get blood out of a turnip, can you?

MRS. MADIGAN: (*Rushing over and shaking him*) Gimme me money, y'oul' reprobate, or I'll shake the worth of it out of you!

BOYLE: Ey, houl' on, there; houl' on, there! You'll wait for your money now, me lassie!

MRS. MADIGAN: (*Looking around the room and seeing the gramophone*) I'll wait for it, will I? Well, I'll not wait long; if I can't get th' cash, I'll get th' worth of it.

(*She catches up the gramophone.*)

BOYLE: Ey, ey, there, wher'r you goin' with that?

MRS. MADIGAN: I'm goin' to th' pawn to get me three quid five shillins; I'll brin' you th' ticket, an' then you can do what you like, me bucko.

BOYLE: You can't touch that, you can't touch that! It's not my property, an' it's not ped for yet!

MRS. MADIGAN: So much th' better. It'll be an ayse to me conscience, for I'm takin' what doesn't belong to you. You're not goin' to be swankin' it like a paycock with Maisie Madigan's money—I'll pull some o' th' gorgeous feathers out o' your tail!

(*She goes off with the gramophone.*)

BOYLE: What's th' world comin' to at all? I ass you, Joxer Daly, is there any morality left anywhere?

JOXER: I wouldn't ha' believed it, only I seen it with me own two eyes. I didn't think Maisie Madigan was that sort of woman; she has either a sup taken, or she's heard somethin'.

BOYLE: Heard somethin'—about what, if it's not any harm to ass you?

JOXER: She must ha' heard some rumour or other that you weren't goin' to get th' money.

BOYLE: Who says I'm not goin' to get th' money?

JOXER: Sure, I don't know—I was only sayin'.

BOYLE: Only sayin' what?

JOXER: Nothin'.

BOYLE: You were goin' to say somethin'—don't be a twisther.

JOXER: (*Angrily*) Who's a twisther?

BOYLE: Why don't you speak your mind, then?

JOXER: You never twisted yourself—no, you wouldn't know how!

BOYLE: Did you ever know me to twist; did you ever know me to twist?

JOXER: (*Fiercely*) Did you ever do anythin' else! Sure, you can't believe a word that comes out o' your mouth.

BOYLE: Here, get out, ower o' this; I always knew you were a prognosticator an' a procrastinator!

JOXER: (*Going out as* JOHNNY *comes in*) The anchor's weighed, farewell, ree . . . mem . . . ber . . . me. Jacky Boyle, Esquire, infernal rogue an' damned liar.

JOHNNY: Joxer an' you at it agen?—when are you goin' to have a little respect for yourself, an' not be always makin' a show of us all?

BOYLE: Are you goin' to lecture me now?

JOHNNY: Is mother back from the doctor yet, with Mary?

(MRS. BOYLE *enters; it is apparent from the serious look on her face that something has happened. She takes off her hat and coat without a word and puts them by. She then sits down near the fire, and there is a few moments' pause.*)

BOYLE: Well, what did the doctor say about Mary?

MRS. BOYLE: (*In an earnest manner and with suppressed agitation*) Sit down here, Jack; I've something to say to you . . . about Mary.

BOYLE: (*Awed by her manner*) About . . . Mary?

MRS. BOYLE: Close that door there and sit down here.

BOYLE: (*Closing the door*) More throuble in our native land, is it? (*He sits down.*) Well, what is it?

MRS. BOYLE: It's about Mary.

BOYLE: Well, what about Mary—there's nothin' wrong with her, is there?

MRS. BOYLE: I'm sorry to say there's a gradle wrong with her.

BOYLE: A gradle wrong with her! (*Peevishly*) First Johnny an' now Mary; is the whole house goin' to become an hospital! It's not consumption, is it?

MRS. BOYLE: No . . . it's not consumption . . . it's worse.

JOHNNY: Worse! Well, we'll have to get her into some place ower this, there's no one here to mind her.

MRS. BOYLE: We'll all have to mind her now. You might as well know now, Johnny, as another time. (*To* BOYLE) D'ye know what the doctor said to me about her, Jack?

BOYLE: How ud I know—I wasn't there, was I?

MRS. BOYLE: He told me to get her married at wanst.

BOYLE: Married at wanst! An' why did he say the like o' that?

MRS. BOYLE: Because Mary's goin' to have a baby in a short time.

BOYLE: Goin' to have a baby!—my God, what'll Bentham say when he hears that?

MRS. BOYLE: Are you blind, man, that you can't see that it was Bentham that has done this wrong to her?

BOYLE: (*Passionately*) Then he'll marry her, he'll have to marry her!

MRS. BOYLE: You know he's gone to England, an' God knows where he is now.

BOYLE: I'll folly him, I'll folly him, an' bring him back, an' make him do her justice. The scoundrel, I might ha' known what he was, with his yogees an' his prawna!

MRS. BOYLE: We'll have to keep it quiet till we see what we can do.

BOYLE: Oh, isn't this a nice thing to come on top o' me, an' the state I'm in! A pretty show I'll be to Joxer an' to that oul' wan, Madigan! Amn't I afther goin' through enough without havin' to go through this!

MRS. BOYLE: What you an' I'll have to go through'll be nothin' to what poor Mary'll have to go through; for you an' me is middlin' old, an' most of our years is spent; but Mary'll have maybe forty years to face an' handle, an' every wan of them'll be tainted with a bitther memory.

BOYLE: Where is she? Where is she till I tell her off? I'm tellin' you when I'm done with her she'll be a sorry girl!

MRS. BOYLE: I left her in me sister's till I came to speak to you. You'll say nothin' to her, Jack; ever since she left school she's earned her livin', an' your fatherly care never throubled the poor girl.

BOYLE: Gwan, take her part agen her father! But I'll let you see whether I'll say nothin' to her or no! Her an' her readin'! That's more o' th' blasted nonsense that has the house fallin' down on top of us! What did th' likes of her, born in a tenement house, want with readin'? Her readin's afther bringin' her to a nice pass—oh, it's madnin', madnin', madnin'!

MRS. BOYLE: When she comes back say nothin' to her, Jack, or she'll leave this place.

BOYLE: Leave this place! Ay, she'll leave this place, an' quick too!

MRS. BOYLE: If Mary goes, I'll go with her.

BOYLE: Well, go with her! Well, go, th' pair o' yous! I lived before I seen yous, an' I can live when yous are gone. Isn't this a nice thing to come rollin' in on top o' me afther all your prayin' to St. Anthony an' The Little Flower! An' she's a Child o' Mary, too—I wonder what'll the nuns think of her now? An' it'll be bellows'd all over th' disthrict before you could say Jack Robinson; an' whenever I'm seen they'll whisper, 'That's th' father of Mary Boyle that had th' kid be th' swank she used to go with; d'ye know, d'ye know?' To be sure they'll know—more about it than I will meself!

JOHNNY: She should be dhriven out o' th' house she's brought disgrace on!

MRS. BOYLE: Hush, you, Johnny. We needn't let it be bellows'd all over the place; all we've got to do is to leave this place quietly an' go somewhere where we're not known an' nobody'll be th' wiser.

BOYLE: You're talkin' like a two-year-oul', woman. Where'll we get a place ou' o' this—places aren't that easily got.

MRS. BOYLE: But, Jack, when we get the money . . .

BOYLE: Money—what money?

MRS. BOYLE: Why, oul' Ellison's money, of course.

BOYLE: There's no money comin' from oul' Ellison, or any one else. Since you've heard of wan throuble, you might as well hear of another. There's no money comin' to us at all—the Will's a wash-out!

MRS. BOYLE: What are you sayin', man—no money?

JOHNNY: How could it be a wash-out?

BOYLE: The boyo that's after doin' it to Mary done it to me as well. The thick made out the Will wrong; he said in th' Will, only first cousin an' second cousin, instead of mentionin' our names, an' now any one that thinks he's a first cousin or second cousin t'oul' Ellison can claim the money as well as me, an' they're springin' up in hundreds, an' comin' from America an' Australia, thinkin' to get their whack out of it, while all the time the lawyers is gobblin' it up, till there's not as much as ud buy a stockin' for your lovely daughter's baby!

MRS. BOYLE: I don't believe it, I don't believe it, I don't believe it!

JOHNNY: Why did you say nothin' about this before?

MRS. BOYLE: You're not serious, Jack; you're not serious!

BOYLE: I'm tellin' you the scholar, Bentham, made a banjax o' th' Will; instead o' sayin', 'th' rest o' me property to be divided between me first cousin, Jack Boyle, an' me second cousin, Mick Finnegan, o' Santhry', he writ down only, 'me first an' second cousins', an' the world an' his wife are after th' property now.

MRS. BOYLE: Now I know why Bentham left poor Mary in th' lurch; I can see it all now—oh, is there not even a middlin' honest man left in th' world?

JOHNNY: (*To* BOYLE) An' you let us run into debt, an' you borreyed money from everybody to fill yourself with beer! An' now you tell us the whole thing's a washout! Oh, if it's thrue, I'm done with you, for you're worse than me sisther Mary!

BOYLE: You hole your tongue, d'ye hear? I'll not take any lip from you. Go an' get Bentham if you want satisfaction for all that's afther happenin' us.

JOHNNY: I won't hole me tongue, I won't hole me tongue! I'll tell you what I think of you, father an' all you are . . . you . . .

MRS. BOYLE: Johnny, Johnny, Johnny, for God's sake, be quiet!

JOHNNY: I'll not be quiet, I'll not be quiet; he's a nice father, isn't he? Is it any wondher Mary went asthray, when . . .

MRS. BOYLE: Johnny, Johnny, for my sake be quiet—for your mother's sake!

BOYLE: I'm goin' out now to have a few dhrinks with th' last few makes I have, an' tell that lassie o' yours not to be here when I come back; for if I lay me eyes on her, I'll lay me hans on her, an' if I lay me hans on her, I won't be accountable for me actions!

JOHNNY: Take care somebody doesn't lay his hans on you—y'oul' . . .

MRS. BOYLE: Johnny, Johnny!

BOYLE: (*At door, about to go out*) Oh, a nice son, an' a nicer daughter, I have. (*Calling loudly upstairs*) Joxer, Joxer, are you there?

JOXER: (*From a distance*) I'm here, More . . . ee . . . aar . . . i . . . tee!

BOYLE: I'm goin' down to Foley's—are you comin'?

JOXER: Come with you? With that sweet call me heart is stirred; I'm only waiting for the word, an' I'll be with you, like a bird!

(BOYLE *and* JOXER *pass the door going out.*)

JOHNNY: (*Throwing himself on the bed*) I've a nice sisther, an' a nice father, there's no bettin' on it. I wish to God a bullet or a bomb had whipped me ou' o' this long ago! Not one o' yous, not one o' yous, have any thought for me!

MRS. BOYLE: (*With passionate remonstrance*) If you don't whisht, Johnny, you'll drive me mad. Who has kep' th' home together for the past few years—only me? An' who'll have to bear th' biggest part o' this throuble but me?—but whinin' an' whingin' isn't goin' to do any good.

JOHNNY: You're to blame yourself for a gradle of it—givin' him his own way in everything, an' never assin' to check him, no matther what he done. Why didn't you look afther th' money? why . . .

(*There is a knock at the door;* MRS. BOYLE *opens it;* JOHNNY *rises on his elbow to look and listen; two men enter.*)

FIRST MAN: We've been sent up be th' Manager of the Hibernian Furnishings Co., Mrs. Boyle, to take back the furniture that was got a while ago.

MRS. BOYLE: Yous'll touch nothin' here—how do I know who yous are?

FIRST MAN: (*Showing a paper*) There's the ordher, ma'am. (*Reading*) A chest o' drawers, a table, wan easy an' two ordinary chairs; wan mirror; wan chestherfield divan, an' a wardrobe an' two vases (*To his comrade*) Come on, Bill, it's afther knockin'-off time already.

JOHNNY: For God's sake, mother, run down to Foley's an' bring father back, or we'll be left without a stick.

(*The men carry out the table.*)

MRS. BOYLE: What good would it be?—you heard what he said before he went out.

JOHNNY: Can't you thry? He ought to be here, an' the like of this goin' on.

(MRS. BOYLE *puts a shawl around her, as* MARY *enters.*)

MARY: What's up, mother? I met men carryin' away the table, an' everybody's talking about us not gettin' the money after all.

MRS. BOYLE: Everythin's gone wrong, Mary, everythin'. We're not gettin' a penny out o' the Will, not a penny—I'll tell you all when I come back; I'm goin' for your father.

(*She runs out.*)

JOHNNY: (*To* MARY, *who has sat down by the fire*) It's a wondher you're not ashamed to show your face here, afther what has happened.

(JERRY *enters slowly; there is a look of earnest hope on his face. He looks at* MARY *for a few moments.*)

JERRY: (*Softly*) Mary!

(MARY *does not answer.*)

JERRY: Mary, I want to speak to you for a few moments, may I?

(MARY *remains silent;* JOHNNY *goes slowly into room on left.*)

JERRY: Your mother has told me everything, Mary, and I have come to you. . . . I have come to tell you, Mary, that my love for you is greater and deeper than ever. . . .

MARY: (*With a sob*) Oh, Jerry, Jerry, say no more; all that is over now; anything like that is impossible now!

JERRY: Impossible? Why do you talk like that, Mary?

MARY: After all that has happened.

JERRY: What does it matter what has happened? We are young enough to be able to forget all those things. (*He catches her hand*) Mary, Mary, I am pleading for your love. With Labour, Mary, humanity is above everything; we are the Leaders in the fight for a new life. I want to forget Bentham, I want to forget that you left me—even for a while.

MARY: Oh, Jerry, Jerry, you haven't the bitter word of scorn for me after all.

JERRY: (*Passionately*) Scorn! I love you, love you, Mary!

MARY: (*Rising, and looking him in the eyes*) Even though . . .

JERRY: Even though you threw me over for another man; even though you gave me many a bitter word!

MARY: Yes, yes, I know; but you love me, even though . . . even though . . . I'm . . . goin' . . . goin' . . . (*He looks at her questioningly, and fear gathers in his eyes*) Ah, I was thinkin' so. . . . You don't know everything!

JERRY: (*Poignantly*) Surely to God, Mary, you don't mean that . . . that . . . that . . .

MARY: Now you know all, Jerry; now you know all!

JERRY: My God, Mary, have you fallen as low as that?

MARY: Yes, Jerry, as you say, I have fallen as low as that.

JERRY: I didn't mean it that way, Mary . . . it came on me so sudden, that I didn't mind what I was sayin'. . . . I never expected this—your mother never told me. . . . I'm sorry . . . God knows, I'm sorry for you, Mary.

MARY: Let us say no more, Jerry; I don't blame you for thinkin' it's terrible. . . . I suppose it is. . . . Everybody'll think the same . . . it's only as I expected—your humanity is just as narrow as the humanity of the others.

JERRY: I'm sorry, all the same. . . . I shouldn't have troubled you. . . . I wouldn't if I'd known. . . . If I can do anything for you . . . Mary . . . I will.

(*He turns to go, and halts at the door.*)

MARY: Do you remember, Jerry, the verses you read when you gave the lecture in the Socialist Rooms some time ago, on Humanity's Strife with Nature?

JERRY: The verses—no; I don't remember them.

MARY: I do. They're runnin' in me head now—

An' we felt the power that fashion'd
All the lovely things we saw,
That created all the murmur
Of an everlasting law,
Was a hand of force an' beauty,
With an eagle's tearin' claw.

Then we saw our globe of beauty
Was an ugly thing as well,
A hymn divine whose chorus
Was an agonizin' yell;
Like the story of a demon,
That an angel had to tell;

Like a glowin' picture by a
Hand unsteady, brought to ruin;
Like her craters, if their deadness
Could give life unto the moon;
Like the agonizing horror
Of a violin out of tune.

(*There is a pause, and* DEVINE *goes slowly out.*)

JOHNNY: (*Returning*) Is he gone?

MARY: Yes.

(*The two men re-enter.*)

FIRST MAN: We can't wait any longer for t'oul' fella—sorry, Miss, but we have to live as well as th' nex' man.

(*They carry out some things.*)

JOHNNY: Oh, isn't this terrible! . . . I suppose you told him everything . . . couldn't you have waited for a few days? . . . he'd have stopped th' takin' of the things, if you'd kep' your mouth shut. Are you burnin' to tell every one of the shame you've brought on us?

MARY: (*Snatching up her hat and coat*) Oh, this is unbearable!

(*She rushes out.*)

FIRST MAN: (*Re-entering*) We'll take the chest o' drawers next—it's the heaviest.

(*The votive light flickers for a moment, and goes out.*)

JOHNNY: (*In a cry of fear*) Mother o' God, the light's afther goin' out!

FIRST MAN: You put the win' up me the way you bawled that time. The oil's all gone, that's all.

JOHNNY: (*With an agonizing cry*) Mother o' God, there's a shot I'm afther gettin'!

FIRST MAN: What's wrong with you, man? Is it a fit you're takin'?

JOHNNY: I'm afther feelin' a pain in me breast, like the tearin' by of a bullet!

FIRST MAN: He's goin' mad—it's a wondher they'd leave a chap like that here by himself.

(TWO IRREGULARS *enter swiftly; they carry revolvers; one goes over to* JOHNNY; *the other covers the two furniture men.*)

FIRST IRREGULAR: (*To the men, quietly and incisively*) Who are you?—what are yous doin' here?—quick!

FIRST MAN: Removin' furniture that's not paid for.

IRREGULAR: Get over to the other end of the room an' turn your faces to the wall—quick!

(*The two men turn their faces to the wall, with their hands up.*)

SECOND IRREGULAR: (*To* JOHNNY) Come on, Sean Boyle, you're wanted; some of us have a word to say to you.

JOHNNY: I'm sick, I can't—what do you want with me?

SECOND IRREGULAR: Come on, come on; we've a distance to go, an' haven't much time—come on.

JOHNNY: I'm an oul' comrade—yous wouldn't shoot an oul' comrade.

SECOND IRREGULAR: Poor Tancred was an oul' comrade o' yours, but you didn't think o' that when you gave him away to the gang that sent him to his grave. But we've no time to waste; come on—here, Dermot, ketch his arm. (*To* JOHNNY) Have you your beads?

JOHNNY: Me beads! Why do you ass me that, why do you ass me that?

SECOND IRREGULAR: Go on, go on, march!

JOHNNY: Are yous goin' to do in a comrade?—look at me arm, I lost it for Ireland.

SECOND IRREGULAR: Commandant Tancred lost his life for Ireland.

JOHNNY: Sacred Heart of Jesus, have mercy on me! Mother o' God, pray for me—be with me now in the agonies o' death! . . . Hail, Mary, full o' grace . . . the Lord is . . . with Thee.

(They drag out JOHNNY BOYLE, *and the curtain falls. When it rises again the most of the furniture is gone.* MARY *and* MRS. BOYLE, *one on each side, are sitting in a darkened room, by the fire; it is an hour later.)*

MRS. BOYLE: I'll not wait much longer . . . what did they bring him away in the mothor for? Nugent says he thinks they had guns . . . is me throubles never goin' to be over? . . . If anything ud happen to poor Johnny, I think I'd lose me mind. . . . I'll go to the Police Station, surely they ought to be able to do somethin'.

(Below is heard the sound of voices.)

MRS. BOYLE: Whisht, is that something? Maybe, it's your father, though when I left him in Foley's he was hardly able to lift his head. Whisht!

(A knock at the door, and the voice of MRS. MADIGAN, *speaking very softly):* Mrs. Boyle, Mrs. Boyle.

*(*MRS. BOYLE *opens the door.)*

MRS. MADIGAN: Oh, Mrs. Boyle, God an' His Blessed Mother be with you this night!

MRS. BOYLE: *(Calmly)* What is it, Mrs. Madigan? It's Johnny—something about Johnny.

MRS. MADIGAN: God send it's not, God send it's not Johnny!

MRS. BOYLE: Don't keep me waitin', Mrs. Madigan; I've gone through so much lately that I feel able for anything.

MRS. MADIGAN: Two polismen below wantin' you.

MRS. BOYLE: Wantin' me; an' why do they want me?

MRS. MADIGAN: Some poor fella's been found, an' they think it's, it's . . .

MRS. BOYLE: Johnny, Johnny!

MARY: *(With her arms round her mother)* Oh, mother, mother, me poor, darlin' mother.

MRS. BOYLE: Hush, hush, darlin'; you'll shortly have your own throuble to bear. *(To* MRS. MADIGAN) An' why do the polis think it's Johnny, Mrs. Madigan?

MRS. MADIGAN: Because one o' the doctors knew him when he was attendin' with his poor arm.

MRS. BOYLE: Oh, it's thrue, then; it's Johnny, it's me son, me own son!

MARY: Oh, it's thrue, it's thrue what Jerry Devine says— there isn't a God, there isn't a God; if there was He wouldn't let these things happen!

MRS. BOYLE: Mary, you mustn't say them things. We'll want all the help we can get from God an' His Blessed Mother now! These things have nothin' to do with the Will o' God. Ah, what can God do agen the stupidity o' men!

MRS. MADIGAN: The polis want you to go with them to the hospital to see the poor body—they're waitin' below.

MRS. BOYLE: We'll go. Come, Mary, an' we'll never come back here agen. Let your father furrage for himself now; I've done all I could an' it was all no use—he'll be hopeless till the end of his days. I've got a little room in me sisther's where we'll stop till your throuble is over, an' then we'll work together for the sake of the baby.

MARY: My poor little child that'll have no father!

MRS. BOYLE: It'll have what's far betther—it'll have two mothers.

A ROUGH VOICE *shouting from below:* Are yous goin' to keep us waitin' for yous all night?

MRS. MADIGAN: *(Going to the door, and shouting down)* Take your hour, there, take your hour! If yous are in such a hurry, skip off, then, for nobody wants you here—if they did yous wouldn't be found. For you're the same as yous were undher the British Government—never where yous are wanted! As far as I can see, the Polis as Polis, in this city, is Null an' Void!

MRS. BOYLE: We'll go, Mary, we'll go; you to see your poor dead brother, an' me to see me poor dead son!

MARY: I dhread it, mother, I dhread it!

MRS. BOYLE: I forgot, Mary, I forgot; your poor oul' selfish mother was only thinkin' of herself. No, no, you mustn't come—it wouldn't be good for you. You go on to me sisther's an' I'll face th' ordeal meself. Maybe I didn't feel sorry enough for Mrs. Tancred when her poor son was found as Johnny's been found now—because he was a Die-hard! Ah, why didn't I remember that then he wasn't a Die-hard or a Stater, but only a poor dead son! It's well I remember all that she said—an' it's my turn to say it now: What was the pain I suffered, Johnny, bringin' you into the world to carry you to your cradle, to the pains I'll suffer carryin' you out o' the world to bring you to your grave! Mother o' God, Mother o' God, have pity on us all! Blessed Virgin, where were you when me darlin' son was riddled with bullets, when me darlin' son was riddled with bullets? Sacred Heart o' Jesus, take away our hearts o' stone, and give us hearts o' flesh! Take away this murdherin' hate, an' give us Thine own eternal love!

(They all go slowly out. There is a pause; then a sound of shuffling steps on the stairs outside. The door opens and BOYLE *and* JOXER, *both of them very drunk, enter.)*

BOYLE: I'm able to go no farther. . . . Two polis, ey . . . what were they doin' here, I wondher? . . . Up to no good, anyhow . . . an' Juno an' that lovely daughter o' mine with them. (*Taking a sixpence from his pocket and looking at it*) Wan single, solitary tanner left out of all I borreyed . . . (*He lets it fall*) The last o' the Mohicans. . . . The blinds is down, Joxer, the blinds is down!

JOXER: (*Walking unsteadily across the room, and anchoring at the bed*) Put all . . . your throubles . . . in your oul' kit-bag . . . an' smile . . . smile . . . smile!

BOYLE: The counthry'll have to steady itself . . . it's goin' . . . to hell. . . . Where'r all . . . the chairs . . . gone to . . . steady itself, Joxer. . . . Chairs'll . . . have to . . . steady themselves. . . . No matther . . . what any one may . . . say. . . . Irelan's sober . . . is Irelan' . . . free.

JOXER: (*Stretching himself on the bed*) Chains . . . an' . . . slaveree . . . that's a darlin' motto . . . a daaarlin' . . . motto!

BOYLE: If th' worst comes . . . to th' worse . . . I can join a . . . flyin' . . . column. . . . I done . . . me bit . . . in Easther Week . . . had no business . . . to . . . be . . . there . . . but Captain Boyle's Captain Boyle!

JOXER: Breathes there a man with soul . . . so . . . de . . . ad . . . this . . . me . . . o . . . wn, me nat . . . ive l . . . an'!

BOYLE: (*Subsiding into a sitting posture on the floor*) Commandant Kelly died . . . in them . . . arms . . . Joxer. . . . Tell me Volunteer Butties . . . says he . . . that . . . I died for . . . Irelan'!

JOXER: D'jever rade Willie . . . Reilly . . . an' his own . . . Colleen . . . Bawn? It's a darlin' story, a daarlin' story!

BOYLE: I'm telling you . . . Joxer . . . th' whole worl's . . . in a terr . . . ible state o' . . . chassis!

CURTAIN

Figure 1. Joxer (John Rogan) and "Captain" Boyle (Norman Rodway) enjoy a surreptitious breakfast in the shabby Dublin tenement in the Royal Shakespeare Company production of *Juno and the Paycock*, directed by Trevor Nunn, 1980. (Photograph: Donald Cooper/Photostage.)

Figure 2. Juno (Judi Dench) tries to comfort Mrs. Tancred (Marie Kean), while neighbors (Frankie Cosgrave, Denyse Alexander, *partially hidden,* and Doreen Keogh) and Juno's daughter Mary (Dearbhla Molloy) look sympathetically at the grieving old woman in the Royal Shakespeare Company production of *Juno and the Paycock,* directed by Trevor Nunn, 1980. (Photograph: Donald Cooper/Photostage.)

Figure 3. Johnny Boyle (Gerard Murphy), frightened and angered after hearing of the betrayal of Mary and the loss of his family's financial hopes, clings to his mother, Juno (Judi Dench), in the Royal Shakespeare Company production of *Juno and the Paycock,* directed by Trevor Nunn, 1980. (Photograph: Donald Cooper/Photostage.)

Staging of *Juno and the Paycock*

REVIEW OF THE ROYAL SHAKESPEARE COMPANY PRODUCTION, 1980, BY DEREK MAHON

There was a group of American undergraduates at the Aldwych on the night I saw the RSC revival of *Juno and the Paycock,* and I wondered if they could have guessed, without being told, that this was one of the great plays of the twentieth century. Amazed by the listlessness of the first act, I took some time to realize that it was intentional, not the result of a virus among the cast. Trevor Nunn's production adopts a radically different approach to O'Casey's masterpiece from the one to which we have long been accustomed. Subduing the star turns in the interest of the whole, he has come up with a slow-moving, low-keyed version which is more insidiously depressing than any I have yet seen, if adequate on its own terms. An interesting line of inquiry perhaps, but not a recipe for artistic success.

Nunn's strategy is mistaken because the play is composed of star turns. It is a play about character, even "characters," as well as circumstances, and to eschew vividness of personality, a vividness the playwright certainly intended, is to lose a vital dimension of the play, and the one that makes it great. The Boyles and their neighbours are victims of circumstance, granted; but they must be allowed to be more than that, or we make of a complex and exhilarating work a piece of doleful social realism. Not even that. The reality of the long-demolished Dublin tenements is not here, or only partly so; as any reader of O'Casey's autobiographies will know, the irrepressible high spirits were, in those surroundings, as much a fact of life as the squalor.

Norman Rodway as Boyle and John Rogan as Joxer are, therefore, not so much disappointing as infuriating. Deflected by the rationale of the production from playing their marvelous parts to the full, they give us, respectively, a dejected and irritable codger apparently endowed with sober self-knowledge, and a whining creep devoid of even superficial charm. When Boyle announces defiantly to Juno, "I've a little spirit left in me still," he is boasting, but it should not be an empty boast, as the liveliness of his fancy and the trenchancy of his self-dramatizing balderdash make clear. Self-dramatizing in a literal sense; for he and Joxer conduct their own little play within the play, oddly prefiguring Estragon and Vladimir, though much of the fun of that goes by the board here.

On the plus side, Gerard Murphy brings more presence to the part of the maimed and frightened Johnny than is usually the case. O'Casey himself, during rehearsals for the original Abbey production, habitually referred to *Juno* as "the play about Johnny Boyle"—meaning, perhaps, that Johnny represented in his own person all the desperation of a people living, like the Boyles, on impossible dreams. Nobody in the play pays him much heed, and the part is too often treated as a nuisance, like Johnny himself; but that isn't the case here. And Judi Dench is a memorable Juno; her bitterness qualified by an essential sweetness, she alone of the cast shines through the doctrinaire opacity.

I described Boyle as "self-dramatizing," and the theme of the play is the price of his self-dramatization—even, it might be said, the price of drama. In terms of the Boyles' family life, that price is disintegration and chaos. So too in the political sphere, where theatrical postures and heightened language have led to civil war. "Give us one of your shut-eyed ones," says Boyle to Joxer during a sing-song; and Joxer forgets the words. "Shut-eyed ones," for O'Casey as for Dr. Cruise O'Brien in our own day, are the source of half the misery of Ireland; yet they are a seemingly indispensable part of the drama: even the RSC permits itself the liberty of introducing and concluding each act with a snatch of the kind of demotic Dublin melody of which O'Casey evidently took a dim view. This is unfortunate; the effect is to cheapen and trivialize the play itself.

It is Juno's distinction that she resists the blandishments of drama and song, and her misfortune that she (and her daughter Mary, despite her half-baked socialism) sees the only alternative in a mirage of middle-class gentility. The power of the play resides in its intellectual battle with its own emotional appeal. Clear-sighted though it may be, *Juno and the Paycock* is also O'Casey's great "shut-eyed one." The struggle within the artefact itself is of central importance, and to tilt the balance so completely in Juno's favour, by denying Boyle his measure of magnetism, however specious, is to forfeit a crucial tension.

I have never seen a better production of *Juno and the Paycock* than Trevor Nunn's, and I do not expect to see one. It had the characteristics of Nunn's work at its best, a sensitivity to detail, rhythm, clarity and self-confidence; but it also lifted Sean O'Casey's play out of that slightly condescending slot of the mind to which many critics, including me, have assigned it. Nobody doubts the power of certain scenes, particularly the accumulation of disasters which leads to Mrs. Boyle's courageous speech in the last act—"Take away this murdherin' hate," and few question either the humor of the Joxer Daly/Captain Boyle scenes, which too easily confirm the British impression of the Irish as a charming, feckless race.

But the combination of tragedy and farce has been queried, as if O'Casey, self-taught, from a poor family, had not acquired the sophistication to distinguish between the two. Some scenes, too, have been held to betray a literary self-consciousness, as if O'Casey wanted to remind his audience that he, like Mary Boyle, has been reading Ibsen. Mrs. Madigan's flattery of Mary— "I remember, as well as I remember yesterday, the day she was born"—recalls the Nurse's speech in *Romeo and Juliet*; while the sing-song at the end of Act Two, where the Boyle family, supposedly enriched by an inheritance, gather with their friends around the new gramophone on the new three-piece suite, can seem like padding, as if O'Casey, uncertain how to complete the scene without anticipating the revelations to come, had resorted to music-hall nostalgia.

For these and other reasons, *Juno and the Paycock* has been regarded as a rich and powerful play, but far from a masterpiece. Nunn's production, however, faultlessly cast, turns the supposed weaknesses into strengths. The contrast between Judi Dench's determination as Juno and Norman Rodway's fecklessness as the Captain are shown as two sides to the Irish despair, one carrying on against the odds while the other gives up too soon. Nunn brings out the family likenesses in the next generation: Dearbhla Molloy's Mary actually looks like a younger Juno, particularly when the two sing together sweetly and shyly, and there is the same impetuousness in love which landed poor Juno with the Captain. If we need a justification for the family sing-song, here it is—the perpetuation of follies, because, on a darker note, Gerard Murphy's Johnny Boyle skulks in fear on the party fringes and the funeral of a neighbor's son interrupts the proceedings. "If you're Irish," runs the record, "Come into the parlour"—and a mourning mother in widow's black does.

The RSC production is rooted in naturalism—the broken bike by the grimy window—but it never slumps into an accumulation of irrelevant details. Nunn has managed to bring the play together so that each moment of each scene fits into the whole, and we are not left just with another sad anecdote from Dublin in the troublesome Twenties, but with an orchestrated hymn against all poverty, despair and hate. It is deeply moving, without being sentimental or sententious, and establishes Nunn as the best British director of our time.

FEDERICO GARCIA LORCA

1898–1936

Before he was executed by the Fascists at the beginning of the Spanish civil war, Lorca had written twelve plays. His last three works—tragedies of rural life— are such powerful evocations of an archetypal conflict between passionate human instincts and traditional codes of behavior that they alone have been sufficient to establish his reputation as the most culturally conscious and theatrically intense dramatist to emerge in Spain during the twentieth century. He was born near the city of Granada, in southern Spain, a region deeply influenced by the Andalusian and gypsy folk traditions of balladry and dance—traditions that left their mark on both his poetry and plays. He was also influenced by his wealthy father and his cultivated mother who evidently encouraged him to develop his widely varied artistic talents, for he was not only a poet and playwright, but also an accomplished pianist and painter. By the time he was eight, he was already improvising plays in the courtyard of his parents' home, and before he entered the University of Granada at the age of sixteen he was writing ballads, poems, and prose descriptions of the Spanish landscape that he subsequently included in published collections of his works. When he entered the University, he planned to study for a career in the law, but he quickly changed his mind and moved on to studies in philosophy and literature, which he continued at the University of Madrid. When he moved to Madrid in 1919, he had already published *Impressions and Landscapes* (1918), an evocative series of impressions based on his travels throughout Spain, and he had in hand a manuscript of poems that he shared with his fellow students in public readings. Lorca, in fact, was an inveterate performer, and throughout his life he evidently took much greater pleasure in reading his works or seeing them produced than in rushing them into print. He usually published his work well after it had been written, and much of it remained unpublished even at the time of his death.

Lorca's playwriting career began in earnest during the 1920s, a period when he experimented in a variety of forms and turned out a number of works, including a parable play about a cockroach who becomes entranced by the enchanting world of a butterfly, a comedy based on the traditional Spanish puppet character Don Cristobal, a series of farces based on the films of Buster Keaton, a surrealist work involving a young man, his fiancée, a mannequin, a dead child, and a cat, a verse play about Mariana Pineda, a nineteenth-century figure who died in the liberation of Madrid, and a tragic farce about an old bachelor who falls in love with a naive and sensual young girl. These works, together with his numerous public readings, as well as the publication of two collections of poems and a collection of ballads, had turned Lorca into a widely celebrated Spanish writer by the end of the 1920s. In 1929, he left Spain temporarily to visit Paris and London, before traveling to America, where he spent a year at Columbia University, but he evidently did not find New York a congenial place, and by 1930 he had left to visit Cuba, Argentina, and other Latin American countries before returning permanently to Spain.

His travel abroad had also apparently turned him away from all the cosmopolitan movements in drama that were then astir in the major theatrical centers, for when he returned to Spain in 1931, he organized a government-sponsored theatrical troupe and began touring the provinces, producing the Spanish classics of the seventeenth century, wherever he could find an audience in small Spanish towns and villages. His sustained immersion in the folk life of the Spanish provinces also must have led him to develop the subjects that resulted in the major works of his career—his three tragedies of rural experience—which he wrote during his last five years. In each of these, he focused on the predicament of characters who are torn between their allegiance to traditional Spanish codes of honor and religious belief, on the one hand, and their passionate human desires, on the other. And, in each case, he dramatized the tragic frustration of natural human impulses that he evidently perceived as the inescapable outcome of being forced to submit to rigid and anachronistic codes of behavior. Lorca's emphasis on such frustration may also reflect a covert attack on a variety of repressive forces in his own life: the dogmatic power of the Catholic church, the political conservatism of the governing Fascists who would execute Lorca in 1936, and the hostility of a predominantly heterosexual society that degraded and ostracized homosexuals like himself.

In the earliest of the tragedies, *Blood Wedding* (1933), a work heavily interspersed with lyric scenes, Lorca dramatized the primal power of the blood in the person of a young woman "burning with desire," who finds herself betrothed and married to a man whom she regards as "a little bit of water." Immediately after the marriage ceremony she runs off with another man, the husband of her cousin, a man whose family had killed the father and brother of her own husband in a blood feud, but a man whom she had always loved because he was for her "a dark river, choked with brush, that brought near me the undertone of its rushes and its whispered song." The two lovers thus violate all the codes of belief and honor in their community and escape into the forest, where they are pursued by the newly married groom, which results in a doubly fatal encounter between the groom and his rival. The bride is thus left "without a single man ever having seen himself in the whiteness of my breasts," a condition that is at once the measure of her conventional purity and her intense frustration. And the mother of the groom, in a final chorus, is seen lamenting the death of her last son at the hands of the same family that had previously killed her husband and her other son. The conflict between traditional codes and human desires is, therefore, presented as bringing profound suffering to all the central characters, old and young, conventional and rebellious alike. In his second tragedy of rural experience, *Yerma* (1934), Lorca examined the plight of a married woman, whose frustrated maternal desire ultimately drives her to the act of killing her impotent and unsympathetic husband—an act that in turn moves her to cry out "I'm going to rest without ever waking to see whether my blood has announced the coming of new blood. My body barren forever."

Like his other mature plays, *The House of Bernarda Alba*, finished in 1936 a few months before Lorca's death but not produced until 1945, is dramatically preoccupied with the frustration of natural human desire. And like these other plays, it dramatizes this problem by focusing on the experience of women, exploring the sentiment voiced by Amelia, "To be born a woman's the worst possible punishment." Indeed, in this play there are no men on stage at all, though every speech resounds either with the memory of Bernarda's recently dead husband or with the yearning of all her daughters for the virile figure of Pepe el Romano. The world of the play, as indicated by its title, is dominated by Bernarda, whose tyrannical honor and pride and piety and repressiveness are epitomized by the starkly white color of her house, by the black colors of mourning she enforces upon her daughters, and by her big stick that thumps over and over again on the stage. The play repeatedly emphasizes repression: Bernarda's announcement of eight years of mourning, Maria Josefa gagged so that she won't shout, the stallion locked in the stall. Even when La Poncia, the earthy maid who is willing to confront Bernarda directly, imagines revenge, she invokes the prevailing sense of a household that is really a prison: "Then I'll lock myself up in a room with her and spit in her face—for a whole year."

Staging a play whose characters almost always seem at emotional breaking points is not easy, but Nuria Espert, a well-known Spanish actress and director, succeeded in her 1986 production (first staged at the Lyric, Hammersmith, then transferred to the West End). As Michael Billington points out in his review, and as a number of other critics noted, the set itself was crucial, its white stone walls and barred windows harshly looming over the black-clad actresses (see Figure 1). Espert's three older actresses, differing noticeably in physical stature, emphasize the conflict between contrasting views of womanhood. Patricia Hayes as Maria Josefa appears always in white (see Figure 3), symbolizing both the bride she wishes to become and the innocence of the lamb she carries in the last act, an innocence her daughter Bernarda has imprisoned and thus distorted into madness. Glenda Jackson's thin angular features and her ramrod-straight posture (see Figure 3) aptly reflect Bernarda's condemnation of everyone beneath her in social standing or in moral outlook. Joan Plowright's rounder features and full curls (see Figure 2) suggest that La Poncia is a woman able to remember her husband with delight, a woman able to understand the sexual longings of Martirio and Adela, longings that Bernarda can only try to repress. Given the irrepressibility of such desires, it's not surprising that Bernarda at the end turns into a screaming banshee, driving off Pepe el Romano (see Figure 4) and thus driving Adela to suicide. She may command her house, but it is a house dominated by death.

THE HOUSE OF BERNARDA ALBA

A Drama about Women in the Villages of Spain

BY FEDERICO GARCIA LORCA / TRANSLATED BY JAMES GRAHAM-LUJÁN AND RICHARD L. O'CONNELL

CHARACTERS

BERNARDA *(age 60)*
MARIA JOSEFA, *Bernarda's Mother (age 80)*
ANGUSTIAS, *Bernarda's Daughter (age 39)*
MAGDALENA, *Bernarda's Daughter (age 30)*
AMELIA, *Bernarda's Daughter (age 27)*
MARTIRIO, *Bernarda's Daughter (age 24)*
ADELA, *Bernarda's Daughter (age 20)*

A MAID *(age 50)*
LA PONCIA, *A Maid (age 60)*
PRUDENCIA *(age 50)*
Women in Mourning

The writer states that these Three Acts are intended as a photographic document.

ACT 1

(A very white room in BERNARDA ALBA'S *house. The walls are white. There are arched doorways with jute curtains tied back with tassels and ruffles. Wicker chairs. On the walls, pictures of unlikely landscapes full of nymphs or legendary kings.*

It is summer. A great brooding silence fills the stage. It is empty when the curtain rises. Bells can be heard tolling outside.)

FIRST SERVANT *(entering)*: The tolling of those bells hits me right between the eyes.

PONCIA *(she enters, eating bread and sausage)*: More than two hours of mumbo jumbo. Priests are here from all the towns. The church looks beautiful. At the first responsory for the dead, Magdalena fainted.

FIRST SERVANT: She's the one who's left most alone.

PONCIA: She's the only one who loved her father. Ay! Thank God we're alone for a little. I came over to eat.

FIRST SERVANT: If Bernarda sees you . . . !

PONCIA: She's not eating today so she'd just as soon we'd all die of hunger! Domineering old tyrant! But she'll be fooled! I opened the sausage crock.

FIRST SERVANT *(with an anxious sadness)*: Couldn't you give me some for my little girl, Poncia?

PONCIA: Go ahead! And take a fistful of peas too. She won't know the difference today.

VOICE *(within)*: Bernarda!

PONCIA: There's the grandmother! Isn't she locked up tight?

FIRST SERVANT: Two turns of the key.

PONCIA: You'd better put the cross-bar up too. She's got the fingers of a lock-picker!

VOICE *(within)*: Bernarda!

PONCIA *(shouting)*: She's coming! *(to the* SERVANT*)* Clean everything up good. If Bernarda doesn't find things shining, she'll pull out the few hairs I have left.

SERVANT: What a woman!

PONCIA: Tyrant over everyone around her. She's perfectly capable of sitting on your heart and watching you die for a whole year without turning off that cold little smile she wears on her wicked face. Scrub, scrub those dishes!

SERVANT: I've got blood on my hands from so much polishing of everything.

PONCIA: She's the cleanest, she's the decentest, she's the highest everything! A good rest her poor husband's earned!

(The bells stop.)

SERVANT: Did all the relatives come?

PONCIA: Just hers. His people hate her. They came to see him dead and make the sign of the cross over him; that's all.

SERVANT: Are there enough chairs?

PONCIA: More than enough. Let them sit on the floor. When Bernarda's father died people stopped coming under this roof. She doesn't want them to see her in her "domain." Curse her!

SERVANT: She's been good to you.

PONCIA: Thirty years washing her sheets. Thirty years eating her leftovers. Nights of watching when she had a cough. Whole days peeking through a crack in the shutters to spy on the neighbors and carry her the tale. Life without secrets one from the other. But in spite of that—curse her! May the "pain of the piercing

234

nail" strike her in the eyes.

SERVANT: Poncia!

PONCIA: But I'm a good watchdog! I bark when I'm told and bite beggars' heels when she sics me on 'em. My sons work in her fields—both of them already married, but one of these days I'll have enough.

SERVANT: And then . . . ?

PONCIA: Then I'll lock myself up in a room with her and spit in her face—a whole year. "Bernarda, here's for this, that and the other!" Till I leave her—just like a lizard the boys have squashed. For that's what she is—she and her whole family! Not that I envy her her life. Five girls are left her, five ugly daughters—not counting Angustias the eldest, by her first husband, who has money—the rest of them, plenty of eyelets to embroider, plenty of linen petticoats, but bread and grapes when it comes to inheritance.

SERVANT: Well, *I'd* like to have what thèy've got!

PONCIA: All we have is our hands and a hole in God's earth.

SERVANT: And that's the only earth they'll ever leave to us—to us who have nothing!

PONCIA (*at the cupboard*): This glass has some specks.

SERVANT: Neither soap nor rag will take them off.

(The bells toll.)

PONCIA: The last prayer! I'm going over and listen. I certainly like the way our priest sings. In the Pater Noster his voice went up, and up—like a pitcher filling with water little by little. Of course, at the end his voice cracked, but it's glorious to hear it. No, there never was anybody like the old Sacristan—Tronchapinos. At my mother's Mass, may she rest in peace, he sang. The walls shook—and when he said "Amen," it was as if a wolf had come into the church.

(Imitating him.)

A-a-a-a-men!

(She starts coughing.)

SERVANT: Watch out—you'll strain your windpipe!

PONCIA: I'd rather strain something else!

(Goes out laughing.)
(The SERVANT *scrubs. The bells toll.)*

SERVANT (*imitating the bells*): Dong, dong, dong. Dong, dong, dong. May God forgive him!

BEGGAR WOMAN (*at the door, with a little girl*): Blessèd be God!

SERVANT: Dong, dong, dong. I hope he waits many years for us! Dong, dong, dong.

BEGGAR (*loudly, a little annoyed*): Blessèd be God!

SERVANT (*annoyed*): Forever and ever!

BEGGAR: I came for the scraps.

(The bells stop tolling.)

SERVANT: You can go right out the way you came in. Today's scraps are for me.

BEGGAR: But you have somebody to take care of you—and my little girl and I are all alone!

SERVANT: Dogs are alone too, and they live.

BEGGAR: They always give them to me.

SERVANT: Get out of here! Who let you in anyway? You've already tracked up the place.

(The BEGGAR WOMAN *and* LITTLE GIRL *leave. The* SERVANT *goes on scrubbing.)*

Floors finished with oil, cupboards, pedestals, iron beds—but us servants, we can suffer in silence—and live in mud huts with a plate and a spoon. I hope someday not a one will be left to tell it.

(The bells sound again.)

Yes, yes—ring away. Let them put you in a coffin with gold inlay and brocade to carry it on— you're no less dead than I'll be, so take what's coming to you, Antonio María Benavides—stiff in your broadcloth suit and your high boots— take what's coming to you! You'll never again lift my skirts behind the corral door!

(From the rear door, two by two, women in mourning with large shawls and black skirts and fans, begin to enter. They come in slowly until the stage is full.)

SERVANT (*breaking into a wail*): Oh, Antonio María Benavides, now you'll never see these walls, nor break bread in this house again! I'm the one who loved you most of all your servants.

(Pulling her hair.)

Must I live on after you've gone? Must I go on living?

(The two hundred women finish coming in, and BERNARDA *and her five daughters enter.* BERNARDA *leans on a cane.)*

BERNARDA (*to the* SERVANT): Silence!

SERVANT (*weeping*): Bernarda!

BERNARDA: Less shrieking and more work. You should have had all this cleaner for the wake. Get out. This isn't your place.

(The SERVANT *goes off crying.)*

The poor are like animals—they seem to be made of different stuff.

FIRST WOMAN: The poor feel their sorrows too.

BERNARDA: But they forget them in front of a plateful of peas.

FIRST GIRL (*timidly*): Eating is necessary for living.

BERNARDA: At your age one doesn't talk in front of older people.

WOMAN: Be quiet, child.

BERNARDA: I've never taken lessons from anyone. Sit down.

(They sit down. Pause. Loudly.)

Magdalena, don't cry. If you want to cry, get under your bed. Do you hear me?

SECOND WOMAN *(to BERNARDA)*: Have you started to work the fields?

BERNARDA: Yesterday.

THIRD WOMAN: The sun comes down like lead.

FIRST WOMAN: I haven't known heat like this for years.

(Pause. They all fan themselves.)

BERNARDA: Is the lemonade ready?

PONCIA: Yes, Bernarda.

(She brings in a large tray full of little white jars which she distributes.)

BERNARDA: Give the men some.

PONCIA: They're already drinking in the patio.

BERNARDA: Let them get out the way they came in. I don't want them walking through here.

A GIRL *(to ANGUSTIAS)*: Pepe el Romano was with the men during the service.

ANGUSTIAS: There he was.

BERNARDA: His mother was there. She saw his mother. Neither she nor I saw Pepe . . .

GIRL: I thought . . .

BERNARDA: The one who *was* there was Darajalí, the widower. Very close to your Aunt. We all of us saw him.

SECOND WOMAN *(aside, in a low voice)*: Wicked, worse than wicked woman!

THIRD WOMAN: A tongue like a knife!

BERNARDA: Women in church shouldn't look at any man but the priest—and him only because he wears skirts. To turn your head is to be looking for the warmth of corduroy.

FIRST WOMAN: Sanctimonious old snake!

PONCIA *(between her teeth)*: Itching for a man's warmth.

BERNARDA *(beating with her cane on the floor)*: Blesséd be God!

ALL *(crossing themselves)*: Forever blesséd and praised.

BERNARDA: Rest in peace with holy company at your head.

ALL: Rest in peace!

BERNARDA: With the Angel Saint Michael, and his sword of justice.

ALL: Rest in peace!

BERNARDA: With the key that opens, and the hand that locks.

ALL: Rest in peace!

BERNARDA: With the most blesséd, and the little lights of the field.

ALL: Rest in peace!

BERNARDA: With our holy charity, and all souls on land and sea.

ALL: Rest in peace!

BERNARDA: Grant rest to your servant, Antonio María Benavides, and give him the crown of your blesséd glory.

ALL: Amen.

BERNARDA *(she rises and chants)*: Requiem aeternam donat eis domine.

ALL *(standing and chanting in the Gregorian fashion)*: Et lux perpetua luce ab eis.

(They cross themselves.)

FIRST WOMAN: May you have health to pray for his soul. *(They start filing out.)*

THIRD WOMAN: You won't lack loaves of hot bread.

SECOND WOMAN: Nor a roof for your daughters.

(They are all filing in front of BERNARDA and going out. ANGUSTIAS leaves by the door to the patio.)

FOURTH WOMAN: May you go on enjoying your wedding wheat.

PONCIA *(she enters, carrying a money bag)*: From the men—this bag of money for Masses.

BERNARDA: Thank them—and let them have a glass of brandy.

GIRL *(to MAGDALENA)*: Magdalena . . .

BERNARDA *(to MAGDALENA, who is starting to cry)*: Sh-h-h-h!

(She beats with her cane on the floor.)
(All the women have gone out.)

BERNARDA *(to the women who have just left)*: Go back to your houses and criticize everything you've seen! I hope it'll be many years before you pass under the archway of my door again.

PONCIA: You've nothing to complain about. The whole town came.

BERNARDA: Yes, to fill my house with the sweat from their wraps and the poison of their tongues.

AMELIA: Mother, don't talk like that.

BERNARDA: What other way is there to talk about this curséd village with no river—this village full of wells where you drink water always fearful it's been poisoned?

PONCIA: Look what they've done to the floor!

BERNARDA: As though a herd of goats had passed through.

(PONCIA cleans the floor.)

Adela, give me a fan.

ADELA: Take this one.

(She gives her a round fan with green and red flowers.)

BERNARDA (*throwing the fan on the floor*): Is that the fan to give to a widow? Give me a black one and learn to respect your father's memory.

MARTIRIO: Take mine.

BERNARDA: And you?

MARTIRIO: I'm not hot.

BERNARDA: Well, look for another, because you'll need it. For the eight years of mourning, not a breath of air will get in this house from the street. We'll act as if we'd sealed up doors and windows with bricks. That's what happened in my father's house—and in my grandfather's house. Meantime, you can all start embroidering your hope-chest linens. I have twenty bolts of linen in the chest from which to cut sheets and coverlets. Magdalena can embroider them.

MAGDALENA: It's all the same to me.

ADELA (*sourly*): If you don't want to embroider them—they can go without. That way yours will look better.

MAGDALENA: Neither mine nor yours. I know I'm not going to marry. I'd rather carry sacks to the mill. Anything except sit here day after day in this dark room.

BERNARDA: That's what a woman is for.

MAGDALENA: Cursed be all women.

BERNARDA: In this house you'll do what I order. You can't run with the story to your father any more. Needle and thread for women. Whiplash and mules for men. That's the way it has to be for people who have certain obligations.

(ADELA *goes out.*)

VOICE: Bernarda! Let me out!

BERNARDA (*calling*): Let her out now!

(*The* FIRST SERVANT *enters.*)

FIRST SERVANT: I had a hard time holding her. In spite of her eighty years, your mother's strong as an oak.

BERNARDA: It runs in the family. My grandfather was the same way.

SERVANT: Several times during the wake I had to cover her mouth with an empty sack because she wanted to shout out to you to give her dishwater to drink at least, and some dogmeat, which is what she says you feed her.

MARTIRIO: She's mean!

BERNARDA (*to* SERVANT): Let her get some fresh air in the patio.

SERVANT: She took her rings and the amethyst earrings out of the box, put them on, and told me she wants to get married.

(*The daughters laugh.*)

BERNARDA: Go with her and be careful she doesn't get near the well.

SERVANT: You don't need to be afraid she'll jump in.

BERNARDA: It's not that— but the neighbors can see her there from their windows.

(*The* SERVANT *leaves.*)

MARTIRIO: We'll go change our clothes.

BERNARDA: Yes, but don't take the kerchiefs from your heads.

(ADELA *enters.*)

And Angustias?

ADELA (*meaningfully*): I saw her looking out through the cracks of the back door. The men had just gone.

BERNARDA: And you, what were *you* doing at the door?

ADELA: I went there to see if the hens had laid.

BERNARDA: But the men had already gone!

ADELA (*meaningfully*): A group of them were still standing outside.

BERNARDA (*furiously*): Angustias! Angustias!

ANGUSTIAS (*entering*): Did you want something?

BERNARDA: For what—and at whom—were you looking?

ANGUSTIAS: Nobody.

BERNARDA: Is it decent for a woman of your class to be running after a man the day of her father's funeral? Answer me! Whom were you looking at?

(*Pause.*)

ANGUSTIAS: I . . .

BERNARDA: Yes, you!

ANGUSTIAS: Nobody.

BERNARDA: Soft! Honeytongue!

(*She strikes her.*)

PONCIA (*running to her*): Bernarda, calm down!

(*She holds her.* ANGUSTIAS *weeps.*)

BERNARDA: Get out of here, all of you!

(*They all go out.*)

PONCIA: She did it not realizing what she was doing—although it's bad, of course. It really disgusted me to see her sneak along to the patio. Then she stood at the window listening to the men's talk, which, as usual, was not the sort one should listen to.

BERNARDA: That's what they come to funerals for. (*With curiosity.*) What were they talking about?

PONCIA: They were talking about Paca la Roseta. Last night they tied her husband up in a stall, stuck her on a horse behind the saddle, and carried her away to the depths of the olive grove.

BERNARDA: And what did she do?

PONCIA: She? She was just as happy—they say her

breasts were exposed and Maximiliano held on to her as if he were playing a guitar. Terrible!

BERNARDA: And what happened?

PONCIA: What had to happen. They came back almost at daybreak. Paca la Roseta with her hair loose and a wreath of flowers on her head.

BERNARDA: She's the only bad woman we have in the village.

PONCIA: Because she's not from here. She's from far away. And those who went with her are the sons of outsiders too. The men from here aren't up to a thing like that.

BERNARDA: No, but they like to see it, and talk about it, and suck their fingers over it.

PONCIA: They were saying a lot more things.

BERNARDA (*looking from side to side with a certain fear*): What things?

PONCIA: I'm ashamed to talk about them.

BERNARDA: And my daughter heard them?

PONCIA: Of course!

BERNARDA: That one takes after her Aunts: white and mealy-mouthed and casting sheep's eyes at any little barber's compliment. Oh, what one has to go through and put up with so people will be decent and not too wild!

PONCIA: It's just that your daughters are of an age when they ought to have husbands. Mighty little trouble they give you. Angustias must be much more than thirty now.

BERNARDA: Exactly thirty-nine.

PONCIA: Imagine. And she's never had a beau . . .

BERNARDA (*furiously*): None of them has ever had a beau and they've never needed one! They get along very well.

PONCIA: I didn't mean to offend you.

BERNARDA: For a hundred miles around there's no one good enough to come near them. The men in this town are not of their class. Do you want me to turn them over to the first shepherd?

PONCIA: You should have moved to another town.

BERNARDA: That's it. To sell them!

PONCIA: No, Bernarda, to change. . . . Of course, any place else, they'd be the poor ones.

BERNARDA: Hold your tormenting tongue!

PONCIA: One can't even talk to you. Do we, or do we not share secrets?

BERNARDA: We do not. You're a servant and I pay you. Nothing more.

PONCIA: But . . .

FIRST SERVANT (*entering*): Don Arturo's here. He's come to see about dividing the inheritance.

BERNARDA: Let's go. (*to the* SERVANT) You start whitewashing the patio. (*to* LA PONCIA) And you start putting all the dead man's clothes away in the chest.

PONCIA: We could give away some of the things.

BERNARDA: Nothing—not a button even! Not even the cloth we covered his face with.

(*She goes out slowly, leaning on her cane. At the door she turns to look at the two servants. They go out. She leaves.*)
(AMELIA *and* MARTIRIO *enter.*)

AMELIA: Did you take the medicine?

MARTIRIO: For all the good it'll do me.

AMELIA: But you took it?

MARTIRIO: I do things without any faith, but like clockwork.

AMELIA: Since the new doctor came you look livelier.

MARTIRIO: I feel the same.

AMELIA: Did you notice? Adelaida wasn't at the funeral.

MARTIRIO: I know. Her sweetheart doesn't let her go out even to the front doorstep. Before, she was gay. Now, not even powder on her face.

AMELIA: These days a girl doesn't know whether to have a beau or not.

MARTIRIO: It's all the same.

AMELIA: The whole trouble is all these wagging tongues that won't let us live. Adelaida has probably had a bad time.

MARTIRIO: She's afraid of our mother. Mother is the only one who knows the story of Adelaida's father and where he got his lands. Everytime she comes here, Mother twists the knife in the wound. Her father killed his first wife's husband in Cuba so he could marry her himself. Then he left her there and went off with another woman who already had one daughter, and then he took up with this other girl, Adelaida's mother, and married her after his second wife died insane.

AMELIA: But why isn't a man like that put in jail?

MARTIRIO: Because men help each other cover up things like that and no one's able to tell on them.

AMELIA: But Adelaida's not to blame for any of that.

MARTIRIO: No. But history repeats itself. I can see that everything is a terrible repetition. And she'll have the same fate as her mother and grandmother—both of them wife to the man who fathered her.

AMELIA: What an awful thing!

MARTIRIO: It's better never to look at a man. I've been afraid of them since I was a little girl. I'd see them in the yard, yoking the oxen and lifting grain sacks, shouting and stamping, and I was always afraid to grow up for fear one of them would suddenly take me in his arms. God has made me weak and ugly and has definitely put such things away from me.

AMELIA: Don't say that! Enrique Humanas was after you and he liked you.

MARTIRIO: That was just people's ideas! One time I stood in my nightgown at the window until day-

break because he let me know through his
shepherd's little girl that he was going to come,
and he didn't. It was all just talk. Then he married someone else who had more money than I.

AMELIA: And ugly as the devil.

MARTIRIO: What do men care about ugliness? All they
care about is lands, yokes of oxen, and a submissive bitch who'll feed them.

AMELIA: Ay!

(MAGDALENA *enters.*)

MAGDALENA: What are you doing?

MARTIRIO: Just here.

AMELIA: And you?

MAGDALENA: I've been going through all the rooms.
Just to walk a little, and look at Grandmother's
needlepoint pictures—the little woolen dog, and
the black man wrestling with the lion—which we
liked so much when we were children. Those
were happier times. A wedding lasted ten days
and evil tongues weren't in style. Today people
are more refined. Brides wear white veils, just as
in the cities, and we drink bottled wine, but we
rot inside because of what people might say.

MARTIRIO: Lord knows what went on then!

AMELIA *(to* MAGDALENA*)*: One of your shoelaces has
come untied.

MAGDALENA: What of it?

AMELIA: You'll step on it and fall.

MAGDALENA: One less!

MARTIRIO: And Adela?

MAGDALENA: Ah! She put on the green dress she
made to wear for her birthday, went out to the
yard, and began shouting: "Chickens! Chickens,
look at me!" I had to laugh.

AMELIA: If Mother had only seen her!

MAGDALENA: Poor little thing! She's the youngest one
of us and still has her illusions. I'd give something to see her happy.

(*Pause.* ANGUSTIAS *crosses the stage, carrying some towels.*)

ANGUSTIAS: What time is it?

MAGDALENA: It must be twelve.

ANGUSTIAS: So late?

AMELIA: It's about to strike.

(ANGUSTIAS *goes out.*)

MAGDALENA *(meaningfully)*: Do you know what?

(*Pointing after* ANGUSTIAS.*)

AMELIA: No.

MAGDALENA: Come on!

MARTIRIO: I don't know what you're talking about!

MAGDALENA: Both of you know it better than I do,
always with your heads together, like two little

sheep, but not letting anybody else in on it. I
mean about Pepe el Romano!

MARTIRIO: Ah!

MAGDALENA *(mocking her)*: Ah! The whole town's talking about it. Pepe el Romano is coming to marry
Angustias. Last night he was walking around the
house and I think he's going to send a declaration soon.

MARTIRIO: I'm glad. He's a good man.

AMELIA: Me too. Angustias is well off.

MAGDALENA: Neither one of you is glad.

MARTIRIO: Magdalena! What do you mean?

MAGDALENA: If he were coming because of Angustias'
looks, for Angustias as a woman, I'd be glad too,
but he's coming for her money. Even though
Angustias is our sister, we're her family here and
we know she's old and sickly, and always has
been the least attractive one of us! Because if she
looked like a dressed-up stick at twenty, what can
she look like now, now that she's forty?

MARTIRIO: Don't talk like that. Luck comes to the one
who least expects it.

AMELIA: But Magdalena's right after all! Angustias
has all her father's money; she's the only rich one
in the house and that's why, now that Father's
dead and the money will be divided, they're coming for her.

MAGDALENA: Pepe el Romano is twenty-five years old
and the best looking man around here. The
natural thing would be for him to be after you,
Amelia, or our Adela, who's twenty—not looking
for the least likely one in this house, a woman
who, like her father, talks through her nose.

MARTIRIO: Maybe he likes that!

MAGDALENA: I've never been able to bear your hypocrisy.

MARTIRIO: Heavens!

(ADELA *enters.*)

MAGDALENA: Did the chickens see you?

ADELA: What did you want me to do?

AMELIA: If Mother sees you, she'll drag you by your
hair!

ADELA: I had a lot of illusions about this dress. I'd
planned to put it on the day we were going to eat
watermelons at the well. There wouldn't have
been another like it.

MARTIRIO: It's a lovely dress.

ADELA: And one that looks very good on me. It's the
best thing Magdalena's ever cut.

MAGDALENA: And the chickens, what did they say to
you?

ADELA: They presented me with a few fleas that riddled my legs.

(*They laugh.*)

MARTIRIO: What you can do is dye it black.

MAGDALENA: The best thing you can do is give it to Angustias for her wedding with Pepe el Romano.

ADELA (*with hidden emotion*): But Pepe el Romano . . .

AMELIA: Haven't you heard about it?

ADELA: No.

MAGDALENA: Well, now you know!

ADELA: But it can't be!

MAGDALENA: Money can do anything.

ADELA: Is that why she went out after the funeral and stood looking through the door?

(*Pause.*)

And that man would . . .

MAGDALENA: Would do anything.

(*Pause.*)

MARTIRIO: What are you thinking, Adela?

ADELA: I'm thinking that this mourning has caught me at the worst moment of my life for me to bear it.

MAGDALENA: You'll get used to it.

ADELA (*bursting out, crying with rage*): I will not get used to it! I can't be locked up. I don't want my skin to look like yours. I don't want my skin's whiteness lost in these rooms. Tomorrow I'm going to put on my green dress and go walking in the streets. I want to go out!

(*The* FIRST SERVANT *enters.*)

MAGDALENA (*in a tone of authority*): Adela!

SERVANT: The poor thing! How she misses her father. . . .

(*She goes out.*)

MARTIRIO: Hush!

AMELIA: What happens to one will happen to all of us.

(ADELA *grows calm.*)

MAGDALENA: The servant almost heard you.

SERVANT (*entering*): Pepe el Romano is coming along at the end of the street.

(AMELIA, MARTIRIO *and* MAGDALENA *run hurriedly.*)

MAGDALENA: Let's go see him!

(*They leave rapidly.*)

SERVANT (*to* ADELA): Aren't you going?

ADELA: It's nothing to me.

SERVANT: Since he has to turn the corner, you'll see him better from the window of your room.

(*The* SERVANT *goes out.* ADELA *is left on the stage, standing doubtfully; after a moment, she also leaves rapidly, going toward her room.* BERNARDA *and* LA PONCIA *come in.*)

BERNARDA: Damned portions and shares.

PONCIA: What a lot of money is left to Angustias!

BERNARDA: Yes.

PONCIA: And for the others, considerably less.

BERNARDA: You've told me that three times now, when you know I don't want it mentioned! Considerably less; a lot less! Don't remind me any more.

(ANGUSTIAS *comes in, her face heavily made up.*)

Angustias!

ANGUSTIAS: Mother.

BERNARDA: Have you dared to powder your face? Have you dared to wash your face on the day of your father's death?

ANGUSTIAS: He wasn't my father. Mine died a long time ago. Have you forgotten that already?

BERNARDA: You owe more to this man, father of your sisters, than to your own. Thanks to him, your fortune is intact.

ANGUSTIAS: We'll have to see about that first!

BERNARDA: Even out of decency! Out of respect!

ANGUSTIAS: Let me go out, mother!

BERNARDA: Let you go out? After I've taken that powder off your face, I will. Spineless! Painted hussy! Just like your aunts!

(*She removes the powder violently with her handkerchief.*)

Now get out!

PONCIA: Bernarda, don't be so hateful!

BERNARDA: Even though my mother is crazy, I still have my five senses and I know what I'm doing.

(*They all enter.*)

MAGDALENA: What's going on here?

BERNARDA: Nothing's "going on here"!

MAGDALENA (*to* ANGUSTIAS): If you're fighting over the inheritance, you're the richest one and can hang on to it all.

ANGUSTIAS: Keep your tongue in your pocketbook!

BERNARDA (*beating on the floor*): Don't fool yourselves into thinking you'll sway me. Until I go out of this house feet first I'll give the orders for myself and for you!

(*Voices are heard and* MARIA JOSEFA, BERNARDA's *mother, enters. She is very old and has decked out her head and breast with flowers.*)

MARIA JOSEFA: Bernarda, where is my mantilla? Nothing, nothing of what I own will be for any of you. Not my rings nor my black moiré dress. Because not a one of you is going to marry—not a one. Bernarda, give me my necklace of pearls.

BERNARDA (*to the* SERVANT): Why did you let her get in here?

SERVANT (*trembling*): She got away from me!

MARIA JOSEFA: I ran away because I want to marry—I

want to get married to a beautiful manly man from the shore of the sea. Because here the men run from women.

BERNARDA: Hush, hush, Mother!

MARIA JOSEFA: No, no—I won't hush. I don't want to see these single women, longing for marriage, turning their hearts to dust; and I want to go to my home town. Bernarda, I want a man to get married to and be happy with!

BERNARDA: Lock her up!

MARIA JOSEFA: Let me go out, Bernarda!

(The SERVANT seizes MARIA JOSEFA.)

BERNARDA: Help her, all of you!

(They all grab the old woman.)

MARIA JOSEFA: I want to get away from here! Bernarda! To get married by the shore of the sea—by the shore of the sea!

(Quick, curtain.)

ACT 2

(A white room in BERNARDA's house. The doors on the left lead to the bedrooms. BERNARDA's DAUGHTERS are seated on low chairs, sewing. MAGDALENA is embroidering. LA PONCIA is with them.)

ANGUSTIAS: I've cut the third sheet.

MARTIRIO: That one goes to Amelia.

MAGDALENA: Angustias, shall I put Pepe's initials here too?

ANGUSTIAS *(dryly)*: No.

MAGDALENA *(calling, from off stage to ADELA)*: Adela, aren't you coming?

AMELIA: She's probably stretched out on the bed.

PONCIA: Something's wrong with that one. I find her restless, trembling, frightened—as if a lizard were between her breasts.

MARTIRIO: There's nothing, more or less, wrong with her than there is with all of us.

MAGDALENA: All of us except Angustias.

ANGUSTIAS: I feel fine, and anybody who doesn't like it can pop.

MAGDALENA: We all have to admit the nicest things about you are your figure and your tact.

ANGUSTIAS: Fortunately, I'll soon be out of this hell.

MAGDALENA: Maybe you won't get out!

MARTIRIO: Stop this talk!

ANGUSTIAS: Besides, a good dowry is better than dark eyes in one's face!

MAGDALENA: All you say just goes in one ear and out the other.

AMELIA *(to LA PONCIA)*: Open the patio door and see if we can get a bit of a breeze.

(LA PONCIA opens the door.)

MARTIRIO: Last night I couldn't sleep because of the heat.

AMELIA: Neither could I.

MAGDALENA: I got up for a bit of air. There was a black storm cloud and a few drops even fell.

PONCIA: It was one in the morning and the earth seemed to give off fire. I got up too. Angustias was still at the window with Pepe.

MAGDALENA *(with irony)*: That late? What time did he leave?

ANGUSTIAS: Why do you ask, if you saw him?

AMELIA: He must have left about one-thirty.

ANGUSTIAS: Yes. How did you know?

AMELIA: I heard him cough and heard his mare's hoofbeats.

PONCIA: But I heard him leave around four.

ANGUSTIAS: It must have been someone else!

PONCIA: No, I'm sure of it!

AMELIA: That's what it seemed to me, too.

MAGDALENA: That's very strange!

(Pause.)

PONCIA: Listen, Angustias, what did he say to you the first time he came by your window?

ANGUSTIAS: Nothing. What should he say? Just talked.

MARTIRIO: It's certainly strange that two people who never knew each other should suddenly meet at a window and be engaged.

ANGUSTIAS: Well, I didn't mind.

AMELIA: I'd have felt very strange about it.

ANGUSTIAS: No, because when a man comes to a window he knows, from all the busybodies who come and go and fetch and carry, that he's going to be told "yes."

MARTIRIO: All right, but he'd have to ask you.

ANGUSTIAS: Of course!

AMELIA *(inquisitively)*: And how did he ask you?

ANGUSTIAS: Why, no way:—"You know I'm after you. I need a good, well brought up woman, and that's you—if it's agreeable."

AMELIA: These things embarrass me!

ANGUSTIAS: They embarrass me too, but one has to go through it!

PONCIA: And did he say anything more?

ANGUSTIAS: Yes, he did all the talking.

MARTIRIO: And you?

ANGUSTIAS: I couldn't have said a word. My heart was almost coming out of my mouth. It was the first time I'd ever been alone at night with a man.

MAGDALENA: And such a handsome man.

ANGUSTIAS: He's not bad looking!

PONCIA: Those things happen among people who have an idea how to do things, who talk and say and move their hand. The first time my husband, Evaristo the Short-tailed, came to my window . . . Ha! Ha! Ha!

AMELIA: What happened?

PONCIA: It was very dark. I saw him coming along

and as he went by he said, "Good evening." "Good evening," I said. Then we were both silent for more than half an hour. The sweat poured down my body. Then Evaristo got nearer and nearer as if he wanted to squeeze in through the bars and said in a very low voice—"Come here and let me feel you!"

(They all laugh. AMELIA *gets up, runs, and looks through the door.)*

AMELIA: Ay, I thought mother was coming!

MAGDALENA: What she'd have done to us!

(They go on laughing.)

AMELIA: Sh-h-h! She'll hear us.

PONCIA: Then he acted very decently. Instead of getting some other idea, he went to raising birds, until he died. You aren't married but it's good for you to know, anyway, that two weeks after the wedding a man gives up the bed for the table, then the table for the tavern, and the woman who doesn't like it can just rot, weeping in a corner.

AMELIA: You liked it.

PONCIA: I learned how to handle him!

MARTIRIO: Is it true that you sometimes hit him?

PONCIA: Yes, and once I almost poked out one of his eyes!

MAGDALENA: All women ought to be like that!

PONCIA: I'm one of your mother's school. One time I don't know what he said to me, and then I killed all his birds—with the pestle!

(They laugh.)

MAGDALENA: Adela, child! Don't miss this.

AMELIA: Adela!

(Pause.)

MAGDALENA: I'll go see!

(She goes out.)

PONCIA: That child is sick!

MARTIRIO: Of course. She hardly sleeps!

PONCIA: What *does* she do, then?

MARTIRIO: How do I know what she does?

PONCIA: You probably know better than we do, since you sleep with just a wall between you.

ANGUSTIAS: Envy gnaws on people.

AMELIA: Don't exaggerate.

AUGUSTIAS: I can tell it in her eyes. She's getting the look of a crazy woman.

MARTIRIO: Don't talk about crazy women. This is one place you're not allowed to say that word.

*(*MAGDALENA *and* ADELA *enter.)*

MAGDALENA: Didn't you say she was asleep?

ADELA: My body aches.

MARTIRIO *(with a hidden meaning)*: Didn't you sleep well last night?

ADELA: Yes.

MARTIRIO: Then?

ADELA *(loudly)*: Leave me alone. Awake or asleep, it's no affair of yours. I'll do whatever I want to with my body.

MARTIRIO: I was just concerned about you!

ADELA: Concerned?—curious! Weren't you sewing? Well, continue! I wish I were invisible so I could pass through a room without being asked where I was going!

SERVANT *(entering)*: Bernarda is calling you. The man with the laces is here.

(All but ADELA *and* LA PONCIA *go out, and as* MARTIRIO *leaves, she looks fixedly at* ADELA.)*

ADELA: Don't look at me like that! If you want, I'll give you my eyes, for they're younger, and my back to improve that hump you have, but look the other way when I go by.

PONCIA: Adela, she's your sister, and the one who most loves you besides!

ADELA: She follows me everywhere. Sometimes she looks in my room to see if I'm sleeping. She won't let me breathe, and always, "Too bad about that face!" "Too bad about that body! It's going to waste!" But I won't let that happen. My body will be for whomever I choose.

PONCIA *(insinuatingly, in a low voice)*: For Pepe el Romano, no?

ADELA *(frightened)*: What do you mean?

PONCIA: What I said, Adela!

ADELA: Shut up!

PONCIA *(loudly)*: Don't you think I've noticed?

ADELA: Lower your voice!

PONCIA: Then forget what you're thinking about!

ADELA: What do you know?

PONCIA: We old ones can see through walls. Where do you go when you get up at night?

ADELA: I wish you were blind!

PONCIA: But my head and hands are full of eyes, where something like this is concerned. I couldn't possibly guess your intentions. Why did you sit almost naked at your window, and with the light on and the window open, when Pepe passed by the second night he came to talk with your sister?

ADELA: That's not true!

PONCIA: Don't be a child! Leave your sister alone. And if you like Pepe el Romano, keep it to yourself.

*(*ADELA *weeps.)*

Besides, who says you can't marry him? Your sister Angustias is sickly. She'll die with her first child. Narrow waisted, old—and out of my experience I can tell you she'll die. Then Pepe will do what all widowers do in these parts: he'll marry the youngest and most beautiful, and that's you. Live on that hope, forget him, anything; but don't go against God's law.

ADELA: Hush!

PONCIA: I won't hush!

ADELA: Mind your own business. Snooper, traitor!

PONCIA: I'm going to stick to you like a shadow!

ADELA: Instead of cleaning the house and then going to bed and praying for the dead, you root around like an old sow about goings on between men and women—so you can drool over them.

PONCIA: I keep watch; so people won't spit when they pass our door.

ADELA: What a tremendous affection you've suddenly conceived for my sister.

PONCIA: I don't have any affection for any of you. I want to live in a decent house. I don't want to be dirtied in my old age!

ADELA: Save your advice. It's already too late. For I'd leap not over you, just a servant, but over my mother to put out this fire I feel in my legs and my mouth. What can you possibly say about me? That I lock myself in my room and will not open the door? That I don't sleep? I'm smarter than you! See if you can catch the hare with your hands.

PONCIA: Don't defy me, Adela, don't defy me! Because I can shout, light lamps, and make bells ring.

ADELA: Bring four thousand yellow flares and set them about the walls of the yard. No one can stop what has to happen.

PONCIA: You like him that much?

ADELA: That much! Looking in his eyes I seem to drink his blood in slowly.

PONCIA: I won't listen to you.

ADELA: Well, you'll have to. I've been afraid of you. But now I'm stronger than you!

(ANGUSTIAS enters.)

ANGUSTIAS: Always arguing!

PONCIA: Certainly. She insists that in all this heat I have to go bring her I don't know what from the store.

ANGUSTIAS: Did you buy me the bottle of perfume?

PONCIA: The most expensive one. And the face powder. I put them on the table in your room.

(ANGUSTIAS goes out.)

ADELA: And be quiet!

PONCIA: We'll see!

(MARTIRIO and AMELIA enter.)

MARTIRIO *(to ADELA)*: Did you see the laces?

AMELIA: Angustias', for her wedding sheets, are beautiful.

ADELA *(to MARTIRIO, who is carrying some lace)*: And these?

MARTIRIO: They're for me. For a nightgown.

ADELA *(with sarcasm)*: One needs a sense of humor around here!

MARTIRIO *(meaningfully)*: But only for me to look at. I don't have to exhibit myself before anybody.

PONCIA: No one ever sees us in our nightgowns.

MARTIRIO *(meaningfully, looking at ADELA)*: Sometimes they don't! But I love nice underwear. If I were rich, I'd have it made of Holland Cloth. It's one of the few tastes I've left.

PONCIA: These laces are beautiful for babies' caps and christening gowns. I could never afford them for my own. Now let's see if Augustias will use them for hers. Once she starts having children, they'll keep her running night and day.

MAGDALENA: I don't intend to sew a stitch on them.

AMELIA: And much less bring up some stranger's children. Look how our neighbors across the road are—making sacrifices for four brats.

PONCIA: They're better off than you. There at least they laugh and you can hear them fight.

MARTIRIO: Well, you go work for them, then.

PONCIA: No, fate has sent me to this nunnery!

(Tiny bells are heard distantly as though through several thicknesses of wall.)

MAGDALENA: It's the men going back to work.

PONCIA: It was three o'clock a minute ago.

MARTIRIO: With this sun!

ADELA *(sitting down)*: Ay! If only we could go out in the fields too!

MAGDALENA *(sitting down)*: Each class does what it has to!

MARTIRIO *(sitting down)*: That's it!

AMELIA *(sitting down)*: Ay!

PONCIA: There's no happiness like that in the fields right at this time of year. Yesterday morning the reapers arrived. Forty or fifty handsome young men.

MAGDALENA: Where are they from this year?

PONCIA: From far, far away. They came from the mountains! Happy! Like weathered trees! Shouting and throwing stones! Last night a woman who dresses in sequins and dances, with an accordion, arrived, and fifteen of them made a deal with her to take her to the olive grove. I saw them from far away. The one who talked with her was a boy with green eyes—tight knit as a sheaf of wheat.

AMELIA: Really?

ADELA: Are you sure?

PONCIA: Years ago another one of those women came here, and I myself gave my eldest son some money so he could go. Men need things like that.

ADELA: Everything's forgiven *them*.

AMELIA: To be born a woman's the worst possible punishment.

MAGDALENA: Even our eyes aren't our own.

(A distant song is heard, coming nearer.)

PONCIA: There they are. They have a beautiful song.

AMELIA: They're going out to reap now.

CHORUS:
> The reapers have set out
> Looking for ripe wheat;
> They'll carry off the hearts
> Of any girls they meet.

(Tambourines and carrañacas are heard. Pause. They all listen in the silence cut by the sun.)

AMELIA: And they don't mind the sun!

MARTIRIO: They reap through flames.

ADELA: How I'd like to be a reaper so I could come and go as I pleased. Then we could forget what's eating us all.

MARTIRIO: What do you have to forget?

ADELA: Each one of us has something.

MARTIRIO *(intensely)*: Each one!

PONCIA: Quiet! Quiet!

CHORUS *(very distantly)*:
> Throw wide your doors and windows,
> You girls who live in the town
> The reaper asks you for roses
> With which to deck his crown.

PONCIA: What a song!

MARTIRIO *(with nostalgia)*:
> Throw wide your doors and windows,
> You girls who live in the town.

ADELA *(passionately)*:
> The reaper asks you for roses
> With which to deck his crown.

(The song grows more distant.)

PONCIA: Now they're turning the corner.

ADELA: Let's watch them from the window of my room.

PONCIA: Be careful not to open the shutters too much because they're likely to give them a push to see who's looking.

(The three leave. MARTIRIO is left sitting on the low chair with her head between her hands.)

AMELIA *(drawing near her)*: What's wrong with you?

MARTIRIO: The heat makes me feel ill.

AMELIA: And it's no more than that?

MARTIRIO: I was wishing it were November, the rainy days, the frost—anything except this unending summertime.

AMELIA: It'll pass and come again.

MARTIRIO: Naturally.

(Pause.)

What time did you go to sleep last night?

AMELIA: I don't know. I sleep like a log. Why?

MARTIRIO: Nothing. Only I thought I heard someone in the yard.

AMELIA: Yes?

MARTIRIO: Very late.

AMELIA: And weren't you afraid?

MARTIRIO: No. I've heard it other nights.

AMELIA: We'd better watch out! Couldn't it have been the shepherds?

MARTIRIO: The shepherds come at six.

AMELIA: Maybe a young, unbroken mule?

MARTIRIO *(to herself, with double meaning)*: That's it! That's it. An unbroken little mule.

AMELIA: We'll have to set a watch.

MARTIRIO: No. No. Don't say anything. It may be I've just imagined it.

AMELIA: Maybe.

(Pause. AMELIA starts to go.)

MARTIRIO: Amelia!

AMELIA *(at the door)*: What?

(Pause.)

MARTIRIO: Nothing.

(Pause.)

AMELIA: Why did you call me?

(Pause.)

MARTIRIO: It just came out. I didn't mean to.

(Pause.)

AMELIA: Lie down for a little.

ANGUSTIAS *(she bursts in furiously, in a manner that makes a great contrast with previous silence)*: Where's that picture of Pepe I had under my pillow? Which one of you has it?

MARTIRIO: No one.

AMELIA: You'd think he was a silver St. Bartholomew.

ANGUSTIAS: Where's the picture?

(PONCIA, MAGDALENA and ADELA enter.)

ADELA: What picture?

ANGUSTIAS: One of you has hidden it from me.

MAGDALENA: Do you have the effrontery to say that?

ANGUSTIAS: I had it in my room, and now it isn't there.

MARTIRIO: But couldn't it have jumped out into the yard at midnight? Pepe likes to walk around in the moonlight.

ANGUSTIAS: Don't joke with me! When he comes I'll tell him.

PONCIA: Don't do that! Because it'll turn up.

(Looking at ADELA.*)*

ANGUSTIAS: I'd like to know which one of you has it.

ADELA *(looking at* MARTIRIO*)*: Somebody has it! But not me!

MARTIRIO *(with meaning)*: Of course not you!

BERNARDA *(entering with her cane)*: What scandal is this in my house in the heat's heavy silence? The neighbors must have their ears glued to the walls.

ANGUSTIAS: They've stolen my sweetheart's picture!

BERNARDA *(fiercely)*: Who? Who?

ANGUSTIAS: They have!

BERNARDA: Which one of you?

(Silence.)

Answer me!

(Silence.) (To LA PONCIA.*)*

Search their rooms! Look in their beds. This comes of not tying you up with shorter leashes. But I'll teach you now! *(to* ANGUSTIAS*)* Are you sure?

ANGUSTIAS: Yes.

BERNARDA: Did you look everywhere?

ANGUSTIAS: Yes, Mother.

(They all stand in an embarrassed silence.)

BERNARDA: At the end of my life—to make me drink the bitterest poison a mother knows. *(to* PONCIA*)* Did you find it?

PONCIA: Here it is.

BERNARDA: Where did you find it?

PONCIA: It was . . .

BERNARDA: Say it! Don't be afraid.

PONCIA *(wonderingly)*: Between the sheets in Martirio's bed.

BERNARDA *(to* MARTIRIO*)*: Is that true?

MARTIRIO: It's true.

BERNARDA *(advancing on her, beating her with her cane)*: You'll come to a bad end yet, you hypocrite! Trouble maker!

MARTIRIO *(fiercely)*: Don't hit me, Mother!

BERNARDA: All I want to!

MARTIRIO: If I let you! You hear me? Get back!

PONCIA: Don't be disrespectful to your mother!

ANGUSTIAS *(holding* BERNARDA*)*: Let her go, please!

BERNARDA: Not even tears in your eyes.

MARTIRIO: I'm not going to cry just to please you.

BERNARDA: Why did you take the picture?

MARTIRIO: Can't I play a joke on my sister? What else would I want it for?

ADELA *(leaping forward, full of jealousy)*: It wasn't a joke! You never liked to play jokes. It was something else bursting in her breast—trying to come out. Admit it openly now.

MARTIRIO: Hush, and don't make me speak; for if I should speak the walls would close together one against the other with shame.

ADELA: An evil tongue never stops inventing lies.

BERNARDA: Adela!

MAGDALENA: You're crazy.

AMELIA: And you stone us all with your evil suspicions.

MARTIRIO: But some others do things more wicked!

ADELA: Until all at once they stand forth stark naked and the river carries them along.

BERNARDA: Spiteful!

ANGUSTIAS: It's not my fault Pepe el Romano chose me!

ADELA: For your money.

ANGUSTIAS: Mother!

BERNARDA: Silence!

MARTIRIO: For your fields and your orchards.

MAGDALENA: That's only fair.

BERNARDA: Silence, I say! I saw the storm coming but I didn't think it'd burst so soon. Oh, what an avalanche of hate you've thrown on my heart! But I'm not old yet—I have five chains for you, and this house my father built, so not even the weeds will know of my desolation. Out of here!

(They go out. BERNARDA *sits down desolately.* LA PONCIA *is standing close to the wall.* BERNARDA *recovers herself, and beats on the floor.)*

I'll have to let them feel the weight of my hand! Bernarda, remember your duty!

PONCIA: May I speak?

BERNARDA: Speak. I'm sorry you heard. A stranger is always out of place in a family.

PONCIA: What I've seen, I've seen.

BERNARDA: Angustias must get married right away.

PONCIA: Certainly. We'll have to get her away from here.

BERNARDA: Not her, him!

PONCIA: Of course. He's the one to get away from here. You've thought it all out.

BERNARDA: I'm not thinking. These are things that shouldn't and can't be thought out. I give orders.

PONCIA: And you think he'll be satisfied to go away?

BERNARDA *(rising)*: What are you imagining now?

PONCIA: He will, of course, marry Angustias.

BERNARDA: Speak up! I know you well enough to see that your knife's out for me.

PONCIA: I never knew a warning could be called murder.

BERNARDA: Have you some "warning" for me?

PONCIA: I'm not making any accusations, Bernarda. I'm only telling you to open your eyes and you'll see.

BERNARDA: See what?

PONCIA: You've always been smart, Bernarda. You've

seen other people's sins a hundred miles away. Many times I've thought you could read minds. But, your children are your children, and now you're blind.

BERNARDA: Are you talking about Martirio?

PONCIA: Well, yes—about Martirio . . .

(With curiosity.)

I wonder why she hid the picture?

BERNARDA *(shielding her daughter)*: After all, she says it was a joke. What else could it be?

PONCIA *(scornfully)*: Do you believe that?

BERNARDA *(sternly)*: I don't merely believe it. It's so!

PONCIA: Enough of this. We're talking about your family. But if we were talking about your neighbor across the way, what would it be?

BERNARDA: Now you're beginning to pull the point of the knife out.

PONCIA *(always cruelly)*: No, Bernarda. Something very grave is happening here. I don't want to put the blame on your shoulders, but you've never given your daughters any freedom. Martirio is lovesick. I don't care what you say. Why didn't you let her marry Enrique Humanas? Why, on the very day he was coming to her window did you send him a message not to come?

BERNARDA *(loudly)*: I'd do it a thousand times over! My blood won't mingle with the Humanas' while I live! His father was a shepherd.

PONCIA: And you see now what's happening to you with these airs!

BERNARDA: I have them because I can afford to. And you don't have them because you know where you came from!

PONCIA *(with hate)*: Don't remind me! I'm old now. I've always been grateful for your protection.

BERNARDA *(emboldened)*: You don't seem so!

PONCIA *(with hate, behind softness)*: Martirio will forget this.

BERNARDA: And if she doesn't—the worse for her. I don't believe this is that "very grave thing" that's happening here. Nothing's happening here. It's just that you wish it would! And if it should happen one day, you can be sure it won't go beyond these walls.

PONCIA: I'm not so sure of that! There are people in town who can also read hidden thoughts, from afar.

BERNARDA: How you'd like to see me and my daughters on our way to a whorehouse!

PONCIA: No one knows her own destiny!

BERNARDA: I know my destiny! And my daughters'! The whorehouse was for a certain woman, already dead. . . .

PONCIA *(fiercely)*: Bernarda, respect the memory of my mother!

BERNARDA: Then don't plague me with your evil thoughts!

(Pause.)

PONCIA: I'd better stay out of everything.

BERNARDA: That's what you ought to do. Work and keep your mouth shut. The duty of all who work for a living.

PONCIA: But we can't do that. Don't you think it'd be better for Pepe to marry Martirio or . . . yes! . . . Adela?

BERNARDA: No, I *don't* think so.

PONCIA *(with meaning)*: Adela! She's Romano's real sweetheart!

BERNARDA: Things are never the way we want them!

PONCIA: But it's hard work to turn them from their destined course. For Pepe to be with Angustias seems wrong to me—and to other people—and even to the wind. Who knows if they'll get what they want?

BERNARDA: There you go again! Sneaking up on me—giving me bad dreams. But I won't listen to you, because if all you say should come to pass—I'd scratch your face.

PONCIA: Frighten someone else with that.

BERNARDA: Fortunately, my daughters respect me and have never gone against my will!

PONCIA: That's right! But, as soon as they break loose they'll fly to the rooftops!

BERNARDA: And I'll bring them down with stones!

PONCIA: Oh, yes! You were always the bravest one!

BERNARDA: I've always enjoyed a good fight!

PONCIA: But aren't people strange. You should see Angustias' enthusiasm for her lover, at her age! And he seems very smitten too. Yesterday my oldest son told me that when he passed by with the oxen at four-thirty in the morning they were still talking.

BERNARDA: At four-thirty?

ANGUSTIAS *(entering)*: That's a lie!

PONCIA: That's what he told me.

BERNARDA *(to ANGUSTIAS)*: Speak up!

ANGUSTIA: For more than a week Pepe has been leaving at one. May God strike me dead if I'm lying.

MARTIRIO *(entering)*: I heard him leave at four too.

BERNARDA: But did you see him with your eyes?

MARTIRIO: I didn't want to look out. Don't you talk now through the side window?

ANGUSTIAS: We talk through my bedroom window.

(ADELA appears at the door.)

MARTIRIO: Then . . .

BERNARDA: What's going on here?

PONCIA: If you're not careful, you'll find out! At least Pepe was at *one* of your windows—and at four in the morning too!

BERNARDA: Are you sure of that?

PONCIA: You can't be sure of anything in this life!

ADELA: Mother, don't listen to someone who wants us to lose everything we have.

BERNARDA: I know how to take care of myself! If the townspeople want to come bearing false witness against me, they'll run into a stone wall! Don't any of you talk about this! Sometimes other people try to stir up a wave of filth to drown us.

MARTIRIO: I don't like to lie.

PONCIA: So there must be something.

BERNARDA: There won't be anything. I was born to have my eyes always open. Now I'll watch without closing them 'til I die.

ANGUSTIAS: I have the right to know.

BERNARDA: You don't have any right except to obey. No one's going to fetch and carry for me. (to LA PONCIA) And don't meddle in our affairs. No one will take a step without my knowing it.

SERVANT (entering): There's a big crowd at the top of the street, and all the neighbors are at their doors!

BERNARDA (to PONCIA): Run see what's happening!

(The GIRLS are about to run out.)

Where are you going? I always knew you for window-watching women and breakers of your mourning. All of you, to the patio!

(They go out. BERNARDA leaves. Distant shouts are heard.)

(MARTIRIO and ADELA enter and listen, not daring to step farther than the front door.)

MARTIRIO: You can be thankful I didn't happen to open my mouth.

ADELA: I would have spoken too.

MARTIRIO: And what were you going to say? Wanting isn't doing!

ADELA: I do what I can and what happens to suit me. You've wanted to, but haven't been able.

MARTIRIO: You won't go on very long.

ADELA: I'll have everything!

MARTIRIO: I'll tear you out of his arms!

ADELA (pleadingly): Martirio, let me be!

MARTIRIO: None of us will have him!

ADELA: He wants me for his house!

MARTIRIO: I saw how he embraced you!

ADELA: I didn't want him to. It's as if I were dragged by a rope.

MARTIRIO: I'll see you dead first!

(MAGDALENA and ANGUSTIAS look in. The tumult is increasing. A SERVANT enters with BERNARDA. PONCIA also enters from another door.)

PONCIA: Bernarda!

BERNARDA: What's happening?

PONCIA: Librada's daughter, the unmarried one, had a child and no one knows whose it is!

ADELA: A child?

PONCIA: And to hide her shame she killed it and hid it under the rocks, but the dogs, with more heart than most Christians, dug it out and, as though directed by the hand of God, left it at her door. Now they want to kill her. They're dragging her through the streets—and down the paths and across the olive groves the men are coming, shouting so the fields shake.

BERNARDA: Yes, let them all come with olive whips and hoe handles—let them all come and kill her!

ADELA: No, not to kill her!

MARTIRIO: Yes—and let us go out too!

BERNARDA: And let whoever loses her decency pay for it!

(Outside a woman's shriek and a great clamor is heard.)

ADELA: Let her escape! Don't you go out!

MARTIRIO (looking at ADELA): Let her pay what she owes!

BERNARDA (at the archway): Finish her before the guards come! Hot coals in the place where she sinned!

ADELA (holding her belly): No! No!

BERNARDA: Kill her! Kill her!

(Curtain.)

ACT 3

(Four white walls, lightly washed in blue, of the interior patio of BERNARDA ALBA's house. The doorways, illumined by the lights inside the rooms, give a tenuous glow to the stage. At the center there is a table with a shaded oil lamp about which BERNARDA and her DAUGHTERS are eating. LA PONCIA serves them. PRUDENCIA sits apart. When the curtain rises, there is a great silence interrupted only by the noise of plates and silverware.)

PRUDENCIA: I'm going. I've made you a long visit.

(She rises.)

BERNARDA: But wait, Prudencia. We never see one another.

PRUDENCIA: Have they sounded the last call to rosary?

PONCIA: Not yet.

(PRUDENCIA sits down again.)

BERNARDA: And your husband, how's he getting on?

PRUDENCIA: The same.

BERNARDA: We never see him either.

PRUDENCIA: You know how he is. Since he quarreled with his brothers over the inheritance, he hasn't used the front door. He takes a ladder and climbs over the back wall.

BERNARDA: He's a real man! And your daughter?

PRUDENCIA: He's never forgiven her.

BERNARDA: He's right.

PRUDENCIA: I don't know what he told you. I suffer because of it.

BERNARDA: A daughter who's disobedient stops being a daughter and becomes an enemy.

PRUDENCIA: I let water run. The only consolation I've left is to take refuge in the church, but, since I'm losing my sight, I'll have to stop coming so the children won't make fun of me.

(A heavy blow is heard against the walls.)

What's that?

BERNARDA: The stallion. He's locked in the stall and he kicks against the wall of the house.

(Shouting.)

Tether him and take him out in the yard!

(In a lower voice.)

He must be too hot.

PRUDENCIA: Are you going to put the new mares to him?

BERNARDA: At daybreak.

PRUDENCIA: You've known how to increase your stock.

BERNARDA: By dint of money and struggling.

PONCIA (*interrupting*): And she has the best herd in these parts. It's a shame that prices are low.

BERNARDA: Do you want a little cheese and honey?

PRUDENCIA: I have no appetite.

(The blow is heard again.)

PONCIA: My God!

PRUDENCIA: It quivered in my chest.

BERNARDA (*rising, furiously*): Do I have to say things twice? Let him out to roll on the straw.

(Pause. Then, as though speaking to the STABLEMAN.*)*

Well then, lock the mares in the corral, but let him run free or he may kick down the walls.

(She returns to the table and sits again.)

Ay, what a life!

PRUDENCIA: You have to fight like a man.

BERNARDA: That's it.

*(*ADELA *gets up from the table.)*

Where are you going?

ADELA: For a drink of water.

BERNARDA (*raising her voice*): Bring a pitcher of cool water. (*to* ADELA) You can sit down. (ADELA *sits down.*)

PRUDENCIA: And Angustias, when will she get married?

BERNARDA: They're coming to ask for her within three days.

PRUDENCIA: You must be happy.

ANGUSTIAS: Naturally!

AMELIA (*to* MAGDALENA): You've spilled the salt!

MAGDALENA: You can't possibly have worse luck than you're having.

AMELIA: It always brings bad luck.

BERNARDA: That's enough!

PRUDENCIA (*to* ANGUSTIAS): Has he given you the ring yet?

ANGUSTIAS: Look at it.

(She holds it out.)

PRUDENCIA: It's beautiful. Three pearls. In my day, pearls signified tears.

ANGUSTIAS: But things have changed now.

ADELA: I don't think so. Things go on meaning the same. Engagement rings should be diamonds.

PONCIA: The most appropriate.

BERNARDA: With pearls or without them, things are as one proposes.

MARTIRIO: Or as God disposes.

PRUDENCIA: I've been told your furniture is beautiful.

BERNARDA: It cost sixteen thousand *reales*.

PONCIA (*interrupting*): The best is the wardrobe with the mirror.

PRUDENCIA: I never saw a piece like that.

BERNARDA: We had chests.

PRUDENCIA: The important thing is that everything be for the best.

ADELA: And that you never know.

BERNARDA: There's no reason why it shouldn't be.

(Bells are heard very distantly.)

PRUDENCIA: The last call. (*to* ANGUSTIAS) I'll be coming back to have you show me your clothes.

ANGUSTIAS: Whenever you like.

PRUDENCIA: Good evening—God bless you!

BERNARDA: Good-bye, Prudencia.

ALL FIVE DAUGHTERS (*at the same time*): God go with you!

(Pause. PRUDENCIA *goes out.)*

BERNARDA: Well, we've eaten.

(They rise.)

ADELA: I'm going to walk as far as the gate to stretch my legs and get a bit of fresh air.

*(*MAGDALENA *sits down in a low chair and leans against the wall.)*

AMELIA: I'll go with you.

MARTIRIO: I too.

ADELA (*with contained hate*): I'm not going to get lost!

AMELIA: One needs company at night.

(They go out. BERNARDA *sits down.* ANGUSTIAS *is clearing the table.)*

BERNARDA: I've told you once already! I want you to talk to your sister Martirio. What happened about the picture was a joke and you must forget it.

ANGUSTIAS: You know she doesn't like me.

BERNARDA: Each one knows what she thinks inside. I don't pry into anyone's heart, but I want to put up a good front and have family harmony. You understand?

ANGUSTIAS: Yes.

BERNARDA: Then that's settled.

MAGDALENA (*she is almost asleep*): Besides, you'll be gone in no time.

(*She falls asleep.*)

ANGUSTIAS: Not soon enough for me.

BERNARDA: What time did you stop talking last night?

ANGUSTIAS: Twelve-thirty.

BERNARDA: What does Pepe talk about?

ANGUSTIAS: I find him absent-minded. He always talks to me as though he were thinking of something else. If I ask him what's the matter, he answers—"We men have our worries."

BERNARDA: You shouldn't ask him. And when you're married, even less. Speak if he speaks, and look at him when he looks at you. That way you'll get along.

ANGUSTIAS: But, Mother, I think he's hiding things from me.

BERNARDA: Don't try to find out. Don't ask him, and above all, never let him see you cry.

ANGUSTIAS: I should be happy, but I'm not.

BERNARDA: It's all the same.

ANGUSTIAS: Many nights I watch Pepe very closely through the window bars and he seems to fade away—as though he were hidden in a cloud of dust like those raised by the flocks.

BERNARDA: That's just because you're not strong.

ANGUSTIAS: I hope so!

BERNARDA: Is he coming tonight?

ANGUSTIAS: No, he went into town with his mother.

BERNARDA: Good, we'll get to bed early. Magdalena!

ANGUSTIAS: She's asleep.

(ADELA, MARTIRIO *and* AMELIA *enter.*)

AMELIA: What a dark night!

ADELA: You can't see two steps in front of you.

MARTIRIO: A good night for robbers, for anyone who needs to hide.

ADELA: The stallion was in the middle of the corral. White. Twice as large. Filling all the darkness.

AMELIA: It's true. It was frightening. Like a ghost.

ADELA: The sky has stars as big as fists.

MARTIRIO: This one stared at them till she almost cracked her neck.

ADELA: Don't you like them up there?

MARTIRIO: What goes on over the roof doesn't mean a thing to me. I have my hands full with what happens under it.

ADELA: Well, that's the way it goes with you!

BERNARDA: And it goes the same for you as for her.

ANGUSTIAS: Good night.

ADELA: Are you going to bed now?

ANGUSTIAS: Yes, Pepe isn't coming tonight.

(*She goes out.*)

ADELA: Mother, why, when a stars falls or lightning flashes, does one say:
Holy Barbara, blessed on high
May your name be in the sky
With holy water written high?

BERNARDA: The old people know many things we've forgotten.

AMELIA: I close my eyes so I won't see them.

ADELA: Not I. I like to see what's quiet and been quiet for years on end, running with fire.

MARTIRIO: But all that has nothing to do with us.

BERNARDA: And it's better not to think about it.

ADELA: What a beautiful night! I'd like to stay up till very late and enjoy the breeze from the fields.

BERNARDA: But we have to go to bed. Magdalena!

AMELIA: She's just dropped off.

BERNARDA: Magdalena!

MAGDALENA (*annoyed*): Leave me alone!

BERNARDA: To bed!

MAGDALENA (*rising, in a bad humor*): You don't give anyone a moment's peace!

(*She goes off grumbling.*)

AMELIA: Good night!

(*She goes out.*)

BERNARDA: You two get along, too.

MARTIRIO: How is it Angustias' sweetheart isn't coming tonight?

BERNARDA: He went on a trip.

MARTIRIO (*looking at* ADELA): Ah!

ADELA: I'll see you in the morning!

(*She goes out.* MARTIRIO *drinks some water and goes out slowly, looking at the door to the yard.* LA PONCIA *enters.*)

PONCIA: Are you still here?

BERNARDA: Enjoying this quiet and not seeing anywhere the "very grave thing" that's happening here—according to you.

PONCIA: Bernarda, let's not go any further with this.

BERNARDA: In this house there's no question of a yes or a no. My watchfulness can take care of anything.

PONCIA: Nothing's happening outside. That's true, all right. Your daughters act and are as though stuck in a cupboard. But neither you nor anyone else can keep watch inside a person's heart.

BERNARDA: My daughters breathe calmly enough.

PONCIA: That's your business, since you're their mother. I have enough to do just with serving you.

BERNARDA: Yes, you've turned quiet now.

PONCIA: I keep my place—that's all.

BERNARDA: The trouble is you've nothing to talk about. If there were grass in this house, you'd make it your business to put the neighbors' sheep to pasture here.

PONCIA: I hide more than you think.

BERNARDA: Do your sons still see Pepe at four in the morning? Are they still repeating this house's evil litany?

PONCIA: They say nothing.

BERNARDA: Because they can't. Because there's nothing for them to sink their teeth in. And all because my eyes keep constant watch!

PONCIA: Bernarda, I don't want to talk about this because I'm afraid of what you'll do. But don't you feel so safe.

BERNARDA: Very safe!

PONCIA: Who knows, lightning might strike suddenly. Who knows but what all of a sudden, in a rush of blood, your heart might stop.

BERNARDA: Nothing will happen here. I'm on guard now against all your suspicions.

PONCIA: All the better for you.

BERNARDA: Certainly, all the better!

SERVANT (entering): I've just finished with the dishes. Is there anything else, Bernarda?

BERNARDA (rising): Nothing. I'm going to get some rest.

PONCIA: What time do you want me to call you?

BERNARDA: No time. Tonight I intend to sleep well.

(She goes out.)

PONCIA: When you're powerless against the sea, it's easier to turn your back on it and not look at it.

SERVANT: She's so proud! She herself pulls the blindfold over her eyes.

PONCIA: I can do nothing. I tried to head things off, but now they frighten me too much. You feel this silence?—in each room there's a thunderstorm—and the day it breaks, it'll sweep all of us along with it. But I've said what I had to say.

SERVANT: Bernarda thinks nothing can stand against her, yet she doesn't know the strength a man has among women alone.

PONCIA: It's not all the fault of Pepe el Romano. It's true last year he was running after Adela; and she was crazy about him—but she ought to keep her place and not lead him on. A man's a man.

SERVANT: And some there are who believe he didn't have to talk many times with Adela.

PONCIA: That's true.

(In a low voice.)

And some other things.

SERVANT: I don't know what's going to happen here.

PONCIA: How I'd like to sail across the sea and leave this house, this battleground, behind!

SERVANT: Bernarda's hurrying the wedding and it's possible nothing will happen.

PONCIA: Things have gone much too far already. Adela is set no matter what comes, and the rest of them watch without rest.

SERVANT: Martirio too . . . ?

PONCIA: That one's the worst. She's a pool of poison. She sees El Romano is not for her, and she'd sink the world if it were in her hand to do so

SERVANT: How bad they all are!

PONCIA: They're women without men, that's all. And in such matters even blood is forgotten. Sh-h-h-h!

(She listens.)

SERVANT: What's the matter?

PONCIA (she rises): The dogs are barking.

SERVANT: Someone must have passed by the back door.

(ADELA enters wearing a white petticoat and corselet.)

PONCIA: Aren't you in bed yet?

ADELA: I want a drink of water.

(She drinks from a glass on the table.)

PONCIA: I imagined you were asleep.

ADELA: I got thirsty and woke up. Aren't you two going to get some rest?

SERVANT: Soon now.

(ADELA goes out.)

PONCIA: Let's go.

SERVANT: We've certainly earned some sleep. Bernarda doesn't let me rest the whole day.

PONCIA: Take the light.

SERVANT: The dogs are going mad.

PONCIA: They're not going to let us sleep.

(They go out. The stage is left almost dark. MARIA JOSEFA enters with a lamb in her arms.)

MARIA JOSEFA (singing):
Little lamb, child of mine,
Let's go to the shore of the sea,
The tiny ant will be at his doorway,
I'll nurse you and give you your bread.
Bernarda, old leopard-face,
And Magdalena, hyena-face,
Little lamb . . .
Rock, rock-a-bye,
Let's go to the palms at Bethlehem's gate.

(She laughs.)

Neither you nor I would want to sleep
The door will open by itself
And on the beach we'll go and hide
In a little coral cabin.
Bernarda, old leopard-face,
And Magdalena, hyena-face,
Little lamb . . .
Rock, rock-a-bye,
Let's go to the palms at Bethlehem's gate.

(She goes off singing.)
(ADELA enters. She looks about cautiously and disappears out the door leading to the corral. MARTIRIO enters by another door and stands in anguished watchfulness near the center of the stage. She also is in petticoats. She covers herself with a small black scarf. MARIA JOSEFA crosses before her.)

MARTIRIO: Grandmother, where are you going?

MARIA JOSEFA: You are going to open the door for me? Who are you?

MARTIRIO: How did you get out here?

MARIA JOSEFA: I escaped. You, who are you?

MARTIRIO: Go back to bed.

MARIA JOSEFA: You're Martirio. Now I see you. Martirio, face of a martyr. And when are you going to have a baby? I've had this one.

MARTIRIO: Where did you get that lamb?

MARIA JOSEFA: I know it's a lamb. But can't a lamb be a baby? It's better to have a lamb than not to have anything. Old Bernarda, leopard-face, and Magdalena, hyena-face!

MARTIRIO: Don't shout.

MARIA JOSEFA: It's true. Everything's very dark. Just because I have white hair you think I can't have babies, but I can—babies and babies and babies. This baby will have white hair, and I'd have *this* baby, and another, and this *one* other; and with all of us with snow white hair we'll be like the waves—one, then another, and another. Then we'll all sit down and all of us will have white heads, and we'll be seafoam. Why isn't there any seafoam here? Nothing but mourning shrouds here.

MARTIRIO: Hush, hush.

MARIA JOSEFA: When my neighbor had a baby, I'd carry her some chocolate and later she'd bring me some, and so on—always and always and always. You'll have white hair, but your neighbors won't come. Now I have to go away, but I'm afraid the dogs will bite me. Won't you come with me as far as the fields? I don't like fields. I like houses, but open houses, and the neighbor women asleep in their beds with their little tiny tots, and the men outside sitting in their chairs. Pepe el Romano is a giant. All of you love him. But he's going to devour you because you're

grains of wheat. No, not grains of wheat. Frogs with no tongues!

MARTIRIO *(angrily)*: Come, off to bed with you.

(She pushes her.)

MARIA JOSEFA: Yes, but then you'll open the door for me, won't you?

MARTIRIO: Of course.

MARIA JOSEFA *(weeping)*:
Little lamb, child of mine,
Let's go to the shore of the sea,
The tiny ant will be at his doorway,
I'll nurse you and give you your bread.

(MARTIRIO locks the door through which MARIA JOSEFA came out and goes to the yard door. There she hesitates, but goes two steps farther.)

MARTIRIO *(in a low voice)*: Adela! *(Pause. She advances to the door. Then, calling.)* Adela!

(ADELA enters. Her hair is disarranged.)

ADELA: And what are you looking for me for?

MARTIRIO: Keep away from him.

ADELA: Who are you to tell me that?

MARTIRIO: That's no place for a decent woman.

ADELA: How you wish *you'd* been there!

MARTIRIO *(shouting)*: This is the moment for me to speak. This can't go on.

ADELA: This is just the beginning. I've had strength enough to push myself forward—the spirit and looks you lack. I've seen death under this roof, and gone out to look for what was mine, what belonged to me.

MARTIRIO: That soulless man came for another woman. You pushed yourself in front of him.

ADELA: He came for the money, but his eyes were always on me.

MARTIRIO: I won't allow you to snatch him away. He'll marry Angustias.

ADELA: You know better than I he doesn't love her.

MARTIRIO: I know.

ADELA: You know because you've seen—he loves me, me!

MARTIRIO *(desperately)*: Yes.

ADELA *(close before her)*: He loves me, *me!* He loves me, *me!*

MARTIRIO: Stick me with a knife if you like, but don't tell me that again.

ADELA: That's why you're trying to fix it so I won't go away with him. It makes no difference to you if he puts his arms around a woman he doesn't love. Nor does it to me. He could be a hundred years with Angustias, but for him to have his arms around me seems terrible to you—because you too love him! You love him!

MARTIRIO (*dramatically*): Yes! Let me say it without hiding my head. Yes! my breast's bitter, bursting like a pomegranate. I love him!

ADELA (*impulsively, hugging her*): Martirio, Martirio, I'm not to blame!

MARTIRIO: Don't put your arms around me! Don't try to smooth it over. My blood's no longer yours, and even though I try to think of you as a sister, I see you as just another woman.

(*She pushes her away.*)

ADELA: There's no way out here. Whoever has to drown—let her drown. Pepe is mine. He'll carry me to the rushes along the river bank. . . .

MARTIRIO: He won't!

ADELA: I can't stand this horrible house after the taste of his mouth. I'll be what he wants me to be. Everybody in the village against me, burning me with their fiery fingers; pursued by those who claim they're decent, and I'll wear, before them all, the crown of thorns that belongs to the mistress of a married man.

MARTIRIO: Hush!

ADELA: Yes, yes. (*In a low voice.*) Let's go to bed. Let's let him marry Angustias. I don't care any more, but I'll go off alone to a little house where he'll come to see me whenever he wants, whenever he feels like it.

MARTIRIO: That'll never happen! Not while I have a drop of blood left in my body.

ADELA: Not just weak you, but a wild horse I could force to his knees with just the strength of my little finger.

MARTIRIO: Don't raise that voice of yours to me. It irritates me. I have a heart full of a force so evil that, without my wanting to be, I'm drowned by it.

ADELA: You show us the way to love our sisters. God must have meant to leave me alone in the midst of darkness because I can see you as I've never seen you before.

(*A whistle is heard and* ADELA *runs toward the door, but* MARTIRIO *gets in front of her.*)

MARTIRIO: Where are you going?

ADELA: Get away from that door!

MARTIRIO: Get by me if you can!

ADELA: Get away!

(*They struggle.*)

MARTIRIO (*shouts*): Mother! Mother!

ADELA: Let me go!

(BERNARDA *enters. She wears petticoats and a black shawl.*)

BERNARDA: Quiet! Quiet! How poor I am without even a man to help me!

MARTIRIO (*pointing to* ADELA): She was with him. Look at those skirts covered with straw!

BERNARDA (*going furiously toward Adela*): That's the bed of a bad woman!

ADELA (*facing her*): There'll be an end to prison voices here! (ADELA *snatches away her mother's cane and breaks it in two.*) This is what I do with the tyrant's cane. Not another step. No one but Pepe commands me!

(MAGDALENA *enters.*)

MAGDALENA: Adela!

(LA PONCIA *and* ANGUSTIAS *enter.*)

ADELA: I'm his. (*to* ANGUSTIAS) Know that—and go out in the yard and tell him. He'll be master in this house.

ANGUSTIAS: My God!

BERNARDA: The gun! Where's the gun?

(*She rushes out.* LA PONCIA *runs ahead of her.* AMELIA *enters and looks on frightened, leaning her head against the wall. Behind her comes* MARTIRIO.)

ADELA: No one can hold me back!

(*She tries to go out.*)

ANGUSTIAS (*holding her*): You're not getting out of here with your body's triumph! Thief! Disgrace of this house!

MAGDALENA: Let her go where we'll never see her again!

(*A shot is heard.*)

BERNARDA (*entering*): Just try looking for him now!

MARTIRIO (*entering*): That does away with Pepe el Romano.

ADELA: Pepe! My God! Pepe!

(*She runs out.*)

PONCIA: Did you kill him?

MARTIRIO: No. He raced away on his mare!

BERNARDA: It was my fault. A woman can't aim.

MAGDALENA: Then, why did you say . . . ?

MARTIRIO: For her! I'd like to pour a river of blood over her head!

PONCIA: Curse you!

MAGDALENA: Devil!

BERNARDA: Although it's better this way!

(*A thud is heard.*)

Adela! Adela!

PONCIA (*at her door*): Open this door!

BERNARDA: Open! Don't think the walls will hide your shame!

SERVANT (*entering*): All the neighbors are up!

BERNARDA (*in a low voice, but like a roar*): Open! Or I'll knock the door down!

(*Pause. Everything is silent.*)

Adela!

(*She walks away from the door.*)

A hammer!

(LA PONCIA *throws herself against the door. It opens and she goes in. As she enters, she screams and backs out.*)

What is it?

PONCIA (*she puts her hands to her throat*): May we never die like that!

(*The* SISTERS *fall back. The* SERVANT *crosses herself.* BERNARDA *screams and goes forward.*)

Don't go in!

BERNARDA: No, not I! Pepe, you're running now, alive in the darkness, under the trees, but another day you'll fall. Cut her down! My daughter died a virgin. Take her to another room and dress her as though she were a virgin. No one will say anything about this! She died a virgin. Tell them, so that at dawn, the bells will ring twice.

MARTIRIO: A thousand times happy she, who had him.

BERNARDA: And I want no weeping. Death must be looked at face to face. Silence!

(*To one daughter.*)

Be still, I said!

(*To another daughter.*)

Tears when you're alone! We'll drown ourselves in a sea of mourning. She, the youngest daughter of Bernarda Alba, died a virgin. Did you hear me? Silence, silence, I said. Silence!

CURTAIN

Figure 1. The entire household of Bernarda Alba and the neighbor women join in mourning for Bernarda's late husband in Nuria Espert's 1986 production at the Lyric, Hammersmith. (Photograph: Donald Cooper / Photostage.)

Figure 2. Poncia (Joan Plowright, *arms outstretched*) tells Angustias (Julie Legrand, *left*), Magdalena (Christine Edmonds), Amelia (Chloe Salaman), and Martirio (Deborah Findlay) about her courtship in Nuria Espert's 1986 production at the Lyric, Hammersmith. (Photograph: Donald Cooper / Photostage.)

Figure 3. Maria Josefa (Patricia Hayes, *center*) insists that she wants to marry; Bernarda (Glenda Jackson) stares at her in anger, and Poncia (Joan Plowright) tries to restrain her in Nuria Espert's 1986 production at the Lyric, Hammersmith. (Photograph: Donald Cooper / Photostage.)

Figure 4. "Just try looking for him now!" screams Bernarda Alba (Glenda Jackson, *center,* with rifle) after firing at Pepe el Romano; Adela (Amanda Root, *standing right*) is about to rush out, distraught, to her death in Nuria Espert's 1986 production (as seen at the Globe Theatre in 1987). (Photograph: Donald Cooper / Photostage.)

Staging of *The House of Bernarda Alba*

REVIEW OF THE LYRIC, HAMMERSMITH,
PRODUCTION, 1988, BY MICHAEL BILLINGTON

The British theatre suddenly seems to be shedding its insularity. Peter James's internationalist policy at the Lyric, Hammersmith, brings us a moving, austerely impressive production of Lorca's 50-year-old *The House of Bernarda Alba,* directed by Nuria Espert, that proves several things: that British actresses can play Spanish tragedy, that Lorca is translatable (at least by Robert David Macdonald), and that a suburban theatre can yield a production that would not disgrace—indeed would enhance—the stages of our national companies.

The set has a lot to do with it. Ezio Frigerio (Strehler's designer) has taken the title literally and made the house one of the stars of the evening. Lorca's play is about the passion and frustration of the five, immured daughters of the widowed, tyrannical Bernarda Alba: and Frigerio has surrounded them by towering, white, age-pocked Granada walls inset with tiny, barred windows and culminating in a grating, flagstone floor.

The impression, simultaneously, is of a prison courtyard, a nunnery and an asylum: and, even if the sense of Andalusian heat is not very strong, the claustrophobia is heightened by the lowering space and by Franca Squarciatino's black costumes giving the women the look of bottled insects.

The difficulty lies in creating, for an English audience, a world dominated by honour, tradition, toil and sexual restraint from which there is only one escape: an arranged marriage has been fixed between the eldest daughter, Angustias, and the unseen Pepe El Romano who, it tragically transpires, is the lover of her youngest sister, Adela.

The power of Lorca's play lies in its portrait of a specific family but even in the canopied courtyard while outside the men go off to harvest. They are enclosed by the house, history, sexual custom and an overpowering sense of fate. "I should be happy but I'm not," says Angustias. "It's all the same either way," her mother replies, sealing their collective doom.

Nuria Espert breaks through Anglo-Saxon optimism to create this sense of entrapment and she does this by assembling a crack company in which no one is allowed to give a selfish-star-performance. Gillian Hanna's Maid, dutifully scrubbing stone floors and driven mad by the noise of the funeral bells, is as vital to the atmosphere as Glenda Jackson's tyrannical matriarch who rules over her brood like a female leopard (she even brandishes a claw at a recalcitrant daughter) and who howls with sadistic relish as an errant village woman is dragged through the streets.

At first hard to distinguish, her five daughters gradually take on individual life: Deborah Findlay's Martirio, caressing a black-stockinged ankle as she talks of the men yoking bullocks in the yard, implies a sensuality balefully repressed, while Amanda Root's Adela in her green dress embodies a dream of freedom.

But the vital tonal contrast is supplied by Joan Plowright in a marvellous performance as the servant Poncia: she is earthy, robust, sensual but the way she smoothes the nap of the folded linen evokes a lifetime of drudgery and suggests she is as much part of a doomed, mechanistic universe as the sisters. Patricia Hayes, stark-naked in a white shift, also gives a highly courageous performance as the mad, locked-in grandmother symbolising the fate awaiting Bernarda's daughters.

A needless interval dissipates the tension. But otherwise this is a vivid realisation of Lorca's play that conveys much of its meaning through a series of resonant images: of the sisters breaking into dreamy, private dances as the men go off to reap and of the family dining in a corner of the courtyard in a state of imprisoned festivity. Nuria Espert has put before us an enclosed world: at the same time, she has opened up the possibility of Lorca on the British stage.

BERTOLT BRECHT

1898–1956

The social and political upheavals of the twentieth century profoundly influenced Brecht's life and his plays. World War I put an end to his medical studies in Munich and marked the beginning of his intense political consciousness, which he expressed in "The Legend of the Dead Soldier" (1918), a poem the Nazis were later to cite as evidence for denying him German citizenship. Shortly after the war, in 1919, he took part in an unsuccessful revolution in his native Bavaria, a bitter experience that provided the basis for his first successful play, *Drums in the Night* (1922). By 1922, Brecht had also become "dramaturg" (a resident playwright and adapter) at the Munich Kammerspiele, a theater for which he wrote *In the Jungle of the Cities* (1923). There, too, he directed *Edward II* (1924), his revision of Marlowe's history play, in a striking production that featured a battle scene with the faces of the soldiers painted starkly white.

But it was in Berlin, where Brecht moved in 1924, that he was to become widely known—and where he was to develop his revolutionary concept of "epic theater": a form of drama and dramatic production intended to provoke spectators into a heightened social and political awareness, rather than involve them emotionally in a realistic or naturalistic situation. To prevent spectators from empathizing with his characters, Brecht advocated an "alienation effect" both in acting and playwriting. Brecht's approach to acting directly countered the method of Stanislavsky. Brecht asked actors to distance themselves from the inner life of a role and not immerse themselves in it, to deliver lines in a mocking or dispassionate tone instead of an emotionally convincing voice, and in general to act a part in a manner that conveyed the awareness of being a performer rather than the involvement of being a character. To jerk spectators into a heightened social and political consciousness, Brecht abandoned the carefully elaborated plots of realistic drama in favor of an episodic structure he learned from reading and viewing of the expressionistic political plays of his German contemporaries. Brecht created this jerky, episodic effect by using short scenes in rapidly changing locales, with frequent shifts from prose to verse to song. And to further awaken the audience to his political message, Brecht incorporated a variety of nonrealistic staging devices used by the radical German producer Erwin Piscator—posters, slide projections, motion pictures, stylized sets, and garish lighting effects.

Brecht synthesized all these elements for the first time in *Man Is Man* (1926), a fiercely anti-colonial, anti-war play, which is set in India during the British imperial rule and depicts the transformation of a poor dock worker into a soldier and military hero—a transformation that also changes him from a human being into a monster of nature. Two years later, Brecht produced his most popular and successful piece of epic theater, *The Threepenny Opera* (1928), a biting attack on capitalistic society, a society in which "money rules the world," and in which "Mankind can keep alive thanks to its brilliance in keeping its humanity repressed." To this political satire, Brecht joins romantic satire, mocking Polly Peachum's naive attachment to the lusty Macheath. The fame and money Brecht gained from this work, the popularity of which derived not just from Brecht's clever reworking of John Gay's *The Beggar's Opera* (1728) but from Kurt Weill's pungent score, gave Brecht the freedom to create a wide variety of theatrical works: his dogmatically Marxist plays, which he called "lehrstücke" (literally, learning pieces), including *The Measures Taken* (1930) and *The Exception and the Rule* (1930); his less dogmatic but still socialist plays, such as *The Mother* (1932) and *St. Joan of the Stockyards* (1932); and his other musical collaborations with Weill, *Happy End* (1929), *The Rise and Fall of the City of Mahagonny* (1929), and *The Seven Deadly Sins* (1933). The overtly didactic message in all these plays was, in essence, a challenge to the audience to change an existing social order that Brecht perceived as enslaving human beings through bureaucracy, war, and capitalism.

In 1933, political upheaval once again altered the course of Brecht's life, for when Hitler came to power Brecht was compelled to flee Nazi Germany—the communist politics of his plays had led to the danger of his being tried for high treason. He stayed briefly in Switzerland, then made his home in Denmark until 1939, when an impending Nazi invasion of that country forced him to move his family and his acting company to Sweden. But in 1940, the fear that Sweden would be invaded drove Brecht and his entourage to Finland. In 1941, he obtained a visa to the United States and settled in Santa Monica, California, where he lived until 1947, when his communist allegiances brought him under investigation by the House Committee on Un-American Activities, and he was forced to return to Germany. He spent his remaining years in East Berlin, where he devoted himself primarily to producing his already written plays and to turning his acting company, the Berliner Ensemble, into one of the most distinguished theatrical groups in the world.

During his exile from Germany, Brecht composed his most powerful plays—among them *Mother Courage and Her Children* (1939), *The Good Woman of Setzuan* (1943), *The Caucasian Chalk Circle* (1945), and *Galileo*, which he wrote and rewrote between 1938 and 1954. In all of these plays, the overt, even strident didacticism of his earlier Marxist plays gives way to a broader socialist message. Oppression is still the enemy, but in these plays it is seen as residing not only in social institutions, but in the acts of individual human beings. And it is in these plays, too, that the split between Brecht's theories of epic theater and his actual practice become most noticeable, for the plays seem to invite an audience to become passionately involved in the problems of their central characters. Although Brecht's notes on Mother Courage repeatedly emphasize the distasteful qualities he had hoped to reveal in her—her pettiness, her moral deformity, her incurable political ignorance—audiences invariably become engaged by her tenacity and idomitability. The female protagonist of *The Good Woman of Setzuan* must adopt male disguise and ruthless behavior in order to enjoy the good fortune which suddenly befalls her, but although Brecht offers no solution to her dilemma (how can one be good and still survive in a grasping, materialistic world?), the strength of Shen Te's idealism still engages the audience's sympathies. And although Brecht's notes to *Galileo* indicate that he meant to portray the famous scientist as having betrayed his calling, the play itself invites a more spacious and sympathetic view of the man.

Brecht's three versions of the play show his continuing fascination with the character of Galileo as well as his perception that Galileo's recantation of his scientific discoveries could be interpreted in a variety of ways. In the first version, written in 1938 and titled *The Earth Moves*, Galileo's revolutionary experiments and discoveries are depicted as profoundly disturbing to the religious authorities because they replace a geocentric view of planetary relationships with a heliocentric one and thereby remove human beings from the center of God's universe—a decentering that challenges the centrality of the Catholic church itself. But after 1945, when American war planes dropped atom bombs on Hiroshima and Nagasaki, Brecht, aided by Charles Laughton, rewrote the play in English to mock not only the institutions of the church but also Galileo himself as a kind of self-serving intellectual who would do anything, even recant his own scientific work, to save his skin. In this version, the play turns into a condemnation of the scientist as a man who might have changed human understanding but who failed to do so and in that failure indirectly contributed to something as horrific as the dropping of the bomb. The play's final version, in German again, is the longest, containing Brecht's bitterest attack on Galileo's failure to resist the Inquisition.

The balance and clarity of the "Laughton version" reflect the unusual working conditions that created the text. Meeting every morning in Laughton's large house overlooking the Pacific Ocean, the famous actor who spoke no German and the famous playwright whose English was limited, communicated through their common language—theatrical gesture. Brecht reports that he would act out a piece of dialogue in "bad English or even in German," Laughton would act it back in "proper English," and finally Brecht would consent to a line which Laughton would then write down.

Photographs from the 1947 New York production show Laughton's ability to convey different facets of Galileo's personality: his wary suspicion of the Inquisitor (Figure 1), his comfortably relaxed enjoyment of his friends (Figure 2), and his intense concentration (Figure 3). In that final photograph, one sees too the pain of the "stony and scientifically accurate self-knowledge" that Irwin Shaw found so memorable. Galileo's chilling view of himself as a man who betrayed his profession seemed for Irwin Shaw "the very core of truth." Yet the play follows Galileo's long speech of self-recrimination with Andrea's view that Galileo's recantation was strategic, something that enabled him to live and continue his writing. Who, then, has the last word? In the play's final scene, Andrea smuggles Galileo's manuscript out of Italy, trying to explain the truth to a young boy just as Galileo had explained it to him. And though the almost-blind Galileo can no longer see the sky, it is nonetheless bright.

GALILEO

BY BERTOLT BRECHT / TRANSLATED BY CHARLES LAUGHTON

It is my opinion that the earth is very noble and admirable by reason of so many and so different alterations and generations which are incessantly made therein.

—GALILEO GALILEI

CHARACTERS

GALILEO GALILEI
ANDREA SARTI, *two actors: boy and man*
MRS. SARTI
LUDOVICO MARSILI
PRIULI, *the curator*
SAGREDO, GALILEO'*s friend*
VIRGINIA GALILEI
TWO SENATORS
MATTI, *an iron founder*
PHILOSOPHER, *later,* RECTOR OF THE UNIVERSITY
ELDERLY LADY
YOUNG LADY
FEDERZONI, *assistant to* GALILEO
MATHEMATICIAN
LORD CHAMBERLAIN
FAT PRELATE
TWO SCHOLARS
TWO MONKS
INFURIATED MONK
OLD CARDINAL
ATTENDANT MONK
CHRISTOPHER CLAVIUS
LITTLE MONK
TWO SECRETARIES
CARDINAL BELLARMIN
CARDINAL BARBERINI
CARDINAL INQUISITOR
YOUNG GIRL
HER FRIEND
GIUSEPPE
STREET SINGER
HIS WIFE
REVELLER
A LOUD VOICE
INFORMER
TOWN CRIER
OFFICIAL
PEASANT
CUSTOMS OFFICER
BOY
SENATORS, OFFICIALS, PROFESSORS, LADIES, GUESTS, CHILDREN

There are two wordless roles: The Doge in scene 2 and Prince Cosmo de Medici in scene 4. The ballad of scene 9 is filled out by a pantomime: among the individuals in the pantomimic crowd are three extras (including the "King of Hungary"), Cobbler's Boy, Three Children, Peasant Woman, Monk, Rich Couple, Dwarf, Beggar, and Girl.

SCENE 1

In the year sixteen hundred and nine
Science' light began to shine.
At Padua City, in a modest house
Galileo Galilei set out to prove
The sun is still, the earth is on the move.

(GALILEO'*s scantily furnished study. Morning.* GALILEO *is washing himself. A barefooted boy,* ANDREA, *son of his housekeeper,* MRS. SARTI, *enters with a big astronomical model.*)

GALILEO: Where did you get that thing?
ANDREA: The coachman brought it.
GALILEO: Who sent it?
ANDREA: It said "From the Court of Naples" on the box.
GALILEO: I don't want their stupid presents. Illuminated manuscripts, a statue of Hercules the size of an elephant—they never send money.
ANDREA: But isn't this an astronomical instrument, Mr. Galilei?
GALILEO: This is an antique too. An expensive toy.
ANDREA: What's it for?

GALILEO: It's a map of the sky according to the wise men of ancient Greece. Bosh! We'll try and sell it to the university. They still teach it there.
ANDREA: How does it work, Mr. Galilei?
GALILEO: It's complicated.
ANDREA: I think I could understand it.
GALILEO (*interested*): Maybe. Let's begin at the beginning. Description!
ANDREA: There are metal rings, a lot of them.
GALILEO: How many?
ANDREA: Eight.
GALILEO: Correct. And?
ANDREA: There are words painted on the bands.
GALILEO: What words?
ANDREA: The names of stars.
GALILEO: Such as?
ANDREA: Here is a band with the sun on it and on the inside band is the moon.
GALILEO: Those metal bands represent crystal globes, eight of them.
ANDREA: Crystal?
GALILEO: Like huge soap bubbles one inside the other and the stars are supposed to be tacked on to them.

Spin the band with the sun on it. (ANDREA *does.*) You see the fixed ball in the middle?

ANDREA: Yes.

GALILEO: That's the earth. For two thousand years man has chosen to believe that the sun and all the host of stars revolve about him. Well. The Pope, the Cardinals, the princes, the scholars, captains, merchants, housewives, have pictured themselves squatting in the middle of an affair like that.

ANDREA: Locked up inside?

GALILEO (*triumphant*): Ah!

ANDREA: It's like a cage.

GALILEO: So you sensed that. (*Against the model.*) I like to think the ships began it.

ANDREA: Why?

GALILEO: They used to hug the coasts and then all of a sudden they left the coasts and spread over the oceans. A new age was coming. I was on to it years ago. I was a young man, in Siena. There was a group of masons arguing. They had to raise a block of granite. It was hot. To help matters, one of them wanted to try a new arrangement of ropes. After five minutes' discussion, out went a method which had been employed for a thousand years. The millennium of faith is ended, said I, this is the millennium of doubt. And we are pulling out of that contraption. The sayings of the wise men won't wash anymore. Everybody, at last, is getting nosy. I predict that in our time astronomy will become the gossip of the marketplace and the sons of fishwives will pack the schools.

ANDREA: You're off again, Mr. Galilei. Give me the towel. (*He wipes some soap from* GALILEO's *back.*)

GALILEO: By that time, with any luck, they will be learning that the earth rolls around the sun, and that their mothers, the captains, the scholars, the princes, and the Pope are rolling with it.

ANDREA: That turning-round-business is no good. I can see with my own eyes that the sun comes up in one place in the morning and goes down in a different place in the evening. It doesn't stand still, I can see it move.

GALILEO: You see nothing, all you do is gawk. Gawking is not seeing. (*He puts the iron washstand in the middle of the room.*) Now: that's the sun. Sit down. (ANDREA *sits on a chair.* GALILEO *stands behind him.*) Where is the sun, on your right or on your left?

ANDREA: Left.

GALILEO: And how will it get to the right?

ANDREA: By your putting it there, of course.

GALILEO: Of course? (*He picks* ANDREA *up, chair and all, and carries him round to the other side of the washstand.*) Now where is the sun?

ANDREA: On the right.

GALILEO: And did it move?

ANDREA: I did.

GALILEO: Wrong. Stupid! The chair moved.

ANDREA: But I was on it.

GALILEO: Of course. The chair is the earth, and you're sitting on it.

(MRS. SARTI, *who has come in with a glass of milk and a roll, has been watching.*)

MRS. SARTI: What are you doing with my son, Mr. Galilei?

ANDREA: Now, mother, you don't understand.

MRS. SARTI: You understand, don't you? Last night he tried to tell me that the earth goes round the sun. You'll soon have him saying that two times two is five.

GALILEO (*eating his breakfast*): Apparently we are on the threshold of a new era, Mrs. Sarti.

MRS. SARTI: Well, I hope we can pay the milkman in this new era. A young gentleman is here to take private lessons and he is well-dressed and don't you frighten him away like you did the others. Wasting your time with Andrea! (*To* ANDREA.) How many times have I told you not to wheedle free lessons out of Mr. Galilei? (MRS. SARTI *goes.*)

GALILEO: So you thought enough of the turning-round-business to tell your mother about it.

ANDREA: Just to surprise her.

GALILEO: Andrea, I wouldn't talk about our ideas outside.

ANDREA: Why not?

GALILEO: Certain of the authorities won't like it.

ANDREA: Why not, if it's the truth?

GALILEO (*laughs*): Because we are like the worms who are little and have dim eyes and can hardly see the stars at all, and the new astronomy is a framework of guesses or very little more—yet.

(MRS. SARTI *shows in* LUDOVICO MARSILI, *a presentable young man.*)

GALILEO: This house is like a marketplace. (*Pointing to the model.*) Move that out of the way! Put it down there!

(LUDOVICO *does.*)

LUDOVICO: Good morning, sir. My name is Ludovico Marsili.

GALILEO (*reading a letter of recommendation he has brought*): You came by way of Holland and your family lives in the Campagna? Private lessons, thirty scudi a month.

LUDOVICO: That's all right, of course, sir.

GALILEO: What is your subject?

LUDOVICO: Horses.

GALILEO: Aha.

LUDOVICO: I don't understand science, sir.

GALILEO: Aha.

LUDOVICO: They showed me an instrument like that in Amsterdam. You'll pardon me, sir, but it didn't make sense to me at all.

GALILEO: It's out of date now.

(ANDREA goes.)

LUDOVICO: You'll have to be patient with me, sir. Nothing in science makes sense to me.

GALILEO: Aha.

LUDOVICO: I saw a brand new instrument° in Amsterdam. A tube affair. "See things five times as large as life!" It had two lenses, one at each end, one lens bulged and the other was like that. (*Gesture.*) Any normal person would think that different lenses cancel each other out. They didn't! I just stood and looked a fool.

GALILEO: I don't quite follow you. What does one see enlarged?

LUDOVICO: Church steeples, pigeons, boats. Anything at a distance.

GALILEO: Did you yourself—see things enlarged?

LUDOVICO: Yes, sir.

GALILEO: And the tube had two lenses? Was it like this? (*He has been making a sketch.*)

(LUDOVICO nods.)

GALILEO: A recent invention?

LUDOVICO: It must be. They only started peddling it on the streets a few days before I left Holland.

GALILEO (*starts to scribble calculations on the sketch; almost friendly*): Why do you bother your head with science? Why don't you just breed horses?

(*Enter* MRS. SARTI. GALILEO *doesn't see her. She listens to the following.*)

LUDOVICO: My mother is set on the idea that science is necessary nowadays for conversation.

GALILEO: Aha. You'll find Latin or philosophy easier. (MRS. SARTI *catches his eye.*) I'll see you on Tuesday afternoon.

LUDOVICO: I shall look forward to it, sir.

GALILEO: Good morning. (*He goes to the window and shouts into the street.*) Andrea! Hey, Redhead, Redhead!

MRS. SARTI: The curator of the museum is here to see you.

---

brand new instrument, The telescope was thought erroneously to have been invented by Hans Lippershey, who made and sold telescopes in Middelburg, Netherlands, in 1608. When he applied for a patent, he was refused on the grounds that the idea was widespread. Telescopes were available for sale in Paris in 1609, then Germany, Italy, and London in the same year. Galileo reinvented the instrument by calculating the mathematical relationship of the focal lengths of lenses. His versions were on the order of ten times more powerful than those available, and they also permitted the viewer to see things right side up, which Lippershey's did not.

GALILEO: Don't look at me like that. I took him, didn't I?

MRS. SARTI: I caught your eye in time.

GALILEO: Show the curator in.

(*She goes. He scribbles something on a new sheet of paper. The* CURATOR *comes in.*)

CURATOR: Good morning, Mr. Galilei.

GALILEO: Lend me a scudo. (*He takes it and goes to the window, wrapping the coin in the paper on which he has been scribbling.*) Redhead, run to the spectacle-maker and bring me two lenses; here are the measurements. (*He throws the paper out of the window. During the following scene* GALILEO *studies his sketch of the lenses.*)

CURATOR: Mr. Galilei, I have come to return your petition for an honorarium. Unfortunately I am unable to recommend your request.

GALILEO: My good sir, how can I make ends meet on five hundred scudi?

CURATOR: What about your private students?

GALILEO: If I spend all my time with students, when am I to study? My particular science is on the threshold of important discoveries. (*He throws a manuscript on the table.*) Here are my findings on the laws of falling bodies. That should be worth two hundred scudi.

CURATOR: I am sure that any paper of yours is of infinite worth, Mr. Galilei. . . .

GALILEO: I was limiting it to two hundred scudi.

CURATOR (*cool*): Mr. Galilei, if you want money and leisure, go to Florence. I have no doubt Prince Cosmo de Medici will be glad to subsidize you, but eventually you will be forbidden to think—in the name of the Inquisition. (GALILEO *says nothing.*) Now let us not make a mountain out of a molehill. You are happy here in the Republic of Venice but you need money. Well, that's human, Mr. Galilei, may I suggest a simple solution? You remember that chart you made for the army to extract cube roots without any knowledge of mathematics? Now that was practical!

GALILEO: Bosh!

CURATOR: Don't say bosh about something that astounded the Chamber of Commerce. Our city elders are businessmen. Why don't you invent something useful that will bring them a little profit?

GALILEO (*playing with the sketch of the lenses; suddenly*): I see. Mr. Priuli, I may have something for you.

CURATOR: You don't say so.

GALILEO: It's not quite there yet, but . . .

CURATOR: You've never let me down yet, Galilei.

GALILEO: You are always an inspiration to me, Priuli.

CURATOR: You are a great man: a discontented man, but I've always said you are a great man.

GALILEO (*tartly*): My discontent, Priuli, is for the most part with myself. I am forty-six years of age and have achieved nothing which satisfies me.

CURATOR: I won't disturb you any further.

GALILEO: Thank you. Good morning.

CURATOR: Good morning. And thank you.

(*He goes.* GALILEO *sighs.* ANDREA *returns, bringing lenses.*)

ANDREA: One scudo was not enough. I had to leave my cap with him before he'd let me take them away.

GALILEO: We'll get it back someday. Give them to me. (*He takes the lenses over to the window, holding them in the relation they would have in a telescope.*)

ANDREA: What are those for?

GALILEO: Something for the senate. With any luck, they will rake in two hundred scudi. Take a look!

ANDREA: My, things look close! I can read the copper letters on the bell in the Campanile. And the washerwomen by the river, I can see their washboards!

GALILEO: Get out of the way. (*Looking through the lenses himself.*) Aha!

SCENE 2

No one's virtue is complete:
Great Galileo liked to eat.
You will not resent, we hope,
The truth about his telescope.

(*The great arsenal of Venice, overlooking the harbor full of ships.* SENATORS *and* OFFICIALS *on one side,* GALILEO, *his daughter* VIRGINIA, *and his friend* SAGREDO *on the other side. They are dressed in formal, festive clothes.* VIRGINIA *is fourteen and charming. She carries a velvet cushion on which lies a brand new telescope. Behind* GALILEO *are some* ARTISANS *from the arsenal. There are onlookers,* LUDOVICO *amongst them.*)

CURATOR (*announcing*): Senators, Artisans of the Great Arsenal of Venice; Mr. Galileo Galilei, professor of mathematics at your University of Padua.

(GALILEO *steps forward and starts to speak.*)

GALILEO: Members of the High Senate! Gentlemen: I have great pleasure, as director of this institute, in presenting for your approval and acceptance an entirely new instrument originating from this our great arsenal of the Republic of Venice. As professor of mathematics at your University of Padua, your obedient servant has always counted it his privilege to offer you such discoveries and inventions as might prove lucrative to the manufacturers and merchants of our Venetian Republic. Thus, in all humility, I tender you this, my optical tube, or telescope, constructed, I assure you, on the most scientific and Christian principles, the product of seventeen years patient research at your University of Padua.

(GALILEO *steps back. The* SENATORS *applaud.*)

SAGREDO (*aside to* GALILEO): Now you will be able to pay your bills.

GALILEO: Yes. It will make money for them. But you realize that it is more than a money-making gadget?—I turned it on the moon last night . . .

CURATOR (*in his best chamber-of-commerce manner*): Gentlemen: Our Republic is to be congratulated not only because this new acquisition will be one more feather in the cap of Venetian culture . . . (*polite applause*) . . . not only because our own Mr. Galilei has generously handed this fresh product of his teeming brain entirely over to you, allowing you to manufacture as many of these highly salable articles as you please. . . . (*Considerable applause.*) But Gentlemen of the Senate, has it occurred to you that—with the help of this remarkable new instrument—the battle fleet of the enemy will be visible to us a full two hours before we are visible to him? (*Tremendous applause.*)

GALILEO (*aside to* SAGREDO): We have been held up three generations for lack of a thing like this. I want to go home.

SAGREDO: What about the moon?

GALILEO: Well, for one thing, it doesn't give off its own light.

CURATOR (*continuing his oration*): And now, Your Excellency, and Members of the Senate, Mr. Galilei entreats you to accept the instrument from the hands of his charming daughter Virginia.

(*Polite applause. He beckons to* VIRGINIA *who steps forward and presents the telescope to the* DOGE.)

CURATOR (*during this*): Mr. Galilei gives his invention entirely into your hands, Gentlemen, enjoining you to construct as many of these instruments as you may please.

(*More applause. The* SENATORS *gather round the telescope, examining it, and looking through it.*)

GALILEO (*aside to* SAGREDO): Do you know what the Milky Way is made of?

SAGREDO: No.

GALILEO: I do.

CURATOR (*interrupting*): Congratulations, Mr. Galilei. Your extra five hundred scudi a year are safe.

GALILEO: Pardon? What? Of course, the five hundred scudi! Yes!

(*A prosperous man is standing beside the* CURATOR.)

CURATOR: Mr. Galilei, Mr. Matti of Florence.

MATTI: You're opening new fields, Mr. Galilei. We could do with you at Florence.

CURATOR: Now, Mr. Matti, leave something to us poor Venetians.

MATTI: It is a pity that a great republic has to seek an excuse to pay its great men their right and proper dues.

CURATOR: Even a great man has to have an incentive. (*He joins the* SENATORS *at the telescope.*)

MATTI: I am an iron founder.

GALILEO: Iron founder!

MATTI: With factories at Pisa and Florence. I wanted to talk to you about a machine you designed for a friend of mine in Padua.

GALILEO: I'll put you on to someone to copy it for you, I am not going to have the time.—How are things in Florence?

(*They wander away.*)

FIRST SENATOR (*peering*): Extraordinary! They're having their lunch on that frigate. Lobsters! I'm hungry!

(*Laughter.*)

SECOND SENATOR: Oh, good heavens, look at her! I must tell my wife to stop bathing on the roof. When can I buy one of these things?

(*Laughter.* VIRGINA *has spotted* LUDOVICO *among the onlookers and drags him to* GALILEO.)

VIRGINIA (*to* LUDOVICO): Did I do it nicely?

LUDOVICO: I thought so.

VIRGINIA: Here's Ludovico to congratulate you, father.

LUDOVICO (*embarrassed*): Congratulations, sir.

GALILEO: I improved it.

LUDOVICO: Yes, sir. I am beginning to understand science.

(GALILEO *is surrounded.*)

VIRGINIA: Isn't father a great man?

LUDOVICO: Yes.

VIRGINIA: Isn't that new thing father made pretty?

LUDOVICO: Yes, a pretty red. Where I saw it first it was covered in green.

VIRGINIA: What was?

LUDOVICO: Never mind. (*A short pause.*) Have you ever been to Holland?

(*They go. All Venice is congratulating* GALILEO, *who wants to go home.*)

SCENE 3

January ten, sixteen ten;
Galileo Galilei abolishes heaven.

(GALILEO'S *study at Padua. It is night.* GALILEO *and* SAGREDO *at a telescope.*)

SAGREDO (*softly*): The edge of the crescent is jagged. All along the dark part, near the shiny crescent, bright particles of light keep coming up, one after the other and growing larger and merging with the bright crescent.

GALILEO: How do you explain those spots of light?

SAGREDO: It can't be true . . .

GALILEO: It *is* true: they are high mountains.

SAGREDO: On a star?

GALILEO: Yes. The shining particles are mountain peaks catching the first rays of the rising sun while the slopes of the mountains are still dark, and what you see is the sunlight moving down from the peaks into the valleys.

SAGREDO: But this gives the lie to all the astronomy that's been taught for the last two thousand years.

GALILEO: Yes. What you are seeing now has been seen by no other man beside myself.

SAGREDO: But the moon can't be an earth with mountains and valleys like our own any more than the earth can be a star.

GALILEO: The moon *is* an earth with mountains and valleys—and the earth *is* a star. As the moon appears to us, so we appear to the moon. From the moon, the earth looks something like a crescent, sometimes like a half-globe, sometimes a full globe, and sometimes it is not visible at all.

SAGREDO: Galileo, this is frightening.

(*An urgent knocking on the door.*)

GALILEO: I've discovered something else, something even more astonishing.

(*More knocking.* GALILEO *opens the door and the* CURATOR *comes in.*)

CURATOR: There it is—your "miraculous optical tube." Do you know that this invention he so picturesquely termed "the fruit of seventeen years research" will be on sale tomorrow for two scudi apiece at every street corner in Venice? A shipload of them has just arrived from Holland.

SAGREDO: Oh, dear!

(GALILEO *turns his back and adjusts the telescope.*)

CURATOR: When I think of the poor gentlemen of the senate who believed they were getting an invention they could monopolize for their own profit. . . . Why, when they took their first look through the glass, it was only by the merest chance that they didn't see a peddler, seven times enlarged, selling tubes exactly like it at the corner of the street.

SAGREDO: Mr. Priuli, with the help of this instrument, Mr. Galilei has made discoveries that will revolutionize our concept of the universe.

CURATOR: Mr. Galilei provided the city with a first rate water pump and the irrigation works he designed function splendidly. How was I to expect this?

GALILEO (*still at the telescope*): Not so fast, Priuli. I may be on the track of a very large gadget. Certain of the stars appear to have regular movements. If there were a clock in the sky, it could be seen from anywhere. That might be useful for your shipowners.

CURATOR: I won't listen to you. I listened to you before, and as a reward for my friendship you have made me the laughingstock of the town. You can laugh—you got your money. But let me tell you this: you've destroyed my faith in a lot of things, Mr. Galilei. I'm disgusted with the world. That's all I have to say. (*He storms out.*)

GALILEO (*embarrassed*): Businessmen bore me, they suffer so. Did you see the frightened look in his eyes when he caught sight of a world not created solely for the purpose of doing business?

SAGREDO: Did you know that telescopes had been made in Holland?

GALILEO: I'd heard about it. But the one I made for the Senators was twice as good as any Dutchman's. Besides, I needed the money. How can I work, with the tax collector on the doorstep? And my poor daughter will never acquire a husband unless she has a dowry, she's not too bright. And I like to buy books—all kinds of books. Why not? And what about my appetite? I don't think well unless I eat well. Can I help it if I get my best ideas over a good meal and a bottle of wine? They don't pay me as much as they pay the butcher's boy. If only I could have five years to do nothing but research! Come on. I am going to show you something else.

SAGREDO: I don't know that I want to look again.

GALILEO: This is one of the brighter nebulae of the Milky Way. What do you see?

SAGREDO: But it's made up of stars—countless stars.

GALILEO: Countless worlds.

SAGREDO (*hesitating*): What about the theory that the earth revolves round the sun? Have you run across anything about that?

GALILEO: No. But I noticed something on Tuesday that might prove a step towards even that. Where's Jupiter? There are four lesser stars near Jupiter. I happened on them on Monday but didn't take any particular note of their position. On Tuesday I looked again. I could have sworn they had moved. They have changed again. Tell me what you see.

SAGREDO: I only see three.

GALILEO: Where's the fourth? Let's get the charts and settle down to work.

(*They work and the lights dim. The lights go up again. It is near dawn.*)

GALILEO: The only place the fourth can be is round at the back of the larger star where we cannot see it. This means there are small stars revolving around a big star. Where are the crystal shells now that the stars are supposed to be fixed to?

SAGREDO: Jupiter can't be attached to anything: there are other stars revolving round it.

GALILEO: There is no support in the heavens. (SAGREDO *laughs awkwardly.*) Don't stand there looking at me as if it weren't true.

SAGREDO: I suppose it is true. I'm afraid.

GALILEO: Why?

SAGREDO: What do you think is going to happen to you for saying that there is another sun around which other earths revolve? And that there are only stars and no difference between earth and heaven? Where is God then?

GALILEO: What do you mean?

SAGREDO: God? Where is God?

GALILEO (*angrily*): Not there! Any more than he'd be here—if creatures from the moon came down to look for him!

SAGREDO: Then where is He?

GALILEO: I'm not a theologian: I'm a mathematician.

SAGREDO: You are a human being! (*Almost shouting.*) Where is God in your system of the universe?

GALILEO: Within ourselves. Or—nowhere.

SAGREDO: Ten years ago a man was burned at the stake for saying that.

GALILEO: Giordano Bruno° was an idiot: he spoke too soon. He would never have been condemned if he could have backed up what he said with proof.

SAGREDO (*incredulously*): Do you really believe proof will make any difference?

GALILEO: I believe in the human race. The only people that can't be reasoned with are the dead. Human beings are intelligent.

SAGREDO: Intelligent—or merely shrewd?

GALILEO: I know they call a donkey a horse when they want to sell it, and a horse a donkey when they want to buy it. But is that the whole story? Aren't they susceptible to truth as well? (*He fishes a small pebble out of his pocket.*) If anybody were to drop a stone . . . (*drops the pebble*) . . . and tell them that it didn't fall, do you think they would keep quiet? The evidence of your own eyes is a very seductive thing. Sooner or later everybody must succumb to it.

SAGREDO: Galileo, I am helpless when you talk.

(*A church bell has been ringing for some time, calling people to Mass. Enter* VIRGINIA, *muffled up for Mass, carrying a candle, protected from the wind by a globe.*)

VIRGINIA: Oh, father, you promised to go to bed tonight, and it's five o'clock again.

GALILEO: Why are you up at this hour?

VIRGINIA: I'm going to Mass with Mrs. Sarti. Ludovico is going too. How was the night, father?

Giordano Bruno, Bruno (1548–1600), one of the most distinguished Italian Renaissance thinkers, lectured in England, France, Germany, and other countries in Europe before being imprisoned for heresy by the Inquisition. After a period of confinement and a lengthy trial, he was burned at the stake. He believed, like Galileo, in the Copernican view of astronomy, which asserted that the earth rotated around the sun.

GALILEO: Bright.

VIRGINIA: What did you find through the tube?

GALILEO: Only some little specks by the side of a star. I must draw attention to them somehow. I think I'll name them after the Prince of Florence. Why not call them the Medicean planets? By the way, we may move to Florence. I've written to His Highness, asking if he can use me as Court Mathematician.

VIRGINIA: Oh, father, we'll be at the court!

SAGREDO (amazed): Galileo!

GALILEO: My dear Sagredo, I must have leisure. My only worry is that His Highness after all may not take me. I'm not accustomed to writing formal letters to great personages. Here, do you think this is the right sort of thing?

SAGREDO (reads and quotes): "Whose sole desire is to reside in Your Highness' presence—the rising sun of our great age." Cosmo de Medici is a boy of nine.

GALILEO: The only way a man like me can land a good job is by crawling on his stomach. Your father, my dear, is going to take his share of the pleasures of life in exchange for all his hard work, and about time too. I have no patience, Sagredo, with a man who doesn't use his brains to fill his belly. Run along to Mass now.

(VIRGINIA goes.)

SAGREDO: Galileo, do not go to Florence.

GALILEO: Why not?

SAGREDO: The monks are in power there.

GALILEO: Going to Mass is a small price to pay for a full belly. And there are many famous scholars at the court of Florence.

SAGREDO: Court monkeys.

GALILEO: I shall enjoy taking them by the scruff of the neck and making them look through the telescope.

SAGREDO: Galileo, you are traveling the road to disaster. You are suspicious and skeptical in science, but in politics you are as naive as your daughter! How can people in power leave a man at large who tells the truth, even if it be the truth about the distant stars? Can you see the Pope scribbling a note in his diary: "10th of January, 1610, Heaven abolished"? A moment ago, when you were at the telescope, I saw you tied to the stake, and when you said you believed in proof, I smelt burning flesh!

GALILEO: I am going to Florence.

(Before the next scene a curtain with the following legend on it is lowered:

By setting the name of Medici in the sky, I am bestowing immortality upon the stars. I commend myself to you as your most faithful and devoted servant, whose sole desire is to reside in Your Highness' presence, the rising sun of our great age.

—GALILEO GALILEI)

SCENE 4

(GALILEO's house at Florence. Well-appointed. GALILEO is demonstrating his telescope to PRINCE COSMO DE MEDICI, a boy of nine, accompanied by his LORD CHAMBERLAIN, LADIES AND GENTLEMEN OF THE COURT, and an assortment of university PROFESSORS. With GALILEO are ANDREA and FEDERZONI, the new assistant (an old man). MRS. SARTI stands by. Before the scene opens the voice of the PHILOSOPHER can be heard.)

VOICE OF THE PHILOSOPHER: Quaedam miracula universi. Orbes mystice canorae, arcus crystallini, circulatio corporum coelestium. Cyclorum epicyclorumque intoxicatio, integritas tabulae chordarum et architectura elata globorum coelestium.

GALILEO: Shall we speak in everyday language? My colleague Mr. Federzoni does not understand Latin.

PHILOSOPHER: Is it necessary that he should?

GALILEO: Yes.

PHILOSOPHER: Forgive me. I thought he was your mechanic.

ANDREA: Mr. Federzoni is a mechanic and a scholar.

PHILOSOPHER: Thank you, young man. If Mr. Federzoni insists . . .

GALILEO: I insist.

PHILOSOPHER: It will not be as clear, but it's your house. Your Highness . . . (The PRINCE is ineffectually trying to establish contact with ANDREA.) I was about to recall to Mr. Galilei some of the wonders of the universe as they are set down for us in the Divine Classics. (The LADIES "ah.") Remind him of the "mystically musical spheres, the crystal arches, the circulation of the heavenly bodies—"

ELDERLY LADY: Perfect poise!

PHILOSOPHER: "—the intoxication of the cycles and epicycles, the integrity of the tables of chords and the enraptured architecture of the celestial globes."

ELDERLY LADY: What diction!

PHILOSOPHER: May I pose the question: Why should we go out of our way to look for things that can only strike a discord in this ineffable harmony?

(The LADIES applaud.)

FEDERZONI: Take a look through here—you'll be interested.

ANDREA: Sit down here, please.

(The PROFESSORS laugh.)

MATHEMATICIAN: Mr. Galilei, nobody doubts that your brain child—or is it your adopted brain child?—is brilliantly contrived.

GALILEO: Your Highness, one can see the four stars as large as life, you know.

(The PRINCE looks to the ELDERLY LADY for guidance.)

MATHEMATICIAN: Ah. But has it occurred to you that an eyeglass through which one sees such phenomena might not be a too reliable eyeglass?

GALILEO: How is that?

MATHEMATICIAN: If one could be sure you would keep your temper, Mr. Galilei, I could suggest that what one sees in the eyeglass and what is in the heavens are two entirely different things.

GALILEO (*quietly*): You are suggesting fraud?

MATHEMATICIAN: No! How could I, in the presence of His Highness?

ELDERLY LADY: The gentlemen are just wondering if Your Highness' stars are really, really there!

(*Pause.*)

YOUNG LADY (*trying to be helpful*): Can one see the claws on the Great Bear?

GALILEO: And everything on Taurus the Bull.

FEDERZONI: Are you going to look through it or not?

MATHEMATICIAN: With the greatest of pleasure.

(*Pause. Nobody goes near the telescope. All of a sudden the boy* ANDREA *turns and marches pale and erect past them through the whole length of the room. The* GUESTS *follow with their eyes.*)

MRS. SARTI (*as he passes her*): What is the matter with you?

ANDREA (*shocked*): They are wicked.

PHILOSOPHER: Your Highness, it is a delicate matter and I had no intention of bringing it up, but Mr. Galilei was about to demonstrate the impossible. His new stars would have broken the outer crystal sphere—which we know of on the authority of Aristotle. I am sorry.

MATHEMATICIAN: The last word.

FEDERZONI: He had no telescope.

MATHEMATICIAN: Quite.

GALILEO (*keeping his temper*): "Truth is the daughter of Time, not of Authority." Gentlemen, the sum of our knowledge is pitiful. It has been my singular good fortune to find a new instrument which brings a small patch of the universe a little bit closer. It is at your disposal.

PHILOSOPHER: Where is all this leading?

GALILEO: Are we, as scholars, concerned with where the truth might lead us?

PHILOSOPHER: Mr. Galilei, the truth might lead us anywhere!

GALILEO: I can only beg you to look through my eyeglass.

MATHEMATICIAN (*wild*): If I understand Mr. Galilei correctly, he is asking us to discard the teachings of two thousand years.

GALILEO: For two thousand years we have been looking at the sky and didn't see the four moons of Jupiter, and there they were all the time. Why defend shaken teachings? You should be doing the shaking. (*The* PRINCE *is sleepy.*) Your Highness! My work in the Great Arsenal of Venice brought me in daily contact with sailors, carpenters, and so on. These men are unread. They depend on the evidence of their senses. But they taught me many new ways of doing things. The question is whether these gentlemen here want to be found out as fools by men who might not have had the advantages of a classical education but who are not afraid to use their eyes. I tell you that our dockyards are stirring with that same high curiosity which was the true glory of Ancient Greece.

(*Pause.*)

PHILOSOPHER: I have no doubt Mr. Galilei's theories will arouse the enthusiasm of the dockyards.

CHAMBERLAIN: Your Highness, I find to my amazement that this highly informative discussion has exceeded the time we had allowed for it. May I remind Your Highness that the State Ball begins in three-quarters of an hour?

(*The* COURT *bows low.*)

ELDERLY LADY: We would really have liked to look through your eyeglass, Mr. Galilei, wouldn't we, Your Highness?

(*The* PRINCE *bows politely and is led to the door.* GALILEO *follows the* PRINCE, CHAMBERLAIN, *and* LADIES *towards the exit. The* PROFESSORS *remain at the telescope.*)

GALILEO (*almost servile*): All anybody has to do is look through the telescope, Your Highness.

(MRS. SARTI *takes a plate with candies to the* PRINCE *as he is walking out.*)

MRS. SARTI: A piece of homemade candy, Your Highness?

ELDERLY LADY: Not now. Thank you. It is too soon before His Highness' supper.

PHILOSOPHER: Wouldn't I like to take that thing to pieces.

MATHEMATICIAN: Ingenious contraption. It must be quite difficult to keep clean. (*He rubs the lens with his handkerchief and looks at the handkerchief.*)

FEDERZONI: We did not paint the Medicean stars on the lens.

ELDERLY LADY (*to the* PRINCE, *who has whispered something to her*): No, no, no, there is nothing the matter with your stars!

CHAMBERLAIN (*across the stage to* GALILEO): His Highness will of course seek the opinion of the greatest living authority: Christopher Clavius, Chief Astronomer to the Papal College in Rome.

SCENE 5

Things take indeed a wondrous turn
When learned men do stoop to learn.

Clavius, we are pleased to say,
Upheld Galileo Galilei.

(*A burst of laughter is heard and the curtains reveal a hall in the Collegium Romanum.* HIGH CHURCHMEN, MONKS, *and* SCHOLARS *standing about talking and laughing.* GALILEO *by himself in a corner.*)

FAT PRELATE (*shaking with laughter*): Hopeless! Hopeless! Hopeless! Will you tell me something people won't believe?

A SCHOLAR: Yes, that you don't love your stomach!

FAT PRELATE: They'd believe that. They only do not believe what's good for them. They doubt the devil, but fill them up with some fiddle-de-dee about the earth rolling like a marble in the gutter and they swallow it hook, line, and sinker. Sancta simplicitas!

(*He laughs until the tears run down his cheeks. The others laugh with him. A group has formed whose members boisterously begin to pretend they are standing on a rolling globe.*)

A MONK: It's rolling fast, I'm dizzy. May I hold on to you, Professor? (*He sways dizzily and clings to one of the* SCHOLARS *for support.*)

THE SCHOLAR: Old Mother Earth's been at the bottle again. Whoa!

MONK: Hey! Hey! We're slipping off! Help!

SECOND SCHOLAR: Look! There's Venus! Hold me, lads. Whee!

SECOND MONK: Don't, don't hurl us off on to the moon. There are nasty sharp mountain peaks on the moon, brethren!

VARIOUSLY: Hold tight! Hold tight! Don't look down! Hold tight! It'll make you giddy!

FAT PRELATE: And we cannot have giddy people in Holy Rome.

(*They rock with laughter. An* INFURIATED MONK *comes out from a large door at the rear holding a Bible in his hand and pointing out a page with his finger.*)

INFURIATED MONK: What does the Bible say—"Sun, stand thou still on Gideon and thou, moon, in the valley of Ajalon." Can the sun come to a standstill if it doesn't ever move? Does the Bible lie?

FAT PRELATE: How did Christopher Clavius, the greatest astronomer we have, get mixed up in an investigation of this kind?

INFURIATED MONK: He's in there with his eye glued to that diabolical instrument.

FAT PRELATE (*to* GALILEO, *who has been playing with his pebble and has dropped it*): Mr. Galilei, something dropped down.

GALILEO: Monsignor, are you sure it didn't drop up?

INFURIATED MONK: As astronomers we are aware that there are phenomena which are beyond us, but man can't expect to understand everything!

(*Enter a very* OLD CARDINAL *leaning on a* MONK *for support. Others move aside.*)

OLD CARDINAL: Aren't they out yet? Can't they reach a decision on that paltry matter? Christopher Clavius ought to know his astronomy after all these years. I am informed that Mr. Galilei transfers mankind from the center of the universe to somewhere on the outskirts. Mr. Galilei is therefore an enemy of mankind and must be dealt with as such. Is it conceivable that God would trust this most precious fruit of His labor to a minor frolicking star? Would He have sent His Son to such a place? How can there be people with such twisted minds that they believe what they're told by the slave of a multiplication table?

FAT PRELATE (*quietly to* CARDINAL): The gentleman is over there.

OLD CARDINAL: So you are the man. You know my eyes are not what they were, but I can see you bear a striking resemblance to the man we burned. What was his name?

MONK: Your Eminence must avoid excitement the doctor said . . .

OLD CARDINAL (*disregarding him*): So you have degraded the earth despite the fact that you live by her and receive everything from her. I won't have it! I won't have it! I won't be a nobody on an inconsequential star briefly twirling hither and thither. I tread the earth, and the earth is firm beneath my feet, and there is no motion to the earth, and the earth is the center of all things, and I am the center of the earth, and the eye of the Creator is upon me. About me revolve, affixed to their crystal shells, the lesser lights of the stars and the great light of the sun, created to give light upon me that God might see me—Man, God's greatest effort, the center of creation. "In the image of God created He him." Immortal . . . (*His strength fails him and he catches for the* MONK *for support.*)

MONK: You mustn't overtax your strength, Your Eminence.

(*At this moment the door at the rear opens and* CHRISTOPHER CLAVIUS *enters followed by his* ASTRONOMERS. *He strides hastily across the hall, looking neither to right nor left. As he goes by we hear him say—*)

CLAVIUS: He is right.

(*Deadly silence. All turn to* GALILEO.)

OLD CARDINAL: What is it? Have they reached a decision?

(*No one speaks.*)

MONK: It is time that Your Eminence went home.

(*The hall is emptying fast. One* LITTLE MONK *who had entered with* CLAVIUS *speaks to* GALILEO.)

LITTLE MONK: Mr. Galilei, I heard Father Clavius say: "Now it's for the theologians to set the heavens right again." You have won.

(*Before the next scene a curtain with the following legend on it is lowered:*

. . . As these new astronomical charts enable us to determine longitudes at sea and so make it possible to reach the new continents by the shortest routes, we would beseech Your Excellency to aid us in reaching Mr. Galilei, mathematician to the Court of Florence, who is now in Rome . . .

—From a letter written by a member of the Genoa Chamber of Commerce and Navigation to the Papal Legation)

SCENE 6

When Galileo was in Rome
A Cardinal asked him to his home
He wined and dined him as his guest
And only made one small request.

(CARDINAL BELLARMIN's *house in Rome. Music is heard and the chatter of many guests. Two* SECRETARIES *are at the rear of the stage at a desk.* GALILEO, *his daughter* VIRGINIA, *now twenty-one and* LUDOVICO MARSILI, *who has become her fiancé, are just arriving. A few* GUESTS, *standing near the entrance with masks in their hands, nudge each other and are suddenly silent.* GALILEO *looks at them. They applaud him politely and bow.*)

VIRGINIA: O father! I'm so happy. I won't dance with anyone but you, Ludovico.

GALILEO (*to a* SECRETARY): I was to wait here for His Eminence.

FIRST SECRETARY: His Eminence will be with you in a few minutes.

VIRGINIA: Do I look proper?

LUDOVICO: You are showing some lace.

(GALILEO *puts his arms around their shoulders.*)

GALILEO (*quoting mischievously*): Fret not, daughter, if perchance
You attract a wanton glance.
The eyes that catch a trembling lace
Will guess the heartbeat's quickened pace.
Lovely woman still may be
Careless with felicity.

VIRGINIA (*to* GALILEO): Feel my heart.

GALILEO (*to* LUDOVICO): It's thumping.

VIRGINIA: I hope I always say the right thing.

LUDOVICO: She's afraid she's going to let us down.

VIRGINIA: Oh, I want to look beautiful.

GALILEO: You'd better. If you don't they'll start saying all over again that the earth doesn't turn.

LUDOVICO (*laughing*): It *doesn't* turn, sir.

(GALILEO *laughs.*)

GALILEO: Go and enjoy yourselves. (*He speaks to one of the* SECRETARIES.) A large fête?

FIRST SECRETARY: Two hundred and fifty guests, Mr. Galilei. We have represented here this evening most of the great families of Italy, the Orsinis, the Villanis, the Nuccolis, the Soldanieris, the Canes, the Lecchis, the Estensis, the Colombinis, the . . .

(VIRGINIA *comes running back.*)

VIRGINIA: Oh father, I didn't tell you: you're famous.

GALILEO: Why?

VIRGINIA: The hairdresser in the Via Vittorio kept four other ladies waiting and took me first. (*Exit.*)

GALILEO (*at the stairway, leaning over the well*): Rome!

(*Enter* CARDINAL BELLARMIN, *wearing the mask of a lamb, and* CARDINAL BARBERINI, *wearing the mask of a dove.*)

SECRETARIES: Their Eminences, Cardinals Bellarmin and Barberini.

(*The* CARDINALS *lower their masks.*)

GALILEO (*to* BELLARMIN): Your Eminence.

BELLARMIN: Mr. Galilei, Cardinal Barberini.

GALILEO: Your Eminence.

BARBERINI: So you are the father of that lovely child!

BELLARMIN: Who is inordinately proud of being her father's daughter.

(*They laugh.*)

BARBERINI (*points his finger at* GALILEO): "The sun riseth and setteth and returneth to its place," saith the Bible. What saith Galilei?

GALILEO: Appearances are notoriously deceptive, Your Eminence. Once when I was so high, I was standing on a ship that was pulling away from the shore and I shouted, "The shore is moving!" I know now that it was the ship which was moving.

BARBERINI (*laughs*): You can't catch that man. I tell you, Bellarmin, his moons around Jupiter are hard nuts to crack. Unfortunately for me I happened to glance at a few papers on astronomy once. It is harder to get rid of than the itch.

BELLARMIN: Let's move with the times. If it makes navigation easier for sailors to use new charts based on a new hypothesis let them have them. We only have to scotch doctrines that contradict Holy Writ.

(*He leans over the balustrade of the well and acknowledges various* GUESTS.)

BARBERINI: But Bellarmin, you haven't caught on to this fellow. The scriptures don't satisfy him. Copernicus does.

GALILEO: Copernicus? "He that withholdeth corn the people shall curse him." Book of Proverbs.

BARBERINI: "A prudent man concealeth knowledge." Also Book of Proverbs.

GALILEO: "Where no oxen are, the stable is clean, but much increase is by the strength of the ox."

BARBERINI: "He that ruleth his spirit is better than he that taketh a city."

GALILEO: "But a broken spirit drieth up the bones." (*Pause.*) "Doth not wisdom cry?"

BARBERINI: "Can one walk on hot coals and his feet not be scorched?"—Welcome to Rome, Friend Galileo. You recall the legend of our city's origin? Two small boys found sustenance and refuge with a she-wolf and from that day we have paid the price for the she-wolf's milk. But the place is not bad. We have everything for your pleasure—from a scholarly dispute with Bellarmin to ladies of high degree. Look at that woman flaunting herself. No? He wants a weighty discussion! All right! (*To* GALILEO.) You people speak in terms of circles and ellipses and regular velocities—simple movements that the human mind can grasp—very convenient—but suppose Almighty God had taken it into his head to make the stars move like that . . . (*he describes an irregular motion with his fingers through the air*) . . . then where would you be?

GALILEO: My good man—the Almighty would have endowed us with brains like that . . . (*repeats the movement*) . . . so that we could grasp the movements . . . (*repeats the movement*) . . . like that. I believe in the brain.

BARBERINI: I consider the brain inadequate. He doesn't answer. He is too polite to tell me he considers *my* brain inadequate. What is one to do with him? Butter wouldn't melt in his mouth. All he wants to do is to prove that God made a few boners in astronomy. God didn't study his astronomy hard enough before he composed Holy Writ. (*To the* SECRETARIES.) Don't take anything down. This is a scientific discussion among friends.

BELLARMIN (*to* GALILEO): Does it not appear more probable—even to you—that the Creator knows more about his work than the created?

GALILEO: In his blindness man is liable to misread not only the sky but also the Bible.

BELLARMIN: The interpretation of the Bible is a matter for the ministers of God. (GALILEO *remains silent.*) At last you are quiet. (*He gestures to the* SECRETARIES. *They start writing.*) Tonight the Holy Office has decided that the theory according to which the earth goes around the sun is foolish, absurd, and a heresy. I am charged, Mr. Galilei, with cautioning you to abandon these teachings. (*To the* FIRST SECRETARY.) Would you repeat that?

FIRST SECRETARY (*reading*): "His Eminence, Cardinal Bellarmin, to the aforesaid Galilei: The Holy Office has resolved that the theory according to which the earth goes around the sun is foolish, absurd, and a

heresy. I am charged, Mr. Galilei, with cautioning you to abandon these teachings."

GALILEO (*rocking on his base*): But the facts!

BARBERINI (*consoling*): Your findings have been ratified by the Papal Observatory, Galilei. That should be most flattering to you . . .

BELLARMIN (*cutting in*): The Holy Office formulated the decree without going into details.

GALILEO (*to* BARBERINI): Do you realize, the future of all scientific research is . . .

BELLARMIN (*cutting in*): Completely assured, Mr. Galilei. It is not given to man to know the truth: it is granted to him to seek after the truth. Science is the legitimate and beloved daughter of the Church. She must have confidence in the Church.

GALILEO (*infuriated*): I would not try confidence by whistling her too often.

BARBERINI (*quickly*): Be careful what you're doing—you'll be throwing out the baby with the bath water, friend Galilei. (*Serious.*) We need you more than you need us.

BELLARMIN: Well, it is time we introduced our distinguished friend to our guests. The whole country talks of him!

BARBERINI: Let us replace our masks, Bellarmin. Poor Galilei hasn't got one.

(*He laughs. They take* GALILEO *out.*)

FIRST SECRETARY: Did you get his last sentence?

SECOND SECRETARY: Yes. Do you have what he said about believing in the brain?

(*Another cardinal—the* INQUISITOR—*enters.*)

INQUISITOR: Did the conference take place?

(*The* FIRST SECRETARY *hands him the papers and the* INQUISITOR *dismisses the* SECRETARIES. *They go. The* INQUISITOR *sits down and starts to read the transcription. Two or three* YOUNG LADIES *skitter across the stage; they see the* INQUISITOR *and curtsy as they go.*)

YOUNG GIRL: Who was that?

HER FRIEND: The Cardinal Inquisitor.

(*They giggle and go. Enter* VIRGINIA. *She curtsies as she goes. The* INQUISITOR *stops her.*)

INQUISITOR: Good evening, my child. Beautiful night. May I congratulate you on your betrothal? Your young man comes from a fine family. Are you staying with us here in Rome?

VIRGINIA: Not now, Your Eminence. I must go home to prepare for the wedding.

INQUISITOR: Ah. You are accompanying your father to Florence. That should please him. Science must be cold comfort in a home. Your youth and warmth will keep him down to earth. It is easy to get lost up there. (*He gestures to the sky.*)

VIRGINIA: He doesn't talk to me about the stars, Your Eminence.

INQUISITOR: No. (*He laughs.*) They don't eat fish in the fisherman's house. I can tell you something about astronomy. My child, it seems that God has blessed our modern astronomers with imaginations. It is quite alarming! Do you know that the earth—which we old fogies supposed to be so large—has shrunk to something no bigger than a walnut, and the new universe has grown so vast that prelates—and even cardinals—look like ants. Why, God Almighty might lose sight of a Pope! I wonder if I know your Father Confessor.

VIRGINIA: Father Christopherus, from Saint Ursula's at Florence, Your Eminence.

INQUISITOR: My dear child, your father will need you. Not so much now perhaps, but one of these days. You are pure, and there is strength in purity. Greatness is sometimes, indeed often, too heavy a burden for those to whom God has granted it. What man is so great that he has no place in a prayer? But I am keeping you, my dear. Your fiancé will be jealous of me, and I am afraid your father will never forgive me for holding forth on astronomy. Go to your dancing and remember me to Father Christopherus.

(VIRGINIA *kisses his ring and runs off. The* INQUISITOR *resumes his reading.*)

SCENE 7

Galileo, feeling grim,
A young monk came to visit him.
The monk was born of common folk.
It was of science that they spoke.

(*Garden of Florentine Ambassador in Rome. Distant hum of a great city.* GALILEO *and the* LITTLE MONK *of scene 5 are talking.*)

GALILEO: Let's hear it. That robe you're wearing gives you the right to say whatever you want to say. Let's hear it.

LITTLE MONK: I have studied physics, Mr. Galilei.

GALILEO: That might help us if it enabled you to admit that two and two are four.

LITTLE MONK: Mr. Galilei, I have spent four sleepless nights trying to reconcile the decree that I have read with the moons of Jupiter that I have seen. This morning I decided to come to see you after I had said Mass.

GALILEO: To tell me that Jupiter has no moons?

LITTLE MONK: No, I found out that I think the decree a wise decree. It has shocked me into realizing that free research has its dangers. I have had to decide to give up astronomy. However, I felt the impulse to confide in you some of the motives which have impelled even a passionate physicist to abandon his work.

GALILEO: Your motives are familiar to me.

LITTLE MONK: You mean, of course, the special powers invested in certain commissions of the Holy Office? But there is something else. I would like to talk to you about my family. I do not come from the great city. My parents are peasants in the Campagna, who know about the cultivation of the olive tree, and not much about anything else. Too often these days when I am trying to concentrate on tracking down the moons of Jupiter, I see my parents. I see them sitting by the fire with my sister, eating their curded cheese. I see the beams of the ceiling above them, which the smoke of centuries has blackened, and I can see the veins stand out on their toil-worn hands, and the little spoons in their hands. They scrape a living, and underlying their poverty there is a sort of order. There are routines. The routine of scrubbing the floors, the routine of the seasons in the olive orchard, the routine of paying taxes. The troubles that come to them are recurrent troubles. My father did not get his poor bent back all at once, but little by little, year by year, in the olive orchard; just as year after year, with unfailing regularity, childbirth has made my mother more and more sexless. They draw the strength they need to sweat with their loaded baskets up the stony paths, to bear children, even to eat, from the sight of the trees greening each year anew, from the reproachful face of the soil, which is never satisfied, and from the little church and Bible texts they hear there on Sunday. They have been told that God relies upon them and that the pageant of the world has been written around them that they may be tested in the important or unimportant parts handed out to them. How could they take it, were I to tell them that they are on a lump of stone ceaselessly spinning in empty space, circling around a second-rate star? What, then, would be the use of their patience, their acceptance of misery? What comfort, then, the Holy Scriptures, which have mercifully explained their crucifixion? The Holy Scriptures would then be proved full of mistakes. No, I see them begin to look frightened. I see them slowly put their spoons down on the table. They would feel cheated. "There is no eye watching over us, after all," they would say. "We have to start out on our own, at our time of life. Nobody has planned a part for us beyond this wretched one on a worthless star. There is no meaning in our misery. Hunger is just not having eaten. It is no test of strength. Effort is just stooping and carrying. It is not a virtue." Can you understand that I read into the decree of the Holy Office a noble motherly pity and a great goodness of the soul?

GALILEO (*embarrasssed*): Hm, well at least you have found out that it is not a question of the satellites of Jupiter, but of the peasants of the Campagna! And don't try to break me down by the halo of beauty that radiates from old age. How does a pearl develop in an oyster? A jagged grain of sand makes its way into the oyster's shell and makes its life unbearable. The oyster exudes slime to cover the grain of sand and the slime eventually hardens into a pearl. The oyster nearly dies in the process. To hell with the pearl, give me the healthy oyster! And virtues are not exclusive to misery. If your parents were prosperous and happy, they might develop the virtues of happiness and prosperity. Today the virtues of exhaustion are caused by the exhausted land. For that my new water pumps could work more wonders than their ridiculous superhuman efforts. Be fruitful and multiply: for war will cut down the population, and our fields are barren! (*A pause.*) Shall I lie to your people?

LITTLE MONK: We must be silent from the highest of motives: the inward peace of less fortunate souls.

GALILEO: My dear man, as a bonus for not meddling with your parents' peace, the authorities are tendering me, on a silver platter, persecution-free, my share of the fat sweated from your parents, who, as you know, were made in God's image. Should I condone this decree, my motives might not be disinterested: easy life, no persecution, and so on.

LITTLE MONK: Mr. Galilei, I am a priest.

GALILEO: You are also a physicist. How can new machinery be evolved to domesticate the river water if we physicists are forbidden to study, discuss, and pool our findings about the greatest machinery of all, the machinery of the heavenly bodies? Can I reconcile my findings on the paths of falling bodies with the current belief in the tracks of witches on broom sticks? (*A pause.*) I am sorry—I shouldn't have said that.

LITTLE MONK: You don't think that the truth, if it is the truth, would make its way without us?

GALILEO: No! No! No! As much of the truth gets through as we push through. You talk about the Campagna peasants as if they were the moss on their huts. Naturally, if they don't get a move on and learn to think for themselves, the most efficient of irrigation systems cannot help them. I can see their divine patience, but where is their divine fury?

LITTLE MONK (*helpless*): They are old!

(GALILEO *stands for a moment, beaten; he cannot meet the* LITTLE MONK's *eyes. He takes a manuscript from the table and throws it violently on the ground.*)

LITTLE MONK: What is that?

GALILEO: Here is writ what draws the ocean when it ebbs and flows. Let it lie there. Thou shalt not read. (LITTLE MONK *has picked up the manuscript.*) Already!

An apple of the tree of knowledge, he can't wait, he wolfs it down. He will rot in hell for all eternity. Look at him, where are his manners?—Sometimes I think I would let them imprison me in a place a thousand feet beneath the earth where no light could reach me, if in exchange I could find out what stuff that is: "Light." The bad thing is that, when I find something, I have to boast about it like a lover or a drunkard or a traitor. That is a hopeless vice and leads to the abyss. I wonder how long I shall be content to discuss it with my dog!

LITTLE MONK (*immersed in the manuscript*): I don't understand this sentence.

GALILEO: I'll explain it to you, I'll explain it to you.

(*They are sitting on the floor.*)

SCENE 8

Eight long years with tongue in cheek
Of what he knew he did not speak.
Then temptation grew too great
And Galileo challenged fate.

(GALILEO's *house in Florence again.* GALILEO *is supervising his* ASSISTANTS—ANDREA, FEDERZONI, *and the* LITTLE MONK—*who are about to prepare an experiment.* MRS. SARTI *and* VIRGINIA *are at a long table sewing bridal linen. There is a new telescope, larger than the old one. At the moment it is covered with a cloth.*)

ANDREA (*looking up a schedule*): Thursday. Afternoon. Floating bodies again. Ice, bowl of water, scales, and it says here an iron needle. Aristotle.

VIRGINIA: Ludovico likes to entertain. We must take care to be neat. His mother notices every stitch. She doesn't approve of father's books.

MRS. SARTI: That's all a thing of the past. He hasn't published a book for years.

VIRGINIA: That's true. Oh Sarti, it's fun sewing a trousseau.

MRS. SARTI: Virginia, I want to talk to you. You are very young, and you have no mother, and your father is putting those pieces of ice in water, and marriage is too serious a business to go into blind. Now you should go to see a real astronomer from the university and have him cast your horoscope so you know where you stand. (VIRGINIA *giggles.*) What's the matter?

VIRGINIA: I've been already.

MRS. SARTI: Tell Sarti.

VIRGINIA: I have to be careful for three months now because the sun is in Capricorn, but after that I get a favorable ascendant, and I can undertake a journey if I am careful of Uranus, as I'm a Scorpion.

MRS. SARTI: What about Ludovico?

VIRGINIA: He's a Leo, the astronomer said. Leos are sensual. (*Giggles.*)

(*There is a knock at the door, it opens. Enter the* RECTOR OF THE UNIVERSITY, *the philosopher of scene 4, bringing a book.*)

RECTOR (*to* VIRGINIA): This is about the burning issue of the moment. He may want to glance over it. My faculty would appreciate his comments. No, don't disturb him now, my dear. Every minute one takes of your father's time is stolen from Italy. (*He goes.*)

VIRGINIA: Federzoni! The rector of the university brought this.

(FEDERZONI *takes it.*)

GALILEO: What's it about?

FEDERZONI (*spelling*): DE MACULIS IN SOLE.

ANDREA: Oh, it's on the sun spots!

(ANDREA *comes to one side, and the* LITTLE MONK *the other, to look at the book.*)

ANDREA: A new one!

(FEDERZONI *resentfully puts the book into their hands and continues with the preparation of the experiment.*)

ANDREA: Listen to this dedication. (*Quotes.*) "To the greatest living authority on physics, Galileo Galilei."—I read Fabricius' paper the other day. Fabricius says the spots are clusters of planets between us and the sun.

LITTLE MONK: Doubtful.

GALILEO (*noncommittal*): Yes?

ANDREA: Paris and Prague hold that they are vapors from the sun. Federzoni doubts that.

FEDERZONI: Me? You leave me out. I said "hm," that was all. And don't discuss new things before me. I can't read the material, it's in Latin. (*He drops the scales and stands trembling with fury.*) Tell me, can I doubt anything?

(GALILEO *walks over and picks up the scales silently. Pause.*)

LITTLE MONK: There is happiness in doubting, I wonder why.

ANDREA: Aren't we going to take this up?

GALILEO: At the moment we are investigating floating bodies.

ANDREA: Mother has baskets full of letters from all over Europe asking his opinion.

FEDERZONI: The question is whether you can afford to remain silent.

GALILEO: I cannot afford to be smoked on a wood fire like a ham.

ANDREA (*surprised*): Ah. You think the sun spots may have something to do with that again? (GALILEO *does not answer.*)

ANDREA: Well, we stick to fiddling about with bits of ice in water. That can't hurt you.

GALILEO: Correct.—Our thesis!

ANDREA: All things that are lighter than water float, and all things that are heavier sink.

GALILEO: Aristotle says—

LITTLE MONK (*reading out of a book, translating*): "A broad and flat disk of ice, although heavier than water, still floats, because it is unable to divide the water."

GALILEO: Well. Now I push the ice below the surface. I take away the pressure of my hands. What happens?

(*Pause.*)

LITTLE MONK: It rises to the surface.

GALILEO: Correct. It seems to be able to divide the water as it's coming up, doesn't it?

LITTLE MONK: Could it be lighter than water after all?

GALILEO: Aha!

ANDREA: Then all things that are lighter than water float, and all things that are heavier sink. Q.e.d.°

GALILEO: Not at all. Hand me that iron needle. Heavier than water? (*They all nod.*) A piece of paper. (*He places the needle on a piece of paper and floats it on the surface of the water. Pause.*) Do not be hasty with your conclusion. (*Pause.*) What happens?

FEDERZONI: The paper has sunk, the needle is floating.

VIRGINIA: What's the matter?

MRS. SARTI: Every time I hear them laugh it sends shivers down my spine.

(*There is a knocking at the outer door.*)

MRS. SARTI: Who's that at the door?

(*Enter* LUDOVICO. VIRGINIA *runs to him. They embrace.* LUDOVICO *is followed by a* SERVANT *with baggage.*)

MRS. SARTI: Well!

VIRGINIA: Oh! Why didn't you write that you were coming?

LUDOVICO: I decided on the spur of the moment. I was over inspecting our vineyards at Bucciole. I couldn't keep away.

GALILEO: Who's that?

LITTLE MONK: Miss Virginia's intended. What's the matter with your eyes?

GALILEO (*blinking*): Oh yes, it's Ludovico, so it is. Well! Sarti, get a jug of that Sicilian wine, the old kind. We celebrate.

Q.e.d., In Latin, *quod erat demonstrandum,* "which was to be demonstrated," the usual ending on a logical examination using Aristotelian logic. The point is that it is not demonstrated; the experiment with the needle and the paper demonstrates the power of surface tension, which contradicts Andrea's earlier statement. Experimentation, in other words, is the final arbiter of what is true, not rules such as Andrea establishes.

(Everybody sits down. MRS. SARTI *has left, followed by* LUDOVICO's SERVANT.*)*

GALILEO: Well, Ludovico, old man. How are the horses?
LUDOVICO: The horses are fine.
GALILEO: Fine.
LUDOVICO: But those vineyards need a firm hand. (*To* VIRGINIA.) You look pale. Country life will suit you. Mother's planning on September.
VIRGINIA: I suppose I oughtn't, but stay here, I've got something to show you.
LUDOVICO: What?
VIRGINIA: Never mind. I won't be ten minutes. (*She runs out.*)
LUDOVICO: How's life these days, sir?
GALILEO: Dull.—How was the journey?
LUDOVICO: Dull.—Before I forget, mother sends her congratulations on your admirable tact over the latest rumblings of science.
GALILEO: Thank her from me.
LUDOVICO: Christopher Clavius had all Rome on its ears. He said he was afraid that the turning-around-business might crop up again on account of these spots on the sun.
ANDREA: Clavius is on the same track! (*To* LUDOVICO.) My mother's baskets are full of letters from all over Europe asking Mr. Galilei's opinion.
GALILEO: I am engaged in investigating the habits of floating bodies. Any harm in that?

*(*MRS. SARTI *reenters, followed by the* SERVANT. *They bring wine and glasses on a tray.*)*

GALILEO (*hands out the wine*): What news from the Holy City, apart from the prospect of my sins?
LUDOVICO: The Holy Father is on his death bed. Hadn't you heard?
LITTLE MONK: My goodness! What about the succession?
LUDOVICO: All the talk is of Barberini.
GALILEO: Barberini?
ANDREA: Mr. Galilei knows Barberini.
LITTLE MONK: Cardinal Barberini is a mathematician.
FEDERZONI: A scientist in the chair of Peter!

(Pause.)

GALILEO (*cheering up enormously*): This means change. We might live to see the day, Federzoni, when we don't have to whisper that two and two are four. (*To* LUDOVICO.) I like this wine. Don't you, Ludovico?
LUDOVICO: I like it.
GALILEO: I know the hill where it is grown. The slope is steep and stony, the grape almost blue. I am fond of this wine.
LUDOVICO: Yes, sir.
GALILEO: There are shadows in this wine. It is almost sweet but just stops short.—Andrea, clear that stuff away, ice, bowl and needle.—I cherish the conso-

lations of the flesh. I have no patience with cowards who call them weaknesses. I say there is a certain achievement in enjoying things.

(The PUPILS *get up and go to the experiment table.)*

LITTLE MONK: What are we to do?
FEDERZONI: He is starting on the sun.

(They begin with clearing up.)

ANDREA (*singing in a low voice*): The Bible proves the earth stands still,
The Pope, he swears with tears:
The earth stands still. To prove it so
He takes it by the ears.
LUDOVICO: What's the excitement?
MRS. SARTI: You're not going to start those hellish goings-on again, Mr. Galilei?
ANDREA: And gentlefolk, they say so too.
Each learned doctor proves,
(If you grease his palm): The earth stands still.
And yet—and yet it moves.
GALILEO: Barberini is in the ascendant, so your mother is uneasy, and you're sent to investigate me. Correct me if I am wrong, Ludovico. Clavius is right: These spots on the sun interest me.
ANDREA: We might find out that the sun also revolves. How would you like that, Ludovico?
GALILEO: Do you like my wine, Ludovico?
LUDOVICO: I told you I did, sir.
GALILEO: You really like it?
LUDOVICO: I like it.
GALILEO: Tell me, Ludovico, would you consider going so far as to accept a man's wine or his daughter without insisting that he drop his profession? I have no wish to intrude, but have the moons of Jupiter affected Virginia's bottom?
MRS. SARTI: That isn't funny, it's just vulgar. I am going for Virginia.
LUDOVICO (*keeps her back*): Marriages in families such as mine are not arranged on a basis of sexual attraction alone.
GALILEO: Did they keep you back from marrying my daughter for eight years because I was on probation?
LUDOVICO: My future wife must take her place in the family pew.
GALILEO: You mean, if the daughter of a bad man sat in your family pew, your peasants might stop paying the rent?
LUDOVICO: In a sort of way.
GALILEO: When I was your age, the only person I allowed to rap me on the knuckles was my girl.
LUDOVICO: My mother was assured that you had undertaken not to get mixed up in this turning-around-business again, sir.

GALILEO: We had a conservative Pope then.

MRS. SARTI: Had! His Holiness is not dead yet!

GALILEO (*with relish*): Pretty nearly.

MRS. SARTI: That man will weigh a chip of ice fifty times, but when it comes to something that's convenient, he believes it blindly. "Is His Holiness dead?"— "Pretty nearly!"

LUDOVICO: You will find, sir, if His Holiness passes away, the new Pope, whoever he turns out to be, will respect the convictions held by the solid families of the country.

GALILEO (*to* ANDREA): That remains to be seen.—Andrea, get out the screen. We'll throw the image of the sun on our screen to save our eyes.

LITTLE MONK: I thought you'd been working at it. Do you know when I guessed it? When you didn't recognize Mr. Marsili.

MRS. SARTI: If my son has to go to hell for sticking to you, that's my affair, but you have no right to trample on your daughter's happiness.

LUDOVICO (*to his* SERVANT): Giuseppe, take my baggage back to the coach, will you?

MRS. SARTI: This will kill her. (*She runs out, still clutching the jug.*)

LUDOVICO (*politely*): Mr. Galilei, if we Marsilis were to countenance teachings frowned on by the church, it would unsettle our peasants. Bear in mind: these poor people in their brute state get everything upside down. They are nothing but animals. They will never comprehend the finer points of astronomy. Why, two months ago a rumor went around, an apple had been found on a pear tree, and they left their work in the fields to discuss it.

GALILEO (*interested*): Did they?

LUDOVICO: I have seen the day when my poor mother has had to have a dog whipped before their eyes to remind them to keep their place. Oh, you may have seen the waving corn from the window of your comfortable coach. You have, no doubt, nibbled our olives, and absentmindedly eaten our cheese, but you can have no idea how much responsibility that sort of thing entails.

GALILEO: Young man, I do not eat my cheese absentmindedly. (*To* ANDREA.) Are we ready?

ANDREA: Yes, sir.

GALILEO (*leaves* LUDOVICO *and adjusts the mirror*): You would not confine your whippings to dogs to remind your peasants to keep their places, would you, Marsili?

LUDOVICO (*after a pause*): Mr. Galilei, you have a wonderful brain, it's a pity.

LITTLE MONK (*astonished*): He threatened you.

GALILEO: Yes. And he threatened you too. We might unsettle his peasants. Your sister, Fulganzio, who works the lever of the olive press, might laugh out loud if she heard the sun is not a gilded coat of arms but a lever too. The earth turns because the sun turns it.

ANDREA: That could interest his steward too and even his money lender—and the seaport towns . . .

FEDERZONI: None of them speak Latin.

GALILEO: I might write in plain language. The work we do is exacting. Who would go through the strain for less than the population at large!

LUDOVICO: I see you have made your decision. It was inevitable. You will always be a slave of your passions. Excuse me to Virginia, I think it's as well I don't see her now.

GALILEO: The dowry is at your disposal at any time.

LUDOVICO: Good afternoon. (*He goes, followed by the* SERVANT.)

ANDREA: Exit Ludovico. To hell with all Marsilis, Villanis, Orsinis, Canes, Nuccolis, Soldanieris . . .

FEDERZONI: . . . who ordered the earth stand still because their castles might be shaken loose if it revolves . . .

LITTLE MONK: . . . and who only kiss the Pope's feet as long as he uses them to trample on the people. God made the physical world, God made the human brain. God will allow physics.

ANDREA: They will try to stop us.

GALILEO: Thus we enter the observation of these spots on the sun in which we are interested, at our own risk, not counting on protection from a problematical new Pope . . .

ANDREA: . . . but with great likelihood of dispelling Fabricius' vapors, and the shadows of Paris and Prague, and of establishing the rotation of the sun . . .

GALILEO: . . . and with *some* likelihood of establishing the rotation of the sun. My intention is not to prove that I was right but to find out *whether* I was right. "Abandon hope all ye who enter—an observation." Before assuming these phenomena are spots, which would suit us, let us first set about proving that they are not—fried fish. We crawl by inches. What we find today we will wipe from the blackboard tomorrow and reject it—unless it shows up again the day after tomorrow. And if we find anything which would suit us, that thing we will eye with particular distrust. In fact, we will approach this observing of the sun with the implacable determination to prove that the earth stands still and only if hopelessly defeated in this pious undertaking can we allow ourselves to wonder if we may not have been right all the time: the earth revolves. Take the cloth off the telescope and turn it on the sun.

(*Quietly they start work. When the corruscating image of the sun is focused on the screen,* VIRGINIA *enters hurriedly, her wedding dress on, her hair disheveled,* MRS. SARTI *with her, carrying her wedding veil. The two women realize what has happened.* VIRGINIA *faints.* ANDREA, LITTLE MONK, *and* GALILEO *rush to her.* FEDERZONI *continues working.*)

SCENE 9

On April Fool's Day, thirty two,
Of science there was much ado.
People had learned from Galilei:
They used his teaching in their way.

(*Around the corner from the marketplace a* STREET
SINGER *and his* WIFE, *who is costumed to represent the
earth in a skeleton globe made of thin bands of brass, are
holding the attention of a sprinkling of representative
citizens, some in masquerade who were on their way to
see the carnival procession. From the marketplace the
noise of an impatient crowd.*)

BALLAD SINGER (*accompanied by his* WIFE *on the gui-
tar*): When the Almighty made the universe
He made the earth and then he made the sun.
Then round the earth he bade the sun to turn—
That's in the Bible, Genesis, Chapter One.
And from that time all beings here below
Were in obedient circles meant to go:

Around the Pope the cardinals
Around the cardinals the bishops
Around the bishops the secretaries
Around the secretaries the aldermen
Around the aldermen the craftsmen
Around the craftsmen the servants
Around the servants the dogs, the chickens, and
the beggars.

(*A conspicuous* REVELLER—*henceforth called the* SPIN-
NER—*has slowly caught on and is exhibiting his idea of
spinning around. He does not lose dignity, he faints with
mock grace.*)

BALLAD SINGER: Up stood the learned Galileo
Glanced briefly at the sun
And said: "Almighty God was wrong
In Genesis, Chapter One!"

Now that was rash, my friends, it is no matter small
For heresy will spread today like foul diseases.
Change Holy Writ, forsooth? What will be left at
all?
Why: each of us would say and do just what he
pleases!

(*Three wretched* EXTRAS, *employed by the chamber of
commerce, enter. Two of them, in ragged costumes, moodily bear a litter with a mock throne. The third sits on the
throne. He wears sacking, a false beard, a prop crown,
he carries a prop orb and sceptre, and around his chest
the inscription* "THE KING OF HUNGARY." *The litter has
a card with* "No. 4" *written on it. The litter bearers dump
him down and listen to the* BALLAD SINGER.)

BALLAD SINGER: Good people, what will come to pass
If Galileo's teachings spread?
No altar boy will serve the Mass
No servant girl will make the bed.

Now that is grave, my friends, it is no matter small:
For independent spirit spreads like foul diseases!
(Yet life is sweet and man is weak and after all—
How nice it is, for a little change, to do just as one
pleases!)

(*The* BALLAD SINGER *takes over the guitar. His* WIFE
*dances around him, illustrating the motion of the earth.
A* COBBLER'S BOY *with a pair of resplendent lacquered
boots hung over his shoulder has been jumping up and
down in mock excitement. There are three more* CHIL-
DREN, *dressed as grownups among the* SPECTATORS, *two
together and a single one with mother. The* COBBLER'S
BOY *takes the three* CHILDREN *in hand, forms a chain,
and leads it, moving to the music, in and out among the*
SPECTATORS, *"whipping" the chain so that the last child
bumps into people. On the way past a* PEASANT WOMAN,
*he steals an egg from her basket. She gestures to him to
return it. As he passes her again he quietly breaks the egg
over her head. The* KING OF HUNGARY *ceremoniously
hands his orb to one of his bearers, marches down with
mock dignity, and chastises the* COBBLER'S BOY. *The
parents remove the three* CHILDREN. *The unseemliness
subsides.*)

BALLAD SINGER: The carpenters take wood and build
Their houses—not the church's pews.
And members of the cobblers' guild
Now boldly walk the streets—in shoes.
The tenant kicks the noble lord
Quite off the land he owned—like that!
The milk his wife once gave the priest
Now makes (at last!) her children fat.

Ts, ts, ts, ts, my friends, this is no matter small
For independent spirit spreads like foul diseases
People must keep their place, some down and some
on top!
(Though it is nice, for a little change, to do just as
one pleases!)

(*The* COBBLER'S BOY *has put on the lacquered boots he
was carrying. He struts off. The* BALLAD SINGER *takes
over the guitar again. His* WIFE *dances around him in
increased tempo. A* MONK *has been standing near a* RICH
COUPLE, *who are in subdued costly clothes, without
masks: shocked at the song, he now leaves. A* DWARF *in
the costume of an astronomer turns his telescope on the
departing* MONK, *thus drawing attention to the* RICH
COUPLE. *In imitation of the* COBBLER'S BOY, *the* SPIN-
NER *forms a chain of grownups. They move to the music,
in and out, and between the* RICH COUPLE. *The* SPINNER
changes the GENTLEMAN'S *bonnet for the ragged hat of
a* BEGGAR. *The* GENTLEMAN *decides to take this in good
part, and a* GIRL *is emboldened to take his dagger. The*
GENTLEMAN *is miffed, throws the* BEGGAR'S *hat back.
The* BEGGAR *discards the* GENTLEMAN'S *bonnet and
drops it on the ground. The* KING OF HUNGARY *has
walked from his throne, taken an egg from the* PEASANT
WOMAN, *and paid for it. He now ceremoniously breaks*

it over the GENTLEMAN's *head as he is bending down to pick up his bonnet. The* GENTLEMAN *conducts the* LADY *away from the scene. The* KING OF HUNGARY, *about to resume his throne, finds one of the* CHILDREN *sitting on it. The* GENTLEMAN *returns to retrieve his dagger. Merriment. The* BALLAD SINGER *wanders off. This is part of his routine. His* WIFE *sings to the* SPINNER.)

WIFE: Now speaking for myself I feel
That I could also do with a change.
You know, for me . . . (*Turning to a reveller*)
. . . *you* have appeal
Maybe tonight we could arrange . . .

(*The* DWARF-ASTRONOMER *has been amusing the people by focusing his telescope on her legs. The* BALLAD SINGER *has returned.*)

BALLAD SINGER: No, no, no, no, no, stop, Galileo, stop!
For independent spirit spreads like foul diseases
People must keep their place, some down and some on top!
(Though it is nice, for a little change, to do just as one pleases!)

(*The* SPECTATORS *stand embarrassed. A* GIRL *laughs loudly.*)

BALLAD SINGER AND HIS WIFE: Good people who have trouble here below
In serving cruel lords and gentle Jesus
Who bids you turn the other cheek just so . . .
(*With mimicry.*)
While they prepare to strike the second blow:
Obedience will never cure your woe
So each of you wake up and do just as he pleases!

(*The* BALLAD SINGER *and his* WIFE *hurriedly start to try to sell pamphlets to the* SPECTATORS.)

BALLAD SINGER: Read all about the earth going round the sun, two centesimi only. As proved by the great Galileo. Two centesimi only. Written by a local scholar. Understandable to one and all. Buy one for your friends, your children and your aunty Rosa, two centesimi only. Abbreviated but complete. Fully illustrated with pictures of the planets, including Venus, two centesimi only.

(*During the speech of the* BALLAD SINGER *we hear the carnival procession approaching followed by laughter. A* REVELLER *rushes in.*)

REVELLER: The procession!

(*The litter bearers speedily joggle out the* KING OF HUNGARY. *The* SPECTATORS *turn and look at the first float of the procession, which now makes its appearance. It bears a gigantic figure of* GALILEO, *holding in one hand an open Bible with the pages crossed out. The other hand points to the Bible, and the head mechanically turns from side to side as if to say "No! No!"*)

A LOUD VOICE: Galileo, the Bible killer!

(*The laughter from the marketplace becomes uproarious. The* MONK *comes flying from the marketplace followed by delighted* CHILDREN.)

SCENE 10

The depths are hot, the heights are chill
The streets are loud, the court is still.

(*Antechamber and staircase in the Medicean palace in Florence.* GALILEO, *with a book under his arm, waits with his* DAUGHTER *to be admitted to the presence of the* PRINCE.)

VIRGINIA: They are a long time.
GALILEO: Yes.
VIRGINIA: Who is that funny-looking man? (*She indicates the* INFORMER *who has entered casually and seated himself in the background, taking no apparent notice of* GALILEO.)
GALILEO: I don't know.
VIRGINIA: It's not the first time I have seen him around. He gives me the creeps.
GALILEO: Nonsense. We're in Florence, not among robbers in the mountains of Corsica.
VIRGINIA: Here comes the Rector.

(*The* RECTOR *comes down the stairs.*)

GALILEO: Gaffone is a bore. He attaches himself to you.

(*The* RECTOR *passes, scarcely nodding.*)

GALILEO: My eyes are bad today. Did he acknowledge us?
VIRGINIA: Barely. (*Pause.*) What's in your book? Will they say it's heretical?
GALILEO: You hang around church too much. And getting up at dawn and scurrying to Mass is ruining your skin. You pray for me, don't you?

(*A* MAN *comes down the stairs.*)

VIRGINIA: Here's Mr. Matti. You designed a machine for his iron foundries.
MATTI: How were the squabs, Mr. Galilei? (*Low.*) My brother and I had a good laugh the other day. He picked up a racy pamphlet against the Bible somewhere. It quoted you.
GALILEO: The squabs, Matti, were wonderful, thank you again. Pamphlets I know nothing about. The Bible and Homer are my favorite reading.
MATTI: No necessity to be cautious with me, Mr. Galilei. I am on your side. I am not a man who knows about the motions of the stars, but you have championed the freedom to teach new things. Take that mechanical cultivator they have in Germany which you described to me. I can tell you, it will never be used in this country. The same circles that are hampering you now will forbid the physicians at Bologna to cut

up corpses for research. Do you know, they have such things as money markets in Amsterdam and in London? Schools for business, too. Regular papers with news. Here we are not even free to make money. I have a stake in your career. They are against iron foundries because they say the gathering of so many workers in one place fosters immorality! If they ever try anything, Mr. Galilei, remember you have friends in all walks of life including an iron founder. Good luck to you. (*He goes.*)

GALILEO: Good man, but need he be so affectionate in public? His voice carries. They will always claim me as their spiritual leader particularly in places where it doesn't help me at all. I have written a book about the mechanics of the firmament, that is all. What they do or don't do with it is not my concern.

VIRGINIA (*loud*): If people only knew how you disagreed with those goings-on all over the country last All Fools' day.

GALILEO: Yes. Offer honey to a bear, and lose your arm if the beast is hungry.

VIRGINIA (*low*): Did the Prince ask you to come here today?

GALILEO: I sent word I was coming. He will want the book, he has paid for it. My health hasn't been any too good lately. I may accept Sagredo's invitation to stay with him in Padua for a few weeks.

VIRGINIA: You couldn't manage without your books.

GALILEO: Sagredo has an excellent library.

VIRGINIA: We haven't had this month's salary yet—

GALILEO: Yes. (*The* CARDINAL INQUISITOR *passes down the staircase. He bows deeply in answer to* GALILEO'*s bow.*) What is he doing in Florence? If they try to do anything to me, the new Pope will meet them with an iron NO. And the Prince is my pupil, he would never have me extradited.

VIRGINIA: Psst. The Lord Chamberlain.

(*The* LORD CHAMBERLAIN *comes down the stairs.*)

LORD CHAMBERLAIN: His Highness had hoped to find time for you, Mr. Galilei. Unfortunately, he has to leave immediately to judge the parade at the Riding Academy. On what business did you wish to see His Highness?

GALILEO: I wanted to present my book to His Highness.

LORD CHAMBERLAIN: How are your eyes today?

GALILEO: So, so. With His Highness' permission, I am dedicating the book . . .

LORD CHAMBERLAIN: Your eyes are a matter of great concern to His Highness. Could it be that you have been looking too long and too often through your marvelous tube? (*He leaves without accepting the book.*)

VIRGINIA (*greatly agitated*): Father, I am afraid.

GALILEO: He didn't take the book, did he? (*Low and resolute.*) Keep a straight face. We are not going home, but to the house of the lens-grinder. There

is a coach and horses in his backyard. Keep your eyes to the front, don't look back at that man.

(*They start. The* LORD CHAMBERLAIN *comes back.*)

LORD CHAMBERLAIN: Oh, Mr. Galilei! His Highness has just charged me to inform you that the Florentine Court is no longer in a position to oppose the request of the Holy Inquisition to interrogate you in Rome.

SCENE 11

The Pope

(*A chamber in the Vatican. The* POPE, URBAN VIII— *formerly* CARDINAL BARBERINI—*is giving audience to the* CARDINAL INQUISITOR. *The trampling and shuffling of many feet is heard throughout the scene from the adjoining corridors. During the scene the* POPE *is being robed for the conclave he is about to attend: at the beginning of the scene he is plainly* BARBERINI, *but as the scene proceeds he is more and more obscured by grandiose vestments.*)

POPE: No! No! No!

INQUISITOR (*referring to the owners of the shuffling feet*): Doctors of all chairs from the universities, representatives of the special orders of the church, representatives of the clergy as a whole who have come believing with childlike faith in the word of God as set forth in the Scriptures, who have come to hear Your Holiness confirm their faith: and Your Holiness is really going to tell them that the Bible can no longer be regarded as the alphabet of truth?

POPE: I will not set myself up against the multiplication table. No!

INQUISITOR: Ah, that is what these people say, that it is the multiplication table. Their cry is, "The figures compel us," but where do these figures come from? Plainly they come from doubt. These men doubt everything. Can society stand on doubt and not on faith? "Thou are my master, but I doubt whether it is for the best." "This is my neighbor's house and my neighbor's wife, but why shouldn't they belong to me?" After the plague, after the new war, after the unparalleled disaster of the Reformation, your dwindling flock look to their shepherd, and now the mathematicians turn their tubes on the sky and announce to the world that you have not the best advice about the heavens either—up to now your only uncontested sphere of influence. This Galilei started meddling in machines at an early age. Now that men in ships are venturing on the great oceans—I am not against that of course—they are putting their faith in a brass bowl they call a compass and not in Almighty God.

POPE: This man is the greatest physicist of our time. He is the light of Italy, and not just any muddlehead.

INQUISITOR: Would we have had to arrest him otherwise? This bad man knows what he is doing, not writing his books in Latin, but in the jargon of the marketplace.

POPE (*occupied with the shuffling feet*): That was not in the best of taste. (*A pause.*) These shuffling feet are making me nervous.

INQUISITOR: May they be more telling than my words, Your Holiness. Shall all these go from you with doubt in their hearts?

POPE: This man has friends. What about Versailles?° What about the Viennese court? They will call Holy Church a cesspool for defunct ideas. Keep your hands off him.

INQUISITOR: In practice it will never get far. He is a man of the flesh. He would soften at once.

POPE: He has more enjoyment in him than any man I ever saw. He loves eating and drinking and thinking. To excess. He indulges in thinking bouts! He cannot say no to an old wine or a new thought. (*Furious.*) I do not want a condemnation of physical facts. I do not want to hear battle cries: Church, church, church! Reason, reason, reason! (*Pause.*) These shuffling feet are intolerable. Has the whole world come to my door?

INQUISITOR: Not the whole world, Your Holiness. A select gathering of the faithful.

(*Pause.*)

POPE (*exhausted*): It is clearly understood: he is not to be tortured. (*Pause.*) At the very most, he may be shown the instruments.

INQUISITOR: That will be adequate, Your Holiness. Mr. Galilei understands machinery.

(*The eyes of* BARBERINI *look helplessly at the* CARDINAL INQUISITOR *from under the completely assembled panoply of* POPE URBAN VIII.)

SCENE 12

June twenty-second, sixteen thirty-three,
A momentous date for you and me.
Of all the days that was the one
An age of reason could have begun.

(*Again the garden of the Florentine Ambassador at Rome, where* GALILEO's *assistants wait the news of the trial. The* LITTLE MONK *and* FEDERZONI *are attempting to concentrate on a game of chess.* VIRGINIA *kneels in a corner, praying and counting her beads.*)

Versailles, The Pope refers to Versailles as the center of the French court, even though Louis XIV's massive palace would not be built until the 1660s.

LITTLE MONK: The Pope didn't even grant him an audience.

FEDERZONI: No more scientific discussions.

ANDREA: The "Discorsi" will never be finished. The sum of his findings. They will kill him.

FEDERZONI (*stealing a glance at him*): Do you really think so?

ANDREA: He will never recant.

(*Silence.*)

LITTLE MONK: You know when you lie awake at night how your mind fastens on to something irrelevant. Last night I kept thinking: if only they would let him take his little stone in with him, the appeal-to-reason-pebble that he always carries in his pocket.

FEDERZONI: In the room *they'll* take him to, he won't have a pocket.

ANDREA: But he will not recant.

LITTLE MONK: How can they beat the truth out of a man who gave his sight in order to see?

FEDERZONI: Maybe they can't.

(*Silence.*)

ANDREA (*speaking about* VIRGINIA): She is praying that he will recant.

FEDERZONI: Leave her alone. She doesn't know whether she's on her head or on her heels since they got hold of her. They brought her Father Confessor from Florence.

(*The* INFORMER *of scene 10 enters.*)

INFORMER: Mr. Galilei will be here soon. He may need a bed.

FEDERZONI: Have they let him out?

INFORMER: Mr. Galilei is expected to recant at five o'clock. The big bell of Saint Marcus will be rung and the complete text of his recantation publicly announced.

ANDREA: I don't believe it.

INFORMER: Mr. Galilei will be brought to the garden gate at the back of the house, to avoid the crowds collecting in the streets. (*He goes.*)

(*Silence.*)

ANDREA: The moon is an earth because the light of the moon is not her own. Jupiter is a fixed star, and four moons turn around Jupiter, therefore we are not shut in by crystal shells. The sun is the pivot of our world, therefore the earth is not the center. The earth moves, spinning about the sun. And he showed us. You can't make a man unsee what he has seen.

(*Silence.*)

FEDERZONI: Five o'clock is one minute.

(VIRGINIA *prays louder.*)

ANDREA: Listen all of you, they are murdering the truth.

(He stops up his ears with his fingers. The two other pupils do the same. FEDERZONI *goes over to the* LITTLE MONK, *and all of them stand absolutely still in cramped positions. Nothing happens. No bell sounds. After a silence, filled with the murmur of* VIRGINIA's *prayers,* FEDERZONI *runs to the wall to look at the clock. He turns around, his expression changed. He shakes his head. They drop their hands.)*

FEDERZONI: No. No bell. It is three minutes after.

LITTLE MONK: He hasn't.

ANDREA: He held true. It is all right, it is all right.

LITTLE MONK: He did not recant.

FEDERZONI: No.

(They embrace each other, they are delirious with joy.)

ANDREA: So force cannot accomplish everything. What has been seen can't be unseen. Man is constant in the face of death.

FEDERZONI: June 22, 1633: dawn of the age of reason. I wouldn't have wanted to go on living if he had recanted.

LITTLE MONK: I didn't say anything, but I was in agony. Oh, ye of little faith!

ANDREA: I was sure.

FEDERZONI: It would have turned our morning to night.

ANDREA: It would have been as if the mountain had turned to water.

LITTLE MONK *(kneeling down, crying)*: Oh God, I thank Thee.

ANDREA: Beaten humanity can lift its head. A man has stood up and said "no."

(At this moment the bell of Saint Marcus begins to toll. They stand like statues. VIRGINIA *stands up.)*

VIRGINIA: The bell of Saint Marcus. He is not damned.

(From the street one hears the TOWN CRIER *reading* GALILEO's *recantation.)*

TOWN CRIER: I, Galileo Galilei, Teacher of Mathematics and Physics, do hereby publicly renounce my teaching that the earth moves. I foreswear this teaching with a sincere heart and unfeigned faith and detest and curse this and all other errors and heresies repugnant to the Holy Scriptures.

(The lights dim; when they come up again the bell of Saint Marcus is petering out. VIRGINIA *has gone but the* SCHOLARS *are still there waiting.)*

ANDREA *(loud)*: The mountain did turn to water.

*(*GALILEO *has entered quietly and unnoticed. He is changed, almost unrecognizable. He has heard* ANDREA. *He waits some seconds by the door for somebody to greet him. Nobody does. They retreat from him. He goes slowly and, because of his bad sight, uncertainly, to the front of the stage where he finds a chair, and sits down.)*

ANDREA: I can't look at him. Tell him to go away.

FEDERZONI: Steady.

ANDREA *(hysterically)*: He saved his big gut.

FEDERZONI: Get him a glass of water.

(The LITTLE MONK *fetches a glass of water for* ANDREA. *Nobody acknowledges the presence of* GALILEO, *who sits silently on his chair listening to the voice of the* TOWN CRIER, *now in another street.)*

ANDREA: I can walk. Just help me a bit.

(They help him to the door.)

ANDREA *(in the door)*: "Unhappy is the land that breeds no hero."

GALILEO: No, Andrea: "Unhappy is the land that needs a hero."

(Before the next scene a curtain with the following legend on it is lowered:

You can plainly see that if a horse were to fall from a height of three or four feet, it could break its bones, whereas a dog would not suffer injury. The same applies to a cat from a height of as much as eight or ten feet, to a grasshopper from the top of a tower, and to an ant falling down from the moon. Nature could not allow a horse to become as big as twenty horses nor a giant as big as ten men, unless she were to change the proportions of all its members, particularly the bones. Thus the common assumption that great and small structures are equally tough is obviously wrong.

—From the *Discorsi)*

SCENE 13

1633–1642.
Galileo Galilei remains a prisoner
of the Inquisition until his death.

(A country house near Florence. A large room simply furnished. There is a huge table, a leather chair, a globe of the world on a stand, and a narrow bed. A portion of the adjoining anteroom is visible, and the front door which opens into it.)

(An OFFICIAL OF THE INQUISITION *sits on guard in the anteroom.)*

(In the large room, GALILEO *is quietly experimenting with a bent wooden rail and a small ball of wood. He is still vigorous but almost blind.)*

(After a while there is a knocking at the outside door. The OFFICIAL *opens it to a* PEASANT *who brings a plucked goose.* VIRGINIA *comes from the kitchen. She is past forty.)*

PEASANT *(handing the goose to* VIRGINIA*)*: I was told to deliver this here.

VIRGINIA: I didn't order a goose.

PEASANT: I was told to say it's from someone who was passing through.

(VIRGINIA *takes the goose, surprised. The* OFFICIAL *takes it from her and examines it suspiciously. Then, reassured, he hands it back to her. The* PEASANT *goes.* VIRGINIA *brings the goose in to* GALILEO.)

VIRGINIA: Somebody who was passing through sent you something.

GALILEO: What is it?

VIRGINIA: Can't you see it?

GALILEO: No. (*He walks over.*) A goose. Any name?

VIRGINIA: No.

GALILEO (*weighing the goose*): Solid.

VIRGINIA (*cautiously*): Will you eat the liver, if I have it cooked with a little apple?

GALILEO: I had my dinner. Are you under orders to finish me off with food?

VIRGINIA: It's not rich. And what is wrong with your eyes again? You should be able to see it.

GALILEO: You were standing in the light.

VIRGINIA: I was not.—You haven't been writing again?

GALILEO (*sneering*): What do you think?

(VIRGINIA *takes the goose out into the anteroom and speaks to the* OFFICIAL.)

VIRGINIA: You had better ask Monsignor Carpula to send the doctor. Father couldn't see this goose across the room.—Don't look at me like that. He has not been writing. He dictates everything to me, as you know.

OFFICIAL: Yes?

VIRGINIA: He abides by the rules. My father's repentance is sincere. I keep an eye on him (*She hands him the goose.*) Tell the cook to fry the liver with an apple and an onion. (*She goes back into the large room.*) And you have no business to be doing that with those eyes of yours, father.

GALILEO: You may read me some Horace.

VIRGINIA: We should go on with your weekly letter to the Archbishop. Monsignor Carpula to whom we owe so much was all smiles the other day because the Archbishop had expressed his pleasure at your collaboration.

GALILEO: Where were we?

VIRGINIA (*sits down to take his dictation*): Paragraph four.

GALILEO: Read what you have.

VIRGINIA: "The position of the church in the matter of the unrest at Genoa. I agree with Cardinal Spoletti in the matter of the unrest among the Venetian ropemakers . . ."

GALILEO: Yes. (*Dictates.*) I agree with Cardinal Spoletti in the matter of the unrest among the Venetian ropemakers: it is better to distribute good nourishing food in the name of charity than to pay them more for their bellropes. It being surely better to strengthen their faith than to encourage their acquisitiveness. St. Paul says: Charity never faileth.—How is that?

VIRGINIA: It's beautiful, father.

GALILEO: It couldn't be taken as irony?

VIRGINIA: No. The Archbishop will like it. It's so practical.

GALILEO: I trust your judgment. Read it over slowly.

VIRGINIA: "The position of the Church in the matter of the unrest . . ."

(*There is a knocking at the outside door.* VIRGINIA *goes into the anteroom. The* OFFICIAL *opens the door. It is* ANDREA.)

ANDREA: Good evening. I am sorry to call so late, I'm on my way to Holland. I was asked to look him up. Can I go in?

VIRGINIA: I don't know whether he will see you. You never came.

ANDREA: Ask him.

(GALILEO *recognizes the voice. He sits motionless.* VIRGINIA *comes in to* GALILEO.)

GALILEO: Is that Andrea?

VIRGINIA: Yes. (*Pause.*) I will send him away.

GALILEO: Show him in.

(VIRGINIA *shows* ANDREA *in.* VIRGINIA *sits,* ANDREA *remains standing.*)

ANDREA (*cool*): Have you been keeping well, Mr. Galilei?

GALILEO: Sit down. What are you doing these days? What are you working on? I heard it was something about hydraulics in Milan.

ANDREA: As he knew I was passing through, Fabricius of Amsterdam asked me to visit you and inquire about your health.

(*Pause.*)

GALILEO: I am very well.

ANDREA (*formally*): I am glad I can report you are in good health.

GALILEO: Fabricius will be glad to hear it. And you might inform him that, on account of the depth of my repentance, I live in comparative comfort.

ANDREA: Yes, we understand that the church is more than pleased with you. Your complete acceptance has had its effect. Not one paper expounding a new thesis has made its appearance in Italy since your submission.

(*Pause.*)

GALILEO: Unfortunately there are countries not under the wing of the church. Would you not say the erroneous condemned theories are still taught—there?

ANDREA (*relentless*): Things are almost at a standstill.

GALILEO: Are they? (*Pause.*) Nothing from Descartes in Paris?

ANDREA: Yes. On receiving the news of your recantation, he shelved his treatise on the nature of light.

GALILEO: I sometimes worry about my assistants whom I led into error. Have they benefited by my example?

ANDREA: In order to work I have to go to Holland.

GALILEO: Yes.

ANDREA: Federzoni is grinding lenses again, back in some shop.

GALILEO: He can't read the books.

ANDREA: Fulganzio, our little monk, has abandoned research and is resting in peace in the church.

GALILEO: So. (*Pause.*) My superiors are looking forward to my spiritual recovery. I am progressing as well as can be expected.

VIRGINIA: You are doing well, father.

GALILEO: Virginia, leave the room.

(VIRGINIA *rises uncertainly and goes out.*)

VIRGINIA (*to the* OFFICIAL): He was his pupil, so now he is his enemy.—Help me in the kitchen.

(*She leaves the anteroom with the* OFFICIAL.)

ANDREA: May I go now, sir?

GALILEO: I do not know why you came, Sarti. To unsettle me? I have to be prudent.

ANDREA: I'll be on my way.

GALILEO: As it is, I have relapses. I completed the "Discorsi."

ANDREA: You completed what?

GALILEO: My "Discorsi."

ANDREA: How?

GALILEO: I am allowed pen and paper. My superiors are intelligent men. They know the habits of a lifetime cannot be broken abruptly. But they protect me from any unpleasant consequences: they lock my pages away as I dictate them. And I should know better than to risk my comfort. I wrote the "Discorsi" out again during the night. The manuscript is in the globe. My vanity has up to now prevented me from destroying it. If you consider taking it, you will shoulder the entire risk. You will say it was pirated from the original in the hands of the Holy Office.

(ANDREA, *as in a trance, has gone to the globe. He lifts the upper half and gets the book. He turns the pages as if wanting to devour them. In the background the opening sentences of the* Discorsi *appear:*

MY PURPOSE IS TO SET FORTH A VERY NEW
SCIENCE DEALING WITH A VERY ANCIENT
SUBJECT—MOTION. . . . AND I HAVE
DISCOVERED BY EXPERIMENT SOME PROPERTIES
OF IT WHICH ARE WORTH KNOWING. . . .)

GALILEO: I had to employ my time somehow.

(*The text disappears.*)

ANDREA: Two new sciences! This will be the foundation stone of a new physics.

GALILEO: Yes. Put it under your coat.

ANDREA: And we thought you had deserted. (*In a low voice.*) Mr. Galilei, how can I begin to express my shame. Mine has been the loudest voice against you.

GALILEO: That would seem to have been proper. I taught you science and I decried the truth.

ANDREA: Did you? I think not. Everything is changed!

GALILEO: What is changed?

ANDREA: You shielded the truth from the oppressor. Now I see! In your dealings with the Inquisition you used the same superb common sense you brought to physics.

GALILEO: Oh!

ANDREA: We lost our heads. With the crowd at the street corners we said: "He will die, he will never surrender!" You came back: "I surrendered but I am alive." We cried: "Your hands are stained!" You say: "Better stained than empty."

GALILEO: "Better stained than empty."—It sounds realistic. Sounds like me.

ANDREA: And I of all people should have known. I was twelve when you sold another man's telescope to the Venetian Senate, and saw you put it to immortal use. Your friends were baffled when you bowed to the Prince of Florence: Science gained a wider audience. You always laughed at heroics. "People who suffer bore me," you said. "Misfortunes are due mainly to miscalculations." And: "If there are obstacles, the shortest line between two points may be the crooked line."

GALILEO: It makes a picture.

ANDREA: And when you stooped to recant in 1633, I should have understood that you were again about your business.

GALILEO: My business being?

ANDREA: Science. The study of the properties of motion, mother of the machines which will themselves change the ugly face of the earth.

GALILEO: Aha!

ANDREA: You gained time to write a book that only you could write. Had you burned at the stake in a blaze of glory they would have won.

GALILEO: They have won. And there is no such thing as a scientific work that only one man can write.

ANDREA: Then why did you recant, tell me that!

GALILEO: I recanted because I was afraid of physical pain.

ANDREA: No!

GALILEO: They showed me the instruments.

ANDREA: It was not a plan?

GALILEO: It was not.

(*Pause.*)

ANDREA: But you have contributed. Science has only

one commandment: contribution. And you have contributed more than any man for a hundred years.

GALILEO: Have I? Then welcome to my gutter, dear colleague in science and brother in treason: I sold out, you are a buyer. The first sight of the book! His mouth watered and his scoldings were drowned. Blessed be our bargaining, whitewashing, death-fearing community!

ANDREA: The fear of death is human.

GALILEO: Even the church will teach you that to be weak is not human. It is just evil.

ANDREA: The church, yes! But science is not concerned with our weaknesses.

GALILEO: No? My dear Sarti, in spite of my present convictions, I may be able to give you a few pointers as to the concerns of your chosen profession.

(*Enter* VIRGINIA *with a platter.*)

In my spare time, I happen to have gone over this case. I have spare time.—Even a man who sells wool, however good he is at buying wool cheap and selling it dear, must be concerned with the standing of the wool trade. The practice of science would seem to call for valor. She trades in knowledge, which is the product of doubt. And this new art of doubt has enchanted the public. The plight of the multitude is old as the rocks, and is believed to be basic as the rocks. But now they have learned to doubt. They snatched the telescopes out of our hands and had them trained on their tormentors: prince, official, public moralist. The mechanism of the heavens was clearer, the mechanism of their courts was still murky. The battle to measure the heavens is won by doubt; by credulity the Roman housewife's battle for milk will always be lost. Word is passed down that this is of no concern to the scientist who is told he will only release such of his findings as do not disturb the peace, that is, the peace of mind of the well-to-do. Threats and bribes fill the air. Can the scientist hold out on the numbers? For what reason do you labor? I take it the intent of science is to ease human existence. If you give way to coercion, science can be crippled, and your new machines may simply suggest new drudgeries. Should you then, in time, discover all there is to be discovered, your progress must then become a progress away from the bulk of humanity. The gulf might even grow so wide that the sound of your cheering at some new achievement would be echoed by a universal howl of horror.—As a scientist I had an almost unique opportunity. In my day astronomy emerged into the marketplace. At that particular time, had one man put up a fight, it could have had wide repercussions. I have come to believe that I was never in real danger; for some years I was as strong as the authorities, and I sur-

rendered my knowledge to the powers that be, to use it, no, not *use* it, *abuse* it, as it suits their ends. I have betrayed my profession. Any man who does what I have done must not be tolerated in the ranks of science.

(VIRGINIA, *who has stood motionless, puts the platter on the table.*)

VIRGINIA: You are accepted in the ranks of the faithful, father.

GALILEO (*sees her*): Correct. (*He goes over to the table.*) I have to eat now.

VIRGINIA: We lock up at eight.

ANDREA: I am glad I came. (*He extends his hand.* GALILEO *ignores it and goes over to his meal.*)

GALILEO (*examining the plate; to* ANDREA): Somebody who knows me sent me a goose. I still enjoy eating.

ANDREA: And your opinion is now that the "new age" was a illusion?

GALILEO: Well.—This age of ours turned out to be a whore, spattered with blood. Maybe, new ages look like blood-spattered whores. Take care of yourself.

ANDREA: Yes. (*Unable to go.*) With reference to your evaluation of the author in question—I do not know the answer. But I cannot think that your savage analysis is the last word.

GALILEO: Thank you, sir.

(OFFICIAL *knocks at the door.*)

VIRGINIA (*showing* ANDREA *out*): I don't like visitors from the past, they excite him.

(*She lets him out. The* OFFICIAL *closes the iron door.* VIRGINIA *returns.*)

GALILEO (*eating*): Did you try and think who sent the goose?

VIRGINIA: Not Andrea.

GALILEO: Maybe not. I gave Redhead his first lesson; when he held out his hand, I had to remind myself he is teaching now.—How is the sky tonight?

VIRGINIA (*at the window*): Bright.

(GALILEO *continues eating.*)

SCENE 14

The great book o'er the border went
And, good folk, that was the end.
But we hope you'll keep in mind
You and I were left behind.

(*Before a little Italian customs house early in the morning.* ANDREA *sits upon one of his traveling trunks at the barrier and reads* GALILEO'*s book. The window of a small house is still lit, and a big grotesque shadow, like an old witch and her cauldron, falls upon the house wall beyond.*

Barefoot CHILDREN *in rags see it and point to the little house.*)

CHILDREN (*singing*): One, two, three, four, five, six,
Old Marina is a witch.
At night, on a broomstick she sits
And on the church steeple she spits.

CUSTOMS OFFICER (*to* ANDREA): Why are you making this journey?

ANDREA: I am a scholar.

CUSTOMS OFFICER (*to his* CLERK): Put down under "reason for leaving the country": Scholar. (*He points to the baggage.*) Books! Anything dangerous in these books?

ANDREA: What is dangerous?

CUSTOMS OFFICER: Religion. Politics.

ANDREA: These are nothing but mathematical formulas.

CUSTOMS OFFICER: What's that?

ANDREA: Figures.

CUSTOMS OFFICER: Oh, figures. No harm in figures. Just wait a minute, sir, we will soon have your papers stamped. (*He exits with* CLERK.)

(*Meanwhile, a little council of war among the* CHILDREN *has taken place.* ANDREA *quietly watches. One of the* BOYS, *pushed forward by the others, creeps up to the little house from which the shadow comes and takes the jug of milk on the doorstep.*)

ANDREA (*quietly*): What are you doing with that milk?

BOY (*stopping in mid-movement*): She is a witch.

(*The other* CHILDREN *run away behind the customs house. One of them shouts, "Run, Paolo!"*)

ANDREA: Hmm!—And because she is a witch she mustn't have milk. Is that the idea?

BOY: Yes.

ANDREA: And how do you know she is a witch?

BOY (*points to shadow on house wall*): Look!

ANDREA: Oh! I see.

BOY: And she rides on a broomstick at night—and she bewitches the coachman's horses. My cousin Luigi looked through the hole in the stable roof, that the snowstorm made, and heard the horses coughing something terrible.

ANDREA: Oh!—How big was the hole in the stable roof?

BOY: Luigi didn't tell. Why?

ANDREA: I was asking because maybe the horses got sick because it was cold in the stable. You had better ask Luigi how big that hole is.

BOY: You are not going to say Old Marina isn't a witch, because you can't.

ANDREA: No, I can't say she isn't a witch. I haven't looked into it. A man can't know about a thing he hasn't looked into, or can he?

BOY: No!—But THAT! (*He points to the shadow.*) She is stirring hell-broth.

ANDREA: Let's see. Do you want to take a look? I can lift you up.

BOY: You lift me to the window, mister! (*He takes a sling shot out of his pocket.*) I can really bash her from there.

ANDREA: Hadn't we better make sure she is a witch before we shoot? I'll hold that.

(*The* BOY *puts the milk jug down and follows him reluctantly to the window.* ANDREA *lifts the boy up so that he can look in.*)

ANDREA: What do you see?

BOY (*slowly*): Just an old girl cooking porridge.

ANDREA: Oh! Nothing to it then. Now look at her shadow, Paolo.

(*The* BOY *looks over his shoulder and back and compares the reality and the shadow.*)

BOY: The big thing is a soup ladle.

ANDREA: Ah! A ladle! You see, I would have taken it for a broomstick, but I haven't looked into the matter as you have, Paolo. Here is your sling.

CUSTOMS OFFICER (*returning with the* CLERK *and handing* ANDREA *his papers*): All present and correct. Good luck, sir.

(ANDREA *goes, reading* GALILEO's *book. The* CLERK *starts to bring his baggage after him. The barrier rises.* ANDREA *passes through, still reading the book. The* BOY *kicks over the milk jug.*)

BOY (*shouting after* ANDREA): She *is* a witch! She *is* a witch!

ANDREA: You saw with your own eyes: think it over!

(*The* BOY *joins the others. They sing.*)

One, two, three, four, five, six,
Old Marina is a witch.
At night, on a broomstick she sits
And on the church steeple she spits.

(*The* CUSTOMS OFFICERS *laugh.* ANDREA *goes.*)

Figure 1. Galileo (Charles Laughton) glances warily at the Inquisitor (John Carradine) while Virginia (Joan McCracken) curtsies demurely in the 1947 New York production directed by Joseph Losey. (Photograph: Billy Rose Theatre Collection. The New York Public Library for the Performing Arts. Astor, Lenox, and Tilden Foundations.)

Figure 2. A relaxed Galileo (Charles Laughton) chats with his co-workers and Ludovico while Mrs. Sarti (Hester Sondergard) looks on disapprovingly. Around the table are Ludovico (Philip Swander), Andrea (Nehemiah Persoff), and the Little Monk (Donald Symington), while Federzoni (Dwight Marfield) stands in the background. The 1947 New York production was directed by Joseph Losey. (Photograph: Billy Rose Theatre Collection. The New York Public Library for the Performing Arts. Astor, Lenox, and Tilden Foundations.)

Figure 3. Almost blind, the imprisoned Galileo (Charles Laughton)
"is experimenting with a bent wooden rail and a small ball of wood"
in the final scene of the 1947 New York production directed by Joseph
Losey. (Photograph: Billy Rose Theatre Collection. The New York
Public Library for the Performing Arts. Astor, Lenox, and Tilden
Foundations.)

Staging of *Galileo*

REVIEW OF THE NEW YORK PRODUCTION, 1947, BY IRWIN SHAW

There has been considerable discussion, some of it quite acrimonious, about the propriety of having an institution called the Experimental Theatre put on a work in which an actor of Charles Laughton's standing plays the leading part. The argument has leaked over to include the Experimental Theatre's next production, "Skipper Next to God," with John Garfield. According to the critics of the enterprise, it would seem that nothing a well-known actor can do on a stage can properly be considered an experiment. This, of course, is nonsense, and the sponsors of the project are to be congratulated for fulfilling handsomely, in Bertolt Brecht's "Galileo," the promise of the organization's title.

The play is noble in theme, relentlessly unconventional in execution, and it permits Laughton to escape, if only for six performances, the absurd, minor warblings which have recently been his lot in Hollywood. Equipped with an abstract set, a fluttering gauze curtain that is drawn at the end of each scene by a small boy with a pole, projections of Renaissance drawings and paintings, and intermittent choruses with music by Hanns Eisler, sung by three choirboys, it could hardly be called a standard Broadway performance.

Aside from its technical innovations, the story of Galileo's martyrdom by Authority is bitterly apposite for today's audiences. The heresy hunters are almost as busy today in Washington as they ever were in Florence, and recantations fill the air in a medieval blizzard of fear. *Time, Life* and Hearst have replaced the rack, and the Representative from New Jersey has donned the Inquisitor's dark satin. The sobbing "I was wrong" of the matinee idol is now to be heard, instead of the "I have sinned" of the old astronomer, but the pattern, as Brecht bleakly points out, is the same. Truth dies with conformity, this year or last.

Cool demands. Brecht's method of saying these things, in accordance with his theories of the "Epic" theater, is abstract, cold and didactic. He assumes the air of the passionless teacher lecturing to students who are not so bright as they should be. He disdains all emotionalism; scornfully, he refuses to amuse us with the usual dramatist's tricks. His characters are symbols, not people; his action the functioning of huge forces, not the clash of human beings. The final effect is interesting, but aggravating. We get the unpleasant feeling that Brecht regards the human race, or at least that part of it which goes to the theater, as animals equipped with only the most rudimentary ability to reason. His Olympian condescension is bound to annoy us, even when we agree with him most heartily.

Joseph Losey's staging meets, I suppose, with Brecht's cool demands, but it is only in three magnificently searching and eloquent scenes in the second half that the play comes really alive. One is in a garden, in which a young monk tells Galileo the reasons of conscience for which he is giving up the study of physics; another is in the Pope's robing room, in which the humanitarian prelate is forced by the logic of his position to agree to the limited torture of the scientist; and the third is the last scene of the play, in which Galileo explores the most profound and complex depths of compromise, cowardice and treachery.

It is in this scene, seated quietly on the almost empty stage, that Laughton gives us one of the most memorable moments of the recent theater. With a stony and scientifically accurate self-knowledge, he appraises himself and the world. Tragically clear, half-victor half-victim, the old giant delivers himself of a monumental monologue, and for a time, on the stage of the Maxine Elliot, we seem to be at the very core of truth.

It is devoutly to be hoped that the commercial theater will rise to the challenge of "Galileo" and put it on the boards where all may see it.

EUGENE O'NEILL

1888–1953

Before his death of a rare degenerative disease that made it almost impossible for him to write during the last several years of his life, O'Neill produced more than fifty plays whose theatrical range and vision have firmly established him as the greatest playwright in the history of American drama. From the very beginning of his life the theater was an inextricable part of his experience, for he was the son of one of America's most famous matinee idols, the romantic actor James O'Neill, who achieved theatrical fame as the star of *The Count of Monte Cristo* and continued to tour in the play until he was well into his sixties. O'Neill himself was born in a hotel in the theater district of New York, and during his early childhood he travelled with his father on theatrical tours that took him throughout the United States. The chaotic life of his father's career and the morphine addiction that his mother developed after taking the drug to alleviate the pain of O'Neill's birth were also an indelible part of his experience, which he reflected in a number of late autobiographical plays that constitute the greatest achievement of his career, among them *Long Day's Journey into Night* (1940) and *A Moon for the Misbegotten* (1943). In these and other late plays, O'Neill confronted the most painful aspects of his family's and his own personal experience—his father's extramarital affairs, his mother's morphine addiction, his brother's inability to hold a job, his father's alcoholism, his brother's alcoholism, his own alcoholism that drove him to attempt suicide at a Bowery bar in 1912, and the endless cycle of bitter accusation and shamefaced apology that consumed the family throughout his life, leaving him obsessively torn between love and hatred for all its members. But the writing of these plays was more than a psychological milestone of honestly confronting his own past, for they also represent the artistic climax to his many years of searching for an appropriate dramatic form in which to convey his vision of modern experience.

O'Neill turned to playwriting in 1912, after a hectic period of several years, during which he got secretly married to a young woman whom he promptly left to go prospecting for gold in Honduras, then returned after a year to join his father as an actor and assistant stage manager on tour, went to sea again for a brief period, returned and took a job as a reporter on a small town newspaper in Connecticut, and then came down with tuberculosis, brought on no doubt by his dissolute life, which forced him to be hospitalized for an extended period of time. During 1912, he became an avid reader of drama and decided to make his career as a dramatist. He began writing plays in 1913, enrolled in a playwriting course at Harvard during 1914, moved to Greenwich Village in 1915, and there joined up with a group of *avant-garde* writers who had formed a repertory company, called the Provincetown Players, which became one of the most influential groups in American theater, largely because of the plays that O'Neill produced for them during his early career.

O'Neill began by writing a series of one-act plays based on his earlier experiences at sea, strictly realistic plays in which he dramatized the illusions and preoccupations of men adrift in the world. By the early 1920s, he had begun writing full-length plays, still drawing on his fascination with the sea, but conveying a complex vision of tragic fate and frustration, as in the Pulitzer Prize-winning *Beyond the Horizon* (1920) and *Anna Christie* (1921). He then began to experiment with expressionistic techniques in *The Emperor Jones* (1920), a one-act psychodrama about a Negro "emperor" who flees a palace revolution and succumbs to his own fantasies and "the Little Formless Fears." The most striking innovation in this play was O'Neill's use of a drumbeat that began at pulse rate and gradually accelerated as Jones came closer and closer to death, ceasing only when he died. In *The Hairy Ape* (1922), O'Neill went even further with expressionist techniques by using contrastive symbolic settings (a furnace room versus fashionable Fifth Avenue), as well as choral speeches, and socially emblematic characters to dramatize the destruction of a young stoker, named Yank, who is unable to move outside of his class.

By the mid-1920s, his fascination with Freudian psychology had already become manifest in *Desire Under the Elms* (1924), a play dramatizing the tragic sexual attraction between a young man and his young stepmother. Then in *The Great God Brown* (1926), he used expressionistic techniques to dramatize what he was later to call the "profound hidden conflicts of the mind," by having the actors wear masks, as in Greek drama, to reflect their assumed personalities. By the late 1920s, his absorption with Freudian psychology had carried him so far into experimental theater that he tried to reveal the inner thoughts of his characters by having them interrupt their dialogue and express their hidden feelings in monologue to the audience, a strategy used in his nine-act play *Strange Interlude* (1928). In *Days without End* (1934), he carried his expressionistic rendering of Freudian themes to the logical extreme by having two actors play the conflicting sides of the main character. Yet even during this period when he was exploring the psychopathology of the human mind, he was also working in more realistic and naturalistic modes that anticipated the style of his late plays. In *Mourning Becomes Electra* (1931), a trilogy based on the *Oresteia* of Aeschylus, O'Neill dramatized the tragic fate of a family across several generations—a fate determined not by pride, as in the Greek drama, but by sexual instincts, psychic guilt, suicide, and remorse. During the early 1930s, he also wrote his only comedy, *Ah, Wilderness* (1933), a nostalgic work in the realistic style that depicts a family very much like his own, but which offers an idyllic family picture that was to be strikingly reversed in the years to follow.

Finally, in the late 1930s, he began to face up to his own past, first with *The Iceman Cometh* (1939), which was set in a saloon very much like the one where he had lived and had tried to kill himself, and which dramatized at length O'Neill's painful awareness of human frailty and self-deception. In *Long Day's Journey into Night* (1940), he was able "to face my dead at last," and he did so by turning the four members of his family—his father, mother, brother Jamie, and himself—into the "four haunted Tyrones," whose love-hate conflicts he completely exposed, but exposed with compassion, understanding, and forgiveness. Finally, in 1943, he completed his last autobiographical play, *A Moon for the Misbegotten*, a work based on the life of his alcoholic brother Jamie. It was the last of O'Neill's plays to be produced during his lifetime, and it almost never got staged at all.

The first production, in 1947, floundered in Columbus, was attacked by the Chamber of Commerce in Pittsburgh, censored by the police in Detroit, and never made it to New York until ten years later in 1957. And when it finally did get to New York, four years after O'Neill had died, the critics treated it as roughly as the businessmen and police had ten years earlier. Only in 1968, in a production at Circle in the Square, did it finally find a receptive audience, though when it was revived again in the mid-1970s critics were ready to recognize it as one of O'Neill's finest plays, possibly even his greatest.

Like his other late autobiographical plays, *A Moon for the Misbegotten* is written in the style of what O'Neill himself called "faithful realism." Yet it is by no means an easy play to witness or produce. It calls for two exceptional performers, one of them a huge woman, "so oversize for a woman that she is almost a freak," and the other an actor capable of sustaining a third act monologue that goes on for several pages. Josie, the oversized virgin, whom everyone thinks of as a whore, gets a bottle of real bourbon, hoping to seduce Jim Tyrone, the cynical New York drunk, and so get him to marry her. But the planned seduction turns into a long confession by Jim, and the embrace that is meant to produce a shotgun marriage produces instead "a strangely tragic picture"—"this big sorrowful woman hugging a haggard-faced, middle-aged drunkard against her breast as if he were a sick child." A theatrically parallel tableau of hopelessness also appears in *A Long Day's Journey into Night*, at the end of the play, when the three drunken Tyrone men sit silently listening to the drugged Mary Tyrone. But *A Moon for the Misbegotten* moves beyond the momentary stasis to the waking-up, both literally and spiritually, when Jim awakens and tries to pretend that his confession did not happen, but then finally admits that he does remember and is glad to remember. Josie's final line is thus full of compassion, when she says gently to an empty stage, "May you have your wish and die in your sleep soon, Jim, darling. May you rest forever in forgiveness and peace."

The most memorable production of the play took place in 1973, when Colleen Dewhurst and Jason Robards, Jr., joined forces with the director José Quintero. Quintero had already directed *Long Day's Journey into Night*, in 1955, and Robards had played the role of Jamie Tyrone in that same production. In Colleen Dewhurst, they found an actress who could encompass Josie, both physically and emotionally. She was capable of the raucous, even coarse behavior that characterizes Josie for much of the first two acts (see Figure 2), and yet she could also show the understanding and compassion necessary as she listens to Jim throughout much of Act 3 (see Figure 3). Miss Dewhurst received rave notices from the critics, as reflected in the review reprinted following the text. The set for that production was an evocative rather than detailed re-creation of the farmhouse where the action of the play is located (see Figure 1), with its base in real objects, in the wooden floor, the rocks, and the chairs, just as the play has its roots in the reality of O'Neill's tormented past. Yet the set was also free of those objects, implying the world beyond, just as the play itself hints at a future free of guilt.

A MOON FOR THE MISBEGOTTEN

BY EUGENE O'NEILL

CHARACTERS

JOSIE HOGAN
PHIL HOGAN, *her father*
MIKE HOGAN, *her brother*
JAMES TYRONE, JR.
T. STEDMAN HARDER

SCENE

ACT 1: *The farmhouse. Around noon. Early September, 1923,* ACT 2: *The same, but with the interior of sitting room revealed—11 o'clock that night;* ACT 3: *The same as Act 1. No time elapses between Acts 2 and 3;* ACT 4: *The same— Dawn of the following morning.*

The play takes place in Connecticut at the home of tenant farmer, Phil Hogan, between the hours of noon on a day in early September, 1923, and the sunrise of the following day.

The house is not, to speak mildly, a fine example of New England architecture, placed so perfectly in its setting that it appears a harmonious part of the landscape, rooted in the earth. It has been moved to its present site, and looks it. An old box-like, clapboarded affair, with a shingled roof and brick chimney, it is propped up about two feet above ground by layers of timber blocks. There are two windows on the lower floor of this side of the house which faces front, and one window on the floor above. These windows have no shutters, curtains or shades. Each has at least one pane missing, a square of cardboard taking its place. The house had once been painted a repulsive yellow with brown trim, but the walls now are a blackened and weathered gray, flaked with streaks and splotches of dim lemon. Just around the left corner of the house, a flight of steps leads to the front door.

To make matters worse, a one-story, one-room addition has been tacked on at right. About twelve feet long by six high, this room which is JOSIE HOGAN'S *bedroom, is evidently homemade. Its walls and sloping roof are covered with tar paper, faded to dark gray. Close to where it joins the house, there is a door with a flight of three unpainted steps leading to the ground. At right of door is a small window.*

From these steps there is a footpath going around an old pear tree, at right-rear, through a field of hay stubble to a patch of woods. The same path also extends left to join a dirt road which leads up from the county highway (about a hundred yards off left) to the front door of the house, and thence back through a scraggly orchard of apple trees to the barn. Close to the house, under the window next to JOSIE'S *bedroom, there is a big boulder with a flat-top.*

ACT 1

(It is just before noon. The day is clear and hot.

The door of JOSIE'S *bedroom opens and she comes out on the steps, bending to avoid bumping her head.*

JOSIE *is twenty-eight. She is so oversize for a woman that she is almost a freak—five feet eleven in her stockings and weighs around one hundred and eighty. Her sloping shoulders are broad, her chest deep with large, firm breasts, her waist wide but slender by contrast with her hips and thighs. She has long smooth arms, immensely strong, although no muscles show. The same is true of her legs.*

She is more powerful than any but an exceptionally strong man, able to do the manual labor of two ordinary men. But there is no mannish quality about her. She is all woman.

The map of Ireland is stamped on her face, with its long upper lip and small nose, thick black eyebrows, black hair as coarse as a horse's mane, freckled, sunburned fair skin, high cheekbones and heavy jaw. It is not a pretty face, but her large dark-blue eyes give it a note of beauty, and her smile, revealing even white teeth, gives it charm.

She wears a cheap, sleeveless, blue cotton dress. Her feet are bare, the soles earth-stained and tough as leather.

She comes down the steps and goes left to the corner of the house and peers around it toward the barn. Then she moves swiftly to the right of the house and looks back.)

JOSIE: Ah, thank God. *(She goes back toward the steps as her brother,* MIKE, *appears hurrying up from right-rear.)*

*(*MIKE HOGAN *is twenty, about four inches shorter than his sister. He is sturdily built, but seems almost puny compared to her. He has a common Irish face, its expression sullen, or slyly cunning, or primly self-righteous. He never forgets that he is a good Catholic, faithful to all the observances, and so is one of the élite of Almighty God in a world of damned sinners composed of Protestants and bad Catholics. In brief,* MIKE *is a New England Irish Catholic Puritan, Grade B, and an extremely irritating youth to have around.)*

*(*MIKE *wears dirty overalls, a sweat-stained brown shirt. He carries a pitchfork.)*

ACT 1

JOSIE: Bad luck to you for a slowpoke. Didn't I tell you half-past eleven?

MIKE: How could I sneak here sooner with him peeking round the corner of the barn to catch me if I took a minute's rest, the way he always does? I had to wait till he went to the pig pen. (*He adds viciously.*) Where he belongs, the old hog! (*JOSIE's right arm strikes with surprising swiftness and her big hand lands on the side of his jaw. She means it to be only a slap, but his head jerks back and he stumbles, dropping the pitchfork, and pleads cringingly.*) Don't hit me, Josie! Don't, now!

Directing Beat

JOSIE (*quietly*): Then keep your tongue off him. He's my father, too, and I like him, if you don't.

MIKE (*out of her reach—sullenly*): You're two of a kind, and a bad kind.

JOSIE (*good naturedly*): I'm proud of it. And I didn't hit you, or you'd be flat on the ground. It was only a love tap to waken your wits, so you'll use them. If he catches you running away, he'll beat you half to death. Get your bag now. I've packed it. It's inside the door of my room with your coat laid over it. Hurry now, while I see what he's doing. (*She moves quickly to peer around the corner of the house at left. He goes up the steps into her room and returns carrying an old coat and a cheap bulging satchel. She comes back.*) There's no sight of him. (*MIKE drops the satchel on the ground while he puts on the coat.*) I put everything in the bag. You can change to your Sunday suit in the can at the station or in the train, and don't forget to wash your face. I know you want to look your best when our brother, Thomas, sees you on his doorstep. (*Her tone becomes derisively amused.*) And him way up in the world, a noble sergeant of the Bridgeport police. Maybe he'll get you on the force. It'd suit you. I can see you leading drunks to the lockup while you give them a lecture on temperance. Or if Thomas can't get you a job, he'll pass you along to our brother, John, the noble barkeep in Meriden. He'll teach you the trade. You'll make a nice one, who'll never steal from the till, or drink, and who'll tell customers they've had enough and better go home just when they're beginning to feel happy. (*She sighs regretfully.*) Ah, well, Mike, you was born a priest's pet, and there's no help for it.

MIKE: That's right! Make fun of me again, because I want to be decent.

JOSIE: You're worse than decent. You're virtuous.

MIKE: Well that's a thing nobody can say about—(*He stops, a bit ashamed, but mostly afraid to finish.*)

JOSIE (*amused*): About me? No, and what's more, they don't. (*She smiles mockingly.*) I know what a trial it's been to you, Mike, having a sister who's the scandal of the neighborhood.

MIKE: It's you that's saying it, not me. I don't want to part with hard feelings. And I'll keep on praying for you.

JOSIE (*roughly*): Och! To hell with your prayers!

MIKE (*stiffly*): I'm going. (*He picks up his bag.*)

JOSIE (*her manner softening*): Wait. (*She comes to him.*) Don't mind my rough tongue, Mike. I'm sorry to see you go, but it's the best thing for you. That's why I'm helping you, the same as I helped Thomas and John. You can't stand up to the Old Man any more than Thomas or John could, and the old divil would always keep you a slave. I wish you all the luck in the world, Mike. I know you'll get on—and God bless you. (*Her voice has softened, and she blinks back tears. She kisses him—then fumbling in the pocket of her dress, pulls out a little roll of one-dollar bills and presses it in his hand.*) Here's a little present over your fare. I took it from his little green bag, and won't he be wild when he finds out! But I can handle him.

MIKE (*enviously*): You can. You're the only one. (*Gratefully moved for a second.*) Thank you, Josie. You've a kind heart. (*Then virtuously.*) But I don't like taking stolen money.

JOSIE: Don't be a bigger jackass than you are already. Tell your conscience it's a bit of the wages he's never given you.

MIKE: That's true, Josie. It's rightfully mine. (*He shoves the money into his pocket.*)

JOSIE: Get along now, so you won't miss the trolley. And don't forget to get off the train at Bridgeport. Give my love to Thomas and John. No, never mind. They've not written me in years. Give them a boot in the tail for me.

MIKE: That's nice talk for a woman. You've a tongue as dirty as the Old Man's.

JOSIE (*impatiently*): Don't start preaching, like you love to, or you'll never go.

MIKE: You're as bad as he is, almost. It's his influence made you what you are, and him always scheming how he'll cheat people, selling them a broken-down nag or a sick cow or pig that he's doctored up to look good for a day or two. It's no better than stealing, and you help him.

JOSIE: I do. Sure, it's grand fun.

MIKE: You ought to marry and have a home of your own away from this shanty and stop your shameless ways with men. (*He adds, not without moral satisfaction.*) Though it'd be hard to find a decent man who'd have you now.

JOSIE: I don't want a decent man, thank you. They're no fun. They're all sticks like you. And I wouldn't marry the best man on earth and be tied down to him alone.

MIKE (*with a cunning leer*): Not even Jim Tyrone, I suppose? (*She stares at him.*) You'd like being tied to money, I know that, and he'll be rich when his mother's estate is settled. (*Sarcastically.*) I suppose

naturalism: philosophical/pessimistic view of realism.

you've never thought of that? Don't tell me! I've watched you making sheep's eyes at him.

JOSIE (*contemptuously*): So I'm leading Jim on to propose, am I?

MIKE: I know it's crazy, but maybe you're hoping if you got hold of him alone when he's mad drunk— Anyway, talk all you please to put me off, I'll bet my last penny you've cooked up some scheme to hook him, and the Old Man put you up to it. Maybe he thinks if he caught you with Jim and had witnesses to prove it, and his shotgun to scare him—

JOSIE (*controlling her anger*): You're full of bright thoughts. I wouldn't strain my brains any more, if I was you.

MIKE: Well, I wouldn't put it past the Old Man to try any trick. And I wouldn't put it past you, God forgive you. You've never cared about your virtue, or what man you went out with. You've always been brazen as brass and proud of your disgrace. You can't deny that, Josie.

JOSIE: I don't. (*Then ominously.*) You'd better shut up now. I've been holding my temper, because we're saying good-bye. (*She stands up.*) But I'm losing patience.

MIKE (*hastily*): Wait till I finish and you won't be mad at me. I was going to say I wish you luck with your scheming, for once. I hate Jim Tyrone's guts, with his quotin' Latin and his high-toned Jesuit College education, putting on airs as if he was too good to wipe his shoes on me, when he's nothing but a drunken bum who never done a tap of work in his life, except acting on the stage while his father was alive to get him the jobs. (*Vindictively.*) I'll pray you'll find a way to nab him, Josie, and skin him out of his last nickel!

JOSIE (*makes a threatening move toward him*): One more word out of you— (*Then contemptuously.*) You're a dirty tick and it'd serve you right if I let you stay gabbing until Father came and beat you to a jelly, but I won't. I'm too anxious to be rid of you. (*Roughly.*) Get out of here, now! Do you think he'll stay all day with the pigs, you gabbing fool? (*She goes left to peer around the corner of the house— with real alarm.*) There he is coming up to the barn. (MIKE *grabs the satchel, terrified. He slinks swiftly around the corner and disappears along the path to the woods, right-rear. She keeps watching her father and does not notice* MIKE's *departure.*) He's looking toward the meadow. He sees you're not working. He's running down there. He'll come here next. You'd better run for your life! (*She peeks around the corner again—with amused admiration.*) Look at my poor old father pelt. He's as spry on his stumpy legs as a yearling—and as full of rage as a nest of wasps! (*She laughs and comes back to look along the path to the woods.*) Well, that's

the last of you, Mike, and good riddance. It was the little boy you used to be that I had to mother, and not you, I stole the money for. (*This dismisses him. She sighs.*) Well, himself will be here in a minute. I'd better be ready. (*She reaches in her bedroom corner by the door and takes out a sawed-off broom handle.*) Not that I need it, but it saves his pride. (*She sits on the steps with the broom handle propped against the steps near her right hand. A moment later, her father,* PHIL HOGAN, *comes running up from left-rear and charges around the corner of the house, his arms pumping up and down, his fists clenched, his face full of fighting fury.*)

(HOGAN *is fifty-five, about five feet six. He has a thick neck, lumpy, sloping shoulders, a barrel-like trunk, stumpy legs, and big feet. His arms are short and muscular, with large hairy hands. His head is round with thinning sandy hair. His face is fat with a snub nose, long upper lip, big mouth, and little blue eyes with bleached lashes and eyebrows that remind one of a white pig's. He wears heavy brogans, filthy overalls, and a dirty short-sleeved undershirt. Arms and face are sunburned and freckled. On his head is an old wide-brimmed hat of coarse straw that would look more becoming on a horse. His voice is high-pitched with a pronounced brogue.*)

HOGAN (*stops as he turns the corner and sees her—furiously*): Where is he? Is he hiding in the house? I'll wipe the floors with him, the lazy bastard! (*Turning his anger against her.*) Haven't you a tongue in your head, you great slut you?

JOSIE (*with provoking calm*): Don't be calling me names, you bad-tempered old hornet, or maybe I'll lose my temper, too.

HOGAN: To hell with your temper, you overgrown cow!

JOSIE: I'd rather be a cow than an ugly little buck goat. You'd better sit down and cool off. Old men shouldn't run around raging in the noon sun. You'll get sunstroke.

JOGAN: To hell with sunstroke! Have you seen him?

JOSIE: Have I seen who?

HOGAN: Mike! Who else would I be after, the Pope? He was in the meadow, but the minute I turned my back he sneaked off. (*He sees the pitchfork.*) There's his pitchfork! Will you stop your lying!

JOSIE: I haven't said I didn't see him.

HOGAN: Then don't try to help him hide from me, or— Where is he?

JOSIE: Where you'll never find him.

HOGAN: We'll soon see! I'll bet he's in your room under the bed, the cowardly lump! (*He moves toward the steps.*)

JOSIE: He's not. He's gone like Thomas and John before him to escape your slave-driving.

HOGAN (*stares at her incredulously*): You mean he's run off to make his own way in the world?

JOSIE: He has. So make up your mind to it, and sit down.

HOGAN (*baffled, sits on the boulder and takes off his hat to scratch his head–with a faint trace of grudging respect*): I'd never dream he had that much spunk. (*His temper rising again.*) And I know damned well he hadn't, not without you to give him the guts and help him, like the great soft fool you are!

JOSIE: Now don't start raging again, Father.

HOGAN (*seething*): You've stolen my satchel to give him, I suppose, like you did before for Thomas and John?

JOSIE: It was my satchel, too. Didn't I help you in the trade for the horse, when you got the Crowleys to throw in the satchel for good measure? I was up all night fixing that nag's forelegs so his knees wouldn't buckle together till after the Crowleys had him a day or two.

HOGAN (*forgets his anger to grin reminiscently*): You've a wonderful way with animals, God bless you. And do you remember the two Crowleys came back to give me a beating, and I licked them both?

JOSIE (*with calculating flattery*): You did. You're a wonderful fighter. Sure, you could give Jack Dempsey himself a run for his money.

HOGAN (*with sharp suspicion*): I could, but don't try to change the subject and fill me with blarney.

JOSIE: All right. I'll tell the truth. They were getting the best of you till I ran out and knocked one of them tail over tin cup against the pigpen.

HOGAN (*outraged*): You're a liar! They was begging for mercy before you came. (*Furiously.*) You thief, you! You stole my fine satchel for that lump! And I'll bet that's not all. I'll bet, like when Thomas and John sneaked off, you— (*He rises from the boulder threateningly.*) Listen, Josie, if you found where I had my little green bag, and stole money to give to that lousy altar boy, I'll—

JOSIE (*rises from the steps with the broom handle in her right hand*): Well, I did. So now what'll you do? Don't be threatening me. You know I'll beat better sense in your skull if you lay a finger on me.

HOGAN: I never yet laid hands on a woman—not when I was sober—but if it wasn't for that club— (*Bitterly.*) A fine curse God put on me when he gave me a daughter as big and strong as a bull, and as vicious and disrespectful. (*Suddenly his eyes twinkle and he grins admiringly.*) Be God, look at you standing there with the club! If you ain't the damnedest daughter in Connecticut, who is? (*He chuckles and sits on the boulder again.*)

JOSIE (*laughs and sits on the steps putting the club away*): And if you ain't the damnedest father in Connecticut, who is?

HOGAN (*takes a clay pipe and plug of tobacco and knife from his pocket. He cuts the plug and stuffs his pipe–without*

rancor): How much did you steal, Josie?

JOSIE: Six dollars only.

HOGAN: *Only!* Well, God grant someone with wits will see that dopey gander at the depot and sell him the railroad for the six. (*Grumbling.*) It isn't the money I mind, Josie—

JOSIE: I know. Sure, what do you care for money? You'd give your last penny to the first beggar you met—if he had a shotgun pointed at your heart!

HOGAN: Don't be teasing. You know what I mean. It's the thought of that pious lump having my money that maddens me. I wouldn't put it past him to drop it in the collection plate next Sunday, he's that big a jackass.

JOSIE: I knew when you'd calmed down you'd think it worth six dollars to see the last of him.

HOGAN (*finishes filling his pipe*): Well, maybe I do. To tell the truth, I never liked him. (*He strikes a match on the seat of his overalls and lights his pipe.*) And I never liked Thomas and John, either.

JOSIE (*amused*): You've the same bad luck in sons I have in brothers.

HOGAN (*puffs ruminatively*): They all take after your mother's family. She was the only one in it had spirit, God rest her soul. The rest of them was a pious lousy lot. They wouldn't dare put food in their mouths before they said grace for it. They was too busy preaching temperance to have time for a drink. They spent so much time confessing their sins, they had no chance to do any sinning. (*He spits disgustedly.*) The scum of the earth! Thank God, you're like me and your mother.

JOSIE: I don't know if I should thank God for being like you. Sure, everyone says you're a wicked old tick, as crooked as a corkscrew.

HOGAN: I know. They're an envious lot, God forgive them. (*They both chuckle. He pulls on his pipe reflectively.*) You didn't get much thanks from Mike, I'll wager, for your help.

JOSIE: Oh, he thanked me kindly. And then he started to preach about my sins—and yours.

HOGAN: Oho, did he? (*Exploding.*) For the love of God, why didn't you hold him till I could give him one good kick for a parting blessing!

JOSIE: I near gave him one myself.

HOGAN: When I think your poor mother was killed bringing that crummy calf into life! (*Vindictively.*) I've never set foot in a church since, and never will. (*A pause. He speaks with a surprising sad gentleness.*) A sweet woman. Do you remember her, Josie? You were only a little thing when she died.

JOSIE: I remember her well. (*With a teasing smile which is half sad.*) She was the one could put you in your place when you'd come home drunk and want to tear down the house for the fun of it.

HOGAN (*with admiring appreciation*): Yes, she could do

it, God bless her. I only raised my hand to her once—just a slap because she told me to stop singing, it was after daylight. The next moment I was on the floor thinking a mule had kicked me. (*He chuckles.*) Since you've grown up, I've had the same trouble. There's no liberty in my own home.

JOSIE: That's lucky—or there wouldn't be any home.

HOGAN (*after a pause of puffing on his pipe*): What did that donkey, Mike, preach to you about?

JOSIE: Oh, the same as ever—that I'm the scandal of the countryside, carrying on with men without a marriage license.

HOGAN (*gives her a strange, embarrassed glance and then looks away. He does not look at her during the following dialogue. His manner is casual*): Hell roast his soul for saying it. But it's true enough.

JOSIE (*defiantly*): It is, and what of it? I don't care a damn for the scandal.

HOGAN: No. You do as you please and to hell with everyone.

JOSIE: Yes, and that goes for you, too, if you are my father. So don't you start preaching too.

HOGAN: Me, preach? Sure, the divil would die laughing. Don't bring me into it. I learned long since to let you go your own way because there's no controlling you.

JOSIE: I do my work and I earn my keep and I've a right to be free.

HOGAN: You have. I've never denied it.

JOSIE: No. You've never. I've often wondered why a man that likes fights as much as you didn't grab at the excuse of my disgrace to beat the lights out of the men.

HOGAN: Wouldn't I look a great fool, when everyone knows any man who tried to make free with you, and you not willing, would be carried off to the hospital? Anyway, I wouldn't want to fight an army. You've had too many sweethearts.

JOSIE (*with a proud toss of her head—boastfully*): That's because I soon get tired of any man and give him his walking papers.

HOGAN: I'm afraid you were born to be a terrible wanton woman. But to tell the truth, I'm well satisfied you're what you are, though I shouldn't say it, because if you was the decent kind, you'd have married some fool long ago, and I'd have lost your company and your help on the farm.

JOSIE (*with a trace of bitterness*): Leave it to you to think of your own interest.

HOGAN (*puffs on his pipe*): What else did my beautiful son, Mike, say to you?

JOSIE: Oh, he was full of stupid gab, as usual. He gave me good advice—

HOGAN (*grimly*): That was kind of him. It must have been good—

JOSIE: I ought to marry and settle down—if I could find a decent man who'd have me, which he was sure I couldn't.

HOGAN (*beginning to boil*): I tell you, Josie, it's going to be the saddest memory of my life I didn't get one last swipe at him!

JOSIE: So the only hope, he thought, was for me to catch some indecent man, who'd have money coming to him I could steal.

HOGAN (*gives her a quick, probing side glance—casually*): He meant Jim Tyrone?

JOSIE: He did. And the dirty tick accused you and me of making up a foxy scheme to trap Jim. I'm to get him alone when he's crazy drunk and lead him on to marry me. (*She adds in a hard, scornful tone.*) As if that would ever work. Sure, all the pretty little tarts on Broadway, New York, must have had a try at that, and much good it did them.

HOGAN (*again with a quick side glance—casually*): They must have, surely. But that's in the city where he's suspicious. You never can tell what he mightn't do here in the country, where he's innocent, with a moon in the sky to fill him with poetry and a quart of bad hootch inside of him.

JOSIE (*turns on him angrily*): Are you taking Mike's scheme seriously, you old goat?

HOGAN: I'm not. I only thought you wanted my opinion. (*She regards him suspiciously, but his face is blank, as if he hadn't a thought beyond enjoying his pipe.*)

JOSIE (*turning away*): And if that didn't work, Mike said maybe we had a scheme that I'd get Jim in bed with me and you'd come with witnesses and a shotgun, and catch him there.

HOGAN: Faith, me darlin' son never learnt that from his prayer book! He must have improved his mind on the sly.

JOSIE: The dirty tick!

HOGAN: Don't call him a tick. I don't like ticks but I'll say this for them, I never picked one off me yet was a hypocrite.

JOSIE: Him daring to accuse us of planning a rotten trick like that on Jim!

HOGAN (*as if he misunderstood her meaning*): Yes, it's as old as the hills. Everyone's heard of it. But it still works now and again, I'm told, and sometimes an old trick is best because it's so ancient no one would suspect you'd try it.

JOSIE (*staring at him resentfully*): That's enough out of you, Father. I never can tell to this day, when you put that dead mug on you, whether you're joking or not, but I don't want to hear any more—

HOGAN (*mildly*): I thought you wanted my honest opinion on the merits of Mike's suggestion.

JOSIE: Och, shut up, will you? I know you're only trying to make game of me. You like Jim and you'd

never play a dirty trick on him, not even if I was
willing.

HOGAN: No—not unless I found he was playing one
on me.

JOSIE: Which he'd never.

HOGAN: No, I wouldn't think of it, but my motto in
life is never trust anyone too far, not even myself.

JOSIE: You've reason for the last. I've often suspected
you sneak out of bed in the night to pick your
own pockets.

HOGAN: I wouldn't call it a dirty trick on him to get
you for a wife.

JOSIE (exasperatedly): God save us, are you off on that
again?

HOGAN: Well, you've put marriage in my head and I
can't help considering the merits of the case, as
they say. Sure, you're two of a kind, both great
disgraces. That would help make a happy marriage because neither of you could look down on
the other.

JOSIE: Jim mightn't think so.

HOGAN: You mean he'd think he was marrying beneath his station? He'd be a damned fool if he
had that notion, for his Old Man who'd worked
up from nothing to be rich and famous didn't
give a damn about station. Didn't I often see him
working on his grounds in clothes I wouldn't put
on a scarecrow, not caring who saw him? (With
admiring affection.) God rest him, he was a true
Irish gentleman.

JOSIE: He was, and didn't you swindle him, and make
me help you at it? I remember when I was a slip
of a girl, and you'd get a letter saying his agent
told him you were a year behind in the rent, and
he'd be damned if he'd stand for it, and he was
coming here to settle the matter. You'd make me
dress up, with my hair brushed and a ribbon in
it, and leave me to soften his heart before he saw
you. So I'd skip down the path to meet him, and
make a courtesy, and hold on to his hand, and
bat my eyes at him and lead him in the house,
and offer him a drink of the good whiskey you
didn't keep for company, and gape at him and
tell him he was the handsomest man in the
world, and the fierce expression he'd put on for
you would go away.

HOGAN (chuckles): You did it wonderful. You should
have gone on the stage.

JOSIE (dryly): Yes, that's what he'd tell me, and he'd
reach in his pocket and take out a half dollar,
and ask me if you hadn't put me up to it. So I'd
say yes, you had.

HOGAN (sadly): I never knew you were such a black
traitor, and you only a child.

JOSIE: And then you'd come and before he could get
a word out of him, you'd tell him you'd vacate

the premises unless he lowered the rent and
painted the house.

HOGAN: Be God, that used to stop him in his tracks.

JOSIE: It didn't stop him from saying you were the
damnedest crook ever came out of Ireland.

HOGAN: He said it with admiration. And we'd start
drinking and telling stories, and singing songs,
and by the time he left we were both too busy
cursing England to worry over the rent. (He grins
affectionately.) Oh, he was a great man entirely.

JOSIE: He was. He always saw through your tricks.

HOGAN: Didn't I know he would? Sure, all I wanted
was to give him the fun of seeing through them
so he couldn't be hard-hearted. That was the real
trick.

JOSIE (stares at him): You old devil, you've always a
trick hidden behind your tricks, so no one can
tell at times what you're after.

HOGAN: Don't be suspicious. Sure, I'd never try to
fool you. You know me too well. But we've gone
off the track. It's Jim we're discussing, not his
father. I was telling you I could see the merit in
your marrying him.

JOSIE (exasperatedly): Och, a cow must have kicked you
in the head this morning.

HOGAN: I'd never give it a thought if I didn't know
you had a soft spot in your heart for him.

JOSIE (resentfully): Well, I haven't! I like him, if that's
what you mean, but it's only to talk to, because
he's educated and quiet-spoken and has politeness even when he's drunkest, and doesn't roar
around cursing and singing, like some I could
name.

HOGAN: If you could see the light in your eyes when
he blarneys you—

JOSIE (roughly): The light in me foot! (Scornfully.) I'm
in love with him, you'll be saying next!

HOGAN (ignores this): And another merit of the case is,
he likes you.

JOSIE: Because he keeps dropping in here lately?
Sure, it's only when he gets sick of the drunks at
the Inn, and it's more to joke with you than see
me.

HOGAN: It's your happiness I'm considering when I
recommend your using your wits to catch him, if
you can.

JOSIE (jeeringly): If!

HOGAN: Who knows? With all the sweethearts you've
had, you must have a catching way with men.

JOSIE (boastfully): Maybe I have. But that doesn't
mean—

HOGAN: If you got him alone tonight—there'll be a
beautiful moon to fill him with poetry and loneliness, and—

JOSIE: That's one of Mike's dirty schemes.

HOGAN: Mike be damned! Sure, that's every woman's
scheme since the world was created. Without it

there'd be no population. (*Persuasively.*) There'd be no harm trying it, anyway.

JOSIE: And no use, either. (*Bitterly.*) Och, Father, don't play the jackass with me. You know, and I know, I'm an ugly overgrown lump of a woman, and the men that want me are no better than stupid bulls. Jim can have all the pretty, painted little Broadway girls he wants—and dancers on the stage, too—when he comes into his estate. That's the kind he likes.

HOGAN: I notice he's never married one. Maybe he'd like a fine strong handsome figure of a woman for a change, with beautiful eyes and hair and teeth and a smile.

JOSIE (*pleased, but jeering*): Thank you kindly for your compliments. Now I know a cow kicked you in the head.

HOGAN: If you think Jim hasn't been taking in your fine points, you're a fool.

JOSIE: You mean you've noticed him? (*Suddenly furious.*) Stop your lying!

HOGAN: Don't fly in a temper. All I'm saying is, there may be a chance in it to better yourself.

JOSIE (*scornfully*): Better myself by being tied down to a man who's drunk every night of his life? No thank you!

HOGAN: Sure, you're strong enough to reform him. A taste of that club you've got, when he came home to you paralyzed, and in a few weeks you'd have him a dirty prohibitionist.

JOSIE (*seriously*): It's true, if I was his wife, I'd cure him of drinking himself to death, if I had to kill him. (*Then angrily.*) Och, I'm sick of your crazy gab, Father! Leave me alone!

HOGAN: Well, let's put it another way. Don't tell me you couldn't learn to love the estate he'll come into.

JOSIE (*resentfully*): Ah, I've been waiting for that. That's what Mike said again. Now we've come to the truth behind all your blather of my liking him or him liking me. (*Her manner changing—defiantly.*) All right then. Of course I'd love the money. Who wouldn't? And why shouldn't I get my hands on it, if I could? He's bound to be swindled out of it, anyway. He'll go back to the Broadway he thinks is heaven, and by the time the pretty little tarts, and the barroom sponges and racetrack touts and gamblers are through with him he'll be picked clean. I'm no saint, God knows, but I'm decent and deserving compared to those scum.

HOGAN (*eagerly*): Be God, now you're using your wits. And where there's a will there's a way. You and me have never been beat when we put our brains together. I'll keep thinking it over, and you do the same.

JOSIE (*with illogical anger*): Well, I won't! And you keep your mad scheming to yourself. I won't listen to it.

HOGAN (*as if he were angry, too*): All right. The divil take you. It's all you'll hear from me. (*He pauses—then with great seriousness, turning to her.*) Except one thing— (*As she starts to shut him up—sharply.*) I'm serious, and you'd better listen, because it's about this farm. which is home to us.

JOSIE (*surprised, stares at him*): What about the farm?

HOGAN: Don't forget, if we have lived on it twenty years, we're only tenants and we could be thrown out on our necks any time. (*Quickly.*) Mind you, I don't say Jim would ever do it, rent or no rent, or let the executors do it, even if they wanted, which they don't, knowing they'd never find another tenant.

JOSIE: What's worrying you, then?

HOGAN: This. I've been afraid lately the minute the estate is out of probate, Jim will sell the farm.

JOSIE (*exasperatedly*): Of course he will! Hasn't he told us and promised you can buy it on easy time payments at the small price you offered?

HOGAN: Jim promises whatever you like when he's full of whiskey. He might forget a promise as easy when he's drunk enough.

JOSIE (*indignantly*): He'd never! And who'd want it except us? No one ever has in all the years—

HOGAN: Someone has lately. The agent got an offer last month, Jim told me, bigger than mine.

JOSIE: Och, Jim loves to try and get your goat. He was kidding you.

HOGAN: He wasn't. I can tell. He said he told the agent to tell whoever it was the place wasn't for sale.

JOSIE: Of course he did. Did he say who'd made the offer?

HOGAN: He didn't know. It came through a real-estate man who wouldn't tell who his client was. I've been trying to guess, but I can't think of anyone crazy enough unless it'd be some damn fool of a millionaire buying up land to make a great estate for himself, like our beautiful neighbor, Harder, the Standard Oil thief, did years ago. (*He adds with bitter fervency.*) May he roast in hell and his Limey superintendent with him!

JOSIE: Amen to that. (*Then, scornfully.*) This land for an estate? And if there was an offer, Jim's refused it, and that ends it. He wouldn't listen to any offer, after he's given his word to us.

HOGAN: Did I say he would—when he's in his right mind? What I'm afraid of is, he might be led into it sometime when he has one of his sneering bitter drunks on and talks like a Broadway crook himself, saying money is the only thing in the world, and everything and anyone can be bought if the price is big enough. You've heard him.

JOSIE: I have. But he doesn't fool me at all. He only acts like he's hard and shameless to get back at life when it's tormenting him—and who doesn't? *(He gives her a quick, curious side glance which she doesn't notice.)*

HOGAN: Or take the other kind of queer drunk he gets on sometimes when, without any reason you can see, he'll suddenly turn strange, and look sad, and stare at nothing as if he was mourning over some ghost inside him, and—

JOSIE: I think I know what comes over him when he's like that. It's the memory of his mother comes back and his grief for her death. *(Pityingly.)* Poor Jim.

HOGAN *(ignoring this)*: And whiskey seems to have no effect on him, like water off a duck's back. He'll keep acting natural enough, and you'd swear he wasn't bad at all, but the next day you find his brain was so paralyzed he don't remember a thing until you remind him? He's done a lot of mad things, when he was that way, he was sorry for after.

JOSIE *(scornfully)*: What drunk hasn't? But he'd never— *(Resentfully.)* I won't have you suspecting Jim without any cause, d'you hear me!

HOGAN: I don't suspect him. All I've said is, when a man gets as queer drunk as Jim, he doesn't know himself what he mightn't do, and we'd be damned fools if we didn't fear the possibility, however small it is, and do all we can to guard against it.

JOSIE: There's no possibility! And how could we guard against it, if there was?

HOGAN: Well, you can put yourself out to be extra nice to him, for one thing.

JOSIE: How nice is extra nice?

HOGAN: You ought to know. But here's one tip. I've noticed when you talk rough and brazen like you do to other men, he may grin like they do, as if he enjoyed it, but he don't. So watch your tongue.

JOSIE *(with a defiant toss of her head)*: I'll talk as I please, and if he don't like it he can lump it! *(Scornfully.)* I'm to pretend I'm a pure virgin, I suppose? That would fool him, wouldn't it, and him hearing all about me from the men at the Inn? *(She gets to her feet, abruptly changing the subject.)* We're wasting the day, blathering. *(Then her face hardening.)* If he ever went back on his word, no matter how drunk he was, I'd be with you in any scheme you made against him, no matter how dirty. *(Hastily.)* But it's all your nonsense. I'd never believe it. *(She comes and picks up the pitchfork.)* I'll go to the meadow and finish Mike's work. You needn't fear you'll miss his help on the farm.

HOGAN: A hell of a help! A weak lazy back and the appetitie of a drove of starving pigs! *(As she turns to go—suddenly bellicose.)* Leaving me, are you? When it's dinner time? Where's my dinner, you lazy cow?

JOSIE: There's stew on the stove, you bad-tempered runt. Go in and help yourself. I'm not hungry. Your gab has bothered my mind. I need hard work in the sun to clear it. *(She starts to go off toward rear-right.)*

HOGAN *(glancing down the road, off left-front)*: You'd better wait. There's a caller coming to the gate—and if I'm not mistaken, it's the light of your eyes himself.

JOSIE *(angrily)*: Shut up! *(She stares off—her face softens and grows pitying.)* Look at him when he thinks no one is watching, with his eyes on the ground. Like a dead man walking slow behind his own coffin. *(Then roughly.)* Faith, he must have a hangover. He sees us now. Look at the bluff he puts up, straightening himself and grinning. *(Resentfully.)* I don't want to meet him. Let him make jokes with you and play the old game about a drink you both think is such fun. That's all he comes for, anyway. *(She starts off again.)*

HOGAN: Are you running away from him? Sure, you must be afraid you're in love. *(JOSIE halts instantly and turns back defiantly. He goes on.)* Go in the house now, and wash your face, and tidy your dress, and give a touch to your hair. You want to look decent for him.

JOSIE *(angrily)*: I'll go in the house, but only to see the stew ain't burned, for I supposed you'll have the foxiness to ask him to have a bit to eat to keep in his good graces.

HOGAN: Why shouldn't I ask him? I know damned well he has no appetite this early in the day, but only a thirst.

JOSIE: Och, you make me sick, you sly miser! *(She goes through her bedroom, slamming the door behind her. HOGAN refills his pipe, pretending he doesn't notice TYRONE approaching, his eyes bright with droll expectation. JIM TYRONE enters along the road from the highway, left.)*

(TYRONE is in his early forties, around five feet nine, broad-shouldered and deep-chested. His naturally fine physique has become soft and soggy from dissipation, but his face is still good-looking despite its unhealthy puffiness and the bags under the eyes. He has thinning dark hair, parted and brushed back to cover a bald spot. His eyes are brown, the whites congested and yellowish. His nose, big and aquiline, gives his face a certain Mephistophelian quality which is accentuated by his habitually cynical expression. But when he smiles without sneering, he still has the ghost of a former youthful irresponsible Irish charm— that of the beguiling ne'er-do-well, sentimental and romantic. It is his humor and charm which have kept him attractive to women, and popular with men as a drinking

companion. He is dressed in an expensive dark-brown suit, tight-fitting and drawn in at the waist, dark-brown made-to-order shoes and silk socks, a white silk shirt, silk handkerchief in breast pocket, a dark tie. This get-up suggests that he follows a style set by well-groomed Broadway gamblers who would like to be mistaken for Wall Street brokers.)

(He has had enough pick-me-ups to recover from morning-after nausea and steady his nerves. During the following dialogue, he and HOGAN *are like players at an old familiar game where each knows the other's moves, but which still amuses them.)*

TYRONE *(approaches and stands regarding* HOGAN *with a sardonic relish.* HOGAN *scratches a match on the seat of his overalls and lights his pipe, pretending not to see him.* TYRONE *recites with feeling):*
"*Fortunate senex, ergo tua rura manebunt, et tibi magna satis, quamvis lapis omnia nudus.*"

HOGAN *(mutters):* It's the landlord again, and my shotgun not handy. *(He looks up at* TYRONE.*)* Is it Mass you're saying, Jim? That was Latin. I know it by ear. What the hell—insult does it mean?

TYRONE: Translated very freely into Irish English, something like this. *(He imitates* HOGAN's *brogue.)* "Ain't you the lucky old bastard to have this beautiful farm, if it is full of nude rocks."

HOGAN: I like that part about the rocks. If cows could eat them this place would make a grand dairy farm. *(He spits.)* It's easy to see you've a fine college education. It must be a big help to you conversing with whores and barkeeps.

TYRONE: Yes, a very valuable worldly asset. I was once offered a job as office boy—until they discovered I wasn't qualified because I had no Bachelor of Arts diploma. There had been a slight misunderstanding just before I was to graduate.

HOGAN: Between you and the Fathers? I'll wager!

TYRONE: I made a bet with another Senior I could get a tart from the Haymarket to visit me, introduce her to the Jebs as my sister—and get away with it.

HOGAN: But you didn't?

TYRONE: Almost. It was a memorable day in the halls of learning. All the students were wise and I had them rolling in the aisles as I showed Sister around the grounds, accompanied by one of the Jebs. He was a bit suspicious at first, but Dutch Maisie—her professional name—had no make-up on, and was dressed in black, and had eaten a pound of Sen-Sen to kill the gin on her breath, and seemed such a devout girl that he forgot his suspicions. *(He pauses.)* Yes, all would have been well, but she was a mischievous minx, and had her own ideas of improving on my joke. When she was saying good-bye to Father Fuller, she added innocently: "Christ, Father, it's nice and quiet out here away from the damned Sixth

Avenue El. I wish to hell I could stay here!" *(Dryly.)* But she didn't, and neither did I.

HOGAN *(chuckles delightedly):* I'll bet you didn't. God bless Dutch Maisie! I'd like to have known her.

TYRONE *(sits down on the steps—with a change of manner):* Well, how's the Duke of Donegal this fine day?

HOGAN: Never better.

TYRONE: Slaving and toiling as usual, I see.

HOGAN: Hasn't a poor man a right to his noon rest without being sneered at by his rich landlord?

TYRONE: "Rich" is good. I would be, if you'd pay up your back rent.

HOGAN: You ought to pay me, instead, for occupying this rockpile, miscalled a farm. *(His eyes twinkling.)* But I have fine reports to give you of a promising harvest. The milkweed and the thistles is in thriving condition, and I never saw the poison ivy so bounteous and beautiful. *(*TYRONE *laughs. Without their noticing,* JOSIE *appears in the doorway behind* TYRONE. *She has tidied up and arranged her hair. She smiles down at* JIM, *her face softening, pleased to hear him laugh.)*

TYRONE: You win. Where did Josie go, Phil? I saw her here—

HOGAN: She ran in the house to make herself beautiful for you.

JOSIE *(breaks in roughly):* You're a liar. *(To* TYRONE, *her manner one of bold, free-and-easy familiarity.)* Hello, Jim.

TYRONE *(starts to stand up):* Hello, Josie.

JOSIE *(puts a hand on his shoulder and pushes him down):* Don't get up. Sure, you know I'm no lady. *(She sits on the top step—banteringly.)* How's my fine Jim this beautiful day? You don't look so bad. You must have stopped at the Inn for an eye-opener—or ten of them.

TYRONE: I've felt worse. *(He looks up at her sardonically.)* And how's my Virgin Queen of Ireland?

JOSIE: Yours, is it? Since when? And don't be miscalling me a virgin. You'll ruin my reputation, if you spread that lie about me. *(She laughs.* TYRONE *is staring at her. She goes on quickly.)* How is it you're around so early? I thought you never got up till afternoon.

TYRONE: Couldn't sleep. One of those heebie-jeebie nights when the booze keeps you awake instead of— *(He catches her giving him a pitying look—irritably.)* But what of it!

JOSIE: Maybe you had no woman in bed with you, for a change. It's a terrible thing to break the habit of years.

TYRONE *(shrugs his shoulders):* Maybe.

JOSIE: What's the matter with the tarts in town, they let you do it? I'll bet the ones you know on Broadway, New York, wouldn't neglect their business.

TYRONE (*pretends to yawn boredly*): Maybe not. (*Then irritably.*) Cut out the kidding, Josie. It's too early.

HOGAN (*who has been taking everything in without seeming to*): I told you not to annoy the gentleman with your rough tongue.

JOSIE: Sure I thought I was doing my duty as hostess making him feel at home.

TYRONE (*stares at her again*): Why all the interest lately in the ladies of the profession, Josie?

JOSIE: Oh, I've been considering joining their union. It's easier living than farming, I'm sure. (*Then resentfully.*) You think I'd starve at it, don't you because your fancy is for dainty dolls of women! But other men like—

TYRONE (*with sudden revulsion*): For God's sake, cut out that kind of talk, Josie! It sounds like hell.

JOSIE (*stares at him startledly–then resentfully*): Oh, it does, does it? (*Forcing a scornful smile.*) I'm shocking you, I suppose? (HOGAN *is watching them both, not missing anything in their faces, while he seems intent on his pipe.*)

TYRONE (*looking a bit sheepish and annoyed at himself for his interest–shrugs his shoulders*): No. Hardly. Forget it. (*He smiles kiddingly.*) Anyway, who told you I fall for the dainty dolls? That's all a thing of the past. I like them tall and strong and voluptuous, now, with beautiful big breasts. (*She blushes and looks confused and is furious with herself for doing so.*)

HOGAN: There you are, Josie, darlin'. Sure he couldn't speak fairer than that.

JOSIE (*recovers herself*): He couldn't, indeed. (*She pats* TYRONE's *head–playfully.*) You're a terrible blarneying liar, Jim, but thank you just the same. (TYRONE *turns his attention to* HOGAN. *He winks at* JOSIE *and begins in an exaggeratedly casual manner.*)

TYRONE: I don't blame you, Mr. Hogan, for taking it easy on such a blazing hot day.

HOGAN (*doesn't look at him. His eyes twinkle*): Hot, did you say? I find it cool, meself. Take off your coat if you're hot, Mister Tyrone.

TYRONE: One of the most stifling days I've ever known. Isn't it, Josie?

JOSIE (*smiling*): Terrible. I know you must be perishing.

HOGAN: I wouldn't call it a damned bit stifling.

TYRONE: It parches the membranes in your throat.

HOGAN: The what? Never mind. I can't have them, for my throat isn't parched at all. If yours is, Mister Tyrone, there's a well full of water at the back.

TYRONE: Water? That's something people wash with, isn't it? I mean, some people.

HOGAN: So I've heard. But, like you, I find it hard to believe. It's a dirty habit. They must be foreigners.

TYRONE: As I was saying, my throat is parched after the long dusty walk I took just for the pleasure of being your guest.

HOGAN: I don't remember inviting you, and the road is hard macadam with divil a speck of dust, and it's less than a quarter mile from the Inn here.

TYRONE: I didn't have a drink at the Inn. I was waiting until I arrived here, knowing that you—

HOGAN: Knowing I'd what?

TYRONE: Your reputation as a generous host—

HOGAN: The world must be full of liars. So you didn't have a drink at the Inn? Then it must be the air itself smells of whiskey today, although I didn't notice it before you came. You've gone on the water-wagon, I suppose? Well, that's fine, and I ask pardon for misjudging you.

TYRONE: I've wanted to go on the wagon for the past twenty-five years, but the doctors have strictly forbidden it. It would be fatal—with my weak heart.

HOGAN: So you've a weak heart? Well, well, and me thinking all along it was your head. I'm glad you told me. I was just going to offer you a drink, but whiskey is the worst thing—

TYRONE: The Docs say it's a matter of life and death. I must have a stimulant—one big drink, at least, whenever I strain my heart walking in the hot sun.

HOGAN: Walk back to the Inn, then, and give it a good strain, so you can buy yourself two big drinks.

JOSIE (*laughing*): Ain't you the fools, playing that old game between you, and both of you pleased as punch!

TYRONE (*gives up with a laugh*): Hasn't he ever been known to loosen up, Josie?

JOSIE: You ought to know. If you need a drink you'll have to buy it from him or die of thirst.

TYRONE: Well, I'll bet this is one time he's going to treat.

HOGAN: Be God, I'll take that bet!

TYRONE: After you've heard the news I've got for you, you'll be so delighted you won't be able to drag out the old bottle quick enough.

HOGAN: I'll have to be insanely delighted.

JOSIE (*full of curiosity*): Shut up, Father. What news, Jim?

TYRONE: I have it off the grapevine that a certain exalted personage will drop in on you before long.

HOGAN: It's the sheriff again. I know by the pleased look on your mug.

TYRONE: Not this time. (*He pauses tantalizingly.*)

JOSIE: Bad luck to you, can't you tell us who?

TYRONE: A more eminent grafter than the sheriff— (*Sneeringly.*) A leading aristocrat in our Land of the Free and Get-Rich-Quick, whose boots are licked by one and all—and one of the Kings of our Republic by Divine Right of Inherited Swag. In short, I refer to your good neighbor, T. Stedman Harder, Standard Oil's sappiest child, whom I know you both love so dearly. *(There is a pause after this announcement.* HOGAN *and* JOSIE *stiffen, and their eyes begin to glitter. But they can't believe their luck at first.)*

HOGAN *(in an ominous whisper)*: Did you say Harder is coming to call on us, Jim?

JOSIE: It's too good to be true.

TYRONE *(watching them with amusement)*: No kidding. The great Mr. Harder intends to stop here on his way back to lunch from a horseback ride.

JOSIE: How do you know?

TYRONE: Simpson told me. I ran into him at the Inn.

HOGAN: That English scum of a superintendent!

TYRONE: He was laughing himself sick. He said he suggested the idea to Harder—told him you'd be overwhelmed with awe if he deigned to interview you in person.

HOGAN: Overwhelmed isn't the word. Is it, Josie?

JOSIE: It isn't indeed, Father.

TYRONE: For once in his life, Simpson is cheering for you. He doesn't like his boss. In fact, he asked me to tell you he hopes you kill him.

HOGAN *(disdainfully)*: To hell with the Limey's good wishes. I'd like both of them to call together.

JOSIE: Ah, well, we can't have everything. *(to* TYRONE*)* What's the reason Mr. Harder decided to notice poor, humble scum the like of us?

TYRONE *(grinning)*: That's right, Josie. Be humble. He'll expect you to know your place.

HOGAN: Will he now? Well, well. *(With a great happy sigh.)* This is going to be a beautiful day entirely.

JOSIE: But what's Harder's reason, Jim?

TYRONE: Well, it seems he has an ice pond on his estate.

HOGAN: Oho! So that's it!

TYRONE: Yes. That's it. Harder likes to keep up the good old manorial customs. He clings to his ice pond. And your pigpen isn't far from his ice pond.

HOGAN: A nice little stroll for the pigs, that's all.

TYRONE: And somehow Harder's fence in that vicinity has a habit of breaking down.

HOGAN: Fences are queer things. You can't depend on them.

TYRONE: Simpson says he's had it repaired a dozen times, but each time on the following night it gets broken down again.

JOSIE: What a strange thing! It must be the bad fairies. I can't imagine who else could have done it. Can you, Father?

HOGAN: I can't, surely.

TYRONE: Well, Simpson can. He knows you did it and he told his master so.

HOGAN *(disdainfully)*: Master is the word. Sure, the

English can't live unless they have a lord's backside to kiss, the dirty slaves.

TYRONE: The result of those breaks in the fence is that your pigs stroll—as you so gracefully put it—stroll through to wallow happily along the shores of the ice pond.

HOGAN: Well, why not? Sure, they're fine ambitious American-born pigs and they don't miss any opportunities. They're like Harders' father who made the money for him.

TYRONE: I agree, but for some strange reason Harder doesn't look forward to the taste of pig in next summer's ice water.

HOGAN: He must be delicate. Remember he's delicate, Josie, and leave your club in the house. *(He bursts into joyful menacing laughter.)* Oh, be God and be Christ in the mountains! I've pined to have a quiet word with Mr. Harder for years, watching him ride past in his big shiny automobile with his snoot in the air, and being tormented always by the complaints of his Limey superintendent. Oh, won't I welcome him!

JOSIE: Won't *we*, you mean. Sure, I love him as much as you.

HOGAN: I'd kiss you, Jim, for this beautiful news, if you wasn't so damned ugly. Maybe Josie'll do it for me. She has a stronger stomach.

JOSIE: I will! He's earned it. *(She pulls* TYRONE'S *head back and laughingly kisses him on the lips. Her expression changes. She looks startled and confused, stirred and at the same time frightened. She forces a scornful laugh.)* Och, there's no spirit in you! It's like kissing a corpse.

TYRONE *(gives her a strange surprised look—mockingly)*: Yes? *(Turning to* HOGAN.*)* Well, how about that drink, Phil? I'll leave it to Josie if drinks aren't on the house.

HOGAN: *I* won't leave it to Josie. She's prejudiced, being in love.

JOSIE *(angrily)*: Shut up, you old liar! *(Then guiltily, forcing a laugh.)* Don't talk nonsense to sneak out of treating Jim.

HOGAN *(sighing)*: All right, Josie. Go get the bottle and one small glass, or he'll never stop nagging me. I can turn my back, so the sight of him drinking free won't break my heart. *(*JOSIE *gets up, laughing, and goes in the house.* HOGAN *peers at the road off left.)* On his way back to lunch you said? Then it's time— *(Fervently.)* O Holy Joseph, don't let the bastard change his mind!

TYRONE *(beginning to have qualms)*: Listen, Phil. Don't get too enthusiastic. He has a big drag around here, and he'll have you pinched, sure as hell, if you beat him up.

HOGAN: Och, I'm no fool. *(*JOSIE *comes out with a bottle and a tumbler.)* Will you listen to this, Josie. He's warning me not to give Harder a beating—as if

I'd dirty my hands on the scum.

JOSIE: As if we'd need to. Sure, all we want is a quiet chat with him.

HOGAN: That's all. As neighbor to neighbor.

JOSIE (hands TYRONE the bottle and tumbler): Here you are, Jim. Don't stint yourself.

HOGAN (mournfully): A fine daughter! I tell you a small glass and you give him a bucket! (As TYRONE pours a big drink, grinning at him, he turns away with a comic shudder.) That's a fifty-dollar drink, at least.

TYRONE: Here's luck, Phil.

HOGAN: I hope you drown. (TYRONE drinks and makes a wry face.)

TYRONE: The best chicken medicine I've ever tasted.

HOGAN: That's gratitude for you! Here, pass me the bottle. A drink will warm up my welcome for His Majesty. (He takes an enormous swig from the bottle.)

JOSIE (looking off left): There's two horseback riders on the county road now.

HOGAN: Praise be to God! It's him and a groom. (He sets the bottle on top of the boulder.)

JOSIE: That's McCabe. An old sweetheart of mine. (She glances at TYRONE provokingly–then suddenly worried and protective.) You get in the house, Jim. If Harder sees you here, he'll lay the whole blame on you.

TYRONE: Nix, Josie. You don't think I'm going to miss this, do you?

JOSIE: You can sit inside by my window and take in everything. Come on, now, don't be stubborn with me. (She puts her hands under his arms and lifts him to his feet as easily as if he was a child–banteringly.) Go into my beautiful bedroom. It's a nice place for you.

TYRONE (kiddingly): Just what I've been thinking for some time, Josie.

JOSIE (boldly): Sure, you've never given me a sign of it. Come up tonight and we'll spoon in the moonlight and you can tell me your thoughts.

TYRONE: That's a date. Remember, now.

JOSIE: It's you who'll forget. Go inside now, before it's too late. (She gives him a shove inside and closes the door.)

HOGAN (has been watching the visitor approach): He's dismounting—as graceful as a scarecrow, and his poor horse longing to give him a kick. Look at Mac grinning at us. Sit down, Josie. (She sits on the steps, he on the boulder.) Pretend you don't notice him. (T. STEDMAN HARDER appears at left. They act as if they didn't see him. HOGAN knocks out his pipe on the palm of his hand.)

(HARDER is in his late thirties but looks younger because his face is unmarked by worry, ambition, or any of the common hazards of life. No matter how long he lives, his four undergraduate years will always be for him the most significant in his life, and the moment of his highest achievement the time he was tapped for an exclusive Senior Society at the Ivy university to which his father had given millions. Since that day he has felt no need for further aspiring, no urge to do anything except settle down on his estate and live the life of a country gentleman, mildly interested in saddle horses and sport models of foreign automobiles. He is not the blatantly silly, playboy heir to millions whose antics make newspaper headlines. He doesn't drink much except when he attends his class reunion every spring–the most exciting episode of each year for him. He doesn't give wild parties, doesn't chase after musical-comedy cuties, is a mildly contented husband and father of three children. A not unpleasant man, affable, good-looking in an ordinary way, sunburnt and healthy, beginning to take on fat, he is simply immature, naturally lethargic, a bit stupid. Coddled from birth, everything arranged and made easy for him, deferred to because of his wealth, he usually has the self-confident attitude of acknowledged superiority, but assumes a supercilious insecure air when dealing with people beyond his ken. He is dressed in a beautifully tailored English tweed coat and whipcord riding breeches, immaculately polished English riding boots with spurs, and carries a riding crop in his hand.)

(It would be hard to find anyone more ill-equipped for combat with the HOGANS. He has never come in contact with anyone like them. To make matters easier for them he is deliberate in his speech, slow on the uptake, and has no sense of humor. The experienced strategy of the HOGANS in verbal battle is to take the offensive at once and never let an opponent get set to hit back. Also, they use a beautifully co-ordinated, bewildering change of pace, switching suddenly from jarring shouts to low, confidential vituperation. And they exaggerate their Irish brogues to confuse an enemy still further.)

HARDER (walks toward HOGAN–stiffly).: Good morning. I want to see the man who runs this farm.

HOGAN (surveys him deliberately, his little pig eyes gleaming with malice): You do, do you? Well, you've seen him. So run along now and play with your horse, and don't bother me. (He turns to JOSIE, who is staring at HARDER, much to his discomfiture, as if she had discovered a cockroach in her soup.) D'you see what I see, Josie? Be God, you'll have to give that damned cat of yours a spanking for bringing it to our doorstep.

HARDER (determined to be authoritative and command respect–curtly): Are you Hogan?

HOGAN (insultingly): I am Mister Philip Hogan—to a gentleman.

JOSIE (glares at HARDER): Where's your manners, you spindle-shanked jockey? Were you brought up in a stable?

HARDER (does not fight with ladies, and especially not with this lady–ignoring her): My name is Harder. (He *obviously expects them to be immediately impressed and apologetic.)*

HOGAN *(contemptuously)*: Who asked you your name, me little man?

JOSIE: Sure, who in the world cares who the hell you are?

HOGAN: But if you want to play politeness, we'll play with you. Let me introduce you to my daughter, Harder—Miss Josephine Hogan.

JOSIE *(petulantly)*: I don't want to meet him, Father. I don't like his silly sheep's face, and I've no use for jockeys, anyway. I'll wager he's no damned good to a woman. *(From inside her bedroom comes a burst of laughter. This revelation of an unseen audience startles HARDER. He begins to look extremely unsure of himself.)*

HOGAN: I don't think he's a jockey. It's only the funny pants he's wearing. I'll bet if you asked his horse, you'd find he's no cowboy either. *(to HARDER, jeeringly)* Come, tell us the truth, me honey. Don't you kiss your horse each time you mount and beg him, please don't throw me today, darlin', and I'll give you an extra bucket of oats. *(He bursts into an extravagant roar of laughter, slapping his thigh, and JOSIE guffaws with him, while they watch the disconcerting effect of this theatrical mirth on HARDER.)*

HARDER *(beginning to lose his temper)*: Listen to me, Hogan! I didn't come here— *(He is going to add "to listen to your damned jokes" or something like that, but HOGAN silences him.)*

HOGAN *(shouts)*: What? What's that you said? *(He stares at the dumbfounded HARDER with droll amazement, as if he couldn't believe his ears.)* You didn't come here? *(He turns to JOSIE—in a whisper.)* Did you hear that, Josie? *(He takes off his hat and scratches his head in comic bewilderment.)* Well, that's a puzzle, surely. How d'you suppose he got here?

JOSIE: Maybe the stork brought him, bad luck to it for a dirty bird. *(Again TYRONE's laughter is heard from the bedroom.)*

HARDER *(so off balance now he can only repeat angrily)*: I said I didn't come here—

HOGAN *(shouts)*: Wait! Wait, now! *(Threateningly.)* We've had enough of that. Say it a third time and I'll send my daughter to telephone the asylum.

HARDER *(forgetting he's a gentleman)*: Damn you, I'm the one who's had enough—!

JOSIE *(shouts)*: Hold your dirty tongue! I'll have no foul language in my presence.

HOGAN: Och, don't mind him, Josie. He's said he isn't here, anyway, so we won't talk to him behind his back. *(He regards HARDER with pitying contempt.)* Sure, ain't you the poor crazy creature? Do you want us to believe you're a ghost?

HARDER *(notices the bottle on the boulder for the first time—tries to be contemptuously tolerant and even to smile*

with condescending disdain): Ah! I understand now. You're drunk. I'll come back sometime when you're sober—or send Simpson— *(He turns away, glad of an excuse to escape.)*

JOSIE *(jumps up and advances on him menacingly)*: No, you don't! You'll apologize first for insulting a lady—insinuating I'm drunk this early in the day—or I'll knock some good breeding in you!

HARDER *(actually frightened now)*: I—I said nothing about you—

HOGAN *(gets up to come between them)*: Aisy now, Josie. He didn't mean it. He don't know what he means, the poor loon. *(to HARDER—pityingly)* Run home, that's a good lad, before your keeper misses you.

HARDER *(hastily)*: Good day. *(He turns eagerly toward left but suddenly HOGAN grabs his shoulder and spins him around—then shifts his grip to the lapel of HARDER's coat.)*

HOGAN *(grimly)*: Wait now, me Honey Boy. I'll have a word with you, if you plaze. I'm beginning to read some sense into this. You mentioned that English bastard, Simpson. I know who you are now.

HARDER *(outraged)*: Take your hands off me, you drunken fool. *(He raises his riding crop.)*

JOSIE *(grabs it and tears it from his hand with one powerful twist—fiercely)*: Would you strike my poor infirm old father, you coward, you!

HARDER *(calling for help)*: McCabe!

HOGAN: Don't think McCabe will hear you, if you blew Gabriel's horn. He knows I or Josie can lick him with one hand. *(Sharply)* Josie! Stand between us and the gate. *(JOSIE takes her stand where the path meets the road. She turns her back for a moment, shaking with suppressed laughter, and waves her hand at MC CABE and turns back. HOGAN releases his hold on HARDER's coat.)* There now. Don't try running away or my daughter will knock you senseless. *(He goes on grimly before HARDER can speak.)* You're the blackguard of a millionaire that owns the estate next to ours, ain't you? I've been meaning to call on you, for I've a bone to pick with you, you bloody tyrant! But I couldn't bring myself to set foot on land bought with Standard Oil money that was stolen from the poor it ground in the dust beneath its dirty heel—land that's watered with the tears of starving widows and orphans—*(He abruptly switches from this eloquence to a matter-of-fact tone.)* But never mind that, now. I won't waste words trying to reform a born crook. *(Fiercely, shoving his dirty unshaven face almost into HARDER's.)* What I want to know is, what the hell d'you mean by your contemptible trick of breaking down your fence to entice my poor pigs to take their death in your ice pond? *(There is a shout of laughter from JOSIE's bedroom, and* JOSIE *doubles up and holds her sides.* HARDER *is so flabbergasted by this mad accusation he cannot even sputter. But* HOGAN *acts as if he'd denied it–savagely.*) Don't lie, now! None of your damned Standard Oil excuses, or be Jaysus, I'll break you in half! Haven't I mended that fence morning after morning, and seen the footprints where you had sneaked up in the night to pull it down again. How many times have I mended that fence, Josie?

JOSIE: If it's once, it's a hundred, Father.

HOGAN: Listen, me little millionaire! I'm a peaceful, mild man that believes in live and let live, and as long as the neighboring scum leaves me alone, I'll let them alone, but when it comes to standing by and seeing my poor pigs murthered one by one—! Josie! How many pigs is it caught their death of cold in his damned ice pond and died of pneumonia?

JOSIE: Ten of them, Father. And ten more died of cholera after drinking the dirty water in it.

HOGAN: All prize pigs, too! I was offered two hundred dollars apiece for them. Twenty pigs at two hundred, that's four thousand. And a thousand to cure the sick and cover funeral expenses for the dead. Call it four thousand you owe me. (*Furiously.*) And you'll pay it, or I'll sue you, so help me Christ! I'll drag you in every court in the land! I'll paste your ugly mug on the front page of every newspaper as a pig-murdering tyrant! Before I'm through with you, you'll think you're the King of England at an Irish wake! (*With a quick change of pace to a wheedling confidential tone.*) Tell me now, if it isn't a secret, whatever made you take such a savage grudge against pigs? Sure, it isn't reasonable for a Standard Oil man to hate hogs.

HARDER (*manages to get in three sputtering words*): I've had enough—!

HOGAN (*with a grin*): Be God, I believe you! (*Switching to fierceness and grabbing his lapel again.*) Look out, now! Keep your place and be soft-spoken to your betters! You're not in your shiny automobile now with your funny nose cocked so you won't smell the poor people. (*He gives him a shake.*) And let me warn you! I have to put up with a lot of pests on this heap of boulders some joker once called a farm. There's a cruel skinflint of a landlord who swindles me out of my last drop of whiskey, and there's poison ivy, and ticks, and potato bugs, and there's snakes and skunks! But, be God, I draw the line somewhere, and I'll be damned if I'll stand for a Standard Oil man trespassing! So will you kindly get the hell out of here before I plant a kick on your backside that'll land you in the Atlantic Ocean! (*He gives* HARDER *a shove.*) Beat it now! (HARDER *tries to make some sort of dis-*

dainfully dignified exit. But he has to get by JOSIE.)

JOSIE (*leers at him idiotically*): Sure, you wouldn't go without a word of good-bye to me, would you, darlin'? Don't scorn me just because you have on your jockey's pants. (*In a hoarse whisper.*) Meet me tonight, as usual, down by the pigpen. (HARDER'S *retreat becomes a rout. He disappears on left, but a second later his voice, trembling with anger, is heard calling back threateningly.*)

HARDER: If you dare touch that fence again, I'll put this matter in the hands of the police!

HOGAN (*shouts derisively*): And I'll put it in my lawyer's hands and in the newspapers! (*He doubles up with glee.*) Look at him fling himself on his nag and spur the poor beast! And look at McCabe behind him! He can hardly stay in the saddle for laughing! (*He slaps his thigh.*) O Jaysus, this is a great day for the poor and oppressed! I'll do no more work! I'll go down to the Inn and spend money and get drunk as Moses!

JOSIE: Small blame to you. You deserve it. But you'll have your dinner first, to give you a foundation. Come on, now. (*They turn back toward the house. From inside another burst of laughter from* TYRONE *is heard.* JOSIE *smiles.*) Listen to Jim still in stitches. It's good to hear him laugh as if he meant it. (TYRONE *appears in the doorway of her bedroom.*)

TYRONE: O God, my sides are sore. (*They all laugh together. He joins them at the left corner of the house.*)

JOSIE: It's dinner time. Will you have a bite to eat with us, Jim? I'll boil you some eggs.

HOGAN: Och, why do you have to mention eggs? Don't you know it's the one thing he might eat? Well, no matter. Anything goes today. (*He gets the bottle of whiskey.*) Come in, Jim. We'll have a drink while Josie's fixing the grub. (*They start to go in the front door,* HOGAN *in the lead.*)

TYRONE (*suddenly–with sardonic amusement*): Wait a minute. Let us pause to take a look at this very valuable property. Don't you notice the change, Phil? Every boulder on the place has turned to solid gold.

HOGAN: What the hell—? You didn't get the D.T.'s from my whiskey, I know that.

TYRONE: No D.T.'s about it. This farm has suddenly become a gold mine. You know that offer I told you about? Well, the agent did a little detective work and he discovered it came from Harder. He doesn't want the damned place but he dislikes you as a neighbor and he thinks the best way to get rid of you would be to become your landlord.

HOGAN: The sneaking skunk! I'm sorry I didn't give him that kick.

TYRONE: Yes. So am I. That would have made the place even more valuable. But as it is, you did nobly. I expect him to double or triple his first offer. In fact, I'll bet the sky is the limit now.

HOGAN (*gives* JOSIE *a meaningful look*): I see your point! But we're not worrying you'd ever forget your promise to us for any price.

TYRONE: Promise? What promise? You know what Kipling wrote: (*Paraphrasing the "Rhyme of the Three Sealers."*) There's never a promise of God or man goes north of ten thousand bucks.

HOGAN: D'you hear him, Josie? We can't trust him.

JOSIE: Och, you know he's kidding.

HOGAN: I don't! I'm becoming suspicious.

TYRONE (*a trace of bitterness beneath his amused tone*): That's wise dope, Phil. Trust and be a sucker. If I were you, I'd be seriously worried. I've always wanted to own a gold mine—so I could sell it.

JOSIE (*bursts out*): Will you shut up your rotten Broadway blather!

TYRONE (*stares at her in surprise*): Why so serious and indignant, Josie? You just told your unworthy Old Man I was kidding. (*to* HOGAN) At last, I've got you by the ears, Phil. We must have a serious chat about when you're going to pay that back rent.

HOGAN (*groans*): A landlord who's a blackmailer! Holy God, what next! (JOSIE *is smiling with relief now.*)

TYRONE: And you, Josie, please remember when I keep that moonlight date tonight I expect you to be very sweet to me.

JOSIE (*with a bold air*): Sure, you don't have to blackmail me. I'd be that to you, anyway.

HOGAN: Are you laying plots in my presence to seduce my only daughter? (*Then philosophically.*) Well, what can I do? I'll be drunk at the Inn, so how could I prevent it? (*He goes up the steps.*) Let's eat, for the love of God. I'm starving. (*He disappears inside the house.*)

JOSIE (*with an awkward playful gesture, takes* TYRONE *by the hand*): Come along, Jim.

TYRONE (*smiles kiddingly*): Afraid you'll lose me? Swell chance! (*His eyes fix on her breasts—with genuine feeling*). You have the most beautiful breasts in the world, do you know it, Josie?

JOSIE (*pleased—shyly*): I don't—but I'm happy if you think— (*Then quickly.*) But I've no time now to listen to your kidding, with my mad old father waiting for his dinner. So come on. (*She tugs at his hand and he follows her up the steps. Her manner changes to worried solicitude.*) Promise me you'll eat something, Jim. You've got to eat. You can't go on the way you are, drinking and never eating, hardly. You're killing yourself.

TYRONE (*sardonically*): That's right. Mother me, Josie, I love it.

JOSIE (*bullyingly*): I will, then. You need one to take care of you. (*They disappear inside the house.*)

ACT 2

(*Scene: The same, with the wall of the living room removed. It is a clear warm moonlight night, around eleven o'clock.*

JOSIE *is sitting on the steps before the front door. She has changed to her Sunday best, a cheap dark-blue dress, black stockings and shoes. Her hair is carefully arranged, and by way of adornment a white flower is pinned on her bosom. She is hunched up, elbows on knees, her chin in her hands. There is an expression on her face we have not seen before, a look of sadness and loneliness and humiliation.*

She sighs and gets slowly to her feet, her body stiff from sitting long in the same position. She goes into the living room, fumbles around for a box of matches, and lights a kerosene lamp on the table.

The living room is small, low-ceilinged, with faded, fly-specked wallpaper, a floor of bare boards. It is cluttered up with furniture that looks as if it had been picked up at a fire sale. There is a table at center, a disreputable old Morris chair beside it; two ugly sideboards, one at left, the other at right-rear; a porch rocking-chair, painted green, with a hole in its cane bottom; a bureau against the rear wall, with two chairs on either side of a door to the kitchen. On the bureau is an alarm clock which shows the time to be five past eleven. At right-front is the door to JOSIE's *bedroom.*)

JOSIE (*looks at the clock—dully*): Five past eleven, and he said he'd be here around nine. (*Suddenly in a burst of humiliated anger, she tears off the flower pinned to her bosom and throws it in the corner.*) To hell with you, Jim Tyrone! (*From down the road, the quiet of the night is shattered by a burst of melancholy song. It is unmistakably* HOGAN's *voice wailing an old Irish lament at the top of his lungs.* JOSIE *starts—then frowns irritably.*) What's bringing him home an hour before the Inn closes? He must be more paralyzed than ever I've known him. (*She listens to the singing—grimly.*) Ah, here you come, do you, as full as a tick! I'll give you a welcome, if you start cutting up! I'm in no mood to put up with you. (*She goes into her bedroom and returns with her broomstick club. Outside the singing grows louder as* HOGAN *approaches the house. He only remembers one verse of the song and he has been repeating it.*)

HOGAN:

Oh the praties they grow small
Over here, over here,
Oh, the praties they grow small
Over here.
Oh the praties they grow small
And we dig them in the fall
And we eat them skins and all
Over here, over here.

(*He enters left-front, weaving and lurching a bit. But*

he is not as drunk as he appears. Or rather, he is one of those people who can drink an enormous amount and be absolutely plastered when they want to be for their own pleasure, but at the same time are able to pull themselves together when they wish and be cunningly clear-headed. Just now, he is letting himself go and getting great satisfaction from it. He pauses and bellows belligerently at the house) Hurroo! Down with all tyrants, male and female! To hell with England, and God damn Standard Oil!

JOSIE *(shouts back)*: Shut up your noise, you crazy old billy goat!

HOGAN *(hurt and mournful)*: A sweet daughter and a sweet welcome home in the dead of night. *(Beginning to boil.)* Old goat! There's respect for you! *(Angrily-starting for the front door.)* Crazy billy goat, is it? Be God, I'll learn you manners! *(He pounds on the door with his fist.)* Open the door! Open this door, I'm saying, before I drive a fist through it, or kick it into flinders! *(He gives it a kick.)*

JOSIE: It's not locked, you drunken old loon! Open it yourself!

HOGAN *(turns the knob and stamps in)*: Drunken old loon, am I? Is that the way to address your father?

JOSIE: No. It's too damned good for him.

HOGAN: It's time I taught you a lesson. Be Jaysus, I'll take you over my knee and spank your tail, if you are as big as a cow! *(He makes a lunge to grab her.)*

JOSIE: Would you, though! Take that, then! *(She raps him smartly, but lightly, on his bald spot with the end of her broom handle.)*

HOGAN *(with an exaggerated howl of pain)*: Ow! *(His anger evaporates and he rubs the top of his head ruefully–with bitter complaint.)* God forgive you, it's a great shame to me I've raised a daughter so cowardly she has to use a club.

JOSIE *(puts her club on the table–grimly)*: Now I've no club.

HOGAN *(evades the challenge)*: I never thought I'd see the day when a daughter of mine would be such a coward as to threaten her old father when he's helpless drunk and can't hit back. *(He slumps down on the Morris chair.)*

JOSIE: Ah, that's better. Now that little game is over. *(Then angrily.)* Listen to me, Father. I have no patience left, so get up from that chair, and go in your room, and go to bed, or I'll take you by the scruff of your neck and the seat of your pants and throw you in and lock the door on you! I mean it now! *(On the verge of angry tears.)* I've had all I can bear this night, and I want some peace and sleep, and not to listen to an old lush!

HOGAN *(appears drunker, his head wagging, his voice thick, his talk rambling)*: That's right. Fight with me. My own daughter has no feelings or sympathy. As if

I hadn't enough after what's happened tonight.

JOSIE *(with angry disgust)*: Och, don't try— *(Then curiously.)* What's happened? I thought something must be queer, you coming home before the Inn closed, but then I thought maybe for once you'd drunk all you could hold. *(Scathingly.)* And, God pity you, if you ain't that full, you're damned close to it.

HOGAN: Go on. Make fun of me. Old lush! You wouldn't feel so comical, if— *(He stops, mumbling to himself.)*

JOSIE: If what?

HOGAN: Never mind. Never mind. I didn't come home to fight, but seek comfort in your company. And if I was singing coming along the road, it was only because there's times you have to sing to keep from crying.

JOSIE: I can see you crying!

HOGAN: You will. And you'll see yourself crying, too, when— *(He stops again and mumbles to himself.)*

JOSIE: When what! *(Exasperatedly.)* Will you stop your whiskey drooling and talk plain?

HOGAN *(thickly)*: No matter. No matter. Leave me alone.

JOSIE *(angrily)*: That's good advice. To hell with you! I know your game. Nothing at all has happened. All you want is to keep me up listening to your guff. Go to your room, I'm saying, before—

HOGAN: I won't. I couldn't sleep with my thoughts tormented the way they are. I'll stay here in this chair, and you go to your room and let me be.

JOSIE *(snorts)*: And have you singing again in a minute and smashing the furniture—

HOGAN: Sing, is it? Are you making fun again? I'd give a keen of sorrow or howl at the moon like an old mangy hound in his sadness if I knew how, but I don't. So rest aisy. You won't hear a sound from me. Go on and snore like a pig to your heart's content. *(He mourns drunkenly.)* A fine daughter! I'd get more comfort from strangers.

JOSIE: Och, for God's sake, dry up! You'll sit in the dark then. I won't leave the lamp lit for you to tip over and burn down the house. *(She reaches out to turn down the lamp.)*

HOGAN *(thickly)*: Let it burn to the ground. A hell of a lot I care if it burns.

JOSIE *(in the act of turning down the lamp, stops and stares at him, puzzled and uneasy)*: I never heard you talk that way before, no matter how drunk you were. *(He mumbles. Her tone becomes persuasive.)* What's happened to you, Father?

HOGAN *(bitterly)*: Ah it's "Father" now, is it, not old billy goat? Well, thank God for small favors. *(With heavy sarcasm.)* Oh, nothing's happened to me at all, at all. A trifle, only. I wouldn't waste your time mentioning it, or keep you up when you want sleep so bad.

JOSIE (*angrily*): Och, you old loon, I'm sick of you. Sleep it off till you get some sense. (*She reaches for the lamp again.*)

HOGAN: Sleep it off? We'll see if you'll sleep it off when you know— (*He lapses into drunken mumbling.*)

JOSIE (*again stares at him*): Know what, Father?

HOGAN (*mumbles*): The son of a bitch!

JOSIE (*trying a light tone*): Sure, there's a lot of those in the neighborhood. Which one do you mean? Is Harder on your mind again?

HOGAN (*thickly*): He's one and a prize one, but I don't mean him. I'll say this for Harder, you know what to expect from him. He's no wolf in sheep's clothing, nor a treacherous snake in the grass who stabs you in the back with a knife—

JOSIE (*apprehensive now—forces a joke*): Sure, if you've found a snake who can stab you with a knife, you'd better join the circus with him and make a pile of money.

HOGAN (*bitterly*): Make jokes, God forgive you! You'll soon laugh from the wrong end of your mouth! (*He mumbles.*) Pretending he's our friend! The lying bastard!

JOSIE (*bristles resentfully*): Is it Jim Tyrone you're calling hard names?

HOGAN: That's right. Defend him, you big soft fool! Faith, you're a prize dunce! You've had a good taste of believing his word, waiting hours for him dressed up in your best like a poor sheep without pride or spirit—

JOSIE (*stung*): Shut up! I was calling him a lying bastard myself before you came, and saying I'd never speak to him again. And I knew all along he'd never remember to keep his date after he got drunk.

HOGAN: He's not so drunk he forgot to attend to business.

JOSIE (*as if she hadn't heard—defiantly*): I'd have stayed up anyway a beautiful night like this to enjoy the moonlight, if there wasn't a Jim Tyrone in the world.

HOGAN (*with heavy sarcasm*): In your best shoes and stockings? Well, well. Sure, the moon must feel flattered by your attentions.

JOSIE (*furiously*): You won't feel flattered if I knock you tail over tincup out of that chair! And stop your whiskey gabble about Jim. I see what you're driving at with your dark hints and curses, and if you think I'll believe— (*With forced assurance.*) Sure, I know what's happened as well as if I'd been there. Jim saw you'd got drunker than usual and you were an easy mark for a joke, and he made a goat of you!

HOGAN (*bitterly*): Goat again! (*He struggles from his chair and stands swaying unsteadily—with offended dignity.*) All right, I won't say another word. There's no use telling the truth to a bad-tempered woman in love.

JOSIE: Love be damned! I hate him now!

HOGAN: Be Christ, you have me stumped. A great proud slut who's played games with half the men around here, and now you act like a numbskull virgin that can't believe a man would tell her a lie!

JOSIE (*threateningly*): If you're going to your room, you'd better go quick!

HOGAN (*fixes his eyes on the door at rear—with dignity*): That's where I'm going, yes—to talk to myself so I'll know someone with brains is listening. Good night to you, Miss Hogan. (*He starts—swerves left—tries to correct this and lurches right and bumps against her, clutching the supporting arm she stretches out.*)

JOSIE: God help you, if you try to go upstairs now, you'll end up in the cellar.

HOGAN (*hanging on to her arm and shoulder—maudlinly affectionate now*): You're right. Don't listen to me. I'm wrong to bother you. You've had sorrow enought this night. Have a good sleep, while you can, Josie, darlin'—and good night and God bless you. (*He tries to kiss her, but she wards him off and steers him back to the chair.*)

JOSIE: Sit down before you split in pieces on the floor and I have to get a wheelbarrow to collect you. (*She dumps him in the chair where he sprawls limply, his chin on his chest.*)

HOGAN (*mumbles dully*): It's too late. It's all settled. We're helpless, entirely.

JOSIE (*really worried now*): How is it all settled? If you're helpless, I'm not. (*Then as he doesn't reply—scornfully.*) It's the first time I ever heard you admit you were licked. And it's the first time I ever saw you so paralyzed you couldn't shake the whiskey from your brains and get your head clear when you wanted. Sure, that's always been your pride—and now look at you, the stupid object you are, mumbling and drooling!

HOGAN (*struggles up in his chair—angrily*): Shut up your insults! Be God, I can get my head clear if I like! (*He shakes his head violently.*) There! It's clear. I can tell you each thing that happened tonight as clear as if I'd not taken a drop, if you'll listen and not keep calling me a liar.

JOSIE: I'll listen, now I see you have hold of your wits.

HOGAN: All right, then. I'll begin at the beginning when him and me left here, and you gave him a sweet smile, and rolled your big beautiful cow's eyes at him, and wiggled your backside, and stuck out your beautiful breasts you know he admires, and said in a sick sheep's voice. "Don't forget our moonlight date, Jim."

JOSIE (*with suppressed fury*): You're a—! I never—! You old—!

HOGAN: And he said: "You bet I won't forget, Josie."

JOSIE: The lying crook!

HOGAN (*his voice begins to sink into a dejected monotone*): We went to the Inn and started drinking whiskey. And I got drunk.

JOSIE (*exasperatedly*): I guessed that! And Jim got drunk, too. And then what?

HOGAN (*dully*): Who knows how drunk he got? He had one of his queer fits when you can't tell. He's the way I told you about this morning, when he talks like a Broadway crook, who'd sell his soul for a price, and there's a sneering divil in him, and he loves to pick out the weakness in people and say cruel, funny things that flay the hide off them, or play cruel jokes on them. (*With sudden rage.*) God's curse on him, I'll wager he's laughing to himself this minute, thinking it's the cutest joke in the world, the fools he made of us. You in particular. Be God, I had my suspicions, at least, but your head was stuffed with mush and love, and you wouldn't—

JOSIE (*furiously*): You'll tell that lie about my love once too often! And I'll play a joke on him yet that'll make him sorry he—

HOGAN (*sunk in drunken defeatism again*): It's too late. You shouldn't have let him get away from you to the Inn. You should have kept him here. Then maybe, if you'd got him drunk enough you could have— (*His head nodding, his eyes blinking–thickly.*) But it's no good talking now—no good at all—no good—

JOSIE (*gives him a shake*): Keep hold of your wits or I'll give you a cuff on both ears! Will you stop blathering like an old woman and tell me plainly what he's done!

HOGAN: He's agreed to sell the farm, that's what! Simpson came to the Inn to see him with a new offer from Harder. Ten thousand, cash.

JOSIE (*overwhelmed*): Ten thousand! Sure, three is all it's worth at most. And two was what you offered that Jim promised—

HOGAN: What's money to Harder? After what we did to him, all he wants is revenge. And here's where he's foxy. Simpson must have put him up to it knowing how Jim hates it here living on a small allowance, and he longs to go back to Broadway and his whores. Jim won't have to wait for his half of the cash till the estate's settled. Harder offers to give him five thousand cash as a loan against the estate the second the sale is made. Jim can take the next train to New York.

JOSIE (*tensely, on the verge of tears*): And Jim accepted? I don't believe it!

HOGAN: Don't then. Be God, you'll believe it tomorrow. Harder proposed that he meet with Jim and the executors in the morning and settle it, and Jim promised Simpson he would.

JOSIE (*desperately*): Maybe he'll get so drunk he'll never remember—

HOGAN: He won't. Harder's coming in his automobile to pick him up and make sure of him. Anyway don't think because he forgot you were waiting—in the moonlight, eating your heart out, that he'd ever miss a date with five thousand dollars, and all the pretty whores of Broadway he can buy with it.

JOSIE (*distractedly*): Will you shut up! (*Angrily.*) And where were you when all this happened? Couldn't you do anything to stop it, you old loon?

HOGAN: I couldn't. Simpson came and sat at the table with us—

JOSIE: And you let him!

HOGAN: Jim invited him. Anyway, I wanted to find out what trick he had up his sleeve, and what Jim would do. When it was all over, I got up and took a swipe at Simpson, but I missed him. (*With drunken sadness.*) I was too drunk—too drunk—too drunk— I missed him, God forgive me! (*His chin sinks on his chest and his eyes shut.*)

JOSIE (*shakes him*): If you don't keep awake, be God, I won't miss you!

HOGAN: I was going to take a swipe at Jim, too, but I couldn't do it. My heart was too broken with sorrow. I'd come to love him like a son—a real son of my heart!—to take the place of that jackass, Mike, and me two other jackasses.

JOSIE (*her face hard and bitter*): I think now Mike was the only one in this house with sense.

HOGAN: I was too drowned in sorrow by his betraying me—and you he'd pretended to like so much. So I only called him a dirty lying skunk of a treacherous bastard, and I turned my back on him and left the Inn, and I made myself sing on the road so he'd hear, and they'd all hear in the Inn, to show them I didn't care a damn.

JOSIE (*scathingly*): Sure, wasn't you the hero! A hell of a lot of good—

HOGAN: Ah, well, I suppose the temptation was too great. He's weak, with one foot in the grave from whiskey. Maybe we shouldn't blame him.

JOSIE (*her eyes flashing*): Not blame him? Well, I blame him, God damn him! Are you making excuses for him, you old fool!

HOGAN: I'm not. He's a dirty snake! But I was thinking how do I know what I wouldn't do for five thousand cash, and how do you know what you wouldn't do?

JOSIE: Nothing could make me betray him! (*Her face grows hard and bitter.*) Or it couldn't before. There's nothing I wouldn't do now. (HOGAN *suddenly begins to chuckle.*) Do you think I'm lying? Just give me a chance—

HOGAN: I remembered something. (*He laughs drunk-*

enly.) Be Christ, Josie, for all his Broadway wisdom about women, you've made a prized damned fool of him and that's some satisfaction!

JOSIE (*bewildered*): How'd you mean?

HOGAN: You'll never believe it. Neither did I, But he kept on until, be God, I saw he really meant it.

JOSIE: Meant what?

HOGAN: It was after he'd turned queer—early in the night before Simpson came. He started talking about you, as if you was on his mind, worrying him—and before he finished I take my oath I began to hope you could really work Mike's first scheme on him, if you got him alone in the moonlight, because all his gab was about his great admiration for you.

JOSIE: Och! The liar!

HOGAN: He said you had great beauty in you that no one appreciated but him.

JOSIE (*shakenly*): You're lying.

HOGAN: Great strength, you had, and great pride, he said—and great goodness, no less! But here's where you've made a prize jackass of him, like I said. (*With a drunken leer.*) Listen now, darlin', and don't drop dead with amazement. (*He leans toward her and whispers.*) He believes you're a virgin! (JOSIE *stiffens as if she'd been insulted.* HOGAN *goes on.*) He does, so help me! He means it, the poor dunce! He thinks you're a poor innocent virgin! He thinks it's all boasting and pretending you've done about being a slut. (*He chuckles.*) A virgin, no less! You!

JOSIE (*furiously*): Stop saying it! Boasting and pretending, am I? The dirty liar!

HOGAN: Faith, you don't have to tell me. (*Then he looks at her in drunken surprise–thickly.*) Are you taking it as an insult? Why the hell don't you laugh? Be God, you ought to see what a stupid sheep that makes him.

JOSIE (*forces a laugh*): I do see it.

HOGAN (*chuckling drunkenly*): Oh, be God, I've just remembered another thing, Josie. I know why he didn't keep his date with you. It wasn't that he'd forgot. He remembered well enough, for he talked about it—

JOSIE: You mean he deliberately, knowing I'd be waiting— (*Fiercely.*) God damn him!

HOGAN: He as much as told me his reason, though he wouldn't come out with it plain, me being your father. His conscience was tormenting him. He's going to leave you alone and not see you again—for your sake, because he loves you! (*He chuckles.*)

JOSIE (*looks stricken and bewildered–her voice trembling*): Loves me? You're making it up.

HOGAN: I'm not. I know it sounds crazy but—

JOSIE: What did he mean, for my sake?

HOGAN: Can't you see? You're a pure virgin to him, but all the same there's things besides your beautiful soul he feels drawn to, like your beautiful hair and eyes, and—

JOSIE (*strickenly*): Och, don't Father! You know I'm only a big—

HOGAN (*as if she hadn't spoken*): So he'll keep away from temptation because he can't trust himself, and it'd be a sin on his conscience if he was to seduce you. (*He laughs drunkenly.*) Oh, be God! If that ain't rich!

JOSIE (*her voice trembles*): So that was his reason— (*Then angrily.*) So he thinks all he has to do is crook a finger and I'll fall for him, does he, the vain Broadway crook!

HOGAN (*chuckling*): Be Jaysus, it was the maddest thing in the world, him gabbing like a soft loon about you—and there at the bar in plain sight was two of the men you've been out with, the gardener at Smith's, and Regan, the chauffeur for Driggs, having a drink together!

JOSIE (*with a twitching smile*): It must have been mad, surely. I wish I'd been there to laugh up my sleeve. (*Angry.*) But what's all his crazy lying blather got to do with him betraying us and selling the place?

HOGAN (*at once, hopelessly dejected again*): Nothing at all. I only thought you'd like to know you'd had that much revenge.

JOSIE: A hell of a revenge! I'll have a better one than that on him— or I'll try to! I'm not like you, owning up I'm beaten and crying wurra-wurra like a coward and getting hopeless drunk! (*She gives him a shake.*) Get your wits about you and answer me this: Did Simpson get him to sign a paper?

HOGAN: No, but what good is that? In the morning he'll sign all they shove in front of him.

JOSIE: It's this good. It means we still have a chance. Or I have.

HOGAN: What chance? Are you going to beg him to take pity on us?

JOSIE: I'll see him in hell first! There's another chance, and a good one. But I'll need your help— (*Angrily.*) And look at you, your brains drowned in whiskey, so I can't depend on you!

HOGAN (*rousing himself*): You can, if there's any chance. Be God, I'll make myself as sober as a judge for you in the wink of an eye! (*Then dejectedly.*) But what can you do now, darlin'? You haven't even got him here. He's down at the Inn sitting alone, drinking and dreaming of the little whores he'll be with tomorrow night on Broadway.

JOSIE: I'll get him here! I'll humble my pride and go down to the Inn for him! And if he doesn't want to come I've a way to make him. I'll raise a scene and pretend I'm in a rage because he forgot his date. I'll disgrace him till he'll be glad to come with me to shut me up. I know his weakness, and it's his vanity about his women. If I was a dainty, pretty tart he'd be proud I'd raise a rumpus about him. But when it's a big, ugly hulk like me— (*She falters and forces herself to go on.*) If he ever was tempted to want me, he'd be ashamed of it. That's the truth behind the lies he told you of his conscience and his fear he might ruin me, God damn him!

HOGAN: No, he meant it, Josie. But never mind that now. Let's say you've got him here. Then what will you do?

JOSIE: I told you this morning if he ever broke his promise to us I'd do anything and not mind how crooked it was. And I will! Your part in it is to come at sunrise with witnesses and catch us in— (*She falters.*)

HOGAN: In bed, is it? Then it's Mike's second scheme you're thinking about?

JOSIE: I told you I didn't care how dirty a trick— (*With a hard bitter laugh.*) The dirtier the better now!

HOGAN: But how'll you get him in bed, with all his honorable scruples, thinking you're a virgin? But I'm forgetting he stayed away because he was afraid he'd be tempted. So maybe—

JOSIE (*tensely*): For the love of God, don't harp on his lies. He won't be tempted at all. But I'll get him so drunk he'll fall asleep and I'll carry him in and put him in bed—

HOGAN: Be God, that's the way! But you'll never do it unless you're more sociable and stop looking at him the way you do, whenever he takes a drink, as if you was praying Almighty God to forgive a poor drunkard. You've got to encourage him. The best way would be for you to drink with him. It would put him at his ease and unsuspecting, and it'd give you courage, too, so you'd act bold for a change instead of giving him brazen talk he's tired of hearing, while you act shy as a mouse.

JOSIE (*gives her father a bitter, resentful look*): You're full of sly advice all of a sudden, ain't you? You dirty little tick!

HOGAN (*angrily*): Didn't you tell me to get hold of my wits? Be God if you want me drunk, I've only to let go. That'd suit me. I want to forget my sorrow, and I've no faith in your scheme because you'll be too full of scruples. Like the drinking. You're such a virtuous teetotaller—

JOSIE: I've told you I'd do anything now! (*Then confusedly.*) All I meant was, it's not right, a father to tell his daughter how to— (*Then angrily.*) I don't need your advice. Haven't I had every man I want around here?

HOGAN: Ah, thank God, that sounds natural! Be God, I thought you'd started playing virgin with me just because the Broadway sucker thinks you're one.

JOSIE (*furiously*): Shut up! I'm not playing anything. And don't worry I can't do my part of the trick.

HOGAN: That's the talk! But let me get it all clear. I come at sunrise with my witnesses, and you've forgot to lock your door, and we walk in, and there's the two of you in bed, and I raise the roof and threaten him if he don't marry you—

JOSIE: Marry him? After what he's done to us? I wouldn't marry him now if he was the last man on earth! All we want is a paper signed by him with witnesses that he'll sell the farm to you for the price you offered, and not to Harder.

HOGAN: Well, that's justice, but that's all it is. I thought you wanted to make him pay for his black treachery against us, the dirty bastard!

JOSIE: I do want! (*She again gives him a bitter resentful glance.*) It's the estate money you're thinking of, isn't it? Leave it to you! (*Hastily.*) Well, so am I! I'd like to get my hooks on it! (*With a hard, brazen air.*) Be God, if I'm to play whore, I deserve my pay! We'll make him sign a paper he owes me ten thousand dollars the minute the estate is settled. (*She laughs.*) How's that? I'll bet none of his tarts on Broadway ever got a thousandth part of that out of him, no matter how dainty and pretty! (*Laughing again.*) And here's what'll be the greatest joke to teach him a lesson. He'll pay for it for nothing! I'll get him in bed but I'll never let him—

HOGAN (*with delighted admiration*): Och, by Jaysus, Josie, that's the best yet! (*He slaps his thigh enthusiastically.*) Oh, that'll teach him to double-cross his friends! That'll show him two can play at tricks! And him believing you so innocent! Be God, you'll make him the prize sucker of the world! Won't I roar inside me when I see his face in the morning! (*He bursts into coarse laughter.*)

JOSIE (*again with illogical resentment*): Stop laughing! You're letting yourself be drunk again. (*Then with a hard, business-like air.*) We've done enough talking. Let's start—

HOGAN: Wait, now. There's another thing. Just what do you want me to threaten him with when I catch you? That we'll sue him for outraging your virtue? Sure, his lawyer would have all your old flames in the witness box, till the jury would think you'd been faithful to the male inhabitants of America. So what threat—I can't think of any he wouldn't laugh at.

JOSIE (*tensely*): Well I can! Do I have to tell you his weakness again? It's his vanity about women, and his Broadway pride he's so wise no woman could fool him. It's the disgrace to his vanity—being caught with the likes of me—(*Falteringly, but forcing herself to go on.*) My mug beside his in all the newspapers—the New York papers, too—he'll see the whole of Broadway splitting their sides laughing at him—and he'll give anything to keep us quiet, I tell you. He will! I know him! So don't worry—(*She ends up on the verge of bitter humiliated tears.*)

HOGAN (*without looking at her–enthusiastic again*): Be God, you're right!

JOSIE (*gives him a bitter glance–fiercely*): Then get the hell out of that chair and let's start it! (*He gets up. She surveys him resentfully.*) You're steady on your pins, ain't you, you scheming old thief, now there's the smell of money around! (*Quickly.*) Well, I'm glad. I know I can depend on you now. You'll walk down to the Inn with me and hide outside until you see me come out with him. Then you can sneak in the Inn yourself and pick the witnesses to stay up with you. But mind you don't get drunk again, and let them get too drunk.

HOGAN: I won't, I take my oath! (*He pats her on the shoulder approvingly.*) Be God, you've got the proud, fighting spirit in you that never says die, and you make me ashamed of my weakness. You're that eager now, be damned if I don't almost think you're glad of the excuse!

JOSIE (*stiffens*): Excuse for what, you old—

HOGAN: To show him no man can get the best of you—what else?—like you showed all the others.

JOSIE: I'll show him to his sorrow! (*Then abruptly, starting for the screen door at left.*) Come on. We've no time to waste. (*But when she gets to the door, she appears suddenly hesitant and timid–hurriedly.*) Wait. I'd better give a look at myself in the mirror. (*In a brazen tone.*) Sure, those in my trade have to look their best! (*She hurries back across the room into her bedroom and closes the door.* HOGAN *stares after her. Abruptly he ceases to look like a drunk who, by an effort, is keeping himself half-sober. He is a man who has been drinking a lot but is still clear-headed and has complete control of himself.*)

HOGAN (*watches the crack under* JOSIE'S *door and speaks half-aloud to himself, shaking his head pityingly*): A look in the mirror and she's forgot to light her lamp! (*Remorsefully.*) God forgive me, it's bitter medicine. But it's the only way I can see that has a chance now. (JOSIE'S *door opens. At once, he is as he was. She comes out, a fixed smile on her lips, her head high, her face set defiantly. But she has evidently been crying.*)

JOSIE (*brazenly*): There, now. Don't I look ten thousand dollars' worth to any drunk?

HOGAN: You look a million, darlin'!

JOSIE (*goes to the screen door and pushes it open with the manner of one who has burned all bridges*): Come

along, then. (*She goes out. He follows close on her heels. She stops abruptly on the first step–startledly.*) Look! There's someone on the road—

HOGAN (*pushes past her down the steps–peering off left-front–as if aloud to himself, in dismay*): Be God, it's him! I never thought—

JOSIE (*as if aloud to herself*): So he didn't forget—

HOGAN (*quickly*): Well, it proves he can't keep away from you, and that'll make it easier for you—(*Then furiously.*) Oh, the dirty, double-crossing bastard! The nerve of him! Coming to call on you, after making you wait for hours, thinking you don't know what he's done to us this night, and it'll be a fine cruel joke to blarney you in the moonlight, and you trusting him like a poor sheep, and never suspecting—

JOSIE (*stung*): Shut up! I'll teach him who's the joker! I'll let him go on as if you hadn't told me what he's done—

HOGAN: Yes, don't let him suspect it, or you wouldn't fool him. He'd know you were after revenge. But he can see me here now. I can't sneak away or he'd be suspicious. We've got to think of a new scheme quick to get me away—

JOSIE (*quickly*): I know how. Pretend you're as drunk as when you came. Make him believe you're so drunk you don't remember what he's done, so he can't suspect you told me.

HOGAN: I will. Be God, Josie, damned if I don't think he's so queer drunk himself he don't remember, or he'd never come here.

JOSIE: The drunker he is the better! (*Lowering her voice–quickly.*) He's turned in the gate where he can hear us. Pretend we're fighting and I'm driving you off till you're sober. Say you won't be back tonight. It'll make him sure he'll have the night alone with me. You start the fight.

HOGAN (*becomes at once very drunk. He shouts*): Put me out of my own home, will you, you undutiful slut!

JOSIE: Celebration or not, I'll have no drunks cursing and singing all night. Go back to the Inn.

HOGAN: I will! I'll get a room and two bottles and stay drunk as long as I please!

JOSIE: Don't come back till you've slept it off, or I'll wipe the floor with you! (TYRONE *enters, left-front. He does not appear to be drunk–that is, he shows none of the usual symptoms. He seems much the same as in Act 1. The only perceptible change is that his eyes have a peculiar fixed, glazed look, and there is a certain vague quality in his manner and speech, as if he were a bit hazy and absent-minded.*)

TYRONE (*dryly*): Just in time for the Big Bout. Or is this the final round?

HOGAN (*whirls on him unsteadily*): Who the hell—(*Peering at him.*) Oh, it's you, is it?

TYRONE: What was the big idea, Phil, leaving me flat?

HOGAN: Leave you flat? Be Jaysus, that reminds me I owe you a swipe on the jaw for something. What was it? Be God, I'm too drunk to remember. But here it is, anyway. (*He turns loose a round-house swing that misses* TYRONE *by a couple of feet, and reels away.* TYRONE *regards him with vague surprise.*)

JOSIE: Stop it, you damned old fool, and get out of here!

HOGAN: Taking his side against your poor old father, are you? A hell of a daughter! (*He draws himself up with drunken dignity.*) Don't expect me home tonight, Miss Hogan, or tomorrow either, maybe. You can take your bad temper out on your sweetheart here. (*He starts off down the road, left-front, with a last word over his shoulder.*) Bad luck to you both. (*He disappears. A moment later he begins to bawl his mournful Irish song.*) "Oh, the praties they grow small, Over here, over here," etc. (*During a part of the following scene the song continues to be heard at intervals, receding as he gets farther off on his way to the Inn.*)

JOSIE: Well, thank God. That's good riddance. (*She comes to* TYRONE, *who stands staring after* HOGAN *with a puzzled look.*)

TYRONE: I've never seen him that stinko before. Must have got him all of a sudden. He didn't seem so lit up at the Inn, but I guess I wasn't paying much attention.

JOSIE (*forcing a playful air*): I should think, if you were a real gentleman, you'd be apologizing to me, not thinking of him. Don't you know you're two hours and a half late? I oughtn't to speak to you, if I had any pride.

TYRONE (*stares at her curiously*): You've got too damn much pride, Josie. That's the trouble.

JOSIE: And just what do you mean by that, Jim?

TYRONE (*shrugs his shoulders*): Nothing. Forget it. I do apologize, Josie. I'm damned sorry. Haven't any excuse. Can't think up a lie. (*Staring at her curiously again.*) Or, now I think of it, I had a damned good honorable excuse, but— (*He shrugs.*) Nuts. Forget it.

JOSIE: Holy Joseph, you're full of riddles tonight. Well, I don't need excuses. I forgive you, anyway, now you're here. (*She takes his hand—playfully.*) Come on now and we'll sit on my bedroom steps and be romantic in the moonlight, like we planned to. (*She leads him there. He goes along in an automatic way, as if only half-conscious of what he is doing. She sits on the top step and pulls him down on the step beneath her. A pause. He stares vaguely at nothing. She bends to give him an uneasy appraising glance.*)

TYRONE (*suddenly, begins to talk mechanically*): Had to get out of the damned Inn. I was going batty alone there. The old heebie-jeebies. So I came to you. (*He pauses—then adds with strange, wondering sincerity.*) I've really begun to love you a lot, Josie.

JOSIE (*blurts out bitterly*): Yes, you've proved that tonight, haven't you? (*Hurriedly regaining her playful tone.*) But never mind. I said I'd forgive you for being so late. So go on about love. I'm all ears.

TYRONE (*as if he hadn't listened*): I thought you'd have given me up and gone to bed. I remember I had some nutty idea I'd get in bed with you—just to lie with my head on your breast.

JOSIE (*moved in spite of herself—but keeps her bold, playful tone*): Well, maybe I'll let you— (*Hurriedly.*) Later on, I mean. The night's young yet, and we'll have it all to ourselves. (*Boldly again.*) But here's for a starter. (*She puts her arms around him and draws him back till his head is on her breast.*) There, now.

TYRONE (*relaxes—simply and gratefully*): Thanks, Josie. (*He closes his eyes. For a moment, she forgets everything and stares down at his face with a passionate, possessive tenderness. A pause. From far-off on the road to the Inn,* HOGAN's *mournful song drifts back through the moonlight quiet: "Oh, the praties they grow small, Over here, over here."* TYRONE *rouses himself and straightens up. He acts embarrassed, as if he felt he'd been making a fool of himself—mockingly.*) Hark, Hark, the Donegal lark! "Thou wast not born for death, immortal bird." Can't Phil sing anything but that damned dirge, Josie? (*She doesn't reply. He goes on hazily.*) Still, it seems to belong tonight—in the moonlight—or in my mind—(*He quotes.*)

"Now more than ever seems it rich to die,
To cease upon the midnight with no pain.
In such an ecstasy!"

(*He has recited this with deep feeling. Now he sneers.*) Good God! Ode to Phil the Irish Nightingale! I must have the D.T.'s.

JOSIE (*her face grown bitter*): Maybe it's only your bad conscience.

TYRONE (*starts guiltily and turns to stare into her face—suspiciously*): What put that in your head? Conscience about what?

JOSIE (*quickly*): How would I know, if you don't? (*Forcing a playful tone.*) For the sin of wanting to be in bed with me. Maybe that's it.

TYRONE (*with strange relief*): Oh. (*A bit shamefacedly.*) Forget that stuff, Josie. I was half nutty.

JOSIE (*bitterly*): Och, for the love of God, don't apologize as if you was ashamed of— (*She catches herself.*)

TYRONE (*with a quick glance at her face*): All right. I certainly won't apologize—if you're not kicking. I was afraid I might have shocked your modesty.

JOSIE (*roughly*): My modesty? Be God, I didn't know I had any left.

TYRONE (*draws away from her–irritably*): Nix, Josie. Lay off that line, for tonight at least. (*He adds slowly.*) I'd like tonight to be different.

JOSIE: Different from what? (*He doesn't answer. She forces a light tone.*) All right. I'll be as different as you please.

TYRONE (*simply*): Thanks, Josie. Just be yourself. (*Again as if he were ashamed, or afraid he had revealed some weakness–off-handedly.*) This being out in the moonlight instead of the lousy Inn isn't a bad bet, at that. I don't know why I hang out in that dump, except I'm even more bored in the so-called good hotels in this hick town.

JOSIE (*trying to examine his face without his knowing*): Well, you'll be back on Broadway soon now, won't you?

TYRONE: I hope so.

JOSIE: Then you'll have all the pretty little tarts to comfort you when you get your sorrowful spell on.

TYRONE: Oh, to hell with the rough stuff, Josie! You promised you'd can it tonight.

JOSIE (*tensely*): You're a fine one to talk of promises!

TYRONE (*vaguely surprised by her tone*): What's the matter? Still sore at me for being late?

JOSIE (*quickly*): I'm not. I was teasing you. To prove there's no hard feelings, how would you like a drink? But I needn't ask. (*She gets up.*) I'll get a bottle of his best.

TYRONE (*mechanically*): Fine. Maybe that will have some kick. The booze at the Inn didn't work tonight.

JOSIE: Well, this'll work. (*She starts to go into her bedroom. He sits hunched up on the step, staring at nothing. She pauses in the doorway to glance back. The hard, calculating expression on her face softens. For a second she stares at him, bewildered by her conflicting feelings. Then she goes inside, leaving the door open. She opens the door from her room to the lighted living room, and is seen going to the kitchen on the way to the cellar. She has left the door from the living room to her bedroom open and the light reveals a section of the bedroom framed in the doorway behind* TYRONE. *The foot of the bed which occupies most of the room can be seen, and that is all except that the walls are unpainted pine boards.* TYRONE *continues to stare at nothing, but becomes restless. His hands and mouth twitch.*)

TYRONE (*suddenly, with intense hatred*): You rotten bastard! (*He springs to his feet–fumbles in his pockets for cigarettes–strikes a match which lights up his face, on which there is now an expression of miserable guilt. His hand is trembling so violently he cannot light the cigarette.*)

ACT 3

(*Scene: The living-room wall has been replaced and all we see now of its lighted interior is through the two win-*

dows. Otherwise, everything is the same, and this Act follows the preceding without any lapse of time. TYRONE *is still trying with shaking hands to get his cigarette lighted. Finally he succeeds, and takes a deep inhale, and starts pacing back and forth a few steps, as if in a cell of his own thought. He swears defensively.*) God damn it. You'll be crying in your beer in a minute. (*He begins to sing sneeringly half under his breath a snatch from an old sob song, popular in the Nineties*)

"And baby's cries can't waken her
In the baggage coach ahead."

(*His sneer changes to a look of stricken guilt and grief*) Christ! (*He seems about to break down and sob but he fights this back*) Cut it out, you drunken fool! (JOSIE *can be seen through the windows, returning from the kitchen. He turns with a look of relief and escape*) Thank God! (*He sits on the boulder and waits.* JOSIE *stops by the table in the living room to turn down the lamp until only a dim light remains. She has a quart of whiskey under her arm, two tumblers, and a pitcher of water. She goes through her bedroom and appears in the outer doorway.* TYRONE *gets up*) Ah! At last the old booze! (*He relieves her of the pitcher and tumblers as she comes down the steps.*)

JOSIE (*with a fixed smile*): You'd think I'd been gone years. You didn't seem so perishing for a drink.

TYRONE (*in his usual, easy, kidding way*): It's you I was perishing for. I've been dying of loneliness—

JOSIE: You'll die of lying some day. But I'm glad you're alive again. I thought when I left you really were dying on me.

TYRONE: No such luck.

JOSIE: Och, don't talk like that. Come on have a drink. We'll use the boulder for a table and I'll be barkeep. (*He puts the pitcher and tumblers on the boulder and she uncorks the bottle. She takes a quick glance at his face–startledly.*) What's come over you, Jim? You look as if you've seen a ghost.

TYRONE (*looks away–dryly*): I have. My own. He's punk company.

JOSIE: Yes, it's the worst ghost of all, your own. Don't I know? But this will keep it in place. (*She pours a tumbler half full of whiskey and hands it to him.*) Here. But wait till I join you. (*She pours the other tumbler half full.*)

TYRONE (*surprised.*): Hello! I thought you never touched it.

JOSIE (*glibly*): I have on occasion. And this is one. I don't want to be left out altogether from celebrating our victory over Harder. (*She gives him a sharp bitter glance. Meeting his eyes, which are regarding her with puzzled wonder, she forces a laugh.*) Don't look at me as if I was up to some game. A drink or two will make me better company, and help me enjoy the moon and the night with you. Here's luck. (*She touches his glass with hers.*)

TYRONE (*shrugs his shoulders*): All right. Here's luck. (*They drink. She gags and sputters. He pours water in her glass. She drinks it. He puts his glass and the pitcher back on the boulder. He keeps staring at her with a puzzled frown.*)

JOSIE: Some of it went down the wrong way.

TYRONE: So I see. That'll teach you to pour out baths instead of drinks.

JOSIE: It's the first time I ever heard you complain a drink was too big.

TYRONE: Yours was too big.

JOSIE: I'm my father's daughter. I've a strong head. So don't worry I'll pass out and you'll have to put me to bed. (*She gives a little bold laugh.*) Sure, that's a beautiful notion. I'll have to pretend I'm—

TYRONE (*irritably*): Nix on the raw stuff, Josie. Remember you said—

JOSIE (*resentment in her kidding*): I'd be different? That's right. I'm forgetting it's your pleasure to have me pretend I'm an innocent virgin tonight.

TYRONE (*in a strange tone that is almost threatening*): If you don't look out, I'll call you on that bluff, Josie. (*He stares at her with a deliberate sensualist's look that undresses her.*) I'd like to. You know that, don't you?

JOSIE (*boldly*): I don't at all. You're the one who's bluffing.

TYRONE (*grabs her in his arms—with genuine passion*): Josie! (*Then as suddenly lets her go.*) Nix. Let's cut it out. (*He turns away. Her face betrays the confused conflict within her of fright, passion, happiness, and bitter resentment. He goes on with an abrupt change of tone.*) How about another drink? That's honest-to-God old bonded Bourbon. How the devil did Phil get hold of it?

JOSIE: Tom Lombardo, the bootlegger, gave him a case for letting him hide a truckload in our barn when the agents were after him. He stole it from a warehouse on faked permits. (*She pours out drinks as she speaks, a half tumblerful for him, a small one for herself.*) Here you are. (*She gives him his drink—smiles at him coquettishly, beginning to show the effect of her big drink by her increasingly bold manners.*) Let's sit down where the moon will be in our eyes and we'll see romance. (*She takes his arm and leads him to her bedroom steps. She sits on the top step, pulling him down beside her but on the one below. She raises her glass.*) Here's hoping before the night's out you'll have more courage and kiss me at least.

TYRONE (*frowns—then kiddingly*): That's a promise. Here's how. (*He drains his tumbler. She drinks half of hers. He puts his glass on the ground beside him. A pause. She tries to read his face without his noticing. He seems to be lapsing again into vague preoccupation.*)

JOSIE: Now don't sink back half-dead-and-alive in dreams the way you were before.

TYRONE (*quickly*): I'm not. I had a good final dose of heebie-jeebies when you were in the house. That's all for tonight. (*He adds a bit maudlinly, his two big drinks beginning to affect him.*) Let the dead past bury its dead.

JOSIE: That's the talk. There's only tonight, and the moon, and us—and the bonded Bourbon. Have another drink, and don't wait for me.

TYRONE: Not now, thanks. They're coming too fast. (*He gives her a curious, cynically amused look.*) Trying to get me soused, Josie?

JOSIE (*starts—quickly*): I'm not. Only to get you feeling happy, so you'll forget all sadness.

TYRONE (*kiddingly*): I might forget all my honorable intentions, too. So look out.

JOSIE: I'll look forward to it—and I hope that's another promise, like the kiss you owe me. If you're suspicious I'm trying to get you soused—well, here goes. (*She drinks what is left in her glass.*) There, now. I must be scheming to get myself soused, too.

TYRONE: Maybe you are.

JOSIE (*resentfully*): If I was, it'd be to make you feel at home. Don't all the pretty little Broadway tarts get soused with you?

TYRONE (*irritably*): There you go again with that old line!

JOSIE: All right, I won't! (*Forcing a laugh.*) I must be eaten up with jealousy for them, that's it.

TYRONE: You needn't be. They don't belong.

JOSIE: And I do?

TYRONE: Yes. You do.

JOSIE: For tonight only, you mean?

TYRONE: We've agreed there is only tonight—and it's to be different from any past night—for both of us.

JOSIE (*in a forced, kidding tone*): I hope it will be. I'll try to control my envy for your Broadway flames. I suppose it's because I have a picture of them in my mind as small and dainty and pretty—

TYRONE: They're just gold-digging tramps.

JOSIE (*as if he hadn't spoken*): While I'm only a big, rough, ugly cow of a woman.

TYRONE: Shut up! You're beautiful.

JOSIE (*jeeringly, but her voice trembles*): God pity the blind!

TYRONE: You're beautiful to me.

JOSIE: It must be the Bourbon—

TYRONE: You're real and healthy and clean and fine and warm and strong and kind—

JOSIE: I have a beautiful soul, you mean?

TYRONE: Well, I don't know much about ladies' souls— (*He takes her hand.*) But I do know you're beautiful. (*He kisses her hand.*) And I love you a lot—in my fashion.

JOSIE (*stammers*): Jim— (*Hastily forcing her playful tone.*) Sure, you're full of fine compliments all of a sudden, and I ought to show you how pleased I am. (*She pulls his head back and kisses him on the lips–a quick, shy kiss.*) That's for my beautiful soul.

TYRONE (*The kiss arouses his physical desire. He pulls her head down and stares into her eyes*): You have a beautiful strong body, too, Josie—and beautiful eyes and hair, and a beautiful smile and beautiful warm breasts. (*He kisses her on the lips. She pulls back frightenedly for a second–then returns his kiss. Suddenly he breaks away–in a tone of guilty irritation.*) Nix! Nix! Don't be a fool, Josie. Don't let me pull that stuff.

JOSIE (*triumphant for a second*): You meant it! I know you meant it! (*Then with resentful bitterness–roughly.*) Be God, you're right I'm a damned fool to let you make me forget you're the greatest liar in the world! (*Quickly.*) I mean, the greatest kidder. And now, how about another drink?

TYRONE (*staring at nothing–vaguely*): You don't get me, Josie. You don't know—and I hope you never will know—

JOSIE (*blurts out bitterly*): Maybe I know more than you think.

TYRONE (*as if she hadn't spoken*): There's always the aftermath that poisons you. I don't want you to be poisoned—

JOSIE: Maybe you know what you're talking about—

TYRONE: And I don't want to be poisoned myself—not again—not with you. (*He pauses–slowly.*) There have been too many nights—and dawns. This must be different. I want— (*His voice trails off into silence.*)

JOSIE (*trying to read his face–uneasily*): Don't get in one of your queer spells, now. (*She gives his shoulder a shake–forcing a light tone.*) Sure, I don't think you know what you want. Except another drink. I'm sure you want that. And I want one, too.

TYRONE (*recovering himself*): Fine! Grand idea. (*He gets up and brings the bottle from the boulder. He picks up his tumbler and pours a big drink. She is holding out her tumbler but he ignores it.*)

JOSIE: You're not polite, pouring your own first.

TYRONE: I said a drink was a grand idea—for me. Not for you. You skip this one.

JOSIE (*resentfully*): Oh, I do, do I? Are you giving me orders?

TYRONE: Yes. Take a big drink of moonlight instead.

JOSIE (*angrily*): You'll pour me a drink, if you please, Jim Tyrone, or—

TYRONE (*stares at her–then shrugs his shoulders*): All right, if you want to take it that way, Josie. It's your funeral. (*He pours a drink into her tumbler.*)

JOSIE (*ashamed but defiant–stiffly*): Thank you kindly. (*She raises her glass–mockingly.*) Here's to tonight. (TYRONE *is staring at her, a strange bitter disgust in his eyes. Suddenly he slaps at her hand. knocking the glass to the ground.*)

TYRONE (*his voice hard with repulsion*): I've slept with drunken tramps on too many nights!

JOSIE (*stares at him, too startled and bewildered to be angry. Her voice trembles with surprising meekness*): All right, Jim, if you don't want me to—

TYRONE (*now looks as bewildered by his action as she does*): I'm sorry, Josie. Don't know what the drink got into me. (*He picks up her glass.*) Here. I'll pour you another.

JOSIE (*still meek*): No, thank you. I'll skip this one. (*She puts the glass on the ground.*) But you drink up.

TYRONE: Thanks. (*He gulps down his drink. Mechanically, as if he didn't know what he was doing, he pours another. Suddenly he blurts out with guilty loathing.*) That fat blonde pig on the train—I got her drunk! That's why— (*He stops guiltily.*)

JOSIE (*uneasily*): What are you talking about? What train?

TYRONE: No train. Don't mind me. (*He gulps down the drink and pours another with the same strange air of acting unconsciously.*) Maybe I'll tell you—later, when I'm— That'll cure you—for all time! (*Abruptly he realizes what he is saying. He gives the characteristic shrug of shoulders–cynically.*) Nuts! The Brooklyn boys are talking again. I guess I'm more stewed than I thought—in the center of the old bean, at least. (*Dully.*) I better beat it back to the Inn and go to bed and stop bothering you, Josie.

JOSIE (*bullyingly–and pityingly*): Well, you won't, not if I have to hold you. Come on now, bring your drink and sit down like you were before. (*He does so. She pats his cheek–forcing a playful air.*) That's a good boy. And I won't take any more whiskey. I've all the effect from it I want already. Everything is far away and doesn't matter—except the moon and its dreams, and I'm part of the dreams—and you are, too. (*She adds with a rueful little laugh.*) I keep forgetting the thing I've got to remember. I keep hoping it's a lie, even though I know I'm a damned fool.

TYRONE (*hazily*): Damned fool about what?

JOSIE: Never mind. (*Forcing a laugh.*) I've just had a thought. If my poor old father had seen you knocking his prize whiskey on the ground—Holy Joseph, he'd have had three paralytic strokes!

TYRONE (*grins*): Yes, I can picture him, (*He pauses–with amused affection.*) But that's all a fake. He loves to play tightwad, but the people he likes know better. He'd give them his shirt. He's a grand old scout, Josie. (*A bit maudlin.*) The only real friend I've got left—except you. I love his guts.

JOSIE (*tensely–sickened by his hypocrisy*): Och, for the love of God—!

TYRONE (*shrugs his shoulders*): Yes, I suppose that does sound like moaning-at-the-bar stuff. But I mean it.

JOSIE: Do you? Well, I know my father's virtues without you telling me.

TYRONE: You ought to appreciate him because he worships the ground you walk on—and he knows you a lot better than you think. *(He turns to smile at her teasingly.)* As well as I do—almost.

JOSIE *(defensively)*: That's not saying much. Maybe I can guess what you think you know— *(Forcing a contemptuous laugh.)* If it's that, God pity you, you're a terrible fool.

TYRONE *(teasingly)*: If it's what? I haven't said anything.

JOSIE: You'd better not, or I'll die laughing at you. *(She changes the subject abruptly.)* Why don't you drink up? It makes me nervous watching you hold it as if you didn't know it was there.

TYRONE: I didn't, at that. *(He drinks.)*

JOSIE: And have another.

TYRONE *(a bit drunkenly)*: Will a whore go to a picnic? Real bonded Bourbon. That's my dish. *(He goes to the boulder for the bottle. He is as steady on his feet as if he were completely sober.)*

JOSIE *(in a light tone)*: Bring the bottle back so it'll be handy and you won't have to leave me. I miss you.

TYRONE *(comes back with the bottle. He smiles at her cynically)*: Still trying to get me soused, Josie?

JOSIE: I'm not such a fool—with your capacity.

TYRONE: You better watch your step. It might work—and then think of how disgusted you'd feel with me lying beside you, probably snoring, as you watched the dawn come. You don't know—

JOSIE *(defiantly)*: The hell I don't! Isn't that the way I've felt with every one of them, after?

TYRONE *(as if he hadn't heard–bitterly)*: But take it from me, I know. I've seen too God-damned many dawns creeping grayly over too many dirty windows.

JOSIE *(ignores this–boldly)*: But it might be different with you. Love could make it different. And I've been head over heels in love ever since you said you loved my beautiful soul. *(Again he doesn't seem to have heard–resentfully.)* Don't stand there like a loon, mourning over the past. Why don't you pour yourself a drink and sit down?

TYRONE *(looks at the bottle and tumbler in his hands, as if he'd forgotten them–mechanically)*: Sure thing. Real bonded Bourbon. I ought to know. If I had a dollar for every drink of it I had before Prohibition, I'd hire our dear bully, Harder, for a valet. *(JOSIE stiffens and her face hardens. TYRONE pours a drink and sets the bottle on the ground. He looks up suddenly into her eyes–warningly.)* You'd better remember I said you had beautiful eyes and hair—and breasts.

JOSIE: I remember you did. *(She tries to be calculatingly enticing.)* So sit down and I'll let you lay your head—

TYRONE: No. If you won't watch your step, I've got to. *(He sits down but doesn't lean back.)* And don't let me get away with pretending I'm so soused I don't know what I'm doing. I always know. Or part of me does. That's the trouble. *(He pauses—then bursts out in a strange threatening tone.)* You better look out, Josie. She was tickled to death to get me pie-eyed. Had an idea she could roll me, I guess. She wasn't so tickled about it—later on.

JOSIE: What she? *(He doesn't reply. She forces a light tone.)* I hope you don't think I'm scheming to roll you.

TYRONE *(vaguely)*: What? *(Coming to—indignantly.)* Of course not. What are you talking about? For God's sake, you're not a tart.

JOSIE *(roughly)*: No, I'm a fool. I'm always giving it away.

TYRONE *(angrily)*: That lousy bluff again, eh? You're a liar! For Christ sake, quit that smut stuff, can't you!

JOSIE *(stung)*: Listen to me, Jim! Drunk or not, don't you talk that way to me or—

TYRONE: How about your not talking the old smut stuff to me? You promised you'd be yourself. *(Pauses—vaguely.)* You don't get it, Josie. You see, she was one of the smuttiest talking pigs I've ever listened to.

JOSIE: What she? Do you mean the blonde on the train?

TYRONE *(starts—sharply)*: Train? Who told you—? *(Quickly.)* Oh—that's right—I did say— *(Vaguely.)* What blonde? What's the difference? Coming back from the Coast. It was long ago. But it seems like tonight. There is no present or future—only the past happening over and over again—now. You can't get away from it. *(Abruptly.)* Nuts! To hell with that crap.

JOSIE: You came back from the Coast about a year ago after—*(She checks herself.)*

TYRONE *(dully)*: Yes. After Mama's death. *(Quickly.)* But I've been to the Coast a lot of times during my career as a third-rate ham. I don't remember which time—or anything much—except I was pie-eyed in a drawing room for the whole four days. *(Abruptly.)* What were we talking about before? What a grand guy Phil is. You ought to be glad you've got him for a father. Mine was an old bastard.

JOSIE: He wasn't! He was one of the finest, kindest gentlemen ever lived.

TYRONE *(sneeringly)*: Outside the family, sure. Inside, he was a lousy tightwad bastard.

JOSIE *(repelled)*: You ought to be ashamed!

TYRONE: To speak ill of the dead? Nuts! He can't hear, and he knows I hated him, anyway—as much as he hated me. I'm glad he's dead. So is he. Or he ought to be. Everyone ought to be, if they have any sense. Out of a bum racket. At peace. (*He shrugs his shoulders.*) Nuts! What of it?

JOSIE (*tensely*): Don't Jim. I hate you when you talk like that. (*Forcing a light tone.*) Do you want to spoil our beautiful moonlight night? And don't be telling me of your old flames, on trains or not. I'm too jealous.

TYRONE (*with a shudder of disgust*): Of that pig? (*He drinks his whiskey as if to wash a bad taste from his mouth—then takes one of her hands in both of his— simply.*) You're a fool to be jealous of anyone. You're the only woman I care a damn about.

JOSIE (*deeply stirred, in spite of herself—trembling*): Jim, don't— (*Forcing a tense little laugh.*) All right, I'll try and believe that—for tonight.

TYRONE (*simply*): Thanks, Josie. (*A pause. He speaks in a tone of random curiosity.*) Why did you say a while ago I'd be leaving for New York soon?

JOSIE (*stiffens—her face hardening*): Well, I was right, wasn't I? (*Unconsciously she tries to pull her hand away.*)

TYRONE: Why are you pulling your hand away?

JOSIE (*stops*): Was I? (*Forcing a smile.*) I suppose because it seems crazy for you to hold my big ugly paw so tenderly. But you're welcome to it, if you like.

TYRONE: I do like. It's strong and kind and warm— like you. (*He kisses it.*)

JOSIE (*tensely*): Och, for the love of God—! (*She jerks her hand away—then hastily forces a joking tone.*) Wasting kisses on my hand! Sure, even the moon is laughing at us.

TYRONE: Nuts for the moon! I'd rather have one light on Broadway than all the moons since Rameses was a pup. (*He takes cigarettes from his pocket and lights one.*)

JOSIE (*her eyes searching his face, lighted up by the match*): You'll be taking a train back to your dear old Broadway tomorrow night, won't you?

TYRONE (*still holding the burning match, stares at her in surprise*): Tomorrow night? Where did you get that?

JOSIE: A little bird told me.

TYRONE (*blows out the match in a cloud of smoke*): You'd better give that bird the bird. By the end of the week, is the right dope. Phil got his dates mixed.

JOSIE (*quickly*): He didn't tell me. He was too drunk to remember anything.

TYRONE: He was sober when I told him. I called up the executors when we reached the Inn after leaving here. They said the estate would be out of probate within a few days. I told Phil the glad tidings and bought drinks for all and sundry. There was quite a celebration. Funny, Phil wouldn't remember that.

JOSIE (*bewildered–not knowing what to believe*): It is— funny.

TYRONE (*shrugs his shoulders*): Well, he's stewed to the ears. That always explains anything. (*Then strangely.*) Only sometimes it doesn't.

JOSIE: No—sometimes it doesn't.

TYRONE (*goes on without real interest, talking to keep from thinking*): Phil certainly has a prize bun on to- night. He never took a punch at me before. And that drivel he talked about owing me one—What got into his head, I wonder.

JOSIE (*tensely*): How would I know, if you don't?

TYRONE: Well, I don't. Not unless—I remember I did try to get his goat. Simpson sat down with us. Harder sent him to see me. You remember after Harder left here I said the joke was on you, that you'd made this place a gold mine. I was kidding, but I had the right dope. What do you think he told Simpson to offer? Ten grand! On the level, Josie.

JOSIE (*tense*): So you accepted?

TYRONE: I told Simpson to tell Harder I did. I de- cided the best way to fix him was to let him think he'd got away with it, and then when he comes tomorrow morning to drive me to the executor's office, I'll tell him what he can do with himself, his bankroll, and tin oil tanks.

JOSIE (*knows he is telling the truth—so relieved she can only stammer stupidly*): So that's—the truth of it.

TYRONE (*smiles*): Of course, I did it to kid Phil, too. He was right there, listening. But I know I didn't fool him.

JOSIE (*weakly*): Maybe you did fool him, for once. But I don't know.

TYRONE: And that's why he took a swing at me? (*He laughs, but there is a forced note to it.*) Well, if so, it's one hell of a joke on him. (*His tone becomes hurt and bitter.*) All the same, I'll be good and sore, Josie. I promised this place wouldn't be sold ex- cept to him. What the hell does he think I am? He ought to know I wouldn't double-cross you and him for ten million!

JOSIE (*giving away at last to her relief and joy*): Don't I know! Oh, Jim, darling! (*She hugs him passionately and kisses him on the lips.*) I knew you'd never—I told him— (*She kisses him again.*) Oh, Jim, I love you.

TYRONE (*again with a strange, simple gratitude*): Thanks, Josie. I mean, for not believing I'm a rotten louse. Everyone else believes it—including myself—for a damned good reason. (*Abruptly changing the subject.*) I'm a fool to let this stuff about Phil get under my skin, but— Why, I re- member telling him tonight I'd even written my brother and got his okay on selling the farm to him. And Phil thanked me. He seemed touched and grateful. You wouldn't think he'd forget that.

JOSIE (*her face hard and bitter*): I wouldn't, indeed. There's a lot of things he'll have to explain when he comes at sun— (*Hastily.*) When he comes back. (*She pauses—then bursts out.*) The damned old schemer, I'll teach him to— (*Again checking herself.*) to act like a fool.

TYRONE (*smiles*): You'll get out the old club, eh? What a bluff you are, Josie. (*Teasingly.*) You and your loves, Messalina—when you've never—

JOSIE (*with a faint spark of her old defiance*): You're a liar.

TYRONE: "Pride is the sin by which the angels fell." Are you going to keep that up—with me?

JOSIE (*feebly*): You think I've never because no one would—because I'm a great ugly cow—

TYRONE (*gently*): Nuts! You could have had any one of them. You kidded them till you were sure they wanted you. That was all you wanted. And then you slapped them groggy when they tried for more. But you had to keep convincing yourself—

JOSIE (*tormentedly*): Don't, Jim.

TYRONE: You can take the truth, Josie—from me. Because you and I belong to the same club. We can kid the world but we can't fool ourselves, like most people, no matter what we do—nor escape ourselves no matter where we run away. Whether it's the bottom of a bottle, or a South Sea Island, we'd find our own ghosts there waiting to greet us— "sleepless with pale commemorative eyes," as Rossetti wrote. (*He sneers to himself.*) The old poetic bull, eh? Crap! (*Reverting to a teasing tone.*) You don't ask how I saw through your bluff, Josie. You pretend too much. And so do the guys. I've listened to them at the Inn. They all lie to each other. No one wants to admit all he got was a slap in the puss, when he thinks a lot of other guys made it. You can't blame them. And they know you don't give a damn how they lie. So—

JOSIE: For the love of God, Jim! Don't!

TYRONE: Phil is wise to you, of course, but although he knew I knew, he would never admit it until tonight.

JOSIE (*startled—vindictively*): So he admitted it, did he? Wait till I get hold of him!

TYRONE: He'll never admit it to you. He's afraid of hurting you.

JOSIE: He is, is he? Well— (*Almost hysterically.*) For the love of God, can't you shut up about him!

TYRONE (*glances up at her, surprised—then shrugs his shoulders*): Oh, all right. I wanted to clear things up, that's all—for Phil's sake as well as yours. You have a hell of a license to be sore. He's the one who ought to be. Don't you realize what a lousy position you've put him in with your brazentrollop act?

JOSIE (*tensely*): No. He doesn't care, except to use me in his scheming. He—

TYRONE: Don't be a damned fool. Of course he cares. And so do I. (*He turns and pulls her head down and kisses her on the lips.*) I care, Josie. I love you.

JOSIE (*with pitiful longing*): Do you, Jim? Do you? (*She forces a trembling smile—faintly.*) Then I'll confess the truth to you. I've been a crazy fool. I am a virgin. (*She begins to sob with a strange forlorn shame and humiliation.*) And now you'll never—and I want you to—now more than ever—because I love you more than ever, after what's happened—(*Suddenly she kisses him with fierce passion.*) But you will! I'll make you! To hell with your honorable scruples! I know you want me! I couldn't believe that until tonight—but now I know. It's in your kisses! (*She kisses him again—with passionate tenderness.*) Oh, you great fool! As if I gave a damn what happened after! I'll have had tonight and your love to remember for the rest of my days! (*She kisses him again.*) Oh, Jim darling, haven't you said yourself there's only tonight? (*She whispers tenderly.*) Come. Come with me. (*She gets to her feet, pulling at his arm—with a little self-mocking laugh.*) But I'll have to make you leave before sunrise. I mustn't forget that.

TYRONE (*a strange change has come over his face. He looks her over now with a sneering cynical lust. He speaks thickly as if he was suddenly very drunk*): Sure thing, Kiddo. What the hell else do you suppose I came for? I've been kidding myself. (*He steps up beside her and puts his arm around her and presses his body to hers.*) You're the goods, Kid. I've wanted you all along. Love, nuts! I'll show you what love is. I know what you want, Bright Eyes. (*She is staring at him now with a look of frightened horror. He kisses her roughly.*) Come on, Baby Doll, let's hit the hay. (*He pushes her back in the doorway.*)

JOSIE (*strickenly*): Jim! Don't! (*She pulls his arms away so violently that he staggers back and would fall down the steps if she didn't grab his arm in time. As it is he goes down on one knee. She is on the verge of collapse herself—brokenly.*) Jim! I'm not a whore.

TYRONE (*remains on one knee—confusedly, as if he didn't know what had happened*): What the hell? Was I trying to rape you, Josie? Forget it. I'm drunk—not responsible. (*He gets to his feet, staggering a bit, and steps down to the ground.*)

JOSIE (*covering her face with her hands*): Oh, Jim! (*She sobs.*)

TYRONE (*with vague pity*): Don't cry. No harm done. You stopped me, didn't you? (*She continues to sob. He mutters vaguely, as if talking to himself.*) Must have drawn a blank for a while. Nuts! Cut out the faking. I knew what I was doing. (*Slowly, staring before him.*) But it's funny. I *was* seeing things. That's the truth, Josie. For a moment I thought you were that blonde pig— (*Hastily.*) The old heebie-jeebies. Hair of the dog. (*He gropes around *for the bottle and his glass.)* I'll have another shot—

JOSIE *(takes her hands from her face—fiercely)*: Pour the whole bottle down your throat, if you like! Only stop talking! *(She covers her face with her hands and sobs again.)*

TYRONE *(stares at her with a hurt and sad expression—dully)*: Can't forgive me, eh? You ought to. You ought to thank me for letting you see— *(He pauses, as if waiting for her to say something, but she remains silent. He shrugs his shoulders, pours out a big drink mechanically.)* Well, here's how. *(He drinks and puts the bottle and glass on the ground—dully.)* That was a nightcap. Our moonlight romance seems to be a flop, Josie. I guess I'd better go.

JOSIE *(dully)*: Yes. You'd better go. Good night.

TYRONE: Not good night. Good-bye.

JOSIE *(lifts her head)*: Good-bye?

TYRONE: Yes. I won't see you again before I leave for New York. I was a damned fool to come tonight. I hoped—But you don't get it. How could you? So what's the good— *(He shrugs his shoulders hopelessly and turns toward the road.)*

JOSIE: Jim!

TYRONE *(turning back—bitter accusation in his tone now)*: Whore? Who said you were a whore? But I warned you, didn't I. if you kept on— Why did you have to act like one, asking me to come to bed? That wasn't what I came here for. And you promised tonight would be different. Why the hell did you promise that, if all you wanted was what all the others want, if that's all love means to you? *(Then guiltily.)* Oh, Christ, I don't mean that, Josie. I know how you feel, and if I could give you happiness— But it wouldn't work. You don't know me. I'd poison it for myself and for you. I've poisoned it already, haven't I, but it would be a million times worse after— No matter how I tried not to. I'd make it like all the other nights—for you, too. You'd lie awake and watch the dawn come with disgust, with nausea retching your memory, and the wine of passion poets blab about, a sour aftertaste in your mouth of Dago red ink! *(He gives a sneering laugh.)*

JOSIE *(distractedly)*: Oh, Jim, don't! Please don't!

TYRONE: You'd hate me and yourself—not for a day or two but for the rest of your life. *(With a perverse, jeering note of vindictive boastfulness in his tone.)* Believe me, Kid, when I poison them, they stay poisoned!

JOSIE *(with dull bitterness)*: Good-bye, Jim.

TYRONE *(miserably hurt and sad for a second—appealingly)*: Josie— *(Gives the characteristic shrug of his shoulders—simply.)* Good-bye. *(He turns toward the road—bitterly.)* I'll find it hard to forgive, too. I came here asking for love—just for this one night, because I thought you loved me. *(Dully.)* Nuts. To hell with it. *(He starts away.)*

JOSIE *(watches him for a second, fighting the love that, in spite of her, responds to his appeal—then she springs up and runs to him—with fierce, possessive, maternal tenderness)*: Come here to me, you great fool, and stop your silly blather. There's nothing to hate you for. There's nothing to forgive. Sure, I was only trying to give you happiness, because I love you. I'm sorry I was so stupid and didn't see— But I see now. and you'll find I have all the love you need. *(She gives him a hug and kisses him. There is passion in her kiss but it is a tender, protective maternal passion, which he responds to with an instant grateful yielding.)*

TYRONE *(simply)*: Thanks, Josie. You're beautiful. I love you. I knew you'd understand.

JOSIE: Of course I do. Come, now. *(She leads him back, her arm around his waist.)*

TYRONE: I didn't want to leave you. You know that.

JOSIE: Indeed I know it. Come now. We'll sit down. *(She sits on the top step and pulls him down on the step below her.)* That's it—with my arm around you. Now lay your head on my breast—the way you said you wanted to do.— *(He lets his head fall back on her breast. She hugs him—gently.)* There, now. Forget all about my being a fool and forgive— *(Her voice trembles—but she goes on determinedly.)* Forgive my selfishness, thinking only of myself. Sure, if there's one thing I owe you tonight, after all my lying and scheming, it's to give you the love you need, and it'll be my pride and my joy— *(Forcing a trembling echo of her playful tone.)* It's easy enough, too, for I have all kinds of love for you—and maybe this is the greatest of all—because it costs so much. *(She pauses, looking down at his face. He has closed his eyes and his haggard, dissipated face looks like a pale mask in the moonlight—at peace as a death mask is at peace. She becomes frightened.)* Jim! Don't look like that!

TYRONE *(opens his eyes—vaguely)*: Like what?

JOSIE *(quickly)*: It's the moonlight. It makes you look so pale, and with your eyes closed—

TYRONE *(simply)*: You mean I looked dead?

JOSIE: No! As if you'd fallen asleep.

TYRONE *(speaks in a tired, empty tone, as if he felt he ought to explain something to her—something which no longer interests him)*: Listen, and I'll tell you a little story, Josie. All my life I had just one dream. From the time I was a kid, I loved race-horses. I thought they were the most beautiful things in the world. I liked to gamble, too. So the big dream was that some day I'd have enough dough to play a cagey system of betting on favorites, and follow the horses south in the winter, and come back north with them in the spring, and be at the track every day. It seemed that would be the ideal life—for me. *(He pauses.)*

JOSIE: Well, you'll be able to do it.

TYRONE: No. I won't be able to do it, Josie. That's the joke. I gave it a try-out before I came up here. I borrowed some money on my share of the estate, and started going to tracks. But it didn't work. I played my system, but I found I didn't care if I won or lost. The horses were beautiful, but I found myself saying to myself, what of it? Their beauty didn't mean anything. I found that every day I was glad when the last race was over, and I could go back to the hotel—and the bottle in my room. (*He pauses, staring into the moonlight with vacant eyes.*)

JOSIE (*uneasily*): Why did you tell me this?

TYRONE (*in the same listless monotone*): You said I looked dead. Well, I am.

JOSIE: You're not! (*She hugs him protectively.*) Don't talk like that!

TYRONE: Ever since Mama died.

JOSIE (*deeply moved—pityingly*): I know. I've felt all along it was that sorrow was making you— (*She pauses—gently.*) Maybe if you talked about your grief for her, it would help you. I think it must be all choked up inside you, killing you.

TYRONE (*in a strange warning tone*): You'd better look out, Josie.

JOSIE: Why?

TYRONE (*quickly, forcing his cynical smile*): I might develop a crying jag, and sob on your beautiful breast.

JOSIE (*gently*): You can sob all you like.

TYRONE: Don't encourage me. You'd be sorry. (*A deep conflict shows in his expression and tone. He is driven to go on in spite of himself.*) But if you're such a glutton for punishment— After all, I said I'd tell you later, didn't I?

JOSIE (*puzzled*): You said you'd tell me about the blonde on the train.

TYRONE: She's part of it. I lied about that. (*He pauses—then blurts out sneeringly.*) You won't believe it could have happened. Or if you did believe it, you couldn't understand or forgive— (*Quickly.*) But you might. You're the one person who might. Because you really love me. And because you're the only woman I've ever met who understands the lousy rotten things a man can do when he's crazy drunk, and draws a blank— especially when he's nutty with grief to start with.

JOSIE (*hugging him tenderly*): Of course I'll understand, Jim, darling.

TYRONE (*stares into the moonlight—hauntedly*): But I didn't draw a blank. I tried to. I drank enough to knock out ten men. But it didn't work. I knew what I was doing. (*He pauses—dully.*) No, I can't tell you, Josie. You'd loathe my guts, and I couldn't blame you.

JOSIE: No! I'll love you no matter what—

TYRONE (*with strange triumphant harshness*): All right! Remember that's a promise! (*He pauses—starts to speak—pauses again.*)

JOSIE (*pityingly*): Maybe you'd better not—if it will make you suffer.

TYRONE: Trying to welch now, eh? It's too late. You've got me started. Suffer? Christ, I ought to suffer! (*He pauses. Then he closes his eyes. It is as if he had to hide from sight before he can begin. He makes his face expressionless. His voice becomes impersonal and objective, as though what he told concerned some man he had known, but had nothing to do with him. This is the only way he can start telling the story.*) When Mama died, I'd been on the wagon for nearly two years. Not even a glass of beer. Honestly. And I know I would have stayed on. For her sake. She had no one but me. The Old Man was dead. My brother had married—had a kid—had his own life to live. She'd lost him. She had only me to attend to things for her and take care of her. She'd always hated my drinking. So I quit. It made me happy to do it. For her. Because she was all I had, all I cared about. Because I loved her. (*He pauses.*) No one would believe that now, who knew— But I did.

JOSIE (*gently*): I know how much you loved her.

TYRONE: We went out to the Coast to see about selling a piece of property the Old Man had bought there years ago. And one day she suddenly became ill. Got rapidly worse. Went into a coma. Brain tumor. The docs said, no hope. Might never come out of coma. I went crazy. Couldn't face losing her. The old booze yen got me. I got drunk and stayed drunk. And I began hoping she'd never come out of the coma, and see I was drinking again. That was my excuse, too—that she'd never know. And she never did. (*He pauses—then sneeringly.*) Nix! Kidding myself again. I know damned well just before she died she recognized me. She saw I was drunk. Then she closed her eyes so she couldn't see, and was glad to die! (*He opens his eyes and stares into the moonlight as if he saw this deathbed scene before him.*)

JOSIE (*soothingly*): Ssshh. You only imagine that because you feel guilty about drinking.

TYRONE (*as if he hadn't heard, closes his eyes again*): After that, I kept so drunk I did draw a blank most of the time, but I went through the necessary motions and no one guessed how drunk— (*He pauses.*) But there are things I can never forget—the undertakers, and her body in a coffin with her face made up. I couldn't hardly recognize her. She looked young and pretty like someone I remembered meeting long ago. Practically a stranger. To who I was a stranger. Cold and indifferent. Not worried about me any more. Free at last. Free from worry. From pain. From me. I stood looking down at her, and something happened to me. I found I couldn't feel anything. I knew I ought to be heartbroken but I couldn't feel anything. I seemed dead, too. I knew I ought to cry. Even a crying jag would look better than just standing there. But I couldn't cry. I cursed to myself, "You dirty bastard, it's Mama. You loved her, and now she's dead. She's gone away from you forever. Never, never again—" But it had no effect. All I did was try to explain to myself, "She's dead. What does she care now if I cry or not, or what I do? It doesn't matter a damn to her. She's happy to be where I can't hurt her ever again. She's rid of me at last. For God's sake, can't you leave her alone even now? For God's sake, can't you let her rest in peace?" (He pauses—then sneeringly.) But there were several people around and I knew they expected me to show something. Once a ham, always a ham! So I put on an act. I flopped on my knees and hid my face in my hands and faked some sobs and cried, "Mama! Mama! My dear mother!" But all the time I kept saying to myself, "You lousy ham! You God-damned lousy ham! Christ, in a minute you'll start singing 'Mother Macree'!" (He opens his eyes and gives a tortured, sneering laugh, staring into the moonlight.)

JOSIE (horrified, but still deeply pitying): Jim! Don't! It's past. You've punished yourself. And you were drunk. You didn't mean—

TYRONE (again closes his eyes): I had to bring her body East to be buried beside the Old Man. I took a drawing room and hid in it with a case of booze. She was in her coffin in the baggage car. No matter how drunk I got, I couldn't forget that for a minute. I found I couldn't stay alone in the drawing room. It became haunted. I was going crazy. I had to go out and wander up and down the train looking for company. I made such a public nuisance of myself that the conductor threatened if I didn't quit, he'd keep me locked in the drawing room. But I'd spotted one passenger who was used to drunks and could pretend to like them, if there was enough dough in it. She had parlor house written all over her—a blonde pig who looked more like a whore than twenty-five whores, with a face like an overgrown doll's and a come-on smile as cold as a polar bear's feet. I bribed the porter to take a message to her and that night she sneaked into my drawing room. She was bound for New York, too. So every night—for fifty bucks a night— (He opens his eyes and now he stares torturedly through the moonlight into the drawing room.)

JOSIE (her face full of revulsion—stammers): Oh, how could you! (Instinctively she draws away, taking her arms from around him.)

TYRONE: How could I? I don't know. But I did. I suppose I had some mad idea she could make me forget—what was in the baggage car ahead.

JOSIE: Don't. (She draws back again so he has to raise his head from her breast. He doesn't seem to notice this.)

TYRONE: No, it couldn't have been that. Because I didn't seem to want to forget. It was like some plot I had to carry out. The blonde—she didn't matter. She was only something that belonged in the plot. It was as if I wanted revenge—because I'd been left alone—because I knew I was lost, without any hope left—that all I could do would be drink myself to death, because no one was left who could help me. (His face hardens and a look of cruel vindictiveness comes into it—with a strange horrible satisfaction in his tone.) No, I didn't forget even in that pig's arms! I remembered the last two lines of a lousy tear-jerker song I'd heard when I was a kid kept singing over and over in my brain.

"And baby's cries can't waken her
In the baggage coach ahead."

JOSIE (distractedly): Jim!

TYRONE: I couldn't stop it singing. I didn't want to stop it!

JOSIE: Jim! For the love of God. I don't want to hear!

TYRONE (after a pause—dully): Well, that's all—except I was too drunk to go to her funeral.

JOSIE: Oh! (She has drawn away from him as far as she can without getting up. He becomes aware of this for the first time and turns slowly to stare at her.)

TYRONE (dully): Don't want to touch me now, eh? (He shrugs his shoulders mechanically.) Sorry. I'm a damned fool. I shouldn't have told you.

JOSIE (her horror ebbing as her love and protective compassion returns—moves nearer him—haltingly): Don't, Jim. Don't say—I don't want to touch you. It's—a lie. (She puts a hand on his shoulder.)

TYRONE (as if she hadn't spoken—with hopeless longing): Wish I could believe in the spiritualists' bunk. If I could tell her it was because I missed her so much and couldn't forgive her for leaving me—

JOSIE: Jim! For the love of God—!

TYRONE (unheeding): She'd understand and forgive me, don't you think? She always did. She was simple and kind and pure of heart. She was beautiful. You're like her deep in your heart. That's why I told you. I thought— (Abruptly his expression becomes sneering and cynical—harshly.) My mistake. Nuts! Forget it. Time I got a move on. I don't like your damned moon, Josie. It's an ad for the past. (He recites mockingly)

"It is the very error of the moon:
She comes more nearer earth than she was wont,
And makes men mad."

(He moves) I'll grab the last trolley for town. There'll be a speak open, and some drunk laughing. I need a laugh. (He starts to get up.)

JOSIE (throws her arms around him and pulls him back—

tensely): No! You won't go! I won't let you! *(She hugs him close—gently.)* I understand now, Jim, darling, and I'm proud you came to me as the one in the world you know loves you enough to understand and forgive—and I do forgive!

TYRONE *(lets his head fall back on her breast—simply)*: Thanks, Josie, I knew you—

JOSIE: As *she* forgives, do you hear me! As *she* loves and understands and forgives!

TYRONE *(simply)*: Yes, I know she— *(His voice breaks.)*

JOSIE *(bends over him with a brooding maternal tenderness)*: That's right. Do what you came for, my darling. It isn't drunken laughter in a speakeasy you want to hear at all, but the sound of yourself crying your heart's repentance against her breast. *(His face is convulsed. He hides it on her breast and sobs rackingly. She hugs him more tightly and speaks softly, staring into the moonlight.)* She hears. I feel her in the moonlight, her soul wrapped in it like a silver mantle, and I know she understand and forgives me, too, and her blessing lies on me. *(A pause. His sobs begin to stop exhaustedly. She looks down at him again and speaks soothingly as she would to a child.)* There. There, now. *(He stops. She goes on in a gentle, bullying tone.)* You're a fine one, wanting to leave me when the night I promised I'd give you has just begun, our night that'll be different from all the others, with a dawn that won't creep over dirty windowpanes but will wake in the sky like a promise of God's peace in the soul's dark sadness. *(She smiles a little amused smile.)* Will you listen to me, Jim! I must be a poet. Who would have guessed it? Sure, love is a wonderful mad inspiration! *(A pause. She looks down. His eyes are closed. His face against her breast looks pale and haggard in the moonlight. Calm with the drained, exhausted peace of death. For a second she is frightened. Then she realizes and whispers softly.)* Asleep. *(In a tender crooning tone like a lullaby.)* That's right. Sleep in peace, my darling. *(Then with sudden anguished longing.)* Oh, Jim, Jim, maybe my love could still save you, if you could want it enough! *(She shakes her head.)* No. That can never be. *(Her eyes leave his face to stare up at the sky. She looks weary and stricken and sad. She forces a defensive, self-derisive smile.)* God forgive me, it's a fine end to all my scheming, to sit here with the dead hugged to my breast, and the silly mug of the moon grinning down, enjoying the joke!

ACT 4

(Scene: Same as Act Three. It is dawn. The first faint streaks of color, heralding the sunrise, appear in the eastern sky at left.

JOSIE *sits in the same position on the steps, as if she had not moved, her arms around* TYRONE. *He is still asleep,* his head on her breast. His face has the same exhausted, death-like repose. JOSIE's *face is set in an expression of numbed, resigned sadness. Her body sags tiredly. In spite of her strength, holding herself like this for hours, for fear of waking him, is becoming too much for her.*

The two make a strangely tragic picture in the wan dawn light—this big sorrowful woman hugging a haggard-faced, middle-aged drunkard against her breast, as if he were a sick child.

HOGAN *appears at left-rear, coming from the barn. He approaches the corner of the house stealthily on tiptoe. Wisps of hay stick to his clothes and his face is swollen and sleepy, but his little pig's eyes are sharply wide awake and sober. He peeks around the corner, and takes in the two on the steps. His eyes fix on* JOSIE's *face in a long, probing stare.)*

JOSIE *(speaks in a low grim tone)*: Stop hiding, Father. I heard you sneak up. *(He comes guiltily around the corner. She keeps her voice low, but her tone is commanding.)* Come here, and be quiet about it. *(He obeys meekly, coming as far as the boulder silently, his eyes searching her face, his expression becoming guilty and miserable at what he sees. She goes on in the same tone, without looking at him.)* Talk low, now. I don't want him wakened— *(She adds strangely.)* Not until the dawn has beauty in it.

HOGAN *(worriedly)*: What? *(He decides it's better for the present to ask no questions. His eyes fall on* TYRONE's *face. In spite of himself, he is startled—in an awed, almost frightened whisper.)* Be god, he looks dead!

JOSIE *(strangely)*: Why wouldn't he? He is.

HOGAN: Is?

JOSIE: Don't be a fool. Can't you see him breathing? Dead asleep, I mean. Don't stand there gawking. Sit down. *(He sits meekly on the boulder. His face betrays a guilty dread of what is coming. There is a pause in which she doesn't look at him but, he keeps glancing at her, growing visibly more uneasy. She speaks bitterly.)* Where's your witnesses?

HOGAN *(guiltily)*: Witnesses? *(Then forcing an amused grin.)* Oh, be God, if that ain't a joke on me! Sure I got so blind drunk at the Inn I forgot all about our scheme and came home and went to sleep in the hayloft.

JOSIE *(her expression harder and more bitter)*: You're a liar.

HOGAN: I'm not. I just woke up. Look at the hay sticking to me. That's proof.

JOSIE: I'm not thinking of that, and well you know it. *(With bitter voice.)* So you just woke up—did you?—and then came sneaking here to see if the scheme behind your scheme had worked!

HOGAN *(guiltily)*: I don't know what you mean.

JOSIE: Don't lie any more, Father. This time, you've told one too many. *(He starts to defend himself but the look on her face makes him think better of it and he remains uneasily silent. A pause.)*

HOGAN (*finally has to blurt out*): Sure, if I'd brought the witnesses, there's nothing for them to witness that—

JOSIE: No. You're right there. There's nothing. Nothing at all. (*She smiles strangely.*) Except a great miracle they'd never believe, or you either.

HOGAN: What miracle?

JOSIE: A virgin who bears a dead child in the night, and the dawn finds her still a virgin. If that isn't a miracle, what is?

HOGAN (*uneasily*): Stop talking so queer. You give me the shivers. (*He attempts a joking tone.*) Is it you who's the virgin? Faith, that *would* be a miracle, no less! (*He forces a chuckle.*)

JOSIE: I told you to stop lying, Father.

HOGAN: What lie? (*He stops and watches her face worriedly. She is silent, as if she were not aware of him now. Her eyes are fixed on the wanton sky.*)

JOSIE (*as if to herself*): It'll be beautiful soon, and I can wake him.

HOGAN (*can't resist his anxiety any longer*): Josie, darlin'! For the love of God, can't you tell me what happened to you?

JOSIE (*her face hard and bitter again*): I've told you once. Nothing.

HOGAN: Nothing? If you could see the sadness in your face—

JOSIE: What woman doesn't sorrow for the man she loved who has died? But there's pride in my heart, too.

HOGAN (*tormentedly*): Will you stop talking as if you'd gone mad in the night! (*Raising his voice—with revengeful anger.*) Listen to me! If Jim Tyrone has done anything to bring you sorrow— (TYRONE *stirs in his sleep and moans, pressing his face against her breast as if for protection. She looks down at him and hugs him close.*)

JOSIE (*croons softly*): There, there, my darling. Rest in peace a while longer. (*Turns on her father angrily and whispers.*) Didn't I tell you to speak low and not wake him! (*She pauses—then quietly.*) He did nothing to bring me sorrow. It was my mistake. I thought there was still hope. I didn't know he'd died already—that it was a damned soul coming to me in the moonlight, to confess and be forgiven and find peace for a night—

HOGAN: Josie! Will you stop!

JOSIE (*after a pause—dully*): He'd never do anything to hurt me. You know it. (*Self-mockingly.*) Sure, hasn't he told me I'm beautiful to him and he loves me—in his fashion. (*Then matter-of-factly.*) All that happened was that he got drunk and he had one of his crazy notions he wanted to sleep the way he is, and I let him sleep. (*With forced roughness.*) And, be God, the night's over. I'm half dead with tiredness and sleepiness. It's that you see in my face, not sorrow.

HOGAN: Don't try to fool me, Josie. I—

JOSIE (*her face hard and bitter—grimly*): Fool you, is it? It's you who made a fool of me with your lies, thinking you'd use me to get your dirty greasy paws on the money he'll have!

HOGAN: No! I swear by all the saints—

JOSIE: You'd swear on a Bible while you were stealing it! (*Grimly.*) Listen to me, Father. I didn't call you here to answer questions about what's none of your business. I called you here to tell you I've seen through all the lies you told last night to get me to— (*As he starts to speak.*) Shut up! I'll do the talking now. You weren't drunk. You were only putting it on as part of your scheme—

HOGAN (*quietly*): I wasn't drunk, no. I admit that, Josie. But I'd had slews of drinks and they were in my head or I'd never have the crazy dreams—

JOSIE (*with biting scorn*): Dreams, is it? The only dream you've ever had, or will have, is of yourself counting a fistful of dirty money, and divil a care how you got it, or who you robbed or made suffer!

HOGAN (*winces—pleadingly*): Josie!

JOSIE: Shut up! (*Scathingly.*) I'm sure you've made up a whole new set of lies and excuses. You're that cunning and clever, but you can save your breath. They wouldn't fool me now. I've been fooled once too often. (*He gives her a frightened look, as if something he had dreaded has happened. She goes on, grimly accusing.*) You lied about Jim selling the farm. You knew he was kidding. You knew the estate would be out of probate in a few days, and he'd go back to Broadway, and you had to do something quick or you'd lose the last chance of getting your greedy hooks on his money.

HOGAN (*miserably*): No. It wasn't that, Josie.

JOSIE: You saw how hurt and angry I was because he'd kept me waiting here, and you used that. You knew I loved him and wanted him and you used that. You used all you knew about me— Oh, you did it clever! You ought to be proud! You worked it so it was me who did all the dirty scheming— You knew I'd find out from Jim you'd lied about the farm, but not before your lie had done its work—made me go after him, get him drunk, get drunk myself so I could be shameless—and when the truth did come out, wouldn't it make me love him all the more and be more shameless and willing? Don't tell me you didn't count on that, and you such a clever schemer! And if he once had me, knowing I was a virgin, didn't you count on his honor and remorse, and his loving me in his fashion, to make him offer to marry me? Sure, why wouldn't he, you thought. It wouldn't hold him. He'd go back to Broadway just the same and never see me again. But there'd be money in it, and when he'd finished killing himself, I'd be his legal widow and get what's left.

HOGAN (*miserably*): No! It wasn't that.

JOSIE: But what's the good of talking? It's all over. I've only one more word for you, Father, and it's this: I'm leaving you today, like my brothers left. You can live alone and work alone your cunning schemes on yourself.

HOGAN (*after a pause—slowly*): I knew you'd be bitter against me, Josie, but I took the chance you'd be so happy you wouldn't care how—

JOSIE (*as if she hadn't heard, looking at the eastern sky which is now glowing with color*): Thank God, it's beautiful. It's time. (*to* HOGAN) Go in the house and stay there till he's gone. I don't want you around to start some new scheme. (*He looks miserable, starts to speak, thinks better of it, and meekly tiptoes past her up the steps and goes in, closing the door quietly after him. She looks down at* TYRONE. *Her face softens with a maternal tenderness—sadly.*) I hate to bring you back to life, Jim, darling. If you could have died in your sleep, that's what you would have liked, isn't it? (*She gives him a gentle shake.*) Wake up, Jim. (*He moans in his sleep and presses more closely against her. She stares at his face.*) Dear God, let him remember that one thing and forget the rest. That will be enough for me. (*She gives him a more vigorous shake.*) Jim! Wake up, do you hear? It's time.

TYRONE (*half wakens without opening his eyes—mutters*): What the hell? (*Dimly conscious of a woman's body—cynically.*) Again, eh? Same old stuff. Who the hell are you, sweetheart? (*Irritably.*) What's the big idea, waking me up? What time is it?

JOSIE: It's dawn.

TYRONE (*still without opening his eyes*): Dawn? (*He quotes drowsily.*)

"But I was desolate and sick of an old passion,
When I awoke and found the dawn was gray."

(*Then with a sneer*) They're all gray. Go to sleep, Kid—and let me sleep. (*He falls asleep again.*)

JOSIE (*tensely*): This one isn't gray, Jim. It's different from all the others—(*She sees he is asleep—bitterly.*) He'll have forgotten. He'll never notice. And I'm the whore on the train to him now, not— (*Suddenly she pushes him away from her and shakes him roughly.*) Will you wake up, for God's sake! I've had all I can bear—

TYRONE (*still half asleep*): Hey! Cut out the rough stuff, Kid. What? (*Awake now, blinking his eyes—with dazed surprise.*) Josie.

JOSIE (*still bitter*): That's who, and none of your damned tarts! (*She pushes him.*) Get up now, so you won't fall asleep again. (*He does so with difficulty, still in a sleepy daze, his body stiff and cramped. She conquers her bitter resentment and puts on her old free-and-easy kidding tone with him, but all the time waiting to see how much he will remember.*) You're stiff and cramped, and no wonder. I'm worse from holding you, if that's any comfort. (*She stretches and rubs her numbed arms, groaning comically.*) Holy Joseph, I'm a wreck entirely. I'll never be the same. (*Giving him a quick glance.*) You look as if you'd drawn a blank and were wondering how you got here. I'll bet you don't remember a thing.

TYRONE (*moving his arms and legs gingerly—sleepily*): I don't know. Wait till I'm sure I'm still alive.

JOSIE: You need an eye-opener. (*She picks up the bottle and glass and pours him a drink.*) Here you are.

TYRONE (*takes the glass mechanically*): Thanks, Josie. (*He goes and sits on the boulder, holding the drink as if he had no interest in it.*)

JOSIE (*watching him*): Drink up or you'll be asleep again.

TYRONE: No, I'm awake now, Josie. Funny. Don't seem to want a drink. Oh, I've got a head all right. But no heebie-jeebies—yet.

JOSIE: That's fine. It must be a pleasant change—

TYRONE: It is. I've got a nice, dreamy peaceful hangover for once—as if I'd had a sound sleep without nightmares.

JOSIE: So you did. Divil a nightmare. I ought to know. Wasn't I holding you and keeping them away?

TYRONE: You mean you— (*Suddenly.*) Wait a minute. I remember now I was sitting alone at a table in the Inn, and I suddenly had a crazy notion I'd come up here and sleep with my head on your— So that's why I woke up in your arms. (*Shamefacedly.*) And you let me get away with it. You're a nut, Josie.

JOSIE: Oh, I didn't mind.

TYRONE: You must have seen how blotto I was, didn't you?

JOSIE: I did. You were as full as a tick.

TYRONE: Then why didn't you give me the bum's rush?

JOSIE: Why would I? I was glad to humor you.

TYRONE: For God's sake, how long was I cramped on you like that?

JOSIE: Oh, a few hours, only.

TYRONE: God, I'm sorry, Josie, but it's your own fault for letting me—

JOSIE: Och, don't be apologizing. I was glad of the excuse to stay awake and enjoy the beauty of the moon.

TYRONE: Yes, I can remember what a beautiful night it was.

JOSIE: Can you? I'm glad of that, Jim. You seemed to enjoy it the while we were sitting here together before you fell asleep.

TYRONE: How long a while was that?

JOSIE: Not long. Less than an hour, anyway.

TYRONE: I suppose I bored the hell out of you with a

lot of drunken drivel.

JOSIE: Not a lot, no. But some. You were full of blarney, saying how beautiful I was to you.

TYRONE (*earnestly*): That wasn't drivel, Josie. You were. You are. You always will be.

JOSIE: You're a wonder, Jim. Nothing can stop you, can it? Even me in the light of dawn, looking like something you'd put in the field to scare the crows from the corn. You'll kid at the Day of Judgment.

TYRONE (*impatiently*): You know damned well it isn't kidding. You're not a fool. You can tell.

JOSIE (*kiddingly*): All right, then, I'm beautiful and you love me—in your fashion.

TYRONE: "In my fashion," eh? Was I reciting poetry to you? That must have been hard to take.

JOSIE: It wasn't. I liked it. It was all about beautiful nights and the romance of the moon.

TYRONE: Well, there was some excuse for that, anyway. It sure was a beautiful night. I'll never forget it.

JOSIE: I'm glad, Jim.

TYRONE: What other bunk did I pull on you—or I mean, did old John Barleycorn pull?

JOSIE: Not much. You were mostly quiet and sad—in a kind of daze, as if the moon was in your wits as well as whiskey.

TYRONE: I remember I was having a grand time at the Inn, celebrating with Phil, and then suddenly, for no reason, all the fun went out of it, and I was more melancholy than ten Hamlets. (*He pauses.*) Hope I didn't tell you the sad story of my life and weep on your bosom, Josie.

JOSIE: You didn't. The one thing you talked a lot about was that you wanted the night with me to be different from all the other nights you'd spent with women.

TYRONE (*with revulsion*): God, don't make me think of those tramps now! (*Then with deep, grateful feeling.*) It sure was different, Josie. I may not remember much, but I know how different it was from the way I feel now. None of my usual morning-after stuff—the damned sick remorse that makes you wish you'd died in your sleep so you wouldn't have to face the rotten things you're afraid you said and did the night before, when you were so drunk you didn't know what you were doing.

JOSIE: There's nothing you said or did last night for you to regret. You can take my word for it.

TYRONE (*as if he hadn't heard—slowly*): It's hard to describe how I feel. It's a new one on me. Sort of at peace with myself and this lousy life—as if all my sins had been forgiven— (*He becomes self conscious—cynically.*) Nuts with that sin bunk, but you know what I mean.

JOSIE (*tensely*): I do, and I'm happy you feel that way, Jim. (*A pause. She goes on.*) You talked about how you'd watched too many dawns come creeping grayly over dirty windowpanes, with some tart snoring beside you—

TYRONE (*winces*): Have a heart. Don't remind me of that now, Josie. Don't spoil this dawn! (*A pause. She watches him tensely. He turns slowly to face the east, where the sky is now glowing with all the colors of an exceptionally beautiful sunrise. He stares, drawing a deep breath. He is profoundly moved but immediately becomes self-conscious and tries to sneer it off— cynically.*) God seems to be putting on quite a display. I like Belasco better. Rise of curtain, Act-Four stuff. (*Her face has fallen into lines of bitter hurt, but he adds quickly and angrily.*) God damn it! Why do I have to pull that lousy stuff? (*With genuine deep feeling.*) God, it's beautiful, Josie! I—I'll never forget it—here with you.

JOSIE (*her face clearing—simply*): I'm glad, Jim. I was hoping you'd feel beauty in it—by way of a token.

TYRONE (*watching the sunrise—mechanically*): Token of what?

JOSIE: Oh, I don't know. Token to me that—never mind. I forget what I meant. (*Abruptly changing the subject.*) Don't think I woke you just to admire the sunrise. You're on a farm, not Broadway, and it's time for me to start work, not go to bed. (*She gets to her feet and stretches. There is a growing strain behind her free-and-easy manner.*) And that's a hint, Jim. I can't stay entertaining you. So go back to the Inn, that's a good boy. I know you'll understand the reason, and not think I'm tired of your company. (*She forces a smile.*)

TYRONE (*gets up*): Of course, I understand. (*He pauses—then blurts out guiltily.*) One more question. You're sure I didn't get out of order last night—and try to make you, or anything like that.

JOSIE: You didn't. You kidded back when I kidded you, the way we always do. That's all.

TYRONE: Thank God for that. I'd never forgive myself if—I wouldn't have asked you except I've pulled some pretty rotten stuff when I was drawing a blank. (*He becomes conscious of the forgotten drink he has in his hand.*) Well, I might as well drink this. The bar at the Inn won't be open for hours. (*He drinks—then looks pleasantly surprised.*) I'll be damned! That isn't Phil's rotgut. That's real, honest-to-God bonded Bourbon. Where— (*This clicks in his mind and suddenly he remembers everything and* JOSIE *sees that he does. The look of guilt and shame and anguish settles over his face. Instinctively he throws the glass away, his first reaction one of loathing for the drink which brought back memory. He feels* JOSIE *staring at him and fights desperately to control his voice and expression.*) Real Bourbon. I remember now you said a bootlegger gave it to Phil. Well, I'll run along and let you do your work. See you later, Josie. (*He turns toward the road.*)

JOSIE (*strickenly*): No! Don't, Jim! Don't go like that! You won't see me later. You'll never see me again now, and I know that's best for us both, but I can't bear to have you ashamed you wanted my love to comfort your sorrow—when I'm so proud I could give it. (*Pleadingly.*) I hoped, for your sake, you wouldn't remember, but now you do, I want you to remember my love for you gave you peace for a while.

TYRONE (*stares at her fighting with himself. He stammers defensively*): I don't know what you're talking about. I don't remember—

JOSIE (*sadly*): All right, Jim. Neither do I then. Good-bye, and God bless you. (*She turns as if to go up the steps into the house.*)

TYRONE (*stammers*): Wait, Josie! (*Coming to her.*) I'm a liar! I'm a louse! Forgive me, Josie. I do remember! I'm glad I remember! I'll never forget your love! (*He kisses her on the lips.*) Never! (*Kissing her again.*) Never, do you hear! I'll always love you, Josie. (*He kisses her again.*) Good-bye—and God bless you! (*He turns away and walks quickly down the road off left without looking back. She stands, watching him go, for a moment, then she puts her hands over her face, her head bent, and sobs.* HOGAN *comes out of her room and stands on top of the steps. He looks after* TYRONE *and his face is hard with bitter anger.*)

JOSIE (*sensing his presence, stops crying and lifts her head—dully*): I'll get your breakfast in a minute, Father.

HOGAN: To hell with my breakfast! I'm not a pig that has no other thought but eating! (*Then pleadingly.*) Listen, darlin'. All you said about my lying and scheming, and what I hoped would happen, is true. But it wasn't his money, Josie. I did see it was the last chance—the only one left to bring the two of you to stop your damned pretending, and face the truth that you loved each other. I wanted you to find happiness—by hook or crook, one way or another, what did I care how? I wanted to save him, and hoped he'd see that only your love could— It was his talk of the beauty he saw in you that made me hope— And I knew he'd never go to bed with you even if you'd let him unless he married you. And if you gave a thought to his money at all, that was the least of it, and why shouldn't I want to have you live in ease and comfort for a change, like you deserve, instead of in this shanty on a lousy farm, slaving for me? (*He pauses—miserably.*) Can't you believe that's the truth, Josie, and not feel so bitter against me?

JOSIE (*her eyes still following* TYRONE—*gently*): I know it's the truth, Father. I'm not bitter now. Don't be afraid I'm going to leave you. I only said it to

punish you for a while.

HOGAN (*with humble gratitude*): Thank God for that, darlin'.

JOSIE (*forces a teasing smile and a little of her old manner*): A ginger-haired, crooked old goat like you to be playing Cupid!

HOGAN (*his face lights up joyfully. He is almost himself again—ruefully*): You had me punished, that's sure. I was thinking after you'd gone I'd drown myself in Harder's ice pond. There was this consolation in it, I knew that the bastard would never look at a piece of ice again without remembering me. (*She doesn't hear this. Her thoughts are on the receding figure of* TYRONE *again.* HOGAN *looks at her sad face worriedly—gently.*) Don't darlin'. Don't be hurting yourself. (*Then as she still doesn't hear, he puts on his old, fuming irascible tone.*) Are you going to moon at the sunrise forever, and me with the sides of my stomach knocking together?

JOSIE (*gently*): Don't worry about me, Father. It's over now. I'm not hurt. I'm only sad for him.

HOGAN: For him? (*He bursts out in a fit of smoldering rage.*) May the blackest curse from the pit of hell—

JOSIE (*with an anguished cry*): Don't, Father! I love him!

HOGAN (*subsides, but his face looks sorrowful and old—dully*): I didn't mean it. I know whatever happened he meant no harm to you. It was life I was cursing— (*With a trace of his natural manner.*) And, be God, that's a waste of breath, if it does deserve it. (*Then as she remains silent—miserably.*) Or maybe I was cursing myself for a damned old scheming fool, like I ought to.

JOSIE (*turns to him, forcing a teasing smile*): Look out. I might say Amen to that. (*Gently.*) Don't be sad, Father. I'm all right—and I'm well content here with you. (*Forcing her teasing manner again.*) Sure, living with you has spoilt me for any other man, anyway. There'd never be the same fun or excitement.

HOGAN (*plays up to this—in his fuming manner*): There'll be excitement if I don't get my breakfast soon, but it won't be fun, I'm warning you!

JOSIE (*forcing her usual reaction to his threats*): Och, don't be threatening me, you bad-tempered old tick. Let's go in the house and I'll get your damned breakfast.

HOGAN: Now you're talking. (*He goes in the house through her room. She follows him as far as the door—then turns for a last look down the road.*)

JOSIE (*her face sad, tender and pitying—gently*): May you have your wish and die in your sleep soon, Jim, darling. May you rest forever in forgiveness and peace. (*She turns slowly and goes into the house.*)

CURTAIN

Figure 1. Josie (Colleen Dewhurst) and Tyrone (Jason Robards) in front of the realistic/symbolic set for the José Quintero production of *A Moon for the Misbegotten*, New York, 1974. (Photograph: Martha Swope.)

Figure 2. Josie (Colleen Dewhurst) and Tyrone (Jason Robards) in the José Quintero production of *A Moon for the Misbegotten*, New York, 1974. (Photograph: Martha Swope.)

Figure 3. Hogan (Ed Flanders) reproves Josie (Colleen Dewhurst) as she cradles Tyrone (Jason Robards) in her arms in the José Quintero production of *A Moon for the Misbegotten*, New York, 1974. (Photograph: Martha Swope.)

Staging of *A Moon for the Misbegotten*

REVIEW OF THE NEW YORK PRODUCTION, 1974,
BY WALTER KERR

Colleen Dewhurst is a beautiful woman giving a beautiful performance in the newest revival of Eugene O'Neill's "A Moon for the Misbegotten" (which also just happens to be a beautiful play, possibly O'Neill's best), and I find nothing more fetching about her performance than her witchlike way with an unfinished sentence.

Unfinished sentences can be hell for actors, often because the playwright has had no thought to complete and has simply handed the performer the task of implying one. They can hang there, limp as on a washline, ready to blow any which way a wind happens along. Not in Miss Dewhurst's firmly ruled kingdom, though. In "A Moon for the Misbegotten" she is, in her shanty-Irish father's words, "big and strong as a bull, and as vicious and disrespectful," and she is waiting, in the early kerosene-lit moonlight, for a visit from one of her betters. The visitor is to be Jason Robards, member of an acting family, handsomely educated, already half-broken by drink. He should be, in the opinion of a canny father, readily seduceable.

In fact, Father Ed Flanders (another stunning performance) has the night's course well planned into the dawn. He will slip off to a bar and get himself drunk enough to be utterly unable to prevent anything Mr. Robards may have in mind. It is Miss Dewhurst's business to see to it that Mr. Robards's mind takes a right turn. At this point in the conniving, the actress suddenly turns on the aged leprechaun who is whispering goat-songs in her ear.

Eyes blazing, her hair pulled taut from a clear forehead, arm ever-ready to take a stick to her mentor, she lets him know what she thinks of "a father telling his daughter how to—" and there lets the sentence die. The special splendor of the moment is that it doesn't die. The obvious finish to the line is "to seduce a man," and, if that were all, it wouldn't be much. By letting it break where O'Neill broke it, and by reaching out to join her playwright creatively, Miss Dewhurst fills the void with a heartful of contending emotions. What is left over, and unsaid, is that she wants the love of the man, that she wants it on her own terms, that she is terribly, terribly afraid she is not going to get it, and that seduction—if she knew anything at all about it—would waste the last ounce of goodness in two malformed lives. That's a lot, but it's all there.

It is difficult to take your eyes off Miss Dewhurst, whether she is smiling or in fury. She has a smile that behaves strangely. Most smiles, when they are about to crack in dismay, crack downward. Hers shatters upward, sustaining the shape of happiness while a telltale quaver makes a lie of the crescent corners of her mouth. Her face seems actually to brighten under the hint of pain, a sense of unruly merriment tries hard to assert itself, a vixenish gaiety becomes permanent companion of disaster.

The effect is enormously touching, and it blends ever so easily with the roustabout humors of her donnybrooks with her father. The racy, fork-tongued, rattle-on chaffings between Miss Dewhurst and Mr. Flanders are exhilaratingly designed by director José Quintero, and they remind you, in case you've forgotten, that when O'Neill wanted to write comedy, he had only to pick up an alternate pen and let another kind of theater-ink flow, an apparently inexhaustible knowhow takeover.

But "A Moon for the Misbegotten" is not, in the end, comedy, which is where Miss Dewhurst's unfinished sentences and upsweep dismays, and Jason Robards come in. Mr. Robards begins brilliantly, self-conscious not only about his natty 1923 clothes but about his need for a drink, his need for a woman who will not turn out to be a whore, his need for nothing so much as an impossible forgiveness.

The shaking hand with which he lights a cigarette as their tryst together is to begin establishes its outcome; the succulent surrender to a first taste of a drink she brings him outlines precisely the one comfort this doomed man can know. The detail—an uneasy balance on a treacherous planet, fingers at his collar, palms scraping the nap of jacket and trousers as though something dirty could be wiped away—is graphic, conscientiously arrived at, intelligently used.

I have one important reservation about the production and feel something of an ingrate for bringing it up. But at the invitational preview I attended, the terrifying "almost" of the third act—the teasing possibility that against all odds two rattled, emotionally starved, yearning and yet distrustful misfits will somehow find a crooked way to an ultimate meeting—simply didn't happen. We know that it *can't* happen, that it was never in the cards; but that is for the fourth act to say. Here, with all of the anger and ugliness and awkward groping allowed for, there must be a rhythm that moves toward fusion, toward a coming-together of the far ends of the earth. Without it, without its momentary false promise, the play is too much of a piece, each movement reiterating the other.

Mr. Robards, possibly out of over-concern that each moment will be technically right, continually aborts that promised rhythm, lurching away in self-disgust and trying to spit from his mouth the venom of lost years so often that the design becomes fragmented, the contrast stalemated. I may have seen an unduly edgy performance; certainly it is a matter that continued performance can correct. But there were times when I wanted to collar the man and order him to stay with the scene, stay with the woman, until O'Neill's play could come as close as it dared to a psychic embrace. *Then* it might be shattered, letting us see the remorse-ridden figure as truly dead. It is the crest of the wave, before it collapses on the beach, that is missing, leaving me with slightly fonder memories of the 1968 production at the downtown Circle in the Square.

If I suggest that "Moon for the Misbegotten" just may be O'Neill's richest work for the theater, it is because the free creative impulse is allowed more play here than in the directly autobiographical "Long Day's Journey Into Night." The Robards role is, of course, rooted in O'Neill's older brother. The other figures, however, draw upon, and demand, vast imaginative resources; life is made on the wing rather than painstakingly remembered. It is an honest life, and for O'Neill, an unusually lyric one; the crafty, the damned, and the forgiving breathe.

ARTHUR MILLER

1915–

Although Miller has written only a dozen or so plays, he is viewed throughout the world as one of America's most eminent contemporary dramatists. His *Death of a Salesman* (1949) is probably the most famous American play of the twentieth century, for it has come to be seen by millions of people as a consummate dramatization of the most disturbing aspects in the modern American version of "success." Theatrical success came relatively early in Miller's own career, yet he worked arduously to achieve it. He was born in Harlem at a time when his father was still struggling to establish a successful clothing manufacturing business, and he was raised in a suburb of Brooklyn after his father's business had become well established. But the depression of 1929 nearly ruined his father, so that when Miller graduated from high school in 1932, he had to take a job in an automobile warehouse to save up enough money to be able to attend college at the University of Michigan. During his four years at Michigan, he studied playwriting and he won a number of playwriting contests that also helped him to work his way through college. After graduating from Michigan, he worked briefly for the playwriting project the federal government was then supporting to help sustain dramatists during the depression, and subsequently he found work writing radio plays for CBS and later for the Cavalcade of America. During the war, he was unable to serve in the military because of a football injury he had suffered in high school, so instead he began writing radio plays and other pieces to help support civilian morale at home. Before the end of the war, he had also completed his first full-length play to be produced on Broadway, *The Man Who Had All the Luck* (1944), and though it closed after only four performances, it clearly anticipated the concern with moral responsibility and guilt that has been central to virtually all of Miller's work for the theater.

Miller's next play, *All My Sons* (1947), won the New York Drama Critics Circle award for the best play of the season, and it quickly established him as a serious playwright in the socially conscious tradition of Ibsen. When the play was first produced, Miller went out of his way in a press interview to declare his concern with moral and social issues:

> In all my plays and books I try to take setting and dramatic situations from life which involve real questions of right and wrong. Then I set out, rather implacably and in the most realistic situations I can find, the moral dilemma and try to point a real, though hard, path out. I don't see how you can write anything decent without using the question of right and wrong as the basis.

And in *All My Sons* he clearly focussed on the issue of moral responsibility by portraying the crisis that is produced when a small armaments manufacturer is discovered by his son to have sold defective airplane parts to the army, making him responsible for the death of a number of wartime pilots. The father, Joe Keller, seeks to justify himself to his son by claiming that he had wanted to preserve the business and support his family, but the son, Chris, maintains that "There's a universe outside and you're responsible to it." When Keller discovers that his other son, an air corps pilot himself, has been driven to suicide by the discovery of his guilt, he finally is forced to acknowledge his moral responsibility for a world beyond the limits of his own family: "I think to him they were all my sons. And I guess they were." And that recognition drives him to commit suicide himself.

Joe Keller's morally blind commitment to "dollars and cents" clearly anticipated Willy Loman's commitment to "success" in *Death of a Salesman,* much as the shattering of Joe Keller's self-delusion anticipated the shattering of Willy's "dream." But in *Death of a Salesman,* Miller did not confine himself to exposing the ramifications of a fatally wrong moral decision, and in the case of Willy Loman he chose to explore the ramifications of a fatally wrong way of life—a way of life distinctively American in its commitment to a naive idea of success. To invest his play with such broad social implications, Miller chose for his protagonist an archetypal figure in American culture—the travelling salesman—and he endowed that figure with all the conventional American aspirations, including not only the desire to succeed by being "well liked," but also the desire to be respected by one's friends, to be loved and admired by one's family, to contribute to the success of one's children, to pay one's bills on time, and to own one's own home. Then, in order to explore the failure of such middle-class values, Miller made the strategic decision of focussing on the archetypal salesman at the most vulnerable moment in his life, when he is "tired to death" by his age and by the disappointment of all his hopes. That, in essence, is the formula for the play, but the play itself goes far beyond the formula, largely because Miller does not confine himself to making an indictment of American cultural values.

The play can, of course, be read as an exposure of the cruelty, the cynicism, the stupidity, and the immorality that result from a blind commitment to American materialistic values, for those qualities are repeatedly displayed in Willy's behavior toward his wife, his sons, his friends, and his boss, as well as in Happy's behavior toward Willy, the boss' behavior toward Willy, and above all in the symbolic spectacle of Willy's brother Ben preaching the law of the jungle to Biff: "Never fight fair with a stranger, boy. You'll never get out of the jungle that way." The play can also be read as a tragedy of the common man—a view of the work that Miller sought to define in an essay he published along with the play, called "Tragedy and the Common Man." In that essay, he sought to challenge the traditional notion of the tragic figure as being necessarily "well placed" or "exalted," arguing that "the very same mental processes" are to be found in the "lowly," in particular, "the underlying fear of being displaced, the disaster inherent in being torn away from our chosen image of what and who we are in the world." And certainly it can be said that Willy displays that archetypal fear throughout the play, much as he displays the indignation that Miller regards as the inevitable result of being displaced: "the fateful wound from which the inevitable events spiral is the wound of indignity, and its dominant force is indignation. Tragedy, then, is the consequence of a man's total compulsion to evaluate himself justly."

But the power of the play, at last, derives less from its socially conscious tragic vision than from the way that Miller dramatizes that vision by concentrating on Willy's mental and emotional experience during the moment of his tragic crisis. Willy would not, after all, be such a compelling figure if he were merely a common social type. He is, in fact, highly particularized through the detailed exposure of his tortured consciousness—through the expressionistic presentation of his mental processes as he repeatedly shifts back and forth between past and present experience, mingling memory with immediate reality with hallucination. When he is shown, for example, in the first act, on the verge of embracing his wife, Linda, only to find himself engulfed by the memory of his adulterous escapade with another woman, Willy is poignantly revealed as a particular human being overwhelmed by guilt and by the painful isolation that it creates between him and his family. His sense of isolation, of course, increases throughout the play as he is incessantly bombarded both by painful memories from the past and disappointments in the present. Yet he does not simply acquiesce to the relentless flow of events in his world and in his mind, but seeks to resist them, indeed to alter them with all the force of his being. And though he is finally driven to relinquish his being in the act of resistance, he does so not out of a will to succeed, or to be "well liked," but out of a wholly selfless love for his family. In doing so, he thus escapes from the enslavement of being a salesman and becomes a person bound by authentic human attachments, free at last "to do the right thing."

In the years immediately following its first appearance, *Death of a Salesman* was interpreted in the United States and throughout the world as being primarily a statement about American culture, but its persistent appeal to audiences suggests that it speaks to even larger concerns—to the dismay that all human beings experience when they find themselves unable to accept what they have done to others, what others have done to them, and what they have become as a consequence. These dimensions of the play have recently moved directors and producers to revive it and stage it so as to emphasize the deeply human struggle that Willy goes through in the process of facing up to his illusions. This approach, for example, was taken by the famous movie and stage actor, George C. Scott, in a production he directed and starred in during 1974. A review of Scott's production, reprinted following the text, explains how he staged the play in order to emphasize the emotional, mental, and psychological struggle that Willy experiences. Photographs of Scott in the role of Willy clearly reveal that he was able to convey the man's fatigue (see Figure 1), his guilt (see Figure 3), his love for his family (see Figure 2), and thus his ultimate dignity.

DEATH OF A SALESMAN

BY ARTHUR MILLER

CHARACTERS

WILLY LOMAN
LINDA
BIFF
HAPPY
BERNARD
THE WOMAN
CHARLEY
UNCLE BEN
HOWARD WAGNER

JENNY
STANLEY
MISS FORSYTHE
LETTA

SCENE

The action takes place in WILLY LOMAN'S *house and yard and in various places he visits in the New York and Boston of today.*

ACT 1

(A melody is heard, played upon a flute. It is small and fine, telling of grass and trees and the horizon. The curtain rises.

Before us is the Salesman's house. We are aware of towering, angular shapes behind it, surrounding it on all sides. Only the blue light of the sky falls upon the house and forestage; the surrounding area shows an angry glow of orange. As more light appears, we see a solid vault of apartment houses around the small, fragile-seeming home. An air of the dream clings to the place, a dream rising out of reality. The kitchen at center seems actual enough, for there is a kitchen table with three chairs, and a refrigerator. But no other fixtures are seen. At the back of the kitchen there is a draped entrance, which leads to the living-room. To the right of the kitchen, on a level raised two feet, is a bedroom furnished only with a brass bedstead and a straight chair. On a shelf over the bed a silver athletic trophy stands. A window opens onto the apartment house at the side.

Behind the kitchen, on a level raised six and a half feet, is the boys' bedroom, at present barely visible. Two beds are dimly seen, and at the back of the room a dormer window. [This bedroom is above the unseen living-room.] At the left a stairway curves up to it from the kitchen.

The entire setting is wholly or, in some places, partially transparent. The roof-line of the house is one-dimensional; under and over it we see the apartment buildings. Before the house lies an apron, curving beyond the forestage into the orchestra. This forward area serves as the back yard as well as the locale of all WILLY'S *imaginings and of his city scenes. Whenever the action is in the present the actors observe the imaginary wall-lines, entering the house only through its door at the left. But in the scenes of the past these boundaries are broken, and characters enter or leave a room by stepping "through" a wall onto the forestage.*

From the right, WILLY LOMAN, *the Salesman, enters, carrying two large sample cases. The flute plays on. He hears but is not aware of it. He is past sixty years of age, dressed quietly. Even as he crosses the stage to the doorway of the house, his exhaustion is apparent. He unlocks the door, comes into the kitchen, and thankfully lets his burden down, feeling the soreness of his palms. A word-sigh escapes his lips—it might be "Oh, boy, oh, boy." He closes the door, then carries his cases out into the living-room, through the draped kitchen doorway.*

LINDA, *his wife, has stirred in her bed at the right. She gets out and puts on a robe, listening. Most often jovial, she has developed an iron repression of her exceptions to* WILLY'S *behavior—she more than loves him, she admires him, as though his mercurial nature, his temper, his massive dreams and little cruelties, served her only as sharp reminders of the turbulent longings within him, longings which she shares but lacks the temperament to utter and follow to their end.)*

LINDA (*hearing* WILLY *outside the bedroom, calls with some trepidation*): Willy!

WILLY: It's all right. I came back.

LINDA: Why? What happened? (*Slight pause.*) Did something happen, Willy?

WILLY: No, nothing happened.

LINDA: You didn't smash the car, did you?

WILLY (*with casual irritation*): I said nothing happened. Didn't you hear me?

LINDA: Don't you feel well?

WILLY: I'm tired to the death. (*The flute has faded away. He sits on the bed beside her, a little numb.*) I couldn't make it. I just couldn't make it, Linda.

LINDA (*very carefully, delicately*): Where were you all day? You look terrible.

WILLY: I got as far as a little above Yonkers. I stopped for a cup of coffee. Maybe it was the coffee.

LINDA: What?

WILLY (*after a pause*): I suddenly couldn't drive any

more. The car kept going off onto the shoulder, y'know?

LINDA (*helpfully*): Oh. Maybe it was the steering again. I don't think Angelo knows the Studebaker.

WILLY: No, it's me, it's me. Suddenly I realize I'm goin' sixty miles an hour and I don't remember the last five minutes. I'm—I can't seem to—keep my mind to it.

LINDA: Maybe it's your glasses. You never went for your new glasses.

WILLY: No, I see everything. I came back ten miles an hour. It took me nearly four hours from Yonkers.

LINDA (*resigned*): Well, you'll just have to take a rest, Willy, you can't continue this way.

WILLY: I just got back from Florida.

LINDA: But you didn't rest your mind. Your mind is overactive, and the mind is what counts, dear.

WILLY: I'll start out in the morning. Maybe I'll feel better in the morning. (*She is taking off his shoes.*) These goddam arch supports are killing me.

LINDA: Take an aspirin. Should I get you an aspirin? It'll soothe you.

WILLY (*with wonder*): I was driving along, you understand? And I was fine. I was even observing the scenery. You can imagine, me looking at scenery, on the road every week of my life. But it's so beautiful up there, Linda, the trees are so thick, and the sun is warm. I opened the windshield and just let the warm air bathe over me. And then all of a sudden I'm goin' off the road! I'm tellin' ya, I absolutely forgot I was driving. If I'd've gone the other way, over the white line I might've killed somebody. So I went on again—and five minutes later I'm dreamin' again, and I nearly—(*He presses two fingers against his eyes.*) I have such thoughts, I have such strange thoughts.

LINDA: Willy, dear. Talk to them again. There's no reason why you can't work in New York.

WILLY: They don't need me in New York. I'm the New England man. I'm vital in New England.

LINDA: But you're sixty years old. They can't expect you to keep traveling every week.

WILLY: I'll have to send a wire to Portland. I'm supposed to see Brown and Morrison tomorrow morning at ten o'clock to show the line. Goddammit, I could sell them! (*He starts putting on his jacket.*)

LINDA (*taking the jacket from him*): Why don't you go down to the place tomorrow and tell Howard you've simply got to work in New York? You're too accommodating, dear.

WILLY: If old man Wagner was alive I'd a been in charge of New York now! That man was a prince, he was a masterful man. But that boy of his, that Howard, he don't appreciate. When I

was north the first time, the Wagner Company didn't know where New England was!

LINDA: Why don't you tell those things to Howard, dear?

WILLY (*encouraged*): I will, I definitely will. Is there any cheese?

LINDA: I'll make you a sandwich.

WILLY: No, go to sleep. I'll take some milk. I'll be up right away. The boys in?

LINDA: They're sleeping. Happy took Biff on a date tonight.

WILLY (*interested*): That so?

LINDA: It was so nice to see them shaving together, one behind the other, in the bathroom. And going out together. You notice? The whole house smells of shaving lotion.

WILLY: Figure it out. Work a lifetime to pay off a house. You finally own it, and there's nobody to live in it.

LINDA: Well, dear, life is a casting off. It's always that way.

WILLY: No, no, some people—some people accomplish something. Did Biff say anything after I went this morning?

LINDA: You shouldn't have criticized him, Willy, especially after he just got off the train. You mustn't lose your temper with him.

WILLY: When the hell did I lose my temper? I simply asked him if he was making any money. Is that a criticism?

LINDA: But, dear, how could he make any money?

WILLY (*worried and angered*): There's such an undercurrent in him. He became a moody man. Did he apologize when I left this morning?

LINDA: He was crestfallen, Willy. You know how he admires you. I think if he finds himself, then you'll both be happier and not fight any more.

WILLY: How can he find himself on a farm? Is that a life? A farmhand? In the beginning, when he was young, I thought, well, a young man, it's good for him to tramp around, take a lot of different jobs. But it's more than ten years now and he has yet to make thirty-five dollars a week!

LINDA: He's finding himself, Willy.

WILLY: Not finding yourself at the age of thirty-four is a disgrace!

LINDA: Shh!

WILLY: The trouble is he's lazy, goddammit!

LINDA: Willy, please!

WILLY: Biff is a lazy bum.

LINDA: They're sleeping. Get something to eat. Go on down.

WILLY: Why did he come home? I would like to know what brought him home.

LINDA: I don't know. I think he's still lost, Willy. I think he's very lost.

WILLY: Biff Loman is lost. In the greatest country in

the world a young man with such—personal attractiveness, gets lost. And such a hard worker. There's one thing about Biff—he's not lazy.

LINDA: Never.

WILLY (*with pity and resolve*): I'll see him in the morning; I'll have a nice talk with him. I'll get him a job selling. He could be big in no time. My God! Remember how they used to follow him around in high school? When he smiled at one of them their faces lit up. When he walked down the street . . . (*He loses himself in reminiscences.*)

LINDA (*trying to bring him out of it*): Willy, dear, I got a new kind of American-type cheese today. It's whipped.

WILLY: Why do you get American when I like Swiss?

LINDA: I just thought you'd like a change—

WILLY: I don't want a change! I want Swiss cheese. Why am I always being contradicted?

LINDA (*with a covering laugh*): I thought it would be a surprise.

WILLY: Why don't you open a window in here, for God's sake?

LINDA (*with infinite patience*): They're all open, dear.

WILLY: The way they boxed us in here. Bricks and windows, windows and bricks.

LINDA: We should've bought the land next door.

WILLY: The street is lined with cars. There's not a breath of fresh air in the neighborhood. The grass don't grow any more, you can't raise a carrot in the back yard. They should've had a law against apartment houses. Remember those two beautiful elm trees out there? When I and Biff hung the swing between them?

LINDA: Yeah, like being a million miles from the city.

WILLY: They should've arrested the builder for cutting those down. They massacred the neighborhood. (*Lost.*) More and more I think of those days, Linda. This time of year it was lilac and wisteria. And then the peonies would come out, and the daffodils. What fragrance in this room!

LINDA: Well, after all, people had to move somewhere.

WILLY: No, there's more people now.

LINDA: I don't think there's more people. I think—

WILLY: There's more people! That's what's ruining this country! Population is getting out of control. The competition is maddening! Smell the stink from that apartment house! And another one on the other side . . . How can they whip cheese?

(*On* WILLY's *last line*, BIFF *and* HAPPY *raise themselves up in their beds, listening.*)

LINDA: Go down, try it. And be quiet.

WILLY (*turning to* LINDA, *guiltily*): You're not worried about me, are you, sweetheart?

BIFF: What's the matter?

HAPPY: Listen!

LINDA: You've got too much on the ball to worry about.

WILLY: You're my foundation and my support, Linda.

LINDA: Just try to relax, dear. You make mountains out of molehills.

WILLY: I won't fight him any more. If he wants to go back to Texas, let him go.

LINDA: He'll find his way.

WILLY: Sure. Certain men just don't get started till later in life. Like Thomas Edison, I think. Or B. F. Goodrich. One of them was deaf. (*He starts for the bedroom doorway.*) I'll put my money on Biff.

LINDA: And Willy—if it's warm Sunday we'll drive in the country. And we'll open the windshield, and take lunch.

WILLY: No, the windshields don't open on the new cars.

LINDA: But you opened it today.

WILLY: Me? I didn't. (*He stops.*) Now isn't that peculiar! Isn't that a remarkable—(*He breaks off in amazement and fright as the flute is heard distantly.*)

LINDA: What, darling?

WILLY: That is the most remarkable thing.

LINDA: What, dear?

WILLY: I was thinking of the Chevvy. (*Slight pause.*) Nineteen twenty-eight . . . when I had that red Chevvy—(*Breaks off.*) That funny? I coulda sworn I was driving that Chevvy today.

LINDA: Well, that's nothing. Something must've reminded you.

WILLY: Remarkable. Ts. Remember those days? The way Biff used to simonize that car? The dealer refused to believe there was eighty thousand miles on it. (*He shakes his head.*) Heh! (*to* LINDA) Close your eyes, I'll be right up. (*He walks out of the bedroom.*)

HAPPY (*to* BIFF): Jesus, maybe he smashed up the car again!

LINDA (*calling after* WILLY): Be careful on the stairs, dear! The cheese is on the middle shelf! (*She turns, goes over to the bed, takes his jacket, and goes out of the bedroom.*)

(*Light has risen on the boys' room. Unseen,* WILLY *is heard talking to himself, "Eighty thousand miles," and a little laugh.* BIFF *gets out of bed, comes downstage a bit, and stands attentively.* BIFF *is two years older than his brother* HAPPY, *well built, but in these days bears a worn air and seems less self-assured. He has succeeded less, and his dreams are stronger and less acceptable than* HAPPY's. HAPPY *is tall, powerfully made. Sexuality is like a visible color on him, or a scent that many women have discovered. He, like his brother, is lost, but in a different way, for he has never allowed himself to turn his face toward defeat and is thus more confused and hard-skinned, although seemingly more content.*)

HAPPY (*getting out of bed*): He's going to get his license taken away if he keeps that up. I'm getting nervous about him, y'know, Biff?

BIFF: His eyes are going.

HAPPY: No, I've driven with him. He sees all right. He just doesn't keep his mind on it. I drove into the city with him last week. He stops at a green light and then it turns red and he goes. (*He laughs.*)

BIFF: Maybe he's color-blind.

HAPPY: Pop? Why he's got the finest eye for color in the business. You know that.

BIFF (*sitting down on his bed*): I'm going to sleep.

HAPPY: You're not still sour on Dad, are you, Biff?

BIFF: He's all right, I guess.

WILLY (*underneath them, in the living-room*): Yes, sir, eighty thousand miles—eighty-two thousand!

BIFF: You smoking?

HAPPY (*holding out a pack of cigarettes*): Want one?

BIFF (*taking a cigarette*): I can never sleep when I smell it.

WILLY: What a simonizing job, heh!

HAPPY (*with deep sentiment*): Funny, Biff, y'know? Us sleeping in here again? The old beds. (*He pats his bed affectionately.*) All the talk that went across those two beds, huh? Our whole lives.

BIFF: Yeah. Lotta dreams and plans.

HAPPY (*with a deep and masculine laugh*): About five hundred women would like to know what was said in this room.

(*They share a soft laugh.*)

BIFF: Remember that big Betsy something—what the hell was her name—over on Bushwick Avenue?

HAPPY (*combing his hair*): With the collie dog!

BIFF: That's the one. I got you in there, remember?

HAPPY: Yeah, that was my first time—I think. Boy, there was a pig! (*They laugh, almost crudely.*) You taught me everything I know about women. Don't forget that.

BIFF: I bet you forgot how bashful you used to be. Especially with girls.

HAPPY: Oh, I still am, Biff.

BIFF: Oh, go on.

HAPPY: I just control it, that's all. I think I got less bashful and you got more so. What happened, Biff? Where's the old humor, the old confidence? (*He shakes* BIFF's *knee.* BIFF *gets up and moves restlessly about the room.*) What's the matter?

BIFF: Why does Dad mock me all the time?

HAPPY: He's not mocking you, he—

BIFF: Everything I say there's a twist of mockery on his face. I can't get near him.

HAPPY: He just wants you to make good, that's all. I wanted to talk to you about Dad for a long time, Biff. Something's—happening to him. He—talks to himself.

BIFF: I noticed that this morning. But he always mumbled.

HAPPY: But not so noticeable. It got so embarrassing I sent him to Florida. And you know something? Most of the time he's talking to you.

BIFF: What's he say about me?

HAPPY: I can't make it out.

BIFF: What's he say about me?

HAPPY: I think the fact that you're not settled, that you're still kind of up in the air . . .

BIFF: There's one or two other things depressing him, Happy.

HAPPY: What do you mean?

BIFF: Never mind. Just don't lay it all to me.

HAPPY: But I think if you just got started—I mean—is there any future for you out there?

BIFF: I tell ya, Hap, I don't know what the future is. I don't know—what I'm supposed to want.

HAPPY: What do you mean?

BIFF: Well, I spent six or seven years after high school trying to work myself up. Shipping clerk, salesman, business of one kind or another. And it's a measly manner of existence. To get on that subway on the hot mornings in summer. To devote your whole life to keeping stock, or making phone calls, or selling or buying. To suffer fifty weeks of the year for the sake of a two-week vacation, when all you really desire is to be outdoors, with your shirt off. And always have to get ahead of the next fella. And still—that's how you build a future.

HAPPY: Well, you really enjoy it on a farm? Are you content out there?

BIFF (*with rising agitation*): Hap, I've had twenty or thirty different kinds of jobs since I left home before the war, and it always turns out the same. I just realized it lately. In Nebraska when I herded cattle, and the Dakotas, and Arizona, and now in Texas. It's why I came home now, I guess, because I realized it. This farm I work on, it's spring there now, see? And they've got about fifteen new colts. There's nothing more inspiring or—beautiful then the sight of a mare and a new colt. And it's cool there now, see? Texas is cool now, and it's spring. And whenever spring comes to where I am, I suddenly get the feeling, my God, I'm not gettin' anywhere! What the hell am I doing, playing around with horses, twenty-eight dollars a week! I'm thirty-four years old, I oughta be makin' my future. That's when I come running home. And now, I get here, and I don't know what to do with myself. (*After a pause.*) I've always made a point of not wasting my life, and everytime I come back here I know that all I've done is to waste my life.

HAPPY: You're a poet, you know that, Biff? You're a—you're an idealist!

BIFF: No, I'm mixed up very bad. Maybe I oughta get married. Maybe I oughta get stuck into something. Maybe that's my trouble. I'm like a boy. I'm not married, I'm not in business, I just—I'm like a boy. Are you content, Hap? You're a success, aren't you? Are you content?

HAPPY: Hell, no!

BIFF: Why? You're making money, aren't you?

HAPPY (moving about with energy, expressiveness): All I can do now is wait for the merchandise manager to die. And suppose I get to be merchandise manager? He's a good friend of mine, and he just built a terrific estate on Long Island. And he lived there about two months and sold it, and now he's building another one. He can't enjoy it once it's finished. And I know that's just what I would do. I don't know what the hell I'm workin' for. Sometimes I sit in my apartment—all alone. And I think of the rent I'm paying. And it's crazy. But then, it's what I always wanted. My own apartment, a car, and plenty of women. And still, goddammit, I'm lonely.

BIFF (with enthusiasm): Listen, why don't you come out West with me?

HAPPY: You and I, heh?

BIFF: Sure, maybe we could buy a ranch. Raise cattle, use our muscles. Men built like we are should be working out in the open.

HAPPY (avidly): The Loman Brothers, heh?

BIFF (with vast affection): Sure, we'd be known all over the counties!

HAPPY (enthralled): That's what I dream about, Biff. Sometimes I want to just rip my clothes off in the middle of the store and outbox that goddam merchandise manager. I mean I can outbox, outrun, and outlift anybody in that store, and I have to take orders from those common, petty sons-of-bitches till I can't stand it any more.

BIFF: I'm tellin' you, kid, if you were with me I'd be happy out there.

HAPPY (enthused): See, Biff, everybody around me is so false that I'm constantly lowering my ideals . . .

BIFF: Baby, together we'd stand up for one another, we'd have someone to trust.

HAPPY: If I were around you—

BIFF: Hap, the trouble is we weren't brought up to grub for money. I don't know how to do it.

HAPPY: Neither can I!

BIFF: Then let's go!

HAPPY: The only thing is—what can you make out there?

BIFF: But look at your friend. Builds an estate and then hasn't the peace of mind to live in it.

HAPPY: Yeah, but when he walks into the store the waves part in front of him. That's fifty-two thousand dollars a year coming through the revolving door, and I got more in my pinky finger than he's got in his head.

BIFF: Yeah, but you just said—

HAPPY: I gotta show some of those pompous, self-important executives over there that Hap Loman can make the grade. I want to walk into the store the way he walks in. Then I'll go with you, Biff. We'll be together yet, I swear. But take those two we had tonight. Now weren't they gorgeous creatures?

BIFF: Yeah, yeah, most gorgeous I've had in years.

HAPPY: I get that any time I want, Biff. Whenever I feel disgusted. The only trouble is, it gets like bowling or something. I just keep knockin' them over and it doesn't mean anything. You still run around a lot?

BIFF: Naa. I'd like to find a girl—steady, somebody with substance.

HAPPY: That's what I long for.

BIFF: Go on! You'd never come home.

HAPPY: I would! Somebody with character, with resistance! Like Mom, y'know? You're gonna call me a bastard when I tell you this. That girl Charlotte I was with tonight is engaged to be married in five weeks. (He tries on his new hat.)

BIFF: No kiddin'!

HAPPY: Sure, the guy's in line for the vice-presidency of the store. I don't know what gets into me, maybe I just have an overdeveloped sense of competition or something, but I went and ruined her, and furthermore I can't get rid of her. And he's the third executive I've done that to. Isn't that a crummy characteristic? And to top it all, I go to their weddings! (Indignantly, but laughing.) Like I'm not supposed to take bribes. Manufacturers offer me a hundred-dollar bill now and then to throw an order their way. You know how honest I am, but it's like this girl, see. I hate myself for it. Because I don't want the girl, and, still, I take it and—I love it!

BIFF: Let's go to sleep.

HAPPY: I guess we didn't settle anything, heh?

BIFF: I just got one idea that I think I'm going to try.

HAPPY: What's that?

BIFF: Remember Bill Oliver?

HAPPY: Sure, Oliver is very big now. You want to work for him again?

BIFF: No, but when I quit he said something to me. He put his arm on my shoulder, and he said, "Biff, if you ever need anything, come to me."

HAPPY: I remember that. That sounds good.

BIFF: I think I'll go to see him. If I could get ten thousand or even seven or eight thousand dollars I could buy a beautiful ranch.

HAPPY: I bet he'd back you. 'Cause he thought highly of you, Biff. I mean, they all do. You're well liked, Biff. That's why I say to come back here, and we both have the apartment. And I'm tellin' you, Biff, any babe you want . . .

BIFF: No, with a ranch I could do the work I like and still be something. I just wonder though. I wonder if Oliver still thinks I stole that carton of basketballs.

HAPPY: Oh, he probably forgot that long ago. It's almost ten years. You're too sensitive. Anyway, he didn't really fire you.

BIFF: Well, I think he was going to. I think that's why I quit. I was never sure whether he knew or not. I know he thought the world of me, though. I was the only one he'd let lock up the place.

WILLY (*below*): You gonna wash the engine, Biff?

HAPPY: Shh!

(BIFF *looks at* HAPPY, *who is gazing down, listening.* WILLY *is mumbling in the parlor.*)

HAPPY: You hear that?

(*They listen.* WILLY *laughs warmly.*)

BIFF (*growing angry*): Doesn't he know Mom can hear that?

WILLY: Don't get your sweater dirty, Biff!

(*A look of pain crosses* BIFF's *face.*)

HAPPY: Isn't that terrible? Don't leave again, will you? You'll find a job here. You gotta stick around. I don't know what to do about him, it's getting embarrassing.

WILLY: What a simonizing job!

BIFF: Mom's hearing that!

WILLY: No kiddin', Biff, you got a date? Wonderful!

HAPPY: Go on to sleep. But talk to him in the morning, will you?

BIFF (*reluctantly getting into bed*): With her in the house. Brother!

HAPPY (*getting into bed*): I wish you'd have a good talk with him.

(*The light on their room begins to fade.*)

BIFF (*to himself in bed*): That selfish, stupid . . .

HAPPY: Sh . . . Sleep, Biff.

(*Their light is out. Well before they have finished speaking,* WILLY's *form is dimly seen below in the darkened kitchen. He opens the refrigerator, searches in there, and takes out a bottle of milk. The apartment houses are fading out, and the entire house and surroundings become covered with leaves. Music insinuates itself as the leaves appear.*)

WILLY: Just wanna be careful with those girls, Biff, that's all. Don't make any promises. No promises of any kind. Because a girl, y'know, they always believe what you tell 'em, and you're very young, Biff, you're too young to be talking seriously to girls.

(*Light rises on the kitchen.* WILLY, *talking, shuts the refrigerator door and comes downstage to the kitchen table. He pours milk into a glass. He is totally immersed in himself, smiling faintly.*)

WILLY: Too young entirely, Biff. You want to watch your schooling first. Then when you're all set, there'll be plenty of girls for a boy like you. (*He smiles broadly at a kitchen chair.*) That so? The girls pay for you? (*He laughs.*) Boy, you must really be makin' a hit.

(WILLY *is gradually addressing—physically—a point offstage, speaking through the wall of the kitchen, and his voice has been rising in volume to that of a normal conversation.*)

WILLY: I been wondering why you polish the car so careful. Ha! Don't leave the hubcaps, boys. Get the chamois to the hubcaps. Happy, use newspaper on the windows, it's the easiest thing. Show him how to do it, Biff! You see, Happy? Pad it up, use it like a pad. That's it, that's it, good work. You're doin' all right, Hap. (*He pauses, then nods in approbation for a few seconds, then looks upward.*) Biff, first thing we gotta do when we get time is clip that big branch over the house. Afraid it's gonna fall in a storm and hit the roof. Tell you what. We get a rope and sling her around, and then we climb up there with a couple of saws and take her down. Soon as you finish the car, boys, I wanna see ya. I got a surprise for you, boys.

BIFF (*offstage*): Whatta ya got, Dad?

WILLY: No, you finish first. Never leave a job till you're finished—remember that. (*Looking toward the "big trees."*) Biff, up in Albany I saw a beautiful hammock. I think I'll buy it next trip, and we'll hang it right between those two elms. Wouldn't that be something? Just swingin' there under those branches. Boy, that would be . . .

(YOUNG BIFF *and* YOUNG HAPPY *appear from the direction* WILLY *was addressing.* HAPPY *carries rags and a pail of water.* BIFF, *wearing a sweater with a block "S," carries a football.*)

BIFF (*pointing in the direction of the car offstage*): How's that, Pop, professional?

WILLY: Terrific. Terrific job, boys. Good work, Biff.

HAPPY: Where's the surprise, Pop?

WILLY: In the back seat of the car.

HAPPY: Boy! (*He runs off.*)

BIFF: What is it, Dad? Tell me, what'd you buy?

WILLY (*laughing, cuffs him*): Never mind, something I want you to have.

BIFF (*turns and starts off*): What is it, Hap?

HAPPY (*offstage*): It's a punching bag!

BIFF: Oh, Pop!

WILLY: It's got Gene Tunney's signature on it!

(HAPPY runs onstage with a punching bag.)

BIFF: Gee, how'd you know we wanted a punching bag?

WILLY: Well, it's the finest thing for the timing.

HAPPY *(lies down on his back and pedals with his feet)*: I'm losing weight, you notice, Pop?

WILLY *(to HAPPY)*: Jumping rope is good too.

BIFF: Did you see the new football I got?

WILLY *(examining the ball)*: Where'd you get a new ball?

BIFF: The coach told me to practice my passing.

WILLY: That so? And he gave you the ball, heh?

BIFF: Well, I borrowed it from the locker room. *(He laughs confidentially.)*

WILLY *(laughing with him at the theft)*: I want you to return that.

HAPPY: I told you he wouldn't like it!

BIFF *(angrily)*: Well, I'm bringing it back!

WILLY *(stopping the incipient argument, to HAPPY)*: Sure, he's gotta practice with a regulation ball, doesn't he? *(to BIFF)* Coach'll probably congratulate you on your initiative!

BIFF: Oh, he keeps congratulating my initiative all the time, Pop.

WILLY: That's because he likes you. If somebody else took that ball there'd be an uproar. So what's the report, boys, what's the report?

BIFF: Where'd you go this time, Dad? Gee we were lonesome for you.

WILLY *(pleased, puts an arm around each boy and they come down to the apron)*: Lonesome, heh?

BIFF: Missed you every minute.

WILLY: Don't say? Tell you a secret, boys. Don't breathe it to a soul. Someday I'll have my own business, and I'll never have to leave home any more.

HAPPY: Like Uncle Charley, heh?

WILLY: Bigger than Uncle Charley! Because Charley is not—liked. He's liked, but he's not—well liked.

BIFF: Where'd you go this time, Dad?

WILLY: Well, I got on the road, and I went north to Providence. Met the Mayor.

BIFF: The Mayor of Providence!

WILLY: He was sitting in the hotel lobby.

BIFF: What'd he say?

WILLY: He said, "Morning!" and I said, "You got a fine city here, Mayor." And then he had coffee with me. And then I went to Waterbury. Waterbury is a fine city. Big clock city, the famous Waterbury clock. Sold a nice bill there. And then Boston—Boston is the cradle of the Revolution. A fine city. And a couple of other towns in Mass., and on to Portland and Bangor and straight home!

BIFF: Gee, I'd love to go with you sometime, Dad.

WILLY: Soon as summer comes.

HAPPY: Promise?

WILLY: You and Hap and I, and I'll show you all the towns. America is full of beautiful towns and fine, upstanding people. And they know me, boys, they know me up and down New England. The finest people. And when I bring you fellas up, there'll be an open sesame for all of us, 'cause one thing, boys: I have friends. I can park my car in any street in New England, and the cops protect it like their own. This summer, heh?

BIFF *and* HAPPY *(together)*: Yeah! You bet!

WILLY: We'll take our bathing suits.

HAPPY: We'll carry your bags, Pop!

WILLY: Oh, won't that be something! Me comin' into the Boston stores with you boys carryin' my bags. What a sensation!

(BIFF is prancing around, practicing passing the ball.)

WILLY: You nervous, Biff, about the game?

BIFF: Not if you're gonna be there.

WILLY: What do they say about you in school, now that they made you captain?

HAPPY: There's a crowd of girls behind him everytime the classes change.

BIFF *(taking WILLY's hand)*: This Saturday, Pop, this Saturday—just for you, I'm going to break through for a touchdown.

HAPPY: You're supposed to pass.

BIFF: I'm takin' one play for Pop. You watch me, Pop, and when I take off my helmet, that means I'm breakin' out. Then you watch me crash through that line!

WILLY *(kisses BIFF)*: Oh, wait'll I tell this in Boston!

(BERNARD enters in knickers. He is younger than BIFF, earnest and loyal, a worried boy.)

BERNARD: Biff, where are you? You're supposed to study with me today.

WILLY: Hey, looka Bernard. What're you lookin' so anemic about, Bernard?

BERNARD: He's gotta study, Uncle Willy. He's got Regents next week.

HAPPY *(tauntingly, spinning BERNARD around)*: Let's box, Bernard!

BERNARD: Biff! *(He gets away from HAPPY.)* Listen, Biff, I heard Mr. Birnbaum say that if you don't start studyin' math he's gonna flunk you, and you won't graduate. I heard him!

WILLY: You better study with him, Biff. Go ahead now.

BERNARD: I heard him!

BIFF: Oh, Pop, you didn't see my sneakers! *(He holds up a foot for WILLY to look at.)*

WILLY: Hey, that's a beautiful job of printing!

BERNARD *(wiping his glasses)*: Just because he printed University of Virginia on his sneakers doesn't mean they've got to graduate him, Uncle Willy!

WILLY (*angrily*): What're you talking about? With scholarships to three universities they're gonna flunk him?

BERNARD: But I heard Mr. Birnbaum say—

WILLY: Don't be a pest, Bernard! (*to his boys*) What an anemic!

BERNARD: Okay, I'm waiting for you in my house, Biff.

(BERNARD *goes off. The* LOMANS *laugh.*)

WILLY: Bernard is not well liked, is he?

BIFF: He's liked, but he's not well liked.

HAPPY: That's right, Pop.

WILLY: That's just what I mean. Bernard can get the best marks in school, y'understand, but when he gets out in the business world, y'understand, you are going to be five times ahead of him. That's why I thank Almighty God you're both built like Adonises. Because the man who makes an appearance in the business world, the man who creates personal interest, is the man who gets ahead. Be liked and you will never want. You take me, for instance. I never have to wait in line to see a buyer. "Willy Loman is here!" That's all they have to know, and I go right through.

BIFF: Did you knock them dead, Pop?

WILLY: Knocked 'em cold in Providence, slaughtered 'em in Boston.

HAPPY (*on his back, pedaling again*): I'm losing weight, you notice, Pop?

(LINDA *enters, as of old, a ribbon in her hair, carrying a basket of washing.*)

LINDA (*with youthful energy*): Hello, dear!

WILLY: Sweetheart!

LINDA: How'd the Chevvy run?

WILLY: Chevrolet, Linda, is the greatest car ever built. (*to the boys*) Since when do you let your mother carry wash up the stairs?

BIFF: Grab hold there, boy!

HAPPY: Where to, Mom?

LINDA: Hang them up on the line. And you better go down to your friends, Biff. The cellar is full of boys. They don't know what to do with themselves.

BIFF: Ah, when Pop comes home they can wait!

WILLY (*laughs appreciatively*): You better go down and tell them what to do, Biff.

BIFF: I think I'll have them sweep out the furnace room.

WILLY: Good work, Biff.

BIFF (*goes through wall-line of kitchen to doorway at back and calls down*): Fellas! Everybody sweep out the furnace room! I'll be right down!

VOICES: All right! Okay, Biff.

BIFF: George and Sam and Frank, come out back! We're hangin' up the wash! Come on, Hap, on

the double! (*He and* HAPPY *carry out the basket.*)

LINDA: The way they obey him!

WILLY: Well, that's training, the training. I'm tellin' you, I was sellin' thousands and thousands, but I had to come home.

LINDA: Oh, the whole block'll be at that game. Did you sell anything?

WILLY: I did five hundred gross in Providence and seven hundred gross in Boston.

LINDA: No! Wait a minute, I've got a pencil. (*She pulls pencil and paper out of her apron pocket.*) That makes your commission . . . Two hundred—my God! Two hundred and twelve dollars!

WILLY: Well, I didn't figure it yet, but . . .

LINDA: How much did you do?

WILLY: Well, I—I did—about a hundred and eighty gross in Providence. Well, no—it came to— roughly two hundred gross on the whole trip.

LINDA (*without hesitation*): Two hundred gross. That's . . . (*She figures.*)

WILLY: The trouble was that three of the stores were half closed for inventory in Boston. Otherwise I woulda broke records.

LINDA: Well, it makes seventy dollars and some pennies. That's very good.

WILLY: What do we owe?

LINDA: Well, on the first there's sixteen dollars on the refrigerator—

WILLY: Why sixteen?

LINDA: Well, the fan belt broke, so it was a dollar eighty.

WILLY: But it's brand new.

LINDA: Well, the man said that's the way it is. Till they work themselves in, y'know.

(*They move through the wall-line into the kitchen.*)

WILLY: I hope we didn't get stuck on that machine.

LINDA: They got the biggest ads of any of them!

WILLY: I know, it's a fine machine. What else?

LINDA: Well, there's nine-sixty for the washing machine. And for the vacuum cleaner there's three and a half due on the fifteenth. Then the roof, you got twenty-one dollars remaining.

WILLY: It don't leak, does it?

LINDA: No, they did a wonderful job. Then you owe Frank for the carburetor.

WILLY: I'm not going to pay that man! That goddam Chevrolet, they ought to prohibit the manufacture of that car!

LINDA: Well, you owe him three and a half. And odds and ends, comes to around a hundred and twenty dollars by the fifteenth.

WILLY: A hundred and twenty dollars! My God, if business don't pick up I don't know what I'm gonna do!

LINDA: Well, next week you'll do better.

WILLY: Oh, I'll knock 'em dead next week. I'll go to

Hartford. I'm very well liked in Hartford. You know, the trouble is, Linda, people don't seem to take to me.

(They move onto the forestage.)

LINDA: Oh, don't be foolish.

WILLY: I know it when I walk in. They seem to laugh at me.

LINDA: Why? Why would they laugh at you? Don't talk that way, Willy.

*(*WILLY *moves to the edge of the stage.* LINDA *goes into the kitchen and starts to darn stockings.)*

WILLY: I don't know the reason for it, but they just pass me by. I'm not noticed.

LINDA: But you're doing wonderful, dear. You're making seventy to a hundred dollars a week.

WILLY: But I gotta be at it ten, twelve hours a day. Other men—I don't know—they do it easier. I don't know why—I can't stop myself—I talk too much. A man oughta come in with a few words. One thing about Charley. He's a man of few words, and they respect him.

LINDA: You don't talk too much, you're just lively.

WILLY *(smiling)*: Well, I figure, what the hell, life is short, a couple of jokes. *(to himself)* I joke too much! *(The smile goes.)*

LINDA: Why? You're—

WILLY: I'm fat. I'm very—foolish to look at, Linda. I didn't tell you, but Christmas time I happened to be calling on F.H. Stewarts, and a salesman I know, as I was going in to see the buyer I heard him say something about—walrus. And I—I cracked him right across the face. I won't take that. I simply will not take that. But they do laugh at me. I know that.

LINDA: Darling . . .

WILLY: I gotta overcome it. I know I gotta overcome it. I'm not dressing to advantage, maybe.

LINDA: Willy, darling, you're the handsomest man in the world—

WILLY: Oh, no, Linda.

LINDA: To me you are. *(Slight pause.)* The handsomest.

(From the darkness is heard the laughter of a woman. Willy doesn't turn to it, but it continues through LINDA's *lines.)*

LINDA: And the boys, Willy. Few men are idolized by their children the way you are.

(Music is heard as behind a scrim, to the left of the house, THE WOMAN, *dimly seen, is dressing.)*

WILLY *(with great feeling)*: You're the best there is, Linda, you're a pal, you know that? On the road—on the road I want to grab you sometimes and just kiss the life outa you.

(The laughter is loud now, and he moves into a brightening area at the left, where THE WOMAN *has come from behind the scrim and is standing, putting on her hat, looking into a "mirror" and laughing.)*

WILLY: 'Cause I get so lonely—especially when business is bad and there's nobody to talk to. I get the feeling that I'll never sell anything again, that I won't make a living for you, or a business, a business for the boys. *(He talks through* THE WOMAN's *subsiding laughter;* THE WOMAN *primps at the "mirror.")* There's so much I want to make for—

THE WOMAN: Me? You didn't make me, Willy. I picked you.

WILLY *(pleased)*: You picked me?

THE WOMAN *(who is quite proper-looking,* WILLY's *age)*: I did. I've been sitting at that desk watching all the salesmen go by, day in, day out. But you've got such a sense of humor, and we do have such a good time together, don't we?

WILLY: Sure, sure. *(He takes her in his arms.)* Why do you have to go now?

THE WOMAN: It's two o'clock . . .

WILLY: No, come on in! *(He pulls her.)*

THE WOMAN: . . . my sisters'll be scandalized. When'll you be back?

WILLY: Oh, two weeks about. Will you come up again?

THE WOMAN: Sure thing. You do make me laugh. It's good for me. *(She squeezes his arm, kisses him.)* And I think you're a wonderful man.

WILLY: You picked me, heh?

THE WOMAN: Sure. Because you're so sweet. And such a kidder.

WILLY: Well, I'll see you next time I'm in Boston.

THE WOMAN: I'll put you right through to the buyers.

WILLY *(slapping her bottom)*: Right, well, bottoms up!

THE WOMAN *(slaps him gently and laughs)*: You just kill me, Willy. *(He suddenly grabs her and kisses her roughly.)* You kill me. And thanks for the stockings. I love a lot of stockings. Well, good night.

WILLY: Good night. And keep your pores open!

THE WOMAN: Oh, Willy!

*(*THE WOMAN *bursts out laughing, and* LINDA's *laughter blends in.* THE WOMAN *disappears into the dark. Now the area at the kitchen table brightens.* LINDA *is sitting where she was at the kitchen table, but now is mending a pair of her silk stockings.)*

LINDA: You are, Willy. The handsomest man. You've got no reason to feel that—

WILLY *(coming out of* THE WOMAN's *dimming area and going over to* LINDA*)*: I'll make it all up to you, Linda, I'll—

LINDA: There's nothing to make up, dear. You're doing fine, better than—

WILLY *(noticing her mending)*: What's that?

LINDA: Just mending my stockings. They're so expensive—

WILLY (*angrily, taking them from her*): I won't have you mending stockings in this house! Now throw them out!

(LINDA *puts the stockings in her pocket.*)

BERNARD (*entering on the run*): Where is he? If he doesn't study!

WILLY (*moving to the forestage, with great agitation*): You'll give him the answers!

BERNARD: I do, but I can't on a Regents! That's a state exam! They're liable to arrest me!

WILLY: Where is he? I'll whip him, I'll whip him!

LINDA: And he'd better give back that football, Willy, it's not nice.

WILLY: Biff! Where is he? Why is he taking everything?

LINDA: He's too rough with the girls, Willy. All the mothers are afraid of him!

WILLY: I'll whip him!

BERNARD: He's driving the car without a license!

(THE WOMAN'S *laugh is heard.*)

WILLY: Shut up!

LINDA: All the mothers—

WILLY: Shut up!

BERNARD (*backing quietly away and out*): Mr. Birnbaum says he's stuck up.

WILLY: Get outa here!

BERNARD: If he doesn't buckle down he'll flunk math! (*He goes off.*)

LINDA: He's right, Willy, you've gotta—

WILLY (*exploding at her*): There's nothing the matter with him! You want him to be a worm like Bernard? He's got spirit, personality . . .

(*As he speaks,* LINDA, *almost in tears, exits into the living-room.* WILLY *is alone in the kitchen, wilting and staring. The leaves are gone. It is night again, and the apartment houses look down from behind.*)

WILLY: Loaded with it. Loaded! What is he stealing? He's giving it back, isn't he? Why is he stealing? What did I tell him? I never in my life told him anything but decent things.

(HAPPY *in pajamas has come down the stairs;* WILLY *suddenly becomes aware of* HAPPY'S *presence.*)

HAPPY: Let's go now, come on.

WILLY (*sitting down at the kitchen table*): Huh! Why did she have to wax the floors herself? Everytime she waxes the floors she keels over. She knows that!

HAPPY: Shh! Take it easy. What brought you back tonight?

WILLY: I got an awful scare. Nearly hit a kid in Yonkers. God! Why didn't I go to Alaska with my brother Ben that time! Ben! That man was a genius, that man was success incarnate! What a mistake! He begged me to go.

HAPPY: Well, there's no use in—

WILLY: You guys! There was a man started with the clothes on his back and ended up with diamond mines!

HAPPY: Boy, someday I'd like to know how he did it.

WILLY: What's the mystery? The man knew what he wanted and went out and got it! Walked into a jungle, and comes out, the age of twenty-one, and he's rich! The world is an oyster, but you don't crack it open on a mattress!

HAPPY: Pop, I told you I'm gonna retire you for life.

WILLY: You'll retire me for life on seventy goddam dollars a week? And your women and your car and your apartment, and you'll retire me for life! Christ's sake, I couldn't get past Yonkers today! Where are you guys, where are you? The woods are burning! I can't drive a car!

(CHARLEY *has appeared in the doorway. He is a large man, slow of speech, laconic, immovable. In all he says, despite what he says, there is pity, and, now, trepidation. He has a robe over pajamas, slippers on his feet. He enters the kitchen.*)

CHARLEY: Everything all right?

HAPPY: Yeah, Charley, everything's . . .

WILLY: What's the matter?

CHARLEY: I heard some noise. I thought something happened. Can't we do something about the walls? You sneeze in here, and in my house hats blow off.

HAPPY: Let's go to bed, Dad, Come on.

(CHARLEY *signals to* HAPPY *to go.*)

WILLY: You go ahead, I'm not tired at the moment.

HAPPY (*to* WILLY): Take it easy, huh? (*He exits.*)

WILLY: What're you doin' up?

CHARLEY (*sitting down at the kitchen table opposite* WILLY): Couldn't sleep good. I had a heartburn.

WILLY: Well, you don't know how to eat.

CHARLEY: I eat with my mouth.

WILLY: No, you're ignorant. You gotta know about vitamins and things like that.

CHARLEY: Come on, let's shoot. Tire you out a little.

WILLY (*hesitantly*): All right. You got cards?

CHARLEY (*taking a deck from his pocket*): Yeah, I got them. Someplace. What is it with those vitamins?

WILLY (*dealing*): They build up your bones. Chemistry.

CHARLEY: Yeah, but there's no bones in a heartburn.

WILLY: What are you talkin' about? Do you know the first thing about it?

CHARLEY: Don't get insulted.

WILLY: Don't talk about something you don't know anything about.

(They are playing. Pause.)

CHARLEY: What're you doin' home?

WILLY: A little trouble with the car.

CHARLEY: Oh. *(Pause.)* I'd like to take a trip to California.

WILLY: Don't say.

CHARLEY: You want a job?

WILLY: I got a job, I told you that. *(After a slight pause.)* What the hell are you offering me a job for?

CHARLEY: Don't get insulted.

WILLY: Don't insult me.

CHARLEY: I don't see no sense in it. You don't have to go on this way.

WILLY: I got a good job. *(Slight pause.)* What do you keep comin' in here for?

CHARLEY: You want me to go?

WILLY *(after a pause, withering)*: I can't understand it. He's going back to Texas again. What the hell is that?

CHARLEY: Let him go.

WILLY: I got nothin' to give him, Charley, I'm clean, I'm clean.

CHARLEY: He won't starve. None a them starve. Forget about him.

WILLY: Then what have I got to remember?

CHARLEY: You take it too hard. To hell with it. When a deposit bottle is broken you don't get your nickel back.

WILLY: That's easy enough for you to say.

CHARLEY: That ain't easy for me to say.

WILLY: Did you see the ceiling I put up in the living-room?

CHARLEY: Yeah, that's a piece of work. To put up a ceiling is a mystery to me. How do you do it?

WILLY: What's the difference?

CHARLEY: Well, talk about it.

WILLY: You gonna put up a ceiling?

CHARLEY: How could I put up a ceiling?

WILLY: Then what the hell are you bothering me for?

CHARLEY: You're insulted again.

WILLY: A man who can't handle tools is not a man. You're disgusting.

CHARLEY: Don't call me disgusting, Willy.

(UNCLE BEN, carrying a valise and an umbrella, enters the forestage from around the right corner of the house. He is a stolid man, in his sixties, with a mustache and an authoritative air. He is utterly certain of his destiny, and there is an aura of far places about him. He enters exactly as WILLY speaks.)

WILLY: I'm getting awfully tired, Ben.

(BEN's music is heard. BEN looks around at everything.)

CHARLEY: Good, keep playing; you'll sleep better. Did you call me Ben?

(BEN looks at his watch.)

WILLY: That's funny. For a second there you reminded me of my brother Ben.

BEN: I only have a few minutes. *(He strolls, inspecting the place. WILLY and CHARLEY continue playing.)*

CHARLEY: You never heard from him again, heh? Since that time?

WILLY: Didn't Linda tell you? Couple of weeks ago we got a letter from his wife in Africa. He died.

CHARLEY: That so.

BEN *(chuckling)*: So this is Brooklyn, eh?

CHARLEY: Maybe you're in for some of his money.

WILLY: Naa, he had seven sons. There's just one opportunity I had with that man . . .

BEN: I must make a train, William. There are several properties I'm looking at in Alaska.

WILLY: Sure, sure! If I'd gone with him to Alaska that time, everything would've been totally different.

CHARLEY: Go on, you'd froze to death up there.

WILLY: What're you talking about?

BEN: Opportunity is tremendous in Alaska, William. Surprised you're not up there.

WILLY: Sure, tremendous.

CHARLEY: Heh?

WILLY: There was the only man I ever met who knew the answers.

CHARLEY: Who?

BEN: How are you all?

WILLY *(taking a pot, smiling)*: Fine, fine.

CHARLEY: Pretty sharp tonight.

BEN: Is Mother living with you?

WILLY: No, she died a long time ago.

CHARLEY: Who?

BEN: That's too bad. Fine specimen of a lady, Mother.

WILLY *(to CHARLEY)*: Heh?

BEN: I'd hoped to see the old girl.

CHARLEY: Who died?

BEN: Heard anything from Father, have you?

WILLY *(unnerved)*: What do you mean, who died?

CHARLEY *(taking a pot)*: What're you talkin' about?

BEN *(looking at his watch)*: William, it's half-past eight!

WILLY *(as though to dispel his confusion he angrily stops CHARLEY's hand)*: That's my build!

CHARLEY: I put the ace—

WILLY: If you don't know how to play the game I'm not gonna throw my money away on you!

CHARLEY *(rising)*: It was my ace, for God's sake!

WILLY: I'm through, I'm through!

BEN: When did Mother die?

WILLY: Long ago. Since the beginning you never knew how to play cards.

CHARLEY *(picks up the cards and goes to the door)*: All right! Next time I'll bring a deck with five aces.

WILLY: I don't play that kind of game!

CHARLEY *(turning to him)*: You ought to be ashamed of yourself!

WILLY: Yeah?

CHARLEY: Yeah! *(He goes out.)*

WILLY *(slamming the door after him)*: Ignoramus!

BEN *(as* WILLY *comes toward him through the wall-line of the kitchen)*: So you're William.

WILLY *(shaking* BEN's *hand)*: Ben! I've been waiting for you so long! What's the answer? How did you do it?

BEN: Oh, there's a story in that.

*(*LINDA *enters the forestage, as of old, carrying the wash basket.)*

LINDA: Is this Ben?

BEN *(gallantly)*: How do you do, my dear.

LINDA: Where've you been all these years? Willy's always wondered why you—

WILLY *(pulling* BEN *away from her impatiently)*: Where is Dad? Didn't you follow him? How did you get started?

BEN: Well, I don't know how much you remember.

WILLY: Well, I was just a baby, of course, only three or four years old—

BEN: Three years and eleven months.

WILLY: What a memory, Ben!

BEN: I have many enterprises, William, and I have never kept books.

WILLY: I remember I was sitting under the wagon in—was it Nebraska?

BEN: It was South Dakota, and I gave you a bunch of wild flowers.

WILLY: I remember you walking away down some open road.

BEN *(laughing)*: I was going to find Father in Alaska.

WILLY: Where is he?

BEN: At that age I had a very faulty view of geography, William. I discovered after a few days that I was heading due south, so instead of Alaska, I ended up in Africa.

LINDA: Africa!

WILLY: The Gold Coast!

BEN: Principally diamond mines.

LINDA: Diamond mines!

BEN: Yes, my dear. But I've only a few minutes—

WILLY: No! Boys! Boys! *(*YOUNG BIFF *and* HAPPY *appear.)* Listen to this. This is your Uncle Ben, a great man! Tell my boys, Ben!

BEN: Why, boys, when I was seventeen I walked into the jungle, and when I was twenty-one I walked out. *(He laughs.)* And by God I was rich.

WILLY *(to the boys)*: You see what I been talking about? The greatest things can happen!

BEN *(glancing at his watch)*: I have an appointment in Ketchikan Tuesday week.

WILLY: No, Ben! Please tell about Dad. I want my boys to hear. I want them to know the kind of stock they spring from. All I remember is a man with a big beard, and I was in Mamma's lap, sitting around a fire, and some kind of high music.

BEN: His flute. He played the flute.

WILLY: Sure, the flute, that's right!

(New music is heard, a high, rollicking tune.)

BEN: Father was a very great and a very wild-hearted man. We would start in Boston, and he'd toss the whole family into the wagon, and then he'd drive the team right across the country; through Ohio, and Indiana, Michigan, Illinois, and all the Western states. And we'd stop in the towns and sell the flutes that he'd made on the way. Great inventor, Father. With one gadget he made more in a week than a man like you could make in a lifetime.

WILLY: That's just the way I'm bringing them up, Ben—rugged, well liked, all-around.

BEN: Yeah? *(to* BIFF*)* Hit that, boy—hard as you can. *(He pounds his stomach.)*

BIFF: Oh, no, sir!

BEN *(taking boxing stance)*: Come on, get to me! *(He laughs.)*

WILLY: Go to it, Biff! Go ahead, show him!

BIFF: Okay! *(He cocks his fists and starts in.)*

LINDA *(to* WILLY*)*: Why must he fight, dear?

BEN *(sparring with* BIFF*)*: Good boy! Good boy!

WILLY: How's that, Ben, heh?

HAPPY: Give him the left, Biff!

LINDA: Why are you fighting?

BEN: Good boy! *(Suddenly comes in, trips* BIFF, *and stands over him, the point of his umbrella poised over* BIFF's *eye.)*

LINDA: Look out, Biff!

BIFF: Gee!

BEN *(patting* BIFF's *knee)*: Never fight fair with a stranger, boy. You'll never get out of the jungle that way. *(Taking* LINDA's *hand and bowing.)* It was an honor and a pleasure to meet you, Linda.

LINDA *(withdrawing her hand coldly, frightened)*: Have a nice—trip.

BEN *(to* WILLY*)*: And good luck with your—what do you do?

WILLY: Selling.

BEN: Yes. Well . . . *(He raises his hand in farewell to all.)*

WILLY: No, Ben, I don't want you to think . . . *(He takes* BEN's *arm to show him.)* It's Brooklyn. I know, but we hunt too.

BEN: Really, now.

WILLY: Oh, sure, there's snakes and rabbits and—that's why I moved out here. Why, Biff can fell any one of these trees in no time! Boys! Go right over to where they're building the apartment house and get some sand. We're gonna rebuild the entire front stoop right now! Watch this, Ben!

BIFF: Yes, sir! On the double, Hap!

HAPPY (*as he and* BIFF *run off*): I lost weight, Pop, you notice?

(CHARLEY *enters in knickers, even before the boys are gone.*)

CHARLEY: Listen, if they steal any more from that building the watchman'll put the cops on them!

LINDA (*to* WILLY): Don't let Biff . . .

(BEN *laughs lustily.*)

WILLY: You shoulda seen the lumber they brought home last week. At least a dozen six-by-tens worth all kinds a money.

CHARLEY: Listen, if that watchman—

WILLY: I gave them hell, understand. But I got a couple of fearless characters there.

CHARLEY: Willy, the jails are full of fearless characters.

BEN (*clapping* WILLY *on the back, with a laugh at* CHARLEY): And the stock exchange, friend!

WILLY (*joining in* BEN'S *laughter*): Where are the rest of your pants?

CHARLEY: My wife bought them.

WILLY: Now all you need is a golf club and you can go upstairs and go to sleep. (*to* BEN) Great athlete! Between him and his son Bernard they can't hammer a nail!

BERNARD (*rushing in*): The watchman's chasing Biff!

WILLY (*angrily*): Shut up! He's not stealing anything!

LINDA (*alarmed, hurrying off left*): Where is he? Biff, dear! (*She exits.*)

WILLY (*moving toward the left, away from* BEN): There's nothing wrong. What's the matter with you?

BEN: Nervy boy. Good!

WILLY (*laughing*): Oh, nerves of iron, that Biff!

CHARLEY: Don't know what it is. My New England man comes back and he's bleedin', they murdered him up there.

WILLY: It's contacts, Charley, I got important contacts!

CHARLEY (*sarcastically*): Glad to hear it, Willy. Come in later, we'll shoot a little casino. I'll take some of your Portland money. (*He laughs at* WILLY *and exits.*)

WILLY (*turning to* BEN): Business is bad, it's murderous. But not for me, of course.

BEN: I'll stop by on my way back to Africa.

WILLY (*longingly*): Can't you stay a few days? You're just what I need, Ben, because I—I have a fine position here, but I—well, Dad left when I was such a baby and I never had a chance to talk to him and I still feel—kind of temporary about myself.

BEN: I'll be late for my train.

(*They are at opposite ends of the stage.*)

WILLY: Ben, my boys—can't we talk? They'd go into the jaws of hell for me, see, but I—

BEN: William, you're being first-rate with your boys. Outstanding, manly chaps!

WILLY (*hanging on to his words*): Oh, Ben, that's good to hear! Because sometimes I'm afraid that I'm not teaching them the right kind of—Ben, how should I teach them?

BEN (*giving great weight to each word, and with a certain vicious audacity*): William, when I walked into the jungle, I was seventeen. When I walked out I was twenty-one. And, by God, I was rich! (*He goes off into darkness around the right corner of the house.*)

WILLY: . . . was rich! That's just the spirit I want to imbue them with! To walk into a jungle! I was right! I was right! I was right!

(BEN *is gone, but* WILLY *is still speaking to him as* LINDA, *in nightgown and robe, enters the kitchen, glances around for* WILLY, *then goes to the door of the house, looks out and sees him. Comes down to his left. He looks at her.*)

LINDA: Willy, dear? Willy?

WILLY: I was right!

LINDA: Did you have some cheese? (*He can't answer.*) It's very late, darling. Come to bed, heh?

WILLY (*looking straight up*): Gotta break your neck to see a star in this yard.

LINDA: You coming in?

WILLY: Whatever happened to that diamond watch fob? Remember? When Ben came from Africa that time? Didn't he give me a watch fob with a diamond in it?

LINDA: You pawned it, dear. Twelve, thirteen years ago. For Biff's radio correspondence course.

WILLY: Gee, that was a beautiful thing. I'll take a walk.

LINDA: But you're in your slippers.

WILLY (*starting to go around the house at the left*): I was right! I was! (*Half to* LINDA, *as he goes, shaking his head.*) What a man! There was a man worth talking to. I was right!

LINDA (*calling after* WILLY): But in your slippers, Willy!

(WILLY *is almost gone when* BIFF, *in his pajamas, comes down the stairs and enters the kitchen.*)

BIFF: What is he doing out there?

LINDA: Sh!

BIFF: God Almighty, Mom, how long has he been doing this?

LINDA: Don't, he'll hear you.

BIFF: What the hell is the matter with him?

LINDA: It'll pass by morning.

BIFF: Shouldn't we do anything?

LINDA: Oh, my dear, you should do a lot of things, but there's nothing to do, so go to sleep.

(HAPPY *comes down the stair and sits on the steps.*)

HAPPY: I never heard him so loud, Mom.

LINDA: Well, come around more often; you'll hear him. (*She sits down at the table and mends the lining of* WILLY's *jacket.*)

BIFF: Why didn't you ever write me about this, Mom?

LINDA: How would I write to you? For over three months you had no address.

BIFF: I was on the move. But you know I thought of you all the time. You know that, don't you, pal?

LINDA: I know, dear, I know. But he likes to have a letter. Just to know that there's still a possibility for better things.

BIFF: He's not like this all the time, is he?

LINDA: It's when you come home he's always the worst.

BIFF: When I come home?

LINDA: When you write you're coming, he's all smiles, and talks about the future, and—he's just wonderful. And then the closer you seem to come, the more shaky he gets, and then, by the time you get here, he's arguing, and he seems angry at you. I think it's just that maybe he can't bring himself to—to open up to you. Why are you so hateful to each other? Why is that?

BIFF (*evasively*): I'm not hateful, Mom.

LINDA: But you no sooner come in the door than you're fighting!

BIFF: I don't know why. I mean to change. I'm tryin', Mom, you understand?

LINDA: Are you home to stay now?

BIFF: I don't know. I want to look around, see what's doin'.

LINDA: Biff, you can't look around all your life, can you?

BIFF: I just can't take hold, Mom. I can't take hold of some kind of a life.

LINDA: Biff, a man is not a bird, to come and go with the springtime.

BIFF: Your hair . . . (*He touches her hair.*) Your hair got so gray.

LINDA: Oh, it's been gray since you were in high school. I just stopped dyeing it, that's all.

BIFF: Dye it again, will ya? I don't want my pal looking old. (*He smiles.*)

LINDA: You're such a boy! You think you can go away for a year and . . . You've got to get it into your head now that one day you'll knock on this door and there'll be strange people here—

BIFF: What are you talking about? You're not even sixty, Mom.

LINDA: But what about your father?

BIFF (*lamely*): Well, I meant him too.

HAPPY: He admires Pop.

LINDA: Biff, dear, if you don't have any feeling for him, then you can't have any feeling for me.

BIFF: Sure I can, Mom.

LINDA: No. You can't just come to see me, because I love him. (*With a threat, but only a threat, of tears.*) He's the dearest man in the world to me, and I won't have anyone making him feel unwanted and low and blue. You've got to make up your mind now, darling, there's no leeway any more. Either he's your father and you pay him that respect, or else you're not to come here. I know he's not easy to get along with—nobody knows that better than me—but . . .

WILLY (*from the left, with a laugh*): Hey, hey, Biffo!

BIFF (*starting to go out after* WILLY): What the hell is the matter with him? (HAPPY *stops him.*)

LINDA: Don't—don't go near him!

BIFF: Stop making excuses for him! He always, always wiped the floor with you. Never had an ounce of respect for you.

HAPPY: He's always had respect for—

BIFF: What the hell do you know about it?

HAPPY (*surlily*): Just don't call him crazy!

BIFF: He's got no character—Charley wouldn't do this. Not in his own house—spewing out that vomit from his mind.

HAPPY: Charley never had to cope with what he's got to.

BIFF: People are worse off than Willy Loman. Believe me, I've seen them!

LINDA: Then make Charley your father, Biff. You can't do that, can you? I don't say he's a great man. Willy Loman never made a lot of money. His name was never in the paper. He's not the finest character that ever lived. But he's a human being, and a terrible thing is happening to him. So attention must be paid. He's not to be allowed to fall into his grave like an old dog. Attention, attention must be finally paid to such a person. You called him crazy—

BIFF: I didn't mean—

LINDA: No, a lot of people think he's lost his—balance. But you don't have to be very smart to know what his trouble is. The man is exhausted.

HAPPY: Sure!

LINDA: A small man can be just as exhausted as a great man. He works for a company thirty-six years this March, opens up unheard-of territories to their trademark, and now in his old age they take his salary away.

HAPPY (*indignantly*): I didn't know that, Mom.

LINDA: You never asked, my dear! Now that you get your spending money someplace else you don't trouble your mind with him.

HAPPY: But I gave you money last—

LINDA: Christmas time, fifty dollars! To fix the hot water it cost ninety-seven fifty! For five weeks he's been on straight commission, like a beginner, an unknown!

BIFF: Those ungrateful bastards!

LINDA: Are they any worse than his sons? When he brought them business, when he was young, they were glad to see him. But now his old friends, the old buyers that loved him so and always found some order to hand him in a pinch—they're all dead, retired. He used to be able to make six, seven calls a day in Boston. Now he takes his valises out of the car and puts them back and takes them out again and he's exhausted. Instead of walking he talks now. He drives seven hundred miles, and when he gets there no one knows him any more, no one welcomes him. And what goes through a man's mind, driving seven hundred miles home without having earned a cent? Why shouldn't he talk to himself? Why? When he has to go to Charley and borrow fifty dollars a week and pretend to me that it's his pay? How long can that go on? How long? You see what I'm sitting here and waiting for? And you tell me he has no character? The man who never worked a day but for your benefit? When does he get the medal for that? Is this his reward—to turn around at the age of sixty-three and find his sons, who he loved better than his life, one a philandering bum—

HAPPY: Mom!

LINDA: That's all you are, my baby! (*to* BIFF) And you! What happened to the love you had for him? You were such pals! How you used to talk to him on the phone every night! How lonely he was till he could come home to you!

BIFF: All right, Mom. I'll live here in my room, and I'll get a job. I'll keep away from him, that's all.

LINDA: No, Biff. You can't stay here and fight all the time.

BIFF: He threw me out of this house, remember that.

LINDA: Why did he do that? I never knew why.

BIFF: Because I know he's a fake and he doesn't like anybody around who knows!

LINDA: Why a fake? In what way? What do you mean?

BIFF: Just don't lay it all at my feet. It's between me and him—that's all I have to say. I'll chip in from now on. He'll settle for half my pay check. He'll be all right. I'm going to bed. (*He starts for the stairs.*)

LINDA: He won't be all right.

BIFF (*turning on the stairs, furiously*): I hate this city and I'll stay here. Now what do you want?

LINDA: He's dying, Biff.

(HAPPY *turns quickly to her, shocked.*)

BIFF (*after a pause*): Why is he dying?

LINDA: He's been trying to kill himself.

BIFF (*with great horror*): How?

LINDA: I live from day to day.

BIFF: What're you talking about?

LINDA: Remember I wrote you that he smashed up the car again? In February?

BIFF: Well?

LINDA: The insurance inspector came. He said that they have evidence. That all these accidents in the last year—weren't—weren't—accidents.

HAPPY: How can they tell that? That's a lie.

LINDA: It seems there's a woman . . . (*She takes a breath as* . . .)

BIFF (*sharply but contained*): What woman?

LINDA (*simultaneously*): . . . and this woman . . .

LINDA: What?

BIFF: Nothing. Go ahead.

LINDA: What did you say?

BIFF: Nothing. I just said what woman?

HAPPY: What about her?

LINDA: Well, it seems she was walking down the road and saw his car. She says that he wasn't driving fast at all, and that he didn't skid. She says he came to that little bridge, and then deliberately smashed into the railing, and it was only the shallowness of the water that saved him.

BIFF: Oh, no, he probably just fell asleep again.

LINDA: I don't think he fell asleep.

BIFF: Why not?

LINDA: Last month . . . (*With great difficulty.*) Oh, boys, it's so hard to say a thing like this! He's just a big stupid man to you, but I tell you there's more good in him than in many other people. (*She chokes, wipes her eyes.*) I was looking for a fuse. The lights blew out, and I went down the cellar. And behind the fuse box—it happened to fall out—was a length of rubber pipe—just short.

HAPPY: No kidding?

LINDA: There's a little attachment on the end of it. I knew right away. And sure enough, on the bottom of the water heater there's a new little nipple on the gas pipe.

HAPPY (*angrily*): That—jerk.

BIFF: Did you have it taken off?

LINDA: I'm—I'm ashamed to. How can I mention it to him? Every day I go down and take away that little rubber pipe. But, when he comes home, I put it back where it was. How can I insult him that way? I don't know what to do. I live from day to day, boys. I tell you, I know every thought in his mind. It sounds so old-fashioned and silly, but I tell you he put his whole life into you and you've turned your backs on him. (*She is bent over in the chair, weeping, her face in her hands.*) Biff, I swear to God! Biff, his life is in your hands!

HAPPY (*to* BIFF): How do you like that damned fool!

BIFF (*kissing her*): All right, pal, all right. It's all settled now. I've been remiss. I know that, Mom. But now I'll stay, and I swear to you, I'll apply myself. (*Kneeling in front of her, in a fever of self-reproach*)

It's just—you see, Mom, I don't fit in business. Not that I won't try. I'll try, and I'll make good.

HAPPY: Sure you will. The trouble with you in business was you never tried to please people.

BIFF: I know, I—

HAPPY: Like when you worked for Harrison's. Bob Harrison said you were tops, and then you go and do some damn fool thing like whistling whole songs in the elevator like a comedian.

BIFF (against HAPPY): So what? I like to whistle sometimes.

HAPPY: You don't raise a guy to a responsible job who whistles in the elevator!

LINDA: Well, don't argue about it now.

HAPPY: Like when you'd go off and swim in the middle of the day instead of taking the line around.

BIFF (his resentment rising): Well, don't you run off? You take off sometimes, don't you? On a nice summer day?

HAPPY: Yeah, but I cover myself!

LINDA: Boys!

HAPPY: If I'm going to take a fade the boss can call any number where I'm supposed to be and they'll swear to him that I just left. I'll tell you something that I hate to say, Biff, but in the business world some of them think you're crazy.

BIFF (angered): Screw the business world!

HAPPY: All right, screw it! Great, but cover yourself!

LINDA: Hap, Hap!

BIFF: I don't care what they think! They've laughed at Dad for years, and you know why? Because we don't belong in this nuthouse of a city! We should be mixing cement on some open plain, or—or carpenters. A carpenter is allowed to whistle!

(WILLY walks in from the entrance of the house, at left.)

WILLY: Even your grandfather was better than a carpenter. (Pause. They watch him.) You never grew up. Bernard does not whistle in the elevator, I assure you.

BIFF (as though to laugh WILLY out of it): Yeah, but you do, Pop.

WILLY: I never in my life whistled in an elevator! And who in the business world thinks I'm crazy!

BIFF: I didn't mean it like that, Pop. Now don't make a whole thing out of it, will ya?

WILLY: Go back to the West! Be a carpenter, a cowboy, enjoy yourself!

LINDA: Willy, he was just saying—

WILLY: I heard what he said!

HAPPY (trying to quiet WILLY): Hey, Pop, come on now . . .

WILLY (continuing over HAPPY's line): They laugh at me, heh? Go to Filene's, go to the Hub, go to Slattery's, Boston. Call out the name Willy Loman and see what happens! Big shot!

BIFF: All right, Pop.

WILLY: Big!

BIFF: All right!

WILLY: Why do you always insult me?

BIFF: I didn't say a word. (to LINDA) Did I say a word?

LINDA: He didn't say anything, Willy.

WILLY (going to the doorway of the living-room): All right, good night, good night.

LINDA: Willy, dear, he just decided . . .

WILLY (to BIFF): If you get tired hanging around tomorrow, paint the ceiling I put up in the living-room.

BIFF: I'm leaving early tomorrow.

HAPPY: He's going to see Bill Oliver, Pop.

WILLY (interestedly): Oliver? For what?

BIFF (with reserve, but trying, trying): He always said he'd stake me. I'd like to go into business, so maybe I can take him up on it.

LINDA: Isn't that wonderful?

WILLY: Don't interrupt. What's wonderful about it? There's fifty men in the City of New York who'd stake him. (to BIFF) Sporting goods?

BIFF: I guess so. I know something about it and—

WILLY: He knows something about it! You know sporting goods better than Spalding, for God's sake! How much is he giving you?

BIFF: I don't know, I didn't even see him yet, but—

WILLY: Then what're you talkin' about?

BIFF (getting angry): Well, all I said was I'm gonna see him, that's all!

WILLY (turning away): Ah, you're counting your chickens again.

BIFF (starting left for the stairs): Oh, Jesus, I'm going to sleep!

WILLY (calling after him): Don't curse in this house!

BIFF (turning): Since when did you get so clean?

HAPPY (trying to stop them): What a . . .

WILLY: Don't use that language to me! I won't have it!

HAPPY (grabbing BIFF, shouts): Wait a minute! I got an idea. I got a feasible idea. Come here, Biff, let's talk this over now, let's talk some sense here. When I was down in Florida last time, I thought of a great idea to sell sporting goods. It just came back to me. You and I, Biff—we have a line, the Loman Line. We train a couple of weeks, and put on a couple of exhibitions, see?

WILLY: That's an idea!

HAPPY: Wait! We form two basketball teams, see? Two water-polo teams. We play each other. It's a million dollars' worth of publicity. Two brothers, see? The Loman Brothers. Displays in the Royal Palms—all the hotels. And banners over the ring and the basketball court; "Loman Brothers." Baby, we could sell sporting goods!

WILLY: This is a one-million-dollar idea!

LINDA: Marvelous!

BIFF: I'm in great shape as far as that's concerned.

HAPPY: And the beauty of it is, Biff, it wouldn't be like a business. We'd be out playin' ball again . . .

BIFF (*enthused*): Yeah, that's . . .

WILLY: Million-dollar . . .

HAPPY: And you wouldn't get fed up with it, Biff. It'd be the family again. There'd be the old honor, and comradeship, and if you wanted to go off for a swim or somethin'—well, you'd do it! Without some smart cooky gettin' up ahead of you!

WILLY: Lick the world! You guys together could absolutely lick the civilized world.

BIFF: I'll see Oliver tomorrow. Hap, if we could work that out . . .

LINDA: Maybe things are beginning to—

WILLY (*wildly enthused, to* LINDA): Stop interrupting! (*To* BIFF) But don't wear sport jacket and slacks when you see Oliver.

BIFF: No, I'll—

WILLY: A business suit, and talk as little as possible, and don't crack any jokes.

BIFF: He did like me. Always liked me.

LINDA: He loved you!

WILLY (*to* LINDA): Will you stop! (*to* BIFF) Walk in very serious. You are not applying for a boy's job. Money is to pass. Be quiet, fine, and serious. Everybody likes a kidder, but nobody lends him money.

HAPPY: I'll try to get some myself, Biff. I'm sure I can.

WILLY: I see great things for you kids. I think your troubles are over. But remember, start big and you'll end big. Ask for fifteen. How much you gonna ask for?

BIFF: Gee, I don't know—

WILLY: And don't say "Gee." "Gee" is a boy's word. A man walking in for fifteen thousand dollars does not say "Gee!"

BIFF: Ten, I think would be top though.

WILLY: Don't be so modest. You always started too low. Walk in with a big laugh. Don't look worried. Start off with a couple of your good stories to lighten things up. It's not what you say, it's how you say it—because personality always wins the day.

LINDA: Oliver always thought the highest of him—

WILLY: Will you let me talk?

BIFF: Don't yell at her, Pop, will ya?

WILLY (*angrily*): I was talking, wasn't I?

BIFF: I don't like you yelling at her all the time, and I'm tellin' you, that's all.

WILLY: What're you, takin' over this house?

LINDA: Willy—

WILLY (*turning on her*): Don't take his side all the time, goddammit!

BIFF (*furiously*): Stop yelling at her!

WILLY (*suddenly pulling on his cheek, beaten down, guilt ridden*): Give my best to Bill Oliver—he may remember me. (*He exits through the living-room doorway.*)

LINDA (*her voice subdued*): What'd you have to start that for? (BIFF *turns away.*) You see how sweet he was as soon as you talked hopefully? (*She goes over to* BIFF.) Come up and say good night to him. Don't let him go to bed that way.

HAPPY: Come on, Biff, let's buck him up.

LINDA: Please, dear. Just say good night. It takes so little to make him happy. Come. (*She goes through the living-room doorway, calling upstairs from within the living-room.*) Your pajamas are hanging in the bathroom, Willy!

HAPPY (*looking toward where* LINDA *went out*): What a woman! They broke the mold when they made her. You know that, Biff?

BIFF: He's off salary. My God, working on commission!

HAPPY: Well, let's face it: he's no hot-shot selling man. Except that sometimes, you have to admit, he's a sweet personality.

BIFF (*deciding*): Lend me ten bucks, will ya? I want to buy some new ties.

HAPPY: I'll take you to a place I know. Beautiful stuff. Wear one of my striped shirts tomorrow.

BIFF: She got gray. Mom got awful old. Gee, I'm gonna go in to Oliver tomorrow and knock him for a—

HAPPY: Come on up. Tell that to Dad. Let's give him a whirl. Come on.

BIFF (*steamed up*): You know, with ten thousand bucks, boy!

HAPPY (*as they go into the living-room*): That's the talk, Biff, that's the first time I've heard the old confidence out of you! (*From within the living-room, fading off.*) You're gonna live with me, kid, and any babe you want just say the word . . . (*The last lines are hardly heard. They are mounting the stairs to their parents' bedroom.*)

LINDA (*entering her bedroom and addressing* WILLY, *who is in the bathroom. She is straightening the bed for him*): Can you do anything about the shower? It drips.

WILLY (*from the bathroom*): All of a sudden everything falls to pieces! Goddam plumbing, oughta be sued, those people. I hardly finished putting it in and the thing . . . (*His words rumble off.*)

LINDA: I'm just wondering if Oliver will remember him. You think he might?

WILLY (*coming out of the bathroom in his pajamas*): Remember him? What's the matter with you, you crazy? If he'd've stayed with Oliver he'd be on top by now! Wait'll Oliver gets a look at him. You don't know the average caliber any more. The average young man today—(*He is getting into bed.*)—is got a caliber of zero. Greatest thing in the world for him was to bum around.

(BIFF *and* HAPPY *enter the bedroom. Slight pause.*)

WILLY (*stops short, looking at* BIFF): Glad to hear it, boy.

HAPPY: He wanted to say good night to you, sport.

WILLY (to BIFF): Yeah. Knock him dead, boy. What'd you want to tell me?

BIFF: Just take it easy, Pop. Good night. (He turns to go.)

WILLY (unable to resist): And if anything falls off the desk while you're talking to him—like a package or something—don't you pick it up. They have office boys for that.

LINDA: I'll make a big breakfast—

WILLY: Will you let me finish? (to BIFF) Tell him you were in the business in the West. Not farm work.

BIFF: All right, Dad.

LINDA: I think everything—

WILLY (going right through her speech): And don't undersell yourself. No less than fifteen thousand dollars.

BIFF (unable to bear him): Okay. Good night, Mom. (He starts moving.)

WILLY: Because you got a greatness in you, Biff, remember that. You got all kinds a greatness . . . (He lies back, exhausted. BIFF walks out.)

LINDA (calling after BIFF): Sleep well, darling!

HAPPY: I'm gonna get married, Mom. I wanted to tell you.

LINDA: Go to sleep, dear.

HAPPY (going): I just wanted to tell you.

WILLY: Keep up the good work. (HAPPY exits.) God . . . remember that Ebbets Field game? The championship of the city?

LINDA: Just rest. Should I sing to you?

WILLY: Yeah. Sing to me. (LINDA hums a soft lullaby.) When that team came out—he was the tallest, remember?

LINDA: Oh, yes. And in gold.

(BIFF enters the darkened kitchen, takes a cigarette and leaves the house. He comes downstage into a golden pool of light. He smokes, staring at the night.)

WILLY: Like a young god. Hercules—something like that. And the sun, the sun all around him. Remember how he waved to me? Right up from the field, with the representatives of three colleges standing by? And the buyers I brought, and the cheers when he came out—Loman, Loman, Loman! God Almighty, he'll be great yet. A star like that, magnificent, can never really fade away!

(The light on WILLY is fading. The gas heater begins to glow through the kitchen wall, near the stairs, a blue flame beneath red coils.)

LINDA (timidly): Willy dear, what has he got against you?

WILLY: I'm so tired. Don't talk any more.

(BIFF slowly returns to the kitchen. He stops, stares toward the heater.)

LINDA: Will you ask Howard to let you work in New York?

WILLY: First thing in the morning. Everything'll be all right.

(BIFF reaches behind the heater and draws out a length of rubber tubing. He is horrified and turns his head toward WILLY's room, still dimly lit, from which the strains of LINDA's desperate but monotonous humming rise.)

WILLY (staring through the window into the moonlight): Gee, look at the moon moving between the buildings!

(BIFF wraps the tubing around his hand and quickly goes up the stairs.)

ACT 2

(Music is heard, gay and bright. The curtain rises as the music fades away. WILLY, in shirt sleeves, is sitting at the kitchen table, sipping coffee, his hat in his lap. LINDA is filling his cup when she can.)

WILLY: Wonderful coffee. Meal in itself.

LINDA: Can I make you some eggs?

WILLY: No. Take a breath.

LINDA: You look so rested, dear.

WILLY: I slept like a dead one. First time in months. Imagine, sleeping till ten on a Tuesday morning. Boys left nice and early, heh?

LINDA: They were out of here by eight o'clock.

WILLY: Good work!

LINDA: It was so thrilling to see them leaving together. I can't get over the shaving lotion in this house!

WILLY (smiling): Mmm—

LINDA: Biff was very changed this morning. His whole attitude seemed to be hopeful. He couldn't wait to get downtown to see Oliver.

WILLY: He's heading for a change. There's no question, there simply are certain men that take longer to get—solidified. How did he dress?

LINDA: His blue suit. He's so handsome in that suit. He could be a—anything in that suit!

(WILLY gets up from the table. LINDA holds his jacket for him.)

WILLY: There's no question, no question at all. Gee, on the way home tonight I'd like to buy some seeds.

LINDA (laughing): That'd be wonderful. But not enough sun gets back there. Nothing'll grow any more.

WILLY: You wait, kid, before it's all over we're gonna get a little place out in the country, and I'll raise some vegetables, a couple of chickens . . .

LINDA: You'll do it yet, dear.

(WILLY walks out of his jacket. LINDA follows him.)

WILLY: And they'll get married, and come for a weekend. I'd built a little guest house. 'Cause I got so many fine tools, all I'd need would be a little lumber and some peace of mind.

LINDA (*joyfully*): I sewed the lining . . .

WILLY: I could build two guest houses, so they'd both come. Did he decide how much he's going to ask Oliver for?

LINDA (*getting him into the jacket*): He didn't mention it, but I imagine ten or fifteen thousand. You going to talk to Howard today?

WILLY: Yeah, I'll put it to him straight and simple. He'll just have to take me off the road.

LINDA: And Willy, don't forget to ask for a little advance, because we've got the insurance premium. It's the grace period now.

WILLY: That's a hundred . . . ?

LINDA: A hundred and eight, sixty-eight. Because we're a little short again.

WILLY: Why are we short?

LINDA: Well, you had the motor job on the car . . .

WILLY: That goddam Studebaker!

LINDA: And you got one more payment on the refrigerator . . .

WILLY: But it just broke again!

LINDA: Well, it's old, dear.

WILLY: I told you we should've bought a well-advertised machine. Charley bought a General Electric and its twenty years old and it's still good, that son-of-a-bitch.

LINDA: But, Willy—

WILLY: Whoever heard of a Hastings refrigerator? Once in my life I would like to own something outright before it's broken! I'm always in a race with the junkyard! I just finished paying for the car and it's on its last legs. The refrigerator consumes belts like a goddamn maniac. They time those things. They time them so when you finally paid for them, they're used up.

LINDA (*buttoning up his jacket as he unbuttons it*): All told, about two hundred dollars would carry us, dear. But that includes the last payment on the mortgage. After this payment, Willy, the house belongs to us.

WILLY: It's twenty-five years!

LINDA: Biff was nine years old when we bought it.

WILLY: Well, that's a great thing. To weather a twenty-five year mortgage is—

LINDA: It's an accomplishment.

WILLY: All the cement, the lumber, the reconstruction I put in this house! There ain't a crack to be found in it any more.

LINDA: Well, it served its purpose.

WILLY: What purpose? Some stranger'll come along, move in, and that's that. If only Biff would take this house, and raise a family . . . (*He starts to go.*) Good-by, I'm late.

LINDA (*suddenly remembering*): Oh, I forgot! You're supposed to meet them for dinner.

WILLY: Me?

LINDA: At Frank's Chop House on Forty-eighth near Sixth Avenue.

WILLY: Is that so! How about you?

LINDA: No, just the three of you. They're gonna blow you to a big meal!

WILLY: Don't say! Who thought of that?

LINDA: Biff came to me this morning, Willy, and he said, "Tell Dad, we want to blow him to a big meal." Be there six o'clock. You and your two boys are going to have dinner.

WILLY: Gee whiz! That's really somethin'. I'm gonna knock Howard for a loop, kid. I'll get an advance, and I'll come home with a New York job. Goddammit, now I'm gonna do it!

LINDA: Oh, that's the spirit, Willy!

WILLY: I will never get behind a wheel the rest of my life!

LINDA: It's changing, Willy, I can feel it changing!

WILLY: Beyond a question. G'by, I'm late. (*He starts to go again.*)

LINDA (*calling after him as she runs to the kitchen table for a handkerchief*): You got your glasses?

WILLY (*feels for them, then comes back in*): Yeah, yeah, got my glasses.

LINDA (*giving him the handkerchief*): And a handkerchief.

WILLY: Yeah, handkerchief.

LINDA: And your saccharine?

WILLY: Yeah, my saccharine.

LINDA: Be careful on the subway stairs.

(*She kisses him, and a silk stocking is seen hanging from her hand. WILLY notices it.*)

WILLY: Will you stop mending stockings? At least while I'm in the house. It gets me nervous. I can't tell you. Please.

(LINDA *hides the stocking in her hand as she follows* WILLY *across the forestage in front of the house.*)

LINDA: Remember, Frank's Chop House.

WILLY (*passing the apron*): Maybe beets would grow out there.

LINDA (*laughing*): But you tried so many times.

WILLY: Yeah. Well, don't work hard today. (*He disappears around the right corner of the house.*)

LINDA: Be careful!

(*As* WILLY *vanishes,* LINDA *waves to him. Suddenly the phone rings. She runs across the stage and into the kitchen and lifts it.*)

LINDA: Hello? Oh, Biff! I'm so glad you called, I just . . . Yes, sure, I just told him. Yes, he'll be there for dinner at six o'clock, I didn't forget. Listen, I was just dying to tell you. You know that little rubber pipe I told you about? That he connected to the gas heater? I finally decided to go down the cellar this morning and take it away and destroy it. But it's gone! Imagine? He took it away himself, it isn't there! *(She listens.)* When? Oh, then you took it. Oh—nothing, it's just that I'd hoped he'd taken it away himself. Oh, I'm not worried, darling, because this morning he left in such high spirits, it was like the old days! I'm not afraid any more. Did Mr. Oliver see you? . . . Well, you wait there then. And make a nice impression on him, darling. Just don't perspire too much before you see him. And have a nice time with Dad. He may have big news too! . . . That's right, a New York job. And be sweet to him tonight, dear. Be loving to him. Because he's only a little boat looking for a harbor. *(She is trembling with sorrow and joy.)* Oh, that's wonderful, Biff, you'll save his life. Thanks, darling. Just put your arm around him when he comes into the restaurant. Give him a smile. That's the boy . . . Good-by, dear. . . . You got your comb? . . . That's fine. Good-by, Biff dear.

(In the middle of her speech, HOWARD WAGNER, *thirty-six, wheels on a small typewriter table on which is a wire-recording machine and proceeds to plug it in. This is on the left forestage. Light slowly fades on* LINDA *as it rises on* HOWARD. HOWARD *is intent on threading the machine and only glances over his shoulder as* WILLY *appears.)*

WILLY: Pst! Pst!

HOWARD: Hello, Willy, come in.

WILLY: Like to have a little talk with you, Howard.

HOWARD: Sorry to keep you waiting. I'll be with you in a minute.

WILLY: What's that, Howard?

HOWARD: Didn't you ever see one of these? Wire recorder.

WILLY: Oh. Can we talk a minute?

HOWARD: Records things. Just got delivery yesterday. Been driving me crazy, the most terrific machine I ever saw in my life. I was up all night with it.

WILLY: What do you do with it?

HOWARD: I bought it for dictation, but you can do anything with it. Listen to this. I had it home last night. Listen to what I picked up. The first one is my daughter. Get this. *(He flicks the switch and "Roll out the Barrel" is heard being whistled.)* Listen to that kid whistle.

WILLY: That is lifelike, isn't it?

HOWARD: Seven years old. Get that tone.

WILLY: Ts, ts. Like to ask a little favor if you . . .

(The whistling breaks off, and the voice of HOWARD'S *daughter is heard.)*

HIS DAUGHTER: "Now you, Daddy."

HOWARD: She's crazy for me! *(Again the same song is*

whistled.) That's me! Ha! *(He winks.)*

WILLY: You're very good!

(The whistling breaks off again. The machine runs silent for a moment.)

HOWARD: Sh! Get this now, this is my son.

HIS SON: "The capital of Alabama is Montgomery; the capital of Arizona is Phoenix; the capital of Arkansas is Little Rock; the capital of California is Sacramento . . ." *(and on, and on.)*

HOWARD *(holding up five fingers)*: Five years old, Willy!

WILLY: He'll make an announcer some day!

HIS SON *(continuing)*: "The capital . . ."

HOWARD: Get that—alphabetical order! *(The machine breaks off suddenly.)* Wait a minute. The maid kicked the plug out.

WILLY: It certainly is a—

HOWARD: Sh, for God's sake!

HIS SON: "It's nine o'clock, Bulova watch time. So I have to go to sleep."

WILLY: That really is—

HOWARD: Wait a minute! The next is my wife.

(They wait.)

HOWARD'S VOICE: "Go on, say something." *(Pause.)* "Well, you gonna talk?"

HIS WIFE: "I can't think of anything."

HOWARD'S VOICE: "Well, talk—it's turning."

HIS WIFE *(shyly, beaten)*: "Hello." *(Silence.)* "Oh, Howard, I can't talk into this . . ."

HOWARD *(snapping the machine off)*: That was my wife.

WILLY: This is a wonderful machine. Can we—

HOWARD: I tell you, Willy, I'm gonna take my camera, and my bandsaw, and all my hobbies, and out they go. This is the most fascinating relaxation I ever found.

WILLY: I think I'll get one myself.

HOWARD: Sure, they're only a hundred and a half. You can't do without it. Supposing you wanna hear Jack Benny, see? But you can't be at home at that hour. So you tell the maid to turn the radio on when Jack Benny comes on, and this automatically goes on with the radio . . .

WILLY: And when you come home you . . .

HOWARD: You can come home twelve o'clock, one o'clock, any time you like, and you get yourself a Coke and sit yourself down, throw the switch, and there's Jack Benny's program in the middle of the night!

WILLY: I'm definitely going to get one. Because lots of time I'm on the road, and I think to myself, what I must be missing on the radio!

HOWARD: Don't you have a radio in the car?

WILLY: Well, yeah, but who ever thinks of turning it on?

HOWARD: Say, aren't you supposed to be in Boston?

WILLY: That's what I want to talk to you about, Howard. You got a minute? (*He draws a chair in from the wing.*)

HOWARD: What happened? What're you doing here?

WILLY: Well . . .

HOWARD: You didn't crack up again, did you?

WILLY: Oh, no. No . . .

HOWARD: Geez, you had me worried there for a minute. What's the trouble?

WILLY: Well, tell you the truth, Howard. I've come to the decision that I'd rather not travel any more.

HOWARD: Not travel! Well, what'll you do?

WILLY: Remember, Christmas time, when you had the party here? You said you'd try to think of some spot for me here in town.

HOWARD: With us?

WILLY: Well, sure.

HOWARD: Oh, yeah, yeah, I remember. Well, I couldn't think of anything for you, Willy.

WILLY: I tell ya, Howard. The kids are all grown up, y'know. I don't need much any more. If I could take home—well, sixty-five dollars a week, I could swing it.

HOWARD: Yeah, but Willy, see I—

WILLY: I tell ya why, Howard. Speaking frankly and between the two of us, y'know—I'm just a little tired.

HOWARD: Oh, I could understand that, Willy. But you're a road man, Willy, and we do a road business. We've only got a half-dozen salesmen on the floor here.

WILLY: God knows, Howard, I never asked a favor of any man. But I was with the firm when your father used to carry you in here in his arms.

HOWARD: I know that, Willy, but—

WILLY: Your father came to me the day you were born and asked me what I thought of the name of Howard, may he rest in peace.

HOWARD: I appreciate that, Willy, but there just is no spot here for you. If I had a spot I'd slam you right in, but I just don't have a single solitary spot.

(*He looks for his lighter.* WILLY *has picked it up and gives it to him. Pause.*)

WILLY (*with increasing anger*): Howard, all I need to set my table is fifty dollars a week.

HOWARD: But where am I going to put you, kid?

WILLY: Look, it isn't a question of whether I can sell merchandise, is it?

HOWARD: No, but it's a business, kid, and everybody's gotta pull his own weight.

WILLY (*desperately*): Just let me tell you a story, Howard—

HOWARD: 'Cause you gotta admit, business is business.

WILLY (*angrily*): Business is definitely business, but just listen for a minute. You don't understand this. When I was a boy—eighteen, nineteen—I was already on the road. and there was a question in my mind as to whether selling had a future for me. Because in those days I had a yearning to go to Alaska. See, there were three gold strikes in one month in Alaska, and I felt like going out. Just for the ride, you might say.

HOWARD (*barely interested*): Don't say.

WILLY: Oh, yeah, my father lived many years in Alaska. He was an adventurous man. We've got quite a little streak of self-reliance in our family. I thought I'd go out with my older brother and try to locate him, and maybe settle in the North with the old man. And I was almost decided to go, when I met a salesman in the Parker House. His name was Dave Singleman. And he was eighty-four years old, and he'd drummed merchandise in thirty-one states. And old Dave, he'd go up to his room, y'understand, put on his green velvet slippers—I'll never forget—and pick up his phone and call the buyers, and without ever leaving his room, at the age of eighty-four, he made his living. And when I saw that, I realized that selling was the greatest career a man could want. 'Cause what could be more satisfying than to be able to go, at the age of eighty-four, into twenty or thirty different cities, and pick up a phone, and be remembered and loved and helped by so many different people? Do you know? when he died—and by the way he died the death of a salesman, in his green velvet slippers in the smoker of the New York, New Haven and Hartford, going into Boston—when he died, hundreds of salesmen and buyers were at his funeral. Things were sad on a lotta trains for months after that. (*He stands up.* HOWARD *has not looked at him.*) In those days there was personality in it, Howard. There was respect, and comradeship, and gratitude in it. Today, it's all cut and dried, and there's no chance for bringing friendship to bear—or personality. You see what I mean? They don't know me any more.

HOWARD (*moving away, to the right*): That's just the thing, Willy.

WILLY: If I had forty dollars a week—that's all I'd need. Forty dollars, Howard.

HOWARD: Kid, I can't take blood from a stone, I—

WILLY (*desperation is on him now*): Howard, the year Al Smith was nominated, your father came to me and—

HOWARD (*starting to go off*): I've got to see some people, kid.

WILLY (*stopping him*): I'm talking about your father! There were promises made across this desk! You mustn't tell me you've got people to see—I put thirty-four years into this firm, Howard, and now I can't pay my insurance! You can't eat the orange and throw the peel away—a man is not a piece of fruit! (*After a pause.*) Now pay attention. Your father—in 1928 I had a big year. I averaged a hundred and seventy dollars a week in commissions.

HOWARD (*impatiently*): Now, Willy, you never averaged—

WILLY (*banging his hand on the desk*): I averaged a hundred and seventy dollars a week in the year of 1928! And your father came to me—or rather, I was in the office here—it was right over this desk—and he put his hand on my shoulder—

HOWARD (*getting up*): You'll have to excuse me, Willy, I gotta see some people. Pull yourself together. (*Going out.*) I'll be back in a little while.

(*On* HOWARD's *exit, the light of his chair grows very bright and strange.*)

WILLY: Pull myself together! What the hell did I say to him! My God, I was yelling at him! How could I! (WILLY *breaks off, staring at the light, which occupies the chair, animating it. He approaches this chair, standing across the desk from it.*) Frank, Frank, don't you remember what you told me that time? How you put your hand on my shoulder, and Frank . . . (*He leans on the desk and as he speaks the dead man's name he accidentally switches on the recorder, and instantly*)

HOWARD'S SON: ". . . of New York is Albany. The capital of Ohio is Cincinnati, the capital of Rhode Island is . . ." (*The recitation continues.*)

WILLY (*leaping away with fright, shouting*): Ha! Howard! Howard! Howard!

HOWARD (*rushing in*): What happened?

WILLY (*pointing at the machine, which contines nasally, childishly, with the capital cities*): Shut it off! Shut it off!

HOWARD (*pulling the plug out*): Look, Willy . . .

WILLY (*pressing his hands to his eyes*): I gotta get myself some coffee. I'll get some coffee . . .

(WILLY *starts to walk out.* HOWARD *stops him.*)

HOWARD (*rolling up the cord*): Willy, Look . . .

WILLY: I'll go to Boston.

HOWARD: Willy, you can't go to Boston for us.

WILLY: Why can't I go?

HOWARD: I don't want you to represent us. I've been meaning to tell you for a long time now.

WILLY: Howard, are you firing me?

HOWARD: I think you need a good long rest, Willy.

WILLY: Howard—

HOWARD: And when you feel better, come back, and we'll see if we can work something out.

WILLY: But I gotta earn money, Howard. I'm in no position to—

HOWARD: Where are your sons? Why don't your sons give you a hand?

WILLY: They're working on a very big deal.

HOWARD: This is no time for false pride, Willy. You go to your sons and you tell them that you're tired. You've got two great boys, haven't you?

WILLY: Oh, no question, no question, but in the meantime . . .

HOWARD: Then that's that, heh?

WILLY: All right, I'll go to Boston tomorrow.

HOWARD: No, no.

WILLY: I can't throw myself on my sons. I'm not a cripple!

HOWARD: Look, kid, I'm busy this morning.

WILLY (*grasping* HOWARD's *arm*): Howard, you've got to let me go to Boston!

HOWARD (*hard, keeping himself under control*): I've got a line of people to see this morning. Sit down, take five minutes, and pull yourself together, and then go home, will ya? I need the office, Willy. (*He starts to go; turns, remembering the recorder, starts to push off the table holding the recorder.*) Oh, yeah. Whenever you can this week, stop by and drop off the samples. You'll feel better, Willy, and then come back and we'll talk. Pull yourself together, kid, there's people outside.

(HOWARD *exits, pushing the table off left.* WILLY *stares into space, exhausted. Now the music is heard*—BEN's *music—first distantly, then closer, closer. As* WILLY *speaks,* BEN *enters from the right. He carries valise and umbrella.*)

WILLY: Oh, Ben, how did you do it? What is the answer? Did you wind up the Alaska deal already?

BEN: Doesn't take much time if you know what you're doing. Just a short business trip. Boarding ship in an hour. Wanted to say good-by.

WILLY: Ben, I've got to talk to you.

BEN (*glancing at his watch*): Haven't the time, William.

WILLY (*crossing the apron to* BEN): Ben, nothing's working out. I don't know what to do.

BEN: Now look here, William. I've bought timberland in Alaska and I need a man to look after things for me.

WILLY: God, timberland! Me and my boys in those grand outdoors!

BEN: You've a new continent at your doorstep, William. Get out of these cities, they're full of talk and time payments and courts of law. Screw on your fists and you can fight for a fortune up there.

WILLY: Yes, yes! Linda, Linda!

(LINDA *enters as of old, with the wash.*)

LINDA: Oh, you're back?

BEN: I haven't much time.

WILLY: No, wait! Linda, he's got a proposition for me in Alaska.

LINDA: But you've got—(to BEN) He's got a beautiful job here.

WILLY: But in Alaska, kid, I could—

LINDA: You're doing well enough, Willy!

BEN (to LINDA): Enough for what, my dear?

LINDA (frightened of BEN and angry at him): Don't say those things to him! Enough to be happy right here, right now. (to WILLY, while BEN laughs) Why must everybody conquer the world? You're well liked, and the boys love you, and someday—(to BEN)—why, old man Wagner told him just the other day that if he keeps it up he'll be a member of the firm, didn't he, Willy?

WILLY: Sure, sure. I am building something with this firm, Ben, and if a man is building something he must be on the right track, mustn't he?

BEN: What are you building? Lay your hand on it. Where is it?

WILLY (hesitantly): That's true, Linda, there's nothing.

LINDA: Why? (to BEN) There's a man eighty-four years old—

WILLY: That's right, Ben, that's right. When I look at that man I say, what is there to worry about?

BEN: Bah!

WILLY: It's true, Ben. All he has to do is go into any city, pick up the phone, and he's making his living and you know why?

BEN (picking up his valise): I've got to go.

WILLY (holding BEN back): Look at this boy!

(BIFF, in his high school sweater, enters carrying suitcase. HAPPY carries BIFF's shoulder guards, gold helmet, and football pants.)

WILLY: Without a penny to his name, three great universities are begging for him, and from there the sky's the limit, because it's not what you do, Ben. It's who you know and the smile on your face! It's contacts, Ben, contacts! The whole wealth of Alaska passes over the lunch table at the Commodore Hotel, and that's the wonder, the wonder of this century, that a man can end with diamonds here on the basis of being liked! (He turns to BIFF.) And that's why when you get out on that field today it's important. Because thousands of people will be rooting for you and loving you. (to BEN, who has again begun to leave) And Ben! when he walks into a business office his name will sound out like a bell and all the doors will open to him! I've seen it, Ben, I've seen it a thousand times! You can't feel it with your hand like timber, but it's there!

BEN: Good-by, William.

WILLY: Ben, am I right? Don't you think I'm right? I value your advice.

BEN: There's a new continent at your doorstep, William. You could walk out rich. Rich! (He is gone.)

WILLY: We'll do it here, Ben! You hear me? We're gonna do it here!

(YOUNG BERNARD rushes in. The gay music of the Boys is heard.)

BERNARD: Oh, gee, I was afraid you left already!

WILLY: Why? What time is it?

BERNARD: It's half-past one!

WILLY: Well, come on, everybody! Ebbets Field next stop! Where's the pennants? (He rushes through the wall-line of the kitchen and out into the living-room.)

LINDA (to BIFF): Did you pack fresh underwear?

BIFF (who has been limbering up): I want to go!

BERNARD: Biff, I'm carrying your helmet, ain't I?

HAPPY: No, I'm carrying the helmet.

BERNARD: Oh, Biff, you promised me.

HAPPY: I'm carrying the helmet.

BERNARD: How am I going to get in the locker room?

LINDA: Let him carry the shoulder guards. (She puts her coat and hat on in the kitchen.)

BERNARD: Can I, Biff? 'Cause I told everybody I'm going to be in the locker room.

HAPPY: In Ebbets Field it's the clubhouse.

BERNARD: I meant the clubhouse, Biff!

HAPPY: Biff!

BIFF (grandly, after a slight pause): Let him carry the shoulder guards.

HAPPY (as he gives BERNARD the shoulder guards): Stay close to us now.

(WILLY rushes in with the pennants.)

WILLY (handing them out): Everybody wave when Biff comes out on the field. (HAPPY and BERNARD run off.) You set now, boy?

(The music has died away.)

BIFF: Ready to go, Pop. Every muscle is ready.

WILLY (at the edge of the apron): You realize what this means?

BIFF: That's right, Pop.

WILLY (feeling BIFF's muscles): You're comin' home this afternoon captain of the All-Scholastic Championship Team of the City of New York.

BIFF: I got it, Pop. And remember, pal, when I take off my helmet, that touchdown is for you.

WILLY: Let's go! (He is starting out, with his arm around BIFF, when CHARLEY enters, as of old, in knickers.) I got no room for you, Charley.

CHARLEY: Room? For what?

WILLY: In the car.

CHARLEY: You goin' for a ride? I wanted to shoot some casino.

WILLY (furiously): Casino! (Incredulously.) Don't you realize what today is?

LINDA: Oh, he knows, Willy. He's just kidding you.

WILLY: That's nothing to kid about!

CHARLEY: No, Linda, what's goin' on?

LINDA: He's playing in Ebbets Field.

CHARLEY: Baseball in this weather?

WILLY: Don't talk to him. Come on, come on! (*He is pushing them out.*)

CHARLEY: Wait a minute, didn't you hear the news?

WILLY: What?

CHARLEY: Don't you listen to the radio? Ebbets Field just blew up.

WILLY: You go to hell! (CHARLEY *laughs. Pushing them out.*) Come on, come on! We're late.

CHARLEY (*as they go*): Knock a homer, Biff, knock a homer!

WILLY (*the last to leave, turning to* CHARLEY): I don't think that was funny, Charley. This is the greatest day of his life.

CHARLEY: Willy, when are you going to grow up?

WILLY: Yeah, heh? When this game is over, Charley, you'll be laughing out of the other side of your face. They'll be calling him another Red Grange. Twenty-five thousand a year.

CHARLEY (*kidding*): Is that so?

WILLY: Yeah, that's so.

CHARLEY: Well, then, I'm sorry, Willy. But tell me something.

WILLY: What?

CHARLEY: Who is Red Grange?

WILLY: Put up your hands. Goddam you, put up your hands!

(CHARLEY, *chuckling, shakes his head and walks away, around the left corner of the stage.* WILLY *follows him. The music rises to a mocking frenzy.*)

WILLY: Who the hell do you think you are, better than everybody else? You don't know everything, you big, ignorant, stupid . . . Put up your hands!

(*Light rises, on the right side of the forestage, on a small table in the reception room of* CHARLEY's *office. Traffic sounds are heard.* BERNARD, *now mature, sits whistling to himself. A pair of tennis rackets and an overnight bag are on the floor beside him.*)

WILLY (*offstage*): What are you walking away for? Don't walk away! If you're going to say something say it to my face! I know you laugh at me behind my back. You'll laugh out of the other side of your goddam face after this game. Touchdown! Touchdown! Eighty thousand people! Touchdown! Right between the goal posts.

(BERNARD *is a quiet, earnest, but self-assured young man.* WILLY's *voice is coming from right upstage now.* BERNARD *lowers his feet off the table and listens.* JENNY, *his father's secretary, enters.*)

JENNY (*distressed*): Say, Bernard, will you go out in the hall?

BERNARD: What is that noise? Who is it?

JENNY: Mr. Loman. He just got off the elevator.

BERNARD (*getting up*): Who's he arguing with?

JENNY: Nobody. There's nobody with him. I can't deal with him any more, and your father gets all upset everytime he comes. I've got a lot of typing to do, and your father's waiting to sign it. Will you see him?

WILLY (*entering*): Touchdown! Touch—(*He sees* JENNY.) Jenny, Jenny, good to see you. How're ya? Workin'? Or still honest?

JENNY: Fine. How've you been feeling?

WILLY: Not much any more, Jenny. Ha, ha! (*He is surprised to see the rackets.*)

BERNARD: Hello, Uncle Willy.

WILLY (*almost shocked*): Bernard! Well, look who's here! (*He comes quickly, guiltily, to* BERNARD *and warmly shakes his hand.*)

BERNARD: How are you? Good to see you.

WILLY: What are you doing here?

BERNARD: Oh, just stopped by to see Pop. Get off my feet till my train leaves. I'm going to Washington in a few minutes.

WILLY: Is he in?

BERNARD: Yes, he's in his office with the accountant. Sit down.

WILLY (*sitting down*): What're you going to do in Washington?

BERNARD: Oh, just a case I've got there, Willy.

WILLY: That so? (*Indicating the rackets.*) You going to play tennis there?

BERNARD: I'm staying with a friend who's got a court.

WILLY: Don't say. His own tennis court. Must be fine people, I bet.

BERNARD: They are, very nice. Dad tells me Biff's in town.

WILLY (*with a big smile*): Yeah, Biff's in. Working on a very big deal, Bernard.

BERNARD: What's Biff doing?

WILLY: Well, he's been doing very big things in the West. But he decided to establish himself here. Very big. We're having dinner. Did I hear your wife had a boy?

BERNARD: That's right. Our second.

WILLY: Two boys! What do you know!

BERNARD: What kind of a deal has Biff got?

WILLY: Well, Bill Oliver—very big sporting-goods man—he wants Biff very badly. Called him in from the West. Long distance, carte blanche, special deliveries. Your friends have their own private tennis court?

BERNARD: You still with the old firm, Willy?

WILLY (*after a pause*): I'm—I'm overjoyed to see how you made the grade, Bernard, overjoyed. It's an encouraging thing to see a young man really—

really—Looks very good for Biff—very—(*He breaks off, then.*) Bernard—(*He is so full of emotion, he breaks off again.*)

BERNARD: What is it, Willy?

WILLY (*small and alone*): What—what's the secret?

BERNARD: What secret?

WILLY: How—how did you? Why didn't he ever catch on?

BERNARD: I wouldn't know that, Willy.

WILLY (*confidentially, desperately*): You were his friend, his boyhood friend. There's something I don't understand about it. His life ended after that Ebbets Field game. From the age of seventeen nothing good ever happened to him.

BERNARD: He never trained himself for anything.

WILLY: But he did, he did. After high school he took so many correspondence courses. Radio mechanics; television; God knows what, and never made the slightest mark.

BERNARD (*taking off his glasses*): Willy, do you want to talk candidly?

WILLY (*rising, faces* BERNARD): I regard you as a very brilliant man, Bernard. I value your advice.

BERNARD: Oh, the hell with the advice, Willy. I couldn't advise you. There's just one thing I've always wanted to ask you. When he was supposed to graduate, and the math teacher flunked him—

WILLY: Oh, that son-of-a-bitch ruined his life.

BERNARD: Yeah, but, Willy, all he had to do was go to summer school and make up that subject.

WILLY: That's right, that's right.

BERNARD: Did you tell him not to go to summer school?

WILLY: Me? I begged him to go. I ordered him to go!

BERNARD: Then why wouldn't he go?

WILLY: Why? Why! Bernard, that question has been trailing me like a ghost for the last fifteen years. He flunked the subject, and laid down and died like a hammer hit him!

BERNARD: Take it easy, kid.

WILLY: Let me talk to you—I got nobody to talk to. Bernard, Bernard, was it my fault? Y'see? It keeps going around in my mind, maybe I did something to him. I got nothing to give him.

BERNARD: Don't take it so hard.

WILLY: Why did he lay down? What is the story there? You were his friend!

BERNARD: Willy, I remember, it was June, and our grades came out. And he'd flunked math.

WILLY: That son-of-a-bitch!

BERNARD: No, it wasn't right then. Biff just got very angry, I remember, and he was ready to enroll in summer school.

WILLY (*surprised*): He was?

BERNARD: He wasn't beaten by it at all. But then, Willy, he disappeared from the block for almost a month. And I got the idea that he'd gone up to New England to see you. Did he have a talk with you then?

(WILLY *stares in silence.*)

BERNARD: Willy?

WILLY (*with a strong edge of resentment in his voice*): Yeah, he came to Boston. What about it?

BERNARD: Well, just that when he came back—I'll never forget this, it always mystifies me. Because I'd thought so well of Biff, even though he'd always taken advantage of me. I loved him, Willy, y'know? And he came back after that month and took his sneakers—remember those sneakers with "University of Virginia" printed on them? He was so proud of those, wore them every day. And he took them down in the cellar, and burned them up in the furnace. We had a fist fight. It lasted at least half an hour. Just the two of us, punching each other down the cellar, and crying right through it. I've often thought of how strange it was that I knew he'd given up his life. What happened in Boston, Willy?

(WILLY *looks at him as at an intruder.*)

BERNARD: I just bring it up because you asked me.

WILLY (*angrily*): Nothing. What do you mean, "What happened?" What's that got to do with anything?

BERNARD: Well, don't get sore.

WILLY: What are you trying to do, blame it on me? If a boy lays down is that my fault?

BERNARD: Now, Willy, don't get—

WILLY: Well, don't—don't talk to me that way! What does that mean, "What happened?"

(CHARLEY *enters. He is in his vest, and he carries a bottle of bourbon.*)

CHARLEY: Hey, you're going to miss that train. (*He waves the bottle.*)

BERNARD: Yeah, I'm going. (*He takes the bottle.*) Thanks, Pop. (*He picks up his rackets and bag.*) Good-by, Willy, and don't worry about it. You know, "If at first you don't succeed . . ."

WILLY: Yes, I believe in that.

BERNARD: But sometimes, Willy, it's better for a man just to walk away.

WILLY: Walk away?

BERNARD: That's right.

WILLY: But if you can't walk away?

BERNARD (*after a slight pause*): I guess that's when it's tough. (*Extending his hand.*) Good-by, Willy.

WILLY (*shaking* BERNARD's *hand*): Good-by, boy.

CHARLEY (*an arm on* BERNARD's *shoulder*): How do you like this kid? Gonna argue a case in front of the Supreme Court.

BERNARD (*protesting*): Pop!

WILLY (*genuinely shocked, pained, and happy*): No! The Supreme Court!

BERNARD: I gotta run. 'By, Dad!

CHARLEY: Knock 'em dead, Bernard!

(*BERNARD goes off.*)

WILLY (*as* CHARLEY *takes out his wallet*): The Supreme Court! And he didn't even mention it!

CHARLEY (*counting out money on the desk*): He don't have to—he's gonna do it.

WILLY: And you never told him what to do, did you? You never took any interest in him.

CHARLEY: My salvation is that I never took any interest in anything. There's some money—fifty dollars. I got an accountant inside.

WILLY: Charley, look . . . (*With difficulty.*) I got my insurance to pay. If you can manage it—I need a hundred and ten dollars.

(*CHARLEY doesn't reply for a moment; merely stops moving.*)

WILLY: I'd draw it from my bank but Linda would know, and I . . .

CHARLEY: Sit down, Willy.

WILLY (*moving toward the chair*): I'm keeping an account of everything, remember. I'll pay every penny back. (*He sits.*)

CHARLEY: Now listen to me, Willy.

WILLY: I want you to know I appreciate . . .

CHARLEY (*sitting down on the table*): Willy, what're you doin'? What the hell is goin' on in your head?

WILLY: Why? I'm simply . . .

CHARLEY: I offered you a job. You can make fifty dollars a week. And I won't send you on the road.

WILLY: I've got a job.

CHARLEY: Without pay? What kind of a job is a job without pay? (*He rises.*) Now, look, kid, enough is enough. I'm no genius but I know when I'm being insulted.

WILLY: Insulted!

CHARLEY: Why don't you want to work for me?

WILLY: What's the matter with you? I've got a job.

CHARLEY: Then what're you walkin' in here every week for?

WILLY (*getting up*): Well, if you don't want me to walk in here—

CHARLEY: I am offering you a job.

WILLY: I don't want your goddam job!

CHARLEY: When the hell are you going to grow up?

WILLY (*furiously*): You big ignoramus, if you say that to me again I'll rap you one! I don't care how big you are! (*He's ready to fight.*)

(*Pause.*)

CHARLEY (*kindly, going to him*): How much do you need, Willy?

WILLY: Charley, I'm strapped, I'm strapped. I don't know what to do. I was just fired.

CHARLEY: Howard fired you?

WILLY: That snotnose. Imagine that? I named him. I named him Howard.

CHARLEY: Willy, when're you gonna realize that them things don't mean anything? You named him Howard, but you can't sell that. The only thing you got in this world is what you can sell. And the funny thing is that you're a salesman, and you don't know that.

WILLY: I've always tried to think otherwise, I guess. I always felt that if a man was impressive, and well liked, that nothing—

CHARLEY: Why must everybody like you? Who liked J. P. Morgan? Was he impressive? In a Turkish bath he'd look like a butcher. But with his pockets on he was very well liked. Now listen, Willy, I know you don't like me, and nobody can say I'm in love with you, but I'll give you a job because—just for the hell of it, put it that way. Now what do you say?

WILLY: I—I just can't work for you, Charley.

CHARLEY: What're you, jealous of me?

WILLY: I can't work for you, that's all, don't ask me why.

CHARLEY (*angered, takes out more bills*): You been jealous of me all your life, you damned fool! Here, pay your insurance. (*He puts the money in* WILLY's *hand.*)

WILLY: I'm keeping strict accounts.

CHARLEY: I've got some work to do. Take care of yourself. And pay your insurance.

WILLY (*moving to the right*): Funny, y'know? After all the highways, and the trains, and the appointments, and the years, you end up worth more dead than alive.

CHARLEY: Willy, nobody's worth nothin' dead. (*After a slight pause.*) Did you hear what I said?

(*WILLY stands still, dreaming.*)

CHARLEY: Willy!

WILLY: Apologize to Bernard for me when you see him. I didn't mean to argue with him. He's a fine boy. They're all fine boys, and they'll end up big—all of them. Someday they'll all play tennis together. Wish me luck, Charley. He saw Bill Oliver today.

CHARLEY: Good luck.

WILLY (*on the verge of tears*): Charley, you're the only friend I got. Isn't that a remarkable thing? (*He goes out.*)

CHARLEY: Jesus!

(*CHARLEY stares after him a moment and follows. All light blacks out. Suddenly raucous music is heard, and a red glow rises behind the screen at right. STANLEY, a young waiter, appears, carrying a table, followed by* HAPPY, *who is carrying two chairs.*)

STANLEY (*putting the table down*): That's all right, Mr. Loman, I can handle it myself. (*He turns and takes the chairs from* HAPPY *and places them at the table.*)

HAPPY (*glancing around*): Oh, this is better.

STANLEY: Sure, in the front there you're in the middle of all kinds a noise. Whenever you got a party, Mr. Loman, you just tell me and I'll put you back here. Y'know, there's a lotta people they don't like it private, because when they go out they like to see a lotta action around them because they're sick and tired to stay in the house by theirself. But I know you, you ain't from Hackensack. You know what I mean?

HAPPY (*sitting down*): So how's it coming, Stanley?

STANLEY: Ah, it's a dog's life. I only wish during the war they'd a took me in the Army. I coulda been dead by now.

HAPPY: My brother's back, Stanley.

STANLEY: Oh, he come back, heh? From the Far West.

HAPPY: Yeah, big cattle man, my brother, so treat him right. And my father's coming too.

STANLEY: Oh, your father too!

HAPPY: You got a couple of nice lobsters?

STANLEY: Hundred per cent, big.

HAPPY: I want them with the claws.

STANLEY: Don't worry, I don't give you no mice. (HAPPY *laughs.*) How about some wine? It'll put a head on the meal.

HAPPY: No. You remember, Stanley, that recipe I brought you from overseas? With the champagne in it?

STANLEY: Oh, yeah, sure. I still got it tacked up yet in the kitchen. But that'll have to cost a buck apiece anyways.

HAPPY: That's all right.

STANLEY: What'd you, hit a number or somethin'?

HAPPY: No, it's a little celebration. My brother is—I think he pulled off a big deal today. I think we're going into business together.

STANLEY: Great! That's the best for you. Because a family business, you know what I mean?—that's the best.

HAPPY: That's what I think.

STANLEY: 'Cause what's the difference? Somebody steals? It's in the family. Know what I mean? (*Sotto voce.*) Like this bartender here. The boss is goin' crazy what kinda leak he's got in the cash register. You put it in but it don't come out.

HAPPY (*raising his head*): Sh!

STANLEY: What?

HAPPY: You notice I wasn't lookin' right or left, was I?

STANLEY: No.

HAPPY: And my eyes are closed.

STANLEY: So what's the—?

HAPPY: Strudel's comin'.

STANLEY (*catching on, looks around*): Ah, no, there's no—

(*He breaks off as a furred, lavishly dressed girl enters and sits at the next table. Both follow her with their eyes.*)

STANLEY: Geez, how'd ya know?

HAPPY: I got radar or something. (*Staring directly at her profile.*) Oooooooo . . . Stanley.

STANLEY: I think that's for you, Mr. Loman.

HAPPY: Look at that mouth. Oh, God. And the binoculars.

STANLEY: Geez, you got a life, Mr. Loman.

HAPPY: Wait on her.

STANLEY (*going to the girl's table*): Would you like a menu, ma'am?

GIRL: I'm expecting someone, but I'd like a—

HAPPY: Why don't you bring her—excuse me, miss, do you mind? I sell champagne, and I'd like you to try my brand. Bring her a champagne, Stanley.

GIRL: That's awfully nice of you.

HAPPY: Don't mention it. It's all company money. (*He laughs.*)

GIRL: That's a charming product to be selling, isn't it?

HAPPY: Oh, gets to be like everything else. Selling is selling, y'know.

GIRL: I suppose.

HAPPY: You don't happen to sell, do you?

GIRL: No, I don't sell.

HAPPY: Would you object to a compliment from a stranger? You ought to be on a magazine cover.

GIRL (*looking at him a little archly*): I have been.

(STANLEY *comes in with a glass of champagne.*)

HAPPY: What'd I say before, Stanley? You see? She's a cover girl.

STANLEY: Oh, I could see, I could see.

HAPPY (*to the* GIRL): What magazine?

GIRL: Oh, a lot of them. (*She takes the drink.*) Thank you.

HAPPY: You know what they say in France, don't you? "Champagne is the drink of the complexion"—Hya, Biff!

(BIFF *has entered and sits with* HAPPY.)

BIFF: Hello, kid. Sorry I'm late.

HAPPY: I just got here. Uh, Miss—?

GIRL: Forsythe.

HAPPY: Miss Forsythe, this is my brother.

BIFF: Is Dad here?

HAPPY: His name is Biff. You might've heard of him. Great football player.

GIRL: Really? What team?

HAPPY: Are you familiar with football?

GIRL: No, I'm afraid I'm not.

HAPPY: Biff is quarterback with the New York Giants.

GIRL: Well, that is nice, isn't it? *(She drinks.)*

HAPPY: Good health.

GIRL: I'm happy to meet you.

HAPPY: That's my name. Hap. It's really Harold, but at West Point they called me Happy.

GIRL *(now really impressed)*: Oh, I see. How do you do? *(She turns her profile.)*

BIFF: Isn't Dad coming?

HAPPY: You want her?

BIFF: Oh, I could never make that.

HAPPY: I remember the time that idea would never come into your head. Where's the old confidence, Biff?

BIFF: I just saw Oliver—

HAPPY: Wait a minute. I've got to see that old confidence again. Do you want her? She's on call.

BIFF: Oh, no. *(He turns to look at the GIRL.)*

HAPPY: I'm telling you. Watch this. *(Turning to the GIRL.)* Honey? *(She turns to him.)* Are you busy?

GIRL: Well, I am . . . but I could make a phone call.

HAPPY: Do that, will you, honey? And see if you can get a friend. We'll be here for a while. Biff is one of the greatest football players in the country.

GIRL *(standing up)*: Well, I'm certainly happy to meet you.

HAPPY: Come back soon.

GIRL: I'll try.

HAPPY: Don't try, honey, try hard.

(The GIRL exits. STANLEY follows, shaking his head in bewildered admiration.)

HAPPY: Isn't that a shame now? A beautiful girl like that? That's why I can't get married. There's not a good woman in a thousand. New York is loaded with them, kid!

BIFF: Hap, look—

HAPPY: I told you she was on call!

BIFF *(strangely unnerved)*: Cut it out, will ya? I want to say something to you.

HAPPY: Did you see Oliver?

BIFF: I saw him all right. Now look, I want to tell Dad a couple of things and I want you to help me.

HAPPY: What? Is he going to back you?

BIFF: Are you crazy? You're out of your goddam head, you know that?

HAPPY: Why? What happened?

BIFF *(breathlessly)*: I did a terrible thing today, Hap. It's been the strangest day I ever went through. I'm all numb, I swear.

HAPPY: You mean he wouldn't see you?

BIFF: Well, I waited six hours for him, see? All day. Kept sending my name in. Even tried to date his secretary so she'd get me to him, but no soap.

HAPPY: Because you're not showin' the old confidence, Biff. He remembered you, didn't he?

BIFF *(stopping HAPPY with a gesture)*: Finally, about five o'clock, he comes out. Didn't remember who I was or anything. I felt like such an idiot, Hap.

HAPPY: Did you tell him my Florida idea?

BIFF: He walked away. I saw him for one minute. I got so mad I could've torn the walls down! How the hell did I ever get the idea I was a salesman there? I even believed myself that I'd been a salesman for him! And then he gave me one look and—I realized what a ridiculous lie my whole life has been! We've been talking in a dream for fifteen years. I was a shipping clerk.

HAPPY: What'd you do?

BIFF *(with great tension and wonder)*: Well, he left, see. And the secretary went out. I was all alone in the waiting-room. I don't know what came over me, Hap. The next thing I know I'm in his office—paneled walls, everything. I can't explain it. I—Hap, I took his fountain pen.

HAPPY: Geez, did he catch you?

BIFF: I ran out. I ran down all eleven flights. I ran and ran and ran.

HAPPY: That was an awful dumb—what'd you do that for?

BIFF *(agonized)*: I don't know, I just—wanted to take something, I don't know. You gotta help me, Hap, I'm gonna tell Pop.

HAPPY: You crazy? What for?

BIFF: Hap, he's got to understand that I'm not the man somebody lends that kind of money to. He thinks I've been spiting him all these years and it's eating him up.

HAPPY: That's just it. You tell him something nice.

BIFF: I can't.

HAPPY: Say you got a lunch date with Oliver tomorrow.

BIFF: So what do I do tomorrow?

HAPPY: You leave the house tomorrow and come back at night and say Oliver is thinking it over. And he thinks it over for a couple of weeks, and gradually it fades away and nobody's the worse.

BIFF: But it'll go on forever!

HAPPY: Dad is never so happy as when he's looking forward to something!

(WILLY enters.)

HAPPY: Hello, scout!

WILLY: Gee, I haven't been here in years!

(STANLEY has followed WILLY in and sets a chair for him. STANLEY starts off but HAPPY stops him.)

HAPPY: Stanley!

(STANLEY stands by, waiting for an order.)

BIFF *(going to WILLY with guilt, as to an invalid)*: Sit down, Pop. You want a drink?

WILLY: Sure, I don't mind.

BIFF: Let's get a load on.

WILLY: You look worried.

BIFF: N-no. *(to* STANLEY*)* Scotch all around. Make it doubles.

STANLEY: Doubles, right. *(He goes.)*

WILLY: You had a couple already, didn't you?

BIFF: Just a couple, yeah.

WILLY: Well, what happened, boy? *(Nodding affirmatively, with a smile.)* Everything go all right?

BIFF *(takes a breath, then reaches out and grasps* WILLY's *hand):* Pal . . . *(He is smiling bravely, and* WILLY *is smiling too.)* I had an experience today.

HAPPY: Terrific, Pop.

WILLY: That so? What happened?

BIFF *(high, slightly alcoholic, above the earth):* I'm going to tell you everything from first to last. It's been a strange day. *(Silence. He looks around, composes himself as best he can, but his breath keeps breaking the rhythm of his voice.)* I had to wait quite a while for him, and—

WILLY: Oliver?

BIFF: Yeah, Oliver. All day, as a matter of cold fact. And a lot of—instances—facts, Pop, facts about my life came back to me. Who was it, Pop? Who ever said I was a salesman with Oliver?

WILLY: Well, you were.

BIFF: No, Dad, I was a shipping clerk.

WILLY: But you were practically—

BIFF *(with determination):* Dad, I don't know who said it first, but I was never a salesman for Bill Oliver.

WILLY: What're you talking about?

BIFF: Let's hold on to the facts tonight, Pop. We're not going to get anywhere bullin' around. I was a shipping clerk.

WILLY *(angrily):* All right, now listen to me—

BIFF: Why don't you let me finish?

WILLY: I'm not interested in stories about the past or any crap of that kind because the woods are burning, boys, you understand? There's a big blaze going on all around. I was fired today.

BIFF *(shocked):* How could you be?

WILLY: I was fired, and I'm looking for a little good news to tell your mother, because the woman has waited and the woman has suffered. The gist of it is that I haven't got a story left in my head, Biff. So don't give me a lecture about facts and aspects. I am not interested. Now what've you got to say to me?

*(*STANLEY *enters with three drinks. They wait until he leaves.)*

WILLY: Did you see Oliver?

BIFF: Jesus, Dad!

WILLY: You mean you didn't go up there?

HAPPY: Sure he went up there.

BIFF: I did. I—saw him. How could they fire you?

WILLY *(on the edge of his chair):* What kind of a welcome did he give you?

BIFF: He won't even let you work on commission?

WILLY: I'm out! *(Driving.)* So tell me, he gave you a warm welcome?

HAPPY: Sure, Pop, sure!

BIFF *(driven):* Well, it was kind of—

WILLY: I was wondering if he'd remember you. *(to* HAPPY*.)* Imagine, man doesn't see him for ten, twelve years, and gives him that kind of a welcome!

HAPPY: Damn right!

BIFF *(trying to return to the offensive):* Pop, look—

WILLY: You know why he remembered you, don't you? Because you impressed him in those days.

BIFF: Let's talk quietly and get this down to the facts, huh?

WILLY *(as though* BIFF *had been interrupting):* Well, what happened? It's great news, Biff. Did he take you into his office or'd you talk in the waiting-room?

BIFF: Well, he came in, see, and—

WILLY *(with a big smile):* What'd he say? Betcha he threw his arm around you.

BIFF: Well, he kinda—

WILLY: He's a fine man. *(to* HAPPY*)* Very hard man to see, y'know.

HAPPY *(agreeing):* Oh, I know.

WILLY *(to* BIFF*):* Is that where you had the drinks?

BIFF: Yeah, he gave me a couple of—no, no!

HAPPY *(cutting in):* He told him my Florida idea.

WILLY: Don't interrupt. *(to* BIFF*)* How'd he react to the Florida idea?

BIFF: Dad, will you give me a minute to explain?

WILLY: I've been waiting for you to explain since I sat down here! What happened? He took you into his office and what?

BIFF: Well—I talked. And—and he listened, see.

WILLY: Famous for the way he listens, y'know. What was his answer?

BIFF: His answer was—*(He breaks off, suddenly angry.)* Dad, you're not letting me tell you what I want to tell you!

WILLY *(accusing, angered):* You didn't see him, did you?

BIFF: I did see him!

WILLY: What'd you insult him or something? You insulted him, didn't you?

BIFF: Listen, will you let me out of it, will you just let me out of it!

HAPPY: What the hell!

WILLY: Tell me what happened!

BIFF *(to* HAPPY*):* I can't talk to him!

(A single trumpet note jars the ear. The light of green leaves stains the house, which holds the air of night and a dream. YOUNG BERNARD *enters and knocks on the door of the house.)*

YOUNG BERNARD *(frantically):* Mrs. Loman, Mrs. Loman!

HAPPY: Tell him what happened!

BIFF (*to* HAPPY): Shut up and leave me alone!

WILLY: No, no! You had to go and flunk math!

BIFF: What math? What're you talking about?

YOUNG BERNARD: Mrs. Loman, Mrs. Loman!

(LINDA *appears in the house, as of old.*)

WILLY (*wildly*): Math, math, math!

BIFF: Take it easy, Pop!

YOUNG BERNARD: Mrs. Loman!

WILLY (*furiously*): If you hadn't flunked you'd've been set by now!

BIFF: Now, look, I'm gonna tell you what happened, and you're going to listen to me.

YOUNG BERNARD: Mrs. Loman!

BIFF: I waited six hours—

HAPPY: What the hell are you saying?

BIFF: I kept sending in my name but he wouldn't see me. So finally he . . . (*He continues unheard as light fades low on the restaurant.*)

YOUNG BERNARD: Biff flunked math!

LINDA: No!

YOUNG BERNARD: Birnbaum flunked him! They won't graduate him!

LINDA: But they have to. He's gotta go to the university. Where is he? Biff! Biff!

YOUNG BERNARD: No, he left. He went to Grand Central.

LINDA: Grand— You mean he went to Boston!

YOUNG BERNARD: Is Uncle Willy in Boston?

LINDA: Oh, maybe Willy can talk to the teacher. Oh, the poor, poor boy!

(*Light on house area snaps out.*)

BIFF (*at the table, now audible, holding up a gold fountain pen*): . . . so I'm washed up with Oliver, you understand? Are you listening to me?

WILLY (*at a loss*): Yeah, sure. If you hadn't flunked—

BIFF: Flunked what? What're you talking about?

WILLY: Don't blame everything on me! I didn't flunk math—you did! What pen?

HAPPY: That was awful dumb, Biff, a pen like that is worth—

WILLY (*seeing the pen for the first time*): You took Oliver's pen?

BIFF (*weakening*): Dad, I just explained it to you.

WILLY: You stole Bill Oliver's fountain pen!

BIFF: I didn't exactly steal it! That's just what I've been explaining to you!

HAPPY: He had it in his hand and just then Oliver walked in, so he got nervous and stuck it in his pocket!

WILLY: My God, Biff!

BIFF: I never intended to do it, Dad!

OPERATOR'S VOICE: Standish Arms, good evening!

WILLY (*shouting*): I'm not in my room!

BIFF (*frightened*): Dad, what's the matter? (*He and* HAPPY *stand up.*)

OPERATOR: Ringing Mr. Loman for you!

WILLY: I'm not there, stop it!

BIFF (*horrified, gets down on one knee before* WILLY): Dad, I'll make good, I'll make good. (WILLY *tries to get to his feet.* BIFF *holds him down.*) Sit down now.

WILLY: No, you're no good, you're no good for anything.

BIFF: I am, Dad, I'll find something else, you understand? Now don't worry about anything. (*He holds up* WILLY'S *face.*) Talk to me, Dad.

OPERATOR: Mr. Loman does not answer. Shall I page him.

WILLY (*attempting to stand, as though to rush and silence the* OPERATOR): No, no, no!

HAPPY: He'll strike something, Pop.

WILLY: No, no . . .

BIFF (*desperately, standing over* WILLY): Pop, listen! Listen to me! I'm telling you something good. Oliver talked to his partner about the Florida idea. You listening? He—he talked to his partner, and he came to me . . . I'm going to be all right, you hear? Dad, listen to me, he said it was just a question of the amount!

WILLY: Then you . . . got it?

HAPPY: He's gonna be terrific, Pop!

WILLY (*trying to stand*): Then you got it, haven't you? You got it! You got it!

BIFF (*agonized, holds* WILLY *down*): No, no. Look, Pop. I'm supposed to have lunch with them tomorrow. I'm just telling you this so you'll know that I can still make an impression, Pop. And I'll make good somewhere, but I can't go tomorrow, see?

WILLY: Why not? You simply—

BIFF: But the pen, Pop!

WILLY: You give it to him and tell him it was an oversight!

HAPPY: Sure, have lunch tomorrow!

BIFF: I can't say that—

WILLY: You were doing a crossword puzzle and accidentally used his pen!

BIFF: Listen, kid, I took those balls years ago, now I walk in with his fountain pen? That clinches it, don't you see? I can't face him like that! I'll try elsewhere.

PAGE'S VOICE: Paging Mr. Loman!

WILLY: Don't you want to be anything?

BIFF: Pop, how can I go back?

WILLY: You don't want to be anything, is that what's behind it?

BIFF (*now angry at* WILLY *for not crediting his sympathy*): Don't take it that way! You think it was easy walking into that office after what I'd done to him? A team of horses couldn't have dragged me back to Bill Oliver!

WILLY: Then why'd you go?

BIFF: Why did I go? Why did I go! Look at you! Look

at what's become of you!

(*Off left,* THE WOMAN *laughs.*)

WILLY: Biff, you're going to go to that lunch tomorrow, or—

BIFF: I can't go. I've got no appointment!

HAPPY: Biff, for . . . !

WILLY: Are you spiting me?

BIFF: Don't take it that way! Goddammit!

WILLY (*strikes* BIFF *and falters away from the table*): You rotten little louse! Are you spiting me?

THE WOMAN: Someone's at the door, Willy!

BIFF: I'm no good, can't you see what I am?

HAPPY (*separating them*): Hey, you're in a restaurant! Now cut it out, both of you! (*The* GIRLS *enter.*) Hello, girls, sit down.

(THE WOMAN *laughs, off left.*)

MISS FORSYTHE: I guess we might as well. This is Letta.

THE WOMAN: Willy, are you going to wake up?

BIFF (*ignoring* WILLY): How're ya, miss, sit down. What do you drink?

MISS FORSYTHE: Letta might not be able to stay long.

LETTA: I gotta get up very early tomorrow. I got jury duty. I'm so excited! Were you fellows ever on a jury?

BIFF: No, but I been in front of them! (*The* GIRLS *laugh.*) This is my father.

LETTA: Isn't he cute? Sit down with us, Pop.

HAPPY: Sit him down, Biff!

BIFF (*going to him*): Come on, slugger, drink us under the table. To hell with it! Come on, sit down, pal.

(*On* BIFF's *last insistence,* WILLY *is about to sit.*)

THE WOMAN (*now urgently*): Willy, are you going to answer the door!

(THE WOMAN's *call pulls* WILLY *back. He starts right, befuddled.*)

BIFF: Hey, where are you going?

WILLY: Open the door.

BIFF: The door?

WILLY: The washroom . . . the door . . . where's the door?

BIFF (*leading* WILLY *to the left*): Just go straight down.

(WILLY *moves left.*)

THE WOMAN: Willy, Willy, are you going to get up, get up, get up, get up?

(WILLY *exits left.*)

LETTA: I think it's sweet you bring your daddy along.

MISS FORSYTHE: Oh, he isn't really your father!

BIFF (*at left, turning to her resentfully*): Miss Forsythe, you've just seen a prince walk by. A fine, troubled prince. A hard-working, unappreciated

prince. A pal, you understand? A good companion. Always for his boys.

LETTA: That's so sweet.

HAPPY: Well, girls, what's the program? We're wasting time. Come on, Biff. Gather round. Where would you like to go?

BIFF: Why don't you do something for him?

HAPPY: Me!

BIFF: Don't you give a damn for him, Hap?

HAPPY: What're you talking about? I'm the one who—

BIFF: I sense it, you don't give a good goddam about him. (*He takes the rolled-up hose from his pocket and puts it on the table in front of* HAPPY.) Look what I found in the cellar, for Christ's sake. How can you bear to let it go on?

HAPPY: Me? Who goes away? Who runs off and—

BIFF: Yeah, but he doesn't mean anything to you. You could help him—I can't! Don't you understand what I'm talking about? He's going to kill himself, don't you know that?

HAPPY: Don't I know it! Me!

BIFF: Hap, help him! Jesus . . . help him . . . Help me, help me, I can't bear to look at his face! (*Ready to weep, he hurries out, up right.*)

HAPPY (*starting after him*): Where are you going?

MISS FORSYTHE: What's he so mad about?

HAPPY: Come on, girls, we'll catch up with him.

MISS FORSYTHE (*as* HAPPY *pushes her out*): Say, I don't like that temper of his!

HAPPY: He's just a little overstrung, he'll be all right!

WILLY (*off left, as* THE WOMAN *laughs*): Don't answer! Don't answer!

LETTA: Don't you want to tell your father—

HAPPY: No, that's not my father. He's just a guy. Come on, we'll catch Biff, and, honey, we're going to paint this town! Stanley, where's the check! Hey, Stanley!

(*They exit.* STANLEY *looks toward left.*)

STANLEY (*calling to* HAPPY *indignantly*): Mr. Loman! Mr. Loman!

(STANLEY *picks up a chair and follows them off. Knocking is heard off left.* THE WOMAN *enters, laughing.* WILLY *follows her. She is in a black slip, he is buttoning his shirt. Raw, sensuous music accompanies their speech.*)

WILLY: Will you stop laughing? Will you stop?

THE WOMAN: Aren't you going to answer the door? He'll wake the whole hotel.

WILLY: I'm not expecting anybody.

THE WOMAN: Whyn't you have another drink, honey, and stop being so damn self-centered?

WILLY: I'm so lonely.

THE WOMAN: You know you ruined me, Willy? From now on, whenever you come to the office, I'll see that you go right through to the buyers. No waiting at my desk any more, Willy. You ruined me.

WILLY: That's nice of you to say that.

THE WOMAN: Gee, you are self-centered! Why so sad? You are the saddest, self-centeredest soul I ever did see-saw. (*She laughs. He kisses her.*) Come on inside, drummer boy. It's silly to be dressing in the middle of the night. (*As knocking is heard.*) Aren't you going to answer the door?

WILLY: They're knocking on the wrong door.

THE WOMAN: But I felt the knocking. And he heard us talking in here. Maybe the hotel's on fire!

WILLY (*his terror rising*): It's a mistake.

THE WOMAN: Then tell him to go away!

WILLY: There's nobody there.

THE WOMAN: It's getting on my nerves, Willy. There's somebody standing out there and it's getting on my nerves!

WILLY (*pushing her away from him*): All right, stay in the bathroom here, and don't come out. I think there's a law in Massachusetts about it, so don't come out. It may be that new room clerk. He looked very mean. So don't come out. It's a mistake, there's no fire.

(*The knocking is heard again. He takes a few steps away from her, and she vanishes into the wing. The light follows him, and now he is facing YOUNG BIFF, who carries a suitcase. BIFF steps toward him. The music is gone.*)

BIFF: Why didn't you answer?

WILLY: Biff! What are you doing in Boston?

BIFF: Why didn't you answer? I've been knocking for five minutes, I called you on the phone—

WILLY: I just heard you. I was in the bathroom and had the door shut. Did anything happen home?

BIFF: Dad—I let you down.

WILLY: What do you mean?

BIFF: Dad . . .

WILLY: Biffo, what's this about? (*Putting his arm around BIFF.*) Come on, let's go downstairs and get you a malted.

BIFF: Dad, I flunked math.

WILLY: Not for the term?

BIFF: The term. I haven't got enough credits to graduate.

WILLY: You mean to say Bernard wouldn't give you the answers?

BIFF: He did, he tried, but I only got a sixty-one.

WILLY: And they wouldn't give you four points?

BIFF: Birnbaum refused absolutely. I begged him, Pop, but he won't give me those points. You gotta talk to him before they close the school. Because if he saw the kind of man you are, and you just talked to him in your way, I'm sure he'd come through for me. The class came right before practice, see, and I didn't go enough. Would you talk to him? He'd like you, Pop. You know the way you could talk.

WILLY: You're on. We'll drive right back.

BIFF: Oh, Dad, good work! I'm sure he'll change it for you!

WILLY: Go downstairs and tell the clerk I'm checkin' out. Go right down.

BIFF: Yes, sir! See, the reason he hates me, Pop—one day he was late for class so I got up at the blackboard and imitated him. I crossed my eyes and talked with a lithp.

WILLY (*laughing*): You did? The kids like it?

BIFF: They nearly died laughing!

WILLY: Yeah? What'd you do?

BIFF: The thquare root of thixthy twee is . . . (WILLY *bursts out laughing;* BIFF *joins him.*) And in the middle of it he walked in!

(WILLY *laughs and* THE WOMAN *joins in offstage.*)

WILLY (*without hesitation*): Hurry downstairs and—

BIFF: Somebody in there?

WILLY: No, that was next door.

(THE WOMAN *laughs offstage.*)

BIFF: Somebody got in your bathroom!

WILLY: No, it's the next room, there's a party—

THE WOMAN (*enters, laughing. She lisps this*): Can I come in? There's something in the bathtub, Willy, and it's moving!

(WILLY *looks at* BIFF, *who is staring open-mouthed and horrified at* THE WOMAN.)

WILLY: Ah—you better go back to your room. They must be finished painting by now. They're painting her room so I let her take a shower here. Go back, go back . . . (*He pushes her.*)

THE WOMAN (*resisting*): But I've got to get dressed Willy, I can't—

WILLY: Get out of here! Go back, go back . . . (*Suddenly striving for the ordinary.*) This is Miss Francis, Biff, she's a buyer. They're painting her room. Go back, Miss Francis, go back . . .

THE WOMAN: But my clothes, I can't go out naked in the hall!

WILLY (*pushing her offstage*): Get outa here! Go back, go back!

(BIFF *slowly sits down on his suitcase as the argument continues offstage.*)

THE WOMAN: Where's my stockings? You promised me stockings, Willy!

WILLY: I have no stockings here!

THE WOMAN: You had two boxes of size nine sheers for me, and I want them!

WILLY: Here, for God's sake, will you get outa here!

THE WOMAN (*enters holding a box of stockings*): I just hope there's nobody in the hall. That's all I hope. (*to* BIFF) Are you football or baseball?

BIFF: Football.

THE WOMAN (*angry, humiliated*): That's me too. G'night. (*She snatches her clothes from* WILLY, *and walks out.*)

WILLY (*after a pause*): Well, better get going. I want to get to the school first thing in the morning. Get my suits out of the closet. I'll get my valise. (*BIFF doesn't move.*) What's the matter? (*BIFF remains motionless, tears falling.*) She's a buyer. Buys for J. H. Simmons. She lives down the hall—they're painting. You don't imagine—(*He breaks off. After a pause.*) Now listen, pal, she's just a buyer. She sees merchandise in her room and they have to keep it looking just so . . . (*Pause. Assuming command.*) All right, get my suits. (*BIFF doesn't move.*) Now stop crying and do as I say. I gave you an order. Biff, I gave you an order! Is that what you do when I give you an order? How dare you cry! (*Putting his arm around* BIFF.) Now look, Biff, when you grow up you'll understand about these things. You mustn't—you mustn't overemphasize a thing like this. I'll see Birnbaum first thing in the morning.

BIFF: Never mind.

WILLY (*getting down beside* BIFF): Never mind! He's going to give you those points. I'll see to it.

BIFF: He wouldn't listen to you.

WILLY: He certainly will listen to me. You need those points for the U. of Virginia.

BIFF: I'm not going there.

WILLY: Heh? If I can't get him to change that mark you'll make it up in summer school. You've got all summer to—

BIFF (*his weeping breaking from him*): Dad . . .

WILLY (*infected by it*): Oh, my boy . . .

BIFF: Dad . . .

WILLY: She's nothing to me, Biff. I was lonely, I was terribly lonely.

BIFF: You—you gave her Mama's stockings! (*His tears break through and he rises to go.*)

WILLY (*grabbing for* BIFF): I gave you an order!

BIFF: Don't touch me, you—liar!

WILLY: Apologize for that!

BIFF: You fake! You phony little fake! You fake! (*Overcome, he turns quickly and weeping fully goes out with his suitcase.* WILLY *is left on the floor on his knees.*)

WILLY: I gave you an order! Biff, come back here or I'll beat you! Come back here! I'll whip you!

(STANLEY *comes quickly in from the right and stands in front of* WILLY.)

WILLY (*shouts at* STANLEY): I gave you an order . . .

STANLEY: Hey, let's pick it up, pick it up, Mr. Loman. (*He helps* WILLY *to his feet.*) Your boys left with the chippies. They said they'll see you home.

(*A second waiter watches some distance away.*)

WILLY: But we were supposed to have dinner together.

(*Music is heard,* WILLY's *theme.*)

STANLEY: Can you make it?

WILLY: I'll—sure, I can make it. (*Suddenly concerned about his clothes.*) Do I—I look all right?

STANLEY: Sure, you look all right. (*He flicks a speck off* WILLY's *lapel.*)

WILLY: Here—here's a dollar.

STANLEY: Oh, your son paid me. It's all right.

WILLY (*putting it in* STANLEY's *hand*): No, take it. You're a good boy.

STANLEY: Oh, no, you don't have to . . .

WILLY: Here—here's some more, I don't need it any more. (*After a slight pause.*) Tell me—is there a seed store in the neighborhood?

STANLEY: Seeds? You mean like to plant?

(*As* WILLY *turns,* STANLEY *slips the money back into his jacket pocket.*)

WILLY: Yes. Carrots, peas . . .

STANLEY: Well, there's hardware stores on Sixth Avenue, but it may be too late now.

WILLY (*anxiously*): Oh, I'd better hurry. I've got to get some seeds. (*He starts off to the right.*) I've got to get some seeds, right away. Nothing's planted. I don't have a thing in the ground.

(WILLY *hurries out as the light goes down.* STANLEY *moves over to the right after him, watches him off. The other waiter has been staring at* WILLY.)

STANLEY (*to the waiter*): Well, whatta you looking at?

(*The waiter picks up the chairs and moves off right. Stanley takes the table and follows him. The light fades on this area. There is a long pause, the sound of the flute coming over. The light gradually rises on the kitchen, which is empty.* HAPPY *appears at the door of the house, followed by* BIFF. HAPPY *is carrying a large bunch of long-stemmed roses. He enters the kitchen, looks around for* LINDA. *Not seeing her, he turns to* BIFF, *who is just outside the house door, and makes a gesture with his hands, indicating "Not here, I guess." He looks into the living-room and freezes. Inside,* LINDA, *unseen, is seated,* WILLY's *coat on her lap. She rises ominously and quietly and moves toward* HAPPY, *who backs up into the kitchen, afraid.*)

HAPPY: Hey, what're you doing up? (LINDA *says nothing but moves toward him implacably.*) Where's Pop? (*He keeps backing to the right, and now* LINDA *is in full view in the doorway to the living-room.*) Is he sleeping?

LINDA: Where were you?

HAPPY (*trying to laugh it off*): We met two girls, Mom, very fine types. Here, we brought you some flowers. (*Offering them to her.*) Put them in your room, Ma.

(She knocks them to the floor at BIFF's feet. He has now come inside and closed the door behind him. She stares at BIFF, silent.)

HAPPY: Now, what'd you do that for? Mom, I want you to have some flowers—

LINDA *(cutting HAPPY off, violently to BIFF)*: Don't you care whether he lives or dies?

HAPPY *(going to the stairs)*: Come upstairs, Biff.

BIFF *(with a flare of digust, to HAPPY)*: Go away from me! *(to LINDA)* What do you mean, lives or dies? Nobody's dying around here, pal.

LINDA: Get out of my sight! Get out of here!

BIFF: I wanna see the boss.

LINDA: You're not going near him!

BIFF: Where is he? *(He moves into the living-room and LINDA follows.)*

LINDA *(shouting after BIFF)*: You invite him for dinner. He looks forward to it all day—*(BIFF appears in his parents' bedroom, looks around, and exits.)*—and then you desert him there. There's no stranger you'd do that to!

HAPPY: Why? He had a swell time with us. Listen, when I—*(LINDA comes back into the kitchen.)*—desert him I hope I don't outlive the day!

LINDA: Get out of here!

HAPPY: Now look, Mom . . .

LINDA: Did you have to go to women tonight? You and your lousy rotten whores!

(BIFF re-enters the kitchen.)

HAPPY: Mom, all we did was follow Biff around trying to cheer him up! *(To BIFF)* Boy, what a night you gave me!

LINDA: Get out of here, both of you, and don't come back! I don't want you tormenting him any more. Go on now, get your things together! *(to BIFF)* You can sleep in his apartment. *(She starts to pick up the flowers and stops herself.)* Pick up this stuff, I'm not your maid any more. Pick it up, you bum, you!

(HAPPY turns his back to her in refusal. BIFF slowly moves over and gets down on his knees, picking up the flowers.)

LINDA: You're a pair of animals! No one, not another living soul would have had the cruelty to walk out on that man in a restaurant.

BIFF *(not looking at her)*: Is that what he said?

LINDA: He didn't have to say anything. He was so humiliated he nearly limped when he came in.

HAPPY: But, Mom, he had a great time with us—

BIFF *(cutting him off violently)*: Shut up!

(Without another word, HAPPY goes upstairs.)

LINDA: You! You didn't even go in to see if he was all right!

BIFF *(still on the floor in front of LINDA, the flowers in his hand; with self-loathing)*: No. Didn't. Didn't do a damned thing. How do you like that, heh? Left him babbling in a toilet.

LINDA: You louse. You . . .

BIFF: Now you hit it on the nose! *(He gets up, throws the flowers in the wastebasket)*. The scum of the earth, and you're looking at him!

LINDA: Get out of here!

BIFF: I gotta talk to the boss, Mom. Where is he?

LINDA: You're not going near him. Get out of this house!

BIFF *(with absolute assurance, determination)*: No. We're gonna have an abrupt conversation, him and me.

LINDA: You're not talking to him!

(Hammering is heard from outside the house, off right. BIFF turns toward the noise.)

LINDA *(suddenly pleading)*: Will you please leave him alone?

BIFF: What's he doing out there?

LINDA: He's planting the garden!

BIFF *(quietly)*: Now? Oh, my God!

(BIFF moves outside, LINDA following. The light dies down on them and comes up on the center of the apron as WILLY walks into it. He is carrying a flashlight, a hoe, and a handful of seed packets. He raps the top of the hoe sharply to fix it firmly, and then moves to the left, measuring off the distance with his foot. He holds the flashlight to look at the seed packets, reading off the instructions. He is in the blue of night.)

WILLY: Carrots . . . quarter-inch apart. Rows . . . one-foot rows. *(He measures it off.)* One foot. *(He puts down a package and measures off.)* Beets. *(He puts down another package and measures again.)* Lettuce. *(He reads the package, puts it down.)* One foot—*(He breaks off as BEN appears at the right and moves slowly down to him.)* What a proposition, ts, ts. Terrific, terrific. 'Cause she's suffered, Ben, the woman has suffered. You understand me? A man can't go out the way he came in, Ben, a man has got to add up to something. You can't, you can't—*(BEN moves toward him as though to interrupt.)* You gotta consider, now. Don't answer so quick. Remember, it's a guaranteed twenty-thousand-dollar proposition. Now look, Ben, I want you to go through the ins and outs of this thing with me. I've got nobody to talk to, Ben, and the woman has suffered, you hear me?

BEN *(standing still, considering)*: What's the proposition?

WILLY: It's twenty thousand dollars on the barrelhead. Guaranteed, gilt-edged, you understand?

BEN: You don't want to make a fool of yourself. They might not honor the policy.

WILLY: How can they dare refuse? Didn't I work like

a coolie to meet every premium on the nose? And now they don't pay off? Impossible!

BEN: It's called a cowardly thing, William.

WILLY: Why? Does it take more guts to stand here the rest of my life ringing up a zero?

BEN (*yielding*): That's a point, William. (*He moves, thinking, turns.*) And twenty thousand—that *is* something one can feel with the hand, it is there.

WILLY (*now assured, with rising power*): Oh, Ben, that's the whole beauty of it! I see it like a diamond, shining in the dark, hard and rough, that I can pick up and touch in my hand. Not like—like an appointment! This would not be another damned-fool appointment, Ben, and it changes all the aspects. Because he thinks I'm nothing, see, and so he spites me. But the funeral— (*Straightening up.*) Ben, that funeral will be massive! They'll come from Maine, Massachusetts, Vermont, New Hampshire! All the old-timers with the strange license plates—that boy will be thunder-struck, Ben, because he never realized—I am known! Rhode Island, New York, New Jersey—I am known, Ben, and he'll see it with his eyes once and for all. He'll see what I am, Ben! He's in for a shock, that boy!

BEN (*coming down to the edge of the garden*): He'll call you a coward.

WILLY (*suddenly fearful*): No, that would be terrible.

BEN: Yes. And a damned fool.

WILLY: No, no, he mustn't, I won't have that! (*He is broken and desperate.*)

BEN: He'll hate you, William.

(*The gay music of the* BOYS *is heard.*)

WILLY: Oh, Ben, how do we get back to all the great times? Used to be so full of light, and comradeship, the sleigh-riding in winter, and the ruddiness on his cheeks. And always some kind of good news coming up, always something nice coming up ahead. And never even let me carry the valises in the house, and simonizing, simonizing that little red car! Why, why can't I give him something and not have him hate me?

BEN: Let me think about it. (*He glances at his watch.*) I still have a little time. Remarkable proposition, but you've got to be sure you're not making a fool of yourself.

(BEN *drifts off upstage and goes out of sight.* BIFF *comes down from the left.*)

WILLY (*suddenly conscious of* BIFF, *turns and looks up at him, then begins picking up the packages of seeds in confusion*): Where the hell is that seed? (*Indignantly*) You can't see nothing out here! They boxed in the whole goddam neighborhood!

BIFF: There are people all around here. Don't you realize that?

WILLY: I'm busy. Don't bother me.

BIFF (*taking the hoe from* WILLY): I'm saying good-by to you, Pop. (WILLY *looks at him, silent, unable to move.*) I'm not coming back any more.

WILLY: You're not going to see Oliver tomorrow?

BIFF: I've got no appointment, Dad.

WILLY: He put his arm around you, and you've got no appointment?

BIFF: Pop, get this now, will you? Everytime I've left it's been a fight that sent me out of here. Today I realized something about myself and I tried to explain it to you and I—I think I'm just not smart enough to make any sense out of it for you. To hell with whose fault it is or anything like that. (*He takes* WILLY's *arm.*) Let's just wrap it up, heh? Come on in, we'll tell Mom. (*He gently tries to pull* WILLY *to left.*)

WILLY (*frozen, immobile, with guilt in his voice*): No, I don't want to see her.

BIFF: Come on! (*He pulls again, and* WILLY *tries to pull away.*)

WILLY (*highly nervous*): No, no, I don't want to face her.

BIFF (*tries to look into* WILLY's *face, as if to find the answer there*): Why don't you want to see her?

WILLY (*more harshly now*): Don't bother me, will you?

BIFF: What do you mean, you don't want to see her? You don't want them calling you yellow, do you? This isn't your fault; it's me, I'm a bum. Now come inside! (WILLY *strains to get away.*) Did you hear what I said to you?

(WILLY *pulls away and quickly goes by himself into the house.* BIFF *follows.*)

LINDA (*to* WILLY): Did you plant, dear?

BIFF (*at the door, to* LINDA): All right, we had it out. I'm going and I'm not writing any more.

LINDA (*going to* WILLY *in the kitchen*): I think that's the best way, dear. 'Cause there's no use drawing it out, you'll just never get along.

(WILLY *doesn't respond.*)

BIFF: People ask where I am and what I'm doing, you don't know, and you don't care. That way it'll be off your mind and you can start brightening up again. All right? That clears it, doesn't it? (WILLY *is silent, and* BIFF *goes to him.*) You gonna wish me luck, scout? (*He extends his hand.*) What do you say?

LINDA: Shake his hand, Willy.

WILLY (*turning to her, seething with hurt*): There's no necessity to mention the pen at all, y'know.

BIFF (*gently*): I've got no appointment, Dad.

WILLY (*erupting fiercely*): He put his arm around . . . ?

BIFF: Dad, you're never going to see what I am, so what's the use of arguing? If I strike oil I'll send you a check. Meantime forget I'm alive.

WILLY (*to* LINDA): Spite, see?

BIFF: Shake hands, Dad.

WILLY: Not my hand.

BIFF: I was hoping not to go this way.

WILLY: Well, this is the way you're going. Good-by.

(BIFF *looks at him a moment, then turns sharply and goes to the stairs.*)

WILLY (*stops him with*): May you rot in hell if you leave this house!

BIFF (*turning*): Exactly what is it that you want from me?

WILLY: I want you to know, on the train, in the mountains, in the valleys, wherever you go, that you cut down your life for spite!

BIFF: No, no.

WILLY: Spite, spite, is the word of your undoing! And when you're down and out, remember what did it. When you're rotting somewhere beside the railroad tracks, remember, and don't you dare blame it on me!

BIFF: I'm not blaming it on you!

WILLY: I won't take the rap for this, you hear?

(HAPPY *comes down the stairs and stands on the bottom step, watching.*)

BIFF: That's just what I'm telling you!

WILLY (*sinking into a chair at the table, with full accusation*): You're trying to put a knife in me—don't think I don't know what you're doing!

BIFF: All right, phony! Then let's lay it on the line. (*He whips the rubber tube out of his pocket and puts it on the table.*)

HAPPY: You crazy—

LINDA: Biff! (*She moves to grab the hose, but* BIFF *holds it down with his hand.*)

BIFF: Leave it there! Don't move it!

WILLY (*not looking at it*): What is that?

BIFF: You know goddam well what that is.

WILLY (*caged, wanting to escape*): I never saw that.

BIFF: You saw it. The mice didn't bring it into the cellar! What is this supposed to do, make a hero out of you? This supposed to make me sorry for you?

WILLY: Never heard of it.

BIFF: There'll be no pity for you, you hear it? No pity!

WILLY (*to* LINDA): You hear the spite!

BIFF: No, you're going to hear the truth—what you are and what I am!

LINDA: Stop it!

WILLY: Spite!

HAPPY (*coming down toward* BIFF): You cut it now!

BIFF (*to* HAPPY): The man don't know who we are! The man is gonna know! (*to* WILLY) We never told the truth for ten minutes in this house!

HAPPY: We always told the truth!

BIFF (*turning on him*): You big blow, are you the assis-

tant buyer? You're one of the two assistants to the assistant, aren't you?

HAPPY: Well, I'm practically—

BIFF: You're practically full of it! We all are! And I'm through with it. (*to* WILLY) Now hear this, Willy, this is me.

WILLY: I know you!

BIFF: You know why I had no address for three months? I stole a suit in Kansas City and I was in jail. (*to* LINDA, *who is sobbing*) Stop crying. I'm through with it.

(LINDA *turns away from them, her hands covering her face.*)

WILLY: I suppose that's my fault!

BIFF: I stole myself out of every good job since high school!

WILLY: And whose fault is that?

BIFF: And I never got anywhere because you blew me so full of hot air I could never stand taking orders from anybody! That's whose fault it is!

WILLY: I hear that!

LINDA: Don't, Biff!

BIFF: It's goddam time you heard that! I had to be boss big shot in two weeks, and I'm through with it!

WILLY: Then hang yourself! For spite, hang yourself!

BIFF: No! Nobody's hanging himself, Willy! I ran down eleven flights with a pen in my hand today. And suddenly I stopped, you hear me? And in the middle of that office building, do you hear this? I stopped in the middle of that building and I saw—the sky. I saw the things that I love in this world. The work and the food and time to sit and smoke. And I looked at the pen and said to myself, what the hell am I grabbing this for? Why am I trying to become what I don't want to be? What am I doing in an office, making a contemptuous, begging fool of myself, when all I want is out there, waiting for me the minute I say I know who I am! Why can't I say that, Willy? (*He tries to make* WILLY *face him, but* WILLY *pulls away and moves to the left.*)

WILLY (*with hatred, threateningly*): The door of your life is wide open!

BIFF: Pop! I'm a dime a dozen, and so are you!

WILLY (*turning on him now in an uncontrolled outburst*): I am not a dime a dozen! I am Willy Loman and you are Biff Loman!

(BIFF *starts for* WILLY, *but is blocked by* HAPPY. *In his fury,* BIFF *seems on the verge of attacking his father.*)

BIFF: I am not a leader of men, Willy, and neither are you. You were never anything but a hard-working drummer who landed in the ash can like all the rest of them! I'm one dollar an hour, Willy! I tried seven states and couldn't raise it. A buck an hour! Do you gather my meaning? I'm not bringing home any prizes any more, and you're going to stop waiting for me to bring them home!

WILLY (*directly to* BIFF): You vengeful, spiteful mut!

(BIFF *breaks from* HAPPY. WILLY, *in fright, starts up the stairs.* BIFF *grabs him.*)

BIFF (*at the peak of his fury*): Pop, I'm nothing! I'm nothing, Pop. Can't you understand that? There's no spite in it any more. I'm just what I am, that's all.

(BIFF's *fury has spent itself, and he breaks down, sobbing, holding on to* WILLY, *who dumbly fumbles for* BIFF's *face.*)

WILLY (*astonished*): What're you doing? What're you doing? (*to* LINDA) Why is he crying?

BIFF (*crying, broken*): Will you let me go, for Christ's sake? Will you take that phony dream and burn it before something happens? (*Struggling to contain himself, he pulls away and moves to the stairs.*) I'll go in the morning. Put him—put him to bed. (*Exhausted,* BIFF *moves up the stairs to his room.*)

WILLY (*after a long pause, astonished, elevated*): Isn't that—isn't that remarkable? Biff—he likes me!

LINDA: He loves you, Willy!

HAPPY (*deeply moved*): Always did, Pop.

WILLY: Oh, Biff! (*Staring wildly.*) He cried! Cried to me. (*He is choking with his love, and now cries out his promise.*) That boy—that boy is going to be magnificent!

(BEN *appears in the light just outside the kitchen.*)

BEN: Yes, outstanding, with twenty thousand behind him.

LINDA (*sensing the racing of his mind, fearfully, carefully*): Now come to bed, Willy. It's all settled now.

WILLY (*finding it difficult not to rush out of the house*): Yes, we'll sleep. Come on. Go to sleep, Hap.

BEN: And it does take a great kind of a man to crack the jungle.

(In accents of dread, BEN's *idyllic music starts up.*)

HAPPY (*his arm around* LINDA): I'm getting married, Pop, don't forget it. I'm changing everything. I'm gonna run that department before the year is up. You'll see, Mom. (*He kisses her.*)

BEN: The jungle is dark but full of diamonds, Willy.

(WILLY *turns, moves, listening to* BEN.)

LINDA: Be good. You're both good boys, just act that way, that's all.

HAPPY: 'Night, Pop. (*He goes upstairs.*)

LINDA (*to* WILLY): Come, dear.

BEN (*with greater force*): One must go in to fetch a diamond out.

WILLY (*to* LINDA, *as he moves slowly along the edge of the kitchen, toward the door*): I just want to get settled down, Linda. Let me sit alone for a little.

LINDA (*almost uttering her fear*): I want you upstairs.

WILLY (*taking her in his arms*): In a few minutes, Linda. I couldn't sleep right now. Go on, you look awful tired. (*He kisses her.*)

BEN: Not like an appointment at all. A diamond is rough and hard to the touch.

WILLY: Go on now. I'll be right up.

LINDA: I think this is the only way, Willy.

WILLY: Sure, it's the best thing.

BEN: Best thing!

WILLY: The only way. Everything is gonna be—go on, kid, go to bed. You look so tired.

LINDA: Come right up.

WILLY: Two minutes.

(LINDA *goes into the living-room, then reappears in her bedroom.* WILLY *moves just outside the kitchen door.*)

WILLY: Loves me. (*Wonderingly.*) Always loved me. Isn't that a remarkable thing? Ben, he'll worship me for it!

BEN (*with promise*): It's dark there, but full of diamonds.

WILLY: Can you imagine that magnificence with twenty thousand dollars in his pocket?

LINDA (*calling from her room*): Willy! Come up!

WILLY (*calling into the kitchen*): Yes! Yes. Coming! It's very smart, you realize that, don't you sweetheart? Even Ben sees it. I gotta go, baby. 'By! 'By! (*Going over to* BEN, *almost dancing*) Imagine? When the mail comes he'll be ahead of Bernard again!

BEN: A perfect proposition all around.

WILLY: Did you see how he cried to me? Oh, if I could kiss him, Ben!

BEN: Time, William, time!

WILLY: Oh, Ben, I always knew one way or another we were gonna make it, Biff and I!

BEN (*looking at his watch*): The boat. We'll be late. (*He moves slowly off into the darkness.*)

WILLY (*elegiacally, turning to the house*): Now when you kick off, boy, I want a seventy-yard boot, and get right down the field under the ball, and when you hit, hit low and hit hard, because it's important, boy. (*He swings around and faces the audience.*) There's all kinds of important people in the stands, and the first thing you know . . .(*Suddenly realizing he is alone.*) Ben! Ben, where do I . . . ? (*He makes a sudden movement of search.*) Ben, how do I . . . ?

LINDA (*calling*): Willy, you coming up?

WILLY (*uttering a gasp of fear, whirling about as if to quiet her*): Sh! (*He turns around as if to find his way; sounds, faces, voices, seem to be swarming in upon him and he flicks at them, crying.*) Sh! Sh! (*Suddenly *music, faint and high, stops him. It rises in intensity, almost to an unbearable scream. He goes up and down on his toes, and rushes off around the house.)* Shhh!

LINDA: Willy?

(There is no answer. LINDA waits. BIFF gets up off his bed. He is still in his clothes. HAPPY sits up. BIFF stands listening.)

LINDA *(with real fear)*: Willy, answer me! Willy!

(There is the sound of a car starting and moving away at full speed.)

LINDA: No!

BIFF *(rushing down the stairs)*: Pop!

(As the car speeds off, the music crashes down in a frenzy of sound, which becomes the soft pulsation of a single cello string. BIFF slowly returns to his bedroom. He and HAPPY gravely don their jackets. LINDA slowly walks out of her room. The music has developed into a dead march. The leaves of day are appearing over everything. CHARLEY and BERNARD, somberly dressed, appear and knock on the kitchen door. BIFF and HAPPY slowly descend the stairs to the kitchen as CHARLEY and BERNARD enter. All stop a moment when LINDA, in clothes of mourning, bearing a little bunch of roses, comes through the draped doorway into the kitchen. She goes to CHARLEY and takes his arm. Now all move toward the audience, through the wall-line of the kitchen. At the limit of the apron, LINDA lays down the flowers, kneels, and sits back on her heels. All stare down at the grave.)

REQUIEM

CHARLEY: It's getting dark, Linda.

(LINDA doesn't react. She stares at the grave.)

BIFF: How about it, Mom? Better get some rest, heh? They'll be closing the gate soon.

(LINDA makes no move. Pause.)

HAPPY *(deeply angered)*: He had no right to do that. There was no necessity for it. We would've helped him.

CHARLEY *(grunting)*: Hmmm.

BIFF: Come along, Mom.

LINDA: Why didn't anybody come?

CHARLEY: It was a very nice funeral.

LINDA: But where are all the people he knew? Maybe they blame him.

CHARLEY: Naa. It's a rough world, Linda. They wouldn't blame him.

LINDA: I can't understand it. At this time especially. First time in thirty-five years we were just about free and clear. He only needed a little salary. He was even finished with the dentist.

CHARLEY: No man only needs a little salary.

LINDA: I can't understand it.

BIFF: There were a lot of nice days. When he'd come home from a trip; or on Sundays, making the stoop; finishing the cellar; putting on the new porch; when he built the extra bathroom; and put up the garage. You know something, Charley, there's more of him in that front stoop than in all the sales he ever made.

CHARLEY: Yeah. He was a happy man with a batch of cement.

LINDA: He was so wonderful with his hands.

BIFF: He had the wrong dreams. All, all, wrong.

HAPPY *(almost ready to fight BIFF)*: Don't say that!

BIFF: He never knew who he was.

CHARLEY *(stopping HAPPY's movement and reply. To BIFF)*: Nobody dast blame this man. You don't understand: Willy was a salesman. And for a salesman, there is no rock bottom to the life. He don't put a bolt to a nut, he don't tell you the law or give you medicine. He's a man way out there in the blue, riding on a smile and a shoeshine. And when they start not smiling back—that's an earthquake. And then you get yourself a couple of spots on your hat, and you're finished. Nobody dast blame this man. A salesman is got to dream, boy. It comes with the territory.

BIFF: Charley, the man didn't know who he was.

HAPPY *(infuriated)*: Don't say that!

BIFF: Why don't you come with me, Happy?

HAPPY: I'm not licked that easily. I'm staying right in this city and I'm gonna beat this racket! *(He looks at BIFF, his chin set.)* The Loman Brothers!

BIFF: I know who I am, kid.

HAPPY: All right, boy. I'm gonna show you and everybody else that Willy Loman did not die in vain. He had a good dream. It's the only dream you can have—to come out number-one man. He fought it out here, and this is where I'm gonna win it for him.

BIFF *(with a hopeless glance at HAPPY, bends toward his mother)*: Let's go, Mom.

LINDA: I'll be with you in a minute. Go on, Charley. *(He hesitates.)* I want to, just for a minute. I never had a chance to say good-by.

(CHARLEY moves away, followed by HAPPY. BIFF remains a slight distance up and left of LINDA. She sits there, summoning herself. The flute begins, not far away, playing behind her speech.)

LINDA: Forgive me, dear, I can't cry. I don't know what it is, but I can't cry. I don't understand it. Why did you ever do that? Help me, Willy, I can't cry. It seems to me that you're just on another trip. I keep expecting you. Willy, dear, I can't cry. Why did you do it? I search and search and I search, and I can't understand it, Willy. I made the last payment on the house today. To-day, dear. And there'll be nobody home. *(A sob rises in her throat.*) We're free and clear. (*Sobbing more fully, released.*) We're free. (BIFF *comes slowly toward her.*) We're free . . . We're free . . .

(BIFF *lifts her to her feet and moves out up right with her in his arms.* LINDA *sobs quietly.* BERNARD *and* CHARLEY *come together and follow them, followed by* HAPPY. *Only the music of the flute is left on the darkening stage as over the house the hard towers of the apartment buildings rise into sharp focus, and*

THE CURTAIN FALLS

Figure 1. Willy (George C. Scott) leans against the refrigerator shortly after returning home from his trip to Yonkers at the opening of the Circle in the Square production of *Death of a Salesman,* directed by George C. Scott, New York, 1975. (Photograph: Inge Morath, Magnum Photos, Inc.)

Figure 2. Willy (George C. Scott), during the enactment of a pleasant memory, tells Young Happy (Harvey Keitel, *left*) and Young Biff (James Farentino, *right*) to help their mother Linda (Teresa Wright) carry up the wash in the Circle in the Square production of *Death of a Salesman,* directed by George C. Scott, New York, 1975. (Photograph: Inge Morath, Magnum Photos, Inc.)

Figure 3. Willy (George C. Scott), during the enactment of a painful memory, tries to explain away the presence of The Woman (Patricia Quinn) with whom he has been discovered by Biff (James Farentino) in the Circle in the Square production of *Death of a Salesman,* directed by George C. Scott, New York, 1975. (Photograph: Inge Morath, Magnum Photos, Inc.)

Staging of *Death of a Salesman*

REVIEW OF THE CIRCLE IN THE SQUARE PRODUCTION, 1975, BY WALTER KERR

Attention has been paid. In reviving Arthur Miller's "Death of a Salesman" at Circle in the Square, and in taking on the part of the self-doomed but perpetually incurable Willy Loman himself, director-star George C. Scott has first of all behaved not as director or as star but as servant of a play, a piece of work in the hand. Furthermore, he has not behaved as though he were serving an old play, a familiar play, a play whose ancient echoes were so overwhelming that a kind of fearful obeisance was the best that could be offered it. He has chosen not to remember it, or to remember other people's remembrances of it, but to pay attention to its undeniably powerful, still most affecting, but extraordinarily ambiguous voice. Not what Elia Kazan once heard in it, not what Lee J. Cobb once heard in it, perceptive and just as they may have been. But, with one sharp ear cocked, what is it saying *now?*

This is not simply a matter of muting the lines we recall all too well. Mr. Scott has a fascinating trick—it is more than a trick, it is a heart-rending trait of character—of burying a phrase like "He's liked, but he's not well liked" by making it part of a compulsive contradiction, hurling it so hot on the heels of the contrary line preceding it that you must take the two in balance and believe neither. Listen to him, without transition, pause, or apparent dishonesty, breathlessly bracketing "I'm very well liked, the only thing is people don't take to me" and making both sense and agony of it. Or, glorying in his talent for regaling his New England buyers. "I'm full of jokes, I tell too many jokes," with the savagery of the latter seeming to bite off his own braggart head.

There is much savagery in Mr. Scott's performance—he comes on like the last bald American eagle dead set for a final reckoning—but it is more than the quite normal savagery of his customary stage deportment, it is a savagery uncovered in the near-manic, electrifying shifts of mood, boast and bile back to back, of Arthur Miller's play. And it completely disrupts my *own* (perhaps faulty) memory of the original production, its original meaning. I remember assuming that Willy Loman had once been a successful salesman, had once done well by his wife and boys, had once made "a smile and a shoeshine" work for him. That the dream (the American dream of success by back-slapping and coming in Number One on all sales charts?) had eventually collapsed of its own essential vacuousness was the pathos of the moment, but the pathos of the moment was a somewhat recent discovery, a realization, not a permanence recognized from the beginning.

With Mr. Scott it is certainly otherwise. Quite apart from absorbing the catch-phrases by which we identify the play into a relentless, run-on "yes-no" that is Willy Loman's never-ending private torment, Mr. Scott makes us hear lines we seem never to have heard before. He is speaking to his outrageously successful brother, Ben, despoiler of the Gold Coast, reaper of fabulous Alaskan harvests. Ben is older than Willie, got started sooner than Willy. Ben even remembers their father, a man who played a flute as he carted the family from state to state across the American landscape.

But the father died before Willy could quite know him, or know himself in relation to any father. "I still feel a little *temporary* about myself," he says, reflectively, with unconscious grief, to the solid, if almost mythical, brother who never felt temporary about anything. Mr. Scott's Willy always had to compensate, to inflate his indeterminate place in the scheme of things, to substitute for his sickened hollowness an equally hollow image in which only others—only his adoring sons—could possibly believe. He has been a shell from the beginning, filling himself with borrowed life, life that could be borrowed from successful salesmen he admired, life that might be borrowed—on a kind of promissory note—from the coming success of his two boys.

This becomes stunningly clear in a scene almost impossible to contemplate, given Mr. Scott's intensely mesmerizing presence. Willy is to recall a day, early in his career, when he listened to a salesman, an 84-year-old master-drummer, in his room at the Parker House, making an ample, indestructible living by doing nothing more than reach for a phone and run up orders by the dozen. He must make us believe that this one eavesdropping image of success has given him his goal in life, a self-image strong enough to sustain him. And he must do it while the man he is talking to, an employer about to fire him now that he is an exhausted 62, is paying no heed at all, incapable of being moved by anything he says.

To begin with, it is unthinkable that anyone within Mr. Scott's feverish, concentrated range should not listen to him. And if we can bring ourselves to believe that the man is not listening, then why should we listen? The essence of the sequence is the deaf dismissal of Mr. Scott's dreams. And yet it happens both ways, creating stage magic of the highest order. Our own absorption in Mr. Scott's passionate recollection of things past is total: we see everything he sees, the room's furnishings, the drummer's posture, the waves of power reaching out to envelope Mr. Scott. At the same time the actor is able to distance himself from his indifferent employer, to isolate himself with *us,* to the point where we hear what no one else can hear, share what no one else can share. The doubleness is devastating; I still don't believe it.

And, at the same time Mr. Scott is alternately drawing his teeth across his lower lip and lifting the corners of his mouth in a mirthless but expansive smile, abruptly shifting from snarl to endearment, Teresa Wright, as his wife, is creating the perfect complement to his instability. Face severely in repose, voice rarely raised, she is both patient and rock-hard in her steadfast coping with home truths. She is not deceived, not even by love. But she does love. And her love has the toughness that will tolerate neither lies nor laments from her failed children.

Their father is an ordinary man; they are to find no blame in him for that. Ordinary men become exhausted as surely as great men do; the exhaustion is just as real, no guilt is to be lodged against it. She has heard her husband letting himself in by night beneath the naked bulb over the back door, sigh as he dropped his satchels, greet her encouragingly, explosively betray his own chagrin in sudden envy of men who have "accomplished something." She knows he has accomplished nothing, hadn't an identity to do it with. The boys are not to say so. "Attention must be paid" to ordinary men, exhausted or not. There is no rhetoric in Miss Wright as she speaks the words, no lumpy quasi-poetry. She is speaking a harsh truth, harshly. Let the boys be "bums," if that is what they are to be. And let them honor their father, who would have honored them if he had only known how. If we are to shed tears, and we do, they fall on granite.

Between Mr. Scott and the superb Miss Wright, "Death of a Salesman" becomes a play of persons, not of social prophecy or some archetypal proclamation of an already failed American myth. It is too richly contradictory, too intimately detailed, too ambiguously loving and desperate, for mere abstraction; its weaknesses and its toughnesses are tangible, not distantly theoretical. If the work now seems tantalizing in its implications, the implications are more nearly those that endlessly badgered O'Neill: it is illusions that destroy. "We never told the truth for one minute in this house" is a cry near the end in a house that cannot stand; to the last, Willy Loman is imagining that, somehow or other, the $20,000 in insurance money that will come with his death will guarantee the successful future of his elder, equally emptied-out son. Death goes right on dreaming.

Mr. Miller's play holds, contains its own complex meaning that is beyond facile ideological analysis, lives and moves and has its being in the mercury of its ravaged, hoping, falsely jovial, forgiving, unforgiving figures. At the preview I saw, the evening's momentum was interrupted at least once, possibly due to an errant light cue; and because the act-endings are insufficiently italicized, I think the production might profit from having a single intermission rather than two, though that may be demanding something too much of Mr. Scott's unhusbanded energies. But the whole is handsomely acted—James Farentino, Harvey Keitel, and Chuck Patterson are particularly fine— and Mr. Scott's staging is as restlessly right as his performance; he is endlessly on his feet though he knows that his feet will betray him before they can ever see him home.

TENNESSEE WILLIAMS

1911–1983

Despite his first name, a nickname he adopted during his college days, Williams was born in Mississippi and lived there until 1918, when his father, a travelling salesman, was promoted to an office in St. Louis. That move to the midwest, according to Williams, was a "tragic" experience. He was mocked for his southern accent, he was pained by the heightened awareness of being poor, and thus he never adjusted to life in St. Louis. Looking back on his childhood there, Williams once described it as "the beginning of the social consciousness which I think has marked most of my writing." Williams lived in St. Louis until his mid-twenties, and those years with his family—with his tyrannical father, his overprotective mother, and his mentally withdrawn sister—evidently gave rise to the acute psychological awareness that has also marked virtually all of his writing. Those years with his family in St. Louis certainly must have given rise to his abiding concern with the painful experience of the outsider: the artist, the dreamer, the physically crippled, the mentally disturbed, and the sexually driven. As a child, he had been afflicted by diptheria, which for many years left him with paralyzed legs and weakened kidneys. As a teenager, he suffered the taunts of his father who repeatedly called him "Miss Nancy" because of his literary inclinations. In his mid-twenties, he worked himself into a nervous and physical breakdown, selling shoes during the day at his father's insistence and writing plays late into the night to escape his miserable existence. During this time he also witnessed the permanent mental breakdown of his introverted sister, with whom he had been close throughout his years in Mississippi and St. Louis.

These painful experiences of his childhood and youth clearly provided Williams with material for his first major stage success, *The Glass Menagerie* (1944), "a memory play," whose protagonist-narrator, Tom Wingfield is clearly modelled on Williams himself, much as Laura Wingfield is modelled on Williams' sister Rose. Tom, for example, is portrayed as a poet and dreamer, yearning for escape from the suffocating world of business, while Laura is depicted as a pathologically shy young woman who lives in a private world of glass animals and old phonograph records. Indeed, it might well be said that Williams has reflected the personality and disposition of his father, or his mother, or his sister, or himself in virtually all his work. His father's personality is echoed in the cynically practical and coarsely domineering men who often figure prominently in his plays, such as Stanley Kowalski of *A Streetcar Named Desire* (1947) or Big Daddy in *Cat on a Hot Tin Roof* (1955). His mother is echoed in the long-suffering women who patiently endure the afflictions of being married to these domineering characters, such as Stella Kowalski or Big Mama. His sister is echoed in psychologically fragile women who have retreated from life, such as Blanche, a faded southern "gentlewoman," who clings desperately to the memory of her lost plantation in *A Streetcar Named Desire,* or Alma, the virginal spinster in *Summer and Smoke* (1948), or Hannah Jelkes, the "ethereal, almost ghostly" figure in *The Night of the Iguana* (1961). And Williams has echoed himself in all his artists, and poets, and dreamers—men and women characters alike—who suffer from the brutality of the coarsely practical worlds they inhabit.

But Williams by no means limited himself to characters modeled on his own family, as is evident simply from all the lusty and vigorous women who figure in his plays, such as Serafina in *The Rose Tattoo* (1950), or Maxine Faulk in *The Night of the Iguana*, or Maggie in *Cat on a Hot Tin Roof*. Indeed, it would be mistaken to regard Williams as a strictly autobiographical dramatist, for he repeatedly transformed his personal experience so that his characters, while echoing aspects of his family, are by no means exactly like them at all. And the aspects that Williams chose to echo are occasioned by his persistent concern with the experience of the outsider in modern society, and with the implications of that experience as it is manifest in human loneliness, in the inability of human beings to communicate with one another, and in the irrepressible need to create illusions through which they can escape from the loneliness and painfulness of their existence.

In dramatizing these aspects of experience, Williams was never content to settle for a strictly realistic method of presentation. In his "Production Notes" to *The Glass Menagerie,* for example, he attacked "the straight realistic play with its genuine frigidaire and authentic ice-cubes" by comparing it to a mere "photographic likeness," which he considered inadequate to convey the truth of human experience. To bring the audience closer to the truth, Williams argued in favor of "expressionism and all other unconventional techniques in drama." In *The Glass Menagerie* he relied heavily on suggestive music, lighting, and pantomime to evoke the memories of Tom Wingfield. His notes to the play reveal that he intended even to convey comments on Tom's staged memories through the device of projecting images or phrases on a screen—a device from the epic theater of Brecht. Although Williams agreed to omitting the screen device in the original production of the play, he has persisted in using other techniques of expressionistic theater to evoke the mood and quality of his characters' experience. In his "Notes for the Designer" at the beginning of *Cat on a Hot Tin Roof,* Williams clearly blends realistic and expressionistic approaches by describing the stage furniture in meticulous detail and then concluding with the direction that "the walls below the ceiling should dissolve mysteriously into air." He even turns the furniture into a form of symbolic statement by noting that Brick's "*huge* console combination of radio-phonograph (hi-fi with three speakers) TV set *and* liquor cabinet . . . is a very complete and compact little shrine to virtually all the comforts and illusions behind which we hide from such things as the characters in the play are faced with".

The entire set for *Cat on a Hot Tin Roof*—the bedroom of Brick and Maggie—is a richly symbolic location, for the "big double bed" that it contains tangibly reflects the frustrating relationship of Maggie and Brick, and the bedroom as a whole evokes the problematic relationship of Skipper and Brick through the memories it contains of its original owners, "a pair of old bachelors who shared this room all their lives together." In fact, the image of the bedroom and all that it begets—or fails to beget—is a central concern for everyone in the play, for Big Daddy and Big Mama, for Gooper and Mae alike. It is thus highly appropriate that all the struggles within the family take place within this haunting room.

Despite its frankly suggestive set, when the play opened, the critic Walter Kerr called it "a beautifully written, perfectly directed, stunningly acted play of evasion: evasion on the part of its principal character, evasion perhaps on the part of its playwright." He was referring, of course, to the play's persistent concern with the relationship of Brick and Skipper, the exact nature of which is never clearly established. Williams knew that the relationship would raise questions as to whether or not it was homosexual, and thus he took the unusual step of inserting an interpretative comment into the middle of the play:

> The bird that I hope to catch in the net of this play is not the solution of one man's psychological problem. I'm trying to catch the true quality of experience in a group of people, that cloudy, flickering, evanescent—fiercely charged!—interplay of live human beings in the thundercloud of a common crisis. Some mystery should be left in the revelation of character in a play, just as a great deal of mystery is always left in the revelation of character in life, even in one's own character to himself. This does not absolve the playwright of his duty to observe and probe as clearly and deeply as he legitimately can: but it should steer him away from "pat" conclusions, facile definitions which make a play just a play, not a snare for the truth of human experience.

In making such remarks, Williams was clearly directing his readers away from focussing on the question of Brick's relationship with Skipper to the more important issue that concerns Brick himself: the issue of "mendacity," which is evidently also the major concern of Williams. Everyone in the play is guilty of mendacity—of lying, betrayal, and manipulation. And the lies persist only because Big Daddy and Big Mama want to believe them, a condition that suggests the root of public lying is the act of lying to oneself. Williams' concern with the wilful perpetuation of illusions is reflected also in the structure of the play, for the first act centers on Maggie trying to get Brick to look at her, while the second act reaches its climax with Big Daddy forcing Brick to look at himself, and the third act derives its power from Brick's final refusal to let Maggie sustain any illusions about him.

Because all the characters in the play are so determinedly bent on their ways, yet so undone by the ways they have chosen for themselves, they require very complex performances from actors and actresses—performances that convey both their wilfulness and their vulnerability. These qualities were evidently achieved by the American Shakespeare Theater when it revived the play in 1974, as can be seen from a review of that production reprinted following the text. Photographs from that production convey the sensuality and the helplessness Elizabeth Ashley brought to the role of Maggie (see Figure 1), much as they reveal the obstinacy and the air of defeat Keir Dullea gave to the role of Brick (see Figures 1 and 2). They also show the blustery power of Fred Gwynne in the role of Big Daddy (see Figures 3 and 4). Although weakened by disease, that power is still seen in the play as being great enough to hobble virtually everyone in his world.

CAT ON A HOT TIN ROOF

BY TENNESSEE WILLIAMS

CHARACTERS

MARGARET

BRICK

MAE, *sometimes called* SISTER WOMAN

BIG MAMA

DIXIE, *a little girl*

BIG DADDY

REVEREND TOOKER

GOOPER, *sometimes called* BROTHER MAN

DOCTOR BAUGH, *pronounced "Baw"*

LACEY, *a Negro servant*

SOOKEY, *another*

CHILDREN

NOTES FOR THE DESIGNER

The set is the bed-sitting room of a plantation home in the Mississippi Delta. It is along an upstairs gallery which probably runs around the entire house; it has two pairs of very wide doors opening onto the gallery, showing white balustrades against a fair summer sky that fades into dusk and night during the course of the play, which occupies precisely the time of its performance, excepting, of course, the fifteen minutes of intermission.

Perhaps the style of the room is not what you would expect in the home of the Delta's biggest cotton-planter. It is Victorian with a touch of the Far East. It hasn't changed much since it was occupied by the original owners of the place, Jack Straw and Peter Ochello, a pair of old bachelors who shared this room all their lives together. In other words, the room must evoke some ghosts; it is gently and poetically haunted by a relationship that must have involved a tenderness which was uncommon. This may be irrelevant or unnecessary, but I once saw a reproduction of a faded photograph of the verandah of Robert Louis Stevenson's home on that Samoan Island where he spent his last years, and there was a quality of tender light on weathered wood, such as porch furniture made of bamboo and wicker, exposed to tropical suns and tropical rains, which came to mind when I thought about the set for this play, bringing also to mind the grace and comfort of light, the reassurance it gives, on a late and fair afternoon in summer, the way that no matter what, even dread of death, is gently touched and soothed by it. For the set is the background for a play that deals with human extremities of emotion, and it needs that softness behind it.

The bathroom door, showing only pale-blue tile and silver towel racks, is in one side wall; the hall door in the opposite wall. Two articles of furniture need mention: a big double bed which staging should make a functional part of the set as often as suitable, the surface of which should be slightly raked to make figures on it seen more easily; and against the wall space between the two huge double doors upstage: a monumental monstrosity peculiar to our times, a huge console combination of radio-phonograph (hi-fi with three speakers) TV set and liquor cabinet, bearing and containing many glasses and bottles, all in one piece, which is a combination of muted silver tones, and the opalescent tones of reflecting glass, a chromatic link, this thing, between the sepia (tawny gold) tones of the interior and the cool (white and blue) tones of the gallery and sky. This piece of furniture (?!), this monument, is a very complete and compact little shrine to virtually all the comforts and illusions behind which we hide from such things as the characters in the play are faced with.

The set should be far less realistic than I have so far implied in this description of it. I think the walls below the ceiling should dissolve mysteriously into air; the set should be roofed by the sky; stars and moon suggested by traces of milky pallor, as if they were observed through a telescope lens out of focus.

Anything else I can think of? Oh, yes, fanlights (transoms shaped like an open glass fan) above all the doors in the set, with panes of blue and amber, and above all, the designer should take as many pains to give the actors room to move about freely (to show their restlessness, their passion for breaking out) as if it were a set for a ballet.

An evening in summer. The action is continuous, with two intermissions.

ACT 1

(At the rise of the curtain someone is taking a shower in the bathroom, the door of which is half open. A pretty young woman, with anxious lines in her face, enters the bedroom and crosses to the bathroom door.)

MARGARET *(shouting above roar of water):* One of those no-neck monsters hit me with a hot buttered biscuit so I have t' change!

(MARGARET's voice is both rapid and drawling. In her long speeches she has the vocal tricks of a priest delivering a liturgical chant, the lines are almost sung, always continuing a little beyond her breath so she has to gasp for another. Sometimes she intersperses the lines with a little wordless singing, such as "da-da-daaa!")

(Water turns off and BRICK calls out to her, but is still unseen. A tone of politely feigned interest, masking indifference, or worse, is characteristic of his speech with MARGARET.)

BRICK: Wha'd you say, Maggie? Water was on s' loud I couldn't hearya. . . .

MARGARET: Well, I!—just remarked that!—one of th' no-neck monsters messed up m' lovely lace dress so I got t'—cha-a-ange. . . . (*She opens and kicks shut drawers of the dresser.*)

BRICK: Why d'ya call Gooper's kiddies no-neck monsters?

MARGARET: Because they've got no necks! Isn't that a good enough reason?

BRICK: Don't they have any necks?

MARGARET: None visible. Their fat little heads are set on their fat little bodies without a bit of connection.

BRICK: That's too bad.

MARGARET: Yes, it's too bad because you can't wring their necks if they've got no necks to wring! Isn't that right, honey? (*She steps out of her dress, stands in a slip of ivory satin and lace.*) Yep, they're no-neck monsters, all no-neck people are monsters . . .

(*Children shriek downstairs.*)

Hear them? Hear them screaming? I don't know where their voice boxes are located since they don't have necks. I tell you I got so nervous at that table tonight I thought I would throw back my head and utter a scream you could hear across the Arkansas border an' parts of Louisiana an' Tennessee. I said to your charming sister-in-law, Mae, honey, couldn't you feed those precious little things at a separate table with an oilcloth cover? They make such a mess an' the lace cloth looks *so* pretty! She made enormous eyes at me and said, "Ohhh, noooooo! On Big Daddy's birthday? Why, he would never forgive me!" Well, I want you to know, Big Daddy hadn't been at the table two minutes with those five no-neck monsters slobbering and drooling over their food before he threw down his fork an' shouted, "Fo' God's sake, Gooper, why don't you put them pigs at a trough in th' kitchen?"—Well, I swear, I simply could have di-ieed!

Think of it, Brick, they've got five of them and number six is coming. They've brought the whole bunch down here like animals to display at a county fair. Why, they have those children doin' tricks all the time! "Junior, show Big Daddy how you do this, show Big Daddy how you do that, say your little piece fo' Big Daddy, Sister. Show your dimples, Sugar. Brother, show Big Daddy how you stand on your head!"—It goes on all the time, along with constant little remarks and innuendos about the fact that you and I have not produced any children, are totally childless and therefore totally useless!—Of course it's comical but it's also disgusting since it's so obvious what they're up to!

BRICK (*without interest*): What are they up to, Maggie?

MARGARET: Why, you know what they're up to!

BRICK (*appearing*): No, I don't know what they're up to.

(*He stands there in the bathroom doorway drying his hair with a towel and hanging onto the towel rack because one ankle is broken, plastered and bound. He is still slim and firm as a boy. His liquor hasn't started tearing him down outside. He has the additional charm of that cool air of detachment that people have who have given up the struggle. But now and then, when disturbed, something flashes behind it, like lightning in a fair sky, which shows that at some deeper level he is far from peaceful. Perhaps in a stronger light he would show some signs of deliquescence, but the fading, still warm, light from the gallery treats him gently.*)

MARGARET: I'll tell you what they're up to, boy of mine!—They're up to cutting you out of your father's estate, and—

(*She freezes momentarily before her next remark. Her voice drops as if it were somehow a personally embarrassing admission.*)

—Now we know that Big Daddy's dyin' of—cancer. . . .

(*There are voices on the lawn below: long-drawn calls across distance.* MARGARET *raises her lovely bare arms and powders her armpits with a light sigh.*)
(*She adjusts the angle of a magnifying mirror to straighten an eyelash, then rises fretfully saying.*)

There's so much light in the room it—

BRICK (*softly but sharply*): Do we?

MARGARET: Do we what?

BRICK: Know Big Daddy's dyin' of cancer?

MARGARET: Got the report today.

BRICK: Oh . . .

MARGARET (*letting down bamboo blinds which cast long, gold-fretted shadows over the room*): Yep, got th' report just now . . . it didn't surprise me, Baby. . . .

(*Her voice has range, and music; sometimes it drops low as a boy's and you have a sudden image of her playing boy's games as a child.*)

I recognized the symptoms soon's we got here last spring, and I'm willin' to bet you that Brother Man and his wife were pretty sure of it, too. That more than likely explains why their usual summer migration to the coolness of the Great Smokies was passed up this summer in favor of—hustlin' down here ev'ry whipstitch with their whole screamin' tribe! And why so many allusions have been made to Rainbow Hill lately. You know what Rainbow Hill is? Place that's famous for treatin' alcoholics an' dope fiends in the movies!

BRICK: I'm not in the movies.

MARGARET: No, and you don't take dope. Otherwise you're a perfect candidate for Rainbow Hill, Baby, and that's where they aim to ship you—over my dead body! Yep, over my dead body they'll ship you there, but nothing would please them better. Then Brother Man could get a-hold of the purse strings and dole out remittances to us, maybe get power of attorney and sign checks for us and cut off our credit wherever, whenever he wanted! Son-of-a-bitch! How'd you like that, Baby?—Well, you've been doin' just about ev'rything in your power to bring it about, you've just been doin' ev'rything you can think of to aid and abet them in this scheme of theirs! Quittin' work, devoting yourself to the occupation of drinkin'!—Breakin' your ankle last night on the high school athletic field: doin' what? Jumpin' hurdles? At two or three in the morning? Just fantastic! Got in the paper. *Clarksdale Register* carried a nice little item about it, human interest story about a well-known former athlete stagin' a one-man track meet on the Glorious Hill High School athletic field last night, but was slightly out of condition and didn't clear the first hurdle! Brother Man Gooper claims he exercised his influence t' keep it from goin' out over AP or UP or every goddam "P."

But, Brick? You still have one big advantage!

(During the above swift flood of words, BRICK has reclined with contrapuntal leisure on the snowy surface of the bed and has rolled over carefully on his side or belly.)

BRICK *(wryly)*: Did you *say* something, Maggie?

MARGARET: Big Daddy dotes on you, honey. And he can't stand Brother Man and Brother Man's wife, that monster of fertility, Mae. Know how I know? By little expressions that flicker over his face when that woman is holding fo'th on one of her choice topics such as—how she refused twilight sleep!—when the twins were delivered! Because she feels motherhood's an experience that a woman ought to experience fully!—in order to fully appreciate the wonder and beauty of it! HAH!—and how she made Brother Man come in an' stand beside her in the delivery room so he would not miss out on the "wonder and beauty" of it either!—producin' those no-neck monsters. . . .

(A speech of this kind would be antipathetic from almost anybody but MARGARET; she makes it oddly funny, because her eyes constantly twinkle and her voice shakes with laughter which is basically indulgent.)

—Big Daddy shares my attitude toward those

two! As for me, well—I give him a laugh now and then and he tolerates me. In fact!—I sometimes suspect that Big Daddy harbors a little unconscious "lech" fo' me. . . .

BRICK: What makes you think that Big Daddy has a lech for you, Maggie?

MARGARET: Way he always drops his eyes down my body when I'm talkin' to him, drops his eyes to my boobs and licks his old chops! Ha ha!

BRICK: That kind of talk is disgusting.

MARGARET: Did anyone ever tell you that you're an ass-aching Puritan, Brick?

I think it's mighty fine that that ole fellow, on the doorstep of death, still takes in my shape with what I think is deserved appreciation!

And you wanta know something else? Big Daddy didn't know how many little Maes and Goopers had been produced! "How many kids have you got?" he asked at the table, just like Brother Man and his wife were new acquaintances to him! Big Mama said he was jokin', but that ole boy wasn't jokin', Lord, no!

And when they infawmed him that they had five already and were turning out number six!—the news seemed to come as a sort of unpleasant surprise . . .

(Children yell below.)

Scream, monsters!

(Turns to BRICK with a sudden, gay, charming smile which fades as she notices that he is not looking at her but into fading gold space with a troubled expression.)
(It is constant rejection that makes her humor "bitchy.")

Yes, you should of been at that supper-table, Baby.

(Whenever she calls him "baby" the word is a soft caress.)

Y'know, Big Daddy, bless his ole sweet soul, he's the dearest ole thing in the world, but he does hunch over his food as if he preferred not to notice anything else. Well, Mae an' Gooper were side by side at the table, direckly across from Big Daddy, watchin' his face like hawks while they jawed an' jabbered about the cuteness an' brilliance of th' no-neck monsters!

(She giggles with a hand fluttering at her throat and her breast and her long throat arched.)
(She comes downstage and recreates the scene with voice and gesture.)

And the no-neck monsters were ranged around the table, some in high chairs and some on th' *Books of Knowledge*, all in fancy little paper caps in honor of Big Daddy's birthday, and all through dinner, well, I want you to know that Brother Man an' his partner never once, for one mo-

ment, stopped exchanging pokes an' pinches an'
kicks an' signs an' signals!—Why, they were like a
couple of cardsharps fleecing a sucker.—Even
Big Mama, bless her ole sweet soul, she isn't th'
quickest an' brightest thing in the world, she finally noticed, at last, an' said to Gooper,
"Gooper, what are you an' Mae makin' all these
signs at each other about?"—I swear t' goodness,
I nearly choked on my chicken!

(MARGARET, *back at the dressing table, still doesn't see*
BRICK. *He is watching her with a look that is not quite
definable—Amused? shocked? contemptuous?—part of
those and part of something else.*)

Y'know—your brother Gooper still cherishes the
illusion he took a giant step up the social ladder
when he married Miss Mae Flynn of the Memphis Flynns.
     But I have a piece of Spanish news for
Gooper. The Flynns never had a thing in this
world but money and they lost that, they were
nothing at all but fairly successful climbers. Of
course, Mae Flynn came out in Memphis eight
years before I made my debut in Nashville, but I
had friends at Ward-Belmont who came from
Memphis and they used to come to see me and I
used to go to see them for Christmas and spring
vacations, and so I know who rates an' who
doesn't rate in Memphis society. Why, y'know ole
Papa Flynn, he barely escaped doing time in the
Federal pen for shady manipulations on th' stock
market when his chain stores crashed, and as for
Mae having been a cotton carnival queen, as they
remind us so often, lest we forget, well, that's one
honor that I don't envy her for!—Sit on a brass
throne on a tacky float an' ride down Main
Street, smilin', bowin', and blowin' kisses to all
the trash on the street—

(*She picks out a pair of jeweled sandals and rushes to the
dressing table.*)

Why, year before last, when Susan McPheeters
was singled out fo' that honor, y' know what
happened to her? Y'know what happened to
poor little Susie McPheeters?
BRICK (*absently*): No. What happened to little Susie
     McPheeters?
MARGARET: Somebody spit tobacco juice in her face.
BRICK (*dreamily*): Somebody spit tobacco juice in her
     face.
MARGARET: That's right, some old drunk leaned out
     of a window in the Hotel Gayoso and yelled,
     "Hey, Queen, hey, hey, there, Queenie!" Poor
     Susie looked up and flashed him a radiant smile
     and he shot out a squirt of tobacco juice right in
     poor Susie's face.
BRICK: Well, what d'you know about that.

MARGARET (*gaily*): What do I know about it? I was
     there, I saw it!
BRICK (*absently*): Must have been kind of funny.
MARGARET: Susie didn't think so. Had hysterics.
     Screamed like a banshee. They had to stop th'
     parade an' remove her from her throne an' go
     on with—

(*She catches sight of him in the mirror, gasps slightly,
wheels about to face him. Count ten.*)

     —Why are you looking at me like that?
BRICK (*whistling softly, now*): Like what, Maggie?
MARGARET (*intensely, fearfully*): The way y' were
     lookin' at me just now, befo' I caught your eye in
     the mirror and you started t' whistle! I don't
     know how t' describe it but it froze my blood!—
     I've caught you lookin' at me like that so often
     lately. What are you thinkin' of when you look at
     me like that?
BRICK: I wasn't conscious of lookin' at you, Maggie.
MARGARET: Well, I was conscious of it! What were
     you thinkin'?
BRICK: I don't remember thinking of anything, Mag-
     gie.
MARGARET: Don't you think I know that—? Don't
     you—?—Think I know that—?
BRICK (*cooly*): Know *what*, Maggie?
MARGARET (*struggling for expression*): That I've gone
     through this—*hideous!*—*transformation*, be-
     come—*hard!* Frantic! (*Then she adds, almost ten-
     derly.*) —*cruel!!*
     That's what you've been observing in me
     lately. How could y' help but observe it? That's
     all right. I'm not—thin-skinned any more, can't
     afford t' be thin-skinned any more. (*She is now
     recovering her power.*) —But Brick? Brick?
BRICK: Did you say something?
MARGARET: I was *goin'* t' say something; that I get—
     lonely. Very!
BRICK: Ev'rybody gets that . . .
MARGARET: Living with someone you love can be
     lonelier—than living entirely *alone!*—if the one
     that y' love doesn't love you. . . .

(*There is a pause.* BRICK *hobbles downstage and asks,
without looking at her.*)

BRICK: Would you like to live alone, Maggie?

(*Another pause: then—after she has caught a quick, hurt
breath.*)

MARGARET: *No!—God!—I wouldn't!*

(*Another gasping breath. She forcibly controls what must
have been an impulse to cry out. We see her deliberately,
very forcibly, going all the way back to the world in which
you can talk about ordinary matters.*)

     Did you have a nice shower?

BRICK: Uh-huh.

MARGARET: Was the water cool?

BRICK: No.

MARGARET: But it made y' feel fresh, huh?

BRICK: Fresher. . . .

MARGARET: I know something would make y' feel *much* fresher!

BRICK: What?

MARGARET: An alcohol rub. Or cologne, a rub with cologne!

BRICK: That's good after a workout but I haven't been workin' out, Maggie.

MARGARET: You've kept in good shape, though.

BRICK (*indifferently*): You think so, Maggie?

MARGARET: I always thought drinkin' men lost their looks, but I was plainly mistaken.

BRICK (*wryly*): Why, thanks, Maggie.

MARGARET: You're the only drinkin' man I know that it never seems t' put fat on.

BRICK: I'm gettin' softer, Maggie.

MARGARET: Well, sooner or later it's bound to soften you up. It was just beginning to soften up Skipper when— (*She stops short.*) I'm sorry. I never could keep my fingers off a sore—I wish you *would* lose your looks. If you did it would make the martyrdom of Saint Maggie a little more bearable. But no such goddam luck. I actually believe you've gotten better looking since you've gone on the bottle. Yeah, a person who didn't know you would think you'd never had a tense nerve in your body or a strained muscle.

(*There are sounds of croquet on the lawn below: the click of mallets, light voices, near and distant.*)

Of course, you always had that detached quality as if you were playing a game without much concern over whether you won or lost, and not that you've lost the game, not lost but just quit playing, you have that rare sort of charm that usually only happens in very old or hopelessly sick people, the charm of the defeated.—You look so cool, so cool, so enviably cool.

REVEREND TOOKER (*off stage right*): Now looka here, boy, lemme show you how to get outa that!

MARGARET: They're playing croquet. The moon has appeared and it's white, just beginning to turn a little bit yellow. . . .

You were a wonderful lover. . . .

Such a wonderful person to go to bed with, and I think mostly because you were really indifferent to it. Isn't that right? Never had any anxiety about it, did it naturally, easily, slowly, with absolute confidence and perfect calm, more like opening a door for a lady or seating her at a table than giving expression to any longing for her. Your indifference made you wonderful at lovemaking—*strange?*—but true. . . .

REVEREND TOOKER: Oh! That's a beauty.

DOCTOR BAUGH: Yeah. I got you boxed.

MARGARET: You know, if I thought you would never, never, *never* make love to me again—I would go downstairs to the kitchen and pick out the longest and sharpest knife I could find and stick it straight into my heart, I swear that I would!

REVEREND TOOKER: Watch out, you're gonna miss it.

DOCTOR BAUGH: You just don't know me, boy!

MARGARET: But one thing I don't have is the charm of the defeated, my hat is still in the ring, and I am determined to win!

(*There is the sound of croquet mallets hitting croquet balls.*)

REVEREND TOOKER: Mmm—You're too slippery for me.

MARGARET: —What is the victory of a cat on a hot tin roof?—I wish I knew. . . .

Just staying on it, I guess, as long as she can. . . .

DOCTOR BAUGH: Jus' like an eel, boy, jus' like an eel!

(*More croquet sounds.*)

MARGARET: Later tonight I'm going to tell you I love you an' maybe by that time you'll be drunk enough to believe me. Yes, they're playing croquet. . . .

Big Daddy is dying of cancer. . . .

What were you thinking of when I caught you looking at me like that? Were you thinking of Skipper?

(BRICK *takes up his crutch, rises.*)

Oh, excuse me, forgive me, but laws of silence don't work! No, laws of silence don't work. . . .

(BRICK *crosses to the bar, takes a quick drink, and rubs his head with a towel.*)

Laws of silence don't work. . . .

When something is festering in your memory or your imagination, laws of silence don't work, it's just like shutting a door and locking it on a house on fire in hope of forgetting that the house is burning. But not facing a fire doesn't put it out. Silence about a thing just magnifies it. It grows and festers in silence, becomes malignant. . . .

(*He drops his crutch.*)

BRICK: Give me my crutch.

(*He has stopped rubbing his hair dry but still stands hanging onto the towel rack in a white towel-cloth robe.*)

MARGARET: Lean on me.

BRICK: No, just give me my crutch.

MARGARET: Lean on my shoulder.

BRICK: *I don't want to lean on your shoulder, I want my crutch!*

(*This is spoken like sudden lightning.*)

Are you going to give me my crutch or do I have to get down on my knees on the floor and—

MARGARET: *Here, here, take it, take it!* (*She has thrust the crutch at him.*)

BRICK (*hobbling out*): Thanks . . .

MARGARET: We mustn't scream at each other, the walls in this house have ears. . . .

(*He hobbles directly to liquor cabinet to get a new drink.*)

—but that's the first time I've heard you raise your voice in a long time, Brick. A crack in the wall?—Of composure?

—I think that's a good sign. . . .
A sign of nerves in a player on the defensive!

(BRICK *turns and smiles at her cooly over his fresh drink.*)

BRICK: It just hasn't happened yet, Maggie.

MARGARET: What?

BRICK: The click I get in my head when I've had enough of this stuff to make me peaceful. . . .
Will you do me a favor?

MARGARET: Maybe I will. What favor?

BRICK: Just, just keep your voice down!

MARGARET (*in a hoarse whisper*): I'll do you that favor, I'll speak in a whisper, if not shut up completely, if *you* will do *me* a favor and make that drink your last one till after the party.

BRICK: What party?

MARGARET: Big Daddy's birthday party.

BRICK: Is this Big Daddy's birthday?

MARGARET: You know this is Big Daddy's birthday!

BRICK: No, I don't, I forgot it.

MARGARET: Well, I remembered it for you. . . .

(*They are both speaking as breathlessly as a pair of kids after a fight, drawing deep exhausted breaths and looking at each other with faraway eyes, shaking and panting together as if they had broken apart from a violent struggle.*)

BRICK: Good for you, Maggie.

MARGARET: You just have to scribble a few lines on this card.

BRICK: You scribble something, Maggie.

MARGARET: It's got to be your handwriting; it's your present, I've given him my present; it's got to be your handwriting!

(*The tension between them is building again, the voices becoming shrill once more.*)

BRICK: I didn't get him a present.

MARGARET: I got one for you.

BRICK: All right. You write the card, then.

MARGARET: And have him know you didn't remember his birthday?

BRICK: I didn't remember his birthday.

MARGARET: You don't have to prove you didn't!

BRICK: I don't want to fool him about it.

MARGARET: Just write "Love, Brick!" for God's—

BRICK: No.

MARGARET: You've *got* to!

BRICK: I don't have to do anything I don't want to do. You keep forgetting the conditions on which I agreed to stay on living with you.

MARGARET (*out before she knows it*): I'm not living with you. We occupy the same cage.

BRICK: You've got to remember the conditions agreed on.

SONNY (*off stage*): Mommy, give it to me. I had it first.

MAE: Hush.

MARGARET: They're impossible conditions!

BRICK: Then why don't you—?

SONNY: I want it, I want it!

MAE: Get away!

MARGARET: HUSH! Who is out there? Is somebody at the door?

(*There are footsteps in hall.*)

MAE (*outside*): May I enter a moment?

MARGARET: OH, *you!* Sure. Come in, Mae.

(MAE *enters bearing aloft the bow of a young lady's archery set.*)

MAE: Brick, is this thing yours?

MARGARET: Why, Sister Woman—that's my Diana Trophy. Won it at the intercollegiate archery contest on the Ole Miss campus.

MAE: It's a mighty dangerous thing to leave exposed round a house full of nawmal rid-blooded children, attracted t'weapons.

MARGARET: "Nawmal rid-blooded children attracted t'weapons" ought t'be taught to keep their hands off things that don't belong to them.

MAE: Maggie, honey, if you had children of your own you'd know how funny that is. Will you please lock this up and put the key out of reach?

MARGARET: Sister Woman, nobody is plotting the destruction of your kiddies. —Brick and I still have our special archers' license. We're goin' deer-huntin' on Moon Lake as soon as the season starts. I love to run with dogs through chilly woods, run, run leap over obstructions— (*She goes into the closet carrying the bow.*)

MAE: How's the injured ankle, Brick?

BRICK: Doesn't hurt. Just itches.

MAE: Oh, my! Brick—Brick, you should've been downstairs after supper! Kiddies put on a show. Polly played the piano, Buster an' Sonny drums, an' then they turned out the lights an' Dixie an' Trixie puhfawmed a toe dance in fairy costume with *spahklus!* Big Daddy just beamed! He just beamed!

MARGARET (*from the closet with a sharp laugh*): Oh, I bet. It breaks my heart that we missed it! (*She reenters.*) But Mae? Why did y'give dawgs' names to all your kiddies?

MAE: *Dogs' names?*

MARGARET (*sweetly*): Dixie, Trixie, Buster, Sonny, Polly!—Sounds like four dogs and a parrot . . .

MAE: Maggie?

(MARGARET *turns with a smile.*)

Why are you so catty?

MARGARET: Cause I'm a cat! But why can't *you* take a joke, Sister Woman?

MAE: Nothin' pleases me more than a joke that's funny. You know the real names of our kiddies. Buster's real name is Robert. Sonny's real name is Saunders. Trixie's real name is Marlene and Dixie's—

(GOOPER *downstairs calls for her. "Hey, Mae! Sister Woman, intermission is over!"—she rushes to door, saying.*)

Intermission is over! See ya later!

MARGARET: I wonder what Dixie's real name is?

BRICK: Maggie, being catty doesn't help things any . . .

MARGARET: I know! *WHY!*—Am I so catty?—Cause I'm consumed with envy an' eaten up with longing?—Brick, I'm going to lay out your beautiful Shantung silk suit from Rome and one of your monogrammed silk shirts. I'll put your cuff links in it, those lovely star sapphires I get you to wear so rarely. . . .

BRICK: I can't get trousers on over this plaster cast.

MARGARET: Yes, you can, I'll help you.

BRICK: I'm not going to get dressed, Maggie.

MARGARET: Will you just put on a pair of white silk pajamas?

BRICK: Yes, I'll do that, Maggie.

MARGARET: *Thank* you, thank you so *much!*

BRICK: Don't mention it.

MARGARET: *Oh, Brick!* How long does it have t' go on? This punishment? Haven't I done time enough, haven't I served my term, can't I apply for a—pardon?

BRICK: Maggie, you're spoiling my liquor. Lately your voice always sounds like you'd been running upstairs to warn somebody that the house was on fire!

MARGARET: Well, no wonder, no wonder. Y'know what I feel like, Brick?

I feel all the time like a cat on a hot tin roof!

BRICK: Then jump off the roof, jump off it, cats can jump off roofs and land on their four feet uninjured!

MARGARET: Oh, yes!

BRICK: Do it!—fo' God's sake, do it . . .

MARGARET: Do what?

BRICK: Take a lover!

MARGARET: I can't see a man but you! Even with my eyes closed, I just see you! Why don't you get ugly, Brick, why don't you please get fat or ugly or something so I could stand it? (*She rushes to hall door, opens it, listens.*) The concert is still going on! Bravo, no-necks, bravo! (*She slams and locks door fiercely.*)

BRICK: What did you lock the door for?

MARGARET: To give us a little privacy for a while.

BRICK: You know better, Maggie.

MARGARET: No, I don't know better. . . .

(*She rushes to gallery doors, draws the rose-silk drapes across them.*)

BRICK: Don't make a fool of yourself.

MARGARET: I don't mind makin' a fool of myself over you!

BRICK: I mind, Maggie. I feel embarrassed for you.

MARGARET: Feel embarrassed! But don't continue my torture. I can't live on and on under these circumstances.

BRICK: You agreed to—

MARGARET: I know but—

BRICK: —Accept that condition!

MARGARET: *I CAN'T! I CAN'T! I CAN'T!* (*She seizes his shoulder.*)

BRICK: Let go!

(*He breaks away from her and seizes the small boudoir chair and raises it like a lion-tamer facing a big circus cat.*)

(*Count five. She stares at him with her fist pressed to her mouth, then bursts into shrill, almost hysterical laughter. He remains grave for a moment, then grins and puts the chair down.*)

(BIG MAMA *calls through closed door.*)

BIG MAMA: Son? Son? Son?

BRICK: What is it, Big Mama?

BIG MAMA (*outside*): Oh, son! We got the most wonderful news about Big Daddy. I just had t' run up an' tell you right this— (*She rattles the knob.*) —What's this door doin', locked, faw? You all think there's robbers in the house?

MARGARET: Big Mama, Brick is dressin', he's not dressed yet.

BIG MAMA: That's all right, it won't be the first time I've seen Brick not dressed. Come on, open this door!

(MARGARET, *with a grimace, goes to unlock and open the hall door, as* BRICK *hobbles rapidly to the bathroom and kicks the door shut.* BIG MAMA *has disappeared from the hall.*)

MARGARET: Big Mama?

(BIG MAMA *appears through the opposite gallery doors behind* MARGARET, *huffing and puffing like an old bulldog. She is a short, stout woman; her sixty years and 170 pounds have left her somewhat breathless most of the time; she's always tensed like a boxer, or rather, a Japanese wrestler. Her "family" was maybe a little superior to* BIG DADDY's *but not much. She wears a black or silver lace dress and at least half a million in flashy gems. She is very sincere.*)

BIG MAMA (*loudly, startling* MARGARET): Here—I come through Gooper's and Mae's gall'ry door. Where's Brick? *Brick*—Hurry on out of there, son, I just have a second and want to give you the news about Big Daddy.—I hate locked doors in a house. . . .

MARGARET (*with affected lightness*): I've noticed you do, Big Mama, but people have got to have *some* moments of privacy, don't they?

BIG MAMA: No, ma'am, not in *my* house. (*Without pause.*) Whacha took off you' dress faw? I thought that little lace dress was so sweet on yuh, honey.

MARGARET: I thought it looked sweet on me, too, but one of m' cute little table-partners used it for a napkin so—!

BIG MAMA (*picking up stockings on floor*): What?

MARGARET: You know, Big Mama, Mae and Gooper's so touchy about those children—thanks, Big Mama . . .

(BIG MAMA *has thrust the picked-up stockings in* MARGARET's *hand with a grunt.*)

—that you just don't dare to suggest there's any room for improvement in their—

BIG MAMA: Brick, hurry out!—Shoot, Maggie, you just don't like children.

MARGARET: I do SO like children! Adore them!—well brought up!

BIG MAMA (*gentle—loving*): Well, why don't you have some and bring them up well, then, instead of all the time pickin' on Gooper's an' Mae's?

GOOPER (*shouting up the stairs*): Hey, hey, Big Mama, Betsy an' Hugh got to go, waitin' t' tell yuh g'by!

BIG MAMA: Tell 'em to hold their hawses, I'll be right down in a jiffy!

GOOPER: Yes ma'am!

(*She turns to the bathroom door and calls out.*)

BIG MAMA: Son? Can you hear me in there?

(*There is a muffled answer.*)

We just got the full report from the laboratory at the Ochsner Clinic, completely negative, son, ev'rything negative, right on down the line! Nothin' a-tall's wrong with him but some little functional thing called a spastic colon. Can you hear me, son?

MARGARET: He can hear you, Big Mama.

BIG MAMA: Then why don't he say something? God Almighty, a piece of news like that should make him shout. It made *me* shout, I can tell you. I shouted and sobbed and fell right down on my knees!—Look! (*She pulls up her skirt.*) See the bruises where I hit my kneecaps? Took both doctors to haul me back on my feet!

(*She laughs—she always laughs like hell at herself.*)

Big Daddy was furious with me! But ain't that wonderful news?

(*Facing bathroom again, she continues.*)

After all the anxiety we been through to git a report like that on Big Daddy's birthday? Big Daddy tried to hide how much of a load that news took off his mind, but didn't fool *me*. He was mighty close to crying about it *himself!*

(*Goodbyes are shouted downstairs, and she rushes to door.*)

GOOPER: Big Mama!

BIG MAMA: *Hold those people down there, don't let them go!*—Now, git dressed, we're comin' up to this room fo' Big Daddy's birthday party because of your ankle.—How's his ankle, Maggie?

MARGARET: Well, he broke it, Big Mama.

BIG MAMA: I know he broke it.

(*A phone is ringing in hall. A Negro voice answers: "Mistuh Polly's res'dence."*)

I mean does it hurt him much still.

MARGARET: I'm afraid I can't give you that information, Big Mama. You'll have to ask Brick if it hurts much still or not.

SOOKEY (*in the hall*): It's Memphis, Mizz Polly, it's Miss Sally in Memphis.

BIG MAMA: Awright, Sookey.

(BIG MAMA *rushes into the hall and is heard shouting on the phone.*)

Hello, Miss Sally. How are you, Miss Sally?—Yes, well, I was just gonna call you about it. *Shoot!*

MARGARET: Brick, don't!

(BIG MAMA *raises her voice to a bellow.*)

BIG MAMA: *Miss Sally? Don't ever call me from the Gayoso Lobby, too much talk goes on in that hotel lobby, no wonder you can't hear me!* Now listen, Miss Sally. They's nothin' serious wrong with Big Daddy. We got the report just now, they's nothin' wrong but a thing called a—spastic! *SPASTIC!*—colon . . . (*She appears at the hall door and calls to* MARGARET.) —Maggie, come out here and talk to that fool on the phone. I'm shouted breathless!

MARGARET (*goes out and is heard sweetly at phone*): Miss Sally? This is Brick's wife, Maggie. So nice to hear your voice. Can you hear *mine*? Well, *good!*—Big Mama just wanted you to know that they've got the report from the Ochsner Clinic and what Big Daddy has is a spastic colon. Yes. Spastic colon, Miss Sally. That's right, spastic colon. *G'bye, Miss Sally, hope I'll see you real soon!*

(*Hangs up a little before* MISS SALLY *was probably ready to terminate the talk. She returns through the hall door.*)

She heard me perfectly. I've discovered with deaf people the thing to do is not shout at them but just enunciate clearly. My rich old Aunt Cornelia was deaf as the dead but I could make her hear me just by sayin' each word slowly, distinctly, close to her ear. I read her the *Commercial Appeal* ev'ry night, read her the classified ads in it, even, she never missed a word of it. But was she a mean ole thing! Know what I got when she died? Her unexpired subscriptions to five magazines and the Book-of-the-Month Club and a LIBRARY full of ev'ry dull book ever written! All else went to her hellcat of a sister . . . meaner than she was, even!

(BIG MAMA *has been straightening things up in the room during this speech.*)

BIG MAMA (*closing closet door on discarded clothes*): Miss Sally sure is a case! Big Daddy says she's always got her hand out fo' something. He's not mistaken. That poor ole thing always has her hand out fo' somethin'. I don't think Big Daddy gives her as much as he should.

GOOPER: Big Mama! Come on now! Betsy and Hugh can't wait no longer!

BIG MAMA (*shouting*): I'm comin'!

(*She starts out. At the hall door, turns and jerks a forefinger, first toward the bathroom door, then toward the liquor cabinet, meaning: "Has* BRICK *been drinking?"* MARGARET *pretends not to understand, cocks her head and raises her brows as if the pantomimic performance was completely mystifying to her.*)
(BIG MAMA *rushes back to* MARGARET.)

Shoot! *Stop playin' so dumb!*—I mean has he been drinkin' that stuff much yet?

MARGARET (*with a little laugh*): Oh! I think he had a highball after supper.

BIG MAMA: Don't laugh about it!—some single men stop drinkin' when they git married and others start! Brick never touched liquor before he—!

MARGARET (*crying out*): *THAT'S NOT FAIR!*

BIG MAMA: Fair or not fair I want to ask you a question, one question: D'you make Brick happy in bed?

MARGARET: Why don't you ask if he makes *me* happy in bed?

BIG MAMA: Because I know that—

MARGARET: *It works both ways!*

BIG MAMA: Something's not right! You're childless and my son drinks!

GOOPER: Come on, Big Mama!

(GOOPER *has called her downstairs and she has rushed to the door on the line above. She turns at the door and points at the bed.*)

—When a marriage goes on the rocks, the rocks are *there*, right *there*!

MARGARET: *That's*—

(BIG MAMA *has swept out of the room and slammed the door.*)

—not—*fair* . . .

(MARGARET *is alone, completely alone, and she feels it. She draws in, hunches her shoulders, raises her arms with fists clenched, shuts her eyes tight as a child about to be stabbed with a vaccination needle. When she opens her eyes again, what she sees is the long oval mirror and she rushes straight to it, stares into it with a grimace and says: "Who are you?"—Then she crouches a little and answers herself in a different voice which is high, thin, mocking: "I am Maggie the Cat!"—Straightens quickly as bathroom door opens a little and* BRICK *calls out to her.*)

BRICK: Has Big Mama gone?

MARGARET: She's gone.

(*He opens the bathroom door and hobbles out, with his liquor glass now empty, straight to the liquor cabinet. He is whistling softly.* MARGARET's *head pivots on her long, slender throat to watch him.*)
(*She raises a hand uncertainly to the base of her throat, as if it was difficult for her to swallow, before she speaks.*)

You know, our sex life didn't just peter out in the usual way, it was cut off short, long before the natural time for it to, and it's going to revive again, just as sudden as that. I'm confident of it. That's what I'm keeping myself attractive for. For the time when you'll see me again like other men see me. Yes, like other men see me. They still see me, Brick, and they like what they see. Uh-huh. Some of them would give their—
Look, Brick!

(*She stands before the long oval mirror, touches her breast and then her hips with her two hands.*)

How high my body stays on me!—Nothing has fallen on me—not a fraction. . . .

(*Her voice is soft and trembling: a pleading child's. At this moment as he turns to glance at her—a look which is like a player passing a ball to another player, third down and goal to go—she has to capture the audience in a grip so tight that she can hold it till the first intermission without any lapse of attention.)*

Other men still want me. My face looks strained, sometimes, but I've kept my figure as well as you've kept yours, and men admire it. I still turn heads on the street. Why, last week in Memphis everywhere that I went men's eyes burned holes in my clothes, at the country club and in restaurants and department stores, there wasn't a man I met or walked by that didn't just eat me up with his eyes and turn around when I passed him and look back at me. Why, at Alice's party for her New York cousins, the best-lookin' man in the crowd—followed me upstairs and tried to force his way in the powder room with me, followed me to the door and tried to force his way in!

BRICK: Why didn't you let him, Maggie?

MARGARET: Because I'm not that common, for one thing. Not that I wasn't almost tempted to. You like to know who it was? It was Sonny Boy Maxwell, that's who!

BRICK: Oh, yeah, Sonny Boy Maxwell, he was a good end-runner but had a little injury to his back and had to quit.

MARGARET: He has no injury now and has no wife and still has a lech for me!

BRICK: I see no reason to lock him out of a powder room in that case.

MARGARET: And have someone catch me at it? I'm not that stupid. Oh, I might sometime cheat on you with someone, since you're so insultingly eager to have me do it!—But if I do, you can be damned sure it will be in a place and a time where no one but me and the man could possibly know. Because I'm not going to give you any excuse to divorce me for being unfaithful or anything else. . . .

BRICK: Maggie, I wouldn't divorce you for being unfaithful or anything else. Don't you know that? Hell. I'd be relieved to know that you'd found yourself a lover.

MARGARET: Well, I'm taking no chances. No, I'd rather stay on this hot tin roof.

BRICK: A hot tin roof's 'n uncomfo'table place t' stay on. . . . *(He starts to whistle softly.)*

MARGARET *(through his whistle):* Yeah, but I can stay on it just as long as I have to.

BRICK: You could leave me, Maggie.

(He resumes whistle. She wheels about to glare at him.)

MARGARET: *Don't want to and will not!* Besides if I did, you don't have a cent to pay for it but what you get from Big Daddy and he's dying of cancer!

(For the first time a realization of BIG DADDY's doom seems to penetrate to BRICK's consciousness, visibly, and he looks at MARGARET.)

BRICK: Big Mama just said he *wasn't*, that the report was okay.

MARGARET: That's what she thinks because she got the same story that they gave Big Daddy. And was just as taken in by it as he was, poor ole things. . . .

But tonight they're going to tell her the truth about it. When Big Daddy goes to bed, they're going to tell her that he is dying of cancer. *(She slams the dresser drawer.)*—It's malignant and it's terminal.

BRICK: Does Big Daddy know it?

MARGARET: Hell, do they *ever* know it? Nobody says, "You're dying." You have to fool them. They have to fool *themselves.*

BRICK: Why?

MARGARET: *Why?* Because human beings dream of life everlasting, that's the reason! But most of them want it on earth and not in heaven.

(He gives a short, hard laugh at her touch of humor.)

Well. . . . *(She touches up her mascara.)* That's how it is, anyhow. . . . *(She looks about.)* Where did I put down my cigarette? Don't want to burn up the home-place, at least not with Mae and Gooper and their five monsters in it!

(She has found it and sucks at it greedily. Blows out smoke and continues.)

So this is Big Daddy's last birthday. And Mae and Gooper, they know it, oh, *they* know it, all right. They got the first information from the Ochsner Clinic. That's why they rushed down here with their no-neck monsters. Because. Do you know something? Big Daddy's made no will? Big Daddy's never made out any will in his life, and so this campaign's afoot to impress him, forcibly as possible, with the fact that you drink and I've borne no children!

(He continues to stare at her a moment, then mutters something sharp but not audible and hobbles rather rapidly out onto the long gallery in the fading, much faded, gold light.)

MARGARET *(continuing her liturgical chant):* Y'know, I'm *fond* of Big Daddy, I am genuinely fond of that old man, I really *am*, you know. . . .

BRICK *(faintly, vaguely):* Yes, I know you are. . . .

MARGARET: I've always sort of admired him in spite of his coarseness, his four-letter words and so forth. Because Big Daddy *is* what he *is*, and he makes no bones about it. He hasn't turned gentleman farmer, he's still a Mississippi redneck, as much of a redneck as he must have been when he was just overseer here on the old Jack Straw and Peter Ochello place. But he got hold of it an' built it into th' biggest an' finest plantation in the Delta.—I've always *liked* Big Daddy. . . .

(*She crosses to the proscenium.*)

Well, this is Big Daddy's last birthday. I'm sorry about it. But I'm facing the facts. It takes money to take care of a drinker and that's the office that I've been elected to lately.

BRICK: You don't have to take care of me.

MARGARET: Yes, I do. Two people in the same boat have got to take care of each other. At least you want money to buy more Echo Spring when this supply is exhausted, or will you be satisfied with a ten-cent beer?

Mae an' Gooper are plannin' to freeze us out of Big Daddy's estate because you drink and I'm childless. But we can defeat that plan. We're *going* to defeat that plan!

Brick, y'know, I've been so God damn disgustingly poor all my life!—That's the *truth*, Brick!

BRICK: I'm not sayin' it isn't.

MARGARET: Always had to suck up to people I couldn't stand because they had money and I was poor as Job's turkey. You don't know what that's like. Well, I'll tell you, it's like you would feel a thousand miles away from Echo Spring!—And had to get back to it on that broken ankle . . . without a crutch!

That's how it feels to be as poor as Job's turkey and have to suck up to relatives that you hated because they had money and all you had was a bunch of hand-me-down clothes and a few old moldy three-per-cent government bonds! My daddy loved his liquor, he fell in love with his liquor the way you've fallen in love with Echo Spring!—And my poor Mama, having to maintain some semblance of social position, to keep appearances up, on an income of one hundred and fifty dollars a month on those old government bonds!

When I came out, the year that I made my debut, I had just two evening dresses! One Mother made me from a pattern in *Vogue*, the other a hand-me-down from a snotty rich cousin I hated!

—The dress that I married you in was my grandmother's weddin' gown. . . .

So that's why I'm like a cat on a hot tin roof!

(BRICK *is still on the gallery. Someone below calls up to him in a warm Negro voice, "Hiya, Mistuh Brick, how yuh feelin'?"* BRICK *raises his liquor glass as if that answered the question.*)

MARGARET: You can be young without money, but you can't be old without it. You've got to be old *with* money because to be old without it is just too awful, you've got to be one or the other, either

young or *with money*, you can't be old and *without* it.—That's the *truth*, Brick. . . .

(BRICK *whistles softly, vaguely.*)

Well, now I'm dressed, I'm all dressed, there's nothing else for me to do. (*Forlornly, almost fearfully.*) I'm dressed, all dressed, nothing else for me to do. . . .

(*She moves about restlessly, aimlessly, and speaks, as if to herself.*)

What am I—? Oh!—my bracelets. . . .

(*She starts working a collection of bracelets over her hands onto her wrists, about six on each, as she talks.*)

I've thought a whole lot about it and now I know when I made my mistake. Yes, I made my mistake when I told you the truth about that thing with Skipper. Never should have confessed it, a fatal error, tellin' you about that thing with Skipper.

BRICK: Maggie, shut up about Skipper. I mean it, Maggie; you got to shut up about Skipper.

MARGARET: You ought to understand that Skipper and I—

BRICK: You don't think I'm serious, Maggie? You're fooled by the fact that I am saying this quiet? Look, Maggie. What you're doing is a dangerous thing to do. You're—you're—you're—foolin' with something that—nobody ought to fool with.

MARGARET: This time I'm going to finish what I have to say to you. Skipper and I made love, if love you could call it, because it made both of us feel a little bit closer to you. You see, you son of a bitch, you asked too much of people, of me, of him, of all the unlucky poor damned sons of bitches that happen to love you, and there was a whole pack of them, yes, there was a pack of them besides me and Skipper, you asked too goddam much of people that loved you, you—superior creature!—you godlike being!—And so we made love to each other to dream it was you, both of us! Yes, yes, yes! Truth, truth! What's so awful about it? I like it, I think the truth is—yeah! I shouldn't have told you. . . .

BRICK (*holding his head unnaturally still and uptilted a bit*): It was Skipper that told me about it. Not you, Maggie.

MARGARET: I told you!

BRICK: After he told me!

MARGARET: What does it matter who—?

DIXIE: I got your mallet, I got your mallet.

TRIXIE: Give it to me, give it to me, IT's mine.

(BRICK *turns suddenly out upon the gallery and calls.*)

BRICK: Little girl! Hey, little girl!

LITTLE GIRL (*at a distance*): What, Uncle Brick?

BRICK: Tell the folks to come up!—Bring everybody upstairs!

TRIXIE: It's mine, it's mine.

MARGARET: I can't stop myself! I'd go on telling you this in front of them all, if I had to!

BRICK: Little girl, Go on, go on, will you? Do what I told you, call them!

DIXIE: Okay.

MARGARET: Because it's got to be told and you, you!—you never let me!

(She sobs, then controls herself, and continues almost calmly.)

It was one of those beautiful, ideal things, they tell about in the Greek legends, it couldn't be anything else, you being you, and that's what made it so sad, and that's what made it so awful, because it was love that never could be carried through to anything satisfying or even talked about plainly.

BRICK: Maggie, you gotta stop this.

MARGARET: Brick, I tell you, you got to believe me, Brick, I *do* understand all about it! I—I think it was—*noble!* Can't you tell I'm sincere when I say I respect it? My only point, the only point that I'm making, is life has got to be allowed to continue even after the *dream* of life is —all— over....

(BRICK is without his crutch. Leaning on furniture, he crosses to pick it up as she continues as if possessed by a will outside herself.)

Why I remember when we double-dated at college, Gladys Fitzgerald and I and you and Skipper, it was more like a date between you and Skipper. Gladys and I were just sort of tagging along as if it was necessary to chaperone you!—to make a good public impression—

BRICK *(turns to face her, half lifting his crutch)*: Maggie, you want me to hit you with this crutch? Don't you know I could kill you with this crutch?

MARGARET: Good, Lord, man, d' you think I'd care if you did?

BRICK: One man has one great good true thing in his life. One great good thing which is true!—I had friendship with Skipper.—You are naming it dirty!

MARGARET: I'm not naming it dirty! I am naming it clean.

BRICK: Not love with you, Maggie, but friendship with Skipper was that one great true thing, and you are naming it dirty!

MARGARET: Then you haven't been listenin', not understood what I'm saying! I'm naming it so damn clean that it killed poor Skipper!—You two had something that had to be kept on ice, yes, incor-ruptible, yes!—and death was the only icebox where you could keep it. . . .

BRICK: I married you, Maggie. Why would I marry you, Maggie, if I was—?

MARGARET: Brick, let me finish!—I know, believe me I know, that it was only Skipper that harbored even any *unconscious* desire for anything not perfectly pure between you two!—Now let me skip a little. You married me early that summer we graduated out of Ole Miss, and we were happy, weren't we, we were blissful, yes, hit heaven together ev'ry time that we loved! But that fall you an' Skipper turned down wonderful offers of jobs in order to keep on bein' football heroes—pro-football heroes. You organized the Dixie Stars that fall, so you could keep on bein' teammates forever! But somethin' was not right with it!—*Me included!*—between you. Skipper began hittin' the bottle . . . you got a spinal injury—couldn't play the Thanksgivin' game in Chicago, watched it on TV from a traction bed in Toledo. I joined Skipper. The Dixie Stars lost because poor Skipper was drunk. We drank together that night all night in the bar of the Blackstone and when cold day was comin' up over the Lake an' we were comin' out drunk to take a dizzy look at it, I said, "SKIPPER! STOP LOVIN' MY HUSBAND OR TELL HIM HE'S GOT TO LET YOU ADMIT IT TO HIM!"—one way or another!

HE SLAPPED ME HARD ON THE MOUTH!—then turned and ran without stopping once, I am sure, all the way back into his room at the Blackstone. . . .

—When I came to his room that night, with a little scratch like a shy little mouse at his door, he made that pitiful, ineffectual little attempt to prove that what I had said wasn't true. . . .

(BRICK strikes at her with crutch, a blow that shatters the gemlike lamp on the table.)

—In this way, I destroyed him, by telling him truth that he and his world which he was born and raised in, yours and his world, had told him could not be told?

From then on Skipper was nothing at all but a receptacle for liquor and drugs. . . .

—*Who shot cock robin? I with my—* *(She throws back her head with tight shut eyes.)* —*merciful arrow!*

(BRICK strikes at her; misses.)

Missed me!—Sorry,—I'm not tryin' to whitewash my behavior, Christ, no! Brick, I'm not good. I don't know why people have to pretend to be good, nobody's good. The rich or the well-to-do can afford to respect moral patterns, conventional moral patterns, but I could never afford to, yeah, but—I'm honest! Give me credit for just that, will you *please*?—Born poor, raised poor, expect to die poor unless I manage to get us something out of what Big Daddy leaves when he dies of cancer! But Brick?!—*Skipper is dead!* *I'm alive!* Maggie the cat is—

(BRICK *hops awkwardly forward and strikes at her again with his crutch.*)

—alive! I am alive, alive! I am . . .

(*He hurls the crutch at her, across the bed she took refuge behind, and pitches forward on the floor as she completes her speech.*)

—alive!

(*A little girl,* DIXIE, *bursts into the room, wearing an Indian war bonnet and firing a cap pistol at* MARGARET *and shouting: "Bang, bang, bang!"*)
(*Laughter downstairs floats through the open hall door.* MARGARET *had crouched gasping to bed at child's entrance. She now rises and says with cool fury.*)

Little girl, your mother or someone should teach you—(*gasping*)—to knock at a door before you come into a room. Otherwise people might think that you—lack—good breeding. . . .

DIXIE: Yanh, yanh, yanh, what is Uncle Brick doin' on th' floor?

BRICK: I tried to kill your Aunt Maggie, but I failed—and I fell. Little girl, give me my crutch so I can get up off th' floor.

MARGARET: Yes, give your uncle his crutch, he's a cripple, honey, he broke his ankle last night jumping hurdles on the high school athletic field!

DIXIE: What were you jumping hurdles for, Uncle Brick?

BRICK: Because I used to jump them, and people like to do what they used to do, even after they've stopped being able to do it. . . .

MARGARET: That's right, that's your answer, now go away, little girl.

(DIXIE *fires cap pistol at* MARGARET *three times.*)

Stop, you stop that, monster! You little no-neck monster! (*She seizes the cap pistol and hurls it through gallery door.*)

DIXIE (*with a precocious instinct for the cruelest thing*): You're *jealous!*—You're just jealous because you can't have babies!

(*She sticks out her tongue at* MARGARET *as she sashays past her with her stomach stuck out, to the gallery.* MARGARET *slams the gallery doors and leans panting against them. There is a pause.* BRICK *has replaced his spilt drink and sits, faraway, on the great four-poster bed.*)

MARGARET: You see?—they gloat over us being child-less, even in front of their five little no-neck monsters!

(*Pause. Voices approach on the stairs.*)

Brick?—I've been to a doctor in Memphis, a—a gynecologist. . . .

I've been completely examined, and there is no reason why we can't have a child whenever we want one. And this is my time by the calendar to conceive. Are you listening to me? Are you? Are you LISTENING TO ME!

BRICK: Yes. I hear you, Maggie. (*His attention returns to her inflamed face.*) —But how in hell on earth do you imagine—that you're going to have a child by a man that can't stand you?

MARGARET: That's a problem that I will have to work out. (*She wheels about to face the hall door.*)

MAE (*off stage left*): Come on, Big Daddy. We're all goin' up to Brick's room.

(*From off stage left, voices:* REVEREND TOOKER, DOCTOR BAUGH, MAE.)

MARGARET: *Here they come!*

(*The lights dim.*)

ACT 2

(*There is no lapse of time.* MARGARET *and* BRICK *are in the same positions they held at the end of Act 1.*)

MARGARET (*at door*): *Here they come!*

(BIG DADDY *appears first, a tall man with a fierce, anxious look, moving carefully not to betray his weakness even, or especially, to himself.*)

GOOPER: I read in the *Register* that you're getting a new memorial window.

(*Some of the people are approaching through the hall, others along the gallery: voices from both directions.* GOOPER *and* REVEREND TOOKER *become visible outside gallery doors, and their voices come in clearly.*)
(*They pause outside as* GOOPER *lights a cigar.*)

REVEREND TOOKER (*vivaciously*): Oh, but St. Paul's in Grenada has three memorial windows, and the latest one is a Tiffany stained-glass window that cost twenty-five hundred dollars, a picture of Christ the Good Shepherd with a Lamb in His arms.

MARGARET: Big Daddy.

BIG DADDY: Well, Brick.

BRICK: Hello Big Daddy.—Congratulations!

BIG DADDY: —Crap. . . .

GOOPER: Who give that window, Preach?

REVEREND TOOKER: Clyde Fletcher's widow. Also presented St. Paul's with a baptismal font.

GOOPER: Y'know what somebody ought t' give your church is a *coolin'* system, Preach.

MAE (*almost religiously*): Let's see now, they've had their *tyyy*-phoid shots, and their tetanus shots, their diptheria shots and their hepatitis shots and their polio shots, they got *those* shots every month from May through September, and—Gooper? Hey! Gooper!—What all have the kiddies been shot faw?

REVEREND TOOKER: Yes, siree, Bob! And y'know what Gus Hamma's family gave in his memory to the church at Two Rivers? A complete new stone parish-house with a basketball court in the basement and a—

BIG DADDY (*uttering a loud barking laugh which is far from truly mirthful*): Hey, Preach! What's all this talk about memorials, Preach? Y' think somebody's about t' kick off around here? 'S that it?

(*Startled by this interjection, REVEREND TOOKER decides to laugh at the question almost as loud as he can.*)
(*How he would answer the question we'll never know, as he's spared that embarrassment by the voice of GOOPER's wife, MAE, rising high and clear as she appears with "DOC" BAUGH, the family doctor, through the hall door.*)

MARGARET (*overlapping a bit*): Turn on the hi-fi, Brick! Let's have some music t' start th' party with!

BRICK: You turn it on, Maggie.

(*The talk becomes so general that the room sounds like a great aviary of chattering birds. Only BRICK remains unengaged, leaning upon the liquor cabinet with his faraway smile, an ice cube in a paper napkin with which he now and then rubs his forehead. He doesn't respond to MARGARET's command. She bounds forward and stoops over the instrument panel of the console.*)

GOOPER: We gave 'em that thing for a third anniversay present, got three speakers in it.

(*The room is suddenly blasted by the climax of a Wagnerian opera or a Beethoven symphony.*)

BIG DADDY: *Turn that dam thing off!*

(*Almost instant silence, almost instantly broken by the shouting charge of BIG MAMA, entering through the hall door like a charging rhino.*)

BIG MAMA: Wha's my Brick, wha's mah precious baby!!
BIG DADDY: Sorry! Turn it back on!

(*Everyone laughs very loud. BIG DADDY is famous for his jokes at BIG MAMA's expense, and nobody laughs louder at these jokes than BIG MAMA herself, though sometimes they're pretty cruel and BIG MAMA has to pick up or fuss with something to cover the hurt that the loud laugh doesn't quite cover.*)
(*On this occasion, a happy occasion because the dread in her heart has also been lifted by the false report on BIG*

DADDY's *condition, she giggles, grotesquely, coyly, in* BIG DADDY's *direction and bears down upon* BRICK, *all very quick and alive.*)

BIG MAMA: Here he is, here's my precious baby! What's that you've got in your hand? You put that liquor down, son, your hand was made fo' holdin' somethin' better than that!

GOOPER: Look at Brick put it down!

(BRICK *has obeyed* BIG MAMA *by draining the glass and handing it to her. Again everyone laughs, some high, some low.*)

BIG MAMA: Oh, you bad boy, you, you're my bad little boy. Give Big Mama a kiss, you bad boy, you!—Look at him shy away, will you? Brick never liked bein' kissed or made a fuss over, I guess because he's always had too much of it!

Son, you turn that thing off!

(BRICK *has switched on the TV set.*)

I can't stand TV, radio was bad enough but TV has gone it one better, I mean—(*plops wheezing in chair*)—one worse, ha ha! Now what'm I sittin' down here faw? I want t' sit next to my sweetheart on the sofa, hold hands with him and love him up a little!

(BIG MAMA *has on a black and white figured chiffon. The large irregular patterns, like the markings of some massive animal, the luster of her great diamonds and many pearls, the brilliants set in the silver frames of her glasses, her riotous voice, booming laugh, have dominated the room since she entered.* BIG DADDY *has been regarding her with a steady grimace of chronic annoyance.*)

BIG MAMA (*still louder*): Preacher, Preacher, hey, Preach! Give me you' hand an' help me up from this chair!

REVEREND TOOKER: None of your tricks, Big Mama!

BIG MAMA: What tricks? You give me you' hand so I can get up an'—

(REVEREND TOOKER *extends her his hand. She grabs it and pulls him into her lap with a shrill laugh that spans an octave in two notes.*)

Ever seen a preacher in a fat lady's lap? Hey, hey, folks! Ever seen a preacher in a fat lady's lap?

(BIG MAMA *is notorious throughout the Delta for this sort of inelegant horseplay.* MARGARET *looks on with indulgent humor, sipping Dubonnet "on the rocks" and watching* BRICK, *but* MAE *and* GOOPER *exchange signs of humorless anxiety over these antics, the sort of behavior which* MAE *thinks may account for their failure to quite get in with the smartest young married set in Memphis, despite all. One of the Negroes,* LACY *or* SOOKEY, *peeks in, cackling. They are waiting for a sign to bring in the cake and champagne. But* BIG DADDY's *not amused. He doesn't understand why, in spite of the infinite mental relief he's received from the doctor's report, he still has these same old fox teeth in his guts. "This spastic condition is something else," he says to himself, but aloud he roars at* BIG MAMA.)

BIG DADDY: *BIG MAMA, WILL YOU QUIT HORSIN'?*—You're too old an' too fat fo' that sort of crazy kid stuff an' besides a woman with your blood pressure—she had two hundred last spring!—is riskin' a stroke when you mess around like that. . . .

(MAE *blows on a pitch pipe.*)

BIG MAMA: *Here comes Big Daddy's birthday!*

(*Negroes in white jackets enter with an enormous birthday cake ablaze with candles and carrying buckets of champagne with satin ribbons about the bottle necks.* MAE *and* GOOPER *strike up song, and everybody, including the* NEGROES *and* CHILDREN, *joins in. Only* BRICK *remains aloof.*)

EVERYONE:
> Happy birthday to you.
> Happy birthday to you.
> Happy birthday, Big Daddy—

(*Some sing: "Dear, Big Daddy!"*)

> Happy birthday to you.

(*Some sing: "How old are you?"*)
(MAE *has come down center and is organizing her children like a chorus. She gives them a barely audible: "One, two, three!" and they are off in the new tune.*)

CHILDREN:
> Skinamarinka—dinka—dink
> Skinamarinka—do
> We love you.
> Skinamarinka—dinka—dink
> Skinamarinka—do.

(*All together, they turn to* BIG DADDY.)

> Big Daddy, you!

(*They turn back front, like a musical comedy chorus.*)

> We love you in the morning;
> We love you in the night.
> We love you when we're with you,
> And we love you out of sight.
> Skinamarinka—dinka—dink
> Skinamarinka—do.

(MAE *turns to* BIG MAMA.)

> Big Mama, too!

(BIG MAMA *bursts into tears. The* NEGROES *leave.*)

BIG DADDY: Now Ida, what the hell is the matter with you?

MAE: She's just so happy.

BIG MAMA: I'm just so happy, Big Daddy, I have to cry or something.

(*Sudden and loud in the hush.*)

Brick, do you know the wonderful news that Doc Baugh got from the clinic about Big Daddy? Big Daddy's one hundred per cent!

MARGARET: Isn't that wonderful?

BIG MAMA: He's just one hundred per cent. Passed the examination with flying colors. Now that we know there's nothing wrong with Big Daddy but a spastic colon, I can tell you something. I was worried sick, half out of my mind, for fear Big Daddy might have a thing like—

(MARGARET *cuts through this speech, jumping up and exclaiming shrilly.*)

MARGARET: Brick, honey, aren't you going to give Big Daddy his birthday present?

(*Passing by him, she snatches his liquor glass from him.*)
(*She picks up a fancily wrapped package.*)

Here it is, Big Daddy, this is from Brick!

BIG MAMA: This is the biggest birthday Big Daddy's ever had, a hundred presents and bushels of telegrams from—

MAE (*at same time*): What is it, Brick?

GOOPER: I bet 500 to 50 that Brick don't *know* what it is.

BIG MAMA: The fun of presents is not knowing what they are till you open the package. Open your present, Big Daddy.

BIG DADDY: Open it you'self. I want to ask Brick somethin'! Come here, Brick.

MARGARET: Big Daddy's callin' you, Brick. (*She is opening the package.*)

BRICK: Tell Big Daddy I'm crippled.

BIG DADDY: I see you're crippled. I want to know how you got crippled.

MARGARET (*making diversionary tactics*): Oh, look, oh, look, why, it's a cashmere robe! (*She holds the robe up for all to see.*)

MAE: You sound surprised, Maggie.

MARGARET: I never saw one before.

MAE: That's funny.—*Hah!*

MARGARET (*turning on her fiercely, with a brilliant smile*): Why is it funny? All my family ever had was family—and luxuries such as cashmere robes still surprise me!

BIG DADDY (*ominously*): Quiet!

MAE (*heedless in her fury*): I don't see how you could be so surprised when you bought it yourself at Loewenstein's in Memphis last Saturday. You know how I know?

BIG DADDY: I said, Quiet!

MAE: —I know because the salesgirl that sold it to you waited on me and said, Oh, Mrs. Pollitt, your sister-in-law just bought a cashmere robe for your husband's father!

MARGARET: Sister Woman! Your talents are wasted as a housewife and mother, you really ought to be with the FBI or—

BIG DADDY: QUIET!

(REVEREND TOOKER's *reflexes are slower than the others'. He finishes a sentence after the bellow.)*

REVEREND TOOKER (*to* DOC BAUGH): —the Stork and the Reaper are running neck and neck!

(He starts to laugh gaily when he notices the silence and BIG DADDY's *glare. His laugh dies falsely.)*

BIG DADDY: Preacher, I hope I'm not butting in on more talk about memorial stained-glass windows, am I, Preacher?

(REVEREND TOOKER *laughs feebly, then coughs dryly in the embarrassed silence.)*

Preacher?

BIG MAMA: Now, Big Daddy, don't you pick on Preacher!

BIG DADDY (*raising his voice*): You ever hear that expression all hawk and no spit? You bring that expression to mind with that little dry cough of yours, all hawk an' no spit. . . .

(The pause is broken only by a short startled laugh from MARGARET, *the only one there who is conscious of and amused by the grotesque.)*

MAE (*raising her arms and jangling her bracelets*): I wonder if the mosquitoes are active tonight?

BIG DADDY: What's that, Little Mama? Did you make some remark?

MAE: Yes, I said I wondered if the mosquitoes would eat us alive if we went out on the gallery for a while.

BIG DADDY: Well, if they do, I'll have your bones pulverized for fertilizer!

BIG MAMA (*quickly*): Last week we had an airplane spraying the place and I think it done some good, at least I haven't had a—

BIG DADDY (*cutting her speech*): Brick, they tell me, if what they tell me is true, that you done some jumping last night on the high school athletic field!

BIG MAMA: Brick, Big Daddy is talking to you, son.

BRICK (*smiling vaguely over his drink*): What was that, Big Daddy?

BIG DADDY: They said you done some jumping on the high school track field last night.

BRICK: That's what they told me, too.

BIG DADDY: Was it jumping or humping that you were doing out there? What were you doing out there at three A.M., layin' a woman on that cinder track?

BIG MAMA: Big Daddy, you are off the sick-list, now, and I'm not going to excuse you for talkin' so—

BIG DADDY: Quiet!

BIG MAMA: —*nasty* in front of Preacher and—

BIG DADDY: *QUIET!*—I ast you, Brick, if you was cuttin' you'self a piece o' poon-tang last night on that cinder track? I thought maybe you were chasin' poon-tang on that track an' tripped over something in the heat of the chase—'sthat it?

(GOOPER *laughs, loud and false, others nervously following suit.* BIG MAMA *stamps her foot, and purses her lips, crossing to* MAE *and whispering something to her as* BRICK *meets his father's hard, intent, grinning stare with a slow, vague smile that he offers all situations from behind the screen of his liquor.)*

BRICK: No, sir, I don't think so. . . .

MAE (*at the same time, sweetly*): Reverend Tooker, let's you and I take a stroll on the widow's walk.

(She and the preacher go out on the gallery as BIG DADDY *says.)*

BIG DADDY: Then what the hell were you doing out there at three o'clock in the morning?

BRICK: Jumping the hurdles, Big Daddy, runnin' and jumpin' the hurdles, but those high hurdles have gotten too high for me, now.

BIG DADDY: Cause you was drunk?

BRICK (*his vague smile fading a little*): Sober I wouldn't have tried to jump the *low* ones. . . .

BIG MAMA (*quickly*): Big Daddy, blow out the candles on your birthday cake!

MARGARET (*at the same time*): I want to propose a toast to Big Daddy Pollitt on his sixty-fifth birthday, the biggest cotton planter in—

BIG DADDY (*bellowing with fury and disgust*): *I told you to stop it, now stop it, quit this—!*

BIG MAMA (*coming in front of* BIG DADDY *with the cake*).: Big Daddy, I will not allow you to talk that way, not even on your birthday, I—

BIG DADDY: I'll talk like I want to on my birthday, Ida, or any other goddam day of the year and anybody here that don't like it knows what they can do!

BIG MAMA: You don't mean that!

BIG DADDY: What makes you think I don't mean it?

(Meanwhile various discreet signals have been exchanged and GOOPER *has also gone out on the gallery.)*

BIG MAMA: I just know you don't mean it.

BIG DADDY: You don't know a goddam thing and you never did!

BIG MAMA: Big Daddy, you don't mean that.

BIG DADDY: Oh, yes, I do, oh, yes, I do, I mean it! I

put up with a whole lot of crap around here because I thought I was dying. And you thought I was dying and you started taking over, well, you can stop taking over now, Ida, because I'm not gonna die, you can just stop now this business of taking over because you're not taking over because I'm not dying, I went through the laboratory and the goddam exploratory operation and there's nothing wrong with me but a spastic colon. And I'm not dying of cancer which you thought I was dying of. Ain't that so? Didn't you think that I was dying of cancer, Ida?

(Almost everybody is out on the gallery but the two old people glaring at each other across the blazing cake.)
(BIG MAMA's chest heaves and she presses a fat fist to her mouth.)
(BIG DADDY continues, hoarsely.)

Ain't that so, Ida? Didn't you have an idea I was dying of cancer and now you could take control of this place and everything on it? I got that impression, I seemed to get that impression. Your loud voice everywhere, your fat old body butting in here and there!

BIG MAMA: Hush! The Preacher!
BIG DADDY: Fuck the goddam preacher!

(BIG MAMA gasps loudly and sits down on the sofa which is almost too small for her.)

Did you hear what I said? I said fuck the goddam preacher!

(Somebody closes the gallery doors from outside just as there is a burst of fireworks and excited cries from the children.)

BIG MAMA: I never seen you act like this before and I can't think what's got in you!
BIG DADDY: I went through all that laboratory and operation and all just so I would know if you or me was boss here! Well, now it turns out that I am and you ain't—and that's my birthday present—and my cake and champagne!—because for three years now you been gradually taking over. Bossing. Talking. Sashaying your fat old body around the place I made! I made this place! I was overseer on it! I was the overseer on the old Straw and Ochello plantation. I quit school at ten! I quit school at ten years old and went to work like a nigger in the fields. And I rose to be overseer of the Straw and Ochello plantation. And old Straw died and I was Ochello's partner and the place got bigger and bigger and bigger and bigger and bigger! I did all that myself with no goddam help from you, and now you think you're just about to take over. Well, I am just about to tell you that you are not just about to take over, you are not just about to take

over a God damn thing. Is that clear to you, Ida? Is that very plain to you, now? Is that understood completely? I been through the laboratory from A to Z. I've had the goddam exploratory operation, and nothing is wrong with me but a spastic colon—made spastic, I guess, by *disgust!* By all the goddam lies and liars that I have had to put up with, and all the goddam hypocrisy that I lived with all these forty years that we been livin' together!

Hey! Ida!! Blow out the candles on the birthday cake! Purse up your lips and draw a deep breath and blow out the goddam candles on the cake!

BIG MAMA: Oh, Big Daddy, oh, oh, oh, Big Daddy!
BIG DADDY: What's the matter with you?
BIG MAMA: *In all these years you never believed that I loved you??*
BIG DADDY: Huh?
BIG MAMA: *And I did. I did so much. I did love you!—I even loved your hate and your hardness, Big Daddy! (She sobs and rushes awkwardly out onto the gallery.)*
BIG DADDY *(to himself)*: *Wouldn't it be funny if that was true....*

(A pause is followed by a burst of light in the sky from the fireworks.)

BRICK! HEY, BRICK!

(He stands over his blazing birthday cake.)
(After some moments, BRICK hobbles in on his crutch, holding his glass. MARGARET follows him with a bright, anxious smile.)

I didn't call you, Maggie. I called Brick.
MARGARET: I'm just delivering him to you.

(She kisses BRICK on the mouth which he immediately wipes with the back of his hand. She flies girlishly back out. BRICK and his father are alone.)

BIG DADDY: Why did you do that?
BRICK: Do what, Big Daddy?
BIG DADDY: Wipe her kiss off your mouth like she'd spit on you.
BRICK: I don't know. I wasn't conscious of it.
BIG DADDY: That woman of yours has a better shape on her than Gooper's but somehow or other they got the same look about them.
BRICK: What sort of look is that, Big Daddy?
BIG DADDY: I don't know how to describe it but it's the same look.
BRICK: They don't look peaceful, do they?
BIG DADDY: No, they sure in hell don't.
BRICK: They look nervous as cats?
BIG DADDY: That's right, they look nervous as cats.
BRICK: Nervous as a couple of cats on a hot tin roof?
BIG DADDY: That's right, boy, they look like a couple

of cats on a hot tin roof. It's funny that you and Gooper being so different would pick out the same type of woman.

BRICK: Both of us married into society, Big Daddy.

BIG DADDY: Crap . . . I wonder what gives them both that look?

BRICK: Well. They're sittin' in the middle of a big piece of land, Big Daddy, twenty-eight thousand acres is a pretty big piece of land and so they're squaring off on it, each determined to knock off a bigger piece of it than the other whenever you let it go.

BIG DADDY: I got a surprise for those women. I'm not gonna let it go for a long time yet if that's what they're waiting for.

BRICK: That's right, Big Daddy. You just sit tight and let them scratch each other's eyes out. . . .

BIG DADDY: You bet your life I'm going to sit tight on it and let those sons of bitches scratch their eyes out, ha ha ha. . . .

But Gooper's wife's a good breeder, you got to admit she's fertile. Hell, at supper tonight she had them all at the table and they had to put a couple of extra leafs in the table to make room for them, she's got five head of them, now, and another one's comin'.

BRICK: Yep, number six is comin'. . . .

BIG DADDY: Six hell, she'll probably drop a litter next time. Brick, you know, I swear to God, I don't know the way it happens?

BRICK: The way what happens, Big Daddy?

BIG DADDY: You git you a piece of land, by hook or crook, an' things start growin' on it, things accumulate on it, and the first thing you know it's completely out of hand, completely out of hand!

BRICK: Well, they say nature hates a vacuum, Big Daddy.

BIG DADDY: That's what they say, but sometimes I think that a vacuum is a hell of a lot better than some of the stuff that nature replaces it with.

Is someone out there by that door?

GOOPER: Hey Mae.

BRICK: Yep.

BIG DADDY: Who? (He has lowered his voice.)

BRICK: Someone int'rested in what we say to each other.

BIG DADDY: Gooper?—GOOPER!

(After a discreet pause, MAE appears in the gallery door.)

MAE: Did you call Gooper, Big Daddy?

BIG DADDY: Aw, it was you.

MAE: Do you want Gooper, Big Daddy?

BIG DADDY: No, and I don't want you. I want some privacy here, while I'm having a confidential talk with my son Brick. Now it's too hot in here to close them doors, but if I have to close those fuckin' doors in order to have a private talk with

my son Brick, just let me know and I'll close 'em. Because I hate eavesdroppers, I don't like any kind of sneakin' an' spyin'.

MAE: Why, Big Daddy—

BIG DADDY: You stood on the wrong side of the moon, it threw your shadow!

MAE: I was just—

BIG DADDY: You was just nothing but *spyin'* an' you *know* it!

MAE (*begins to sniff and sob*): Oh, Big Daddy, you're so unkind for some reason to those that really love you!

BIG DADDY: Shut up, shut up, shut up! I'm going to move you and Gooper out of that room next to this! It's none of your goddam business what goes on in here at night between Brick an' Maggie. You listen at night like a couple of rutten peekhole spies and go and give a report on what you hear to Big Mama an' she comes to me and says they say such and such and so and so about what they heard goin' on between Brick an' Maggie, and Jesus, it makes me sick. I'm goin' to move you an' Gooper out of that room, I can't stand sneakin' an' spyin', it makes me puke. . . .

(MAE *throws back her head and rolls her eyes heavenward and extends her arms as if invoking God's pity for this unjust martyrdom; then she presses a handkerchief to her nose and flies from the room with a loud swish of skirts.*)

BRICK (*now at the liquor cabinet*): They listen, do they?

BIG DADDY: Yeah. They listen and give reports to Big Mama on what goes on in here between you and Maggie. They say that— (*He stops as if embarrassed.*) —You won't sleep with her, that you sleep on the sofa. Is that true or not true? If you don't like Maggie, get rid of Maggie!—What are you doin' there now?

BRICK: Fresh'nin up my drink.

BIG DADDY: Son, you know you got a real liquor problem?

BRICK: Yes, sir, yes, I know.

BIG DADDY: Is that why you quit sports-announcing, because of this liquor problem?

BRICK: Yes, sir, yes, sir, I guess so.

(*He smiles vaguely and amiably at his father across his replenished drink.*)

BIG DADDY: Son, don't guess about it, it's too important.

BRICK (*vaguely*): Yes, sir.

BIG DADDY: And listen to me, don't look at the damn chandelier. . . .

(*Pause.* BIG DADDY'*s voice is husky.*)

—Somethin' else we picked up at th' big fire sale in Europe.

(Another pause.)

Life is important. There's nothing else to hold
onto. A man that drinks is throwing his life away.
Don't do it, hold onto your life. There's nothing
else to hold onto. . . .

Sit down over here so we don't have to raise
our voices, the walls have ears in this place.

BRICK *(hobbling over to sit on the sofa beside him)*: All
right, Big Daddy.

BIG DADDY: Quit!—how'd that come about? Some
disappointment?

BRICK: I don't know. Do you?

BIG DADDY: I'm askin' you, God damn it! How in hell
would I know if you don't?

BRICK: I just got out there and found that I had a
mouth full of cotton. I was always two or three
beats behind what was goin' on on the field and
so I—

BIG DADDY: Quit!

BRICK *(amiably)*: Yes, quit.

BIG DADDY: Son?

BRICK: Huh?

BIG DADDY *(inhales loudly and deeply from his cigar; then
bends suddenly a little forward, exhaling loudly and
raising a hand to his forehead)*: Whew!—ha ha!—I
took in too much smoke, it made me a little
lightheaded. . . .

(The mantel clock chimes.)

Why is it so damn hard for people to talk?

BRICK: Yeah. . . .

*(The clock goes on sweetly chiming till it has completed the
stroke of ten.)*

—Nice peaceful-soundin' clock, I like to hear it
all night. . . .

(He slides low and comfortable on the sofa; BIG DADDY
*sits straight and rigid with some unspoken anxiety. All his
gestures are tense and jerky as he talks. He wheezes and
pants and sniffs through his nervous speech, glancing
quickly, shyly, from time to time, at his son.)*

BIG DADDY: We got that clock the summer we wint to
Europe, me an' Big Mama on that damn Cook's
Tour, never had such an awful time in my life.
I'm tellin' you, son, those gooks over there, they
gouge your eyeballs out in their grand hotels.
And Big Mama bought more stuff than you
could haul in a couple of boxcars, that's no crap.
Everywhere she wint on this whirlwind tour, she
bought, bought, bought. Why, half that stuff she
bought is still crated up in the cellar, under water
last spring! *(He laughs.)*

That Europe is nothin' on earth but a great
big auction, that's all it is, that bunch of old
worn-out places, it's just a big firesale, the whole
fuckin' thing, an' Big Mama wint wild in it, why,
you couldn't hold that woman with a mule's harness! Bought, bought, bought!—lucky I'm a rich
man, yes siree, Bob, an' half that stuff is mildew-
in' in th' basement. It's lucky I'm a rich man, it
sure is lucky, well, I'm a rich man, Brick, yep, I'm
a mighty rich man. *(His eyes light up for a moment.)*

Y'know how much I'm worth? Guess, Brick!
Guess how much I'm worth!

*(*BRICK *smiles vaguely over his drink.)*

Close on ten million in cash an' blue-chip stocks,
outside, mind you, of twenty-eight thousand
acres of the richest land this side of the valley
Nile!

But a man can't buy his life with it, he can't
buy back his life with it when his life has been
spent, that's one thing not offered in the Europe
fire-sale or in the American markets or any markets on earth, a man can't buy his life with it, he
can't buy back his life when his life is finished.

That's a sobering thought, a very sobering
thought, and that's a thought that I was turning
over in my head, over and over and over—until
today. . . .

I'm wiser and sadder, Brick, for this experience which I just gone through. They's one thing
else that I remember in Europe.

BRICK: What is that, Big Daddy?

BIG DADDY: The hills around Barcelona in the country of Spain and the children running over those
bare hills in their bare skins beggin' like starvin'
dogs with howls and screeches, and how fat the
priests are on the streets of Barcelona, so many
of them and so fat and so pleasant, ha ha!—
Y'know I could feed that country? I got money
enough to feed that goddam country, but the
human animal is a selfish beast and I don't
reckon the money I passed out there to those
howling children in the hills around Barcelona
would more than upholster the chairs in this
room, I mean pay to put a new cover on this
chair!

Hell, I threw them money like you'd scatter
feed corn for chickens, I threw money at them
just to get rid of them long enought to climb
back into th' car and—drive away. . . .

And then in Morocco, them Arabs, why, I remember one day in Marrakech, that old walled
Arab city, I set on a broken-down wall to have a
cigar, it was fearful hot there and this Arab
woman stood in the road and looked at me till I
was embarrassed, she stood stock still in the
dusty hot road and looked at me till I was embarrassed. But listen to this. She had a naked child
with her, a little naked girl with her, barely able
to toddle, and after a while she set this child on

the ground and give her a push and whispered something to her.

This child come toward me, barely able t' walk, come toddling up to me and—

Jesus, it makes you sick to' remember a thing like this!

It stuck out its hand and tried to unbutton my trousers!

That child was not yet five! Can you believe me? Or do you think that I am making this up? I wint back to the hotel and said to Big Mama, Git packed! We're clearing out of this country. . . .

BRICK: Big Daddy, you're on a talkin' jag tonight.

BIG DADDY (*ignoring this remark*): Yes, sir, that's how it is, the human animal is a beast that dies but the fact that he's dying don't give him pity for others, no, sir, it—

—Did you say something?

BRICK: Yes.

BIG DADDY: What?

BRICK: Hand me over that crutch so I can get up.

BIG DADDY: Where you goin'?

BRICK: I'm takin' a little short trip to Echo Spring.

BIG DADDY: To where?

BRICK: Liquor cabinet. . . .

BIG DADDY: Yes, sir, boy— (*He hands* BRICK *the crutch*) —the human animal is a beast that dies and if he's got money he buys and buys and buys and I think the reason he buys everything he can buy is that in the back of his mind he has the crazy hope that one of his purchases will be life everlasting!—Which it never can be. . . . The human animal is a beast that—

BRICK (*at the liquor cabinet*): Big Daddy, you sure are shootin' th' breeze here tonight.

(*There is a pause and voices are heard outside.*)

BIG DADDY: I been quiet here lately, spoke not a word, just sat and stared into space. I had something heavy weighing on my mind but tonight that load was took off me. That's why I'm talking.—The sky looks diff'rent to me. . . .

BRICK: You know what I like to hear most?

BIG DADDY: What?

BRICK: Solid quiet. Perfect unbroken quiet.

BIG DADDY: Why?

BRICK: Because it's more peaceful.

BIG DADDY: Man, you'll hear a lot of that in the grave. (*He chuckles agreeably.*)

BRICK: Are you through talkin' to me?

BIG DADDY: Why are you so anxious to shut me up?

BRICK: Well, sir, ever so often you say to me, Brick, I want to have a talk with you, but when we talk, it never materializes. Nothing is said. You sit in a chair and gas about this and that and I look like I listen. I try to look like I listen, but I don't listen, not much. Communication is—awful hard be-

tween people an'—somehow between you and me, it just don't—happen.

BIG DADDY: Have you ever been scared? I mean have you ever felt downright terror of something? (*He gets up.*) Just one moment. (*He looks off as if he were going to tell an important secret.*)

Brick?

BRICK: What?

BIG DADDY: Son, I thought I had it!

BRICK: Had what? Had what, Big Daddy?

BIG DADDY: Cancer!

BRICK: Oh . . .

BIG DADDY: I thought the old man made out of bones had laid his cold and heavy hand on my shoulder!

BRICK: Well, Big Daddy, you kept a tight mouth about it.

BIG DADDY: A pig squeals. A man keeps a tight mouth about it, in spite of a man not having a pig's advantage.

BRICK: What advantage is that?

BIG DADDY: Ignorance—of mortality—is a comfort. A man don't have that comfort, he's the only living thing that conceives of death, that knows what it is. The others go without knowing which is the way that anything living should go, go without knowing, without any knowledge of it, and yet a pig squeals, but a man sometimes, he can keep a tight mouth about it. Sometimes he—

(*There is a deep smoldering ferocity in the old man.*)

—can keep a tight mouth about it. I wonder if—

BRICK: What, Big Daddy?

BIG DADDY: A whiskey highball would injure this spastic condition?

BRICK: No, sir, it might do it good.

BIG DADDY (*grins suddenly, wolfishly*): Jesus, I can't tell you! The sky is open! Christ, it's open again! It's open boy, it's open!

(BRICK *looks down at his drink.*)

BRICK: You feel better, Big Daddy?

BIG DADDY: Better? Hell! I can breathe!—All of my life I been like a doubled up fist. . . . (*He pours a drink.*) —Poundin', smashin', drivin'!—now I'm going to loosen these doubled-up hands and touch things *easy* with them. . . .

(*He spreads his hands as if caressing the air.*)

You know what I'm contemplating?

BRICK (*vaguely*): No, sir. What are you contemplating?

BIG DADDY: Ha ha!—*Pleasure!*—pleasure with *women!*

(BRICK's *smile fades a little but lingers.*)

—Yes, boy. I'll tell you something that you might

not guess. I still have desire for women and this is my sixty-fifth birthday.

BRICK: I think that's mighty remarkable, Big Daddy.

BIG DADDY: Remarkable?

BRICK: *Admirable*, Big Daddy.

BIG DADDY: You're damn right it is, remarkable and admirable both. I realize now that I never had me enough. I let many chances slip by because of scruples about it, scruples, convention—crap. . . . All that stuff is bull, bull, bull!—It took the shadow of death to make me see it. Now that shadow's lifted, I'm going to cut loose and have, what is it they call it, have me a—ball!

BRICK: A ball, huh?

BIG DADDY: That's right, a ball, a ball! Hell!—I slept with Big Mama till, let's see, five years ago, till I was sixty and she was fifty-eight, and never even liked her, never did!

(The phone has been ringing down the hall. BIG MAMA *enters, exclaiming.)*

BIG MAMA: Don't you men hear that phone ring? I heard it way out on the gall'ry.

BIG DADDY: There's five rooms off this front gall'ry that you could go through. Why do you go through this one?

*(*BIG MAMA *makes a playful face as she bustles out the hall door.)*

Hunh!—Why, when Big Mama goes out of a room, I can't remember what that woman looks like—

BIG MAMA: Hello.

BIG DADDY: But when Big Mama comes back into the room, boy, then I see what she looks like, and I wish I didn't.

(Bends over laughing at this joke till it hurts his guts and he straightens with a grimace. The laugh subsides to a chuckle as he puts the liquor glass a little distrustfully down the table.)

BIG MAMA: Hello, Miss Sally.

*(*BRICK *has risen and hobbled to the gallery doors.)*

BIG DADDY: Hey! Where you goin'?

BRICK: Out for a breather.

BIG DADDY: Not yet you ain't. Stay here till this talk is finished, young fellow.

BRICK: I thought it was finished, Big Daddy.

BIG DADDY: It ain't even begun.

BRICK: My mistake. Excuse me. I just wanted to feel that river breeze.

BIG DADDY: Set back in that chair.

*(*BIG MAMA's *voice rises, carrying down the hall.)*

BIG MAMA: Miss Sally, you're a case! You're a caution, Miss Sally.

BIG DADDY: Jesus, she's talking to my old maid sister again.

BIG MAMA: Why didn't you give me a chance to explain it to you?

BIG DADDY: Brick, this stuff burns me.

BIG MAMA: Well, goodbye, now, Miss Sally. You come down real soon. Big Daddy's dying to see you.

BIG DADDY: Crap!

BIG MAMA: Yaiss, goodbye, Miss Sally. . . .

(She hangs up and bellows with mirth. BIG DADDY *groans and covers his ears as she approaches.)*
(Bursting in)

Big Daddy, that was Miss Sally callin' from Memphis again! You know what she done, Big Daddy? She called her doctor in Memphis to git him to tell her what that spastic thing is! Ha-HAAAA!—And called back to tell me how relieved she was that—Hey! Let me in!

*(*BIG DADDY *has been holding the door half closed against her.)*

BIG DADDY: Naw I ain't. I told you not to come and go through this room You just back out and go through those five other rooms.

BIG MAMA: Big Daddy? Big Daddy? Oh, Big Daddy!—You didn't mean those things you said to me, did you?

(He shuts door firmly against her but she still calls.)

Sweetheart? Sweetheart? Big Daddy? You didn't mean those awful things you said to me?—I know you didn't. I know you didn't mean those things in your heart. . . .

(The childlike voice fades with a sob and her heavy footsteps retreat down the hall. BRICK *has risen once more on his crutches and starts for the gallery again.)*

BIG DADDY: All I ask of that woman is that she leave me alone. But she can't admit to herself that she makes me sick. That comes of having slept with her too many years. Should of quit much sooner but that old woman she never got enough of it—and I was good in bed . . . I never should of wasted so much of it on her. . . . They say you got just so many and each one is numbered. Well, I got a few left in me, a few, and I'm going to pick me a good one to spend 'em on! I'm going to pick me a choice one, I don't care how much she costs, I'll smother her in—minks! Ha ha! I'll strip her naked and smother her in minks and choke her with diamonds! Ha ha! I'll strip her naked and choke her with diamonds and smother her with minks and hump her from hell to breakfast. *Ha aha ha ha ha!*

MAE *(gaily at door)*: Who's that laughin' in there?

GOOPER: Is Big Daddy laughin' in there?

BIG DADDY: Crap!—them two—*drips*. . . .

(He goes over and touches BRICK's *shoulder.)*

Yes, son. Brick, boy.—I'm *happy!* I'm happy, son, I'm happy!

(He chokes a little and bites his under lip, pressing his head quickly, shyly against his son's head and then, coughing with embarrassment, goes uncertainly back to the table where he set down the glass. He drinks and makes a grimace as it burns his guts. BRICK *sighs and rises with effort.)*

What makes you so restless? Have you got ants in your britches?

BRICK: Yes, sir . . .

BIG DADDY: Why?

BRICK: —Something—hasn't happened. . . .

BIG DADDY: Yeah? What is that!

BRICK *(sadly)*: —the click. . . .

BIG DADDY: Did you say click?

BRICK: Yes, click.

BIG DADDY: What click?

BRICK: A click that I get in my head that makes me peaceful.

BIG DADDY: I sure in hell don't know what you're talking about, but it disturbs me.

BRICK: It's just a mechanical thing.

BIG DADDY: What is a mechanical thing?

BRICK: This click that I get in my head that makes me peaceful. I got to drink till I get it. It's just a mechanical thing, something like a—like a—like a—

BIG DADDY: Like a—

BRICK: Switch clicking off in my head, turning the hot light off and the cool night on and— *(He looks up, smiling sadly.)* —all of a sudden there's —peace!

BIG DADDY *(whistles long and soft with astonishment; he goes back to* BRICK *and clasps his son's two shoulders)* Jesus! I didn't know it had gotten that bad with you. Why, boy, you're—*alcoholic!*

BRICK: That's the truth, Big Daddy. I'm alcoholic.

BIG DADDY: This shows how I—let things go!

BRICK: I have to hear that little click in my head that makes me peaceful. Usually I hear it sooner than this, sometimes as early as—noon, but— —Today it's—dilatory. . . . —I just haven't got the right level of alcohol in my bloodstream yet!

(This last statement is made with energy as he freshens his drink.)

BIG DADDY: Uh—huh. Expecting death made me blind. I didn't have no idea that a son of mine was turning into a drunkard under my nose.

BRICK *(gently)*: Well, now you do, Big Daddy, the news has penetrated. . . .

BIG DADDY: Uh-huh, yes, now I do. The news has penetrated.

BRICK: And so if you'll excuse me—

BIG DADDY: No, I won't excuse you.

BRICK: —I'd better sit by myself till I hear that click in my head, it's just a mechanical thing but it don't happen except when I'm alone or talking to no one. . . .

BIG DADDY: You got a long, long time to sit still, boy, and talk to no one, but now you're talkin' to me. At least I'm talking to you. And you set there and listen until I tell you the conversation is over!

BRICK: But this talk is like all the others we've ever had together in our lives! It's nowhere, nowhere!—it's—it's *painful*, Big Daddy. . . .

BIG DADDY: All right, then let it be painful, but don't you move from that chair!—I'm going to remove that crutch. . . . *(He seizes the crutch and tosses it across room.)*

BRICK: I can hop on one foot, and if I fall, I can crawl!

BIG DADDY: If you ain't careful you're gonna crawl off this plantation and then, by Jesus, you'll have to hustle your drinks along Skid Row!

BRICK: That'll come, Big Daddy.

BIG DADDY: Naw, it won't. You're my son and I'm going to straighten you out; now that *I'm* straightened out, I'm going to straighten out you!

BRICK: Yeah?

BIG DADDY: Today the report come in from Ochsner Clinic. Y'know what they told me? *(His face glows with triumph.)* The only thing that they could detect with all the instruments of science in that great hospital is a little spastic condition of the colon! And nerves torn to pieces by all that worry about it.

(A little girl bursts into room with a sparkler clutched in each fist, hops and shrieks like a monkey gone mad and rushes back out again as BIG DADDY *strikes at her.)*
(Silence. The two men stare at each other. A woman laughs gaily outside.)

I want you to know I breathed a sigh of relief almost as powerful as the Vicksburg tornado!

(There is laughter outside, running footsteps, the soft, plushy sound and light of exploding rockets.)
*(*BRICK *stares at him soberly for a long moment; then makes a sort of startled sound in his nostrils and springs up on one foot and hops across the room to grab his crutch, swinging on the furniture for support. He gets the crutch and flees as if in horror for the gallery. His father seizes him by the sleeve of his white silk pajamas.)*

Stay here, you son of a bitch!—till I say go!

BRICK: I can't.

BIG DADDY: You sure in hell will, God damn it.

BRICK: No, I can't. We talk, you talk, in—circles! We get no where, no where! It's always the same, you say you want to talk to me and don't have a fuckin' thing to say to me!

BIG DADDY: Nothin' to say when I'm tellin' you I'm going to live when I thought I was dying?!

BRICK: Oh—*that*—Is that what you have to say to me?

BIG DADDY: Why, you son of a bitch! Ain't that, ain't that—*important?!*

BRICK: Well, you said that, that's said, and now I—

BIG DADDY: Now you set back down.

BRICK: You're all balled up, you—

BIG DADDY: I ain't balled up!

BRICK: You are, you're all balled up!

BIG DADDY: Don't tell me what I am, you drunken whelp! I'm going to tear this coat sleeve off you if you don't set down!

BRICK: Big Daddy—

BIG DADDY: Do what I tell you! I'm the boss here, now! I want you to know I'm back in the driver's seat now!

(BIG MAMA *rushes in, clutching her great heaving bosom.*)

BIG MAMA: Big Daddy!

BIG DADDY: What in hell do you want in here, Big Mama?

BIG MAMA: Oh, Big Daddy! Why are you shouting like that? I just cain't *stainnnnnnnd*—it. . . .

BIG DADDY (*raising the back of his hand above his head*): GIT!—outa here.

(*She rushes back out, sobbing.*)

BRICK (*softly, sadly*): Christ. . . .

BIG DADDY (*fiercely*): Yeah! Christ!—is right . . .

(BRICK *breaks loose and hobbles toward the gallery.*)
(BIG DADDY *jerks his crutch from under* BRICK *so he steps with the injured ankle. He utters a hissing cry of anguish, clutches a chair and pulls it over on top of him on the floor.*)

Son of a—tub of—hog fat. . . .

BRICK: Big Daddy! Give me my crutch.

(BIG DADDY *throws the crutch out of reach.*)

Give me that crutch, Big Daddy.

BIG DADDY: Why do you drink?

BRICK: Don't know, give me my crutch!

BIG DADDY: You better think why you drink or give up drinking!

BRICK: Will you please give me my crutch so I can get up off this floor?

BIG DADDY: First you answer my question. Why do you drink? Why are you throwing your life away, boy, like somethin' disgusting you picked up on the street?

BRICK (*getting onto his knees*): Big Daddy, I'm in pain, I stepped on that foot.

BIG DADDY: Good! I'm glad you're not too numb with the liquor in you to feel some pain!

BRICK: You—spilled my—drink . . .

BIG DADDY: I'll make a bargain with you. You tell me why you drink and I'll hand you one. I'll pour the liquor myself and hand it to you.

BRICK: Why do I drink?

BIG DADDY: Yea! Why?

BRICK: Give me a drink and I'll tell you.

BIG DADDY: Tell me first!

BRICK: I'll tell you in one word.

BIG DADDY: What word?

BRICK: DISGUST!

(*The clock chimes softly, sweetly.* BIG DADDY *gives it a short, outraged glance.*)

Now how about that drink?

BIG DADDY: What are you disgusted with? You got to tell me that, first. Otherwise being disgusted don't make no sense!

BRICK: Give me my crutch.

BIG DADDY: You heard me, you got to tell me what I asked you first.

BRICK: I told you, I said to kill my disgust!

BIG DADDY: DISGUST WITH WHAT!

BRICK: You strike a hard bargain.

BIG DADDY: What are you disgusted with?—an' I'll pass you the liquor.

BRICK: I can hop on one foot, and if I fall, I can crawl.

BIG DADDY: You want liquor that bad?

BRICK (*dragging himself up, clinging to bedstead*): Yeah, I want it that bad.

BIG DADDY: If I give you a drink, will you tell me what it is you're disgusted with, Brick?

BRICK: Yes, sir, I will try to.

(*The old man pours him a drink and solemnly passes it to him.*)
(*There is a silence as* BRICK *drinks.*)

Have you ever heard the word "mendacity"?

BIG DADDY: Sure. Mendacity is one of them five dollar words that cheap politicians throw back and forth at each other.

BRICK: You know what it means?

BIG DADDY: Don't it mean lying and liars?

BRICK: Yes, sir, lying and liars.

BIG DADDY: Has someone been lying to you?

CHILDREN (*chanting in chorus offstage*):
We want Big Dad-dee!
We want Big Dad-dee

(GOOPER *appears in the gallery door.*)

GOOPER: Big Daddy, the kiddies are shouting for you out there.

BIG DADDY (*fiercely*): Keep out, Gooper!

GOOPER: 'Scuse *me!*

(BIG DADDY *slams the doors after* GOOPER.)

BIG DADDY: Who's been lying to you, has Margaret been lying to you, has your wife been lying to you about something, Brick?

BRICK: Not her. That wouldn't matter.

BIG DADDY: Then who's been lying to you, and what about?

BRICK: No one single person and no one lie. . . .

BIG DADDY: Then what, what then, for Christ's sake?

BRICK: The whole, the whole—thing. . . .

BIG DADDY: Why are you rubbing your head? You got a headache?

BRICK: No, I'm tryin' to—

BIG DADDY: —Concentrate, but you can't because your brain's all soaked with liquor, is that the trouble? Wet brain! (*He snatches the glass from* BRICK'*s hand.*) What do you know about this mendacity thing? Hell! I could write a book on it! Don't you know that? I could write a book on it and still not cover the subject. Well, I could, I could write a goddam book on it and still not cover the subject anywhere near enough!!— Think of all the lies I got to put up with!— Pretenses! Ain't that mendacity? Having to pretend stuff you don't think or feel or have any idea of? Having for instance to act like I care for Big Mama!—I haven't been able to stand the sight, sound, or smell of that woman for forty years now!—even when I *laid* her!—regular as a piston. . . .

Pretend to love that son of a bitch of a Gooper and his wife Mae and those five same screechers out there like parrots in a jungle? Jesus! Can't stand to look at 'em!

Church!—it bores the bejesus out of me but I go!—I go an' sit there and listen to the fool preacher!

Clubs!—Elks! Masons! Rotary!—*crap!*

(*A spasm of pain makes him clutch his belly. He sinks into a chair and his voice is softer and hoarser.*)

You I *do* like for some reason, did always have some kind of real feeling for—affection— respect—yes, always. . . .

You and being a success as a planter is all I ever had any devotion to in my whole life!—and that's the truth. . . .

I don't know why, but it is!

I've lived with mendacity!—Why can't *you* live with it? Hell, you *got* to live with it, there's nothing *else* to *live* with except mendacity, is there?

BRICK: Yes, sir. Yes, sir there is something else that you can live with!

BIG DADDY: What?

BRICK (*lifting his glass*): This!—Liquor. . . .

BIG DADDY: That's not living, that's dodging away from life.

BRICK: I want to dodge away from it.

BIG DADDY: Then why don't you kill yourself, man?

BRICK: I like to drink. . . .

BIG DADDY: Oh, God, I can't talk to you. . . .

BRICK: I'm sorry, Big Daddy.

BIG DADDY: Not as sorry as I am. I'll tell you something. A little while back when I thought my number was up—

(*This speech should have torrential pace and fury.*)

—before I found out it was just this—spastic— colon. I thought about you. Should I or should I not, if the jig was up, give you this place when I go—since I hate Gooper an' Mae an' know that they hate me, and since all five same monkeys are little Maes an' Goopers.—And I thought, No!—Then I thought, Yes!—I couldn't make up my mind. I hate Gooper and his five same monkeys and that bitch Mae! Why should I turn over twenty-eight thousand acres of the richest land this side of the valley Nile to not my kind?—But why in hell, on the other hand, Brick—should I subsidize a goddam fool on the bottle?—Liked or not liked, well, maybe even—*loved!*—Why should I do that?—Subsidize worthless behavior? Rot? Corruption?

BRICK (*smiling*): I understand.

BIG DADDY: Well, if you do, you're smarter than I am. God damn it, because I don't understand. And this I will tell you frankly. I didn't make up my mind at all on that question and still to this day I ain't made out no will!—Well, now I don't *have* to. The pressure is gone. I can just wait and see if you pull yourself together or if you don't.

BRICK: That's right, Big Daddy.

BIG DADDY: You sound like you thought I was kidding.

BRICK (*rising*): No, sir, I know you're not kidding.

BIG DADDY: But you don't care—?

BRICK (*hobbling toward the gallery door*): No, sir, I don't care. . . .

(*He stands in the gallery doorway as the night sky turns pink and green and gold with successive flashes of light.*)

BIG DADDY: *WAIT!*—Brick. . . .

(*His voice drops. Suddenly there is something shy, tender, in his restraining gesture.*)

Don't let's—leave it like this, like them other talks we've had, we've always—talked around things, we've—just talked around things for some fuckin' reason. I don't know what, it's always like something was left not spoken, something avoided because neither of us was honest enough with the—other. . . .

BRICK: I never lied to you, Big Daddy.

BIG DADDY: Did I ever to *you?*

BRICK: No, sir. . . .

BIG DADDY: Then there is at least two people that never lied to each other.

BRICK: But we've never *talked* to each other.

BIG DADDY: We can *now.*

BRICK: Big Daddy, there don't seem to be anything much to say.

BIG DADDY: You say that you drink to kill your disgust with lying.

BRICK: You said to give you a reason.

BIG DADDY: Is liquor the only thing that'll kill this disgust?

BRICK: Now. Yes.

BIG DADDY: But not once, huh?

BRICK: Not when I was still young an' believing. A drinking man's someone who wants to forget he isn't still young an' believing.

BIG DADDY: Believing what?

BRICK: Believing. . . .

BIG DADDY: Believing *what?*

BRICK (*stubbornly evasive*): Believing. . . .

BIG DADDY: I don't know what the hell you mean by believing and I don't think you know what you mean by believing, but if you still got sports in your blood, go back to sports announcing and—

BRICK: Sit in a glass box watching games I can't play? Describing what I can't do while players do it? Sweating out their disgust and confusion in contests I'm not fit for? Drinkin' a coke, half bourbon, so I can stand it? That's no goddam good any more, no help—time just outran me, Big Daddy—got there first . . .

BIG DADDY: I think you're passing the buck.

BRICK: You know many drinkin' men?

BIG DADDY (*with a slight, charming smile*): I have known a fair number of that species.

BRICK: Could any of them tell you why he drank?

BIG DADDY: Yep, you're passin' the buck to things like time and disgust with "mendacity" and—crap!— if you got to use that kind of language about a thing, it's ninety-proof bull, and I'm not buying any.

BRICK: I had to give you a reason to get a drink!

BIG DADDY: You started drinkin' when your friend Skipper died.

(*Silence for five beats. Then* BRICK *makes a startled movement, reaching for his crutch.*)

BRICK: What are you suggesting?

BIG DADDY: I'm suggesting nothing.

(*The shuffle and clop of* BRICK's *rapid hobble away from*

his father's steady, grave attention.*)

—But Gooper an' Mae suggested that there was something not right exactly in your—

BRICK (*stopping short downstage as if backed to a wall*): "Not right"?

BIG DADDY: Not, well, exactly *normal* in your friendship with—

BRICK: They suggested that, too? I thought that was Maggie's suggestion.

(BRICK's *detachment is at last broken through. His heart is accelerated; his forehead sweat-beaded; his breath becomes more rapid and his voice hoarse. The thing they're discussin, timidly and painfully on the side of* BIG DADDY, *fiercely, violently on* BRICK's *side, is the inadmissible thing that* SKIPPER *died to disavow between them. The fact that if it existed it had to be disavowed to "keep face" in the world they lived in, may be at the heart of the "mendacity" that* BRICK *drinks to kill his disgust with. It may be the root of his collapse. Or maybe it is only a single manifestation of it, not even the most important. The bird that I hope to catch in the net of this play is not the solution of one man's psychological problem. I'm trying to catch the true quality of experience in a group of people, that cloudy, flickering, evanescent—fiercely charged!—interplay of live human beings in the thundercloud of a common crisis. Some mystery should be left in the revelation of characters in a play, just as a great deal of mystery is always left in the revelation of character in life, even in one's own character to himself. This does not absolve the playwright of his duty to observe and probe as clearly and deeply as he legitimately can: but it should steer him away from "pat" conclusions, facile definitions which make a play just a play, not a snare for the truth of human experience.*)

(*The following scene should be played with great concentration, with most of the power leashed but palpable in what is left unspoken.*)

Who else's suggestion is it, is it *yours?* How many others thought that Skipper and I were—

BIG DADDY (*gently*): Now, hold on, hold on a minute, son.—I knocked around in my time.

BRICK: What's that got to do with—

BIG DADDY: I said "Hold on!"—I bummed, I bummed this country till I was—

BRICK: Whose suggestion, who else's suggestion is it?

BIG DADDY: Slept in hobo jungles and railroad Y's and flophouses in all cities before I—

BRICK: Oh, *you* think so, too, you call me your son and a queer. Oh! Maybe that's why you put Maggie and me in this room that was Jack Straw's and Peter Ochello's, in which that pair of old sisters slept in a double bed where both of 'em died!

BIG DADDY: *Now just don't go throwing rocks at—*

(*Suddenly* REVEREND TOOKER *appears in the gallery doors, his head slightly, playfully, fatuously cocked, with a practised clergyman's smile, sincere as a bird call blown on a hunter's whistle, the living embodiment of the pious, conventional lie.)*

(BIG DADDY gasps a little at this perfectly timed, but incongruous, apparition.)

—What're you lookin' for, Preacher?

REVEREND TOOKER: The gentleman's lavatory, ha ha!—heh, heh . . .

BIG DADDY *(with strained courtesy)*: —Go back out and walk down to the other end of the gallery, Reverend Tooker, and use the bathroom connected with my bedroom, and if you can't find it, ask them where it is!

REVEREND TOOKER: Ah, thanks. *(He goes out with a deprecatory chuckle.)*

BIG DADDY: It's hard to talk in this place . . .

BRICK: Son of a—!

BIG DADDY *(leaving a lot unspoken)*: —I seen all things and understood a lot of them, till 1910. Christ, the year that—I had worn my shoes through, hocked my—I hopped off a yellow dog freight car half a mile down the road, slept in a wagon of cotton outside the gin—Jack Straw an' Peter Ochello took me in. Hired me to manage this place which grew into this one.—When Jack Straw died—why, old Peter Ochello quit eatin' like a dog does when its master's dead, and died, too!

BRICK: Christ!

BIG DADDY: I'm just saying I understand such—

BRICK *(violently)*: Skipper is dead. I have not quit eating!

BIG DADDY: No, but you started drinking.

(BRICK wheels on his crutch and hurls his glass across the room shouting.)

BRICK: YOU THINK SO, TOO?

(Footsteps run on the gallery. There are women's calls.)
(BIG DADDY goes toward the door.)
(BRICK is transformed, as if a quiet mountain blew suddenly up in volcanic flame.)

BRICK: You think so, too? You think so, too? You think me an' Skipper did, did, did!—sodomy!—together?

BIG DADDY: Hold—!

BRICK: That what you—

BIG DADDY: —ON—a minute!

BRICK: You think we did dirty things between us, Skipper an'—

BIG DADDY: Why are you shouting like that? Why are you—

BRICK: —Me, is that what you think of Skipper, is that—

BIG DADDY: —so excited? I don't think nothing. I don't know nothing. I'm simply telling you what—

BRICK: You think that Skipper and me were a pair of dirty old men?

BIG DADDY: Now that's—

BRICK: Straw? Ochello? A couple of—

BIG DADDY: Now just—

BRICK: —fucking sissies? Queers? Is that what you—

BIG DADDY: Shhh.

BRICK: —think?

(He loses his balance and pitches to his knees without noticing the pain. He grabs the bed and drags himself up.)

BIG DADDY: Jesus!—Whew. . . . Grab my hand!

BRICK: Naw, I don't want your hand. . . .

BIG DADDY: Well, I want yours. Git up!

(He draws him up, keeps an arm about him with concern and affection.)

You broken out in a sweat! You're panting like you'd run a race with—

BRICK *(freeing himself from his father's hold)*: Big Daddy, you shock me, Big Daddy, you, you—*shock* me! Talkin' so— *(He turns away from his father.)* —casually!—about a—thing like that . . .

—Don't you know how people *feel* about things like that? How, how *disgusted* they are by things like that? Why, at Ole Miss when it was discovered a pledge to our fraternity, Skipper's and mine, did a, *attempted* to do a, unnatural thing with—

We not only dropped him like a hot rock!— We told him to git off the campus, and he did, he got!—All the way to— *(He halts, breathless.)*

BIG DADDY: —Where?

BRICK: —North Africa, last I heard!

BIG DADDY: Well, I have come back from further away than that, I have just now returned from the other side of the moon, death's country, son, and I'm not easy to shock by anything here. *(He comes downstage and faces out.)* Always, anyhow, lived with too much space around me to be infected by ideas of other people. One thing you can grow on a big place more important than cotton!—is *tolerance!*—I grown it. *(He returns toward BRICK.)*

BRICK: Why can't exceptional friendship, *real, real, deep, deep friendship!* between two men be respected as something clean and decent without being thought of as—

BIG DADDY: It can, it is, for God's sake.

BRICK: —Fairies. . . .

(In his utterance of this word, we gauge the wide and profound reach of the conventional mores he got from the world that crowned him with early laurel.)

BIG DADDY: I told Mae an' Gooper—

BRICK: Frig Mae and Gooper, frig all dirty lies and liars!—Skipper and me had a clean, true thing between us!—had a clean friendship, practically all our lives, till Maggie got the idea you're talking about. Normal? No!—it was too rare to be normal, any true thing between two people is too rare to be normal. Oh, once in a while he put his hand on my shoulder or I'd put mine on his, oh, maybe even, when we were touring the country in pro-football an' shared hotel-rooms we'd reach across the space between the two beds and shake hands to say goodnight, yeah, one or two times we—

BIG DADDY: Brick, nobody thinks that that's not normal!

BRICK: Well, they're mistaken, it was! It was a pure an' true thing an' that's not normal.

MAE (off stage): Big Daddy, they're startin' the fireworks.

(They both stare straight at each other for a long moment. The tension breaks and both turn away as if tired.)

BIG DADDY: Yeah, it's—hard t'—talk. . . .

BRICK: All right, then, let's—let it go. . . .

BIG DADDY: Why did Skipper crack up? Why have you?

(BRICK looks back at his father again. He has already decided, without knowing that he has made this decision, that he is going to tell his father that he is dying of cancer. Only this could even the score between them: one inadmissible thing in return for another.)

BRICK (ominously): All right. You're asking for it, Big Daddy. We're finally going to have that real true talk you wanted. It's too late to stop it, now, we got to carry it through and cover every subject.

(He hobbles back to the liquor cabinet.)

Uh-huh.

(He opens the ice bucket and picks up the silver tongs with slow admiration of their frosty brightness.)

Maggie declares that Skipper and I went into pro-football after we left "Ole Miss" because we were scared to grow up . . .

(He moves downstage with the shuffle and clop of a cripple on a crutch. As MARGARET did when her speech became "recitative," he looks out into the house, commanding its attention by his direct, concentrated gaze—a broken, "tragically elegant" figure telling simply as much as he knows of "the Truth.")

—Wanted to—keep on tossing—those long, long!—high, high!—passes that—couldn't be intercepted except by time, the aerial attack that made us famous! And so we did, we did, we kept it up for one season, that aerial attack, we held it high!—Yeah, but—

—that summer, Maggie, she laid the law down to me, said, Now or never, and so I married Maggie. . . .

BIG DADDY: How was Maggie in bed?

BRICK (wryly): Great! the greatest!

(BIG DADDY nods as if he thought so.)

She went on the road that fall with the Dixie Stars. Oh, she made a great show of being the world's best sport. She wore a—wore a—tall bearskin cap! A shako, they call it, a dyed moleskin coat, a moleskin coat dyed red!—Cut up crazy! Rented hotel ballrooms for victory celebrations, wouldn't cancel them when it—turned out—defeat. . . .

MAGGIE THE CAT! Ha ha!

(BIG DADDY nods.)

—But Skipper, he had some fever which came back on him which doctors couldn't explain and I got that injury—turned out to be just a shadow on the X-ray plate—and a touch of bursitis. . . .

I lay in a hospital bed, watched our games on TV, saw Maggie on the bench next to Skipper when he was hauled out of a game for stumbles, fumbles!—Burned me up the way she hung on his arm!—Y'know, I think that Maggie had always felt sort of left out because she and me never got any closer together than two people just get in bed, which is not much closer than two cats on a—fence humping. . . .

So! She took this time to work on poor dumb Skipper. He was a less than average student at Ole Miss, you know that, don't you?!—Poured in his mind the dirty, false idea that what we were, him and me, was a frustrated case of that ole pair of sisters that lived in this room, Jack Straw and Peter Ochello!—He, poor Skipper, went to bed with Maggie to prove it wasn't true, and when it didn't work out, he thought it was true!— Skipper broke in two like a rotten stick—nobody ever turned so fast to a lush—or died of it so quick. . . .

—Now are you satisfied?

(BIG DADDY has listened to this story, dividing the grain from the chaff. Now he looks at his son.)

BIG DADDY: Are you satisfied?

BRICK: With what?

BIG DADDY: That half-ass story!

BRICK: What's half-ass about it?

BIG DADDY: Something's left out of that story. What did you leave out?

(The phone has started ringing in the hall.)

GOOPER *(off stage):* Hello.

(As if it reminded him of something BRICK *glances suddenly toward the sound and says.)*

BRICK: Yes!—I left out a long-distance call which I had from Skipper—

GOOPER: Speaking, go ahead.

BRICK: —In which he made a drunken confession to me and on which I hung up!

GOOPER: No.

BRICK: Last time we spoke to each other in our lives . . .

GOOPER: No, sir.

BIG DADDY: You musta said something to him before you hung up.

BRICK: What could I say to him?

BIG DADDY: Anything. Something.

BRICK: Nothing.

BIG DADDY: Just hung up?

BRICK: Just hung up.

BIG DADDY: Uh-huh. Anyhow now!—we have tracked down the lie with which you're disgusted and which you are drinking to kill your disgust with, Brick. You been passing the buck. This disgust with mendacity is disgust with yourself.

You!—dug the grave of your friend and kicked him in it!—before you'd face truth with him!

BRICK: *His* truth, not *mine!*

BIG DADDY: His truth, okay! But you wouldn't face it with him!

BRICK: Who *can* face truth? Can *you?*

BIG DADDY: Now don't start passin' the rotten buck again, boy!

BRICK: *How about these birthday congratulations, these many, many happy returns of the day, when ev'rybody knows there won't be any except you!*

*(*GOOPER, *who has answered the hall phone, lets out a high, shrill laugh; the voice becomes audible saying: "No, no, you got it all wrong! Upside down. Are you crazy?")*
*(*BRICK *suddenly catches his breath as he realizes that he has made a shocking disclosure. He hobbles a few paces, then freezes, and without looking at his father's shocked face, says.)*

Let's, let's—go out, now, and—watch the fireworks. Come on, Big Daddy.

*(*BIG DADDY *moves suddenly forward and grabs hold of the boy's crutch like it was a weapon for which they were fighting for possession.)*

BIG DADDY: Oh, no, no! No one's going out! What did you start to say?

BRICK: I don't remember.

BIG DADDY: "Many happy returns when they know there won't be any"?

BRICK: Aw, hell, Big Daddy, forget it. Come on out on the gallery and look at the fireworks they're shooting off for your birthday. . . .

BIG DADDY: First you finish that remark you were makin' before you cut off. "Many happy returns when they know there won't be any"?—Ain't that what you just said?

BRICK: Look, now. I can get around without that crutch if I have to but it would be a lot easier on the furniture an' glassware if I didn' have to go swinging along like Tarzan of th'—

BIG DADDY: FINISH! WHAT YOU WAS SAYIN'!

(An eerie green glow shows in sky behind him.)

BRICK *(sucking the ice in his glass, speech becoming thick):* Leave th' place to Gooper and Mae an' their five little same little monkeys. All I want is—

BIG DADDY: "LEAVE TH' PLACE," did you say?

BRICK *(vaguely):* All twenty-eight thousand acres of the richest land this side of the valley Nile.

BIG DADDY: Who said I was "leaving the place" to Gooper or anybody? This is my sixty-fifth birthday! I got fifteen years or twenty years left in me! I'll outlive *you!* I'll bury you an' have to pay for your coffin!

BRICK: Sure. Many happy returns. Now let's go watch the fireworks, come on, let's—

BIG DADDY: Lying, have they been lying? About the report from th'—clinic? Did they, did they—find something—*Cancer.* Maybe?

BRICK: Mendacity is a system that we live in. Liquor is one way out an' death's the other. . . .

(He takes the crutch from BIG DADDY's *loose grip and swings out on the gallery leaving the doors open.)*
(A song, "Pick a Bale of Cotton," is heard.)

MAE *(appearing in door):* Oh, Big Daddy, the field hands are singin' fo' you!

BRICK: I'm sorry, Big Daddy. My head don't work any more and it's hard for me to understand how anybody could care if he lived or died or was dying or cared about anything but whether or not there was liquor left in the bottle and so I said what I said without thinking. In some ways I'm no better than the others, in some ways worse because I'm less alive. Maybe it's being alive that makes them lie, and being almost *not* alive makes me sort of accidentally truthful—I don't know but—anyway—we've been friends . . .

—And being friends is telling each other the truth. . . .

(There is a pause.)

You told *me!* I told *you!*

BIG DADDY *(slowly and passionately)*: CHRIST—DAMN—

GOOPER *(off stage)*: Let her go!

(Fireworks off stage right.)

BIG DADDY: —ALL—LYING SONS OF—LYING BITCHES!

(He straightens at last and crosses to the inside door. At the door he turns and looks back as if he had some desperate question he couldn't put into words. Then he nods reflectively and says in a hoarse voice.)

Yes, all liars, all liars, all lying dying liars!

(This is said slowly, slowly, with a fierce revulsion. He goes on out.)

—Lying! Dying! Liars!

(BRICK remains motionless as the lights dim out and the curtain falls.)

ACT 3

(There is no lapse of time. BIG DADDY is seen leaving as at the end of ACT 2.)

BIG DADDY: ALL LYIN'—DYIN'!—LIARS!—LIARS!—LIARS!

(MARGARET enters.)

MARGARET: Brick, what in the name of God was goin' on in this room?

(DIXIE and TRIXIE enter through the doors and circle around MARGARET shouting. MAE enters from the lower gallery window.)

MAE: Dixie, Trixie, you quit that!

(GOOPER enters through the doors.)

Gooper, will y' please get these kiddies to bed right now!

GOOPER: Mae, you seen Big Mama?

MAE: Not yet.

(GOOPER and kids exit through the doors. REVEREND TOOKER enters through the windows.)

REVEREND TOOKER: Those kiddies are so full of vitality. I think I'll have to be starting back to town.

MAE: Not yet, Preacher. You know we regard you as a member of this family, one of our closest an' dearest, so you just got t' be with us when Doc Baugh gives Big Mama th' actual truth about th' report from the clinic.

MARGARET: Where do you think you're going?

BRICK: Out for some air.

MARGARET: Why'd Big Daddy shout "Liars"?

MAE: Has Big Daddy gone to bed, Brick?

GOOPER *(entering)*: Now where is that old lady?

REVEREND TOOKER: I'll look for her. *(He exits to the gallery.)*

MAE: Cain'tcha find her, Gooper?

GOOPER: She's avoidin' this talk.

MAE: I think she senses somethin'.

MARGARET *(going out to the gallery to BRICK)*: Brick, they're goin' to tell Big Mama the truth about Big Daddy and she's goin' to need you.

DOCTOR BAUGH: This is going to be painful.

MAE: Painful things cain't always be avoided.

REVEREND TOOKER: I see Big Mama.

GOOPER: Hey, Big Mama, come here.

MAE: Hush, Gooper, don't holler.

BIG MAMA *(entering)*: Too much smell of burnt fireworks makes me feel a little bit sick at my stomach.—Where is Big Daddy?

MAE: That's what I want to know, where has Big Daddy gone?

BIG MAMA: He must have turned in, I reckon he went to baid . . .

GOOPER: Well, then, now we can talk.

BIG MAMA: What *is* this talk, *what* talk?

(MARGARET appears on the gallery, talking to DOCTOR BAUGH.)

MARGARET *(musically)*: My family freed their slaves ten years before abolition. My great-great-grandfather gave his slaves their freedom five years before the War between the States started!

MAE: Oh, for God's sake! Maggie's climbed back up in her family tree!

MARGARET *(sweetly)*: What, Mae?

(The pace must be very quick: great Southern animation.)

BIG MAMA *(addressing them all)*: I think Big Daddy was just worn out. He loves his family, he loves to have them around him, but it's a strain on his nerves. He wasn't himself tonight, Big Daddy wasn't himself, I could tell he was all worked up.

REVEREND TOOKER: I think he's remarkable.

BIG MAMA: Yaisss! Just remarkable. Did you all notice the food he ate at that table? Did you all notice the supper he put away? Why he ate like a hawss!

GOOPER: I hope he doesn't regret it.

BIG MAMA: What? Why that man—ate a huge piece of cawn bread with molasses on it! Helped himself twice to hoppin' John.

MARGARET: Big Daddy loves hoppin' John.—We had a real country dinner.

BIG MAMA *(overlapping MARGARET)*: Yaiss, he simply adores it! an' candied yams? Son? That man put away enough food at that table to stuff a *field* hand!

GOOPER *(with grim relish)*: I hope he don't have to pay for it later on . . .

BIG MAMA (*fiercely*): What's *that*, Gooper?

MAE: Gooper says he hopes Big Daddy doesn't suffer tonight.

BIG MAMA: Oh, shoot, Gooper says, Gooper says! Why should Big Daddy suffer for satisfying a normal appetite? There's nothin' wrong with that man but nerves, he's sound as a dollar! And now he knows he is an' that's why he ate such a supper. He had a big load off his mind, knowin' he wasn't doomed t'—what he thought he was doomed to . . .

MARGARET (*sadly and sweetly*): Bless his old sweet soul . . .

BIG MAMA (*vaguely*): Yais, bless his heart, where's Brick?

MAE: Outside.

GOOPER: —Drinkin' . . .

BIG MAMA: I know he's drinkin'. Cain't I see he's drinkin' without you continually tellin' me that boy's drinkin'?

MARGARET: Good for you, Big Mama! (*She applauds.*)

BIG MAMA: Other people *drink* and *have* drunk an' will *drink*, as long as they make that stuff an' put it in bottles.

MARGARET: That's the truth. I never trusted a man that didn't drink.

BIG MAMA: *Brick? Brick!*

MARGARET: He's still on the gall'ry. I'll go bring him in so we can talk.

BIG MAMA (*worriedly*): I don't know what this mysterious family conference is about.

(*Awkward silence.* BIG MAMA *looks from face to face, then belches slightly and mutters, "Excuse me . . ." She opens an ornamental fan suspended about her throat. A black lace fan to go with her black lace gown, and fans her wilting corsage, sniffing nervously and looking from face to face in the uncomfortable silence as* MARGARET *calls "Brick?" and* BRICK *sings to the moon on the gallery.*)

MARGARET: Brick, they're gonna tell Big Mama the truth an' she's gonna need you.

BIG MAMA: I don't know what's wrong here, you all have such long faces! Open that door on the hall and let some air circulate through here, will you please, Gooper?

MAE: I think we'd better leave that door closed, Big Mama, till after the talk.

MARGARET: Brick!

BIG MAMA: Reveren' Tooker, will *you* please open that door?

REVEREND TOOKER: I sure will, Big Mama.

MAE: I just didn't think we ought t' take any chance of Big Daddy hearin' a word of this discussion.

BIG MAMA: *I swan!* Nothing's going to be said in Big Daddy's house that he cain't hear if he want to!

GOOPER: Well, Big Mama, it's—

(MAE *gives him a quick, hard poke to shut him up. He glares at her fiercely as she circles before him like a burlesque ballerina, raising her skinny bare arms over her head, jangling her bracelets, exclaiming.*)

MAE: A breeze! A breeze!

REVEREND TOOKER: I think this house is the coolest house in the Delta.—Did you all know that Halsey Bank's widow put air-conditioning units in the church and rectory at Friar's Point in memory of Halsey?

(*General conversation has resumed; everybody is chatting so that the stage sounds like a bird cage.*)

GOOPER: Too bad nobody cools your church off for you. I bet you sweat in that pulpit these hot Sundays, Reverend Tooker.

REVEREND TOOKER: Yes, my vestments are drenched. Last Sunday the gold in my chasuble faded into the purple.

GOOPER: Reveren', you musta been preachin' hell's fire last Sunday.

MAE (*at the same time to* DOCTOR BAUGH): You reckon those vitamin B12 injections are what they're cracked up t' be, Doc Baugh?

DOCTOR BAUGH: Well if you want to be stuck with something I guess they're as good to be stuck with as anything else.

BIG MAMA (*at the gallery door*): *Maggie, Maggie, aren't you comin' with Brick?*

MAE (*suddenly and loudly, creating a silence*): I have a strange feeling, I have a peculiar feeling!

BIG MAMA (*turning from the gallery*): What feeling?

MAE: That Brick said somethin' he shouldn't of said t' Big Daddy.

BIG MAMA: Now what on earth could Brick of said t' Big Daddy that he shouldn't say?

GOOPER: Big Mama, there's somethin'—

MAE: NOW, WAIT!

(*She rushes up to* BIG MAMA *and gives her a quick hug and kiss.* BIG MAMA *pushes her impatiently off.*)

DOCTOR BAUGH: In my day they had what they call the Keeley cure for heavy drinkers.

BIG MAMA: Shoot!

DOCTOR BAUGH: But now I understand they just take some kind of tablets.

GOOPER: They call them "Annie Bust" tablets.

BIG MAMA: *Brick* don't need to take *nothin'*.

(BRICK *and* MARGARET *appear in gallery doors.* BIG MAMA *unaware of his presence behind her.*)

That boy is just broken up over Skipper's death. You know how poor Skipper died. They gave him a big, big dose of that sodium amytal stuff at his home and then they called the ambulance and give him another big, big dose of it at the hospital and that and all of the alcohol in his system fo' months an' months just proved too much for his heart . . . I'm scared of needles! I'm more scared of a needle than the knife . . . I think more people have been needled out of this world than— (*She stops short and wheels about.*) Oh—here's Brick! My precious baby—

(*She turns upon* BRICK *with short, fat arms extended, at the same time uttering a loud, short sob, which is both comic and touching.* BRICK *smiles and bows slightly, making a burlesque gesture of gallantry for* MARGARET *to pass before him into the room. Then he hobbles on his crutch directly to the liquor cabinet and there is absolute silence, with everybody looking at* BRICK *as everybody has always looked at* BRICK *when he spoke or moved or appeared. One by one he drops ice cubes in his glass, then suddenly, but not quickly looks back over his shoulder with a wry, charming smile, and says.*)

BRICK: I'm sorry! Anyone else?

BIG MAMA (*sadly*): No, son, I *wish* you wouldn't!

BRICK: I wish I didn't have to, Big Mama, but I'm still waiting for that click in my head which makes it all smooth out!

BIG MAMA: Ow, Brick, you—BREAK MY HEART!

MARGARET (*at same time*): Brick, go sit with Big Mama!

BIG MAMA: I just cain't staiiiiiii-nnnnnnnd-it . . . (*She sobs.*)

MAE: Now that we're all assembled—

GOOPER: We kin talk . . .

BIG MAMA: Breaks my heart . . .

MARGARET: Sit with Big Mama, Brick, and hold her hand.

(BIG MAMA *sniffs very loudly three times, almost like three drumbeats in the pocket of silence.*)

BRICK: You do that, Maggie. I'm a restless cripple. I got to stay on my crutch.

(BRICK *hobbles to the gallery door; leans there as if waiting.*)
(MAE *sits beside* BIG MAMA, *while* GOOPER *moves in front and sits on the end of the couch, facing her.* REVEREND TOOKER *moves nervously into the space between them; on the other side,* DOCTOR BAUGH *stands looking at nothing in particular and lights a cigar.* MARGARET *turns away.*)

BIG MAMA: Why're you all *surroundin'* me—like this? Why're you all starin' at me like this an' makin' signs at each other?

(REVEREND TOOKER *steps back startled.*)

MAE: Calm yourself, Big Mama.

BIG MAMA: Calm you'self, *you'self*, Sister Woman. How could I calm myself with everyone starin' at me as if big drops of blood had broken out on m'face? What's this all about, annh! What?

(GOOPER *coughs and takes a center position.*)

GOOPER: Now, Doc Baugh.

MAE: Doc Baugh?

GOOPER: Big Mama wants to know the complete truth about the report we got from the Ochsner Clinic.

MAE (*eagerly*): —on Big Daddy's condition!

GOOPER: Yais, on Big Daddy's condition, we got to face it.

DOCTOR BAUGH: Well . . .

BIG MAMA (*terrified, rising*): Is there? Something? Something that I? Don't—know?

(*In these few words, this startled, very soft question,* BIG MAMA *reviews the history of her forty-five years with* BIG DADDY, *her great almost embarrassingly true-hearted and simple-minded devotion to* BIG DADDY, *who must have had something* BRICK *has, who made himself loved so much by the "simple expedient" of not loving enough to disturb his charming detachment, also once coupled, like* BRICK, *with virile beauty.*)
(BIG MAMA *has a dignity at this moment; she almost stops being fat.*)

DOCTOR BAUGH (*after a pause, uncomfortably*): Yes?— Well—

BIG MAMA: I!!!—want to—knowwwwww . . .

(*Immediately she thrusts her fist to her mouth as if to deny that statement. Then for some curious reason, she snatches the withered corsage from her breast and hurls it on the floor and steps on it with her short, fat feet.*)

Somebody must be lyin'!—I want to know!

MAE: Sit down, Big Mama, sit down on this sofa.

MARGARET: Brick, go sit with Big Mama.

BIG MAMA: *What is it, what is it?*

DOCTOR BAUGH: I never have seen a more thorough examination than Big Daddy Pollitt was given in all my experience with the Ochsner Clinic.

GOOPER: It's one of the best in the country.

MAE: It's THE best in the country—bar *none!*

(*For some reason she gives* GOOPER *a violent poke as she goes past him. He slaps at her hand without removing his eyes from his mother's face.*)

DOCTOR BAUGH: Of course they were ninety-nine and nine-tenths per cent sure before they even started.

BIG MAMA: Sure of what, sure of what, sure of— what?—what?

(*She catches her breath in a startled sob.* MAE *kisses her quickly. She thrusts* MAE *fiercely away from her, staring at the* DOCTOR.)

MAE: Mommy, be a brave girl!

BRICK (*in the doorway, softly*): "By the light, by the light, Of the sil-ve-ry moo-oo-n . . ."

GOOPER: Shut up!—Brick.

BRICK: Sorry . . . (*He wanders out on the gallery.*)

DOCTOR BAUGH: But, now, you see, Big Mama, they

cut a piece off this growth, a specimen of the tissue and—

BIG MAMA: Growth? You told Big Daddy—

DOCTOR BAUGH: Now wait.

BIG MAMA *(fiercely)*: You told me and Big Daddy there wasn't a thing wrong with him but—

MAE: Big Mama, they always—

GOOPER: Let Doc Baugh talk, will yuh?

BIG MAMA: —little spastic condition of—*(Her breath gives out in a sob.)*

DOCTOR BAUGH: Yes, that's what we told Big Daddy. But we had this bit of tissue run through the laboratory and I'm sorry to say the test was positive on it. It's—well—malignant . . .

(Pause.)

BIG MAMA: Cancer?! Cancer?!

*(*DOCTOR BAUGH *nods gravely.* BIG MAMA *gives a long gasping cry.)*

MAE AND GOOPER: Now, now, now. Big Mama, you had to know . . .

BIG MAMA: WHY DIDN'T THEY CUT IT OUT OF HIM? HANH? HANH?

DOCTOR BAUGH: Involved too much, Big Mama, too many organs affected.

MAE: Big Mama, the liver's affected and so's the kidneys, both! It's gone way past what they call a—

GOOPER: A surgical risk.

MAE: —Uh-huh . . .

*(*BIG MAMA *draws a breath like a dying gasp.)*

REVEREND TOOKER: Tch, tch, tch, tch, tch!

DOCTOR BAUGH: Yes, it's gone past the knife.

MAE: *That's why he's turned yellow, Mommy!*

BIG MAMA: *Git away from me, git away from me, Mae! (She rises abruptly.) I want Brick! Where's Brick? Where is my only son?*

MAE: Mama! Did she say "*only* son"?

GOOPER: What does that make *me?*

MAE: A sober responsible man with five precious children!—*Six!*

BIG MAMA: I want Brick to tell me! Brick! Brick!

MARGARET *(rising from her reflections in a corner)*: Brick was so upset he went back out.

BIG MAMA: *Brick!*

MARGARET: Mama, let *me* tell you!

BIG MAMA: No, no, leave me alone, you're not my blood!

GOOPER: *Mama, I'm your son!* Listen to *me!*

MAE: Gooper's your son, he's your first-born!

BIG MAMA: Gooper never liked Daddy.

MAE *(as if terribly shocked)*: *That's not TRUE!*

(There is a pause. The minister coughs and rises.)

REVEREND TOOKER *(to* MAE*)*: I think I'd better slip away at this point. *(Discreetly.)* Good night, good

night, everybody, and God bless you all . . . on this place . . .

(He slips out.)

*(*MAE *coughs and points at* BIG MAMA.*)*

DOCTOR BAUGH: Well, Big Mama . . . *(He sighs.)*

BIG MAMA: It's all a mistake, I know it's just a bad dream.

DOCTOR BAUGH: We're gonna keep Big Daddy as comfortable as we can.

BIG MAMA: Yes, it's just a bad dream, that's all it is, it's just an awful dream.

GOOPER: In my opinion Big Daddy is having some pain but won't admit that he has it.

BIG MAMA: Just a dream, a bad dream.

DOCTOR BAUGH: That's what lots of them do, they think if they don't admit they're having the pain they can sort of escape the fact of it.

GOOPER *(with relish)*: Yes, they get sly about it, they get real sly about it.

MAE: Gooper and I think—

GOOPER: Shut up, Mae! Big Mama, I think—Big Daddy ought to be started on morphine.

BIG MAMA: Nobody's going to give Big Daddy morphine.

DOCTOR BAUGH: Now, Big Mama, when that pain strikes it's going to strike mighty hard and Big Daddy's going to need the needle to bear it.

BIG MAMA: I tell you, nobody's going to give him morphine.

MAE: Big Mama, you don't want to see Big Daddy suffer, you know you—

*(*GOOPER, *standing beside her, gives her a savage poke.)*

DOCTOR BAUGH *(placing a package on the table)*: I'm leaving this stuff here, so if there's a sudden attack you all won't have to send out for it.

MAE: I know how to give a hypo.

BIG MAMA: Nobody's gonna give Big Daddy morphine.

GOOPER: Mae took a course in nursing during the war.

MARGARET: Somehow I don't think Big Daddy would want Mae to give him a hypo.

MAE: You think he'd want *you* to do it?

DOCTOR BAUGH: Well . . .

*(*DOCTOR BAUGH *rises.)*

GOOPER: Doctor Baugh is goin'.

DOCTOR BAUGH: Yes, I got to be goin'. Well, keep your chin up, Big Mama.

GOOPER *(with jocularity)*: She's gonna keep *both* chins up, aren't you, Big Mama?

*(*BIG MAMA *sobs.)*

Now stop that, Big Mama.

GOOPER *(at the door with* DOCTOR BAUGH*)*: Well, Doc,

we sure do appreciate all you done. I'm telling you, we're surely obligated to you for—

(DOCTOR BAUGH *has gone out without a glance at him.*)

—I guess that doctor has got a lot on his mind but it wouldn't hurt him to act a little more human . . .

(BIG MAMA *sobs.*)

Now be a brave girl Mommy.

BIG MAMA: It's not true, I know that it's just not true!

GOOPER: Mama, those tests are infallible!

BIG MAMA: Why are you so determined to see your father daid?

MAE: Big Mama!

MARGARET (*gently*): I know what Big Mama means.

MAE (*fiercely*): Oh, do you?

MARGARET (*quietly and very sadly*): Yes, I think I do.

MAE: For a newcomer in the family you sure do show a lot of understanding.

MARGARET: Understanding is needed on this place.

MAE: I guess you must have needed a lot of it in your family, Maggie, with your father's liquor problem and now you've got Brick with his!

MARGARET: Brick does not have a liquor problem at all. Brick is devoted to Big Daddy. This thing is a terrible strain on him.

BIG MAMA: Brick is Big Daddy's boy, but he drinks too much and it worries me and Big Daddy, and, Margaret, you've got to cooperate with us, you've got to cooperate with Big Daddy and me in getting Brick straightened out. Because it will break Big Daddy's heart if Brick don't pull himself together and take hold of things.

MAE: Take hold of *what* things, Big Mama?

BIG MAMA: The place.

(*There is a quick violent look between* MAE *and* GOOPER.)

GOOPER: Big Mama, you've had a shock.

MAE: Yais, we've all had a shock, but . . .

GOOPER: Let's be realistic—

MAE: Big Daddy would never, would *never*, be foolish enough to—

GOOPER: —put this place in irresponsible hands!

BIG MAMA: Big Daddy ain't going to leave the place in anybody's hands; Big Daddy is *not* going to die. I want you to get that in your heads, all of you!

MAE: Mommy, Mommy, Big Mama, we're just as hopeful an' optimistic as you are about Big Daddy's prospects, we have faith in *prayer*—but nevertheless there are certain matters that have to be discussed an' dealt with, because otherwise—

GOOPER: Eventualities have to be considered and now's the time . . . Mae, will you please get my brief case out of our room?

MAE: Yes, honey. (*She rises and goes out through the hall door.*)

GOOPER (*standing over* BIG MAMA): Now, Big Mom. What you said just now was not at all true and you know it. I've always loved Big Daddy in my own quiet way. I never made a show of it, and I know that Big Daddy has always been fond of me in a quiet way, too, and he never made a show of it neither.

(MAE *returns with* GOOPER'*s brief case.*)

MAE: Here's your brief case, Gooper, honey.

GOOPER (*handing the brief case back to her*): Thank you . . . Of cou'se, my relationship with Big Daddy is different from Brick's.

MAE: You're eight years older'n Brick an' always had t' carry a bigger load of th' responsibilities than Brick ever had t' carry. He never carried a thing in his life but a football or a highball.

GOOPER: Mae, will y' let me talk, please?

MAE: Yes, honey.

GOOPER: Now, a twenty-eight-thousand-acre plantation's a mighty big thing t' run.

MAE: Almost singlehanded.

(MARGARET *has gone onto the gallery and can be heard calling softly to* BRICK.)

BIG MAMA: You never had to run this place! What are you talking about? As if Big Daddy was dead and in his grave, you had to run it? Why, you just helped him out with a few business details and had your law practice at the same time in Memphis!

MAE: Oh, Mommy, Mommy, Big Mommy! Let's be fair!

MARGARET: Brick!

MAE: Why, Gooper has given himself body and soul to keeping this place up for the past five years since Big Daddy's health started failing.

MARGARET: Brick!

MAE: Gooper won't say it, Gooper never thought of it as a duty, he just did it. And what did Brick do? Brick kept living in his past glory at college! Still a football player at twenty-seven!

MARGARET (*returning alone*): Who are you talking about now? Brick? A football player? He isn't a football player and you know it. Brick is a sports announcer on T.V. and one of the best-known ones in the country!

MAE: I'm talking about what he was.

MARGARET: Well, I wish you would just stop talking about my husband.

GOOPER: I've got a right to discuss my brother with other members of MY OWN family, which don't include *you.* Why don't you go out there and drink with Brick?

MARGARET: I've never seen such malice toward a brother.

GOOPER: How about his for me? Why, he can't stand to be in the same room with me!

MARGARET: This is a deliberate campaign of vilification for the most disgusting and sordid reason on earth, and I know what it is! It's *avarice, greed, greed!*

BIG MAMA: *Oh, I'll scream! I will scream in a moment unless this stops!*

(GOOPER *has stalked up to* MARGARET *with clenched fists at his sides as if he would strike her.* MAE *distorts her face again into a hideous grimace behind* MARGARET'S *back.*)

BIG MAMA (*sobs*): Margaret. Child. Come here. Sit next to Big Mama.

MARGARET: Precious Mommy. I'm sorry, I'm, sorry, I—!

(*She bends her long graceful neck to press her forehead to* BIG MAMA'S *bulging shoulder under its black chiffon.*)

MAE: How beautiful, how touching, this display of devotion! Do you know why she's childless? She's childless because that big beautiful athlete husband of hers won't go to bed with her!

GOOPER: You jest won't let me do this in a nice way, will yah? Aw right—I don't give a goddam if Big Daddy likes me or don't like me or did or never did or will or will never! I'm just appealing to a sense of common decency and fair play. I'll tell you the truth. I've resented Big Daddy's partiality to Brick ever since Brick was born, and the way I've been treated like I was just barely good enough to spit on and sometimes not even good enough for that. Big Daddy is dying of cancer, and it's spread all through him and it's attacked all his vital organs including the kidneys and right now he is sinking into uremia, and you all know what uremia is, it's poisoning of the whole system due to the failure of the body to eliminate its poisons.

MARGARET (*to herself, downstage, hissingly*): *Poisons, poisons! Venomous thoughts and words! In hearts and minds!—That's poisons!*

GOOPER (*overlapping her*): I am asking for a square deal, and by God, I expect to get one. But if I don't get one, if there's any peculiar shenanigans going on around here behind my back, well, I'm not a corporation lawyer for nothing, I know how to protect my own interests.

(BRICK *enters from the gallery with a tranquil, blurred smile, carrying an empty glass with him.*)

BRICK: Storm coming up.

GOOPER: Oh! A late arrival!

MAE: Behold the conquering hero comes!

GOOPER: The fabulous Brick Pollitt! Remember him?—Who could forget him!

MAE: He looks like he's been injured in a game!

GOOPER: Yep, I'm afraid you'll have to warm the bench at the Sugar Bowl this year, Brick!

(MAE *laughs shrilly.*)

Or was it the Rose Bowl that he made that famous run in?—

(*Thunder.*)

MAE: The punch bowl, honey. It was in the punch bowl, the cut-glass punch bowl!

GOOPER: Oh, that's right, I'm getting the bowls mixed up!

MARGARET: Why don't you stop venting your malice and envy on a sick boy?

BIG MAMA: *Now you two hush, I mean it, hush, all of you, hush!*

DAISY, SOOKEY: Storm! Storm comin'! Storm! Storm!

LACEY: Brightie, close them shutters.

GOOPER: Lacey, put the top up on my Cadillac, will yuh?

LACEY: Yes, suh, Mistah Pollitt!

GOOPER (*at the same time*): Big Mama, you know it's necessary for me t' go back to Memphis in th' mornin' t' represent the Parker estate in a lawsuit.

(MAE *sits on the bed and arranges papers she has taken from the brief case.*)

BIG MAMA: Is it, Gooper?

MAE: Yaiss.

GOOPER: That's why I'm forced to—to bring up a problem that—

MAE: Somethin' that's too important t' be put off!

GOOPER: If Brick was sober, he ought to be in on this.

MARGARET: Brick is present; we're present.

GOOPER: Well, good. I will now give you this outline my partner, Tom Bullitt, an' me have drawn up—a sort of dummy—trusteeship.

MARGARET: Oh, that's it! You'll be in charge an' dole out remittances, will you?

GOOPER: This we did as soon as we got the report on Big Daddy from th' Ochsner Laboratories. We did this thing, I mean we drew up this dummy outline with the advice and assistance of the Chairman of the Boa'd of Directors of th' Southern Plantahs Bank and Trust Company in Memphis, C. C. Bellowes, a man who handles estates for all th' prominent fam'lies in West Tennessee and th' Delta.

BIG MAMA: Gooper?

GOOPER (*crouching in front of* BIG MAMA): Now this is not—not final, or anything like it. This is just a preliminary outline. But it does provide a basis—a design—a—possible, feasible—*plan!*

MARGARET: Yes, I'll bet it's a plan.

(*Thunder.*)

MAE: It's a plan to protect the biggest estate in the Delta from irresponsibility an'—

BIG MAMA: Now you listen to me, all of you, you listen here? They's not goin' to be any more catty talk in my house! And Gooper, you put that away before I grab it out of your hand and tear it right up! I don't know what the hell's in it, and I don't want to know what the hell's in it. I'm talkin' in Big Daddy's language now; I'm his *wife* not his *widow,* I'm still his *wife!* And I'm talkin' to you in his language an'—

GOOPER: Big Mama, what I have here is—

MAE (*at the same time*): Gooper explained that it's just a plan . . .

BIG MAMA: I don't care what you got there. Just put it back where it came from, an' don't let me see it again, not even the outside of the envelope of it! Is that understood? Basis! Plan! Preliminary! Design! I say—what is it Big Daddy always says when he's disgusted?

BRICK (*from the bar*): Big Daddy says "crap" when he's disgusted.

BIG MAMA (*rising*): That's right!—CRAP! I say CRAP too, like Big Daddy!

(*Thunder.*)

MAE: Coarse language doesn't seem called for in this—

GOOPER: Somethin' in me is *deeply outraged* by hearin' you talk like this.

BIG MAMA: *Nobody's goin' to take nothin'!*—till Big Daddy lets go of it—maybe, just possibly, not— not even then! No, not even then!

(*Thunder.*)

MAE: Sookey, hurry up an' git that po'ch furniture covahed; want th' paint to come off?

GOOPER: Lacey, put mah car away!

LACEY: Caint, Mistah Pollitt, you got the keys!

GOOPER: Naw, you got 'em, man. Where th' keys to th' car, honey?

MAE: You got 'em in your pocket!

BRICK: "You can always hear me singin' this song, Show me the way to go home."

(*Thunder distantly.*)

BIG MAMA: Brick! Come here, Brick, I need you. Tonight Brick looks like he used to look when he was a little boy, just like he did when he played wild games and used to come home when I hollered myself hoarse for him, all sweaty and pink cheeked and sleepy, with his—red curls shining . . .

(BRICK *draws aside as he does from all physical contact and continues the song in a whisper, opening the ice bucket and dropping in the ice cubes one by one as if he were mixing some important chemical formula.*)

(*Distant thunder.*)

Time goes by so fast. Nothin' can outrun it. Death commences too early—almost before you're half acquainted with life—you meet the other . . . Oh, you know we just got to love each other an' stay together, all of us, just as close as we can, especially now that such a *black* thing has come and moved into this place without invitation.

(*Awkwardly embracing* BRICK, *she presses her head to his shoulder.*)

(*A dog howls off stage.*)

Oh, Brick, son of Big Daddy, Big Daddy does so love you. Y'know what would be his fondest dream come true? If before he passed on, if Big Daddy has to pass on . . .

(*A dog howls.*)

. . . you give him a child of yours, a grandson as much like his son as his son is like Big Daddy . . .

MARGARET: I know that's Big Daddy's dream.

BIG MAMA: That's his dream.

MAE: Such a pity that Maggie and Brick can't oblige.

BIG DADDY (*off down stage right on the gallery*): Looks like the wind was takin' liberties with this place.

SERVANT (*off stage*): Yes, sir, Mr. Pollitt.

MARGARET (*crossing to the right door*): Big Daddy's on the gall'ry.

(BIG MAMA *has turned toward the hall door at the sound of* BIG DADDY'S *voice on the gallery.*)

BIG MAMA: I can't stay here. He'll see somethin' in my eyes.

(BIG DADDY *enters the room from up stage right.*)

BIG DADDY: Can I come in?

(*He puts his cigar in an ash tray.*)

MARGARET: Did the storm wake you up, Big Daddy?

BIG DADDY: Which stawm are you talkin' about—th' one outside or th' hullaballoo in here?

(GOOPER *squeezes past* BIG DADDY.)

GOOPER: 'Scuse me.

(MAE *tries to squeeze past* BIG DADDY *to join* GOOPER, *but* BIG DADDY *puts his arm firmly around her.*)

BIG DADDY: I heard some mighty loud talk. Sounded like somethin' important was bein' discussed. What was the powwow about?

MAE (*flustered*): Why—nothin', Big Daddy . . .

BIG DADDY (*crossing to extreme left center, taking* MAE *with him*): What is that pregnant-lookin' envelope you're puttin' back in your brief case, Gooper?

GOOPER (*at the foot of the bed, caught, as he stuffs papers into envelope*): That? Nothin', suh—nothin' much of anythin' at all . . .

BIG DADDY: Nothin'? It looks like a whole lot of nothin'!

(*He turns up stage to the group.*)

You all know th' story about th' young married couple—

GOOPER: Yes, sir!

BIG DADDY: Hello, Brick—

BRICK: Hello, Big Daddy.

(*The group is arranged in a semicircle above* BIG DADDY, MARGARET *at the extreme right, then* MAE *and* GOOPER, *then* BIG MAMA, *with* BRICK *at the left.*)

BIG DADDY: Young married couple took Junior out to th' zoo one Sunday, inspected all of God's creatures in their cages, with satisfaction.

GOOPER: Satisfaction.

BIG DADDY (*crossing to up stage center, facing front*): This afternoon was a warm afternoon in spring an' that ole elephant had somethin' else on his mind which was bigger'n peanuts. You know this story, Brick?

(GOOPER *nods.*)

BRICK: No, sir, I don't know it.

BIG DADDY: Y'see, in th' cage adjoinin' they was a young female elephant in heat!

BIG MAMA (*at* BIG DADDY's *shoulder*): Oh, Big Daddy!

BIG DADDY: What's the matter, preacher's gone, ain't he? All right. That female elephant in the next cage was permeatin' the atmosphere about her with a powerful and excitin' odor of female fertility! Huh! Ain't that a nice way to put it, Brick?

BRICK: Yes, sir, nothin' wrong with it!

BIG DADDY: Brick says th's nothin' wrong with it!

BIG MAMA: Oh, Big Daddy!

BIG DADDY (*crossing to down stage center*): So this ole bull elephant still had a couple of fornications left in him. He reared back his trunk an' got a whiff of that elephant lady next door!—began to paw at the dirt in his cage an' butt his head against the separatin' partition and, first thing y'know, there was a conspicuous change in his *profile*—very *conspicuous!* Ain't I tellin' this story in decent language, Brick?

BRICK: Yes, sir, too fuckin' decent!

BIG DADDY: So, the little boy pointed at it and said, "What's that?" His mama said, "Oh, that's—nothin'!"—His papa said, "She's spoiled!"

(BIG DADDY *crosses to* BRICK *at left.*)

You didn't laugh at that story, Brick.

(BIG MAMA *crosses to down stage right crying.* MARGARET *goes to her.* MAE *and* GOOPER *hold up stage right center.*)

BRICK: No, sir, I didn't laugh at that story.

BIG DADDY: What is the smell in this room? Don't you notice it, Brick? Don't you notice a powerful and obnoxious odor of mendacity in this room?

BRICK: Yes, sir, I think I do, sir.

GOOPER: Mae, Mae . . .

BIG DADDY: There is nothing more powerful. Is there, Brick?

BRICK: No, sir. No, sir there isn't, an' nothin' more obnoxious.

BIG DADDY: Brick agrees with me. The odor of mendacity is a powerful and obnoxious odor an' the stawm hasn't blown it away from this room yet. You notice it, Gooper?

GOOPER: What, sir?

BIG DADDY: How about you, Sister Woman? You notice the unpleasant odor of mendacity in this room?

MAE: Why, Big Daddy, I don't even know what that is.

BIG DADDY: You can smell it. Hell it smells like death!

(BIG MAMA *sobs.* BIG DADDY *looks toward her.*)

What's wrong with that fat woman over there, loaded with diamonds? Hey, what's-you-name, what's the matter with you?

MARGARET (*crossing toward* BIG DADDY): She had a slight dizzy spell, Big Daddy.

BIG DADDY: You better watch that, Big Mama. A stroke is a bad way to go.

MARGARET (*crossing to* BIG DADDY *at center*): Oh, Brick, Big Daddy has on your birthday present to him, Brick, he has on your cashmere robe, the softest material I have ever felt.

BIG DADDY: Yeah, this is my soft birthday, Maggie . . . Not my gold or my silver birthday, but my soft birthday, everything's got to be soft for Big Daddy on this soft birthday.

(MAGGIE *kneels before* BIG DADDY *at center.*)

MARGARET: Big Daddy's got on his Chinese slippers that I gave him, Brick. Big Daddy, I haven't given you my big present yet, but now I will, now's the time for me to present it to you! I have an announcement to make!

MAE: What? What kind of announcement?

GOOPER: A sports announcement, Maggie?

MARGARET: Announcement of life beginning! A child is coming, sired by Brick, and out of Maggie the

Cat! I have Brick's child in my body, an' that's my birthday present to Big Daddy on this birthday!

(BIG DADDY *looks at* BRICK *who crosses behind* BIG DADDY *to down stage portal, left.*)

BIG DADDY: Get up, girl, get up off your knees, girl.

(BIG DADDY *helps* MARGARET *to rise. He crosses above her, to her right, bites off the end of a fresh cigar, taken from his bathrobe pocket, as he studies* MARGARET.)

Uh-huh, this girl has life in her body, that's no lie!

BIG MAMA: BIG DADDY'S DREAM COME TRUE!

BRICK: JESUS!

BIG DADDY (*crossing right below wicker stand*): Gooper, I want my lawyer in the mornin'.

BRICK: Where are you goin', Big Daddy?

BIG DADDY: Son, I'm goin' up on the roof, to the belvedere on th' roof to look over my kingdom before I give up my kingdom—twenty-eight thousand acres of th' richest land this side of the valley Nile!

(*He exits through right doors, and down right on the gallery.*)

BIG MAMA (*following*): Sweetheart, sweetheart, sweetheart—can I come with you?

(*She exits down stage right.*)
(MARGARET *is down stage center in the mirror area.* MAE *has joined* GOOPER *and she gives him a fierce poke, making a low hissing sound and a grimace of fury.*)

GOOPER (*pushing her aside.*): Brick, could you possibly spare me one small shot of that liquor?

BRICK: Why, help yourself, Gooper boy.

GOOPER: I will.

MAE (*shrilly*): Of course we know that this is—a lie.

GOOPER: *Be still, Mae.*

MAE: I won't be still! I know she's made this up!

GOOPER: Goddam it, I said shut up!

MARGARET: Gracious! I didn't know that my little announcement was going to provoke such a storm!

MAE: *That* woman isn't *pregnant!*

GOOPER: Who said she was?

MAE: *She* did.

GOOPER: The doctor didn't. Doc Baugh didn't.

MARGARET: I haven't gone to Doc Baugh.

GOOPER: Then who'd you go to, Maggie?

MARGARET: One of the best gynecologists in the South.

GOOPER: Uh huh, uh huh!—I see . . . (*He takes out a pencil and notebook.*) —May we have his name, please?

MARGARET: No, you may not, Mister Prosecuting Attorney!

MAE: He doesn't have any name, he doesn't exist!

MARGARET: Oh, he exists all right, and so does my child, Brick's baby!

MAE: You can't conceive a child by a man that won't sleep with you unless you think you're—

(BRICK *has turned on the phonograph. A scat song cuts* MAE's *speech.*)

GOOPER: *Turn that off!*

MAE: We know it's a lie because we hear you in here; he won't sleep with you, we hear you! So don't imagine you're going to put a trick over on us, to fool a dying man with a—

(*A long drawn cry of agony and rage fills the house.* MARGARET *turns the phonograph down to a whisper. The cry is repeated.*)

MAE: Did you hear that, Gooper, did you hear that?

GOOPER: Sounds like the pain has struck.

MAE: Go see, Gooper!

GOOPER: Come along and leave these lovebirds together in their nest!

(*He goes out first.* MAE *follows but turns at the door, contorting her face and hissing at* MARGARET.)

MAE: *Liar!*

(*She slams the door.*)
(MARGARET *exhales with relief and moves a little unsteadily to catch hold of* BRICK's *arm.*)

MARGARET: Thank you for—keeping still . . .

BRICK: O.K., Maggie.

MARGARET: It was gallant of you to save my face!

(*He now pours down three shots in quick succession and stands waiting, silent. All at once he turns with a smile and says.*)

BRICK: *There!*

MARGARET: What?

BRICK: The *click* . . .

(*His gratitude seems almost infinite as he hobbles out on the gallery with a drink. We hear his crutch as he swings out of sight. Then, at some distance, he begins singing to himself a peaceful song.* MARGARET *holds the big pillow forlornly as if it were her only companion, for a few moments, then throws it on the bed. She rushes to the liquor cabinet, gathers all the bottles in her arms, turns about undecidedly, then runs out of the room with them, leaving the door ajar on the dim yellow hall.* BRICK *is heard hobbling back along the gallery, singing his peaceful song. He comes back in, sees the pillow on the bed, laughs lightly, sadly, picks it up. He has it under his arm as* MARGARET *returns to the room.* MARGARET *softly shuts the door and leans against it, smiling softly at* BRICK.)

MARGARET: Brick, I used to think that you were stronger than me and I didn't want to be overpowered by you. But now, since you've taken to liquor—you know what?—I guess it's bad, but now I'm stronger than you and I can love you more truly! Don't move that pillow, I'll move it right back if you do!—Brick?

(She turns out all the lamps but a single rose-silk-shaded one by the bed.)

I really have been to a doctor and I know what to do and—Brick?—this is my time by the calendar to conceive?

BRICK: Yes, I understand, Maggie. But how are you going to conceive a child by a man in love with his liquor?

MARGARET: By locking his liquor up and making him satisfy my desire before I unlock it!

BRICK: Is that what you've done, Maggie?

MARGARET: Look and see. That cabinet's mighty empty compared to before!

BRICK: Well, I'll be a son of a—

(He reaches for his crutch but she beats him to it and rushes out on the gallery, hurls the crutch over the rail and comes back in, panting.)

MARGARET: And so tonight we're going to make the lie true, and when that's done, I'll bring the liquor back here and we'll get drunk together, here, tonight, in this place that death has come into . . . —What do you say?

BRICK: I don't say anything. I guess there's nothing to say.

MARGARET: Oh, you weak people, you weak, beautiful people who give up with such grace. What you want is someone to—

(She turns out the rose-silk lamp.)

—take hold of you.—Gently, gently with love hand your life back to you, like somethin' gold you let go of. I do love you, Brick, I do!

BRICK (smiling with charming sadness): Wouldn't it be funny if that was true?

Figure 1. Maggie (Elizabeth Ashley) and Brick (Keir Dullea) in the American Shakespeare Theater production of *Cat on a Hot Tin Roof*, directed by Michael Kahn and designed by John Conklin, New York, 1974. (Photograph: Martha Swope.)

Figure 2. Brick (Keir Dullea) and Big Daddy (Fred Gwynne) in the American Shakespeare Theater production of *Cat on a Hot Tin Roof*, directed by Michael Kahn and designed by John Conklin, New York, 1974. (Photograph: Martha Swope.)

Figure 3. Mae (Joan Pape, *standing center*), Gooper (Charles Siebert), and their five children perform a musical chorus to celebrate the birthday of Big Daddy (Fred Gwynne), while *(left to right)* Reverend Tooker (Wyman Pendleton), Doctor Baugh (William Larsen), Big Mama (Kate Reid), Sookey (Sarallen), and Lacey look on in the American Shakespeare Theater production of *Cat on a Hot Tin Roof,* directed by Michael Kahn and designed by John Conklin, New York, 1974. This photograph also shows the realistic/expressionistic set with walls that "dissolve mysteriously into air," as Williams specified in his "Notes to the Designer." (Photograph: Martha Swope.)

Figure 4. Big Daddy (Fred Gwynne) tells the story of the "ole bull elephant" to Mae (Joan Pape), Big Mama (Kate Reid), and Maggie (Elizabeth Ashley) in the American Shakespeare Theater production of *Cat on a Hot Tin Roof,* directed by Michael Kahn and designed by John Conklin, New York, 1974. (Photograph: Martha Swope.)

Staging of *Cat on a Hot Tin Roof*

**REVIEW OF THE AMERICAN SHAKESPEARE
THEATER PRODUCTION, 1974, BY CLIVE BARNES**

People used to think that Tennessee Williams's plays were about sex and violence. How wrong they were—they are about love and survival. Mr. Williams's "Cat on a Hot Tin Roof" is now 20 years old, and in its first day it was regarded as something of a shocker. Now even though a certain four-letter word has been restored where a euphemism once reigned stupidly supreme, I doubt whether anyone is going to be shocked . . . . But I hope they will be affected. This is a gripping and intensely moving play, a play that can hold its own with anything written in the post-O'Neill American theater.

The Cat is Maggie—a Southern beauty of indefinite lineage. She is married to Brick, a handsome, former football player, now TV sportscaster. The marriage could be perfect, but Brick is an impotent alcoholic who fears that he failed his best friend, apparently a homosexual. Brick's father, Big Daddy, a self-made Southern millionaire, is dying of cancer. He doesn't know it. His wife doesn't know it. But the family, including Brick's brother and sister-in-law, they know it. It is Big Daddy's 65th, and last, birthday.

Michael Kahn's new staging, which opened at the ANTA Theater last night for a limited run, really is new. It originated at the American Shakespeare Theater in Connecticut this summer, and it offers a rewarding new variant on the original play.

As is well known the Broadway version, directed by Elia Kazan, incorporated in its last act a number of Mr. Kazan's own ideas. Indeed in most printed versions of the play the last act exists in two versions, the so-called "Broadway" version, and the original. In the latter Big Daddy does not appear and Brick, faced with some faint prospect of fatherhood, changes somewhat in his character. Mr. Kahn, presumably with the playwright's permission, seems to have taken the best of both acts—following Mr. Kazan in his inclusion of Big Daddy in the last act (and Kazan was right in his thinking there), and yet following the original in its far more sensitive handling of the final relationship between Brick and Maggie. The result seems to be a definitive version of the play.

Twenty years ago everyone made much of the symbolism in Tennessee Williams, and undoubtedly the symbolism is here. The magnolia scented bedroom that used to belong to the old-maidish bachelors that once owned the plantation, the concept of the bed itself as Maggie's territory, or Brick's possible latent homosexuality symbolized by his hazy impotence—yes, all these are symbols of the sexual warfare that underlies the story. But the story itself, and the compassion Mr. Williams brings to the telling of it, is what really matters.

Mr. Williams has the one vital gift a playwright must possess—he holds the interest. He makes you care by showing you a world. His characters are drawn with rough strokes, for Mr. Williams always demonstrates by exaggeration. He is also a playwright who wants to be very popular (or, rather, very much loved) and this sometimes leads him into cheapness. But he is a master. His plays have a time, a place, a development and ring true.

He is lucky with Mr. Kahn, whose direction seems directly aimed at lowering the play's hot-house temperature, and at making a domestic drama rather than an eternal triangle between a woman, a reluctant man and a bed. As a result Big Daddy becomes rather more important than before.

The imaginative setting by John Conklin, the cleverly evocative costumes by Jane Greenwood and the dappled lighting by Marc B. Weiss, are all splendid, but if Mr. Williams has been fortunate in Mr. Kahn and his collaborators, Mr. Kahn has been equally fortunate in his cast, or at least clever in his casting.

Elizabeth Ashley was much praised for her Maggie in Connecticut, but even then she was sold short. Sensuous, withdrawn, composed and determined, Miss Ashley's Maggie vibrantly combines charm with grit. She can stand outside a conversation like a cobra, or flutter in like a bird. Splendid.

Keir Dullea's ironic, embittered Brick makes her the perfect partner. He has precisely "the charm of the defeated," with his alcoholic eyes staring into the mid-distance of half-forgotten memory, still waiting for the click of oblivion. Both this Brick and this Maggie are oddly vulnerable, which is also the special quality of Fred Gwynne's blustering, hollowed out Big Daddy. These three performances are so right that they detract from the more shallow playing of the rest of the cast, including Kate Reid, slightly too shrill as a miscast Big Mama.

This is a glowing play, memorably staged. It gets Broadway's dramatic season off to a flying start.

CONTEMPORARY THEATER

Most periods in the history of drama are associated with distinctive theatrical structures—the classical Greek with outdoor amphitheaters; the middle ages with pageant wagons and platform stages; the renaissance English with multi-level open-air theaters; the neoclassical with indoor theaters, proscenium stages, and perspective backdrops; the modern with fan-shaped auditoriums and box sets. During the contemporary period, variety is the rule in theatrical structures and staging conventions. The fan-shaped auditorium and the box set of realistic theater (see pages 2 and 4) continue to flourish in many amateur and professional houses. Yet, in addition to this now common pattern, other theatrical arrangements have developed, reflecting a renewed interest in earlier methods of staging. In an attempt to reclaim and combine elements of the classical Greek and renaissance English theaters, mid-twentieth-century designers created the thrust stage (see Figure 1), in which the audience is seated on rising tiers around three sides of a platform, the fourth side being occupied by a permanent setting that contains multiple acting surfaces. And somewhat earlier in the century, designers reclaimed the medieval style of theater-in-the-round and turned it into the arena stage (see Figure 2), an arrangement placing the audience on all four sides of the actors and using the aisles for entrances and exits. The theatrical freedom of the arena stage has also prompted directors and producers to reclaim another medieval heritage by putting on plays in the street, in public squares, or any other open space that will bring actors and spectators closer to each other than is possible in the traditional theater.

Contemporary set design has been equally flexible, ranging from a total abandonment of settings, set pieces, and props to the use of highly elaborate set designs in a realistic or symbolic style. In part, of course, various styles in set design have been determined by the nature of the theatrical environment. Arena stages and thrust stages clearly do not invite the use of box sets or painted backdrops. But even in a conventional modern theater, where the realism of the box set has been readily accessible, designers have taken the liberty of blending and modifying a combination of styles to achieve unique dramatic effects. Harold Pinter's stage direction for *The Homecoming* (1965) asks for "An old house in North London. A large room, extending the width of the stage" but also specifies that "The back wall, which contained the door, has been removed. A square arch shape remains." Such a direction, and the resulting design by John Bury, clearly portrayed a house both real and unreal, familiar and strange, a setting in which individual props, such as the glass of water about which Lenny and Ruth talk, seem to take on symbolic weight far greater than they might have in a more conventional set.

The freedom in contemporary theater to choose among a variety of styles has also made it possible for dramatists to reject realistic conventions altogether, as did the playwrights of the most influential movement of the 1950s and 1960s,

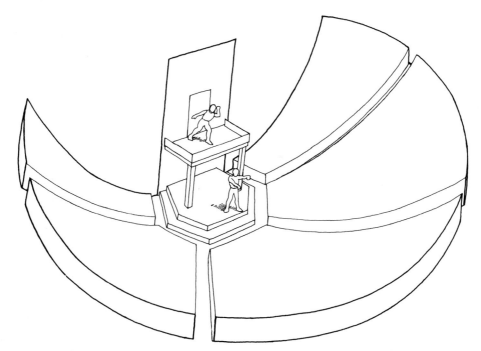

Figure 1. The contemporary thrust stage, showing the multiple acting surfaces adapted from the renaissance English theater, surrounded on three sides by the rising tiers of seats adapted from the classical Greek theater.

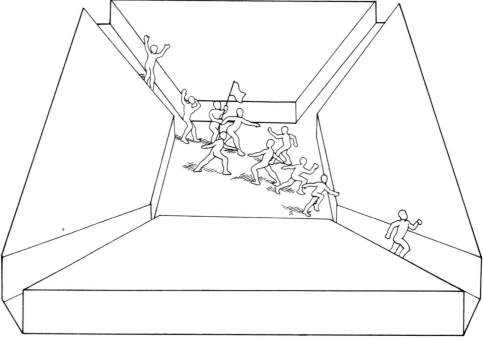

Figure 2. The contemporary arena stage.

the "Theater of the Absurd," a movement defined and named by the critic Martin Esslin. The absurdists—most notably Samuel Beckett, Eugène Ionesco, and Jean Genet—rejected such realistic conventions as psychologically motivated characters and plots, logically consistent dialogue, and familiar styles of presentation, for, as Esslin explained, "The Theatre of the Absurd has renounced arguing about the absurdity of the human condition; it merely presents it in being—that is, in terms of the concrete stage images of the absurdity of existence." Given their acute sense of the malignancy, or meaninglessness, or sterility of existence, the absurdists deliberately favor stage actions and images that will clearly evoke such a view of experience, whether it is the garbage can residents of Beckett's *Endgame* (1957) or the rhinoceros that takes over the world in Ionesco's *Rhinoceros* (1959). The drama that Esslin has labelled absurdist has its roots in avant-garde theater of the early twentieth century, in such plays as Alfred Jarry's *Ubu Roi* (1896), a scatological and seemingly nonsensical play about a brutal and whimsical ruler, or Guillaume Apollinaire's *The Breasts of Tiresias* (1917), which features a dancing news-kiosk and a woman turning into a man when her breasts float away as balloons. Absurdism derives as well from the radical ideas of Antonin Artaud, who in 1938 expounded a "theater of cruelty" which he based on the assumption that "Everything that acts is a cruelty. It is upon this idea of extreme action, pushed beyond all limits, that theatre must be rebuilt." Although absurdist drama, strictly speaking, does not exemplify the theater of cruelty, it does clearly push drama to extreme actions and images.

Not only is absurdist drama a striking instance of the stylistic freedom in contemporary theater, it has also been an influence nurturing even greater experimentation among playwrights, directors, actors, and set designers. After seeing Beckett's *Waiting for Godot* (1952), for example, the dramatist William Saroyan said, "It will make it easier for me and everyone else to write freely in the theatre." Unhampered by expectations about what drama should be, contemporary playwrights have constantly experimented with symbolic and image-centered drama, as indicated by the metaphoric titles of their plays, such as *Endgame, Dutchman, Professional Foul,* and *Temptation.* The dramatic inventions of the playwrights have, in turn, stimulated designers, such as Eiko Ishioka who created the curving ramp that swirls around the stage in *M. Butterfly.* And the actors themselves, of course, have been forced to develop nonrealistic styles of performance, a challenge that has provoked them to explore the arts of dance, mime, and vaudeville. How, after all, is it possible for an actor to portray "realistically" the process of a man turning into a rhinoceros, or of a mute, in *Waiting for Godot,* suddenly unleashing a torrent of speech? The need to find new acting styles and to make sense of these plays for an audience has ultimately led to a greatly increased emphasis on the imaginative leadership of the director.

Indeed, contemporary theater, whether it has taken the form of realism, modified realism, or absurdism, has often been determined not only by a playwright's script but also by a director's creative influence upon the script. Max Stafford-Clark, artistic director of England's Royal Court Theatre, a nationally subsidized theater devoted to the production of new plays, furnished not only financial support and a stage for *Our Country's Good* but the inspiration as well. After reading *The Playmaker,* a novel about a production of *The Recruiting Officer* in Australia in 1789, he commissioned Timberlake Wertenbaker to do an ad-

aptation of the novel that would run in repertory with *The Recruiting Officer.*
The creative influence of the director is reflected by August Wilson's tribute in
Fences to "Lloyd Richards, who adds to whatever he touches," a public acknowledgment of Wilson's debt to the Yale Repertory Theatre director who has
directed all of his major works.

Perhaps the most striking example of the creative director in contemporary
theater is the Englishman, Peter Brook, whose productions of Shakespeare have
moved critics to speak of "Brook's *King Lear*" and "Brook's *A Midsummer Night's
Dream,*" rather than Shakespeare's. Brook first came to public notice in the early
1940s and 1950s as a "boy genius" directing major productions of Shakespeare
in London and Stratford. But his sensational reputation as a revolutionary
director did not get established until 1962 when he produced *King Lear* in a
style heavily influenced by the starkly expressionistic techniques of Brecht's epic
theater. Brook was further influenced by Artaud's theater of cruelty, which led
him to argue that cruelty is a necessary "form of self-discipline" for performers;
he thus entered into an intense period of physical exercises and improvisations
with a group of selected actors, a project culminating in his 1964 production of
Peter Weiss's *Marat/Sade,* an elaborate play-within-a-play that features the inmates of a mental asylum staging the events of the French Revolution. Brook's
highly disciplined actors kept the stage in a continuous state of theatrical disarray
in order to convey the deranged experience of a mental asylum—the actors
performing as inmates never stopped moving and drooling and acting out their
fantasies. And at the play's conclusion, when the inmates begin attacking the
onstage audience who have watched the play, Brook added a final inventive
touch: as the audience applauded, the actors lined up and steadily, smirkingly,
rhythmically applauded back. Since his work in the 1960s with the Royal Shakespeare Company, Brook has formed his own theater company and established
himself in Paris, where he has presented productions as varied as *The Cherry
Orchard* (see page 113), a reworking of Bizet's opera *Carmen,* and a ten-hour
adaptation of the great Indian epic, *The Mahabharata.*

The revolution in contemporary theater has been carried to its logical extreme
by directors who have formed repertory groups committed to a radical alteration
of virtually all the traditional conventions of drama. During the late 1960s, for
example, the Living Theater of Julian Beck and Judith Malina staged a series
of works stressing political activism—an activism they sought to dramatize by
deliberately breaking the barrier that has traditionally separated actors from
spectators. Members of the Living Theater routinely talked to, touched, and
even invited the audience onstage during their performances, and one of their
productions, *Paradise Now,* actually climaxed with a "love pile" or "group grope"
for both actors and those members of the audience who still remained in the
theater. By contrast, Jerzy Grotowski and the Polish Laboratory Theatre deliberately sought to isolate members of the audience, bringing each person in a
forty- or fifty-person group into the acting space one by one, sometimes even
seating them behind raised walls. Furthermore, by abandoning a permanent
stage and choosing to redesign the acting space for each play, by discarding
makeup, costumes, props, and music, Grotowski created what has been known
as "poor theater," in order to focus on "the personal and scenic technique of
the actor as the core of theater art." Other experimental groups of the 1960s

and 1970s have applied the rituals of yoga and meditation to theatrical performance, and still others have staged productions in slow motion, creating barely moving visual images in works that run from three to twelve hours in length. Perhaps the most remarkable element in all these experimental groups is not their assault upon theatrical conventions, nor their intense fascination with sound and movement, but their abandonment of scripted plays in favor of improvisation—a phenomenon reminiscent of Artaud's manifesto calling for "No More Masterpieces!"

The 1980s may have brought about a closer working relationship between playwright, director, and actors, especially when one considers the plays of Caryl Churchill, the most notable of which grew out of workshops with actors and directors, or the productions of Ariane Mnouchkine in Paris, whose company of actors and musicians, like that of Peter Brook, has worked with established writers to create the script for productions such as an eight-hour play about Cambodia and Prince Sihanouk. Great Britain's long tradition of repertory companies has led to these groups either commissioning plays or sometimes creating elaborate adaptations, such as a two-part, eight-and-a-half-hour version of Dickens' *Nicholas Nickleby*, which grew out of a collaboration between directors Trevor Nunn and John Caird, playwright David Edgar, and forty-some actors of the Royal Shakespeare Company. In America, several regional theaters have been particularly important in developing new plays and playwrights. The Actors Theater of Louisville and its artistic director, Jon Jory, have been crucial in the development of Marsha Norman's work, just as the Yale Repertory Theatre and its director, Lloyd Richards, have been central to the career of August Wilson.

While contemporary drama has developed through a series of collaborative theatrical ventures, it also reflects and challenges the most popular art forms of our day, film and television. Because film and television can attract such large audiences, contemporary drama must contend with these popular forms of entertainment. One strategy is to create something entirely different: contemporary drama is often sparse where film is lush, abstract where television is realistic. In Beckett's *Endgame*, people live with only the barest remnants of ordinary life; in Shange's *spell #7*, the performers sometimes wear masks to reflect stereotypes; in Wertenbaker's *Our Country's Good*, everyone in the cast plays at least two roles, with women convicts sometimes appearing as male soldiers. But contemporary drama also *uses* the realism associated with film and television. Neil Simon's phenomenally successful career reflects his particular talent for finding humor in details from domestic life and in his characters' inability to cope with such details. The same reliance on realistic detail appears in Marsha Norman's *'night, Mother*, though in this play Jessie's insistence on dealing with the minutiae of everyday life throws into horrifying relief her lack of control over everything else. Much as contemporary drama has drawn on the techniques of film and television, so contemporary dramatists often write for both stage and screen: Harold Pinter and Sam Shepard are successful filmscript writers; Tom Stoppard created *Professional Foul* for BBC television. Film and television scripts usually involve many short scenes, perhaps because the medium allows for such fast cutting from one place to another, while realistic stage scripts have often opted for a single set. Yet the blending of the two approaches is also frequent in contemporary drama, as in the many short scenes of both *M. Butterfly* and *Our Country's Good*, scenes that shift the audience's focus not only from one group of characters to another but from one place to another.

Such "fragmentary" structures are not unique to film or television. Elizabethan drama often juxtaposed short scenes, frequently contrasting social classes or geographic locales. Indeed, one might argue that what is new in contemporary theater is really an echo of what is old. Just as contemporary theatrical design reflects a variety of staging techniques from the classical, medieval, and renaissance periods, so the contemporary experimental fascination with sound and movement recalls the religious rituals from which drama first arose. In fact, contemporary drama both implicitly and explicitly alludes to and revises earlier drama, whether we hear Hamm in *Endgame* mimicking Shakespearean characters or the scientist Foustka in *Temptation* summoning a devil, Fistula, much as Marlowe's Faustus summoned Mephistophilis. The last two plays in this collection could not exist without their predecessors: *M. Butterfly* rewrites and quotes Puccini's opera *Madame Butterfly*, while *Our Country's Good* rehearses and extends relationships from Farquhar's *The Recruiting Officer*. Thus the history of theater seems to follow a cyclical pattern, though perhaps it would be more accurate to say, as Peter Brook has, that the theater is not static or unchanging, that "truth in the theater is always on the move." Such movement is inherent in drama, on any stage, at any stage of history, for drama is a living form of art; it draws its life from live actors and a live audience coming together to create the performance.

EUGÈNE IONESCO

1912–

When Martin Esslin coined the phrase "the theatre of the absurd," he adopted Albert Camus's notion of a human being as a stranger, "an irremediable exile," caught in the absurd and painful predicament of having neither a past to remember nor a future to hope for. Eugène Ionesco, born in Bucharest, Rumania, to a Rumanian father and a French mother, has in a sense always been an exile. When he was very young, his parents took him to France where he lived first in Paris, and then, because he developed anemia, on a farm in the country, a place he would later describe as his lost paradise. In 1925, the family returned to Rumania where, at the age of thirteen, Ionesco learned his native language for the first time. As a young literary critic, he published an attack on three Rumanian writers, only to bring out a second essay a few days later praising the very same authors; then under the title *No!*, he published the two essays together, a first glimpse of the confusing and often contradictory experience that his plays would later dramatize. Ionesco taught French for two years in Bucharest but then returned to France, planning to write a doctoral thesis on contemporary French poetry. Instead he wrote about his childhood, began a novel, and to support himself, worked in a publishing house. The outbreak of World War II in 1939 compelled him to remain in France, together with his wife and baby daughter.

How then did Ionesco become a playwright? Already fluent in both French and Rumanian, Ionesco decided in 1948 to learn English. Picking up a self-study course in dialogue form, "L'Anglais Sans Peine" ("English without difficulty"), he became fascinated by the conversation between the characters: "To my astonishment, Mrs. Smith informed her husband that they had several children, that they lived in the vicinity of London, that their name was Smith, that Mr. Smith was a clerk, that they had a servant, Mary—English, like themselves." As Ionesco copied out the sentences, he found a "tragedy of language" in this conversation so full of clichés as to be meaningless—and thus drafted his "anti-play," *La Cantatrice chauve* (*The Bald Soprano*). The friends to whom he read this play found it not tragic but very funny, so much so that one of them helped to get it produced at a small avant-garde theater. In Ionesco's exuberant adaptation of the English lessons, not only do the Smiths inform each other of facts that they must already know, but their dinner guests, Mr. and Mrs. Martin, begin by addressing each other as strangers but eventually discover that they are married to each other. After building to a crescendo of nonsense words and syllables, the play then begins again, this time with the Martins speaking the lines of the Smiths.

Though *The Bald Soprano* ran for only six weeks in 1950, Ionesco continued to write absurdist plays and to get them produced: *The Lesson* (1951), *The Chairs* (1952), *Amédée, or How to Get Rid of It* (1954), *Jack or the Submission* (1955). Most of these were one-acts, although *Amédée*, which features a corpse that keeps growing and finally floats away into space carrying Amédée with it, is a three-act play, as is *The Killer* (1959). In *The Killer*, whose French title, *Tueur sans gages*, implies that the killer works without payment and thus kills almost randomly, Ionesco presents a world clearly echoing the memories of his idyllic childhood in the French countryside, a "radiant city" where it is always springtime, but a city now deserted because of the mysterious killer. In the last act, the protagonist, Bérenger, tries to appeal to the killer, but hears only chuckling. The ineffectiveness of Bérenger's arguments against such meaningless murder represents Ionesco's most despairing view of humanity. Such helplessness also underlies his next major play, *Rhinoceros* (1960), in which Bérenger, again the protagonist, resists the forces of social/political conformity as represented by the rhinoceros. While *The Killer* shows Bérenger gradually succumbing both to the killer's inexorable chuckling and, in Ionesco's words, to "the vacuity of his own rather commonplace morality," *Rhinoceros* presents at least the possibility that an individual human being might triumph over the thundering menace of mass thinking. Two major productions of *Rhinoceros* in 1960 (the first in Paris, starring the great French actor-manager, Jean-Louis Barrault, the second in London, directed by Orson Welles and starring Laurence Olivier) both reflected and contributed to Ionesco's growing public stature.

To many critics, the take-over by the rhinoceroses and the willingness of everyone in the play, except for Bérenger, to change into a rhinoceros, was a parable about the success of the Nazi movement. Ionesco had seen the violence of the Nazis when he lived in Rumania, and had felt for himself the difficulty of challenging Fascist doctrine: "When you're twenty years old and you have teachers who offer you scientific or pseudo-scientific theories and explanations, when you have newspapers, when you have a whole atmosphere, doctrines, a whole movement against you, it's really very hard to resist, hard not to let yourself be convinced." And, as the reference to teachers suggests, Ionesco held major doubts about his own life both as a student and then as a teacher.

All of the major themes in Ionesco's plays—the meaningless aspect of language, the human being's tendency to violence, the destructive power of collective thinking—find chilling expression in *The Lesson*. At first, *The Lesson* seems a comedy about education as the young woman coming for a private tutorial with the Professor can hardly remember the capital of France but wishes to qualify for a doctorate in just three weeks. Comically, too, the tutorial begins with arithmetic (the Pupil can't subtract but she can multiply two ten-digit numbers correctly) and then moves to linguistics and comparative philology. Just as Ionesco delights in exposing linguistic clichés in *The Bald Soprano*, so in *The Lesson* the Professor explains how languages differ from one another through "something intangible that one is able to perceive only after very long study, with a great deal of trouble and after the broadest experience." The Professor's discussion of the names of countries, while ridiculous on one level, is also a painful echo of Ionesco's own confusion when he moved from France to Rumania: "At primary school, in France, I'd been taught that French—which was my language—was the most beautiful language in the world, that the French were the bravest people in the world. . . . When I got to Bucharest, my teachers explained that my language was Rumanian, that the most beautiful language in the world was not French but Rumanian. . . ."

By the end of the play, when the Professor attacks the Pupil not only with words but with a knife, Ionesco's perception of the world as one in which "the comic is terrifying, the comic is tragic," becomes frighteningly clear. The donning of an armband with a swastika implies political violence, just as the description of the attack on the Pupil implies not only murder but also rape. The explicit onstage attack, similar to the endings of Albee's *The Zoo Story* and Baraka's *Dutchman*, dramatizes the struggle for power in terms of sexual relationships. Indeed, more recent plays, such as Robert Athayde's *Miss Margarida's Way* (first American production, 1977) and David Mamet's highly controversial *Oleanna* (1992), have taken the teacher/student relationship and used it, as Ionesco does, as a metaphor for political, social, and sexual domination.

In performance, *The Lesson* has seemed both opaque and accessible, as reflected in reviews of the 1958 New York production. Brooks Atkinson, writing in the *New York Times*, seemed willing to accept *The Chairs* and *The Lesson* as "odd, elliptical fantastifications" and to enjoy a "diverting evening," without feeling bothered by the fact that he couldn't "explain the cosmic significance of M. Ionesco's theme." Walter Kerr, whose review is reprinted following the text, was bothered by the "defiant mindlessness" of both plays, and felt he had followed "a long, tortured, circuitous, pretentious road to a nice, round zero that might be drawn at once." Yet Kerr still responded to the power of the production, with most of his reservations coming afterwards when he thought about what he had seen. The theatrical energy of the performance, so strikingly evoked in Kerr's description of Max Adrian and Joan Plowright (see Figure 1), is thus balanced by the "black despair" of the playwright's vision, as the maid comforts the murderous Professor (see Figure 2) and then calmly ushers in the forty-first pupil and the forty-first victim.

THE LESSON
A Comic Drama

BY EUGÈNE IONESCO

THE CHARACTERS

THE PROFESSOR, *aged fifty to sixty*
THE YOUNG PUPIL, *aged eighteen*
THE MAID, *aged forty-five to fifty*

SCENE

The office of the old professor, which also serves as a dining room. To the left, a door opens onto the apartment stairs; upstage, to the right, another door opens onto a corridor of the apartment. Upstage, a little left of center, a window, not very large, with plain curtains; on the outside sill of the window are ordinary potted plants. The low buildings with red roofs of a small town can be seen in the distance. The sky is grayish-blue. On the right stands a provincial buffet. The table doubles as a desk, it stands at stage center. There are three chairs around the table, and two more stand on each side of the window. Light-colored wallpaper, some shelves with books.

(When the curtain rises the stage is empty, and it remains so for a few moments. Then we hear the doorbell ring.)

VOICE OF THE MAID *(from the corridor)*: Yes. I'm coming.

(The MAID *comes in, after having run down the stairs. She is stout, aged forty-five to fifty, red-faced, and wears a peasant woman's cap. She rushes in, slamming the door to the right behind her, and dries her hands on her apron as she runs towards the door on the left. Meanwhile we hear the doorbell ring again.)*

MAID: Just a moment, I'm coming.

(She opens the door. A young PUPIL, *aged eighteen, enters. She is wearing a gray student's smock, a small white collar, and carries a student's satchel under her arm.)*

MAID: Good morning, miss.

PUPIL: Good morning, madam. Is the Professor at home?

MAID: Have you come for the lesson?

PUPIL: Yes, I have.

MAID: He's expecting you. Sit down for a moment. I'll tell him you're here.

PUPIL: Thank you.

(She seats herself near the table, facing the audience; the hall door is to her left; her back is to the other door, through which the MAID *hurriedly exits, calling:)*

MAID: Professor, come down please, your pupil is here.

VOICE OF THE PROFESSOR *(rather reedy)*: Thank you. I'm coming . . . in just a moment . . .

(The MAID *exits; the* PUPIL *draws in her legs, holds her satchel on her lap, and waits demurely. She casts a glance or two around the room, at the furniture, at the ceiling too. Then she takes a notebook out of her satchel, leafs through it, and stops to look at a page for a moment as though reviewing a lesson, as though taking a last look at her homework. She seems to be a well-brought-up girl, polite, but lively, gay, dynamic; a fresh smile is on her lips. During the course of the play she progressively loses the lively rhythm of her movement and her carriage, she becomes withdrawn. From gay and smiling she becomes progressively sad and morose; from very lively at the beginning, she becomes more and more fatigued and somnolent. Towards the end of the play her face must clearly express a nervous depression; her way of speaking shows the effects of this, her tongue becomes thick, words come to her memory with difficulty and emerge from her mouth with as much difficulty; she comes to have a manner vaguely paralyzed, the beginning of aphasia.° Firm and determined at the beginning, so much so as to appear to be almost aggressive, she becomes more and more passive, until she is almost a mute and inert object, seemingly inanimate in the* PROFESSOR's *hands, to such an extent that when he makes his final gesture, she no longer reacts. Insensible, her reflexes deadened, only her eyes in an expressionless face will show inexpressible astonishment and fear. The transition from one manner to the other must of course be made imperceptibly.)*

(The PROFESSOR *enters. He is a little old man with a little white beard. He wears pince-nez,° a black skull cap, a long black schoolmaster's coat, trousers and shoes of black, detachable white collar, a black tie. Excessively polite, very timid, his voice deadened by his timidity, very proper, very much the teacher. He rubs his hands together constantly; occasionally a lewd gleam comes into his eyes and is quickly repressed.)*

(During the course of the play his timidity will disappear progressively, imperceptibly; and the lewd gleams in his eyes will become a steady devouring flame in the end.

---

aphasia, loss of the power of using or understanding words. **pince-nez,** eyeglasses attached to the nose by a spring-clip.

From a manner that is inoffensive at the start, the PRO-
FESSOR *becomes more and more sure of himself, more
and more nervous, aggressive, dominating, until he is
able to do as he pleases with the* PUPIL, *who has become,
in his hands, a pitiful creature. Of course, the voice of
the* PROFESSOR *must change too, from thin and reedy, to
stronger and stronger, until at the end it is extremely
powerful, ringing, sonorous, while the* PUPIL's *voice
changes from the very clear and ringing tones that she
has at the beginning of the play until it is almost inau-
dible. In these first scenes the* PROFESSOR *might stammer
very slightly.)*

PROFESSOR: Good morning, young lady. You . . . I expect that you . . . that you are the new pupil?

PUPIL *(turns quickly with a lively and self-assured manner;
she gets up, goes toward the* PROFESSOR, *and gives him
her hand)*: Yes, Professor. Good morning, Professor. As you see, I'm on time. I didn't want to be
late.

PROFESSOR: That's fine, miss. Thank you, you didn't
really need to hurry. I am very sorry to have kept
you waiting . . . I was just finishing up . . . well . . .
I'm sorry . . . You will excuse me, won't you?

PUPIL: Oh, certainly, Professor. It doesn't matter at all,
Professor.

PROFESSOR: Please excuse me . . . Did you have any
trouble finding the house?

PUPIL: No . . . Not at all. I just asked the way. Everybody
knows you around here.

PROFESSOR: For thirty years I've lived in this town.
You've not been here for long? How do you find
it?

PUPIL: It's all right. The town is attractive and even
agreeable, there's a nice park, a boarding school, a
bishop, nice shops and streets . . .

PROFESSOR: That's very true, young lady. And yet, I'd
just as soon live somewhere else. In Paris, or at least
Bordeaux.

PUPIL: Do you like Bordeaux?

PROFESSOR: I don't know. I've never seen it.

PUPIL: But you know Paris?

PROFESSOR: No, I don't know it either, young lady, but
if you'll permit me, can you tell me, Paris is the
capital city of . . . miss?

PUPIL *(searching her memory for a moment, then, happily
guessing)*: Paris is the capital city of . . . France?

PROFESSOR: Yes, young lady, bravo, that's very good,
that's perfect. My congratulations. You have your
French geography at your finger tips. You know
your chief cities.

PUPIL: Oh! I don't know them all yet, Professor, it's not
quite that easy, I have trouble learning them.

PROFESSOR: Oh! it will come . . . you mustn't give up . . .
young lady . . . I beg your pardon . . . have patience
. . . little by little . . . You will see, it will come in
time . . . What a nice day it is today . . . or rather,
not so nice . . . Oh! but then yes it is nice. In short,

it's not too bad a day, that's the main thing . . . ahem
. . . ahem . . . it's not raining and it's not snowing
either.

PUPIL: That would be most unusual, for it's summer
now.

PROFESSOR: Excuse me, miss, I was just going to say so
. . . but as you will learn, one must be ready for
anything.

PUPIL: I guess so, Professor.

PROFESSOR: We can't be sure of anything, young lady,
in this world.

PUPIL: The snow falls in the winter. Winter is one of
the four seasons. The other three are . . . uh . . .
spr . . .

PROFESSOR: Yes?

PUPIL: . . . ing, and then summer . . . and . . . uh . . .

PROFESSOR: It begins like "automobile," miss.

PUPIL: Ah, yes, autumn . . .

PROFESSOR: That's right, miss. That's a good answer,
that's perfect. I am convinced that you will be a
good pupil. You will make real progress. You are
intelligent, you seem to me to be well informed,
and you've a good memory.

PUPIL: I know my seasons, don't I, Professor?

PROFESSOR: Yes, indeed, miss . . . or almost. But it will
come in time. In any case, you're coming along.
Soon you'll know all the seasons, even with your
eyes closed. Just as I do.

PUPIL: It's hard.

PROFESSOR: Oh, no. All it takes is a little effort, a little
good will, miss. You will see. It will come, you may
be sure of that.

PUPIL: Oh, I do hope so, Professor. I have a great thirst
for knowledge. My parents also want me to get an
education. They want me to specialize. They consider a little general culture, even if it is solid, is no
longer enough, in these times.

PROFESSOR: Your parents, miss, are perfectly right. You
must go on with your studies. Forgive me for saying
so, but it is very necessary. Our contemporary life
has become most complex.

PUPIL: And so very complicated too . . . My parents are
fairly rich, I'm lucky. They can help me in my work,
help me in my very advanced studies.

PROFESSOR: And you wish to qualify for . . . ?

PUPIL: Just as soon as possible, for the first doctor's
orals. They're in three weeks' time.

PROFESSOR: You already have your high school diploma, if you'll pardon the question?

PUPIL: Yes, Professor, I have my science diploma and
my arts diploma, too.

PROFESSOR: Ah, you're very far advanced, even perhaps
too advanced for your age. And which doctorate
do you wish to qualify for? In the physical sciences
or in moral philosophy?

PUPIL: My parents are very much hoping—if you think
it will be possible in such a short time—they very
much hope that I can qualify for the total doctorate.

PROFESSOR: The total doctorate? . . . You have great courage, young lady, I congratulate you sincerely. We will try, miss, to do our best. In any case, you already know quite a bit, and at so young an age too.

PUPIL: Oh, Professor.

PROFESSOR: Then, if you'll permit me, pardon me, please, I do think that we ought to get to work. We have scarcely any time to lose.

PUPIL: Oh, but certainly, Professor, I want to. I beg you to.

PROFESSOR: Then, may I ask you to sit down . . . there . . . Will you permit me, miss, that is if you have no objections, to sit down opposite you?

PUPIL: Oh, of course, Professor, please do.

PROFESSOR: Thank you very much, miss. (*They sit down facing each other at the table, their profiles to the audience.*) There we are. Now have you brought your books and notebooks?

PUPIL (*taking notebooks and books out of her satchel*): Yes, Professor. Certainly, I have brought all that we'll need.

PROFESSOR: Perfect, miss. This is perfect. Now, if this doesn't bore you . . . shall we begin?

PUPIL: Yes, indeed, Professor, I am at your disposal.

PROFESSOR: At my disposal? (*A gleam comes into his eyes and is quickly extinguished; he begins to make a gesture that he suppresses at once.*) Oh, miss, it is I who am at your disposal. I am only your humble servant.

PUPIL: Oh, Professor . . .

PROFESSOR: If you will . . . now . . . we . . . we . . . I . . . I will begin by making a brief examination of your knowledge, past and present, so that we may chart our future course . . . Good. How is your perception of plurality?

PUPIL: It's rather vague . . . confused.

PROFESSOR: Good. We shall see.

(*He rubs his hands together. The* MAID *enters, and this appears to irritate the* PROFESSOR. *She goes to the buffet and looks for something, lingering.*)

PROFESSOR: Now, miss, would you like to do a little arithmetic, that is if you want to . . .

PUPIL: Oh, yes, Professor. Certainly, I ask nothing better.

PROFESSOR: It is rather a new science, a modern science, properly speaking, it is more a method than a science . . . And it is also a therapy. (*To the* MAID:) Have you finished, Marie?

MAID: Yes, Professor, I've found the plate. I'm just going . . .

PROFESSOR: Hurry up then. Please go along to the kitchen, if you will.

MAID: Yes, Professor, I'm going. (*She starts to go out.*) Excuse me, Professor, but take care, I urge you to remain calm.

PROFESSOR: You're being ridiculous, Marie. Now, don't worry.

MAID: That's what you always say.

PROFESSOR: I will not stand for your insinuations. I know perfectly well how to comport myself. I am old enough for that.

MAID: Precisely, Professor. You will do better not to start the young lady on arithmetic. Arithmetic is tiring, exhausting.

PROFESSOR: Not at my age. And anyhow, what business is it of yours? This is my concern. And I know what I'm doing. This is not your department.

MAID: Very well, Professor. But you can't say that I didn't warn you.

PROFESSOR: Marie, I can get along without your advice.

MAID: As you wish, Professor. (*She exits.*)

PROFESSOR: Miss, I hope you'll pardon this absurd interruption . . . Excuse this woman . . . She is always afraid that I'll tire myself. She fusses over my health.

PUPIL: Oh, that's quite all right, Professor. It shows that she's very devoted. She loves you very much. Good servants are rare.

PROFESSOR: She exaggerates. Her fears are stupid. But let's return to our arithmetical knitting.

PUPIL: I'm following you, Professor.

PROFESSOR (*wittily*): Without leaving your seat!

PUPIL (*appreciating his joke*): Like you, Professor.

PROFESSOR: Good. Let us arithmetize a little now.

PUPIL: Yes, gladly, Professor.

PROFESSOR: It wouldn't be too tiresome for you to tell me . . .

PUPIL: Not at all, Professor, go on.

PROFESSOR: How much are one and one?

PUPIL: One and one make two.

PROFESSOR (*marveling at the* PUPIL'S *knowledge*): Oh, but that's very good. You appear to me to be well along in your studies. You should easily achieve the total doctorate, miss.

PUPIL: I'm so glad. Especially to have someone like you tell me this.

PROFESSOR: Let's push on: how much are two and one?

PUPIL: Three.

PROFESSOR: Three and one?

PUPIL: Four.

PROFESSOR: Four and one?

PUPIL: Five.

PROFESSOR: Five and one?

PUPIL: Six.

PROFESSOR: Six and one?

PUPIL: Seven.

PROFESSOR: Seven and one?

PUPIL: Eight.

PROFESSOR: Seven and one?

PUPIL: Eight again.

PROFESSOR: Very well answered. Seven and one?

PUPIL: Eight once more.

PROFESSOR: Perfect. Excellent. Seven and one?

PUPIL: Eight again. And sometimes nine.

PROFESSOR: Magnificent. You are magnificent. You are

exquisite. I congratulate you warmly, miss. There's scarcely any point in going on. At addition you are a past master. Now, let's look at subtraction. Tell me, if you are not exhausted, how many are four minus three?

PUPIL: Four minus three? . . . Four minus three?

PROFESSOR: Yes. I mean to say: subtract three from four.

PUPIL: That makes . . . seven?

PROFESSOR: I am sorry but I'm obliged to contradict you. Four minus three does not make seven. You are confused: four plus three makes seven, four minus three does not make seven . . . This is not addition anymore, we must subtract now.

PUPIL (trying to understand): Yes . . . yes . . .

PROFESSOR: Four minus three makes . . . How many? . . . How many?

PUPIL: Four?

PROFESSOR: No, miss, that's not it.

PUPIL: Three, then.

PROFESSOR: Not that either, miss . . . Pardon, I'm sorry . . . I ought to say, that's not it . . . excuse me.

PUPIL: Four minus three . . . Four minus three . . . Four minus three? . . . But now doesn't that make ten?

PROFESSOR: Oh, certainly not, miss. It's not a matter of guessing, you've got to think it out. Let's try to deduce it together. Would you like to count?

PUPIL: Yes, Professor. One . . . two . . . uh . . .

PROFESSOR: You know how to count? How far can you count up to?

PUPIL: I can count to . . . infinity.

PROFESSOR: That's not possible, miss.

PUPIL: Well then, let's say to sixteen.

PROFESSOR: That is enough. One must know one's limits. Count then, if you will, please.

PUPIL: One . . . two . . . and after two, comes three . . . then four . . .

PROFESSOR: Stop there, miss. Which number is larger? Three or four?

PUPIL: Uh . . . three or four? Which is the larger? The larger of three or four? In what sense larger?

PROFESSOR: Some numbers are smaller and others are larger. In the large numbers there are more units than in the small . . .

PUPIL: Than in the small numbers?

PROFESSOR: Unless the small ones have smaller units. If they are very small, then there might be more units in the small numbers than in the large . . . if it is a question of other units . . .

PUPIL: In that case, the small numbers can be larger than the large numbers?

PROFESSOR: Let's not go into that. That would take us much too far. You must realize simply that more than numbers are involved here . . . there are also magnitudes, totals, there are groups, there are heaps, heaps of such things as plums, trucks, geese, prune pits, etc. To facilitate our work, let's merely suppose that we have only equal numbers, then the bigger numbers will be those that have the most units.

PUPIL: The one that has the most is the biggest? Ah, I understand, Professor, you are identifying quality with quantity.

PROFESSOR: That is too theoretical, miss, too theoretical. You needn't concern yourself with that. Let us take an example and reason from a definite case. Let's leave the general conclusions for later. We have the number four and the number three, and each has always the same number of units. Which number will be larger, the smaller or the larger?

PUPIL: Excuse me, Professor . . . What do you mean by the larger number? Is it the one that is not so small as the other?

PROFESSOR: That's it, miss, perfect. You have understood me very well.

PUPIL: Then, it is four.

PROFESSOR: What is four—larger or smaller than three?

PUPIL: Smaller . . . no, larger.

PROFESSOR: Excellent answer. How many units are there between three and four? . . . Or between four and three, if you prefer?

PUPIL: There aren't any units, Professor, between three and four. Four comes immediately after three; there is nothing at all between three and four!

PROFESSOR: I haven't made myself very well understood. No doubt, it is my fault. I've not been sufficiently clear.

PUPIL: No, Professor, it's my fault.

PROFESSOR: Look here. Here are three matches. And here is another one, that makes four. Now watch carefully—we have four matches. I take one away, now how many are left?

(We don't see the matches, nor any of the objects that are mentioned. The PROFESSOR gets up from the table, writes on the imaginary blackboard with an imaginary piece of chalk, etc.)

PUPIL: Five. If three and one make four, four and one make five.

PROFESSOR: That's not it. That's not it at all. You always have a tendency to add. But one must be able to subtract too. It's not enough to integrate, you must also disintegrate. That's the way life is. That's philosophy. That's science. That's progress, civilization.

PUPIL: Yes, Professor.

PROFESSOR: Let's return to our matches. I have four of them. You see, there are really four. I take one away, and there remain only . . .

PUPIL: I don't know, Professor.

PROFESSOR: Come now, think. It's not easy, I admit. Nevertheless, you've had enough training to make the intellectual effort required to arrive at an understanding. So?

PUPIL: I can't get it, Professor. I don't know, Professor.

PROFESSOR: Let us take a simpler example. If you had

two noses, and I pulled one of them off . . . how many would you have left?

PUPIL: None.

PROFESSOR: What do you mean, none?

PUPIL: Yes, it's because you haven't pulled off any, that's why I have one now. If you had pulled it off, I wouldn't have it anymore.

PROFESSOR: You've not understood my example. Suppose that you have only one ear.

PUPIL: Yes, and then?

PROFESSOR: If I gave you another one, how many would you have then?

PUPIL: Two.

PROFESSOR: Good. And if I gave you still another ear. How many would you have then?

PUPIL: Three ears.

PROFESSOR: Now, I take one away . . . and there remain . . . how many ears?

PUPIL: Two.

PROFESSOR: Good. I take away still another one, how many do you have left?

PUPIL: Two.

PROFESSOR: No. You have two, I take one away, I eat one up, then how many do you have left?

PUPIL: Two.

PROFESSOR: I eat one of them . . . one.

PUPIL: Two.

PROFESSOR: One.

PUPIL: Two.

PROFESSOR: One!

PUPIL: Two!

PROFESSOR: One!!!

PUPIL: Two!!!

PROFESSOR: One!!!

PUPIL: Two!!!

PROFESSOR: One!!!

PUPIL: Two!!!

PROFESSOR: No. No. That's not right. The example is not . . . it's not convincing. Listen to me.

PUPIL: Yes, Professor.

PROFESSOR: You've got . . . you've got . . . you've got . . .

PUPIL: Ten fingers!

PROFESSOR: If you wish. Perfect. Good. You have then ten fingers.

PUPIL: Yes, Professor.

PROFESSOR: How many would you have if you had only five of them?

PUPIL: Ten, Professor.

PROFESSOR: That's not right!

PUPIL: But it is, Professor.

PROFESSOR: I tell you it's not!

PUPIL: You just told me that I had ten . . .

PROFESSOR: I also said, immediately afterwards, that you had five!

PUPIL: I don't have five, I've got ten!

PROFESSOR: Let's try another approach . . . for purposes of subtraction let's limit ourselves to the numbers from one to five . . . Wait now, miss, you'll soon see. I'm going to make you understand.

(*The* PROFESSOR *begins to write on the imaginary blackboard. He moves it closer to the* PUPIL, *who turns around in order to see it.*)

PROFESSOR: Look here, miss . . . (*He pretends to draw a stick on the blackboard and the number 1 below the stick; then two sticks and the number 2 below, then three sticks and the number 3 below, then four sticks with the number 4 below.*) You see . . .

PUPIL: Yes, Professor.

PROFESSOR: These are sticks, miss, sticks. This is one stick, these are two sticks, and three sticks, then four sticks, then five sticks. One stick, two sticks, three sticks, four and five sticks, these are numbers. When we count the sticks, each stick is a unit, miss . . . What have I just said?

PUPIL: "A unit, miss! What have I just said?"

PROFESSOR: Or a figure! Or a number! One, two, three, four, five, these are the elements of numeration, miss.

PUPIL (*hesitant*): Yes, Professor. The elements, figures, which are sticks, units and numbers . . .

PROFESSOR: At the same time . . . that's to say, in short— the whole of arithmetic is there.

PUPIL: Yes, Professor. Good, Professor. Thanks, Professor.

PROFESSOR: Now, count, if you will please, using these elements . . . add and subtract . . .

PUPIL (*as though trying to impress them on her memory*): Sticks are really figures and numbers are units?

PROFESSOR: Hmm . . . so to speak. And then?

PUPIL: One could subtract two units from three units, but can one subtract two twos from three threes? And two figures from four numbers? And three numbers from one unit?

PROFESSOR: No, miss.

PUPIL: Why, Professor?

PROFESSOR: Because, miss.

PUPIL: Because why, Professor? Since one is the same as the other?

PROFESSOR: That's the way it is, miss. It can't be explained. This is only comprehensible through internal mathematical reasoning. Either you have it or you don't.

PUPIL: So much the worse for me.

PROFESSOR: Listen to me, miss, if you don't achieve a profound understanding of these principles, these arithmetical archetypes, you will never be able to perform correctly the functions of a polytechnician. Still less will you be able to teach a course in a polytechnical school . . . or the primary grades. I realize that this is not easy, it is very, very abstract . . . obviously . . . but unless you can comprehend the primary elements, how do you expect to be able to calculate mentally—and this is the least of the things that even an ordinary engineer must be able to do—how much, for example, are three billion seven hundred fifty-five million nine hundred ninety-eight thousand two hundred fifty one, multiplied by five billion one hundred sixty-two million three hundred and three thousand five hundred and eight?

PUPIL *(very quickly)*: That makes nineteen quintillion three hundred ninety quadrillion two trillion eight hundred forty-four billion two hundred nineteen million one hundred sixty-four thousand five hundred and eight . . .

PROFESSOR *(astonished)*: No. I don't think so. That must make nineteen quintillion three hundred ninety quadrillion two trillion eight hundred forty-four billion two hundred nineteen million one hundred sixty-four thousand five hundred and nine . . .

PUPIL: . . . No . . . five hundred and eight . . .

PROFESSOR *(more and more astonished, calculating mentally)*: Yes . . . you are right . . . the result is indeed . . . *(He mumbles unintelligibly:)* . . . quintillion, quadrillion, trillion, billion, million . . . *(Clearly:)* one hundred sixty-four thousand five hundred and eight . . . *(Stupefied:)* But how did you know that, if you don't know the principles of arithmetical reasoning?

PUPIL: It's easy. Not being able to rely on my reasoning, I've memorized all the products of all possible multiplications.

PROFESSOR: That's pretty good . . . However, permit me to confess to you that that doesn't satisfy me, miss, and I do not congratulate you: in mathematics and in arithmetic especially, the thing that counts—for in arithmetic it is always necessary to count—the thing that counts is, above all, understanding . . . It is by mathematical reasoning, simultaneously inductive and deductive, that you ought to arrive at this result—as well as at any other result. Mathematics is the sworn enemy of memory, which is excellent otherwise, but disastrous, arithmetically speaking! . . . That's why I'm not happy with this . . . this won't do, not at all . . .

PUPIL *(desolated)*: No, Professor.

PROFESSOR: Let's leave it for the moment. Let's go on to another exercise . . .

PUPIL: Yes, Professor.

MAID *(entering)*: Hmm, hmm, Professor . . .

PROFESSOR *(who doesn't hear her)*: It is unfortunate, miss, that you aren't further along in specialized mathematics . . .

MAID *(taking him by the sleeve)*: Professor! Professor!

PROFESSOR: I hear that you will not be able to qualify for the total doctor's orals . . .

PUPIL: Yes, Professor, it's too bad!

PROFESSOR: Unless you . . . *(To the* MAID*:)* Let me be, Marie . . . Look here, why are you bothering me?

Go back to the kitchen! To your pots and pans! Go away! Go away! *(To the* PUPIL*:)* We will try to prepare you at least for the partial doctorate . . .

MAID: Professor! . . . Professor! . . . *(She pulls his sleeve.)*

PROFESSOR *(to the* MAID*)*: Now leave me alone! Let me be! What's the meaning of this? . . . *(To the* PUPIL*:)* I must therefore teach you, if you really do insist on attempting the partial doctorate . . .

PUPIL: Yes, Professor.

PROFESSOR: . . . The elements of linguistics and of comparative philology° . . .

MAID: No, Professor, no! . . . You mustn't do that! . . .

PROFESSOR: Marie, you're going too far!

MAID: Professor, especially not philology, philology leads to calamity . . .

PUPIL *(astonished)*: To calamity? *(Smiling, a little stupidly:)* That's hard to believe.

PROFESSOR *(to the* MAID*)*: That's enough now! Get out of here!

MAID: All right, Professor, all right. But you can't say that I didn't warn you! Philology leads to calamity!

PROFESSOR: I'm an adult, Marie!

PUPIL: Yes, Professor.

MAID: As you wish.

(She exits.)

PROFESSOR: Let's continue, miss.

PUPIL: Yes, Professor.

PROFESSOR: I want you to listen now with the greatest possible attention to a lecture I have prepared . . .

PUPIL: Yes, Professor!

PROFESSOR: . . . Thanks to which, in fifteen minutes' time, you will be able to acquire the fundamental principles of the linguistic and comparative philology of the neo-Spanish languages.

PUPIL: Yes, Professor, oh good!

(She claps her hands.)

PROFESSOR *(with authority)*: Quiet! What do you mean by that?

PUPIL: I'm sorry, Professor.

(Slowly, she replaces her hands on the table.)

PROFESSOR: Quiet! *(He gets up, walks up and down the room, his hands behind his back; from time to time he stops at stage center or near the* PUPIL*, and underlines his words with a gesture of his hand; he orates, but without being too emotional. The* PUPIL *follows him with her eyes, occasionally with some difficulty, for she has to turn her head far around; once or twice, not more, she turns around completely.)* And now, miss, Spanish is truly the mother tongue which gave birth to all the neo-Spanish languages, of which Spanish, Latin, Italian,

---

philology, study of language.

our own French, Portuguese, Romanian, Sardinian or Sardanapalian, Spanish and neo-Spanish—and also, in certain of its aspects, Turkish which is otherwise very close to Greek, which is only logical, since it is a fact that Turkey is a neighbor of Greece and Greece is even closer to Turkey than you are to me—this is only one more illustration of the very important linguistic law which states that geography and philology are twin sisters . . . You may take notes, miss.

PUPIL (in a dull voice): Yes, Professor!

PROFESSOR: That which distinguishes the neo-Spanish languages from each other and their idioms from the other linguistic groups, such as the group of languages called Austrian and neo-Austrian or Hapsburgian, as well as the Esperanto, Helvetian, Monacan, Swiss, Andorran, Basque, and jai alai° groups, and also the groups of diplomatic and technical languages—that which distinguishes them, I repeat, is their striking resemblance which makes it so hard to distinguish them from each other—I'm speaking of the neo-Spanish languages which one is able to distinguish from each other, however, only thanks to their distinctive characteristics, absolutely indisputable proofs of their extraordinary resemblance, which renders indisputable their common origin, and which, at the same time, differentiates them profoundly—through the continuation of the distinctive traits which I've just cited.

PUPIL: Oooh! Ye-e-e-s-s-s, Professor!

PROFESSOR: But let's not linger over generalities . . .

PUPIL (regretfully, but won over): Oh, Professor . . .

PROFESSOR: This appears to interest you. All the better, all the better.

PUPIL: Oh, yes, Professor . . .

PROFESSOR: Don't worry, miss. We will come back to it later . . . That is if we come back to it at all. Who can say?

PUPIL (enchanted in spite of everything): Oh, yes, Professor.

PROFESSOR: Every tongue—you must know this, miss, and remember it until the hour of your death . . .

PUPIL: Oh! yes, Professor, until the hour of my death . . . Yes, Professor . . .

PROFESSOR: . . . And this, too, is a fundamental principle, every tongue is at bottom nothing but language, which necessarily implies that it is composed of sounds, or . . .

PUPIL: Phonemes . . .

PROFESSOR: Just what I was going to say. Don't parade your knowledge. You'd do better to listen.

PUPIL: All right, Professor. Yes, Professor.

PROFESSOR: The sounds, miss, must be seized on the wing as they fly so that they'll not fall on deaf ears. As a result, when you set out to articulate, it is recommended, insofar as possible, that you lift up your neck and chin very high, and rise up on the tips of your toes, you see, this way . . .

PUPIL: Yes, Professor.

PROFESSOR: Keep quiet. Remain seated, don't interrupt me . . . And project the sounds very loudly with all the force of your lungs in conjunction with that of your vocal cords. Like this, look: "Butterfly," "Eureka," "Trafalgar," "Papaya." This way, the sounds become filled with a warm air that is lighter than the surrounding air so that they can fly without danger of falling on deaf ears, which are veritable voids, tombs of sonorities. If you utter several sounds at an accelerated speed, they will automatically cling to each other, constituting thus syllables, words, even sentences, that is to say groupings of various importance, purely irrational assemblages of sounds, denuded of all sense, but for that very reason the more capable of maintaining themselves without danger at a high altitude in the air. By themselves, words charged with significance will fall, weighted down by their meaning, and in the end they always collapse, fall . . .

PUPIL: . . . On deaf ears.

PROFESSOR: That's it, but don't interrupt . . . and into the worst confusion . . . Or else burst like balloons. Therefore, miss . . . (The PUPIL suddenly appears to be unwell.) What's the matter?

PUPIL: I've got a toothache, Professor.

PROFESSOR: That's not important. We're not going to stop for anything so trivial. Let us go on . . .

PUPIL (appearing to be in more and more pain): Yes, Professor.

PROFESSOR: I draw your attention in passing to the consonants that change their nature in combinations. In this case f becomes v, d becomes t, g becomes k, and vice versa, as in these examples that I will cite for you: "That's all right," "hens and chickens," "Welsh rabbit," "lots of nothing," "not at all."°

PUPIL: I've got a toothache.

PROFESSOR: Let's continue.

PUPIL: Yes.

PROFESSOR: To resume: it takes years and years to learn to pronounce. Thanks to science, we can achieve this in a few minutes. In order to project words, sounds and all the rest, you must realize that it is necessary to pitilessly expel air from the lungs, and make it pass delicately, caressingly, over the vocal cords, which, like harps or leaves in the wind, will suddenly shake, agitate, vibrate, vibrate, vibrate or uvulate, or fricate or jostle against each other, or sibilate, sibilate, placing everything in movement, the uvula, the tongue, the palate, the teeth . . .

PUPIL: I have a toothache.

---

jai alai, handball-like game.

All to be heavily elided.—Translator's note.

PROFESSOR: . . . And the lips . . . Finally the words come out through the nose, the mouth, the ears, the pores, drawing along with them all the organs that we have named, torn up by the roots, in a powerful, majestic flight, which is none other than what is called, improperly, the voice, whether modulated in singing or transformed into a terrible symphonic storm with a whole procession . . . of garlands of all kinds of flowers, of sonorous artifices: labials, dentals, occlusives, palatals, and others, some caressing, some bitter or violent.

PUPIL: Yes, Professor, I've got a toothache.

PROFESSOR: Let's go on, go on. As for the neo-Spanish languages, they are closely related, so closely to each other, that they can be considered as true second cousins. Moreover, they have the same mother: Spanishe, with a mute *e*. That is why it is so difficult to distinguish them from one another. That is why it is so useful to pronounce carefully, and to avoid errors in pronunciation. Pronunciation itself is worth a whole language. A bad pronunciation can get you into trouble. In this connection, permit me, parenthetically, to share a personal experience with you. *(Slight pause. The* PROFESSOR *goes over his memories for a moment; his features mellow, but he recovers at once.)* I was very young, little more than a child. It was during my military service. I had a friend in the regiment, a vicomte, who suffered from a rather serious defect in his pronunciation: he could not pronounce the letter *f*. Instead of *f*, he said *f*. Thus, instead of "Birds of a feather flock together," he said: "Birds of a feather flock together." He pronounced filly instead of filly, Firmin instead of Firmin, French bean instead of French bean, go frig yourself instead of go frig yourself, farrago instead of farrago, fee fi fo fum instead of fee fi fo fum, Philip instead of Philip, fictory instead of fictory, February instead of February, March-April instead of March-April, Gerard de Nerval and not as is correct—Gerard de Nerval, Mirabeau instead of Mirabeau, etc., instead of etc., and thus instead of etc., instead of etc., and thus and so forth. However, he managed to conceal his fault so effectively that, thanks to the hats he wore, no one ever noticed it.

PUPIL: Yes, I've got a toothache.

PROFESSOR *(abruptly changing his tone, his voice hardening)*: Let's go on. We'll first consider the points of similarity in order the better to apprehend, later on, that which distinguishes all these languages from each other. The differences can scarcely be recognized by people who are not aware of them. Thus, all the words of all the languages . . .

PUPIL: Uh, yes? . . . I've got a toothache.

PROFESSOR: Let's continue . . . are always the same, just as all the suffixes, all the prefixes, all the terminations, all the roots . . .

PUPIL: Are the roots of words square?

PROFESSOR: Square or cube. That depends.

PUPIL: I've got a toothache.

PROFESSOR: Let's go on. Thus, to give you an example which is little more than an illustration, take the word "front" . . .

PUPIL: How do you want me to take it?

PROFESSOR: However you wish, so long as you take it, but above all do not interrupt.

PUPIL: I've got a toothache.

PROFESSOR: Let's continue . . . I said: Let's continue. Take now the word "front." Have you taken it?

PUPIL: Yes, yes, I've got it. My teeth, my teeth . . .

PROFESSOR: The word "front" is the root of "frontispiece." It is also to be found in "affronted." "Ispiece" is the suffix, and "af" the prefix. They are so called because they do not change. They don't want to.

PUPIL: I've got a toothache.

PROFESSOR: Let's go on *(Rapidly:)* These prefixes are of Spanish origin. I hope you noticed that, did you?

PUPIL: Oh, how my tooth aches.

PROFESSOR: Let's continue. You've surely also noticed that they've not changed in French. And now, young lady, nothing has succeeded in changing them in Latin either, nor in Italian, nor in Portuguese, nor in Sardanapalian, nor in Sardanapali, nor in Romanian, nor in neo-Spanish, nor in Spanish, nor even in the Oriental: front, frontispiece, affronted, always the same word, invariably with the same root, the same suffix, the same prefix, in all the languages I have named. And it is always the same for all words.

PUPIL: In all languages, these words mean the same thing? I've got a toothache.

PROFESSOR: Absolutely. Moreover, it's more a notion than a word. In any case, you have always the same signification, the same composition, the same sound structure, not only for this word, but for all conceivable words, in all languages. For one single notion is expressed by one and the same word, and its synonyms, in all countries. Forget about your teeth.

PUPIL: I've got a toothache. Yes, yes, yes.

PROFESSOR: Good, let's go on. I tell you, let's go on . . . How would you say, for example, in French: the roses of my grandmother are as yellow as my grandfather who was Asiatic?

PUPIL: My teeth ache, ache, ache.

PROFESSOR: Let's go on, let's go on, go ahead and answer, anyway.

PUPIL: In French?

PROFESSOR: In French.

PUPIL: Uhh . . . I should say in French: the roses of my grandmother are . . . ?

PROFESSOR: As yellow as my grandfather who was Asiatic . . .

PUPIL: Oh well, one would say, in French, I believe, the roses . . . of my . . . how do you say "grandmother" in French?

PROFESSOR: In French? Grandmother.

PUPIL: The roses of my grandmother are as yellow—in in French, is it "yellow"?

PROFESSOR: Yes, of course!

PUPIL: Are as yellow as my grandfather when he got angry.

PROFESSOR: No . . . who was A . . .

PUPIL: . . . siatic . . . I've got a toothache.

PROFESSOR: That's it.

PUPIL: I've got a tooth . . .

PROFESSOR: Ache . . . so what . . . let's continue! And now translate the same sentence into Spanish, then into neo-Spanish . . .

PUPIL: In Spanish . . . this would be: the roses of my grandmother are as yellow as my grandfather who was Asiatic.

PROFESSOR: No. That's wrong.

PUPIL: And in neo-Spanish: the roses of my grandmother are as yellow as my grandfather who was Asiatic.

PROFESSOR: That's wrong. That's wrong. That's wrong. You have inverted it, you've confused Spanish with neo-Spanish, and neo-Spanish with Spanish . . . Oh . . . no . . . it's the other way around . . .

PUPIL: I've got a toothache. You're getting mixed up.

PROFESSOR: You're the one who is mixing me up. Pay attention and take notes. I will say the sentence to you in Spanish, then in neo-Spanish, and finally, in Latin. You will repeat after me. Pay attention, for the resemblances are great. In fact, they are identical resemblances. Listen, follow carefully . . .

PUPIL: I've got a tooth . . .

PROFESSOR: . . . Ache.

PUPIL: Let us go on . . . Ah! . . .

PROFESSOR: . . . In Spanish: the roses of my grandmother are as yellow as my grandfather who was Asiatic; in Latin: the roses of my grandmother are as yellow as my grandfather who was Asiatic. Do you detect the differences? Translate this into . . . Romanian.

PUPIL: The . . . how do you say "roses" in Romanian?

PROFESSOR: But "roses," what else?

PUPIL: It's not "roses"? Oh, how my tooth aches!

PROFESSOR: Certainly not, certainly not, since "roses" is a translation in Oriental of the French word "roses," in Spanish "roses," do you get it? In Sardanapali, "roses" . . .

PUPIL: Excuse me, Professor, but . . . Oh, my toothache! . . . I don't get the difference.

PROFESSOR: But it's so simple! So simple! It's a matter of having a certain experience, a technical experience and practice in these diverse languages, which are so diverse in spite of the fact that they present wholly identical characteristics. I'm going to try to give you a key . . .

PUPIL: Toothache . . .

PROFESSOR: That which differentiates these languages, is neither the words, which are absolutely the same, nor the structure of the sentence which is everywhere the same, nor the intonation, which does not offer any differences, nor the rhythm of the language . . . that which differentiates them . . . are you listening?

PUPIL: I've got a toothache.

PROFESSOR: Are you listening to me, young lady? Aah! We're going to lose our temper.

PUPIL: You're bothering me, Professor. I've got a toothache.

PROFESSOR: Son of a cocker spaniel! Listen to me!

PUPIL: Oh well . . . yes . . . yes . . . go on . . .

PROFESSOR: That which distinguishes them from each other, on the one hand, and from their mother, Spanishe with its mute *e*, on the other hand . . . is . . .

PUPIL (*grimacing*): Is what?

PROFESSOR: Is an intangible thing. Something intangible that one is able to perceive only after very long study, with a great deal of trouble and after the broadest experience . . .

PUPIL: Ah?

PROFESSOR: Yes, young lady. I cannot give you any rule. One must have a feeling for it, and well, that's it. But in order to have it, one must study, study, and then study some more.

PUPIL: Toothache.

PROFESSOR: All the same, there are some specific cases where words differ from one language to another . . . but we cannot base our knowledge on these cases, which are, so to speak, exceptional.

PUPIL: Oh, yes? . . . Oh, Professor, I've got a toothache.

PROFESSOR: Don't interrupt! Don't make me lose my temper! I can't answer for what I'll do. I was saying, then . . . Ah, yes, the exceptional cases, the so-called easily distinguished . . . or facilely distinguished . . . or conveniently . . . if you prefer . . . I repeat, if you prefer, for I see that you're not listening to me . . .

PUPIL: I've got a toothache.

PROFESSOR: I say then: in certain expressions in current usage, certain words differ totally from one language to another, so much so that the language employed is, in this case, considerably easier to identify. I'll give you an example: the neo-Spanish expression, famous in Madrid: "My country is the new Spain," becomes in Italian: "My country is . . .

PUPIL: The new Spain.

PROFESSOR: No! "My country is Italy." Tell me now, by simple deduction, how do you say "Italy" in French?

PUPIL: I've got a toothache.

PROFESSOR: But it's so easy: for the word "Italy," in French we have the word "France," which is an exact translation of it. My country is France. And "France" in Oriental: "Orient!" My country is the Orient. And "Orient" in Portuguese: "Portugal!" The Oriental expression: My country is the Orient is translated then in the same fashion into Portuguese: My country is Portugal! And so on . . .

PUPIL: Oh, no more, no more. My teeth . . .

PROFESSOR: Ache! ache! ache! . . . I'm going to pull them out, I will! One more example. The word "capital"—it takes on, according to the language one speaks, a different meaning. That is to say that when a Spaniard says: "I reside in the capital," the word "capital" does not mean at all the same thing that a Portuguese means when he says: "I reside in the capital." All the more so in the case of a Frenchman, a neo-Spaniard, a Romanian, a Latin, a Sardanapali . . . Whenever you hear it, young lady—young lady, I'm saying this for you! Pooh! Whenever you hear the expression: "I reside in the capital," you will immediately and easily know whether this is Spanish or Spanish, neo-Spanish, French, Oriental, Romanian, or Latin, for it is enough to know which metropolis is referred to by the person who pronounces the sentence . . . at the very moment he pronounces it . . . But these are almost the only precise examples that I can give you . . .

PUPIL: Oh dear! My teeth . . .

PROFESSOR: Silence! Or I'll bash in your skull!

PUPIL: Just try to! Skulldugger!°

(The PROFESSOR *seizes her wrist and twists it.)*

PUPIL: Oww!

PROFESSOR: Keep quiet now! Not a word!

PUPIL *(whimpering)*: Toothache . . .

PROFESSOR: One thing that is the most . . . how shall I say it? . . . the most paradoxical . . . yes . . . that's the word . . . the most paradoxical thing, is that a lot of people who are completely illiterate speak these different languages . . . do you understand? What did I just say?

PUPIL: . . . "Speak these different languages! What did I just say?"

PROFESSOR: You were lucky that time! . . . The common people speak a Spanish full of neo-Spanish words that they are entirely unaware of, all the while believing that they are speaking Latin . . . or they speak Latin, full of Oriental words, all the while believing that they're speaking Romanian . . . or Spanish, full of neo-Spanish, all the while believing that they're speaking Sardanapali, or Spanish . . . Do you understand?

PUPIL: Yes! yes! yes! yes! What more do you want . . . ?

PROFESSOR: No insolence, my pet, or you'll be sorry . . . *(In a rage:)* But the worst of all, young lady, is that certain people, for example, in a Latin that they suppose is Spanish, say: "Both my kidneys are of the same kidney," in addressing themselves to a Frenchman who does not know a word of Spanish,

but the latter understands it as if it were his own language. For that matter he thinks it is his own language. And the Frenchman will reply, in French: "Me too, sir, mine are too," and this will be perfectly comprehensible to a Spaniard, who will feel certain that the reply is in pure Spanish and that Spanish is being spoken . . . when, in reality, it was neither Spanish nor French, but Latin in the neo-Spanish dialect . . . Sit still, young lady, don't fidget, stop tapping your feet . . .

PUPIL: I've got a toothache.

PROFESSOR: How do you account for the fact that, in speaking without knowing which language they speak, or even while each of them believes that he is speaking another, the common people understand each other at all?

PUPIL: I wonder.

PROFESSOR: It is simply one of the inexplicable curiosities of the vulgar empiricism of the common people—not to be confused with experience!—a paradox, a non-sense, one of the aberrations of human nature, it is purely and simply instinct—to put it in a nutshell . . . That's what is involved here.

PUPIL: Hah! hah!

PROFESSOR: Instead of staring at the flies while I'm going to all this trouble . . . you would do much better to try to be more attentive . . . it is not I who is going to qualify for the partial doctor's orals . . . I passed mine a long time ago . . . and I've won my total doctorate, too . . . and my super-total diploma . . . Don't you realize that what I'm saying is for your own good?

PUPIL: Toothache!

PROFESSOR: Ill-mannered . . . It can't go on like this, it won't do, it won't do, it won't do . . .

PUPIL: I'm . . . listening . . . to you . . .

PROFESSOR: Ahah! In order to learn to distinguish all the different languages, as I've told you, there is nothing better than practice . . . Let's take them up in order. I am going to try to teach you all the translations of the word "knife."

PUPIL: Well, all right . . . if you want . . .

PROFESSOR *(calling the* MAID): Marie! Marie! She's not there . . . Marie! Marie! . . . Marie, where are you? *(He opens the door on the right.)* Marie! . . .

(He exits. The PUPIL *remains alone several minutes, staring into space, wearing a stupefied expression.)*

PROFESSOR *(offstage, in a shrill voice)*: Marie! What are you up to? Why don't you come! When I call you, you must come! *(He re-enters, followed by* MARIE.) It is I who gives the orders, do you hear? *(He points at the* PUPIL:) She doesn't understand anything, that girl. She doesn't understand!

MAID: Don't get into such a state, sir, you know where it'll end! You're going to go too far, you're going to go too far.

PROFESSOR: I'll be able to stop in time.

Skulldugger, contemptible person.

MAID: That's what you always say. I only wish I could see it.

PUPIL: I've got a toothache.

MAID: You see, it's starting, that's the symptom!

PROFESSOR: What symptom? Explain yourself? What do you mean?

PUPIL (*in a spiritless voice*): Yes, what do you mean? I've got a toothache.

MAID: The final symptom! The chief symptom!

PROFESSOR: Stupid! stupid! stupid! (*The* MAID *starts to exit.*) Don't go away like that! I called you to help me find the Spanish, neo-Spanish, Portuguese, French, Oriental, Romanian, Sardanapali, Latin and Spanish knives.

MAID (*severely*): Don't ask me. (*She exits.*)

PROFESSOR (*makes a gesture as though to protest, then refrains, a little helpless. Suddenly, he remembers*): Ah! (*He goes quickly to the drawer where he finds a big knife, invisible or real according to the preference of the director. He seizes it and brandishes it happily.*) Here is one, young lady, here is a knife. It's too bad that we only have this one, but we're going to try to make it serve for all the languages, anyway! It will be enough if you will pronounce the word "knife" in all the languages, while looking at the object, very closely, fixedly, and imagining that it is in the language that you are speaking.

PUPIL: I've got a toothache.

PROFESSOR (*almost singing, chanting*): Now, say "kni," like "kni," "fe," like "fe" . . . And look, look, look at it, watch it . . .

PUPIL: What is this one in? French, Italian or Spanish?

PROFESSOR: That doesn't matter now . . . That's not your concern. Say: "kni."

PUPIL: "Kni."

PROFESSOR: . . . "fe" . . . Look.

(*He brandishes the knife under the* PUPIL's *eyes.*)

PUPIL: "fe" . . .

PROFESSOR: Again . . . Look at it.

PUPIL: Oh, no! My God! I've had enough. And besides, I've got a toothache, my feet hurt me, I've got a headache.

PROFESSOR (*abruptly*): Knife . . . look . . . knife . . . look . . . knife . . . look . . .

PUPIL: You're giving me an earache, too. Oh, your voice! It's so piercing!

PROFESSOR: Say: knife . . . kni . . . fe . . .

PUPIL: No! My ears hurt, I hurt all over . . .

PROFESSOR: I'm going to tear them off, your ears, that's what I'm going to do to you, and then they won't hurt you anymore, my pet.

PUPIL: Oh . . . you're hurting me, oh, you're hurting me . . .

PROFESSOR: Look, come on, quickly, repeat after me: "kni" . . .

PUPIL: Oh, since you insist . . . knife . . . knife . . . (*In a lucid moment, ironically:*) Is that neo-Spanish . . . ?

PROFESSOR: If you like, yes, it's neo-Spanish, but hurry up . . . we haven't got time . . . And then, what do you mean by that insidious question? What are you up to?

PUPIL (*becoming more and more exhausted, weeping, desperate, at the same time both exasperated and in a trance*): Ah!

PROFESSOR: Repeat, watch. (*He imitates a cuckoo:*) Knife, knife . . . knife, knife . . . knife, knife . . . knife, knife . . .

PUPIL: Oh, my head . . . aches . . . (*With her hand she caressingly touches the parts of her body as she names them:*) . . . My eyes . . .

PROFESSOR (*like a cuckoo*): Knife, knife . . . knife, knife . . . (*They are both standing. The* PROFESSOR *still brandishes his invisible knife, nearly beside himself, as he circles around her in a sort of scalp dance, but it is important that this not be exaggerated and that his dance steps be only suggested. The* PUPIL *stands facing the audience, then recoils in the direction of the window, sickly, languid, victimized.*)

PROFESSOR: Repeat, repeat: knife . . . knife . . . knife . . .

PUPIL: I've got a pain . . . my throat, neck . . . oh, my shoulders . . . my breast . . . knife . . .

PROFESSOR: Knife . . . knife . . . knife . . .

PUPIL: My hips . . . knife . . . my thighs . . . kni . . .

PROFESSOR: Pronounce it carefully . . . knife . . . knife . . .

PUPIL: Knife . . . my throat . . .

PROFESSOR: Knife . . . knife . . .

PUPIL: Knife . . . my shoulders . . . my arms, my breast, my hips . . . knife . . . knife . . .

PROFESSOR: That's right . . . Now, you're pronouncing it well . . .

PUPIL: Knife . . . my breast . . . my stomach . . .

PROFESSOR (*changing his voice*): Pay attention . . . don't break my window . . . the knife kills . . .

PUPIL (*in a weak voice*): Yes, yes, . . . the knife kills?

PROFESSOR (*striking the* PUPIL *with a very spectacular blow of the knife*): Aaah! That'll teach you!

(PUPIL *also cries* "Aah!" *then falls, flopping in an immodest position onto a chair which, as though by chance, is near the window. The murderer and his victim shout* "Aaah!" *at the same moment. After the first blow of the knife, the* PUPIL *flops onto the chair, her legs spread wide and hanging over both sides of the chair. The* PROFESSOR *remains standing in front of her, his back to the audience. After the first blow, he strikes her dead with a second slash of the knife, from bottom to top. After that blow a noticeable convulsion shakes his whole body.*)

PROFESSOR (*winded, mumbling*): Bitch . . . Oh, that's good, that does me good . . . Ah! Ah! I'm exhausted . . . I can scarcely breathe . . . Aah! (*He breathes with difficulty; he falls—fortunately a chair is there; he mops his brow, mumbles some incomprehensible words; his breathing becomes normal. He gets up, looks at the knife in his hand, looks at the young girl, then as though he were waking up, in a panic:)* What have I done! What's going to happen to me now! What's going to happen! Oh! dear! Oh dear, I'm in trouble! Young lady, young lady, get up! *(He is agitated, still holding onto the invisible knife, which he doesn't know what to do with.)* Come now, young lady, the lesson is over . . . you may go . . . you can pay another time . . . Oh! she is dead . . . dea-ead . . . And by my knife . . . She is dea-ead . . . It's terrible. *(He calls the* MAID:*)* Marie! Marie! My good Marie, come here! Ah! Ah! *(The door on the right opens a little and* MARIE *appears.)* No . . . don't come in . . . I made a mistake . . . I don't need you, Marie . . . I don't need you anymore . . . do you understand? . . .

*(*MAID *enters wearing a stern expression, without saying a word. She sees the corpse.)*

PROFESSOR *(in a voice less and less assured)*: I don't need you, Marie . . .

MAID *(sarcastic)*: Then, you're satisfied with your pupil, she's profited by your lesson?

PROFESSOR *(holding the knife behind his back)*: Yes, the lesson is finished . . . but . . . she . . . she's still there . . . she doesn't want to leave . . .

MAID *(very harshly)*: Is that a fact? . . .

PROFESSOR *(trembling)*: It wasn't I . . . it wasn't I . . . Marie . . . No . . . I assure you . . . it wasn't I, my little Marie . . .

MAID: And who was it? Who was it then? Me?

PROFESSOR: I don't know . . . maybe . . .

MAID: Or the cat?

PROFESSOR: That's possible . . . I don't know . . .

MAID: And today makes it the fortieth time! . . . And every day it's the same thing! Every day! You should be ashamed, at your age . . . and you're going to make yourself sick! You won't have any pupils left. That will serve you right.

PROFESSOR *(irritated)*: It wasn't my fault! She didn't want to learn! She was disobedient! She was a bad pupil! She didn't want to learn!

MAID: Liar! . . .

PROFESSOR *(craftily approaching the* MAID, *holding the knife behind his back)*: It's none of your business! *(He tries to strike her with a great blow of the knife; the* MAID *seizes his wrist in mid-gesture and twists it; the* PROFESSOR *lets the knife fall to the floor)*: . . . I'm sorry!

MAID *(gives him two loud, strong slaps; the* PROFESSOR *falls onto the floor, on his prat; he sobs)*: Little murderer! bastard! You're disgusting! You wanted to do that to me? I'm not one of your pupils, not me! *(She pulls him up by the collar, picks up his skullcap and puts it on his head; he's afraid she'll slap him again and holds his arm up to protect his face, like a child.)* Put the knife back where it belongs, go on! *(The* PROFESSOR *goes and puts it back in the drawer of the buffet, then comes back to her.)* Now didn't I warn you, just a little while

ago: arithmetic leads to philology, and philology leads to crime . . .

PROFESSOR: You said "to calamity"!

MAID: It's the same thing.

PROFESSOR: I didn't understand you. I thought that "calamity" was a city and that you meant that philology leads to the city of Calamity . . .

MAID: Liar! Old fox! An intellectual like you is not going to make a mistake in the meanings of words. Don't try to pull the wool over my eyes.

PROFESSOR *(sobbing)*: I didn't kill her on purpose!

MAID: Are you sorry at least?

PROFESSOR: Oh, yes, Marie, I swear it to you!

MAID: I can't help feeling sorry for you! Ah! you're a good boy in spite of everything! I'll try to fix this. But don't start it again . . . It could give you a heart attack . . .

PROFESSOR: Yes, Marie! What are we going to do, now?

MAID: We're going to bury her . . . along with the thirty-nine others . . . that will make forty coffins . . . I'll call the undertakers and my lover, Father Auguste . . . I'll order the wreaths . . .

PROFESSOR: Yes, Marie, thank you very much.

MAID: Well, that's that. And perhaps it won't be necessary to call Auguste, since you yourself are something of a priest at times, if one can believe the gossip.

PROFESSOR: In any case, don't spend too much on the wreaths. She didn't pay for her lesson.

MAID: Don't worry . . . The least you can do is cover her up with her smock, she's not decent that way. And then we'll carry her out . . .

PROFESSOR: Yes, Marie, yes. *(He covers up the body.)* There's a chance that we'll get pinched° . . . with forty coffins . . . Don't you think . . . people will be surprised . . . Suppose they ask us what's inside them?

MAID: Don't worry so much. We'll say that they're empty. And besides, people won't ask questions, they're used to it.

PROFESSOR: Even so . . .

MAID *(she takes out an armband with an insignia, perhaps the Nazi swastika)*: Wait, if you're afraid, wear this, then you won't have anything more to be afraid of. *(She puts the armband around his arm.)* . . . That's good politics.

PROFESSOR: Thanks, my little Marie. With this, I won't need to worry . . . You're a good girl, Marie . . . very loyal . . .

MAID: That's enough. Come on, sir. Are you all right?

PROFESSOR: Yes, my little Marie. *(The* MAID *and the* PROFESSOR *take the body of the young girl, one by the shoulders, the other by the legs, and move towards the door on the right.)* Be careful. We don't want to hurt her.

---

pinched, caught, or arrested.

(They exit. The stage remains empty for several moments. We hear the doorbell ring at the left.)

VOICE OF THE MAID: Just a moment, I'm coming!

(She appears as she was at the beginning of the play, and goes towards the door. The doorbell rings again.)

MAID *(aside)*: She's certainly in a hurry, this one! *(Aloud:)* Just a moment! *(She goes to the door on the left, and opens it.)* Good morning, miss! You are the new pupil? You have come for the lesson? The Professor is expecting you. I'll go tell him that you've come. He'll be right down. Come in, miss, come in!

Figure 1. The Professor (Max Adrian) begins to lecture the Pupil (Joan Plowright) on linguistics and comparative philology while the Maid (Paula Bauersmith) looks on with stern disapproval in the 1958 Phoenix Theatre production, directed by Tony Richardson. (Photograph: Yale Collection of American Literature. Beinecke Rare Book and Manuscript Collection. Yale University.)

Figure 2. After killing the Pupil, the Professor (Max Adrian) clings "like a child" to the comforting Maid (Paula Bauersmith) in the 1958 Phoenix Theatre production, directed by Tony Richardson. (Photograph: Yale Collection of American Literature. Beinecke Rare Book and Manuscript Collection. Yale University.)

Staging of *The Lesson*

REVIEW OF THE PHOENIX THEATRE
PRODUCTION, NEW YORK, 1958,
BY WALTER KERR

I once knew a man who wanted to write a play on the meaninglessness of meaning. I hope he isn't still working on it, for Eugène Ionesco has beaten him to the punch with at least two such treasures, "The Chairs" and "The Lesson," both of which were passionately and perhaps even properly produced at the Phoenix last night.

The first, and far more nerve-wracking, of the pair takes place in what I took to be a lighthouse, beyond which the waters of the sea ripple gently and vacantly. Two toothless and arthritic creatures, played with cackling enthusiasm and considerable skill by Joan Plowright and Eli Wallach, nurse each other's daydreams and blow each other's noses while they wait for a company of invisible friends to assemble so that the old fellow's terribly important "message to mankind" can be delivered by an Orator hired for the occasion.

Before the non-company comes, Mr. Wallach sits on Miss Plowright's lap: she is both his wife and his "mummy." Once the guests are not occupying the several dozens of chairs hurtled onto the stage for them, Miss Plowright explains to her portion of empty air that their only son left them at the age of seven ("the age of discretion"), while Mr. Wallach confides to his vacuum that they have never had any children. When all of the absent guests are assembled, the Orator—looking like Lon Chaney in the role of the Mad Hatter—appears. In a spastic grinding of teeth and tongue, the message is delivered: it is gibberish.

"The Lesson," which affords the extremely adaptable and really talented Miss Plowright an opportunity to wipe off the makeup and appear as a sunny little monster with a toothache, begins with a stoop-shouldered, feverishly intense tutor (Max Adrian, in brilliant form) opening the door to a student who can count to infinity or to 16, whichever is easier. The fact that the child can add but not subtract throws Mr. Adrian into a frenzy ("Integration alone is not enough—disintegration is necessary, too"). The pursuit of mathematics leads the increasingly shaken Adrian to the brink of some secret malaise; as they proceed to the study of words he is toppled over the brink, for "philology is the worst of all." He cuts Miss Plowright's throat, tidies the body away, and opens the door to the next pupil: Miss Plowright. (I wouldn't tell you this if I wasn't pretty certain you'd guess it).

In the course of these two calculated journeys into unreason, some astonishing theatrical effects are spun by director Tony Richardson's ingenious hand: a nightmare cyclone of flapping doors, spinning bodies (only two, it seems like twenty), and whining musical strings; a blur of purple color bleeding downward over the set; a red-and-green electrical storm while confetti uncoils from the heavens. The simple shock value of these violent images is enormous; and the players seem honestly to inherit the wind.

What bothers me about both these exercises, aside from a slight headache that is going away now, is their delicate, insistent assault upon form. I'm not thinking now of the arrogant and fanciful "irregularities" that dot the surface every inch of the way, but of the destiny to which we are being so ruthlessly led: to the defiant mindlessness that is the "answer" in each case. And is, inevitably, "nothing"—intellectual opposites mean the same thing, the only possible message is literally without content: if anything begins over again it is nothing that is beginning again. A philosophy of nihilism is perfectly possible to grasp. But its elaboration into theatrical non-sequiturs becomes a long, tortured, circuitous, pretentious road to a nice, round zero that might be drawn at once. Not the complexity, but the almost juvenile simplicity, of the evening's course is, I think, its undoing.

It is quite as though Lewis Carroll had gone about his work with no playfulness at all, but in black despair, believing hopelessly in every "Off with his head!"

SAMUEL BECKETT

1906–1989

Beckett did not start writing plays until his early forties, but by his mid-fifties he had become internationally recognized as one of the most revolutionary, influential, and philosophically significant dramatists of the contemporary period. Born near Dublin to a wealthy family, he was sent away at the age of fourteen to an Irish boarding school, and from there went on to Trinity College, Dublin, where he proved himself an exceptional student of French and Italian. In 1928, he went to Paris as an exchange teacher and there became acquainted with the most famous Irish author of his day, James Joyce, whose radically new fiction stimulated Beckett to experiment with avant-garde methods of poetry and fiction writing. He returned briefly to Dublin to serve as lecturer in French and to receive his master's degree in 1931 for a study of Marcel Proust, but by the mid-1930s he was on the move again in France and Germany, supporting himself at odd jobs, while he continued to write fiction and poetry. Then, in 1937, he settled in Paris, and when World War II began he worked for the French resistance movement. Shortly after the end of the war, having taken up permanent residence in Paris, he wrote his first play, *Waiting for Godot*. When it was produced in 1953, it quickly turned into an international sensation.

Waiting for Godot startled audiences and reviewers because it challenged most of their assumptions about the nature of dramatic form. It undercut their ideas of plot with its persistently illogical and purposeless activity; it questioned their ideas of dialogue with its endless contradictions between language and action; it defied their ideas of spectacle with its stage bare except for a tree that is also bare until the second act when it has somehow acquired "four or five leaves." And in all his subsequent plays, Beckett continued to challenge audiences by stripping away more and more of the conventions associated with theater, as if he were seeking to discover how much can be taken away from drama without forsaking the essence of dramatic experience.

In seeking to discover the limits of drama, Beckett progressively stripped away virtually all the elements of theater. Physical action decreased as Beckett's protagonists became less and less mobile. In *Waiting for Godot,* two of the characters are roped to one another, and though everyone can walk they frequently fall down. In *Endgame* (1957), Nagg and Nell are confined to ashbins, Hamm is confined to a wheelchair, and Clov, the only mobile character, hobbles around the stage. In *Happy Days,* Winnie is buried up to her waist in a mound, and by Act 2 the mound has reached her neck. In *Play* (1964), all three characters are immobilized in urns and speak only when a light shines upon them. And in *Not I* (1972), the only visible action is the mouth of a woman speaking. Characters likewise decrease from the five in *Waiting for Godot* to one (and his tape recorder) in *Krapp's Last Tape* (1958). Even language disappears in Beckett's shorter pieces. *Act without Words I* (1957) and *II* (1960) are mime pieces, and *Breath* (1970) lasts for one minute of cries and breaths. Consequently many audiences and reviewers have often been moved in witnessing Beckett's plays to echo the words of

Estragon in *Waiting for Godot*: "Nothing happens, nobody comes, nobody goes, it's awful."

Today, however, *Waiting for Godot* and *Endgame* are recognized as two of the most important plays in contemporary drama, and they have been performed throughout the world to appreciative audiences in Paris and London, on Broadway and off, at San Quentin Prison, and even in community churches. The two couples of *Waiting for Godot*—the tramps Vladimir and Estragon, and the master and his slave, Pozzo and Lucky—have been examined, annotated, and allegorized, yet they still survive. In fact, survival—or existence, to use a more neutral term—is the action of the play. Stranded on a bare stage, in a barren existence, Vladimir and Estragon "wait for Godot," and while they wait they tell stories to each other, they reminisce, they contemplate suicide, they munch carrots and radishes, they pull their boots on and off, and they go through many other routines that Beckett appears to have drawn from the vaudeville world of Charlie Chaplin, Buster Keaton, and the Marx brothers. Estragon sums up their existence when he says, "We always find something, eh Didi, to give us the impression we exist?" Although Godot does not arrive at the end of the first act, nor at the end of the second—though their world grows increasingly meaningless—they sustain themselves through their continued inventiveness. And in contrast to Pozzo and Lucky, who are tied to one another by a rope, Vladimir and Estragon are bound to each other by a friendship that survives repeated separations and quarrels. *Endgame* is a grimmer and tighter play. The two acts of *Godot* have shrunk to a single long act. The two pairs of characters are still present but the emphasis has been drastically changed; the master-slave pair, the blind Hamm and the hobbling Clov, dominate the play, while Nagg and Nell, who are reminiscent of Vladimir and Estragon in their exchanging of memories and food, are confined to ashbins and appear only occasionally. Instead of a road on which the characters might come and go, there is only a room, and the world outside does not appear to contain any sign of life, not even a tree with a few leaves on it.

Endgame has repeatedly tempted critics to define its meaning, in part because it so insistently appears to deny itself significance—Hamm, for example, says "We're not beginning to . . . to . . . mean something?" and Clov replies, "Mean something! You and I, mean something!"—in part because it implicitly alludes to so many interpretative contexts. The chess metaphor of the title is echoed in the physical action of Hamm, the king who can move only in limited ways, and in the "very red faces" of Hamm and Clov contrasted to the "very white faces" of Nagg and Nell. Allusions to Shakespeare abound throughout the play: Hamm's name seems to be a shortened form of Hamlet; he sees himself as a deposed king, like Lear and Richard II; he parodies Richard III's final words when he calls out "My kingdom for a nightman"; and he directly quotes Prospero, "Our revels now are ended," and then throws away his gaff, much as Prospero breaks his magic wand at the end of *The Tempest*. The theatrical metaphor running throughout the play provides another interpretative context. Hamm's first words, for example, are "Me—*(he yawns)*—to play." Clov looks out at the auditorium and comments, ironically, "I see . . . a multitude . . . in transports . . . of joy." Hamm speaks of the "dialogue," worries that the small boy may provide an "underplot," grumbles when Clov reacts to "an aside," and announces, "I'm warming up for my last soliloquy." Clov starts to leave the stage with the line, "This is what we call making an exit." Thus the stage is, it seems, the only place of life in a world Clov calls "corpsed." And that reference to death is only one of innumerable references to it from the title to the final tableau.

Yet in the theater, as indicated by the review of the Paris premiere following the text, *Endgame* also turns out to be a highly comic experience, in spite of, or perhaps because of, its grim situation. Clov may find his repeated taunting of Hamm amusing (see Figure 1), even if Hamm does not. Yet at moments Clov and Hamm join together in comic routines, as when Clov thinks he has discovered a flea; Hamm's fear that "humanity might start from there all over again" leads to Clov searching for the insecticide powder he winds up sprinkling in his trousers. Even the two old people in the ashbins take part in the vaudeville routines:

NAGG: Can you hear me?
NELL: Yes. And you?
NAGG: Yes.

(Pause)

Our hearing hasn't failed.
NELL: Our what?
NAGG: Our hearing.

Even moments that might well be solemn, such as Hamm's order, "Let us pray to God" (see Figure 2), are interrupted by Clov's interest in getting back to rat-extermination and Nagg's cry for "me sugar-plum." Nell seems to have the final word on the play's theatrical meaning when she says, "Nothing is funnier than unhappiness, I grant you that."

ENDGAME
A Play in One Act

BY SAMUEL BECKETT

CHARACTERS

NAGG
NELL
HAMM
CLOV

SCENE

Bare interior. Grey light. Left and right back, high up, two small windows, curtains drawn. Front right, a door.

Hanging near door, its face to wall, a picture. Front left, touching each other, covered with an old sheet, two ashbins. Center, in an armchair on castors, covered with an old sheet, HAMM. Motionless by the door, his eyes fixed on HAMM, CLOV. Very red face. Brief tableau.

(CLOV goes and stands under window left. Stiff, staggering walk. He looks up at window left. He turns and looks at window right. He goes and stands under window right. He looks up at window right. He turns and looks at window left. He goes out, comes back immediately with a small step-ladder, carries it over and sets it down under window left, gets up on it, draws back curtain. He gets down, takes six steps (for example) towards window right, goes back for ladder, carries it over and sets it down under window right, gets up on it, draws back curtain. He gets down, takes three steps towards window left, goes back for ladder, carries it over and sets it down under window left, gets up on it, looks out of window. Brief laugh. He gets down, goes with ladder towards ashbins, halts, turns, carries back ladder and sets it down under window right, goes to ashbins, removes sheet covering them, folds it over his arm. He raises one lid, stoops and looks into bin. Brief laugh. He closes lid. Same with other bin. He goes to HAMM, removes sheet covering him, folds it over his arm. In a dressing-gown, a stiff toque on his head, a large blood-stained handkerchief over his face, a whistle hanging from his neck, a rug over his knees, thick socks on his feet, HAMM seems to be asleep. CLOV looks him over. Brief laugh. He goes to door, halts, turns towards auditorium.)

CLOV (fixed gaze, tonelessly): Finished, it's finished, nearly finished, it must be nearly finished.

(Pause.)

Grain upon grain, one by one, and one day, suddenly, there's a heap, a little heap, the impossible heap.

(Pause.)

I can't be punished any more.

(Pause.)

I'll go now to my kitchen, ten feet by ten feet by ten feet, and wait for him to whistle me.

(Pause.)

Nice dimensions, nice proportions, I'll lean on the table, and look at the wall, and wait for him to whistle me.

(He remains a moment motionless, then goes out. He comes back immediately, goes to window right, takes up the ladder and carries it out. Pause. HAMM stirs. He yawns under the handkerchief. He removes the handkerchief from his face. Very red face. Black glasses.)

HAMM: Me—(He yawns.)—to play.

(He holds the handkerchief spread out before him.)

Old stancher!

(He takes off his glasses, wipes his eyes, his face, the glasses, puts them on again, folds the handkerchief and puts it back neatly in the breast-pocket of his dressing-gown. He clears his throat, joins the tips of his fingers.)

Can there be misery—(He yawns.)—loftier than mine? No doubt. Formerly. But now?

(Pause.)

My father?

(Pause.)

My mother?

(Pause.)

My . . . dog?

(Pause.)

Oh I am willing to believe they suffer as much as

such creatures can suffer. But does that mean their sufferings equal mine? No doubt.

(*Pause.*)

No, all is a—(*He yawns.*)—bsolute, (*Proudly.*) the bigger a man is the fuller he is.

(*Pause. Gloomily.*)

And the emptier.

(*He sniffs.*)

Clov!

(*Pause.*)

No, alone.

(*Pause.*)

What dreams! Those forests!

(*Pause.*)

Enough, it's time it ended, in the shelter too.

(*Pause.*)

And yet I hesitate, I hesitate to . . . to end. Yes, there it is, it's time it ended and yet I hesitate to—(*He yawns.*)—to end. (*Yawns.*)

God, I'm tired, I'd be better off in bed.

(*He whistles. Enter* CLOV *immediately. He halts beside the chair.*)

You pollute the air!

(*Pause.*)

Get me ready. I'm going to bed.

CLOV: I've just got you up.

HAMM: And what of it?

CLOV: I can't be getting you up and putting you to bed every five minutes, I have things to do.

(*Pause.*)

HAMM: Did you ever see my eyes?

CLOV: No.

HAMM: Did you never have the curiosity, while I was sleeping, to take off my glasses and look at my eyes?

CLOV: Pulling back the lids?

(*Pause.*)

No.

HAMM: One of these days I'll show them to you.

(*Pause.*)

It seems they've gone all white.

(*Pause.*)

What time is it?

CLOV: The same as usual.

HAMM (*gestures toward window right*): Have you looked?

CLOV: Yes

HAMM: Well?

CLOV: Zero.

HAMM: It'd need to rain.

CLOV: It won't rain.

(*Pause.*)

HAMM: Apart from that, how do you feel?

CLOV: I don't complain.

HAMM: You feel normal?

CLOV (*irritably*): I tell you I don't complain.

HAMM: I feel a little queer.

(*Pause.*)

Clov!

CLOV: Yes.

HAMM: Have you not had enough?

CLOV: Yes.

(*Pause.*)

Of what?

HAMM: Of this . . . this . . . thing.

CLOV: I always had.

(*Pause*)

Not you?

HAMM (*gloomily*): Then there's no reason for it to change.

CLOV: It may end.

(*Pause.*)

All life long the same questions, the same answers.

HAMM: Get me ready.

(CLOV *does not move.*)

Go and get the sheet.

(CLOV *does not move.*)

Clov!

CLOV: Yes.

HAMM: I'll give you nothing more to eat.

CLOV: Then we'll die.

HAMM: I'll give you just enough to keep you from dying. You'll be hungry all the time.

CLOV: Then we won't die.

(*Pause.*)

I'll go and get the sheet.

(*He goes toward the door.*)

HAMM: No!

(CLOV *halts.*)

I'll give you one biscuit per day.

(*Pause.*)

One and a half.

(*Pause.*)

Why do you stay with me?
CLOV: Why do you keep me?
HAMM: There's no one else.
CLOV: There's nowhere else.

(*Pause.*)

HAMM: You're leaving me all the same.
CLOV: I'm trying.
HAMM: You don't love me.
CLOV: No.
HAMM: You loved me once.
CLOV: Once!
HAMM: I've made you suffer too much.

(*Pause.*)

Haven't I?
CLOV: It's not that.
HAMM (*shocked*): I haven't made you suffer too much?
CLOV: Yes!
HAMM (*relieved*): Ah you gave me a fright!

(*Pause. Coldly.*)

Forgive me.

(*Pause. Louder.*)

I said, Forgive me.
CLOV: I heard you.

(*Pause.*)

Have you bled?
HAMM: Less.

(*Pause.*)

Is it not time for my pain-killer?
CLOV: No.

(*Pause.*)

HAMM: How are your eyes?
CLOV: Bad.
HAMM: How are your legs?
CLOV: Bad.
HAMM: But you can move.
CLOV: Yes.
HAMM (*violently*): Then move!

(CLOV *goes to back wall, leans against it with his forehead and hands.*)

Where are you?

CLOV: Here.
HAMM: Come back!

(CLOV *returns to his place beside the chair.*)

Where are you?
CLOV: Here.
HAMM: Why don't you kill me?
CLOV: I don't know the combination of the cupboard.

(*Pause.*)

HAMM: Go and get two bicycle-wheels.
CLOV: There are no more bicycle-wheels.
HAMM: What have you done with your bicycle?
CLOV: I never had a bicycle.
HAMM: The thing is impossible.
CLOV: When there were still bicycles I wept to have one. I crawled at your feet. You told me to go to hell. Now there are none.
HAMM: And your rounds? When you inspected my paupers. Always on foot?
CLOV: Sometimes on horse.

(*The lid of one of the bins lifts and the hands of* NAGG *appear, gripping the rim. Then his head emerges. Night-cap. Very white face.* NAGG *yawns, then listens.*)

I'll leave you, I have things to do.
HAMM: In your kitchen?
CLOV: Yes.
HAMM: Outside of here it's death.

(*Pause.*)

All right, be off.

(*Exit* CLOV. *Pause.*)

We're getting on.
NAGG: Me pap!
HAMM: Accursed progenitor!
NAGG: Me pap!
HAMM: The old folks at home! No decency left! Guzzle, guzzle, that's all they think of.

(*He whistles. Enter* CLOV. *He halts beside the chair.*)

Well! I thought you were leaving me.
CLOV: Oh not just yet, not just yet.
NAGG: Me pap!
HAMM: Give him his pap.
CLOV: There's no more pap.
HAMM (*to* NAGG): Do you hear that? There's no more pap. You'll never get any more pap.
NAGG: I want me pap!
HAMM: Give him a biscuit.

(*Exit* CLOV.)

Accursed fornicator! How are your stumps?
NAGG: Never mind me stumps.

(*Enter* CLOV *with biscuit.*)

CLOV: I'm back again, with the biscuit.

(*He gives biscuit to* NAGG *who fingers it, sniffs it.*)

NAGG (*plaintively*): What is it?
CLOV: Spratt's medium.
NAGG (*as before*): It's hard! I can't!
HAMM: Bottle him!

(CLOV *pushes* NAGG *back into the bin, closes the lid.*)

CLOV (*returning to his place beside the chair*): If age but knew!
HAMM: Sit on him!
CLOV: I can't sit.
HAMM: True. And I can't stand.
CLOV: So it is.
HAMM: Every man his specialty.

(*Pause.*)

No phone calls?

(*Pause.*)

Don't we laugh?
CLOV (*after reflection*): I don't feel like it.
HAMM (*after reflection*): Nor I.

(*Pause.*)

Clov!
CLOV: Yes.
HAMM: Nature has forgotten us.
CLOV: There's no more nature.
HAMM: No more nature! You exaggerate.
CLOV: In the vicinity.
HAMM: But we breathe, we change! We lose our hair, our teeth! Our bloom! Our ideals!
CLOV: Then she hasn't forgotten us.
HAMM: But you say there is none.
CLOV (*sadly*): No one that ever lived ever thought so crooked as we.
HAMM: We do what we can.
CLOV: We shouldn't.

(*Pause.*)

HAMM: You're a bit of all right, aren't you?
CLOV: A smithereen.

(*Pause.*)

HAMM: This is slow work.

(*Pause.*)

Is it not time for my pain-killer?
CLOV: No.

(*Pause.*)

I'll leave you, I have things to do.

HAMM: In your kitchen?
CLOV: Yes.
HAMM: What, I'd like to know.
CLOV: I look at the wall.
HAMM: The wall! And what do you see on your wall? Mene, mene? Naked bodies?
CLOV: I see my light dying.
HAMM: Your light dying! Listen to that! Well, it can die just as well here, *your* light. Take a look at me and then come back and tell me what you think of *your* light.

(*Pause.*)

CLOV: You shouldn't speak to me like that.

(*Pause.*)

HAMM (*coldly*): Forgive me.

(*Pause. Louder.*)

I said, Forgive me.
CLOV: I heard you.

(*The lid of* NAGG's *bin lifts. His hands appear, gripping the rim. Then his head emerges. In his mouth the biscuit. He listens.*)

HAMM: Did your seeds come up?
CLOV: No.
HAMM: Did you scratch round them to see if they had sprouted?
CLOV: They haven't sprouted.
HAMM: Perhaps it's still too early.
CLOV: If they were going to sprout they would have sprouted.

(*Violently.*)

They'll never sprout!

(*Pause.* NAGG *takes biscuit in his hand.*)

HAMM: This is not much fun.

(*Pause.*)

But that's always the way at the end of the day, isn't it, Clov?
CLOV: Always.
HAMM: It's the end of the day like any other day, isn't it, Clov?
CLOV: Looks like it.

(*Pause.*)

HAMM (*anguished*): What's happening, what's happening?
CLOV: Something is taking its course.

(*Pause.*)

HAMM: All right, be off.

(He leans back in his chair, remains motionless. CLOV *does not move, heaves a great groaning sigh.* HAMM *sits up.)*

I thought I told you to be off.

CLOV: I'm trying.

(He goes to door, halts.)

Ever since I was whelped.

(Exit CLOV.*)*

HAMM: We're getting on.

(He leans back in his chair, remains motionless. NAGG *knocks on the lid of the other bin. Pause. He knocks harder. The lid lifts and the hands of* NELL *appear, gripping the rim. Then her head emerges. Lace cap. Very white face.)*

NELL: What is it, my pet?

(Pause.)

Time for love?

NAGG: Were you asleep?

NELL: Oh no!

NAGG: Kiss me.

NELL: We can't.

NAGG: Try.

(Their heads strain toward each other, fail to meet, fall apart again.)

NELL: Why this farce, day after day?

(Pause.)

NAGG: I've lost me tooth.

NELL: When?

NAGG: I had it yesterday.

NELL *(elegiac):* Ah yesterday!

(They turn painfully toward each other.)

NAGG: Can you see me?

NELL: Hardly. And you?

NAGG: What?

NELL: Can you see me?

NAGG: Hardly.

NELL: So much the better, so much the better.

NAGG: Don't say that.

(Pause.)

Our sight has failed.

NELL: Yes.

(Pause. They turn away from each other.)

NAGG: Can you hear me?

NELL: Yes, And you?

NAGG: Yes.

(Pause.)

Our hearing hasn't failed.

NELL: Our what?

NAGG: Our hearing.

NELL: No.

(Pause.)

Have you anything else to say to me?

NAGG: Do you remember—

NELL: No.

NAGG: When we crashed on our tandem and lost our shanks.

(They laugh heartily.)

NELL: It was in the Ardennes.

(They laugh less heartily.)

NAGG: On the road to Sedan.

(They laugh still less heartily.)

Are you cold?

NELL: Yes, perished. And you?

NAGG *(pause):* I'm freezing.

(Pause.)

Do you want to go in?

NELL: Yes.

NAGG: Then go in.

*(*NELL *does not move.)*

Why don't you go in?

NELL: I don't know.

(Pause.)

NAGG: Has he changed your sawdust?

NELL: It isn't sawdust.

(Pause. Wearily.)

Can you not be a little accurate, Nagg?

NAGG: Your sand then. It's not important.

NELL: It is important.

(Pause.)

NAGG: It was sawdust once.

NELL: Once!

NAGG: And now it's sand.

(Pause.)

From the shore.

(Pause. Impatiently.)

Now it's sand he fetches from the shore.

NELL: Now it's sand.

NAGG: Has he changed yours?

NELL: No.

NAGG: Nor mine.

(Pause.)

I won't have it!

(Pause. Holding up the biscuit.)

Do you want a bit?

NELL: No.

(Pause.)

Of what?

NAGG: Biscuit. I've kept you half.

(He looks at the biscuit. Proudly.)

Three quarters. For you. Here.

(He proffers the biscuit.)

No?

(Pause.)

Do you not feel well?

HAMM *(wearily)*: Quiet, quiet, you're keeping me awake.

(Pause.)

Talk softer.

(Pause.)

If I could sleep I might make love. I'd go into the woods. My eyes would see . . . the sky, the earth. I'd run, run, they wouldn't catch me.

(Pause.)

Nature!

(Pause.)

There's something dripping in my head.

(Pause.)

A heart, a heart in my head.

(Pause.)

NAGG *(softly)*: Do you hear him? A heart in his head!

(He chuckles cautiously.)

NELL: One mustn't laugh at those things, Nagg. Why must you always laugh at them?

NAGG: Not so loud!

NELL *(without lowering her voice)*: Nothing is funnier than unhappiness, I grant you that. But—

NAGG *(shocked)*: Oh!

NELL: Yes, yes, it's the most comical thing in the world. And we laugh, we laugh, with a will, in the beginning. But it's always the same thing. Yes, it's like the funny story we have heard too often, we still find it funny, but we don't laugh any more.

(Pause.)

Have you anything else to say to me?

NAGG: No.

NELL: Are you quite sure?

(Pause.)

Then I'll leave you.

NAGG: Do you not want your biscuit?

(Pause.)

I'll keep it for you.

(Pause.)

I thought you were going to leave me.

NELL: I am going to leave you.

NAGG: Could you give me a scratch before you go?

NELL: No.

(Pause.)

Where?

NAGG: In the back.

NELL: No.

(Pause.)

Rub yourself against the rim.

NAGG: It's lower down. In the hollow.

NELL: What hollow?

NAGG: The hollow!

(Pause.)

Could you not?

(Pause.)

Yesterday you scratched me there.

NELL *(elegaic)*: Ah yesterday!

NAGG: Could you not?

(Pause.)

Would you like me to scratch you?

(Pause.)

Are you crying again?

NELL: I was trying.

(Pause)

HAMM: Perhaps it's a little vein.

(Pause.)

NAGG: What was that he said?

NELL: Perhaps it's a little vein.

NAGG: What does that mean?

(Pause.)

That means nothing.

(Pause.)

Will I tell you the story of the tailor?

NELL: No.

(Pause.)

What for?

NAGG: To cheer you up.

NELL: It's not funny.

NAGG: It always made you laugh.

(Pause.)

The first time I thought you'd die.

NELL: It was on Lake Como.

(Pause.)

One April afternoon.

(Pause.)

Can you believe it?

NAGG: What?

NELL: That we once went out rowing on Lake Como.

(Pause.)

One April afternoon.

NAGG: We had got engaged the day before.

NELL: Engaged!

NAGG: You were in such fits that we capsized. By rights we should have been drowned.

NELL: It was because I felt happy.

NAGG *(indignant)*: It was not, it was not, it was my story and nothing else. Happy! Don't you laugh at it still? Every time I tell it. Happy!

NELL: It was deep, deep. And you could see down to the bottom. So white. So clean.

NAGG: Let me tell it again.

(Raconteur's voice.)

An Englishman, needing a pair of striped trousers in a hurry for the New Year festivities, goes to his tailor who takes his measurements.

(Tailor's voice.)

"That's the lot, come back in four days, I'll have it ready." Good. Four days later.

(Tailor's voice.)

"So sorry, come back in a week. I've made a mess of the seat." Good, that's all right, a neat seat can be very ticklish. A week later.

(Tailor's voice.)

"Frightfully sorry, come back in ten days, I've made a hash of the crotch." Good, can't be helped, a snug crotch is always a teaser. Ten days later.

(Tailor's voice.)

"Dreadfully sorry, come back in a fortnight, I've made a balls of the fly." Good, at a pinch, a smart fly is a stiff proposition.

(Pause. Normal voice.)

I never told it worse.

(Pause. Gloomy.)

I tell this story worse and worse.

(Pause. Raconteur's voice.)

Well, to make it short, the bluebells are blowing and he ballockses the buttonholes.

(Customer's voice.)

"God damn you to hell, Sir, no, it's indecent, there are limits! In six days, do you hear me, six days, God made the world. Yes Sir, no less Sir, the WORLD! And you are not bloody well capable of making me a pair of trousers in three months!"

(Tailor's voice, scandalized.)

"But my dear Sir, my dear Sir, look—

(Disdainful gesture, disgustedly.)

—at the world—

(Pause.)

and look—

(Loving gesture, proudly.)—at my TROUSERS!"

(Pause. He looks at NELL who has remained impassive, her eyes unseeing, breaks into a high forced laugh, cuts it short, pokes his head towards NELL, launches his laugh again.)

HAMM: Silence!

(NAGG starts, cuts short his laugh.)

NELL: You could see down to the bottom.

HAMM *(exasperated)*: Have you not finished? Will you never finish?

(With sudden fury.)

Will this never finish?

(NAGG disappears into his bin, closes the lid behind him. NELL does not move. Frenziedly.)

My kingdom for a nightman!

(He whistles. Enter CLOV.)

Clear away this muck! Chuck it in the sea!

(CLOV goes to bins, halts.)

NELL: So white.

HAMM: What? What's she blathering about?

(CLOV stoops, takes NELL's hand, feels her pulse.)

NELL *(to CLOV)*: Desert!

(CLOV lets go her hand, pushes her back in the bin, closes the lid.)

CLOV *(returning to his place beside the chair)*: She has no pulse.

HAMM: What was she drivelling about?

CLOV: She told me to go away, into the desert.

HAMM: Damn busybody! Is that all?

CLOV: No.

HAMM: What else?

CLOV: I didn't understand.

HAMM: Have you bottled her?

CLOV: Yes.

HAMM: Are they both bottled?

CLOV: Yes

HAMM: Screw down the lids.

(CLOV *goes toward door.*)

Time enough.

(CLOV *halts.*)

My anger subsides, I'd like to pee.

CLOV (*with alacrity*): I'll go and get the catheter.

(*He goes toward door.*)

HAMM: Time enough.

(CLOV *halts.*)

Give me my pain-killer.

CLOV: It's too soon.

(*Pause.*)

It's too soon on top of your tonic, it wouldn't act.

HAMM: In the morning they brace you up and in the evening they calm you down. Unless it's the other way round.

(*Pause.*)

That old doctor, he's dead naturally?

CLOV: He wasn't old.

HAMM: But he's dead?

CLOV: Naturally.

(*Pause.*)

You ask *me* that?

(*Pause.*)

HAMM: Take me for a little turn.

(CLOV *goes behind the chair and pushes it forward.*)

Not too fast!

(CLOV *pushes chair.*)

Right round the world!

(CLOV *pushes chair.*)

Hug the walls, then back to the center again.

(CLOV *pushes chair.*)

I was right in the center, wasn't I?

CLOV (*pushing*): Yes.

HAMM: We'd need a proper wheel-chair. With big wheels. Bicycle wheels!

(*Pause.*)

Are you hugging?

CLOV (*pushing*): Yes.

HAMM (*groping for wall*): It's a lie! Why do you lie to me?

CLOV (*bearing close to wall*): There! There!

HAMM: Stop!

(CLOV *stops chair close to back wall.* HAMM *lays his hand against the wall.*)

Old wall!

(*Pause.*)

Beyond is the . . . other hell.

(*Pause. Violently.*)

Closer! Closer! Up against!

CLOV: Take away your hand.

(HAMM *withdraws his hand.* CLOV *rams chair against wall.*)

There!

(HAMM *leans toward wall, applies his ear to it.*)

HAMM: Do you hear?

(*He strikes the wall with his knuckles.*)

Do you hear? Hollow bricks!

(*He strikes again.*)

All that's hollow!

(*Pause. He straightens up. Violently.*)

That's enough. Back!

CLOV: We haven't done the round.

HAMM: Back to my place!

(CLOV *pushes chair back to center.*)

Is that my place?

CLOV: Yes, that's your place.

HAMM: Am I right in the center?

CLOV: I'll measure it.

HAMM: More or less! More or less!

CLOV (*moving chair slightly*): There!

HAMM: I'm more or less in the center?

CLOV: I'd say so.

HAMM: You'd say so! Put me right in the center!

CLOV: I'll go and get the tape.

HAMM: Roughly! Roughly!

(CLOV *moves chair slightly.*)

Bang in the center!

CLOV: There!

(*Pause.*)

HAMM: I feel a little too far to the left.

(CLOV *moves chair slightly.*)

Now I feel a little too far to the right.

(CLOV *moves chair slightly.*)

I feel a little too far forward.

(CLOV *moves chair slightly.*)

Now I feel a little too far back.

(CLOV *moves chair slightly.*)

Don't stay there, (*i.e., behind the chair*) you give me the shivers.

(CLOV *returns to his place beside the chair.*)

CLOV: If I could kill him I'd die happy.

(*Pause.*)

HAMM: What's the weather like?
CLOV: As usual.
HAMM: Look at the earth.
CLOV: I've looked.
HAMM: With the glass?
HAMM: No need of the glass.
HAMM: Look at it with the glass.
CLOV: I'll go and get the glass.

(*Exit* CLOV.)

HAMM: No need of the glass!

(*Enter* CLOV *with telescope.*)

CLOV: I'm back again, with the glass.

(*He goes to window right, looks up at it.*)

I need the steps.
HAMM: Why? Have you shrunk?

(*Exit* CLOV *with telescope.*)

I don't like that, I don't like that.

(*Enter* CLOV *with ladder, but without telescope.*)

CLOV: I'm back again, with the steps.

(*He sets down ladder under window right, gets up on it, realizes he has not the telescope, gets down.*)

I need the glass.

(*He goes toward door.*)

HAMM (*violently*): But you have the glass!
CLOV (*halting, violently*): No, I haven't the glass!

(*Exit* CLOV.)

HAMM: This is deadly.

(*Enter* CLOV *with telescope. He goes toward ladder.*)
CLOV: Things are livening up.

(*He gets up on a ladder, raises the telescope, lets it fall.*)

I did it on purpose.

(*He gets down, picks up the telescope, turns it on auditorium.*)

I see . . . a multitude . . . in transports . . . of joy.

(*Pause.*)

That's what I call a magnifier.

(*He lowers the telescope, turns toward* HAMM.)

Well? Don't we laugh?
HAMM (*after reflection*): I don't.
CLOV (*after reflection*): Nor I.

(*He gets up on ladder, turns the telescope on the without.*)

Let's see.

(*He looks, moving the telescope.*)

Zero . . . (*He looks.*) . . . zero . . . (*He looks*) . . . and zero.
HAMM: Nothing stirs. All is—
CLOV: Zer—
HAMM (*violently*): Wait till you're spoken to!

(*Normal voice.*)

All is . . . all is . . . all is what?

(*Violently.*)

All is what?
CLOV: What all is? In a word? Is that what you want to know? Just a moment.

(*He turns the telescope on the without, looks, lowers the telescope, turns toward* HAMM.)

Corpsed.

(*Pause.*)

Well? Content?
HAMM: Look at the sea.
CLOV: It's the same.
HAMM: Look at the ocean!

(CLOV *gets down, takes a few steps toward window left, goes back for ladder, carries it over and sets it down under window left, gets up on it, turns the telescope on the without, looks at length. He starts, lowers the telescope, examines it, turns it again on the without.*)

CLOV: Never seen anything like that!
HAMM (*anxiously*): What? A sail? A fin? Smoke?
CLOV (*looking*): The light is sunk.
HAMM (*relieved*): Pah! We all knew that.
CLOV (*looking*): There was a bit left.
HAMM: The base.
CLOV (*looking*): Yes.
HAMM: And now?
CLOV (*looking*): All gone.
HAMM: No gulls?
CLOV (*looking*): Gulls!

HAMM: And the horizon? Nothing on the horizon?
CLOV (*lowering the telescope, turning toward* HAMM, *exasperatedly*): What in God's name could there be on the horizon?

(*Pause.*)

HAMM: The waves, how are the waves?
CLOV: The waves?

(*He turns the telescope on the waves.*)

Lead.
HAMM: And the sun?
CLOV (*looking*): Zero.
HAMM: But it should be sinking. Look again.
CLOV (*looking*): Damn the sun.
HAMM: Is it night already then?
CLOV (*looking*): No.
HAMM: Then what is it?
CLOV (*looking*): Gray.

(*Lowering the telescope, turning toward* HAMM, *louder.*)

Gray!

(*Pause. Still louder.*)

GRRAY!

(*Pause. He gets down, approaches* HAMM *from behind, whispers in his ear.*)

HAMM (*starting*): Gray! Did I hear you say gray?
CLOV: Light black. From pole to pole.
HAMM: You exaggerate.

(*Pause.*)

Don't stay there, you give me the shivers.

(CLOV *returns to his place beside the chair.*)

CLOV: Why this farce, day after day?
HAMM: Routine. One never knows.

(*Pause.*)

Last night I saw inside my breast. There was a big sore.
CLOV: Pah! You saw your heart.
HAMM: No, it was living.

(*Pause. Anguished.*)

Clov!
CLOV: Yes.
HAMM: What's happening?
CLOV: Something is taking its course.

(*Pause.*)

HAMM: Clov!
CLOV (*impatiently*): What is it?
HAMM: We're not beginning to . . . to . . . mean something?
CLOV: Mean something! You and I, mean something!

(*Brief laugh.*)

Ah that's a good one!
HAMM: I wonder.

(*Pause.*)

Imagine if a rational being came back to earth, wouldn't he be liable to get ideas into his head if he observed us long enough.

(*Voice of rational being.*)

Ah, good, now I see what it is, yes, now I understand what they're at!

(CLOV *starts, drops the telescope and begins to scratch his belly with both hands. Normal voice.*)

And without going so far as that, we ourselves . . . (*With emotion.*) . . . we ourselves . . . at certain moments . . . (*Vehemently.*) To think perhaps it won't all have been for nothing!
CLOV (*anguished, scratching himself*): I have a flea!
HAMM: A flea! Are there still fleas?
CLOV: On me, there's one.

(*Scratching.*)

Unless it's a crablouse.
HAMM (*very perturbed*): But humanity might start from there all over again! Catch him, for the love of God!
CLOV: I'll go and get the powder.

(*Exit* CLOV.)

HAMM: A flea! This is awful! What a day!

(*Enter* CLOV *with a sprinkling-tin.*)

CLOV: I'm back again, with the insecticide.
HAMM: Let him have it!

(CLOV *loosens the top of his trousers, pulls it forward and shakes powder into the aperture. He stoops, looks, waits, starts, frenziedly shakes more powder, stoops, looks, waits.*)

CLOV: The bastard!
HAMM: Did you get him?
CLOV: Looks like it.

(*He drops the tin and adjusts his trousers.*)

Unless he's laying doggo.
HAMM: Laying! Lying you mean. Unless he's *lying* doggo.
CLOV: Ah? One says lying? One doesn't say laying?
HAMM: Use your head, can't you. If he was laying we'd be bitched.
CLOV: Ah.

(*Pause.*)

What about that pee?
HAMM: I'm having it.
CLOV: Ah that's the spirit, that's the spirit!

(Pause.)

HAMM *(with ardour)*: Let's go from here, the two of us! South! You can make a raft and the currents will carry us away, far away, to other . . . mammals!

CLOV: God forbid!

HAMM: Alone, I'll embark alone! Get working on that raft immediately. Tomorrow I'll be gone for ever.

CLOV *(hastening toward door)*: I'll start straight away.

HAMM: Wait!

(CLOV halts.)

Will there be sharks, do you think?

CLOV: Sharks? I don't know. If there are there will be.

(He goes toward door.)

HAMM: Wait!

(CLOV halts.)

Is it not yet time for my pain-killer?

CLOV *(violently)*: No!

(He goes toward door.)

HAMM: Wait!

(CLOV halts.)

How are your eyes?

CLOV: Bad.

HAMM: But you can see.

CLOV: All I want.

HAMM: How are your legs?

CLOV: Bad.

HAMM: But you can walk.

CLOV: I come . . . and go.

HAMM: In my house.

(Pause. With prophetic relish.)

One day you'll be blind, like me. You'll be sitting there, a speck in the void, in the dark, for ever, like me.

(Pause.)

One day you'll say to yourself, I'm tired, I'll sit down, and you'll go and sit down. Then you'll say, I'm hungry, I'll get up and get something to eat. But you won't get up. You'll say, I shouldn't have sat down, but since I have I'll sit on a little longer, then I'll get up and get something to eat. But you won't get up and you won't get anything to eat.

(Pause.)

You'll look at the wall a while, then you'll say, I'll close my eyes, perhaps have a little sleep, after that I'll feel better, and you'll close them. And when you open them again there'll be no wall any more.

(Pause.)

Infinite emptiness will be all around you, all the resurrected dead of all the ages wouldn't fill it, and there you'll be like a little bit of grit in the middle of the steppe.

(Pause.)

Yes, one day you'll know what it is, you'll be like me, except that you won't have anyone with you, because you won't have had pity on anyone and because there won't be anyone left to have pity on.

(Pause.)

CLOV: It's not certain.

(Pause.)

And there's one thing you forget.

HAMM: Ah?

CLOV: I can't sit down.

HAMM *(impatiently)*: Well you'll lie down then, what the hell! Or you'll come to a standstill, simply stop and stand still, the way you are now. One day you'll say, I'm tired, I'll stop. What does the attitude matter?

(Pause.)

CLOV: So you all want me to leave you.

HAMM: Naturally.

CLOV: Then I'll leave you.

HAMM: You can't leave us.

CLOV: Then I won't leave you.

(Pause.)

HAMM: Why don't you finish us?

(Pause.)

I'll tell you the combination of the cupboard if you promise to finish me.

CLOV: I couldn't finish you.

HAMM: Then you won't finish me.

(Pause.)

CLOV: I'll leave you, I have things to do.

HAMM: Do you remember when you came here?

CLOV: No. Too small, you told me.

HAMM: Do you remember your father?

CLOV *(wearily)*: Same answer.

(Pause.)

You've asked me these questions millions of times.

HAMM: I love the old questions.

(With fervour.)

Ah the old questions, the old answers, there's nothing like them!

(Pause.)

It was I was a father to you.

CLOV: Yes.

(He looks at HAMM *fixedly.)*

You were that to me.

HAMM: My house a home for you.

CLOV: Yes.

(He looks about him.)

This was that for me.

HAMM *(proudly)*: But for me, *(Gesture toward himself.)* no father. But for Hamm, *(Gesture toward surroundings.)* no home.

(Pause.)

CLOV: I'll leave you.

HAMM: Did you ever think of one thing?

CLOV: Never.

HAMM: That here we're down in a hole.

(Pause.)

But beyond the hills? Eh? Perhaps it's still green. Eh?

(Pause.)

Flora! Pomona!

(Ecstatically.)

Ceres!

(Pause.)

Perhaps you won't need to go very far.

CLOV: I can't go very far.

(Pause.)

I'll leave you.

HAMM: Is my dog ready?

CLOV: He lacks a leg.

HAMM: Is he silky?

CLOV: He's a kind of Pomeranian.

HAMM: Go and get him.

CLOV: He lacks a leg.

HAMM: Go and get him!

(Exit CLOV.*)*

We're getting on.

(Enter CLOV *holding by one of its three legs a black toy dog.)*

CLOV: Your dogs are here.

(He hands the dog to HAMM *who feels it, fondles it.)*

HAMM: He's white, isn't he?

CLOV: Nearly.

HAMM: What do you mean, nearly? Is he white or isn't he?

CLOV: He isn't.

(Pause.)

HAMM: You've forgotten the sex.

CLOV *(vexed)*: But he isn't finished. The sex goes at the end.

(Pause.)

HAMM: You haven't put on his ribbon.

CLOV *(angrily)*: But he isn't finished, I tell you! First you finish your dog and then you put on his ribbon!

(Pause.)

HAMM: Can he stand?

CLOV: I don't know.

HAMM: Try.

(He hands the dog to CLOV *who places it on the ground.)*

Well?

CLOV: Wait!

(He squats down and tries to get the dog to stand on its three legs, fails, lets it go. The dog falls on its side.)

HAMM *(impatiently)*: Well?

CLOV: He's standing.

HAMM *(groping for the dog)*: Where? Where is he?

*(*CLOV *holds up the dog in a standing position.)*

CLOV: There.

(He takes HAMM*'s hand and guides it toward the dog's head.)*

HAMM *(his hand on the dog's head)*: Is he gazing at me?

CLOV: Yes.

HAMM *(proudly)*: As if he were asking me to take him for a walk?

CLOV: If you like.

HAMM *(as before)*: Or as if he were begging me for a bone.

(He withdraws his hand.)

Leave him like that, standing there imploring me.

*(*CLOV *straightens up. The dog falls on its side.)*

CLOV: I'll leave you.

HAMM: Have you had your visions?

CLOV: Less.

HAMM: Is Mother Pegg's light on?

CLOV: Light! How could anyone's light be on?

HAMM: Extinguished!

CLOV: Naturally it's extinguished. If it's not on it's extinguished.

HAMM: No, I mean Mother Pegg.

CLOV: But naturally she's extinguished!

(Pause.)

What's the matter with you today?

HAMM: I'm taking my course.

(Pause.)

Is she buried?

CLOV: Buried! Who would have buried her?

HAMM: You.

CLOV: Me! Haven't I enough to do without burying people?

HAMM: But you'll bury me.

CLOV: No I won't bury you.

(Pause.)

HAMM: She was bonny once, like a flower of the field.

(With reminiscent leer.)

And a great one for the men!

CLOV: We too were bonny—once. It's a rare thing not to have been bonny—once.

(Pause.)

HAMM: Go and get the gaff.

(CLOV goes to door, halts.)

CLOV: Do this, do that, and I do it. I never refuse. Why?

HAMM: You're not able to.

CLOV: Soon I won't do it any more.

HAMM: You won't be able to any more.

(Exit CLOV.)

Ah the creatures, the creatures, everything has to be explained to them.

(Enter CLOV with gaff.)

CLOV: Here's your gaff. Stick it up.

(He gives the gaff to HAMM who, wielding it like a puntpole, tries to move his chair.)

HAMM: Did I move?

CLOV: No.

(HAMM throws down the gaff.)

HAMM: Go and get the oilcan.

CLOV: What for?

HAMM: To oil the castors.

CLOV: I oiled them yesterday.

HAMM: Yesterday! What does that mean? Yesterday!

CLOV (violently): That means that bloody awful day long ago, before this bloody awful day. I use the words you taught me. If they don't mean anything any more, teach me others. Or let me be silent.

(Pause.)

HAMM: I once knew a madman who thought the end of the world had come. He was a painter—and engraver. I had a great fondness for him. I used to go and see him, in the asylum. I'd take him by the hand and drag him to the window. Look! There! All that rising corn. And there! Look! The sails of the herring fleet! All that loveliness!

(Pause.)

He'd snatch away his hand and go back into his corner. Appalled. All he had seen was ashes.

(Pause.)

He alone had been spared.

(Pause.)

Forgotten.

(Pause.)

It appears the case is . . . was not so . . . so unusual.

CLOV: A madman? When was that?

HAMM: Oh way back, way back, you weren't in the land of the living.

CLOV: God be with the days!

(Pause. HAMM raises his toque.)

HAMM: I had a great fondness for him.

(Pause. He puts on his toque again.)

He was a painter—and engraver.

CLOV: There are so many terrible things.

HAMM: No, no, there are not so many now.

(Pause.)

Clov!

CLOV: Yes.

HAMM: Do you not think this has gone on long enough?

CLOV: Yes!

(Pause.)

What?

HAMM: This . . . this . . . thing.

CLOV: I've always thought so.

(Pause.)

You not?

HAMM (gloomily): Then it's a day like any other day.

CLOV: As long as it lasts.

(Pause.)

All life long the same inanities.

HAMM: I can't leave you.

CLOV: I know. And you can't follow me.

(Pause.)

HAMM: If you leave me how shall I know?

CLOV *(briskly)*: Well you simply whistle me and if I don't come running it means I've left you.

(Pause.)

HAMM: You won't come and kiss me goodbye?

CLOV: Oh I shouldn't think so.

(Pause.)

HAMM: But you might be merely dead in your kitchen.

CLOV: The result would be the same.

HAMM: Yes, but how would I know, if you were merely dead in your kitchen?

CLOV: Well . . . sooner or later I'd start to stink.

HAMM: You stink already. The whole place stinks of corpses.

CLOV: The whole universe.

HAMM *(angrily)*: To hell with the universe.

(Pause.)

Think of something.

CLOV: What?

HAMM: An idea, have an idea.

(Angrily.)

A bright idea!

CLOV: Ah good.

(He starts pacing to and fro, his eyes fixed on the ground, his hands behind his back. He halts.)

The pains in my legs! It's unbelievable! Soon I won't be able to think any more.

HAMM: You won't be able to leave me.

(CLOV resumes his pacing.)

What are you doing?

CLOV: Having an idea.

(He paces.)

Ah!

(He halts.)

HAMM: What a brain!

(Pause.)

Well?

CLOV: Wait!

(He meditates. Not very convinced.)

Yes . . .

(Pause. More convinced.)

Yes!

(He raises his head.)

I have it! I set the alarm.

(Pause.)

HAMM: This is perhaps not one of my bright days, but frankly—

CLOV: You whistle me. I don't come. The alarm rings. I'm gone. It doesn't ring. I'm dead.

(Pause.)

HAMM: Is it working?

(Pause. Impatiently.)

The alarm, is it working?

CLOV: Why wouldn't it be working?

HAMM: Because it's worked too much.

CLOV: But it's hardly worked at all.

HAMM *(angrily)*: Then because it's worked too little!

CLOV: I'll go and see.

(Exit CLOV. Brief ring of alarm off. Enter CLOV with alarm-clock. He holds it against HAMM's ear and releases alarm. They listen to it ringing to the end. Pause.)

Fit to wake the dead! Did you hear it?

HAMM: Vaguely.

CLOV: The end is terrific!

HAMM: I prefer the middle.

(Pause.)

Is it not time for my pain-killer?

CLOV: No!

(He goes to door, turns.)

I'll leave you.

HAMM: It's time for my story. Do you want to listen to my story.

CLOV: No.

HAMM: Ask my father if he wants to listen to my story.

(CLOV goes to bins, raises the lid of NAGG's, stoops, looks into it. Pause. He straightens up.)

CLOV: He's asleep.

HAMM: Wake him.

(CLOV stoops, wakes NAGG with the alarm. Unintelligible words. CLOV straightens up.)

CLOV: He doesn't want to listen to your story.

HAMM: I'll give him a bon-bon.

(CLOV stoops. As before.)

CLOV: He wants a sugar-plum.

HAMM: He'll get a sugar-plum.

(CLOV stoops. As before.)

CLOV: It's a deal.

(*He goes toward door.* NAGG's *hands appear, gripping the rim. Then the head emerges.* CLOV *reaches door, turns.*)

Do you believe in the life to come?
HAMM: Mine was always that.

(*Exit* CLOV.)

Got him that time!
NAGG: I'm listening.
HAMM: Scoundrel! Why did you engender me?
NAGG: I didn't know.
HAMM: What? What didn't you know?
NAGG: That it'd be you.

(*Pause.*)

You'll give me a sugar-plum?
HAMM: After the audition.
NAGG: You swear?
HAMM: Yes.
NAGG: On what?
HAMM: My honor.

(*Pause. They laugh heartily.*)

NAGG: Two.
HAMM: One.
NAGG: One for me and one for—
HAMM: One! Silence!

(*Pause.*)

Where was I?

(*Pause. Gloomily.*)

It's finished, we're finished.

(*Pause.*)

Nearly finished.

(*Pause.*)

There'll be no more speech.

(*Pause.*)

Something dripping in my head, ever since the fontanelles.

(*Stifled hilarity of* NAGG.)

Splash, splash, always on the same spot.

(*Pause.*)

Perhaps it's a little vein.

(*Pause.*)

A little artery.

(*Pause. More animated.*)

Enough of that, it's story time, where was I?

(*Pause. Narrative tone.*)

The man came crawling towards me, on his belly. Pale, wonderfully pale and thin, he seemed on the point of—

(*Pause. Normal tone.*)

No, I've done that bit.

(*Pause. Narative tone.*)

I calmly filled my pipe—the meerschaum, lit it with . . . let us say a vesta, drew a few puffs. Aah!

(*Pause.*)

Well, what is it *you* want?

(*Pause.*)

It was an extra-ordinarily bitter day, I remember, zero by the thermometer. But considering it was Christmas Eve there was nothing . . . extra-ordinary about that. Seasonable weather, for once in a way.

(*Pause.*)

Well, what ill wind blows you my way? He raised his face to me, black with mingled dirt and tears.

(*Pause. Normal tone.*)

That should do it.

(*Narrative tone.*)

No, no, don't look at me, don't look at me. He dropped his eyes and mumbled something, apologies I presume.

(*Pause.*)

I'm a busy man, you know, the final touches, before the festivities. You know what it is.

(*Pause. Forcibly.*)

Come on now, what is the object of this invasion?

(*Pause.*)

It was a glorious bright day, I remember, fifty by the heliometer, but already the sun was sinking down into the . . . down among the dead.

(*Normal tone.*)

Nicely put, that.

(*Narrative tone.*)

Come on now, come on, present your petition and let me resume my labors.

(*Pause. Normal tone.*)

There's English for you. Ah well . . .

(*Narrative tone.*)

It was then he took the plunge. It's my little one, he said. Tsstss, a little one, that's bad. My little boy, he said, as if the sex mattered. Where did he come from? He named the hole. A good half-day, on horse. What are you insinuating? That the place is still inhabited? No, no, not a soul except himself and the child—assuming he existed. Good. I enquired about the situation at Kov, beyond the gulf. Not a sinner. Good. And you expect me to believe you have left your little one back there, all alone, and alive into the bargain? Come now!

(Pause.)

It was a howling wild day, I remember, a hundred by the anenometer. The wind was tearing up the dead pines and sweeping them . . . away.

(Pause. Normal tone.)

A bit feeble, that.

(Narrative tone.)

Come on, man, speak up, what is you want from me. I have to put up my holly.

(Pause.)

Well to make it short it finally transpired that what he wanted from me was . . . bread for his brat? Bread? But I have no bread, it doesn't agree with me. Good. Then perhaps a little corn?

(Pause. Normal tone.)

That should do it.

(Narrative tone.)

Corn, yes, I have corn, it's true, in my granaries. But use your head. I give you some corn, a pound, a pound and a half, you bring it back to your child and you make him—if he's still alive—a nice pot of porridge,

(NAGG reacts.)

a nice pot and a half of porridge, full of nourishment. Good. The colors come back into his little cheeks—perhaps. And then?

(Pause.)

I lost patience.

(Violently.)

Use your head, can't you, use your head, you're on earth, there's no cure for that!

(Pause.)

It was an exceedingly dry day, I remember, zero by the hygrometer. Ideal weather, for my lumbago.

(Pause. Violently.)

But what in God's name do you imagine? That the earth will awake in spring? That the rivers and seas will run with fish again? That there's manna in heaven still for imbeciles like you?

(Pause.)

Gradually I cooled down, sufficiently at least to ask him how long he had taken on the way. Three whole days. Good. In what condition he had left the child. Deep in sleep.

(Forcibly.)

But deep in what sleep, deep in what sleep already?

(Pause.)

Well to make it short I finally offered to take him into my service. He had touched a chord. And then I imagined already that I wasn't much longer for this world.

(He laughs. Pause.)

Well?

(Pause.)

Well? Here if you were careful you might die a nice natural death, in peace and comfort.

(Pause.)

Well?

(Pause.)

In the end he asked me would I consent to take in the child as well—if he were still alive.

(Pause.)

It was the moment I was waiting for.

(Pause.)

Would I consent to take the child . . .

(Pause.)

I can see him still, down on his knees, his hands flat on the ground, glaring at me with his mad eyes, in defiance of my wishes.

(Pause. Normal tone.)

I'll soon have finished with this story.

(Pause.)

Unless I bring in other characters.

(Pause.)

But where would I find them?

(*Pause.*)

Where would I look for them?

(*Pause. He whistles. Enter* CLOV.)

Let us pray to God.

NAGG: Me sugar-plum!

CLOV: There's a rat in the kitchen!

HAMM: A rat! Are there still rats?

CLOV: In the kitchen there's one.

HAMM: And you haven't exterminated him?

CLOV: Half. You disturbed us.

HAMM: He can't get away?

CLOV: No.

HAMM: You'll finish him later. Let us pray to God.

CLOV: Again!

NAGG: Me sugar-plum!

HAMM: God first!

(*Pause.*)

Are you right?

CLOV (*resigned*): Off we go.

HAMM (*to* NAGG): And you?

NAGG (*clasping his hands, closing his eyes, in a gabble*): Our Father which art—

HAMM: Silence! In silence! Where are your manners?

(*Pause.*)

Off we go.

(*Attitudes of prayer. Silence. Abandoning his attitude, discouraged.*)

Well?

CLOV (*abandoning his attitude*): What a hope! And you?

HAMM: Sweet damn all! (*to* NAGG) And you?

NAGG: Wait!

(*Pause. Abandoning his attitude.*)

Nothing doing!

HAMM: The bastard! He doesn't exist!

CLOV: Not yet.

NAGG: Me sugar-plum!

HAMM: There are no more sugar-plums!

(*Pause.*)

NAGG: It's natural. After all I'm your father. It's true if it hadn't been me it would have been someone else. But that's no excuse.

(*Pause.*)

Turkish Delight, for example, which no longer exists, we all know that, there is nothing in the world I love more. And one day I'll ask you for some, in return for a kindness, and you'll promise it to me. One must live with the times.

(*Pause.*)

Whom did you call when you were a tiny boy, and were frightened, in the dark? Your mother? No. Me. We let you cry. Then we moved you out of earshot, so that we might sleep in peace.

(*Pause.*)

I was asleep, as happy as a king, and you woke me up to have me listen to you. It wasn't indispensable, you didn't really need to have me listen to you.

(*Pause.*)

I hope the day will come when you'll really need to have me listen to you, and need to hear my voice, any voice.

(*Pause.*)

Yes, I hope I'll live till then, to hear you calling me like when you were a tiny boy, and were frightened, in the dark, and I was your only hope.

(*Pause.* NAGG *knocks on lid of* NELL's *bin. Pause.*)

Nell!

(*Pause. He knocks louder. Pause. Louder.*)

Nell!

(*Pause.* NAGG *sinks back into his bin, closes the lid behind him. Pause.*)

HAMM: Our revels now are ended.

(*He gropes for the dog.*)

The dog's gone.

CLOV: He's not a real dog, he can't go.

HAMM (*groping*): He's not there.

CLOV: He's lain down.

HAMM: Give him to me.

(CLOV *picks up the dog and gives it to* HAMM. HAMM *holds it in his arms. Pause.* HAMM *throws away the dog.*)

Dirty brute!

(CLOV *begins to pick up the objects lying on the ground.*)

What are you doing?

CLOV: Putting things in order.

(*He straightens up. Fervently.*)

I'm going to clear everything away!

(*He starts picking up again.*)

HAMM: Order!

CLOV (*straightening up*): I love order. It's my dream. A world where all would be silent and still and each thing in its last place, under the last dust.

(He starts picking up again.)

HAMM *(exasperated)*: What in God's name do you think you are doing?

CLOV *(straightening up)*: I'm doing my best to create a little order.

HAMM: Drop it!

*(*CLOV *drops the objects he has picked up.)*

CLOV: After all, there or elsewhere.

(He goes toward door.)

HAMM *(irritably)*: What's wrong with your feet?

CLOV: My feet?

HAMM: Tramp! Tramp!

CLOV: I must have put on my boots.

HAMM: Your slippers were hurting you?

(Pause.)

CLOV: I'll leave you.

HAMM: No!

CLOV: What is there to keep me here?

HAMM: The dialogue.

(Pause.)

I've got on with my story.

(Pause.)

I've got on with it well.

(Pause. Irritably.)

Ask me where I've got to.

CLOV: Oh, by the way, your story?

HAMM *(surprised)*: What story?

CLOV: The one you've been telling yourself all your days.

HAMM: Ah you mean my chronicle?

CLOV: That's the one.

(Pause.)

HAMM *(angrily)*: Keep going, can't you, keep going!

CLOV: You've got on with it, I hope.

HAMM *(modestly)*: Oh not very far, not very far.

(He sighs.)

There are days like that, one isn't inspired.

(Pause.)

Nothing you can do about it, just wait for it to come.

(Pause.)

No forcing, no forcing, it's fatal.

(Pause.)

I've got on with it a little all the same.

(Pause.)

Technique, you know.

(Pause. Irritably.)

I say I've got on with it a little all the same.

CLOV *(admiringly)*: Well I never! In spite of everything you were able to get on with it!

HAMM *(modestly)*: Oh not very far, you know, not very far, but nevertheless, better than nothing.

CLOV: Better than nothing! Is it possible?

HAMM: I'll tell you how it goes. He comes crawling on his belly—

CLOV: Who?

HAMM: What?

CLOV: Who do you mean, he?

HAMM: Who do I mean! Yet another.

CLOV: Ah him! I wasn't sure.

HAMM: Crawling on his belly, whining for bread for his brat. He's offered a job as gardener. Before—

*(*CLOV *bursts out laughing.)*

What is there so funny about that?

CLOV: A job as gardener!

HAMM: Is that what tickles you?

CLOV: It must be that.

HAMM: It wouldn't be the bread?

CLOV: Or the brat.

(Pause.)

HAMM: The whole thing is comical, I grant you that. What about having a good guffaw the two of us together?

CLOV *(after reflection)*: I couldn't guffaw again today.

HAMM *(after reflection)*: Nor I.

(Pause.)

I continue then. Before accepting with gratitude he asks if he may have his little boy with him.

CLOV: What age?

HAMM: Oh tiny.

CLOV: He would have climbed the trees.

HAMM: All the little odd jobs.

CLOV: And then he would have grown up.

HAMM: Very likely.

(Pause.)

CLOV: Keep going, can't you, keep going!

HAMM: That's all. I stopped there.

(Pause.)

CLOV: Do you see how it goes on.

HAMM: More or less.

CLOV: Will it not soon be the end?

HAMM: I'm afraid it will.

CLOV: Pah! You'll make up another.

HAMM: I don't know.

(Pause.)

I feel rather drained.

(Pause.)

The prolonged creative effort.

(Pause.)

If I could drag myself down to the sea! I'd make a pillow of sand for my head and the tide would come.

CLOV: There's no more tide.

(Pause.)

HAMM: Go and see is she dead.

(CLOV goes to bins, raises the lid of NELL's, stoops, looks into it. Pause.)

CLOV: Looks like it.

(He closes the lid, straightens up. HAMM raises his toque. Pause. He puts it on again.)

HAMM *(with his hand to his toque)*: And Nagg?

(CLOV raises lid of NAGG's bin, stoops, looks into it. Pause.)

CLOV: Doesn't look like it.

(He closes the lid, straightens up.)

HAMM *(letting go his toque)*: What's he doing?

(CLOV raises lid of NAGG's bin, stoops, looks into it. Pause.)

CLOV: He's crying.

(He closes lid, straightens up.)

HAMM: Then he's living.

(Pause.)

Did you ever have an instant of happiness?
CLOV: Not to my knowledge.

(Pause.)

HAMM: Bring me under the window.

(CLOV goes toward chair.)

I want to feel the light on my face.

(CLOV pushes chair.)

Do you remember, in the beginning, when you took me for a turn? You used to hold the chair too high. At every step you nearly tipped me out.

(With senile quaver.)

Ah great fun, we had, the two of us, great fun.

(Gloomily.)

And then we got into the way of it.

(CLOV stops the chair under window right.)

There already?

(Pause. He tilts back his head.)

Is it light?
CLOV: It isn't dark.
HAMM *(angrily)*: I'm asking you is it light.
CLOV: Yes.

(Pause.)

HAMM: The curtain isn't closed?
CLOV: No.
HAMM: What window is it?
CLOV: The earth.
HAMM: I knew it!

(Angrily.)

But there's no light there! The other!

(CLOV pushes the chair toward window left.)

The earth!

(CLOV stops the chair under window left. HAMM tilts back his head.)

That's what I call light!

(Pause.)

Feels like a ray of sunshine.

(Pause.)

No?
CLOV: No.
HAMM: It isn't a ray of sunshine I feel on my face?
CLOV: No.

(Pause.)

HAMM: Am I very white?

(Pause. Angrily.)

I'm asking you am I very white!
CLOV: Not more so than usual.

(Pause.)

HAMM: Open the window.
CLOV: What for?
HAMM: I want to hear the sea.
CLOV: You wouldn't hear it.
HAMM: Even if you opened the window?
CLOV: No.
HAMM: Then it's not worth while opening it?
CLOV: No.
HAMM *(violently)*: Then open it!

(CLOV gets up on the ladder, opens the window. Pause.)

Have you opened it?

CLOV: Yes.

(Pause.)

HAMM: You swear you've opened it?

CLOV: Yes.

(Pause.)

HAMM: Well . . . !

(Pause.)

It must be very calm.

(Pause. Violently.)

I'm asking you is it very calm!

CLOV: Yes.

HAMM: It's because there are no more navigators.

(Pause.)

You haven't much conversation all of a sudden. Do you not feel well?

CLOV: I'm cold.

HAMM: What month are we?

(Pause.)

Close the window, we're going back.

(CLOV closes the window, gets down, pushes the chair back to its place, remains standing behind it, head bowed.)

Don't stay there, you give me the shivers!

(CLOV returns to his place beside the chair.)

Father!

(Pause. Louder.)

Father!

(Pause.)

Go and see did he hear me.

(CLOV goes to NAGG's bin, raises the lid, stoops. Unintelligible words. CLOV straightens up.)

CLOV: Yes.

HAMM: Both times?

(CLOV stops. As before.)

CLOV: Once only.

HAMM: The first time or the second?

(CLOV stoops. As before.)

CLOV: He doesn't know.

HAMM: It must have been the second.

CLOV: We'll never know.

(He closes lid.)

HAMM: Is he still crying?

CLOV: No.

HAMM: The dead go fast.

(Pause.)

What's he doing?

CLOV: Sucking his biscuit.

HAMM: Life goes on.

(CLOV returns to his place beside the chair.)

Give me a rug, I'm freezing.

CLOV: There are no more rugs.

(Pause.)

HAMM: Kiss me.

(Pause.)

Will you not kiss me?

CLOV: No.

HAMM: On the forehead.

CLOV: I won't kiss you anywhere.

(Pause.)

HAMM *(holding out his hand)*: Give me your hand at least.

(Pause.)

Will you not give me your hand?

CLOV: I won't touch you.

(Pause.)

HAMM: Give me the dog.

(CLOV looks round for the dog.)

No!

CLOV: Do you not want your dog?

HAMM: No.

CLOV: Then I'll leave you.

HAMM *(head bowed, absently)*: That's right.

(CLOV goes to door, turns.)

CLOV: If I don't kill that rat he'll die.

HAMM *(as before)*: That's right.

(Exit CLOV. Pause.)

Me to play.

(He takes out his handkerchief, unfolds it, holds it spread out before him.)

We're getting on.

(Pause.)

You weep, and weep, for nothing, so as not to laugh, and little by little . . . you begin to grieve.

(He folds the handkerchief, he puts it back in his pocket, raises his head.)

All those I might have helped.

(Pause.)

Helped!

(Pause.)

Saved.

(Pause.)

Saved!

(Pause.)

The place was crawling with them!

(Pause. Violently.)

Use your head, can't you, use your head, you're on earth, there's no cure for that!

(Pause.)

Get out of here and love one another! Lick your neighbor as yourself!

(Pause. Calmer.)

When it wasn't bread they wanted it was crumpets.

(Pause. Violently.)

Out of my sight and back to your petting parties!

(Pause.)

All that, all that!

(Pause.)

Not even a real dog!

(Calmer.)

The end is in the beginning and yet you go on.

(Pause.)

Perhaps I could go on with my story, end it and begin another.

(Pause.)

Perhaps I could throw myself out on the floor.

(He pushes himself painfully off his seat, falls back again.)

Dig my nails into the cracks and drag myself forward with my fingers.

(Pause.)

It will be the end and there I'll be, wondering what can have brought it on and wondering what can have . . . *(He hesitates.)* . . . why it was so long coming.

(Pause.)

There I'll be, in the old shelter, alone against the silence and . . . *(He hesitates.)* . . . the stillness. If I can hold my peace, and sit quiet, it will be all over with sound, and motion, all over and done with.

(Pause.)

I'll have called my father and I'll have called my . . . *(He hesitates.)* . . . my son. And even twice, or three times, in case they shouldn't have heard me, the first time, or the second.

(Pause.)

I'll say to myself. He'll come back.

(Pause.)

And then?

(Pause.)

And then?

(Pause.)

He couldn't, he has gone too far.

(Pause.)

And then?

(Pause. Very agitated.)

All kinds of fantasies! That I'm being watched! A rat! Steps! Breath held and then . . .

(He breathes out.)

Then babble, babble, words, like the solitary child who turns himself into children, two, three, so as to be together, and whisper together in the dark.

(Pause.)

Moment upon moment, pattering down, like the millet grains of . . . *(He hesitates.)* . . . that old Greek, and all life long you wait for that to mount up to a life.

(Pause. He opens his mouth to continue, renounces.)

Ah let's get it over!

(He whistles. Enter CLOV *with alarm-clock. He halts beside the chair.)*

What? Neither gone nor dead?

CLOV: In spirit only.

HAMM: Which?

CLOV: Both.

HAMM: Gone from me you'd be dead.

CLOV: And vice versa.

HAMM: Outside of here it's death!

(Pause.)

And the rat?

CLOV: He's got away.

HAMM: He can't go far.

(*Pause. Anxious.*)

Eh?

CLOV: He doesn't need to go far.

(*Pause.*)

HAMM: Is it not time for my pain-killer?

CLOV: Yes.

HAMM: Ah! At last! Give it to me! Quick!

(*Pause.*)

CLOV: There's no more pain-killer.

(*Pause.*)

HAMM (*appalled*): Good . . . !

(*Pause.*)

No more pain-killer!

CLOV: No more pain-killer. You'll never get any more pain-killer.

(*Pause.*)

HAMM: But the little round box. It was full!

CLOV: Yes. But now it's empty.

(*Pause.* CLOV *starts to move about the room. He is looking for a place to put down the alarm-clock.*)

HAMM (*soft*): What'll I do?

(*Pause. In a scream.*)

What'll I do?

(CLOV *sees the picture, takes it down, stands it on the floor with its face to the wall, hangs up the alarm-clock in its place.*)

What are you doing?

CLOV: Winding up.

HAMM: Look at the earth.

CLOV: Again!

HAMM: Since it's calling to you.

CLOV: Is your throat sore?

(*Pause.*)

Would you like a lozenge?

(*Pause.*)

No.

(*Pause.*)

Pity.

(CLOV *goes, humming, toward window right, halts before it, looks up at it.*)

HAMM: Don't sing.

CLOV (*turning toward* HAMM): One hasn't the right to sing any more?

HAMM: No.

CLOV: Then how can it end?

HAMM: You want it to end?

CLOV: I want to sing.

HAMM: I can't prevent you.

(*Pause.* CLOV *turns toward window right.*)

CLOV: What did I do with that steps?

(*He looks around for ladder.*)

You didn't see that steps?

(*He sees it.*)

Ah, about time.

(*He goes toward window left.*)

Sometimes I wonder if I'm in my right mind. Then it passes over and I'm as lucid as before.

(*He gets up on ladder, looks out of window.*)

Christ, she's under water!

(*He looks.*)

How can that be?

(*He pokes forward his head, his hand above his eyes.*)

It hasn't rained.

(*He wipes the pane, looks. Pause.*)

Ah what a fool I am! I'm on the wrong side!

(*He gets down, takes a few steps towards window right.*)

Under water!

(*He goes back for ladder.*)

What a fool I am!

(*He carries ladder toward window right.*)

Sometimes I wonder if I'm in my right senses. Then it passes off and I'm as intelligent as ever.

(*He sets down ladder under window right, gets up on it, looks out of window. He turns toward* HAMM.)

Any particular sector you fancy? Or merely the whole thing?

HAMM: Whole thing.

CLOV: The general effect? Just a moment.

(*He looks out of window. Pause.*)

HAMM: Clov.

CLOV (*absorbed*): Mmm.

HAMM: Do you know what it is?

CLOV (*as before*): Mmm.

HAMM: I was never there.

(*Pause.*)

Clov!

CLOV (*turning toward* HAMM, *exasperated*): What is it?
HAMM: I was never there.
CLOV: Lucky for you.

(*He looks out of window.*)

HAMM: Absent, always. It all happened without me. I don't know what's happened.

(*Pause.*)

Do you know what's happened?

(*Pause.*)

Clov!
CLOV (*turning toward* HAMM, *exasperated*): Do you want me to look at this muckheap, yes or no?
HAMM: Answer me first.
CLOV: What?
HAMM: Do you know what's happened?
CLOV: When? Where?
HAMM (*violently*): When! What's happened? Use your head, can't you? What has happened?
CLOV: What for Christ's sake does it matter?

(*He looks out of window.*)

HAMM: I don't know.

(*Pause.* CLOV *turns toward* HAMM.)

CLOV (*harshly*): When old Mother Pegg asked you for oil for her lamp and you told her to get out to hell, you knew what was happening then, no?

(*Pause.*)

You know what she died of, Mother Pegg? Of darkness.
HAMM (*feebly*): I hadn't any.
CLOV (*as before*): Yes, you had.

(*Pause.*)

HAMM: Have you the glass?
CLOV: No, it's clear enough as it is.
HAMM: Go and get it.

(*Pause.* CLOV *casts up his eyes, brandishes his fists. He loses balance, clutches on to the ladder. He starts to get down, halts.*)

CLOV: There's one thing I'll never understand.

(*He gets down.*)

Why I always obey you. Can you explain that to me?
HAMM: No. . . . Perhaps it's compassion.

(*Pause.*)

A kind of compassion.

(*Pause.*)

Oh you won't find it easy, you won't find it easy.

(*Pause.* CLOV *begins to move about the room in search of the telescope.*)

CLOV: I'm tired of our goings on, very tired.

(*He searches.*)

You're not sitting on it?

(*He moves the chair, looks at the place where it stood, resumes his search.*)

HAMM (*anguished*): Don't leave me there!

(*Angrily* CLOV *restores the chair to its place.*)

Am I right in the center?
CLOV: You'd need a microscope to find this—

(*He sees the telescope.*)

Ah, about time.

(*He picks up the telescope, gets up on the ladder, turns the telescope on the without.*)

HAMM: Give me the dog.
CLOV (*looking*): Quiet!
HAMM (*angrily*): Give me the dog!

(CLOV *drops the telescope, clasps his hands to his head. Pause. He gets down precipitately, looks for the dog, sees it, picks it up, hastens toward* HAMM *and strikes him violently on the head with the dog.*)

CLOV: There's your dog for you!

(*The dog falls to the ground. Pause.*)

HAMM: He hit me!
CLOV: You drive me mad, I'm mad!
HAMM: If you must hit me, hit me with the axe.

(*Pause.*)

Or with the gaff, hit me with the gaff. Not with the dog. With the gaff. Or with the axe.

(CLOV *picks up the dog and gives it to* HAMM *who takes it in his arms.*)

CLOV (*imploringly*): Let's stop playing!
HAMM: Never!

(*Pause.*)

Put me in my coffin.
CLOV: There are no more coffins.
HAMM: Then let it end!

(CLOV *goes toward ladder.*)

With a bang!

(CLOV *gets up on ladder, gets down again, looks for telescope, sees it, picks it up, gets up on ladder, raises telescope.*)

Of darkness! And me? Did anyone ever have pity on me?

CLOV *(lowering the telescope, turning toward* HAMM*)*: What?

(Pause.)

Is it me you're referring to?

HAMM *(angrily)*: An aside, ape! Did you never hear an aside before?

(Pause.)

I'm warming up for my last soliloquy.

CLOV: I warn you. I'm going to look at this filth since it's an order. But it's the last time.

(He turns the telescope on the without.)

Let's see.

(He moves the telescope.)

Nothing . . . nothing . . . good . . . good . . . nothing . . . goo—

(He starts, lowers the telescope, examines it, turns it again on the without. Pause.)

Bad luck to it!

HAMM: More complications!

(CLOV gets down.)

Not an underplot, I trust.

(CLOV moves ladder nearer window, gets up on it, turns telescope on the without.)

CLOVE *(dismayed)*: Looks like a small boy!

HAMM *(sarcastic)*: A small . . . boy!

CLOV: I'll go and see.

(He gets down, drops the telescope, goes toward door, turns.)

I'll take the gaff.

(He looks for the gaff, sees it, picks it up, hastens toward door.)

HAMM: No!

(CLOV halts.)

CLOV: No? A potential procreator?

HAMM: If he exists he'll die there or he'll come here. And if he doesn't . . .

(Pause.)

CLOV: You don't believe me? You think I'm inventing?

(Pause.)

HAMM: It's the end, Clov, we've come to the end. I don't need you any more.

(Pause.)

CLOV: Lucky for you.

(He goes toward door.)

HAMM: Leave me the gaff.

(CLOV gives him the gaff, goes toward door, halts, looks at alarm-clock, takes it down, looks round for a better place to put it, goes to bins, puts it on lid of NAGG's bin. Pause.)

CLOV: I'll leave you.

(He goes toward door.)

HAMM: Before you go . . .

(CLOV halts near door.)

. . . say something.

CLOV: There is nothing to say.

HAMM: A few words . . . to ponder . . . in my heart.

CLOV: Your heart!

HAMM: Yes.

(Pause. Forcibly.)

Yes!

(Pause.)

With the rest, in the end, the shadows, the murmurs, all the trouble, to end up with.

(Pause.)

Clov. . . . He never spoke to me. Then, in the end, before he went, without my having asked him, he spoke to me. He said . . .

CLOV *(despairingly)*: Ah. . . !

HAMM: Something . . . from your heart.

CLOV: My heart!

HAMM: A few words . . . from your heart.

(Pause.)

CLOV *(fixed gaze, tonelessly, toward auditorium)*: They said to me, That's love, yes, yes, not a doubt, now you see how—

HAMM: Articulate!

CLOV *(as before)*: How easy it is. They said to me, That's friendship, yes, yes, no question, you've found it. They said to me, Here's the place, stop, raise your head and look at all that beauty. That order! They said to me, Come now, you're not a brute beast, think upon these things and you'll see how all becomes clear. And simple! They said to me, What skilled attention they get, all these dying of their wounds.

HAMM: Enough!

CLOV *(as before)*: I say to myself—sometimes, Clov, you must learn to suffer better than that if you want them to weary of punishing you—one day. I say to myself—sometimes, Clov, you must be there better than that if you want them to let you go—one day. But I feel too old, and too far, to form new habits. Good, it'll never end, I'll never go.

(*Pause.*)

Then one day, suddenly, it ends, it changes, I don't understand, it dies, or it's me, I don't understand, that either. I ask the words that remain—sleeping, waking, morning, evening. They have nothing to say.

(*Pause.*)

I open the door of the cell and go. I am so bowed I only see my feet, if I open my eyes, and between my legs a little trail of black dust. I say to myself that the earth is extinguished, though I never saw it lit.

(*Pause.*)

It's easy going.

(*Pause.*)

When I fall I'll weep for happiness.

(*Pause. He goes toward door.*)

HAMM: Clov!

(CLOV *halts, without turning.*)

Nothing.

(CLOV *moves on.*)

Clov!

(CLOV *halts, without turning.*)

CLOV: This is what we call making an exit.
HAMM: I'm obliged to you, Clov. For your services.
CLOV (*turning, sharply*): Ah pardon, it's I am obliged to you.
HAMM: It's we are obliged to each other.

(*Pause.* CLOV *goes toward door.*)

One thing more.

(CLOV *halts.*)

A last favor.

(*Exit* CLOV.)

Cover me with the sheet.

(*Long pause.*)

No? Good.

(*Pause.*)

Me to play.

(*Pause. Wearily.*)

Old endgame lost of old, play and lose and have done with losing.

(*Pause. More animated.*)

Let me see.

(*Pause.*)

Ah yes!

(*He tries to move the chair, using the gaff as before. Enter* CLOV, *dressed for the road. Panama hat, tweed coat, raincoat over his arm, umbrella, bag. He halts by the door and stands there, impassive and motionless, his eyes are fixed on* HAMM, *till the end.* HAMM *gives up.*)

Good.

(*Pause.*)

Discard.

(*He throws away the gaff, makes to throw away the dog, thinks better of it.*)

Take it easy.

(*Pause.*)

And now?

(*Pause.*)

Raise hat.

(*He raises his toque.*)

Peace to our . . . arses.

(*Pause.*)

And put on again.

(*He puts on his toque.*)

Deuce.

(*Pauses. He takes off his glasses.*)

Wipe.

(*He takes out his handkerchief and, without unfolding it, wipes his glasses.*)

And put on again.

(*He puts on his glasses, puts back the handkerchief in his pocket.*)

We're coming. A few more squirms like that and I'll call.

(*Pause.*)

A little poetry.

(*Pause.*)

You prayed—

(*Pause. He corrects himself.*)

You CRIED for night; it comes—

(*Pause, He corrects himself.*)

It FALLS: now cry in darkness.

(*He repeats, chanting.*)

You cried for night; it falls; now cry in darkness.

(*Pause.*)

Nicely put, that.

(*Pause.*)

And now?

(*Pause.*)

Moments for nothing, now as always, time was never and time is over, reckoning closed and story ended.

(*Pause. Narrative tone.*)

If he could have his child with him. . . .

(*Pause.*)

It was the moment I was waiting for.

(*Pause.*)

You don't want to abandon him? You want him to bloom while you are withering? Be there to solace your last million last moments?

(*Pause.*)

He doesn't realize, all he knows is hunger, and cold, and death to crown it all. But you! You ought to know what the earth is like, nowadays. Oh I put him before his responsibilities!

(*Pause. Normal tone.*)

Well, there we are, there I am, that's enough.

(*He raises the whistle to his lips, hesitates, drops it. Pause.*)

Yes, truly!

(*He whistles. Pause. Louder. Pause.*)

Good.

(*Pause.*)

Father!

(*Pause. Louder.*)

Father!

(*Pause.*)

Good.

(*Pause.*)

We're coming.

(*Pause.*)

And to end up with?

(*Pause.*)

Discard.

(*He throws away the dog. He tears the whistle from his neck.*)

With my compliments.

(*He throws whistle toward auditorium. Pause. He sniffs. Soft.*)

Clov!

(*Long pause.*)

No? Good.

(*He takes out the handkerchief.*)

Since that's the way we're playing it . . . (*He unfolds handkerchief.*) . . . let's play it that way . . . (*He unfolds.*) . . . and speak no more about it . . . (*He finishes unfolding.*) . . . speak no more.

(*He holds handkerchief spread out before him.*)

Old stancher!

(*Pause.*)

You . . . remain.

(*Pause. He covers his face with handkerchief, lowers his arms to armrests, remains motionless.*)
(*Brief tableau.*)

CURTAIN

Figure 1. Hamm (Roger Blin) and Clov (Jean Martin) in the Studio des Champs-Élysées production of *Endgame*, directed by Roger Blin and designed by Jacques Noel, Paris, 1957. (Photograph: Roger Pic.)

Figure 2. Nagg (Georges Adet) asks for his sugar-plum while Hamm
(Roger Blin) and Clov (Jean Martin) pray to God in the Studio des
Champs-Élysées production of *Endgame,* directed by Roger Blin and
designed by Jacques Noel, Paris, 1957. (Photograph: Roger Pic.)

Staging of *Endgame*

REVIEW OF THE STUDIO DES CHAMPS-ÉLYSÉES PRODUCTION, 1957, BY JACQUES LEMARCHAND

"Endgame" by Samuel Beckett lends a theatrical reality, a frightening reality, to a certain daydream that I imagine we have all yielded to at one time or another: some day, it matters little under what conditions, there will no longer be any men on Earth; nor will there be any Earth then either. One short moment, no more, in the entire universe, when a single man, the very last man, will have the task of feeling the last emotion, the last sensation, of speaking the last word—and that word will not be historic. To young people this seems, if I remember correctly, frightening, dizzying. To those not so young it can seem more like a pleasant reassurance that one should not attach a great deal of importance to winning literary prizes, nor fret too much about honors granted to imbeciles. This is a rather peaceful daydream, blending a fair amount of humor into the inevitable terror that the end of *everything* arouses in man.

And this terror and comedy have never been presented on stage in a manner so immediately perceptible, and with so little rhetoric as well as so much persuasive power, as in this "Endgame," playing at the Studio des Champs-Élysées, to its infinite honor. It is easy, and legitimate, to seek and to find in "Endgame" some sort of sequel to, or echo of, "Waiting for Godot." In fact, Beckett's second play, although it bears the undeniable stamp of its author—that clown-like naiveté, with which the characters juggle, to all appearances innocently, our most secret and serious anxieties—is a play entirely different from "Waiting for Godot." Godot has absolutely refused to come, and no one is waiting for him any more; what they are waiting for is to "make an exit"; and words of waiting, hope, and desire have lost all meaning: the characters of "Endgame" simply consent to something they know is inevitable.

These protagonists have been criticized for not being very attractive young men. It is true that Beckett's play is lacking in young leads. One could just as well criticize them for having names that are rather uncommon in the boulevard theaters. They are called Hamm, Clov, Nagg and Nell, names reeking of the circus and lacking in distinction. But after all, this is the very last day of the human race, and it is permissible to imagine that the saints of the calendar have withdrawn. It is no less true that these characters are in poor health: Hamm is paralyzed and cannot leave his armchair; Clov, his slave, has difficulty walking and shakes with palsy; as for Nagg and his wife Nell, their situation is quite simple: they are legless cripples, and each lives in an ashbin, comfortably, it seems, considering their smaller size; these four characters are shut in a sort of bunker, in which they will certainly have to die. The two windows of the shelter look out upon a leaden sea and empty land, equally forsaken by humanity. This is hardly a pleasant situation, I admit, but it can surely be granted that is eminently dramatic.

Among these four human beings there is no other solidarity than that arising from self-interest. Nagg and Nell, who are Hamm's parents, depend on him for the last few mouthfuls of pap that will prolong their mediocre lives; Hamm depends on his servant-son, Clov, for the attentions required by his condition; and if Clov refrains from dispatching Hamm, it is simply because he does not have the "combination to the cupboard" where the last few biscuits are locked up. And yet there is not one of these human beings who does not have his dream, a dream he tries to make the others share, to communicate to them: and this need to communicate is as vital to their lives as is the diminishing store of biscuits. From one ashbin to the other, Nagg and Nell allusively exchange their memories: that of rowing a boat one April afternoon on Lake Como, or even the evocation of the accident that crippled them, draws them closer together; from time to time Hamm pursues the fabrication of a long drawn-out literary story, for which, like a true man of letters, he requires an audience. Clov announces his own imminent departure, though he knows it to be impossible, and does all he can to convince himself that his departure depends on his will alone.

It is the spectacle of a game that is coming to an end, of an endgame, that is presented to us in Beckett's play. The fact that this may be the very game we play all the time, without ever believing it to be as close as it is to its end, is made constantly apparent by the way relations among the four characters are stripped down and reduced to an elemental level. The humor of this grim play—vigorous, savage, never gratuitous, provoking brusque outbreaks of laughter—arises also from flashes of confrontation between the actual situation of these characters and the tremendous futility of their malice as well as of their moments of tenderness. It arises too from the frenzy we discover in these characters, which they reveal in their furious acceptance of their fate: the distant apparition of what they take to be a human figure, the discovery of a live rat or a live flea horrifies them. "But humanity might start from there all over again," says Hamm. "Catch him, for the love of God!" Black humor indeed, but of a kind that arises spontaneously from felicitous and unexpected phrases, from a latent tragicomicality that suddenly becomes enormously ludicrous. A humor whose power is in no way increased by one obscene pun and two or three instances of coarse language.

I have limited myself to describing only the exterior aspect of "Endgame": a poem in dialogue, full of surprises and verbal successes, a play that moves and progresses, despite its immobile protagonists and subtle repetitions, towards a poignant and beautiful ending. As for any metaphysical conclusions it may imply, naturally it is for each spectator to understand them to his own liking; the author leaves them complete latitude, and this is not the least of the reasons for the fascination one experiences at a performance of "Endgame."

Jacques Noel's set, that bare bunker in which the human race is coming to an end, is stifling; assuredly just as Beckett must have conceived it. Roger Blin (Hamm), who ensured the meticulous direction of the play, and Jean Martin (Clov) are its extremely impressive protagonists; Germane de France (Nell) and Georges Adet (Nagg), emerging from their Diogenesque ashbins, succeed in being at once ludicrous and pathetic.

The performance ends with an "Act Without Words," by Beckett—a pantomime for one actor, carried through to its termination with the sureness of a great artist by Deryk Mendel—who, amid silence punctuated by blasts from a whistle, shows the same qualities of humor and cruelty we enjoyed in "Endgame." (Translated by Jean M. Sommermeyer)

EDWARD ALBEE

1928–

Twice in *The Zoo Story*, Jerry asserts: "sometimes a person has to go a very long distance out of his way to come back a short distance correctly." Perhaps Jerry speaks for his creator, Edward Albee, whose first theatrical success, *The Zoo Story*, which he wrote in 1958, was originally turned down by various New York producers, then via a circuitous route of being sent from one friend to another was initially performed in Berlin in 1959 and only after its German success was finally produced in New York in January 1960. Before those two productions Albee's life itself seems to have been a complex blend of privilege and insecurity, of opportunity and failure, beginning with his adoption at two weeks old; he was thus a child both wanted and unwanted, a paradox he would return to in his plays. Young Albee attended, and was dismissed from, three different prep schools before he finally settled down at Choate, a prestigious Connecticut private school, where he published short stories, poems, and essays in the school literary magazine. He entered Trinity College in Connecticut in 1946 and took part in amateur theatrical groups, but was dismissed three semesters later. By 1948, Albee was living in New York City and working in a variety of jobs—office boy, sales clerk, luncheonette counterperson, and Western Union messenger. Yet, because he was supported by a trust fund from his grandmother, he was able to travel to Italy in 1952 and take time to write several unpublished plays, to visit the McDowell Colony for writers, and to study briefly at Columbia University.

In 1959, with the world premiere of *The Zoo Story*, which won the Berlin Festival Award, Albee's theatrical career began and moved swiftly from one striking success to another, resulting in the production of four new plays in one year. A double bill of Samuel Beckett's *Krapp's Last Tape* and Albee's *The Zoo Story* opened at the Provincetown Playhouse in New York's Greenwich Village; this combination of plays by the already well-known Beckett and the newly visible Albee ran for 582 performances. In April 1960, Albee had another premiere in Berlin, this time for *The Death of Bessie Smith*. In May, his fourteen-minute play, *The Sandbox*, opened at the Jazz Gallery in New York, and by the end of May, Albee received both the Obie (Off-Broadway) and the Vernon Rice awards for *The Zoo Story*. Later that year, in August, a sketch called *FAM and YAM*, a dialogue between a new playwright and a more established one, played in Connecticut and then off-Broadway. And just a year after *The Zoo Story* opened in New York, Albee's *The American Dream*, his bitterly funny attack on the American family and its cruelty towards both young and old, began a run of 360 performances at the York Theatre.

The capstone to this amazing record of successful new plays came with Albee's first full-length work, *Who's Afraid of Virginia Woolf?*, which opened on Broadway on October 13, 1962. In the savage marital battles that Albee dramatizes in this major work, he forces his four characters, hosts George and Martha, as well as guests Nick and Honey, to spend the early hours of the morning drinking themselves into a frightening recognition of the truths about themselves and their marriages. Thus an evening that begins with "Fun and Games" (the title of the first act), then turns into a "Walpurgisnacht" (the title of the second act, which refers to the orgiastic and nightmarish celebrations that once took place the evening before May Day), and concludes with "The Exorcism" (the title of the third and final act)—an exorcism fraught with social and psychological significance. But whether one considers *Who's Afraid of Virginia Woolf?* to be a study in truth and illusion, or an uncompromising analysis of the psychological and social games people play, or a veiled attack on American values (the names George and Martha recall the first president and his wife), the play's power derives from the combination of its biting humor, and, unforgettably, its seering and often vicious dialogue. In 1963, the play won almost every award possible, with the exception of the Pulitzer Prize; two members of the Pulitzer committee, the drama critic John Mason Brown, and the scholar John Gassner, resigned in protest when the Pulitzer trustees refused to award the prize to Albee because of the play's subject and its language. In London, the play won the *Evening Standard* Award in 1964, and in 1966, the film of the play starred a couple already famous for their own offstage brawls, Richard Burton and Elizabeth Taylor.

None of Albee's later plays (*Tiny Alice*, 1964; *A Delicate Balance*, 1966; *Box* and *Quotations from Chairman Mao Tse-tung*, 1968; *All Over*, 1971; *Seascape*, 1975; *Counting the Ways*, 1976) has ever achieved the popular success of his early ones, though the Pulitzer committee did award the drama prize to both *A Delicate Balance* and *Seascape*. For many critics, Albee's later plays seem more abstract and detached, while the early ones, in George's words, "peel the labels," working through the emotional skin, muscle, bones, and marrow of the characters. And of the short plays, it is *The Zoo Story* that accomplishes that process of dissection with the greatest urgency and pathos.

As Henry Hewes points out in his review following the text, *The Zoo Story* seems very simple: a park bench, two men, conversation. At first, Jerry's questions to Peter may seem merely annoying and only slightly threatening. The audience, like Peter, may think that Jerry is planning to rob Peter, or, given the number of references to homosexuals, attempting a sexual pickup. But while the continuing questions and the hesitant answers reveal Peter's life of compromise, it is Jerry's desperate longing to make contact that drives the play forward: "every once in a while I like to talk to somebody, really *talk*; like to get to know somebody, know all about him." Peter, sitting alone on a "sun-drenched Sunday afternoon," may not know that he is escaping from his conventional existence, but Jerry recognizes in him another lonely figure. Albee's awareness that relationships may be both mutually sustaining and mutually destructive underlies not only *Who's Afraid of Virginia Woolf?* but also *The Zoo Story*. Jerry and Peter, one a "permanent transient," the other with a wife, two daughters, two cats, and two parakeets, need each other, a need acted out in the gesture of violence and sexuality which ends the play.

When *The Zoo Story* was first performed, it attracted much praise as a first play, though a number of critics called the ending melodramatic and sentimental. Yet both Henry Hewes, in the accompanying review, and Harold Clurman, the noted director-critic, found the ending one of success, whether read as Jerry's achievement of connection, albeit in death (Clurman) or Jerry's ability to shake Peter out of his "deep modern lethargy" (Hewes). No matter how one interprets the ending, the central strength of the play still lies in the fascination/repulsion that flows between Jerry and Peter (see Figure 1). Whether Jerry is shocking Peter with his description of his "laughably small room" or tickling him into hysterical laughter (see Figure 2), he is always compelling. He may be the nightmare of the middle class brought to life as a nonstop talker, or he may be a parodic savior, or a demonic version of life imitating the violence reported on television news. Gradually he invades Peter's physical space and, in so doing, invades the audience's mental space. Peter's bench is no longer a refuge, and the theater is not a safe place; the animals have left their cages.

THE ZOO STORY

BY EDWARD ALBEE

THE PLAYERS

PETER, *A man in his early forties, neither fat nor gaunt, neither handsome nor homely. He wears tweeds, smokes a pipe, carries horn-rimmed glasses. Although he is moving into middle age, his dress and his manner would suggest a man younger.*

JERRY, *A man in his late thirties, not poorly dressed, but carelessly. What was once a trim and lightly muscled body has begun to go to fat; and while he is no longer handsome, it is evident that he once was. His fall from physical grace should not suggest debauchery; he has, to come closest to it, a great weariness.*

THE SCENE

It is Central Park; a Sunday afternoon in summer; the present. There are two park benches, one toward either side of the stage; they both face the audience. Behind them: foliage, trees, sky. At the beginning, PETER *is seated on one of the benches.*

STAGE DIRECTIONS

As the curtain rises, PETER *is seated on the bench stage-right. He is reading a book. He stops reading, cleans his glasses, goes back to reading.* JERRY *enters.*

JERRY: I've been to the zoo. (PETER *doesn't notice*) I said, I've been to the zoo. MISTER, I'VE BEEN TO THE ZOO!

PETER: Hm? . . . What? . . . I'm sorry, were you talking to me?

JERRY: I went to the zoo, and then I walked until I came here. Have I been walking north?

PETER (*Puzzled*): North? Why . . . I . . . I think so. Let me see.

JERRY (*Pointing past the audience*): Is that Fifth Avenue?

PETER: Why yes; yes, it is.

JERRY: And what is that cross street there; that one, to the right?

PETER: That? Oh, that's Seventy-fourth Street.

JERRY: And the zoo is around Sixty-fifth Street; so, I've been walking north.

PETER (*Anxious to get back to his reading*): Yes; it would seem so.

JERRY: Good old north.

PETER (*Lightly, by reflex*): Ha, ha.

JERRY (*After a slight pause*): But not due north.

PETER: I . . . well, no, not due north; but, we . . . call it north. It's northerly.

JERRY (*Watches as* PETER, *anxious to dismiss him, prepares his pipe*): Well, boy; *you're* not going to get lung cancer, are you?

PETER (*Looks up, a little annoyed, then smiles*): No, sir. Not from this.

JERRY: No, sir. What you'll probably get is cancer of the mouth, and then you'll have to wear one of those things Freud wore after they took one whole side of his jaw away. What do they call those things?

PETER (*Uncomfortable*): A prosthesis?

JERRY: The very thing! A prosthesis. You're an educated man, aren't you? Are you a doctor?

PETER: Oh, no; no. I read about it somewhere; *Time* magazine, I think. (*He turns to his book*)

JERRY: Well, *Time* magazine isn't for blockheads.

PETER: No, I suppose not.

JERRY (*After a pause*): Boy, I'm glad that's Fifth Avenue there.

PETER (*Vaguely*): Yes.

JERRY: I don't like the west side of the park much.

PETER: Oh? (*Then, slightly wary, but interested*) Why?

JERRY (*Offhand*): I don't know.

PETER: Oh. (*He returns to his book*)

JERRY (*He stands for a few seconds, looking at* PETER, *who finally looks up again, puzzled*): Do you mind if we talk?

PETER (*Obviously minding*): Why . . . no, no.

JERRY: Yes you do; you do.

PETER (*Puts his book down, his pipe out and away, smiling*): No, really; I don't mind.

JERRY: Yes you do.

PETER (*Finally decided*): No; I don't mind at all, really.

JERRY: It's . . . it's a nice day.

PETER (*Stares unnecessarily at the sky*): Yes. Yes, it is; lovely.

JERRY: I've been to the zoo.

PETER: Yes, I think you said so . . . didn't you?

JERRY: You'll read about it in the papers tomorrow, if you don't see it on your TV tonight. You have TV, haven't you?

PETER: Why yes, we have two; one for the children.

JERRY: You're married!

PETER (*With pleased emphasis*): Why, certainly.

JERRY: It isn't a law, for God's sake.

PETER: No . . . no, of course not.

JERRY: And you have a wife.

PETER (*Bewildered by the seeming lack of communication*): Yes!

JERRY: And you have children.

PETER: Yes; two.

JERRY: Boys?

PETER: No, girls . . . both girls.

JERRY: But you wanted boys.

PETER: Well . . . naturally, every man wants a son, but . . .

JERRY (*Lightly mocking*): But that's the way the cookie crumbles?

PETER (*Annoyed*): I wasn't going to say that.

JERRY: And you're not going to have any more kids, are you?

PETER (*A bit distantly*): No. No more. (*Then back, and irksome*) Why did you say that? How would you know about that?

JERRY: The way you cross your legs, perhaps; something in the voice. Or maybe I'm just guessing. Is it your wife?

PETER (*Furious*): That's none of your business! (*A silence*) Do you understand? (JERRY *nods.* PETER *is quiet now*) Well, you're right. We'll have no more children.

JERRY (*Softly*): That *is* the way the cookie crumbles.

PETER (*Forgiving*): Yes . . . I guess so.

JERRY: Well, now; what else?

PETER: What were you saying about the zoo . . . that I'd read about it, or see . . . ?

JERRY: I'll tell you about it, soon. Do you mind if I ask you questions?

PETER: Oh, not really.

JERRY: I'll tell you why I do it; I don't talk to many people—except to say like: give me a beer, or where's the john, or what time does the feature go on, or keep your hands to yourself, buddy. You know—things like that.

PETER: I must say I don't . . .

JERRY: But every once in a while I like to talk to somebody, really *talk;* like to get to know somebody, know all about him.

PETER (*Lightly laughing, still a little uncomfortable*): And am I the guinea pig for today?

JERRY: On a sun-drenched Sunday afternoon like this? Who better than a nice married man with two daughters and . . . uh . . . a dog? (PETER *shakes his head*) No? Two dogs. (PETER *shakes his head again*) Hm. No dogs? (PETER *shakes his head, sadly*) Oh, that's a shame. But you look like an animal man. CATS? (PETER *nods his head, ruefully*) Cats! But, that can't be your idea. No, sir. Your wife and daughters? (PETER *nods his head*) Is there anything else I should know?

PETER (*He has to clear his throat*): There are . . . there are two parakeets. One . . . uh . . . one for each of my daughters.

JERRY: Birds.

PETER: My daughters keep them in a cage in their bedroom.

JERRY: Do they carry disease? The birds.

PETER: I don't believe so.

JERRY: That's too bad. If they did you could set them loose in the house and the cats could eat them and die, maybe. (PETER *looks blank for a moment, then laughs*) And what else? What do you do to support your enormous household?

PETER: I . . . uh . . . I have an executive position with a . . . a small publishing house. We . . . uh . . . we publish textbooks.

JERRY: That sounds nice; very nice. What do you make?

PETER (*Still cheerful*): Now look here!

JERRY: Oh, come on.

PETER: Well, I make around eighteen thousand a year, but I don't carry more than forty dollars at any one time . . . in case you're a . . . a holdup man . . . ha, ha, ha.

JERRY (*Ignoring the above*): Where do you live? (PETER *is reluctant*) Oh, look; I'm not going to rob you, and I'm not going to kidnap your parakeets, your cats, or your daughters.

PETER (*Too loud*): I live between Lexington and Third Avenue, on Seventy-fourth Street.

JERRY: That wasn't so hard, was it?

PETER: I didn't mean to seem . . . ah . . . it's that you don't really carry on a conversation; you just ask questions. And I'm . . . I'm normally . . . uh . . . reticent. Why do you just stand there?

JERRY: I'll start walking around in a little while, and eventually I'll sit down. (*Recalling*) Wait until you see the expression on his face.

PETER: What? Whose face? Look here; is this something about the zoo?

JERRY (*Distantly*): The what?

PETER: The zoo; the zoo. Something about the zoo.

JERRY: The zoo?

PETER: You've mentioned it several times.

JERRY (*Still distant, but returning abruptly*): The zoo? Oh, yes; the zoo. I was there before I came here. I told you that. Say, what's the dividing line between upper-middle-middle-class and lower-upper-middle-class?

PETER: My dear fellow, I . . .

JERRY: Don't my dear fellow me.

PETER (*Unhappily*): Was I patronizing? I believe I was; I'm sorry. But, you see, your question about the classes bewildered me.

JERRY: And when you're bewildered you become patronizing?

PETER: I . . . I don't express myself too well, sometimes. (*He attempts a joke on himself*) I'm in publishing, not writing.

JERRY (*Amused, but not at the humor*): So be it. The truth is: *I* was being patronizing.

PETER: Oh, now; you needn't say that.

(*It is at this point that* JERRY *may begin to move about the stage with slowly increasing determination and authority, but pacing himself, so that the long speech about the dog comes at the high point of the arc*)

JERRY: All right. Who are your favorite writers? Baudelaire° and J. P. Marquand?°

PETER *(Wary)*: Well, I like a great many writers; I have a considerable . . . catholicity of taste, if I may say so. Those two men are fine, each in his way. *(Warming up)* Baudelaire, of course . . . uh . . . is by far the finer of the two, but Marquand has a place . . . in our . . . uh . . . national . . .

JERRY: Skip it.

PETER: I . . . sorry.

JERRY: Do you know what I did before I went to the zoo today? I walked all the way up Fifth Avenue from Washington Square; all the way.

PETER: Oh: you live in the Village!° *(This seems to enlighten* PETER*)*

JERRY: No, I don't. I took the subway down to the Village so I could walk all the way up Fifth Avenue to the zoo. It's one of those things a person has to do; sometimes a person has to go a very long distance out of his way to come back a short distance correctly.

PETER *(Almost pouting)*: Oh, I thought you lived in the Village.

JERRY: What were you trying to do? Make sense out of things? Bring order? The old pigeonhole bit? Well, that's easy; I'll tell you. I live in a four-story brownstone roominghouse on the upper West Side between Columbus Avenue and Central Park West. I live on the top floor; rear; west. It's a laughably small room, and one of my walls is made of beaverboard; this beaverboard separates my room from another laughably small room, so I assume that the two rooms were once one room, a small room, but not necessarily laughable. The room beyond my beaverboard wall is occupied by a colored queen who always keeps his door open; well, not always, but *always* when he's plucking his eyebrows, which he does with Buddhist concentration. This colored queen has rotten teeth, which is rare, and he has a Japanese kimono, which is also pretty rare; and he wears this kimono to and from the john in the hall, which is pretty frequent. I mean, he goes to the john a lot. He never bothers me, and he never brings anyone up to his room. All he does is pluck his eyebrows, wear his kimono and go to the john. Now, the two front rooms on my floor are a little larger, I guess; but they're pretty small, too. There's a Puerto Rican family in one of them, a husband, a wife, and some kids; I don't know how many. These people entertain a lot. And in the other front room, there's somebody living there, but I don't know who it is. I've never seen who it is. Never. Never ever.

PETER *(Embarrassed)*: Why . . . why do you live there?

JERRY *(From a distance again)*: I don't know.

PETER: It doesn't sound like a very nice place . . . where you live.

JERRY: Well, no; it isn't an apartment in the East Seventies. But, then again, I don't have one wife, two daughters, two cats and two parakeets. What I do have, I have toilet articles, a few clothes, a hot plate that I'm not supposed to have, a can opener, one that works with a key, you know; a knife, two forks, and two spoons, one small, one large; three plates, a cup, a saucer, a drinking glass, two picture frames, both empty, eight or nine books, a pack of pornographic playing cards, regular deck, an old Western Union typewriter that prints nothing but capital letters, and a small strongbox without a lock which has in it . . . what? Rocks! Some rocks . . . searounded rocks I picked up on the beach when I was a kid. Under which . . . weighed down . . . are some letters . . . please letters . . . please why don't you do this, and please when will you do that letters. And when letters, too. When will you write? When will you come? When? These letters are from more recent years.

PETER *(Stares glumly at his shoes, then)*: About those two empty picture frames . . . ?

JERRY: I don't see why they need any explanation at all. Isn't it clear? I don't have pictures of anyone to put in them.

PETER: Your parents . . . perhaps . . . a girl friend . . .

JERRY: You're a very sweet man, and you're possessed of a truly enviable innocence. But good old Mom and good old Pop are dead . . . you know? . . . I'm broken up about it, too . . . I mean really. BUT. That particular vaudeville act is playing the cloud circuit now, so I don't see how I can look at them, all neat and framed. Besides, or, rather, to be pointed about it, good old Mom walked out on good old Pop when I was ten and a half years old; she embarked on an adulterous turn of our southern states . . . a journey of a year's duration . . . and her most constant companion . . . among others, among many others . . . was a Mr. Barleycorn.° At least, that's what good old Pop told me after he went down . . . came back . . . brought her body north. We'd received the news between Christmas and New Year's, you see, that good old Mom had parted with the ghost in some dump in Alabama. And, without the ghost . . . she was less welcome. I mean, what was she? A stiff . . . a northern stiff. At any

---

Baudelaire, French poet and critic (1821–1867), best known for his poems published in *Les Fleurs du Mal (The Flowers of Evil);* some of the poems were condemned for obscenity. **J. P. Marquand,** American novelist (1893–1960), whose writing focused primarily on upper-class New England society. **Village,** Greenwich Village, residential area in New York City, associated with artistic and "bohemian" life.

Mr. Barleycorn, jocular name for whiskey.

rate, good old Pop celebrated the New Year for an even two weeks and then slapped into the front of a somewhat moving city omnibus, which sort of cleaned things out family-wise. Well no; then there was Mom's sister, who was given neither to sin nor the consolations of the bottle. I moved in on her, and my memory of her is slight excepting I remember still that she did all things dourly: sleeping, eating, working, praying. She dropped dead on the stairs to her apartment, my apartment then, too, on the afternoon of my high school graduation. A terribly middle-European joke, if you ask me.

PETER: Oh, my; oh, my.

JERRY: Oh, your what? But that was a long time ago, and I have no feeling about any of it that I care to admit to myself. Perhaps you can see, though, why good old Mom and good old Pop are frameless. What's your name? Your first name?

PETER: I'm Peter.

JERRY: I'd forgotten to ask you. I'm Jerry.

PETER (With a slight, nervous laugh): Hello, Jerry.

JERRY (Nods his hello): And let's see now; what's the point of having a girl's picture, especially in two frames? I have two picture frames, you remember. I never see the pretty little ladies more than once, and most of them wouldn't be caught in the same room with a camera. It's odd, and I wonder if it's sad.

PETER: The girls?

JERRY: No. I wonder if it's sad that I never see the little ladies more than once. I've never been able to have sex with, or how is it put? . . . make love to anybody more than once. Once; that's it. . . . Oh, wait; for a week and a half, when I was fifteen . . . and I hang my head in shame that puberty was late . . . I was a h-o-m-o-s-e-x-u-a-l. I mean, I was queer . . . (Very fast) . . . queer, queer, queer . . . with bells ringing, banners snapping in the wind. And for those eleven days, I met at least twice a day with the park superintendent's son . . . a Greek boy, whose birthday was the same as mine, except he was a year older. I think I was very much in love . . . maybe just with sex. But that was the jazz of a very special hotel, wasn't it? And now; oh, do I love the little ladies; really, I love them. For about an hour.

PETER: Well, it seems perfectly simple to me. . . .

JERRY (Angry): Look! Are you going to tell me to get married and have parakeets?

PETER (Angry himself): Forget the parakeets! And stay single if you want to. It's no business of mine. I didn't start this conversation in the . . .

JERRY: All right, all right. I'm sorry. All right? You're not angry?

PETER (Laughing): No, I'm not angry.

JERRY (Relieved): Good. (Now back to his previous tone) Interesting that you asked me about the picture frames. I would have thought that you would have asked me about the pornographic playing cards.

PETER (With a knowing smile): Oh, I've seen those cards.

JERRY: That's not the point. (Laughs) I suppose when you were a kid you and your pals passed them around, or you had a pack of your own.

PETER: Well, I guess a lot of us did.

JERRY: And you threw them away just before you got married.

PETER: Oh, now; look here. I didn't need anything like that when I got older.

JERRY: No?

PETER (Embarrassed): I'd rather not talk about these things.

JERRY: So? Don't. Besides, I wasn't trying to plumb your post-adolescent sexual life and hard times; what I wanted to get at is the value difference between pornographic playing cards when you're a kid, and pornographic playing cards when you're older. It's that when you're a kid you use the cards as a substitute for a real experience, and when you're older you use real experience as a substitute for the fantasy. But I imagine you'd rather hear about what happened at the zoo.

PETER (Enthusiastic): Oh, yes; the zoo. (Then, awkward) That is . . . if you. . . .

JERRY: Let me tell you about why I went . . . well, let me tell you some things. I've told you about the fourth floor of the roominghouse where I live. I think the rooms are better as you go down, floor by floor. I guess they are; I don't know. I don't know any of the people on the third and second floors. Oh, wait! I do know that there's a lady living on the third floor, in the front. I know because she cries all the time. Whenever I go out or come back in, whenever I pass her door, I always hear her crying, muffled, but . . . very determined. Very determined indeed. But the one I'm getting to, and all about the dog, is the landlady. I don't like to use words that are too harsh in describing people. I don't like to. But the landlady is a fat, ugly, mean, stupid, unwashed, misanthropic, cheap, drunken bag of garbage. And you may have noticed that I very seldom use profanity, so I can't describe her as well as I might.

PETER: You describe her . . . vividly.

JERRY: Well, thanks. Anyway, she has a dog, and I will tell you about the dog, and she and her dog are the gatekeepers of my dwelling. The woman is bad enough; she leans around in the entrance hall, spying to see that I don't bring in things or people, and when she's had her mid-afternoon pint of lemon-flavored gin she always stops me in the hall, and grabs ahold of my coat or my arm, and she presses her disgusting body up against me to keep me in a corner so she can talk to me. The smell of her body and her breath . . . you can't imagine it . . . and somewhere, somewhere in the back of that pea-sized brain of hers, an organ developed just enough to let her eat, drink, and emit, she has some foul parody of sexual desire. And I, Peter, I am the object of her sweaty lust.

PETER: That's disgusting. That's . . . horrible.

JERRY: But I have found a way to keep her off. When she talks to me, when she presses herself to my body and mumbles about her room and how I should come there, I merely say: but, Love; wasn't yesterday enough for you, and the day before? Then she puzzles, she makes slits of her tiny eyes, she sways a little, and then, Peter . . . and it is at this moment that I think I might be doing some good in that tormented house . . . a simple-minded smile begins to form on her unthinkable face, and she giggles and groans as she thinks about yesterday and the day before; as she believes and relives what never happened. Then, she motions to that black monster of a dog she has, and she goes back to her room. And I am safe until our next meeting.

PETER: It's so . . . unthinkable. I find it hard to believe that people such as that really *are*.

JERRY (*Lightly mocking*): It's for reading about, isn't it?

PETER (*Seriously*): Yes.

JERRY: And fact is better left to fiction. You're right, Peter. Well, what I have been meaning to tell you about is the dog; I shall, now.

PETER (*Nervously*): Oh, yes; the dog.

JERRY: Don't go. You're not thinking of going, are you?

PETER: Well . . . no, I don't think so.

JERRY (*As if to a child*): Because after I tell you about the dog, do you know what then? Then . . . then I'll tell you about what happened at the zoo.

PETER (*Laughing faintly*): You're . . . you're full of stories, aren't you?

JERRY: You don't *have* to listen. Nobody is holding you here; remember that. Keep that in your mind.

PETER (*Irritably*): I know that.

JERRY: You do? Good.

(*The following long speech, it seems to me, should be done with a great deal of action, to achieve a hypnotic effect on* PETER, *and on the audience, too. Some specific actions have been suggested, but the director and the actor playing* JERRY *might best work it out for themselves*)

ALL RIGHT. (*As if reading from a huge billboard*) THE STORY OF JERRY AND THE DOG! (*Natural again*) What I am going to tell you has something to do with how sometimes it's necessary to go a long distance out of the way in order to come back a short distance correctly; or, maybe I only think that it has something to do with that. But, it's why I went to the zoo today, and why I walked north . . . northerly, rather . . . until I came here. All right. The dog, I think I told you, is a black monster of a beast: an oversized head, tiny, tiny ears, and eyes . . . bloodshot, infected, maybe; and a body you can see the ribs through the skin. The dog is black, all black; all black except for the bloodshot eyes, and . . . yes . . . and an open sore on its . . . *right* forepaw; that is red, too. And, oh yes; the poor monster, and I do believe it's an old dog . . .

it's certainly a misused one . . . almost always has an erection . . . of sorts. That's red, too. And . . . what else? . . . oh, yes; there's a gray-yellow-white color, too, when he bares his fangs. Like this: Grrrrrr! Which is what he did when he saw me for the first time . . . the day I moved in. I worried about that animal the very first minute I met him. Now, animals don't take to me like Saint Francis had birds hanging off him all the time. What I mean is: animals are indifferent to me . . . like people (*He smiles slightly*) . . . most of the time. But this dog wasn't indifferent. From the very beginning he'd snarl and then go for me, to get one of my legs. Not like he was rabid, you know; he was sort of a stumbly dog, but he wasn't half-assed, either. It was a good, stumbly run; but I always got away. He got a piece of my trouser leg, look, you can see right here, where it's mended; he got that the second day I lived there; but, I kicked free and got upstairs fast, so that was that. (*Puzzles*) I still don't know to this day how the other roomers manage it, but you know what I *think*: I think it had to do only with me. Cozy. So. Anyway, this went on for over a week, whenever I came in; but never when I went out. That's funny. Or, it *was* funny. I could pack up and live in the street for all the dog cared. Well, I thought about it up in my room one day, one of the times after I'd bolted upstairs, and I made up my mind. I decided: First, I'll kill the dog with kindness, and if that doesn't work . . . I'll just kill him. (PETER *winces*) Don't react, Peter; just listen. So, the next day I went out and bought a bag of hamburgers, medium rare, no catsup, no onion; and on the way home I threw away all the rolls and kept just the meat.

(*Action for the following, perhaps*)

When I got back to the roominghouse the dog was waiting for me. I half opened the door that led into the entrance hall, and there he was; waiting for me. It figured. I went in, very cautiously, and I had the hamburgers, you remember; I opened the bag, and I set the meat down about twelve feet from where the dog was snarling at me. Like so! He snarled; stopped snarling; sniffed; moved slowly; then faster; then faster toward the meat. Well, when he got to it he stopped, and he looked at me. I smiled; but tentatively, you understand. He turned his face back to the hamburgers, smelled, sniffed some more, and then . . . RRRAAAAGGGGGHHHH, like that . . . he tore into them. It was as if he had never eaten anything in his life before, except like garbage. Which might very well have been the truth. I don't think the landlady ever eats anything but garbage. But. He ate all the hamburgers, almost all at once, making sounds in his throat like a woman. *Then*, when he'd finished the meat, the hamburger, and tried to eat the paper, too, he sat down and smiled. I think he smiled; I know cats do. It was a very gratifying few moments. Then, BAM, he snarled and made for me again. He didn't get me this time, either. So, I got upstairs, and I lay down on my bed and started to think about the dog again. To be truthful, I was offended, and I was damn mad, too. It was six perfectly good hamburgers with not enough pork in them to make it disgusting. I was offended. But, after a while, I decided to try it for a few more days. If you think about it, this dog had what amounted to an antipathy toward me; really. And, I wondered if I mightn't overcome this antipathy. So, I tried it for five more days, but it was always the same: snarl, sniff; move; faster; stare; gobble; RAAGGGHHH; smile; snarl; BAM. Well, now; by this time Columbus Avenue was strewn with hamburger rolls and I was less offended than disgusted. So, I decided to kill the dog.

(PETER *raises a hand in protest*)

Oh, don't be so alarmed, Peter; I didn't succeed. The day I tried to kill the dog I bought only one hamburger and what I thought was a murderous portion of rat poison. When I bought the hamburger I asked the man not to bother with the roll, all I wanted was the meat. I expected some reaction from him, like: we don't sell no hamburgers without rolls; or, wha' d'ya wanna do, eat it out'a ya han's? But no; he smiled benignly, wrapped up the hamburger in waxed paper, and said: A bite for ya pussy-cat? I wanted to say: No, not really; it's part of a plan to poison a dog I know. But, you can't say "a dog I know" without sounding funny; so I said, a little too loud, I'm afraid, and too formally: YES, A BITE FOR MY PUSSY-CAT. People looked up. It always happens when I try to simplify things; people look up. But that's neither hither nor thither. So. On my way back to the roominghouse, I kneaded the hamburger and the rat poison together between my hands, at that point feeling as much sadness as disgust. I opened the door to the entrance hall, and there the monster was, waiting to take the offering and then jump me. Poor bastard; he never learned that the moment he took to smile before he went for me gave me time enough to get out of range. BUT, there he was; malevolence with an erection, waiting. I put the poison patty down, moved toward the stairs and watched. The poor animal gobbled the food down as usual, smiled, which made me almost sick, and then, BAM. But, I sprinted up the stairs, as usual, and the dog didn't get me, as usual. AND IT CAME TO PASS THAT THE BEAST WAS DEATHLY ILL. I knew this because he no longer attended me, and because the landlady sobered up. She stopped me in the hall the same evening of the attempted murder and confided the information that God had struck her puppy-dog a surely fatal blow. She had

forgotten her bewildered lust, and her eyes were wide open for the first time. They looked like the dog's eyes. She sniveled and implored me to pray for the animal. I wanted to say to her: Madam, I have myself to pray for, the colored queen, the Puerto Rican family, the person in the front room whom I've never seen, the woman who cries deliberately behind her closed door, and the rest of the people in all roominghouses, everywhere; besides, Madam, I don't understand how to pray. But . . . to simplify things . . . I told her I would pray. She looked up. She said that I was a liar, and that I probably wanted the dog to die. I told her, and there was so much truth here, that I didn't want the dog to die. I didn't, and not just because I'd poisoned him. I'm afraid that I must tell you I wanted the dog to live so that I could see what our new relationship might come to.

(PETER *indicates his increasing displeasure and slowly growing antagonism*)

Please understand, Peter; that sort of thing is important. You must believe me; it *is* important. We have to know the effect of our actions. (*Another deep sigh*) Well, anyway; the dog recovered. I have no idea why, unless he was a descendant of the puppy that guarded the gates of hell° or some such resort. I'm not up on my mythology. (*He pronounces the word myth-o-logy*) Are you?

(PETER *sets to thinking, but* JERRY *goes on*)

At any rate, and you've missed the eight-thousand-dollar question, Peter; at any rate, the dog recovered his health and the landlady recovered her thirst, in no way altered by the bow-wow's deliverance. When I came home from a movie that was playing on Forty-second Street, a movie I'd seen, or one that was very much like one or several I'd seen, after the landlady told me puppykins was better, I was so hoping for the dog to be waiting for me. I was . . . well, how would you put it . . . enticed? . . . fascinated? . . . no, I don't think so . . . heart-shatteringly anxious, that's it; I was heart-shatteringly anxious to confront my friend again.

(PETER *reacts scoffingly*)

Yes, Peter; friend. That's the only word for it. I was heart-shatteringly et cetera to confront my doggy friend again. I came in the door and advanced, unafraid, to the center of the entrance hall. The beast was there . . . looking at me. And, you know, he looked better for his scrape with the nevermind. I stopped; I looked at him; he looked at me. I think

---

puppy that guarded the gates of hell, Cerberus, a fierce, three-headed dog.

. . . I think we stayed a long time that way . . . still, stone-statue . . . just looking at one another. I looked more into his face than he looked into mine. I mean, I can concentrate longer at looking into a dog's face than a dog can concentrate at looking into mine, or into anybody else's face, for that matter. But during that twenty seconds or two hours that we looked into each other's face, we made contact. Now, here is what I had wanted to happen: I loved the dog now, and I wanted him to love me. I had tried to love, and I had tried to kill, and both had been unsuccessful by themselves. I hoped . . . and I don't really know why I expected the dog to understand anything, much less my motivations . . . I hoped that the dog would understand.

(PETER *seems to be hypnotized*)

It's just . . . it's just that . . . (JERRY *is abnormally tense, now*) . . . it's just that if you can't deal with people, you have to make a start somewhere. WITH ANIMALS! (*Much faster now, and like a conspirator*) Don't you see? A person has to have some way of dealing with SOMETHING. If not with people . . . if not with people . . . SOMETHING. With a bed, with a cockroach, with a mirror . . . no, that's too hard, that's one of the last steps. With a cockroach, with a . . . with a . . . with a carpet, a roll of toilet paper . . . no, not that, either . . . that's a mirror, too; always check bleeding. You see how hard it is to find things? With a street corner, and too many lights, all colors reflecting on the oily-wet streets . . . with a wisp of smoke, a wisp . . . of smoke . . . with . . . with pornographic playing cards, with a strongbox . . . WITHOUT A LOCK . . . with love, with vomiting, with crying, with fury because the pretty little ladies aren't pretty little ladies, with making money with your body which is an act of love and I could prove it, with howling because you're alive; with God. How about that? WITH GOD WHO IS A COLORED QUEEN WHO WEARS A KIMONO AND PLUCKS HIS EYE-BROWS, WHO IS A WOMAN WHO CRIES WITH DETERMINATION BEHIND HER CLOSED DOOR . . . with God who, I'm told, turned his back on the whole thing some time ago . . . with . . . some day, with people. (JERRY *sighs the next word heavily*) People. With an idea; a concept. And where better, where ever better in this humiliating excuse for a jail, where better to communicate one single, simple-minded idea than in an entrance hall? Where? It would be A START! Where better to make a beginning . . . to understand and just possibly be understood . . . a beginning of an understanding, than with . . .

(Here JERRY *seems to fall into almost grotesque fatigue*)

. . . than with A DOG. Just that; a dog.

(*Here there is a silence that might be prolonged for a moment or so; then* JERRY *wearily finishes his story*)

A dog. It seemed like a perfectly sensible idea. Man is a dog's best friend, remember. So: the dog and I looked at each other. I longer than the dog. And what I saw then has been the same ever since. Whenever the dog and I see each other we both stop where we are. We regard each other with a mixture of sadness and suspicion, and then we feign indifference. We walk past each other safely; we have an understanding. It's very sad, but you'll have to admit that it is an understanding. We had made many attempts at contact, and we had failed. The dog has returned to garbage, and I to solitary but free passage. I have not returned. I mean to say, I have *gained* solitary free passage, if that much further loss can be said to be gain. I have learned that neither kindness nor cruelty by themselves, independent of each other, creates any effect beyond themselves; and I have learned that the two combined, together, at the same time, are the teaching emotion. And what is gained is loss. And what has been the result: the dog and I have attained a compromise; more of a bargain, really. We neither love nor hurt because we do not try to reach each other. And, *was* trying to feed the dog an act of love? And, perhaps, was the dog's attempt to bite me *not* an act of love? If we can so misunderstand, well then, why have we invented the word love in the first place?

(*There is silence.* JERRY *moves to* PETER's *bench and sits down beside him. This is the first time* JERRY *has sat down during the play*)

The Story of Jerry and the Dog: the end.

(PETER *is silent*)

Well, Peter? (JERRY *is suddenly cheerful*) Well, Peter? Do you think I could sell that story to the *Reader's Digest* and make a couple of hundred bucks for *The Most Unforgettable Character I've Ever Met*? Huh?

(JERRY *is animated, but* PETER *is disturbed*)

Oh, come on now, Peter; tell me what you think.
PETER (*Numb*): I . . . I don't understand what . . . I don't think I . . . (*Now, almost tearfully*) Why did you tell me all of this?
JERRY: Why not?
PETER: I DON'T UNDERSTAND!
JERRY (*Furious, but whispering*): That's a lie.
PETER: No. No, it's not.
JERRY (*Quietly*): I tried to explain it to you as I went along. I went slowly; it all has to do with . . .
PETER: I DON'T WANT TO HEAR ANY MORE. I don't understand you, or your landlady, or her dog . . .
JERRY: *Her* dog! I thought it was my . . . No. No, you're

right. It *is* her dog. (*Looks at* PETER *intently, shaking his head*) I don't know what I was thinking about; of course you don't understand. (*In a monotone, wearily*) I don't live in your block; I'm not married to two parakeets, or whatever your setup is. I am a *permanent transient,* and my home is the sickening roominghouses on the West Side of New York City, which is the greatest city in the world. Amen.

PETER: I'm . . . I'm sorry; I didn't mean to . . .

JERRY: Forget it. I suppose you don't quite know what to make of me, eh?

PETER (*A joke*): We get all kinds in publishing. (*Chuckles*)

JERRY: You're a funny man. (*He forces a laugh*) You know that? You're a very . . . a richly comic person.

PETER (*Modestly, but amused*): Oh, now, not really. (*Still chuckling*)

JERRY: Peter, do I annoy you, or confuse you?

PETER (*Lightly*): Well, I must confess that this wasn't the kind of afternoon I'd anticipated.

JERRY: You mean, I'm not the gentleman you were expecting.

PETER: I wasn't expecting anybody.

JERRY: No, I don't imagine you were. But I'm here, and I'm not leaving.

PETER (*Consulting his watch*): Well, you may not be, but I must be getting home soon.

JERRY: Oh, come on; stay a while longer.

PETER: I really should get home; you see . . .

JERRY (*Tickles* PETER's *ribs with his fingers*): Oh, come on.

PETER (*He is very ticklish; as* JERRY *continues to tickle him his voice becomes falsetto*): No, I . . . OHHHHH! Don't do that. Stop, Stop. Ohhh, no, no.

JERRY: Oh, come on.

PETER (*As* JERRY *tickles*): Oh, hee, hee, hee. I must go. I . . . hee, hee, hee. After all, stop, stop, hee, hee, hee, after all, the parakeets will be getting dinner ready soon. Hee, hee. And the cats are setting the table. Stop, stop, and, and . . . (PETER *is beside himself now*) . . . and we're having . . . hee, hee . . . uh . . . ho, ho, ho.

(JERRY *stops tickling* PETER, *but the combination of the tickling and his own mad whimsy has* PETER *laughing almost hysterically. As his laughter continues, then subsides,* JERRY *watches him, with a curious fixed smile*)

JERRY: Peter?

PETER: Oh, ha, ha, ha, ha, ha. What? What?

JERRY: Listen, now.

PETER: Oh, ho, ho. What . . . what is it, Jerry? Oh, my.

JERRY (*Mysteriously*): Peter, do you want to know what happened at the zoo?

PETER: Ah, ha, ha. The what? Oh, yes; the zoo. Oh, ho, ho. Well, I had my own zoo there for a moment with . . . hee, hee, the parakeets getting dinner ready, and the . . . ha, ha, whatever it was, the . . .

JERRY (*Calmly*): Yes, that was very funny, Peter. I wouldn't have expected it. But do you want to hear about what happened at the zoo, or not?

PETER: Yes. Yes, by all means; tell me what happened at the zoo. Oh, my. I don't know what happened to me.

JERRY: Now I'll let you in on what happened at the zoo; but first, I should tell you why I went to the zoo. I went to the zoo to find out more about the way people exist with animals, and the way animals exist with each other, and with people too. It probably wasn't a fair test, what with everyone separated by bars from everyone else, the animals for the most part from each other, and always the people from the animals. But, if it's a zoo, that's the way it is. (*He pokes* PETER *on the arm*) Move over.

PETER (*Friendly*): I'm sorry, haven't you enough room? (*He shifts a little*)

JERRY (*Smiling slightly*): Well, all the animals are there, and all the people are there, and it's Sunday and all the children are there. (*He pokes* PETER *again*) Move over.

PETER (*Patiently, still friendly*): All right.

(*He moves some more, and* JERRY *has all the room he might need*)

JERRY: And it's a hot day, so all the stench is there, too, and all the balloon sellers, and all the ice cream sellers, and all the seals are barking, and all the birds are screaming. (*Pokes* PETER *harder*) Move over!

PETER (*Beginning to be annoyed*): Look here, you have more than enough room! (*But he moves more, and is now fairly cramped at one end of the bench*)

JERRY: And I am there, and it's feeding time at the lions' house, and the lion keeper comes into the lion cage, one of the lion cages, to feed one of the lions. (*Punches* PETER *on the arm, hard*) MOVE OVER!

PETER (*Very annoyed*): I can't move over any more, and stop hitting me. What's the matter with you?

JERRY: Do you want to hear the story? (*Punches* PETER's *arm again*)

PETER (*Flabbergasted*): I'm not so sure! I certainly don't want to be punched in the arm.

JERRY (*Punches* PETER's *arm again*): Like that?

PETER: Stop it! What's the matter with you?

JERRY: I'm crazy, you bastard.

PETER: That isn't funny.

JERRY: Listen to me, Peter. I want this bench. You go sit on the bench over there, and if you're good I'll tell you the rest of the story.

PETER (*Flustered*): But . . . whatever for? What *is* the matter with you? Besides, I see no reason why I should give up this bench. I sit on this bench almost every Sunday afternoon, in good weather. It's secluded here; there's never anyone sitting here, so I have it all to myself.

JERRY (*Softly*): Get off this bench, Peter; I want it.

PETER (*Almost whining*): No.

JERRY: I said I want this bench, and I'm going to have it. Now get over there.

PETER: People can't have everything they want. You should know that; it's a rule; people can have some of the things they want, but they can't have every-thing.

JERRY (*Laughs*): Imbecile! You're slow-witted!

PETER: Stop that!

JERRY: You're a vegetable! Go lie down on the ground.

PETER (*Intense*): Now *you* listen to me. I've put up with you all afternoon.

JERRY: Not really.

PETER: LONG ENOUGH. I've put up with you long enough. I've listened to you because you seemed . . . well, because I thought you wanted to talk to somebody.

JERRY: You put things well; economically, and, yet . . . oh, what is the word I want to put justice to your . . . JESUS, you make me sick . . . get off here and give me my bench.

PETER: MY BENCH!

JERRY (*Pushes* PETER *almost, but not quite, off the bench*): Get out of my sight.

PETER (*Regaining his position*): God da . . . mn you. That's enough! I've had enough of you. I will not give up this bench; you can't have it, and that's that. Now, go away.

(JERRY *snorts but does not move*)

Go away, I said.

(JERRY *does not move*)

Get away from here. If you don't move on . . . you're a bum . . . that's what you are. . . . If you don't move on, I'll get a policeman here and make you go.

(JERRY *laughs, stays*)

I warn you, I'll call a policeman.

JERRY (*Softly*): You won't find a policeman around here; they're all over on the west side of the park chasing fairies down from trees or out of the bushes. That's all they do. That's their function. So scream your head off; it won't do you any good.

PETER: POLICE! I warn you, I'll have you arrested. POLICE! (*Pause*) I said POLICE! (*Pause*) I feel ri-diculous.

JERRY: You look ridiculous: a grown man screaming for the police on a bright Sunday afternoon in the park with nobody harming you. If a policeman *did* fill his quota and come sludging over this way he'd probably take you in as a nut.

PETER (*With disgust and impotence*): Great God, I just came here to read, and now you want me to give up the bench. You're mad.

JERRY: Hey, I got news for you, as they say. I'm on your precious bench, and you're never going to have it for yourself again.

PETER (*Furious*): Look, you; get off my bench. I don't care if it makes any sense or not. I want this bench to myself; I want you OFF IT!

JERRY (*Mocking*): Aw . . . look who's mad.

PETER: GET OUT!

JERRY: No.

PETER: I WARN YOU!

JERRY: Do you know how ridiculous you look *now*?

PETER (*His fury and self-consciousness have possessed him*): It doesn't matter. (*He is almost crying*) GET AWAY FROM MY BENCH!

JERRY: Why? You have everything in the world you want; you've told me about your home, and your family, and *your own* little zoo. You have everything, and now you want this bench. Are these the things men fight for? Tell me, Peter, is this bench, this iron and this wood, is this your honor? Is this the thing in the world you'd fight for? Can you think of anything more absurd?

PETER: Absurd? Look, I'm not going to talk to you about honor, or even try to explain it to you. Besides, it isn't a question of honor; but even if it were, you wouldn't understand.

JERRY (*Contemptuously*): You don't even know what you're saying, do you? This is probably the first time in your life you've had anything more trying to face than changing your cats' toilet box. Stupid! Don't you have any idea, not even the slightest, what other people *need*?

PETER: Oh, boy, listen to you; well, you don't need this bench. That's for sure.

JERRY: Yes; yes, I do.

PETER (*Quivering*): I've come here for years; I have hours of great pleasure, great satisfaction, right here. And that's important to a man. I'm a respon-sible person, and I'm a GROWNUP. This is my bench, and you have no right to take it away from me.

JERRY: Fight for it, then. Defend yourself; defend your bench.

PETER: You've *pushed* me to it. Get up and fight.

JERRY: Like a man?

PETER (*Still angry*): Yes, like a man, if you insist on mock-ing me even further.

JERRY: I'll have to give you credit for one thing: you *are* a vegetable, and a slightly nearsighted one, I think . . .

PETER: THAT'S ENOUGH. . . .

JERRY: . . . but, you know, as they say on TV all the time—you know—and I mean this, Peter, you have a certain dignity; it surprises me. . . .

PETER: STOP!

JERRY (*Rises lazily*): Very well, Peter, we'll battle for the bench, but we're not evenly matched.

(*He takes out and clicks open an ugly-looking knife*)

PETER (*Suddenly awaking to the reality of the situation*): You *are* mad! You're stark raving mad! YOU'RE GOING TO KILL ME!

(*But before* PETER *has time to think what to do,* JERRY *tosses the knife at* PETER'S *feet*)

JERRY: There you go. Pick it up. You have the knife and we'll be more evenly matched.

PETER (*Horrified*): No!

JERRY (*Rushes over to* PETER, *grabs him by the collar;* PETER *rises; their faces almost touch*): Now you pick up that knife and you fight with me. You fight for your self-respect; you fight for that goddamned bench.

PETER (*Struggling*): No! Let . . . let go of me! He . . . Help!

JERRY (*Slaps* PETER *on each "fight"*): You fight, you miserable bastard; fight for that bench; fight for your parakeets; fight for your cats, fight for your two daughters; fight for your wife; fight for your manhood, you pathetic little vegetable. (*Spits in* PETER'S *face*) You couldn't even get your wife with a male child.

PETER (*Breaks away, enraged*): It's a matter of genetics, not manhood, you . . . you monster.

(*He darts down, picks up the knife and backs off a little; he is breathing heavily*)

I'll give you one last chance; get out of here and leave me alone!

(*He holds the knife with a firm arm, but far in front of him, not to attack, but to defend*)

JERRY (*Sighs heavily*): So be it!

(*With a rush he charges* PETER *and impales himself on the knife. Tableau: For just a moment, complete silence,* JERRY *impaled on the knife at the end of* PETER'S *still firm arm. Then* PETER *screams, pulls away, leaving the knife in* JERRY. JERRY *is motionless, on point. Then he, too, screams, and it must be the sound of an infuriated and fatally wounded animal. With the knife in him, he stumbles back to the bench that* PETER *had vacated. He crumbles there, sitting, facing* PETER, *his eyes wide in agony, his mouth open*)

PETER (*Whispering*): Oh my God, oh my God, oh my God . . .

(*He repeats these words many times, very rapidly*)

JERRY (JERRY *is dying; but now his expression seems to change. His features relax, and while his voice varies, sometimes wrenched with pain, for the most part he seems removed from his dying. He smiles*): Thank you, Peter. I mean that, now; thank you very much.

(PETER'S *mouth drops open. He cannot move; he is transfixed*)

Oh, Peter, I was so afraid I'd drive you away. (*He laughs as best he can*) You don't know how afraid I was you'd go away and leave me. And now I'll tell you what happened at the zoo. I think . . . I think this is what happened at the zoo . . . I think. I think that while I was at the zoo I decided that I would walk north . . . northerly, rather . . . until I found you . . . or somebody . . . and I decided that I would talk to you . . . I would tell you things . . . and things that I would tell you would . . . Well, here we are. You see? Here we *are*. But . . . I don't know . . . could I have planned all this? No . . . no, I couldn't have. But I think I did. And now I've told you what you wanted to know, haven't I? And now you know all about what happened at the zoo. And now you know what you'll see in your TV, and the face I told you about . . . you remember . . . the face I told you about . . . my face, the face you see right now. Peter . . . Peter? . . . Peter . . . thank you. I came unto you (*He laughs, so faintly*) and you have comforted me. Dear Peter.

PETER (*Almost fainting*): Oh my God!

JERRY: You'd better go now. Somebody might come by, and you don't want to be here when anyone comes.

PETER (*Does not move, but begins to weep*): Oh my God, oh my God.

JERRY (*Most faintly, now; he is very near death*): You won't be coming back here any more, Peter; you've been dispossessed. You've lost your bench, but you've defended your honor. And Peter, I'll tell you something now; you're not really a vegetable; it's all right, you're an animal. You're an animal, too. But you'd better hurry now, Peter. Hurry, you'd better go . . . see?

(JERRY *takes a handkerchief and with great effort and pain wipes the knife handle clean of fingerprints*)

Hurry away, Peter.

(PETER *begins to stagger away*)

Wait . . . wait, Peter. Take your book . . . book. Right here . . . beside me . . . on your bench . . . my bench, rather. Come . . . take your book.

(PETER *starts for the book, but retreats*)

Hurry . . . Peter.

(PETER *rushes to the bench, grabs the book, retreats*)

Very good, Peter . . . very good. Now . . . hurry away.

(PETER *hesitates for a moment, then flees, stage-left*)

Hurry away. . . . (*His eyes are closed now*) Hurry away, your parakeets are making the dinner . . . the cats . . . are setting the table . . .

PETER (*Off stage*): (*A pitiful howl*) OH MY GOD!

JERRY (*His eyes still closed, he shakes his head and speaks; a combination of scornful mimicry and supplication*): Oh . . . my . . . God.

(*He is dead*)

CURTAIN

Figure 1. Jerry (Mark Richman, who took over the role from George Maharis) questions a wary and reserved Peter (William Daniels) in the Provincetown Playhouse production of *The Zoo Story*, directed by Milton Katselas. (Photograph: Billy Rose Theatre Collection. The New York Public Library for the Performing Arts. Astor, Lenox, and Tilden Foundations.)

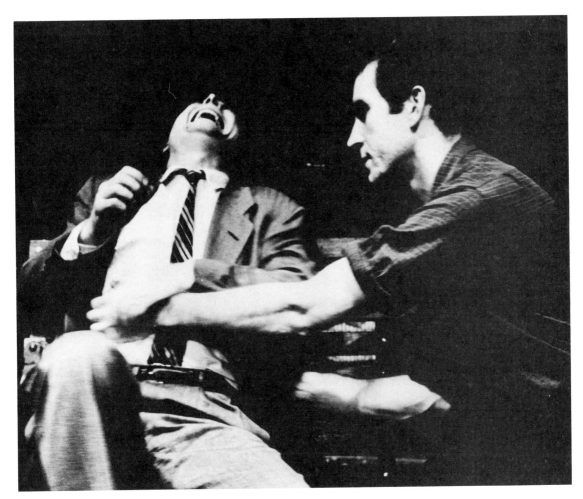

Figure 2. Peter (William Daniels) responds with hysterical laughter as Jerry (Mark Richman) calmly tickles him in the Provincetown Play-house production of *The Zoo Story*, directed by Milton Katselas. (Photograph: Billy Rose Theatre Collection. The New York Public Library for the Performing Arts. Astor, Lenox, and Tilden Foundations.)

Staging of *The Zoo Story*

**REVIEW OF THE PROVINCETOWN PLAYHOUSE
PRODUCTION, 1960, BY HENRY HEWES**

Last week these columns were devoted mainly to a discussion of Samuel Beckett's rich and poetic playlet, *Krapp's Last Tape*. This play is the first half of a twin bill currently at the Provincetown Playhouse. The second play there, titled *The Zoo Story*, is equally exciting, not only because it is compelling theatre, but also because it introduces Edward Albee, a young (circa thirty) playwright of considerable potentiality.

Mr. Albee's play is quite simple in form. A dull, respectable man with that upper-middle-middle expression on his face is reading on a park bench when an obnoxious stranger approaches him with irritating personal questions and remarks. The stranger has a desperate need to make contact with someone, and as a last resort pushes his listener to violence.

The details of these events are made fascinating by the actors George Maharis and William Daniels. To the role of Jerry, the beatnik, Mr. Maharis brings a quietly hypnotic rhythm that comes across as theatrically colorful yet integrated with his own personality. And as Peter, the square, Mr. Daniels provides a genuine humor. He is at his best in the early part of the play where the tone *is* humorous, as Jerry ridicules the clichés he is able to smoke out of Peter's Madison Avenue existence. Of course, this ridicule has itself become a cliché, and if unimaginatively played would seem merely tired and predictable satire. But director Milton Katselas has permitted each actor an awareness of the situation and of what the dialogue means to one who speaks it. Jerry tends to have this awareness at the precise moment he speaks. And Peter has it a second or two after he has said his line. Even an ordinary interchange (JERRY: "Well, *Time* magazine isn't for blockheads." PETER: "No, I suppose not.") becomes subtly hilarious when given this particular treatment. And it is not just funny, for as he considers each random question, Peter becomes more and more aware of inadequacies not really faced before.

Jerry, on the other hand, seems compelled by an inner, not quite understood drive, an unwillingness to stop short of scraping out the last layer of truth. And even when he is using such colorful language as "But that was the jazz of a very special hotel," it is not done for effect, but rather because that is the best way he knows to express his nostalgia without oversentimentalization. The high point of his performance is reached when he tells "The Story of Jerry and the Dog." In the parable Jerry attempts first kindness and then cruelty to a dog that tries to bite him every time he comes into his boarding house. The result is an eventual compromise in which both Jerry and the dog arrive at a state in which they neither love nor hurt because they no longer try to reach each other. This state—the basis of so many relationships in modern adult society—is what has driven Jerry into his present pilgrimage up Fifth Avenue to the zoo where he had hoped to find out more about the way people exist with animals, animals with each other, and animals with people. As he tells Peter the story of what he saw at the zoo, Jerry attempts, through cruelty, to provoke some animal feeling in Peter, and though the ending is melodramatic and violent, Jerry—like Christ—succeeds at the cost of his life in arousing the human soul out of its deep modern lethargy to an awareness of its animal self.

The Zoo Story is done so well that we can afford to point out that Mr. Katselas might have made this production even more effective if he had been able to highlight some of the author's points more distinctly and had found a more interesting way of expressing the animal stirring within Peter at the play's melodramatic end. We can also afford to wonder if Mr. Albee's suggestion that Jerry's boarding house is a West Side purgatory in which God is a queen who plucks his eyebrows and goes to the john is not one that needs the fuller development he might give it in a longer play. And doesn't his description of Jerry's deceased mother ("She embarked on an adulterous turn of our Southern states . . . and her most constant companion among others, among many others, was a Mr. Barleycorn") owe something to Tennessee Williams? No matter. Mr. Albee has written an extraordinary first play, which, next to Jack Gelber's *The Connection*, constitutes the finest new achievement in the theatre this season. Thank God for Off-Broadway, and, I guess, thank God for beatniks.

IMAMU AMIRI BARAKA

1934–

Between March and December 1964, Baraka, who was then still writing under his original name of LeRoi Jones, had four one-act plays produced off-Broadway, one of which, *Dutchman*, won the Obie award for the best off-Broadway play of 1963–64. That production record would be considered astonishing for any playwright, particularly for a young African-American playwright until then known only as a writer of essays and poems. Baraka was born in Newark, New Jersey, where he attended public school and then began college at Rutgers University, later transferring to Howard University, one of America's historically black colleges. Subsequently, he served in the United States Air Force, from 1954 to 1957, and then settled in New York City where, with Hettie Cohen, whom he married in 1958, he edited a literary magazine, publishing avant-garde writers such as William Burroughs, Gregory Corso, Allen Ginsburg, Jack Kerouac, Charles Olson, and himself. His sudden fame after the success of *Dutchman* led him to teaching positions at Columbia University and the New School for Social Research, as well as to the award of a Guggenheim Fellowship in 1965. It was also in 1965 that he changed his name to Imamu Amiri Baraka, roughly translatable as Priest-Warrior-Blessing, and wrote his well-known manifesto, "The Revolutionary Theater." In it he asserted that theater "should force change, it should be change," that it "must EXPOSE! Show up the insides of these humans, look into black skulls. White men will cower before this theater because it hates them." And in his subsequent plays, Baraka followed up on his manifesto, for they are all essentially political in purpose, aimed at stirring African-American audiences to radical action, and thus similar in intent to the "learning plays" that Brecht was writing during the late 1920s and early 1930s.

Although *Dutchman* was written before Baraka became explicitly associated with "revolutionary theater," it is clearly a revolutionary play, particularly when it is seen in the context of the African-American drama that had preceded it. African Americans had written plays during the nineteenth century, yet their works did not achieve prominence until the 1920s with the plays of Garland Anderson, Wallace Thurman, and Willis Richardson. The Federal Theater project of the 1930s gave special encouragement to African-American dramatists and led, in particular, to the plays of Langston Hughes, one of the leading figures of the Harlem Renaissance, whose works include *Mulatto* (1935), *Don't You Want to Be Free* (1936), a long-running historical panorama, and *Emperor of Haiti* (1938). In Chicago, the Federal Theater Unit sponsored the first production of Theodore Ward's *Big White Fog* (1938), a play that shows a family's struggle to attain a new life in the context of urban society through the political movement known as "back-to-Africa." Ward's later play, *Our Lan'* (1941), was even more successful with its depiction of newly freed blacks trying to live on an island off the Georgia coast. At the end of the 1950s, Lorraine Hansberry's *A Raisin in the Sun* (1959) became a major Broadway success by taking up once again the theme of the "new life," this time by showing a protagonist who maintains his individual and racial pride by moving out of the slums and into a white middle-class neighborhood, a neighborhood that had tried to buy him off to keep him from moving in.

All these plays concerned themselves with the social and political problems of African Americans, yet most concentrated almost exclusively on issues within that community, with only a few venturing to deal directly with confrontations between black and white characters. Not until the plays of Baraka did such confrontations become insistently—and violently—central. In *The Slave* (1964), Baraka shows a black leader, Walker Vessels, engaged in a long argument with two white liberals, Grace and Bradford Easley, about their conflicting ideologies. In *The Toilet* (1964), a group of African-American boys beat up a white boy, a Puerto Rican, who has sent a "love letter" to the leader of their group. And in *Dutchman*, Baraka dramatizes the ultimate confrontation in a sexual encounter between a black man and a white woman, a confrontation that leads to a violent conclusion, in which the black man becomes the victim. In *Dutchman*, too, Baraka moved away from the realistic style that had prevailed in earlier African-American plays toward a symbolic style, immediately announced by its title.

This title is meant to evoke the legend of the Flying Dutchman, the man doomed to sail the seas forever until he found a woman who would be faithful to him, and the subway in which the play is set reflects that ceaseless and meaningless voyaging. The title also alludes to the Dutch ships that brought black slaves to North America, and in this context Lula may be seen as a relentless traveler and destroyer, embodying the way that whites have always treated blacks. Baraka himself claimed that the situation rather than the characters was meant to be symbolic, an interpretation stressing the ceaselessness of racial violence. Apart from the title, the play's mythic quality is emphasized by Baraka's stage direction, "The subway heaped in modern myth," by the appearance of Lula eating an apple, by her later remark that "Eating apples is always the first step," and by Clay's name, which echoes Adam's formation "out of the dust of the ground." The interweaving of the realistic and the symbolic can also be seen in the dialogue of the play, which begins essentially with everyday conversation but quickly turns into metaphor, when Lula tells Clay that "You look like death eating a soda cracker." Lula then turns into a mock prophet in her litany at the end of the first scene, and finally a chanter of vicious and obscene litanies, meant to goad Clay into action.

When she does finally arouse him to the violent action and speech audiences yearn for after her relentless taunting, the effect is devastating, for he destroys any myths that whites may have about blacks, ending as he does with an explicit threat about what will happen when blacks are "accepted" by whites:

> They'll murder you, and have very rational explanations. Very much like your own. They'll cut your throats, and drag you out to the edge of your cities, so the flesh can fall away from your bones, in sanitary isolation.

But instead of the physical assault that might be expected from Clay after this speech, Baraka creates an even more frightening conclusion in Lula's stabbing of him, an act that grotesquely inverts and parodies the sexual act they have been discussing. Her comment, "Get this man off me!" continues the sexual subtext. And when a young African American of twenty next enters the subway car, her act of turning and giving him a long slow look clearly indicates that the destructive cycle will begin again, repeating itself endlessly like the travels of the subway and the flying Dutchman.

When the play was first produced, critics were both impressed and defensive, as revealed in the two reviews reprinted following the text. But they also noted the symbolic significance of the play, as indicated by Harold Clurman's remarks about Lula: "She is our neurosis. Not a neurosis in regard to the Negro, but the absolute neurosis of American society." Jennifer West's performance conveyed that neurosis in her move from demure sexuality (see Figure 1) to uncontrollable aggression. When the play was turned into a film in 1967, critics found it stagey and dull, for the real subway car seemed much less effective as a frame for the play's violence than the make-believe one. On stage, the play still shocks, still continues to explode, precisely because the subway car is only a set while the anger, the cruelty, and the hatred are real.

DUTCHMAN

BY IMAMU AMIRI BARAKA

CHARACTERS

CLAY, *twenty-year-old Negro*
LULA, *thirty-year-old white woman*
RIDERS OF COACH, *white and black*
YOUNG NEGRO
CONDUCTOR

SCENE

In the flying underbelly of the city. Steaming hot, and summer on top, outside. Underground. The subway heaped in modern myth.

Opening scene is a man sitting in a subway seat, holding a magazine but looking vacantly just above its wilting pages. Occasionally he looks blankly toward the window on his right. Dim lights and darkness whistling by against the glass. (Or paste the lights, as admitted props, right on the subway windows. Have them move, even dim and flicker. But give the sense of speed. Also stations, whether the train is stopped or the glitter and activity of these stations merely flashes by the windows.)

The man is sitting alone. That is, only his seat is visible, though the rest of the car is outfitted as a complete subway car. But only his seat is shown. There might be, for a time, as the play begins, a loud scream of the actual train. And it can recur throughout the play, or continue on a lower key once the dialogue starts.

The train slows after a time, pulling to a brief stop at one of the stations. The man looks idly up, until he sees a woman's face staring at him through the window; when it realizes that the man has noticed the face, it begins very premeditatedly to smile. The man smiles too, for a moment, without a trace of self-consciousness. Almost an instinctive though undesirable response. Then a kind of awkwardness or embarrassment sets in, and the man makes to look away, is further embarrassed, so he brings back his eyes to where the face was, but by now the train is moving again, and the face would seem to be left behind by the way the man turns his head to look back through the other windows at the slowly fading platform. He smiles then; more comfortably confident, hoping perhaps that his memory of this brief encounter will be pleasant. And then he is idle again.

SCENE 1

(*Train roars. Lights flash outside the windows.*

LULA *enters from the rear of the car in bright, skimpy summer clothes and sandals. She carries a net bag full of paper books, fruit, and other anonymous articles. She is wearing sunglasses, which she pushes up on her forehead from time to time.* LULA *is a tall, slender, beautiful woman with long red hair hanging straight down her back, wearing only loud lipstick in somebody's good taste. She is eating an apple, very daintily. Coming down the car toward* CLAY.

She stops beside CLAY'S *seat and hangs languidly from the strap, still managing to eat the apple. It is apparent that she is going to sit in the seat next to* CLAY, *and that she is only waiting for him to notice her before she sits.*

CLAY *sits as before, looking just beyond his magazine, now and again pulling the magazine slowly back and forth in front of his face in a hopeless effort to fan himself. Then he sees the woman hanging there beside him and he looks up into her face, smiling quizzically.*)

LULA: Hello.
CLAY: Uh, hi're you?
LULA: I'm going to sit down. . . . O.K.?
CLAY: Sure.
LULA (*swings down onto the seat, pushing her legs straight out as if she is very weary*): Oooof! Too much weight.

CLAY: Ha, doesn't look like much to me.

(*Leaning back against the window, a little surprised and maybe stiff.*)

LULA: It's so anyway.

(*And she moves her toes in the sandals, then pulls her right leg up on the left knee, better to inspect the bottoms of the sandals and the back of her heel. She appears for a second not to notice that* CLAY *is sitting next to her or that she has spoken to him just a second before.* CLAY *looks at the magazine, then out the black window. As he does this, she turns very quickly toward him.*)

Weren't you staring at me through the window?
CLAY (*wheeling around and very much stiffened*): What?
LULA: Weren't you staring at me through the window? At the last stop?
CLAY: Staring at you? What do you mean?
LULA: Don't you know what staring means?
CLAY: I saw you through the window . . . if that's what it means. I don't know if I was staring. Seems to me you were staring through the window at me.
LULA: I was. But only after I'd turned around and saw you staring through that window down in the vicinity of my ass and legs.
CLAY: Really?
LULA: Really. I guess you were just taking those idle

potshots. Nothing else to do. Run your mind over people's flesh.

CLAY: Oh boy. Wow, now I admit I was looking in your direction. But the rest of that weight is yours.

LULA: I suppose.

CLAY: Staring through train windows is weird business. Much weirder than staring very sedately at abstract asses.

LULA: That's why I came looking through the window . . . so you'd have more than that to go on. I even smiled at you.

CLAY: That's right.

LULA: I even got into this train, going some other way than mine. Walked down the aisle . . . searching you out.

CLAY: Really? That's pretty funny.

LULA: That's pretty funny. . . . God, you're dull.

CLAY: Well, I'm sorry, lady, but I really wasn't prepared for party talk.

LULA: No, you're not. What are you prepared for?

(Wrapping the apple core in a Kleenex and dropping it on the floor.)

CLAY *(takes her conversation as pure sex talk. He turns to confront her squarely with this idea)*: I'm prepared for anything. How about you?

LULA *(laughing loudly and cutting it off abruptly)*: What do you think you're doing?

CLAY: What?

LULA: You think I want to pick you up, get you to take me somewhere and screw me, huh?

CLAY: Is that the way I look?

LULA: You look like you been trying to grow a beard. That's exactly what you look like. You look like you live in New Jersey with your parents and are trying to grow a beard. That's what. You look like you've been reading Chinese poetry and drinking lukewarm sugarless tea. *(Laughs, uncrossing and recrossing her legs.)* You look like death eating a soda cracker.

CLAY *(cocking his head from one side to the other, embarrassed and trying to make some comeback, but also intrigued by what the woman is saying . . . even the sharp city coarseness of her voice, which is still a kind of gentle sidewalk throb)*: Really? I look like all that?

LULA: Not all of it.

(She feints a seriousness to cover an actual somber tone.)

I lie a lot. *(Smiling.)* It helps me control the world.

CLAY *(relieved and laughing louder than the humor)*: Yeah, I bet.

LULA: But it's true, most of it, right? Jersey? Your bumpy neck?

CLAY: How'd you know all that? Huh? Really, I mean about Jersey . . . and even the beard. I met you

before? You know Warren Enright?

LULA: You tried to make it with your sister when you were ten. *(CLAY leans back hard against the back of the seat, his eyes opening now, still trying to look amused.)* But I succeeded a few weeks ago. *(She starts to laugh again.)*

CLAY: What're you talking about? Warren tell you that? You're a friend of Georgia's?

LULA: I told you I lie. I don't know your sister. I don't know Warren Enright.

CLAY: You mean you're just picking these things out of the air?

LULA: Is Warren Enright a tall skinny black black boy with a phony English accent?

CLAY: I figured you knew him.

LULA: But I don't. I just figured you would know somebody like that. *(Laughs.)*

CLAY: Yeah, yeah.

LULA: You're probably on your way to his house now.

CLAY: That's right.

LULA *(putting her hand on CLAY's closest knee, drawing it from the knee up to the thigh's hinge, then removing it, watching his face very closely, and continuing to laugh, perhaps more gently than before)*: Dull, dull, dull. I bet you think I'm exciting.

CLAY: You're O.K.

LULA: Am I exciting you now?

CLAY: Right. That's not what's supposed to happen?

LULA: How do I know? *(She returns her hand, without moving it, then takes it away and plunges it in her bag to draw out an apple.)* You want this?

CLAY: Sure.

LULA *(she gets one out of the bag for herself)*: Eating apples together is always the first step. Or walking up uninhabited Seventh Avenue in the twenties on weekends. *(Bites and giggles, glancing at CLAY and speaking in loose sing-song.)* Can get you involved . . . boy! Get us involved. Um-huh. *(Mock seriousness.)* Would you like to get involved with me, Mister Man?

CLAY *(trying to be as flippant as LULA, whacking happily at the apple)*: Sure. Why not? A beautiful woman like you. Huh, I'd be a fool not to.

LULA: And I bet you're sure you know what you're talking about. *(Taking him a little roughly by the wrist, so he cannot eat the apple, then shaking the wrist.)* I bet you're sure of almost everything anybody ever asked you . . . right? *(Shakes his wrist harder.)* Right?

CLAY: Yeah, right. . . . Wow, you're pretty strong, you know? Whatta you, a lady wrestler or something?

LULA: What's wrong with lady wrestlers? And don't answer because you never knew any. Huh. *(Cynically.)* That's for sure. They don't have any lady wrestlers in that part of Jersey. That's for sure.

CLAY: Hey, you still haven't told me how you know so much about me.

LULA: I told you I didn't know anything about *you* . . . you're a well-known type.

CLAY: Really?

LULA: Or at least I know the type very well. And your skinny English friend too.

CLAY: Anonymously?

LULA (*settles back in seat, single-mindedly finishing her apple and humming snatches of rhythm and blues song*): What?

CLAY: Without knowing us specifically?

LULA: Oh boy. (*Looking quickly at* CLAY.) What a face. You know, you could be a handsome man.

CLAY: I can't argue with you.

LULA (*vague, off-center response*): What?

CLAY (*raising his voice, thinking the train noise has drowned part of his sentence*): I can't argue with you.

LULA: My hair is turning gray. A gray hair for each year and type I've come through.

CLAY: Why do you want to sound so old?

LULA: But it's always gentle when it starts. (*Attention drifting.*) Hugged against tenements, day or night.

CLAY: What?

LULA (*refocusing*): Hey, why don't you take me to that party you're going to?

CLAY: You must be a friend of Warren's to know about the party.

LULA: Wouldn't you like to take me to the party? (*Imitates clinging vine.*) Oh, come on, ask me to your party.

CLAY: Of course I'll ask you to come with me to the party. And I'll bet you're a friend of Warren's.

LULA: Why not be a friend of Warren's? Why not? (*Taking his arm.*) Have you asked me yet?

CLAY: How can I ask you when I don't know your name?

LULA: Are you talking to my name?

CLAY: What is it, a secret?

LULA: I'm Lena the Hyena.

CLAY: The famous woman poet?

LULA: Poetess! the same!

CLAY: Well, you know so much about me . . . what's my name?

LULA: Morris the Hyena.

CLAY: The famous woman poet?

LULA: The same. (*Laughing and going into her bag.*) You want another apple?

CLAY: Can't make it, lady. I only have to keep one doctor away a day.

LULA: I bet your name is . . . something like . . . uh, Gerald or Walter. Huh?

CLAY: God, no.

LULA: Lloyd, Norman? One of those hopeless colored names creeping out of New Jersey. Leonard? Gag. . . .

CLAY: Like Warren?

LULA: Definitely. Just exactly like Warren. Or Everett.

CLAY: Gag. . . .

LULA: Well, for sure, it's not Willie.

CLAY: It's Clay.

LULA: Clay? Really? Clay what?

CLAY: Take your pick. Jackson, Johnson, or Williams.

LULA: Oh, really? Good for you. But it's got to be Williams. You're too pretentious to be a Jackson or Johnson.

CLAY: Thass right.

LULA: But Clay's O.K.

CLAY: So's Lena.

LULA: It's Lula.

CLAY: Oh?

LULA: Lula the Hyena.

CLAY: Very good.

LULA (*starts laughing again*): Now you say to me, "Lula, Lula, why don't you go to this party with me tonight?" It's your turn, and let those be your lines.

CLAY: Lula, why don't you go to this party with me tonight, Huh?

LULA: Say my name twice before you ask, and no huh's.

CLAY: Lula, Lula, why don't you go to this party with me tonight?

LULA: I'd like to go, Clay, but how can you ask me to go when you barely know me?

CLAY: That is strange, isn't it?

LULA: What kind of reaction is that? You're supposed to say, "Aw, come on, we'll get to know each other better at the party."

CLAY: That's pretty corny.

LULA: What are you into anyway? (*Looking at him half sullenly but still amused.*) What thing are you playing at, Mister? Mister Clay Williams? (*Grabs his thigh, up near the crotch.*) What are *you* thinking about?

CLAY: Watch it now, you're gonna excite me for real.

LULA (*taking her hand away and throwing her apple core through the window*): I bet. (*She slumps in the seat and is heavily silent.*)

CLAY: I thought you knew everything about me? What happened? (LULA *looks at him, then looks slowly away, then over where the other aisle would be. Noise of the train. She reaches in her bag and pulls out one of the paper books. She puts it on her leg and thumbs the pages listlessly.* CLAY *cocks his head to see the title of the book. Noise of the train.* LULA *flips pages and her eyes drift. Both remain silent.*) Are you going to the party with me, Lula?

LULA (*bored and not even looking*): I don't even know you.

CLAY: You said you know my type.

LULA (*strangely irritated*): Don't get smart with me,

Buster. I know you like the palm of my hand.

CLAY: The one you eat the apples with?

LULA: Yeh. And the one I open doors late Saturday evening with. That's my door. Up at the top of the stairs. Five flights. Above a lot of Italians and lying Americans. And scrape carrots with. Also . . . (*Looks at him.*) the same hand I unbutton my dress with, or let my skirt fall down. Same hand. Lover.

CLAY: Are you angry about something? Did I say something wrong?

LULA: Everything you say is wrong. (*Mock smile.*) That's what makes you so attractive. Ha. In that funnybook jacket with all the buttons. (*More animate, taking hold of his jacket.*) What've you got that jacket and tie on in all this heat for? And why're you wearing a jacket and tie like that? Did your people ever burn witches or start revolutions over the price of tea? Boy, those narrow-shoulder clothes come from a tradition you ought to feel oppressed by. A three-button suit. What right do you have to be wearing a three-button suit and striped tie? Your father was a slave, he didn't go to Harvard.

CLAY: My grandfather was a night watchman.

LULA: And you went to a colored college where everybody thought they were Averell Harriman.

CLAY: All except me.

LULA: And who did you think you were? Who do you think you are now?

CLAY (*laughs as if to make light of the whole trend of the conversation*): Well, in college I thought I was Baudelaire. But I've slowed down since.

LULA: I bet you never once thought you were a black nigger. (*Mock serious, then she howls with laughter.* CLAY *is stunned but after initial reaction, he quickly tries to appreciate the humor.* LULA *almost shrieks.*) A black Baudelaire.

CLAY: That's right.

LULA: Boy, are you corny. I take back what I said before. Everything you say is not wrong. It's perfect. You should be on television.

CLAY: You act like you're on television already.

LULA: That's because I'm an actress.

CLAY: I thought so.

LULA: Well, you're wrong. I'm no actress. I told you I always lie. I'm nothing, honey, and don't you ever forget it. (*Lighter.*) Although my mother was a Communist. The only person in my family ever to amount to anything.

CLAY: My mother was a Republican.

LULA: And your father voted for the man rather than the party.

CLAY: Right!

LULA: Yea for him. Yea, yea for him.

CLAY: Yea!

LULA: And yea for America where he is free to vote for the mediocrity of his choice! Yea!

CLAY: Yea!

LULA: And yea for both your parents who even though they differ about so crucial a matter as the body politic still forged a union of love and sacrifice that was destined to flower at the birth of the noble Clay . . . what's your middle name?

CLAY: Clay.

LULA: A union of love and sacrifice that was destined to flower at the birth of the noble Clay Clay Williams. Yea! And most of all yea yea for you, Clay Clay. The Black Baudelaire! Yes! (*And with knifelike cynicism.*) My Christ. My Christ.

CLAY: Thank you, ma'am.

LULA: May the people accept you as a ghost of the future. And love you, that you might not kill them when you can.

CLAY: What?

LULA: You're a murderer, Clay, and you know it. (*Her voice darkening with significance.*) You know god-damn well what I mean.

CLAY: I do?

LULA: So we'll pretend the air is light and full of perfume.

CLAY (*sniffing at her blouse*): It is.

LULA: And we'll pretend the people cannot see you. That is, the citizens. And that you are free of your own history. And I am free of my history. We'll pretend that we are both anonymous beauties smashing along through the city's entrails. (*She yells as loud as she can.*) GROOVE!

SCENE 2

(*Scene is the same as before, though now there are other seats visible in the car. And throughout the scene other people get on the subway. There are maybe one or two seated in the car as the scene opens, though neither* CLAY *or* LULA *notices them.* CLAY'S *tie is open.* LULA *is hugging his arm.*)

CLAY: The party!

LULA: I know it'll be something good. You can come in with me, looking casual and significant. I'll be strange, haughty, and silent, and walk with long slow strides.

CLAY: Right.

LULA: When you get drunk, pat me once, very lovingly on the flanks, and I'll look at you cryptically, licking my lips.

CLAY: It sounds like something we can do.

LULA: You'll go around talking to young men about your mind, and to old men about your plans. If you meet a very close friend who is also with someone like me, we can stand together, sipping our drinks and exchanging codes of lust. The atmosphere will be slithering in love and half-love and very open moral decision.

CLAY: Great. Great.

LULA: And everyone will pretend they don't know your name, and then . . . (*She pauses heavily.*) later, when they have to, they'll claim a friendship that denies your sterling character.

CLAY (*kissing her neck and fingers*): And then what?

LULA: Then? Well, then we'll go down the street, late night, eating apples and winding very deliberately toward my house.

CLAY: Deliberately?

LULA: I mean, we'll look in all the shopwindows, and make fun of the queers. Maybe we'll meet a Jewish Buddhist and flatten his conceits over some very pretentious coffee.

CLAY: In honor of whose God?

LULA: Mine.

CLAY: Who is . . . ?

LULA: Me . . . and you?

CLAY: A corporate Godhead.

LULA: Exactly. Exactly. (*Notices one of the other people entering.*)

CLAY: Go on with the chronicle. Then what happens to us?

LULA (*a mild depression, but she still makes her description triumphant and increasingly direct*): To my house, of course.

CLAY: Of course.

LULA: And up the narrow steps of the tenement.

CLAY: You live in a tenement?

LULA: Wouldn't live anywhere else. Reminds me specifically of my novel form of insanity.

CLAY: Up the tenement stairs.

LULA: And with my apple-eating hand I push open the door and lead you, my tender big-eyed prey, into my . . . God, what can I call it . . . into my hovel.

CLAY: Then what happens?

LULA: After the dancing and games, after the long drinks and long walks, the real fun begins.

CLAY: Ah, the real fun. (*Embarrassed, in spite of himself.*) Which is . . . ?

LULA (*laughs at him*): Real fun in the dark house. Hah! Real fun in the dark house, high up above the street and the ignorant cowboys. I lead you in, holding your wet hand gently in my hand . . .

CLAY: Which is not wet?

LULA: Which is dry as ashes.

CLAY: And cold?

LULA: Don't think you'll get out of your responsibility that way. It's not cold at all. You Fascist! Into my dark living room. Where we'll sit and talk endlessly, endlessly.

CLAY: About what?

LULA: About what? About your manhood, what do you think? What do you think we've been talking about all this time?

CLAY: Well, I didn't know it was that. That's for sure. Every other thing in the world but that. (*Notices another person entering, looks quickly, almost involuntarily up and down the car, seeing the other people in the car.*) Hey, I didn't even notice when those people got on.

LULA: Yeah, I know.

CLAY: Man, this subway is slow.

LULA: Yeah, I know.

CLAY: Well, go on. We were talking about my manhood.

LULA: We still are. All the time.

CLAY: We were in your living room.

LULA: My dark living room. Talking endlessly.

CLAY: About my manhood.

LULA: I'll make you a map of it. Just as soon as we get to my house.

CLAY: Well, that's great.

LULA: One of the things we do while we talk. And screw.

CLAY (*trying to make his smile broader and less shaky*): We finally got there.

LULA: And you'll call my rooms black as a grave. You'll say, "This place is like Juliet's tomb."

CLAY (*laughs*): I might.

LULA: I know. You've probably said it before.

CLAY: And is that all? The whole grand tour?

LULA: Not all. You'll say to me very close to my face, many, many times, you'll say, even whisper, that you love me.

CLAY: Maybe I will.

LULA: And you'll be lying.

CLAY: I wouldn't lie about something like that.

LULA: Hah. It's the only kind of thing you will lie about. Especially if you think it'll keep me alive.

CLAY: Keep you alive? I don't understand.

LULA (*bursting out laughing, but too shrilly*): Don't understand? Well, don't look at me. It's the path I take, that's all. Where both feet take me when I set them down. One in front of the other.

CLAY: Morbid. Morbid. You sure you're not an actress? All that self-aggrandizement.

LULA: Well, I told you I wasn't an actress . . . but I also told you I lie all the time. Draw your own conclusions.

CLAY: Morbid. Morbid. You sure you're not an actress. All scribed? There's no more?

LULA: I've told you all I know. Or almost all.

CLAY: There's no funny parts?

LULA: I thought it was all funny.

CLAY: But you mean peculiar, not ha-ha.

LULA: You don't know what I mean.

CLAY: Well, tell me the almost part then. You said almost all. What else? I want the whole story.

LULA (*searching aimlessly through her bag. She begins to talk breathlessly, with a light and silly tone*): All stories are whole stories. All of 'em. Our whole story . . . nothing but change. How could things go on like that forever? Huh? (*Slaps him on the shoulder, begins finding things in her bag, taking them out and throwing them over her shoulder into the aisle.*) Except I do go on as I do. Apples and long walks with deathless intelligent lovers. But you mix it up. Look out the window, all the time. Turning pages. Change change change. Till, shit, I don't know you. Wouldn't, for that matter. You're too serious. I bet you're even too serious to be psychoanalyzed. Like all those Jewish poets from Yonkers, who leave their mothers looking for other mothers, or others' mothers, on whose baggy tits they lay their fumbling heads. Their poems are always funny, and all about sex.

CLAY: They sound great. Like movies.

LULA: But you change. (*Blankly.*) And things work on you till you hate them.

(*More people come into the train. They come closer to the couple, some of them not sitting, but swinging drearily on the straps, staring at the two with uncertain interest.*)

CLAY: Wow. All these people, so suddenly. They must all come from the same place.

LULA: Right. That they do.

CLAY: Oh? You know about them too?

LULA: Oh yeah. About them more than I know about you. Do they frighten you?

CLAY: Frighten me? Why should they frighten me?

LULA: 'Cause you're an escaped nigger.

CLAY: Yeah?

LULA: 'Cause you crawled through the wire and made tracks to my side.

CLAY: Wire?

LULA: Don't they have wire around plantations?

CLAY: You must be Jewish. All you can think about is wire. Plantations didn't have any wire. Plantations were big open whitewashed places like heaven, and everybody on 'em was grooved to be there. Just strummin' and hummin' all day.

LULA: Yes, yes.

CLAY: And that's how the blues was born.

LULA: Yes, yes. And that's how the blues was born. (*Begins to make up a song that becomes quickly hysterical. As she sings she rises from her seat, still throwing things out of her bag into the aisle, beginning a rhythmical shudder and twistlike wiggle, which she continues up and down the aisle, bumping into many of the standing people and tripping over the feet of those sitting. Each time she runs into a person she lets out a very vicious piece of profanity, wiggling and stepping all the time.*) And that's how the blues was born. Yes. Yes. Son of a bitch, get out of the way. Yes.

Quack. Yes. Yes. And that's how the blues was born. Ten little niggers sitting on a limb, but none of them ever looked like him. (*Points to CLAY, returns toward the seat, with her hands extended for him to rise and dance with her.*) And that's how the blues was born. Yes. Come on, Clay. Let's do the nasty. Rub bellies. Rub bellies.

CLAY (*waves his hands to refuse. He is embarrassed, but determined to get a kick out of the proceedings*): Hey, what was in those apples? Mirror, mirror on the wall, who's the fairest one of all? Snow White, baby, and don't you forget it.

LULA (*grabbing for his hands, which he draws away*): Come on, Clay. Let's rub bellies on the train. The nasty. The nasty. Do the gritty grind, like your ol' rag-head mammy. Grind till you lose your mind. Shake it, shake it, shake it, shake it! OOOOweeee! Come on, Clay. Let's do the choo-choo train shuffle, the navel scratcher.

CLAY: Hey, you coming on like the lady who smoked up her grass skirt.

LULA (*becoming annoyed that he will not dance, and becoming more animated as if to embarrass him still further*): Come on, Clay . . . let's do the thing. Uhh! Uhh! Clay! Clay! You middle-class black bastard. Forget your social-working mother for a few seconds and let's knock stomachs. Clay, you liver-lipped white man. You would-be Christian. You ain't no nigger, you're just a dirty white man. Get up, Clay. Dance with me, Clay.

CLAY: Lula! Sit down, now. Be cool.

LULA (*mocking him, in wild dance*): Be cool. Be cool. That's all you know . . . shaking that wildroot cream-oil on your knotty head, jackets buttoning up to your chin, so full of white man's words. Christ. God. Get up and scream at these people. Like scream meaningless shit in these hopeless faces. (*She screams at people in train, still dancing.*) Red trains cough Jewish underwear for keeps! Expanding smells of silence. Gravy snot whistling like sea birds. Clay, Clay, you got to break out. Don't sit there dying the way they want you to die. Get up.

CLAY: Oh, sit the fuck down. (*He moves to restrain her.*) Sit down, goddamn it.

LULA (*twisting out of his reach*): Screw yourself, Uncle Tom. Thomas Woolly-head. (*Begins to dance a kind of jig, mocking CLAY with loud forced humor*) There is Uncle Tom . . . I mean, Uncle Thomas Woolly-Head. With old white matted mane. He hobbles on his wooden cane. Old Tom. Old Tom. Let the white man hump his ol' mama and he jes' shuffle off in the woods and hide his gentle gray head. Ol' Thomas Woolly-Head.

(*Some of the other riders are laughing now. A drunk gets*

up and joins LULA *in her dance, singing, as best he can, her "song."* CLAY *gets up out of his seat and visibly scans the faces of the other riders.)*

CLAY: Lula! Lula! *(She is dancing and turning, still shouting as loud as she can. The drunk too is shouting, and waving his hands wildly.)* Lula . . . you dumb bitch. Why don't you stop it? *(He rushes half stumbling from his seat, and grabs one of her flailing arms.)*

LULA: Let me go! You black son of a bitch. *(She struggles against him.)* Let me go! Help!

*(*CLAY *is dragging her toward her seat, and the drunk seeks to interfere. He grabs* CLAY *around the shoulders and begins wrestling with him.* CLAY *clubs the drunk to the floor without releasing* LULA, *who is still screaming.* CLAY *finally gets her to the seat and throws her into it.)*

CLAY: Now you shut the hell up. *(Grabbing her shoulders.)* Just shut up. You don't know what you're talking about. You don't know anything. So just keep your stupid mouth closed.

LULA: You're afraid of white people. And your father was. Uncle Tom Big Lip!

CLAY *(slaps her as hard as he can, across the mouth.* LULA's *head bangs against the back of the seat. When she raises it again,* CLAY *slaps her again)*: Now shut up and let me talk. *(He turns toward the other riders, some of whom are sitting on the edge of their seats. The drunk is on one knee, rubbing his head, and singing softly the same song. He shuts up too when he sees* CLAY *watching him. The others go back to newspapers or stare out the window)* Shit, you don't have any sense, Lula, nor feelings either. I could murder you now. Such a tiny ugly throat. I could squeeze it flat, and watch you turn blue, on a humble. For dull kicks. And all these weak-faced ofays squatting around here, staring over their papers at me. Murder them too. Even if they expected it. That man there . . . *(Points to well-dressed man.)* I could rip that *Times* right out of his hand, as skinny and middle-classed as I am, I could rip that paper out of his hand and just as easily rip out his throat. It takes no great effort. For what? To kill you soft idiots? You don't understand anything but luxury.

LULA: You fool!

CLAY *(pushing her against the seat)*: I'm not telling you again, Tallulah Bankhead! Luxury. In your face and your fingers. You telling me what I ought to do. *(Sudden scream frightening the whole coach.)* Well, don't! Don't you tell me anything! If I'm a middle-class fake white man . . . let me be. And let me be in the way I want. *(Through his teeth.)* I'll rip your lousy breasts off! Let me be who I feel like being. Uncle Tom. Thomas. Whoever. It's none of your business. You don't know anything except what's there for you to see. An act. Lies. Device. Not the pure heart, the pumping black heart. You don't ever know that. And I sit here, in this buttoned-up suit, to keep myself from cutting all your throats. I mean wantonly. You great liberated whore! You fuck some black man and right away you're an expert on black people. What a lotta shit that is. The only thing you know is that you come if he bangs you hard enough. And that's all. The belly rub? You wanted me to do the belly rub? Shit, you don't even know how. You don't know that. That ol' dipty-dip shit you do, rolling your ass like an elephant. That's not my kind of belly rub. Belly rub is not Queens. Belly rub is dark places, with big hats and overcoats held up with one arm. Belly rub hates you. Old bald-headed four-eyed ofays popping their fingers . . . and don't know yet what they're doing. They say, "I love Bessie Smith." And don't even understand that Bessie Smith is saying, "Kiss my ass, kiss my black unruly ass." Before love, suffering, desire, anything you can explain, she's saying, and very plainly, "Kiss my black ass." And if you don't know that, it's you that's doing the kissing.

Charlie Parker? Charlie Parker. All the hip white boys scream for Bird. And Bird saying, "Up your ass, feeble-minded ofay! Up your ass." And they sit there talking about the tortured genius of Charlie Parker. Bird would've played not a note of music if he just walked up to East Sixty-seventh Street and killed the first ten white people he saw. Not a note! And I'm the great would-be poet. Yes. That's right! Poet. Some kind of bastard literature . . . all it needs is a simple knife thrust. Just let me bleed you, you loud whore, and one poem vanished. A whole people of neurotics, struggling to keep from being sane. And the only thing that would cure the neurosis would be your murder. Simple as that. I mean if I murdered you, then other white people would begin to understand me. You understand? No. I guess not. If Bessie Smith had killed some white people she wouldn't have needed that music. She could have talked very straight and plain about the world. No metaphors. No grunts. No wiggles in the dark of her soul. Just straight two and two are four. Money. Power. Luxury. Like that. All of them. Crazy niggers turning their backs on sanity. When all it needs is that simple act. Murder. Just murder! Would make us all sane. *(Suddenly weary.)* Ahhh. Shit. But who needs it? I'd rather be a fool. Insane. Safe with my words, and no deaths, and clean, hard thoughts, urging me to new conquests. My people's madness. Hah! That's a laugh. My people. They don't need me to claim them. They got legs and arms of their own. Personal insanities. Mirrors. They don't need all those words. They don't need any defense. But listen, though, one more thing. And you tell this to your father, who's probably the kind of man who needs to know at once. So he can plan ahead. Tell him not to preach so much rationalism and cold logic to these niggers. Let them alone. Let them sing curses at you in code and see your filth as simple lack of style. Don't make the mistake, through some irresponsible surge of Christian charity, of talking too much about the advantages of Western rationalism, or the great intellectual legacy of the white man, or maybe they'll begin to listen. And then, maybe one day, you'll find they actually do understand exactly what you are talking about, all these fantasy people. All these blues people. And on that day, as sure as shit, when you really believe you can "accept" them into your fold, as half-white trusties late of the subject peoples. With no more blues, except the very old ones, and not a watermelon in sight, the great missionary heart will have triumphed, and all of those ex-coons will be stand-up Western men, with eyes for clean hard useful lives, sober, pious and sane, and they'll murder you. They'll murder you, and have very rational explanations. Very much like your own. They'll cut your throats, and drag you out to the edge of your cities so the flesh can fall away from your bones, in sanitary isolation.

LULA (*her voice takes on a different, more businesslike quality*): I've heard enough.

CLAY (*reaching for his books*): I bet you have. I guess I better collect my stuff and get off this train. Looks like we won't be acting out that little pageant you outlined before.

LULA: No. We won't. You're right about that, at least.

(*She turns to look quickly around the rest of the car.*) All right! (*The others respond.*)

CLAY (*bending across the girl to retrieve his belongings*): Sorry, baby, I don't think we could make it.

(*As he is bending over her, the girl brings up a small knife and plunges it into* CLAY's *chest. Twice. He slumps across her knees, his mouth working stupidly.*)

LULA: Sorry is right. (*Turning to the others in the car who have already gotten up from their seats.*) Sorry is the rightest thing you've said. Get this man off me! Hurry, now! (*The others come and drag* CLAY's *body down the aisle.*) Open the door and throw his body out. (*They throw him off.*) And all of you get off at the next stop.

(LULA *busies herself straightening her things. Getting everything in order. She takes out a notebook and makes a quick scribbling note. Drops it in her bag. The train apparently stops and all the others get off, leaving her alone in the coach. Very soon a young Negro of about twenty comes into the coach, with a couple of books under his arms. He sits a few seats in back of* LULA. *When he is seated she turns and gives him a long slow look. He looks up from his book and drops the book on his lap. Then an old Negro conductor comes into the car, doing a sort of restrained soft shoe, and half mumbling the words of some song. He looks at the young man, briefly, with a quick greeting.*)

CONDUCTOR: Hey, brother!

YOUNG MAN: Hey.

(*The conductor continues down the aisle with his little dance and the mumbled song.* LULA *turns to stare at him and follows his movements down the aisle. The conductor tips his hat when he reaches her seat, and continues out the car.*)

CURTAIN

Figure 1. Lula (Jennifer West) munches her apple and provocatively crosses her legs while Clay (Robert Hooks) looks at his magazine in the opening moments of the Cherry Lane Theater production of *Dutchman*, directed by Edward Parone, New York, 1964. (Photograph: Alix Jeffry. Billy Rose Theatre Collection. The New York Public Library for the Performing Arts. Astor, Lenox, and Tilden Foundations.)

Staging of *Dutchman*

REVIEW OF THE CHERRY LANE THEATER PRODUCTION, 1964, BY HAROLD CLURMAN

It is altogether likely that the folk who go down to the Cherry Lane Theatre to see the three one-act plays now being given there are witnesses to a signal event: the emergence of an outstanding dramatist—LeRoi Jones.

His is a turbulent talent. While turbulence is not always a sign of power or of valuable meaning, I have a hunch that Leroi Jones's fire will burn ever higher and clearer if our theatre can furnish an adequate vessel to harbor his flame. We need it.

He is very angry. Anger alone may merely make a loud noise, confuse, sputter and die. For anger to burn to useful effect, it must be guided by an idea. With the "angry young men" of England one was not always certain of the source of dissatisfaction nor of its goal. With Leroi Jones it is easy to say that the plight of the Negro ignited the initial rage—justification enough—and that the rage will not be appeased until there is no more black and white, no more color except as differences in hue and accent are part of the world's splendid spectacle. But there is more to his ferocity than a protest against the horrors of racism.

Dutchman, the first of Jones's plays to reach the professional stage, is a stylized account of a subway episode. A white girl picks up a young Negro who at first is rather embarrassed and later piqued by her advances. There is a perversity in her approach which finally provokes him to a hymn of hate. With lyrical obscenity he declares that murder is in his and every Negro's heart and were it to reach the point of action there would be less "singin' of the blues," less of that delightful folk music and hot jazz which beguile the white man's fancy, more calm in the Negro soul. Meanwhile, it is the black man who is murdered.

What we must not overloook in seeing the play is that, while this explosion of fury is its rhetorical and emotional climax, the crux of its significance resides in the depiction of the white girl whose relevance to the play's situation does not lie in her whiteness but in her representative value as a token of our civilization. She is our neurosis. Not a neurosis in regard to the Negro, but the absolute neurosis of American society.

She is "hep": she has heard about everything, understands and feels nothing. She twitches, jangles, jitters with a thin but inexhaustible energy, propelled by the vibrations from millions of ads, television quiz programs, newspaper columns, intellectual jargon culled from countless digests, panel discussions, illustrated summaries, smatterings of gossip on every conceivable subject (respectable and illicit), epithets, wisecracks, formulas, slogans, cynicisms, cures and solutions. She is the most "informed" person in the world and the most ignorant. (The information feeds the ignorance.) She is the bubbling, boiling garbage cauldron newly produced by our progress. She is a calculating machine gone berserk; she is the real killer. What she destroys is not men of a certain race but mankind. She is the compendium in little of the universal mess.

If *Dutchman* (a title I don't understand) has a fault, it is its completeness. Its ending is somewhat too pat, too pointed in its symbolism. If one has caught the drift of the play's meaning before its final moment, the ending is supererogatory; if one has failed to do so, it is probably useless.

Dutchman is very well played by Jennifer West and Robert Hooks.

REVIEW OF THE CHERRY LANE THEATER PRODUCTION, 1964, BY HOWARD TAUBMAN

Everything about LeRoi Jones's "Dutchman" is designed to shock—its basic idea, its language and its murderous rage.

This half-hour-long piece, the last of three one-act plays being performed at the Cherry Lane Theater, is an explosion of hatred rather than a play. It puts into the mouth of its principal Negro character a scathing denunciation of all the white man's good works, pretensions and condescensions.

If this is the way the Negroes really feel about the

white world around them, there's more rancor buried in the breasts of colored conformists than anyone can imagine. If this is the way even one Negro feels, there is ample cause for guilt as well as alarm, and for a hastening of change.

As an extended metaphor of bitterness and fury, "Dutchman" is transparently simple in structure. Clay, a Negro who wears a three-button suit and is reserved and well-spoken, is accosted by a white female on a train. Lula is a liar, a slut, essentially an agent provocateur of a Caucasian society.

After she disarms Clay with her wild outbursts and sinuous attentions, she turns on him in challenging contempt. His answer is to drop the mask of conformity and to spew out all the anger that has built up in him and his fellow Negroes. When this outburst of violent resentment has finished and Clay has left the train, Lula notices that another Negro has boarded and she sets her slinky charms for him.

Mr. Jones writes with a kind of sustained frenzy. His little work is a mélange of sardonic images and undisciplined filth. The impact of his ferocity would be stronger if he did not work so hard and persistently to be shocking.

Jennifer West in a straight, tight-fitting dress striped like a prisoner's suit plays Lula with a rousing mixture of sultriness and insolence. Robert Hooks as Clay is impressive as he shifts from patient tolerance to savage wrath. Edward Parone's staging is mordant, and intense.

HAROLD PINTER

1930–

Pinter, whose drama has come to be internationally known by critics as the "comedy of menace," is the son of a Portuguese-Jewish tailor who emigrated to London by way of eastern Europe early in the twentieth century. Pinter was born and raised in London's East End, where he attended the local grammar school and during his teens began writing poems, short stories, and dialogues for little magazines, as well as taking part in school theatrical productions. During the late 1940s, he spent a couple of terms at the Royal Academy of Dramatic Art, but he was put off by the sophistication of his fellow students and thus withdrew to start a professional career in acting, first in radio work during 1950, then with a professional company touring Ireland during 1951 and 1952. On returning to England, he continued acting in London and the provinces, under the pseudonym of David Baron, until 1957, when he wrote his first play, *The Room,* a one-act piece he did at the suggestion of a friend who was then studying drama at Bristol University. This eerie little play, which depicts an old couple suddenly beset by menacing visits and messages, clearly anticipated the inexplicably threatening situations that Pinter has dramatized repeatedly in his subsequent plays. During 1957, Pinter also wrote his first full-length work for the stage, *The Birthday Party,* and this time the menacing situation took the form of humiliating physical and verbal games inflicted on a retired pianist by two sinister men who turn up at his room on the afternoon of his birthday, then subject him to their birthday party games that evening, and finally carry him off with them the next morning.

When *The Birthday Party* opened in London in 1958, most critics found it "opaque" and charged that the characters spoke "in non-sequiturs, half-gibberish, and lunatic ravings." Although it closed after one week, *The Birthday Party* was revived six years later by the Royal Shakespeare Company in a highly successful production directed by Pinter himself. By then, Pinter had already achieved his first popular success with *The Caretaker* (1960), which dramatizes the comic but convulsive quarrels and competition that develop in a run-down house among the owner, his brain-damaged brother, and a devious tramp whom the brother has befriended. Several of his shorter plays, including *The Room, The Dumb Waiter* (1957), and *A Slight Ache* (1961) had also been successfully staged, while others, such as *A Night Out* (1960), *Night School* (1960), *The Collection* (1961), and *The Lover* (1963) had been filmed for television. By the mid-1960s, Pinter's screenplays for *The Servant* (1962) and *The Pumpkin Eater* (1964) had received major awards, and in 1965, *The Homecoming* opened in London, again in a highly successful production by the Royal Shakespeare Company. Given these astonishing dramatic accomplishments, it is hardly surprising that in 1966, Pinter was awarded the C.B.E. (Commander of the Order of the British Empire) by the Queen, All of Pinter's major plays have now received major productions first in London, then in New York, and his work is now no longer regarded as being quite so baffling and frustrating as it seemed some thirty years ago.

Years of discerning criticism about other dramatists of the absurd, such as Beckett, Genet, and Ionesco, have helped readers and playgoers to recognize Pinter's work as part of a widespread movement in contemporary drama away from clearly motivated characters and plots, as well as from entirely logical dialogue and events, to a theater in which the actions and utterances of characters, however preposterous or alarming, are interesting, even fascinating, because they can and do take place on stage. Pinter himself has also talked openly and helpfully about this aspect of his plays. For the audiences who came to the Royal Court Theater in 1960 to see *The Room* and *The Dumb Waiter,* he offered this brief statement revealing his approach to characterization:

> A character on the stage who can present no convincing argument or information as to his past experience, his present behaviour or his aspirations, nor give a comprehensive analysis of his motives is as legitimate and as worthy of attention as one who, alarmingly, can do all these things.

Pinter's view of character and motive also accounts for his special view of dialogue, which he also announced in his program notes for the Royal Court Theater:

> The more acute the experience, the less articulate its expression.

Given this concept of inarticulateness in the theater, Pinter was naturally led to his famous statement about "the two silences," which he formulated in a speech to a student drama festival in Bristol, in 1962:

> There are two silences. One when no word is spoken. The other when perhaps a torrent of language is employed. This speech is speaking of a language locked beneath it. That is its continual reference. The speech we hear is an indication of that we don't hear. It is a necessary avoidance, a violent, shy, anguished, or mocking smoke-screen which keeps the other in its place. When true silence falls we are still left with echo but are nearer nakedness. One way of looking at speech is to say it is a constant stratagem to cover nakedness.

Both these kinds of silence are, of course, true to general human experience, as Chekhov had clearly recognized in the dialogue of his plays seventy years earlier, but only in drama of the absurd, particularly in the plays of Pinter, have they become a pervasive theatrical element.

Both these silences occur throughout *The Homecoming,* and thus a recognition of them will usually help to make sense of what is happening in the play and between the characters. For example, when Lenny tells Ruth, whom he has just met, about "a certain lady" and "a certain proposal," both of which he rejected, he is not only telling a long anecdote, but also letting her know of his involvement in the world of pimps and prostitutes, and thus of his capacity for violence. His "torrent of language" is not only a reference to something else about himself, but also a tacit assertion of his having recognized her own lascivious disposition, even before she has said or done anything to reveal it. And when Ruth responds by saying quietly, "Have a sip. Go on. Have a sip from my glass. Sit on my lap. Take a long cool sip. Put your head back and open your mouth," she is not really talking about a glass of water, but returning his implicit sexual proposal. The other kind of silence, "when no word is spoken," may be seen near the beginning of the play, when Teddy returns home after being away for six years and first encounters his younger brother Lenny:

TEDDY: Hullo, Lenny.
LENNY: Hullo, Teddy.
    (Pause.)

The brevity of their greeting followed by that pause, that silence, quickly reveals their indifference, even their hostility, to one another.

Pinter's plays are distinguished not only by his use of language and silence, but also by his fascination with the dramatic situation of "two people sitting in a room." His early works, particularly *The Room, The Birthday Party,* and *The Caretaker,* are all set in a single room and explore the tensions that explode in that closed place and the menace that can intrude without warning. In commenting on this basic situation, Pinter has clearly related its application to ordinary human experience:

> A door can open at any moment and someone will come in. We'd love to know who it is, we'd love to know exactly what he has on his mind and why he comes in, but how often do we know what someone has on his mind or who this somebody is, and what goes to make him and make him what he is, and what his relationship is to others?

And throughout *The Homecoming,* he dramatizes the unanswerability of such questions. Why, for example, do Teddy and his wife, Ruth, suddenly come home to his father's house? Why does his father, Max, not know about his marriage to Ruth, not to mention their children? How does Max really feel about the son he insults and then offers to "cuddle and kiss"? And how does he feel about Ruth whom he labels "a stinking pox-ridden slut" when he first meets her and later praises as a "charming woman," "an intelligent and sympathetic woman"? Why does Teddy stand by silently when his brother Joey proceeds to make love to Ruth on the couch? Indeed, as the play proceeds, the questions about motivation and human relationships become even more troublesome. Why, for example, does Ruth so calmly and in such a businesslike way proceed to negotiate for a position of being resident prostitute to her husband's family? Why does Teddy offer no resistance at all, no plea for her to change her mind? These questions, Pinter would say, cannot really be answered. What is important and dramatically unforgettable in *The Homecoming* is that the events, bizarre as they may seem, do happen. And, in happening, they reveal a disturbing aspect of human experience, or at least a disturbing possibility in human experience.

When *The Homecoming* opened in London and later in New York, critics and audiences alike struggled to find explanations for the behavior they witnessed. Reviews of the New York production, reprinted following the text, reflect two contrasting views of the play: one believes that Pinter is "simply cheating us," the other argues that if we are willing to follow Pinter's vision, "we will have overcome our deadly habit of wanting what we expect." Two of the play's unexpected situations are pictured in photographs of the New York production, one showing Ruth about to offer Lenny a sip of water (see Figure 1), the other of Max insulting Ruth during their first encounter (see Figure 2). Debate about these and the other unexpected situations in the play raged for several months after it came to New York, and the *New York Times* went so far as to print a symposium of opinions under the title "What does *The Homecoming* Mean?" (February 5, 1967). Pinter's reply to that question can be found, perhaps, in the words of Ruth, when she breaks into a pseudophilosophical argument that Lenny and Teddy are having about a table: "My lips move. Why don't you restrict . . . your observations to that? Perhaps the fact that they move is more significant . . . than the words which come through them. You must bear that . . . possibility . . . in mind."

THE HOMECOMING

BY HAROLD PINTER

CHARACTERS

MAX, *a man of seventy*
LENNY, *a man in his early thirties*
SAM, *a man of sixty-three*
JOEY, *a man in his middle twenties*
TEDDY, *a man in his middle thirties*
RUTH, *a woman in her early thirties*

SCENE

Summer. An old house in North London.
A large room, extending the width of the stage.

The back wall, which contained the door, has been removed. A square arch shape remains. Beyond it, the hall. In the hall a staircase ascending upper left, well in view. The front door upper right. A coatstand, hooks, etc.

In the room, a window, right. Odd tables, chairs. Two large armchairs. A large sofa, left. Against right wall a large sideboard, the upper half of which contains a mirror. Upper left, a radiogram.

ACT 1

(Evening.

LENNY *is sitting on the sofa with a newspaper, a pencil in his hand. He wears a dark suit. He makes occasional marks on the back page.*

MAX *comes in, from the direction of the kitchen. He goes to sideboard, opens top drawer, rummages in it, closes it.*

He wears an old cardigan and a cap, and carries a stick.

He walks downstage, stands, looks about the room.)

MAX: What have you done with the scissors?

(Pause.)

I said I'm looking for the scissors. What have you done with them?

(Pause.)

Did you hear me? I want to cut something out of the paper.

LENNY: I'm reading the paper.

MAX: Not that paper. I haven't read that paper. I'm talking about last Sunday's paper. I was just having a look at it in the kitchen.

(Pause.)

Do you hear what I'm saying? I'm talking to you! Where's the scissors?

LENNY *(looking up, quietly.)*: Why don't you shut up, you daft prat?

*(*MAX *lifts his stick and points it at him.)*

MAX: Don't you talk to me like that. I'm warning you.

(He sits in large armchair.)

There's an advertisement in the paper about flannel vests. Cut price. Navy surplus. I could do with a few of them.

(Pause.)

I think I'll have a fag. Give me a fag.

(Pause.)

I just asked you to give me a cigarette.

(Pause.)

Look what I'm lumbered with.

(He takes a crumpled cigarette from his pocket.)

I'm getting old, my word of honour.

(He lights it.)

You think I wasn't a tearaway? I could have taken care of you, twice over. I'm still strong. You ask your Uncle Sam what I was. But at the same time I always had a kind heart. Always.

(Pause.)

I used to knock about with a man called Mac-Gregor. I called him Mac. You remember Mac? Eh?

(Pause.)

Huhh! We were two of the worst hated men in the West End of London. I tell you, I still got the scars. We'd walk into a place, the whole room'd stand up, they'd make way to let us pass. You never heard such silence. Mind you, he was a big man, he was over six foot tall. His family were all MacGregors, they came all the way from Aberdeen, but he was the only one they called Mac.

(Pause.)

520

He was very fond of your mother, Mac was. Very fond. He always had a good word for her.

(Pause.)

Mind you, she wasn't such a bad woman. Even though it made me sick just to look at her rotten stinking face, she wasn't such a bad bitch. I gave her the best bleeding years of my life, anyway.

LENNY: Plug it, will you, you stupid sod, I'm trying to read the paper.

MAX: Listen! I'll chop your spine off, you talk to me like that! You understand? Talking to your lousy filthy father like that!

LENNY: You know what, you're getting demented.

(Pause.)

What do you think of Second Wind for the three-thirty?

MAX: Where?

LENNY: Sandown Park.

MAX: Don't stand a chance.

LENNY: Sure he does.

MAX: Not a chance.

LENNY: He's the winner.

(LENNY ticks the paper.)

MAX: He talks to me about horses.

(Pause.)

I used to live on the course. One of the loves of my life. Epsom? I knew it like the back of my hand. I was one of the best-known faces down at the paddock. What a marvellous open-air life.

(Pause.)

He talks to me about horses. You only read their names in the papers. But I've stroked their manes, I've held them, I've calmed them down before a big race. I was the one they used to call for. Max, they'd say, there's a horse here, he's highly strung, you're the only man on the course who can calm him. It was true. I had a . . . I had an instinctive understanding of animals. I should have been a trainer. Many times I was offered the job—you know, a proper post, by the Duke of . . . I forget his name . . . one of the Dukes. But I had family obligations, my family needed me at home.

(Pause.)

The times I've watched those animals thundering past the post. What an experience. Mind you, I didn't lose, I made a few bob out of it, and you know why? Because I always had the smell of a good horse. I could smell him. And not only the colts but the fillies. Because the fillies are more highly strung than the colts, they're more unreliable, did you know that? No, what do you know? Nothing. But I was always able to tell a good filly by one particular trick. I'd look her in the eye. You see? I'd stand in front of her and look her straight in the eye, it was a kind of hypnotism, and by the look deep down in her eye I could tell whether she was a stayer or not. It was a gift. I had a gift.

(Pause.)

And he talks to me about horses.

LENNY: Dad, do you mind if I change the subject?

(Pause.)

I want to ask you something. That dinner we had before, what was the name of it? What do you call it?

(Pause.)

Why don't you buy a dog? You're a dog cook. Honest. You think you're cooking for a lot of dogs.

MAX: If you don't like it get out.

LENNY: I am going out. I'm going out to buy myself a proper dinner.

MAX: Well, get out! What are you waiting for?

(LENNY looks at him.)

LENNY: What did you say?

MAX: I said shove off out of it, that's what I said.

LENNY: You'll go before me, Dad, if you talk to me in that tone of voice.

MAX: Will I, you bitch?

(MAX grips his stick.)

LENNY: Oh, Daddy, you're not going to use your stick on me, are you? Eh? Don't use your stick on me, Daddy. No, please. It wasn't my fault, it was one of the others. I haven't done anything wrong, Dad, honest. Don't clout me with that stick, Dad.

(Silence.
MAX sits hunched. LENNY reads the paper.
SAM comes in the front door. He wears a chauffeur's uniform. He hangs his hat on a hook in the hall and comes into the room. He goes to a chair, sits in it and sighs.)

Hullo, Uncle Sam.

SAM: Hullo.

LENNY: How are you, Uncle!

SAM: Not bad. A bit tired.

LENNY: Tired? I bet you're tired. Where you been?

SAM: I've been to London Airport.

LENNY: All the way up to London Airport? What, right up the M4?

SAM: Yes, all the way up there.

LENNY: Tch, tch, tch. Well, I think you're entitled to be tired, Uncle.

SAM: Well, it's the drivers.

LENNY: I know. That's what I'm talking about. I'm talking about the drivers.

SAM: Knocks you out.

(Pause.)

MAX: I'm here, too, you know.

(SAM looks at him.)

I said I'm here, too. I'm sitting here.

SAM: I know you're here.

(Pause.)

SAM: I took a Yankee out there today . . . to the Airport.

LENNY: Oh, a Yankee, was it?

SAM: Yes, I been with him all day. Picked him up at the Savoy at half past twelve, took him to the Caprice for his lunch. After lunch I picked him up again, took him down to a house in Eaton Square—he had to pay a visit to a friend there—and then round about tea-time I took him right the way out to the Airport.

LENNY: Had to catch a plane there, did he?

SAM: Yes. Look what he gave me. He gave me a box of cigars.

(SAM takes a box of cigars from his pocket.)

MAX: Come here. Let's have a look at them.

(SAM shows MAX the cigars. MAX takes one from the box, pinches it and sniffs it.)

It's a fair cigar.

SAM: Want to try one?

(MAX and SAM light cigars.)

You know what he said to me? He told me I was the best chauffeur he'd ever had. The best one.

MAX: From what point of view?

SAM: Eh?

MAX: From what point of view?

LENNY: From the point of view of his driving, Dad, and his general sense of courtesy, I should say.

MAX: Thought you were a good driver, did he, Sam? Well, he gave you a first-class cigar.

SAM: Yes, he thought I was the best he'd ever had. They all say that, you know. They won't have anyone else, they only ask for me. They say I'm the best chauffeur in the firm.

LENNY: I bet the other drivers tend to get jealous, don't they, Uncle?

SAM: They do get jealous. They get very jealous.

MAX: Why?

(Pause.)

SAM: I just told you.

MAX: No, I just can't get it clear, Sam. Why do the other drivers get jealous?

SAM: Because (a) I'm the best driver, and because . . . (b) I don't take liberties.

(Pause.)

I don't press myself on people, you see. These big businessmen, men of affairs, they don't want the driver jawing all the time, they like to sit in the back, have a bit of peace and quiet. After all, they're sitting in a Humber Super Snipe, they can afford to relax. At the same time, though, this is what really makes me special . . . I do know how to pass the time of day when required.

(Pause.)

For instance, I told this man today I was in the second world war. Not the first. I told him I was too young for the first. But I told him I fought in the second.

(Pause.)

So did he, it turned out.

(LENNY stands, goes to the mirror and straightens his tie.)

LENNY: He was probably a colonel or something in the American Air Force.

SAM: Yes.

LENNY: Probably a navigator, or something like that, in a Flying Fortress. Now he's most likely a high executive in a worldwide group of aeronautical engineers.

SAM: Yes.

LENNY: Yes, I know the kind of man you're talking about.

(LENNY goes out, turning to his right.)

SAM: After all, I'm experienced. I was driving a dust cart at the age of nineteen. Then I was in long-distance haulage. I had ten years as a taxi-driver and I've had five as a private chauffeur.

MAX: It's funny you never got married, isn't it? A man with all your gifts.

(Pause.)

Isn't it? A man like you?

SAM: There's still time.

MAX: Is there?

(Pause.)

SAM: You'd be surprised.

MAX: What you been doing, banging away at your lady customers, have you?

SAM: Not me.

MAX: In the back of the Snipe? Been having a few crafty reefs in a layby, have you?

SAM: Not me.

MAX: On the back seat? What about the armrest, was it up or down?

SAM: I've never done that kind of thing in my car.

MAX: Above all that kind of thing, are you, Sam?

SAM: Too true.

MAX: Above having a good bang on the back seat, are you?

SAM: Yes, I leave that to others.

MAX: You leave it to others? What others? You paralysed prat!

SAM: I don't mess up my car! Or my . . . my boss's car! Like other people.

MAX: Other people? What other people?

(Pause.)

What other people?

(Pause.)

SAM: Other people.

(Pause.)

MAX: When you find the right girl, Sam, let your family know, don't forget, we'll give you a number one send-off, I promise you. You can bring her to live here, she can keep us all happy. We'd take it in turns to give her a walk round the park.

SAM: I wouldn't bring her here.

MAX: Sam, it's your decision. You're welcome to bring your bride here, to the place where you live, or on the other hand you can take a suite at the Dorchester. It's entirely up to you.

SAM: I haven't got a bride.

(SAM stands, goes to the sideboard, takes an apple from the bowl, bites into it.)

Getting a bit peckish.

(He looks out of the window.)

Never get a bride like you had, anyway. Nothing like your bride . . . going about these days. Like Jessie.

(Pause.)

After all, I escorted her once or twice, didn't I? Drove her round once or twice in my cab. She was a charming woman.

(Pause.)

All the same, she was your wife. But still . . . they were some of the most delightful evenings I've ever had. Used to just drive her about. It was my pleasure.

MAX *(softly, closing his eyes)*: Christ.

SAM: I used to pull up at a stall and buy her a cup of coffee. She was a very nice companion to be with.

(Silence.
JOEY *comes in the front door. He walks into the room,*

takes his jacket off, throws it on a chair and stands. Silence.)

JOEY: Feel a bit hungry.

SAM: Me, too.

MAX: Who do you think I am, your mother? Eh? Honest. They walk in here every time of the day and night like bloody animals. Go and find yourself a mother.

(LENNY walks into the room, stands.)

JOEY: I've been training down at the gym.

SAM: Yes, the boy's been working all day and training all night.

MAX: What do you want, you bitch? You spend all the day sitting on your arse at London Airport, buy yourself a jamroll. You expect me to sit here waiting to rush into the kitchen the moment you step in the door? You've been living sixty-three years, why don't you learn to cook?

SAM: I can cook.

MAX: Well, go and cook!

LENNY: What the boys want, Dad, is your own special brand of cooking, Dad. That's what the boys look forward to. The special understanding of food, you know, that you've got.

MAX: Stop calling me Dad. Just stop all that calling me Dad, do you understand?

LENNY: But I'm your son. You used to tuck me up in bed every night. He tucked you up, too, didn't he, Joey?

(Pause.)

He used to like tucking up his sons.

(LENNY turns and goes toward the front door.)

MAX: Lenny.

LENNY *(turning)*: What?

MAX: I'll give you a proper tuck up one of these nights, son. You mark my word.

(They look at each other.
LENNY *opens the front door and goes out. Silence.)*

JOEY: I've been training with Bobby Dodd.

(Pause.)

And I had a good go at the bag as well.

(Pause.)

I wasn't in bad trim.

MAX: Boxing's a gentleman's game.

(Pause.)

I'll tell you what you've got to do. What you've got to do is you've got to learn how to defend yourself, and you've got to learn how to attack.

That's your only trouble as a boxer. You don't know how to defend yourself, and you don't know how to attack.

(*Pause.*)

Once you've mastered those arts you can go straight to the top.

(*Pause.*)

JOEY: I've got a pretty good idea . . . of how to do that.

(JOEY *looks round for his jacket, picks it up, goes out of the room and up the stairs.*
Pause.)

MAX: Sam . . . why don't you go, too, eh? Why don't you just go upstairs? Leave me quiet. Leave me alone.

SAM: I want to make something clear about Jessie, Max. I want to. I do. When I took her out in the cab, round the town, I was taking care of her, for you. I was looking after her for you, when you were busy, wasn't I? I was showing her the West End.

(*Pause.*)

You wouldn't have trusted any of your other brothers. You wouldn't have trusted Mac, would you? But you trusted me. I want to remind you.

(*Pause.*)

Old Mac died a few years ago, didn't he? Isn't he dead?

(*Pause.*)

He was a lousy stinking rotten loudmouth. A bastard uncouth sodding runt. Mind you, he was a good friend of yours.

(*Pause.*)

MAX: Eh, Sam . . .
SAM: What?
MAX: Why do I keep you here? You're just an old grub.
SAM: Am I?
MAX: You're a maggot.
SAM: Oh yes?
MAX: As soon as you stop paying your way here, I mean when you're too old to pay your way, you know what I'm going to do? I'm going to give you the boot.
SAM: You are, eh?
MAX: Sure. I mean, bring in the money and I'll put up with you. But when the firm gets rid of you—you can flake off.
SAM: This is my house as well, you know. This was our mother's house.

MAX: One lot after the other. One mess after the other.
SAM: Our father's house.
MAX: Look what I'm lumbered with. One cast-iron bunch of crap after another. One flow of stinking pus after another.

(*Pause.*)

Our father? I remember him. Don't worry. You kid yourself. He used to come over to me and look down at me. My old man did. He'd bend right over me, then he'd pick me up. I was only that big. Then he'd dandle me. Give me the bottle. Wipe me clean. Give me a smile. Pat me on the bum. Pass me around, pass me from hand to hand. Toss me up in the air. Catch me coming down. I remember my father.

(BLACKOUT.
LIGHTS UP.
Night.)

(TEDDY *and* RUTH *stand at the threshold of the room. They are both well dressed in light summer suits and light raincoats. Two suitcases are by their side. They look at the room.* TEDDY *tosses the key in his hand, smiles.*)

TEDDY: Well, the key worked.

(*Pause.*)

They haven't changed the lock.

(*Pause.*)

RUTH: No one's here.
TEDDY (*looking up*): They're asleep.

(*Pause.*)

RUTH: Can I sit down?
TEDDY: Of course.
RUTH: I'm tired.

(*Pause.*)

TEDDY: Then sit down.

(*She does not move.*)

That's my father's chair.
RUTH: That one?
TEDDY (*smiling*): Yes, that's it. Shall I go up and see if my room's still there?
RUTH: It can't have moved.
TEDDY: No, I mean if my bed's still there.
RUTH: Someone might be in it.
TEDDY: No. They've got their own beds.

(*Pause.*)

RUTH: Shouldn't you wake someone up? Tell them you're here?
TEDDY: Not at this time of night. It's too late.

(Pause.)

Shall I go up?

(He goes into the hall, looks up the stairs, comes back.)

Why don't you sit down?

(Pause.)

I'll just go up . . . have a look.

(He goes up the stairs, stealthily.
RUTH *stands, then slowly walks across the room.*
TEDDY *returns.)*

It's still there. My room. Empty. The bed's there. What are you doing?

(She looks at him.)

Blankets, no sheets. I'll find some sheets. I could hear snores. Really. They're all still here, I think. They're all snoring up there. Are you cold?
RUTH: No.
TEDDY: I'll make something to drink, if you like. Something hot.
RUTH: No, I don't want anything.

(TEDDY walks about.)

TEDDY: What do you think of the room? Big, isn't it? It's a big house. I mean, it's a fine room, don't you think? Actually there was a wall, across there . . . with a door. We knocked it down . . . years ago . . . to make an open living area. The structure wasn't affected, you see. My mother was dead.

(RUTH sits.)

Tired?
RUTH: Just a little.
TEDDY: We can go to bed if you like. No point in waking anyone up now. Just go to bed. See them all in the morning . . . see my father in the morning. . . .

(Pause.)

RUTH: Do you want to stay?
TEDDY: Stay?

(Pause.)

We've come to stay. We're bound to stay . . . for a few days.
RUTH: I think . . . the children . . . might be missing us.
TEDDY: Don't be silly.
RUTH: They might.
TEDDY: Look, we'll be back in a few days, won't we?

(He walks about the room.)

Nothing's changed. Still the same.

(Pause.)

Still, he'll get a surprise in the morning, won't he? The old man. I think you'll like him, very much. Honestly. He's a . . . well, he's old, of course. Getting on.

(Pause.)

I was born here, do you realize that?
RUTH: I know.

(Pause.)

TEDDY: Why don't you go to bed? I'll find some sheets. I feel . . . wide awake, isn't it odd? I think I'll stay up for a bit. Are you tired?
RUTH: No.
TEDDY: Go to bed. I'll show you the room.
RUTH: No, I don't want to.
TEDDY: You'll be perfectly all right up there without me. Really you will. I mean, I won't be long. Look, it's just up there. It's the first door on the landing. The bathroom's right next door. You . . . need some rest, you know.

(Pause.)

I just want to walk about for a few minutes. Do you mind?
RUTH: Of course I don't.
TEDDY: Well . . . Shall I show you the room?
RUTH: No, I'm happy at the moment.
TEDDY: You don't have to go to bed. I'm not saying you have to. I mean, you can stay up with me. Perhaps I'll make a cup of tea or something. The only thing is we don't want to make too much noise, we don't want to wake anyone up.
RUTH: I'm not making any noise.
TEDDY: I know you're not.

(He goes to her.)

(Gently.) Look, it's all right, really. I'm here. I mean . . . I'm with you. There's no need to be nervous. Are you nervous?
RUTH: No.
TEDDY: There's no need to be.

(Pause.)

They're very warm people, really. Very warm. They're my family. They're not ogres.

(Pause.)

Well, perhaps we should go to bed. After all, we have to be up early, see Dad. Wouldn't be quite right if he found us in bed, I think. *(He chuckles.)* Have to be up before six, come down, say hullo.

(Pause.)

RUTH: I think I'll have a breath of air.

TEDDY: Air?

(Pause.)

What do you mean?

RUTH (standing): Just a stroll.

TEDDY: At this time of night? But we've . . . only just got here. We've got to go to bed.

RUTH: I just feel like some air.

TEDDY: But I'm going to bed.

RUTH: That's all right.

TEDDY: But what am I going to do?

(Pause.)

The last thing I want is a breath of air. Why do you want a breath of air?

RUTH: I just do.

TEDDY: But it's late.

RUTH: I won't go far. I'll come back.

(Pause.)

TEDDY: I'll wait up for you.

RUTH: Why?

TEDDY: I'm not going to bed without you.

RUTH: Can I have the key?

(He gives it to her.)

Why don't you go to bed?

(He puts his arms on her shoulders and kisses her. They look at each other, briefly. She smiles.)

I won't be long.

(She goes out of the front door.
TEDDY goes to the window, peers out after her, half turns from the window, stands, suddenly chews his knuckles.
LENNY walks into the room from upper left. He stands. He wears pyjamas and dressing-gown. He watches TEDDY.
TEDDY turns and sees him.
Silence.)

TEDDY: Hullo, Lenny.

LENNY: Hullo, Teddy.

(Pause.)

TEDDY: I didn't hear you come down the stairs.

LENNY: I didn't.

(Pause.)

I sleep down here now. Next door. I've got a kind of study, workroom cum bedroom next door now, you see.

TEDDY: Oh. Did I . . . wake you up?

LENNY: No. I just had an early night tonight. You know how it is. Can't sleep. Keep waking up.

(Pause.)

TEDDY: How are you?

LENNY: Well, just sleeping a bit restlessly, that's all. Tonight, anyway.

TEDDY: Bad dreams?

LENNY: No, I wouldn't say I was dreaming. It's not exactly a dream. It's just that something keeps waking me up. Some kind of tick.

TEDDY: A tick?

LENNY: Yes.

TEDDY: Well, what is it?

LENNY: I don't know.

(Pause.)

TEDDY: Have you got a clock in your room?

LENNY: Yes.

TEDDY: Well, maybe it's the clock.

LENNY: Yes, could be, I suppose.

(Pause.)

Well, if it's the clock I'd better do something about it. Stifle it in some way, or something.

(Pause.)

TEDDY: I've . . . just come back for a few days.

LENNY: Oh yes? Have you?

(Pause.)

TEDDY: How's the old man?

LENNY: He's in the pink.

(Pause.)

TEDDY: I've been keeping well.

LENNY: Oh, have you?

(Pause.)

Staying the night then, are you?

TEDDY: Yes.

LENNY: Well, you can sleep in your old room.

TEDDY: Yes, I've been up.

LENNY: Yes, you can sleep there.

(LENNY yawns.)

Oh well.

TEDDY: I'm going to bed.

LENNY: Are you?

TEDDY: Yes, I'll get some sleep.

LENNY: Yes, I'm going to bed, too.

(TEDDY picks up the cases.)

I'll give you a hand.

TEDDY: No, they're not heavy.

(TEDDY goes into the hall with the cases.
LENNY turns out the light in the room.
The light in the hall remains on.
LENNY follows into the hall.)

LENNY: Nothing you want?

TEDDY: Mmmm?

LENNY: Nothing you might want, for the night? Glass of water, anything like that?

TEDDY: Any sheets anywhere?

LENNY: In the sideboard in your room.

TEDDY: Oh, good.

LENNY: Friends of mine occasionally stay there, you know, in your room, when they're passing through this part of the world.

(LENNY *turns out the hall light and turns on the first landing light.*
TEDDY *begins to walk up the stairs.*)

TEDDY: Well, I'll see you at breakfast, then.

LENNY: Yes, that's it. Ta-ta.

(TEDDY *goes upstairs.*
LENNY *goes off left.*
Silence.
The landing light goes out.
Slight night light in the hall and room.
LENNY *comes back into the room, goes to the window and looks out.*
He leaves the window and turns on a lamp.
He is holding a small clock.
He sits, places the clock in front of him, lights a cigarette and sits.
RUTH *comes in the front door.*
She stands still. LENNY *turns his head, smiles. She walks slowly into the room.*)

LENNY: Good evening.

RUTH: Morning, I think.

LENNY: You're right there.

(*Pause.*)

My name's Lenny. What's yours?

RUTH: Ruth.

(*She sits, puts her coat collar around her.*)

LENNY: Cold?

RUTH: No.

LENNY: It's been a wonderful summer, hasn't it? Remarkable.

(*Pause.*)

Would you like something? Refreshment of some kind? An aperitif, anything like that?

RUTH: No, thanks.

LENNY: I'm glad you said that. We haven't got a drink in the house. Mind you, I'd soon get some in, if we had a party or something like that. Some kind of celebration . . . you know.

(*Pause.*)

You must be connected with my brother in some way. The one who's been abroad.

RUTH: I'm his wife.

LENNY: Eh listen, I wonder if you can advise me. I've been having a bit of a rough time with this clock. The tick's been keeping me up. The trouble is I'm not all that convinced it was the clock. I mean there are lots of things which tick in the night, don't you find that? All sorts of objects, which, in the day, you wouldn't call anything else but commonplace. They give you no trouble. But in the night any given one of a number of them is liable to start letting out a bit of a tick. Whereas you look at these objects in the day and they're just commonplace. They're as quiet as mice during the daytime. So . . . all things being equal . . . this question of me saying it was the clock that woke me up, well, that could very easily prove something of a false hypothesis.

(*He goes to the sideboard, pours from a jug into a glass, takes the glass to* RUTH.)

Here you are. I bet you could do with this.

RUTH: What is it?

LENNY: Water.

(*She takes it, sips, places the glass on a small table by her chair.*
LENNY *watches her.*)

Isn't it funny? I've got my pyjamas on and you're fully dressed?

(*He goes to the sideboard and pours another glass of water.*)

Mind if I have one? Yes, it's funny seeing my old brother again after all these years. It's just the sort of tonic my Dad needs, you know. He'll be chuffed to his bollocks in the morning, when he sees his eldest son. I was surprised myself when I saw Teddy, you know. Old Ted. I thought he was in America.

RUTH: We're on a visit to Europe.

LENNY: What, both of you?

RUTH: Yes.

LENNY: What, you sort of live with him over there, do you?

RUTH: We're married.

LENNY: On a visit to Europe, eh? Seen much of it?

RUTH: We've just come from Italy.

LENNY: Oh, you went to Italy first, did you? And then he brought you over here to meet the family, did he? Well, the old man'll be pleased to see you, I can tell you.

RUTH: Good.

LENNY: What did you say?

RUTH: Good.

(*Pause.*)

LENNY: Where'd you go to in Italy?

RUTH: Venice.

LENNY: Not dear old Venice? Eh? That's funny. You

know, I've always had a feeling that if I'd been a soldier in the last war—say in the Italian campaign—I'd probably have found myself in Venice. I've always had that feeling. The trouble was I was too young to serve, you see. I was only a child, I was too small, otherwise I've got a pretty shrewd idea I'd probably have gone through Venice. Yes, I'd almost certainly have gone through it with my battalion. Do you mind if I hold your hand?

RUTH: Why?

LENNY: Just a touch.

(He stands and goes to her.)

Just a tickle.

RUTH: Why?

(He looks down at her.)

LENNY: I'll tell you why.

(Slight pause.)

One night, not too long ago, one night down by the docks, I was standing alone under an arch, watching all the men jibbing the boom, out in the harbour, and playing about with the yardarm, when a certain lady came up to me and made me a certain proposal. This lady had been searching for me for days. She'd lost track of my whereabouts. However, the fact was she eventually caught up with me, and when she caught up with me she made me this certain proposal. Well, this proposal wasn't entirely out of order and normally I would have subscribed to it. I mean I would have subscribed to it in the normal course of events. The only trouble was she was falling apart with the pox. So I turned it down. Well, this lady was very insistent and started taking liberties with me down under this arch, liberties which by any criterion I couldn't be expected to tolerate, the facts being what they were, so I clumped her one. It was on my mind at the time to do away with her, you know, to kill her, and the fact is, that as killings go, it would have been a simple matter, nothing to it. Her chauffeur, who had located me for her, he'd popped round the corner to have a drink, which just left this lady and myself, you see, alone, standing underneath this arch, watching all the steamers steaming up, no one about, all quiet on the Western Front, and there she was up against this wall—well, just sliding down the wall, following the blow I'd given her. Well, to sum up, everything was in my favour, for a killing. Don't worry about the chauffeur. The chauffeur would never have spoken. He was an old friend of the family. But . . . in the end I thought . . . Aaah, why go to all the bother . . . you know, getting rid of the corpse and all that, getting yourself into a state of tension. So I just gave her another belt in the nose and a couple of turns of the boot and sort of left it at that.

RUTH: How did you know she was diseased?

LENNY: How did I know?

(Pause.)

I decided she was.

(Silence.)

You and my brother are newly-weds, are you?

RUTH: We've been married six years.

LENNY: He's always been my favourite brother, old Teddy. Do you know that? And my goodness we are proud of him here, I can tell you. Doctor of Philosophy and all that . . . leaves quite an impression. Of course, he's a very sensitive man, isn't he? Ted. Very. I've often wished I was as sensitive as he is.

RUTH: Have you?

LENNY: Oh yes. Oh yes, very much so. I mean, i'm not saying I'm not sensitive. I am. I could just be a bit more so, that's all.

RUTH: Could you?

LENNY: Yes, just a bit more so, that's all.

(Pause.)

I mean, I am very sensitive to atmosphere, but I tend to get desensitized, if you know what I mean, when people make unreasonable demands on me. For instance, last Christmas I decided to do a bit of snow-clearing for the Borough Council, because we had a heavy snow over here that year in Europe. I didn't have to do this snow-clearing—I mean I wasn't financially embarrassed in any way—it just appealed to me, it appealed to something inside me. What I anticipated with a good deal of pleasure was the brisk cold bite in the air in the early morning. And I was right. I had to get my snowboots on and I had to stand on a corner, at about five-thirty in the morning, to wait for the lorry to pick me up, to take me to the allotted area. Bloody freezing. Well, the lorry came, I jumped on the tailboard, headlights on, dipped, and off we went. Got there, shovels up, fags on, and off we went, deep into the December snow, hours before cockcrow. Well, that morning, while I was having my mid-morning cup of tea in a neighbouring cafe, the shovel standing by my chair, an old lady approached me and asked me if I would give her a hand with her iron mangle. Her brother-in-law, she said, had left it for her, but he'd left it in the wrong room, he'd left it in the front room. Well, naturally, she wanted it in the back room. It was a present he'd given her, you see, a mangle, to iron out the washing. But he'd left it in the wrong room, he'd left it in the front room, well that was a silly place to leave it, it couldn't stay there. So I took time off to give her a hand. She only lived up the road. Well, the only trouble was when I got there I couldn't move this mangle. It must have weighed about half a ton. How this brother-in-law got it up there in the first place I can't even begin to envisage. So there I was, doing a bit of shoulders on with the mangle, risking a rupture, and this old lady just standing there, waving me on, not even lifting a little finger to give me a helping hand. So after a few minutes I said to her, now look here, why don't you stuff this iron mangle up your arse? Anyway, I said, they're out of date, you want to get a spin drier. I had a good mind to give her a workover there and then, but as I was feeling jubilant with the snow-clearing I just gave her a short-arm jab to the belly and jumped on a bus outside. Excuse me, shall I take this ashtray out of your way?

RUTH: It's not in my way.

LENNY: It seems to be in the way of your glass. The glass was about to fall. Or the ashtray. I'm rather worried about the carpet. It's not me, it's my father. He's obsessed with order and clarity. He doesn't like a mess. So, as I don't believe you're smoking at the moment, I'm sure you won't object if I move the ashtray.

(He does so.)

And now perhaps I'll relieve you of your glass.

RUTH: I haven't quite finished.

LENNY: You've consumed quite enough, in my opinion.

RUTH: No, I haven't.

LENNY: Quite sufficient, in my opinion.

RUTH: Not in mine, Leonard.

(Pause.)

LENNY: Don't call me that, please.

RUTH: Why not?

LENNY: That's the name my mother gave me.

(Pause.)

Just give me the glass.

RUTH: No.

(Pause.)

LENNY: I'll take it, then.

RUTH: If you take the glass . . . I'll take you.

(Pause.)

LENNY: How about me taking the glass without you taking me?

RUTH: Why don't I just take you?

(Pause.)

LENNY: You're joking.

(Pause.)

You're in love, anyway, with another man. You've had a secret liaison with another man. His family didn't even know. Then you come here without a word of warning and start to make trouble.

(She picks up the glass and lifts it toward him.)

RUTH: Have a sip. Go on. Have a sip from my glass.

(He is still.)

Sit on my lap. Take a long cool sip.

*(She pats her lap. Pause.
She stands, moves to him with the glass.)*

Put your head back and open your mouth.

LENNY: Take that glass away from me.

RUTH: Lie on the floor. Go on. I'll pour it down your throat.

LENNY: What are you doing, making me some kind of proposal?

(She laughs shortly, drains the glass.)

RUTH: Oh, I was thirsty.

*(She smiles at him, puts the glass down, goes into the hall and up the stairs.
He follows into the hall and shouts up the stairs.)*

LENNY: What was that supposed to be? Some kind of proposal?

*(Silence.
He comes back into the room, goes to his own glass, drains it.
A door slams upstairs.
The landing light goes on.
MAX comes down the stairs, in pyjamas and cap. He comes into the room.)*

MAX: What's going on here? You drunk?

(He stares at LENNY.)

What are you shouting about? You gone mad?

(LENNY pours another glass of water.)

Prancing about in the middle of the night shouting your head off. What are you, a raving lunatic?

LENNY: I was thinking aloud.

MAX: Is Joey down here? You been shouting at Joey?

LENNY: Didn't you hear what I said, Dad? I said I was thinking aloud.

MAX: You were thinking so loud you got me out of bed.

LENNY: Look, why don't you just . . . pop off, eh?

MAX: Pop off? He wakes me up in the middle of the night, I think we got burglars here, I think he's got a knife stuck in him, I come down here, he tells me to pop off.

(LENNY *sits down.*)

He was talking to someone. Who could he have been talking to? They're all asleep. He was having a conversation with someone. He won't tell me who it was. He pretends he was thinking aloud. What are you doing, hiding someone here?

LENNY: I was sleepwalking. Get out of it, leave me alone, will you?

MAX: I want an explanation, you understand? I asked you who you got hiding here.

(*Pause.*)

LENNY: I'll tell you what, Dad, since you're in the mood for a bit of a . . . chat, I'll ask you a question. It's a question I've been meaning to ask you for some time. That night . . . you know . . . the night you got me . . . that night with Mum, what was it like? Eh? When I was just a glint in your eye. What was it like? What was the background to it? I mean, I want to know the real facts about my background, I mean, for instance, is it a fact that you had me in mind all the time, or is it a fact that I was the last thing you had in mind?

(*Pause.*)

I'm only asking this in a spirit of inquiry, you understand that, don't you? I'm curious. And there's lots of people of my age share that curiosity, you know that, Dad? They often ruminate, sometimes singly, sometimes in groups, about the true facts of that particular night—the night they were made in the image of those two people *at it*. It's a question long overdue, from my point of view, but as we happen to be passing the time of day here tonight I thought I'd pop it to you.

(*Pause.*)

MAX: You'll drown in your own blood.

LENNY: If you prefer to answer the question in writing I've got no objection.

(MAX *stands.*)

I should have asked my dear mother. Why didn't I ask my dear mother? Now it's too late. She's passed over to the other side.

(MAX *spits at him.*
LENNY *looks down at the carpet.*)

Now look what you've done. I'll have to Hoover that in the morning, you know.

(MAX *turns and walks up the stairs.*
LENNY *sits still.*
BLACKOUT.
LIGHTS UP.
Morning.
JOEY *in front of the mirror. He is doing some slow limbering-up exercises. He stops, combs his hair, carefully. He then shadowboxes, heavily, watching himself in the mirror.*
MAX *comes in from upper left.*
Both MAX *and* JOEY *are dressed.* MAX *watches* JOEY *in silence.* JOEY *stops shadowboxing, picks up a newspaper and sits.*
Silence.)

MAX: I hate this room.

(*Pause.*)

It's the kitchen I like. It's nice in there. It's cosy.

(*Pause.*)

But I can't stay in there. You know why? Because he's always washing up in there, scraping the plates, driving me out of the kitchen, that's why.

JOEY: Why don't you bring your tea in here?

MAX: I don't want to bring my tea in here. I hate it here. I want to drink my tea in there.

(*He goes into the hall and looks toward the kitchen.*)

What's he doing in there?

(*He returns.*)

What's the time?

JOEY: Half past six.

MAX: Half past six.

(*Pause.*)

I'm going to see a game of football this afternoon. You want to come?

(*Pause.*)

I'm talking to you.

JOEY: I'm training this afternoon. I'm doing six rounds with Blackie.

MAX: That's not till five o'clock. You've got time to see a game of football before five o'clock. It's the first game of the season.

JOEY: No, I'm not going.

MAX: Why not?

(*Pause.*
MAX *goes into the hall.*)

Sam! Come here!

(MAX *comes back into the room.*

SAM *enters with a cloth.*)

SAM: What?

MAX: What are you doing in there?

SAM: Washing up.

MAX: What else?

SAM: Getting rid of your leavings.

MAX: Putting them in the bin, eh?

SAM: Right in.

MAX: What point you trying to prove?

SAM: No point.

MAX: Oh yes, you are. You resent making my break-fast, that's what it is, isn't it? That's why you bang round the kitchen like that, scraping the frying-pan, scraping all the leavings into the bin, scrap-ing all the plates, scraping all the tea out of the teapot . . . that's why you do that, every single stinking morning. I know. Listen, Sam. I want to say something to you. From my heart.

(He moves closer.)

I want you to get rid of these feelings of resent-ment you've got towards me. I wish I could understand them. Honestly, have I ever given you cause? Never. When Dad died he said to me, Max, look after your brothers. That's exactly what he said to me.

SAM: How could he say that when he was dead?

MAX: What?

SAM: How could he speak if he was dead?

(Pause.)

MAX: Before he died, Sam. Just before. They were his last words. His last sacred words, Sammy. A split second after he said those words . . . he was a dead man. You think I'm joking? You think when my father spoke—on his death-bed—I wouldn't obey his words to the last letter? You hear that, Joey? He'll stop at nothing. He's even prepared to spit on the memory of our Dad. What kind of son were you, you wet wick? You spent half your time doing crossword puzzles! We took you into the butcher's shop, you couldn't even sweep the dust off the floor. We took MacGregor into the shop, he could run the place by the end of a week. Well, I'll tell you one thing. I respected my father not only as a man but as a number one butcher! And to prove it I followed him into the shop. I learned to carve a carcass at his knee. I commemorated his name in blood. I gave birth to three grown men! All on my own bat. What have you done?

(Pause.)

What have you done? You tit!

SAM: Do you want to finish the washing up? Look, here's the cloth.

MAX: So try to get rid of these feelings of resentment, Sam. After all, we are brothers.

SAM: Do you want the cloth? Here you are. Take it.

(TEDDY and RUTH come down the stairs. They walk across the hall and stop just inside the room. The others turn and look at them. JOEY stands. TEDDY and RUTH are wearing dressing-gowns. Silence. TEDDY smiles.)

TEDDY: Hullo . . . Dad . . . We overslept.

(Pause.)

What's for breakfast?

(Silence.)
(TEDDY chuckles.)

Huh. We overslept.

(MAX turns to SAM.)

MAX: Did you know he was here?

SAM: No.

(MAX turns to JOEY.)

MAX: Did you know he was here?

(Pause.)

I asked you if you knew he was here.

JOEY: No.

MAX: Then who knew?

(Pause.)

Who knew?

(Pause.)

I didn't know.

TEDDY: I was going to come down, Dad, I was going to . . . be here, when you came down.

(Pause.)

How are you?

(Pause.)

Uh . . . look, I'd . . . like you to meet . . .

MAX: How long you been in this house?

TEDDY: All night.

MAX: All night? I'm a laughing-stock. How did you get in?

TEDDY: I had my key.

(MAX whistles and laughs.)

MAX: Who's this?

TEDDY: I was just going to introduce you.

MAX: Who asked you to bring tarts in here?

TEDDY: Tarts?

MAX: Who asked you to bring dirty tarts into this house?

TEDDY: Listen, don't be silly—

MAX: You been here all night?

TEDDY: Yes, we arrived from Venice—

MAX: We've had a smelly scrubber in my house all night. We've had a stinking pox-ridden slut in my house all night.

TEDDY: Stop it! What are you talking about?

MAX: I haven't seen the bitch for six years, he comes home without a word, he brings a filthy scrubber off the street, he shacks up in my house!

TEDDY: She's my wife! We're married!

(Pause.)

MAX: I've never had a whore under this roof before. Ever since your mother died. My word of honour. (to JOEY) Have you ever had a whore here? Has Lenny ever had a whore here. They come back from America, they bring the slopbucket with them. They bring the bedpan with them. *(to* TEDDY*)* Take that disease away from me. Get her away from me.

TEDDY: She's my wife.

MAX *(to* JOEY*)*: Chuck them out.

(Pause.)

A Doctor of Philosophy. Sam, you want to meet a Doctor of Philosophy? *(to* JOEY*)* I said chuck them out.

(Pause.)

What's the matter? You deaf?

JOEY: You're an old man. *(to* TEDDY*)* He's an old man.

(LENNY walks into the room, in a dressing-gown.
He stops.
They all look round.
MAX *turns back, hits* JOEY *in the stomach with all his might.*
JOEY *contorts, staggers across the stage.* MAX, *with the exertion of the blow, begins to collapse. His knees buckle. He clutches his stick.*
SAM *moves forward to help him.*
MAX *hits him across the head with his stick.* SAM *sits, head in hands.*
JOEY, *hands pressed to his stomach, sinks down at the feet of* RUTH.
She looks down at him.
LENNY *and* TEDDY *are still.*
JOEY *slowly stands. He is close to* RUTH. *He turns from* RUTH, *looks round at* MAX.
SAM *clutches his head.*
MAX *breathes heavily, very slowly gets to his feet.*
JOEY *moves to him.*
They look at each other.
Silence.
MAX *moves past* JOEY, *walks toward* RUTH. *He gestures with his stick.)*

MAX: Miss.

*(*RUTH *walks toward him.)*

RUTH: Yes?

(He looks at her.)

MAX: You a mother?

RUTH: Yes.

MAX: How many you got?

RUTH: Three.

(He turns to TEDDY.*)*

MAX: All yours, Ted?

(Pause.)

Teddy, why don't we have a nice cuddle and kiss, eh? Like the old days? What about a nice cuddle and kiss, eh?

TEDDY: Come on, then.

(Pause)

MAX: You want to kiss your old father? Want a cuddle with your old father?

TEDDY: Come on, then.

*(*TEDDY *moves a step toward him.)*

Come on.

(Pause.)

MAX: You still love your old Dad, eh?

(They face each other.)

TEDDY: Come on, Dad. I'm ready for the cuddle.

*(*MAX *begins to chuckle, gurgling.*
He turns to the family and addresses them.)

MAX: He still loves his father!

ACT 2

(Afternoon. MAX, TEDDY, LENNY *and* SAM *are about the stage, lighting cigars.*
JOEY *comes in from upper left with a coffee tray, followed by* RUTH. *He puts the tray down.* RUTH *hands coffee to all the men. She sits with her cup.* MAX *smiles at her.)*

RUTH: That was a very good lunch.

MAX: I'm glad you liked it. *(to the others)* Did you hear that? *(to* RUTH*)* Well, I put my heart and soul into it, I can tell you. *(He sips.)* And this is a lovely cup of coffee.

RUTH: I'm glad.

(Pause.)

MAX: I've got the feeling you're a first-rate cook.

RUTH: I'm not bad.

MAX: No, I've got the feeling you're a number one cook. Am I right, Teddy?

TEDDY: Yes, she's a very good cook.

(Pause.)

MAX: Well, it's a long time since the whole family was together, eh? If only your mother was alive. Eh, what do you say, Sam? What would Jessie say if she was alive? Sitting here with her three sons. Three fine grown-up lads. And a lovely daughter-in-law. The only shame is her grandchildren aren't here. She'd have petted them and cooed over them, wouldn't she, Sam? She'd have fussed over them and played with them, told them stories, tickled them—I tell you she'd have been hysterical. *(to RUTH)* Mind you, she taught those boys everything they know. She taught them all the morality they know. I'm telling you. Every single bit of the moral code they live by—was taught to them by their mother. And she had a heart to go with it. What a heart. Eh, Sam? Listen, what's the use of beating round the bush? That woman was the backbone to this family. I mean, I was busy working twenty-four hours a day in the shop. I was going all over the country to find meat, I was making my way in the world, but I left a woman at home with a will of iron, a heart of gold and a mind. Right, Sam?

(Pause.)

What a mind.

(Pause.)

Mind you, I was a generous man to her. I never left her short of a few bob. I remember one year I entered into negotiations with a top-class group of butchers with continental connections. I was going into association with them. I remember the night I came home, I kept quiet. First of all I gave Lenny a bath, then Teddy a bath, then Joey a bath. What fun we used to have in the bath, eh, boys? Then I came downstairs and I made Jessie put her feet up on a pouffe—what happened to that pouffe, I haven't seen it for years—she put her feet up on the pouffe and I said to her, Jessie, I think our ship is going to come home, I'm going to treat you to a couple of items, I'm going to buy you a dress in pale corded blue silk, heavily encrusted in pearls, and for casual wear, a pair of pantaloons in lilac flowered taffeta. Then I gave her a drop of cherry brandy. I remember the boys came down, in their pyjamas, all their hair shining, their faces pink, it was before they started shaving, and they knelt down at our feet, Jessie's and mine. I tell you, it was like Christmas.

(Pause.)

RUTH: What happened to the group of butchers?

MAX: The group? They turned out to be a bunch of criminals like everyone else.

(Pause.)

This is a lousy cigar.

*(He stubs it out.
He turns to SAM.)*

What time you going to work?

SAM: Soon.

MAX: You've got a job on this afternoon, haven't you?

SAM: Yes, I know.

MAX: What do you mean, you know? You'll be late. You'll lose your job? What are you trying to do, humiliate me?

SAM: Don't worry about me.

MAX: It makes the bile come up in my mouth. The bile—you understand? *(to RUTH)* I worked as a butcher all my life, using the chopper and the slab, the slab, you know what I mean, the chopper and the slab! To keep my family in luxury. Two families! My mother was bedridden, my brothers were all invalids. I had to earn the money for the leading psychiatrists. I had to read books! I had to study the disease, so that I could cope with an emergency at every stage. A crippled family, three bastard sons, a slutbitch of a wife—don't talk to me about the pain of childbirth—I suffered the pain, I've still got the pangs—when I give a little cough my back collapses—and here I've got a lazy idle bugger of a brother won't even get to work on time. The best chauffeur in the world. All his life he's sat in the front seat giving lovely hand signals. You call that work? This man doesn't know his gearbox from his arse!

SAM: You go and ask my customers! I'm the only one they ever ask for.

MAX: What do the other drivers do, sleep all day?

SAM: I can only drive one car. They can't all have me at the same time.

MAX: Anyone could have you at the same time. You'd bend over for half a dollar on Blackfriars Bridge.

SAM: Me!

MAX: For two bob and a toffee apple.

SAM: He's insulting me. He's insulting his brother. I'm driving a man to Hampton Court at four forty-five.

MAX: Do you want to know who could drive? MacGregor! MacGregor was a driver.

SAM: Don't you believe it.

(MAX points his stick at SAM.)

MAX: He didn't even fight in the war. This man didn't even fight in the bloody war!

SAM: I did!

MAX: Who did you kill?

(Silence.

SAM gets up, goes to RUTH, *shakes her hand and goes out of the front door.*

MAX *turns to* TEDDY.)

Well, how you been keeping, son?

TEDDY: I've been keeping very well, Dad.

MAX: It's nice to have you with us, son.

TEDDY: It's nice to be back, Dad.

(Pause.)

MAX: You should have told me you were married, Teddy. I'd have sent you a present. Where was the wedding, in America?

TEDDY: No. Here. The day before we left.

MAX: Did you have a big function?

TEDDY: No, there was no one there.

MAX: You're mad. I'd have given you a white wedding. We'd have had the cream of the cream here. I'd have been only too glad to bear the expense, my word of honour.

(Pause.)

TEDDY: You were busy at the time. I didn't want to bother you.

MAX: But you're my own flesh and blood. You're my first born. I'd have dropped everything. Sam would have driven you to the reception in the Snipe, Lenny would have been your best man, and then we'd have all seen you off on the boat. I mean, you don't think I disapprove of marriage, do you? Don't be daft. *(to* RUTH) I've been begging my two youngsters for years to find a nice feminine girl with proper credentials—it makes life worth living. *(to* TEDDY) Anyway, what's the difference, you did it, you made a wonderful choice, you've got a wonderful family, a marvellous career . . . so why don't we let bygones be bygones?

(Pause.)

You know what I'm saying? I want you both to know that you have my blessing.

TEDDY: Thank you.

MAX: Don't mention it. How many other houses in the district have got a Doctor of Philosophy sitting down drinking a cup of coffee?

(Pause.)

RUTH: I'm sure Teddy's very happy . . . to know that you're pleased with me.

(Pause.)

I think he wondered whether you would be pleased with me.

MAX: But you're a charming woman.

(Pause.)

RUTH: I was . . .

MAX: What?

(Pause.)

What she say?

(They all look at her.)

RUTH: I was . . . different . . . when I met Teddy . . . first.

TEDDY: No you weren't. You were the same.

RUTH: I wasn't.

MAX: Who cares? Listen, live in the present, what are you worrying about? I mean, don't forget the earth's about five thousand million years old, at least. Who can afford to live in the past?

(Pause.)

TEDDY: She's a great help to me over there. She's a wonderful wife and mother. She's a very popular woman. She's got lots of friends. It's a great life, at the University . . . you know . . . it's a very good life. We've got a lovely house . . . we've got all . . . we've got everything we want. It's a very stimulating environment.

(Pause.)

My department . . . is highly successful.

(Pause.)

We've got three boys, you know.

MAX: All boys? Isn't that funny, eh? You've got three, I've got three. You've got three nephews, Joey. Joey! You're an uncle, do you hear? You could teach them how to box.

(Pause.)

JOEY *(to* RUTH): I'm a boxer. In the evenings, after work. I'm in demolition in the daytime.

RUTH: Oh?

JOEY: Yes. I hope to be full time, when I get more bouts.

MAX *(to* LENNY): He speaks so easily to his sister-in-law, do you notice. That's because she's an intelligent and sympathetic woman.

(He leans to her.)

Eh, tell me, do you think the children are missing their mother?

(She looks at him.)

TEDDY: Of course they are. They love her. We'll be seeing them soon.

(Pause.)

LENNY (*to* TEDDY): Your cigar's gone out.
TEDDY: Oh, yes.
LENNY: Want a light?
TEDDY: No. No.

(*Pause.*)

So has yours.
LENNY: Oh, yes.

(*Pause.*)

Eh, Teddy, you haven't told us much about your Doctorship of Philosophy. What do you teach?
TEDDY: Philosophy.
LENNY: Well, I want to ask you something. Do you detect a certain logical incoherence in the central affirmations of Christian theism?
TEDDY: That question doesn't fall within my province.
LENNY: Well, look at it this way . . . you don't mind my asking you some questions, do you?
TEDDY: If they're within my province.
LENNY: Well, look at it this way. How can the unknown merit reverence? In other words, how can you revere that of which you're ignorant? At the same time, it would be ridiculous to propose that what we *know* merits reverence. What we know merits any one of a number of things, but it stands to reason reverence isn't one of them. In other words, apart from the known and the unknown, what else is there?

(*Pause.*)

TEDDY: I'm afraid I'm the wrong person to ask.
LENNY: But you're a philosopher. Come on, be frank. What do you make of all this business of being and not-being?
TEDDY: What do you make of it?
LENNY: Well, for instance, take a table. Philosophically speaking. What is it?
TEDDY: A table.
LENNY: Ah. You mean it's nothing else but a table. Well, some people would envy your certainty, wouldn't they, Joey? For instance, I've got a couple of friends of mine, we often sit round the Ritz Bar having a few liqueurs, and they're always saying things like that, you know, things like: Take a table, take it. All right, I say, *take* it, *take* a table, but once you've taken it, what are you going to do with it? Once you've got hold of it, where you going to take it?
MAX: You'd probably sell it.
LENNY: You wouldn't get much for it.
JOEY: Chop it up for firewood.

(LENNY *looks at him and laughs.*)

RUTH: Don't be too sure though. You've forgotten something. Look at me. I . . . move my leg.

That's all it is. But I wear . . . underwear . . . which moves with me . . . it . . . captures your attention. Perhaps you misinterpret. The action is simple. It's a leg . . . moving. My lips move. Why don't you restrict . . . your observations to that? Perhaps the fact that they move is more significant . . . than the words which come through them. You must bear that . . . possibility . . . in mind.

(*Silence.*
TEDDY *stands.*)

I was born quite near here.

(*Pause.*)

Then . . . six years ago, I went to America.

(*Pause.*)

It's all rock. And sand. It stretches . . . so far . . . everywhere you look. And there's lots of insects there.

(*Pause.*)

And there's lots of insects there.

(*Silence.*
She is still.
MAX *stands.*)

MAX: Well, it's time to go to the gym. Time for your workout, Joey.
LENNY (*standing.*): I'll come with you.

(JOEY *sits looking at* RUTH.)

MAX: Joe.

(JOEY *stands. The three go out.*
TEDDY *sits by* RUTH, *holds her hand.*
She smiles at him.
Pause.)

TEDDY: I think we'll go back. Mmnn?

(*Pause.*)

Shall we go home?
RUTH: Why?
TEDDY: Well, we were only here for a few days, weren't we? We might as well . . . cut it short, I think.
RUTH: Why? Don't you like it here?
TEDDY: Of course I do. But I'd like to go back and see the boys now.

(*Pause.*)

RUTH: Don't you like your family?
TEDDY: Which family?
RUTH: Your family here.
TEDDY: Of course I like them. What are you talking about?

(*Pause.*)

RUTH: You don't like them as much as you thought you did?

TEDDY: Of course I do. Of course I . . . like them. I don't know what you're talking about.

(*Pause.*)

Listen. You know what time of the day it is there now, do you?

RUTH: What?

TEDDY: It's morning. It's about eleven o'clock.

RUTH: Is it?

TEDDY: Yes, they're about six hours behind us . . . I mean . . . behind the time here. The boys'll be at the pool . . . now . . . swimming. Think of it. Morning over there. Sun. We'll go anyway, mmnn? It's so clean there.

RUTH: Clean.

TEDDY: Yes.

RUTH: Is it dirty here?

TEDDY: No, of course not. But it's cleaner there.

(*Pause.*)

Look, I just brought you back to meet the family, didn't I? You've met them, we can go. The fall semester will be starting soon.

RUTH: You find it dirty here?

TEDDY: I didn't say I found it dirty here.

(*Pause.*)

I didn't say that.

(*Pause.*)

Look. I'll go and pack. You rest for a while. Will you? They won't be back for at least an hour. You can sleep. Rest. Please.

(*She looks at him.*)

You can help me with my lectures when we get back. I'd love that. I'd be so grateful for it, really. We can bathe till October. You know that. Here, there's nowhere to bathe, except the swimming bath down the road. You know what it's like? It's like a urinal. A filthy urinal!

(*Pause.*)

You liked Venice, didn't you? It was lovely, wasn't it? You had a good week. I mean . . . I took you there. I can speak Italian.

RUTH: But if I'd been a nurse in the Italian campaign I would have been there before.

(*Pause.*)

TEDDY: You just rest. I'll go and pack.

(TEDDY *goes out and up the stairs.*
(*She closes her eyes.*
LENNY *appears from upper left.*

He walks into the room and sits near her.
She opens her eyes.
Silence.)

LENNY: Well, the evenings are drawing in.

RUTH: Yes, it's getting dark.

(*Pause.*)

LENNY: Winter'll soon be upon us. Time to renew one's wardrobe.

(*Pause.*)

RUTH: That's a good thing to do.

LENNY: What?

(*Pause.*)

RUTH: I always . . .

(*Pause.*)

Do you like clothes?

LENNY: Oh, yes. Very fond of clothes.

(*Pause.*)

RUTH: I'm fond . . .

(*Pause.*)

What do you think of my shoes?

LENNY: They're very nice.

RUTH: No, I can't get the ones I want over there.

LENNY: Can't get them over there, eh?

RUTH: No . . . you don't get them there.

(*Pause.*)

I was a model before I went away.

LENNY: Hats?

(*Pause.*)

I bought a girl a hat once. We saw it in a glass case, in a shop. I tell you what it had. It had a bunch of daffodils on it, tied with a black satin bow, and then it was covered with a cloche of black veiling. A cloche. I'm telling you. She was made for it.

RUTH: No . . . I was a model for the body. A photographic model for the body.

LENNY: Indoor work?

RUTH: That was before I had . . . all my children.

(*Pause.*)

No, not always indoors.

(*Pause.*)

Once or twice we went to a place in the country, by train. Oh, six or seven times. We used to pass a . . . a large white water tower. This place . . . this house . . . was very big . . . the trees . . . there was a lake, you see . . . we used to change and walk down towards the lake . . . we went down a path . . . on stones . . . there were . . . on this path. Oh, just . . . wait . . . yes . . . when we changed in the house we had a drink. There was a cold buffet.

(Pause.)

Sometimes we stayed in the house but . . . most often . . . we walked down to the lake . . . and did our modelling there.

(Pause.)

Just before we went to America I went down there. I walked from the station to the gate and then I walked up the drive. There were lights on . . . I stood in the drive . . . the house was very light.

(TEDDY comes down the stairs with the cases. He puts them down, looks at LENNY.)

TEDDY: What have you been saying to her?

(He goes to RUTH.)

Here's your coat.

(LENNY goes to the radiogram and puts on a record of slow jazz.)

Ruth. Come on. Put it on.

LENNY *(to RUTH)*: What about one dance before you go?

TEDDY: We're going.

LENNY: Just one.

TEDDY: No. We're going.

LENNY: Just one dance, with her brother-in-law, before she goes.

(LENNY bends to her.)

Madam?

(RUTH stands. They dance, slowly.
TEDDY stands, with RUTH's coat.
MAX and JOEY come in the front door and into the room. They stand.
LENNY kisses RUTH. They stand, kissing.)

JOEY: Christ, she's wide open. Dad, look at that.

(Pause.)

She's a tart.

(Pause.)

Old Lenny's got a tart in here.

(JOEY goes to them. He takes RUTH's arm. He smiles at LENNY. He sits with RUTH on the sofa, embraces and kisses her.
He looks up at LENNY.)

Just up my street.

(He leans her back until she lies beneath him. He kisses her.
He looks up at TEDDY and MAX.)

It's better than a rubdown, this.

(LENNY sits on the arm of the sofa. He caresses RUTH's hair as JOEY embraces her.
MAX comes forward, looks at the cases.)

MAX: You going, Teddy? Already?

(Pause.)

Well, when you coming over again, eh? Look, next time you come over, don't forget to let us know beforehand whether you're married or not. I'll always be glad to meet the wife. Honest. I'm telling you.

(JOEY lies heavily on RUTH.
They are almost still.
LENNY caresses her hair.)

Listen, you think I don't know why you didn't tell me you were married? I know why. You were ashamed. You thought I'd be annoyed because you married a woman beneath you. You should have known me better. I'm broadminded. I'm a broadminded man.

(He peers to see RUTH's face under JOEY, turns back to TEDDY.)

Mind you, she's a lovely girl. A beautiful woman. And a mother too. A mother of three. You've made a happy woman out of her. It's something to be proud of. I mean, we're talking about a woman of quality. We're talking about a woman of feeling.

(JOEY and RUTH roll off the sofa on to the floor.
JOEY clasps her. LENNY moves to stand above them. He looks down on them. He touches RUTH gently with his foot.
RUTH suddenly pushes JOEY away.
She stands up.
JOEY gets to his feet, stares at her.)

RUTH: I'd like something to eat. *(To LENNY.)* I'd like a drink. Did you get any drink?

LENNY: We've got drink.

RUTH: I'd like one, please.

LENNY: What drink?

RUTH: Whisky.

LENNY: I've got it.

(Pause.)

RUTH: Well, get it.

(LENNY goes to the sideboard, takes out bottle and glasses.
JOEY moves toward her.)

Put the record off.

(He looks at her, turns, puts the record off.)

I want something to eat.

(Pause.)

JOEY: I can't cook. *(Pointing to* MAX.*)* He's the cook.

(LENNY brings her a glass of whisky.)

LENNY: Soda on the side?

RUTH: What's this glass? I can't drink out of this. Haven't you got a tumbler?

LENNY: Yes.

RUTH: Well, put it in a tumbler.

(He takes the glass back, pours whisky into a tumbler, brings it to her.)

LENNY: On the rocks. Or as it comes?

RUTH: Rocks? What do you know about rocks?

LENNY: We've got rocks. But they're frozen stiff in the fridge.

(RUTH drinks.
LENNY looks round at the others.)

Drinks all round?

(He goes to the sideboard and pours drinks.
JOEY moves closer to RUTH.*)*

JOEY: What food do you want?

(RUTH walks round the room.)

RUTH *(to* TEDDY*)*: Have your family read your critical works?

MAX: That's one thing I've never done. I've never read one of his critical works.

TEDDY: You wouldn't understand them.

(LENNY hands drinks all round.)

JOEY: What sort of food do you want? I'm not the cook, anyway.

LENNY: Soda, Ted? Or as it comes?

TEDDY: You wouldn't understand my works. You wouldn't have the faintest idea of what they were about. You wouldn't appreciate the points of reference. You're way behind. All of you. There's no point in my sending you my works. You'd be lost. It's nothing to do with the question of intelligence. It's a way of being able to look at the world. It's a question of how far you can operate on things and not in things. I mean it's a question of your capacity to ally the two, to relate the two, to balance the two. To see, to be able to *see*! I'm the one who can see. That's why I can write my critical works. Might do you good . . . have a look at them . . . see how certain people can view . . . things . . . how certain people can maintain . . . intellectual equilibrium. Intellec-

tual equilibrium. You're just objects. You just . . . move about. I can observe it. I can see what you do. It's the same as I do. But you're lost in it. You won't get me being . . . I won't be lost in it.

*(*BLACKOUT.*
LIGHTS UP.
Evening.
TEDDY sitting, in his coat, the cases by him. SAM.
Pause.)*

SAM: Do you remember MacGregor, Teddy?

TEDDY: Mac?

SAM: Yes.

TEDDY: Of course I do.

SAM: What did you think of him? Did you take to him?

TEDDY: Yes. I liked him. Why?

(Pause.)

SAM: You know, you were always my favourite, of the lads. Always.

(Pause.)

When you wrote to me from America I was very touched, you know. I mean you'd written to your father a few times but you'd never written to me. But then, when I got that letter from you . . . well, I was very touched. I never told him. I never told him I'd heard from you.

(Pause.)

(Whispering.) Teddy, shall I tell you something? You were always your mother's favourite. She told me. It's true. You were always the . . . you were always the main object of her love.

(Pause.)

Why don't you stay for a couple more weeks, eh? We could have a few laughs.

(LENNY comes in the front door and into the room.)

LENNY: Still here, Ted? You'll be late for your first seminar.

(He goes to the sideboard, opens it, peers in it, to the right and the left, stands.)

Where's my cheese-roll?

(Pause.)

Someone's taken my cheese-roll. I left it there. *(To* SAM.*)* You been thieving?

TEDDY: I took your cheese-roll, Lenny.

(Silence.
SAM *looks at them, picks up his hat and goes out of the front door.*
Silence.)*

LENNY: You took my cheese-roll?

TEDDY: Yes.

LENNY: I made that roll myself. I cut it and put the butter on. I sliced a piece of cheese and put it in between. I put it on a plate and I put it in the sideboard. I did all that before I went out. Now I come back and you've eaten it.

TEDDY: Well, what are you going to do about it?

LENNY: I'm waiting for you to apologize.

TEDDY: But I took it deliberately, Lenny.

LENNY: You mean you didn't stumble on it by mistake?

TEDDY: No, I saw you put it there. I was hungry, so I ate it.

(Pause.)

LENNY: Barefaced audacity.

(Pause.)

What led you to be so . . . vindictive against your own brother? I'm bowled over.

(Pause.)

Well, Ted, I would say this is something approaching the naked truth, isn't it? It's a real cards on the table stunt. I mean, we're in the land of no holds barred now. Well, how else can you interpret it? To pinch your younger brother's specially made cheese-roll when he's out doing a spot of work, that's not equivocal, it's unequivocal.

(Pause.)

Mind you, I will say you do seem to have grown a bit sulky during the last six years. A bit sulky. A bit inner. A bit less forthcoming. It's funny, because I'd have thought that in the United States of America, I mean with the sun and all that, the open spaces, on the old campus, in your position, lecturing, in the centre of all the intellectual life out there, on the old campus, all the social whirl, all the stimulation of it all, all your kids and all that, to have fun with, down by the pool, the Greyhound buses and all that, tons of iced water, all the comfort of those Bermuda shorts and all that, on the old campus, no time of the day or night you can't get a cup of coffee or a Dutch gin, I'd have thought you'd have grown more forthcoming, not less. Because I want you to know that you set a standard for us, Teddy. Your family looks up to you, boy, and you know what it does? It does its best to follow the example you set. Because you're a great source of pride to us. That's why we were so glad to see you come back, to welcome you back to your birthplace. That's why.

(Pause.)

No, listen, Ted, there's no question that we live a less rich life here than you do over there. We live a closer life. We're busy, of course. Joey's busy with his boxing, I'm busy with my occupation, Dad still plays a good game of poker, and he does the cooking as well, well up to his old standard, and Uncle Sam's the best chauffeur in the firm. But nevertheless we do make up a unit, Teddy, and you're an integral part of it. When we all sit round the backyard having a quiet gander at the night sky, there's always an empty chair standing in the circle, which is in fact yours. And so when you at length return to us, we do expect a bit of grace, a bit of je ne sais quoi, a bit of generosity of mind, a bit of liberality of spirit, to reassure us. We do expect that. But do we get it? Have we got it? Is that what you've given us?

(Pause.)

TEDDY: Yes.

(JOEY comes down the stairs and into the room, with a newspaper.)

LENNY *(to JOEY)*: How'd you get on?

JOEY: Er . . . not bad.

LENNY: What do you mean?

(Pause.)

What do you mean?

JOEY: Not bad.

LENNY: I want to know what you *mean*—by not bad.

JOEY: What's it got to do with you?

LENNY: Joey, you tell your brother everything.

(Pause.)

JOEY: I didn't get all the way.

LENNY: You didn't get all the way?

(Pause.)

(With emphasis.) You didn't get all the way? But you've had her up there for two hours.

JOEY: Well?

LENNY: You didn't get all the way and you've had her up there for two hours!

JOEY: What about it?

(LENNY moves closer to him.)

LENNY: What are you telling me?

JOEY: What do you mean?

LENNY: Are you telling me she's a tease?

(Pause.)

She's a tease!

(Pause.)

What do you think of that, Ted? Your wife turns out to be a tease. He's had her up there for two hours and he didn't go the whole hog.

JOEY: I didn't say she was a tease.

LENNY: Are you joking? It sounds like a tease to me, don't it to you, Ted?

TEDDY: Perhaps he hasn't got the right touch.

LENNY: Joey? Not the right touch? Don't be ridiculous. He's had more dolly than you've had cream cakes. He's irresistible. He's one of the few and far between. Tell him about the last bird you had, Joey.

(Pause.)

JOEY: What bird?

LENNY: The last bird! When we stopped the car . . .

JOEY: Oh, that . . . yes . . . well, we were in Lenny's car one night last week . . .

LENNY: The Alfa.

JOEY: And er . . . bowling down the road . . .

LENNY: Up near the Scrubs.

JOEY: Yes, up over by the Scrubs . . .

LENNY: We were doing a little survey of North Paddington.

JOEY: And er . . . it was pretty late, wasn't it?

LENNY: Yes, it was late. Well?

(Pause.)

JOEY: And then we . . . well, by the kerb, we saw this parked car . . . with a couple of girls in it.

LENNY: And their escorts.

JOEY: Yes, there were two geezers in it. Anyway . . .

(Pause.)

What we do then?

LENNY: We stopped the car and got out!

JOEY: Yes . . . we got out . . . and we told the . . . two escorts . . . to go away . . . which they did . . . and then we . . . got the girls out of the car . . .

LENNY: We didn't take them over the Scrubs.

JOEY: Oh, no. Not over the Scrubs. Well, the police would have noticed us there . . . you see. We took them over a bombed site.

LENNY: Rubble. In the rubble.

JOEY: Yes, plenty of rubble.

(Pause.)

Well . . . you know . . . then we had them.

LENNY: You've missed out the best bit. He's missed out the best bit!

JOEY: What bit?

LENNY (to TEDDY): His bird says to him, I don't mind, she says, but I've got to have some protection. I've got to have some contraceptive protection. I haven't got any contraceptive protection, old Joey says to her. In that case I won't do it, she says. Yes you will, says Joey, never mind about the contraceptive protection.

(LENNY laughs.)

Even my bird laughed when she heard that. Yes, even she gave out a bit of a laugh. So you can't say old Joey isn't a bit of a knockout when he gets going, can you? And here he is upstairs with your wife for two hours and he hasn't even been the whole hog. Well, your wife sounds like a bit of a tease to me, Ted. What do you make of it, Joey? You satisfied? Don't tell me you're satisfied without going the whole hog?

(Pause.)

JOEY: I've been the whole hog plenty of times. Sometimes . . . you can be happy . . . and not go the whole hog. Now and again . . . you can be happy . . . without going any hog.

(LENNY stares at him.

MAX and SAM come in the front door and into the room.)

MAX: Where's the whore? Still in bed? She'll make us all animals.

LENNY: The girl's a tease.

MAX: What?

LENNY: She's had Joey on a string.

MAX: What do you mean?

TEDDY: He had her up there for two hours and he didn't go the whole hog.

(Pause.)

MAX: My Joey? She did that to my boy?

(Pause.)

To my youngest son? Tch, tch, tch, tch. How you feeling, son? Are you all right?

JOEY: Sure I'm all right.

MAX (to TEDDY): Does she do that to you, too?

TEDDY: No.

LENNY: He gets the gravy.

MAX: You think so?

JOEY: No he don't.

(Pause.)

SAM: He's her lawful husband. She's his lawful wife.

JOEY: No he don't! He don't get no gravy! I'm telling you. I'm telling all of you. I'll kill the next man who says he gets the gravy.

MAX: Joey . . . what are you getting so excited about? (to LENNY) It's because he's frustrated. You see what happens?

JOEY: Who is?

MAX: Joey. No one's saying you're wrong. In fact everyone's saying you're right.

(Pause.

MAX *turns to the others.)*

You know something? Perhaps it's not a bad idea to have a woman in the house. Perhaps it's a good thing. Who knows? Maybe we should keep her.

(Pause.)

Maybe we'll ask her if she wants to stay.

(Pause.)

TEDDY: I'm afraid not, Dad. She's not well, and we've got to get home to the children.

MAX: Not well? I told you, I'm used to looking after people who are not so well. Don't worry about that. Perhaps we'll keep her here.

(Pause.)

SAM: Don't be silly.

MAX: What's silly?

SAM: You're talking rubbish.

MAX: Me?

SAM: She's got three children.

MAX: She can have more! If she's so keen.

TEDDY: She doesn't want any more.

MAX: What do you know about what she wants, eh, Ted?

TEDDY *(smiling)*: The best thing for her is to come home with me, Dad. Really. We're married, you know.

(MAX walks about the room, clicks his fingers.)

MAX: We'd have to pay her, of course. You realize that? We can't leave her walking about without any pocket money. She'll have to have a little allowance.

JOEY: Of course we'll pay her. She's got to have some money in her pocket.

MAX: That's what I'm saying. You can't expect a woman to walk about without a few bob to spend on a pair of stockings.

(Pause.)

LENNY: Where's the money going to come from?

MAX: Well, how much is she worth? What we talking about three figures?

LENNY: I asked you where the money's going to come from. It'll be an extra mouth to feed. It'll be an extra body to clothe. You realize that?

JOEY: I'll buy her clothes.

LENNY: What with?

JOEY: I'll put in a certain amount out of my wages.

MAX: That's it. We'll pass the hat round. We'll make a donation. We're all grown-up people, we've got a sense of responsibility. We'll put a little in the hat. It's democratic.

LENNY: It'll come to a few quid, Dad.

(Pause.)

I mean, she's not a woman who likes walking around in second-hand goods. She's up to the latest fashion. You wouldn't want her walking about in clothes which don't show her off at her best, would you?

MAX: Lenny, do you mind if I make a little comment? It's not meant to be critical. But I think you're concentrating too much on the economic considerations. There are other considerations. There are the human considerations. You understand what I mean? There are the human considerations. Don't forget them.

LENNY: I won't.

MAX: Well don't.

(Pause.)

Listen, we're bound to treat her in something approximating, at least, to the manner in which she's accustomed. After all, she's not someone off the street, she's my daughter-in-law!

JOEY: That's right.

MAX: There you are, you see. Joey'll donate, Sam'll donate. . . .

(SAM looks at him.)

I'll put in a few bob out of my pension, Lenny'll cough up. We're laughing. What about you, Ted? How much you going to put in the kitty?

TEDDY: I'm not putting anything in the kitty.

MAX: What? You won't even help to support your own wife? I thought he was a son of mine. You lousy stinkpig. Your mother would drop dead if she heard you take that attitude.

LENNY: Eh, Dad.

(LENNY walks forward.)

I've got a better idea.

MAX: What?

LENNY: There's no need for us to go to all this expense. I know these women. Once they get started they ruin your budget. I've got a better idea. Why don't I take her up with me to Greek Street?

(Pause.)

MAX: You mean put her on the game?

(Pause.)

We'll put her on the game. That's a stroke of genius, that's a marvellous idea. You mean she can earn the money herself—on her back?

LENNY: Yes.

MAX: Wonderful. The only thing is, it'll have to be

short hours. We don't want her out of the house all night.

LENNY: I can limit the hours.

MAX: How many?

LENNY: Four hours a night.

MAX (*dubiously*): Is that enough?

LENNY: She'll bring in a good sum for four hours a night.

MAX: Well, you should know. After all, it's true, the last thing we want to do is wear the girl out. She's going to have her obligations this end as well. Where you going to put her in Greek Street?

LENNY: It doesn't have to be right in Greek Street, Dad. I've got a number of flats all around that area.

MAX: You have? Well, what about me? Why don't you give me one?

LENNY: You're sexless.

JOEY: Eh, wait a minute, what's all this?

MAX: I know what Lenny's saying. Lenny's saying she can pay her own way. What do you think, Teddy? That'll solve all our problems.

JOEY: Eh, wait a minute. I don't want to share her.

MAX: What did you say?

JOEY: I don't want to share her with a lot of yobs!

MAX: Yobs! You arrogant git! What arrogance. (*to* LENNY) Will you be supplying her with yobs?

LENNY: I've got a very distinguished clientèle, Joey. They're more distinguished than you'll ever be.

MAX: So you can count yourself lucky we're including you in.

JOEY: I didn't think I was going to have to share her!

MAX: Well, you *are* going to have to share her! Otherwise she goes straight back to America. You understand?

(*Pause.*)

It's tricky enough as it is, without you shoving your oar in. But there's something worrying me. Perhaps she's not so up to the mark. Eh? Teddy, you're the best judge. Do you think she'd be up to the mark?

(*Pause.*)

I mean what about all this teasing? Is she going to make a habit of it? That'll get us nowhere.

(*Pause.*)

TEDDY: It was just love play . . . I suppose . . . that's all I suppose it was.

MAX: Love play? Two bleeding hours? That's a bloody long time for love play!

LENNY: I don't think we've got anything to worry about on that score, Dad.

MAX: How do you know?

LENNY: I'm giving you a professional opinion.

(LENNY *goes to* TEDDY.)

LENNY: Listen, Teddy, you could help us, actually. If I were to send you some cards, over to America . . . you know, very nice ones, with a name on, and a telephone number, very discreet, well, you could distribute them . . . to various parties, who might be making a trip over here. Of course, you'd get a little percentage out of it.

MAX: I mean, you needn't tell them she's your wife.

LENNY: No, we'd call her something else. Dolores, or something.

MAX: Or Spanish Jacky.

LENNY: No, you've got to be reserved about it, Dad. We could call her something nice . . . like Cynthia . . . or Gillian.

(*Pause.*)

JOEY: Gillian.

(*Pause.*)

LENNY: No, what I mean, Teddy, you must know lots of professors, heads of departments, men like that. They pop over here for a week at the Savoy, they need somewhere they can go to have a nice quiet poke. And of course you'd be in a position to give them inside information.

MAX: Sure. You can give them proper data. You know, the kind of thing she's willing to do. How far she'd be prepared to go with their little whims and fancies. Eh, Lenny. To what extent she's various. I mean if you don't know, who does?

(*Pause.*)

I bet you before two months we'd have a waiting list.

LENNY: You could be our representative in the States.

MAX: Of course. We're talking in international terms! By the time we've finished Pan-American'll give us a discount.

(*Pause.*)

TEDDY: She'd get old . . . very quickly.

MAX: No . . . not in this day and age! With the health service? Old! How could she get old? She'll have the time of her life.

(RUTH *comes down the stairs, dressed.*
She comes into the room.
She smiles at the gathering, and sits.
Silence.)

TEDDY: Ruth . . . the family have invited you to stay, for a little while longer. As a . . . as a kind of guest. If you like the idea I don't mind. We can manage very easily at home . . . until you come back.

RUTH: How very nice of them.

(Pause.)

MAX: It's an offer from our heart.

RUTH: It's very sweet of you.

MAX: Listen . . . it would be our pleasure.

(Pause.)

RUTH: I think I'd be too much trouble.

MAX: Trouble? What are you talking about? What trouble? Listen, I'll tell you something. Since poor Jessie died, eh, Sam? we haven't had a woman in the house. Not one. Inside this house. And I'll tell you why. Because their mother's image was so dear any other woman would have . . . tarnished it. But you . . . Ruth . . . you're not only lovely and beautiful, but you're kin. You're kith. You belong here.

(Pause.)

RUTH: I'm very touched.

MAX: Of course you're touched. I'm touched.

(Pause.)

TEDDY: But Ruth, I should tell you . . . that you'll have to pull your weight a little, if you stay. Financially. My father isn't very well off.

RUTH *(to MAX)*: Oh, I'm sorry.

MAX: No, you'd just have to bring in a little, that's all. A few pennies. Nothing much. It's just that we're waiting for Joey to hit the top as a boxer. When Joey hits the top . . . well . . .

(Pause.)

TEDDY: Or you can come home with me.

LENNY: We'd get you a flat.

(Pause.)

RUTH: A flat?

LENNY: Yes.

RUTH: Where?

LENNY: In town.

(Pause.)

But you'd live here, with us.

MAX: Of course you would. This would be your home. In the bosom of the family.

LENNY: You'd just pop up to the flat a couple of hours a night, that's all.

MAX: Just a couple of hours, that's all. That's all.

LENNY: And you make enough money to keep you going here.

(Pause.)

RUTH: How many rooms would this flat have?

LENNY: Not many.

RUTH: I would want at least three rooms and a bathroom.

LENNY: You wouldn't need three rooms and a bathroom.

MAX: She'd need a bathroom.

LENNY: But not three rooms.

(Pause.)

RUTH: Oh, I would. Really.

LENNY: Two would do.

RUTH: No. Two wouldn't be enough.

(Pause.)

I'd want a dressing-room, a rest-room, and a bedroom.

(Pause.)

LENNY: All right, we'll get you a flat with three rooms and a bathroom.

RUTH: With what kind of conveniences?

LENNY: All conveniences.

RUTH: A personal maid?

LENNY: Of course.

(Pause.)

We'd finance you, to begin with, and then, when you were established, you could pay us back, in instalments.

RUTH: Oh, no, I wouldn't agree to that.

LENNY: Oh, why not?

RUTH: You would have to regard your original outlay simply as a capital investment.

(Pause.)

LENNY: I see. All right.

RUTH: You'd supply my wardrobe, of course?

LENNY: We'd supply everything. Everything you need.

RUTH: I'd need an awful lot. Otherwise I wouldn't be content.

LENNY: You'd have everything.

RUTH: I would naturally want to draw up an inventory of everything I would need, which would require your signatures in the presence of witnesses.

LENNY: Naturally.

RUTH: All aspects of the agreement and conditions of employment would have to be clarified to our mutual satisfaction before we finalized the contract.

LENNY: Of course.

(Pause.)

RUTH: Well, it might prove a workable arrangement.

LENNY: I think so.

MAX: And you'd have the whole of your daytime free, of course. You could do a bit of cooking here if you wanted to.

LENNY: Make the beds.

MAX: Scrub the place out a bit.

TEDDY: Keep everyone company.

(SAM *comes forward.*)

SAM (*in one breath*): MacGregor had Jessie in the back of my cab as I drove them along.

(*He croaks and collapses.*
He lies still.
They look at him.)

MAX: What's he done? Dropped dead?

LENNY: Yes.

MAX: A corpse? A corpse on my floor? Get him out of here! Clear him out of here!

(JOEY *bends over* SAM.)

JOEY: He's not dead.

LENNY: He probably was dead, for about thirty seconds.

MAX: He's not even dead!

(LENNY *looks down at* SAM.)

LENNY: Yes, there's still some breath there.

MAX (*pointing at* SAM): You know what that man had?

LENNY: Has.

MAX: Has! A diseased imagination.

(*Pause.*)

RUTH: Yes, it sounds a very attractive idea.

MAX: Do you want to shake on it now, or do you want to leave it till later?

RUTH: Oh, we'll leave it till later.

(TEDDY *stands.*
He looks down at SAM.)

TEDDY: I was going to ask him to drive me to London Airport.

(*He goes to the cases, picks one up.*)

Well, I'll leave your case, Ruth. I'll just go up the road to the Underground.

MAX: Listen if you go the other way, first left, first right, you remember, you might find a cab passing there.

TEDDY: Yes, I might do that.

MAX: Or you can take the tube to Piccadilly Circus, won't take you ten minutes, and pick up a cab from there out to the Airport.

TEDDY: Yes, I'll probably do that.

MAX: Mind you, they'll charge you double fare. They'll charge you for the return trip. It's over the six-mile limit.

TEDDY: Yes. Well, bye-bye, Dad. Look after yourself.

(*They shake hands.*)

MAX: Thanks, son. Listen. I want to tell you something. It's been wonderful to see you.

(*Pause.*)

TEDDY: It's been wonderful to see you.

MAX: Do your boys know about me? Would they like to see a photo, do you think, of their grandfather?

TEDDY: I know they would.

(MAX *brings out his wallet.*)

MAX: I've got one on me. I've got one here. Just a minute. Here you are. Will they like that one?

TEDDY (*taking it*): They'll be thrilled.

(*He turns to* LENNY.)

Good-bye, Lenny.

(*They shake hands.*)

LENNY: Ta-ta, Ted. Good to see you. Have a good trip.

TEDDY: Bye-bye, Joey.

(JOEY *does not move.*)

JOEY: Ta-ta.

(TEDDY *goes to the front door.*)

RUTH: Eddie.

(TEDDY *turns.*
Pause.)

Don't become a stranger.

(TEDDY *goes, shuts the front door.*
Silence.
The three men stand.
RUTH *sits relaxed in her chair.*
SAM *lies still.*
JOEY *walks slowly across the room.*
He kneels at her chair.
She touches his head, lightly.
He puts his head in her lap.
MAX *begins to move above them, backwards and forwards.*
LENNY *stands still.*
MAX *turns to* LENNY.)

MAX: I'm too old, I suppose. She thinks I'm an old man.

(*Pause.*)

I'm not such an old man.

(*Pause.*)

(*To* RUTH) You think I'm too old for you?

(Pause.)

Listen. You think you're just going to get that big slag all the time? You think you're just going to have him . . . you're going to just have him all the time? You're going to have to work! You'll have to take them on, you understand?

(Pause.)

Does she realize that?

(Pause.)

Lenny, do you think she understands . . .

(He begins to stammer.)

What . . . what . . . what . . . we're getting at? What . . . we've got in mind? Do you think she's got it clear?

(Pause.)

I don't think she's got it clear.

(Pause.)

You understand what I mean? Listen, I've got a funny idea she'll do the dirty on us, you want to bet? She'll use us, she'll make use of us, I can tell you that! I can smell it! You want to bet?

(Pause.)

She won't . . . be adaptable!

(He falls to his knees, whimpers, begins to moan and sob. He stops sobbing, crawls past SAM's *body round her chair, to the other side of her.)*

I'm not an old man.

(He looks up at her.)

Do you hear me?

(He raises his face to her.)

Kiss me.

(She continues to touch JOEY's *head, lightly.* LENNY *stands, watching.)*

CURTAIN

Figure 1. Lenny (Ian Holm) offers Ruth (Vivien Merchant) a glass of water in the Royal Shakespeare Company production of *The Homecoming*, directed by Peter Hall, New York, 1967. (Photograph: Friedman-Abeles.)

Figure 2. Max (Paul Rogers, *left*) insults Ruth (Vivien Merchant) while *(left to right)* Joey (Terence Rigby), Sam (John Normington), Teddy (Michael Craig), and Lenny (Ian Holm) listen in the Royal Shakespeare Company production of *The Homecoming*, directed by Peter Hall, New York, 1967. (Photograph: Friedman-Abeles.)

Staging of *The Homecoming*

REVIEW OF THE ROYAL SHAKESPEARE COMPANY PRODUCTION, 1967, BY WALTER KERR

Harold Pinter's "The Homecoming" consists of a single situation that the author refuses to dramatize until he has dragged us all, aching, through a half-drugged dream.

The situation, when it is arrived at, is interesting in the way that Pinter's numbed fantasies are almost always interesting. A Doctor of Philosophy who actually teaches philosophy returns with his wife to the family home in North London, a home that looks like an emptied-out wing of the British Museum gone thoroughly to seed. (The few pieces of furniture are lonely in this cavern. The molding along the walls breaks off and gives up before it can reach the doorways, the carpet could be made of cement.)

A father and two brothers take one look at the wife and mistake (or do not mistake) her for a whore. She is silent, poised, leggy, self-contained. In due time the family decides that they would rather like to have a whore around, whatever about her husband and about the three children she has left behind in America. She might very well be kept available in a room at the top of the steep, forbidding staircase, and she could always pay her own keep by renting herself out a few nights a week.

They put the proposition to her, matter-of-factly, after she has obliged them by moving into trance-like dance with one of the brothers, brushing unfinished kisses across his lips and then obligingly draping herself to another brother's needs across a cold and impersonal sofa.

It is at this point that Mr. Pinter's most curious and most characteristic abilities as a diviner of unspecified demons come effectively into play. We are in an unconventional situation, and of course we know that. But our habits of mind—our compulsive attempts to try to deal with the world by slide rule—still continue to function, stubbornly. We expect even so bizarre a crisis to provoke logical responses: the husband will be humiliated or outraged, the wife will prove herself either a genuine wife or a genuine whore, and so on. We have the probabilities all ready in our heads.

But Mr. Pinter is not interested in the rational probabilities of the moment. He is interested in what *might* happen if our controlling expectations were suddenly junked, if flesh and heart and moving bone were freed from preconditioning and allowed simply to behave, existentially. The world might go another way—a surprising and ultimately unexplained way—if it went its own way, indifferent to philosophers.

Just how the tangle at the Music Box rearranges itself I won't say, because saying nails down what is meant to continue as movement. It's enough to report that for approximately 20 minutes during the final third of "The Homecoming" the erratic energies onstage display their own naked authority by forcing us to accept the unpredictable as though it were the natural shape of things.

During this time Vivien Merchant, as the wife who is hard-headed as she is enigmatic, cooly and with great reserve points out that her legs move, her underwear moves with her, her lips move. ("Perhaps the fact that they move is more significant than the words that come through them.") Husband Michael Craig draws on his donnish pipe with opaque detachment ("I won't be lost in it"), father Paul Rogers leers through sucked-in teeth that seem to have been borrowed from Bert Lahr, and poltergeist Iam Holm grins maliciously at the thought of all the tables that can be turned. The performing is cagey, studied, bristling with overtones. (A good half of Mr. Pinter's suspense invariably comes from the question that sticks in our heads: "What are these people *not* mentioning?").

Until the final moments of the evening, however, the playwright is simply cheating us, draining away our interest with his deliberate delay. He has no more vital material to offer here than he had, say, in the very much shorter "A Slight Ache," to which "The Homecoming" bears a strong resemblance.

But he is determined that we shall have two hours worth of improvisational feinting, and it leads him into a good bit of coy teasing giggly echoes of Ionesco ("You liked Venice, didn't you? You had a good week. I mean, I took you there. I can speak Italian") and calculated incidental violence that is without cumulative effect (the father spits at one son, rams another in the gut, canes his own paraffin-coated dullard of a brother).

Because none of this is of any growing importance to the ultimate confrontation, *everything* must seem to have its own arbitrary and artificial importance: the clink of a sugar lump on a saucer, the stiff, ritual crossing of trousered legs, the huddled lighting of four cigars, the effortful pronunciation of so much as a single word.

Holding too much back for too long, the play comes to seem afflicted by an arthritic mind and tongue, and while Peter Hall has directed the visiting members of England's Royal Shakespeare Company to make sleep-walking and strangled speech constitute a theatrical effect in and for itself, we are not engrossed by the eternal hesitation waltz, but seriously put off by it. The play agonizes over finding its starting point, and we share the prolonged agony without being certain that the conundrum is approaching a real core.

Mr. Pinter is one of the most naturally gifted dramatists to have come out of England since the war. I think he is making the mistake, just now, of supposing that the elusive kernel of impulse that will do for a 40-minute play will serve just as handily and just as suspensefully for an all-day outing. "The Homecoming," to put the matter as simply as possible, needs a second situation: We could easily take an additional act if the author would only scrap the interminable first. The tide must come in at least twice if we are to be fascinated so long by the shoreline.

REVIEW OF THE ROYAL SHAKESPEARE COMPANY PRODUCTION, 1967, BY RICHARD GILMAN

In all his plays, from *The Room*, which was written in 1957 as a more or less naïve exercise in the kind of drama Beckett and Ionesco had already made known, to his latest work, *The Homecoming*, Harold Pinter has been engaged with the question of what drama really is. It might be thought that the playwright, of all people, would know; yet if twentieth-century aesthetic developments have taught us anything, it is that the artist, rather than the public—which knows what it knows—is in continuing doubt about the nature of art. And since the theatre is the most immovable of all the arts, the most resistant to change, it is the playwright who has had to struggle most strenuously for new forms, against the heavy, unyielding conviction of nearly everybody else that there is no mystery about what plays are.

Plays are sequences of imagined events, recognizable to one degree or another as analogous to the events of life, and these events are participated in by "characters," whose interest and credibility are also measured by their potential actuality, their being possible to imagine in one or another way as existing in the world outside the drama. Beyond that, plays must "develop," must move steadily along, generally to a "higher" or "deeper" level, and must not, on pain of murderous responses from the audience, stop at any point—to give opportunity for reflection to gather new kinds of momentum, to simply be still, circular, without linear progression. What plays must do (the last stronghold of realism) is to trace a parabola for which life is thought to have provided the model.

Such, tightly stated, are the sovereign notions that still rule audiences, reviewers and commonplace playwrights alike. They learn nothing from the fact that nearly all the interesting drama of any period has taken place outside the textbook definitions. The complaint is still made against a play like *The Homecoming* that it is slow, illogical, unlifelike, wasteful of its opportunities—which are to be fast, logical, lifelike—and that its characters are not the sort one would expect or want to meet on one's daily round. (Get me Ivan Karamazov: Ivan, baby, we're having a party and we'd love you to . . .)

In Pinter's growth as a dramatist, which in a central way means progress toward colonizing hitherto unconsidered territories of the dramatic, shaping a redefinition, *on the stage*, of character, plot, action, etc., he has come unevenly but significantly to redirect procedures and techniques that had early threatened to congeal into mere negatives. His capacity for extracting ranges of implication from the most conventional varieties of speech themselves—incantatory, often, dreamlike yet anchored in the sharpest accuracy about how people really talk—his use of the most commonplace objects to undermine our complacency about the material world: all this was for the most part unsupported by imposing intellectual structure, any more solid knowledge or intuition than that traditions of perception and experience were not to be relied on.

From his first impact here, by way of rumor and the published early plays and then through *The Caretaker* when it arrived, we spoke of Pinter as a new presence, the master of striking if not quite trustworthy, because seemingly autonomous, effects. The world, his plays announced, is arbitrary, everything menaces, nothing is what it seems; he had broken into a new universe of drama, one in which language seldom coheres with gesture, terror is the obverse of humor, and habits of action conceal other kinds of action we can sense but never know.

In this universe, he once wrote in a program note, "there are no hard distinctions between what is real and what is unreal, nor between what is true and what is false." It is precisely its tendency to assume at some point that it knows what is real and unreal (which means what has up to now been *considered* so) that compels every art including drama continually to remonstrate with its own past, to repudiate its own inertia. This is the least that so-called avant-garde art does—but it has to do more. The peculiar giddiness, the sensations of disequilibrium and disturbed orientation which Pinter induced through his dislocations of the familiar—these, while enormously valuable, were not fully satisfying. For what was being let in through the holes he had punched in conventional dramaturgy? Not what meaning but what new and substanceful drama of his own?

The Homecoming, though flawed and marked by aesthetic problems not yet overcome, is the impressive culmination of a subtle process of change that set in midway in Pinter's career. It was toward a seemingly greater realism, a filling in the vacancies, in which abstract menace and unspecific fear lurked, that had resulted from his abandonment of accepted thematic developments, of ordinary psychologies and sociologies and the sequential narratives in which the stage has traditionally encased them. But this realism had nothing to do with an imitation of life or the conventions of popular drama, except that, in the latter case, it made a canny and partly ironic use of them.

The shift can be studied through Pinter's changing *mises en scène*. Moving into domestic settings, usually middle- or upper-middle class, he largely withdrew from those alarming locales of his earlier plays—the basement room of *The Dumbwaiter*, the seedy rooming house of *The Birthday Party*, the dementedly cluttered room of *The Caretaker*.

These theatrical sites were objectively disturbing, menacing in their own right, physical metaphors of violence which meant that their atmospheres tended to carry a disproportionate share of the plays' effects, tended in fact to consolidate those effects as the very essence of the works.

The setting of *The Homecoming* still possesses disquieting features in its great gray sparsely furnished room. But something crucial has happened. This new Pinter room no longer largely dictates what is to happen to its inhabitants but only reflects what has happened and will happen to them; its walls and furnishings have soaked up their emanations, for the center of dramatic reality has passed to them.

Yet it doesn't lie in them now in any way which we can organically connect with what we think of as domestic drama. If you think during the opening moments that you are watching a familiar battle scene, on the order of *Virginia Woolf*, or *Cat on a Hot Tin Roof*, you will be unprepared for what is to come and you may grow disgruntled, having expected, in the second act, denouement, completion, some satisfying rich ripe finale. But the play moves to its own logic, and it is not a tale; its characters are only tactically engaged in representing potentially real people, their strategic task being to incarnate, along the lines of the "characters" in *The Brothers Karamazov*, certain human faculties, dividing among themselves fundamental possibilities of attitude and approach to existence. They are their figures in a drama of the mind, which is not to say an intellectual drama, but one which makes no pretense (or only a pretense) of being a replica of actuality.

The relationship of the four men who occupy the stage at first is savage, almost cannibalistic, at the same time that it is self-lacerating. "Mind you she wasn't such a bad woman," Max, the roaring foulmouthed old man, says of his dead wife, "even though it made me sick just to look at her rotten stinking face, she wasn't a bad bitch." And he berates his coldly ironic son Lenny, the master of a stable of prostitutes, for "talking to your lousy filthy father like that."

Yet however straightforward, if extreme, their dialogue seems at first, its purpose is not to frame character or psychology, not as an English critic has pointed out, to reveal "inner life or intentions." Pinter's marvelously funny, splendidly violent or consciously banal dialogue is a matter of *kinds* of speech and therefore archetypes of being, warring with one another—Max's scatology, Lenny's wit, Max's pallid brother Sam's pinched rhetoric—as the faculties incarnated by the personages of the play similarly war. And the dialogue is there to serve the play, to serve its mostly immobile, nonanecdotal, ritualistic vision, not its presumed thesis, its "story" or concatenation of events.

That there is to be no plausible story quickly becomes apparent with the entrance of Teddy, Max's oldest son; a philosophy professor at an American university, he is returning for the first time in six years, with his wife Ruth, whom the others do not know of. Cooly elegant, enigmatic, sensual, Ruth immediately shifts the play to a new dimension. In the most Pinteresque of scenes, where language, objects and gestures unite to reinforce one another's elliptical and mythic condition, Ruth and Lenny clash. "I'll take it [a glass of water he has given her]," Lenny says, unaccountably threatening, to which she replies with deadly calm, "If you take the glass . . . I'll take *you*."

From then on the play is about who takes whom,

that is to say, whose presence triumphs or yields, who, in the game of existence—not in that of society—are winners or losers. What loses most decisively is on-looking spectatorship, the propriety of consciousness when pitted against the absolutism of the physical self. In a world beyond morality, what is being sought for is a condition of authenticity, an immersion in what is. And to accomplish this, the play now leaves irrevocably behind it (the point at which the public grumbling starts) all verisimilitude, all pretense of being about a family, a social situation, people like you and me. Pinter is at the heart of his vision here, and if we follow him into it—attending to these characters who can no longer be mistaken for types or personalities but only seen as incarnations of possibility, of desire and refusal—we will have overcome our deadly habit of wanting what we expect.

When Ruth engages Lenny, and afterwards Joey, the naïve strongboy younger brother, in a sexual embrace which Teddy, her husband, watches with pipe-smoking professorial detachment, and when later the family proposes that Ruth stay with them, working for her keep as a prostitute—a proposal which leaves Teddy as unruffled as before—we are not in the presence of social behavior but of a dance of death—and life. Ruth's acceptance of the proposal is a movement toward the greater authenticity of the family, their closer proximity to genuine being. For Teddy is an abstract man, a figure of pure consciousness, an observer, while she is almost pure instinct and physicality.

In the key monologue of the play, the central speech which, as in all Pinter's work, offers the one irradiation of intention to light the rest of the play, Teddy tells the others:

"You wouldn't understand my works . . . You wouldn't appreciate the points of reference. You're way behind . . . It's nothing to do with the question of intelligence. It's a way of being able to look at the world. It's a question of how far you can operate on things and not in things . . . To see, to be able to *see!* I'm the one who can see . . . [I have] intellectual equilibrium . . . You're just objects. You just . . . move about. I can observe it. I can see what you do. It's the same as I do. But you're lost in it. You won't get me being . . . I won't be lost in it."

It is a brilliant piece of writing, one almost no other English-speaking playwright would be capable of. Fusing the most exact and compressed meanings with the most intense feeling, colloquial at the same time that it stretches to a more inclusive and nonrealistic level of speech, it exemplifies what is never considered in our public chatter about the theatre: that language can itself be dramatic, can *be* the play, not merely the means of advancing an anecdote, a decoration, or the emblem of something thought to be realer than itself.

Teddy's speech is followed by a longer one of Lenny's, an equally masterly piece of writing, opposing another rhythm and another mode of language as action to its predecessor. In it Lenny, the wit, the implicated observer, moral consciousness corrupted but still alive, throws at Teddy an image of America which in the conditions of the play, entirely transcends social criticism to become the truest kind of poetic fact:

"I will say you do seem to have grown a bit sulky . . . I'd have thought that in the United States of America, I mean with the sun and all that, the open spaces, on the old campus, in your position, lecturing, in the center of all the intellectual life out there, on the old campus, all the social whirl, all the stimulation of it all, all your kids and all that, to have fun with, down by the pool, the Greyhound buses and all that, tons of iced water, all the comforts of those Bermuda shorts and all that, on the old campus . . . I'd have thought you'd have grown more forthcoming . . . Listen, Ted, there's no question we lead a less rich life here than you do over there . . . We lead a closer life."

In the final movement of the play, this closer life is revealed to be partly one of fantasy. There is something crowded, rushed into being, somewhat arbitrary about this last section. Ruth takes command, promising in the manner of a contemporary fairy godmother to be whatever the men want her to be: for Joey a madonna figure, for Lenny, a whore, for Max a young and rejuvenating wife. A whole allegorical structure now rises shadowily into view. But it is too late, it has not been fully prepared for and therefore comes as an afterthought. Yet the main action of the play has been completed with Ruth's move toward the family and Teddy's devastating acceptance of it; to wish to do more, to want his dense, specific, precisely nonallegorical vision to yield up such further tenuous meanings is evidence that Pinter has not yet solved his major problem. And that is how to fuse meaning so securely with language, gesture and setting that it cannot be extrapolated from them. The taints of the old worn-out dramatic procedures—characters who represent action that points to something else—are still discernible in his work.

Yet, they are taints, not major infections. A struggle for the new is always more interesting than a successful appropriation of the old. *The Homecoming* is such a struggle, and nothing on Broadway in recent years comes close to matching it for the kind of excitement that our debased ad-man's vocabulary of critical appreciation ("*The Odd Couple* is the funniest play ever!") has so thoroughly disillusioned us about. The play itself, Peter Hall's direction and the Royal Shakespeare Company's acting ensemble offer examples of work in a dimension beyond anything we have been accustomed to.

TOM STOPPARD

1937–

When Tom Stoppard told critic Ronald Hayman "the only useful metaphor I can think of for the way I think I write my plays is convergences of different threads," he chose a metaphor that also describes his complex personal heritage. Named Tomas Straussler by his natural father, a shoe-company doctor, he was born in Czechoslovakia, raised in Singapore and Darjeeling, and moved to England when he was nine years old. Adopting the name of his stepfather, a British Army major, he became Tom Stoppard: public school student, reporter, drama critic, and then nationally acclaimed playwright. In 1977, Stoppard visited Russia and his native Czechoslovakia, met with the dissident playwright Václav Havel, and saw for himself what political repression meant; the return to his past inspired his powerful television play, *Professional Foul,* broadcast in September of the same year.

Stoppard's success began ten years earlier, with his first professionally produced play, *Rosencrantz and Guildenstern Are Dead* (1967). Stoppard irreverently retells the events of *Hamlet* from the perspective of two minor characters, emphasizing what *Hamlet* only implies, namely that the two characters are indistinguishable, even to themselves. But at the same time that he rewrites past literature, Stoppard places himself within the main currents of twentieth-century theater and its persistent concern with problematic issues of existence. Rosencrantz and Guildenstern's verbal game-playing and anxious waiting for Hamlet to appear make them cousins to Samuel Beckett's tramps, Vladimir and Estragon, waiting for Godot. And their bantering comments on the relationship between life and art recall Luigi Pirandello's obsessive treatment of that subject. The play also reflects Stoppard's debt to nineteenth-century British drama, particularly farce, with the epigrammatic thrust of Stoppard's lines echoing Oscar Wilde's *The Importance of Being Earnest* (1895). But, on a larger scale, Stoppard is, like Bernard Shaw, combining farcical action with intellectual conversation and philosophy.

That Shavian combination appears even more noticeably in Stoppard's next major play, *Jumpers* (1972), which blends philosophical speculation, acrobats, popular songs, a murder mystery, possible adultery, and references to the moon landing. The opening image of *Jumpers* seems to have been inspired by a brief exchange from *Rosencrantz and Guildenstern Are Dead,* in which Rosencrantz asks "Shouldn't we be doing something—constructive?" and Guildenstern answers sardonically, "What did you have in mind? . . . A short, blunt human pyramid . . . ?" In *Jumpers* Stoppard gave physical shape to that pyramid, had one of the participating acrobats shot, and found "I didn't know who he was or who had shot him or why or what to do with the body." But, as Stoppard also pointed out when discussing this play with Ronald Hayman, he knew he "wanted to write a play about a professor of moral philosophy, and it's the work of a moment to think that there was a metaphor at work in the play already between acrobatics, mental acrobatics, and so on." George Moore, his philosopher, spends most of *Jumpers* trying to answer the question "is God?" in a never-quite-finished speech, while never quite sorting out the similarly baffling questions of who killed the acrobat, what his wife is doing with his boss, and where his pet rabbit, Thumper, might be.

Stoppard's device in *Rosencrantz and Guildenstern Are Dead,* of taking minor figures from literature and making them protagonists, twists in a new direction in *Travesties* (1974), where historical figures become characters on stage. Having discovered that the novelist James Joyce, the Dadaist artist Tristan Tzara, and the Russian revolutionary Lenin all lived in Zurich in 1918, Stoppard decided to bring them together. Characteristically, his approach to these major figures of art and politics is oblique, for the central character in *Travesties* is a fiction-alized Henry Carr (when a young clerk in the British Consul's office), with whom Joyce quarreled violently because of the money he spent for his costume in an amateur production of *The Importance of Being Earnest.* Like *Rosencrantz and Guildenstern Are Dead* (and *The Real Inspector Hound,* Stoppard's 1968 parody of stage murder-mysteries), *Travesties* offers a feast of allusions for literate play-goers. But it also raises uncomfortable questions about the role of the artist and the meaning, if any, of art itself. Carr and Tzara debate the subject, Lenin (perhaps predictably) attacks bourgeois art, and Carr ends the play with a speech implying that art and politics are opposed and yet interchangeable:

> I learned three things in Zurich during the war. I wrote them down. Firstly, you're either a revolu-tionary or you're not, and if you're not you might as well be an artist as anything else. Secondly, if you can't be an artist, you might as well be a revolutionary . . . I forget the third thing.

That "third thing"—the joining of artistic endeavor and revolutionary zeal—becomes the key to Stoppard's work after 1975. Though he previously had denied any interest in writing "political" drama, stating his preference for multiple and, by implication, less simplistic perspectives, two short plays from 1977 mark a distinct shift in his dramatic intentions: *Every Good Boy Deserves Favor* (written for actors and orchestra, centering on the imprisonment of Russian dissenters in mental hospitals), and *Professional Foul,* written for Am-nesty International's Prisoner of Conscience Year. They were, one sees in ret-rospect, plays that Stoppard discovered the necessity of writing. In an interview published in the *New York Times,* he describes the "linking threads" for *Profes-sional Foul* as "my desire to write something about human rights, the combination of my birth, my trips to Russia, my interest in [Václav] Havel and his arrest, the appearance of Charter 77."

Other "linking threads" connect *Professional Foul* to his previous plays. The central character, Anderson, is, like George in *Jumpers,* a professor of philosophy and, like George, scheduled to give a lecture. Like most Stoppard characters, Anderson relishes the games he can play with language. When another philos-ophy professor going to the same conference doesn't recognize Anderson and comments that Anderson's "photograph is younger," Anderson is quick to reply "It must be an old photograph" and then muses "Young therefore old. Old therefore young." And, like Rosencrantz and Guildenstern, George, and Henry Carr, Anderson seems naive about the world in which he lives. He has come to Prague, ostensibly to talk about "Ethical Fictions as Ethical Foundations," but actually to see a soccer match, the World Cup qualifier round. Given such two-sided motives, he is not surprisingly somewhat insensitive to the "dubious things happening in Czechoslovakia" in the wake of the Czechoslovakian government's violation of the 1975 Helsinki Agreement on human rights. His confrontation with the political reality he dismisses so easily forms the central action of the play—just as later Stoppard plays (especially *Night and Day,* 1978, and *The Real Thing,* 1982) show protagonists confronting political and emotional realities they have tried to avoid.

Though *Professional Foul* both continues and extends Stoppard's preoccupations, it also shows Stoppard adapting to the possibilities created by a script for television. Most of Stoppard's plays before 1977 have one or, at most, two settings; such limitations are common in the professional theater where the economics of production work against a multi-set play. But the sixteen scenes of *Professional Foul* require eighteen different locations. And the scenes are noticeably shorter than in Stoppard's stage plays, with some involving only action, and no words. Even the turning point of the play, Anderson's speech to the conference, is interrupted by camera cuts to backstage areas, so that we see how the "authorities" try to cope with Anderson's unexpected text.

Just as television creates new possibilities and perhaps a different style for the writer, so too it necessitates changes for the actor. Peter Barkworth, who played Professor Anderson, defined the difference between acting in the theater and acting in front of the camera in his book *About Acting*: "In the theatre you need to widen your performance so the whole audience can see you, whereas for the cameras you need to narrow it down." The review by David Pryce-Jones, reprinted following the text, notes Barkworth's ability to suggest with "tiny shrugs, wrinkles of surprise, an all-compassionate tilting of the head" the kind of public persona, feigning interest where none exists, that we see in the photograph of Anderson with McKendrick, another philosophy professor attending the conference (see Figure 1). The look on Anderson's face and the gesture toward Hollar in their corridor conversation (see Figure 2) gives us a much more involved character, someone who is trying to explain a complicated point. Even so, he is still the philosophy professor giving a mini-lecture rather than a human being confronting the ugly reality of political repression. The thoughtfulness of Barkworth's expression in Figure 3 suggests the journey he has traveled, a journey which mirrors Stoppard's own.

PROFESSIONAL FOUL
A Play for Television

BY TOM STOPPARD

TO VÁCLAV HAVEL

CHARACTERS

ANDERSON	POLICEMAN. MAN 3
MCKENDRICK	POLICEMAN, MAN 4
CHETWYN	POLICEMAN, MAN 5
HOLLAR	MRS. HOLLAR
BROADBENT	SACHA, *ten years old*
CRISP	GRAYSON
STONE	CHAMBERLAIN
CAPTAIN, MAN 6	FRENCHMAN
POLICEMAN, MAN 1	CHAIRMAN
POLICEMAN, MAN 2	CLERK, LIFT OPERATORS, CONCIERGES,
	INTERPRETERS, CUSTOMS, POLICE, *etc.*

1. Int. airplane. In flight

(*The tourist class cabin of a passenger jet.*

We are mainly concerned with two passengers. ANDERSON *is an Oxbridge don, a professor. He is middle-aged, or more. He is sitting in an aisle seat, on the left as we look down the gangway towards the tail.* MCKENDRICK *is also in an aisle seat, but across the gangway and one row nearer the tail.* MCKENDRICK *is about forty. He is also a don, but where* ANDERSON *gives a somewhat fastidious impression,* MCKENDRICK *is a rougher sort of diamond.*

MCKENDRICK *is sitting in the first row of smokers' seats, and* ANDERSON *in the last row of the non-smokers' seats looking aft.*

The plane is by no means full. The three seats across the aisle from ANDERSON *are vacant. The seat next to* ANDERSON *on his right is also vacant but the seat beyond that, by the window, accommodates a* SLEEPING MAN.

On the vacant seat between ANDERSON *and the* SLEEPING MAN *is lying a sex magazine of the* Penthouse *type. The magazine, however, is as yet face down.*

The passengers are coming to the end of a meal. They have trays of airplane food in front of them.

MCKENDRICK *puts down his fork and lights a cigarette.*

ANDERSON *dabs at his mouth with his napkin and puts it down. He glances around casually and notes the magazine next to him. He notes the* SLEEPING MAN.

MCKENDRICK *has a briefcase on the seat next to him, and from this he takes a glossy brochure. In fact, this is quite an elaborate publication associated with a philosophical congress. The cover of this program is seen to read: "Colloquium Philosophicum Prague 77."*)

ANDERSON *slides out from under his lunch tray a brochure identical to* MCKENDRICK's. *He glances at it for a mere moment and loses interest. He turns his attention back to the magazine on the seat. He turns the magazine over and notes the naked woman on its cover. He picks the magazine up, with a further glance at the* SLEEPING MAN, *and opens it to a spread of color photographs. Consciously or unconsciously he is holding the brochure in such a way as to provide a shield for the magazine.*

MCKENDRICK *casually glancing round, sees the twin to his own brochure.*)

MCKENDRICK: Snap.

(ANDERSON *looks up guiltily.*)

ANDERSON: Ah . . .

(ANDERSON *closes the magazine and slides it face-up under his lunch tray.*
MCKENDRICK's *manner is extrovert. Almost breezy.*
ANDERSON's *manner is a little vague.*)

MCKENDRICK: I wasn't sure it was you. Not a very good likeness.

ANDERSON: I assure you this is how I look.

MCKENDRICK: I mean your photograph. (*He flips his brochure open. It contains small photographs and pen portraits of various men and women who are in fact to be speakers at the colloquium.*) The photograph is younger.

ANDERSON: It must be an old photograph.

(MCKENDRICK *gets up and comes to sit in the empty seat across the aisle from* ANDERSON.)

MCKENDRICK: (*Changing seats*) Bill McKendrick.
ANDERSON: How odd.
MCKENDRICK: Is it?
ANDERSON: Young therefore old. Old therefore young. Only odd at first glance.
MCKENDRICK: Oh yes.

(ANDERSON *takes a notebook, with pencil attached, from his pocket and writes in it as he speaks.*)

ANDERSON: The second glance is known as linguistic analysis. A lot of chaps pointing out that we don't always mean what we say, even when we manage to say what we mean. Personally I'm quite prepared to believe it. (*He finishes writing and closes the notebook. He glances uneasily out of the window.*) Have you noticed the way the wings keep *wagging*? I try to look away and think of something else but I am drawn back irresistibly . . . I wouldn't be nervous about flying if the wings didn't wag. Solid steel. Thick as a bank safe. Flexing like tree branches. It's not natural. There is a coldness around my heart as though I'd seen your cigarette smoke knock against the ceiling and break in two like a bread stick. By the way, that is a non-smoking seat.
MCKENDRICK: Sorry.

(MCKENDRICK *stubs out his cigarette.* ANDERSON *puts his notebook back into his pocket.*)

ANDERSON: Yes, I like to collect little curiosities for the language chaps. It's like handing round a bag of licorice allsorts. They're terribly grateful. (*A thought strikes him.*) Oh, you're not a language chap yourself?

(*The question seems to surprise* MCKENDRICK, *and amuse him.*)

MCKENDRICK: No. I'm McKendrick.
ANDERSON: You'll be giving a paper?
MCKENDRICK: Yes. Nothing new, actually. More of a summing-up of my corner. My usual thing, you know . . . ?

(MCKENDRICK *is fishing but* ANDERSON *doesn't seem to notice.*)

ANDERSON: Jolly good.
MCKENDRICK: Perhaps you've come across some of my stuff . . . ?

(ANDERSON *now wakes up to the situation and is contrite.*)

ANDERSON: Clearly that is a reasonable expectation. I *am* sorry. I'm sure I know your name. I don't read the philosophical journals as much as I should, and hardly ever go to these international bunfights. No time nowadays. They shouldn't call us professors. It's more like being the faculty almoner.

MCKENDRICK: At least my paper will be new to you. We are the only English, actually singing for our supper, I mean. I expect there'll be a few others going for the free trip and the social life. In fact, I see we've got one on board. At the back.

(MCKENDRICK *jerks his head towards the back of the plane.* ANDERSON *turns round to look. The object of attention is* CHETWYN, *asleep in the back row, on the aisle.* CHETWYN *is younger than* MCKENDRICK *and altogether frailer and neater.* ANDERSON *squints down the plane at* CHETWYN.)

Do you know Prague?
ANDERSON: (*Warily*) Not personally. I know the name. (*Then he wakes up to that.*) Oh, *Prague*. Sorry. No, I've never been there. (*Small pause.*) Or have I? I got an honorary degree at Bratislava once. We changed planes in Prague. (*Pause.*) It might have been Vienna actually. (*Pause. He looks at the window.*) Wag, wag.
MCKENDRICK: It's Andrew Chetwyn. Do you know him?
ANDERSON: (*Warily*) Not personally.
MCKENDRICK: I don't know him *personally*. Do you know his line at all?
ANDERSON: Not as such.
MCKENDRICK: (*Suspiciously*) Have you *heard* of him?
ANDERSON: No. In a word.
MCKENDRICK: Oh. He's been quite public recently.
ANDERSON: He's an ethics chap is he?
MCKENDRICK: His line is that Aristotle got it more or less right, and St. Augustine brought it up to date.
ANDERSON: I can see that that might make him conspicuous.
MCKENDRICK: Oh, it's not *that*. I mean politics. Letters to *The Times* about persecuted professors with unpronounceable names. I'm surprised the Czechs gave him a visa.
ANDERSON: There are some rather dubious things happening in Czechoslovakia. Ethically.
MCKENDRICK: Oh yes. No doubt.
ANDERSON: We must not try to pretend otherwise.
MCKENDRICK: Oh quite. I mean I don't. My work is pretty political. I mean by implication, of course. As yours is. I'm looking forward to hearing you.
ANDERSON: Thank you. I'm sure your paper will be very interesting too.
MCKENDRICK: As a matter of fact I think there's a lot of juice left in the fictions problem.
ANDERSON: Is that what you're speaking on?
MCKENDRICK: No—you are.
ANDERSON: Oh, am I? (*He looks in his brochure briefly.*) So I am.
MCKENDRICK: "Ethical Fictions as Ethical Foundations."
ANDERSON: Yes. To tell you the truth I have an ulterior motive for coming to Czechoslovakia at this time. I'm being a tiny bit naughty.
MCKENDRICK: Naughty?

ANDERSON: Unethical. Well, I am being paid for by the Czech government, after all.

MCKENDRICK: And what . . . ?

ANDERSON: I don't think I'm going to tell you. You see, if I tell you I make you a co-conspirator whether or not you would have wished to be one. Ethically I should give you the opportunity of choosing to be one or not.

MCKENDRICK: Then why don't you give me the opportunity?

ANDERSON: I can't without telling you. An impasse.

(MCKENDRICK *is already putting two and two together and cannot hide his curiosity.*)

MCKENDRICK: Look . . . Professor Anderson . . . if it's political in any way I'd really be very interested.

ANDERSON: Why, are you a politics chap?

MCKENDRICK: One is naturally interested in what is happening in these places. And I have an academic interest—my field is the philosophical assumptions of social science.

ANDERSON: How fascinating. What is that exactly?

MCKENDRICK: (*Slightly hurt*) Perhaps my paper tomorrow afternoon will give you a fair idea.

ANDERSON: (*Mortified*) Tomorrow afternoon? I say, what rotten luck. That's exactly when I have to play truant. I *am* sorry.

MCKENDRICK: (*Coldly*) That's all right.

ANDERSON: I expect they'll have copies.

MCKENDRICK: I expect so.

ANDERSON: The science of social philosophy, eh?

MCKENDRICK: (*Brusquely*) More or less.

ANDERSON: (*With polite interest*) McCarthy.

MCKENDRICK: McKendrick.

ANDERSON: And how are things at . . . er . . .

MCKENDRICK: Stoke.

ANDERSON: (*Enthusiastically*) Stoke! An excellent university, I believe.

MCKENDRICK: You know perfectly well you wouldn't be seen dead in it.

(ANDERSON *considers this.*)

ANDERSON: Even if that were true, my being seen dead in a place has never so far as I know been thought a condition of its excellence.

(MCKENDRICK *despite himself laughs, though somewhat bitterly.*)

MCKENDRICK: Very good.

(*An* AIR HOSTESS *is walking down the aisle removing people's lunch trays. She removes* ANDERSON's *tray, revealing the cover of the sexy magazine, in the middle of* MCKENDRICK's *next speech and passes down the aisle.*)

Wit and paradox. Verbal felicity. An occupation for gentlemen. A higher civilization alive and well in the older universities. I see you like tits and bums, by the way.

ANDERSON: (*Embarrassed*) Ah . . .

(*The turning of tables cheers* MCKENDRICK *up considerably.*)

MCKENDRICK: They won't let you in with that you know. You'll have to hide it.

ANDERSON: As a matter of fact it doesn't belong to me.

MCKENDRICK: Western decadence you see. Marxists are a terrible lot of prudes. I can say that because I'm a bit that way myself.

ANDERSON: You surprise me.

MCKENDRICK: Mind you, when I say I'm a Marxist . . .

ANDERSON: Oh, I see.

MCKENDRICK: . . . I don't mean I'm an apologist for everything done in the name of Marxism.

ANDERSON: No, no quite. There's nothing anti-socialist about it. Quite the reverse. The rich have always had it to themselves.

MCKENDRICK: On the contrary. That's why I'd be really very interested in any extracurricular activities which might be going. I have an open mind about it.

ANDERSON: (*His wires crossed*) Oh, yes, indeed, so have I.

MCKENDRICK: I sail pretty close to the wind, Marx-wise.

ANDERSON: Mind you, it's an odd thing but travel broadens the mind in a way that the proverbialist didn't quite intend. It's only at airports and railway stations that one finds in oneself a curiosity about er—er—erotica, um, girly magazines.

(MCKENDRICK *realizes that they've had their wires crossed.*)

MCKENDRICK: Perhaps you've come across some of my articles.

ANDERSON: (*Amazed and fascinated*) You mean you write for—? (*He pulls himself up and together.*) Oh—your—er articles—I'm afraid as I explained I'm not very good at keeping up with the philosophical. . . .

(MCKENDRICK *has gone back to his former seat to fish about in his briefcase. He emerges with another girly magazine and hands it along the aisle to* ANDERSON.)

MCKENDRICK: I've got one here. Page sixty-one. The Science Fiction short story. Not a bad life. Science Fiction and sex. And, of course, the philosophical assumptions of social science.

ANDERSON: (*Faintly*) Thank you very much.

MCKENDRICK: Keep it by all means.

(ANDERSON *cautiously thumbs through pages of naked women.*)

I wonder if there'll be any decent women?

2. Int. hotel lobby. Prague

(*We are near the reception desk.* ANDERSON, MCKENDRICK *and* CHETWYN *have just arrived together. Perhaps* with other people. *Their luggage consists only of small overnight suitcases and briefcases.*

MCKENDRICK *is at the desk half-way through his negotiations. The lobby ought to be rather large, with lifts, etc. It should be large enough to make inconspicuous a* MAN *who is carefully watching the three Englishmen. This* MAN *is aged thirty-five or younger. He is poorly dressed, but not tramp-like. His name is* PAVEL HOLLAR. *The lobby contains other people and a poorly equipped newsstand.*

We catch up with ANDERSON *talking to* CHETWYN.)

ANDERSON: (*Enthusiastically*) Birmingham! Excellent university. Some very good people.

(*The desk* CLERK *comes to the counter where* MCKENDRICK *is first in the queue. The* CLERK *and other Czech people in this script obviously speak with an accent but there is no attempt here to reproduce it.*)

CLERK: Third floor. Dr. McKendrick.
MCKENDRICK: Only of philosophy.
CLERK: Your baggage is there?
MCKENDRICK: (*Hastily*) Oh, I'll see to that. Can I have the key, please?
CLERK: Third floor. Dr. Anderson. Ninth floor. A letter for you.

(*The* CLERK *gives* ANDERSON *a sealed envelope and also a key.* ANDERSON *seems to have been expecting the letter. He thanks the* CLERK *and takes it.*)

Dr. Chetwyn ninth floor.

(*The three philosophers walk towards the lifts.* PAVEL *watches them go. When they reach the lift* ANDERSON *glances round and sees two men some way off across the lobby, perhaps at the newsstand. These men are called* CRISP *and* BROADBENT. CRISP *looks very young, he is twenty-two. He wears a very smart, slightly flashy suit and tie.* BROADBENT *balding but young, in his thirties. He wears flannels and a blazer.* CRISP *is quite small.* BROADBENT *is big and heavy. But both look fit.*)

ANDERSON: I say, look who's over there . . . Broadbent and Crisp.

(*The lift now opens before them.* ANDERSON *goes in showing his key to the middle-aged* WOMAN *in charge of the lift.* MCKENDRICK *and* CHETWYN *do likewise. Over this:*)

CHETWYN: Who? (*He sees them and recognizes them.*) Oh yes.
MCKENDRICK: (*Sees them.*) Who?
CHETWYN: Crisp and Broadbent. They must be staying here too.
MCKENDRICK: Crisp? Broadbent? That kid over by the newsstand?
ANDERSON: That's Crisp.
MCKENDRICK: My God, they get younger all the time.

(*The lift doors close.*
Inside the lift.)

ANDERSON: Crisp is twenty-two. Broadbent is past his peak but Crisp is the next genius in my opinion.
MCKENDRICK: Do you know him?
ANDERSON: Not personally. I've been watching him for a couple of years.
CHETWYN: He's Newcastle, isn't he?
ANDERSON: Yes.
MCKENDRICK: I've never heard of him. What's his role there?
ANDERSON: He's what used to be called left wing. Broadbent's in the center. He's an opportunist more than anything.

(*The lift has stopped at the third floor.*)
(*To* MCKENDRICK.) This is you—see you later.
(MCKENDRICK *steps out of the lift and looks round.*)

MCKENDRICK: Do you think the rooms are bugged?

(*The lift doors shut him off.*
Inside the lift, ANDERSON *and* CHETWYN *ride up in silence for a few moments.*)

ANDERSON: What was it Aristotle said about the higher you go the further you fall . . . ?
CHETWYN: He was talking about tragic heroes.

(*The lift stops at the ninth floor.* ANDERSON *and* CHETWYN *leave the lift.*)

I'm this way. There's a restaurant downstairs. The menu is very limited but it's all right.
ANDERSON: You've been here before?
CHETWYN: Yes. Perhaps see you later then, sir.

(CHETWYN *goes down a corridor away from* ANDERSON'S *corridor.*)

ANDERSON: (*To himself*) Sir?

(ANDERSON *follows the arrow towards his own room number.*)

3. Int. Anderson's hotel room

(*The room contains a bed, a wardrobe, a chest. A telephone. A bathroom containing a bath leads off through a door,*
ANDERSON *is unpacking. He puts some clothes into a drawer and closes it. His suitcase is open on the bed.* ANDERSON *turns his attention to his briefcase and brings out* MCKENDRICK'S *magazine. He looks round wondering what to do with it. There is a knock on the door.* ANDERSON *tosses the girly magazine into his suitcase and closes the case. He goes to open the door. The caller is* PAVEL HOLLAR.)

ANDERSON: Yes?
HOLLAR: I am Pavel Hollar.
ANDERSON: Yes?
HOLLAR: Professor Anderson.

(HOLLAR *is Czech and speaks with an accent.*)

ANDERSON: Hollar? Oh, heavens, yes. How extraordinary. Come in.

HOLLAR: Thank you. I'm sorry to—

ANDERSON: No, no—what a pleasant surprise. I've only just arrived as you can see. Sit where you can. How are you? What are you doing? You live in Prague?

HOLLAR: Oh yes.

(ANDERSON *closes the door.*)

ANDERSON: Well, well. Well, well, well, well. How are you? Must be ten years.

HOLLAR: Yes. It is ten. I took my degree in sixty-seven.

ANDERSON: You got a decent degree, too, didn't you?

HOLLAR: Yes, I got a first.

ANDERSON: Of course you did. Well done, well done. Are you still in philosophy?

HOLLAR: No, unfortunately.

ANDERSON: Ah. What are you doing now?

HOLLAR: I am a what do you say—a cleaner.

ANDERSON: (*With intelligent interest*) A cleaner? What is that?

HOLLAR: (*Surprised*) Cleaning. Washing. With a brush and a bucket. I am a cleaner at the bus station.

ANDERSON: You wash buses?

HOLLAR: No, not buses—the lavatories, the floors where people walk and so on.

ANDERSON: Oh. I see. You're a *cleaner*.

HOLLAR: Yes.

(*Pause.*)

ANDERSON: Are you married now, or anything?

HOLLAR: Yes. I married. She was almost my fiancée when I went to England. Irma. She is a country girl. No English. No philosophy. We have a son who is Sacha. That is Alexander.

ANDERSON: I see.

HOLLAR: And Mrs. Anderson?

ANDERSON: She died. Did you meet her ever?

HOLLAR: No.

ANDERSON: (*Pause*) I don't know what to say.

HOLLAR: Did she die recently?

ANDERSON: No, I mean—a cleaner.

HOLLAR: I had one year graduate research. My doctorate studies were on certain connections with Thomas Paine and Locke. But then, since sixty-nine. . . .

ANDERSON: Cleaning lavatories.

HOLLAR: First I was in a bakery. Later on construction, building houses. Many other things. It is the way it is for many people.

ANDERSON: Is it all right for you to be here talking to me?

HOLLAR: Of course. Why not? You are my old professor.

(HOLLAR *is carrying a bag or briefcase. He puts this down and opens it.*)

I have something here.

(*From the bag he takes out the sort of envelope which would contain about thirty typewritten foolscap pages. He also takes out a child's "magic eraser" pad, the sort of pad on which one scratches a message and then slides it out to erase it.*)

You understand these things of course?

ANDERSON: (*Nonplussed*) Er . . .

HOLLAR: (*Smiling*) Of course.

(HOLLAR *demonstrates the pad briefly, then writes on the pad while* ANDERSON *watches.*)

ANDERSON: (*Stares at him*) To England?

(HOLLAR *abandons the use of the pad, and whispers in* ANDERSON's *ear.*)

HOLLAR: Excuse me.

(HOLLAR *goes to the door and opens it for* ANDERSON. HOLLAR *carries his envelope but leaves his bag in the room.* ANDERSON *goes out of the door baffled.* HOLLAR *follows him. They walk a few paces down the corridor.*)

Thank you. It is better to be careful.

ANDERSON: Why? You don't seriously suggest that my room is bugged?

HOLLAR: It is better to assume it.

ANDERSON: Why?

(*Just then the door of the room next to* ANDERSON's *opens and a* MAN *comes out. He is about forty and wears a dark rather shapeless suit. He glances at* ANDERSON *and* HOLLAR. *And then walks off in the opposite direction towards the lifts and passes out of sight.* HOLLAR *and* ANDERSON *instinctively pause until the* MAN *has gone.*)

I hope you're not getting me into trouble.

HOLLAR: I hope not. I don't think so. I have friends in trouble.

ANDERSON: I know, it's dreadful—but . . . well, what is it?

(HOLLAR *indicates his envelope.*)

HOLLAR: My doctoral thesis. It is mainly theoretical. Only ten thousand words, but very formally arranged.

ANDERSON: My goodness . . . ten years in the writing.

HOLLAR: No. I wrote it this month—when I heard of this congress here and you coming. I decided. Everyday in the night.

ANDERSON: Of course. I'd be very happy to read it.

HOLLAR: It is in Czech.

ANDERSON: Oh . . . well . . . ?

HOLLAR: I'm afraid so. But Peter Volkansky—he was with me, you remember—we came together in sixty-three—

ANDERSON: Oh yes—Volkansky—yes, I do remember him. He never came back here.

HOLLAR: No. He didn't come back. He was a realist.

ANDERSON: He's at Reading or somewhere like that.

HOLLAR: Lyster.

ANDERSON: Leicester. Exactly. Are you in touch with him?

HOLLAR: A little. He will translate it and try to have it published in English. If it's good. I think it is good.

ANDERSON: But can't you publish it in Czech? . . . (*This catches up on him and he shakes his head.*) Oh, Hollar . . . now, you know, really, I'm a guest of the government here.

HOLLAR: They would not search you.

ANDERSON: That's not the point. I'm sorry . . . I mean it would be bad manners, wouldn't it?

HOLLAR: Bad manners?

ANDERSON: I know it sounds rather lame. But ethics and manners are interestingly related. The history of human calumny is largely a series of breaches of good manners. . . . (*Pause.*) Perhaps if I said correct behavior it wouldn't sound so ridiculous. You do see what I mean. I am sorry. . . . Look, can we go back . . . I ought to unpack.

HOLLAR: My thesis is about correct behavior.

ANDERSON: Oh yes?

HOLLAR: Here you know, individual correctness is defined by what is correct for the State.

ANDERSON: Yes, I know.

HOLLAR: I ask how collective right can have meaning by itself. I ask where it comes from, the idea of a collective ethic.

ANDERSON: Yes.

HOLLAR: I reply, it comes from the individual. One man's dealings with another man.

ANDERSON: Yes.

HOLLAR: The collective ethic can only be the individual ethic writ big.

ANDERSON: Writ large.

HOLLAR: Writ large, precisely. The ethics of the State must be judged against the fundamental ethic of the individual. The human being, not the citizen. I conclude there is an obligation, a human responsibility, to fight against the State correctness. Unfortunately that is not a safe conclusion.

ANDERSON: Quite. The difficulty arises when one asks oneself how the *individual* ethic can have any meaning by itself. Where does *that* come from? In what sense is it intelligible, for example, to say that a man has certain inherent, individual rights? It is much easier to understand how a community of individuals can decide to give each other certain rights. These rights may or may not include, for example, the right to publish something. In that situation, the individual ethic would flow from the collective ethic, just as the State says it does.

(*Pause.*)

I only mean it is a question you would have to deal with.

HOLLAR: I mean, it is not safe for me.

ANDERSON: (*Still misunderstanding*) Well yes, but for example, you could say that such an arrangement between a man and the State is a sort of contract, and it is the essence of a contract that both parties enter into it freely. And you have not entered into it freely. I mean, that would be one line of attack.

HOLLAR: It is not the main line. You see, to me the idea of an inherent right is intelligible. I believe that we have such rights, and they are paramount.

ANDERSON: Yes, I see you do, but how do you justify the assertion?

HOLLAR: I observe. I observe my son for example.

ANDERSON: Your son?

HOLLAR: For example.

(*Pause.*)

ANDERSON: Look, there's no need to stand out here. There's . . . no point. I was going to have a bath and change . . . meeting some of my colleagues later. . . .

(ANDERSON *moves to go but* HOLLAR *stops him with a touch on the arm.*)

HOLLAR: I am not a famous dissident. A writer, a scientist. . . .

ANDERSON: No.

HOLLAR: If I am picked up—on the way home, let us say—there is no fuss. A cleaner. I will be one of hundreds. It's all right. In the end it must change. But I have something to say—that is all. If I leave my statement behind, then it's O.K. You understand?

ANDERSON: Perhaps the correct thing for me to have done is not to have accepted their invitation to speak here. But I did accept it. It is a contract, as it were, freely entered into. And having accepted their hospitality I cannot in all conscience start smuggling. . . . It's just not ethical.

HOLLAR: But if you didn't know you were smuggling it—

ANDERSON: Smuggling entails knowledge.

HOLLAR: If I hid my thesis in your luggage, for instance.

ANDERSON: That's childish. Also, you could be getting me into trouble, and your quarrel is not with me. Your action would be unethical on your own terms—one man's dealings with another man. I am sorry.

(ANDERSON *goes back towards his door, which* HOLLAR *had left ajar.* HOLLAR *follows him.*)

HOLLAR: No, it is I who must apologize. The man next door, is he one of your group?

ANDERSON: No. I don't know him.

(ANDERSON *opens his bedroom door. He turns as if to say good-bye.*)

HOLLAR: My bag.

ANDERSON: Oh yes.

(HOLLAR *follows* ANDERSON *into the room.*)

HOLLAR: You will have a bath . . . ?
ANDERSON: I thought I would.

(HOLLAR *turns into the bathroom.* ANDERSON *stays in the bedroom, surprised.*
He hears the bath water being turned on. The bath water makes a rush of sound. ANDERSON *enters the bathroom and sees* HOLLAR *sitting on the edge of the bath.*
Interior bathroom.)

HOLLAR: (*Quietly*) I have not yet made a copy.
ANDERSON: (*Loudly*) What?

(HOLLAR *goes up to* ANDERSON *and speaks close to* ANDERSON's *ear. The bath taps make a loud background noise.*)

HOLLAR: I have not yet made a copy. I have a bad feeling about carrying this home. (*He indicates his envelope.*) I did not expect to take it away. I ask a favor. (*Smiles.*) Ethical.
ANDERSON: (*Quietly now*) What is it?
HOLLAR: Let me leave this here and you can bring it to my apartment tomorrow—I have a safe place for it there.

(HOLLAR *takes a piece of paper and a pencil from his pocket and starts writing his address in capital letters.*)

ANDERSON: But you know my time here is very crowded—(*Then he gives in.*) Do you live nearby?
HOLLAR: It is not far. I have written my address.

(HOLLAR *gives* ANDERSON *the paper.*)

ANDERSON: (*Forgetting to be quiet*) Do you seriously—

(HOLLAR *quiets* ANDERSON.)

Do you seriously expect to be searched on the way home?
HOLLAR: I don't know, but it is better to be careful. I wrote a letter to Mr. Husak. Also some other things. So sometimes they follow me.
ANDERSON: But you weren't worried about bringing the thesis with you.
HOLLAR: No. If anybody watches me they want to know what books *you* give *me*.
ANDERSON: I see. Yes, all right, Hollar. I'll bring it tomorrow.
HOLLAR: Please don't leave it in your room when you go to eat. Take your briefcase.

(*They go back into the bedroom.* ANDERSON *puts* HOLLAR's *envelope into his briefcase.*)

(*Normal voice*) So perhaps you will come and meet my wife.
ANDERSON: Yes. Should I telephone?
HOLLAR: Unfortunately my telephone is removed. I am home all day. Saturday.

ANDERSON: Oh yes.
HOLLAR: Good-bye.
ANDERSON: Good-bye.

(HOLLAR *goes to the door carrying his bag.*)

HOLLAR: I forgot—welcome to Prague.

(HOLLAR *leaves closing the door.*
ANDERSON *stands still for a few moments. Then he hears footsteps approaching down the corridor. The footsteps appear to stop outside his room. But then the door to the next room is opened and the unseen man enters the room next door and loudly closes the door behind him.*)

4. Int. Anderson's room. Morning.

(*Close-up of the colloquium brochure. It is lying on* ANDERSON's *table. Then* ANDERSON *picks it up. His dress and appearance, and the light outside the window, tell us that it is morning. Dressed to go out,* ANDERSON *picks up his briefcase and leaves the room.*
In the corridor he walks towards the lifts.
At the lifts he finds CRISP *waiting.* ANDERSON *stands next to* CRISP *silently for a few moments.*)

ANDERSON: Good morning. (*Pause.*) Mr. Crisp . . . my name is Anderson. I'm a very great admirer of yours.
CRISP: (*Chewing gum*) Oh . . . ta.
ANDERSON: Good luck this afternoon.
CRISP: Thanks. Bloody useless, the lifts in this place.
ANDERSON: Are you all staying in this hotel?

(CRISP *doesn't seem to hear this.* CRISP *sees* BROADBENT *emerging from a room.* BROADBENT *carries a zipped bag,* CRISP *has a similar bag.*)

CRISP: (*Shouts*) Here you are, Roy—it's waiting for you.

(BROADBENT *arrives.*)

ANDERSON: Good morning. Good luck this afternoon.
BROADBENT: Right. Thanks. Are you over for the match?
ANDERSON: Yes. Well, partly. I've got my ticket.

(ANDERSON *takes out of his pocket the envelope he received from the hotel* CLERK *and shows it.*)

CRISP: (*Quietly*) You didn't pull her, then?
BROADBENT: No chance.
CRISP: They don't trust you, do they?
BROADBENT: Well, they're right, aren't they? Remember Milan.
CRISP: (*Laughing*) Yeah—

(*The bell sounds to indicate that the lift is arriving.*)

About bloody time.
ANDERSON: I see from yesterday's paper that they've brought in Jirasek for Vladislav.

BROADBENT: Yes, that's right. Six foot eight, they say.

ANDERSON: He's not very good in the air unless he's got lots of space.

(BROADBENT *looks at him curiously. The lift doors open and the three of them get in. There is no one else in the lift except the female* OPERATOR.
Interior lift.)

BROADBENT: You've seen him, have you?

ANDERSON: I've seen him twice. In the UFA Cup a few seasons ago. . . . I happened to be in Berlin for the Hegel Colloquium, er, bunfight. And then last season I was in Bratislava to receive an honorary degree.

CRISP: Tap his ankles for him. Teach him to be six foot eight.

BROADBENT: Leave off— (*He nods at the lift* OPERATOR.) You never know, do you?

CRISP: Yeah, maybe the lift's bugged.

ANDERSON: He scored both times from the same move, and came close twice more—

BROADBENT: Oh yes?

(*Pause.*)

ANDERSON: (*In a rush*) I realize it's none of my business— I mean you may think I'm an absolute ass, but—

(*Pause.*)

Look, if Halas takes a corner he's going to make it short—almost certainly—push it back to Deml or Kautsky, who pulls the defense out. Jirasek hangs about for the chip to the far post. They'll do the same thing from a set piece. Three or four times in the same match. *Really.* Short corners and free kicks.

(*The lift stops at the third floor.* BROADBENT *and* CRISP *are staring at* ANDERSON.)

(*Lamely.*) Anyway, that's why they've brought Jirasek back, in my opinion.

(*The lift doors open and* MCKENDRICK *gets in.* MCKEN-DRICK's *manner is breezy and bright.*)

MCKENDRICK: Good morning! You've got together then?

ANDERSON: A colleague. Mr. McKendrick . . .

MCKENDRICK: You're Crisp. (*He takes* CRISP's *hand and shakes it.*) Bill McKendrick. I hear you're doing some very interesting work in Newcastle. Great stuff. I still like to think of myself as a bit of a left-winger at Stoke. Of course, my stuff is largely empirical— I leave epistemological questions to the scholastics—eh, Anderson? (*He pokes* ANDERSON *in the ribs.*)

ANDERSON: McKendrick . . .

BROADBENT: Did you say *Stoke?*

(*The lift arrives at the ground floor.*)

MCKENDRICK: (*To* BROADBENT) We've met, haven't we? Your face is familiar . . .

(BROADBENT, CRISP, *and* MCKENDRICK *in close attend-ance leave the lift.* ANDERSON *is slow on the uptake but follows.*)

ANDERSON: McKendrick—?

MCKENDRICK: (*Prattling*) There's a choice of open fo-rums tonight—neo-Hegelians or Quinian neo-Posi-tivists. Which do you fancy? Pity Quine couldn't be here. And Hegel for that matter.

(MCKENDRICK *laughs brazenly in the lobby.* BROADBENT *and* CRISP *eye him warily.* ANDERSON *winces.*)

5. Int. The Colloquium

(*The general idea is that a lot of philosophers sit in a sort of theater while on stage one of their number reads a paper from behind a lectern, with a* CHAIRMAN *in attendance behind him. The set up however is quite complicated. To one side are three glassed-in booths, each one containing "simultaneous interpreters." These interpreters have ear-phones and microphones. They also have a copy of the lecture being given. One of these interpreters is translating into Czech, another into French, another into German. The audience is furnished either with earphones or with those hand-held phones which are issued in theaters sometimes. Each of these phones can tune into any of the three inter-preters depending upon the language of the listener. For our purposes it is better to have the hand-held phones.*

It is important to the play, specifically to a later scene when ANDERSON *is talking, that the hall and the audience should be substantial.*

At the moment ANDERSON *is in the audience, sitting next to* MCKENDRICK. MCKENDRICK *is still discomforted.* CHET-WYN *is elsewhere in the audience.*

We begin however with a large close-up of the speaker who is an American called STONE. *After the first sentence or two of* STONE's *speech, the camera will acquaint us with the situation. At different points during* STONE's *speech, there is conversation between* ANDERSON *and* MCKEN-DRICK. *In this script, these conversations are placed im-mediately after that part of* STONE's *speech which they will cover. This applies also to any other interpolations. Ob-viously,* STONE *does not pause to let these other things in.*)

STONE: The confusion which often arises from the am-biguity of ordinary language raises special prob-lems for a logical language. This is especially so when the ambiguity is not casual and inadvertent— but when it's contrived. In fact, the limitations of a logical language are likely to appear when we ask ourselves whether it can accommodate a literature, or whether poetry can be reduced to a logical lan-guage. It is here that deliberate ambiguity for effect makes problems.

ANDERSON: Perfectly understandable mistake.

STONE: Nor must we confuse ambiguity, furthermore, with mere synonymity. When we say that a politician ran for office, that is not an ambiguous statement, it is merely an instance of a word having different applications, literal, idiomatic and so on.

MCKENDRICK: I said I knew his face.

ANDERSON: Match of the Day.

STONE: The intent is clear in each application. The show ran well on Broadway. Native Dancer ran well at Kentucky, and so on.

(In the audience a Frenchman expresses dismay and bewilderment as his earphones give out a literal translation of "a native dancer" running well at Kentucky. Likewise a German listener has the same problem.)

And what about this word "Well"? Again, it is applied as a qualifier with various intent—the show ran for a long time, the horse ran fast, and so on.

MCKENDRICK: So this pressing engagement of yours is a football match.

ANDERSON: A World Cup qualifier is not just a football match.

STONE: Again, there is no problem here so long as these variations are what I propose to call reliable. "You eat well" says Mary to John, "You cook well" says John to Mary. We know that when Mary says "You *eat* well" she does not mean that John eats *skillfully*. Just as we know that when John says "You cook well" he does not mean that Mary cooks *abundantly*.

ANDERSON: But I'm sorry about missing your paper, I really am.

STONE: I say that we know this, but I mean only that our general experience indicates it. The qualifier takes its meaning from the contextual force of the verb it qualifies. But it is the mark of a sound theory that it should take account not merely of our general experience, but also of the particular experience, and not merely of the particular experience but also of the unique experience, and not merely of the unique experience but also of the hypothetical experience. It is when we consider the world of *possibilities*, hypothetical experience, that we get closer to ambiguity. "You cook well" says John to Mary. "You eat well" says Mary to John.

MCKENDRICK: Do you ever wonder whether all this is worthwhile?

ANDERSON: No.

MCKENDRICK: I know what you mean.

(CHETWYN is twisting the knob on his translation phone, to try all this out in different languages. He is clearly bored. He looks at his watch.)

STONE: No problems there. But I ask you to imagine a competition when what is being judged is table manners.

(Insert FRENCH INTERPRETER's box—interior.)

INTERPRETER: *. . . bonne tenue à table . . .*

STONE: John enters this competition and afterwards Mary says, "Well, you certainly ate well!" Now Mary seems to be saying that John ate *skillfully—with refinement*. And again, I ask you to imagine a competition where the amount of food eaten is taken into account along with refinement of table manners. *Now* Mary says to John, "Well, you didn't eat very well, but at least you ate well."

INTERPRETER: *Alors, vous n'avez pas bien mangé . . . mais . . .*

(All INTERPRETERS baffled by this.)

STONE: Now clearly there is no way to tell whether Mary means that John ate abundantly but clumsily, or that John ate frugally but elegantly. Here we have a genuine ambiguity. To restate Mary's sentence in a logical language we would have to ask her what she meant.

MCKENDRICK: By the way, I've got you a copy of my paper.

ANDERSON: Oh, many thanks.

MCKENDRICK: It's not a long paper. You could read it comfortably during half-time.

(MCKENDRICK gives ANDERSON his paper.)

STONE: But this is to assume that Mary exists. Let us say she is a fictitious character in a story I have written. Very well, you say to me, the author, "What did Mary mean?" Well I might reply—"I don't know what she meant. Her ambiguity makes the necessary point of my story." And here I think the idea of a logical language which can *only* be unambiguous, breaks down.

(ANDERSON opens his briefcase and puts MCKENDRICK's paper into it. He fingers HOLLAR's envelope and broods over it. STONE has concluded. He sits down to applause. The CHAIRMAN, who has been sitting behind him, has stood up.)

ANDERSON: I'm going to make a discreet exit—I've got a call to make before the match.

(ANDERSON stands up.)

CHAIRMAN: Yes—Professor Anderson I think . . . ?

(ANDERSON is caught like a rabbit in the headlights. MCKENDRICK enjoys his predicament and becomes interested in how ANDERSON will deal with it.)

ANDERSON: Ah . . . I would only like to offer Professor Stone the observation that language is not the only level of human communication, and perhaps not the most important level. Whereof we cannot speak, thereof we are by no means silent.

(MCKENDRICK smiles "Bravo.")

Verbal language is a technical refinement of our capacity for communication, rather than the *fons et origo* of that capacity. The likelihood is that language develops in an *ad hoc* way, so there is no reason to expect its development to be logical. (*A thought strikes him.*) The importance of language is overrated. It allows me and Professor Stone to show off a bit, and it is very useful for communicating detail—but the important truths are simple and monolithic. The essentials of a given situation speak for themselves, and language is as capable of obscuring the truth as of revealing it. Thank you.

(ANDERSON *edges his way out towards the door.*)

CHAIRMAN: (*Uncertainly*) Professor Stone . . .

STONE: Well, what was the question?

6. Ext. Front door of the Hollar apartment

(*The apartment is one of two half-way up a large old building. The stairwell is dirty and uncared for. The* HOLLAR *front door is on a landing, and the front door of another flat is across the landing. Stairs go up and down.* ANDERSON *comes up the stairs and finds the right number on the door and rings the bell. He is carrying his briefcase.*

All the men in this scene are Czech plainclothes POLICEMEN. *They will be identified in this text merely by number.* MAN 3 *is the one in charge.* MAN 1 *comes to the door.*)

ANDERSON: I'm looking for Mr. Hollar.

(MAN 1 *shakes his head. He looks behind him.* MAN 2 *comes to the door.*)

MAN 2: (*In Czech*) Yes? Who are you?

ANDERSON: English? Um. *Parlez-vous francais?* Er. *Spreckanzydoitch?*

MAN 2: (*In German*) *Deutch? Ein Bischen.*

ANDERSON: Actually I don't. Does Mr. Hollar live here? Apartment Hollar?

(MAN 2 *speaks to somebody behind him.*)

MAN 2: (*In Czech*) An Englishman. Do you know him?

(MRS. HOLLAR *comes to the door. She is about the same age as* HOLLAR.)

ANDERSON: Mrs. Hollar?

(MRS. HOLLAR *nods.*)

Is your husband here? Pavel . . .

MRS. HOLLAR: (*In Czech*) Pavel is arrested.

(*Inside, behind the door,* MAN 3 *is heard shouting, in Czech.*)

MAN 3: (*Not seen*) What's going on there?

(MAN 3 *comes to the door.*)

ANDERSON: I am looking for Mr. Hollar. I am a friend from England. His Professor. My name is Anderson.

MAN 3: (*In English*) Not here. (*In Czech to* MRS. HOLLAR) He says he is a friend of your husband. Anderson.

ANDERSON: He was my student.

(MRS. HOLLAR *calls out.*)

MAN 3: (*In Czech*) Shut up.

ANDERSON: Student. Philosophy.

(MRS. HOLLAR *calls out.*)

MAN 3: Shut up.

(MAN 3 *and* MAN 2 *come out of the flat on to the landing, closing the door behind them.*)

ANDERSON: I just came to see him. Just to say hello. For a minute. I have a taxi waiting. Taxi.

MAN 3: Taxi.

ANDERSON: Yes. I can't stay.

MAN 3: (*In English*) Moment. O.K.

ANDERSON: I can't stay.

(MAN 3 *rings the bell of the adjacent flat. A rather scared woman opens the door.* MAN 3 *asks, in Czech, to use the phone.* MAN 3 *goes inside the other flat.* ANDERSON *begins to realize the situation.*)

Well, look, if you don't mind—I'm on my way to—an engagement. . . .

MAN 2: (*In Czech*) Stay here.

(*Pause.* ANDERSON *looks at his watch. Then from inside the flat* MRS. HOLLAR *is shouting in Czech.*)

MRS. HOLLAR: (*Unseen*) I'm entitled to a witness of my choice.

(*The door is opened violently and immediately slammed.* ANDERSON *becomes agitated.*)

ANDERSON: What's going on in there?

MAN 2: (*In Czech*) Stay here, he won't be a minute.

(ANDERSON *can hear* MRS. HOLLAR *shouting.*)

ANDERSON: Now look here—

(ANDERSON *rings the doorbell. The door is opened by* MAN 4.)

I demand to speak to Mrs. Hollar.

(*Upstairs and downstairs doors are opening and people are shouting, in Czech, "What's going on?" And so on. There is also shouting from inside the flat.* MAN 2 *shouts up and down the staircase, in Czech.*)

MAN 2: (*In Czech*) Go inside!

ANDERSON: Now look here, I am the J. S. Mill Professor of Ethics at the University of Cambridge and I demand that I am allowed to leave or to telephone the British Ambassador!

MAN 4: (*In Czech*) Bring him inside.

MAN 2: (*In Czech*) In.

(*He pushes* ANDERSON *into the flat. Interior flat. The hallway. Inside it is apparent that the front door leads to more than one flat. Off the very small dirty hall there is a kitchen, a lavatory, and two other doors, not counting the door to the* HOLLAR *rooms.*)

MAN 4: (*In Czech*) Stay with him.

(*The* HOLLAR *interior door is opened from inside by* MRS. HOLLAR.)

MRS. HOLLAR: (*In Czech*) If he's my witness he's allowed in here.

MAN 4: (*In Czech*) Go inside—he's not your witness.

(MAN 4 *pushes* MRS. HOLLAR *inside and closes the door from within. This leaves* ANDERSON *and* MAN 2 *in the little hall. Another door now opens, and a small girl, poorly dressed, looks round it. She is jerked back out of sight by someone and the door is pulled closed. The* HOLLAR *door is flung open again, by* MRS. HOLLAR.)

MRS. HOLLAR: (*In Czech*) I want this door open.

MAN 2: (*In Czech*) Leave it open then. He'll be back in a minute.

(MAN 4 *disappears back inside the flat.* MRS. HOLLAR *is heard.*)

MRS. HOLLAR: (*Unseen. In Czech*) Bastards.

(ANDERSON *stands in the hallway. He can hear* MRS. HOLLAR *starting to cry.* ANDERSON *looks completely out of his depth.*)

ANDERSON: My God. . . .

(*Then the doorbell rings.* MAN 2 *opens it to let in* MAN 3.)

MAN 2: (*In Czech*) We had to come in to shut her up.

MAN 3: (*In Czech*) Well, he's coming over. (*In English to* ANDERSON) Captain coming. Speak English.

ANDERSON: I would like to telephone the British Ambassador.

MAN 3: (*In English*) O.K. Captain coming.

ANDERSON: How long will he be? I have an appointment. (*He looks at his watch.*) Yes, by God! I do have an engagement and it starts in half an hour—

MAN 3: (*In English*) Please.

(*A lavatory flushes. From the other interior door an* OLD MAN *comes out.* MAN 3 *nods curtly at the* OLD MAN. *The* OLD MAN *shuffles by looking at* ANDERSON. MAN 3 *becomes uneasy at being in the traffic. He decides to bring* ANDERSON *inside the flat. He does so.*

Interior HOLLAR's *room. There are two connecting rooms.*

Beyond this room is a door leading to a bedroom. This door is open. The rooms seem full of people. The rooms are small and shabby. They are being thoroughly searched, and obviously have been in this process for

hours. *The searchers do not spoil or destroy anything. There are no torn cushions or anything like that. However, the floor of the first room is almost covered in books. The bookcases which line perhaps two of the walls are empty. The rug could be rolled up, and there could be one or two floorboards up.*

MAN 1 *is going through the books, leafing through each one and looking along the spine. He is starting to put books back on the shelves one by one.* MAN 5 *has emptied drawers of their contents and is going through a pile of papers.* MRS. HOLLAR *stands in the doorway between the two rooms. Beyond her* MAN 2 *can be seen searching.* [MAN 4 *is out of sight in the bedroom.*] MAN 3 *indicates a chair on which* ANDERSON *should sit.* ANDERSON *sits putting his briefcase on the floor by his feet. He looks around. He sees a clock showing 2:35.*

Mix to clock showing 2:55.

ANDERSON *is where he was.* MAN 1 *is still on the books.* MAN 5 *is still looking through papers.* MAN 3 *is examining the inside of a radio set.*

Voices are heard faintly on the stairs. There is a man remonstrating. A woman's voice too.

The doorbell rings.

MAN 3 *leaves the room, closing the door.* ANDERSON *hears him go to the front door. There is some conversation. The front door closes again and* MAN 3 *re-enters the room.*)

MAN 3: (*In English to* ANDERSON) Taxi.

ANDERSON: Oh—I forgot him. Dear me.

MAN 3: O.K.

ANDERSON: I must pay him.

(ANDERSON *takes out his wallet.* MAN 3 *takes it from him without snatching.*)

MAN 3: O.K.

(MAN 3 *looks through the wallet.*)

ANDERSON: Give that back— (*Furious*) Now, you listen to me—this has gone on quite long enough—I demand—to be allowed to leave. . . .

(ANDERSON *has stood up.* MAN 3 *gently pushes him back into the chair. In* ANDERSON's *wallet* MAN 3 *finds his envelope and discovers the football ticket. He puts it back. He looks sympathetically at* ANDERSON.)

MAN 3: (*In Czech*) The old boy's got a ticket for the England match. No wonder he's furious. (*He gives the wallet back to* ANDERSON. *In English*) Taxi O.K. No money. He go. Football no good.

ANDERSON: Serve me right.

MAN 5: (*In Czech*) It's on the radio. Let him have it on.

(MAN 3 *returns to the radio and turns it on.* MRS. HOLLAR *enters quickly from the bedroom and turns it off.*)

MRS. HOLLAR: (*In Czech*) That's my radio.

MAN 3: (*In Czech*) Your friend wants to listen to the match.

(MRS. HOLLAR *looks at* ANDERSON. *She turns the radio on. The radio is talking about the match which is just about to begin.*)

MAN 3: (*In English*) Is good. O.K.?

(ANDERSON, *listening, realizes that the radio is listing the names of the English team.*
Then the match begins.
Mix to:
The same situation about half an hour later. The radio is still on. MAN 1 *is still on the books. He has put aside three or four English books.* MAN 5 *has disappeared.* MAN 2 *is sorting out the fluff from a carpet sweeper.* MAN 4 *is standing on a chair examining the inside of a ventilation grating.*
ANDERSON *gets up off his chair and starts to walk towards the bedroom. The three* MEN *in the room look up but don't stop him.* ANDERSON *enters the bedroom.*
Interior bedroom
MAN 3 *is going through pockets in a wardrobe.* MAN 5 *is looking under floorboards.* MRS. HOLLAR *is sitting on the bed watching them.*)

ANDERSON: It's half-past three. I demand to be allowed to leave or to telephone the British—

MAN 3: Please—too slow.

ANDERSON: I demand to leave—

MAN 3: O.K. Who wins football?

ANDERSON: (*Pause*) No score.

(*The doorbell goes.*
MAN 3 *goes into the other room and to the door.* ANDERSON *follows him as far as the other room. On the way through* MAN 3 *signals to turn off the radio.* MAN 2 *turns off the radio.* MRS. HOLLAR *comes in and turns the radio on.*)

MRS. HOLLAR: (*In Czech*) Show me where it says I can't listen to my own radio.

(MAN 3 *returns from the front door with* MAN 6. MAN 6 *enters the room saying:*)

MAN 6: (*In Czech*) I said don't let him leave—I didn't say bring him inside. (*To* ANDERSON *in English*) Professor Anderson? I'm sorry your friend Mr. Hollar has got himself into trouble.

ANDERSON: Thank Christ—now listen to me—I am a professor of philosophy. I am a guest of the Czechoslovakian government. I might almost say an honored guest. I have been invited to speak at the Colloquium in Prague. My connections in England reach up to the highest in the land—

MAN 6: Do you know the Queen?

ANDERSON: Certainly. (*But he has rushed into that.*) No, I do not know the Queen—but I speak the truth when I say that I am personally acquainted with two members of the government, one of whom has been to my house, and I assure you that unless I am allowed to leave this building immediately there is going to be a major incident about the way my liberty has been impeded by your men. I do not know what they are doing here, I do not care what they are doing here—

MAN 6: Excuse me. Professor. There is some mistake. I thought you were here as a friend of the Hollar family.

ANDERSON: I know Pavel Hollar, certainly.

MAN 6: Absolutely. You are here as a friend, at Mrs. Hollar's request.

ANDERSON: I just dropped in to—what do you mean?

MAN 6: Mr. Hollar unfortunately has been arrested for a serious crime against the State. It is usual for the home of an accused person to be searched for evidence, and so on. I am sure the same thing happens in your country. Well, under our law Mrs. Hollar is entitled to have a friendly witness present during the search. To be frank she is entitled to two witnesses. So if, for example, an expensive vase is broken by mistake, and the police claim it was broken before, it will not just be her word against theirs. And so on. I think you will agree that's fair.

ANDERSON: Well?

MAN 6: Well, my understanding is that she asked you to be her witness. (*In Czech to* MRS. HOLLAR) Did you ask him to be your witness?

MRS. HOLLAR: (*In Czech*) Yes, I did.

MAN 6: (*In English to* ANDERSON) Yes. Exactly so. (*Pause.*) You are Mr. Hollar's friend, aren't you?

ANDERSON: I taught him in Cambridge after he left Czechoslovakia.

MAN 6: A brave man.

ANDERSON: Yes . . . a change of language . . . and culture . . .

MAN 6: He walked across a minefield. In 1962. Brave.

ANDERSON: Perhaps he was simply desperate.

MAN 6: Perhaps a little ungrateful. The State, you know, educated him, fed him, for eighteen years. "Thank you very much—good-bye."

ANDERSON: Well he came back, in the Spring of sixty-eight.

MAN 6: Oh yes.

ANDERSON: A miscalculation.

MAN 6: How do you mean?

ANDERSON: Well, really . . . there are a lot of things wrong in England but it is still not "a serious crime against the State" to put forward a philosophical view which does not find favor with the Government.

MAN 6: Professor. . . . Hollar is charged with currency offenses. There is a black market in hard currency. It is illegal. We do not have laws about philosophy. He is an ordinary criminal.

(*Pause.*
The radio commentary has continued softly. But in this pause it changes pitch. It is clear to ANDERSON, *and to*

us, that something particular has occurred in the match.
MAN 6 *is listening.)*

(In English.) Penalty. *(He listens for a moment)* For us,
I'm afraid.

ANDERSON: Yes, I can hear.

*(This is because it is clear from the crowd noise that it's
a penalty for the home side.* MAN 6 *listens again.)*

MAN 6: *(In English)* Broadbent—a bad tackle when Deml
had a certain goal . . . a what you call it?—a necessary
foul.

ANDERSON: A professional foul.

MAN 6: Yes.

*(On the radio the goal is scored. This is perfectly clear
from the crowd reaction.)*

Not good for you.

*(*MAN 6 *turns off the radio. Pause.* MAN 6 *considers*
ANDERSON.*)*

So you have had a philosophical discussion with Hollar.

ANDERSON: I believe you implied that I was free to go.
(He stands up.) I am quite sure you know that Hollar
visited me at my hotel last night. It was a social call,
which I was returning when I walked into this. And
furthermore, I understood nothing about being a
witness—I was prevented from leaving. I only came
to say hello, and meet Pavel's wife, on my way to
the football—

MAN 6: *(With surprise)* So you came to Czechoslovakia to
go to the football match, Professor?

(This rattles ANDERSON.*)*

ANDERSON: Certainly not. Well, the afternoon of the
Colloquium was devoted to—well, it was not a condition of my invitation that I should attend all the
sessions. *(Pause.)* I was invited to *speak,* not to listen.
I am speaking tomorrow morning.

MAN 6: Why should I know Hollar visited you at the
hotel?

ANDERSON: He told me he was often followed.

MAN 6: Well, when a man is known to be engaged in
meeting foreigners to buy currency—

ANDERSON: I don't believe any of that—he was being
harassed because of his letter to Husak—

MAN 6: A letter to President Husak? What sort of letter?

ANDERSON: *(Flustered)* Your people knew about it—

MAN 6: It is not a crime to write to the President—

ANDERSON: No doubt that depends on what is written.

MAN 6: You mean he wrote some kind of slander?

ANDERSON: *(Heatedly)* I insist on leaving now.

MAN 6:. Of course. You know, your taxi driver has made
a complaint against you.

ANDERSON: What are you talking about?

MAN 6: He never got paid.

ANDERSON: Yes, I'm sorry but—

MAN 6: You are not to blame. My officer told him to go.

ANDERSON: Yes, that's right.

MAN 6: Still, he is very unhappy. You told him you
would be five minutes, you were delivering something—

ANDERSON: How could I have told him that? I don't
speak Czech.

MAN 6: You showed him five on your watch, and you
did all the things people do when they talk to each
other without a language. He was quite certain you
were delivering something in your briefcase.

(Pause.)

ANDERSON: Yes. All right. But it was not money.

MAN 6: Of course not. You are not a criminal.

ANDERSON: Quite so. I promised to bring Pavel one or
two of the Colloquium papers. He naturally has an
interest in philosophy and I assume it is not illegal.

MAN 6: Naturally not. Then you won't mind showing me.

*(*ANDERSON *hesitates then opens the briefcase and takes
out* MCKENDRICK's *paper and his own and passes them
over.* MAN 6 *takes them and reads their English titles.)*

"Ethical Fictions as Ethical Foundations" . . . "Philosophy and the Catastrophe Theory."

*(*MAN 6 *gives the papers back to* ANDERSON.*)*

MAN 6: You wish to go to the football match? You will
see twenty minutes, perhaps more.

ANDERSON: No. I'm going back to the university, to the
Colloquium.

MRS. HOLLAR: *(In Czech)* Is he leaving?

MAN 6: Mrs. Hollar would like you to remain.

ANDERSON: *(To* MRS. HOLLAR*)* No, I'm sorry. *(A thought
strikes him.)* If you spoke to the taxi driver you would
have known perfectly well I was going to the England match.

*(*MAN 6 *doesn't reply to this either in word or expression.*
ANDERSON *closes his briefcase.*
The doorbell rings and MAN 3 *goes to open the door.*
From the bedroom MAN 5 *enters with a small parcel
wrapped in old newspaper.)*

MAN 5: *(In Czech)* I found this, Chief, under the floorboards.

*(*MAN 5 *gives the parcel to* MAN 6 *who unwraps it to
reveal a bundle of American dollars.*

MRS. HOLLAR *watches this with disbelief and there is
an outburst.)*

MRS. HOLLAR: *(In Czech)* He's lying! *(To* ANDERSON*)* It's
a lie—

(The door reopens for MAN 3. SACHA HOLLAR, *aged ten,
comes in with him. He is rather a tough little boy. He
runs across to his mother, who is crying and shouting,*

and embraces her. It is rather as though he were a small adult comforting her.)

ANDERSON: Oh my God . . . Mrs. Hollar . . .

(ANDERSON, out of his depth and afraid, decides abruptly to leave and does so. MAN 3 isn't sure whether to let him go but MAN 6 nods at him and ANDERSON leaves.)

7. Int. hotel corridor. Evening

(ANDERSON approaches his room. He is worn out. When he gets to his door and fumbles with his key he realizes that he can hear a voice in the room next door to his. He puts his ear to this other door.)

GRAYSON: (*Inside*) Yes, a new top for the running piece—O.K.—Prague, Saturday.

(GRAYSON speaks not particularly slowly but with great deliberation enunciating every consonant and splitting syllables up where necessary for clarity. He is, of course, dictating to a fast typist.)

There'll be Czechs bouncing in the streets of Prague tonight as bankruptcy stares English football in the face, stop, new par.

(ANDERSON knocks on the door.)

(*Inside*) It's open!

(ANDERSON opens the door and looks into the room. Interior room. It is of course a room very like ANDERSON's own room, if not identical. Its occupant, the man we had seen leave the room earlier, is GRAYSON, a sports reporter from England. He is on the telephone as ANDERSON cautiously enters the room.)

Make no mistake, comma, the four-goal credit which these slick Slovaks netted here this afternoon will keep them in the black through the second leg of the World Cup Eliminator at Wembley next month, stop. New par— (*To ANDERSON.*) Yes? (*Into phone*) You can bank on it.

ANDERSON: I'm next door.

GRAYSON: (*Into phone*) —bank on it. New par— (*To ANDERSON.*) Look, can you come back? (*Into phone*) But for some determined saving by third-choice Jim Bart in the injury hyphen jinxed England goal, we would have been overdrawn by four more when the books were closed, stop. Maybe Napoleon was wrong when he said we were a nation of shopkeepers, stop. Today England looked like a nation of goalkeepers, stop. Davey, Petherbridge, and Shell all made saves on the line. New par.

ANDERSON: Do you mind if I listen—I missed the match.

(GRAYSON waves him to a chair. ANDERSON sits on a chair next to a door which is in fact a connecting door into the next room. Not ANDERSON's own room but the room on the other side of GRAYSON's room.)

GRAYSON: (*Into phone*) Dickenson and Pratt were mostly left standing by Wolker, with a W, and Deml, D dog, E Edward, M mother, L London—who could go round the halls as a telepathy act, stop. Only Crisp looked as if he had a future outside Madame Tussauds—a.u.d.s.—stop. He laid on the two best chances, comma, both wasted by Pratt who skied one and stubbed his toe on the other, stop. Crisp's, apostrophe s. comment from where I was sitting looked salt and vinegar flavored . . .

(ANDERSON has become aware that another voice is cutting in from the next room. The door between the two rooms is not quite closed. During GRAYSON's last speech ANDERSON gently pushes open the door and looks behind him and realizes that a colleague of GRAYSON's is also dictating in the next room. ANDERSON stands up and looks into the next room and is drawn into it by the rival report.
This room belongs to CHAMBERLAIN.
Interior CHAMBERLAIN's room. CHAMBERLAIN on phone.)

CHAMBERLAIN: Wilson, who would like to be thought the big bad man of the English defense, merely looked slow-footed and slow-witted stop. Deml— D.E.M. mother L.—Deml got round him five times on the trot, bracket, literally, close bracket, using the same swerve, comma, making Wilson look elephantine in everything but memory, stop. On the fifth occasion there was nothing to prevent Deml scoring except what Broadbent took it on himself to do, which was to scythe Deml down from behind, stop. Halas scored from the penalty, stop.

(ANDERSON sighs and sits down on the equivalent chair in CHAMBERLAIN's room. CHAMBERLAIN sees him.)

Can I help you—?

ANDERSON: Sorry—I'm from next door.

CHAMBERLAIN: (*Into phone*) New paragraph— (*To ANDERSON.*) I won't be long— (*Into phone*) This goal emboldened the Czechs to move Bartok, like the composer, forward and risk the consequences, stop. Ten minutes later, just before half time, comma, he was the man left over to collect a short corner from Halas and it was his chip which Jirasek rose to meet for a simple goal at the far post—

ANDERSON: I knew it!

(CHAMBERLAIN turns to look at him.)

CHAMBERLAIN: (*Into phone*) New paragraph. As with tragic opera, things got worse after the interval . . .

(ANDERSON has stood up to leave. He leaves through GRAYSON's room. GRAYSON is on the phone saying:)

GRAYSON: (*Into the phone*) . . . Jirasek, unmarked at the far post, flapped into the air like a great stork, and rising a yard higher than Bart's outstretched hands, he put Czechoslovakia on the road to victory.

(ANDERSON *leaves the room without looking at* GRAYSON *or being noticed.*)

8. Int. hotel dining room

(*The cut is to gay Czech music.*

The dining room has a stage. A small group of Czech musicians and singers in the tourist version of peasant costume is performing.

It is evening. At one of the tables STONE, *the American, and a* FRENCHMAN *are sitting next to each other and sharing the table are* ANDERSON, MCKENDRICK, *and* CHETWYN. *The three of them are, for different reasons, subdued.* STONE *is unsubdued. They are reaching the end of the meal.*)

STONE: Hell's bells. Don't you understand English? When I say to you, "Tell me what you mean," you can only reply, "I would wish to say so and so." "Never mind what you would wish to say," I reply. "Tell me what you *mean*."

FRENCHMAN: *Mais oui,* but if you ask me in French, you must say, "*Qu'est-ce que vous voulez dire?*"—"What is that which you wish to say?" *Naturellement,* it is in order for me to reply, "*Je veux dire etcetera.*"

STONE: (*Excitedly*) But you are making *my* point—don't you see?

MCKENDRICK: What do you think the chances are of meeting a free and easy woman in a place like this?

STONE: I *can't* ask you in French.

MCKENDRICK: I don't mean free, necessarily.

FRENCHMAN: *Pourquoi non? Qu'est-ce que vous voulez dire? Voila!*—now I have asked you.

CHETWYN: You don't often see goose on an English menu.

(CHETWYN *is the last to finish his main course. They have all eaten the main course. There are drinks and cups of coffee on the table.*)

STONE: The French have no verb meaning "I mean."

CHETWYN: Why's that I wonder.

STONE: They just don't.

CHETWYN: People are always eating goose in Dickens.

MCKENDRICK: Do you think it will be safe?

FRENCHMAN: *Par exemple. Je vous dis, "Qu'est-ce que vous voulez dire?"*

MCKENDRICK: I mean one wouldn't want to be photographed through a two-way mirror.

STONE: I don't want to ask you what you would wish to say. I want to ask you what you *mean*. Let's assume there is a difference.

ANDERSON: We do have goose liver. What do they do with the rest of the goose?

STONE: Now assume that you say one but mean the other.

FRENCHMAN: *Je dis quelque chose, mais je veux dire—*

STONE: Right.

MCKENDRICK: (*To* STONE) Excuse me, Brad.

STONE: Yes?

MCKENDRICK: You eat well but you're a lousy eater.

(*This is a fair comment.* STONE *has spoken with his mouth full of bread, cake, coffee, etc., and he is generally messy about it.* STONE *smiles forgivingly but hardly pauses.*)

STONE: Excuse us.

FRENCHMAN: *A bientôt.*

(STONE *and the* FRENCHMAN *get up to leave.*)

STONE: (*Leaving*) You see, what you've got is an incorrect statement which when corrected looks like itself.

(*There is a pause.*)

MCKENDRICK: Did you have a chance to read my paper?

ANDERSON: I only had time to glance at it. I look forward to reading it carefully.

CHETWYN: I read it.

ANDERSON: Weren't you there for it?

MCKENDRICK: No, he sloped off for the afternoon.

ANDERSON: Well, you sly devil, Chetwyn. I bet you had a depressing afternoon. It makes the heart sick, doesn't it.

CHETWYN: Yes, it does rather. We don't know we've been born.

MCKENDRICK: He wasn't at the football match.

CHETWYN: Oh—is that where you were?

ANDERSON: No, I got distracted.

MCKENDRICK: He's being mysterious. I think it's a woman.

ANDERSON: (*To* CHETWYN) What were you doing?

CHETWYN: I was meeting some friends.

MCKENDRICK: He's being mysterious. I don't think it's a woman.

CHETWYN: I have friends here, that's all.

ANDERSON: (*To* MCKENDRICK) Was your paper well received?

MCKENDRICK: No. They didn't get it. I could tell from the questions that there'd been some kind of communications failure.

ANDERSON: The translation phones?

MCKENDRICK: No, no—they simply didn't understand the line of argument. Most of them had never heard of catastrophe theory, so they weren't ready for what is admittedly an audacious application of it.

ANDERSON: I must admit I'm not absolutely clear about it.

MCKENDRICK: It's like a reverse gear—no—it's like a breaking point. The mistake that people make is, they think a moral principle is indefinitely extendible, that it holds good for any situation, a straight line cutting across the graph of our actual situation—here you are, you see— (*He uses a knife to score a line in front of him straight across the table cloth, left to right in front of him.*) "Morality" down there; running parallel to "Immorality" up here— (*He scores a parallel line.*) —and never the twain shall meet. They think that is what a principle means.

ANDERSON: And isn't it?

MCKENDRICK: No. The two lines are on the same plane. (*He holds out his flat hand, palm down, above the scored lines.*) They're the edges of the same plane—it's in three dimensions, you see—and if you twist the plane in a certain way, into what we call the catastrophe curve, you get a model of the sort of behavior we find in the real world. There's a point—the catastrophe point—where your progress along one line of behavior jumps you into the opposite line; the principle reverses itself at the point where a rational man would abandon it.

CHETWYN: Then it's not a principle.

MCKENDRICK: There aren't any principles in your sense. There are only a lot of principled people trying to behave as if there were.

ANDERSON: That's the same thing, surely.

MCKENDRICK: You're a worse case than Chetwyn and his primitive Greeks. At least he has the excuse of *believing* in goodness and beauty. You know they're fictions but you're so hung up on them you want to treat them as if they were God-given absolutes.

ANDERSON: I don't see how else they would have any practical value—

MCKENDRICK: So you end up using a moral principle as your excuse for acting against a moral interest. It's a sort of funk—

(ANDERSON, *under pressure, slams his cup back on to its saucer in a very uncharacteristic and surprising way. His anger is all the more alarming for that.*)

ANDERSON: You make your points altogether too easily, McKendrick. What need have you of moral courage when your principles reverse themselves so conveniently?

MCKENDRICK: All right! I've gone too far. As usual. Sorry. Let's talk about something else. There's quite an attractive woman hanging about outside, loitering in the vestibule.

(*The dining room door offers a view of the lobby.*)

Do you think it is a trap? My wife said to me—now, Bill, don't do anything daft, you know what you're like, if a blonde knocked on your door with the top three buttons of her police uniform undone and asked for a cup of sugar you'd convince yourself she was a bus conductress brewing up in the next room.

ANDERSON: (*Chastened*) I'm sorry . . . you're right up to a point. There would be no moral dilemmas if moral principles worked in straight lines and never crossed each other. One meets test situations which

have troubled much cleverer men than us.

CHETWYN: A good rule, I find, is to try them out on men much *less* clever than us. I often ask my son what *he* thinks.

ANDERSON: Your son?

CHETWYN: Yes. He's eight.

MCKENDRICK: She's definitely glancing this way—seriously, do you think one could chat her up?

(ANDERSON *turns round to look through the door and we see now that the woman is* MRS. HOLLAR.)

ANDERSON: Excuse me.

(*He gets up and starts to leave but then comes back immediately and takes his briefcase from under the table and then leaves. We stay with the table.* MCKENDRICK *watches* ANDERSON *meet* MRS. HOLLAR *and shake her hand and they disappear.*)

MCKENDRICK: Bloody hell, it *was* a woman. Crafty old beggar.

9. Ext. street. Night

(ANDERSON *and* MRS. HOLLAR *walking.*
A park. A park bench. SACHA HOLLAR *sitting on the bench.* ANDERSON *and* MRS. HOLLAR *arrive.*)

MRS. HOLLAR: (*In Czech*) Here he is. (*To* ANDERSON) Sacha. (*In Czech*) Thank him for coming.

SACHA: She is saying thank you that you come.

MRS. HOLLAR: (*In Czech*) We're sorry to bother him.

SACHA: She is saying sorry for the trouble.

ANDERSON: No, no I am sorry about . . . everything. Do you learn English at school?

SACHA: Yes. I am learning English two years. With my father also.

ANDERSON: You are very good.

SACHA: Not good. You are a friend of my father. Thank you.

ANDERSON: I'm afraid I've done nothing.

SACHA: You have his writing?

ANDERSON: His thesis? Yes. It's in here. (*He indicates his briefcase.*)

SACHA: (*In Czech*) It's all right, he's still got it.

(MRS. HOLLAR *nods.*)

MRS. HOLLAR: (*In Czech*) Tell him I didn't know who he was today.

SACHA: My mother is not knowing who you are, tomorrow at the apartment.

ANDERSON: Today.

SACHA: Today. Pardon. So she is saying, "Come here! Come here! Come inside the apartment!" Because she is not knowing. My father is not telling her. He is telling me only.

ANDERSON: I see. What did he tell you?

SACHA: He will go see his friend the English professor. He is taking the writing.

ANDERSON: I see. Did he return home last night?

SACHA: No. He is arrested outside hotel. Then in the night they come to make search.

ANDERSON: Had they been there all night?

SACHA: At eleven o'clock they are coming. They search twenty hours.

ANDERSON: My God.

SACHA: In morning I go to Bartolomesskaya to be seeing him.

MRS. HOLLAR: (*Explains*) Police.

SACHA: But I am not seeing him. They say go home. I am waiting. Then I am going home. Then I am seeing you.

ANDERSON: What were they looking for?

SACHA: (*Shrugs*) Western books. Also my father is writing things. Letters, politics, philosophy. They find nothing. Some English books they don't like but really nothing. But the dollars, of course, they pretend to find.

(MRS. HOLLAR *hears the word dollars.*)

MRS. HOLLAR: (*In Czech*) Tell him the dollars were put there by the police.

SACHA: Not my father's dollars. He is having no monies.

ANDERSON: Yes. I know.

SACHA: They must arrest him for dollars because he does nothing. No bad things. He is signing something. So they are making trouble.

ANDERSON: Yes.

MRS. HOLLAR: (*In Czech*) Tell him about Jan.

SACHA: You must give back my father's thesis. Not now. The next days. My mother cannot take it.

ANDERSON: He asked me to take it to England.

SACHA: Not possible now. But thank you.

ANDERSON: He asked me to take it.

SACHA: Not possible. Now they search you, I think. At the airport. Because they are seeing you coming to the apartment and you have too much contact. Maybe they are seeing us now.

(ANDERSON *looks around him.*)

Is possible.

ANDERSON: (*Uncomfortably*) I ought to tell you . . . (*Quickly.*) I came to the apartment to give the thesis back. I refused him. But he was afraid he might be stopped—I thought he just meant searched, not arrested—

SACHA: Too quick—too quick—

(*Pause.*)

ANDERSON: What do you want me to do?

SACHA: My father's friend—he is coming to Philosophy Congress today.

ANDERSON: Tomorrow.

SACHA: Yes tomorrow. You give him the writing. Is called Jan. Is O.K. Good friend.

(ANDERSON *nods.*)

ANDERSON: Jan.

SACHA: (*In Czech*) He'll bring it to the university hall for Jan tomorrow. (SACHA *stands up.*) We go home now.

(MRS. HOLLAR *gets up and shakes hands with* ANDERSON.)

ANDERSON: I'm sorry . . . What will happen to him?

MRS. HOLLAR: (*In Czech*) What was that?

SACHA: (*In Czech*) He wants to know what will happen to Daddy.

MRS. HOLLAR: Ruzyne.

SACHA: That is the prison. Ruzyne.

(*Pause.*)

ANDERSON: I will, of course, try to help in England. I'll write letters. The Czech Ambassador . . . I have friends, too, in our government—

(ANDERSON *realizes that the boy has started to cry. He is specially taken aback because he has been talking to him like an adult.*)

Now listen—I am personally friendly with important people—the Minister of Education—people like that.

MRS. HOLLAR: (*In Czech but to* ANDERSON) Please help Pavel—

ANDERSON: Mrs. Hollar—I will do everything I can for him.

(*He watches* MRS. HOLLAR *and* SACHA *walk away into the dark.*)

10. Int. Anderson's room. Night

(ANDERSON *is lying fully dressed on the bed. His eyes open. Only light from the window. There are faint voices from* GRAYSON's *room. After a while* ANDERSON *gets up and leaves his room and knocks on* GRAYSON's *door.*

Exterior GRAYSON's *room.*

GRAYSON *opens his door.*)

GRAYSON: Oh hello. Sorry, are we making too much noise?

ANDERSON: No, it's all right, but I heard you were still up and I wondered if I could ask a favor of you. I wonder if I could borrow your typewriter.

GRAYSON: My typewriter?

ANDERSON: Yes.

GRAYSON: Well, I'm leaving in the morning.

ANDERSON: I'll let you have it back first thing. I'm leaving on the afternoon plane myself.

GRAYSON: Oh—all right then.

ANDERSON: That's most kind.

(*During the above the voices from the room have been semi-audible.*

MCKENDRICK's *voice, rather drunk, but articulate, is heard.*)

MCKENDRICK: (*His voice only, heard underneath the above dialogue*) Now, listen to me, I'm a professional philosopher. You'll do well to listen to what I have to say.

ANDERSON: That sounds as if you've got McKendrick in there.

GRAYSON: Oh—is he one of yours?

ANDERSON: I wouldn't put it like that.

GRAYSON: He's getting as tight as a tick.

ANDERSON: Yes.

GRAYSON: You couldn't collect him, could you? He's going to get clouted in a minute.

ANDERSON: Go ahead and clout him, if you like.

GRAYSON: It's not me. It's Broadbent and a couple of the lads. Your pal sort of latched on to us in the bar. He really ought to be getting home.

ANDERSON: I'll see what I can do.

(ANDERSON *follows* GRAYSON *into the room.*)

MCKENDRICK: How can you expect the kids to be little gentlemen when their heroes behave like yobs—answer me that—no—you haven't answered my question—if you've got yobs on the fields you're going to have yobs on the terraces.

(*Interior* GRAYSON's *room.*

MCKENDRICK *is the only person standing up. He is holding court, with a bottle of whisky in one hand and his glass in the other. Around this small room are* BROADBENT, CRISP, CHAMBERLAIN, *and perhaps one or two members of the England squad. Signs of a bottle party.*)

GRAYSON: (*Closing his door*) I thought philosophers were quiet, studious sort of people.

ANDERSON: Well, some of us are.

MCKENDRICK: (*Shouts*) Anderson! You're the very man I want to see! We're having a philosophical discussion about the yob ethics of professional footballers—

BROADBENT: You want to watch it, mate.

MCKENDRICK: Roy here is sensitive because he gave away a penalty today, by a deliberate foul. To stop a certain goal he hacked a chap down. After all, a penalty might be saved and broken legs are quite rare—

(BROADBENT *stands up but* MCKENDRICK *pacifies him with a gesture.*)

it's perfectly all right—you were adopting the utilitarian values of the game, for the good of the team, for England! But I'm not talking about particular acts of expediency. No, I'm talking about the whole *ethos*.

ANDERSON: McKendrick, don't you think it's about time we retired?

MCKENDRICK: (*Ignoring him*) Now, I've played soccer for years. Years and *years*. I played soccer from the age of *eight* until I was *thirteen*. At which point I went to

a rugger school. Even so, Tommy here will tell you that I still consider myself something of a left winger. (*This is to* CRISP.) Sorry about that business in the lift, by the way, Tommy. Well, one thing I remember clearly from my years and *years* of soccer is that if two players go for a ball which then goes into touch, there's never any doubt *among those players* which of them touched the ball last. I can't remember one occasion in all those years and *years* when the player who touched the ball last didn't realize it. So, what I want to know *is*—why is it that on Match of the Day, every time the bloody ball goes into touch, *both* players claim the throw-in for their own side? I merely ask for information. Is it because they are very, very stupid or is it because a dishonest advantage is as welcome as an honest one?

CHAMBERLAIN: Well, look, it's been a long evening, old chap—

ANDERSON: Tomorrow is another day, McKendrick.

MCKENDRICK: Tomorrow, in my experience, is usually the same day. Have a drink—

ANDERSON: No thank you.

MCKENDRICK: Here's a question for anthropologists. Name me a tribe which organizes itself into teams for sporting encounters and greets every score against their opponents with paroxysms of childish glee, whooping, dancing and embracing in an ecstasy of crowing self-congratulation in the very midst of their disconsolate fellows?—Who are these primitives who pile all their responses into the immediate sensation, unaware or uncaring of the long undulations of life's fortunes? Yes, you've got it! (*He chants the Match of the Day signature tune.*) It's the yob-of-the-month competition, entries on a postcard please. But the question is—is it because they're working class, or is it because financial greed has corrupted them? Or is it both?

ANDERSON: McKendrick, you are being offensive.

MCKENDRICK: Anderson is one of life's cricketers. Clap, clap. (*He claps in a well-bred sort of way and puts on a well-bred voice.*) Well played, sir. Bad luck, old chap. The comparison with cricket may suggest to you that yob ethics are working class.

(BROADBENT *comes up to* MCKENDRICK *and pushes him against the wall.* MCKENDRICK *is completely unconcerned, escapes and continues without pause.*)

But you would be quite wrong. Let me refer you to a typical rugby team of Welsh miners. A score is acknowledged with pride but with restraint, the scorer himself composing his features into an expressionless mask lest he might be suspected of exulting in his opponents' misfortune—my God, it does the heart good, doesn't it? I conclude that yob ethics are caused by financial greed.

ANDERSON: Don't be such an ass.

(MCKENDRICK *takes this as an intellectual objection.*)

MCKENDRICK: You think it's the adulation, perhaps? (*To* CRISP) Is it the adulation, Tommy, which has corrupted you?

CRISP: What's he flaming on about?

CHAMBERLAIN: Well I think it's time for my shut-eye.

CRISP: No, I want to know what he's saying about me. He's giving me the needle.

ANDERSON: (*To* MCKENDRICK) May I remind you that you profess to be something of a pragmatist yourself in matters of ethics—

MCKENDRICK: Ah yes—I see—you think that because I don't believe in reliable signposts on the yellow brick road to rainbowland, you think I'm a bit of a yob myself—the swift kick in the kneecap on the way up the academic ladder—the Roy Broadbent of Stoke— (*To* BROADBENT) Stoke's my team, you know.

BROADBENT: Will you tell this stupid bugger his philosophy is getting up my nostrils.

GRAYSON: You're not making much sense, old boy.

MCKENDRICK: Ah! Grayson here has a fine logical mind. He has put his finger on the flaw in my argument, namely that the reason footballers are yobs may be nothing to do with being working class, or with financial greed, or with adulation, or even with being footballers. It may be simply that football attracts a certain kind of person, namely yobs—

(*This is as far as he gets when* BROADBENT *smashes him in the face.* MCKENDRICK *drops.*)

CRISP: Good on you, Roy.

(ANDERSON *goes to* MCKENDRICK *who is flat on the floor.*)

ANDERSON: McKendrick . . .

CHAMBERLAIN: Well, I'm going to bed.

(CHAMBERLAIN *goes through the connecting door into his own room and closes the door.*)

BROADBENT: He can't say that sort of thing and get away with it.

GRAYSON: Where's his room?

ANDERSON: On the third floor.

GRAYSON: Bloody hell.

CRISP: He's waking up.

BROADBENT: He's all right.

ANDERSON: Come on McKendrick.

(*They all lift* MCKENDRICK *to his feet.* MCKENDRICK *makes no protest. He's just about able to walk.*)

I'll take him down in the lift. (*He sees the typewriter in its case and says to* GRAYSON) I'll come back for the typewriter.

(*He leads* MCKENDRICK *towards the door.*)

MCKENDRICK: (*Mutters*) All right. I went too far. Let's talk about something else.

(*But* MCKENDRICK *keeps walking or staggering.* ANDERSON *opens* GRAYSON's *door.*)

BROADBENT: Here. That bloody Jirasek. Just like you said.

ANDERSON: Yes.

BROADBENT: They don't teach you nothing at that place then.

ANDERSON: No.

(ANDERSON *helps* MCKENDRICK *out and closes the door.*)

11. The Colloquium

(ANDERSON *comes to the lectern. There is a Czech* CHAIRMAN *behind him.*

CHETWYN *is in the audience but* MCKENDRICK *is not. We arrive as* ANDERSON *approaches the microphone.* ANDERSON *lays a sheaf of typewritten paper on the lectern.*)

ANDERSON: I propose in this paper to take up a problem which many have taken up before me, namely the conflict between the rights of individuals and the rights of the community. I will be making a distinction between rights and rules.

(*We note that the* CHAIRMAN, *listening politely and intently, is suddenly puzzled. He himself has some papers and from these he extracts one, which is in fact the official copy of* ANDERSON's *official paper. He starts looking at it. It doesn't take him long to satisfy himself that* ANDERSON *is giving a different paper. These things happen while* ANDERSON *speaks. At the same time the three* INTERPRETERS *in their booths, while speaking into their microphones as* ANDERSON *speaks, are also in some difficulty because they have copies of* ANDERSON's *official paper.*)

I will seek to show that rules, in so far as they are related to rights, are a secondary and consequential elaboration of primary rights, and I will be associating rules generally with communities and rights generally with individuals. I will seek to show that a conflict between the two is generally a pseudo-conflict arising out of one side or the other pressing a pseudo-right. Although claiming priority for rights over rules—where they are in conflict—I will be defining rights as fictions acting as incentives to the adoption of practical values; and I will further propose that although these rights are fictions there is an obligation to treat them as if they were truths; and further, that although this obligation can be shown to be based on values which are based on fictions, there is an obligation to treat *that* obligation as though it were based on truth; and so on *ad infinitum*.

(*At this point the* CHAIRMAN *interrupts him.*)

CHAIRMAN: Pardon me—Professor—this is not your paper—

ANDERSON: In what sense? I am indisputably giving it.

CHAIRMAN: But it is not the paper you were invited to give.

ANDERSON: I wasn't invited to give a particular paper.

CHAIRMAN: You offered one.

ANDERSON: That's true.

CHAIRMAN: But this is not it.

ANDERSON: No. I changed my mind.

CHAIRMAN: But it is irregular.

ANDERSON: I didn't realize it mattered.

CHAIRMAN: It is a discourtesy.

ANDERSON: (*Taken aback*) Bad manners? I am sorry.

CHAIRMAN: You cannot give this paper. We do not have copies.

ANDERSON: Do you mean that philosophical papers require some sort of clearance?

CHAIRMAN: The interpreters cannot work without copies.

ANDERSON: Don't worry. It is not a technical paper. I will speak a little slower if you like. (ANDERSON *turns back to the microphone.*) If we decline to define rights as fictions, albeit with the force of truths, there are only two senses in which humans could be said to have rights. Firstly, humans might be said to have certain rights if they had collectively and mutually agreed to give each other these rights. This would merely mean that humanity is a rather large club with club rules, but it is not what is generally meant by human rights. It is not what Locke meant, and it is not what the American Founding Fathers meant when, taking the hint from Locke, they held certain rights to be unalienable—among them, life, liberty and the pursuit of happiness. The early Americans claimed these as the endowment of God—which is the *second* sense in which humans might be said to have rights. This is a view more encouraged in some communities than in others. I do not wish to dwell on it here except to say that it *is* a view and not a deduction, and that I do not hold it myself.

What strikes us is the consensus about an individual's rights put forward both by those who invoke God's authority and by those who invoke no authority at all other than their own idea of what is fair and sensible. The first Article of the American Constitution, guaranteeing freedom of religious observance, of expression, of the press, and of assembly, is closely echoed by Articles 28 and 32 of the no less admirable Constitution of Czechoslovakia, our generous hosts on this occasion. Likewise, protection from invasion of privacy, from unreasonable search and from interference with letters and correspondence guaranteed to the American people by Article 4 is likewise guaranteed to the Czech people by Article 31.

(*The CHAIRMAN, who has been more and more uncomfortable, leaves the stage at this point. He goes into the*

"wings." *At some distance from ANDERSON, but still just in earshot of ANDERSON, i.e. one can hear ANDERSON's words clearly if faintly, is a telephone. Perhaps in a stage manager's office. We go with the CHAIRMAN but we can still hear ANDERSON.*)

Is such a consensus remarkable? Not at all. If there is a God, we his creations would doubtless subscribe to his values. And if there is not a God, he, our creation, would undoubtedly be credited with values which we think to be fair and sensible. But what is fairness? What is sense? What are these values which we take to be self-evident? And why are they values?

12. Int. McKendrick's room

(*MCKENDRICK is fully dressed and coming round from a severe hangover. His room is untidier than ANDERSON's. Clothes are strewn about. His suitcase, half full, is open. His briefcase is also in evidence. MCKENDRICK looks at his watch, but it has stopped. He goes to the telephone and dials.*)

13. Int. Anderson's room

(*The phone starts to ring. The camera pulls back from the phone and we see that there are two men in the room, plainclothes POLICEMEN, searching the room. They look at the phone but only for a moment, and while it rings they continue quietly. They search the room very discreetly. We see one carefully slide open a drawer and we cut away.*)

14. The Colloquium

(*We have returned to ANDERSON's paper. There is no CHAIRMAN on stage.*)

ANDERSON: Ethics were once regarded as a sort of monument, a ghostly Eiffel Tower constructed of Platonic entities like honesty, loyalty, fairness, and so on, all bolted together and consistent with each other, harmoniously stressed so as to keep the edifice standing up: an ideal against which we measured our behavior. The tower has long been demolished. In our own time linguistic philosophy proposes that the notion of, say, justice has no existence outside the ways in which we choose to employ the word, and indeed *consists* only of the way in which we employ it. In other words, that ethics are not the inspiration of our behavior but merely the creation of our utterances.

(*Over the latter part of this we have gone back to the CHAIRMAN who is on the telephone. The CHAIRMAN is doing little talking and some listening.*)

And yet common observation shows us that this view demands qualification. A small child who cries "that's not fair" when punished for something done by his brother or sister is apparently appealing to an idea of justice which is, for want of a better word, natural. And we must see that natural justice, however illusory, does inspire many people's behavior much of the time. As an ethical utterance it seems to be an attempt to define a sense of rightness which is not simply derived from some other utterance elsewhere.

(We cut now to a backstage area, but ANDERSON'S *voice is continuous, heard through the sort of P.A. system which one finds backstage at theaters.*

The CHAIRMAN *hurries along the corridor, seeking, and now finding a uniformed "*FIREMAN,*" a backstage official. During this* ANDERSON *speaks.)*

Now a philosopher exploring the difficult terrain of right and wrong should not be over impressed by the argument "a child would know the difference." But when, let us say, we are being persuaded that it is ethical to put someone in prison for reading or writing the wrong books, it is well to be reminded that you can persuade a man to believe almost anything provided he is clever enough, but it is much more difficult to persuade someone less clever. There is a sense of right and wrong which precedes utterance. It is individually experienced and it concerns one person's dealings with another person. From this experience we have built a system of ethics which is the sum of individual acts of recognition of individual right.

(During this we have returned to ANDERSON *in person. And at this point the* CHAIRMAN *re-enters the stage and goes and sits in his chair.* ANDERSON *continues, ignoring him.)*

If this is so, the implications are serious for a collective or State ethic which finds itself in conflict with individual rights, and seeks, in the name of the people, to impose its values on the very individuals who comprise the State. The illogic of this maneuver is an embarrassment to totalitarian systems. An attempt is sometimes made to answer it by consigning the whole argument to "bourgeois logic," which is a concept no easier to grasp than bourgeois physics or bourgeois astronomy. No, the fallacy must lie elsewhere—

(At this point loud bells, electric bells, ring. The fire alarm. The CHAIRMAN *leaps up and shouts.)*

CHAIRMAN: *(In Czech)* Don't panic! There appears to be a fire. Please leave the hall in an orderly manner. *(In English)* Fire! Please leave quietly!

(The philosophers get to their feet and start heading for the exit. ANDERSON *calmly gathers his papers up and leaves the stage.)*

15. Int. airport

(People leaving the country have to go through a baggage check. There are at least three separate but adjacent benches at which customs men and women search the baggage of travellers. The situation here is as follows:

At the first bench CHETWYN *is in mid-search.*

At the second bench ANDERSON *is in mid-search.*

At the third bench a traveller is in mid-search.

There is a short queue of people waiting for each bench. The leading man in the queue waiting for the third bench is MCKENDRICK. *The search at this third bench is cursory.*

However, ANDERSON *is being searched very thoroughly. We begin on* ANDERSON. *We have not yet noted* CHETWYN.

At ANDERSON'S *bench a uniformed customs* WOMAN *is examining the contents of his suitcase, helped by a uniformed customs* MAN. *At the same time a plainclothes* PO-LICEMAN *is very carefully searching everything in* ANDER-SON'S *briefcase.*

We see the customs MAN *take a cellophane wrapped box of chocolates from* ANDERSON'S *case. He strips off the cellophane and looks at the chocolates and then he digs down to look at the second layer of chocolates.* ANDERSON *watches this with amazement. The chocolate box is closed and put back in the case. Meanwhile a nest of wooden dolls, the kind in which one doll fits inside another, is reduced to its components.*

The camera moves to find MCKENDRICK *arriving at the third desk. There is no plainclothes man there. The customs* OFFICER *there opens his briefcase and flips, in a rather cursory way, through* MCKENDRICK'S *papers. He asks* MCKENDRICK *to open his case. He digs about for a moment in* MCKENDRICK'S *case.*

Back at ANDERSON'S *bench the plainclothes* MAN *is taking* ANDERSON'S *wallet from* ANDERSON'S *hand. He goes through every piece of paper in the wallet.*

We go back to MCKENDRICK'S *bench to find* MCKEN-DRICK *closing his case and being moved on.* MCKENDRICK *turns round to* ANDERSON *to speak.)*

MCKENDRICK: You picked the wrong queue, old man. Russian roulette. And Chetwyn.

(We now discover CHETWYN *who is going through a similar search to* ANDERSON'S. *He has a plainclothes* MAN *too. This* MAN *is looking down the spine of a book from* CHETWYN'S *suitcase. We now return to* ANDERSON'S *bench. We find that the customs* MAN *has discovered a suspicious bulge in the zipped compartment on the underside of the lid of* ANDERSON'S *suitcase.* ANDERSON'S *face tells us that he has a spasm of anxiety. The bulge suggests something about the size of* HOLLAR'S *envelope. The customs* MAN *zips open the compartment and extracts the copy of* MCKENDRICK'S *girly magazine.* ANDERSON *is embarrassed. We return to* CHETWYN *whose briefcase is being searched paper by paper. The customs* OFFICIAL *searching his suitcase finds a laundered shirt, nicely ironed and folded. He opens the shirt up and discovers about half a dozen sheets of writing-paper. Thin paper*

with typewriting on it. Also a photograph of a man. The plainclothes MAN *joins the customs* OFFICIAL *and he starts looking at these pieces of paper. He looks up at* CHETWYN *whose face has gone white.)*

16. Int. airplane

(The plane is taxiing.
MCKENDRICK *and* ANDERSON *are sitting together.*
MCKENDRICK *looks shocked.)*

MCKENDRICK: Silly bugger. Honestly.

ANDERSON: It's all right—they'll put him on the next plane.

MCKENDRICK: To Siberia.

ANDERSON: No, no, don't be ridiculous. It wouldn't look well for them, would it? All the publicity. I don't think there's anything in Czech law about being in possession of letters to Amnesty International and the U.N. and that sort of thing. They couldn't treat Chetwyn as though he were a Czech national anyway.

MCKENDRICK: Very unpleasant for him though.

ANDERSON: Yes.

MCKENDRICK: He took a big risk.

ANDERSON: Yes.

MCKENDRICK: I wouldn't do it. Would you?

ANDERSON: No. He should have known he'd be searched.

MCKENDRICK: Why did they search you?

ANDERSON: They thought I might have something.

MCKENDRICK: Did you have anything?

ANDERSON: I did in a way.

MCKENDRICK: What was it?

ANDERSON: A thesis. Apparently rather slanderous from the State's point of view.

MCKENDRICK: Where did you hide it?

ANDERSON: In your briefcase.

(Pause.)

MCKENDRICK: You what?

ANDERSON: Last night. I'm afraid I reversed a principle.

*(*MCKENDRICK *opens his briefcase and finds* HOLLAR'S *envelope.* ANDERSON *takes it from him.* MCKENDRICK *is furious.)*

MCKENDRICK: You utter bastard.

ANDERSON: I thought you would approve.

MCKENDRICK: Don't get clever with me. (*He relapses, shaking.*) Jesus. It's not quite playing the game is it?

ANDERSON: No, I suppose not. But they were very unlikely to search *you.*

MCKENDRICK: That's not the bloody point.

ANDERSON: I thought it was. But you could be right. Ethics is a very complicated business. That's why they have these congresses.

(The plane picks up speed on the runway towards take-off.)

Figure 1. Anderson (Peter Barkworth) and McKendrick (John Shrapnel) wait for the hotel clerk in the BBC TV production of *Professional Foul*, directed by Michael Lindsay-Hogg. (Photograph: BBC.)

Figure 2. Anderson (Peter Barkworth), seemingly unflustered by having to talk in the hotel corridor because his room may be bugged, discusses ethical questions with his former student, Pavel Hollar (Stephen Rea), in the BBC TV production of *Professional Foul,* directed by Michael Lindsay-Hogg. (Photograph: BBC.)

Figure 3. Anderson (Peter Barkworth) pauses before opening his brief-case to show the Czech plainclothes policeman some of the philosophical papers he is carrying, while concealing the fact that he is also carrying Hollar's thesis in the BBC TV production of *Professional Foul*, directed by Michael Lindsay-Hogg. (Photograph: BBC.)

Staging of *Professional Foul*

REVIEW OF THE BBC PRODUCTION, 1977, BY DAVID PRYCE-JONES

"Some rather dubious things are happening in Czechoslovakia, ethically. We must try not to pretend otherwise." So speaks the Cambridge Professor of Ethics, Professor Anderson, at the beginning of Tom Stoppard's new play, *Professional Foul* (BBC2). This latest in the line of dotty professors whom Tom Stoppard loves to tease is on his way to a philosophers' congress in Prague. His bearded red-brick colleague sums up his own *curriculum vitae* with the retort, "I sail pretty close to the wind, Marx-wise." And an English football team is about to play a World Cup match there at the same time. Professor Anderson devotes the middle regions of his mind to studying the sport; he is reading a paper to the Prague congress only in order to attend the match.

Peter Barkworth is an expert guide to the liberal soul of Professor Anderson. Tiny shrugs, wrinkles of surprise, an all-compassionate tilting of the head tell the rest of the world that it goes wrong insofar as it does not have Cambridge ethics and manners. In the hotel, a former Czech pupil visits him, a dissident unimportant in himself, but nevertheless forbidden the pursuit of philosophy. And will the professor please take out the manuscript of a suppressed thesis? A suggestion most regrettably unethical for Cambridge.

All the same, the professor can recognize a fact of life when he sees one. Before the football kicks off, he slips away to his pupil's flat to return the manuscript, and arrives at the very moment when the secret police have arrested the young man on trumped-up currency charges, and are intimidating his wife and child. The professor knows Shirley Williams, he has access to the highest in the land, and still he is deprived of his football and is within a whisker of falling after his pupil into the meat-grinding machinery.

A lesser playwright might have been satisfied with putting the wind up Professor Anderson. Mr. Stoppard at this point backs away from damning the man, and turns him on to the offensive. On the football field, England has been shamed by tackles which gave away penalty goals. The professor will improvise a paper on human rights, and he reads it until the Czechs commit an even more horrible tackle on him by sounding a false fire alarm to foreclose the proceedings of the congress. And still that forbidden manuscript is taken out safely, stowed without his knowledge in the baggage of the "Marx-wise" colleague.

A happy ending, then, almost slapstick, with its immensely satisfying symmetry. The comeuppance counted for a good deal. Current hypocrisies and evasions are not going to get past Mr. Stoppard. He will be the death of radical chic. *Professional Foul* is another step towards releasing the liberal from the attitudes in which he has been deep-frozen for such ages, like the Siberian mammoth, dead but not decayed, while life passes him by.

MARIA IRENE FORNES

1930–

For thirty years, Maria Irene Fornes has been a vital force in American drama as playwright, director, designer, teacher, and theatrical administrator. Born in Havana, Cuba, in 1930, she emigrated to the United States in 1945 and became a citizen in 1951. Her first artistic interest was in painting and textile design, an interest which led to work as a costume designer at the Judson Poets Theatre in New York, one of the most successful Off-Off Broadway production groups. Fornes's subsequent playwriting career may be divided roughly by decades: the 1960s, when she wrote and directed a series of nonrealistic and often light-hearted works; the 1970s, when she wrote fewer plays because of her work as president of New York Theatre Strategy, a playwrights' organization supporting the development of experimental work throughout the United States; and the 1980s, when her plays took on noticeably darker and more overtly political tones. Thus far Fornes has written some thirty plays and adaptations, working with material that ranges widely over styles and cultures: the ritual for a Vietnamese wedding served as the basis for a staged reading in 1967 protesting American involvement in Vietnam; the diary of a servant in New Hampshire became *Evelyn Brown: A Diary* (1980); and her own Cuban background informed her first play, *The Widow* (1961) as well as later plays such as *Sarita* (1984). She has won the Obie Award (Off-Broadway) six times, including a special Obie in 1982 for "Sustained Achievement," and she continues an active teaching, writing, and directing career, working both in professional repertory theaters around the country and on university campuses.

Commenting on her unusual creative process in *Drama Review* (December 1977), Fornes reveals her willingness to accept the accidental and her distrust of the deliberate: "When something happens by accident, I trust that the play is making its own point." So, too, she describes herself as a transmitter of messages rather than a creator of ideas: "Thoughts come to my mind at any point, anywhere—I could be on the subway—and if I am alert enough and I have a pencil and paper, I write these *messages* that come." And, like the painter she once was, Fornes talks about her work in visual terms, noting that as a play and its characters take shape, she sees the characters, the set, and, most importantly, the colors. At that point, the play exists, and Fornes sees herself as the reporter: "I just listen to it. I move along with it. I let it write itself." Yet once the first draft has "written itself," analysis and rewriting become central.

One of Fornes's earliest experimental successes, *Promenade* (1965), a play with music by Al Carmines of the Judson Poets Theatre, actually grew out of an exercise in seemingly random composition. Fornes wrote down a set of characters on one group of cards and a list of places on another, picked her first "character" card—which said "Aristocrats"—and her first place card—"The Prison"—and then tried to deal with the difficulty of writing about aristocrats in prison. Her solution was to have them dig their way out, and so the adventures of Prisoners 105 and 106 begin. Chased by their jailer, they gatecrash an elaborate society banquet, evade capture by putting their jackets on a man injured in a car accident, are reunited with their mother, take part in a military battle, and finally return to their jail cell. The ending blends social criticism and gentleness, for though the mother sings a lullaby that alludes to poverty and homelessness, the two aristocratic prisoners seem untouched by the pain they have witnessed.

Other plays from the 1960s, such as *The Successful Life of 3* (1965) and *Molly's Dream* (1968) use the movies as a constant point of reference, thus exploiting the popular clichés by which people imagine their lives, particularly their romantic relationships, and, thereby, revealing the emptiness of such clichés. The two men and one woman of *The Successful Life of 3* see themselves as figures from the movies (gangsters, Zorro-type romantic heroes, attractive sex objects) as they move through ten short scenes spread out over sixteen years, scenes that often have no transition but simply "cut" from one locale and time to another. *Molly's Dream* is set entirely in a stereotypical Hollywood saloon, and for much of the play Molly adopts a German accent and gestures reminiscent of Marlene Dietrich. But while all of these characters allude to, and even imitate, actual or fictional characters from Hollywood, they also can see that their lives are much less glamorous. In *Molly's Dream*, for example, when the lights dim and the music begins, a spotlight comes up on Molly, but she undercuts this theatrical cliché by saying, "No. I'm not breaking into song. The moment is too sad."

By contrast, the characters in Fornes's plays of the 1980s seem utterly trapped, unable to break out of the relationships and obsessions that imprison them. Susan Sontag, introducing the second published volume of Fornes's plays, aptly comments that *Mud* (1983) is "about the unsuccessful life of three," since *Mud*, like *The Successful Life of 3*, focuses on two men and the woman they both want. But whereas the earlier play ends with the three characters reunited and singing together, *Mud* ends with Mae's attempt to leave the bleak wooden room where both Henry and Lloyd compete for her, only to be brought back, bleeding and dying, after Lloyd shoots her. While *Molly's Dream* surrealistically depicts the notion of women obsessively clinging to men by surrounding the sexy young man, Jim, with a chorus of five "Hanging Women" who never let go of him, *Sarita* (1984) offers a much more frightening vision of sexual obsession. Sarita first appears as a schoolgirl of thirteen, staring at fortune-telling cards to find out if Julio loves her; eight years later, after a series of reunions and desertions, she can free herself only by stabbing Julio. *The Danube* (1982) and *The Conduct of Life* (1985) also focus on imprisoning worlds and relationships, fraught with disturbing political implications. *The Danube*, which begins in 1938 shortly before World War II, seems at first a rewriting of Ionesco's *The Bald Soprano*, with the "well-meaning American" Paul Green learning Hungarian by repeating phrases from an English/Hungarian language tape. But it turns increasingly sinister as the tyranny of stilted language evokes political repression, particularly when the central characters are replaced by puppets. Even more oppressive is *The Conduct of Life*, set in a Latin American country of the present, with its central character a military commander who imprisons a twelve-year-old girl, first in an empty warehouse, then in his cellar, and repeatedly rapes her. The sexual violence onstage embodies the political violence offstage, since the play's dialogue gradually reveals that the commander is in charge of torturing political prisoners.

Fefu and Her Friends (1977), Fornes's best-known and most widely performed play, is sometimes zanily surreal like her earlier plays, but like her later plays, it is also intensely serious. Fefu's opening line is meant to shake up both onstage and offstage listeners, "My husband married me to have a constant reminder of how loathsome women are," as is the moment soon after when she casually refers to her husband, Phillip, then aims a shotgun out the French doors and shoots at him (though it turns out that the shot was a blank). While Fefu's announced plan for the weekend is the rehearsal of a fund-raising program, with such apparently bland topics as "the stifling conditions of primary school education" or "Art as a Tool for Learning," the actual process of education is revealed to be more like turning over a smooth stone and finding underneath "another life that is parallel to the one we manifest," a life with "worms crawling on it." Thus the seemingly aimless dialogue reveals the disturbing quality of women's existence, particularly the extent to which men, though completely absent from the cast of eight women, still dominate their lives. Nowhere is the domination more evident than in Julia's soliloquy, in which she first speaks of herself as if she's being tortured and then, to save herself from further pain, recites a "prayer" defining men as human and women as not-human and evil. Julia's submission to such perverted thoughts is, Fornes suggests, literally as well as mentally paralyzing, since she must use a wheelchair because of a freak accident, though for an eerie moment in the final scene, she gets up and walks.

While Fefu and Julia are the women whose inner lives are most fully revealed, each of the eight gets a chance to present her feelings to the others and to the audience. Indeed, because of Fornes's unusual staging requirements, the audience is put into the position of snooping on a series of private conversations since the four middle scenes are set in four separate acting spaces, requiring the audience to move in separate groups from scene to scene, while the actors repeat each scene four times. The choice, Fornes explains, came about because she accidentally found the spaces in the process of writing the play and directing the play. Erika Munk, whose review is reprinted following the text, saw the repetition of scenes as a metaphor for "entire trapped lifetimes." But the physical involvement of the audience in its performance also creates a special kind of intimacy, mirroring the relationships found in the play. Those relationships embody or display both playfulness (Figures 1 and 3) and intensity (Figures 2 and 4), just as the play begins with a gunshot that is partially a joke and ends with a gunshot that forces the audience to question what is real and what is hallucination. In these and other boldly dramatic ways, *Fefu* disconcerts and startles us, asking us to rethink, or even re-imagine, our own conventional lives.

FEFU AND HER FRIENDS

BY MARIA IRENE FORNES

CHARACTERS

FEFU
CINDY
CHRISTINA
JULIA
EMMA
PAULA
SUE
CECILIA

New England, Spring 1935.
Part 1: Noon. The living room. The entire audience watches from the main auditorium.

Part 2: Afternoon. The lawn, the study, the bedroom, the kitchen. The audience is divided into four groups. Each group is led to the spaces. These scenes are performed simultaneously. When the scenes are completed the audience moves to the next space and the scenes are performed again. This is repeated four times until each group has seen all four scenes. Then the audience is led back to the main auditorium.
Part 3: Evening. The living room. The entire audience watches from the main auditorium.

PART 1

(The living room of a country house in New England. The decor is a tasteful mixture of styles. To the right is the foyer and the main door. To the left, French doors leading to a terrace, the lawn and a pond. At the rear, there are stairs that lead to the upper floor, the entrance to the kitchen, and the entrance to other rooms on the ground floor. A couch faces the audience. There is a coffee table, two chairs on each side of the table. Upstage right there is a piano. Against the right wall there is an open liquor cabinet. Besides bottles of liquor there are glasses, an ice bucket, and a seltzer bottle. A double barrel shotgun leans on the wall near the French doors. On the table there is a dish with chocolates. On the couch there is a throw. FEFU *stands on the landing.* CINDY *lies on the couch.* CHRISTINA *sits on the chair to the right.)*

FEFU: My husband married me to have a constant reminder of how loathsome women are.
CINDY: What?
FEFU: Yup.
CINDY: That's just awful.
FEFU: No, it isn't.
CINDY: It isn't awful?
FEFU: No.
CINDY: I don't think anyone would marry for that reason.
FEFU: He did.
CINDY: Did he say so?
FEFU: He tells me constantly.
CINDY: Oh, dear.
FEFU: I don't mind. I laugh when he tells me.
CINDY: You laugh?
FEFU: I do.
CINDY: How can you?
FEFU: It's funny.—And it's true. That's why I laugh.
CINDY: What is true?

FEFU: That women are loathsome.
CINDY: . . . Fefu!
FEFU: That shocks you.
CINDY: It does. I don't feel loathsome.
FEFU: I don't mean that you are loathsome.
CINDY: You don't mean that I'm loathsome.
FEFU: No . . . It's something to think about. It's a thought.
CINDY: It's a hideous thought.
FEFU: I take it all back.
CINDY: Isn't she incredible?
FEFU: Cindy, I'm not talking about anyone in particular. It's something to think about.
CINDY: No one in particular, just women.
FEFU: Yes.
CINDY: In that case I am relieved. I thought you were referring to us.
FEFU: *(Affectionately.)* You are being stupid.
CINDY: Stupid and loathsome. *(To* CHRISTINA.) Have you ever heard anything so outrageous.
CHRISTINA: I am speechless.
FEFU: Why are you speechless?
CHRISTINA: I think you are outrageous.
FEFU: Don't be offended. I don't take enough care to be tactful. I know I don't. But don't be offended. Cindy is not offended. She pretends to be, but she isn't really. She understands what I mean.
CINDY: I do not.
FEFU: Yes, you do.—I like exciting ideas. They give me energy.
CHRISTINA: And how is women being loathsome an exciting idea?
FEFU: *(With mischief.)* It revolts me.
CHRISTINA: You find revulsion exciting?
FEFU: Don't you?
CHRISTINA: No.

FEFU: I do. It's something to grapple with.—What do you do with revulsion?

CHRISTINA: I avoid anything that's revolting to me.

FEFU: Hmmm. (*To* CINDY.) You too?

CINDY: Yes.

FEFU: Hmm. Have you ever turned a stone over in damp soil?

CHRISTINA: Ahm.

FEFU: And when you turn it there are worms crawling on it?

CHRISTINA: Ahm.

FEFU: And it's damp and full of fungus?

CHRISTINA: Ahm.

FEFU: Were you revolted?

CHRISTINA: Yes.

FEFU: Were you fascinated?

CHRISTINA: I was.

FEFU: There you have it! You too are fascinated with revulsion.

CHRISTINA: Hmm.

FEFU: You see, that which is exposed to the exterior . . . is smooth and dry and clean. That which is not . . . underneath, is slimy and filled with fungus and crawling with worms. It is another life that is parallel to the one we manifest. It's there. The way worms are underneath the stone. If you don't recognize it . . . (*Whispering.*) it eats you. That is my opinion. Well, who is ready for lunch?

CINDY: I'll have some fried worms with lots of pepper.

FEFU: (*To* CHRISTINA.) You?

CHRISTINA: I'll have mine in a sandwich with mayonnaise.

FEFU: And to drink?

CHRISTINA: Just some dirty dishwater in a tall glass with ice.

(FEFU *looks at* CINDY.)

CINDY: That sounds fine.

FEFU: I'll go dig them up. (FEFU *walks to the French doors. Beckoning* CHRISTINA.) Pst! (FEFU *gets the gun as* CHRISTINA *goes to the French doors.*) You haven't met Phillip. Have you?

CHRISTINA: No.

FEFU: That's him.

CHRISTINA: Which one?

FEFU: (*Aims and shoots.*) That one!

(CHRISTINA *and* CINDY *scream.* FEFU *smiles proudly. She blows on the mouth of the barrel. She puts down the gun and looks out again.*)

CINDY: Christ, Fefu.

FEFU: There he goes. He's up. It's a game we play. I shoot and he falls. Whenever he hears the blast he falls. No matter where he is, he falls. One time he fell in a puddle of mud and his clothes were a mess. (*She looks out.*) It's not too bad. He's just dusting off some stuff. (*She waves to* PHILLIP *and starts to go upstairs.*) He's all right. Look.

CINDY: A drink?

CHRISTINA: Yes.

(CINDY *goes to the liquor cabinet.*)

CINDY: What would you like?

CHRISTINA: Bourbon and soda . . . (CINDY *puts ice and bourbon in a glass. As she starts to squirt the soda . . .*) lots of soda. Just soda. (CINDY *starts with a fresh glass. She starts to squirt soda just as* CHRISTINA *speaks.*) Wait. (CINDY *stops squirting, but not soon enough.*) I'll have an ice cube with a few drops of bourbon. (CINDY *starts with a fresh glass.*)

CINDY: One or two ice cubes?

CHRISTINA: One. Something to suck on.

CINDY: She's unique. There's no one like her.

CHRISTINA: Thank God.

(CINDY *gives the drink to* CHRISTINA.)

CINDY: But she is lovely you know. She really is.

CHRISTINA: She's crazy.

CINDY: A little. She has a strange marriage.

CHRISTINA: Strange? It's revolting.—What is he like?

CINDY: He's crazy too. They drive each other crazy. They are not crazy really. They drive each other crazy.

CHRISTINA: Why do they stay together?

CINDY: They love each other.

CHRISTINA: Love?

CINDY: It's love.

CHRISTINA: Who are the other two men?

CINDY: Fefu's younger brother, John. And the gardener. His name is Tom.—The gun is not loaded.

CHRISTINA: How do you know?

CINDY: It's not. Why should it be loaded?

CHRISTINA: It seemed to be loaded a moment ago.

CINDY: That was just a blank.

CHRISTINA: It sounded like a cannon shot.

CINDY: That was just gun powder. There's no bullet in a blank.

CHRISTINA: The blast alone could kill you. One can die of fright, you know.

CINDY: True.

CHRISTINA: My heart is still beating.

CINDY: That's just fright. You're being a scaredy cat.

CHRISTINA: Of course it's just fright. It's fright.

CINDY: I mean, you were just scared. You didn't get hurt.

CHRISTINA: Just scared. I guess I was lucky I didn't get shot.

CINDY: Fefu won't shoot you. She only shoots Phillip.

CHRISTINA: That's nice of her. Put the gun away, I don't like looking at it.

FEFU: (*As she appears on the landing.*) I just fixed the toilet in your bathroom.

CINDY: You did?

FEFU: I did. The water stopper didn't work. It drained. I adjusted it. I'm waiting for the tank to fill up. Make sure it all works.

CHRISTINA: You do your own plumbing?

FEFU: I just had to bend the metal that supports the rubber stopper so it falls right over the hole. What happened was it fell to the side so the water wouldn't stop running into the bowl. (FEFU *sits near* CINDY.) He scared me this time, you know. He looked like he was really hurt.

CINDY: I thought the guns were not loaded.

FEFU: I'm never sure.

CHRISTINA: What?

CINDY: Fefu, what do you mean?

FEFU: He told me one day he'll put real bullets in the guns. He likes to make me nervous. (*There is a moment's silence.*) I have upset you . . . I don't mean to upset you. That's the way we are with each other. We always go to extremes but it's not anything to be upset about.

CHRISTINA: You scare me.

FEFU: That's all right. I scare myself too, sometimes. But there's nothing wrong with being scared . . . it makes you stronger.—It does me.—He won't put real bullets in the guns.—It suits our relationship . . . the game, I mean. If I didn't shoot him with blanks, I might shoot him for real. Do you see the sense of it?

CHRISTINA: I think you're crazy.

FEFU: I'm not. I'm sane.

CHRISTINA: (*Gently.*) You're very stupid.

FEFU: I'm not. I'm very bright.

CHRISTINA: (*Gently.*) You depress me.

FEFU: Don't be depressed. Laugh at me if you don't agree with me. Say I'm ridiculous. I know I'm ridiculous. Come on, laugh. I hate to think I'm depressing to you.

CHRISTINA: All right. I'll laugh.

FEFU: I'll make you a drink.

CHRISTINA: No, I'm just sucking on the ice.

FEFU: Don't you feel well?

CHRISTINA: I'm all right.

FEFU: What are you drinking?

CHRISTINA: Bourbon.

FEFU: (*Getting* CHRISTINA's *glass and going to the liquor cabinet.*) Would you like some more? I'll get you some.

CHRISTINA: Just a drop.

FEFU: (*With great care pours a single drop of bourbon on the ice cube.*) Like that?

CHRISTINA: Yes, thank you.

FEFU: (*Gives* CHRISTINA *the drink and watches her put the cube to her lips.*) That's the cutest thing I've ever seen. It's cold. (CHRISTINA *nods.*) You need a stick in the ice, like a popsicle stick. You hold the stick and your fingers won't get cold. I have some sticks. I'll do some for you.

CHRISTINA: Don't trouble yourself.

FEFU: It won't be any trouble. You might want some later.—I'm strange, Christina. But I am fortunate in that I don't mind being strange. It's hard on others sometimes. But not that hard. Is it, Cindy? Those who love me, love me precisely because I am the way I am. (*To* CINDY.) Isn't that so? (CINDY *smiles and nods.*)

CINDY: I would love you even if you weren't the way you are.

FEFU: You wouldn't know it was me if I weren't the way I am.

CINDY: I would still know it was you underneath.

FEFU: (*To* CHRISTINA.) You see?—There are some good things about me.—I'm never angry, for example.

CHRISTINA: But you make everyone else angry.

(FEFU *thinks a moment.*)

FEFU: No.

CHRISTINA: You've made me furious.

FEFU: I know. And I might make you angry again. Still I would like it if you liked me.—You think it's unlikely.

CHRISTINA: I don't know.

FEFU: . . . We'll see. (FEFU *goes to the doors. She stands there briefly and speaks reflectively.*) I still like men better than women.—I envy them. I like being like a man. Thinking like a man. Feeling like a man.—They are well together. Women are not. Look at them. They are checking the new grass mower. . . . Out in the fresh air and the sun, while we sit here in the dark. . . . Men have natural strength. Women have to find their strength, and when they do find it, it comes forth with bitterness and it's erratic. . . . Women are restless with each other. They are like live wires . . . either chattering to keep themselves from making contact, or else, if they don't chatter, they avert their eyes . . . like Orpheus° . . . as if a god once said "and if they shall recognize each other, the world will be blown apart." They are always eager for the men to arrive. When they do, they can put themselves at rest, tranquilized and in a mild stupor. With the men they feel safe. The danger is gone. That's the closest they can be to feeling wholesome. Men are muscle that cover the raw nerve. They are the insulators. The danger is gone, but the price is the mind and the spirit. . . . High price.—I've never understood it. Why?— What is feared?—Hmm. Well . . .—Do you know? Perhaps the heavens would fall.—Have I offended you again?

CHRISTINA: No. I too have wished for that trust men have for each other. The faith the world puts in them and they in turn put in the world. I know I don't have it.

FEFU: Hmm. Well, I have to see how my toilet is doing. (FEFU *goes to the landing and exits. She puts her head*

Orpheus, mythic Greek musician who tried to bring his wife back from the underworld by leading her back to the living without looking at her.

out. She smiles.) Plumbing is more important than you think.

(CHRISTINA *falls off her chair in a mock faint.* CINDY *goes to her.)*

CINDY: What do you think?

CHRISTINA: Think? I hurt. I'm all shreds inside.

CINDY: Anything I can do?

CHRISTINA: Sing.

(CINDY *sings "Winter Wonderland."* CHRISTINA *harmonizes. There is the sound of a horn.* FEFU *enters.)*

FEFU: It's Julia. *(To* CHRISTINA, *who is on the floor.)* Are you all right?

CHRISTINA: Yes. *(*FEFU *exits through the foyer.)* Darn it!

(CHRISTINA *starts to stand.)*

FEFU: *(Off-stage.)* Julia . . . let me help you.

JULIA: I can manage. I'm much stronger now.

FEFU: There you go.

JULIA: You have my bag.

FEFU: Yes.

(JULIA *and* FEFU *enter.* JULIA *is in a wheelchair.)*

JULIA: Hello Cindy.

CINDY: Hello darling. How are you?

JULIA: I'm very well now. I'm driving now. You must see my car. It's very clever the way they worked it all out. You might want to drive it. It's not hard at all. *(Turning to* CHRISTINA.) Christina.

CHRISTINA: Hello Julia.

JULIA: I'm glad to see you.

FEFU: I'll take this to your room. You're down here, if you want to wash up.

(FEFU *exits through the upstage exit.* JULIA *follows her.)*

CINDY: I can't get used to it.

CHRISTINA: She's better. Isn't she?

CINDY: Not really.

CHRISTINA: Was she actually hit by the bullet?

CINDY: No . . . I was with her.

CHRISTINA: I know.

CINDY: I thought the bullet hit her, but it didn't.—How do you know if a person is hit by a bullet?

CHRISTINA: Cindy . . . there's a wound and . . . there's a bullet.

CINDY: Well, the hunter aimed . . . at the deer. He shot.

CHRISTINA: He?

CINDY: Yes.

CHRISTINA: *(Pointing in the direction of* FEFU.) It wasn't . . . ?

CINDY: Fefu? . . . No. She wasn't even there. She used to hunt but she doesn't hunt any more. She loves animals.

CHRISTINA: Go on.

CINDY: He shot. Julia and the deer fell. The deer was dead . . . dying. Julia was unconscious. She had convulsions . . . like the deer. He died and she didn't. I screamed for help and the hunter came

and examined Julia. He said, "She is not hurt." Julia's forehead was bleeding. He said, "It is a surface wound. I didn't hurt her." I know it wasn't he who hurt her. It was someone else. He went for help and Julia started talking. She was delirious.—Apparently there was a spinal nerve injury. She hit her head and she suffered a concussion. She blanks out and that is caused by the blow on the head. It's a scar in the brain. It's called the petit mal.°

(FEFU *enters.)*

CHRISTINA: What was it she said?

CINDY: Hmm? . . .

CHRISTINA: When she was delirious.

CINDY: When she was delirious? That she was persecuted.—That they tortured her. . . . That they had tried her and that the shot was her execution. That she recanted because she wanted to live. . . . That if she talked about it . . . to anyone . . . she would be tortured further and killed. And I have not mentioned this before because . . . I fear for her.

CHRISTINA: It doesn't make any sense, Cindy.

CINDY: It makes sense to me. You heard? *(*FEFU *goes to* CINDY *and holds her.)*

FEFU: Who hurt her?

CINDY: I don't know.

FEFU: *(To* CHRISTINA.) Did you know her?

CHRISTINA: I met her once years ago.

FEFU: You remember her then as she was. . . . She was afraid of nothing. . . . Have you ever met anyone like that? . . . She knew so much. She was so young and yet she knew so much. . . . How did she learn all that? . . . *(To* CINDY.) Did you ever wonder? Well, I still haven't checked my toilet. Can you believe that. I still haven't checked it. *(*FEFU *goes upstairs.)*

CHRISTINA: How long ago was the accident?

CINDY: A year . . . a little over a year.

CHRISTINA: Is she in pain?

CINDY: I don't think so.

CHRISTINA: We are made of putty. Aren't we?

(There is the sound of a car. Car doors opening and closing. A house window opening.)

FEFU: *(Off-stage.)* Emma! What is that you're wearing. You look marvelous.

EMMA: *(Off-stage.)* I got it in Turkey.

FEFU: Hi Paula, Sue.

PAULA: Hi.

SUE: Hi.

(CINDY *goes out to greet them.* JULIA *enters. She wheels herself to the downstage area.)*

FEFU: I'll be right down! Hey, my toilet works.

EMMA: Stephany. Mine does too.

---

petit mal, comparatively mild form of epilepsy.

FEFU: Don't be funny.

EMMA: Come down.

(FEFU *enters as* EMMA, SUE, *and* PAULA *enter.* EMMA *and* FEFU *embrace.*)

FEFU: How are you?

EMMA: Good . . . good . . . good . . . (*Still embracing* FEFU, EMMA *sees* JULIA.) Julia! (*She runs to* JULIA *and sits on her lap.*)

FEFU: Emma!

JULIA: It's all right.

EMMA: Take me for a ride. (JULIA *wheels the chair in a circle.* EMMA *waves as they ride.*) Hi, Cindy, Paula, Sue, Fefu.

JULIA: Do you know Christina?

EMMA: How do you do.

CHRISTINA: How do you do.

EMMA: (*Pointing.*) Sue . . . Paula . . .

SUE: Hello.

PAULA: Hello.

CHRISTINA: Hello.

PAULA: (*To* FEFU.) I liked your talk at Flossie Crit.

FEFU: Oh god, don't remind me. I thought I was awful. Come, I'll show you your rooms. (*She starts to go up.*)

PAULA: I thought you weren't. I found it very stimulating.

EMMA: When was that? . . . What was it on?

FEFU: Aviation.

PAULA: It wasn't on aviation. It was on Voltairine de Cleyre.°

JULIA: I wish I had known.

FEFU: It wasn't important.

JULIA: I would have gone, Fefu.

FEFU: Really, it wasn't worth the trouble.

EMMA: Now you'll have to tell Julia and me all about Voltairine de Cleyre.

FEFU: You know all about Voltairine de Cleyre.

EMMA: I don't.

FEFU: I'll tell you at lunch.

EMMA: I had lunch.

JULIA: You can sit and listen while we eat.

EMMA: I will. When do we start our meeting?

FEFU: After lunch. We'll have something to eat and then we'll have our meeting. Who's ready for lunch?

(*The following lines are said almost simultaneously.*)

CINDY: I am.

JULIA: I'm not really hungry.

CHRISTINA: I could eat now.

PAULA: I'm ready.

SUE: I'd rather wait.

EMMA: I'll have coffee.

FEFU: . . . Well . . . we'll take a vote later.

CINDY: What are we doing exactly?

FEFU: About lunch?

CINDY: That too, but I meant the agenda.

SUE: Well, I thought we should first discuss what each of us is going to talk about, so we don't duplicate what someone else is saying, and then we have a review of it, a sort of rehearsal, so we know in what order we should speak and how long it's going to take.

EMMA: We should do a rehearsal in costume. What color should each wear. It matters. Do you know what you're wearing?

PAULA: I haven't thought about it. What color should I wear?

EMMA: Red.

PAULA: Red!

EMMA: Cherry red or white.

SUE: And I?

EMMA: Dark green.

CINDY: The treasurer should wear green.

EMMA: It suits her too.

SUE: And then we'll speak in order of color.

EMMA: Right. Who else wants to know? (CINDY *and* JULIA *raise their hands. To* CINDY.) For you lavender. (*To* JULIA.) Purpura.° (FEFU *raises her hand.*) For you, all the gold in Persia.

FEFU: There is no gold in Persia.

EMMA: In Peru. I brought my costume. I'll put it on later.

FEFU: You're not in costume?

EMMA: No. This is just a dress. My costume is . . . dramatic. I won't tell you any more about it. You'll see it.

SUE: I had no idea we were going to do theatre.

EMMA: Life is theatre. Theatre is life. If we're showing what life is, can be, we must do theatre.

SUE: Will I have to act?

EMMA: It's not acting. It's being. It's springing forth with the powers of the spirit. It's breathing.

JULIA: I'll do a dance.

EMMA: I'll stage a dance for you.

JULIA: Sitting?

EMMA: On a settee.

JULIA: I'm game.

EMMA: (*Takes a deep breath and walks through the French doors.*) Phillip! What are you doing?—Hello.—Hello, John.—What? I'm staging a dance for Julia!

FEFU: We'll never see her again.—Come.

(FEFU, PAULA, *and* SUE *go upstairs.* JULIA *goes to the gun, takes it and smells the mouth of the barrel. She looks at* CINDY.)

CINDY: It's a blank.

Voltairine de Cleyre, American anarchist/feminist/poet (1866–1912).

Purpura, purple.

(JULIA *takes the remaining slug out of the gun. She lets it fall on the floor.*)

JULIA: She's hurting herself. (JULIA *looks blank and is motionless.* CINDY *picks up the slug. She notices* JULIA'S *condition.*)

CINDY: Julia. *(To* CHRISTINA.*)* She's absent.

CHRISTINA: What do we do?

CINDY: Nothing, she'll be all right in a moment. *(She takes the gun from* JULIA. JULIA *comes to.*)

JULIA: It's a blank . . .

CINDY: It is.

JULIA: She's hurting herself. (JULIA *lets out a strange whimper. She goes to the coffee table, takes a piece of chocolate, puts it in her mouth and goes toward her room. After she crosses the threshold, she stops.*) I must lie down a while.

CINDY: Call me if you need anything.

JULIA: I will. *(She exits.* CINDY *tries to put the slug in the rifle. There is the sound of a car, a car door opening, closing.*)

CINDY: Do you know how to do this?

CHRISTINA: Of course not.

(CINDY *succeeds in putting the slug in the gun.* CECILIA *stands in the threshold of the foyer.*)

CECILIA: I am Cecilia Johnson. Do I have the right place?

CINDY: Yes.

(CINDY *locks the gun. Lights fade all around* CECILIA. *Only her head is lit. The light fades.*)

PART 2

On the Lawn

(There is a bench or a tree stump. FEFU *and* EMMA *bring boxes of potatoes, carrots, beets, winter squash, and other vegetables from a root cellar and put them in a small wagon.* FEFU *wears a hat and gardening gloves.*)

EMMA: *(Re-enters carrying a box as* FEFU *exits.)* Do you think about genitals all the time?

FEFU: Genitals? No, I don't think about genitals all the time.

EMMA: *(Starting to exit.)* I do, and it drives me crazy. Each person I see in the street, anywhere at all . . . I keep thinking of their genitals, what they look like, what position they are in. I think it's odd that everyone has them. Don't you?

FEFU: *(Crossing* EMMA.*)* No, I think it'd be odder if they didn't have them.

(EMMA *laughs.* FEFU *re-enters.*)

EMMA: I mean, people act as if they don't have genitals.

FEFU: How do people with genitals act?

EMMA: I mean, how can business men and women stand in a room and discuss business without even one reference to their genitals. I mean everybody has them. They just pretend they don't.

FEFU: I see. *(Shifting her glance from left to right with a fiendish look.)* You mean they should do this all the time.

(EMMA *laughs.*)

EMMA: No, I don't mean that. Think of it. Don't you think I'm right?

FEFU: Yes, I think you're right. (FEFU *sits.*) Oh, Emma, EmmaEmmaEmma.

EMMA: That's m'name.—Well, you see, it's generally believed that you go to heaven if you are good. If you are bad you go to hell. That is correct. However, in heaven they don't judge goodness the way we think. They don't. They have a divine registry of sexual performance. In that registry they mark down every little sexual activity in your life. If your faith is not entirely in it, if you just perform as an obligation and you don't feel the most profound devotion, if your spirit, your heart, and your flesh is not religiously delivered to it, you are condemned. They put you down in the black list and you don't go to heaven. Heaven is populated with divine lovers. And in hell live the duds.

FEFU: That's probably true.

EMMA: I knew you'd see it that way.

FEFU: Oh, I do. I do. You see, on earth we are judged by public acts, and sex is a private act. The partner cannot be said to be the public, since both partners are engaged. So naturally, it stands to reason that it's angels who judge our sexual life.

EMMA: Naturally.

(Pause.)

FEFU: You always bring joy to me.

EMMA: Thank you.

FEFU: I thank you. *(FEFU becomes distressed. She sits.)* I am in constant pain. I don't want to give in to it. If I do I am afraid I will never recover. . . . It's not physical, and it's not sorrow. It's very strange Emma, I can't describe it, and it's very frightening. . . . It is as if normally there is a lubricant . . . not in the body . . . a spiritual lubricant . . . it's hard to describe . . . and without it, life is a nightmare, and everything is distorted.—A black cat started coming to my kitchen. He's awfully mangled and big. He is missing an eye and his skin is diseased. At first I was repelled by him, but then, I thought, this is a monster that has been sent to me and I must feed him. And I fed him. One day he came and shat all over my kitchen. Foul diarrhea. He still comes and I still feed him.—I am afraid of him. (EMMA *kisses* FEFU.*)* How about a little lemonade?

EMMA: Yes.

FEFU: How about a game of croquet?

EMMA: Fine.

(FEFU exits. EMMA improvises an effigy of FEFU. She puts FEFU's hat and gloves on it.)

> Not from the stars do I my judgment pluck.
> And yet methinks I have astronomy;
> But not to tell of good or evil luck,
> Of plagues, of dearths, or seasons' quality;
> Nor can I fortune to brief minutes tell,
> Pointing to each his thunder, rain, and wind,
> Or say with princes if it shall go well
> By oft predict that I in heaven find.
> But from thine eyes my knowledge I derive.
> And, constant stars, in them I read such art
> As truth and beauty shall together thrive
> If from thyself to store thou wouldst convert:
> > Or else of thee this I prognosticate,
> > Thy end is truth's and beauty's doom and date.°

(If FEFU's entrance is delayed, EMMA will sing a popular song of the period. FEFU re-enters with a pitcher and two glasses.)

In the Study

(There are books on the walls, a desk, Victorian chairs, a rug on the floor. CHRISTINA sits behind the desk. She reads a French text book. She mumbles French sentences. CINDY sits to the left of the desk with her feet up on a chair. She looks at a magazine. A few moments pass.)

CHRISTINA: *(Practicing.)* Etes-vous externe ou demi-pensionnaire? La cuisine de votre cantine est-elle bonne, passable ou mauvaise?° *(She continues reading almost inaudibly. A moment passes.)*

CINDY: *(Reading.)* A lady in Africa divorced her husband because he was a cheetah.

CHRISTINA: Oh, dear. *(They laugh. They go back to their reading. A moment passes.)* Est-ce que votre professeur interroge souvant les eleves?° *(They go back to their reading. A moment passes.)*

CINDY: I suppose . . . when a person is swept off their feet . . . the feet remain and the person goes off . . . with the broom.

CHRISTINA: No . . . when a person is swept off their feet . . . there is no broom.

CINDY: What does the sweeping?

CHRISTINA: An emotion . . . a feeling.

CINDY: Then emotions have bristles?

CHRISTINA: Yes.

CINDY: Now I understand. Do the feet remain?

CHRISTINA: No, the feet fly also . . . but separate from the body. At the end of the leap, just before the landing, they join the ankles and one is complete again.

CINDY: Oh, that sounds nice.

CHRISTINA: It is. Being swept off your feet is nice. Anything else?

CINDY: Not for now. *(They go back to their reading. A moment passes.)* Are you having a good time?

CHRISTINA: Yes, I'm very glad I came.

CINDY: Do you like everybody?

CHRISTINA: Yes.

CINDY: Do you like Fefu?

CHRISTINA: I do . . . She confuses me a little.—I try to be honest . . . and I wonder if she is . . . I don't mean that she doesn't tell the truth. I know she does. I mean a kind of integrity. I know she has integrity too. . . . But I don't know if she's careful with life . . . something bigger than the self . . . I suppose I don't mean with life but more with convention. I think she is an adventurer in a way. Her mind is adventurous. I don't know if there is dishonesty in that. But in adventure there is taking chances and risks, and then one has to, somehow, have less regard or respect for things as they are. That is, regard for a kind of convention, I suppose. I am probably ultimately a conformist, I think. And I suppose I do hold back for fear of being disrespectful or destroying something—and I admire those who are not. But I also feel they are dangerous to me. I don't think they are dangerous to the world; they are more useful than I am, more important, but I feel some of my life is endangered by their way of thinking. Do you understand?

CINDY: Yes, I do.

CHRISTINA: I guess I am proud and I don't like thinking that I am thoughtful of things that have no value.—I like her.

CINDY: I had a terrible dream last night.

CHRISTINA: What was it?

CINDY: I was at a dance. And there was a young doctor I had seen in connection with my health. We all danced in a circle and he identified himself and said that he had spoken to Mike about me, but that it was all right, that he had put it so that it was all right. I was puzzled as to why Mike would mind and why he had spoken to him. Then, suddenly everybody sat down on the floor and pretended they were having singing lessons and one person was practicing Italian. The singing professor was being tested by two secret policemen. They were having him correct the voice of someone they had brought. He apparently didn't know how to do it. Then, one of the policemen put his hands on his vocal cords and kicked him out the door. Then he grabbed me and felt my throat from behind with his thumbs while he rubbed my nipples with his pinkies. Then, he pushed me out the door. Then,

---

Not from the stars . . . doom and date, Shakespeare's Sonnet 14. **Etes-vous externe . . . mauvaise?** Do you eat all your meals away or have lunch at school? The cooking of your school cafeteria—is it good, fair, or bad? **Est-ce que votre professeur . . . eleves?** Does your teacher often question the students?

the young doctor started cursing me. His mouth moved like the mouth of a horse. I was on an upper level with a railing and I said to him, "Stop and listen to me." I said it so strongly that he stopped. Everybody turned to me in admiration because I had made him stop. Then, I said to him, "Restrain yourself." I wanted to say respect me. I wasn't sure whether the words coming out of my mouth were what I wanted to say. I turned to ask my sister. The young man was bending over and trembling in mad rage. Another man told me to run before the young man tried to kill me. Meg and I ran downstairs. She asked me if I wanted to go to her place. We grabbed a taxi, but before the taxi got enough speed he came out and ran to the taxi and was on the verge of opening the door when I woke up.

(The door opens. FEFU *looks in. Her entrance may interrupt* CINDY's *speech at any point according to how long it takes her to reach the kitchen.)*

FEFU: Who's for a game of croquet?
CINDY: In a little while.
FEFU: See you outside.
CHRISTINA: That was quite a dream.
CINDY: What do you think it means?
CHRISTINA: I think it means you should go to a different doctor.
CINDY: He's not my doctor. I never saw him before.
CHRISTINA: Well good. I'm sure he's not a good doctor.

(At the end of the fourth repeat, when FEFU *invites them for croquet,* CINDY *says, "Oh let's play croquet" and they follow* FEFU.)*

In the Bedroom

(A plain unpainted room. Perhaps a room that was used for storage and was set up as a sleeping place for JULIA. *There is a mattress on the floor. To the right of the mattress there is a small table, to the left is* JULIA's *wheelchair. There is a sink on the wall. There are dry leaves on the floor although the time is not fall. The sheets are linen.* JULIA *lies in bed covered to her shoulders. She wears a white hospital gown.* JULIA *hallucinates. However, her behavior should not be the usual behavior attributed to a mad person. It should be rather still and luminous. There will be aspects of her hallucinations that frighten her, but hallucinating itself does not.)*

JULIA: They clubbed me. They broke my head. They broke my will. They broke my hands. They tore my eyes out. They took my voice away. They didn't do anything to my heart because I didn't bring my heart with me. They clubbed me again, but my head did not fall off in pieces. That was because they were so good and they felt sorry for me. The judges. You didn't know the judges?—I was good and quiet. I never dropped my smile. I smiled to everyone. If I stopped smiling I would get clubbed be-

cause they love me. They say they love me. I go along with that because if I don't . . .

(With her finger she indicates her throat being cut and makes the sound that usually accompanies that gesture.)

I told them the stinking parts of the body are the important ones: the genitals, the anus, the mouth, the armpit. All important parts except the armpits. And who knows, maybe the armpits are important too. That's what I said. *(Her voice becomes gravelly and tight in imitation of the judges.)* He said that all those parts must be kept clean and put away. He said that women's entrails are heavier than anything on earth and to see a woman running creates a disparate and incongruous image in the mind. It's anti-aesthetic. Therefore women should not run. Instead they should strike positions that take into account the weight of their entrails. Only if they do, can they be aesthetic. He said, for example, Goya's Maja.° He said Rubens'° women are not aesthetic. Flesh. He said that a woman's bottom should be in a cushion, otherwise it's revolting. He said there are exceptions. Ballet dancers are exceptions. They can run and lift their legs because they have no entrails. Isadora Duncan° had entrails, that's why she should not have danced. But she danced and for this reason became crazy. *(Her voice is back to normal.)* She wasn't crazy.

(She moves her hand as if guarding from a blow.)

She was. He said that I had to be punished because I was getting too smart. I'm not smart. I never was. Neither is Fefu smart. They are after her too. Well, she's still walking!

(She guards from a blow. Her eyes close.)

Wait! I'll say my prayer. I'm saying it.

(She mumbles. She opens her eyes with caution.)

You don't think I'm going to argue with them, do you? I repented. I told them exactly what they wanted to hear. They killed me. I was dead. The bullet didn't hit me. It hit the deer. But I died. He didn't. Then I repented and the deer died and I lived. *(With a gravelly voice.)* They said, "Live but crippled. And if you tell . . ."

(She repeats the throat cutting gesture.)

Why do you have to kill Fefu, for she's only a joker? *(With a gravelly voice.)* "Not kill, cure. Cure her." Will it hurt?

Goya's Maja, Spanish painter Francisco Goya (1746–1828); the painting is *The Naked Maja.* ***Rubens,*** Flemish painter Peter Paul Rubens (1577–1640), often featured heavily built women in his paintings. ***Isadora Duncan,*** American dancer (1878–1927), one of the great figures in modern dance.

(She whimpers.)

Oh, dear, dear, my dear, they want your light. Your light my dear. Your precious light. Oh dear, my dear.

(Her head moves as if slapped.)

Not cry. I'll say my prayer. I'll say it. Right now. Look.

(She sits up as if pulled by an invisible force.)

The human being is of the masculine gender. The human being is a boy as a child and grown up he is a man. Everything on earth is for the human being, which is man. To nourish him.—There are evil things on earth, and noxious things. Evil and noxious things are on earth for man also. For him to fight with, and conquer and turn its evil into good. So that it too can nourish him.—There are Evil Plants, Evil Animals, Evil Minerals, and Women are Evil.—Woman is not a human being. She is: 1—A mystery. 2—Another species. 3—As yet undefined. 4—Unpredictable; therefore wicked and gentle and evil and good which is evil.—If a man commits an evil act, he must be pitied. The evil comes from outside him, through him and into the act. Woman generates the evil herself.—God gave man no other mate but woman. The oxen is good but it is not a mate for man. The sheep is good but it is not a mate for man. The mate for man is woman and that is the cross man must bear.—Man is not spiritually sexual, he therefore can enjoy sexuality. His sexuality is physical which means his spirit is pure. Women's spirit is sexual. That is why after coitus they dwell in nefarious feelings. Because that is their natural habitat. That is why it is difficult for them to return to the human world. Their sexual feelings remain with them till they die. And they take those feelings with them to the afterlife where they corrupt the heavens, and they are sent to hell where through suffering they may shed those feelings and return to earth as man.

(Her head moves as if slapped.)

Don't hit me. Didn't I just say my prayer?

(A smaller slap.)

I believe it.

(She lies back.)

They say when I believe the prayer I will forget the judges. And when I forget the judges I will believe the prayer. They say both happen at once. And all women have done it. Why can't I?

(SUE enters with a bowl of soup on a tray.)

SUE: Julia, are you asleep?

(Short pause.)

JULIA: No.
SUE: I brought your soup.
JULIA: Put it down. I'm getting up in a moment.

(SUE puts the soup down.)

SUE: Do you want me to help you?
JULIA: No, I can manage. Thank you, Sue.

(SUE goes to the door.)

SUE: You're all right?
JULIA: Yes.
SUE: I'll see you later.
JULIA: Thank you, Sue.

(SUE exits. JULIA closes her eyes. As soon as each audience group leaves, the tray is removed, if possible through a back door.)

In the Kitchen

(A fully equipped kitchen. There is a table and chairs and a high cutting table. On a counter next to the stove there is a tray with a soup dish and a spoon. There is also a ladle. On the cutting table there are two empty glasses. Soup is heating on a burner. A kettle with water sits on an unlit burner. In the refrigerator there is an ice tray with wooden sticks in each cube. The sticks should rest on the edge of the tray forming two parallel rows, like a caterpillar lying on its back. In the refrigerator there are also two pitchers, one with water, one with lemonade. PAULA sits at the table. She is writing on a pad. SUE waits for the soup to heat.)

PAULA: I have it all figured out.
SUE: What?
PAULA: A love affair lasts seven years and three months.
SUE: It does?
PAULA: *(Reading.)* 3 months of love. 1 year saying: It's all right. This is just a passing disturbance. 1 year trying to understand what's wrong. 2 years knowing the end had come. 1 year finding the way to end it. After the separation, 2 years trying to understand what happened. 7 years, 3 months. *(No longer reading.)* At any point the sequence might be interrupted by another love affair that has the same sequence. That is, it's not really interrupted, the new love affair relegates the first one to a second plane and both continue their sequence at the same time.

(SUE looks over PAULA's shoulder.)

SUE: You really added it up.
PAULA: Sure.
SUE: What do you want to drink?
PAULA: Water. The old love affair may fade, so you are not aware the process goes on. A year later it may surface and you might find yourself figuring out what's wrong with the new one while trying to end the old one.
SUE: So how do you solve the problem?

PAULA: Celibacy?

SUE: (Going to the refrigerator.) Celibacy doesn't solve anything.

PAULA: That's true.

SUE: (Taking out the ice tray with the sticks.) What's this? (PAULA shakes her head.) Dessert. (PAULA shrugs her shoulders. SUE takes an ice cube and places it against her forehead.) For a headache. (She takes another cube and moves her arms in a Judo style.) Eskimo wrestling. (She places one stick behind her ear.) Brain cooler. That's when you're thinking too much. You could use one. (She tries to put the ice cube behind PAULA's ear. They wrestle and laugh. She puts the stick in her own mouth. She takes it out to speak.) This is when you want to keep chaste. No one will kiss you. (She puts it back in to demonstrate. Then takes it out.) That's good for celibacy. If you walk around with one of these in your mouth for seven years you can keep all your sequences straight. Finish one before you start the other. (She puts the ice cube in the tray and looks at it.) A frozen caterpillar. (She puts the tray away.)

PAULA: You're leaving that ice cube in there?

SUE: I'm clean. (Looking at the soup.) So what else do you have on love? (SUE places a bowl and spoon on the table and sits as she waits for the soup to heat.)

PAULA: Well, the break-up takes place in parts. The brain, the heart, the body, mutual things, shared things. The mind leaves but the heart is still there. The heart has left but the body wants to stay. The body leaves but the things are still at the apartment. You must come back. You move everything out of the apartment but the mind stays behind. Memory lingers in the place. Seven years later, perhaps seven years later, it doesn't matter any more. Perhaps it takes longer. Perhaps it never ends.

SUE: It depends.

PAULA: Yup. It depends.

SUE: (Pouring soup in the bowl.) Something's bothering you.

PAULA: No.

SUE: (Taking the tray.) I'm going to take this to Julia.

PAULA: Go ahead.

(As SUE exits, CECILIA enters.)

CECILIA: May I come in?

PAULA: Yes . . . Would you like something to eat?

CECILIA: No, I ate lunch.

PAULA: I didn't eat lunch. I wasn't very hungry.

CECILIA: I know.

PAULA: Would you like some coffee?

CECILIA: I'll have tea.

PAULA: I'll make some.

CECILIA: No, you sit. I'll make it. (CECILIA looks for tea.)

PAULA: Here it is. (She gets the tea and gives it to CECILIA.)

CECILIA: (As she lights the burner.) I've been meaning to call you.

PAULA: It doesn't matter. I know you're busy.

CECILIA: Still I would have called you but I really didn't find the time.

PAULA: Don't worry.

CECILIA: I wanted to see you again. I want to see you often.

PAULA: There's no hurry. Now we know we can see each other.

CECILIA: Yes, I'm glad we can.

PAULA: I have thought a great deal about my life since I saw you. I have questioned my life. I can't help doing that. It's been many years and I wondered how you see me now.

CECILIA: You're the same.

PAULA: I felt small in your presence . . . I haven't done all that I could have. All I wanted to do. Our lives have gone in such different directions I cannot help but review what those years have been for me. I gave up, almost gave up. I have missed you in my life. . . . I became lazy. I lost the drive. You abandoned me and I kept going. But after a while I didn't know how to. I didn't know how to go on. I knew why when I was with you. To give you pleasure. So we could laugh together. So we could rejoice together. To bring beauty to the world. . . . Now we look at each other like strangers. We are guarded. I speak and you don't understand my words. I remember every day.

(FEFU enters. She takes the lemonade pitcher from the refrigerator and two glasses from the top of the refrigerator.)

FEFU: Emma and I are going to play croquet. You want to join us? . . . No. You're having a serious conversation.

PAULA: Very serious. (PAULA smiles at CECILIA in a conciliatory manner.) Too serious.

FEFU: (As she exits.) Come.

PAULA: I'm sorry. Let's go play croquet.—I'm not reproaching you.

CECILIA: (Reaching for PAULA's hand.) I know. I've missed you too.

(They exit. As soon as the audience leaves the props are reset.)

PART 3

(The living room. It is dusk. As the audience enters, two or three of the women are around the piano playing and singing Schubert's "Who Is Silvia?"[5] They exit. EMMA enters, checks the lights in the room on her hand, looks around the room and goes upstairs. The rest enter through the rear. CECILIA enters speaking.)

Schubert's "Who Is Silvia?" setting of famous song from Shakespeare's *The Two Gentlemen of Verona*, IV.ii.

CECILIA: Well, we each have our own system of receiving information, placing it, responding to it. *(She sits in the center of the couch; the rest sit around her.)* That system can function with such a bias that it could take any situation and translate it into one formula. That is, I think, the main reason for stupidity or even madness, not being able to tell the difference between things.

SUE: Like?

CECILIA: Like . . . this person is screaming at me. He's a bully. I don't like being screamed at. Another person or the same person screams in a different situation. But you know you have done something that provokes him to scream. He has a good reason. They are two different things, the screaming of one and the screaming of the other. Often that distinction is not made. We cannot survive in a vacuum. We must be part of a community, perhaps 10, 100, 1000. It depends on how strong you are. But even the strongest will need a dozen, three, even one who sees, thinks, and feels as he does. The greater the need for that kind of reassurance, the greater the number that he needs to identify with. Some need to identify with the whole nation. Then, the greater the number the more limited the number of responses and thoughts. A common denominator must be reached. Thoughts, emotions that fit all, have to be limited to a small number. That is, I feel, the concern of the educator—to teach how to be sensitive to the differences in ourselves as well as outside ourselves, not to supervise the memorization of facts. *(EMMA's head appears in the doorway to the stairs.)* Otherwise the unusual in us will perish. As we grow we feel we are strange and fear any thought that is not shared with everyone.

JULIA: As I feel I am perishing. My hallucinations are madness, of course, but I wish I could be with others who hallucinate also. I would still know I am mad but I would not feel so isolated.—Hallucinations are real, you know. They are not like dreams. They are as real as all of you here. I have actually asked to be hospitalized so I could be with other nuts. But the doctors don't want to. They can't diagnose me. That makes me even more isolated. *(There is a moment's silence.)* You see, right now, it's an awful moment because you don't know what to say or do. If I were with other people who hallucinate, they would say, "Oh yeah. Sure. It's awful. Those dummies, they don't see anything." *(The others begin to relax.)* It's not so bad, really. I can laugh at it. . . . Emma is ready. We should start. *(The others are hesitant. JULIA speaks to FEFU.)* Come on.

FEFU: Sure. *(FEFU begins to move the table. Others help move the table and enough furniture to clear a space in the center. They sit in a semicircle downstage on the floor facing upstage. CECILIA sits on a chair to the left of the semicircle.)* All right. I start. Right?

CINDY: Right.

(FEFU goes to center and faces the others. EMMA sits on the steps. Only her head and legs are visible.)

FEFU: I talk about the stifling conditions of primary school education, etc. . . . etc. . . . The project . . . I know what I'm going to say but I don't want to bore you with it. We all know it by heart. Blah blah blah blah. And so on and so on. And so on and so on. Then I introduce Emma . . . And now Miss Emma Blake. *(They applaud. EMMA shakes her head.)* What.

EMMA: Paula goes next.

FEFU: Does it matter?

EMMA: Of course it matters. Dra-ma-tics. It has to build. I'm in costume.

FEFU: Oh. And now, ladies and gentlemen, Miss Paula Cori will speak on Art as a Tool for Learning. And I tell them the work you have done at the Institute, community centers, essays, etc. Miss Paula Cori.

(They applaud. PAULA goes to center.)

PAULA: Ladies and gentlemen, I, like my fellow educator and colleague, Stephany Beckmann . . .

FEFU: I am not an educator.

PAULA: What are you?

FEFU: . . . a do gooder, a girl scout.

PAULA: Well, I, like my fellow girl scout Stephany Beckmann say blah blah blah blah, blah blah blah and I offer the jewels of my wisdom and experience, which I will write down and memorize, otherwise I would just stand there and stammer and go blank. And even after I memorize it I'm sure I will just stand there and stammer and go blank.

EMMA: I'll work with you on it.

PAULA: However, after our other colleague Miss Emma Blake works with me on it . . . *(In imitation of EMMA she brings her hands together and opens her arms as she moves her head back and speaks.)* My impulses will burst forth through a symphony of eloquence.

EMMA: Breathe . . . in . . . *(PAULA inhales slowly.)* And bow. *(PAULA bows. They applaud.)*

PAULA: *(Coming up from the bow.)* Oh, I liked that. *(She sits.)*

EMMA: Good . . .

(They applaud.)

FEFU: And now, ladies and gentlemen, the one and only, the incomparable, our precious, dear Emma Blake.

(EMMA walks to center. She wears a robe which hangs from her arms to the floor.)

EMMA: From the prologue to "The Science of Educational Dramatics" by Emma Sheridan Fry.° *(She takes*

Emma Sheridan Fry taught acting to children at the Educational Alliance in New York from 1903 to 1909. In 1917, her book *Educational Dramatics* was published by Lloyd Adams Noble. The text of Emma's speech is taken from the prologue.

a dramatic pose and starts. The whole speech is dramatized by interpretive gestures and movements that cover the stage area.)

Environment knocks at the gateway of the senses. A rain of summons beats upon us day and night. . . . We do not answer. Everything around us shouts against our deafness, struggles with our unwillingness, batters our walls, flashes into our blindness, strives to sieve through us at every pore, begging, fighting, insisting. It shouts, "Where are you? Where are you?" But we are deaf. The signals do not reach us.

Society restricts us, school straight jackets us, civilization submerges us, privation wrings us, luxury feather-beds us. The Divine Urge is checked. The Winged Horse balks on the road, and we, discouraged, defeated, dismount and burrow into ourselves. The gates are closed and Divine Urge is imprisoned at Center. Thus we are taken by indifference that is death.

Environment finding the gates closed tries to break in. Turned away, it comes another way. Kept back, it stretches its hands to us. Always scheming to reach us. Never was suitor more insistent than Environment, seeking admission, claiming recognition, signaling to be seen, shouting to be heard. And through the ages we sit inside ourselves deaf, dumb and blind, and will not stir. . . .

. . . Maybe you are not deaf. . . . Perhaps signals reach you. Maybe you stir. . . . The gates give. . . . Eternal Urge pushes through the stupor of our senses, making paths to meet the challenging suitor, windows through which to see him, ears through which to hear him. Environment shouting, "Where are you?" and Center battering at the inner side of the wall crying, "Here I am," and dragging down bars, wrenching gates, prying at port-holes. Listening at cracks, reaching everywhere, and demanding that sense gates be flung open. The gates are open! Eternal Urge stands at the threshold signaling with venturous flag. An imperious instinct lets us know that "all" is ours, and that whatever anyone has ever known, or may ever have or know, we will call and claim. A sense of life universal surges through our life individual. We attack the feast of this table with an insatiable appetite that cries for all.

What are we? A creation of God's consciousness coming now slowly and painfully into recognition of ourselves.

What is Personality? A small part of us. The whole of us is behind that hungry rush at the gates of Senses.

What is Civilization? A circumscribed order in which the whole has not entered.

What is Environment? Our mate, our true mate that clamors for our reunion.

We will meet him. We will seize all, learn all, know all here, that we may fare further on the great quest! The task of Now is only a step toward the task of the Whole! Let us then seek the laws governing real life forces, that coming into their own, they may create, develop and reconstruct. Let us awaken life dormant! Let us, boldly, seizing the star of our intent, lift it as the lantern of our necessity, and let it shine over the darkness of our compliance. Come! The light shines. Come! It brightens our way. Come! Don't let its glorious light pass you by! Come! The day has come!

(EMMA throws herself on the couch. PAULA embraces her.)

Oh, it's so beautiful.

JULIA: It is, Emma. It is.

(They applaud.)

CINDY: Encore! Encore!

(EMMA stands.)

EMMA: Environment knocks at the gateway . . . *(She laughs and joins the others in the semicircle. PAULA remains seated on the couch.)* What's next.
FEFU: *(Going center.)* I introduce Cecilia. I don't think I should introduce Cecilia. She should just come after Emma. Now things don't need introduction. *(Imitating EMMA as she goes to her seat.)* They are happening.
EMMA: Right!

(CECILIA goes to center.)

CECILIA: Well, as we say in the business, that's a very hard act to follow.
EMMA: Not *very* hard. It's a hard act to follow.
CECILIA: Right. I should say my name first.
FEFU: Yes.
CECILIA: I should breathe too. *(She takes a breath. All except PAULA start singing "Cecilia." CECILIA is perplexed and walks backwards till she sits on the couch. She is next to PAULA. Unaware of who she is next to, she puts her hand on PAULA's leg. At the end of the song CECILIA realizes she is next to PAULA and stands.)* I should go before Emma. I don't think anyone should speak after Emma.
CINDY: Right. It should be Fefu, Paula, Cecilia, then Emma, and then Sue explaining the finances and asking for pledges. And the money should roll in. It's very good. *(They applaud.)* Sue . . . *(SUE goes to center.)*
SUE: Yes, blahblahblahblah, pledges and money. *(She does a few balletic moves and bows. They applaud.)*
FEFU: *(As SUE returns to her seat.)* Who's ready for coffee?
CINDY: *(As she stands.)* And dishes.
CHRISTINA: *(As she stands.)* I'll help.
EMMA: *(As she stands.)* Me too.
FEFU: Don't all come. Sit. Sit. You have done enough, relax.

(They put the furniture back as EMMA *and* SUE *jump over the couch making loud warlike sounds. As they exit to the kitchen,* SUE *tries to get ahead of* EMMA. EMMA *speeds ahead of her. All except* JULIA *jump over the couch. All except* CINDY *and* JULIA *exit.)*

JULIA: I should go do the dishes. I haven't done anything.

CINDY: You can do them tomorrow.

JULIA: True.—So how have you been?

CINDY: Hmm.

JULIA: Let me see. I can tell by looking at your face. Not so bad.

CINDY: Not so bad.

(There is the sound of laughter from the kitchen. CHRISTINA *runs in.)*

CHRISTINA: They're having a water fight over who's going to do the dishes.

CINDY: Emma?

CHRISTINA: And Paula, and Sue, all of them. Fefu was getting into it when I left. Cecilia got out the back door.

*(*CHRISTINA *walks back to the kitchen with some caution. She runs back and lies on the couch covering her head with the throw.* EMMA *enters with a pan of water in her hand. She is wet.* CINDY *and* JULIA *point to the lawn.* EMMA *runs to the lawn. There is the sound of knocking from upstairs. While the following conversation goes on,* EMMA, SUE, CINDY, *and* JULIA *engage in water fights in and out of the living room. The screams, laughter, and water splashing may drown the words.)*

PAULA: Open up.

FEFU: There's no one here.

PAULA: Open up you coward.

FEFU: I can't. I'm busy.

PAULA: What are you doing?

FEFU: I have a man here. Ah ah ah ah ah.

PAULA: O.K. I'll wait. Take your time.

FEFU: It's going to take quite a while.

PAULA: It's all right. I'll wait.

FEFU: Do me a favor?

PAULA: Sure. Open up and I'll do you a favor.

(There is the sound of a pot falling, a door slamming.)

FEFU: Fill it up for me.

PAULA: O.K.

FEFU: Thank you.

PAULA: Here's water. Open up.

FEFU: Leave it there. I'll come out in a minute.

PAULA: O.K. Here it is. I'm leaving now.

(Loud steps. PAULA *comes down with a filled pan.* EMMA *hides by the entrance to the steps.* EMMA *splashes water on* PAULA. PAULA *splashes water on* EMMA. SUE *appears with a full pan.)*

PAULA: Truce!

SUE: Who's the winner?

PAULA: You are. You do the dishes.

SUE: I'm the winner. You do the dishes.

FEFU: *(From the landing.)* Line up!

SUE: Psst. *(*PAULA *and* EMMA *look.* SUE *splashes water on them.)* Gotcha!

EMMA: Please don't.

PAULA: Truce. Truce.

FEFU: O.K. Line up. *(Pointing to the kitchen.)* Get in there! *(They all go to the kitchen.)* Start doing those dishes. *(There is a moment's pause.)*

JULIA: It's over.

CINDY: We're safe.

JULIA: *(To* CHRISTINA.*)* You can come up now. *(*CHRISTINA *stays down.)* You rather wait a while. *(*CHRISTINA *nods.)*

CHRISTINA: *(Playful.)* I feel danger lurking.

CINDY: She's been hiding all day.

*(*FEFU *enters. She is wet.)*

FEFU: I won. I got them working.

JULIA: I thought the fight was over who'd do the dishes.

FEFU: Yes. *(Starting to go.)* I have to change. I'm soaked.

CHRISTINA: They forgot what the fight was about.

FEFU: We did?

JULIA: That's usually the way it is.

FEFU: *(Going to* CHRISTINA *and lifting the cover from her face.)* Are you ready for an ice cube?

*(*FEFU *exits upstairs.* CHRISTINA *runs upstairs. There is silence.)*

CINDY: So.—And how have you been?

JULIA: All right. I've been taking care of myself.

CINDY: You look well.

JULIA: I do not. . . . Have you seen Mike?

CINDY: No, not since Christmas.

JULIA: I'm sorry.

CINDY: I'm O.K.—And how's your love life?

JULIA: Far away. . . . I have no need for it.

CINDY: I'm sorry.

JULIA: Don't be. I'm very morbid these days. I think of death all the time.

PAULA: *(Standing in the doorway.)* Anyone for coffee? *(They raise their hands.)* Anyone take milk? *(They raise their hands.)*

JULIA: Should we go in?

PAULA: I'll bring it out. *(*PAULA *exits.)*

JULIA: I feel we are constantly threatened by death, every second, every instant, it's there. And every moment something rescues us. Something rescues us from death every moment of our lives. For every moment we live we have to thank something. We have to be grateful to something that fights for us and saves us. I have felt lifeless and in the face of death. Death is not anything. It's being lifeless and I have felt lifeless sometimes for a brief moment, but I have been rescued by these . . . guardians. I am not sure who these guardians are. I only know they exist because I have felt their absence. I think we have come to know them as life, and we have become familiar with certain forms they take. Our sight is a form they take. That is why we take pleasure in seeing things, and we find some things beautiful. The sun is a guardian. Those things we take pleasure in are usually guardians. We enjoy looking at the sunlight when it comes through the window. Don't we? We, as people, are guardians to each other when we give love. And then of course we have white cells and antibodies protecting us. Those moments when I feel lifeless have occurred, and I am afraid one day the guardians won't come in time and I will be defenseless. I will die . . . for no apparent reason.

(Pause. PAULA *stands in the doorway with a bottle of milk.)*

PAULA: *(In a low-keyed manner.)* Anyone take rotten milk? *(Pause.)* I'm kidding. This one is no good but there's more in there . . . *(Remaining in good spirits.)* Forget it. It's not a good joke.
JULIA: It's good.
PAULA: In there it seemed funny but here it isn't. *(As she exits and shrugging her shoulders.)* It's a kitchen joke. Bye.
JULIA: *(After her.)* It is funny, Paula. *(To* CINDY.) It was funny.
CINDY: It's all right, Paula doesn't mind.
JULIA: I'm sure she minds. I'll go see . . . *(*JULIA *starts to go.* PAULA *appears in the doorway.)*
PAULA: *(In a low-keyed manner.)* Hey, who was that lady I saw you with?—That was no lady. That was my rotten wife. That one wasn't good either, was it? *(Exiting.)* Emma. . . . That one was no good either.

*(*SUE *starts to enter carrying a tray with sugar, milk, and two cups of coffee. She stops at the doorway to look at* PAULA *and* EMMA *who are behind the wall.)*

SUE: *(Whispering.)* What are you doing?—What?—O.K., O.K. *(She enters whispering.* SUE *puts the tray down.)* They're plotting something.

*(*PAULA *appears in the doorway.)*

PAULA: *(In a low-keyed manner.)* Ladies and gentlemen. Ladies, since our material is too shocking and avant-garde, we have decided to uplift our subject matter so it's more palatable to the sensitive public. *(*PAULA *takes a pose.* EMMA *enters. She lifts an imaginary camera to her face.)*
EMMA: Say cheese.
PAULA: Cheese. *(They both turn front and smile. The others applaud.)* Ah, success, success. Make it clean and you'll succeed.—Coffee's in the kitchen.
SUE: Oh, I brought theirs out.
PAULA: Oh, shall we have it here?

JULIA: We can all go in the kitchen. *(They each take their coffee and go to the kitchen.* SUE *takes the tray to the kitchen. The sugar remains on the table.)*
PAULA: Either here or there. *(She sits on the couch.)* I'm exhausted.

*(*CECILIA *enters from the lawn.)*

CECILIA: Is the war over?
PAULA: Yes.
CECILIA: It's nice out. *(*PAULA *nods in agreement.)* Where's everybody?
PAULA: In the kitchen, having coffee.
CECILIA: We must talk. *(*PAULA *starts to speak.)* Not now. I'll call you. *(*CECILIA *starts to go.)*
PAULA: When?
CECILIA: I don't know.
PAULA: I don't want you, you know.
CECILIA: I know.
PAULA: No, you don't. I'm not lusting after you.
CECILIA: I know that. *(She starts to go.)* I'll call you.
PAULA: When?
CECILIA: As soon as I can.
PAULA: I won't be home then.
CECILIA: When will you be home?
PAULA: I'll check my book and let you know.
CECILIA: Do that.—I'll be leaving after coffee. I'll say goodbye now.
PAULA: Goodbye. *(*CECILIA *goes towards the kitchen.* PAULA *starts towards the steps.* FEFU *comes down the steps.)*
FEFU: You're still wet.
PAULA: I'm going to change now.
FEFU: Do you need anything?
PAULA: No, I have something I can change to. Thank you.

*(*PAULA *goes upstairs.* FEFU *stands by the steps. She is downcast. As the lights shift to an eerie tone,* JULIA *enters in slow motion, walking. She goes to the coffee table, gets the sugar bowl, lifts it in* FEFU's *direction, takes the cover off, puts it back on and walks to the kitchen. As soon as* JULIA *exits,* SUE's *voice is heard speaking the following lines. Immediately after,* JULIA *re-enters wheeled by* SUE. CINDY, CHRISTINA, EMMA, *and* CECILIA *are with them. On the arms of the wheelchair rests a tray with a coffee pot and cups. As they reach the couch and chairs they sit.* SUE *puts the tray on the table.* FEFU *stares at* JULIA.)*

SUE: I was terribly exhausted and run down. I lived on coffee so I could stay up all night and do my work. And they used to give us these medical check-ups all the time. But all they did was ask how we felt and we'd say "Fine," and they'd check us out. In the meantime I looked like a ghost. I was all bones. Remember Susan Austin? She was very naive and when they asked her how she felt, she said she was nervous and she wasn't sleeping well. So she had to see a psychiatrist from then on.
EMMA: Well, she was crazy.

(FEFU *exits.*)

SUE: No, she wasn't.—Oh god, those were awful days. . . . Remember Julie Brooks?

EMMA: Sure.

SUE: She was a beautiful girl.

EMMA: Ah yes, she was gorgeous.

(PAULA *comes down the stairs as soon as she has changed. She sits on the steps half way down.*)

SUE: At the end of the first semester they called her in because she had been out with 28 men and they thought that was awful. And the worst thing was that after that, she thought there was something wrong with her.

CINDY: (*Jokingly.*) She was a nymphomaniac, that's all.

SUE: She was not. She was just very beautiful so all the boys wanted to go out with her. And if a boy asked her to go have a cup of coffee she'd sign out and write in the name of the boy. None of us did of course. All she did was go for coffee or go to a movie. She was really very innocent.

EMMA: And Gloria Schuman? She wrote a psychology paper the faculty decided she didn't write and they called her in to try to make her admit she hadn't written it. She insisted she wrote it and they sent her to a psychiatrist also.

JULIA: Everybody ended going to the psychiatrist.

(FEFU *enters through the foyer.*)

EMMA: After a few visits the psychiatrist said: Don't you think you know me well enough now that you can tell me the truth about the paper? He almost drove her crazy. They just couldn't believe she was so smart.

SUE: Those were difficult times.

PAULA: We were young. That's why it was difficult. On my first year I thought you were all very happy. I had been so deprived in my childhood that I believed the rich were all happy. During the summer you spent your vacations in Europe or the Orient. I went to work and I resented that. But then I realized that many lives are ruined by poverty and many lives are ruined by wealth. I was always able to manage. And I think I enjoyed myself as much when I went to Revere Beach on my day off as you did when you visited the Taj Mahal. (CECILIA *enters from the foyer. She stands there and listens.* PAULA *doesn't acknowledge her.*) Then, when I stopped feeling envy, I started noticing the waste. I began feeling contempt for those who, having everything a person can ask for, make such a mess of it. I resented them because they were not better than the poor. If you have all you need you should be generous. If you can afford to go to school your mind should be better. If you didn't have to fight for your place on earth you should be nobler. But I saw them cheating and grabbing like the kids in the slums, or wasting away with self-indulgence. And I saw them be plain stupid. If there is a reason why some are rich while others starve it must be so they put everything they have at the service of others. They should take the responsibility of everything that happens in the world. They are the only ones who can influence things. The poor don't have the power to change things. I think we should teach the poor and let the rich take care of themselves. I'm sorry, I know that's what we're doing. That's what Emma has been doing. I'm sorry . . . I guess I feel it's not enough. (PAULA *sobs.*) I'll wash my face. I'll be right back. (*She starts to go towards the kitchen.*) I think highly of all of you. (CECILIA *follows her.* PAULA *turns.* CECILIA *opens her arms and puts them around* PAULA, *engulfing her. She kisses* PAULA *on the lips.* PAULA *steps back. She is fearful.* CECILIA *follows her.* FEFU *enters from the lawn.*)

FEFU: Have you been out? The sky is full of stars.

(EMMA, SUE, CHRISTINA, *and* CINDY *exit.*)

JULIA: What's the matter?

(FEFU *shakes her head.* JULIA *starts to go toward the door.*)

FEFU: Stay a moment, will you?

JULIA: Of course.

FEFU: Did you have enough coffee?

JULIA: Yes.

FEFU: Did you find the sugar?

JULIA: Yes. There was sugar in the kitchen. What's the matter?

FEFU: Can you walk? (JULIA *is hurt. She opens her arms implying she hides nothing.*) I am sorry, my dear.

JULIA: What is the matter?

FEFU: I don't know, Julia. Every breath is painful for me. I don't know. (FEFU *turns* JULIA's *head to look into her eyes.*) I think you know.

(JULIA *breaks away from* FEFU.)

JULIA: (*Avoiding* FEFU's *glance.*) No, I don't know. I haven't seen much of you lately. I have thought of you a great deal. I always think of you. Cindy tells me how you are. I always ask her. How is Phillip? Things are not well with Phillip?

FEFU: No.

JULIA: What's wrong?

FEFU: A lot is wrong.

JULIA: He loves you.

FEFU: He can't stand me.

JULIA: He loves you.

FEFU: He's left me. His body is here but the rest is gone. I exhaust him. I torment him and I torment myself. I need him, Julia.

JULIA: I know you do.

FEFU: I need his touch. I need his kiss. I need the person he is. I can't give him up. (*She looks into* JULIA's *eyes.*)

I look into your eyes and I know what you see. (JULIA *closes her eyes.*) It's death. (JULIA *shakes her head.*) Fight!

JULIA: I can't.

FEFU: I saw you walking.

JULIA: No. I can't walk.

FEFU: You came for sugar, Julia. You came for sugar. Walk!

JULIA: You know I can't walk.

FEFU: Why not? Try! Get up! Stand up!

JULIA: What is wrong with you?

FEFU: You have given up!

JULIA: I get tired! I get exhausted! I am exhausted!

FEFU: What is it you see? (JULIA *doesn't answer.*) What is it you see! Where is it you go that tires you so?

JULIA: I can't spend time with others! I get tired!

FEFU: What is it you see!

JULIA: You want to see it too?

FEFU: No, I don't. You're nuts, and willingly so.

JULIA: You know I'm not.

FEFU: And you're contagious. I'm going mad too.

JULIA: I try to keep away from you.

FEFU: Why?

JULIA: I might be harmful to you.

FEFU: Why?

JULIA: I am contagious. I can't be what I used to be.

FEFU: You have no courage.

JULIA: You're being cruel.

FEFU: I want to rest, Julia. How does a person rest. I want to put my mind at rest. I am frightened. (JULIA *looks at* FEFU.) Don't look at me. (*She covers* JULIA's *eyes with her hand.*) I lose my courage when you look at me.

JULIA: May no harm come to your head.

FEFU: Fight!

JULIA: May no harm come to your will.

FEFU: Fight, Julia!

(FEFU *starts shaking the wheelchair and pulling* JULIA *off the wheelchair.*)

JULIA: I have no life left.

FEFU: Fight, Julia!

JULIA: May no harm come to your hands.

FEFU: I need you to fight.

JULIA: May no harm come to your eyes.

FEFU: Fight with me!

JULIA: May no harm come to your voice.

FEFU: Fight with me!

JULIA: May no harm come to your heart.

(CHRISTINA *enters.* FEFU *sees* CHRISTINA, *releases* JULIA. *To* CHRISTINA.)

FEFU: Now I have done it. Haven't I. You think I'm a monster. (*She turns to* JULIA *and speaks to her with kindness.*) Forgive me if you can. (JULIA *nods.*)

JULIA: I forgive you.

(FEFU *gets the gun.*)

CHRISTINA: What in the world are you doing with that gun!

FEFU: I'm going to clean it!

CHRISTINA: I think you better not!

FEFU: You're silly!

(CECILIA *appears on the landing.*)

CHRISTINA: I don't care if you shoot yourself! I just don't like the mess you're making!

(FEFU *starts to go to the lawn and turns.*)

FEFU: I enjoy betting it won't be a real bullet! You want to bet!

CHRISTINA: No! (FEFU *exits.* CHRISTINA *goes to* JULIA.) Are you all right?

JULIA: Yes.

CHRISTINA: Can I get you anything?

JULIA: Water. (CECILIA *goes to the liquor cabinet for water.*) Put some sugar in it. Could I have a damp cloth for my forehead? (CHRISTINA *goes toward the kitchen.* JULIA *speaks front.*) I didn't tell her anything. Did I? I didn't.

CECILIA: (*Going to* JULIA *with the water.*) About what?

JULIA: She knew.

(*There is the sound of a shot.* CHRISTINA *and* CECILIA *run out.* JULIA *puts her hand to her forehead. Her hand goes down slowly. There is blood on her forehead. Her head falls back.* FEFU *enters holding a dead rabbit.*)

FEFU: I killed it . . . I just shot . . . and killed it. . . . Julia . . .

(*Dropping the rabbit,* FEFU *walks to* JULIA *and stands behind the chair as she looks at* JULIA. SUE *and* CINDY *enter from the foyer,* EMMA *and* PAULA *from the kitchen,* CHRISTINA *and* CECILIA *from the lawn. They surround* JULIA. *The lights fade.*)

Figure 1. Fefu (Rebecca Schull, *right*) pours one drop of bourbon "with great care" for Christina (Elizabeth Perry, *left*) while Cindy (Dorothy Lyman) watches in the 1978 American Place Theatre production of *Fefu and Her Friends*, directed by the author. (Photograph: Martha Holmes.)

Figure 2. Emma (Gordana Rashovich) holds Fefu's hand (Rebecca Schull) to comfort her in the 1978 American Place Theatre production of *Fefu and Her Friends*, directed by the author. (Photograph: Martha Holmes.)

Figure 3. Sue (Arleigh Richards) demonstrates possible ways of using an ice cube on a stick for Paula (Connie LoCurto Cicone, *seated*) in the 1978 American Place Theatre production of *Fefu and Her Friends*, directed by the author. (Photograph: Martha Holmes.)

Figure 4. Fefu (Rebecca Schull) confronts the tired Julia (Margaret Harrington) in the last act of the 1978 American Place Theatre production of *Fefu and Her Friends*, directed by the author. (Photograph: Martha Holmes.)

Staging of *Fefu and Her Friends*

REVIEW OF THE AMERICAN PLACE THEATRE
PRODUCTION, 1977, BY ERIKA MUNK

My reactions to Irene Fornes's new play and the Manhattan Theatre Club's evening of readings were peculiarly self-conscious because I had just received some disagreeable letters protesting an April review of Kay Carney's show about Off-Off-Broadway. The angriest was from a playwright, Judith Katz, who claimed that because I criticized Megan Terry's recent work as sentimental and said that Fornes had not developed into a "major" force while Sam Shepard has, I denied an entire American theatre movement and its audience, "trashed" Katz's artistic mothers, and worst of all, was a "male-identified" critic, unable to recognize that "women writers were like women which means that we write emotionally . . . what better place [than the theatre] to have your heart hugged!"

It was tempting to poke fun at this squishy image of blood and veins all tangled on stage as the poor pump tried to beat despite those encircling arms—but the basic indictment filled me with resentment and dismay. Feminism and socialism have made me suspicious of, while easily guilt-stricken by, accusations of bad faith and trafficking with the enemy. Sometimes "male-identified" seems, idiotically, to mean one collaborates through heterosexuality, or having children, or working with men: only the ghetto can be pure. At other times it applies to one's mental style and processes: that is, the degree to which heart-hugging is found inadequate as art or politics. But because reviewing is a profession easily suspect as a form of egotism and always wound about with self-doubt (why am I doing this of all things? am I doing it honestly? what *is* doing it honestly?) I saw the Fornes and heard the readings wary of smart-ass opinions, cute judgments, and simultaneously watching myself for sloppy identification and trashy uplifting of consciousness.

The MTC's evening turned out to be a celebration of Honor Moore's just-published anthology. *The New Women's Theatre*, which includes plays by 10 writers of whom six read from their work: Alice Childress, Tina Howe, Corinne Jacker, Myrna Lamb, Moore herself, and Ruth Wolff. Still brooding about the letters, I found it ironic that the basic premise of Moore's collection pretty well dismissed the eminent women playwrights of the '60s (Drexler, Kennedy, Yankowitz, Owens, as well as Terry and Fornes). Her introduction says: "During the '60s, much of the theatre did not touch real women in spite of the number of female dramatists. But in the '70s, with the shift away from 'absurdism' and back to a kind of realism, women have begun to write from their own experience." The assumption that a nonnaturalistic

style is less "real" or less reflective of experience than a naturalistic one is left unexamined. Moore gently criticizes Lillian Hellman's plays for containing no autobiographical characters or "expressions of need"; she says that Gertrude Stein is "not as important as a reinventor of language and syntax as she is as a woman writer who knew women profoundly and expressed that knowledge." Moore rightly calls for "woman-centered" plays, and then says Martha Graham is "perhaps the most important woman dramatist who ever lived," which gives up on words with a '60s-ish vengeance; oddly, from a poet.

The playwrights themselves were less confessional and didactic than this would lead one to expect, though none seemed deeply interested in formal experimentation. When they talked about their working lives and beliefs, Childress and Wolff were models of how to fight back and stay human: both had special battles, Childress because she is black, Wolff, less seriously (think of all the money!) because a major movie was made from the corpse of her play after its feminist heart had been cut out. I don't want to review the readings—you can look at the book. But when I read it in its entirety, Tina Howe's *Birth and After Birth*, a satiric and exterior play, moved me most, perhaps because it's rather coarse and mean, and deals with the pain we inflict on small children and they on us: a subject I have never seen written for stage so precisely (*not* naturalistically).

Yet I do not see how these plays, in all their various virtues and failings, are more woman-centered than those of the '60s; only that their realistic surfaces are more useful for consciousness-raising and television adaptations. I wonder at the historical perspective behind the claim that women have finally "begun" to write from their own experiences, and was bemused by the slight self-congratulatory aura of the event.

Irene Fornes's nuanced and mysterious play is about a middle-aged woman who has invited a group of friends to her country house; it is the '30s, and these women, each at some crucial point in the development of her spirit, are unconscious pioneers of feminism. The house itself, the sense of interior action its rooms engender, holds the play together.

The first scene is conventional enough: The audience sits on bleachers facing a living room. Fefu's friends gather slowly: a sophisticate amused at her hostess's strong eccentricities; a drinker, who finds a lurking sense of menace; a young lesbian couple; a spirited and beautiful but very actressy actress; a woman in a wheelchair, her face like a death's head, who phases in and out of paranoid hallucinations; finally, a chic woman in black—it is like the country house gatherings of a '30s' mystery story.

Fefu has a husband, whom we never see. Now and then she aims a gun into the garden and shoots at him: the game is that she doesn't know whether he has replaced the gun's blanks with bullets. Of this husband, she says: "He married me as a constant reminder how loathsome women are." And his role is strange but clear: "If women shall recognize each other, the world shall blow us apart. Men remove the danger, but the price is the mind and the spirit."

In the second scene the conventions disappear. The audience is divided into four groups, each of which goes to a different room. All end up seeing the same events, in different order. Mine was: (1) in a real kitchen— apparently a large living loft has been made over to accommodate the play—the lesbian couple have a wry conversation about affairs; one leaves; the woman in black comes in and talks with regret and subdued anger to the other, her former lover. (2) On the lawn Fefu and the actress play croquet and also talk of love, but wittily—the scene exists in a golden haze of deep friendship. (3) In the study, two guests talk desultorily, telling dreams, reading bits from magazines; there is a stifling sense of ennui and the unspoken. (4) In a bedroom the crippled woman lies under a sheet like a corpse, sunk in self-loathing visions of woman's evil and man's torture. One sees each scene knowing that another group has just seen it and a new one will see it next, and that the order of scenes does not matter; this enclosed repetitiveness sums up entire trapped lifetimes.

In the third scene, we return to the living room. The women are released into games and theatre. But suddenly we find out that the crippled woman can walk, though she herself does not seem to know she can. This self-deception leads to the end, in which, of course (for the author is mocking the conventions of three-act thinking), the gun is shot, and there's a real bullet. It kills an animal outside—but at the moment the animal is hit, blood streams from the crippled woman's head, and she dies. Fornes is a delicate writer and I reduce this event to a message at some risk—but: if you kill the external enemy the hysteric inside dies, too. For Fornes, at least here, such freedom comes at the price of women being only with women. Yet, however much I may disagree with this message, the play itself is not a polemic but a lovely piece of theatre.

NTOZAKE SHANGE

1948–

sing a black girl's song
bring her out
to know herself
to know you

How does an upper-middle-class "black girl" get to know herself? For Paulette Williams, born into an educated and culturally sophisticated family (her father was a surgeon, her mother a psychiatric social worker), the process involved continual exploration and an unwillingness to settle for a life of privilege. Though her family was wealthy enough to afford a live-in maid, young Paulette also experienced the frightening experience of being one of the first African Americans in St. Louis's previously all-white public school system. After a B.A. from Barnard and an M.A. from the University of Southern California, both in American Studies, she moved to San Francisco and taught humanities and women's studies at various colleges in the area. In San Francisco, she also found a series of artistic and literary communities that challenged and nurtured her: Third World Communications (The Woman's Collective), a group sponsoring poetry readings by women; the Women's Studies Program at Sonoma State College; dance classes with Raymond Sawyer and Ed Mock, who joined folk traditions of Africa and the Caribbean to American dance traditions; and finally the Spirit of Dance, a dance troupe incorporating Cuban, Caribbean, and African styles. "Knowing a woman's mind & spirit had been allowed me, with dance I discovered my body more intimately than I had imagined possible. With the acceptance of the ethnicity of my thighs & backside, came a clearer understanding of my voice as a woman & as a poet." Thus Shange explains how she came to know herself, from accepting her body to freeing her poetic voice.

Part of that liberating process came by embracing her African heritage, which she signified when she was still a graduate student by taking a new name: Ntozake Shange (pronounced "en-toe-zah-key" "shang-gay") meaning "she who brings her own things" and "one who walks with lions." She also freed herself by rejecting many of the grammatical and mechanical rules of writing. In her poems and plays, Shange deliberately uses abbreviations and phonetic spellings, avoids standard punctuation and capitalization, and forges her own distinctive style as a way of declaring her independence. To break the rules is for her a political act: "in murdering the King's English we free ourselves." Yet, as she makes clear, a writer should take such a step only from a position of complete control. "I insist that my students and my colleagues do master the King's English or the King's French, because then it becomes the same thing that you do in military combat: You know your enemy so well that you're able to do something with his weapon."

Shange's artistic liberation expresses itself not only in the mechanics of her sentences but also in the structure of her plays. Her first play, and still her best-known work, *for colored girls who have considered suicide/when the rainbow is enuf* (1975) began as a series of poems and dances that Shange created together with another dancer (Paula Moss), a horn trio, and a blues band. First performed in bars and cafés, as well as on campuses, "the show" moved from California to New York, expanding and refining itself through performance. Starting with seven poems, Shange developed what she calls a "choreopoem," with twenty poems for seven performers. Joseph Papp of the New York Shakespeare Festival produced this musical play first at the Public Theater and then on Broadway; it won both an Obie (Off-Broadway) award and the New York Drama Critics Circle Award.

Focusing on the experience of women, particularly "women of color"—a term Shange puns on in the title and in the identification of the seven performers only through their differently colored costumes—the play reflects both sexual and racial stereotyping, often with pain and anger but also with humor. The Lady in Brown speaks as a young girl who finds both her adult and racial identity simultaneously by rejecting the choices she finds in the children's room of the public library because they concern "only pioneer girls & magic rabbits/ & big city white boys." In the "ADULT READING ROOM" she finds a book about TOUSSAINT L'OUVERTURE:

> TOUSSAINT waz a blk man a negro like my mama say
> who refused to be a slave
> & he spoke french
> & didn't low no white man to tell him nothin

The child's delight in finding a person who represents black strength and independence leads her to read "15 books in three weeks." Other encounters in the play are less liberating, especially the climactic monologue in which the Lady in Red tells about the tortured relationship between Beau Willie Brown, the ex-Vietnam vet, and Crystal, the mother of his two children. This monologue builds to a frightening conclusion as Beau Willie's rage at Crystal's refusal to marry him leads him to dangle the children out the window. At that moment, the Lady in Red virtually identifies herself with the agonized mother in her story:

> i stood by beau in the window/ with naomi reachin
> for me/ & kwame screaming mommy mommy from the fifth
> story/ but i cd only whisper/ & he dropped em

While public response to *for colored girls* was primarily positive, the harrowing effect of "beau willie brown," as well as the number of other violent male-female relationships described in the play raised questions about Shange's racial sensitivity: how could an African-American woman so thoroughly attack African-American men? Were they the only enemies? What about the dominant "other," the entire white community? Shange's 1979 play, *spell #7*, seems to answer those questions by looking not just at the experience of women of color, but of all persons of color ("technologically stressed third world people"), and especially those trapped by the stereotypes created by the white community. In addressing such issues, Shange joins writers such as Alice Childress (1920–), Lorraine Hansberry (1930–1965), and Adrienne Kennedy (1931–) all of whom see all African Americans as continually struggling with the problems of identity. In *Trouble in Mind* (1955), Childress, who worked as an actress and director, examines the problems of a black actress fighting against the degrading stereotype she is asked to play—a mother who would consciously allow her son to turn himself in and be lynched. In *Raisin in the Sun* (1959), Lorraine Hansberry focuses on the conflict between racial pride and the American dream of middle-class security; her protagonist, Walter Lee Younger, seems at first willing to play the subservient "black man" but finally rejects that role to move into a white neighborhood that has tried to exclude him and his family. And in *Funnyhouse of a Negro* (1964) and *The Owl Answers* (1965), Adrienne Kennedy uses surrealist theatrical images and language to explore the distorted views of the African-American culture confronted by her protagonists, "Negro-Sarah" and "She who is Clara Passmore."

Like Kennedy, who deliberately rejects the realistic drama of Childress and Hansberry, Shange begins *spell #7* with a striking theatrical image, "a huge black-face mask" and actors "in tattered fieldhand garb, blackface, and the countenance of stepan fetchit when he waz frightened" (see Figure 1). She thus shows the grinning lie of the minstrel show substituted for the truth of oppression. The opening monologue of Lou, the magician, promises both reality and transformation:

> & i'm fixin you up good/ fixin you up good & colored
> & you gonna be colored all yr life
> & you gonna love it/ bein colored/ all yr life/ colored & love it
> love it/ bein colored. SPELL #7!

Just as *for colored girls* moved through the despair of Crystal's loss to the final choral affirmation, "i found god in myself/ & i loved her/ i loved her fiercely," so *spell #7* progresses towards acceptance though the path to that acceptance is anything but easy. Natalie's first-act monologue about "sue-jean" who "always wanted to have a baby/ a lil boy/ named myself" indicates that bringing a child into the world seems not merely painful but self-destructive; the birth of the child is followed by the death of the child and the minstrel mask that had lifted for most of the act is slowly lowered into place. By the end of the second act, the difficulty of self-acceptance becomes even more pronounced with two bitterly disturbing monologues that explore the consequences of racial stereotyping and oppression.

Yet on stage, the unquenchable vitality of the performers who celebrate the heritage of artists of color make it possible to believe the final line, "colored & love it." The stage directions call for an opening dance drawn from "every period of afro-american entertainment: from acrobats, comedians, tap-dancers, calindy dancers, cotton club choruses, apollo theatre du-wop groups." The text constantly evokes the energetic creativity of popular artists—Tina Turner, Chuck Berry, Butch Morris, Bob Marley, Stevie Wonder. On one level, the nine actors must adopt the presentational style of singer-dancers, putting on a show, telling stories, entertaining each other as well as the audience. But though they begin as masked, stereotyped, imprisoned look-alikes (Figure 1), they gradually reveal the heartfelt reality of individuals caught in immensely personal human dramas (see Figure 2). The return of the minstrel mask at the end forces the audience to confront the contradictions. Shange does not suggest that stereotypes disappear, but she does argue for the possibility that they may be transformed.

spell #7
geechee jibara quik magic trance manual for technologically stressed third world people

A THEATER PIECE BY NTOZAKE SHANGE

CAST *(in order of appearance)*

LOU, *a practicing magician*
ALEC, *a frustrated, angry actor's actor*
DAHLIA, *young gypsy (singer/dancer)*
ELI, *a bartender who is also a poet*
BETTINA, DAHLIA's *co-worker in a chorus*
LILY, *an unemployed actress working as a barmaid*

NATALIE, *a not too successful performer*
ROSS, *guitarist-singer with* NATALIE
MAXINE, *an experienced actress*

this show is dedicated to my great aunt marie, aunt lizzie, aunt jane and my grandma, viola benzena, and her buddy, aunt effie, and the lunar year.

ACT 1

(there is a huge black-face mask hanging from the ceiling of the theater as the audience enters. in a way the show has already begun, for the members of the audience must integrate this grotesque, larger-than-life misrepresentation of life into their preshow chatter. slowly the house lights fade, but the mask looms even larger in the darkness.

once the mask is all that can be seen, LOU, *the magician, enters. he is dressed in the traditional costume of Mr. Interlocutor: tuxedo, bow tie, top hat festooned with all kinds of whatnots that are obviously meant for good luck, he does a few catchy "soft-shoe" steps & begins singing a traditional version of a black play song)*

LOU: *(singing.)*

10 lil picaninnies all in bed
one fell out and the other nine said:
i sees yr hiney
all black & shiny
i see yr hiney
all black & shiny/ shiny

(as a greeting.)

yes/ yes/ yes   isnt life wonderful

(confidentially.)

my father is a retired magician
which accounts for my irregular behavior
everything comes outta magic hats
or bottles wit no bottoms & parakeets
  are as easy to get as a couple a rabbits
or 3 fifty-cent pieces/ 1958
my daddy retired from magic & took
up another trade cuz this friend of mine

from the 3rd grade/ asked to be made white
on the spot

what cd any self-respectin colored american magician
do wit such an outlandish request/ cept
put all them razzamatazz hocus pocus zippity-
  doo-dah
thingamajigs away   cuz
colored chirren believin in magic
waz becomin politically dangerous for the race
& waznt nobody gonna be made white
on the spot
from a clap of my daddy's hands
& the reason i'm so peculiar's
cuz i been studyin up on my daddy's technique
& everything i do is magic these days
& it's very colored/ very now you see it/ now you
dont mess with me

(boastfully.)

                    i come from a family of retired
sorcerers/ active houngans & pennyante fortune
  tellers
wit 41 million spirits/ critturs & celestial bodies
on our side
        i'll listen to yr problems
        help wit yr career/ yr lover/ yr wanderin
          spouse
        make yr grandma's stay in heaven more
        gratifyin
        ease yr mother thru menopause &
          show yr son
        how to clean his room

608

(*while* LOU *has been easing the audience into acceptance of his appearance & the mask* [*his father, the ancestors, our magic*], *the rest of the company enters in tattered fieldhand garb, blackface, and the countenance of stepan fetchit when he waz frightened. their presence belies the magician's promise that "you'll be colored n love it," just as the minstrel shows were lies, but* LOU *continues.*)

YES YES YES 3 wishes is all you get
        scarlet ribbons for yr hair
        a farm in mississippi
        someone to love you madly
all things are possible
but aint no colored magician in his right mind
gonna make you   white
i mean
               this is blk magic
you lookin at
& i'm fixin you up good/ fixin you up good &
   colored
& you gonna be colored all yr life
& you gonna love it/ bein colored/ all yr life/
   colored & love it
love it/ bein colored. SPELL #7!

(LOU *claps his hands, & the company which had been absolutely still til this moment/ jumps up. with a rhythm set on a washboard carried by one of them/ they begin a series of steps that identify every period of afro-american entertainment: from acrobats, comedians, tap-dancers, calindy dancers, cotton club choruses, apollo theatre du-wop groups, til they reach a frenzy in the midst of "ham-bone, hambone where ya been"/ & then take a bow à la bert williams/ the lights bump up abruptly.*

the magician, LOU, *walks through the black-faced fig-ures in their kneeling poses, arms outstretched as if they were going to sing "mammy." he speaks now* [*as a com-panion of the mask*] *to the same audience who fell so easily into his hands & who were so aroused by the way the black-faced figures "sang n danced."*)

LOU: why don't you go on & integrate a german-amer-
     ican school in st. louis mo./ 1955/ better yet why
     dont ya go on & be a red niggah in a blk school in
     1954/ i got it/ try & make one friend at camp in the
     ozarks in 1957/ crawl thru one a jesse james' caves
     wit a class of white kids waitin outside to see the
     whites of yr eyes/ why dontcha invade a clique of
     working class italians trying to be protestant in a
     jewish community/ & come up a spade/ be a lil too
     dark/ lips a lil too full/ hair entirely too nappy/ to
     be beautiful/ be a smart child trying to be dumb/
     you go meet somebody who wants/ always/ a lil less/
     be cool when yr body says hot/ & more/ be a mistake
     in racial integrity/ an error in white folks' most
     absurd fantasies/ be a blk kid in 1954/ who's not blk
     enuf to lovingly ignore/ not beautiful enuf to leave
     alone/ not smart enuf to move outta the way/ not

bitter enuf to die at an early age/ why dontchu
c'mon & live my life for me/ since the dreams aint
enuf/ go on & live my life for me/ i didnt want
certain moments at all/ i'd give em to anybody . . .
,awright. alec.

(*the black-faced* ALEC *gives his minstrel mask to* LOU *when he hears his name/* ALEC *rises. the rest of the com-pany is intimidated by this figure daring to talk without the protection of black-face. they move away from him/ or move in place as if in mourning.*)

ALEC: st. louis/ such a colored town/ a whiskey black
      space of history & neighborhood/ forever ours to
      lawrenceville/ where the only road open to me waz
      cleared by colonial slaves/ whose children never
      moved/ never seems like mended the torments of
      the Depression or the stains of demented spittle/
      dropped from the lips of crystal women/ still makin
      independence flags/
        st. louis/ on a halloween's eve to the veiled
      prophet/ usurpin the mystery of mardi gras/ i made
      it mine tho the queen waz always fair/ that parade
      of pagan floats & tambourines/ commemorates me/
      unlike the lonely walks wit liberal trick or treaters/
      back to my front door/ bag half empty/
        my face enuf to scare anyone i passed/ gee/ a
      colored kid/ whatta gas. here/ a tree/ wanderin the
      horizon/ dipped in blues/ untended bones/ usedta
      hugs drawls rhythm & decency here a tree/ waitin
      to be hanged
        summer high school/ squat & pale on the corner/
      like our vision waz to be vague/ our memory of the
      war/ that made us free/ to be forgotten/ becomin
      paler/ linear movement from sous' carolina to mis-
      souri/ freedmen/ landin in jackie wilson's yelp/
      daughters of the manumitted swimmin in tina tur-
      ner's grinds/ this is chuck berry's town disavowin
      miscega-nation/ in any situation/ & they let us be/
      electric blues & bo didley/ the rockin pneumonia &
      boogie-woogie flu/ the slop & short fried heads/
      runnin always to the river chambersburg/ lil italy/ i
      passed everyday at the sweet shoppe/ & waz afraid/
      the cops raided truants/ regularly/ & after dark i
      wd not be seen wit any other colored/ sane & lovin
      my life

(*shouts n cries that are those of a white mob are heard, very loud . . . the still black-faced figures try to move away from the menacing voices & memories.*)

VOICES: hey niggah/ over here
ALEC: behind the truck lay five hands claspin chains
VOICES: hey niggah/ over here
ALEC: round the trees/ 4 more sucklin steel
VOICES: hey niggah/ over here
ALEC: this is the borderline
VOICE: hey niggah/ over here
ALEC: a territorial dispute

VOICES: hey niggah/ over here

ALEC: *(crouched on floor.)*

> cars loaded with families/ fellas from the factory/
> one or two practical nurses/ become our
>   trenches/
> some dig into cement wit elbows/ under engines/
> do not be seen in yr hometown
> after sunset/ we suck up our shadows

(finally moved to tear off their "shadows," all but two of the company leave with their true faces bared to the audience. DAHLIA has, as if by some magical cause, shed not only her mask, but also her hideous overalls & picaninny-buckwheat wig, to reveal a finely laced unitard/ the body of a modern dancer. she throws her mask to ALEC, who tosses it away. DAHLIA begins a lyrical but pained solo as ALEC speaks for them.)

ALEC:

> we will stand here
> our shoulders embrace an enormous spirit
> my dreams waddle in my lap
> run round to miz bertha's
> where lil richard gets his process
> run backward to the rosebushes
> & a drunk man lyin
> down the block to the nuns
> in pink habits/ prayin in a pink chapel
> my dreams run to meet aunt marie
> my dreams haunt me like the little geechee river
> our dreams draw blood from old sores
> this is our space
> we are not movin

(DAHLIA finishes her movement/ ALEC is seen reaching for her/ lights out. in the blackout they exit as LOU enters. lights come up on LOU who repeats bitterly his challenge to the audience.)

LOU:

> why dontchu go on & live my life for me
> i didnt want certain moments at all
> i'd give them to anybody

(LOU waves his hand commanding the minstrel mask to disappear, which it does. he signals to his left & again by magic, the lights come up higher revealing the interior of a lower manhattan bar & its bartender, ELI, setting up for the night. ELI greets LOU as he continues to set up tables, chairs, candles, etc., for the night's activities. LOU goes over to the jukebox, & plays "we are family" by sister sledge. LOU starts to tell us exactly where we are, but ELI takes over as characters are liable to do. throughout ELI's poem, the other members of the company enter the bar in their street clothes, & doing steps reminiscent of their solos during the minstrel sequence. as each enters, the audience is made aware that these ordinary people are the minstrels. the company continues to dance individually as ELI speaks.)

> this is . . .

ELI:

> MY kingdom
> there shall be no trespassers/ no marauders
> no tourists in my land
> you nurture these gardens   or   be shot on
>   sight
> carelessness & other priorities
> are not permitted within these walls
> i am mantling an array of strength & beauty
> no one shall interfere with this
> the construction of myself
> my city   my theater
> my bar   come to my poems
> but understand we speak english carefully
> & perfect antillean french
> our toilets are disinfected
> the plants here sing to me each morning
> come to my kitchen my parlor even my bed
> i sleep on satin   surrounded by hand made
> infants who bring me good luck & warmth
> come even to my door
> the burglar alarm/ armed guards vault from the
>   east side
> if i am in danger   a siren shouts
> you are welcome
> to my kingdom   my city   my self
> but yr presence must not disturb these inhabit-
>   ants
> leave nothing out of place/ push no dust under
>   my rugs
> leave not a crack in my wine glasses
> no finger prints
> clean up after yrself in the bathroom
> there are no maids here   no days off
> for healing   no insurance policies
> for dislocation of the psyche
> aliens/ foreigners/ are granted resident status
> we give them a little green card
> as they prove themselves non-injurious
> to the joy of my nation
> i sustain no intrusions/ no double-entendre ro-
>   mance
> no soliciting of sadness   in my life
> are those who love me well
> the rest are denied their visas . . .
> is everyone ready to boogie

(finally, when ELI calls for a boogie, the company does a dance that indicates these people have worked & played together a long time. as dance ends, the company sits &

chats at the tables & at the bar. this is now a safe haven for these "minstrels" off from work. here they are free to be themselves, to reveal secrets, fantasies, nightmares, or hope. it is safe because it is segregated & magic reigns.

LILI, the waitress, is continually moving abt the bar, taking orders for drinks & generally staying on top of things.)

ALEC: gimme a triple bourbon/ & a glass of angel dust these thursday nite audiences are abt to kill me

(ELI goes behind bar to get drinks.)

DAHLIA: why do i drink so much?

BETTINA, LILY, NATALIE. *(in unison.):* who cares?

DAHLIA: but i'm an actress. i have to ask myself these questions

LILY: that's a good reason to drink

DAHLIA: no/ i mean the character/ alec, you're a director/ give me some motivation

ALEC: motivation/ if you didn't drink you wd remember that you're not workin

LILY: i wish i cd get just one decent part

LOU: say as lady macbeth or mother courage

ELI: how the hell is she gonna play lady macbeth and macbeth's a white dude?

LILY: ross & natalie/ why are you countin pennies like that?

NATALIE: we had to wait on our money again

ROSS: and then we didnt get it

BETTINA: maybe they think we still accept beads & ribbons

NATALIE: i had to go around wit my tambourine just to get subway fare

ELI: dont worry abt it/ have one on me

NATALIE: thank you eli

BETTINA: *(falling out of her chair.)* oh . . .

ALEC: cut her off eli/ dont give her no more

LILY: what's the matter bettina/ is yr show closin?

BETTINA: *(gets up, resets chair.)* no/ my show is not closin/ but if that director asks me to play it any blacker/ i'm gonna have to do it in a mammy dress

LOU: you know/ countin pennies/ looking for parts/ breakin tambourines/ we must be outta our minds for doin this

BETTINA: no we're not outta our minds/ we're just sorta outta our minds

LILY: no/ we're not outta our minds/ we've been doing this shit a long time . . . ross/ captain theophilis conneau/ in *a slaver's logbook/* says that "youths of both sexes wear rings in the nose and lower lip and stick porcupine quills thru the cartilage of the ear." ross/ when ringlin' bros. comes to madison square garden/ dontcha know the white people just go

ROSS: in their cb radios

DAHLIA: in their mcdonald's hats

ELI: with their save america t-shirts & those chirren who score higher on IQ tests for the white chirren who speak english

ALEC: when the hockey games absorb all america's attention in winter/ they go with their fists clenched & their tongues battering their women who dont know a puck from a 3-yr-old harness racer

BETTINA: they go & sweat in fierce anger

ROSS: these factories

NATALIE: these middle management positions

ROSS: make madison square garden

BETTINA: the temple of the primal scream

(LILY gets money from cash register & heads toward jukebox.)

LILY: oh how they love blood

NATALIE: & how they dont even dress for the occasion/ all inconspicuous & pink

ELI: now if willie colon come there

BETTINA: if/ we say/ the fania all stars gonna be there in that nasty fantasy of the city council

ROSS: where the hot dogs are not even hebrew national

LILY: and the bread is stale

ROSS: even in such a place where dance is an obscure notion

BETTINA: where one's joy is good cause for a boring chat with the pinkerton guard

DAHLIA: where the halls lead nowhere

ELI: & "back to yr seat/ folks"

LILY: when all one's budget for cruisin

LOU: one's budget for that special dinner with you know who

LILY: the one you wd like to love you

BETTINA: when yr whole reasonable allowance for leisure activity/ buys you a seat where what's going on dont matter

DAHLIA: cuz you so high up/ you might be in seattle

LILY: even in such a tawdry space

ELI: where vorster & his pals wd spit & expect black folks to lick it up

ROSS: *(stands on chair.)* in such a place i've seen miracles

ALL: oh yeah/ aw/ ross

ROSS: the miracles

("music for the love of it," by butch morris, comes up on the jukebox/ this is a catchy uptempo rhythm & blues post WW II. as they speak the company does a dance that highlights their ease with one another & their familiarity with "all the new dance steps.")

LILY: the commodores

DAHLIA: muhammad ali

NATALIE: bob marley

ALEC: & these folks who upset alla 7th avenue with their glow/ how the gold in their braids is new in this world of hard hats & men with the grace of wounded buffalo/ how these folks in silk & satin/ in bodies reekin of good love comin/ these pretty muthafuckahs

DAHLIA: make this barn

LILY: this insult to good taste

BETTINA: a foray into paradise

DAHLIA, LILY, ALEC, NATALIE, & ROSS: (in unison.) we dress up

BETTINA, ELI, & LOU: (in unison.) we dress up

DAHLIA: cuz we got good manners

ROSS: cd you really ask dr. funkenstein to come all that way & greet him in the clothes you sweep yr kitchen in?

ALL: NO!

BETTINA: cd you say to muhammad ali/ well/ i just didnt have a chance to change/ you see i have a job/ & then i went jogging & well, you know its just madison square garden

LOU: my dear/ you know that wont do

NATALIE: we honor our guests/ if it costs us all we got

DAHLIA: when stevie wonder sings/ he don't want us lookin like we ain't got no common sense/ he wants us to be as lovely as we really are/ so we strut & reggae

ELI: i seen some doing the jump up/ i myself just got happy/ but i'm tellin you one thing for sure

LILY: we fill up where we at

BETTINA: no police

NATALIE: no cheap beer

DAHLIA: no nasty smellin bano

ROSS: no hallways fulla derelicts & hustlers

NATALIE: gonna interfere wit alla this beauty

ALEC: if it wasnt for us/ in our latino chic/ our rasta-fare our outer space funk suits & all the rest i have never seen

BETTINA: tho my daddy cd tell you bout them fox furs & stacked heels/ the diamonds & marie antoinette wigs

ELI: it's not cuz we got money

NATALIE: it's not cuz if we had money we wd spend it on luxury

LILY: it's just when you gotta audience with the pope/ you look yr best

BETTINA: when you gonna see the queen of england/ you polish yr nails

NATALIE: when you gonna see one of them/ & you know who i mean

ALEC: they gotta really know

BETTINA: we gotta make em feel

ELI: we dont do this for any old body

LOU: we're doin this for you

NATALIE: we dress up

ALEC: is our way of sayin/ you getting the very best

DAHLIA: we cant do less/ we love too much to be stingy

ROSS: they give us too much to be loved ordinary

LILY: we simply have good manners

ROSS: & an addiction to joy

FEMALE CAST MEMBERS: (in unison.) WHEE . . .

DAHLIA: we dress up

MALE CAST MEMBERS: (in unison.) HEY . . .

BETTINA: we gotta show the world/ we gotta corner on the color

ROSS: happiness just jumped right outta us/ & we are lookin good

(everyone in the bar is having so much fun/ that MAXINE takes on an exaggerated character as she enters/ in order to bring them to attention. the company freezes, half in respect/ half in parody.)

MAXINE: cognac!

(the company relaxes, goes to tables or the bar. in the meantime, ROSS has remained in the spell of the character that MAXINE had introduced when she came in. he goes over to MAXINE who is having a drink/ & begins an improvisation.)

ROSS: she left the front gate open/ not quite knowing she wanted someone to walk on thru the wrought iron fence/ scrambled in whiskey bottles broken round old bike spokes/ some nice brown man to wind up in her bed/ she really didnt know/ the sombrero that enveloped her face was a lil too much for an april nite on the bowery/ & the silver halter dug out from summer cookouts near riis beach/ didnt sparkle with the intensity of her promise to have one good time/ before the children came back from carolina. brooklyn cd be such a drag. every street cept flatbush & nostrand/ reminiscent of europe during the plague/ seems like nobody but sickness waz out walkin/ drivels & hypes/ a few youngsters lookin for more than they cd handle/ & then there waz fay/

(MAXINE rises, begins acting the story out.)

waitin for a cab, anyone of the cars inchin along the boulevard cd see fay waznt no whore/ just a good clean woman out for the nite/ & tho her left titty jumped out from under her silver halter/ she didnt notice cuz she waz lookin for a cab. the dank air fondled her long saggin bosom like a possible companion/ she felt good. she stuck her tin-ringed hand on her waist & watched her own ankles dance in the nite. she waz gonna have a good time tonight/ she waz awright/ a whole lotta woman/ wit that special brooklyn bottom strut. knowin she waznt comin in til dawn/ fay covered herself/ sorta/ wit a light kacky jacket that just kept her titties from rompin in the wind/ & she pulled it closer to her/ the winds waz comin/ from nowhere jabbin/ & there waznt no cabs/ the winds waz beatin her behind/ whisperin/ gigglin/ you aint goin noplace/ you an ol bitch/ shd be at home wit ur kids. fay beat off the voices/ & an EBONY-TRUE-TO-YOU cab climbed the curb to get her. (as cabdriver.)

hope you aint plannin on stayin in brooklyn/ after 8:00 you dead in brooklyn. (as narrator.)

she let her titty shake like she thot her mouth oughtta bubble like/ wd she take off her panties/ i'd take her anywhere.

MAXINE: *(as in cab.)* i'm into havin a good time/ yr arms/ veins burstin/ like you usedta lift tobacco onto trucks or cut cane/ i want you to be happy/ long as we dont haveta stay in brooklyn

ROSS: & she made like she waz gypsy rose lee/ or the hotsy totsy girls in the carnival round from way-cross/ when it waz segregated

MAXINE: what's yr name?

ROSS: my name is raphael

MAXINE: oh that's nice

ROSS: & fay moved where i cd see her out the rear view mirror/ waz tellin me all bout her children & big eddie who waz away/ while we crossed the manhattan bridge/ i kept smilin. *(as cabdriver.)* where exactly you going?

MAXINE: i dont really know. i just want to have a good time. take me where i can see famous people/ & act bizarre like sinatra at the kennedys/ maybe even go round & beat up folks like jim brown/ throw somebody offa balcony/ you know/ for a good time

ROSS: the only place i knew/ i took her/ after i kisst the spaces she'd been layin open to me. fay had alla her $17 cuz i hadn't charged her nothin/ turned the meter off/ said it waz wonderful to pick up a lady like her on atlantic avenue/ i saw nobody but those goddamn whores/ & fay

(MAXINE moves in to ROSS & gives him a very long kiss.)

now fay waz a gd clean woman/ & waz burstin with pride & enthusiasm when she walked into the place where I swore/ all the actresses & actors hung out

(the company joins in ROSS's story; responding to MAXINE as tho she waz entering their bar.)

oh yes/ there were actresses in braids & lipsticks/ wigs & winged tip pumps/ fay assumed the posture of someone she'd always admired/ etta james/ the waitress asked her to leave cuz she waz high/ & fay knew better than that

MAXINE: *(responding to LILY's indication of throwing her out.)* i aint high/ i'm enthusiastic/ and i'm gonna have me a gooooooood/ ol time

ROSS: she waz all dressed up/ she came all the way from brooklyn/ she must look high cuz i/ the taxi-man/ well i got her a lil excited/ that waz all/ but she waz gonna cool out/ cuz she waz gonna meet her friends/ at this place/ yes. she knew that/ & she pushed a bunch of rhododendrum/ outta her way so she cd get over to that table/ & stood over the man with the biggest niggah eyes & warmest smellin mouth

MAXINE: please/ let me join you/ i come all the way from brooklyn/ to have a good time/ you dont think i'm high do ya/ cd i please join ya/ i just wanna have a good ol time

ROSS: *(as BETTINA turns away.)* the woman sipped chablis & looked out the window hopin to see one of the bowery drunks fall down somewhere/ fay's voice hoverin/ flirtin wit hope

LOU: *(turning to face MAXINE.)* why dont you go downstairs & put yr titty in yr shirt/ you cant have no good time lookin like that/ now go on down & then come up & join us

(BETTINA & LOU rise & move to another table.)

ROSS: fay tried to shove her flesh anywhere/ she took off her hat/ bummed a kool/ swallowed somebody's cognac/ & sat down/ waitin/ for a gd time

MAXINE: *(rises & hugs ROSS.)* aw ross/ when am i gonna get a chance to feel somethin like that/ i got into this business cuz i wanted to feel things all the time/ & all they want me to do is put my leg in my face/ smile/ &

LILY: you better knock on some wood/ maxine/ at least yr workin

BETTINA: & at least yr not playin a whore/ if some other woman comes in here & tells me she's playin a whore/ i think i might kill her

ELI: you'd kill her so you cd say/ oh dahlia died & i know all her lines

BETTINA: aw hush up eli/ dnt you know what i mean?

ELI: no miss/ i dont/ are you in the theater?

BETTINA: mr. bartender/ poet sir/ i am theater

DAHLIA: well miss theater/ that's a surprise/ especially since you fell all over the damn stage in the middle of my solo

LILY: she did

ELI: miss theater herself fell down?

DAHLIA: yeah/ she cant figure out how to get attention without makin somebody else look bad

MAXINE: now dahlia/ it waznt that bad/ i hardly noticed her

DAHLIA: it waz my solo/ you werent sposed to notice her at all!

BETTINA: you know dahlia/ i didnt do it on purpose/ i cda hurt myself

DAHLIA: that wd be unfortunate

BETTINA: well miss thing with those big ass hips you got/ i dont know why you think you do the ballet anyway

(the company breaks; they're expecting a fight.)

DAHLIA: *(crossing to BETTINA.)* i got this

(demonstrates her leg extension.)

& alla this

(DAHLIA turns her back to BETTINA/ & slaps her own backside. BETTINA grabs DAHLIA, turns her around & they begin a series of finger snaps that are a paraphrase of ailey choreography for very dangerous fights. ELI comes to break up the impending altercation.)

ELI: ladies ladies ladies

(ELI separates the two.)

ELI:

people keep tellin me to put my feet on the
    ground
i get mad & scream/ there is no ground
only shit pieces from dogs horses & men who
    dont live
anywhere/ they tell me think straight & make
    myself
somethin/ i shout & sigh/ i am a poet/ i write
    poems
i make words cartwheel & somersault down
    pages
outta my mouth come visions distilled like boot-
    leg
whiskey/ i am like a radio but i am a channel of
    my own
i keep sayin i write poems/ & people keep askin
    me
what do i do/ what in the hell is going on?
people keep tellin me these are hard times/ what
    are
you gonna be doin ten years from now/
what in the hell do you think/ i am gonna be
    writin poems
i will have poems inchin up the walls of the
    lincoln tunnel/
i am gonna feed my children poems on rye bread
    with horseradish/
i am gonna send my mailman off with a poem
    for his wagon/
give my doctor a poem for his heart/ i am a poet/
i am not a part-time poet/ i am not a amateur
    poet/
i dont even know what that person cd be/
    whoever that is
authorizing poetry as an avocation/ is a fraud/
put yr own feet on the ground

BETTINA: i'm sorry eli/ i just dont want to be a gypsy
all my life

(the bar returns to normal humming & sipping. the lights
change to focus on LILY/ who begins to say what's really
been on her mind. the rest of the company is not aware
of LILY's private thoughts. only BETTINA responds to
LILY, but as a partner in fantasy, not as a voyeur.)

LILY: (illustrating her words with movement.) i'm gonna
simply brush my hair. rapunzel pull yr tresses back
into the tower. & lady godiva give up horseback
riding. i'm gonna alter my social & professional life
dramatically. i will brush 100 strokes in the morn-
ing/ 100 strokes midday & 100 strokes before retir-
ing. i will have a very busy schedule. between the
local trains & the express/ i'm gonna brush. i brush
between telephone calls. at the disco i'm gonna
brush on the slow songs/ i dont slow dance with

strangers. i'ma brush my hair before making love
& after. i'll brush my hair in taxis. while window-
shopping. when i have visitors over the kitchen
table/ i'ma brush. i brush my hair while thinking
abt anything. mostly i think abt how it will be when
i get my full heada hair. like lifting my head in the
morning will become a chore. i'll try to turn my
cheek & my hair will weigh me down

(LILY falls to the floor. BETTINA helps lift her to her
knees, then begins to dance & mime as LILY speaks.)

i dream of chaka khan/ chocolate from graham
central station with all seven wigs/ & medusa. i
brush & brush. i use olive oil hair food/ & posner's
vitamin E. but mostly i brush & brush. i may lose
contact with most of my friends. i cd lose my job/
but i'm on unemployment & brush while waiting
on line for my check. i'm sure i get good recom-
mendations from my social worker: such a fastidious woman/ that lily/ always brushing her hair.
nothing in my dreams suggests that hair brushing/
per se/ has anything to do with my particular heada
hair. a therapist might say that the head fulla hair
has to do with something else/ like: a symbol of lily's
unconscious desires. but i have no therapist

(she takes imaginary pen from BETTINA, who was pretending to be a therapist/ & sits down at table across from
her.)

& my dreams mean things to me/ like if you
dreamed abt tobias/ then something has happened
to tobias/ or he is gonna show up. if you dream abt
yr grandma who's dead/ then you must be doing
something she doesnt like/ or she wdnta gone to all
the trouble to leave heaven like that. if you dream
something red/ you shd stop. if you dream something green/ you shd keep doing it. if a blue person
appears in yr dreams/ then that person is yr true
friend

& that's how i see my dreams. & this head full
hair i have in my dreams is lavender & nappy as a
3-yr-old's in a apple tree. i can fry an egg & see the
white of the egg spreadin in the grease like my hair
is gonna spread in the air/ but i'm not egg-yolk
yellow/ i am brown & the egg white isnt white at all/
it is my actual hair/ & it wd go on & on forever/
irregular like a rasta-man's hair. irregular/ gargan-
tuan & lavender. nestled on blue satin pillows/ pillows like the sky. & so i fry my eggs. i buy daisies
dyed lavender & laced lavender tablemats & lavender nail polish. though i never admit it/ i really
do believe in magic/ & can do strange things when
something comes over me. soon everything around
me will be lavender/ fluffy & consuming. i will know
not a moment of bitterness/ through all the wrist
aching & tennis elbow from brushing/ i'll smile. no
regrets/ "je ne regrette rien" i'll sing like edith piaf.
when my friends want me to go see tina turner or

pacheco/ i'll croon "sorry/ i have to brush my hair."

i'll find ambrosia. my hair'll grow pomegranates & soil/ rich as round the aswan/ i wake in my bed to bananas/ avocados/ collard greens/ the tramps' latest disco hit/ fresh croissant/ pouilly fuissé/ ishmael reed's essays/ charlotte carter's stories/ all stream from my hair.

& with the bricks that plop from where a 9-year-old's top braid wd be/ i will brush myself a house with running water & a bidet. i'll have a closet full of clean bed linen & the lil girl from the castro convertible commercial will come & open the bed repeatedly & stay on as a helper to brush my hair. lily is the only person i know whose every word leaves a purple haze on the tip of yr tongue. when this happens i says clouds are forming/ & i has to close the windows. violet rain is hard to remove from blue satin pillows

(LOU, *the magician, gets up, he points to* LILY *sitting very still. he reminds us that it is only thru him that we are able to know these people without the "masks"/ the lies/ & he cautions that all their thoughts are not benign. they are not safe from what they remember or imagine.*)

LOU: you have t come with me/ to this place where magic is/ to hear my song/ some times i forget & leave my tune in the corner of the closet under all the dirty clothes/ in this place/ magic asks me where i've been/ how i've been singin/ lately i leave my self in all the wrong hands/ in this place where magic is involved in undoin our masks/ i am able to smile & answer that. in this place where magic always asks for me i discovered a lot of other people who talk without mouths who listen to what you say/ by watchin yr jewelry dance & in this place where magic stays you can let yrself in or out but when you leave yrself at home/ burglars & daylight thieves pounce on you & sell yr skin/ at cut-rates on tenth avenue

(ROSS *has been playing the acoustic guitar softly as* LOU *spoke.* ALEC *picks up on the train of* LOU's *thoughts & tells a story that in turn captures* NATALIE's *attention. slowly,* NATALIE *becomes the woman* ALEC *describes.*)

ALEC: she had always wanted a baby/ never a family/ never a man/ she had always wanted a baby/ who wd suckle & sleep a baby boy who wd wet/ & cry/ & smile suckle & sleep when she sat in bars/ on the stool/ near the door/ & cross from the juke box/ with her legs straddled & revealin red lace pants/ & lil hair smashed under the stockings/ she wd think how she wanted this baby & how she wd call the baby/ "myself" & as she thot/ bout this brown lil thing/ she ordered another bourbon/ double & tilted her head as if to cuddle some infant/ not present/ the men in the bar never imagined her as someone's mother/ she rarely tended her own self carefully/

(NATALIE *rises slowly, sits astride on the floor.*)

just enough to exude a languid sexuality that teased the men off work/ & the bartender/ ray who waz her only friend/ women didnt take to her/ so she spent her afternoons with ray/ in the bar round the corner from her lil house/ that shook winsomely in a hard wind/ surrounded by three weepin willows

NATALIE: my name is sue-jean & i grew here/ a ordinary colored girl with no claims to any thing/ or anyone/ i drink now/ bourbon/ in harder times/ beer/ but i always wanted to have a baby/ a lil boy/ named myself

ALEC: one time/ she made it with ray

NATALIE: & there waz nothin special there/ only a hot rough bangin/ a brusque barrelin throwin of torso/ legs & sweat/ ray wanted to kiss me/ but i screamed/ cuz i didnt like kissin/ only fuckin/ & we rolled round/ i waz a peculiar sorta woman/ wantin no kisses/ no caresses/ just power/ heat & no eaziness of thrust/ ray pulled himself outa me/ with no particular exclamation/ he smacked me on my behind/ i waz grinnin/ & he took that as a indication of his skill/ he believed he waz a good lover/ & a woman like me/ didnt never want nothin but a hard dick/ & everyone believed that/ tho no one in town really knew

ALEC: so ray/ went on behind the bar cuz he had got his

NATALIE: & i lay in the corner laughin/ with my drawers/ twisted round my ankles & my hair standin every which way/ i waz laughin/ knowin i wd have this child/ myself/ & no one wd ever claim him/ cept me cuz i waz a low-down thing/ layin in sawdust & whiskey stains/ i laughed & had a good time masturbatin in the shadows.

ALEC: sue-jean ate starch for good luck

NATALIE: like mamma kareena/ tol me

ALEC: & she planted five okras/ five collards/ & five tomatoes

NATALIE: for good luck too/ i waz gonna have this baby/ i even went over to the hospital to learn prenatal care/ & i kept myself clean

ALEC: sue-jean's lanky body got ta spreadin & her stomach waz taut & round high in her chest/ a high pregnancy is sure to be a boy/ & she smiled

NATALIE: i stopped goin to the bar

ALEC: started cannin food

NATALIE: knittin lil booties

ALEC: even goin to church wit the late nite radio evangelist

NATALIE: i gotta prayer cloth for the boy/ myself waz gonna be safe from all that his mama/ waz prey to

ALEC: sure/ sue-jean waz a scandal/ but that waz to be expected/ cuz she waz always a po criterish chile

NATALIE: & wont no man bout step my way/ ever/ just cuz i hadda bad omen on me/ from the very womb/ i waz bewitched is what the old women usedta say

ALEC: sue-jean waz born on a full moon/ the year of the flood/ the night the river raised her skirts & sat over alla the towns & settlements for 30 miles in each direction/ the nite the river waz in labor/ gruntin & groanin/ splittin trees & families/ spillin cupboards over the ground/ waz the nite sue-jean waz born

NATALIE: & my mother died/ drownin/ holdin me up over the mud crawlin in her mouth

ALEC: somebody took her & she lived to be the town's no one/ now with the boy achin & dancin in her belly/ sue-jean waz a gay & gracious woman/ she made pies/ she baked cakes & left them on the stoop of the church she had never entered just cuz she wanted/ & she grew plants & swept her floors/ she waz someone she had never known/ she waz herself with child/ & she waz a wonderful bulbous thing

NATALIE: the nite/ myself waz born/ ol mama kareena from the hills came down to see bout me/ i hollered & breathed/ i did exactly like mama kareena said/ & i pushed & pushed & there waz a earthquake up in my womb/ i wanted to sit up & pull the tons of logs trapped in my crotch out/ so i cd sleep/ but it wdnt go way/ i pushed & thot i saw 19 horses runnin in my pussy/ i waz sure there waz a locomotive stalled up in there burnin coal & steamin & pushin gainst a mountain

ALEC: finally the child's head waz within reach & mama kareena/ brought the boy into this world

NATALIE: & he waz awright/ with alla his toes & his fingers/ his lil dick & eyes/ elbows that bent/ & legs/ straight/ i wanted a big glassa bourbon/& mama kareena brought it/ right away/ we sat drinkin the bourbon/ & lookin at the child whose name waz myself/ like i had wanted/ & the two of us ate placenta stew . . . i waznt really sure . . .

ALEC: sue-jean you werent really sure you wanted myself to wake up/ you always wanted him to sleep/ or at most to nurse/ the nites yr dreams were disturbed by his cryin

NATALIE: i had no one to help me

ALEC: so you were always with him/ & you didnt mind/ you knew this waz yr baby/ myself/ & you cuddled him/ carried him all over the house with you all day/ no matter/ what

NATALIE: everythin waz goin awright til/ myself wanted to crawl

ALEC: (moving closer to NATALIE.) & discover a world of his own/ then you became despondent/ & yr tits began to dry & you lost the fullness of yr womb/ where myself/ had lived

NATALIE: i wanted that back

ALEC: you wanted back the milk

NATALIE: & the tight gourd of a stomach i had when myself waz bein in me

ALEC: so you slit his wrists

NATALIE: he waz sleepin

ALEC: sucked the blood back into yrself/ & waited/ myself shriveled up in his crib

NATALIE: a dank lil blk thing/ i never touched him again

ALEC: you were always holdin yr womb/ feelin him kick & sing to you bout love/ & you wd hold yr tit in yr hand

NATALIE: like i always did when i fed him

ALEC: & you waited & waited/ for a new myself. tho there were labor pains

NATALIE: & i screamed in my bed

ALEC: yr legs pinnin to the air

NATALIE: spinnin sometimes like a ferris wheel/ i cd get no child to fall from me

ALEC: & she forgot abt the child bein born/ & waz heavy & full all her life/ with "myself"

NATALIE: who'll be out/ any day now

(ELI moves from behind the bar to help NATALIE/ or to clean tables. he doesnt really know. he stops suddenly.)

ELI: aint that a goddamn shame/ aint that a way to come into the world sometimes i really cant write sometimes i cant even talk

(the minstrel mask comes down very slowly. blackout, except for lights on the big minstrel mask which remains visible throughout intermission.)

ACT 2

(all players onstage are frozen, except LOU, who makes a motion for the big minstrel mask to disappear again. as the mask flies up, LOU begins.)

LOU: in this place where magic stays you can let yrself in or out

(he makes a magic motion. a samba is heard from the jukebox & activity is begun in the bar again. DAHLIA, NATALIE & LILY enter, apparently from the ladies room.)

NATALIE: i swear we went to that audition in good faith/ & that man asked us where we learned to speak english so well/ i swear this foreigner/ asked us/ from the city of new york/ where we learned to speak english.

LILY: all i did was say "bom dia/ como vai"/ and the englishman got red in the face.

LOU: (as the englishman.) yr from the states/ aren't you?

LILY: "sim"/ i said/ in good portuguese

LOU: but you speak portuguese

LILY: "sim" i said/ in good portuguese

LOU: how did you pick that up?

LILY: i hadda answer so simple/ i cdnt say i learned it/ cuz niggahs cant learn & that wda been too hard on the man/ so i said/ in good english: i held my ear to the ground & listened to the samba from bélim

DAHLIA: you should have said: i make a lotta phone calls to casçais, portugao

BETTINA: i gotta bahiano boyfriend

NATALIE: how abt: i waz an angolan freedom fighter

MAXINE: no/ lily/ tell him: i'm a great admirer of zeza motto & leci brandao

LILY: when the japanese red army invaded san juan/ they poisoned the papaya with portuguese. i eat a lotta papaya. last week/ i developed a strange schizophrenic condition/ with 4 manifest personalities: one spoke english & understood nothing/ one spoke french & had access to the world/ one spoke spanish & voted against statehood for puerto rico/ one spoke portuguese. "eu naõ falo ingles entaõ y voce"/ i dont speak english anymore/ & you?

(all the women in the company have been doing samba steps as the others spoke/ now they all dance around a table in their own ritual/ which stirs ALEC & LOU *to interrupt this female segregation. the women scatter to different tables, leaving the two interlopers alone. so,* ALEC & LOU *begin their conversation.)*

ALEC: not only waz she without a tan, but she held her purse close to her hip like a new yorker. someone who rode the paris métro or listened to mariachis in plaza santa cecilia. she waz not from here

(he sits at table.)

LOU: *(following suit.)* but from there

ALEC: some there where coloureds/ mulattoes/ negroes/ blacks cd make a living big enough to leave there to come here/ where no one went there much any more for all sorts of reasons

LOU: the big reasons being immigration restrictions & unemployment. nowadays, immigration restrictions of every kind apply to any non-european persons who want to go there from here

ALEC: some who want to go there from here risk fetching trouble with the customs authority there

LOU: or later with the police, who can tell who's not from there cuz the shoes are pointed & laced strange

ALEC: the pants be for august & yet it's january

LOU: the accent is patterned for pétionville, but working in crown heights

ALEC: what makes a person comfortably ordinary here cd make him dangerously conspicuous there.

LOU: so some go to london or amsterdam or paris/ where they are so abounding no one tries to tell who is from where

ALEC: still the far right wing of every there prints lil pamphlets that say everyone from there shd leave & go back where they came from

LOU: this is manifest legally thru immigration restrictions & personally thru unemployment

ALEC: anyway the yng woman waz from there/ & she waz alone. that waz good. cuz if a person had no big brother in gronigen/ no aunt in rouen

LOU: no sponsor in chicago

ALEC: this brown woman from there might be a good idea. everybody in the world/ european & non-european alike/ everybody knows that rich white

girls are hard to find. some of them joined the weather underground/ some the baader-meinhof gang.

LOU: a whole bunch of them gave up men entirely

ALEC: so the exotic lover in the sun routine becomes more difficult to swing/ if she wants to talk abt plastic explosives & the resistance of the black masses to socialism/ instead of giving head as the tide slips in or lending money

LOU: just for the next few days

ALEC: is hard to find a rich white girl who is so dumb/ too

LOU: anyway. the whole world knows/ european & non-european alike/ the whole world knows that nobody loves the black woman like they love farrah fawcett-majors. the whole world dont turn out for a dead black woman like they did for marilyn monroe.

ALEC: actually/ the demise of josephine baker waz an international event

LOU: but she waz a war hero the worldwide un-beloved black woman is a good idea/ if she is from there & one is a young man with gd looks/ piercing eyes/ & knowledge of several romantic languages

(throughout this conversation, ALEC & LOU *will make attempts to seduce, cajole, & woo the women of the bar as their narrative indicates. the women play the roles as described, being so moved by romance.)*

ALEC: the best dancing spots/ the hill where one can see the entire bay at twilight

LOU: the beach where the seals & pelicans run free/ the hidden "local" restaurants

ALEC: "aw babee/ you so pretty" begins often in the lobby of hotels where the bright handsome yng men wd be loiterers

LOU: were they not needed to tend the needs of the black women from there

ALEC: tourists are usually white people or asians who didnt come all this way to meet a black woman who isnt even foreign

LOU: so hotel managers wink an eye at the yng men in the lobby or by the bar who wd be loitering/ but are gonna help her have a gd time

ALEC: maybe help themselves too

LOU: everybody in the world/ european & non-european alike/ everybody knows the black woman from there is not treated as a princess/ as a jewel/ a cherished lover

ALEC: that's not how sapphire got her reputation/ nor how mrs. jefferson perceives the world

LOU: you know/ babee/ you dont act like them. aw babee/ you so pretty

ALEC: the yng man in the hotel watches the yng blk woman sit & sit & sit/ while the european tourists dance with each other/ & the dapper local fellas mambo frenetically with secretaries from arizona/ in search of the missing rich white girl. our girl sits &

FEMALE CAST MEMBERS: *(in unison.)* sits & sits & sits

ALEC: *(to* DAHLIA *&* NATALIE, *who move to the music.)* maybe she is courageous & taps her foot. maybe she is bold & enjoys the music/ smiling/ shaking shoulders. let her sit & let her know she is unwanted

LOU: she is not white & she is not from here

ALEC: let her know she is not pretty enuf to dance the next merengue. then appear/ mysteriously/ in the corner of the bar. stare at her. just stare. when stevie wonder's song/ "isnt she lovely"/ blares thru the red-tinted light/ ask her to dance & hold her as tyrone power wda. hold her & stare

*(*ROSS *&* ELI *sing the chorus to stevie wonder's "isn't she lovely.")*

LOU: dance yr ass off. she has been discovered by the non-european fred astaire

ALEC: let her know she is a surprise/ an event. by the look on yr face you've never seen anyone like this black woman from there. you say: "aw/ you not from here?"/ totally astonished. she murmurs that she is from there. as if to apologize for her unfortunate place of birth

LOU: you say

ALEC: aw babee/ you so pretty. & it's all over

LOU: a night in a pension near the sorbonne. pick her up from the mattress. throw her gainst the wall in a show of exotic temper & passion: "maintenant/ tu es ma femme. nous nous sommes mariés."° unions of this sort are common wherever the yng black women travel alone. a woman traveling alone is an affront to the non-european man who is known the world over/ to european & non-european alike/ for his way with women

ALEC: his sense of romance/ how he can say:

LOU: aw babee/ you so pretty . . . and even a beautiful woman will believe no one else ever recognized her loveliness

ELI: or else/ he comes to a cafe in willemstad in the height of the sunset. an able-bodied/ sinewy yng man who wants to buy one beer for the yng woman. after the first round/ he discovers he has run out of money/ so she must buy the next round/ when he discovers/ what beautiful legs you have/ how yr mouth is like the breath of tiger lilies. we shall make love in the/ how you call it/ yes in the earth/ in the dirt/ i will have you in my/ how you say/ where things grow/ aw/ yes/ i will have you in the soil. probably under the stars & smelling of wire/ an unforgettable international affair can be consummated

(the company sings "tara's theme" as ELI *ends his speech.* ELI *&* BETTINA *take a tango walk to the bar, while*

MAXINE *mimics a 1930s photographer, shooting them as they sail off into the sunset.)*

MAXINE: at 11:30 one evening i waz at the port authority/ new york/ united states/ myself. now i waz there & i spoke english & waz holding approximately $7 american currency/ when a yng man from there came up to me from the front of the line of people waiting for the princeton new jersey united states local bus. i mean to say/ he gave up his chance for a good seat to come say to me:

ROSS: i never saw a black woman reading nietzsche

MAXINE: i waz demure enough/ i said i have to for a philosophy class. but as the night went on i noticed this yng man waz so much like the other yng men from here/ who use their bodies as bait & their smiles as passport alternatives. anyway the night did go on. we were snuggled together in the rear of the bus going down the jersey turnpike. he told me in english/ that he had spoken all his life in st. louis/ where he waz raised:

ROSS: i've wanted all my life to meet someone like you. i want you to meet my family/ who haven't seen me in a long time/ since i left missouri looking for opportunity . . .

(he is lost for words.)

LOU: *(stage whisper.)* opportunity to sculpt

ROSS: thank you/ opportunity to sculpt

MAXINE: he had been everyplace/ he said

ROSS: you arent like any black woman i've ever met anywhere

MAXINE: here or there

ROSS: i had to come back to new york cuz of immigration restrictions & high unemployment among black american sculptors abroad

MAXINE: just as we got to princeton/ he picked my face up from his shoulder & said:

ROSS: aw babee/ you so pretty

MAXINE: aw babee/ you so pretty. i believe that night i must have looked beautiful for a black woman from there/ though i cd be asked at any moment to tour the universe/ to climb a 6-story walkup with a brilliant & starving painter/ to share kadushi/ to meet mama/ to getta kiss each time the swing falls toward the willow branch/ to imagine where he say he from/ & more. i cd/ i cd have all of it/ but i cd not be taken/ long as i don't let a stranger be the first to say:

LOU: aw babee/ you so pretty

MAXINE: after all/ immigration restrictions & unemployment cd drive a man to drink or to lie

(she breaks away from ROSS.*)*

so if you know yr beautiful & bright & cherishable awready/ when he say/ in whatever language:

ALEC: *(to* NATALIE.*)* aw babee/ you so pretty

MAXINE: you cd say:

NATALIE: i know. thank you

° *"maintenant . . . mariés,"* now/ you are my wife. we are married.

MAXINE: then he'll smile/ & you'll smile. he'll say:

ELI: *(stroking* BETTINA's *thigh.)* what nice legs you have

MAXINE: you can say:

BETTINA: *(removing his hand.)* yes. they run in the family

MAXINE: oh! whatta universe of beautiful & well traveled women!

MALE CAST MEMBERS: *(in unison.)* aw babee/ i've never met anyone like you

FEMALE CAST MEMBERS: *(in unison, pulling away from men to stage edges.)* that's strange/ there are millions of us!

(men all cluster after unsuccessful attempts to persuade their women to talk. ALEC *gets the idea to serenade the women;* ROSS *takes the first verse, with men singing back-up. song is "ooh baby," by smokey robinson.)*

ROSS: *(singing.)*

>   i did you wrong/ my heart went out to play/ but in the game
>   i lost you/what a price to pay/ i'm cryin . . .

MALE PLAYERS: *(singing.)* oo oo oo/ baby baby. . . . oo oo oo/ baby baby

(this brings no response from the women; the men elect ELI *to lead the second verse.)*

ELI:

>   mistakes i know i've made a few/ but i'm only human/ you've made mistakes too/ i'm cryin . . .
>   oo oo oo/ baby baby . . . oo oo oo/ baby baby

(the women slowly forsake their staunch indignation/ returning to the arms of their partners. all that is except LILY, *who walks abt the room of couples awkwardly)*

MALE CAST MEMBERS & LILY: *(singing.)*

>   i'm just about at the end of my rope
>   but i can't stop trying/ i cant give up hope
>   cause i/ i believe one day/ i'll hold you near
>   whisper i love you/ until that day is here
>   i'm cryin . . . oo oo oo/ baby baby

*(*LILY *begins as the company continues to sing.)*

LILY:

>   unfortunately
>   the most beautiful man in the world
>   is unavailable
>   that's what he told me
>   i saw him wandering abt/ said well this is one of a kind
>   & i might be able to help him out
>   so alone & pretty in all this ganja & bodies melting
>   he danced with me & i cd become that

>   a certain way to be held that's considered in advance
>   a way a thoughtful man wd kiss a woman who
>   cd be offended easily/ but waznt cuz
>   of course the most beautiful man in the world
>   knows exactly what to do
>   with someone who knows that's who he is/
>   these dreads fallin thru my dress
>   so my nipples just stood up
>   these hands playin the guitar on my back
>   the lips somewhere between my neck
>   & my forehead
>   talking bout ocho rios & how i really must go
>   marcus garvey cda come in the door & we/
>   we wd still be dancin that dance
>   the motion that has more to do with kinetic energy
>   than shootin stars/ more to do with the impossibility
>   of all this/ & how it waz awready bein too much
>   our reason failed
>   we tried to go away & be just together
>   aside from the silence that weeped
>   with greed/ we didnt need/ anything/ but one another
>   for tonite
>   but he is the most beautiful man in the world
>   says he's unavailable/
>   & this man whose eyes made me
>   half-naked & still & brazen/ was singin with me
>   since we cd not talk/ we sang

*(*MALE PLAYERS *end their chorus with a flourish.)*

LILY:

>   we sang with bob marley
>   this man/ surely the most beautiful man in the world/ &
>   i
>   sang/ "i wanna love you & treat you right/

(the couples begin different kinds of reggae dances.)

>   i wanna love you every day & every night"

THE COMPANY: *(dancing & singing.)*

>   we'll be together with
>   the roof right over our heads
>   we'll share the shelter of my single bed
>   we'll share the same room/ jah provide the bread

DAHLIA: *(stops dancing during conversation.)* i tell you it's not just the part that makes me love you so much

LOU: what is it/ wait/ i know/ you like my legs

DAHLIA: yes/ uh huh/ yr legs & yr arms/ & . . .

LOU: but that's just my body/ you started off saying you loved me & now i see it's just my body

DAHLIA: oh/ i didn't mean that/ it's just i dont know you/

except as the character i'm sposed to love/ & well i know rehearsal is over/ but i'm still in love with you

(they go to the bar to get drinks, then sit at a table.)

ROSS: but baby/ you have to go on the road. we need the money

NATALIE: i'm not going on the road so you can fuck all these aspiring actresses

ROSS: aw/ just some of them/ baby

NATALIE: that's why i'm not going

ROSS: if you dont go on the road i'll still be fuckin em/ but you & me/ we'll be in trouble/ you understand?

NATALIE: *(stops dancing.)* no i dont understand

ROSS: well let me break it down to you

NATALIE: please/ break it down to me

BETTINA: *(stops dancing.)* hey/ natalie/ why dont you make him go on the road/ they always want us to be so goddamned conscientious

ALEC: *(stops dancing.)* dont you think you shd mind yr own bizness?

NATALIE: yeah bettina/ mind yr own bizness

(she pulls ROSS to the table with her.)

BETTINA: *(to ALEC.)* no/ i'm tired of having to take any & every old job to support us/ & you get to have artistic integrity & refuse parts that are beneath you

ALEC: thats right/ i'm not playing the fool or the black buck pimp circus/ i'm an actor not a stereotype/ i've been trained. you know i'm a classically trained actor

BETTINA: & just what do you think we are?

MAXINE: well/ i got offered another whore part downtown

ELI: you gonna take it?

MAXINE: yeah

LILY: if you dont/ i know someone who will

ALEC: *(to BETTINA.)* i told you/ we arent gonna get anyplace/ by doin every bit part for a niggah that someone waves in fronta my face

BETTINA: & we arent gonna live long on nothin/ either/ cuz i'm quittin my job

ALEC: be in the real world for once & try to understand me

BETTINA: you mean/ i shd understand that you are the great artist & i'm the trouper.

ALEC: i'm not sayin that we cant be gigglin & laughin all the time dancin around/ but i cant stay in these "hate whitey" shows/ cuz they arent true

BETTINA: a failure of imagination on yr part/ i take it

ALEC: no/ an insult to my person

BETTINA: oh i see/ you wanna give the people some more make-believe

ALEC: i cd always black up again & do minstrel work/ wd that make you happy?

BETTINA: there is nothin niggardly abt a decent job. work is honorable/ work!

ALEC: well/ i got a problem. i got lots of problems/ but i got one i want you to fix & if you can fix it/ i'll do

anything you say. last spring this niggah from the midwest asked for president carter to say he waz sorry for that forgettable phenomenon/ slavery/ which brought us all together. i never did get it/ none of us ever got no apology from no white folks abt not bein considered human beings/ that makes me mad & tired. someone told me "roots" was the way white folks worked out their guilt/ the success of "roots" is the way white folks assuaged their consciences/ i dont know this/ this is what i waz told. i dont get any pleasure from nobody watchin me trying to be a slave i once waz/ who got away/ when we all know they had an emancipation proclamation/ that the civil war waz not fought over us. we all know that we/ actually dont exist unless we play football or basketball or baseball or soccer/ pélé/ see they still import a strong niggah to earn money. art here/ isnt like in the old country/ where we had some spare time & did what we liked to do/ i dont know this either/ this is also something i've been told. i just want to find out why no one has even been able to sound a gong & all the reporters recite that the gong is ringin/ while we watch all the white people/ immigrants & invaders/ conquistadors & relatives of london debtors from georgia/ kneel & apologize to us/ just for three or four minutes. now/ this is not impossible/ & someone shd make a day where a few minutes of the pain of our lives is acknowledged. i have never been very interested in what white people did/ cuz i waz able/ like most of us/ to have very lil to do with them/ but if i become a success that means i have to talk to white folks more than in high school/ they are everywhere/ you know how they talk abt a neighborhood changin/ we suddenly become all over the place/ they are now all over my life/ & i dont like it. i am not talkin abt poets & painters/ not abt women & lovers of beauty/ i am talkin abt that proverbial white person who is usually a man who just/ turns yr body around/ looks at yr teeth & yr ass/ who feels yr calves & back/ & agrees on a price. we are/ you see/ now able to sell ourselves/ & i am still a person who is tired/ a person who is not into his demise/ just three minutes for our lives/ just three minutes of silence & a gong in st. louis/ oakland/ in los angeles . . .

(the entire company looks at him as if he's crazy/ he tries to leave the bar/ but BETTINA stops him.)

BETTINA: you're still outta yr mind. ain't no apologies keeping us alive.

LOU: what are you gonna do with white folks kneeling all over the country anyway/ man

(LOU signals everyone to kneel.)

LILY: they say i'm too light to work/ but when i asked him what he meant/ he said i didnt actually look black. but/ i said/ my mama knows i'm black & my daddy/ damn sure knows i'm black/ & he is the only one who has a problem thinkin i'm black/ i said so let me play a white girl/ i'm a classically trained actress & i need the work & i can do it/ he said that wdnt be very ethical of him. can you imagine that shit/ not ethical

NATALIE: as a red-blooded white woman/ i cant allow you all to go on like that

(NATALIE *starts jocularly.*)

cuz today i'm gonna be a white girl/ i'll retroactively wake myself up/ ah low & behold/ a white girl in my bed/ but first i'll haveta call a white girl i know to have some more accurate information/ what's the first thing white girls think in the morning/ do they get up being glad they aint niggahs/ do they re-member mama/ or worry abt gettin to work/ do they work?/ do they play isdora & wrap themselves in sheets & go tip toeing to the kitchen to make maxwell house coffee/ oh i know/ the first thing a white girl does in the morning is fling her hair/

So now i'm done with that/ i'm gonna water my plants/ but am i a po white trash white girl with a old jellyjar/ or am i a sophisticated & protestant suburbanite with 2 valiums slugged awready & a porcelain water carrier leading me up the stairs strewn with heads of dolls & nasty smellin white husband person's underwear/ if i was really pro-tected from the niggahs/ i might go to early morn-ing mass & pick up a tomato pie on the way home/ so i cd eat it during the young & the restless. in williams arizona as a white girl/ i cd push the navaho women outta my way in the supermarket & push my nose in the air so i wdnt haveta smell them. coming from bay ridge on the train i cd smile at all the black & puerto rican people/ & hope they cant tell i want them to go back where they came from/ or at least be invisible.

i'm still in my kitchen/ so i guess i'll just have to fling my hair again & sit down. i shd pinch my cheeks to bring the color back/ i wonder why the colored lady hasn't arrived to clean my house yet/ so i cd go to the beauty parlor & sit under a sunlamp to get some more color back/ it's terrible how god gave those colored women such clear complexions/ it take em years to develop wrinkles/ but beauty can be bought & flattered into the world.

as a white girl on the street/ i can assume since i am a white girl on the streets/ that everyone notices how beautiful i am/ especially lil black & caribbean boys/ they love to look at me/ i'm exotic/ no one in their families looks like me/ poor things. if i waz one of those white girls who loves one of those grown black fellas/ i cd say with my eyes wide open/ totally sincere/ oh i didnt know that/ i cd say i didnt know/ i cant/ i dont know how/ cuz i'ma white girl & i dont have to do much of anything.

all of this is the fault of the white man's sexism/ oh how i loathe tight-assed-thin-lipped pink white

men/ even the football players lack a certain relaxed virility. that's why my heroes are either just like my father/ who while he still cdnt speak english knew enough to tell me how the niggers shd go back where they came from/ or my heroes are psychotic faggots who are white/ or else they are/ oh/ you know/ colored men.

being a white girl by dint of my will/ is much more complicated than i thought it wd be/ but i wanted to try it cuz so many men like white girls/ white men/ black men/ latin men/ jewish men/ asians/ everybody. so i thought if i waz a white girl for a day i might understand this better/ after all ger-trude stein wanted to know abt the black women/ alice adams wrote *thinking abt billie*/ joyce carol oates has three different black characters all with the same name/ i guess cuz we are underdeveloped individuals or cuz we are all the same/ at any rate i'm gonna call this thinkin abt white girls/ cuz hel-mut newton's awready gotta book called *white women*/ see what i mean/ that's a best seller/ one store i passed/ hadda sign said/

WHITE WOMEN
SOLD OUT

---

it's this kinda pressure that forces us white girls to be so absolutely pathological abt the other women in the world/ who now that they're not all servants or peasants want to be considered beautiful too. we simply krinkle our hair/ learn to dance the woogie dances/ slant our eyes with make-up or surgery/ learn spanish & claim argentinian background/ or as a real trump card/ show up looking like a real white girl. you know all western civilization depends on us/

i still havent left my house. i think i'll fling my hair once more/ but this time with a pout/ cuz i think i havent been fair to the sisterhood/ women's movement faction of white girls/ although/ they always ask what do you people really want. as if the colored woman of the world were a strange sort of neutered workhorse/ which isnt too far from real-ity/ since i'm still waiting for my cleaning lady & the lady who takes care of my children & the lady who caters my parties & the lady who accepts quarters at the bathroom in sardi's. those poor creatures shd be sterilized/ no one shd have to live such a life. cd you hand me a towel/ thank-you caroline. i've left all of maxime's last winter clothes in a pile for you by the back door. they have to be cleaned but i hope yr girls can make gd use of them.

oh/ i'm still not being fair/ all the white women in

the world dont wake up being glad they aint niggahs/ only some of them/ the ones who dont/ wake up thinking how can i survive another day of this culturally condoned incompetence. i know i'll play a tenor horn & tell all the colored artists i meet/ that now i'm just like them/ i'm colored i'll say cuz i have a struggle too. or i cd punish this white beleagered body of mine with the advances of a thousand ebony bodies/ all built like franco harris or peter tosh/ a thousand of them may take me & do what they want/ cuz i'm so sorry/ yes i'm so sorry they were born niggahs. but then if i cant punish myself to death for being white/ i certainly cant in good conscience keep waiting for the cleaning lady/ & everytime i attempt even the smallest venture into the world someone comes to help me/ like if i do anything/ anything at all i'm extending myself as a white girl/ cuz part of being a white girl is being absent/ like those women who are just with a man but whose names the black people never remember/ they just say oh yeah his white girl waz with him/. or a white girl got beat & killed today/ why someone will say/ cuz some niggah told her to give him her money & she said no/ cuz she thought she realized that she waz a white girl/ & he did know but he didnt care/ so he killed her & took the money/ but the cops knew she waz a white girl & cdnt be killed by a niggah especially/ when she had awready said no. the niggah was sposed to hop round the corner backwards/ you dig/ so the cops/ found the culprit within 24 hours/ cuz just like emmett till/ niggahs do not kill white girls.

i'm still in my house/ having flung my hair-do for the last time/ what with having to take 20 valium a day/ to consider the ERA/ & all the men in the world/ & my ignorance of the world/ it is overwhelming. i'm so glad i'm colored. boy i cd wake up in the morning & think abt anything. i can remember emmett till & not haveta smile at anybody.

MAXINE: *(compelled to speak by* NATALIE'S *pain.)* whenever these things happened to me/ & i waz young/ i wd eat a lot/ or buy new fancy underwear with rhinestones & lace/ or go to the movies/ maybe call a friend/ talk to made-up boyfriends till dawn. this waz when i waz under my parents' roof/ & trees that grew into my room had to be cut back once a year/ this waz when the birds sometimes flew thru the halls of the house as if the ceilings were sky & i/simply another winged creature. yet no one around me noticed me especially. no one around saw anything but a precocious brown girl with peculiar ideas. like during the polio epidemic/ i wanted to have a celebration/ which nobody cd understand since iron lungs & not going swimming waznt nothing to celebrate. but i explained that i waz celebrating the bounty of the lord/ which more people didnt understand/ til i went on to say that/ it waz obvious that god had protected the colored

folks from polio/ nobody understood that. i did/ if god had made colored people susceptible to polio/ then we wd be on the pictures & the television with the white children. i knew only white folks cd get that particular disease/ & i celebrated. that's how come i always commemorated anything that affected me or the colored people. according to my history of the colored race/ not enough attention was paid to small victories or small personal defeats of the colored. i celebrated the colored trolley driver/ the colored basketball team/ the colored blues singer/ & the colored light heavy weight champion of the world. then too/ i had a baptist child's version of high mass for the slaves in new orleans whom i had read abt/ & i tried to grow watermelons & rice for the dead slaves from the east. as a child i took on the burden of easing the ghost-colored folks' souls & trying hard to keep up with the affairs of my own colored world.

when i became a woman, my world got smaller. my grandma closed up the windows/ so the birds wdnt fly in the house any more. waz bad luck for a girl so yng & in my condition to have the shadows of flying creatures over my head. i didn't celebrate the trolley driver anymore/ cuz he might know i waz in this condition. i didnt celebrate the basketball team anymore/ cuz they were yng & handsome/ & yng & handsome cd mean trouble. but trouble waz when white kids called you names or beat you up cuz you had no older brother/ trouble waz when someone died/ or the tornado hit yr house/ now trouble meant something abt yng & handsome/ & white or colored. if he waz yng & handsome that meant trouble. seemed like every one who didnt have this condition/ so birds cdnt fly over yr head/ waz trouble. as i understood it/ my mama & my grandma were sending me out to be with trouble/ but not to get into trouble. the yng & handsome cd dance with me & call for sunday supper/ the yng & handsome cd write my name on their notebooks/ cd carry my ribbons on the field for gd luck/ the uncles cd hug me & chat for hours abt my growing up/ so i counted all 492 times this condition wd make me victim to this trouble/ before i wd be immune to it/ the way colored folks were immune to polio.

i had discovered innumerable manifestations of trouble: jealousy/ fear/ indignation & recurring fits of vulnerability that lead me right back to the contradiction i had never understood/ even as a child/ how half the world's population cd be bad news/ be yng & handsome/ & later/ eligible & interested/ & trouble.

plus/ according to my own version of the history of the colored people/ only white people hurt little colored girls or grown colored women/ my mama told me only white people had social disease & molested children/ and my grandma told me only white people committed unnatural acts. that's how come i knew only white folks got polio/ muscular dystrophy/ sclerosis/ & mental illness/ this waz all verified by the television. but i found out that the colored folks knew abt the same vicious & disease-ridden passions that the white folks knew.

the pain i succumbed to each time a colored person did something that i believed only white people did waz staggering. my entire life seems to be worthless/ if my own folks arent better than white folks/ then surely the sagas of slavery & the jim crow hadnt convinced anyone that we were better than them. i commenced to buying pieces of gold/ 14 carat/ 24 carat/ 18 carat gold/ every time some black person did something that waz beneath him as a black person & more like a white person. i bought gold cuz it came from the earth/ & more than likely it came from south africa/ where the black people are humiliated & oppressed like in slavery. i wear all these things at once/ to remind the black people that it cost a lot for us to be here/ our value/ can be known instinctively/ but since so many black people are having a hard time not being like white folks/ i wear these gold pieces to protest their ignorance/ their disconnect from history. i buy gold with a vengeance/ each time someone appropriates my space or my time without permission/ each time someone is discourteous or actually cruel to me/ if my mind is not respected/ my body toyed with/ i buy gold/ & weep. i weep as i fix the chains round my neck/ my wrists/ my ankles. i weep cuz all my childhood ceremonies for the ghost-slaves have been in vain. colored people can get polio & mental illness. slavery is not unfamiliar to me. no one on this planet knows/ what i know abt gold/ abt anything hard to get & beautiful/ anything lasting/ wrought from pain. no one understands that sur-

viving the impossible is sposed to accentuate the positive aspects of a people.

(ALEC *is the only member of the company able to come immediately to* MAXINE. *when he reaches her,* LOU, *in his full magician's regalia, freezes the whole company*)

LOU:

yes yes yes   3 wishes is all you get
    scarlet ribbons for yr hair
    a farm in mississippi
    someone to love you madly
all things are possible
but aint no colored magician in his right mind
gonna make you white
cuz this is blk magic you lookin at
& i'm fixin you up good/ fixin you up good &
    colored
& you gonna be colored all yr life
& you gonna love it/ bein colored/ all yr life
colored & love it/ love it/ bein colored

(LOU *beckons the others to join him in the chant,* "colored & love it." *it becomes a serious celebration, like church/ like home/ but then* LOU *freezes them suddenly.*)

LOU:

crackers are born with the right to be
alive/ i'm making ours up right here
in yr face/ & we gonna be
colored & love it

(*the huge minstrel mask comes down as company continues to sing* "colored & love it/ love it being colored." *blackout/ but the minstrel mask remains visible. the company is singing* "colored & love it being colored" *as audience exits*)

Figure 1. The opening tableau of *spell #7* shows all nine performers in exaggerated makeup representing the minstrel-show stereotype while the huge minstrel mask looms behind them in the 1979 New York Shakespeare Festival production, directed by Oz Scott. (Photograph: Martha Swope.)

Figure 2. Natalie (La Tanya Richardson, *foreground*) and Alec (Avery Brooks, *left*) tell the story of "sue-jean" and the baby "myself" while Ross (Reyno) strums his guitar. At the bar are Maxine (Mary Alice) and Eli (Ellis Williams) in the 1979 New York Shakespeare Festival production, directed by Oz Scott. (Photograph: Martha Swope.)

Staging of *spell #7*

**REVIEW OF THE NEW YORK SHAKESPEARE
FESTIVAL PRODUCTION, 1979,
BY RICHARD EDER**

Poetry is as contagious as poison ivy though less prevalent. Look at the response these days to the dramatic poems in Ntozake Shange's remarkable "Spell No. 7." When I went to see the new revised version at the Public Theater the other night, the sketches—lyrical, wry, painful and comically prosaic by turn—lapped over the Anspacher stage and invaded the audience. The place was alive with response, but it wasn't the ordinary applause or laughter of an audience that is pleased or moved. There was a kind of rumination, a repeating of lines, even a few tentative essays at embroidering them.

From two women sitting behind me there was an insistent whispering all through the evening. Sometimes it was one of those counter-accented phrases—"oh yes"—of a revival meeting. When Larry Marshall, as the gleeful *compere*, sets out the long line "you're going to be colored all your life, and you're going to love it being colored," the whispering took up with "and we *do* love it." When Mary Alice chanted references to South Africa, the whisper, in its use of the inconsequential to express strong emotion, could have been designed by Miss Shange herself. "Check it out," the whisper came back giddily, after each fierce line.

I mentioned a revival meeting, and sometimes the springy rhetoric and response of these poetic vignettes about how it feels to be black do have the liveliness and stem-winding buildup of first rate preaching. But if there is any event that Miss Shange's best work approaches, it is something more familiar in other countries—particularly the Soviet Union—than in this one. I am thinking of those highly charged poetry recitals in which a Voznesensky would advance toward the emotions of his audiences head-on, not merely giving words to what was buried or half-buried inside them, but providing them with the public emblem of a man speaking out.

Miss Shange's performers enter as if they were actors gathering in an after-hours bar, but under the tutelage of Mr. Marshall's *compere*, they hurl themselves into their poetic representations. Mr. Marshall has announced that he is the son of a magician who gave up his trade when a black child asked him to perform a spell to make him white. Mr. Marshall proposes a different kind of spell: setting his performers to speaking, he will demonstrate that there is pride and rejoicing in being black. Poetry, of course, demonstrates nothing, not even rejoicing; but it can transmit it. Miss Shange's does, and not only to the black members of the audience.

The bar is a naturalistic setting, a refuge where the performers rest, drink and talk while waiting to assume their roles and deliver their recitations. Although each performer speaks out several times, in different characters, there is little sense of separation between performer and poem. Ellis Williams, corpulent, bearded and bouncy, shifts imperceptibly from serving the drinks in his bar to becoming the particular voice of Miss Shange asserting the commitment to poetry. "I feed my children poems on rye bread."

Mary Alice can become a housewife on a hilarious spree, or the suffering protagonist in a search for black responsibility, but the effect is as if she were moving in and out of her own vision and memory. The visions, of course, are Miss Shange's, but when the performers are not embodying them they are listening to the others embody them. They are each other's audience, linking us, the real audience, to the transformations on the stage.

They speak out with a pyramiding effect. Miss Shange's vignettes proceed with excess, that of the classic tall story, an image is taken, worked up comically, exaggerated and blown up some more. Each vignette is a circus vehicle, clown after clown climbs out, past all reasonable capacity. First they are comic clowns, then ironic clowns, and finally their message is pure pain; or would be except that art redeems the burden it carries by the raffishness with which it carries it.

Take the skittish, wide-eyed swoop with which Mary Alice begins what may be the finest sketch in the play. Flapping her arms, her elbows close to her side, she is a dizzy parody of a skipping child but her beaming innocence is only the first step in a crooked, comical hopscotch into deepening anger.

As a child, she says, she thought that black people had a providential immunity to serious disease, since the handicapped children on the television appeals were always white. (This is certainly true no longer, and I don't know if it ever was, but there is a suggestive truth about the conceit.) She grew up convinced that black people enjoyed a natural edge on virtue and talent.

It was white men who did bad things, her grandmothers told her; and now Mary Alice's face grows heavy as a middle section of the poem explores the disillusioning realization of the hurt that blacks inflict upon each other. The heaviness gives way to a glittering wildness.

"I buy gold," she cries out, shaking her gold necklaces and bracelets. It is the most stunning image of the evening. Gold is mined in South Africa and so, whenever she hears of her own people doing bad things she flaunts the symbol of the country where blacks are most publicly cast down.

We have been angled, played along by Shange's bubbling images, her gift for sprightly ludicrousness; and suddenly we are harpooned right through the gills.

There is a similar power though not quite the same delicate, shifting complexity in the sketch of a young black woman killing her baby. But there is a moving, startling thought contained in it. The woman, suffering and abused, has loved the child to the point of ecstasy as long as she was carrying it in her womb. It is part of her, preserved from any part of the world that has meant so much pain. Once it is born and outside her, it becomes one of the enemy.

There is a great deal more: the lyrically ironic sketch of a black girl, a ferocious gamin played by Laurie Carlos, brushing her knotted hair and insisting that all the fabled rewards of the good life will come once she gets it long and silky. There is a comical, musical collage of black Lotharios and their skeptical and susceptible victims.

Since its first workshop production earlier this summer, a number of adjustments, both of script and cast, have been made. Many of them are improvements, others are not. Despite some convincing individual transitions, there is still awkwardness in relating the recitations, which are the heart of the piece, to the anecdotal mood of the barful of players.

It seems likely that the adjustments will continue. It will certainly be worth it. This is not only a triumph for Miss Shange, director Oz Scott and a splendid cast. It is the triumph of an uneven season for the New York Shakespeare Festival and it is even more than that. Miss Shange, after her success with "For Colored Girls," had a poorish time with her second Festival work, "Photograph." Nothing so justifies the Festival's policy or long-range nurturing of its artists as this lovely new advance for her.

ATHOL FUGARD

1932–

Although Fugard's plays deal almost exclusively with the world of South African experience, they have engaged and challenged audiences throughout the world, for in bearing witness to the inhumanity of his country's long-standing racist policy of "apartheid" (literally, separateness), Fugard persistently creates characters and situations that lamentably reflect an international condition. Even with the legal dismantling of "apartheid," South Africa is still a country divided, often violently, between the white minority and the black majority, as well as between political factions on both sides. Fugard himself grew up in a family that was sharply divided in its view of racial affairs: his father, a hard-drinking jazz pianist of English and Irish descent, was, as Fugard remembers him, "full of pointless, unthought-out prejudices," whereas his mother, an Afrikaner of Dutch colonial stock, had a limitless "capacity for rising above the South African situation and seeing people as people." Thus he speaks of his mother as having "paced my emancipation from prejudice and bigotry."

Born in Middleburg, a village in the semidesert region of South Africa, where his father once led a small band called the Orchestral Jazzonians, Fugard became so alcoholic and indolent that his mother was compelled to support the family, first by running a small boarding house, the Jubilee Hotel, then by operating a café, the St. George's Park Tea Room, which is the setting for Fugard's highly autobiographical play, *"Master Harold" . . . and the Boys* (1982). As an adolescent, Fugard, like the character Hally who is modelled on him (indeed, who bears his childhood nickname), developed a close friendship with one of his mother's black waiters, a man named Sam Semela. Despite the racial gulf and the difference of some twenty years in their ages, they became so close that Fugard thinks of Semela as "the most significant—the only—friend of my boyhood years." Like Hally in the play, Fugard vividly remembers a kite-flying experience with Sam as one of his most precious boyhood experiences. Similarly, Fugard shared his reading and academic learning with Sam, and Sam shared his worldly experience and wisdom with Fugard. And when he was ten years old, Fugard had an argument with his friend (the cause of which he does not remember), and as he bicycled past Sam shortly after the argument "spat in his face." Looking back upon that event years later in his notebooks, Fugard did not imagine he would "ever deal with the shame that overwhelmed me the second after I had done that."

Though the play reflects Fugard's overwhelming sense of shame about that incident, it does not show another prominent side of his adolescence, namely the fact that he was, like his friend Sam, a highly accomplished ballroom dancer. Indeed, he and his sister Glenda were junior ballroom dancing champions several times during his teenage years. As a teenager, he also attended the equivalent of technical high school, evidently planning to become a mechanic, but was so academically gifted that he won a scholarship to the University of Cape Town, where he majored in philosophy and did some lightweight boxing on the side. By the time of his senior year, however, he "had a sense of horizons *shrinking*," so he quit school before graduation and started hitchhiking north in the hopes of eventually reaching Cairo. But after running out of money in Port Sudan, he took a job as the only white seaman on a ship bound for Japan, and during the next two years developed several friendships with blacks and Asians that called into question the racial prejudices of his native land. In his spare time aboard ship, Fugard spent hundreds of hours working on a novel based on his mother's life—he "wanted to write the great South African novel"—but eventually became discouraged with the manuscript and threw it overboard. When he returned to South Africa, however, he could not imagine any other line of working than writing, so his mother bought him a typewriter, and he began writing articles for the local paper, then news bulletins for the national radio in Cape Town.

As a journalist, Fugard was evidently impatient with the task of objective reporting—"my work was always too colored by emotion." So, when in 1956 he met and married an actress, Sheila Meiring, he was naturally inclined to become "more and more involved in theater." He turned out a few highly artificial one-acts, but after witnessing the rebellious drama of the English playwright John Osborne, as well as reading the "*unashamedly* regional" fiction of William Faulkner, Fugard came to realize "how many bloody good South African stories there were to be told." Fugard's decision to focus his plays on South African life was also fuelled by his dismaying experience as a clerk in the Johannesburg office of the Native Commissioner's Court, where he witnessed firsthand the impersonal and oppressive imposition of South Africa's passbook laws, which severely restrict the lives and livelihood of black South Africans. Out of this experience and his encounters with several black South African writers in their segregated shantytowns, Fugard wrote his first full-length play, *No-Good Friday* (1958), which bears witness to both the idealistic impulses and the oppressed lives of black South Africans in the townships. As with many of his subsequent works, Fugard directed *No-Good Friday* and acted in it together with a cast of non-professional black actors, including Zakes Mokae, who has since come to assume a leading role in many of Fugard's plays.

After a brief and frustrating period in London, where Fugard and his wife had gone seeking further theatrical experience, they decided to return home in 1960, to be among friends and to lend support to the anti-apartheid movement after a massacre of peacefully protesting blacks took place in Sharpesville, South Africa. During 1961, drawing on a notebook of literary quotations, personal observations, and theatrical ideas that he had begun keeping in London, Fugard wrote his first highly successful play, *Blood Knot,* which explores the psychologically complex love-hate relationship between two "coloured" (the South African term for people of mixed race) half brothers—the light-skinned and guilt-ridden Morrie (performed by Fugard himself) and the dark-skinned, envious, and bitter Zach (performed by Zakes Mokae). Following their performance of the play for an enthusiastic audience of invited friends, critics, writers, and actors, Fugard and Mokae took the play throughout South Africa, segregated while on trains, but together on stage. A London production of *Blood Knot* did not fare so well, but in 1964 an off-Broadway production starring

James Earl Jones as Zach ran for seven months and established Fugard's reputation in America.

Like *Blood Knot* most of Fugard's subsequent plays have focused on two or three characters complexly related to each other not only by blood, friendship, or marriage, but also by the racially divided world of South African life. Among the most successful of these highly concentrated works are *Boesman and Lena* (1968), which details the wretched life and abusive marriage of a coloured husband and wife wandering across the veld; *The Island* (1972), which dramatizes the heroic effort of two black political prisoners to transcend the brutality of the prison by producing the Greek play *Antigone* in an adaptation that applies the civil disobedience of its heroine to the state of affairs in South Africa; *Sizwe Bansi Is Dead* (1972), which focuses on an unemployed black man whose fear of being arrested because his passbook is not in order drives him to steal the passbook, and thus the identity, of a dead man; *Statements after an Arrest under the Immorality Act* (1974), which explores the multifaceted relationship between a white female librarian and a coloured teacher to whom she first lends books secretly and with whom she then falls in love; *A Lesson from Aloes* (1978), which features the story of an activist white bus driver, suspected of being a political informer, his emotionally distressed wife, and the inspiration he draws from the endurance of his aloe plants to remain true to his own moral convictions; and *The Road to Mecca* (1984), which centers on several days in the life of an eccentric white sculptress as she faces the terror both of losing her artistic inspiration and of being committed to an old folks' rest home.

"Master Harold" . . . and the Boys, widely regarded as Fugard's finest play, also focuses intensely on just a few characters. But in this case, the focal relationship of the play does not involve racially identical persons—blacks, coloureds, or whites—as do most of Fugard's earlier works. Instead *"Master Harold,"* like *Statements after an Arrest,* centers on a relationship involving racially different persons, in particular the long-standing friendship between a black waiter and the white son of his employer. In this respect, it depicts a special relationship that seems to transcend the racial tension and conflict engendered by the South African policy of "apartheid." But as the play unfolds, we discover that loving relationship to be painfully, indeed shockingly, subverted by the complex familial and cultural situation within which it is deeply rooted. For just as Fugard drew on Sam Semela to create the play's Sam, so too he made Hally's offstage father, like his own father, an alcoholic and a cripple. Hally's rejection of his natural father, his turning to a black "father-figure," and his attack on both when he spits on Sam thus come not only out of Fugard's life, but also out of his understanding that racial hatred can be seen, in part, as each individual's own psychological choice. In this fundamental sense, *"Master Harold,"* as Frank Rich notes in the review following the text, is concerned not just with South African apartheid, but with the capacity for cruelty that divides human beings everywhere.

The two major insults of the play—Sam baring his rump to Hally and Hally spitting at Sam—are so arresting and intense, especially following upon the earlier warmth and camaraderie between the two characters (see Figure 1), that one can readily understand how difficult it is for actors to perform them, even in rehearsal. Indeed when Fugard was directing his play for the Yale Repertory Theatre premiere, he had to shock the actors into these insulting gestures by performing them himself, first baring his own backside to Zakes Mokae, the actor playing Sam, and then repeatedly spitting at him. The risk Fugard took in re-enacting the moment of shame—a moment that he thought he would never deal with—was ultimately liberating both for himself and for the actors. Political theater can ask for no greater success, and Fugard's plays, though written out of a specific political reality, nonetheless speak to audiences everywhere. Perhaps they do so because they root the political in the personal, as Sam eloquently displays when he sternly rebukes Hally for mocking his father (see Figure 2), or when he says to Hally, late in the play, "I've got no right to tell you what being a man means if I don't behave like one myself, and I'm not doing so well at that this afternoon. Should we try again, Hally?" Though Hally can't give him a positive answer, Sam's willingness to try again reflects Fugard's hope that solutions, both personal and political, may yet be found.

"MASTER HAROLD" . . . AND THE BOYS

BY ATHOL FUGARD

CHARACTERS

WILLIE
SAM
HALLY

The St. George's Park Tea Room on a wet and windy Port Elizabeth afternoon.

Tables and chairs have been cleared and are stacked on one side except for one which stands apart with a single chair. On this table a knife, fork, spoon and side plate in anticipation of a simple meal, together with a pile of comic books.

Other elements: a serving counter with a few stale cakes under glass and a not very impressive display of sweets, cigarettes and cool drinks, etc.; a few cardboard advertising handouts—Cadbury's Chocolate, Coca-Cola—and a blackboard on which an untrained hand has chalked up the prices of Tea, Coffee, Scones, Milkshakes—all flavors— and Cool Drinks; a few sad ferns in pots; a telephone; an old-style jukebox.

There is an entrance on one side and an exit into a kitchen on the other.

Leaning on the solitary table, his head cupped in one hand as he pages through one of the comic books, is Sam. A black man in his mid-forties. He wears the white coat of a waiter. Behind him on his knees, mopping down the floor with a bucket of water and a rag, is Willie. Also black and about the same age as Sam. He has his sleeves and trousers rolled up.

The year: 1950.

WILLIE: (*Singing as he works*)

> "She was scandalizin' my name,
> She took my money
> She called me honey
> But she was scandalizin' my name.
> Called it love but was playin' a game. . . ."

(He gets up and moves the bucket. Stands thinking for a moment, then, raising his arms to hold an imaginary partner, he launches into an intricate ballroom dance step. Although a mildly comic figure, he reveals a reasonable degree of accomplishment.)

Hey, Sam.

(SAM, absorbed in the comic book, does not respond.)

Hey, Boet Sam!

(SAM looks up.)

I'm getting it. The quickstep. Look now and tell me. (*He repeats the step.*) Well?
SAM: (*Encouragingly*) Show me again.
WILLIE: Okay, count for me.
SAM: Ready?
WILLIE: Ready.
SAM: Five, six, seven, eight. . . . (*Willie starts to dance.*) A-n-d one two three four . . . and one two three four. . . . (*Ad libbing as WILLIE dances.*) Your shoulders, Willie . . . your shoulders! Don't look down! Look happy, Willie! Relax, Willie!
WILLIE: (*Desperate but still dancing*) I am relax.
SAM: No, you're not.
WILLIE: (*He falters*) Ag no man, Sam! Mustn't talk. You make me make mistakes.
SAM: But you're stiff.
WILLIE: Yesterday I'm not straight . . . today I'm too stiff!
SAM: Well, you are. You asked me and I'm telling you.
WILLIE: Where?
SAM: Everywhere. Try to glide through it.
WILLIE: Glide?
SAM: Ja, make it smooth. And give it more style. It must look like you're enjoying yourself.
WILLIE: (*Emphatically*) I wasn't.
SAM: Exactly.
WILLIE: How can I enjoy myself? Not straight, too stiff and now it's also glide, give it more style, make it smooth. . . . Haai! Is hard to remember all those things, Boet Sam.
SAM: That's your trouble. You're trying too hard.
WILLIE: I try hard because it *is* hard.
SAM: But don't let me see it. The secret is to make it look easy. Ballroom must look happy, Willie, not like hard work. It must. . . . Ja! . . . it must look like romance.
WILLIE: Now another one! What's romance?
SAM: Love story with happy ending. A handsome man

633

in tails, and in his arms, smiling at him, a beautiful lady in evening dress!

WILLIE: Fred Astaire, Ginger Rogers.

SAM: You got it. Tapdance or ballroom, it's the same. Romance. In two weeks' time when the judges look at you and Hilda, they must see a man and a woman who are dancing their way to a happy ending. What I saw was you holding her like you were frightened she was going to run away.

WILLIE: Ja! Because that is what she wants to do! I got no romance left for Hilda anymore, Boet Sam.

SAM: Then pretend. When you put your arms around Hilda, imagine she is Ginger Rogers.

WILLIE: With no teeth? You try.

SAM: Well, just remember, there's only two weeks left.

WILLIE: I know, I know! (*To the jukebox.*) I do it better with music. You got sixpence for Sarah Vaughan?

SAM: That's a slow foxtrot. You're practicing the quickstep.

WILLIE: I'll practice slow foxtrot.

SAM: (*Shaking his head*) It's your turn to put money in the jukebox.

WILLIE: I only got bus fare to go home. (*He returns disconsolately to his work.*) Love story and happy ending! She's doing it all right, Boet Sam, but is not me she's giving happy endings. Fuckin' whore! Three nights now she doesn't come practice. I wind up gramophone, I get record ready and I sit and wait. What happens? Nothing. Ten o'clock I start dancing with my pillow. You try and practice romance by yourself, Boet Sam. Struesgod, she doesn't come tonight I take back my dress and ballroom shoes and I find me new partner. Size twenty-six. Shoes size seven. And now she's also making trouble for me with the baby again. Reports me to Child Wellfred, that I'm not giving her money. She lies! Every week I am giving her money for milk. And how do I know is my baby? Only his hair looks like me. She's fucking around all the time I turn my back. Hilda Samuels is a bitch! (*Pause.*) Hey, Sam!

SAM: Ja.

WILLIE: You listening?

SAM: Ja.

WILLIE: So what you say?

SAM: About Hilda?

WILLIE: Ja.

SAM: When did you last give her a hiding?

WILLIE: (*Reluctantly*) Sunday night.

SAM: And today is Thursday.

WILLIE: (*He knows what's coming*) Okay.

SAM: Hiding on Sunday night, then Monday, Tuesday, and Wednesday she doesn't come to practice . . . and you are asking me why?

WILLIE: I said okay, Boet Sam!

SAM: You hit her too much. One day she's going to leave you for good.

WILLIE: So? She makes me the hell-in too much.

SAM: (*Emphasizing his point*) Too much and *too* hard. You had the same trouble with Eunice.

WILLIE: Because she also make the hell-in, Boet Sam. She never got the steps right. Even the waltz.

SAM: Beating her up every time she makes a mistake in the waltz? (*Shaking his head.*) No, Willie! That takes the pleasure out of ballroom dancing.

WILLIE: Hilda is not too bad with the waltz, Boet Sam. Is the quickstep where the trouble starts.

SAM: (*Teasing him gently*) How's your pillow with the quickstep?

WILLIE: (*Ignoring the tease*) Good! And why? Because it got no legs. That's her trouble. She can't move them quick enough, Boet Sam. I start the record and before halfway Count Basie is already winning. Only time we catch up with him is when gramophone runs down. (*Sam laughs.*) Haaikona, Boet Sam, is not funny.

SAM: (*Snapping his fingers*) I got it! Give her a handicap.

WILLIE: What's that?

SAM: Give her a ten-second start and then let Count Basie go. Then I put my money on her. Hot favorite in the Ballroom Stakes: Hilda Samuels ridden by Willie Malopo.

WILLIE: (*Turning away*) I'm not talking to you no more.

SAM: (*Relenting*) Sorry, Willie. . . .

WILLIE: It's finish between us.

SAM: Okay, okay . . . I'll stop.

WILLIE: You can also fuck off.

SAM: Willie, listen! I want to help you!

WILLIE: No more jokes?

SAM: I promise.

WILLIE: Okay. Help me.

SAM: (*His turn to hold an imaginary partner*) Look and learn. Feet together. Back straight. Body relaxed. Right hand placed gently in the small of her back and wait for the music. Don't start worrying about making mistakes or the judges or the other competitors. It's just you, Hilda and the music, and you're going to have a good time. What Count Basie do you play?

WILLIE: "You the cream in my coffee, you the salt in my stew."

SAM: Right. Give it to me in strict tempo.

WILLIE: Ready?

SAM: Ready.

WILLIE: A-n-d . . . (*Singing.*)

"You the cream in my coffee.
You the salt in my stew.
You will always be my necessity.
I'd be lost without you. . . ." (etc.)

(SAM *launches into the quickstep. He is obviously a much more accomplished dancer than* WILLIE. HALLY *enters. A seventeen-year-old white boy. Wet raincoat and school case. He stops and watches* SAM. *The demonstration comes to an end with a flourish. Applause from* HALLY *and* WILLIE.)

HALLY: Bravo! No question about it. First place goes to Mr. Sam Semela.

WILLIE: (*In total agreement*) You was gliding with style, Boet Sam.

HALLY: (*Cheerfully*) How's it, chaps?

SAM: Okay, Hally.

WILLIE: (*Springing to attention like a soldier and saluting*) At your service, Master Harold!

HALLY: Not long to the big event, hey!

SAM: Two weeks.

HALLY: You nervous?

SAM: No.

HALLY: Think you stand a chance?

SAM: Let's just say I'm ready to go out there and dance.

HALLY: It looked like it. What about you, Willie?

(WILLIE *groans.*)

What's the matter?

SAM: He's got leg trouble.

HALLY: (*Innocently*) Oh, sorry to hear that, Willie.

WILLIE: Boet Sam! You promised. (WILLIE *returns to his work.*)

(HALLY *deposits his school case and takes off his raincoat. His clothes are a little neglected and untidy: black blazer with school badge, gray flannel trousers in need of an ironing, khaki shirt and tie, black shoes.* SAM *has fetched a towel for* HALLY *to dry his hair.*)

HALLY: God, what a lousy bloody day. It's coming down cats and dogs out there. Bad for business, chaps. . . . (*Conspiratorial whisper.*) . . . but it also means we're in for a nice quiet afternoon.

SAM: You can speak loud. Your Mom's not here.

HALLY: Out shopping?

SAM: No. The hospital.

HALLY: But it's Thursday. There's no visiting on Thursday afternoons. Is my Dad okay?

SAM: Sounds like it. In fact, I think he's going home.

HALLY: (*Stopped short by* SAM's *remark*) What do you mean?

SAM: The hospital phoned.

HALLY: To say what?

SAM: I don't know. I just heard your Mom talking.

HALLY: So what makes you say he's going home?

SAM: It sounded as if they were telling her to come and fetch him.

(HALLY *thinks about what* SAM *has said for a few seconds.*)

HALLY: When did she leave?

SAM: About an hour ago. She said she would phone you. Want to eat?

(HALLY *doesn't respond.*)

Hally, want your lunch?

HALLY: I suppose so. (*His mood has changed.*) What's on the menu? . . . as if I don't know.

SAM: Soup, followed by meat pie and gravy.

HALLY: Today's?

SAM: No.

HALLY: And the soup?

SAM: Nourishing pea soup.

HALLY: Just the soup. (*The pile of comic books on the table.*) And these?

SAM: For your Dad. Mr. Kempston brought them.

HALLY: You haven't been reading them, have you?

SAM: Just looking.

HALLY: (*Examining the comics*) Jungle Jim . . . Batman and Robin . . . Tarzan . . . God, what rubbish! Mental pollution. Take them away.

(SAM *exits waltzing into the kitchen.* HALLY *turns to* WILLIE.)

HALLY: Did you hear my Mom talking on the telephone, Willie?

WILLIE: No, Master Hally. I was at the back.

HALLY: And she didn't say anything to you before she left?

WILLIE: She said I must clean the floors.

HALLY: I mean about my Dad.

WILLIE: She didn't say nothing to me about him, Master Hally.

HALLY: (*With conviction*) No! It can't be. They said he needed at least another three weeks of treatment. Sam's definitely made a mistake. (*Rummages through his school case, finds a book and settles down at the table to read.*) So, Willie!

WILLIE: Yes, Master Hally! Schooling okay today?

HALLY: Yes, okay. . . . (*He thinks about it.*) . . . No, not really. Ag, what's the difference? I don't care. And Sam says you've got problems.

WILLIE: Big problems.

HALLY: Which leg is sore?

(WILLIE *groans.*)

Both legs.

WILLIE: There is nothing wrong with my legs. Sam is just making jokes.

HALLY: So then you *will* be in the competition.

WILLIE: Only if I can find a partner.

HALLY: But what about Hilda?

SAM: (*Returning with a bowl of soup*) She's the one who's got trouble with her legs.

HALLY: What sort of trouble, Willie?

SAM: From the way he describes it, I think the lady has gone a bit lame.

HALLY: Good God! Have you taken her to see a doctor?

SAM: I think a vet would be better.

HALLY: What do you mean?

SAM: What do you call it again when a racehorse goes very fast?

HALLY: Gallop?

SAM: That's it!

WILLIE: Boet Sam!

HALLY: "A gallop down the homestretch to the winning post." But what's that got to do with Hilda?

SAM: Count Basie always gets there first.

(WILLIE *lets fly with his slop rag. It misses* SAM *and hits* HALLY.)

HALLY: (*Furious*) For Christ's sake, Willie! What the hell do you think you're doing?

WILLIE: Sorry, Master Hally, but it's him....

HALLY: Act your bloody age! (*Hurls the rag back at* WILLIE.) Cut out the nonsense now and get on with your work. And you too, Sam. Stop fooling around.

(SAM *moves away.*)

No. Hang on. I haven't finished! Tell me exactly what my Mom said.

SAM: I have. "When Hally comes, tell him I've gone to the hospital and I'll phone him."

HALLY: She didn't say anything about taking my Dad home?

SAM: No. It's just that when she was talking on the phone....

HALLY: (*Interrupting him*) No, Sam. They can't be discharging him. She would have said so if they were. In any case, we saw him last night and he wasn't in good shape at all. Staff nurse even said there was talk about taking more X-rays. And now suddenly today he's better? If anything, it sounds more like a bad turn to me . . . which I sincerely hope it isn't. Hang on . . . how long ago did you say she left?

SAM: Just before two . . . (*His wrist watch.*) . . . hour and a half.

HALLY: I know how to settle it. (*Behind the counter to the telephone. Talking as he dials.*) Let's give her ten minutes to get to the hospital, ten minutes to load him up, another ten, at the most, to get home, and another ten to get him inside. Forty minutes. They should have been home for at least half an hour already. (*Pause—he waits with the receiver to his ear.*) No reply, chaps. And you know why? Because she's at his bedside in hospital helping him pull through a bad turn. You definitely heard wrong.

SAM: Okay.

(*As far as* HALLY *is concerned, the matter is settled. He returns to his table, sits down, and divides his attention between the book and his soup. Sam is at his school case and picks up a textbook.*)

Modern Graded Mathematics for Standards Nine and Ten.

(*Opens it at random and laughs at something he sees.*) Who is this supposed to be?

HALLY: Old fart-face Prentice.

SAM: Teacher?

HALLY: Thinks he is. And believe me, that is not a bad likeness.

SAM: Has he seen it?

HALLY: Yes.

SAM: What did he say?

HALLY: Tried to be clever, as usual. Said I was no Leonardo da Vinci and that bad art had to be punished. So, six of the best, and his are bloody good.

SAM: On your bum?

HALLY: Where else? The days when I got them on my hands are gone forever, Sam.

SAM: With your trousers down!

HALLY: No. He's not quite that barbaric.

SAM: That's the way they do it in jail.

HALLY: (*Flicker of morbid interest*) Really?

SAM: Ja. When the magistrate sentences you to "strokes with a light cane."

HALLY: Go on.

SAM: They make you lie down on a bench. One policeman pulls down your trousers and holds your ankles, another one pulls your shirt over your head and holds your arms....

HALLY: Thank you! That's enough.

SAM: . . . and the one that gives you the strokes talks to you gently and for a long time between each one. (*He laughs.*)

HALLY: I've heard enough. Sam! Jesus! It's a bloody awful world when you come to think of it. People can be real bastards.

SAM: That's the way it is, Hally.

HALLY: It doesn't *have* to be that way. There is something called progress, you know. We don't exactly burn people at the stake anymore.

SAM: Like Joan of Arc.

HALLY: Correct. If she was captured today, she'd be given a fair trial.

SAM: And then the death sentence.

HALLY: (*A world-weary sigh*) I know, I know! I oscillate between hope and despair for this world as well, Sam. But things will change, you wait and see. One day somebody is going to get up and give history a kick up the backside and get it going again.

SAM: Like who?

HALLY: (*After thought*) They're called social reformers. Every age, Sam, has got its social reformer. My history book is full of them.

SAM: So where's ours?

HALLY: Good question. And I hate to say it, but the answer is: I don't know. Maybe he hasn't even been born yet. Or is still only a babe in arms at his mother's breast. God, what a thought.

SAM: So we just go on waiting.

HALLY: Ja, looks like it. (*Back to his soup and the book.*)

SAM: (*Reading from the textbook*) "Introduction: In some mathematical problems only the magnitude...." (*He mispronounces the word "magnitude."*)

HALLY: (*Correcting him without looking up*) Magnitude.

SAM: What's it mean?

HALLY: How big it is. The size of the thing.

SAM: (*Reading*) ". . . magnitude of the quantities is of importance. In other problems we need to know whether these quantities are negative or positive. For example, whether there is a debit or credit bank balance . . ."

HALLY: Whether you're broke or not.

SAM: ". . . whether the temperature is above or below Zero. . . ."

HALLY: Naught degrees. Cheerful state of affairs! No cash and you're freezing to death. Mathematics won't get you out of that one.

SAM: "All these quantities are called . . ." (*Spelling the word*) . . . s-c-a-l. . . .

HALLY: Scalars.

SAM: Scalars! (*Shaking his head with a laugh.*) You understand all that?

HALLY: (*Turning a page*) No. And I don't intend to try.

SAM: So what happens when the exams come?

HALLY: Failing a maths exam isn't the end of the world, Sam. How many times have I told you that examination results don't measure intelligence?

SAM: I would say about as many times as you've failed one of them.

HALLY: (*Mirthlessly*) Ha, ha, ha.

SAM: (*Simultaneously*) Ha, ha, ha.

HALLY: Just remember Winston Churchill didn't do particularly well at school.

SAM: You've also told me that one many times.

HALLY: Well, it just so happens to be the truth.

SAM: (*Enjoying the word*) Magnitude! Magnitude! Show me how to use it.

HALLY: (*After thought*) An intrepid social reformer will not be daunted by the magnitude of the task he has undertaken.

SAM: (*Impressed*) Couple of jaw-breakers in there!

HALLY: I gave you three for the price of one. Intrepid, daunted, and magnitude. I did that once in an exam. Put five of the words I had to explain in one sentence. It was half a page long.

SAM: Well, I'll put my money on you in the English exam.

HALLY: Piece of cake. Eighty percent without even trying.

SAM: (*Another textbook from Hally's case*) And history?

HALLY: So-so. I'll scrape through. In the fifties if I'm lucky.

SAM: You didn't do too badly last year.

HALLY: Because we had World War One. That at least has some action. You try to find that in the South African Parliamentary system.

SAM: (*Reading from the history textbook*) "Napoleon and the principle of equality." Hey! This sounds interesting. "After concluding peace with Britain in 1802, Napoleon used a brief period of calm to insti-tute . . ."

HALLY: Introduce.

SAM: ". . . many reforms. Napoleon regarded all people

as equal before the law and wanted them to have equal opportunities for advancement. All ves-ti-ges of the feu-dal sys-tem with its oppression of the poor were abol-ished." Vestiges, feudal system, and abolished. I'm all right on oppression.

HALLY: I'm thinking. He swept away . . . abolished . . . the last remains . . . vestiges . . . of the bad old days . . . feudal system.

SAM: Ha! There's the social reformer we're waiting for. He sounds like a man of some magnitude.

HALLY: I'm not so sure about that. It's a damn good title for a book, though. A man of magnitude!

SAM: He sounds pretty big to me, Hally.

HALLY: Don't confuse historical significance with greatness. But maybe I'm being a bit prejudiced. Have a look in there and you'll see he's two chapters long. And hell! . . . has he only got dates, Sam, all of which you've got to remember! This campaign and that campaign, and then, because of all the fighting, the next thing is we get Peace Treaties all over the place. And what's the end of the story? Battle of Waterloo, which he loses. Wasn't worth it. No, I don't know about him as a man of magnitude.

SAM: Then who would you say was?

HALLY: To answer that, we need a definition of greatness, and I suppose that would be somebody who . . . somebody who benefited all mankind.

SAM: Right. But like who?

HALLY: (*He speaks with total conviction*) Charles Darwin. Remember him? That big book from the library. *The Origin of the Species.*

SAM: Him?

HALLY: Yes. For his Theory of Evolution.

SAM: You didn't finish it.

HALLY: I ran out of time. I didn't finish it because my two weeks was up. But I'm going to take it out again after I've digested what I read. It's safe. I've hidden it away in the Theology section. Nobody ever goes in there. And anyway who are you to talk? You hardly even looked at it.

SAM: I tried. I looked at the chapters in the beginning and I saw one called "The Struggle for an Existence." Ah ha, I thought. At last! But what did I get? Something called the mistiltoe which needs the apple tree and there's too many seeds and all are going to die except one . . . ! No, Hally.

HALLY: (*Intellectually outraged*) What do you mean, No! The poor man had to start somewhere. For God's sake, Sam, he revolutionized science. Now we know.

SAM: What?

HALLY: Where we come from and what it all means.

SAM: And that's a benefit to mankind? Anyway, I still don't believe it.

HALLY: God, you're impossible. I showed it to you in black and white.

SAM: Doesn't mean I got to believe it.

HALLY: It's the likes of you that kept the Inquisition in

business. It's called bigotry. Anyway, that's my man of magnitude. Charles Darwin! Who's yours?

SAM: (*Without hesitation*) Abraham Lincoln.

HALLY: I might have guessed as much. Don't get sentimental, Sam. You've never been a slave, you know. And anyway we freed your ancestors here in South Africa long before the Americans. But if you want to thank somebody on their behalf, do it to Mr. William Wilberforce. Come on. Try again. I want a real genius.

(*Now enjoying himself, and so is* SAM. HALLY *goes behind the counter and helps himself to a chocolate.*)

SAM: William Shakespeare.

HALLY: (*No enthusiasm*) Oh. So you're also one of them, are you? You're basing that opinion on only one play, you know. You've only read my *Julius Caesar* and even I don't understand half of what they're talking about. They should do what they did with the old Bible: bring the language up to date.

SAM: That's all you've got. It's also the only one *you've* read.

HALLY: I know. I admit it. That's why I suggest we reserve our judgment until we've checked up on a few others. I've got a feeling, though, that by the end of this year one is going to be enough for me, and I can give you the names of twenty-nine other chaps in the Standard Nine class of the Port Elizabeth Technical College who feel the same. But if you want him, you can have him. My turn now. (*Pacing.*) This is a damned good exercise, you know! It started off looking like a simple question and here it's got us really probing into the intellectual heritage of our civilization.

SAM: So who is it going to be?

HALLY: My next man . . . and he gets the title on two scores: social reform and literary genius . . . is Leo Nikolaevich Tolstoy.

SAM: That Russian.

HALLY: Correct. Remember the picture of him I showed you?

SAM: With the long beard.

HALLY: (*Trying to look like Tolstoy*) And those burning, visionary eyes. My God, the face of a social prophet if ever I saw one! And remember my words when I showed it to you? Here's a *man*, Sam!

SAM: Those were words, Hally.

HALLY: Not many intellectuals are prepared to shovel manure with the peasants and then go home and write a "little book" called *War and Peace*. Incidentally, Sam, he was somebody else who, to quote, ". . . did not distinguish himself scholastically."

SAM: Meaning?

HALLY: He was also no good at school.

SAM: Like you and Winston Churchill.

HALLY: (*Mirthlessly*) Ha, ha, ha.

SAM: (*Simultaneously*) Ha, ha, ha.

HALLY: Don't get clever, Sam. That man freed his serfs of his own free will.

SAM: No argument. He was somebody, all right. I accept him.

HALLY: I'm sure Count Tolstoy will be very pleased to hear that. Your turn. Shoot. (*Another chocolate from behind the counter.*) I'm waiting, Sam.

SAM: I've got him.

HALLY: Good. Submit your candidate for examination.

SAM: Jesus.

HALLY: (*Stopped dead in his tracks*) Who?

SAM: Jesus Christ.

HALLY: Oh, come on, Sam!

SAM: The Messiah.

HALLY: Ja, but still . . . No, Sam. Don't let's get started on religion. We'll just spend the whole afternoon arguing again. Suppose I turn around and say Mohammed?

SAM: All right.

HALLY: You can't have them both on the same list!

SAM: Why not? You like Mohammed, I like Jesus.

HALLY: I *don't* like Mohammed. I never have. I was merely being hypothetical. As far as I'm concerned, the Koran is as bad as the Bible. No. Religion is out! I'm not going to waste my time again arguing with you about the existence of God. You know perfectly well I'm an atheist . . . and I've got homework to do.

SAM: Okay, I take him back.

HALLY: You've got time for one more name.

SAM: (*After thought*) I've got one I know we'll agree on. A simple straightforward great Man of Magnitude . . . and no arguments. And *he* really *did* benefit all mankind.

HALLY: I wonder. After your last contribution I'm beginning to doubt whether anything in the way of an intellectual agreement is possible between the two of us. Who is he?

SAM: Guess.

HALLY: Socrates? Alexandre Dumas? Karl Marx, Dostoevsky? Nietzsche?

(SAM *shakes his head after each name.*)

Give me a clue.

SAM: The letter *P* is important. . . .

HALLY: Plato!

SAM: . . . and his name begins with an *F*.

HALLY: I've got it. Freud and Psychology.

SAM: No. I didn't understand him.

HALLY: That makes two of us.

SAM: Think of moldy apricot jam.

HALLY: (*After a delighted laugh*) Penicillin and Sir Alexander Fleming! And the title of the book: *The Microbe Hunters.* (*Delighted.*) Splendid, Sam! Splendid. For once we are in total agreement. The major breakthrough in medical science in the Twentieth Century. If it wasn't for him, we might have lost the Second World War. It's deeply gratifying, Sam, to know that I haven't been wasting my time in talking to you. (*Strutting around proudly.*) Tolstoy may have educated his peasants, but I've educated you.

SAM: Standard Four to Standard Nine.

HALLY: Have we been at it as long as that?

SAM: Yep. And my first lesson was geography.

HALLY: (*Intrigued*) Really? I don't remember.

SAM: My room there at the back of the old Jubilee Boarding House. I had just started working for your Mom. Little boy in short trousers walks in one afternoon and asks me seriously: "Sam, do you want to see South Africa?" Hey man! Sure I wanted to see South Africa!

HALLY: Was that me?

SAM: . . . So the next thing I'm looking at a map you had just done for homework. It was your first one and you were very proud of yourself.

HALLY: Go on.

SAM: Then came my first lesson. "Repeat after me, Sam: Gold in the Transvaal, mealies in the Free State, sugar in Natal, and grapes in the Cape." I still know it!

HALLY: Well, I'll be buggered. So that's how it all started.

SAM: And your next map was one with all the rivers and the mountains they came from. The Orange, the Vaal, the Limpopo, the Zambezi. . . .

HALLY: You've got a phenomenal memory!

SAM: You should be grateful. That is why you started passing your exams. You tried to be better than me.

(*They laugh together.* WILLIE *is attracted by the laughter and joins them.*)

HALLY: The old Jubilee Boarding House. Sixteen rooms with board and lodging, rent in advance and one week's notice. I haven't thought about it for donkey's years . . . and I don't think that's an accident. God, was I glad when we sold it and moved out. Those years are not remembered as the happiest ones of an unhappy childhood.

WILLIE: (*Knocking on the table and trying to imitate a woman's voice*) "Hally, are you there?"

HALLY: Who's that supposed to be?

WILLIE: "What you doing in there, Hally? Come out at once!"

HALLY: (*To* SAM) What's he talking about?

SAM: Don't you remember?

WILLIE: "Sam, Willie . . . is he in there with you boys?"

SAM: Hiding away in our room when your mother was looking for you.

HALLY: (*Another good laugh*) Of course! I used to crawl and hide under your bed! But finish the story, Willie. Then what used to happen? You chaps would give the game away by telling her I was in there with you. So much for friendship.

SAM: We couldn't lie to her. She knew.

HALLY: Which meant I got another rowing for hanging around the "servants' quarters." I think I spent more time in there with you chaps than anywhere else in that dump. And do you blame me? Nothing but bloody misery wherever you went. Somebody was always complaining about the food, or my mother was having a fight with Micky Nash because she'd caught her with a petty officer in her room. Maud Meiring was another one. Remember those two? They were prostitutes, you know. Soldiers and sailors from the troopships. Bottom fell out of the business when the war ended. God, the flotsam and jetsam that life washed up on our shores! No joking, if it wasn't for your room, I would have been the first certified ten-year-old in medical history. Ja, the memories are coming back now. Walking home from school and thinking: "What can I do this afternoon?" Try out a few ideas, but sooner or later I'd end up in there with you fellows. I bet you I could still find my way to your room with my eyes closed. (*He does exactly that.*) Down the corridor . . . telephone on the right, which my Mom keeps locked because somebody is using it on the sly and not paying . . . past the kitchen and unappetizing cooking smells . . . around the corner into the backyard, hold my breath again because there are more smells coming when I pass your lavatory, then into that little passageway, first door on the right and into your room. How's that?

SAM: Good. But, as usual, you forgot to knock.

HALLY: Like that time I barged in and caught you and Cynthia . . . at it. Remember? God, was I embarrassed! I didn't know what was going on at first.

SAM: Ja, that taught you a lesson.

HALLY: And about a lot more than knocking on doors, I'll have you know, and I don't mean geography either. Hell, Sam, couldn't you have waited until it was dark?

SAM: No.

HALLY: Was it that urgent?

SAM: Yes, and if you don't believe me, wait until your time comes.

HALLY: No, thank you. I am not interested in girls. (*Back to his memories. . . . Using a few chairs he re-creates the room as he lists the items.*) A gray little room with a cold cement floor. Your bed against that wall . . . and I now know why the mattress sags so much! . . . Willie's bed . . . it's propped up on bricks because one leg is broken . . . that wobbly little table with the washbasin and jug of water . . . Yes! . . . stuck to the wall above it are some pin-up pictures from magazines. Joe Louis. . . .

WILLIE: Brown Bomber. World Title. (*Boxing pose.*) Three rounds and knockout.

HALLY: Against who?

SAM: Max Schmeling.

HALLY: Correct. I can also remember Fred Astaire and Ginger Rogers, and Rita Hayworth in a bathing costume which always made me hot and bothered when I looked at it. Under Willie's bed is an old suitcase with all his clothes in a mess, which is why I never hide there. Your things are neat and tidy in a trunk next to your bed, and on it there is a picture of you and Cynthia in your ballroom clothes, your first silver cup for third place in a competition and an old radio which doesn't work anymore. Have I left out anything?

SAM: No.

HALLY: Right, so much for the stage directions. Now the characters. (SAM *and* WILLIE *move to their appropriate positions in the bedroom.*) Willie is in bed, under his blankets with his clothes on, complaining non-stop about something, but we can't make out a word of what he's saying because he's got his head under the blankets as well. You're on your bed trimming your toenails with a knife—not a very edifying sight—and as for me. . . . What am I doing?

SAM: You're sitting on the floor giving Willie a lecture about being a good loser while you get the checkerboard and pieces ready for a game. Then you go to Willie's bed, pull off the blankets and make him play with you first because you know you're going to win, and that gives you the second game with me.

HALLY: And you certainly were a bad loser, Willie!

WILLIE: Haai!

HALLY: Wasn't he, Sam? And so slow! A game with you almost took the whole afternoon. Thank God I gave up trying to teach you how to play chess.

WILLIE: You and Sam cheated.

HALLY: I never saw Sam cheat, and mine were mostly the mistakes of youth.

WILLIE: Then how is it you two was always winning?

HALLY: Have you ever considered the possibility, Willie, that it was because we were better than you?

WILLIE: Every time better?

HALLY: Not every time. There were occasions when we deliberately let you win a game so that you would stop sulking and go on playing with us. Sam used to wink at me when you weren't looking to show me it was time to let you win.

WILLIE: So then you two didn't play fair.

HALLY: It was for your benefit, Mr. Malopo, which is more than being fair. It was an act of self-sacrifice. (*To* SAM.) But you know what my best memory is, don't you?

SAM: No.

HALLY: Come on, guess. If your memory is so good, you must remember it as well.

SAM: We got up to a lot of tricks in there, Hally.

HALLY: This one was special, Sam.

SAM: I'm listening.

HALLY: It started off looking like another of those use-less nothing-to-do afternoons. I'd already been down to Main Street looking for adventure, but nothing had happened. I didn't feel like climbing trees in the Donkin Park or pretending I was a private eye and following a stranger . . . so as usual: See what's cooking in Sam's room. This time it was you on the floor. You had two thin pieces of wood and you were smoothing them down with a knife. It didn't look particularly interesting, but when I asked you what you were doing, you just said, "Wait and see, Hally. Wait . . . and see" . . . in that secret sort of way of yours, so I knew there was a surprise coming. You teased me, you bugger, by being deliberately slow and not answering my questions!

(SAM *laughs.*)

And whistling while you worked away! God, it was infuriating! I could have brained you! It was only when you tied them together in a cross and put that down on the brown paper that I realized what you were doing. "Sam is making a kite?" And when I asked you and you said "Yes" . . . ! (*Shaking his head with disbelief.*) The sheer audacity of it took my breath away. I mean, seriously, what the hell does a black man know about flying a kite? I'll be honest with you, Sam, I had no hopes for it. If you think I was excited and happy, you got another guess coming. In fact, I was shit-scared that we were going to make fools of ourselves. When we left the boarding house to go up onto the hill, I was praying quietly that there wouldn't be any other kids around to laugh at us.

SAM: (*Enjoying the memory as much as* HALLY) Ja, I could see that.

HALLY: I made it obvious, did I?

SAM: Ja. You refused to carry it.

HALLY: Do you blame me? Can you remember what the poor thing looked like? Tomato-box wood and brown paper! Flour and water for glue! Two of my mother's old stockings for a tail, and then all those bits and pieces of string you made me tie together so that we could fly it! Hell, no, that was now only asking for a miracle to happen.

SAM: Then the big argument when I told you to hold the string and run with it when I let go.

HALLY: I was prepared to run, all right, but straight back to the boarding house.

SAM: (*Knowing what's coming*) So what happened?

HALLY: Come on, Sam, you remember as well as I do.

SAM: I want to hear it from you.

(HALLY *pauses. He wants to be as accurate as possible.*)

HALLY: You went a little distance from me down the hill, you held it up ready to let it go. . . . "This is it," I thought. "Like everything else in my life, here comes another fiasco." Then you shouted, "Go, Hally!" and I started to run. (*Another pause.*) I don't know how to describe it, Sam. Ja! The miracle happened! I was running, waiting for it to crash to the ground, but instead suddenly there was something alive behind me at the end of the string, tugging at it as if it wanted to be free. I looked back . . . (*Shakes his head.*) . . . I still can't believe my eyes. It was flying! Looping around and trying to climb even higher into the sky. You shouted to me to let it have more string. I did, until there was none left and I was just holding that piece of wood we had tied it to. You came up and joined me. You were laughing.

SAM: So were you. And shouting, "It works, Sam! We've done it!"

HALLY: And we had! I was so proud of us! It was the most splendid thing I had ever seen. I wished there were hundreds of kids around to watch us. The part that scared me, though, was when you showed me how to make it dive down to the ground and then just when it was on the point of crashing, swoop up again!

SAM: You didn't want to try yourself.

HALLY: Of course not! I would have been suicidal if anything had happened to it. Watching you do it made me nervous enough. I was quite happy just to see it up there with its tail fluttering behind it. You left me after that, didn't you? You explained how to get it down, we tied it to the bench so that I could sit and watch it, and you went away. I wanted you to stay, you know. I was a little scared of having to look after it by myself.

SAM: (*Quietly*) I had work to do, Hally.

HALLY: It was sort of sad bringing it down, Sam. And it looked sad again when it was lying there on the ground. Like something that had lost its soul. Just tomato-box wood, brown paper and two of my mother's old stockings! But, hell, I'll never forget that first moment when I saw it up there. I had a stiff neck the next day from looking up so much.

(SAM *laughs.* HALLY *turns to him with a question he never thought of asking before.*)

Why did you make that kite, Sam?

SAM: (*Evenly*) I can't remember.

HALLY: Truly?

SAM: Too long ago, Hally.

HALLY: Ja, I suppose it was. It's time for another one, you know.

SAM: Why do you say that?

HALLY: Because it feels like that. Wouldn't be a good day to fly it, though.

SAM: No. You can't fly kites on rainy days.

HALLY: (*He studies* SAM. *Their memories have made him conscious of the man's presence in his life.*)

How old are you, Sam?

SAM: Two score and five.

HALLY: Strange, isn't it?

SAM: What?

HALLY: Me and you.

SAM: What's strange about it?

HALLY: Little white boy in short trousers and a black man old enough to be his father flying a kite. It's not every day you see that.

SAM: But why strange? Because the one is white and the other black?

HALLY: I don't know. Would have been just as strange, I suppose, if it had been me and my Dad . . . cripple man and a little boy! Nope! There's no chance of me flying a kite without it being strange. (*Simple statement of fact—no self-pity.*) There's a nice little short story there. "The Kite-Flyers." But we'd have to find a twist in the ending.

SAM: Twist?

HALLY: Yes. Something unexpected. The way it ended with us was too straightforward . . . me on the bench and you going back to work. There's no drama in that.

WILLIE: And me?

HALLY: You?

WILLIE: Yes me.

HALLY: You want to get into the story as well, do you? I got it! Change the title: "Afternoons in Sam's Room" . . . expand it and tell all the stories. It's on its way to being a novel. Our days in the old Jubilee. Sad in a way that they're over. I almost wish we were still in that little room.

SAM: We're still together.

HALLY: That's true. It's just that life felt the right size in there . . . not too big and not too small. Wasn't so hard to work up a bit of courage. It's got so bloody complicated since then.

(*The telephone rings.* SAM *answers it.*)

SAM: St. George's Park Tea Room . . . Hello, Madam . . . Yes, Madam, he's here. . . . Hally, it's your mother.

HALLY: Where is she phoning from?

SAM: Sounds like the hospital. It's a public telephone.

HALLY: (*Relieved*) You see! I told you. (*The telephone.*) Hello, Mom . . . Yes . . . Yes no fine. Everything's under control here. How's things with poor old Dad? . . . Has he had a bad turn? . . . What? . . . Oh, God! . . . Yes, Sam told me, but I was sure he'd made a mistake. But what's this all about, Mom? He didn't look at all good last night. How can he get better so quickly? . . . Then very obviously you must say no. Be firm with him. You're the boss. . . . You know what it's going to be like if he comes home. . . . Well then, don't blame me when I fail my exams at the end of the year. . . . Yes! How am I expected to be fresh for school when I spend half the night massaging his gammy leg? . . . So am I! . . . So tell him a white lie. Say Dr. Colley wants more X-rays of his stump. Or bribe him. We'll sneak in double tots of brandy in future. . . . What? . . . Order him to get back into bed at once! If he's going to behave like a child, treat him like one. . . . All right, Mom! I was just trying to . . . I'm sorry. . . . I said I'm sorry. . . . Quick, give me your number. I'll phone you back. (*He hangs up and waits a few seconds.*) Here we go again! (*He dials.*) I'm sorry, Mom. . . . Okay. . . . But now listen to me carefully. All it needs is for you to put your foot down. Don't take no for an answer. . . . Did you hear me? And whatever you do, don't discuss it with him. . . . Because I'm frightened you'll give in to him. . . . Yes, Sam gave me lunch. . . . I ate all of it! . . . No, Mom not a soul. It's still raining here. . . . Right, I'll tell them. I'll just do some homework and then lock up. . . . But remember now, Mom. Don't listen to anything he says. And phone me back and let me know what happens. . . . Okay. Bye, Mom. (*He hangs up. The men are staring at him.*) My Mom says that when you're finished with the floors you must do the windows. (*Pause.*) Don't misunderstand me, chaps. All I want is for him to get better. And if he was, I'd be the first person to say: "Bring him home." But he's not, and we can't give him the medical care and attention he needs at home. That's what hospitals are there for. (*Brusquely.*) So don't just stand there! Get on with it!

(*Sam clears Hally's table.*)

You heard right. My Dad wants to go home.

SAM: Is he better?

HALLY: (*Sharply*) No! How the hell can he be better when last night he was groaning with pain? This is not an age of miracles!

SAM: Then he should stay in hospital.

HALLY: (*Seething with irritation and frustration*) Tell me something I don't know, Sam. What the hell do you think I was saying to my Mom? All I can say is fuck-it-all.

SAM: I'm sure he'll listen to your Mom.

HALLY: You don't know what she's up against. He's already packed his shaving kit and pajamas and is sitting on his bed with his crutches, dressed and ready to go. I know him when he gets in that mood. If she tries to reason with him, we've had it. She's no match for him when it comes to a battle of words. He'll tie her up in knots. (*Trying to hide his true feelings.*)

SAM: I suppose it gets lonely for him in there.

HALLY: With all the patients and nurses around? Regular visits from the Salvation Army? Balls! It's ten times worse for him at home. I'm at school and my mother is here in the business all day.

SAM: He's at least got you at night.

HALLY: (*Before he can stop himself*) And we've got him! Please! I don't want to talk about it anymore. (*Unpacks his school case, slamming down books on the table.*) Life is just a plain bloody mess, that's all. And people are fools.

SAM: Come on, Hally.

HALLY: Yes, they are! They bloody well deserve what they get.

SAM: Then don't complain.

HALLY: Don't try to be clever, Sam. It doesn't suit you. Anybody who thinks there's nothing wrong with this world needs to need his head examined. Just when things are going along all right, without fail someone or something will come along and spoil everything. Somebody should write that down as a fundamental law of the Universe. The principle of perpetual disappointment. If there is a God who created this world, he should scrap it and try again.

SAM: All right, Hally, all right. What you got for homework?

HALLY: Bullshit, as usual. (*Opens an exercise book and reads.*) "Write five hundred words describing an annual event of cultural or historical significance."

SAM: That should be easy enough for you.

HALLY: And also plain bloody boring. You know what he wants, don't you? One of their useless old ceremonies. The commemoration of the landing of the 1820 Settlers, or if it's going to be culture, Carols by Candlelight every Christmas.

SAM: It's an impressive sight. Make a good description, Hally. All those candles glowing in the dark and the people singing hymns.

HALLY: And it's called religious hysteria. (*Intense irritation.*) Please, Sam! Just leave me alone and let me get on with it. I'm not in the mood for games this afternoon. And remember my Mom's orders . . . you're to help Willie with the windows. Come on now, I don't want any more nonsense in here.

SAM: Okay, Hally, okay.

(HALLY *settles down to his homework; determined preparations . . . pen, ruler, exercise book, dictionary, another cake . . . all of which will lead to nothing.*)

(SAM *waltzes over to* WILLIE *and starts to replace tables and chairs. He practices a ballroom step while doing so.* WILLIE *watches. When* SAM *is finished,* WILLIE *tries.*)

Good! But just a little bit quicker on the turn and only move in to her after she's crossed over. What about this one?

(*Another step. When* SAM *is finished,* WILLIE *again has a go.*)

Much better. See what happens when you just relax and enjoy yourself? Remember that in two weeks' time and you'll be all right.

WILLIE: But I haven't got partner, Boet Sam.

SAM: Maybe Hilda will turn up tonight.

WILLIE: No, Boet Sam. (*Reluctantly.*) I gave her a good hiding.

SAM: You mean a bad one.

WILLIE: Good bad one.

SAM: Then you mustn't complain either. Now you pay the price for losing your temper.

WILLIE: I also pay two pounds ten shilling entrance fee.

SAM: They'll refund you if you withdraw now.

WILLIE: (Appalled) You mean, don't dance?

SAM: Yes.

WILLIE: No! I wait too long and I practice too hard. If I find me new partner, you think I can be ready in two weeks? I ask Madam for my leave now and we practice every day.

SAM: Quickstep nonstop for two weeks. World record, Willie, but you'll be mad at the end.

WILLIE: No jokes, Boet Sam.

SAM: I'm not joking.

WILLIE: So then what?

SAM: Find Hilda. Say you're sorry and promise you won't beat her again.

WILLIE: No.

SAM: Then withdraw. Try again next year.

WILLIE: No.

SAM: Then I give up.

WILLIE: Haaikona, Boet Sam, you can't.

SAM: What do you mean, I can't? I'm telling you: I give up.

WILLIE: (Adamant) No! (Accusingly.) It was you who start me ballroom dancing.

SAM: So?

WILLIE: Before that I use to be happy. And is you and Miriam who bring me to Hilda and say here's partner for you.

SAM: What are you saying, Willie?

WILLIE: You!

SAM: But me what? To blame?

WILLIE: Yes.

SAM: Willie . . . ? (Bursts into laughter.)

WILLIE: And now all you do is make jokes at me. You wait. When Miriam leaves you is my turn to laugh. Ha! Ha! Ha!

SAM: (He can't take WILLIE seriously any longer) She can leave you tonight! I know what to do. (Bowing before an imaginary partner.) May I have the pleasure? (He dances and sings.)

"Just a fellow with his pillow . . .
Dancin' like a willow . . .
In an autumn breeze. . . ."

WILLIE: There you go again! (SAM goes on dancing and singing.) Boet Sam!

SAM: There's the answer to your problem! Judges' announcement in two weeks' time: "Ladies and gentlemen, the winner in the open section . . . Mr. Willie Malopo and his pillow!"

(This is too much for a now really angry WILLIE. He goes for SAM, but the latter is too quick for him and puts HALLY's table between the two of them.)

HALLY: (Exploding) For Christ's sake, you two!

WILLIE: (Still trying to get at SAM) I donner you, Sam! Struesgod!

SAM: (Still laughing) Sorry, Willie . . . Sorry. . . .

HALLY: Sam! Willie! (Grabs his ruler and gives WILLIE a vicious whack on the bum.) How the hell am I supposed to concentrate with the two of you behaving like bloody children!

WILLIE: Hit him too!

HALLY: Shut up, Willie.

WILLIE: He started jokes again.

HALLY: Get back to your work. You too, Sam. (His ruler.) Do you want another one, Willie?

(SAM and WILLIE return to their work. HALLY uses the opportunity to escape from his unsuccessful attempt at homework. He struts around like a little despot, ruler in hand, giving vent to his anger and frustration.)

Suppose a customer had walked in then? Or the Park Superintendent. And seen the two of you behaving like a pair of hooligans. That would have been the end of my mother's license, you know. And your jobs? Well, this is the end of it. From now on there will be no more of your ballroom nonsense in here. This is a business establishment, not a bloody New Brighton dancing school. I've been far too lenient with the two of you. (Behind the counter for a green cool drink and a dollop of ice cream. He keeps up his tirade as he prepares it.) But what really makes me bitter is that I allow you chaps a little freedom in here when business is bad and what do you do with it? The foxtrot! Specially you, Sam. There's more to life than trotting around a dance floor and I thought at least you knew it.

SAM: It's a harmless pleasure, Hally. It doesn't hurt anybody.

HALLY: It's also a rather simple one, you know.

SAM: You reckon so? Have you ever tried?

HALLY: Of course not.

SAM: Why don't you? Now.

HALLY: What do you mean? Me dance?

SAM: Yes. I'll show you a simple step—the waltz—then you try it.

HALLY: What will that prove?

SAM: That it might not be as easy as you think.

HALLY: I didn't say it was easy. I said it was simple—like in simple-minded, meaning mentally retarded. You can't exactly say it challenges the intellect.

SAM: It does other things.

HALLY: Such as?

SAM: Make people happy.

HALLY: (The glass in his hand) So do American cream sodas with ice cream. For God's sake, Sam, you're not asking me to take ballroom dancing serious, are you?

SAM: Yes.

HALLY: (Sigh of defeat) Oh, well, so much for trying to give you a decent education. I've obviously achieved nothing.

SAM: You still haven't told me what's wrong with admiring something that's beautiful and then trying to do it yourself.

HALLY: Nothing. But we happen to be talking about a foxtrot, not a thing of beauty.

SAM: But that is just what I'm saying. If you were to see two champions doing, two masters of the art . . . !

HALLY: Oh God, I give up. So now it's also art!

SAM: Ja.

HALLY: There's a limit, Sam. Don't confuse art and entertainment.

SAM: So then what is art?

HALLY: You want a definition?

SAM: Ja.

HALLY: (*He realizes he has got to be careful. He gives the matter a lot of thought before answering.*) Philosophers have been trying to do that for centuries. What is Art? What is Life? But basically I suppose it's . . . the giving of meaning to matter.

SAM: Nothing to do with beautiful?

HALLY: It goes beyond that. It's the giving of form to the formless.

SAM: Ja, well, maybe it's not art, then. But I still say it's beautiful.

HALLY: I'm sure the word you mean to use is entertaining.

SAM: (*Adamant*) No. Beautiful. And if you want proof come along to the Centenary Hall in New Brighton in two weeks' time.

(*The mention of the Centenary Hall draws* WILLIE *over to them.*)

HALLY: What for? I've seen the two of you prancing around in here often enough.

SAM: (*He laughs*) This isn't the real thing, Hally. We're just playing around in here.

HALLY: So? I can use my imagination.

SAM: And what do you get?

HALLY: A lot of people dancing around and having a so-called good time.

SAM: That all?

HALLY: Well, basically, it is that, surely.

SAM: No, it isn't. Your imagination hasn't helped you at all. There's a lot more to it than that. We're getting ready for the championships, Hally, not just another dance. There's going to be a lot of people, all right, and they're going to have a good time, but they'll only be spectators, sitting around and watching. It's just the competitors out there on the dance floor. Party decorations and fancy lights all around the walls! The ladies in beautiful evening dresses!

HALLY: My mother's got one of those, Sam, and, quite frankly, it's an embarrassment every time she wears it.

SAM: (*Undeterred*) Your imagination left out the excitement.

(HALLY *scoffs.*)

Oh, yes. The finalists are not going to be out there

just to have a good time. One of those couples will be the 1950 Eastern Province Champions. And your imagination left out the music.

WILLIE: Mr. Elijah Gladman Guzana and his Orchestral Jazzonions.

SAM: The sound of the big band, Hally. Trombone, trumpet, tenor and alto sax. And then, finally, your imagination also left out the climax of the evening when the dancing is finished, the judges have stopped whispering among themselves and the Master of Ceremonies collects their scorecards and goes up onto the stage to announce the winners.

HALLY: All right. So you make it sound like a bit of a do. It's an occasion. Satisfied?

SAM: (*Victory*) So you admit that!

HALLY: Emotionally yes, intellectually no.

SAM: Well, I don't know what you mean by that, all I'm telling you is that it is going to be *the* event of the year in New Brighton. It's been sold out for two weeks already. There's only standing room left. We've got competitors coming from Kingwilliamstown, East London, Port Alfred.

(HALLY *starts pacing thoughtfully.*)

HALLY: Tell me a bit more.

SAM: I thought you weren't interested . . . intellectually.

HALLY: (*Mysteriously*) I've got my reasons.

SAM: What do you want to know?

HALLY: It takes place every year?

SAM: Yes. But only every third year in New Brighton. It's East London's turn to have the championships next year.

HALLY: Which, I suppose, makes it an even more significant event.

SAM: Ah ha! We're getting somewhere. Our "occasion" is now a "significant event."

HALLY: I wonder.

SAM: What?

HALLY: I wonder if I would get away with it.

SAM: But what?

HALLY: (*To the table and his exercise book*) "Write five hundred words describing an annual event of cultural or historical significance." Would I be stretching poetic license a little too far if I called your ballroom championships a cultural event?

SAM: You mean . . . ?

HALLY: You think we could get five hundred words out of it, Sam?

SAM: Victor Sylvester has written a whole book on ballroom dancing.

WILLIE: You going to write about it, Master Hally?

HALLY: Yes, gentlemen, that is precisely what I am considering doing. Old Doc Bromely—he's my English teacher—is going to argue with me, of course. He doesn't like natives. But I'll point out to him that in strict anthropological terms the culture of a primitive black society includes its dancing and singing. To put my thesis in a nutshell: The war-dance has been replaced by the waltz. But it still amounts to the same thing: the release of primitive emotions through movement. Shall we give it a go?

SAM: I'm ready.

WILLIE: Me also.

HALLY: Ha! This will teach the old bugger a lesson. (*Decision taken.*) Right. Let's get ourselves organized. (*This means another cake on the table. He sits.*) I think you've given me enough general atmosphere, Sam, but to build the tension and suspense I need facts. (*Pencil poised.*)

WILLIE: Give him facts, Boet Sam.

HALLY: What you called the climax . . . how many finalists?

SAM: Six couples.

HALLY: (*Making notes*) Go on. Give me the picture.

SAM: Spectators seated right around the hall. (WILLIE *becomes a spectator.*)

HALLY: . . . and it's a full house.

SAM: At one end, on the stage, Gladman and his Orchestral Jazzonions. At the other end is a long table with the three judges. The six finalists go onto the dance floor and take up their positions. When they are ready and the spectators have settled down, the Master of Ceremonies goes to the microphone. To start with, he makes some jokes to get people laughing. . . .

HALLY: Good touch. (*As he writes.*) ". . . creating a relaxed atmosphere which will change to one of tension and drama as the climax is approached."

SAM: (*Onto a chair to act out the M.C.*) "Ladies and gentlemen, we come now to the great moment you have all been waiting for this evening. . . . The finals of the 1950 Eastern Province Open Ballroom Dancing Championships. But first let me introduce the finalists! Mr. and Mrs. Welcome Tchabalala from Kingwilliamstown . . ."

WILLIE: (*He applauds after every name*) Is when the people clap their hands and whistle and make a lot of noise, Master Hally.

SAM: "Mr. Mulligan Njikelane and Miss Nomhle Nkonyeni of Grahamstown; Mr. and Mrs. Norman Nchinga from Port Alfred; Mr. Fats Bokolane and Miss Dina Plaatjies from East London; Mr. Sipho Dugu and Mrs. Mable Magada from Peddie; and from New Brighton our very own Mr. Willie Malopo and Miss Hilda Samuels."

(WILLIE *can't believe his ears. He abandons his role as spectator and scrambles into position as a finalist.*)

WILLIE: Relaxed and ready to romance!

SAM: The applause dies down. When everybody is silent, Gladman lifts up his sax, nods at the Orchestral Jazzonions. . . .

WILLIE: Play the jukebox please, Boet Sam!

SAM: I also only got bus fare, Willie.

HALLY: Hold it, everybody. (*Heads for the cash register behind the counter.*) How much is in the till, Sam?

SAM: Three shillings. Hally . . . Your Mom counted it before she left.

(HALLY *hesitates.*)

HALLY: Sorry, Willie. You know how she carried on the last time I did it. We'll just have to pool our combined imaginations and hope for the best. (*Returns to the table.*) Back to work. How are the points scored, Sam?

SAM: Maximum of ten points each for individual style, deportment, rhythm, and general appearance.

WILLIE: Must I start?

HALLY: Hold it for a second, Willie. And penalties?

SAM: For what?

HALLY: For doing something wrong. Say you stumble or bump into somebody . . . do they take off any points?

SAM: (*Aghast*) Hally . . . !

HALLY: When you're dancing. If you and your partner collide into another couple.

(HALLY *can get no further.* SAM *has collapsed with laughter. He explains to* WILLIE.)

SAM: If me and Miriam bump into you and Hilda. . . .

(WILLIE *joins him in another good laugh.*)

Hally, Hally . . . !

HALLY: (*Perplexed*) Why? What did I say?

SAM: There's no collisions out there, Hally. Nobody trips or stumbles or bumps into anybody else. That's what that moment is all about. To be one of those finalists on that dance floor is like . . . like being in a dream about a world in which accidents don't happen.

HALLY: (*Genuinely moved by* SAM's *image*) Jesus, Sam! That's beautiful!

WILLIE: (*Can endure waiting no longer*) I'm starting!

(WILLIE *dances while* SAM *talks.*)

SAM: Of course it is. That's what I've been trying to say to you all afternoon. And it's beautiful because that is what we want life to be like. But instead, like you said, Hally, we're bumping into each other all the time. Look at the three of us this afternoon: I've bumped into Willie, the two of us have bumped into you, you've bumped into your mother, she bumping into your Dad. . . . None of us knows the steps and there's no music playing. And it doesn't stop with us. The whole world is doing it all the time. Open a newspaper and what do you read? America has bumped into Russia, England is bumping into India, rich man bumps into poor man. Those are big collisions, Hally. They make for a lot of bruises. People get hurt in all that bumping, and we're sick and tired of it now. It's been going on for too long. Are we never going to get it right? . . . Learn to dance life like champions instead of always being just a bunch of beginners at it?

HALLY: (*Deep and sincere admiration of the man*) You've got a vision, Sam!

SAM: Not just me. What I'm saying to you is that everybody's got it. That's why there's only standing room left for the Centenary Hall in two weeks' time. For as long as the music lasts, we are going to see six couples get it right, the way we want life to be.

HALLY: But is that the best we can do, Sam . . . watch six finalists dreaming about the way it should be?

SAM: I don't know. But it starts with that. Without the dream we won't know what we're going for. And anyway I reckon there are a few people who have got past just dreaming about it and are trying for something real. Remember that thing we read once in the paper about the Mahatma Gandhi? Going without food to stop those riots in India?

HALLY: You're right. He certainly was trying to teach people to get the steps right.

SAM: And the Pope.

HALLY: Yes, he's another one. Our old General Smuts as well, you know. He's also out there dancing. You know, Sam, when you come to think of it, that's what the United Nations boils down to . . . a dancing school for politicians!

SAM: And let's hope they learn.

HALLY: (*A little surge of hope*) You're right. We mustn't despair. Maybe there's some hope for mankind after all. Keep it up, Willie. (*Back to his table with determination.*) This is a lot bigger than I thought. So what have we got? Yes, our title: "A World Without Collisions."

SAM: That sounds good! "A World Without Collisions."

HALLY: Subtitle: "Global Politics on the Dance Floor." No. A bit too heavy, hey? What about "Ballroom Dancing as a Political Vision"?

(*The telephone rings.* SAM *answers it.*)

SAM: St. George's Park Tea Room . . . Yes, Madam . . . Hally, it's your Mom.

HALLY: (*Back to reality*) Oh, God, yes! I'd forgotten all about that. Shit! Remember my words, Sam? Just when you're enjoying yourself, someone or something will come along and wreck everything.

SAM: You haven't heard what she's got to say yet.

HALLY: Public telephone?

SAM: No.

HALLY: Does she sound happy or unhappy?

SAM: I couldn't tell. (*Pause.*) She's waiting, Hally.

HALLY: (*To the telephone*) Hello, Mom . . . No, everything is okay here. Just doing my homework. . . . What's your news? . . . You've what? . . . (*Pause. He takes the receiver away from his ear for a few seconds. In the course of* HALLY's *telephone conversation,* SAM *and* WILLIE *discreetly position the stacked tables and chairs.* HALLY *places the receiver back to his ear.*) Yes, I'm still here. Oh, well, I give up now. Why did you do it, Mom? . . . Well, I just hope you know what you've let us in

for. . . . (*Loudly.*) I said I hope you know what you've let us in for! It's the end of the peace and quiet we've been having. (*Softly.*) Where is he? (*Normal voice.*) He can't hear us from in there. But for God's sake, Mom, what happened? I told you to be firm with him. . . . Then you and the nurses should have held him down, taken his crutches away. . . . I know only too well he's my father! . . . I'm not being disrespectful, but I'm sick and tired of emptying stinking chamber pots full of phlegm and piss. . . . Yes, I do! When you're not there, he asks *me* to do it. . . . If you really want to know the truth, that's why I've got no appetite for my food. . . . Yes! There's a lot of things you don't know about. For your information, I still haven't got that science textbook I need. And you know why? He borrowed the money you gave me for it. . . . Because I didn't want to start another fight between you two. . . . He says that every time. . . . All right, Mom! (*Viciously.*) Then just remember to start hiding your bag away again, because he'll be at your purse before long for money for booze. And when he's well enough to come down here, you better keep an eye on the till as well, because that is also going to develop a leak. . . . Then don't complain to me when he starts his old tricks. . . . Yes, you do. I get it from you on one side and from him on the other, and it makes life hell for me. I'm not going to be the peacemaker anymore. I'm warning you now: when the two of you start fighting again, I'm leaving home. . . . Mom, if you start crying, I'm going to put down the receiver. . . . Okay. . . . (*Lowering his voice to a vicious whisper.*) Okay, Mom. I heard you. (*Desperate.*) No. . . . Because I don't want to. I'll see him when I get home! Mom! . . . (*Pause. When he speaks again, his tone changes completely. It is not simply pretense. We sense a genuine emotional conflict.*) Welcome home, chum! . . . What's that? . . . Don't be silly, Dad. You being home is just about the best news in the world. . . . I bet you are. Bloody depressing there with everybody going on about their ailments, hey! . . . How you feeling? . . . Good. . . . Here as well, pal. Coming down cats and dogs. . . . That's right. Just the day for a kip and a toss in your old Uncle Ned. . . . Everything's just hunky-dory on my side, Dad. . . . Well, to start with, there's a nice pile of comics for you on the counter. . . . Yes, old Kemple brought them in. *Batman and Robin, Submariner* . . . just your cup of tea. . . . I will. . . . Yes, we'll spin a few yarns tonight. . . . Okay, chum, see you in a little while. . . . No, I promise. I'll come straight home. . . . (*Pause—his mother comes back on the phone.*) Mom? Okay. I'll lock up now. . . . What? . . . Oh, the brandy . . . Yes, I'll remember! . . . I'll put it in my suitcase now, for God's sake. I know well enough what will happen if he doesn't get it. . . . (*Places a bottle of brandy on the counter.*) I *was* kind to him, Mom. I didn't say anything nasty! . . . All right. Bye. (*End of telephone conversation. A desolate* HALLY *doesn't move. A strained silence.*)

SAM: (*Quietly*) That sounded like a bad bump, Hally.

HALLY: (*Having a hard time controlling his emotions. He speaks carefully.*) Mind your own business, Sam.

SAM: Sorry, I wasn't trying to interfere. Shall we carry on? Hally? (*He indicates the exercise book. No response from* HALLY.)

WILLIE: (*Also trying*) Tell him about when they give out the cups, Boet Sam.

SAM: Ja! That's another big moment. The presentation of the cups after the winners have been announced. You've got to put that in.

(*Still no response from* HALLY.)

WILLIE: A big silver one, Master Hally, called floating trophy for the champions.

SAM: We always invite some big-shot personality to hand them over. Guest of honor this year is going to be His Holiness Bishop Jabulani of the All African Free Zionist Church.

(HALLY *gets up abruptly, goes to his table, and tears up the page he was writing on.*)

HALLY: So much for a bloody world without collisions.

SAM: Too bad. It was on its way to being a good composition.

HALLY: Let's stop bullshitting ourselves, Sam.

SAM: Have we been doing that?

HALLY: Yes! That's what all our talk about a decent world has been . . . just so much bullshit.

SAM: We did say it was still only a dream.

HALLY: And a bloody useless one at that. Life's a fuckup and it's never going to change.

SAM: Ja, maybe that's true.

HALLY: There's no maybe about it. It's a blunt and brutal fact. All we've done this afternoon is waste our time.

SAM: Not if we'd got your homework done.

HALLY: I don't give a shit about my homework, so, for Christ's sake, just shut up about it. (*Slamming books viciously into his school case.*) Hurry up now and finish your work. I want to lock up and get out of here. (*Pause.*) And then go where? Home-sweet-fucking-home. Jesus, I hate that word.

(HALLY *goes to the counter to put the brandy bottle and comics in his school case. After a moment's hesitation, he smashes the bottle of brandy. He abandons all further attempts to hide his feelings.* SAM *and* WILLIE *work away as unobtrusively as possible.*)

Do you want to know what is really wrong with your lovely little dream, Sam? It's not just that we are all bad dancers. That does happen to be perfectly true, but there's more to it than just that. You left out the cripples.

SAM: Hally!

HALLY: (*Now totally reckless*) Ja! Can't leave them out, Sam. That's why we always end up on our backsides on the dance floor. They're also out there dancing . . . like a bunch of broken spiders trying to do the quickstep! (*An ugly attempt at laughter.*) When you come to think of it, it's a bloody comical sight. I mean, it's bad enough on two legs . . . but one and a pair of crutches! Hell, no, Sam. That's guaranteed to turn that dance floor into a shambles. Why you shaking your head? Picture it, man. For once this afternoon let's use our imaginations sensibly.

SAM: Be careful, Hally.

HALLY: Of what? The truth? I seem to be the only one around here who is prepared to face it. We've had the pretty dream, it's time now to wake up and have a good long look at the way things really are. Nobody knows the steps, there's no music, the cripples are also out there tripping up everybody and trying to get into the act, and it's all called the All-Comers-How-to-Make-a-Fuckup-of-Life Championships. (*Another ugly laugh.*) Hang on, Sam! The best bit is still coming. Do you know what the winner's trophy is? A beautiful big chamber pot with roses on the side, and it's full to the brim with piss. And guess who I think is going to be this year's winner.

SAM: (*Almost shouting*) Stop now!

HALLY: (*Suddenly appalled by how far he has gone*) Why?

SAM: Hally? It's your father you're talking about.

HALLY: So?

SAM: Do you know what you've been saying?

(HALLY *can't answer. He is rigid with shame.* SAM *speaks to him sternly.*)

No, Hally, you mustn't do it. Take back those words and ask for forgiveness! It's a terrible sin for a son to mock his father with jokes like that. You'll be punished if you carry on. Your father is your father, even if he is a . . . cripple man.

WILLIE: Yes, Master Hally. Is true what Sam say.

SAM: I understand how you are feeling, Hally, but even so. . . .

HALLY: No, you don't!

SAM: I think I do.

HALLY: And I'm telling you you don't. Nobody does. (*Speaking carefully as his shame turns to rage at* SAM.) It's your turn to be careful, Sam. Very careful! You're treading on dangerous ground. Leave me and my father alone.

SAM: I'm not the one who's been saying things about him.

HALLY: What goes on between me and my Dad is none of your business!

SAM: Then don't tell me about it. If that's all you've got to say about him, I don't want to hear.

(*For a moment* HALLY *is at loss for a response.*)

HALLY: Just get on with your bloody work and shut up.

SAM: Swearing at me won't help you.

HALLY: Yes, it does! Mind your own fucking business and shut up!

SAM: Okay. If that's the way you want it, I'll stop trying.

(He turns away. This infuriates HALLY *even more.)*

HALLY: Good. Because what you've been trying to do is meddle in something you know nothing about. All that concerns you in here, Sam, is to try and do what you get paid for—keep the place clean and serve the customers. In plain words, just get on with your job. My mother is right. She's always warning me about allowing you to get too familiar. Well, this time you've gone too far. It's going to stop right now.

(No response from SAM.*)*

You're only a servant in here, and don't forget it.

(Still no response. HALLY *is trying hard to get one.)*

And as far as my father is concerned, all you need to remember is that he is your boss.

SAM: *(Needled at last)* No, he isn't. I get paid by your mother.

HALLY: Don't argue with me, Sam!

SAM: Then don't say he's my boss.

HALLY: He's a white man and that's good enough for you.

SAM: I'll try to forget you said that.

HALLY: Don't! Because you won't be doing me a favor if you do. I'm telling you to remember it.

(A pause. SAM *pulls himself together and makes one last effort.)*

SAM: Hally, Hally . . . ! Come on now. Let's stop before it's too late. You're right. We *are* on dangerous ground. If we're not careful, somebody is going to get hurt.

HALLY: It won't be me.

SAM: Don't be so sure.

HALLY: I don't know what you're talking about, Sam.

SAM: Yes, you do.

HALLY: *(Furious)* Jesus, I wish you would stop trying to tell me what I do and what I don't know.

*(*SAM *gives up. He turns to* WILLIE.*)*

SAM: Let's finish up.

HALLY: Don't turn your back on me! I haven't finished talking.

(He grabs SAM *by the arm and tries to make him turn around.* SAM *reacts with a flash of anger.)*

SAM: Don't do that, Hally! *(Facing the boy.)* All right, I'm listening. Well? What do you want to say to me?

HALLY: *(Pause as* HALLY *looks for something to say)* To begin with, why don't you also start calling me Master Harold, like Willie.

SAM: Do you mean that?

HALLY: Why the hell do you think I said it?

SAM: And if I don't?

HALLY: You might just lose your job.

SAM: *(Quietly and very carefully)* If you make me say it once, I'll never call you anything else again.

HALLY: So? *(The boy confronts the man.)* Is that meant to be a threat?

SAM: Just telling you what will happen if you make me do that. You must decide what it means to you.

HALLY: Well, I have. It's good news. Because that is exactly what Master Harold wants from now on. Think of it as a little lesson in respect, Sam, that's long overdue, and I hope you remember it as well as you do your geography. I can tell you now that somebody who will be glad to hear I've finally given it to you will be my Dad. Yes! He agrees with my Mom. He's always going on about it as well. "You must teach the boys to show you more respect, my son."

SAM: So now you can stop complaining about going home. Everybody is going to be happy tonight.

HALLY: That's perfectly correct. You see, you mustn't get the wrong idea about me and my Dad, Sam. We also have our good times together. Some bloody good laughs. He's got a marvelous sense of humor. Want to know what our favorite joke is? He gives out a big groan, you see, and says: "It's not fair, is it, Hally?" Then I have to ask: "What, chum?" And then he says: "A nigger's arse" . . . and we both have a good laugh.

(The men stare at him with disbelief.)

What's the matter, Willie? Don't you catch the joke? You always were a bit slow on the uptake. It's what is called a pun. You see, fair means both light in color and to be just and decent. *(He turns to* SAM.*)* I thought *you* would catch it, Sam.

SAM: Oh ja, I catch it all right.

HALLY: But it doesn't appeal to your sense of humor.

SAM: Do you really laugh?

HALLY: Of course.

SAM: To please him? Make him feel good?

HALLY: No, for heaven's sake! I laugh because I think it's a bloody good joke.

SAM: You're really trying hard to be ugly, aren't you? And why drag poor old Willie into it? He's done nothing to you except show you the respect you want so badly. That's also not being fair, you know . . . and *I* mean just or decent.

WILLIE: It's all right, Sam. Leave it now.

SAM: It's me you're after. You should just have said "Sam's arse" . . . because that's the one you're trying to kick. Anyway, how do you know it's not fair? You've never seen it. Do you want to? *(He drops his trousers and underpants and presents his backside for* HALLY's *inspection.)* Have a good look. A real Basuto arse . . . which is about as nigger as they can come.

Satisfied? (*Trousers up.*) Now you can make your Dad even happier when you go home tonight. Tell him I showed you my arse and he is quite right. It's not fair. And if it will give him an even better laugh next time, I'll also let *him* have a look. Come, Willie, let's finish up and go.

(SAM *and* WILLIE *start to tidy up the tea room.* HALLY *doesn't move. He waits for a moment when* SAM *passes him.*)

HALLY: (*Quietly*) Sam . . .

(SAM *stops and looks expectantly at the boy.* HALLY *spits in his face. A long and heartfelt groan from* WILLIE. *For a few seconds* SAM *doesn't move.*)

SAM: (*Taking out a handkerchief and wiping his face*) It's all right, Willie.

(*To* HALLY.)

Ja, well, you've done it . . . Master Harold. Yes, I'll start calling you that from now on. It won't be difficult anymore. You've hurt yourself, Master Harold. I saw it coming. I warned you, but you wouldn't listen. You've just hurt yourself *bad.* And you're a coward, Master Harold. The face you should be spitting in is your father's . . . but you used mine, because you think you're safe inside your fair skin . . . and this time I don't mean just or decent. (*Pause, then moving violently toward* HALLY.) Should I hit him, Willie?

WILLIE: (*Stopping* SAM) No, Boet Sam.

SAM: (*Violently*) Why not?

WILLIE: It won't help, Boet Sam.

SAM: I don't want to help! I want to hurt him.

WILLIE: You also hurt yourself.

SAM: And if he had done it to you, Willie?

WILLIE: Me? Spit at me like I was a dog? (*A thought that had not occurred to him before. He looks at* HALLY.) Ja. Then I want to hit him. I want to hit him hard!

(*A dangerous few seconds as the men stand staring at the boy.* WILLIE *turns away, shaking his head.*)

But maybe all I do is go cry at the back. He's little boy, Boet Sam. Little *white* boy. Long trousers now, but he's still little boy.

SAM: (*His violence ebbing away into defeat as quickly as it flooded*) You're right. So go on, then: groan again, Willie. You do it better than me. (*To* HALLY.) You don't know all of what you've just done . . . Master Harold. It's not just that you've made me feel dirtier than I've ever been in my life . . . I mean, how do I wash off yours and your father's filth? . . . I've also failed. A long time ago I promised myself I was going to try and do something, but you've just shown me . . . Master Harold . . . that I've failed. (*Pause.*) I've also got a memory of a little white boy when he was still wearing short trousers and a black man, but they're not flying a kite. It was the old Jubilee days, after dinner one night. I was in my room. You came in and just stood against the wall, looking down at the ground, and only after I'd asked you what you wanted, what was wrong, I don't know how many times, did you speak and even then so softly I almost didn't hear you. "Sam, please help me to go and fetch my Dad." Remember? He was dead drunk on the floor of the Central Hotel Bar. They'd phoned for your Mom, but you were the only one at home. And do you remember how we did it? You went in first by yourself to ask permission for me to go into the bar. Then I loaded him onto my back like a baby and carried him back to the boarding house with you following behind carrying his crutches. (*Shaking his head as he remembers.*) A crowded Main Street with all the people watching a little white boy following his drunk father on a nigger's back! I felt for that little boy . . . Master Harold. I felt for him. After that we still had to clean him up, remember? He'd messed in his trousers, so we had to clean him up and get him into bed.

HALLY: (*Great pain*) I love him, Sam.

SAM: I know you do. That's why I tried to stop you from saying these things about him. It would have been so simple if you could have just despised him for being a weak man. But he's your father. You love him and you're ashamed of him. You're ashamed of so much! . . . And now that's going to include yourself. That was the promise I made to myself: to try and stop that happening. (*Pause.*) After we got him to bed you came back with me to my room and sat in a corner and carried on just looking down at the ground. And for two days after that! You hadn't done anything wrong, but you went around as if you owed the world an apology for being alive. I didn't like seeing that! That's not the way a boy grows up to be a man! . . . But the one person who should have been teaching you what that means was the cause of your shame. If you really want to know, that's why I made you that kite. I wanted you to look up, be proud of something, of yourself . . . (*Bitter smile at the memory*) . . . and you certainly were that when I left you with it up there on the hill. Oh, ja . . . something else! . . . If you ever do write it as a short story, there *was* a twist in our ending. I couldn't sit down there and stay with you. It was a "Whites Only" bench. You were too young, too excited to notice then. But not anymore. If you're not careful . . . Master Harold . . . you're going to be sitting up there by yourself for a long time to come, and there won't be a kite in the sky. (SAM *has got nothing more to say. He exits into the kitchen, taking off his waiter's jacket.*)

WILLIE: Is bad. Is all bad in here now.

HALLY: (*Books into his school case, raincoat on*) Willie . . . (*It is difficult to speak.*) Will you lock up for me and look after the keys?

WILLIE: Okay.

(SAM *returns.* HALLY *goes behind the counter and collects the few coins in the cash register. As he starts to leave. . . .*)

SAM: Don't forget the comic books.

(HALLY *returns to the counter and puts them in his case. He starts to leave again.*)

SAM: (*To the retreating back of the boy*) Stop . . . Hally. . . .

(HALLY *stops, but doesn't turn to face him.*)

Hally . . . I've got no right to tell you what being a man means if I don't behave like one myself, and I'm not doing so well at that this afternoon. Should we try again, Hally?

HALLY: Try what?

SAM: Fly another kite, I suppose. It worked once, and this time I need it as much as you do.

HALLY: It's still raining, Sam. You can't fly kites on rainy days, remember.

SAM: So what do we do? Hope for better weather tomorrow?

HALLY: (*Helpless gesture*) I don't know. I don't know anything anymore.

SAM: You sure of that, Hally? Because it would be pretty hopeless if that was true. It would mean nothing has been learnt in here this afternoon, and there was a hell of a lot of teaching going on . . . one way or the other. But anyway, I don't believe you. I reckon there's one thing you know. You don't *have* to sit up there by yourself. You know what that bench means now, and you can leave it any time you choose. All you've got to do is stand up and walk away from it.

(HALLY *leaves.* WILLIE *goes up quietly to* SAM.)

WILLIE: Is okay, Boet Sam. You see. Is . . . (*He can't find any better words*) . . . is going to be okay tomorrow. (*Changing his tone.*) Hey, Boet Sam! (*He is trying hard.*) You right. I think about it and you right. Tonight I find Hilda and say sorry. And make promise I won't beat her no more. You hear me, Boet Sam?

SAM: I hear you, Willie.

WILLIE: And when we practice I relax and romance with her from beginning to end. Nonstop! You watch! Two weeks' time: "First prize for promising newcomers: Mr. Willie Malopo and Miss Hilda Samuels." (*Sudden impulse.*) To hell with it! I walk home. (*He goes to the jukebox, puts in a coin and selects a record. The machine comes to life in the gray twilight, blushing its way through a spectrum of soft, romantic colors.*) How did you say it, Boet Sam? Let's dream. (WILLIE *sways with the music and gestures for* SAM *to dance.*)

(*Sarah Vaughan sings.*)

> "*Little man you're crying,*
> *I know why you're blue,*
> *Someone took your kiddy car away;*
> *Better go to sleep now,*
> *Little man you've had a busy day.*" (*etc., etc.*)

You lead. I follow.

(*The men dance together.*)

> "*Johnny won your marbles,*
> *Tell you what we'll do;*
> *Dad will get you new ones right away;*
> *Better go to sleep now,*
> *Little man you've had a busy day.*"

Figure 1. Hally (Lonny Price) and Willie (Danny Glover) listen to Sam (Zakes Mokae) describing the dancing championships in the Yale Repertory Theatre production of *"Master Harold" . . . and the Boys,* directed by Athol Fugard, 1982. (Photograph: Martha Swope.)

Figure 2. Sam (Zakes Mokae) rebukes Hally (Lonny Price) for mocking his father, while Willie (Danny Glover) looks on in surprise, in the Yale Repertory Theatre production of *"Master Harold" . . . and the Boys,* directed by Athol Fugard, 1982. (Photograph: Martha Swope.)

Staging of *"Master Harold"* . . . and the Boys

REVIEW OF THE YALE REPERTORY THEATRE PRODUCTION, 1982, FRANK RICH

There may be two or three living playwrights in the world who can write as well as Athol Fugard, but I'm not sure that any of them has written a recent play that can match *"Master Harold"* . . . *and the Boys*. Mr. Fugard's drama—lyrical in design, shattering in impact—is likely to be an enduring part of the theater long after most of this Broadway season has turned to dust.

"Master Harold," which opened at the Lyceum last night following its March premiere at the Yale Repertory Theater, may even outlast the society that spawned it—the racially divided South Africa of apartheid. Though Mr. Fugard's play is set there in 1950, it could take place nearly anywhere at any time. The word "apartheid" is never mentioned; the South African references are minimal. The question that Mr. Fugard raises—how can men of all kinds find the courage to love one another?—is dealt with at such a profound level that *"Master Harold"* sweeps quickly beyond the transitory specifics of any one nation. It's not for nothing that this is the first play Mr. Fugard has chosen to open away from home.

What's more, the author deals with his issue without attitudinizing, without sentimentality, without lecturing the audience. *"Master Harold"* isn't another problem play in which people stand for ideological positions. By turns funny and tragic, it uncovers its moral imperatives by burrowing deeply into the small, intimately observed details of its three characters' lives.

We meet those characters on a rainy afternoon, as they josh and chat in a fading tea room. Two of them, Sam (Zakes Mokae) and Willie (Danny Glover), are black waiters who rehearse for a coming ballroom dancing contest while tidying up the restaurant. Because they only have enough money for bus fare home, they can't put Sarah Vaughan on the jukebox: they imagine the music, as well as their Ginger Rogers–like partners, as they twirl about. Eventually they are joined by Hally (Lonny Price), who is the son of the tea room's owner. A precocious white prep-school student on the verge of manhood, Hally has stopped by to eat lunch and work on an English essay.

The black servants are the boy's second family: they have been employed by his parents since Hally was in short trousers. But, for all the easy camaraderie and tender memories that unite master and servants, there's a slight distance in their relationship, too. As the waiters practice their steps, Hally playfully but condescendingly calls them "a pair of hooligans." To the boy, such danc-

ing is a "simple-minded" reflection of "the culture of primitive black society"—only now "the war dance has been replaced by the waltz."

But the articulate Sam, an unacknowledged mentor to Hally since childhood, patiently sets the boy to thinking otherwise. Dancing, Sam contends, "is like being in a dream about a world where accidents don't happen"— where white and black, rich and poor, men and women don't bump into one another. Hally is so taken with this theory that he decides to write his essay about it. Maybe, he postulates, "the United Nations is a dancing school for politicians." Maybe "there is hope for mankind after all."

It's a lovely, idyllic metaphor, and there is much joy in *"Master Harold"* as the characters imagine their utopian "world without collisions." Yet the joy soon dissipates. Mr. Fugard has structured his intermissionless 100-minute play much as Sam describes a dance contest: "a relaxed atmosphere changes to one of tension and drama as the climax approaches." When the tension erupts in *"Master Harold,"* it rips through the audience so mercilessly that the Lyceum falls into an almost deathly hush.

The drama is catalyzed by a series of phone calls Hally receives from his real-life family offstage. Hally's father, we learn, is a drunk, a cripple and a racist; his mother is his long-suffering victim. Hally is caught between them, and, as old wounds are ripped open, the bitterness of his entire childhood comes raging to the surface. The boy is soon awash in tearful self-pity and, in the absence of his real father, takes out his anger on his surrogate father, Sam. What follows is an unstoppable, almost unwatchable outpouring of ugliness, in which Hally humiliates the black man he loves by insisting that he call him "Master Harold," by mocking their years of shared secrets, by spitting in his face.

Mr. Fugard's point is simple enough: Before we can practice compassion—before we can, as Sam says, "dance life like champions"—we must learn to respect ourselves. It is Hally's self-hatred that leads him to strike at the black man and his crippled Dad and, in this sense, the boy is typical of anyone who attacks the defenseless to bolster his own self-esteem.

But *"Master Harold,"* unlike many works that deal with the genesis of hatred, forces us to identify with the character who inflicts the cruelty. We like Hally so much in the play's early stages, and empathize with his familial sorrow so keenly later on, that it's impossible to pull back once he lashes out. And because we can't sever ourselves from Hally, we're forced to confront our own capacity for cruelty—and to see all too clearly just who it is we really hurt when we give in to it.

Mr. Fugard can achieve this effect because he has the guts to face his own shame: Hally, a fledgling artist who believes in social reform, is too richly drawn not to be a ruthlessly honest portrait of the playwright as a young man. But if Mr. Fugard's relentless conscience gives "Master Harold" its remarkable moral center, his brilliance as an artist gives the play its classic esthetic simplicity.

This work is totally without pretension. As Sam says that the trick of dancing is to "make it look easy," so Mr. Fugard understands that the same is true in the theater. The dialogue is light and easy, full of lilting images that gradually warp as the darkness descends. After Hally relives the exultant childhood experience of flying his first kite with Sam, the kite comes down to the ground, "like something that has lost its soul." Sam's description of graceful waltzers is usurped by the boy's vision of "cripples dancing like a bunch of broken spiders."

Like the script, the production has been deftly choreographed by the author: you don't know you're entering the center of a storm until you're there. The one newcomer to the cast since Yale, Mr. Price, will be at the level of his predecessor, Zeljko Ivanek, as soon as he tones down his overly cute youthful friskiness in Hally's early scenes. Once the protagonist falls apart, Mr. Price takes the audience right with him on his bottomless descent to self-immolation.

As the easygoing Willie, Mr. Glover is a paragon of sweet kindliness—until events leave him whipped and sobbing in a chair, his low moans serving as forlorn counterpoint to the play's main confrontation. Mr. Mokae's Sam is a transcendental force—an avuncular, hearty figure who slowly withdraws into dignified serenity as Hally taunts him. Though the boy has repaid the servant's lifelong instruction in tolerance by making him feel "dirty," Mr. Mokae still glows with his dream of a world of perfect dancers—one that's like "a love story with a happy ending."

The author doesn't provide that happy ending, of course—it's not his to confer. But if "Master Harold" finally lifts us all the way from pain to hope, it's because Mr. Fugard insists that that ending can be—must be—ours to write.

CARYL CHURCHILL

1938–

When asked if she thought there was a "female aesthetic," Caryl Churchill responded: "I don't see how you can tell until there are so many plays by women that you can begin to see what they have in common that's different from the way men have written, and there are still relatively so few." But among those "relatively few," the thirty-two dramas of Caryl Churchill, ranging from radio and television scripts to stage plays, have put her unquestionably into the ranks of major contemporary playwrights.

An only child, Churchill began writing stories at an early age, attended school in London and then in Montreal, and returned to England to study at Oxford University where she started writing plays for student productions. Marriage in 1961 to David Harter, a lawyer, took her to London and to her initial work on radio and television plays. As Churchill put it, she turned to radio plays in part because she liked radio but also because the process of bearing and raising children made it virtually impossible to do anything but shorter pieces. After her third child was born, Churchill felt she needed more time for her writing, and briefly hired a nanny to care for her youngest child—that "a woman must have money and a room of her own if she is to write fiction" seems just as true for Churchill as it was when Virginia Woolf issued her famous manifesto in 1929.

Churchill has said that her 1972 play *Owners* was the beginning of the second part of her career, since it marked the start of her almost total commitment to theater, instead of radio and television. That play, like *Objections to Sex and Violence* (1975) and *Traps* (1977), opened originally at London's Royal Court Theatre, the home since 1956 for many new British plays. Churchill's plays show men and women caught in social, political, gender-based, and personal "traps," from which they try to escape in a variety of ways, including through terrorism and suicide. Perhaps the major influence on Churchill's work came in 1976 when she began working with experimental theater groups in the process of conceiving and drafting her plays. For *Light Shining in Buckinghamshire* (1976), which she developed in collaboration with Joint Stock, Churchill and her director first decided on their subject—the millennial movement during the English Civil War, an essentially working-class movement based on the belief that fighting the king (Charles I) would lead to the second coming of Christ. Then the crucial part of the creative process was, according to Churchill, a three-week workshop with the Joint Stock actors where, "through talk, reading, games, and improvisation, we tried to get closer to the issues and the people." She next spent nine weeks writing a script and worked with the company for another six weeks of rehearsal. Given such extensive collaboration, she acknowledges that, while the actors did not write the lines, "many of the characters and scenes were based on ideas that came from improvisation at the workshop and during rehearsal."

Churchill's reading in seventeenth-century material also fostered her work with Monstrous Regiment, a feminist/socialist theater group with whom she had agreed to do a play about witches. Her research convinced her that she "wanted to write a play about witches with no witches in it; a play not about evil, hysteria, and possession by the devil but about poverty, humiliation, and prejudice, and how the women accused of witchcraft saw themselves." For this play, *Vinegar Tom* (1976), she first talked with the group, drafted the play in three days, went off to work with Joint Stock, came back to Monstrous Regiment in the autumn, and expanded the play to create a new character, in part because a new actress had joined the company, and in part because discussion with the actors indicated that a certain kind of character was needed. Not only did both of these plays come out of similar working conditions and deal with (roughly) the same historical period, but both show Churchill's move into a less realistic kind of drama than she had previously written. The plays call for large casts, yet each production uses only a small group of actors: twenty-five roles in *Light Shining in Buckinghamshire* were played by six actors, while fourteen roles in *Vinegar Tom* were played by nine actors. What may have started as a financial necessity—a limit on the number of actors the group could support—turns into a highly suggestive mode of staging, since, as Churchill points out, "When different actors play the parts what comes over is a large event involving many people, whose characters resonate in a way they wouldn't if they were more clearly defined." The events and their political significance become central rather than the psychology of the characters or the star quality of the actors.

Most of Churchill's major plays since the 1976 collaborative ventures show the influence of that experience, for *Cloud Nine* (1979), *Fen* (1983), and *Serious Money* (1987) have also been developed out of workshops with the original actors. These plays, as well as *Top Girls* (1982) and *Softcops* (1984), call for actors to play multiple roles, and increasingly Churchill stresses the connection of the actor with the role. Thus, in *Cloud Nine*, a black farce which examines the similarities between colonial and sexual repression, the casting of a man in the role of Betty, the wife of the white colonial administrator in Africa, represents for Churchill the idea that Betty "wants to be what men want her to be." Similarly, the black servant, Joshua, is played by a white man, and Edward, the young son whose homosexual tendencies are both repressed and revealed, by a woman. In the second act, which moves forward 100 years to contemporary London, with the characters only twenty-five years older, Churchill asks for different gender castings, again to make points about the changing self-perceptions of men and women; thus Betty "is now played by a woman, as she gradually becomes real to herself, " but Cathy, a child of five, is to be played by a man, "partly, as with Edward, to show more clearly the issues involved in learning what is considered correct behavior for a girl."

Churchill's preoccupation with the past and its relation to the present is most dazzlingly represented in the first scene of *Top Girls*. In a contemporary London restaurant, Marlene, the new managing director of the Top Girls Employment Agency, hosts a dinner to celebrate her promotion, and her dinner guests, who span centuries and continents, include both real women and women imagined by men. Thus, the Victorian traveler Isabella Bird, the Japanese-courtesan-turned-nun Lady Nijo, and the Italian Pope Joan join Marlene along with Dull

Gret, a woman in apron and armor from Brueghel's painting "Dulle Griet," and Patient Griselda, the much-abused heroine of Chaucer's "The Clerk's Tale" (see Figure 1). Not only does Churchill blend the real and the imaginary with the medieval, Renaissance, Victorian, and modern worlds, but she invents an overlapping style, so that characters speak over each other, or continue their speeches without noticing that another character has spoken on a seemingly different topic. Although these women from the past look unrelated, their stories link together in that they show the painful experiences women suffer in dealing with men, with children, and with their own sexual identity. Even Dull Gret, who speaks in monosyllables for most of the scene, suddenly bursts into a long speech which recounts the Brueghel painting from her own point of view, showing that her anger springs from a mother's outrage rather than from the plundering instincts of an unwomanly woman.

Churchill devotes the rest of the play to Marlene's story, gradually detailing what she has become in order to run Top Girls, and the price she has paid for her success. Marlene is the only role not switched or shared, a theatrical choice which may also suggest that she can't escape into another life. The fifteen other characters are played by only six actresses, often with ironic juxtapositions. The intrepid traveler Isabella Bird turns into Marlene's sister Joyce, who, unlike Marlene and Isabella, is trapped at home, visiting their sick mother once a week, and taking care of Angie, a "slow" sixteen-year-old, who turns out to be Marlene's daughter rather than her niece. Angie, less surprisingly, is played by the actress who played Dull Gret, both characters who seem to have little to say. And Patient Griselda, who has taken so much abuse from her husband, becomes a client interviewed by Marlene, showing the same vacuous adaptability as the character from the past.

When the play opened in 1982, reviews commented extensively on the play's elaborate dinner scene (see Figure 1), but also on the quality of the acting of the seven women taking the sixteen roles. While reactions to the play ranged widely ("articulate, eloquent, alive" or "predictable and, at times, rather trite" or "a strange play, disturbing and intriguing"), most reviewers agreed that Churchill had created a feast of acting opportunities, fully realized in performance. Though all of the actresses received praise, frequent attention went most often to Carole Hayman's "lovely, humane performance" of Angie, who is "a bit thick." Angie's existence, and Marlene's attempt to hide from her true relationship to the girl, posed the question for one reviewer: "What use is female emancipation, Churchill asks, if it transforms the clever women into predators and does nothing for the stupid, weak, and helpless?" Thus it seems especially appropriate that the exotic worlds conjured up in the play's first scene shrink to the rooms of the employment agency and Joyce's backyard, where Angie and her friend Kit play "squashed together" in "a shelter made of junk" (see Figure 2). No matter what dreams women have had, have enacted, have yet to dream, Churchill reminds us in the play's final lines of today's reality. Marlene comforts Angie, who has suddenly awakened: "Did you have a bad dream? What happened in it? Well you're awake now, aren't you pet?" Angie's answer may reflect Churchill's: "Frightening."

TOP GIRLS

BY CARYL CHURCHILL

CHARACTERS

MARLENE
WAITRESS/KIT/SHONA
ISABELLA BIRD/JOYCE/MRS. KIDD
LADY NIJO/WIN
DULL GRET/ANGIE
POPE JOAN/LOUISE
PATIENT GRISELDA/NELL/JEANINE

ACT 1
Scene 1: *A Restaurant.*
Scene 2: *Top Girls' Employment Agency, London.*
Scene 3: *Joyce's backyard in Suffolk.*

ACT 2
Scene 1: *Top Girls' Employment Agency.*
Scene 2: *A Year Earlier. Joyce's kitchen.*

Production Note: *The seating order for Act 1, Scene 1 in the original production at the Royal Court was (from right) Gret, Nijo, Marlene, Joan, Griselda, Isabella.*

THE CHARACTERS

ISABELLA BIRD (1831–1904): Lived in Edinburgh, traveled extensively between the ages of forty and seventy.

LADY NIJO (b. 1258): Japanese, was an Emperor's courtesan and later a Buddhist nun who traveled on foot through Japan.

DULL GRET: Is the subject of the Brueghel painting *Dulle Griet,* in which a woman in an apron and armor leads a crowd of women charging through hell and fighting the devils.

POPE JOAN: Disguised as a man, is thought to have been pope between 854 and 856.

PATIENT GRISELDA: Is the obedient wife whose story is told by Chaucer in "The Clerk's Tale" of *The Canterbury Tales.*

THE LAYOUT: *A speech usually follows the one immediately before it but: (1) When one character starts speaking before the other has finished, the point of interruption is marked "/."* E.g.,

ISABELLA: This is the Emperor of Japan? / I once met the Emperor of Morocco.
NIJO: In fact he was the ex-Emperor.

(2) A character sometimes continues speaking right through another's speech. E.g.,

ISABELLA: When I was forty I thought my life was over. / Oh I was pitiful. I was
NIJO: I didn't say I felt it for twenty years. Not every minute.
ISABELLA: sent on a cruise for my health and felt even worse. Pains in my bones, pins and needles . . . etc.

(3) Sometimes a speech follows on from a speech earlier than the one immediately before it, and continuity is marked *. E.g.,*

GRISELDA: I'd seen him riding by, we all had. And he'd seen me in the fields with the sheep.*
ISABELLA: I would have been well suited to minding sheep.
NIJO: And Mr. Nugent went riding by.
ISABELLA: Of course not, Nijo, I mean a healthy life in the open air.
JOAN: *He just rode up while you were minding the sheep and asked you to marry him?

where "in the fields with the sheep" is the cue to both "I would have been" and "He just rode up."

ACT 1 / SCENE 1

(Restaurant. Saturday night. There is a table with a white cloth set for dinner with six places. The lights come up on MARLENE and the WAITRESS.)

MARLENE: Excellent, yes, table for six. One of them's going to be late but we won't wait. I'd like a bottle of Frascati straight away if you've got one really cold. *(The WAITRESS goes. ISABELLA BIRD arrives.)* Here we are. Isabella.
ISABELLA: Congratulations, my dear.
MARLENE: Well, it's a step. It makes for a party. I haven't time for a holiday. I'd like to go somewhere exotic like you but I can't get away. I don't know how you could bear to leave Hawaii. / I'd like to lie
ISABELLA: I did think of settling.
MARLENE: in the sun forever, except of course I can't bear sitting still.
ISABELLA: I sent for my sister Hennie to come and join me. I said, Hennie we'll live here forever and help the natives. You can buy two sirloins of beef for what a pound of chops cost in Edinburgh. And Hennie wrote back, the dear, that yes, she would come to Hawaii if I wished, but I said she had far better stay where she was. Hennie was suited to life in Tobermory.
MARLENE: Poor Hennie.

ISABELLA: Do you have a sister?

MARLENE: Yes in fact.

ISABELLA: Hennie was happy. She was good. I did miss its face, my own pet. But I couldn't stay in Scotland. I loathed the constant murk.

(Lady NIJO *arrives.)*

MARLENE: *(Seeing her)* Ah! Nijo! *(The* WAITRESS *enters with the wine.)*

NIJO: Marlene! *(To* ISABELLA.) So excited when Marlene told me / you were coming.

ISABELLA: I'm delighted / to meet you.

MARLENE: I think a drink while we wait for the others. I think a drink anyway. What a week. (MARLENE *seats* NIJO. *The* WAITRESS *pours the wine.)*

NIJO: It was always the men who used to get so drunk. I'd be one of the maidens, passing the sake.

ISABELLA: I've had sake. Small hot drink. Quite fortifying after a day in the wet.

NIJO: One night my father proposed three rounds of three cups, which was normal, and then the Emperor should have said three rounds of three cups, but he said three rounds of nine cups, so you can imagine. Then the Emperor passed his sake cup to my father and said, "Let the wild goose come to me this spring."

MARLENE: Let the what?

NIJO: It's a literary allusion to a tenth-century epic, / His Majesty was very cultured.

ISABELLA: This is the Emperor of Japan? / I once met the Emperor of Morocco.

NIJO: In fact he was the ex-Emperor.

MARLENE: But he wasn't old? / Did you, Isabella?

NIJO: Twenty-nine.

ISABELLA: Oh it's a long story.

MARLENE: Twenty-nine's an excellent age.

NIJO: Well I was only fourteen and I knew he meant something but I didn't know what. He sent me an eight-layered gown and I sent it back. So when the time came I did nothing but cry. My thin gowns were badly ripped. But even that morning when he left / he'd a green

MARLENE: Are you saying he raped you?

NIJO: robe with a scarlet lining and very heavily embroidered trousers, I already felt different about him. It made me uneasy. No, of course not, Marlene, I belonged to him, it was what I was brought up for from a baby. I soon found I was sad if he stayed away. It was depressing day after day not knowing when he would come. I never enjoyed taking other women to him.

ISABELLA: I certainly never saw my father drunk. He was a clergyman. / And I didn't get married till I was fifty. *(The* WAITRESS *brings the menus.)*

NIJO: Oh, my father was a very religious man. Just before he died he said to me, "Serve His Majesty, be respectful, if you lose his favor enter holy orders."

MARLENE: But he meant stay in a convent, not go wandering round the country.

NIJO: Priests were often vagrants, so why not a nun? You think I shouldn't / I still did what my father wanted.

MARLENE: No no, I think you should. / I think it was wonderful.

*(*DULL GRET *arrives.)*

ISABELLA: I tried to do what my father wanted.

MARLENE: Gret, good. Nijo. Gret / I know Griselda's going to be late, but should we wait for Joan? / Let's get you a drink.

ISABELLA: Hello, Gret! *(She continues to* NIJO.) I tried to be a clergyman's daughter. Needlework, music, charitable schemes. I had a tumor removed from my spine and spent a great deal of time on the sofa. I studied the metaphysical poets and hymnology. / I thought I enjoyed intellectual pursuits.

NIJO: Ah, you like poetry. I come of a line of eight generations of poets. Father had a poem / in the anthology.

ISABELLA: My father taught me Latin although I was a girl. / But really I was

MARLENE: They didn't have Latin at my school.

ISABELLA: more suited to manual work. Cooking, washing, mending, riding horses. / Better than reading

NIJO: Oh but I'm sure you're very clever.

ISABELLA: books, eh Gret? A rough life in the open air.

NIJO: I can't say I enjoyed my rough life. What I enjoyed most was being the Emperor's favorite / and wearing thin silk.

ISABELLA: Did you have any horses, Gret?

GRET: Pig.

*(*POPE JOAN *arrives.)*

MARLENE: Oh Joan, thank God, we can order. Do you know everyone? We were just talking about learning Latin and being clever girls. Joan was by way of an infant prodigy. Of course you were. What excited you when you were ten?

JOAN: Because angels are without matter they are not individuals. Every angel is a species.

MARLENE: There you are. *(They laugh. They look at the menus.)*

ISABELLA: Yes, I forgot all my Latin. But my father was the mainspring of my life and when he died I was so grieved. I'll have the chicken, please, / and the soup.

NIJO: Of course you were grieved. My father was saying his prayers and he dozed off in the sun. So I touched his knee to rouse him. "I wonder what will happen," he said, and then he was dead before he finished the sentence. / If he'd

MARLENE: What a shock.

NIJO: died saying his prayers he would have gone straight to heaven. / Waldorf salad.

JOAN: Death is the return of all creatures to God.

NIJO: I shouldn't have woken him.

JOAN: Damnation only means ignorance of the truth. I was always attracted by the teachings of John the Scot, though he was inclined to confuse / God and the world.

ISABELLA: Grief always overwhelmed me at the time.

MARLENE: What I fancy is a rare steak. Gret?

ISABELLA: I am of course a member of the / Church of England.

MARLENE: Gret?

GRET: Potatoes.

MARLENE: I haven't been to church for years. / I like Christmas carols.

ISABELLA: Good works matter more than church attendance.

MARLENE: Make that two steaks and a lot of potatoes. Rare. But I don't do good works either.

JOAN: Canelloni, please, / and a salad.

ISABELLA: Well, I tried, but oh dear. Hennie did good works.

NIJO: The first half of my life was all sin and the second / all repentance.*

MARLENE: Oh what about starters?

GRET: Soup.

JOAN: *And which did you like best?

MARLENE: Were your travels just a penance? Avocado vinaigrette. Didn't you / enjoy yourself?

JOAN: Nothing to start with for me, thank you.

NIJO: Yes, but I was very unhappy. / It hurt to remember the past.

MARLENE: And the wine list.

NIJO: I think that was repentance.

MARLENE: Well I wonder.

NIJO: I might have just been homesick.

MARLENE: Or angry.

NIJO: Not angry, no, / why angry?

GRET: Can we have some more bread?

MARLENE: Don't you get angry? I get angry.

NIJO: But what about?

MARLENE: Yes let's have two more Frascati. And some more bread, please. (*The* WAITRESS *exits.*)

ISABELLA: I tried to understand Buddhism when I was in Japan but all this birth and death succeeding each other through eternities just filled me with the most profound melancholy. I do like something more active.

NIJO: You couldn't say I was inactive. I walked every day for twenty years.

ISABELLA: I don't mean walking. / I mean in the head.

NIJO: I vowed to copy five Mahayana sutras.° / Do you know how long they are?

MARLENE: I don't think religious beliefs are something we have in common. Activity yes. (GRET *empties the bread basket into her apron.*)

Mahayana sutras, Buddhist religious texts.

NIJO: My head was active. / My head ached.

JOAN: It's no good being active in heresy.

ISABELLA: What heresy? She's calling the Church of England / a heresy.

JOAN: There are some very attractive / heresies.

NIJO: I had never heard of Christianity. Never / heard of it. Barbarians.

MARLENE: Well I'm not a Christian. / And I'm not a Buddhist.

ISABELLA: You have heard of it?

MARLENE: We don't all have to believe the same.

ISABELLA: I knew coming to dinner with a Pope we should keep off religion.

JOAN: I always enjoy a theological argument. But I won't try to convert you, I'm not a missionary. Anyway I'm a heresy myself.

ISABELLA: There are some barbaric practices in the east.

NIJO: Barbaric?

ISABELLA: Among the lower classes.

NIJO: I wouldn't know.

ISABELLA: Well theology always made my head ache.

MARLENE: Oh good, some food. (*The* WAITRESS *brings the first course, serves it during the following, then exits.*)

NIJO: How else could I have left the court if I wasn't a nun? When father died I had only His Majesty. So when I fell out of favor I had nothing. Religion is a kind of nothing / and I dedicated what was left of me to nothing.

ISABELLA: That's what I mean about Buddhism. It doesn't brace.

MARLENE: Come on, Nijo, have some wine.

NIJO: Haven't you ever felt like that? You've all felt / like that. Nothing will ever happen again. I am dead already.

ISABELLA: You thought your life was over but it wasn't.

JOAN: You wish it was over.

GRET: Sad.

MARLENE: Yes, when I first came to London I sometimes . . . and when I got back from America I did. But only for a few hours. Not twenty years.

ISABELLA: When I was forty I thought my life was over. / Oh I was pitiful. I was sent

NIJO: I didn't say I felt it for twenty years. Not every minute.

ISABELLA: on a cruise for my health and I felt even worse. Pains in my bones, pins and needles in my hands, swelling behind the ears, and—oh, stupidity. I shook all over, indefinable terror. And Australia seemed to me a hideous country, the acacias stank like drains. / I

NIJO: You were homesick. (GRET *steals a bottle of wine.*)

ISABELLA: had a photograph taken for Hennie but I told her I wouldn't send it, my hair had fallen out and my clothes were crooked, I looked completely insane and suicidal.

NIJO: So did I, exactly, dressed as a nun. / I was wearing walking shoes for the first time.

ISABELLA: I longed to go home, / but home to what? Houses are so perfectly dismal.*

NIJO: I longed to go back ten years.

MARLENE: *I thought traveling cheered you both up.

ISABELLA: Oh it did / of course. It was on

NIJO: I'm not a cheerful person, Marlene. I just laugh a lot.

ISABELLA: the trip from Australia to the Sandwich Isles, I fell in love with the sea. There were rats in the cabin and ants in the food but suddenly it was like a new world. I woke up every morning happy, knowing there would be nothing to annoy me. No nervousness. No dressing.

NIJO: Don't you like getting dressed? I adored my clothes. / When I was chosen

MARLENE: You had prettier colors than Isabella.

NIJO: to give sake to His Majesty's brother, the Emperor Kameyana, on his formal visit, I wore raw silk pleated trousers and a seven-layered gown in shades of red, and two outer garments, / yellow lined with green

MARLENE: Yes, all that silk must have been very— (*The* WAITRESS *enters, clears the first course and exits.*)

JOAN: I dressed as a boy when I left home.*

NIJO: and a light green jacket. Lady Betto had a five-layered gown in shades of green and purple.

ISABELLA: *You dressed as a boy?

MARLENE: Of course, / for safety.

JOAN: It was easy, I was only twelve. / Also women weren't allowed in the library. We wanted to study in Athens.

MARLENE: You ran away alone?

JOAN: No, not alone, I went with my friend. / He was

NIJO: Ah, an elopement.

JOAN: sixteen but I thought I knew more science than he did and almost as much philosophy.

ISABELLA: Well I always traveled as a lady and I repudiated strongly any suggestion in the press that I was other than feminine.

MARLENE: I don't wear trousers in the office. / I could but I don't.

ISABELLA: There was no great danger to a woman of my age and appearance.

MARLENE: And you got away with it, Joan?

JOAN: I did then. (*The* WAITRESS *brings in the main course.*)

MARLENE: And nobody noticed anything?

JOAN: They noticed I was a very clever boy. / And

MARLENE: I couldn't have kept pretending for so long.

JOAN: when I shared a bed with my friend, that was ordinary—two poor students in a lodging house. I think I forgot I was pretending.

ISABELLA: Rocky Mountain Jim, Mr. Nugent, showed me no disrespect. He found it interesting, I think, that I could make scones and also lasso cattle. Indeed he declared his love for me, which was most distressing.

NIJO: What did he say? / We always sent poems first.

MARLENE: What did you say?

ISABELLA: I urged him to give up whiskey, / but he said it was too late.

MARLENE: Oh Isabella.

ISABELLA: He had lived alone in the mountains for many years.

MARLENE: But did you—? (*The* WAITRESS *goes.*)

ISABELLA: Mr. Nugent was a man that any woman might love but none could marry. I came back to England.

NIJO: Did you write him a poem when you left? / Snow on the mountains. My sleeves

MARLENE: Did you never see him again?

ISABELLA: No, never.

NIJO: are wet with tears. In England no tears, no snow.

ISABELLA: Well, I say never. One morning very early in Switzerland, it was a year later, I had a vision of him as I last saw him / in his trapper's clothes with his

NIJO: A ghost!

ISABELLA: hair round his face, and that was the day, / I learned later, he died with a

NIJO: Ah!

ISABELLA: bullet in his brain. / He just bowed to me and vanished.

MARLENE: Oh Isabella.

NIJO: When your lover dies—One of my lovers died. / The priest Ariake.

JOAN: My friend died. Have we all got dead lovers?

MARLENE: Not me, sorry.

NIJO: (*To* ISABELLA) I wasn't a nun, I was still at court, but he was a priest, and when he came to me he dedicated his whole life to hell. / He knew that when he died he would fall into one of the three lower realms. And he died, he did die.

JOAN: (*To* MARLENE) I'd quarreled with him over the teachings of John the Scot,° who held that our ignorance of God is the same as his ignorance of himself. He only knows what he creates because he creates everything he knows but he himself is above being—do you follow?

MARLENE: No, but go on.

NIJO: I couldn't bear to think / in what shape would he be reborn.*

JOAN: St. Augustine maintained that the Neo-Platonic Ideas are indivisible

ISABELLA: *Buddhism is really most uncomfortable.

JOAN: from God, but I agreed with John that the created world is essences derived from Ideas which derived from God. As Denys the Areopagite° said— the pseudo-Denys—first we give God a name, then deny it, / then reconcile the contradiction

---

John the Scot, John Scotus Erigena (c. 810–866), Irish scholastic philosopher. **Denys the Areopagite,** the "pseudo-Denys" is the author of influential Neoplatonic philosophical texts dating from the late fifth or early sixth century.

NIJO: In what shape would he return?

JOAN: by looking beyond / those terms—

MARLENE: Sorry, what? Denys said what?

JOAN: Well we disagreed about it, we quarreled. And next day he was ill, / I was so annoyed with him

NIJO: Misery in this life and worse in the next, all because of me.

JOAN: all the time I was nursing him I kept going over the arguments in my mind. Matter is not a means of knowing the essence. The source of the species is the Idea. But then I realized he'd never understand my arguments again, and that night he died. John the Scot held that the individual disintegrates / and there is no personal immortality.

ISABELLA: I wouldn't have you think I was in love with Jim Nugent. It was yearning to save him that I felt.

MARLENE: (*To* JOAN) So what did you do?

JOAN: First I decided to stay a man. I was used to it. And I wanted to devote my life to learning. Do you know why I went to Rome? Italian men didn't have beards.

ISABELLA: The loves of my life were Hennie, my own pet, and my dear husband the doctor, who nursed Hennie in her last illness. I knew it would be terrible when Hennie died but I didn't know how terrible. I felt half of myself had gone. How could I go on my travels without that sweet soul waiting at home for my letters? It was Doctor Bishop's devotion to her in her last illness that made me decide to marry him. He and Hennie had the same sweet character. I had not.

NIJO: I thought His Majesty had sweet character because when he found out about Ariake he was so kind. But really it was because he no longer cared for me. One night he even sent me out to a man who had been pursuing me. / He lay awake on the other side of the screens and listened.

ISABELLA: I did wish marriage had seemed more of a step. I tried very hard to cope with the ordinary drudgery of life. I was ill again with carbuncles on the spine and nervous prostration. I ordered a tricycle, that was my idea of adventure then. And John himself fell ill, with erysipelas and anemia. I began to love him with my whole heart but it was too late. He was a skeleton with transparent white hands. I wheeled him on various seafronts in a bathchair. And he faded and left me. There was nothing in my life. The doctors said I had gout / and my heart was much affected.

NIJO: There was nothing in my life, nothing, without the Emperor's favor. The Empress had always been my enemy, Marlene, she said I had no right to wear three-layered gowns. / But I was the adopted daughter of my grandfather the Prime Minister. I had been publicly granted permission to wear thin silk.

JOAN: There was nothing in my life except my studies. I was obsessed with pursuit of the truth. I taught

at the Greek School in Rome, which St. Augustine had made famous. I was poor, I worked hard, I spoke apparently brilliantly, I was still very young, I was a stranger, suddenly I was quite famous, I was everyone's favorite. Huge crowds came to hear me. The day after they made me cardinal I fell ill and lay two weeks without speaking, full of terror and regret. / But then I got up determined to

MARLENE: Yes, success is very . . .

JOAN: go on. I was seized again / with a desperate longing for the absolute.

ISABELLA: Yes, yes, to go on. I sat in Tobermory among Hennie's flowers and sewed a complete outfit in Jaeger flannel. / I was fifty-six years old.

NIJO: Out of favor but I didn't die. I left on foot, nobody saw me go. For the next twenty years I walked through Japan.

GRET: Walking is good. (*Meanwhile, the* WAITRESS *enters, pours lots of wine, then shows* MARLENE *the empty bottle.*)

JOAN: Pope Leo died and I was chosen. All right then. I would be Pope. I would know God. I would know everything.

ISABELLA: I determined to leave my grief behind and set off for Tibet.

MARLENE: Magnificent all of you. We need some more wine, please, two bottles I think, Griselda isn't even here yet, and I want to drink a toast to you all. (*The* WAITRESS *exits.*)

ISABELLA: To yourself surely, / we're here to celebrate your success.

NIJO: Yes, Marlene.

JOAN: Yes, what is it exactly, Marlene?

MARLENE: Well it's not Pope but it is managing director.*

JOAN: And you find work for people.

MARLENE: Yes, an employment agency.

NIJO: *Over all the women you work with. And the men.

ISABELLA: And very well deserved too. I'm sure it's just the beginning of something extraordinary.

MARLENE: Well it's worth a party.

ISABELLA: To Marlene.*

MARLENE: And all of us.

JOAN: *Marlene.

NIJO: Marlene.

GRET: Marlene.

MARLENE: We've all come a long way. To our courage and the way we changed our lives and our extraordinary achievements. (*They laugh and drink a toast.*)

ISABELLA: Such adventures. We were crossing a mountain pass at seven thousand feet, the cook was all to pieces, the muleteers suffered fever and snow blindness. But even though my spine was agony I managed very well.*

MARLENE: Wonderful.

NIJO: *Once I was ill for four months lying alone at an inn. Nobody to offer a horse to Buddha. I had to live for myself, and I did live.

ISABELLA: Of course you did. It was far worse returning

to Tobermory. I always felt dull when I was station-
ary. / That's why I could never stay anywhere.

NIJO: Yes, that's it exactly. New sights. The shrine by
the beach, the moon shining on the sea. The goddess had vowed to save all living things. / She would
even save the fishes. I was full of hope.

JOAN: I had thought the Pope would know everything.
I thought God would speak to me directly. But of
course he knew I was a woman.

MARLENE: But nobody else even suspected? (*The* WAIT-
RESS *brings more wine and then exits.*)

JOAN: In the end I did take a lover again.*

ISABELLA: In the Vatican?

GRET: *Keep you warm.

NIJO: *Ah, lover.

MARLENE: *Good for you.

JOAN: He was one of my chamberlains. There are such
a lot of servants when you're Pope. The food's very
good. And I realized I did know the truth. Because
whatever the Pope says, that's true.

NIJO: What was he like, the chamberlain?*

GRET: Big cock.

ISABELLA: Oh, Gret.

MARLENE: *Did he fancy you when he thought you were
a fella?

NIJO: What was he like?

JOAN: He could keep a secret.

MARLENE: So you did know everything.

JOAN: Yes, I enjoyed being Pope. I consecrated bishops
and let people kiss my feet. I received the King of
England when he came to submit to the church.
Unfortunately there were earthquakes, and some
village reported it had rained blood, and in France
there was a plague of giant grasshoppers, but I
don't think that can have been my fault, do you?*
(*Laughter.*) The grasshoppers fell on the English
Channel / and were washed up on shore

NIJO: I once went to sea. It was very lonely. I realized it
made very little difference where I went.

JOAN: and their bodies rotted and poisoned the air and
everyone in those parts died. (*Laughter.*)

ISABELLA: *Such superstition! I was nearly murdered
in China by a howling mob. They thought the barbarians ate babies and put them under railway
sleepers to make the tracks steady, and ground up
their eyes to make the lenses of cameras. / So they
were shouting,

MARLENE: And you had a camera!

ISABELLA: "Child-eater, child-eater." Some people tried
to sell girl babies to Europeans for cameras or stew!
(*Laughter.*)

MARLENE: So apart from the grasshoppers it was a great
success.

JOAN: Yes, if it hadn't been for the baby I expect I'd
have lived to an old age like Theodora of Alexan-
dria, who lived as a monk. She was accused by a girl
/ who fell in love with her of being the father of her
child and—

NIJO: But tell us what happened to your baby. I had
some babies.

MARLENE: Didn't you think of getting rid of it?

JOAN: Wouldn't that be a worse sin than having it? / But
a Pope with a child was about as bad as possible.

MARLENE: I don't know, you're the Pope.

JOAN: But I wouldn't have known how to get rid of it.

MARLENE: Other Popes had children, surely.

JOAN: They didn't give birth to them.

NIJO: Well you were a woman.

JOAN: Exactly and I shouldn't have been a woman.
Women, children, and lunatics can't be Pope.

MARLENE: So the only thing to do / was to get rid of it
somehow.

NIJO: You had to have it adopted secretly.

JOAN: But I didn't know what was happening. I thought
I was getting fatter, but then I was eating more and
sitting about, the life of a Pope is quite luxurious. I
don't think I'd spoken to a woman since I was
twelve. The chamberlain was the one who realized.

MARLENE: And by then it was too late.

JOAN: Oh I didn't want to pay attention. It was easier
to do nothing.

NIJO: But you had to plan for having it. You had to say
you were ill and go away.

JOAN: That's what I should have done I suppose.

MARLENE: Did you want them to find out?

NIJO: I too was often in embarrassing situations, there's
no need for a scandal. My first child was His Majesty's, which unfortunately died, but my second was
Akebono's. I was seventeen. He was in love with me
when I was thirteen, he was very upset when I had
to go to the Emperor, it was very romantic, a lot of
poems. Now His Majesty hadn't been near me for
two months so he thought I was four months pregnant when I was really six, so when I reached the
ninth month / I announced I was seriously ill,

JOAN: I never knew what month it was.

NIJO: and Akebono announced he had gone on a religious retreat. He held me round the waist and lifted
me up as the baby was born. He cut the cord with
a short sword, wrapped the baby in white and took
it away. It was only a girl but I was sorry to lose it.
Then I told the Emperor that the baby had miscar-
ried because of my illness, and there you are. The
danger was past.

JOAN: But, Nijo, I wasn't used to having a woman's
body.

ISABELLA: So what happened?

JOAN: I didn't know of course that it was near the time.
It was Rogation Day,° there was always a procession.
I was on the horse dressed in my robes and a cross
was carried in front of me, and all the cardinals

Rogation Day, day set aside for solemn procession to
invoke God's mercy; the major Rogation Day was April 25.

were following, and all the clergy of Rome, and a huge crowd of people. / We set off from St. Peter's° to go

MARLENE: Total Pope. (GRET *pours the wine and steals the bottle.*)

JOAN: to St. John's.° I had felt a slight pain earlier, I thought it was something I'd eaten, and then it came back, and came back more often. I thought when this is over I'll go to bed. There were still long gaps when I felt perfectly all right and I didn't want to attract attention to myself and spoil the ceremony. Then I suddenly realized what it must be. I had to last out till I could get home and hide. Then something changed, my breath started to catch. I couldn't plan things properly anymore. We were in a little street that goes between St. Clement's° and the Colosseum, and I just had to get off the horse and sit down for a minute. Great waves of pressure were going through my body, I heard sounds like a cow lowing, they came out of my mouth. Far away I heard people screaming, "The Pope is ill, the Pope is dying." And the baby just slid out on to the road.*

MARLENE: The cardinals / won't have known where to put themselves.

NIJO: Oh dear, Joan, what a thing to do! In the street!

ISABELLA: *How embarrassing.

GRET: In a field, yah. (*They are laughing.*)

JOAN: One of the cardinals said, "The Antichrist!" and fell over in a faint. (*They all laugh.*)

MARLENE: So what did they do? They weren't best pleased. •

JOAN: They took me by the feet and dragged me out of town and stoned me to death. (*They stop laughing.*)

MARLENE: Joan, how horrible.

JOAN: I don't really remember.

NIJO: And the child died too?

JOAN: Oh yes, I think so, yes. (*The* WAITRESS *enters to clear the plates. Pause. They start talking very quietly.*)

ISABELLA: (*To* JOAN) I never had any children. I was very fond of horses.

NIJO: (*To* MARLENE) I saw my daughter once. She was three years old. She wore a plum-red / small sleeved gown. Akebono's wife

ISABELLA: Birdie was my favorite. A little Indian bay mare I rode in the Rocky Mountains.

NIJO: had taken the child because her own died. Everyone thought I was just a visitor. She was being brought up carefully so she could be sent to the palace like I was. (GRET *steals her empty plate.*)

ISABELLA: Legs of iron and always cheerful, and such a pretty face. If a stranger led her she reared up like a bronco.

NIJO: I never saw my third child after he was born, the son of Ariake the priest. Ariake held him on his lap the day he was born and talked to him as if he could understand, and cried. My fourth child was Ariake's too. Ariake died before he was born. I didn't want to see anyone, I stayed alone in the hills. It was a boy again, my third son. But oddly enough I felt nothing for him.

MARLENE: How many children did you have, Gret?

GRET: Ten.

ISABELLA: Whenever I came back to England I felt I had so much to atone for. Hennie and John were so good. I did no good in my life. I spent years in self-gratification. So I hurled myself into committees, I nursed the people of Tobermory in the epidemic of influenza, I lectured the Young Women's Christian Association on Thrift. I talked and talked explaining how the East was corrupt and vicious. My travels must do good to someone besides myself. I wore myself out with good causes.

MARLENE: (*Pause*) Oh god, why are we all so miserable?

JOAN: (*Pause*) The procession never went down that street again.

MARLENE: They rerouted it specially?

JOAN: Yes they had to go all round to avoid it. And they introduced a pierced chair.

MARLENE: A pierced chair?

JOAN: Yes, a chair made out of solid marble with a hole in the seat / and it was

MARLENE: You're not serious.

JOAN: in the Chapel of the Savior, and after he was elected the Pope had to sit in it.

MARLENE: And someone looked up his skirts? / Not really!

ISABELLA: What an extraordinary thing.

JOAN: Two of the clergy / made sure he was a man.

NIJO: On their hands and knees!

MARLENE: A pierced chair!

GRET: Balls!

(GRISELDA *arrives unnoticed.*)

NIJO: Why couldn't he just pull up his robe?

JOAN: He had to sit there and look dignified.

MARLENE: You could have made all your chamberlains sit in it.*

GRET: Big one. Small one.

NIJO: Very useful chair at court.

ISABELLA: *Or the Laird of Tobermory in his kilt.

(*They are quite drunk. They get the giggles.* MARLENE *notices* GRISELDA *and gets up to welcome her. The others go on talking and laughing.* GRET *crosses to* JOAN *and* ISABELLA *and pours them wine from her stolen bottles. The* WAITRESS *gives out the menus.*)

MARLENE: Griselda! / There you are. Do you want to eat?

GRISELDA: I'm sorry I'm so late. No, no, don't bother.

MARLENE: Of course it's no bother. / Have you eaten?

St. Peter's, St. John's, major churches in Rome. **St. Clement's,** church in Rome.

GRISELDA: No really, I'm not hungry.

MARLENE: Well have some pudding.

GRISELDA: I never eat pudding.

MARLENE: Griselda, I hope you're not anorexic. We're having pudding, I am, and getting nice and fat.

GRISELDA: Oh if everyone is. I don't mind.

MARLENE: Now who do you know? This is Joan who was Pope in the ninth century, and Isabella Bird, the Victorian traveler, and Lady Nijo from Japan, Emperor's concubine and Buddhist nun, thirteenth century, nearer your own time, and Gret who was painted by Brueghel. Griselda's in Boccaccio and Petrarch and Chaucer because of her extraordinary marriage. I'd like profiteroles because they're disgusting.

JOAN: Zabaglione,° please.

ISABELLA: Apple pie / and cream.

NIJO: What's this?

MARLENE: Zabaglione, it's Italian, it's what Joan's having, / it's delicious.

NIJO: A Roman Catholic / dessert? Yes please.

MARLENE: Gret?

GRET: Cake.

GRISELDA: Just cheese and biscuits, thank you. (*The* WAITRESS *exits.*)

MARLENE: Yes, Griselda's life is like a fairy story, except it starts with marrying the prince.

GRISELDA: He's only a marquis, Marlene.

MARLENE: Well everyone for miles around is his liege and he's absolute lord of life and death and you were the poor but beautiful peasant girl and he whisked you off. / Near enough a prince.

NIJO: How old were you?

GRISELDA: Fifteen.

NIJO: I was brought up in court circles and it was still a shock. Had you ever seen him before?

GRISELDA: I'd seen him riding by, we all had. And he'd seen me in the fields with the sheep.*

ISABELLA: I would have been well suited to minding sheep.

NIJO: And Mr. Nugent riding by.

ISABELLA: Of course not, Nijo, I mean a healthy life in the open air.

JOAN: *He just rode up while you were minding the sheep and asked you to marry him?

GRISELDA: No, no, it was on the wedding day. I was waiting outside the door to see the procession. Everyone wanted him to get married so there'd be an heir to look after us when he died, / and at last he

MARLENE: I don't think Walter wanted to get married. It is Walter? Yes.

GRISELDA: announced a day for the wedding but nobody knew who the bride was, we thought it must

be a foreign princess, we were longing to see her. Then the carriage stopped outside our cottage and we couldn't see the bride anywhere. And he came and spoke to my father.

NIJO: And your father told you to serve the Prince.

GRISELDA: My father could hardly speak. The Marquis said it wasn't an order, I could say no, but if I said yes I must always obey him in everything.

MARLENE: That's when you should have suspected.

GRISELDA: But of course a wife must obey her husband. / And of course I must obey the Marquis.*

ISABELLA: I swore to obey dear John, of course, but it didn't seem to arise. Naturally I wouldn't have wanted to go abroad while I was married.

MARLENE: *Then why bother to mention it at all? He'd got a thing about it, that's why.

GRISELDA: I'd rather obey the Marquis than a boy from the village.

MARLENE: Yes, that's a point.

JOAN: I never obeyed anyone. They all obeyed me.

NIJO: And what did you wear? He didn't make you get married in your own clothes? That would be perverse.*

MARLENE: Oh, you wait.

GRISELDA: *He had ladies with him who undressed me and they had a white silk dress and jewels for my hair.

MARLENE: And at first he seemed perfectly normal?

GRISELDA: Marlene, you're always so critical of him. / Of course he was normal, he was very kind.

MARLENE: But, Griselda, come on, he took your baby.

GRISELDA: Walter found it hard to believe I loved him. He couldn't believe I would always obey him. He had to prove it.

MARLENE: I don't think Walter likes women.

GRISELDA: I'm sure he loved me, Marlene, all the time.

MARLENE: He just had a funny way / of showing it.

GRISELDA: It was hard for him too.

JOAN: How do you mean he took away your baby?

NIJO: Was it a boy?

GRISELDA: No, the first one was a girl.

NIJO: Even so it's hard when they take it away. Did you see it at all?

GRISELDA: Oh yes, she was six weeks old.

NIJO: Much better to do it straight away.

ISABELLA: But why did your husband take the child?

GRISELDA: He said all the people hated me because I was just one of them. And now I had a child they were restless. So he had to get rid of the child to keep them quiet. But he said he wouldn't snatch her, I had to agree and obey and give her up. So when I was feeding her a man came in and took her away. I thought he was going to kill her even before he was out of the room.

MARLENE: But you let him take her? You didn't struggle?

GRISELDA: I asked him to give her back so I could kiss her. And I asked him to bury her where no animals

---

Zabaglione, frothy dessert of beaten eggs, sugar, wine.

could dig her up. / It was Walter's child to do what he

ISABELLA: Oh, my dear.

GRISELDA: liked with.*

MARLENE: Walter was bonkers.°

GRET: Bastard.

ISABELLA: *But surely, murder.

GRISELDA: I had promised.

MARLENE: I can't stand this. I'm going for a pee.

(MARLENE goes out. The WAITRESS brings the dessert, serves it during the following, then exits.)

NIJO: No, I understand. Of course you had to, he was your life. And were you in favor after that?

GRISELDA: Oh yes, we were very happy together. We never spoke about what had happened.

ISABELLA: I can see you were doing what you thought was your duty. But didn't it make you ill?

GRISELDA: No, I was very well, thank you.

NIJO: And you had another child?

GRISELDA: Not for four years, but then I did, yes, a boy.

NIJO: Ah a boy. / So it all ended happily.

GRISELDA: Yes he was pleased. I kept my son till he was two years old. A peasant's grandson. It made the people angry. Walter explained.

ISABELLA: But surely he wouldn't kill his children / just because—

GRISELDA: Oh it wasn't true. Walter would never give in to the people. He wanted to see if I loved him enough.

JOAN: He killed his children / to see if you loved him enough?

NIJO: Was it easier the second time or harder?

GRISELDA: It was always easy because I always knew I would do what he said. *(Pause. They start to eat.)*

ISABELLA: I hope you didn't have any more children.

GRISELDA: Oh no, no more. It was twelve years till he tested me again.

ISABELLA: So whatever did he do this time? / My poor John, I never loved him enough, and he would never have dreamt . . .

GRISELDA: He sent me away. He said the people wanted him to marry someone else who'd give him an heir and he'd got special permission from the Pope. So I said I'd go home to my father. I came with nothing / so I went with nothing. I took

NIJO: Better to leave if your master doesn't want you.

GRISELDA: off my clothes. He let me keep a slip so he wouldn't be shamed. And I walked home barefoot. My father came out in tears. Everyone was crying except me.

NIJO: At least your father wasn't dead. / I had nobody.

ISABELLA: Well it can be a relief to come home. I loved to see Hennie's sweet face again.

GRISELDA: Oh yes, I was perfectly content. And quite soon he sent for me again.

JOAN: I don't think I would have gone.

GRISELDA: But he told me to come. I had to obey him. He wanted me to help prepare his wedding. He was getting married to a young girl from France / and nobody except me knew how to arrange things the way he liked them.

NIJO: It's always hard taking him another woman. (MARLENE comes back.)

JOAN: I didn't live a woman's life. I don't understand it.

GRISELDA: The girl was sixteen and far more beautiful than me. I could see why he loved her. / She had her younger brother with her as a page. *(The WAITRESS enters.)*

MARLENE: Oh God, I can't bear it. I want some coffee. Six coffees. Six brandies. / Double brandies. Straightaway. *(The WAITRESS exits.)*

GRISELDA: They all went into the feast I'd prepared. And he stayed behind and put his arms round me and kissed me. / I felt half asleep with the shock.

NIJO: Oh, like a dream.

MARLENE: And he said, "This is your daughter and your son."

GRISELDA: Yes.

JOAN: What?

NIJO: Oh. Oh I see. You got them back.

ISABELLA: I did think it was remarkably barbaric to kill them but you learn not to say anything. / So he had them brought up secretly I suppose.

MARLENE: Walter's a monster. Weren't you angry? What did you do?

GRISELDA: Well I fainted. Then I cried and kissed the children. / Everyone was making a fuss of me.

NIJO: But did you feel anything for them?

GRISELDA: What?

NIJO: Did you feel anything for the children?

GRISELDA: Of course, I loved them.

JOAN: So you forgave him and lived with him?

GRISELDA: He suffered so much all those years.

ISABELLA: Hennie had the same sweet nature.

NIJO: So they dressed you again?

GRISELDA: Cloth of gold.

JOAN: I can't forgive anything.

MARLENE: You really are exceptional, Griselda.

NIJO: Nobody gave me back my children. *(She cries.)*

(The WAITRESS brings the brandies and then exits. During the following, JOAN goes to NIJO.)

ISABELLA: I can never be like Hennie. I was always so busy in England, a kind of business I detested. The very presence of people exhausted my emotional reserves. I could not be like Hennie however I tried. I tried and was as ill as could be. The doctor suggested a steel net to support my head, the weight of my own head was too much for my diseased spine. It is dangerous to put oneself in depressing circumstances. Why should I do it?

---

bonkers, crazy.

JOAN: (*To* NIJO) Don't cry.

NIJO: My father and the Emperor both died in the autumn. So much pain.

JOAN: Yes, but don't cry.

NIJO: They wouldn't let me into the palace when he was dying. I hid in the room with his coffin, then I couldn't find where I'd left my shoes, I ran after the funeral procession in bare feet, I couldn't keep up. When I got there it was over, a few wisps of smoke in the sky, that's all that was left of him. What I want to know is, if I'd still been at court, would I have been allowed to wear full mourning?

MARLENE: I'm sure you would.

NIJO: Why do you say that? You don't know anything about it. Would I have been allowed to wear full mourning?

ISABELLA: How can people live in this dim pale island and wear our hideous clothes? I cannot and will not live the life of a lady.

NIJO: I'll tell you something that made me angry. I was eighteen, at the Full Moon Ceremony. They make a special rice gruel and stir it with their sticks, and then they beat their women across the loins so they'll have sons and not daughters. So the Emperor beat us all / very hard as

MARLENE: What a sod. (*The* WAITRESS *enters with the coffees.*)

NIJO: usual—that's not it, Marlene, that's normal, what made us angry he told his attendants they could beat us too. Well they had a wonderful time. / So Lady Genki and I made a plan, and the ladies

MARLENE: I'd like another brandy, please. Better make it six. (*The* WAITRESS *exits.*)

NIJO: all hid in his rooms, and Lady Mashimizu stood guard with a stick at the door, and when His Majesty came in Genki seized him and I beat him till he cried out and promised he would never order anyone to hit us again. Afterward there was a terrible fuss. The nobles were horrified. "We wouldn't even dream of stepping on Your Majesty's shadow." And I had hit him with a stick. Yes, I hit him with a stick.

(*The* WAITRESS *brings the brandy bottle and tops up the glasses.* JOAN *crosses in front of the table and back to her place while drunkenly reciting:*)

JOAN:

Suave, mari magno turantibus aequora ventis,
e terra magnum alterius spectare laborem;
non quia vexari quemquamst iucunda voluptas,
sed quibus ipse malis careas quia cernere suave est.
Suave etiam belli certamina magna tueri
per campos instructa tua sine parte pericli.
Sed nil dulcius est, bene quam munita tenere
edita doctrina sapientum templa serena, /

despicere unde queas alios passimque videre
errare atque viam palantis quaerere vitae,°

GRISELDA: I do think—I do wonder—it would have been nicer if Walter hadn't had to.

ISABELLA: Why should I? Why should I?

MARLENE: Of course not.

NIJO: I hit him with a stick.

JOAN:

certare ingenio, contendere nobilitate,
noctes atque dies niti praestante labore
ad summas emergere opes rerumque potiri.
O miseras hominum mentis, / o pectora caeca!*°

ISABELLA: O miseras!

NIJO: *Pectora caeca!

JOAN:

qualibus in tenebris vitae quantisque periclis
degitur hoc aevi quodcumquest! / nonne videre
nil aliud sibi naturam latrare, nisi utqui
corpore seiunctus dolor absit, mente fruatur° . . .
(*She subsides.*)

GRET: We come to hell through a big mouth. Hell's black and red. / It's

MARLENE: (*To* JOAN) Shut up, pet.

GRISELDA: Hush, please.

Suave, . . . quaerere vitae, This passage opens the second book of the long poem, *De Rerum Natura* (*On the Nature of Things*) by the Roman stoic philosopher Lucretius (97?–54 BCE). The speaker begins by contrasting the privilege of calm observation with the turmoil of dangerous involvement. Translation by Rolfe Humphries. "How sweet it is, when whirlwinds roil great ocean, / To watch, from land, the danger of another, / Not that to see some other person suffer / Brings great enjoyment, but the sweetness lies / In watching evils you yourself are free from. / How sweet, again, to see the clash of battle / Across the plains, yourself immune to danger. / But nothing is more sweet than full possession / Of those calm heights, well built, well fortified / By wise men's teaching, to look down from here / At others wandering below, men lost, / Confused, in hectic search for the right road." ***certare . . . caeca!*** Lucretius continues: "The strife of wits, the wars for precedence / The everlasting struggle, night and day, / To win towards heights of wealth and power. O wretched, / O wretched minds of men! O hearts in darkness!" ***qualibus . . . mente fruatur*** . . . , "Under what shadows and among what dangers / Your lives are spent, such as they are. But look— / Your nature snarls, yaps, barks for nothing, really, / Except that pain be absent from the body / And mind enjoy delight. . . ."

ISABELLA: Listen, she's been to hell.

GRET: like the village where I come from. There's a river and a bridge and houses. There's places on fire like when the soldiers come. There's a big devil sat on a roof with a big hole in his arse and he's scooping stuff out of it with a big ladle and it's falling down on us, and it's money, so a lot of the women stop and get some. But most of us is fighting the devils. There's lots of little devils, our size, and we get them down all right and give them a beating. There's lots of funny creatures round your feet, you don't like to look, like rats and lizards, and nasty things, a bum° with a face, and fish with legs, and faces on things that don't have faces on. But they don't hurt, you just keep going. Well we'd had worse, you see, we'd had the Spanish. We'd all had family killed. My big son die on a wheel. Birds eat him. My baby, a soldier run her through with a sword. I'd had enough, I was mad, I hate the bastards. I come out of my front door that morning and shout till my neighbors come out and I said, "Come on, we're going where the evil come from and pay the bastards out." And they all come out just as they was / from baking or

NIJO: All the ladies come.

GRET: washing in their aprons, and we push down the street and the ground opens up and we go through a big mouth into a street just like ours but in hell. I've got a sword in my hand from somewhere and I fill a basket with gold cups they drink out of down there. You just keep running on and fighting, / you didn't stop for nothing. Oh we give them devils such a beating.*

NIJO: Take that, take that.

JOAN:

> *Something something something mortisque timores
> tum vacuum pectus—damn.
> Quod si ridicula—
> something something on and on and on
> and something splendorem purpureai.°

ISABELLA: I thought I would have a last jaunt up the west river in China. Why not? But the doctors were

so very grave I just went to Morocco. The sea was so wild I had to be landed by ship's crane in a coal bucket. / My horse was a terror to me, a powerful black charger.

GRET: Coal bucket good.

JOAN:

> *nos in luce timemus
> something
> terrorem°*

(NIJO *is laughing and crying.* JOAN *gets up and is sick.* GRISELDA *looks after her.*)

GRISELDA: Can I have some water, please? (*The* WAITRESS *exits.*)

ISABELLA: So off I went to visit the Berber sheikhs in full blue trousers and great brass spurs. I was the only European woman ever to have seen the Emperor of Morocco. I was (*The* WAITRESS *brings the water*) seventy years old. What lengths to go to for a last chance of joy. I knew my return of vigor was only temporary, but how marvelous while it lasted.

ACT 1 / SCENE 2

(*"Top Girls" Employment Agency. Monday morning. The lights come up on* MARLENE *and* JEANINE.)

MARLENE: Right, Jeanine, you are Jeanine aren't you? Let's have a look. O's and A's.° / No A's, all those

JEANINE: Six O's.

MARLENE: O's you probably could have got an A. / Speeds, not brilliant, not too bad.

JEANINE: I wanted to go to work.

MARLENE: Well, Jeanine, what's your present job like?

JEANINE: I'm a secretary.

MARLENE: Secretary or typist?

JEANINE: I did start as a typist but the last six months I've been a secretary.

MARLENE: To?

JEANINE: To three of them, really, they share me.

---

bum, buttocks. ***Something . . . splendorem purpureai,*** Joan is still quoting from Lucretius, this time in fragments. The passage she is attempting to remember is this: "And does all this frighten religious terror / In panic from your heart? does the great fear / Of death depart, and leave you comforted? / What vanity, what nonsense! If men's fears, / Anxieties, pursuing horrors, move, / Indifferent to any clash of arms, / Untroubled among lords and monarchs, bow / Before no gleam of gold, no crimson robe [*splendorem purpureai*], / Why do you hesitate, why doubt that reason / Alone has absolute power?"

Nos in luce . . . terrorem, The passage Joan is trying to remember ends with an appeal to reason, though she gets only to the notion of "terrors": "As children tremble and fear everything / In their dark shadows, we, in the full light, / Fear things that really are not one bit more awful / Than what poor babies shudder at in darkness, / The horrors they imagine to be coming. / Our terrors and our darknesses of mind / Must be dispelled, then, not by sunshine's rays, / . . . / But by insight into nature, and a scheme / Of systematic contemplation." ***O's and A's,*** standardized exams in the British educational system. O-levels (Ordinary) are usually taken at sixteen and A-levels (Advanced) are usually taken at eighteen.

There's Mr. Ashford, he's the office manager, and Mr. Philby / is sales, and—

MARLENE: Quite a small place?

JEANINE: A bit small.

MARLENE: Friendly?

JEANINE: Oh it's friendly enough.

MARLENE: Prospects?

JEANINE: I don't think so, that's the trouble. Miss Lewis is secretary to the managing director and she's been there forever, and Mrs. Bradford / is—

MARLENE: So you want a job with better prospects?

JEANINE: I want a change.

MARLENE: So you'll take anything comparable?

JEANINE: No, I do want prospects. I want more money.

MARLENE: You're getting—?

JEANINE: Hundred.

MARLENE: It's not bad you know. You're what? Twenty?

JEANINE: I'm saving to get married.

MARLENE: Does that mean you don't want a long-term job, Jeanine?

JEANINE: I might do.

MARLENE: Because where do the prospects come in? No kids for a bit?

JEANINE: Oh no, not kids, not yet.

MARLENE: So you won't tell them you're getting married?

JEANINE: Had I better not?

MARLENE: It would probably help.

JEANINE: I'm not wearing a ring. We thought we wouldn't spend on a ring.

MARLENE: Saves taking it off.

JEANINE: I wouldn't take it off.

MARLENE: There's no need to mention it when you go for an interview. / Now, Jeanine, do you have a feel

JEANINE: But what if they ask?

MARLENE: for any particular kind of company?

JEANINE: I thought advertising.

MARLENE: People often do think advertising. I have got a few vacancies but I think they're looking for something glossier.

JEANINE: You mean how I dress? / I can

MARLENE: I mean experience.

JEANINE: dress different. I dress like this on purpose for where I am now.

MARLENE: I have a marketing department here of a knitwear manufacturer. / Marketing is near enough

JEANINE: Knitwear?

MARLENE: advertising. Secretary to the marketing manager, he's thirty-five, married, I've sent him a girl before and she was happy, left to have a baby, you won't want to mention marriage there. He's very fair I think, good at his job, you won't have to nurse him along. Hundred and ten, so that's better than you're doing now.

JEANINE: I don't know.

MARLENE: I've a fairly small concern here, father and two sons, you'd have more say potentially, secretarial and reception duties, only a hundred but the

job's going to grow with the concern and then you'll be in at the top with new girls coming in underneath you.

JEANINE: What is it they do?

MARLENE: Lampshades. / This would be my first choice for you.

JEANINE: Just lampshades?

MARLENE: There's plenty of different kinds of lampshade. So we'll send you there, shall we, and the knitwear second choice. Are you free to go for an interview any day they call you?

JEANINE: I'd like to travel.

MARLENE: We don't have any foreign clients. You'd have to go elsewhere.

JEANINE: Yes I know. I don't really . . . I just mean . . .

MARLENE: Does your fiancé want to travel?

JEANINE: I'd like a job where I was here in London and with him and everything but now and then—I expect it's silly. Are there jobs like that?

MARLENE: There's personal assistant to a top executive in a multinational. If that's the idea you need to be planning ahead. Is that where you want to be in ten years?

JEANINE: I might not be alive in ten years.

MARLENE: Yes but you will be. You'll have children.

JEANINE: I can't think about ten years.

MARLENE: You haven't got the speeds anyway. So I'll send you to these two shall I? You haven't been to any other agency? Just so we don't get crossed wires. Now, Jeanine, I want you to get one of these jobs, all right? If I send you that means I'm putting myself on the line for you. Your presentation's OK, you look fine, just be confident and go in there convinced that this is the best job for you and you're the best person for the job. If you don't believe it they won't believe it.

JEANINE: Do you believe it?

MARLENE: I think you could make me believe it if you put your mind to it.

JEANINE: Yes, all right.

ACT 1 / SCENE 3

(JOYCE's back yard. Sunday afternoon. The house with a back door is upstage. Downstage is a shelter made of junk, made by children. The lights come up on two girls, ANGIE and KIT, who are squashed together in the shelter. ANGIE is sixteen, KIT is twelve. They cannot be seen from the house.)

JOYCE: (Off, calling from the house) Angie. Angie, are you out there?

(Silence. They keep still and wait. When nothing else happens they relax.)

ANGIE: Wish she was dead.

KIT: Wanna watch The Exterminator?

ANGIE: You're sitting on my leg.

KIT: There's nothing on telly. We can have an ice cream. Angie?

ANGIE: Shall I tell you something?

KIT: Do you wanna watch *The Exterminator*?

ANGIE: It's X, innit?

KIT: I can get into Xs.

ANGIE: Shall I tell you something?

KIT: We'll go to something else. We'll go to Ipswich. What's on the Odeon?°

ANGIE: She won't let me, will she?

KIT: Don't tell her.

ANGIE: I've no money.

KIT: I'll pay.

ANGIE: She'll moan though, won't she?

KIT: I'll ask her for you if you like.

ANGIE: I've no money, I don't want you to pay.

KIT: I'll ask her.

ANGIE: She don't like you.

KIT: I still got three pounds birthday money. Did she say she don't like me? I'll go by myself then.

ANGIE: Your mum don't let you. I got to take you.

KIT: She won't know.

ANGIE: You'd be scared who'd sit next to you.

KIT: No I wouldn't. She does like me anyway. Tell me then.

ANGIE: Tell you what?

KIT: It's you she doesn't like.

ANGIE: Well I don't like her so tough shit.

JOYCE: (*Off*) Angie. Angie. Angie. I know you're out there. I'm not coming out after you. You come in here. (*Silence. Nothing happens.*)

ANGIE: Last night when I was in bed. I been thinking yesterday could I make things move. You know, make things move by thinking about them without touching them. Last night I was in bed and suddenly a picture fell down off the wall.

KIT: What picture?

ANGIE: My gran, that picture. Not the poster. The photograph in the frame.

KIT: Had you done something to make it fall down?

ANGIE: I must have done.

KIT: But were you thinking about it?

ANGIE: Not about it, but about something.

KIT: I don't think that's very good.

ANGIE: You know the kitten?

KIT: Which one?

ANGIE: There only is one. The dead one.

KIT: What about it?

ANGIE: I heard it last night.

KIT: Where?

ANGIE: Out here. In the dark. What if I left you here in the dark all night?

KIT: You couldn't. I'd go home.

ANGIE: You couldn't.

KIT: I'd / go home.

ANGIE: No you couldn't, not if I said.

KIT: I could.

ANGIE: Then you wouldn't see anything. You'd just be ignorant.

KIT: I can see in the daytime.

ANGIE: No you can't. You can't hear it in the daytime.

KIT: I don't want to hear it.

ANGIE: You're scared that's all.

KIT: I'm not scared of anything.

ANGIE: You're scared of blood.

KIT: It's not the same kitten anyway. You just heard an old cat. / you just heard some old cat.

ANGIE: You don't know what I heard. Or what I saw. You don't know nothing because you're a baby.

KIT: You're sitting on me.

ANGIE: Mind my hair / you silly cunt.

KIT: Stupid fucking cow, I hate you.

ANGIE: I don't care if you do.

KIT: You're horrible.

ANGIE: I'm going to kill my mother and you're going to watch.

KIT: I'm not playing.

ANGIE: You're scared of blood. (KIT *puts her hand under dress, brings it out with blood on her finger.*)

KIT: There, see, I got my own blood, so. (ANGIE *takes* KIT's *hand and licks her finger.*)

ANGIE: Now I'm a cannibal. I might turn into a vampire now.

KIT: That picture wasn't nailed up right.

ANGIE: You'll have to do that when I get mine.

KIT: I don't have to.

ANGIE: You're scared.

KIT: I'll do it, I might do it. I don't have to just because you say. I'll be sick on you.

ANGIE: I don't care if you are sick on me, I don't mind sick. I don't mind blood. If I don't get away from here I'm going to die.

KIT: I'm going home.

ANGIE: You can't go through the house. She'll see you.

KIT: I won't tell her.

ANGIE: Oh great, fine.

KIT: I'll say I was by myself. I'll tell her you're at my house and I'm going there to get you.

ANGIE: She knows I'm here, stupid.

KIT: Then why can't I go through the house?

ANGIE: Because I said not.

KIT: My mum don't like you anyway.

ANGIE: I don't want her to like me. She's a slag.°

KIT: She is not.

ANGIE: She does it with everyone.

KIT: She does not.

ANGIE: You don't even know what it is.

KIT: Yes I do.

Odeon, popular chain of cinemas.

slag, slut.

ANGIE: Tell me then.

KIT: We get it all at school, cleverclogs. It's on television. You haven't done it.

ANGIE: How do you know?

KIT: Because I know you haven't.

ANGIE: You know wrong then because I have.

KIT: Who with?

ANGIE: I'm not telling you / who with.

KIT: You haven't anyway.

ANGIE: How do you know?

KIT: Who with?

ANGIE: I'm not telling you.

KIT: You said you told me everything.

ANGIE: I was lying wasn't I.

KIT: Who with? You can't tell me who with because / you never—

ANGIE: Sh.

(JOYCE *has come out of the house. She stops halfway across the yard and listens. They listen.*)

JOYCE: You there Angie? Kit? You there Kitty? Want a cup of tea? I've got some chocolate biscuits. Come on now I'll put the kettle on. Want a choccy biccy, Angie? (*They all listen and wait.*) Fucking rotten little cunt. You can stay there and die. I'll lock the door.

(*They all wait.* JOYCE *goes back to the house.* ANGIE *and* KIT *sit in silence for a while.*)

KIT: When there's a war, where's the safest place?

ANGIE: Nowhere.

KIT: New Zealand is, my mum said. Your skin's burned right off. Shall we go to New Zealand?

ANGIE: I'm not staying here.

KIT: Shall we go to New Zealand?

ANGIE: You're not old enough.

KIT: You're not old enough.

ANGIE: I'm old enough to get married.

KIT: You don't want to get married.

ANGIE: No but I'm old enough.

KIT: I'd find out where they were going to drop it and stand right in the place.

ANGIE: You couldn't find out.

KIT: Better than walking round with your skin dragging on the ground. Eugh. / Would you like walking round with your skin dragging on the ground?

ANGIE: You couldn't find out, stupid, it's a secret.

KIT: Where are you going?

ANGIE: I'm not telling you.

KIT: Why?

ANGIE: It's a secret.

KIT: But you tell me all your secrets.

ANGIE: Not the true secrets.

KIT: Yes you do.

ANGIE: No I don't.

KIT: I want to go somewhere away from the war.

ANGIE: Just forget the war.

KIT: I can't.

ANGIE: You have to. It's so boring.

KIT: I'll remember it at night.

ANGIE: I'm going to do something else anyway.

KIT: What? Angie, come on. Angie.

ANGIE: It's a true secret.

KIT: It can't be worse than the kitten. And killing your mother. And the war.

ANGIE: Well I'm not telling you so you can die for all I care.

KIT: My mother says there's something wrong with you playing with someone my age. She says why haven't you got friends your own age. People your own age know there's something funny about you. She says you're a bad influence. She says she's going to speak to your mother. (ANGIE *twists* KIT's *arm till she cries out.*)

ANGIE: Say you're a liar.

KIT: She said it not me.

ANGIE: Say you eat shit.

KIT: You can't make me. (ANGIE *lets go.*)

ANGIE: I don't care anyway. I'm leaving.

KIT: Go on then.

ANGIE: You'll all wake up one morning and find I've gone.

KIT: Good.

ANGIE: I'm not telling you when.

KIT: Go on then.

ANGIE: I'm sorry I hurt you.

KIT: I'm tired.

ANGIE: Do you like me?

KIT: I don't know.

ANGIE: You do like me.

KIT: I'm going home. (*She gets up.*)

ANGIE: No you're not.

KIT: I'm tired.

ANGIE: She'll see you.

KIT: She'll give me a chocolate biscuit.

ANGIE: Kitty.

KIT: Tell me where you're going.

ANGIE: Sit down.

KIT: (*Sitting down again*) Go on then.

ANGIE: Swear?

KIT: Swear.

ANGIE: I'm going to London. To see my aunt.

KIT: And what?

ANGIE: That's it.

KIT: I see my aunt all the time.

ANGIE: I don't see my aunt.

KIT: What's so special?

ANGIE: It is special. She's special.

KIT: Why?

ANGIE: She is.

KIT: Why?

ANGIE: She is.

KIT: Why?

ANGIE: My mother hates her.

KIT: Why?

ANGIE: Because she does.

KIT: Perhaps she's not very nice.

ANGIE: She is nice.

KIT: How do you know?

ANGIE: Because I know her.

KIT: You said you never see her.

ANGIE: I saw her last year. You saw her.

KIT: Did I?

ANGIE: Never mind.

KIT: I remember her. That aunt. What's so special?

ANGIE: She gets people jobs.

KIT: What's so special?

ANGIE: I think I'm my aunt's child. I think my mother's really my aunt.

KIT: Why?

ANGIE: Because she goes to America, now shut up.

KIT: I've been to London.

ANGIE: Now give us a cuddle and shut up because I'm sick.

KIT: You're sitting on my arm.

(They curl up in each other's arms. Silence. JOYCE *comes out of the house and comes up to them quietly.)*

JOYCE: Come on.

KIT: Oh hello.

JOYCE: Time you went home.

KIT: We want to go to the Odeon.

JOYCE: What time?

KIT: Don't know.

JOYCE: What's on?

KIT: Don't know.

JOYCE: Don't know much do you?

KIT: That all right then?

JOYCE: Angie's got to clean her room first.

ANGIE: No I don't.

JOYCE: Yes you do, it's a pigsty.

ANGIE: Well I'm not.

JOYCE: Then you're not going. I don't care.

ANGIE: Well I am going.

JOYCE: You've no money, have you?

ANGIE: Kit's paying anyway.

JOYCE: No she's not.

KIT: I'll help you with your room.

JOYCE: That's nice.

ANGIE: No you won't. You wait here.

KIT: Hurry then.

ANGIE: I'm not hurrying. You just wait. (ANGIE *goes slowly into the house. Silence.)*

JOYCE: I don't know. *(Silence.)* How's school then?

KIT: All right.

JOYCE: What are you now? Third year?

KIT: Second year.

JOYCE: Your mum says you're good at English. *(Silence.)* Maybe Angie should've stayed on.

KIT: She didn't like it.

JOYCE: I didn't like it. And look at me. If your face fits at school it's going to fit other places too. It wouldn't make no difference to Angie. She's not going to get a job when jobs are hard to get. I'd be sorry for anyone in charge of her. She'd better get married. I don't know who'd have her, mind. She's one of those girls might never leave home. What do you want to be when you grow up, Kit?

KIT: Physicist.

JOYCE: What?

KIT: Nuclear physicist.

JOYCE: Whatever for?

KIT: I could, I'm clever.

JOYCE: I know you're clever, pet. *(Silence.)* I'll make a cup of tea. *(Silence.)* Looks like it's going to rain. *(Silence.)* Don't you have friends your own age?

KIT: Yes.

JOYCE: Well then.

KIT: I'm old for my age.

JOYCE: And Angie's simple is she? She's not simple.

KIT: I love Angie.

JOYCE: She's clever in her own way.

KIT: You can't stop me.

JOYCE: I don't want to.

KIT: You can't, so.

JOYCE: Don't be cheeky, Kitty. She's always kind to little children.

KIT: She's coming so you better leave me alone.

*(ANGIE *comes out. She has changed into an old best dress, slightly small for her.)*

JOYCE: What you put that on for? Have you done your room? You can't clean your room in that.

ANGIE: I looked in the cupboard and it was there.

JOYCE: Of course it was there, it's meant to be there. Is that why it was a surprise, finding something in the right place? I should think she's surprised, wouldn't you, Kit, to find something in her room in the right place.

ANGIE: I decided to wear it.

JOYCE: Not today, why? To clean your room? You're not going to the pictures till you've done your room. You can put your dress on after if you like. (ANGIE *picks up a brick.)* Have you done your room? You're not getting out of it, you know.

KIT: Angie, let's go.

JOYCE: She's not going till she's done her room.

KIT: It's starting to rain.

JOYCE: Come on, come on then. Hurry and do your room, Angie, and then you can go to the cinema with Kit. Oh it's wet, come on. We'll look up the time in the paper. Does your mother know, Kit, it's going to be a late night for you, isn't it? Hurry up, Angie. You'll spoil your dress. You make me sick. (JOYCE *and* KIT *run into the house.* ANGIE *stays where she is. There is the sound of rain.* KIT *comes out of the house.)*

KIT: *(Shouting)* Angie. Angie, come on, you'll get wet. *(She comes back to* ANGIE.)*

ANGIE: I put on this dress to kill my mother.

KIT: I suppose you thought you'd do it with a brick.

ANGIE: You can kill people with a brick. (*She puts the brick down.*)

KIT: Well you didn't, so.

ACT 2 / SCENE 1

(*"Top Girls" Employment Agency. Monday morning. There are three desks in the main office and a separate small interviewing area. The lights come up in the main office on* WIN *and* NELL *who have just arrived for work.*)

NELL: Coffee coffee coffee coffee / coffee.

WIN: The roses were smashing. / Mermaid.

NELL: Ohhh.

WIN: Iceberg. He taught me all their names. (NELL *has some coffee now.*)

NELL: Ah. Now then.

WIN: He has one of the finest rose gardens in West Sussex. He exhibits.

NELL: He what?

WIN: His wife was visiting her mother. It was like living together.

NELL: Crafty, you never said.

WIN: He rang on Saturday morning.

NELL: Lucky you were free.

WIN: That's what I told him.

NELL: Did you hell.

WIN: Have you ever seen a really beautiful rose garden?

NELL: I don't like flowers. / I like swimming pools.

WIN: Marilyn. Esther's Baby. They're all called after birds.

NELL: Our friend's late. Celebrating all weekend I bet you.

WIN: I'd call a rose Elvis. Or John Conteh.°

NELL: Is Howard in yet?

WIN: If he is he'll be bleeping us with a problem.

NELL: Howard can just hang on to himself.

WIN: Howard's really cut up.

NELL: Howard thinks because he's a fella the job was his as of right. Our Marlene's got far more balls than Howard and that's that.

WIN: Poor little bugger.

NELL: He'll live.

WIN: He'll move on.

NELL: I wouldn't mind a change of air myself.

WIN: Serious?

NELL: I've never been a staying-put lady. Pastures new.

WIN: So who's the pirate?

NELL: There's nothing definite.

WIN: Inquiries?

NELL: There's always inquiries. I'd think I'd got bad breath if there stopped being inquiries. Most of them can't afford me. Or you.

WIN: I'm all right for the time being. Unless I go to Australia.

NELL: There's not a lot of room upward.

WIN: Marlene's filled it up.

NELL: Good luck to her. Unless there's some prospects moneywise.

WIN: You can but ask.

NELL: Can always but ask.

WIN: So what have we got? I've got a Mr. Holden I saw last week.

NELL: Any use?

WIN: Pushy. Bit of a cowboy.

NELL: Goodlooker?

WIN: Good dresser.

NELL: High flyer?°

WIN: That's his general idea certainly but I'm not sure he's got it up there.

NELL: Prestel° wants six flyers and I've only seen two and a half.

WIN: He's making a bomb on the road but he thinks it's time for an office. I sent him to IBM but he didn't get it.

NELL: Prestel's on the road.

WIN: He's not overbright.

NELL: Can he handle an office?

WIN: Provided his secretary can punctuate he should go far.

NELL: Bear Prestel in mind then, I might put my head round the door. I've got that poor little nerd I should never have said I could help. Tender heart me.

WIN: Tender like old boots. How old?

NELL: Yes well forty-five.

WIN: Say no more.

NELL: He knows his place, he's not after calling himself a manager, he's just a poor little bod wants a better commission and a bit of sunshine.

WIN: Don't we all.

NELL: He's just got to relocate. He's got a bungalow in Dymchurch.

WIN: And his wife says.

NELL: The lady wife wouldn't care to relocate. She's going through the change.

WIN: It's his funeral, don't waste your time.

NELL: I don't waste a lot.

WIN: Good weekend you?

NELL: You could say.

WIN: Which one?

NELL: One Friday, one Saturday.

WIN: Aye—aye.

NELL: Sunday night I watched telly.

WIN: Which of them do you like best really?

NELL: Sunday was best, I like the Ovaltine.°

John Conteh, popular boxer and model.

High flyer, someone who is succeeding by moving up in a chosen field. **Prestel,** television and computer stock market information service. **Ovaltine,** hot chocolate malt drink.

WIN: Holden, Barker, Gardner, Duke.

NELL: I've a lady here thinks she can sell.

WIN: Taking her on?

NELL: She's had some jobs.

WIN: Services?

NELL: No, quite heavy stuff, electric.

WIN: Tough bird like us.

NELL: We could do with a few more here.

WIN: There's nothing going here.

NELL: No but I always want the tough ones when I see them. Hang on to them.

WIN: I think we're plenty.

NELL: Derek asked me to marry him again.

WIN: He doesn't know when he's beaten.

NELL: I told him I'm not going to play house, not even in Ascot.

WIN: Mind you, you could play house.

NELL: If I chose to play house I would play house ace.°

WIN: You could marry him and go on working.

NELL: I could go on working and not marry him.

(MARLENE arrives.)

MARLENE: Morning ladies. (WIN *and* NELL *cheer and whistle.*) Mind my head.

NELL: Coffee coffee coffee.

WIN: We're tactfully not mentioning you're late.

MARLENE: Fucking tube.°

WIN: We've heard that one.

NELL: We've used that one.

WIN: It's the top executive doesn't come in as early as the poor working girl.

MARLENE: Pass the sugar and shut your face, pet.

WIN: Well I'm delighted.

NELL: Howard's looking sick.

WIN: Howard is sick. He's got ulcers and heart. He told me.

NELL: He'll have to stop then, won't he?

WIN: Stop what?

NELL: Smoking, drinking, shouting. Working.

WIN: Well, working.

NELL: We're just looking through the day.

MARLENE: I'm doing some of Pam's ladies. They've been piling up while she's away.

NELL: Half a dozen little girls and an arts graduate who can't type.

WIN: I spent the whole weekend at his place in Sussex.

NELL: She fancies his rose garden.

WIN: I had to lie down in the back of the car so the neighbors wouldn't see me go in.

NELL: You're kidding.

WIN: It was funny.

NELL: Fuck that for a joke.

WIN: It was funny.

MARLENE: Anyway they'd see you in the garden.

---

ace, slang for "first-class." *tube,* London subway.

WIN: The garden has extremely high walls.

NELL: I think I'll tell the wife.

WIN: Like hell.

NELL: She might leave him and you could have the rose garden.

WIN: The minute it's not a secret I'm out on my ear.

NELL: Don't know why you bother.

WIN: Bit of fun.

NELL: I think it's time you went to Australia.

WIN: I think it's pushy Mr. Holden time.

NELL: If you've any really pretty bastards, Marlene, I want some for Prestel.

MARLENE: I might have one this afternoon. This morning it's all Pam's secretarial.

NELL: Not long now and you'll be upstairs watching over us all.

MARLENE: Do you feel bad about it?

NELL: I don't like coming second.

MARLENE: Who does?

WIN: We'd rather it was you than Howard. We're glad for you, aren't we, Nell?

NELL: Oh yes. Aces.

(LOUISE enters the interviewing area. The lights cross-fade to WIN and LOUISE in the interviewing area. NELL exits.)

WIN: Now, Louise, hello, I have your details here. You've been very loyal to the one job I see.

LOUISE: Yes I have.

WIN: Twenty-one years is a long time in one place.

LOUISE: I feel it is. I feel it's time to move on.

WIN: And you are what age now?

LOUISE: I'm in my early forties.

WIN: Exactly?

LOUISE: Forty-six.

WIN: It's not necessarily a handicap, well it is of course we have to face that, but it's not necessarily a disabling handicap, experience does count for something.

LOUISE: I hope so.

WIN: Now between ourselves is there any trouble, any reason why you're leaving that wouldn't appear on the form?

LOUISE: Nothing like that.

WIN: Like what?

LOUISE: Nothing at all.

WIN: No long-term understandings come to a sudden end, making for an insupportable atmosphere?

LOUISE: I've always completely avoided anything like that at all.

WIN: No personality clashes with your immediate superiors or inferiors?

LOUISE: I've always taken care to get on very well with everyone.

WIN: I only ask because it can affect the reference and it also affects your motivation, I want to be quite clear why you're moving on. So I take it the job itself no longer satisfies you. Is it the money?

LOUISE: It's partly the money. It's not so much the money.

WIN: Nine thousand is very respectable. Have you dependants?

LOUISE: No, no dependants. My mother died.

WIN: So why are you making a change?

LOUISE: Other people make changes.

WIN: But why are you, now, after spending most of your life in the one place?

LOUISE: There you are, I've lived for that company, I've given my life really you could say because I haven't had a great deal of social life, I've worked in the evenings. I haven't had office entanglements for the very reason you just mentioned and if you are committed to your work you don't move in many other circles. I had management status from the age of twenty-seven and you'll appreciate what that means. I've built up a department. And there it is, it works extremely well, and I feel I'm stuck there. I've spent twenty years in middle management. I've seen young men who I trained go on, in my own company or elsewhere, to higher things. Nobody notices me, I don't expect it, I don't attract attention by making mistakes, everybody takes it for granted that my work is perfect. They will notice me when I go, they will be sorry I think to lose me, they will offer me more money of course, I will refuse. They will see when I've gone what I was doing for them.

WIN: If they offer you more money you won't stay?

LOUISE: No I won't.

WIN: Are you the only woman?

LOUISE: Apart from the girls of course, yes. There was one, she was my assistant, it was the only time I took on a young woman assistant, I always had my doubts. I don't care greatly for working with women, I think I pass as a man at work. But I did take on this young woman, her qualifications were excellent, and she did well, she got a department of her own, and left the company for a competitor where she's now on the board and good luck to her. She has a different style, she's a new kind of attractive well dressed—I don't mean I don't dress properly. But there is a kind of woman who is thirty now who grew up in a different climate. They are not so careful. They take themselves for granted. I have had to justify my existence every minute, and I have done so, I have proved—well.

WIN: Let's face it, vacancies are ones where you'll be in competition with younger men. And there are companies that will value your experience enough that you'll be in with a chance. There are also fields that are easier for a woman, there is a cosmetic company here where your experience might be relevant. It's eight and a half, I don't know if that appeals.

LOUISE: I've proved I can earn money. It's more important to get away. I feel it's now or never. I sometimes / think—

WIN: You shouldn't talk too much at an interview.

LOUISE: I don't. I don't normally talk about myself. I know very well how to handle myself in an office situation. I only talk to you because it seems to me this is different, it's your job to understand me, surely. You asked the questions.

WIN: I think I understand you sufficiently.

LOUISE: Well good, that's good.

WIN: Do you drink?

LOUISE: Certainly not. I'm not a teetotaler, I think that's very suspect, it's seen as being an alcoholic if you're teetotal. What do you mean? I don't drink. Why?

WIN: I drink.

LOUISE: I don't.

WIN: Good for you.

(The lights crossfade to the main office with MARLENE *sitting at her desk.* WIN *and* LOUISE *exit.* ANGIE *arrives in the main office.)*

ANGIE: Hello.

MARLENE: Have you an appointment?

ANGIE: It's me. I've come.

MARLENE: What? It's not Angie?

ANGIE: It was hard to find this place. I got lost.

MARLENE: How did you get past the receptionist? The girl on the desk, didn't she try to stop you?

ANGIE: What desk?

MARLENE: Never mind.

ANGIE: I just walked in. I was looking for you.

MARLENE: Well you found me.

ANGIE: Yes.

MARLENE: So where's your mum? Are you up in town for the day?

ANGIE: Not really.

MARLENE: Sit down. Do you feel all right?

ANGIE: Yes thank you.

MARLENE: So where's Joyce?

ANGIE: She's at home.

MARLENE: Did you come up on a school trip then?

ANGIE: I've left school.

MARLENE: Did you come up with a friend?

ANGIE: No. There's just me.

MARLENE: You came up by yourself, that's fun. What have you been doing? Shopping? Tower of London?

ANGIE: No, I just come here. I come to you.

MARLENE: That's very nice of you to think of paying your aunty a visit. There's not many nieces make that the first port of call. Would you like a cup of coffee?

ANGIE: No thank you.

MARLENE: Tea, orange?

ANGIE: No thank you.

MARLENE: Do you feel all right?

ANGIE: Yes thank you.

MARLENE: Are you tired from the journey?

ANGIE: Yes, I'm tired from the journey.

MARLENE: You sit there for a bit then. How's Joyce?

ANGIE: She's all right.

MARLENE: Same as ever.

ANGIE: Oh yes.

MARLENE: Unfortunately you've picked a day when I'm rather busy, if there's ever a day when I'm not, or I'd take you out to lunch and we'd go to Madame Tussaud's.° We could go shopping. What time do you have to be back? Have you got a day return?

ANGIE: No.

MARLENE: So what train are you going back on?

ANGIE: I came on the bus.

MARLENE: So what bus are you going back on? Are you staying the night?

ANGIE: Yes.

MARLENE: Who are you staying with? Do you want me to put you up for the night, is that it?

ANGIE: Yes please.

MARLENE: I haven't got a spare bed.

ANGIE: I can sleep on the floor.

MARLENE: You can sleep on the sofa.

ANGIE: Yes please.

MARLENE: I do think Joyce might have phoned me. It's like her.

ANGIE: This is where you work is it?

MARLENE: It's where I have been working the last two years but I'm going to move into another office.

ANGIE: It's lovely.

MARLENE: My new office is nicer than this. There's just the one big desk in it for me.

ANGIE: Can I see it?

MARLENE: Not now, no, there's someone else in it now. But he's leaving at the end of next week and I'm going to do his job.

ANGIE: Is that good?

MARLENE: Yes, it's very good.

ANGIE: Are you going to be in charge?

MARLENE: Yes I am.

ANGIE: I knew you would be.

MARLENE: How did you know?

ANGIE: I knew you'd be in charge of everything.

MARLENE: Not quite everything.

ANGIE: You will be.

MARLENE: Well we'll see.

ANGIE: Can I see it next week then?

MARLENE: Will you still be here next week?

ANGIE: Yes.

MARLENE: Don't you have to go home?

ANGIE: No.

MARLENE: Why not?

ANGIE: It's all right.

MARLENE: Is it all right?

ANGIE: Yes, don't worry about it.

MARLENE: Does Joyce know where you are?

ANGIE: Yes of course she does.

MARLENE: Well does she?

ANGIE: Don't worry about it.

MARLENE: How long are you planning to stay with me then?

ANGIE: You know when you came to see us last year?

MARLENE: Yes, that was nice wasn't it.

ANGIE: That was the best day of my whole life.

MARLENE: So how long are you planning to stay?

ANGIE: Don't you want me?

MARLENE: Yes yes, I just wondered.

ANGIE: I won't stay if you don't want me.

MARLENE: No, of course you can stay.

ANGIE: I'll sleep on the floor. I won't be any bother.

MARLENE: Don't get upset.

ANGIE: I'm not, I'm not. Don't worry about it.

(MRS. KIDD *comes in.*)

MRS. KIDD: Excuse me.

MARLENE: Yes.

MRS. KIDD: Excuse me.

MARLENE: Can I help you?

MRS. KIDD: Excuse me bursting in on you like this but I have to talk to you.

MARLENE: I am engaged at the moment. / If you could go to reception—

MRS. KIDD: I'm Rosemary Kidd, Howard's wife, you don't recognize me but we did meet, I remember you of course / but you wouldn't—

MARLENE: Yes of course, Mrs. Kidd, I'm sorry, we did meet. Howard's about somewhere I expect, have you looked in his office?

MRS. KIDD: Howard's not about, no. I'm afraid it's you I've come to see if I could have a minute or two.

MARLENE: I do have an appointment in five minutes.

MRS. KIDD: This won't take five minutes. I'm very sorry. It is a matter of some urgency.

MARLENE: Well of course. What can I do for you?

MRS. KIDD: I just wanted a chat, an informal chat. It's not something I can simply—I'm sorry if I'm interrupting your work. I know office work isn't like housework / which is all interruptions.

MARLENE: No no, this is my niece. Angie. Mrs. Kidd.

MRS. KIDD: Very pleased to meet you.

ANGIE: Very well thank you.

MRS. KIDD: Howard's not in today.

MARLENE: Isn't he?

MRS. KIDD: He's feeling poorly.

MARLENE: I didn't know. I'm sorry to hear that.

MRS. KIDD: The fact is he's in a state of shock. About what's happened.

MARLENE: What has happened?

MRS. KIDD: You should know if anyone. I'm referring to you being appointed managing director instead of Howard. He hasn't been at all well all weekend. He hasn't slept for three nights. I haven't slept.

MARLENE: I'm sorry to hear that, Mrs. Kidd. Has he thought of taking sleeping pills?

Madame Tussaud's, London waxworks museum.

MRS. KIDD: It's very hard when someone has worked all these years.

MARLENE: Business life is full of little setbacks. I'm sure Howard knows that. He'll bounce back in a day or two. We all bounce back.

MRS. KIDD: If you could see him you'd know what I'm talking about. What's it going to do to him working for a woman? I think if it was a man he'd get over it as something normal.

MARLENE: I think he's going to have to get over it.

MRS. KIDD: It's me that bears the brunt. I'm not the one that's been promoted. I put him first every inch of the way. And now what do I get? You women this, you women that. It's not my fault. You're going to have to be very careful how you handle him. He's very hurt.

MARLENE: Naturally I'll be tactful and pleasant to him, you don't start pushing someone around. I'll consult him over any decisions affecting his department. But that's no different, Mrs. Kidd, from any of my other colleagues.

MRS. KIDD: I think it is different, because he's a man.

MARLENE: I'm not quite sure why you came to see me.

MRS. KIDD: I had to do something.

MARLENE: Well you've done it, you've seen me. I think that's probably all we've time for. I'm sorry he's been taking it out on you. He really is a shit, Howard.

MRS. KIDD: But he's got a family to support. He's got three children. It's only fair.

MARLENE: Are you suggesting I give up the job to him then?

MRS. KIDD: It had crossed my mind if you were unavailable after all for some reason, he would be the natural second choice I think, don't you? I'm not asking.

MARLENE: Good.

MRS. KIDD: You mustn't tell him I came. He's very proud.

MARLENE: If he doesn't like what's happening here he can go and work somewhere else.

MRS. KIDD: Is that a threat?

MARLENE: I'm sorry but I do have some work to do.

MRS. KIDD: It's not that easy, a man of Howard's age. You don't care. I thought he was going too far but he's right. You're one of these ballbreakers, / that's what you

MARLENE: I'm sorry but I do have some work to do.

MRS. KIDD: are. You'll end up miserable and lonely. You're not natural.

MARLENE: Could you please piss off?

MRS. KIDD: I thought if I saw you at least I'd be doing something. (MRS. KIDD goes.)

MARLENE: I've got to go and do some work now. Will you come back later?

ANGIE: I think you were wonderful.

MARLENE: I've got to go and do some work now.

ANGIE: You told her to piss off.

MARLENE: Will you come back later?

ANGIE: Can't I stay here?

MARLENE: Don't you want to go sightseeing?

ANGIE: I'd rather stay here.

MARLENE: You can stay here I suppose, if it's not boring.

ANGIE: It's where I most want to be in the world.

MARLENE: I'll see you later then.

(MARLENE goes. SHONA and NELL enter the interviewing area. ANGIE sits at WIN's desk. The lights crossfade to NELL and SHONA in the interviewing area.)

NELL: Is this right? You are Shona?

SHONA: Yeh.

NELL: It says here you're twenty-nine.

SHONA: Yeh.

NELL: Too many late nights, me. So you've been where you are for four years, Shona, you're earning six basic and three commission. So what's the problem?

SHONA: No problem.

NELL: Why do you want a change?

SHONA: Just a change.

NELL: Change of product, change of area?

SHONA: Both.

NELL: But you're happy on the road?

SHONA: I like driving.

NELL: You're not after management status?

SHONA: I would like management status.

NELL: You'd be interested in titular management status but not come off the road?

SHONA: I want to be on the road, yeh.

NELL: So how many calls have you been making a day?

SHONA: Six.

NELL: And what proportion of those are successful?

SHONA: Six.

NELL: That's hard to believe.

SHONA: Four.

NELL: You find it easy to get the initial interest do you?

SHONA: Oh yeh, I get plenty of initial interest.

NELL: And what about closing?

SHONA: I close, don't I?

NELL: Because that's what an employer is going to have doubts about with a lady as I needn't tell you, whether she's got the guts to push through to a closing situation. They think we're too nice. They think we listen to the buyer's doubts. They think we consider his needs and his feelings.

SHONA: I never consider people's feelings.

NELL: I was selling for six years, I can sell anything, I've sold in three continents, and I'm jolly as they come but I'm not very nice.

SHONA: I'm not very nice.

NELL: What sort of time do you have on the road with the other reps? Get on all right? Handle the chat?

SHONA: I get on. Keep myself to myself.

NELL: Fairly much of a loner are you?

SHONA: Sometimes.

NELL: So what field are you interested in?

SHONA: Computers.

NELL: That's a top field as you know and you'll be up against some very slick fellas there, there's some very pretty boys in computers, it's an American-style field.

SHONA: That's why I want to do it.

NELL: Video systems appeal? That's a high-flying situation.

SHONA: Video systems appeal OK.

NELL: Because Prestel have half a dozen vacancies I'm looking to fill at the moment. We're talking in the area of ten to fifteen thousand here and upwards.

SHONA: Sounds OK.

NELL: I've half a mind to go for it myself. But it's good money here if you've got the top clients. Could you fancy it do you think?

SHONA: Work here?

NELL: I'm not in a position to offer, there's nothing officially going just now, but we're always on the lookout. There's not that many of us. We could keep in touch.

SHONA: I like driving.

NELL: So the Prestel appeals?

SHONA: Yeh.

NELL: What about ties?

SHONA: No ties.

NELL: So relocation wouldn't be a problem.

SHONA: No problem.

NELL: So just fill me in a bit more could you about what you've been doing.

SHONA: What I've been doing. It's all down there.

NELL: The bare facts are down here but I've got to present you to an employer.

SHONA: I'm twenty-nine years old.

NELL: So it says here.

SHONA: We look young. Youngness runs in the family in our family.

NELL: So just describe your present job for me.

SHONA: My present job at present. I have a car. I have a Porsche. I go up the M1° a lot. Burn up the M1 a lot. Straight up the M1 in the fast lane to where the clients are, Staffordshire, Yorkshire, I do a lot in Yorkshire. I'm selling electric things. Like dish-washers, washing machines, stainless steel tubs are a feature and the reliability of the program. After sales service, we offer a very good after sales service, spare parts, plenty of spare parts. And fridges, I sell a lot of fridges specially in the summer. People want to buy fridges in the summer because of the heat melting the butter and you get fed up standing the milk in a basin of cold water with a cloth over, stands to reason people don't want to do that in this day and age. So I sell a lot of them. Big ones with big freezers. Big freezers. And I stay in hotels at night when I'm away from home. On my expense

---

M1, expressway running from London to Yorkshire.

account. I stay in various hotels. They know me, the ones I go to. I check in, have a bath, have a shower. Then I go down to the bar, have a gin and tonic, have a chat. Then I go into the dining room and have dinner. I usually have fillet steak and mushrooms, I like mushrooms. I like smoked salmon very much. I like having a salad on the side. Green salad. I don't like tomatoes.

NELL: Christ what a waste of time.

SHONA: Beg your pardon?

NELL: Not a word of this is true, is it?

SHONA: How do you mean?

NELL: You just filled in the form with a pack of lies.

SHONA: Not exactly.

NELL: How old are you?

SHONA: Twenty-nine.

NELL: Nineteen?

SHONA: Twenty-one.

NELL: And what jobs have you done? Have you done any?

SHONA: I could though, I bet you.

(The lights crossfade to the main office with ANGIE sitting as before. WIN comes in to the main office. SHONA and NELL exit.)

WIN: Who's sitting in my chair?

ANGIE: What? Sorry.

WIN: Who's been eating my porridge?

ANGIE: What?

WIN: It's all right, I saw Marlene. Angie, isn't it? I'm Win. And I'm not going out for lunch because I'm knackered. I'm going to set me down here and have a yogurt. Do you like yogurt?

ANGIE: No.

WIN: That's good because I've only got one. Are you hungry?

ANGIE: No.

WIN: There's a café on the corner.

ANGIE: No thank you. Do you work here?

WIN: How did you guess?

ANGIE: Because you look as if you might work here and you're sitting at the desk. Have you always worked here?

WIN: No I was headhunted. That means I was working for another outfit like this and this lot came and offered me more money. I broke my contract, there was a hell of a stink. There's not many top ladies about. Your aunty's a smashing bird.

ANGIE: Yes I know.

MARLENE: Fan are you? Fan of your aunty's?

ANGIE: Do you think I could work here?

WIN: Not at the moment.

ANGIE: How do I start?

WIN: What can you do?

ANGIE: I don't know. Nothing.

WIN: Type?

ANGIE: Not very well. The letters jump up when I do

capitals. I was going to do a CSE° in commerce but I didn't.

WIN: What have you got?

ANGIE: What?

WIN: CSE's, O's.

ANGIE: Nothing, none of that. Did you do all that?

WIN: Oh yes, all that, and a science degree funnily enough. I started out doing medical research but there's no money in it. I thought I'd go abroad. Did you know they sell Coca Cola in Russia and Pepsi-Cola in China? You don't have to be qualified as much as you might think. Men are awful bullshitters, they like to make out jobs are harder than they are. Any job I ever did I started doing it better than the rest of the crowd and they didn't like it. So I'd get unpopular and I'd have a drink to cheer myself up. I lived with a fella and supported him for four years, he couldn't get work. After that I went to California. I like the sunshine. Americans know how to live. This country's too slow. Then I went to Mexico, still in sales, but it's no country for a single lady. I came home, went bonkers for a bit, thought I was five different people, got over that all right, the psychiatrist said I was perfectly sane and highly intelligent. Got married in a moment of weakness and he's inside° now, he's been inside four years, and I've not been to see him too much this last year. I like this better than sales, I'm not really that aggressive. I started thinking sales was a good job if you want to meet people, but you're meeting people that don't want to meet you. It's no good if you like being liked. Here your clients want to meet you because you're the one doing them some good. They hope. (ANGIE *has fallen asleep.* NELL *comes in.*)

NELL: You're talking to yourself, sunshine.

WIN: So what's new?

NELL: Who is this?

WIN: Marlene's little niece.

NELL: What's she got, brother, sister? She never talks about her family.

WIN: I was telling her my life story.

NELL: Violins?

WIN: No, success story.

NELL: You've heard Howard's had a heart attack?

WIN: No, when?

NELL: I heard just now. He hadn't come in, he was at home, he's gone to hospital. He's not dead. His wife was here, she rushed off in a cab.

WIN: Too much butter, too much smoke. We must send him some flowers. (MARLENE *comes in.*) You've heard about Howard?

MARLENE: Poor sod.

NELL: Lucky he didn't get the job if that's what his health's like.

MARLENE: Is she asleep?

WIN: She wants to work here.

MARLENE: Packer in Tesco° more like.

WIN: She's a nice kid. Isn't she?

MARLENE: She's a bit thick. She's a bit funny.

WIN: She thinks you're wonderful.

MARLENE: She's not going to make it.

ACT 2 / SCENE 2

(JOYCE'S *kitchen. Sunday evening, a year earlier. The lights come up on* JOYCE, ANGIE, *and* MARLENE. MARLENE *is taking presents out of bright carrier bag.* ANGIE *has already opened a box of chocolates.*)

MARLENE: Just a few little things. / I've

JOYCE: There's no need.

MARLENE: no memory for birthdays have I, and Christmas seems to slip by. So I think I owe Angie a few presents.

JOYCE: What do you say?

ANGIE: Thank you very much. Thank you very much, Aunty Marlene. (*She opens a present. It is the dress from Act 1, new.*) Oh look, Mum, isn't it lovely?

MARLENE: I don't know if it's the right size. She's grown up since I saw her. / I knew she was always

ANGIE: Isn't it lovely?

MARLENE: tall for her age.

JOYCE: She's a big lump.

MARLENE: Hold it up, Angie, let's see.

ANGIE: I'll put it on, shall I?

MARLENE: Yes, try it on.

JOYCE: Go on to your room then, we don't want / a strip show thank you.

ANGIE: Of course I'm going to my room, what do you think. Look, Mum, here's something for you. Open it, go on. What is it? Can I open it for you?

JOYCE: Yes, you open it, pet.

ANGIE: Don't you want to open it yourself? / Go on.

JOYCE: I don't mind, you can do it.

ANGIE: It's something hard. It's—what is it? A bottle. Drink is it? No, it's what? Perfume, look. What a lot. Open it, look, let's smell it. Oh it's strong. It's lovely. Put it on me. How do you do it? Put it on me.

JOYCE: You're too young.

ANGIE: I can play wearing it like dressing up.

JOYCE: And you're too old for that. Here, give it here, I'll do it, you'll tip the whole bottle over yourself / and we'll have you smelling all summer.

CSE, Certificate of Secondary Education, similar to O-levels, but less prestigious. *inside,* in jail.

Packer in Tesco, shelf-stocker in major grocery store.

ANGIE: Put it on you. Do I smell? Put it on Aunty too. Put it on Aunty too. Let's all smell.

MARLENE: I didn't know what you'd like.

JOYCE: There's no danger I'd have it already, / that's one thing.

ANGIE: Now we all smell the same.

MARLENE: It's a bit of nonsense.

JOYCE: It's very kind of you Marlene, you shouldn't.

ANGIE: Now I'll put on the dress and then we'll see. (ANGIE goes.)

JOYCE: You've caught me on the hop with the place in a mess. / If you'd let me

MARLENE: That doesn't matter.

JOYCE: know you was coming I'd have got something in to eat. We had our dinner dinnertime. We're just going to have a cup of tea. You could have an egg.

MARLENE: No, I'm not hungry. Tea's fine.

JOYCE: I don't expect you take sugar.

MARLENE: Why not?

JOYCE: You take care of yourself.

MARLENE: How do you mean you didn't know I was coming?

JOYCE: You could have written. I know we're not on the phone but we're not completely in the dark ages, / we do have a postman.

MARLENE: But you asked me to come.

JOYCE: How did I ask you to come?

MARLENE: Angie said when she phoned up.

JOYCE: Angie phoned up, did she.

MARLENE: Was it just Angie's idea?

JOYCE: What did she say?

MARLENE: She said you wanted me to come and see you. / It was a couple of

JOYCE: Ha.

MARLENE: weeks ago. How was I to know that's a ridiculous idea? My diary's always full a couple of weeks ahead so we fixed it for this weekend. I was meant to get here earlier but I was held up. She gave me messages from you.

JOYCE: Didn't you wonder why I didn't phone you myself?

MARLENE: She said you didn't like using the phone. You're shy on the phone and can't use it. I don't know what you're like, do I?

JOYCE: Are there people who can't use the phone?

MARLENE: I expect so.

JOYCE: I haven't met any.

MARLENE: Why should I think she was lying?

JOYCE: Because she's like what she's like.

MARLENE: How do I know / what she's like?

JOYCE: It's not my fault you don't know what she's like. You never come and see her.

MARLENE: Well I have now / and you don't seem over the moon.*

JOYCE: Good. *Well I'd have got a cake if she'd told me. (Pause.)

MARLENE: I did wonder why you wanted to see me.

JOYCE: I didn't want to see you.

MARLENE: Yes, I know. Shall I go?

JOYCE: I don't mind seeing you.

MARLENE: Great, I feel really welcome.

JOYCE: You can come and see Angie any time you like, I'm not stopping you. / You

MARLENE: Ta ever so.°

JOYCE: know where we are. You're the one went away, not me. I'm right here where I was. And will be a few years yet I shouldn't wonder.

MARLENE: All right. All right. (JOYCE gives MARLENE a cup of tea.)

JOYCE: Tea.

MARLENE: Sugar? (JOYCE passes MARLENE the sugar.) It's very quiet down here.

JOYCE: I expect you'd notice it.

MARLENE: The air smells different too.

JOYCE: That's the scent.

MARLENE: No, I mean walking down the lane.

JOYCE: What sort of air you get in London then?

(ANGIE comes in, wearing the dress. It fits.)

MARLENE: Oh, very pretty. / You do look pretty, Angie.

JOYCE: That fits all right.

MARLENE: Do you like the color?

ANGIE: Beautiful. Beautiful.

JOYCE: You better take it off, / you'll get it dirty.

ANGIE: I want to wear it. I want to wear it.

MARLENE: It is for wearing after all. You can't just hang it up and look at it.

ANGIE: I love it.

JOYCE: Well if you must you must.

ANGIE: If someone asks me what's my favorite color I'll tell them it's this. Thank you very much, Aunty Marlene.

MARLENE: You didn't tell your mum you asked me down.

ANGIE: I wanted it to be a surprise.

JOYCE: I'll give you a surprise / one of these days.

ANGIE: I thought you'd like to see her. She hasn't been here since I was nine. People do see their aunts.

MARLENE: Is it that long? Doesn't time fly.

ANGIE: I wanted to.

JOYCE: I'm not cross.

ANGIE: Are you glad?

JOYCE: I smell nicer anyhow, don't I?

(KIT comes in without saying anything, as if she lived there.)

MARLENE: I think it was a good idea, Angie, about time. We are sisters after all. It's a pity to let that go.

JOYCE: This is Kitty, / who lives up the road. This is Angie's Aunty Marlene.

KIT: What's that?

ANGIE: It's a present. Do you like it?

Ta ever so, Thanks ever so much.

KIT: It's all right. / Are you coming out?*

MARLENE: Hello, Kitty.

ANGIE: *No.

KIT: What's that smell?

ANGIE: It's a present.

KIT: It's horrible. Come on.*

MARLENE: Have a chocolate.

ANGIE: *No, I'm busy.

KIT: Coming out later?

ANGIE: No.

KIT: (*To* MARLENE) Hello. (KIT *goes without a chocolate.*)

JOYCE: She's a little girl Angie sometimes plays with because she's the only child lives really close. She's like a little sister to her really. Angie's good with little children.

MARLENE: Do you want to work with children, Angie? / Be a teacher or a nursery nurse?

JOYCE: I don't think she's ever thought of it.

MARLENE: What do you want to do?

JOYCE: She hasn't an idea in her head what she wants to do. / Lucky to get anything.

MARLENE: Angie?

JOYCE: She's not clever like you. (*Pause.*)

MARLENE: I'm not clever, just pushy.

JOYCE: True enough. (MARLENE *takes a bottle of whiskey out of the bag.*) I don't drink spirits.

ANGIE: You do at Christmas.

JOYCE: It's not Christmas, is it?

ANGIE: It's better than Christmas.

MARLENE: Glasses?

JOYCE: Just a small one then.

MARLENE: Do you want some, Angie?

ANGIE: I can't, can I?

JOYCE: Taste it if you want. You won't like it. (ANGIE *tastes it.*)

ANGIE: Mmm.

MARLENE: We got drunk together the night your grandfather died.

JOYCE: We did not get drunk.

MARLENE: I got drunk. You were just overcome with grief.

JOYCE: I still keep up the grave with flowers.

MARLENE: Do you really?

JOYCE: Why wouldn't I?

MARLENE: Have you seen Mother?

JOYCE: Of course I've seen Mother.

MARLENE: I mean lately.

JOYCE: Of course I've seen her lately, I go every Thursday.

MARLENE: (*To* ANGIE) Do you remember your grandfather?

ANGIE: He got me out of the bath one night in a towel.

MARLENE: Did he? I don't think he ever gave me a bath. Did he give you a bath, Joyce? He probably got soft in his old age. Did you like him?

ANGIE: Yes of course.

MARLENE: Why?

ANGIE: What?

MARLENE: So what's the news? How's Mrs. Paisley? Still going crazily? / And Dorothy. What happened to Dorothy?*

ANGIE: Who's Mrs. Paisley?

JOYCE: *She went to Canada.

MARLENE: Did she? What to do?

JOYCE: I don't know. She just went to Canada.

MARLENE: Well / good for her.

ANGIE: Mr. Connolly killed his wife.

MARLENE: What, Connolly at Whitegates?

ANGIE: They found her body in the garden. / Under the cabbages.

MARLENE: He was always so proper.

JOYCE: Stuck up git,° Connolly. Best lawyer money could buy but he couldn't get out of it. She was carrying on with Matthew.

MARLENE: How old's Matthew then?

JOYCE: Twenty-one. / He's got a motorbike.

MARLENE: I think he's about six.

ANGIE: How can he be six? He's six years older than me. / If he was six I'd be nothing, I'd be just born this minute.

JOYCE: Your aunty knows that, she's just being silly. She means it's so long since she's been here she's forgotten about Matthew.

ANGIE: You were here for my birthday when I was nine. I had a pink cake. Kit was only five then, she was four, she hadn't started school yet. She could read already when she went to school. You remember my birthday? / You remember me?

MARLENE: Yes, I remember the cake.

ANGIE: You remember me?

MARLENE: Yes, I remember you.

ANGIE: And Mum and Dad was there, and Kit was.

MARLENE: Yes, how is your dad? Where is he tonight? Up the pub?

JOYCE: No, he's not here.

MARLENE: I can see he's not here.

JOYCE: He moved out.

MARLENE: What? When did he? / Just recently?*

ANGIE: Didn't you know that? You don't know much.

JOYCE: *No, it must be three years ago. Don't be rude, Angie.

ANGIE: I'm not, am I, Aunty? What else don't you know?

JOYCE: You was in America or somewhere. You sent a postcard.

ANGIE: I've got that in my room. It's the Grand Canyon. Do you want to see it? Shall I get it? I can get it for you.

MARLENE: Yes, all right. (ANGIE *goes.*)

JOYCE: You could be married with twins for all I know. You must have affairs and break up and I don't need to know about any of that so I don't see what the fuss is about.

---

git, idiot.

MARLENE: What fuss? (ANGIE *comes back with the postcard.*)

ANGIE: "Driving across the states for a new job in L.A. It's a long way but the car goes very fast. It's very hot. Wish you were here. Love from Aunty Marlene."

JOYCE: Did you make a lot of money?

MARLENE: I spent a lot.

ANGIE: I want to go to America. Will you take me?

JOYCE: She's not going to America, she's been to America, stupid.

ANGIE: She might go again, stupid. It's not something you do once. People who go keep going all the time, back and forth on jets. They go on Concorde and Laker and get jet lag. Will you take me?

MARLENE: I'm not planning a trip.

ANGIE: Will you let me know?

JOYCE: Angie, / you're getting silly.

ANGIE: I want to be American.

JOYCE: It's time you were in bed.

ANGIE: No it's not. / I don't have to go to bed at all tonight.

JOYCE: School in the morning.

ANGIE: I'll wake up.

JOYCE: Come on now, you know how you get.

ANGIE: How do I get? / I don't get anyhow.*

JOYCE: Angie. *Are you staying the night?

MARLENE: Yes, if that's all right. / I'll see you in the morning.

ANGIE: You can have my bed. I'll sleep on the sofa.

JOYCE: You will not, you'll sleep in your bed. / Think

ANGIE: Mum.

JOYCE: I can't see through that? I can just see you going to sleep / with us talking.

ANGIE: I would, I would go to sleep, I'd love that.

JOYCE: I'm going to get cross, Angie.

ANGIE: I want to show her something.

JOYCE: Then bed.

ANGIE: It's a secret.

JOYCE: Then I expect it's in your room so off you go. Give us a shout when you're ready for bed and your aunty'll be up and see you.

ANGIE: Will you?

MARLENE: Yes of course. (ANGIE *goes. Silence.*) It's cold tonight.

JOYCE: Will you be all right on the sofa? You can / have my bed.

MARLENE: The sofa's fine.

JOYCE: Yes the forecast said rain tonight but it's held off.

MARLENE: I was going to walk down to the estuary but I've left it a bit late. Is it just the same?

JOYCE: They cut down the hedges a few years back. Is that since you were here?

MARLENE: But it's not changed down the end, all the mud? And the reeds? We used to pick them up when they were bigger than us. Are there still lapwings?

JOYCE: You get strangers walking there on a Sunday. I

expect they're looking at the mud and the lapwings, yes.

MARLENE: You could have left.

JOYCE: Who says I wanted to leave?

MARLENE: Stop getting at me then, you're really boring.

JOYCE: How could I have left?

MARLENE: Did you want to?

JOYCE: I said how, / how could I?

MARLENE: If you'd wanted to you'd have done it.

JOYCE: Christ.

MARLENE: Are we getting drunk?

JOYCE: Do you want something to eat?

MARLENE: No, I'm getting drunk.

JOYCE: Funny time to visit, Sunday evening.

MARLENE: I came this morning. I spent the day—

ANGIE: (*Off*) Aunty! Aunty Marlene!

MARLENE: I'd better go.

JOYCE: Go on then.

MARLENE: All right.

ANGIE: (*Off*) Aunty! Can you hear me? I'm ready.

(MARLENE *goes.* JOYCE *goes on sitting, clears up, sits again.* MARLENE *comes back.*)

JOYCE: So what's the secret?

MARLENE: It's a secret.

JOYCE: I know what it is anyway.

MARLENE: I bet you don't. You always said that.

JOYCE: It's her exercise book.

MARLENE: Yes, but you don't know what's in it.

JOYCE: It's some game, some secret society she has with Kit.

MARLENE: You don't know the password. You don't know the code.

JOYCE: You're really in it, aren't you. Can you do the handshake?

MARLENE: She didn't mention a handshake.

JOYCE: I thought they'd have a special handshake. She spends hours writing that but she's useless at school. She copies things out of books about black magic, and politicians out of the paper. It's a bit childish.

MARLENE: I think it's a plot to take over the world.

JOYCE: She's been in the remedial class the last two years.

MARLENE: I came up this morning and spent the day in Ipswich. I went to see Mother.

JOYCE: Did she recognize you?

MARLENE: Are you trying to be funny?

JOYCE: No, she does wander.

MARLENE: She wasn't wandering at all, she was very lucid thank you.

JOYCE: You were very lucky then.

MARLENE: Fucking awful life she's had.

JOYCE: Don't tell me.

MARLENE: Fucking waste.

JOYCE: Don't talk to me.

MARLENE: Why shouldn't I talk? Why shouldn't I talk to you? / Isn't she my mother too?

JOYCE: Look, you've left, you've gone away, / we can do without you.

MARLENE: I left home, so what, I left home. People do leave home / it is normal.

JOYCE: We understand that, we can do without you.

MARLENE: We weren't happy. Were you happy?

JOYCE: Don't come back.

MARLENE: So it's just your mother is it, your child, you never wanted me round, / you were jealous

JOYCE: Here we go.

MARLENE: of me because I was the little one and I was clever.

JOYCE: I'm not clever enough for all this psychology / if that's what it is.

MARLENE: Why can't I visit my own family / without

JOYCE: Aah.

MARLENE: all this?

JOYCE: Just don't go on about Mum's life when you haven't been to see her for how many years. / I go

MARLENE: It's up to me.

JOYCE: and see her every week.

MARLENE: Then don't go and see her every week.

JOYCE: Somebody has to.

MARLENE: No they don't. / Why do they?

JOYCE: How would I feel if I didn't go?

MARLENE: A lot better.

JOYCE: I hope you feel better.

MARLENE: It's up to me.

JOYCE: You couldn't get out of here fast enough. (*Pause.*)

MARLENE: Of course I couldn't get out of here fast enough. What was I going to do? Marry a dairyman who'd come home pissed? / Don't you fucking this

JOYCE: Christ.

MARLENE: fucking that fucking bitch fucking tell me what to fucking do fucking.

JOYCE: I don't know how you could leave your own child.

MARLENE: You were quick enough to take her.

JOYCE: What does that mean?

MARLENE: You were quick enough to take her.

JOYCE: Or what? Have her put in a home? Have some stranger / take her would you rather?

MARLENE: You couldn't have one so you took mine.

JOYCE: I didn't know that then.

MARLENE: Like hell, / married three years.

JOYCE: I didn't know that. Plenty of people / take that long.

MARLENE: Well it turned out lucky for you, didn't it?

JOYCE: Turned out all right for you by the look of you. You'd be getting a few less thousand a year.

MARLENE: Not necessarily.

JOYCE: You'd be stuck here / like you said.

MARLENE: I could have taken her with me.

JOYCE: You didn't want to take her with you. It's no good coming back now, Marlene, / and saying—

MARLENE: I know a managing director who's got two children, she breastfeeds in the board room, she pays a hundred pounds a week on domestic help alone and she can afford that because she's an extremely high-powered lady earning a great deal of money.

JOYCE: So what's that got to do with you at the age of seventeen?

MARLENE: Just because you were married and had somewhere to live—

JOYCE: You could have lived at home. / Or live

MARLENE: Don't be stupid.

JOYCE: with me and Frank. / You

MARLENE: You never suggested.

JOYCE: said you weren't keeping it. You shouldn't have had it / if you wasn't

MARLENE: Here we go.

JOYCE: going to keep it. You was the most stupid, / for someone so clever you was the most stupid, get yourself pregnant, not go to the doctor, not tell.

MARLENE: You wanted it, you said you were glad, I remember the day, you said I'm glad you never got rid of it, I'll look after it, you said that down by the river. So what are you saying, sunshine, you don't want her?

JOYCE: Course I'm not saying that.

MARLENE: Because I'll take her, / wake her up and pack now.

JOYCE: You wouldn't know how to begin to look after her.

MARLENE: Don't you want her?

JOYCE: Course I do, she's my child.

MARLENE: Then what are you going on about / why did I have her?

JOYCE: You said I got her off you / when you didn't—

MARLENE: I said you were lucky / the way it—

JOYCE: Have a child now if you want one. You're not old.

MARLENE: I might do.

JOYCE: Good. (*Pause.*)

MARLENE: I've been on the pill so long / I'm probably sterile.

JOYCE: Listen when Angie was six months I did get pregnant and I lost it because I was so tired looking after your fucking baby / because she cried so

MARLENE: You never told me.

JOYCE: much—yes I did tell you— / and the doctor

MARLENE: Well I forgot.

JOYCE: said if I'd sat down all day with my feet up I'd've kept it / and that's the only chance I ever had because after that—

MARLENE: I've had two abortions, are you interested? Shall I tell you about them? Well I won't, it's boring, it wasn't a problem. I don't like messy talk about blood / and what a bad time we all had. I

JOYCE: If I hadn't had your baby. The doctor said.

MARLENE: don't want a baby. I don't want to talk about gynecology.

JOYCE: Then stop trying to get Angie off of me.

MARLENE: I come down here after six years. All night you've been saying I don't come often enough. If I don't come for another six years she'll be twenty-one, will that be OK?

JOYCE: That'll be fine, yes, six years would suit me fine. (*Pause.*)

MARLENE: I was afraid of this. I only came because I thought you wanted . . . I just want . . . (*She cries.*)

JOYCE: Don't grizzle,° Marlene, for God's sake. Marly? Come on, pet. Love you really. Fucking stop it, will you? (*She goes to* MARLENE.)

MARLENE: No, let me cry. I like it. (*They laugh,* MARLENE *begins to stop crying.*) I knew I'd cry if I wasn't careful.

JOYCE: Everyone's always crying in this house. Nobody takes any notice.

MARLENE: You've been wonderful looking after Angie.

JOYCE: Don't get carried away.

MARLENE: I can't write letters but I do think of you.

JOYCE: You're getting drunk. I'm going to make some tea.

MARLENE: Love you. (JOYCE *goes to make tea.*)

JOYCE: I can see why you'd want to leave. It's a dump here.

MARLENE: So what's this about you and Frank?

JOYCE: He was always carrying on, wasn't he. And if I wanted to go out in the evening he'd go mad, even if it was nothing, a class, I was going to go to an evening class. So he had this girlfriend, only twenty-two poor cow, and I said go on, off you go, hoppit. I don't think he even likes her.

MARLENE: So what about money?

JOYCE: I've always said I don't want your money.

MARLENE: No, does he send you money?

JOYCE: I've got four different cleaning jobs. Adds up. There's not a lot round here.

MARLENE: Does Angie miss him?

JOYCE: She doesn't say.

MARLENE: Does she see him?

JOYCE: He was never that fond of her to be honest.

MARLENE: He tried to kiss me once. When you were engaged.

JOYCE: Did you fancy him?

MARLENE: No, he looked like a fish.

JOYCE: He was lovely then.

MARLENE: Ugh.

JOYCE: Well I fancied him. For about three years.

MARLENE: Have you got someone else?

JOYCE: There's not a lot round here. Mind you, the minute you're on your own, you'd be amazed how your friends' husbands drop by. I'd sooner do without.

MARLENE: I don't see why you couldn't take my money.

JOYCE: I do, so don't bother about it.

MARLENE: Only got to ask.

JOYCE: So what about you? Good job?

MARLENE: Good for a laugh. / Got back

JOYCE: Good for more than a laugh I should think.

MARLENE: from the US of A a bit wiped out and slotted into this speedy employment agency and still there.

JOYCE: You can always find yourself work then?

MARLENE: That's right.

JOYCE: And men?

MARLENE: Oh there's always men.

JOYCE: No one special?

MARLENE: There's fellas who like to be seen with a high-flying lady. Shows they've got something really good in their pants. But they can't take the day to day. They're waiting for me to turn into the little woman. Or maybe I'm just horrible of course.

JOYCE: Who needs them.

MARLENE: Who needs them. Well I do. But I need adventures more. So on on into the sunset. I think the eighties are going to be stupendous.

JOYCE: Who for?

MARLENE: For me. / I think I'm going up up up.

JOYCE: Oh for you. Yes, I'm sure they will.

MARLENE: And for the country, come to that. Get the economy back on its feet and whoosh. She's a tough lady, Maggie.° I'd give her a job. / She just needs to hang

JOYCE: You voted for them, did you?

MARLENE: in there. This country needs to stop whining. / Monetarism is not

JOYCE: Drink your tea and shut up, pet.

MARLENE: stupid. It takes time, determination. No more slop. / And

JOYCE: Well I think they're filthy bastards.

MARLENE: who's got to drive it on? First woman prime minister. Terrifico. Aces. Right on. / You must admit. Certainly gets my vote.

JOYCE: What good's first woman if it's her? I suppose you'd have liked Hitler if he was a woman. Ms. Hitler. Got a lot done, Hitlerina. / Great adventures.

MARLENE: Bosses still walking on the workers' faces? Still dadda's little parrot? Haven't you learned to think for yourself? I believe in the individual. Look at me.

JOYCE: I am looking at you.

MARLENE: Come on, Joyce, we're not going to quarrel over politics.

JOYCE: We are though.

MARLENE: Forget I mentioned it. Not a word about the slimy unions will cross my lips. (*Pause.*)

JOYCE: You say Mother had a wasted life.

MARLENE: Yes I do. Married to that bastard.

JOYCE: What sort of life did he have? /

---

grizzle, whine.

Maggie, Margaret Thatcher, former prime minister (1979–1991).

MARLENE: Violent life?

JOYCE: Working in the fields like an animal. / Why

MARLENE: Come off it.

JOYCE: wouldn't he want a drink? You want a drink. He couldn't afford whiskey.

MARLENE: I don't want to talk about him.

JOYCE: You started, I was talking about her. She had a rotten life because she had nothing. She went hungry.

MARLENE: She was hungry because he drank the money. / He used to hit her.

JOYCE: It's not all down to him. / Their

MARLENE: She didn't hit him.

JOYCE: lives were rubbish. They were treated like rubbish. He's dead and she'll die soon and what sort of life / did they have?

MARLENE: I saw him one night. I came down.

JOYCE: Do you think I didn't? / They

MARLENE: I still have dreams.

JOYCE: didn't get to America and drive across it in a fast car. / Bad nights, they had bad days.

MARLENE: America, America, you're jealous. / I had to get out, I knew when I

JOYCE: Jealous?

MARLENE: was thirteen, out of their house, out of them, never let that happen to me, / never let him, make my own way, out.

JOYCE: Jealous of what you've done, you'd be ashamed of me if I came to your office, your smart friends, wouldn't you, I'm ashamed of you, think of nothing but yourself, you've got on, nothing's changed for most people, / has it?

MARLENE: I hate the working class / which is what

JOYCE: Yes you do.

MARLENE: you're going to go on about now, it doesn't exist any more, it means lazy and stupid. / I don't

JOYCE: Come on, now we're getting it.

MARLENE: like the way they talk. I don't like beer guts and football vomit and saucy tits / and brothers and sisters—

JOYCE: I spit when I see a Rolls Royce, scratch it with my ring / Mercedes it was.

MARLENE: Oh very mature—

JOYCE: I hate the cows I work for / and their dirty dishes with blanquette of fucking veau.

MARLENE: and I will not be pulled down to their level by a flying picket and I won't be sent to Siberia / or a loony bin just because I'm original. And I support

JOYCE: No, you'll be on a yacht, you'll be head of Coca Cola and you wait, the eighties is going to be stupendous all right because we'll get you lot off our backs—

MARLENE: Reagan even if he is a lousy movie star because the reds are swarming up his map and I want to be free in a free world—

JOYCE: What? / What?

MARLENE: I know what I mean / by that—not shut up here.

JOYCE: So don't be round here when it happens because if someone's kicking you I'll just laugh. (Silence.)

MARLENE: I don't mean anything personal. I don't believe in class. Anyone can do anything if they've got what it takes.

JOYCE: And if they haven't?

MARLENE: If they're stupid or lazy or frightened, I'm not going to help them get a job, why should I?

JOYCE: What about Angie?

MARLENE: What about Angie?

JOYCE: She's stupid, lazy, and frightened, so what about her?

MARLENE: You run her down too much. She'll be all right.

JOYCE: I don't expect so, no. I expect her children will say what a wasted life she had. If she has children. Because nothing's changed and it won't with them in.

MARLENE: Them, them. / Us and them?

JOYCE: And you're one of them.

MARLENE: And you're us, wonderful us, and Angie's us / and Mum and Dad's us.

JOYCE: Yes, that's right, and you're them.

MARLENE: Come on, Joyce, what a night. You've got what it takes.

JOYCE: I know I have.

MARLENE: I didn't really mean all that.

JOYCE: I did.

MARLENE: But we're friends anyway.

JOYCE: I don't think so, no.

MARLENE: Well it's lovely to be out in the country. I really must make the effort to come more often. I want to go to sleep. I want to go to sleep. (JOYCE gets blankets for the sofa.)

JOYCE: Goodnight then. I hope you'll be warm enough.

MARLENE: Goodnight. Joyce—

JOYCE: No, pet. Sorry. (JOYCE goes. MARLENE sits wrapped in a blanket and has another drink. ANGIE comes in.)

ANGIE: Mum?

MARLENE: Angie? What's the matter?

ANGIE: Mum?

MARLENE: No, she's gone to bed. It's Aunty Marlene.

ANGIE: Frightening.

MARLENE: Did you have a bad dream? What happened in it? Well you're awake now, aren't you, pet?

ANGIE: Frightening.

Figure 1. Marlene (Gwen Taylor, *seated center*) hosts a dinner for her guests. They are (*left to right*): Lady Nijo (Lindsay Duncan), Dull Gret (Carole Hayman), Pope Joan (Selina Cadell), Patient Griselda (Lesley Manville), and Isabella Bird (Deborah Findlay). The Royal Court production of *Top Girls,* was directed by Max Stafford-Clark, 1982. (Photograph: Donald Cooper/ Photostage.)

Figure 2. Kit (Lou Wakefield) and Angie (Carole Hayman) share confidences in "a shelter made of junk, made by children" in the Royal Court production of *Top Girls,* directed by Max Stafford-Clark, 1982. (Photograph: Donald Cooper/Photostage.)

Staging of *Top Girls*

**REVIEW OF THE ROYAL COURT THEATRE
PREMIERE, 1982, BY ROBERT CUSHMAN**

Last week Caryl Churchill's *Top Girls* opened on the Royal Court's main stage, while Louise Page's *Salonika* ended its run upstairs. For a short time the Court housed the two most interesting new plays of the year, both of them written by women. A chap has to take notice.

Miss Churchill's last play, *Cloud Nine,* had a complicated time-scheme, simplicity itself compared to what happens in *Top Girls.* In the first scene Marlene, who has just been made managing director of an employment agency, hosts a dinner party at a London restaurant called La Prima Donna. Her guests are various historical prima donnas: Isabella Bird, Scots Victorian lady traveler; Lady Nijo, thirteenth-century Japanese courtesan turned Buddhist nun, and also a traveler; Dull Gret, kitchenmaid in armor, centerpiece of a Bruegel painting depicting a female invasion of Hell; Pope Joan; Patient Griselda.

These are all ladies who have suffered. Joan, for example, may have been Pope, but she ended up stoned to death, having ill-advisedly given birth. On the other hand they are all, in some sense, successes. Even Griselda, as Marlene points out, made it into three bestsellers through the terrible psychological battering she took from her husband.

They all profess devotion to the men in their lives: fathers, emperors, lovers actual or platonic, even husbands. This shocks Marlene; she wants them all as her patron saints, but she can't stomach Griselda, who typically arrives late and will only order cheese and biscuits. At first we share her irritation; after all, she's modern and they're archaic. Then our feelings slide.

Dull Gret doesn't say much. She's the real subversive. She—if you except an even more silent waitress—is the only person present not, by birth or adoption, upper class. She is played by Carole Hayman, who appears in the rest of the play as a modern girl similarly disinherited: someone who has dreams but no prospects.

This girl is presented to us as Marlene's niece. The bulk of the play is split between Marlene's London office and her East Anglian roots. The office is revealing, since not only is Marlene a success herself, but she is in the business of sniffing out success in other people, and of mercilessly weeding out failure. The play here goes down intriguing side-turnings, showing us two of Marlene's juniors, both self-consciously tough, and a variety of their clients.

One of them is nervous and middle-aging, aware of having suppressed her sexuality to survive on men's terms in their world. She is played by Selina Cadell, who has already scored a booming success as Pope Joan. Another is differently androgynous, with salesman fantasies.

Meanwhile there is Marlene's sister, who stayed at home. (Isabella Bird's sister also stayed home, though I confess I failed to pick up this thread at the time.) She points out that Marlene's upward mobility has changed nothing for most women, or indeed most men. Marlene declares herself a Thatcherite, which we might have deduced for ourselves. Her sister's political stance comes as a surprise, and seems manufactured for the occasion.

But the play runs thin nowhere else. Thoroughly personal in tone and structure, it manages to be an amazingly full polygonal presentation of a feminist predicament: career women behaving like career men. The situation is (mostly) deplored, but sympathy is withheld from no one. Miss Churchill also does for overlapping dialogue on stage what Robert Altman has done in the movies.

The seven actresses are terrific. Gwen Taylor, in her third play on socially sundered sisters (she's also played Mrs. Thatcher), is Marlene; Lindsay Duncan is gorgeous as Lady Nijo, wrestling simultaneously with the ways of Western woman and her first zabaglione. Max Stafford-Clark directed; I congratulate him, and wonder how he felt at rehearsals.

SAM SHEPARD

1943–

Sam Shepard has always been on the move, beginning with his early days as an Air Force child: "By the time I was six I had lived or spent time in Illinois, Wisconsin, Florida, North and South Dakota, Iowa, Washington, Indiana, Idaho, Michigan, the Marianas Islands, and finally California, where I stayed more or less until the age of eighteen." After high school, a year at junior college, and a variety of jobs in California (stable hand, herdsman, orange picker, sheep shearer), Shepard joined the Bishop's Company Repertory Players and hit the road again, touring New England and finally ending up in New York City. There, in addition to the commercial theater on Broadway, and the lively world of Off-Broadway, a new movement was flourishing, financed by playwrights and actors, usually in nontheatrical settings (churches, restaurants, even a hardware store), known collectively as Off-Off-Broadway. Shepard made his way into that world by a happy coincidence of timing and employment. Working as a bus boy at the Village Gate, a nightclub specializing in jazz, he met the head waiter, Ralph Cook, just as Cook was planning a new Off-Off venture at St. Mark's Church (located in New York's Bowery). Prophetically named Theatre Genesis, the new company opened its doors with a double bill of Shepard's *Cowboys* and *The Rock Garden* (1964). Shepard's prolific output (six short plays in 1965 alone) found a highly supportive environment in Theatre Genesis. Not only did he drop his family name (he was originally named Samuel Shepard Rogers III) but he quickly established his theatrical identity.

Though many now well-known playwrights were associated with Off-Off Broadway in the 1960s—John Guare, Maria Irene Fornes, Megan Terry, Jean-Claude van Itallie, Leonard Melfi, Rochelle Owens, Lanford Wilson, to name a few—Shepard's astonishing output and his compellingly surrealist visions of America distinguished him as a playwright of extraordinary talent. His plays moved from Theatre Genesis to the American Place Theatre where *La Turista*, produced in 1967, won him the first of nine Obie awards; *The Unseen Hand* (1969) was produced at the La Mama Experimental Theatre Club, one of the still surviving venues of Off-Off Broadway; and in 1970, his most scenically complex and longest play to date, *Operation Sidewinder*, opened at Lincoln Center's Vivian Beaumont Theater, with a large cast, and, in the center of the stage, a six-foot sidewinder rattlesnake, which was also an Air Force computer. Such arresting theatrical images helped Shepard's plays gain recognition from audiences and critics alike, as well as support for himself from prestigious foundations; he won a Rockefeller grant in 1967 and a Guggenheim fellowship in 1968.

But the real turning point in Shepard's playwriting came during his extended stay in England from 1971 to 1974: "It wasn't until I came to England that I found out what it means to be an American." Having discovered his cultural roots, he immediately embodied them in *The Tooth of Crime* (1972), a recasting of the Western shoot-out as a confrontation between the established rock star, Hoss, and the "gypsy" challenger, Crow. Combining the mythology of the Western and popular music, the use of a referee and pom-pom–waving cheerleaders, Shepard drew not only on his own intermittent musical career (as a drummer), but even more on his fascination with language, since the climactic duel between Hoss and Crow involves a variety of linguistic styles, which in turn create striking physical gestures. Working in a similarly eclectic cultural vein, Shepard to date has written over forty plays—short pieces, full-length works, collaborative efforts, and film scripts. Not since Eugene O'Neill has an American playwright been so prolific. And, like O'Neill, who went through an extended period of experimenting with symbolic drama before turning in his last autobiographical plays to a much more realistic style, Shepard too has moved from symbolic settings such as the junkyard of Azusa ("Everything from 'A' to 'Z' in the USA") in *The Unseen Hand* or the snake-dominated desert of *Operation Sidewinder* to settings that people might actually live in. Thus, the stage directions in *Curse of the Starving Class* (1978) call for "a very plain breakfast table with a red oilcloth covering it" as well as "a working refrigerator and a small gas stove." In *Buried Child* (1979), the action takes place in an old farmhouse, sparsely furnished, but with realistic items such as a couch and a television set. In *True West* (1980), the set combines kitchen and living room, and Shepard insists in his stage directions that "the set should be constructed realistically" and that "the costumes should be exactly representative of who the characters are."

Though the worlds of these three plays—like those of *Fool for Love* (1983) and *A Lie of the Mind* (1985)—may seem more realistic than those depicted in his earlier work, certain thematic and structural motifs link them to the early plays. Drawing on his unrooted childhood and on his adolescence in California, a state that is literally the last frontier of America, Shepard constantly shows people living on the edge, sometimes physically, but always emotionally. *Curse of the Starving Class* takes place in Southern California, where the lushness of the surroundings throws into sharp relief the barrenness of family relationships ("I could smell the avocado blossoms" says one character while another later unloads a bagful of artichokes into a mostly empty refrigerator). *True West* also takes place in Southern California, where the smooth glittery world of Hollywood, both as a real place and as a world of dreams and fictions, is constantly threatened by the conflict between two brothers. And in *Fool for Love*, the setting is significantly a "stark, low-rent motel room *on the edge of the Mojave Desert*" [emphasis added]. All of these Western settings picture an America teetering on the verge of emotional and social annihilation. In the nineteenth century, the West lured adventurers, speculators, outcasts, and pioneers and thus became the mythic place for America to reinvent itself. In the twentieth century, Shepard evokes that myth as a way of showing how desperately America—and its people—need to find themselves again.

That need for self-definition and identity creates one of Shepard's most noticeable stylistic traits, the monologue. In one sense, Shepard's characters speak in monologue because they are isolated and, like Jerry in Edward Albee's *The Zoo Story*, can't easily make contact. Blue Morphan in *The Unseen Hand* sits in a junked Chevy convertible and talks to an imaginary driver because there is no one else for him to talk to. Halie, the mother in *Buried Child*, lives in emotional isolation, focusing on her dead son, Ansel, and imagining how different her barren life would have been if Ansel had lived, ignoring the two men on stage with her. And in *Fool for Love*, Eddie's monologue about his missing father and May's monologue about her mother lead finally to the revelation that they are half-brother and sister.

Repeatedly, Shepard sees his characters linked in mutual dependence and mutual estrangement or hostility. The story of the eagle who picked up a tomcat ends *Curse of the Starving Class* with a metaphoric statement that reverberates through many of Shepard's plays: "They fight like crazy in the middle of the sky. That cat's tearing his chest out, and the eagle's trying to drop him, but the cat won't let go because he knows if he falls he'll die." Usually the linkage is a violent one, as Shepard finds many ways to represent the violence that seems inherent in both people and places. There is literal violence, with offstage explosions such as the car blowing up at the end of *Curse of the Starving Class* and Eddie's horse trailer catching fire at the end of *Fool for Love*. There is symbolic violence when Bradley puts his fingers into Shelly's mouth in *Buried Child* or Eddie systematically ropes the bedposts in *Fool for Love*. There is the physical violence of a set turned from a neat apartment to "a desert junkyard" in *True West*. And in *Fool for Love*, Shepard requires that his actors not only slam doors (carefully miked so that the slam reverberates) but actually hit the walls with their bodies. Thus the motel room becomes a prison in which Eddie and May must confront feelings that both pull them together and drive them apart; they can't live with each other, but they also can't live without each other.

The insistent physicality of *Fool for Love* grows not only from Shepard's vision but also from the collaboration of the actors who first performed Eddie and May—namely, Ed Harris and Kathy Baker—with Shepard, who directed the first two productions in San Francisco and in New York. The actors' willingness to throw themselves—often literally—into their roles exemplifies the powerful hold this destructive relationship can create. After four performances on a weekend, said Ed Harris, "there's a desperation about it. The play is like that. It's the characters' last hour and a half together." May's clinging to Eddie in the opening moments (see Figure 1) powerfully embodies her need for him, while the violence that permeates their relationship is expressed not only through body language but through props such as the shotgun that Eddie carefully dismantles (see Figure 2). Though the motel room is bleakly empty (see Figure 3), such emptiness is filled with the desperation and energy of both characters and actors as they create what Shepard calls "a certain kind of emotional terrain that was true to itself," a territory not of land but of feeling.

FOOL FOR LOVE
for Billy Pearson

BY SAM SHEPARD

"*The proper response to love is to accept it. There is nothing to* do."

—Archbishop Anthony Bloom

This play is to be performed relentlessly without a break.

SCENE

Stark, low-rent motel room on the edge of the Mojave Desert. Faded green plaster walls. Dark brown linoleum floor. No rugs. Cast iron four poster single bed, slightly off center favoring stage right, set horizontally to audience. Bed covered with faded blue chenille bedspread. Metal table with well-worn yellow Formica top. Two matching metal chairs in the fifties "S" shape design with yellow plastic seats and backs, also well-worn. Table set extreme down left (from actor's p.o.v.). Chairs set upstage and down right of table. Nothing on the table. Faded yellow exterior door in the center of the stage-left wall. When this door is opened, a small orange porch light shines into room. Yellow bathroom door up right of the stage-right wall. This door slightly ajar to begin with, revealing part of an old style porcelain sink, white towels, a general clutter of female belongings and allowing a yellow light to bleed onto stage. Large picture window dead center of upstage wall, framed by dirty, long, dark green plastic curtains. Yellow-orange light from a streetlamp shines thru window.

Extreme down left, next to the table and chairs is a small extended platform on the same level as the stage. The floor is black and it's framed by black curtains. The only object on the platform is an old maple rocking chair facing upstage right. A pillow with no slipcover rests on the seat. An old horse blanket with holes is laced to the back of the rocker. The color of the blanket should be subdued—grays and blacks.

Lights fade to black on set. In the dark, Merle Haggard's tune "Wake Up" from his The Way I Am *album is heard. Lights begin to rise slowly on stage in the tempo of the song. Volume swells with the lights until they arrive at their mark. The platform remains in darkness with only a slight spill from the stage lights. Three actors are revealed.*

CHARACTERS

THE OLD MAN *sits in the rocker facing up right so he's just slightly profile to the audience. A bottle of whiskey sits on the floor beside him. He picks up bottle and pours whiskey into a Styrofoam cup and drinks. He has a scraggly red beard, wears an old stained "open-road" Stetson hat (the kind with the short brim), a sun-bleached, dark quilted jacket with the stuffing coming out at the elbows, black-and-white checkered slacks that are too short in the legs, beat up, dark western boots, an old vest and a pale green shirt. He exists only in the minds of* MAY *and* EDDIE, *even though they might talk to him directly and acknowledge his physical presence.* THE OLD MAN *treats them as though they all existed in the same time and place.*

MAY *sits on the edge of bed facing audience, feet on floor, legs apart, elbows on knees, hands hanging limp and crossed between her knees, head hanging forward, face staring at floor. She is absolutely still and maintains this attitude until she speaks. She wears a blue denim full skirt, baggy white T-shirt and bare feet with a silver ankle bracelet. She's in her early thirties.*

EDDIE *sits in the upstage chair by the table, facing* MAY. *He wears muddy, broken-down cowboy boots with silver gaffer's tape wrapped around them at the toe and instep, well-worn, faded, dirty jeans that smell like horse sweat. Brown western shirt with snaps. A pair of spurs dangles from his belt. When he walks, he limps slightly and gives the impression he's rarely off a horse. There's a peculiar broken-down quality about his body in general, as though he's aged long before his time. He's in his late thirties. On the floor, between his feet, is a leather bucking strap like bronc riders use. He wears a bucking glove on his right hand and works resin into the glove from a small white bag. He stares at* MAY *as he does this and ignores* THE OLD MAN. *As the song nears the end of its fade, he leans over, sticks his gloved hand into the handle of the bucking strap and twists it so that it makes a weird stretching sound from the friction of the resin and leather. The song ends, lights up full. He pulls his hand out and removes glove.*

EDDIE: *(seated, tossing glove on the table. Short pause)* May, look. May? I'm not goin' anywhere. See? I'm right here. I'm not gone. Look. *(she won't)* I don't know why you won't just look at me. You know it's me.

Who else do you think it is. *(pause)* You want some water or somethin'? Huh? *(he gets up slowly, goes cautiously to her, strokes her head softly, she stays still)* May? Come on. You can't just sit around here like this. How long you been sittin' here anyway? You want me to go outside and get you something? Some potato chips or something? *(she suddenly grabs his closest leg with both arms and holds tight burying her head between his knees)* I'm not gonna' leave. Don't worry. I'm not gonna' leave. I'm stayin' right here. I already told ya' that. *(she squeezes tighter to his leg, he just stands there, strokes her head softly)* May? Let go, okay? Honey? I'll put you back in bed. Okay? *(she grabs his other leg and holds on tight to both)* Come on. I'll put you in bed and make you some hot tea or somethin'. You want some tea? *(she shakes her head violently, keeps holding on)* With lemon? Some Ovaltine? May, you gotta' let go of me now, okay? *(pause, then she pushes him away and returns to her original position)* Now just lay back and try to relax. *(he starts to try to push her back gently on the bed as he pulls back the blankets. She erupts furiously, leaping off bed and lashing out at him with her fists. He backs off. She returns to bed and stares at him wild-eyed and angry, faces him squarely)*

EDDIE: *(after pause)* You want me to go?

(She shakes her head.)

MAY: No!
EDDIE: Well, what do you want then?
MAY: You smell.
EDDIE: I smell.
MAY: You do.
EDDIE: I been drivin' for days.
MAY: Your fingers smell.
EDDIE: Horses.
MAY: Pussy.
EDDIE: Come on, May.
MAY: They smell like metal.
EDDIE: I'm not gonna' start this shit.
MAY: Rich pussy. Very clean.
EDDIE: Yeah, sure.
MAY: You know it's true.
EDDIE: I came to see if you were all right.
MAY: I don't need you!
EDDIE: Okay. *(turns to go, collects his glove and bucking strap)* Fine.
MAY: Don't go!
EDDIE: I'm goin'.

(He exits stage-left door, slamming it behind him; the door booms.)

MAY: *(agonized scream)* Don't go!!!

(She grabs pillow, clutching it to her chest, then throws herself face down on bed, moaning and moving from one end of bed to the other on her elbows and knees. EDDIE is heard returning to stage-left door outside. She leaps

off bed clutching pillow, stands upstage right of bed, facing stage-left door. EDDIE enters stage-left door, banging it behind him. He's left the glove and bucking strap offstage. They stand there facing each other for a second. He makes a move toward her. MAY retreats to extreme upstage-right corner of room clutching pillow to her chest. EDDIE stays against left wall, facing her.)*

EDDIE: What am I gonna' do? Huh? What am I supposed to do?
MAY: You know.
EDDIE: What.
MAY: You're gonna' erase me.
EDDIE: What're you talkin' about?
MAY: You're either gonna' erase me or have me erased.
EDDIE: Why would I want that? Are you kidding?
MAY: Because I'm in the way.
EDDIE: Don't be stupid.
MAY: I'm smarter than you are and you know it. I can smell your thoughts before you even think 'em.

(EDDIE moves along wall to upstage-left corner. MAY holds her ground in opposite corner.)

EDDIE: May, I'm tryin' to take care of you. All right?
MAY: No, you're not. You're just guilty. Gutless and guilty.
EDDIE: Great.

(He moves down left to table, sticking close to wall. Pause.)

MAY: *(quietly, staying in corner)* I'm gonna' kill her ya' know.
EDDIE: Who?
MAY: Who.
EDDIE: Don't talk like that.

(MAY slowly begins to move downstage right as EDDIE simultaneously moves up left. Both of them press the walls as they move.)

MAY: I am. I'm gonna' kill her and then I'm gonna' kill you. Systematically. With sharp knives. Two separate knives. One for her and one for you. *(she slams wall with her elbow. Wall resonates)* So the blood doesn't mix. I'm gonna' torture her first though. Not you. I'm just gonna' let you have it. Probably in the midst of a kiss. Right when you think everything's been healed up. Right in the moment when you're sure you've got me buffaloed. That's when you'll die.

(She arrives extreme down right at the very limits of the set. EDDIE in the extreme up left corner. Pause.)

EDDIE: You know how many miles I went outa' my way just to come here and see you? You got any idea?
MAY: Nobody asked you to come.
EDDIE: Two thousand, four hundred and eighty.
MAY: Yeah? Where were you, Katmandu or something?

EDDIE: Two thousand, four hundred and eighty miles.

MAY: So what!

(He drops his head, stares at floor. Pause. She stares at him. He begins to move slowly down left, sticking close to wall as he speaks.)

EDDIE: I missed you. I did. I missed you more than anything I ever missed in my whole life. I kept thinkin' about you the whole time I was driving. Kept seeing you. Sometimes just a part of you.

MAY: Which part?

EDDIE: Your neck.

MAY: My neck?

EDDIE: Yeah.

MAY: You missed my neck?

EDDIE: I missed all of you but your neck kept coming up for some reason. I kept crying about your neck.

MAY: Crying?

EDDIE: *(he stops by stage-left door. She stays down right)* Yeah. Weeping. Like a little baby. Uncontrollable. It would just start up and stop and then start up all over again. For miles. I couldn't stop it. Cars would pass me on the road. People would stare at me. My face was all twisted up. I couldn't stop my face.

MAY: Was this before or after your little fling with the Countess?

EDDIE: *(he bangs his head into the wall. Wall booms)* There wasn't any fling with any Countess!

MAY: You're a liar.

EDDIE: I took her out to dinner once, okay?

MAY: Ha!

(She moves upstage-right wall.)

EDDIE: Twice.

MAY: You were bumping her on a regular basis! Don't gimme that shit.

EDDIE: You can believe whatever you want.

MAY: *(she stops by bathroom door, opposite Eddie)* I'll believe the truth! It's less confusing.

(Pause.)

EDDIE: I'm takin' you back, May.

(She tosses pillow on bed and moves to upstage-right corner.)

MAY: I'm not going back to that idiot trailer if that's what you think.

EDDIE: I'm movin' it. I got a piece of ground up in Wyoming.

MAY: Wyoming? Are you crazy? I'm not moving to Wyoming. What's up there? Marlboro Men?

EDDIE: You can't stay here.

MAY: Why not? I got a job. I'm a regular citizen here now.

EDDIE: You got a job?

MAY: *(she moves back down to head of bed)* Yeah. What'd you think, I was helpless?

EDDIE: No. I mean—it's been a long time since you had a job.

MAY: I'm a cook.

EDDIE: A cook? You can't even flip an egg, can you?

MAY: I'm not talkin' to you anymore!

(She turns away from him, runs into the bathroom, slams door behind her. EDDIE goes after her, tries door, but she's locked it.)

EDDIE: *(at bathroom door)* May, I got everything worked out. I been thinkin' about this for weeks. I'm gonna' move the trailer. Build a little pipe corral to keep the horses. Have a big vegetable garden. Some chickens maybe.

MAY'S VOICE: *(unseen, behind bathroom door)* I hate chickens! I hate horses! I hate all that shit! You know that. You got me confused with somebody else. You keep comin' up here with this lame country dream life with chickens and vegetables and I can't stand any of it. It makes me puke to even think about it.

EDDIE: *(EDDIE has crossed stage left during this, stops at table)* You'll get used to it.

MAY: *(enters from bathroom)* You're unbelievable!

(She slams bathroom door, crosses upstage to window.)

EDDIE: I'm not lettin' go of you this time, May.

(He sits in chair upstage of table.)

MAY: You never had ahold of me to begin with. *(pause)* How many times have you done this to me?

EDDIE: What.

MAY: Suckered me into some dumb little fantasy and then dropped me like a hot rock. How many times has that happened?

EDDIE: It's no fantasy.

MAY: It's all a fantasy.

EDDIE: And I never dropped you either.

MAY: No, you just disappeared!

EDDIE: I'm here now aren't I?

MAY: Well, praise Jesus God!

EDDIE: I'm gonna' take care of you, May. I am. I'm gonna' stick with you no matter what. I promise.

MAY: Get outa' here.

(Pause.)

EDDIE: What'd you have to go and run off for anyway.

MAY: Run off? Me?

EDDIE: Yeah. Why couldn't you just stay put. You knew I was comin' back to get you.

MAY: *(crossing down to head of bed)* What do you think it's like sittin' in a tin trailer for weeks on end with the wind ripping through it? Waitin' around for the butane to arrive. Hiking down to the Laundromat in the rain. Do you think that's thrilling or somethin'?

EDDIE: *(still sitting)* I bought you all those magazines.

MAY: What magazines?

EDDIE: I bought you a whole stack of those fashion magazines before I left. I thought you liked those. Those French kind.

MAY: Yeah, I especially liked the one with the Countess on the cover. That was real cute.

(Pause.)

EDDIE: All right.

(He stands.)

MAY: All right, what.

(He turns to go out stage-left door.)

MAY: Where are you going?

EDDIE: Just to get my stuff outa' the truck. I'll be right back.

MAY: What're you movin' in now or something?

EDDIE: Well, I thought I'd spend the night if that's okay.

MAY: Are you kidding?

EDDIE: *(opens door)* Then I'll just leave, I guess.

MAY: *(she stands)* Wait.

(He closes door. They stand there facing each other for a while. She crosses slowly to him. She stops. He takes a few steps toward her. Stops. They both move closer. Stop. Pause as they look at each other. They embrace. Long, tender kiss. They are very soft with each other. She pulls away from him slightly. Smiles. She looks him straight in the eyes, then suddenly knees him in the groin with tremendous force. EDDIE doubles over and drops like a rock. She stands over him. Pause.)

MAY: You can take it, right. You're a stunt man.

(She exits into bathroom, stage right, slams the door behind her. The door is amplified with microphones and a bass drum hidden in the frame so that each time an actor slams it, the door booms loud and long. Same is true for the stage-left door. EDDIE remains on the floor holding his stomach in pain. Stage lights drop to half their intensity as a spot rises softly on THE OLD MAN. He speaks directly to EDDIE.)

THE OLD MAN: I thought you were supposed to be a fantasist, right? Isn't that basically the deal with you? You dream things up. Isn't that true?

EDDIE: *(stays on floor)* I don't know.

THE OLD MAN: You don't know. Well, if you don't know I don't know who the hell else does. I wanna' show you somethin'. Somethin' real, okay? Somethin' actual.

EDDIE: Sure.

THE OLD MAN: Take a look at that picture on the wall over there. *(he points at wall stage-right. There is no picture but EDDIE stares at the wall.)* Ya' see that? Take a good look at that. Ya' see it?

EDDIE: *(staring at wall)* Yeah.

THE OLD MAN: Ya' know who that is?

EDDIE: I'm not sure.

THE OLD MAN: Barbara Mandrell. That's who that is. Barbara Mandrell. You heard a' her?

EDDIE: Sure.

THE OLD MAN: Well, would you believe me if I told ya' I was married to her?

EDDIE: *(pause)* No.

THE OLD MAN: Well, see, now that's the difference right there. That's realism. I am actually married to Barbara Mandrell in my mind. Can you understand that?

EDDIE: Sure.

THE OLD MAN: Good. I'm glad we have an understanding.

(THE OLD MAN drinks from his cup. Spot slowly fades to black as stage lights come back up full. These light changes are cued to the opening and closing of doors. MAY enters from bathroom, closes door quietly. She is carrying a sleek red dress, panty hose, a pair of black high heels, a black shoulder purse and a hairbrush. She crosses to foot of bed and throws the clothes on it. Hangs the purse on a bedpost, sits on foot of bed her back to EDDIE and starts brushing her hair. EDDIE remains on floor. She finishes brushing her hair, throws brush on bed, then starts taking off her clothes and changing into the clothes she brought onstage. As she speaks to EDDIE and changes into the new clothes, she gradually transforms from her former tough drabness into a very sexy woman. This occurs almost unnoticeably in the course of her speech.)

MAY: *(very cold, quick, almost monotone voice like she's writing him a letter)* I don't understand my feelings. I really don't. I don't understand how I could hate you so much after so much time. How, no matter how much I'd like to not hate you, I hate you even more. It grows. I can't even see you now. All I see is a picture of you. You and her. I don't even know if the picture's real anymore. I don't even care. It's a made-up picture. It invades my head. The two of you. And this picture stings even more than if I'd actually seen you with her. It cuts me. It cuts me so deep I'll never get over it. And I can't get rid of this picture either. It just comes. Uninvited. Kinda' like a little torture. And I blame you more for this little torture than I do for what you did.

EDDIE: *(standing slowly)* I'll go.

MAY: You better.

EDDIE: Why?

MAY: You just better.

EDDIE: I thought you wanted me to stay.

MAY: I got somebody coming to get me.

EDDIE: *(short pause, on his feet)* Here?

MAY: Yeah, here. Where else?

EDDIE: *(makes a move toward her upstage)* You been seeing somebody?

MAY: *(she moves quickly down left, crosses right)* When was the last time we were together, Eddie? Huh? Can you remember that far back?

EDDIE: Who've you been seeing?

(He moves violently toward her.)

MAY: Don't you touch me! Don't you even think about it.

EDDIE: How long have you been seeing him!

MAY: What difference does it make!

(Short pause. He stares at her, then turns suddenly and exits out the stage-left door and slams it behind him. Door booms.)

MAY: Eddie! Where are you going? Eddie!

(Short pause. She looks after EDDIE, then turns fast, moves upstage to window. She parts the Venetian blinds, looks out window, turns back into room. She rushes to upstage side of bed, gets down on hands and knees, pulls a suitcase out from under bed, throws it on top of bed, opens it. She rushes into bathroom, disappears, leaving door open. She comes back in with various items of clothing, throws stuff into suitcase, turns as if to go back into bathroom. Stops. She hears EDDIE off left. She quickly shuts suitcase, slides it under bed again, rushes around to downstage side of bed. Sits on bed. Stands again. Rushes back into bathroom, returns with hairbrush, slams bathroom door. Starts brushing her hair as though that's what she's been doing all along. She sits on bed brushing her hair. EDDIE enters stage left, slams door behind him, door booms. He stands there holding a ten gauge shotgun in one hand and a bottle of tequila in the other. He moves toward bed, tosses shotgun on bed beside her.)

MAY: *(she stands, moves upstage, stops brushing her hair)* Oh, wonderful. What're you gonna' do with that?

EDDIE: Clean it.

(He opens the bottle.)

EDDIE: You got any glasses?

MAY: In the bathroom.

EDDIE: What're they doin' in the bathroom?

(EDDIE crosses toward bathroom door with bottle.)

MAY: I keep everything in the bathroom. It's safer.

EDDIE: You want some a' this?

MAY: I'm on the wagon.

EDDIE: Good. 'Bout time.

(He exits into bathroom. MAY moves back to bed, stares at shotgun.)

MAY: Eddie, this is a very friendly person who's coming over here. He's not malicious in any way. *(pause)* Eddie?

EDDIE'S VOICE: *(off right)* Where's the damn glasses?

MAY: In the medicine cabinet!

EDDIE'S VOICE: What the hell're they doin' in the medicine cabinet!

(Sound of medicine cabinet being opened and slammed shut off right.)

MAY: There's no germs in the medicine cabinet!

EDDIE'S VOICE: Germs.

MAY: Eddie, did you hear me?

(EDDIE enters with a glass, pouring tequila into it slowly until it's full as he crosses to table down left.)

MAY: Did you hear what I said, Eddie?

EDDIE: About what?

MAY: About the man who's coming over here.

EDDIE: What man?

MAY: Oh, brother.

(EDDIE sets bottle of tequila on table then sits in upstage chair. Takes a long drink from glass. He ignores THE OLD MAN.)

EDDIE: First off, it can't be very serious.

MAY: Oh, really? And why is that?

EDDIE: Because you call him a "man."

MAY: What am I supposed to call him?

EDDIE: A "guy" or something. If you called him a "guy," I'd be worried about it but since you call him a "man" you give yourself away. You're in a dumb situation with this guy by calling him a "man." You put yourself below him.

MAY: What in the hell do you know about it.

EDDIE: This guy's gotta' be a twerp. He's gotta' be a punk chump in a two dollar suit or somethin'.

MAY: Anybody who doesn't half kill themselves falling off horses or jumping on steers is a twerp in your book.

EDDIE: That's right.

MAY: And what're you supposed to be, a "guy" or a "man"?

(EDDIE lowers his glass slowly. Stares at her. Pause. He smiles then speaks low and deliberately.)

EDDIE: I'll tell you what. We'll just wait for this "man" to come over here. The two of us. We'll just set right here and wait. Then I'll let you be the judge.

MAY: Why is everything a big contest with you? He's not competing with you. He doesn't even know you exist.

EDDIE: You can introduce me.

MAY: I'm not introducing you. I am definitely not introducing you. He'd be very embarrassed to find me here with somebody else. Besides, I've only just met him.

EDDIE: Embarrassed?

MAY: Yes! Embarrassed. He's a very gentle person.

EDDIE: Is that right. Well, I'm a very gentle person myself. My feelings get easily damaged.

MAY: What feelings.

(EDDIE falls silent, takes a drink, then gets up slowly with glass, leaves bottle on table, crosses to bed, sits on bed, sets glass on floor, picks up shotgun and starts dismantling it. MAY watches him closely.)

MAY: You can't keep messing me around like this. It's been going on too long. I can't take it anymore. I get sick everytime you come around. Then I get sick when you leave. You're like a disease to me. Besides, you got no right being jealous of me after all the bullshit I've been through with you.

(Pause. EDDIE *keeps his attention on shotgun as he talks to her.)*

EDDIE: We've got a pact.

MAY: Oh, God.

EDDIE: We made a pact.

MAY: There's nothing between us now!

EDDIE: Then what're you so excited about?

MAY: I'm not excited.

EDDIE: You're beside yourself.

MAY: You're driving me crazy. You're driving me totally crazy!

EDDIE: You know we're connected, May. We'll always be connected. That was decided a long time ago.

MAY: Nothing was decided! You made all that up.

EDDIE: You know what happened.

MAY: You promised me that was finished. You can't start that up all over again. You promised me.

EDDIE: A promise can't stop something like that. It happened.

MAY: Nothing happened! Nothing ever happened!

EDDIE: Innocent to the last drop.

MAY: *(pause, controlled)* Eddie—will you please leave? Now.

EDDIE: You're gonna' find out one way or the other.

MAY: I want you to leave.

EDDIE: You didn't want me to leave before.

MAY: I want you to leave now. And it's not because of this man. It's just—

EDDIE: What.

MAY: Stupid. You oughta' know that by now.

EDDIE: You think so, huh?

MAY: It'll be the same thing over and over again. We'll be together for a little while and then you'll be gone.

EDDIE: I'll be gone.

MAY: You will. You know it. You just want me now because I'm seeing somebody else. As soon as that's over, you'll be gone again.

EDDIE: I didn't come here because you were seein' somebody else! I don't give a damn who you're seeing! You'll never replace me and you know it!

MAY: Get outa' here!

(Long silence. EDDIE *lifts his glass and toasts her, then slowly drinks it dry. He sets glass down softly on floor.)*

EDDIE: *(smiles at her)* All right.

(He rises slowly, picks up the sections of his shotgun. He stands there looking down at the shotgun pieces for a second. MAY *moves slightly toward him.)*

MAY: Eddie—

(His head jerks up and stares at her. She stops cold.)

EDDIE: You're a traitor.

(He exits left with shotgun. Slams door. Door booms. MAY *runs toward door.)*

MAY: Eddie!!

(She throws herself against stage-left door. Her arms reach out and hug the walls. She weeps and slowly begins to move along the stage-left wall upstage to the corner, embracing the wall as she moves and weeps. THE OLD MAN *begins to tell his story as* MAY *moves slowly along the wall. He tells it directly to her as though she's a child.* MAY *remains involved with her emotion of loss and keeps moving clear around the room, hugging the walls during the course of the story until she arrives in the extreme downstage-right corner of the room. She sinks to her knees.)*

(Slowly, in the course of MAY's *mourning, the spotlight softly rises on* THE OLD MAN *and the stage lights decrease to half again.)*

THE OLD MAN: Ya' know, one thing I'll never forget. I'll never forget this as long as I live—and I don't even know why I remember it exactly. We were drivin' through southern Utah once, I think it was. Me, you and your mother—in that old Plymouth we had. You remember that Plymouth? Had a white plastic hood ornament on it. Replica of the *Mayflower* I think it was. Some kind a' ship. Anyway, we'd been drivin' all night and you were sound asleep in the front. And all of a sudden you woke up crying. Just bustin' a gut over somethin'. I don't know what it was. Nightmare or somethin'. Woke your mom right up and she climbed over the seat in back there with you to try to get you settled down. But you wouldn't shut up for hell or high water. Just kept wailing away. So I stopped the Plymouth by the side of the road. Middle a' nowhere. I can't even remember where it was exactly. Pitch black. I picked you up outa' the back seat there and carried you into this field. Thought the cold air might quiet you down a little bit. But you just kept on howling away. Then, all of a sudden, I saw somethin' move out there. Somethin' bigger than both of us put together. And it started to move toward us kinda' slow.

*(*MAY *begins to crawl slowly on her hands and knees from down-right corner toward bed. When she reaches bed, she grabs pillow and embraces it, still on her knees. She rocks back and forth embracing pillow as* THE OLD MAN *continues.)*

And then it started to get joined up by some other things just like it. Same shape and everything. It was so black out there I could hardly make out my own hand. But these things started to kinda' move in on us from all directions in a big circle. And I stopped dead still and turned back to the car to see if your mother was all right. But I couldn't see the car anymore. So I called out to her. I called her name loud and clear. And she answered me back from outa' the darkness. She yelled back to me. And just then these things started to "moo." They all started "mooing" away.

(He makes the sound of a cow.)

And it turns out, there we were, standin' smack in the middle of a goddamn herd of cattle. Well, you never heard a baby pipe down so fast in your life. You never made a peep after that. The whole rest of the trip.

(MAY stops rocking abruptly. Suddenly MAY hears EDDIE off left. Stage lights pop back up. Spot on THE OLD MAN cuts to black. She leaps to her feet, completely dropping her grief, hesitates a second, then rushes to chair upstage of table and sits. She takes a drink straight from the bottle, slams bottle down on table, leans back in the chair and stares at the bottle as though she's been sitting like that the whole time since he left. EDDIE enters fast from stage-left door carrying two steer ropes. He slams door. Door booms. He completely ignores MAY. She completely ignores him and keeps staring at the bottle. He crosses upstage of bed, throws one of the ropes on bed and starts building a loop in the other rope, feeding it with the left hand so that it makes a snakelike zipping sound as it passes through the honda. Now he begins to pay attention to MAY as he continues fooling with the rope. She remains staring at the bottle of tequila.)

EDDIE: Decided to jump off the wagon, huh?

(He spins the rope above his head in a flat horn-loop, then ropes one of the bedposts, taking up the slack with a sharp snap of the right hand. He takes the loop off the bedpost, rebuilds it, swings and ropes another bedpost. He continues this right around the bed, roping every post and never missing. MAY takes another drink and sets bottle down quietly.)

MAY: *(still not looking at him)* What're you doing?

EDDIE: Little practice. Gotta' stay in practice these days. There's kids out there ropin' calves in six seconds dead. Can you believe that? Six and no change. Flyin' off the saddle on the right hand side like a bunch a' Spider Monkeys. I'm tellin' ya', they got it down to a science.

(He continues roping bedposts, making his way around the bed in a circle.)

MAY: *(flatly, staring at bottle)* I thought you were leaving. Didn't you say you were leaving?

EDDIE: *(as he ropes)* Well, yeah, I was gonna'. But then it suddenly occurred to me in the middle of the parking lot out there that there probably isn't any man comin' over here at all. There probably isn't any

"guy" or any "man" or anybody comin' over here. You just made all that up.

MAY: Why would I do that?

EDDIE: Just to get even.

(She turns to him slowly in chair, takes a drink, stares at him, then sets bottle on table.)

MAY: I'll never get even with you.

(He laughs, crosses to table, takes a deep drink from bottle, cocks his head back, gargles, swallows, then does a back-flip across stage and crashes into stage-right wall.)

MAY: So, now we're gonna' get real mean and sloppy, is that it? Just like old times.

EDDIE: Well, I haven't dropped the reins in quite a while ya' know. I've been real good. I have. No hooch. No slammer. No women. No nothin'. I been a pretty boring kind of a guy actually. I figure I owe it to myself. Once a once.

(He returns to roping the bedposts. She just stares at him from the chair.)

MAY: Why are you doing this?

EDDIE: I already told ya'. I need the practice.

MAY: I don't mean that.

EDDIE: Well, say what ya' mean then, honey.

MAY: Why are you going through this whole thing again like you're trying to impress me or something. Like we just met. This is the same crap you laid on me in high school.

EDDIE: *(still roping)* Well, it's just a little testimony of my love, see, baby. I mean if I stopped trying to impress you, that'd mean it was all over, wouldn't it?

MAY: It *is* all over.

EDDIE: You're trying to impress me, too, aren't you?

MAY: You know me inside and out. I got nothing new to show you.

EDDIE: You got this guy comin' over. This new guy. That's very impressive. I woulda' thought you'd be hung out to dry by now.

MAY: Oh, thanks a lot.

EDDIE: What is he, a "younger man" or something?

MAY: It's none of your damn business.

EDDIE: Have you balled him yet?

(She throws him a mean glare and just pins him with her eyes.)

EDDIE: Have you? I'm just curious. *(pause)* You don't have to tell me. I already know.

MAY: You're just like a little kid, you know that? A jealous little snot-nosed kid.

(EDDIE laughs, spits, makes a snot-nosed-kid face, keeps roping bedposts.)

EDDIE: I hope this guy comes over. I really hope he does. I wanna' see him walk through that door.

MAY: What're you gonna' do?

(He stops roping, turns to her. He smiles.)

EDDIE: I'm gonna' nail his ass to the floor. Directly.

(He suddenly ropes chair downstage, right next to MAY. *He takes up slack and drags chair violently back toward bed. Pause. They stare at each other.* MAY *suddenly stands, goes to bedpost, grabs her purse, slings it on her shoulder and heads for stage-left door.)*

MAY: I'm not sticking around for this.

(She exits stage-left door, leaving it open. EDDIE *runs offstage after her.)*

EDDIE: Where're you goin'?

MAY: *(off left)* Take your hands offa' me!

EDDIE: *(off left)* Wait a second, wait a second. Just a second, okay?

*(*MAY *screams.* EDDIE *carries her back onstage screaming and kicking. He sets her down, slams door shut. She walks away from him stage right, straightening her dress.)*

EDDIE: Tell ya' what. I'll back off. I'll be real nice. I will. I promise. I'll be just like a little ole pussycat, okay? You can introduce me to him as your brother or something. Well—maybe not your brother.

MAY: Maybe not.

EDDIE: Your cousin. Okay? I'll be your cousin. I just wanna' meet him is all. Then I'll leave. Promise.

MAY: Why do you want to meet him? He's just a friend.

EDDIE: Just to see where you stand these days. You can tell a lot about a person by the company they keep.

MAY: Look. I'm going outside. I'm going to the pay phone across the street. I'm calling him up and I'm telling him to forget about the whole thing. Okay?

EDDIE: Good. I'll pack up your stuff while you're gone.

MAY: I'm not going with you, Eddie!

(Suddenly headlights arc across the stage from upstage right, through the window. They slash across the audience, then dissolve off left. These should be two intense beams of piercing white light and not "realistic" headlights.)

MAY: Oh, great.

(She rushes upstage to window, looks out. EDDIE *laughs, takes a drink.)*

EDDIE: Why don't ya' run out there. Go ahead. Run on out. Throw yourself into his arms or somethin'. Blow kisses in the moonlight.

*(*EDDIE *laughs, moves to bed, pulls a pair of old spurs off his belt. Sits. Starts putting spurs on his boots. It's important these spurs look old and used, with small rowels—not cartoon "cowboy" spurs.* MAY *goes into bathroom, leaving door open.)*

MAY: *(off right)* What're you doing?

EDDIE: Puttin' my hooks on. I wanna' look good for this "man." Give him the right impression. I'm yer cousin, after all.

MAY: *(entering from bathroom)* If you hurt him, Eddie—

EDDIE: I'm not gonna' hurt him. I'm a nice guy. Very sensitive, too. Very civilized.

MAY: He's just a date, you know. Just an ordinary date.

EDDIE: Yeah? Well, I'm gonna turn him into a fig.

(He starts laughing so hard at his own joke that he rolls off the bed and crashes to the floor. He goes into a fit of laughter, pounding his fists into the floor. MAY *makes a move toward the door, then stops and turns to* EDDIE.*)*

MAY: Eddie! Do me a favor. Just this once, okay?

EDDIE: *(laughing hard)* Anything you want, honey. Anything you want.

(He goes on laughing hysterically.)

MAY: *(turning away from him)* Shit.

(She goes to stage-left door and throws it open. Pitch black outside with only the porch light glowing. She stands in the doorway, staring out. Pause as EDDIE *slowly gains control of himself and stops laughing. He stares at* MAY.*)*

EDDIE: *(still on floor)* What're you doing? *(Pause.* MAY *keeps looking out)* May?

MAY: *(staring out open door)* It's not him.

EDDIE: It's not, huh?

MAY: No, it's not.

EDDIE: Well, who is it then?

MAY: Somebody else.

EDDIE: *(slowly getting up and sitting on bed)* Yeah. It's probably not ever gonna' be "him." What're you tryin' to make me jealous for? I know you've been livin' alone.

MAY: It's a big, huge, extra-long, black Mercedes-Benz.

EDDIE: *(pause)* Well, this is a motel, isn't it? People are allowed to park in front of a motel if they're stayin' here.

MAY: People who stay here don't drive a big, huge, extra-long, black Mercedes-Benz.

EDDIE: You don't, but somebody else might.

MAY: *(still at door)* This is not a black Mercedes-Benz type of motel.

EDDIE: Well, close the damn door then and get back inside.

MAY: Somebody's sitting out there in that car looking straight at me.

EDDIE: *(stands fast)* What're they doing?

MAY: It's not a "they," It's a "she."

*(*EDDIE *drops to floor behind bed.)*

EDDIE: Well, what's she doing, then?

MAY: Just sitting there. Staring at me.

EDDIE: Get away from the door, May.

MAY: *(turning toward him slowly)* You don't know anybody with a black Mercedes-Benz by any chance, do you?

EDDIE: Get away from the door!

(Suddenly the white headlight beams slash across the stage through the open door. EDDIE *rushes to door, slams it*

shut and pushes MAY *aside. Just as he slams the door the sound of a large caliber magnum pistol explodes off left, followed immediately by the sound of shattering glass, then a car horn blares and continues on one relentless note.)*

MAY: *(yelling over the sound of the horn)* Who is that! Who in the hell is that out there!

EDDIE: How should I know.

*(*EDDIE *flips the light switch off by stage-left door. Stage lights go black. Bathroom light stays on.)*

MAY: Eddie!

EDDIE: Just get down will ya'! Get down on the floor!

*(*EDDIE *grabs her and tries to pull her down on the floor beside the bed.* MAY *struggles in the dark with him. Car horn keeps blaring. Headlights start popping back and forth from high beam to low beam, slashing across stage through the window now.)*

MAY: Who is that? Did you bring her with you! You sonofabitch!

(She starts lashing out at EDDIE, *fighting with him as he tries to drag her down on the floor.)*

EDDIE: I didn't bring anybody with me! I don't know who she is! I don't know where she came from! Just get down on the floor, will ya'!

MAY: She followed you here! Didn't she! You told her where you were going and she followed you.

EDDIE: I didn't tell anybody where I was going. I didn't know where I was going till I got here.

MAY: You are gonna' pay for this! I swear to God. You are gonna' pay.

*(*EDDIE *finally pulls her down and rolls over on top of her so she can't get up. She slowly gives up struggling as he keeps her pinned to the floor. Car horn suddenly stops. Headlights snap off. Long pause. They listen in the dark.)*

MAY: What do you think she's doing?

EDDIE: How should I know.

MAY: Don't pretend you don't know her. That's the kind of car a Countess drives. That's the kind of car I always pictured her in. *(she starts struggling again)*

EDDIE: *(holding her down)* Just stay put.

MAY: I'm not gonna' lay here on my back with you on top of me and get shot by some dumb rich twat. Now lemme up, Eddie!

(Sound of tires burning rubber off left. Headlights arc back across the stage again from left to right. A car drives off. Sound fades.)

EDDIE: Just stay down!

MAY: I'm down!

(Long pause in the dark. They listen.)

MAY: How crazy is this chick anyway?

EDDIE: She's pretty crazy.

MAY: Have you balled her yet? *(pause)*

*(*EDDIE *gets up slowly, hunched over, crosses upstage to window cautiously, parts Venetian blinds and peeks outside.)*

EDDIE: *(looking out)* Shit, she's blown the windshield outa' my truck. Goddammit.

MAY: *(still on floor)* Eddie?

EDDIE: *(still looking out window)* What?

MAY: Is she gone?

EDDIE: I don't know. I can't see any headlights. *(pause)* I don't believe it.

MAY: *(gets up, crosses to light switch)* Yeah, you shoulda' thought of the consequences before you got in her pants.

(She switches the light back on. EDDIE *whirls around toward her. He stands.)*

EDDIE: *(moving toward her)* Turn the lights off! Keep the lights off!

(He rushes to light switch and turns lights back off. Stage goes back to darkness. MAY *shoves past him and turns the lights back on again. Stage lit.)*

MAY: This is my place!

EDDIE: Look, she's gonna' come back here. I know she's gonna' come back. We either have to get outa' here now or you have to keep the fuckin' lights off.

MAY: I thought you said you didn't know her!

EDDIE: Get your stuff! We're gettin' outa' here.

MAY: I'm not leaving! This is your mess, not mine.

EDDIE: I came here to get you! Whatsa' matter with you! I came all this way to get you! Do you think I'd do that if I didn't love you! Huh? That bitch doesn't mean anything to me! Nuthin'. I got no reason to be here but you.

MAY: I'm not goin', Eddie.

(Pause. EDDIE *stares at her.)*

(Spot rises on THE OLD MAN. *Stage lights stay the same.* EDDIE *and* MAY *just stand there staring at each other through the duration of* THE OLD MAN'*s words. They are not "frozen," they just stand there and face each other in a suspended moment of recognition.)*

THE OLD MAN: Amazing thing is, neither one a' you look a bit familiar to me. Can't figure that one out. I don't recognize myself in either one a' you. Never did. 'Course your mothers both put their stamp on ya'. That's plain to see. But my whole side a' the issue is absent, in my opinion. Totally unrecognizable. You could be anybody's. Probably are. I can't even remember the original circumstances. Been so long. Probably a lot a' things I forgot. Good thing I got out when I did though. Best thing I ever did.

(Spot fades on THE OLD MAN. *Stage lights come back up.* EDDIE *picks up his rope and starts to coil it up.* MAY *watches him.)*

EDDIE: I'm not leavin'. I don't care what you think any-more. I don't care what you feel. None a' that mat-ters. I'm not leavin'. I'm stayin' right here. I don't care if a hundred "dates" walk through that door—I'll take every one of 'em on. I don't care if you hate my guts. I don't care if you can't stand the sight of me or the sound of me or the smell of me. I'm never leavin'. You'll never get rid of me. You'll never escape me either. I'll track you down no matter where you go. I know exactly how your mind works. I've been right every time. Every single time.

MAY: You've gotta' give this up, Eddie.

EDDIE: I'm not giving it up!

(Pause.)

MAY: *(calm)* Okay. Look. I don't understand what you've got in your head anymore. I really don't. I don't get it. *Now* you desperately need me. *Now* you can't live without me. *NOW* you'll do anything for me. Why should I believe it this time?

EDDIE: Because it's true.

MAY: It was supposed to have been true every time before. Every other time. Now it's true again. You've been jerking me off like this for fifteen years. Fifteen years I've been a yo-yo for you. I've never been split. I've never been two ways about you. I've either loved you or not loved you. And now I just plain don't love you. Understand? Do you understand that? I don't love you. I don't need you. I don't want you. Do you get that? Now if you can still stay, then you're either crazy or pathetic.

(She crosses down left to table, sits in upstage chair facing audience, takes slug of tequila from bottle, slams it down on table. Headlights again come slashing across the stage from up right, across audience, then disappear off left. EDDIE rushes to light switch, flips it off. Stage goes black. Exterior lights shine through.)

EDDIE: *(taking her by shoulder)* Get in the bathroom!

MAY: *(pulls away)* I'm not going in the bathroom! I'm not gonna' hide in my own house! I'm gonna' go out there. I'm gonna' go out there and tear her damn head off! I'm gonna' wipe her out!

(She moves toward stage-left door. EDDIE stops her. She screams. They struggle as MAY yells at stage-left door.)

MAY: *(yelling at door)* Come on in here! Come on in here and bring your dumb gun! You hear me? Bring all your weapons and your skinny silly self! I'll eat you alive!

(Suddenly the stage-left door bursts open and MARTIN crashes onstage in the darkness. He's in his mid-thirties, solidly built, wears a green plaid shirt, baggy work pants with suspenders, heavy work boots. MAY and EDDIE pull apart. MARTIN tackles EDDIE around the waist and the two of them go crashing into the stage-right bathroom door. The door booms. MAY rushes to light switch, flips it

on. Lights come back up onstage. MARTIN stands over EDDIE who's crumpled up against the wall on the floor. MARTIN is about to smash EDDIE in the face with his fist. MAY stops him with her voice.)

MAY: Martin, wait!

(Pause. MARTIN turns and looks at MAY. EDDIE is dazed, remains on floor. MAY goes to MARTIN and pulls him away from EDDIE.)

MAY: It's okay, Martin. It's uh—it's okay. We were just having a kind of an argument. Really. Just take it easy. All right?

(MARTIN moves back away from EDDIE. EDDIE stays on floor. Pause.)

MARTIN: Oh. I heard you screaming when I drove up and then all the lights went off. I thought somebody was trying to—

MAY: It's okay. This is my uh—cousin. Eddie.

MARTIN: *(stares at EDDIE)* Oh. I'm sorry.

EDDIE: *(grins at MARTIN)* She's lying.

MARTIN: *(looks at MAY)* Oh.

MAY: *(moving to table)* Everything's okay, Martin. You want a drink or something? Why don't you have a drink.

MARTIN: Yeah. Sure.

EDDIE: *(stays on floor)* She's lying through her teeth.

MAY: I gotta' get some glasses.

(MAY exits quickly into bathroom, stepping over EDDIE. MARTIN stares at EDDIE. EDDIE grins back. Pause.)

EDDIE: She keeps the glasses in the bathroom. Isn't that weird?

(MAY comes back on with two glasses. She goes to table, pours two drinks from bottle.)

MAY: I was starting to think you weren't going to show up, Martin.

MARTIN: Yeah, I'm sorry. I had to water the football field down at the high school. Forgot all about it.

EDDIE: Forgot all about what?

MARTIN: I mean I forgot all about watering. I was half-way here when I remembered. Had to go back.

EDDIE: Oh, I thought you meant you forgot all about her.

MARTIN: Oh, no.

EDDIE: How far was halfway?

MARTIN: Excuse me?

EDDIE: How far were you when it was halfway here?

MARTIN: Oh—uh—I don't know. I guess a couple miles or so.

EDDIE: Couple miles? That's all? Couple a' lousy little miles? You wanna' know how many miles I came? Huh?

MAY: We've been drinking a little bit, Martin.

EDDIE: She hasn't touched a drop.

(Pause.)

MAY: (*offering drink to* MARTIN) Here.

EDDIE: Yeah, that's my tequila, Martin.

MARTIN: Oh.

EDDIE: I don't care if you drink it. I just want you to know where it comes from.

MARTIN: Thanks.

EDDIE: You don't have to thank me. Thank the Mexicans. They made it.

MARTIN: Oh.

EDDIE: You should thank the entire Mexican nation in fact. We owe everything to Mexico down here. Do you realize that? You probably don't realize that, do ya'. We're sittin' on Mexican ground right now. It's only by chance that you and me aren't Mexican ourselves. What kinda' people do you hail from anyway, Martin?

MARTIN: Me? Uh—I don't know. I was adopted.

EDDIE: Oh. You must have a lotta' problems then, huh?

MARTIN: Well—not really, no.

EDDIE: No? You orphans are supposed to steal a lot aren't ya'? Shoplifting and stuff. You're also supposed to be the main group responsible for bumping off our Presidents.

MARTIN: Really? I never heard that.

EDDIE: Well, you oughta' read the papers, Martin.

(*Pause.*)

MARTIN: I'm really sorry I knocked you over. I mean, I thought she was in trouble or something.

EDDIE: She is in trouble.

MARTIN: (*looks at* MAY) Oh.

EDDIE: She's in big trouble.

MARTIN: What's the matter, May?

MAY: (*moves to bed with drink, sits*) Nothing.

MARTIN: How come you had the lights off?

MAY: We were uh—just about to go out.

MARTIN: You were?

MAY: Yeah—well, I mean, we were going to come back.

(MARTIN *stands there between them. He looks at* EDDIE, *then back to* MAY. *Pause.*)

EDDIE: (*laughs*) No, no, no. That's not what we were gonna' do. Your name's Martin, right?

MARTIN: Yeah, right.

EDDIE: That's not what we were gonna' do, Marty.

MARTIN: Oh.

EDDIE: Could you hand me that bottle, please?

MARTIN: (*crossing to bottle at table*) Sure.

EDDIE: Thanks.

(MARTIN *moves back to* EDDIE *with bottle and hands it to him.* EDDIE *drinks.*)

EDDIE: (*after drink*) We were actually having an argument about you. That's what we were doin'.

MARTIN: About me?

EDDIE: Yeah. We were actually in the middle of a big huge argument about you. It got so heated up we had to turn the lights off.

MARTIN: What was it about?

EDDIE: It was about whether or not you're actually a man or not. Ya' know? Whether you're a "man" or just a "guy."

(*Pause.* MARTIN *looks at* MAY. MAY *smiles politely.* MARTIN *looks back to* EDDIE.)

EDDIE: See, she says you're a man. That's what she calls you. A "man." Did you know that? That's what she calls you.

MARTIN: (*looks back to* MAY) No.

MAY: I never called you a man, Martin. Don't worry about it.

MARTIN: It's okay. I don't mind or anything.

EDDIE: No, but see I uh—told her she was fulla' shit. I mean I told her that way before I even saw you. And now that I see you I can't exactly take it back. Ya' see what I mean, Martin?

(*Pause,* MAY *stands.*)

MAY: Martin, do you want to go to the movies?

MARTIN: Well, yeah—I mean, that's what I thought we were going to do.

MAY: So let's go to the movies.

(*She crosses fast to bathroom, steps over* EDDIE, *goes into bathroom, slams door, door booms. Pause as* MARTIN *stares at bathroom door.* EDDIE *stays on floor, grins at* MARTIN.)

MARTIN: She's not mad or anything is she?

EDDIE: You got me, buddy.

MARTIN: I didn't mean to make her mad.

(*Pause.*)

EDDIE: What're you gonna' go see, Martin?

MARTIN: I can't decide.

EDDIE: What d'ya' mean you can't decide? You're supposed to have all that worked out ahead of time aren't ya'?

MARTIN: Yeah, but I'm not sure what she likes.

EDDIE: What's that got to do with it? You're takin' her out to the movies, right?

MARTIN: Yeah.

EDDIE: So you pick the movie, right? The guy picks the movie. The guy's always supposed to pick the movie.

MARTIN: Yeah, but I don't want to take her to see something she doesn't want to see.

EDDIE: How do you know what she wants to see?

MARTIN: I don't. That's the reason I can't decide. I mean what if I take her to something she's already seen before?

EDDIE: You miss the whole point, Martin. The reason you're taking her out to the movies isn't to see something she hasn't seen before.

MARTIN: Oh.

EDDIE: The reason you're taking her out to the movies is because you just want to be with her. Right? You just wanna' be close to her. I mean you could take her just about anywhere.

MARTIN: I guess.

EDDIE: I mean after a while you probably wouldn't have to take her out at all. You could just hang around here.

MARTIN: What would we do here?

EDDIE: Well, you could uh—tell each other stories.

MARTIN: Stories?

EDDIE: Yeah.

MARTIN: I don't know any stories.

EDDIE: Make 'em up.

MARTIN: That'd be lying wouldn't it?

EDDIE: No, no. Lying's when you believe it's true. If you already know it's a lie, then it's not lying.

MARTIN: (after pause) Do you want some help getting up off the floor?

EDDIE: I like it down here. Less tension. You notice how when you're standing up, there's a lot more tension?

MARTIN: Yeah. I've noticed that. A lot of times when I'm working, you know, I'm down on my hands and knees.

EDDIE: What line a' work do you follow, Martin?

MARTIN: Yard work mostly. Maintenance.

EDDIE: Oh, lawns and stuff?

MARTIN: Yeah.

EDDIE: You do lawns on your hands and knees?

MARTIN: Well—edging. You know, trimming around the edges.

EDDIE: Oh.

MARTIN: And weeding around the sprinkler heads. Stuff like that.

EDDIE: I get ya'.

MARTIN: But I've always noticed how much more relaxed I get when I'm down low to the ground like that.

EDDIE: Yeah. Well, you could get down on your hands and knees right now if you want to. I don't mind.

MARTIN: (grins, gets embarrassed, looks at bathroom door) Naw, I'll stand. Thanks.

EDDIE: Suit yourself. You're just gonna' get more and more tense.

(Pause.)

MARTIN: You're uh—May's cousin, huh?

EDDIE: See now, right there. Askin' me that. Right there. That's a result of tension. See what I mean?

MARTIN: What?

EDDIE: Askin' me if I'm her cousin. That's because you're tense you're askin' me that. You already know I'm not her cousin.

MARTIN: Well, how would I know that?

EDDIE: Do I look like her cousin.

MARTIN: Well, she said that you were.

EDDIE: (grins) She's lying.

(Pause.)

MARTIN: Well—what are you then?

EDDIE: (laughs) Now you're really gettin' tense, huh?

MARTIN: Look, maybe I should just go or something. I mean—

(MARTIN makes a move to exit stage left. EDDIE rushes to stage-left door and beats MARTIN to it. MARTIN freezes, then runs to window upstage, opens it and tries to escape. EDDIE runs to him and catches him by the back of the pants, pulls him out of the window, slams him up against stage-right wall, then pulls him slowly down the wall as he speaks. They arrive at down-right corner.)

EDDIE: No, no. Don't go, Martin. Don't go. You'll just get all blue and lonely out there in the black night. I know. I've wandered around lonely like that myself. Awful. Just eats away at ya'. (he puts his arm around MARTIN's shoulder and leads him to table down left) Now just come on over here and sit down and we'll have us a little drink. Okay?

MARTIN: (as he goes with EDDIE) Uh—do you think she's okay in there?

EDDIE: Sure she's okay. She's always okay. She just likes to take her time. Just to torture you.

MARTIN: Well—we were supposed to go to the movies.

EDDIE: She'll be out. Don't worry about it. She likes the movies.

(They sit at table, down left. EDDIE pulls out the down-right chair and seats MARTIN in it, then he goes to the upstage chair and sits so that he's now partially facing THE OLD MAN. Spot rises softly on THE OLD MAN but MARTIN does not acknowledge his presence. Stage lights stay the same. MARTIN sets his glass on table. EDDIE fills it up with the bottle. THE OLD MAN's left arm slowly descends and reaches across the table holding out his empty Styrofoam cup for a drink. EDDIE looks THE OLD MAN in the eye for a second, then pours him a drink, too. All three of them drink. EDDIE takes his from the bottle.)

MARTIN: What exactly's the matter with her anyway?

EDDIE: She's in a state a' shock.

(THE OLD MAN chuckles to himself. Drinks.)

MARTIN: Shock? How come?

EDDIE: Well, we haven't seen each other in a long time. I mean—me and her, we go back quite a ways, see. High school.

MARTIN: Oh. I didn't know that.

EDDIE: Yeah. Lotta' miles.

MARTIN: And you're not really cousins?

EDDIE: No. Not really. No.

MARTIN: You're—her husband?

EDDIE: No. She's my sister. (he and THE OLD MAN look at each other, then he turns back to MARTIN) My half-sister.

(Pause. EDDIE and THE OLD MAN drink.)

MARTIN: Your sister?

EDDIE: Yeah.

MARTIN: Oh. So—you knew each other even before high school then, huh?

EDDIE: No, see, I never knew I had a sister until it was too late.

MARTIN: How do you mean?

EDDIE: Well, by the time I found out we'd already—you know—fooled around.

(THE OLD MAN *shakes his head, drinks. Long pause.* MARTIN *just stares at* EDDIE.)

EDDIE: (*grins*) Whatsa' matter, Martin?

MARTIN: You fooled around?

EDDIE: Yeah.

MARTIN: Well—um—that's illegal, isn't it?

EDDIE: I suppose so.

THE OLD MAN: (*to* EDDIE) Who is this guy?

MARTIN: I mean—is that true? She's really your sister?

EDDIE: Half. Only half.

MARTIN: Which half?

EDDIE: Top half. In horses we call that the "topside."

THE OLD MAN: Yeah, and the mare's what? The mare's uh—"distaff," isn't it? Isn't that the bottom half? "Distaff." Funny I should remember that.

MARTIN: And you fooled around in high school together?

EDDIE: Yeah. Sure. Everybody fooled around in high school. Didn't you?

MARTIN: No. I never did.

EDDIE: Maybe you should have, Martin.

MARTIN: Well, not with my sister.

EDDIE: No, I wouldn't recommend that.

MARTIN: How could that happen? I mean—

EDDIE: Well, see—(*pause, he stares at* THE OLD MAN)—our daddy fell in love twice. That's basically how it happened. Once with my mother and once with her mother.

THE OLD MAN: It was the same love. Just got split in two, that's all.

MARTIN: Well, how come you didn't know each other until high school then?

EDDIE: He had two separate lives. That's how come. Two completely separate lives. He'd live with me and my mother for a while and then he'd disappear and go live with her and her mother for a while.

THE OLD MAN: Now don't be too hard on me, boy. It can happen to the best of us.

MARTIN: And you never knew what was going on?

EDDIE: Nope. Neither did my mother.

THE OLD MAN: She knew.

EDDIE: (*to* MARTIN) She never knew.

MARTIN: She must've suspected something was going on.

EDDIE: Well, if she did she never let on to me. Maybe she was afraid of finding out. Or maybe she just loved him. I don't know. He'd disappear for months at a time and she never once asked him where he went. She was always glad to see him when he came back. The two of us used to go running out of the house to meet him as soon as we saw the Studebaker coming across the field.

THE OLD MAN: (*to* EDDIE) That was no Studebaker, that was a Plymouth. I never owned a goddamn Studebaker.

EDDIE: This went on for years. He kept disappearing and reappearing. For years that went on. Then, suddenly, one day it stopped. He stayed home for a while. Just stayed in the house. Never went outside. Just sat in his chair. Staring. Then he started going on these long walks. He'd walk all day. Then he'd walk all night. He'd walk out across the fields. In the dark. I used to watch him from my bedroom window. He'd disappear in the dark with his overcoat on.

MARTIN: Where was he going?

EDDIE: Just walking.

THE OLD MAN: I was making a decision.

(EDDIE *gets* MARTIN *to his feet and takes him on a walk around the entire stage as he tells the story.* MARTIN *is reluctant but* EDDIE *keeps pulling him along.*)

EDDIE: But one night I asked him if I could go with him. And he took me. We walked straight out across the fields together. In the dark. And I remember it was just plowed and our feet sank down in the powder and the dirt came up over the tops of my shoes and weighed me down. I wanted to stop and empty my shoes out but he wouldn't stop. He kept walking straight ahead and I was afraid of losing him in the dark so I just kept up as best I could. And we were completely silent the whole time. Never said a word to each other. We could barely see a foot in front of us, it was so dark. And these white owls kept swooping down out of nowhere, hunting for jackrabbits. Diving right past our heads, then disappearing. And we just kept walking silent like that for miles until we got to town. I could see the drive-in movie way off in the distance. That was the first thing I saw. Just square patches of color shifting. Then vague faces began to appear. And, as we got closer, I could recognize one of the faces. It was Spencer Tracy. Spencer Tracy moving his mouth. Speaking without words. Speaking to a woman in a red dress. Then we stopped at a liquor store and he made me wait outside in the parking lot while he bought a bottle. And there were all these Mexican migrant workers standing around a pickup truck with red mud all over the tires. They were drinking beer and laughing and I remember being jealous of them and I didn't know why. And I remember seeing the old man through the glass door of the liquor store as he paid for the bottle. And I remember feeling sorry for him and I didn't know why. Then he came outside with the bottle wrapped in a brown paper sack and as soon as he came out, all the Mexican men stopped laughing. They just stared at us as we walked away.

(During the course of the story the lights shift down very slowly into blues and greens—moonlight.)

EDDIE: And we walked right through town. Past the donut shop, past the miniature golf course, past the Chevron station. And he opened the bottle up and offered it to me. Before he even took a drink, he offered it to me first. And I took it and drank it and handed it back to him. And we just kept passing it back and forth like that as we walked until we drank the whole thing dry. And we never said a word the whole time. Then, finally, we reached this little white house with a red awning, on the far side of town. I'll never forget the red awning because it flapped in the night breeze and the porch light made it glow. It was a hot, desert breeze and the air smelled like new-cut alfalfa. We walked right up to the front porch and he rang the bell and I remember getting real nervous because I wasn't expecting to visit anybody. I thought we were just out for a walk. And then this woman comes to the door. This real pretty woman with red hair. And she throws herself into his arms. And he starts crying. He just breaks down right there in front of me. And she's kissing him all over the face and holding him real tight and he's just crying like a baby. And then through the doorway, behind them both, I see this girl.

(The bathroom door very slowly and silently swings open revealing MAY, standing in the doorframe backlit with yellow light in her red dress. She just watches EDDIE as he keeps telling story. He and MARTIN are unaware of her presence.)

EDDIE: She just appears. She's just standing there, staring at me and I'm staring back at her and we can't take our eyes off each other. It was like we knew each other from somewhere but we couldn't place where. But the second we saw each other, that very second, we knew we'd never stop being in love.

(MAY slams bathroom door behind her. Door booms. Lights bang back up to their previous setting.)

MAY: *(to EDDIE)* Boy, you really are incredible! You're unbelievable! Martin comes over here. He doesn't know you from Adam and you start telling him a story like that. Are you crazy? None of it's true, Martin. He's had this weird, sick idea for years now and it's totally made up. He's nuts. I don't know where he got it from. He's completely nuts.

EDDIE: *(to MARTIN)* She's kinda' embarrassed about the whole deal, see. You can't blame her really.

MARTIN: I didn't even know you could hear us out here, May. I—

MAY: I heard every word. I followed it very carefully. He's told me that story a thousand times and it always changes.

EDDIE: I never repeat myself.

MAY: You do nothing but repeat yourself. That's all you do. You just go in a big circle.

MARTIN: *(standing)* Well, maybe I should leave.

EDDIE: NO! You sit down.

(Silence. MARTIN slowly sits again.)

EDDIE: *(quietly to MARTIN, leaning toward him)* Did you think that was a story, Martin? Did you think I made that whole thing up?

MARTIN: No. I mean, at the time you were telling it, it seemed real.

EDDIE: But now you're doubting it because she says it's a lie?

MARTIN: Well—

EDDIE: She suggests it's a lie to you and all of a sudden you change your mind? Is that it? You go from true to false like that, in a second?

MARTIN: I don't know.

MAY: Let's go to the movies, Martin.

(MARTIN stands again.)

EDDIE: Sit down!

(MARTIN sits back down. Long pause.)

MAY: Eddie—

(Pause.)

EDDIE: What?

MAY: We want to go to the movies.

Pause. EDDIE just stares at her.)

MAY: I want to go out to the movies with Martin. Right now.

EDDIE: Nobody's going to the movies. There's not a movie in this town that can match the story I'm gonna' tell. I'm gonna' finish this story.

MAY: Eddie—

EDDIE: You wanna' hear the rest of the story, don't ya', Martin?

MARTIN: *(pause. He looks at MAY, then back to EDDIE)* Sure.

MAY: Martin, let's go. Please.

MARTIN: I—

(Long pause. EDDIE and MARTIN stare at each other.)

EDDIE: You what?

MARTIN: I don't mind hearing the rest of it if you want to tell the rest of it.

THE OLD MAN: *(to himself)* I'm dyin' to hear it myself.

(EDDIE leans back in his chair. Grins.)

MAY: *(to EDDIE)* What do you think this is going to do? Do you think this is going to change something?

EDDIE: No.

MAY: Then what's the point?

EDDIE: It's absolutely pointless.

MAY: Then why put everybody through this. Martin doesn't want to hear this bullshit. *I* don't want to hear it.

EDDIE: I know *you* don't wanna' hear it.

MAY: Don't try to pass it off on me! You got it all turned around, Eddie. You got it all turned around. You don't even know which end is up anymore. Okay. Okay. I don't need either of you. I don't need any of it because I already know the rest of the story. I know the whole rest of the story, see *(she speaks directly to* EDDIE, *who remains sitting)* I know it just exactly the way it happened. Without any little tricks added onto it.

*(*THE OLD MAN *leans over to* EDDIE, *confidentially.)*

THE OLD MAN: What does she know?

EDDIE: *(to* THE OLD MAN*)* She's lying.

(Lights begin to shift down again in the course of MAY's *story. She moves very slowly downstage, then crosses toward* THE OLD MAN *as she tells it.)*

MAY: You want me to finish the story for you, Eddie? Huh? You want me to finish this story?

(Pause as MARTIN *sits again.)*

MAY: See, my mother—the pretty red-haired woman in the little white house with the red awning—was desperately in love with the old man. Wasn't she, Eddie? You could tell that right away. You could see it in her eyes. She was obsessed with him to the point where she couldn't stand being without him for even a second. She kept hunting for him from town to town. Following little clues that he left behind, like a postcard maybe, or a motel on the back of a matchbook. *(to* MARTIN*)* He never left her a phone number or an address or anything as simple as that because my mother was his secret, see. She hounded him for years and he kept trying to keep her at a distance because the closer these two separate lives drew together, these two separate women, these two separate kids, the more nervous he got. The more filled with terror that the two lives would find out about each other and devour him whole. That his secret would take him by the throat. But finally she caught up with him. Just by a process of elimination she dogged him down. I remember the day we discovered the town. She was on fire. "This is it!" she kept saying; "this is the place!" Her whole body was trembling as we walked through the streets, looking for the house where he lived. She kept squeezing my hand to the point where I thought she'd crush the bones in my fingers. She was terrified she'd come across him by accident on the street because she knew she was trespassing. She knew she was crossing this forbidden zone but she couldn't help herself. We walked all day through that stupid hick town. All day long. We went through every neighborhood, peering through every open window, looking in at every dumb family, until finally we found him.

(Rest.)

It was just exactly suppertime and they were all sitting down at the table and they were having fried chicken. That's how close we were to the window. We could see what they were eating. We could hear their voices but we couldn't make out what they were saying. Eddie and his mother were talking but the old man never said a word. Did he, Eddie? Just sat there eating his chicken in silence.

THE OLD MAN: *(to* EDDIE*)* Boy, is she ever off the wall with this one. You gotta' do somethin' about this.

MAY: The funny thing was, that almost as soon as we'd found him—he disappeared. She was only with him about two weeks before he just vanished. Nobody saw him after that. Ever. And my mother—just turned herself inside out. I never could understand that. I kept watching her grieve, as though somebody'd died. She'd pull herself up into a ball and just stare at the floor. And I couldn't understand that because I was feeling the exact opposite feeling. I was in love, see. I'd come home after school, after being with Eddie, and I was filled with this joy and there she'd be—standing in the middle of the kitchen staring at the sink. Her eyes looked like a funeral. And I didn't know what to say. I didn't even feel sorry for her. All I could think of was him.

THE OLD MAN: *(to* EDDIE*)* She's gettin' way outa' line, here.

MAY: And all he could think of was me. Isn't that right, Eddie. We couldn't take a breath without thinking of each other. We couldn't eat if we weren't together. We couldn't sleep. We got sick at night when we were apart. Violently sick. And my mother even took me to see a doctor. And Eddie's mother took him to see the same doctor but the doctor had no idea what was wrong with us. He thought it was the flu or something. And Eddie's mother had no idea what was wrong with him. But my mother—my mother knew exactly what was wrong. She knew it clear down to her bones. She recognized every symptom. And she begged me not to see him but I wouldn't listen. Then she begged Eddie not to see me but he wouldn't listen. Then she went to Eddie's mother and begged her. And Eddie's mother— *(pause. She looks straight at* EDDIE*)*—Eddie's mother blew her brains out. Didn't she, Eddie? Blew her brains right out.

THE OLD MAN: *(standing. He moves from the platform onto the stage, between* EDDIE *and* MAY*)* Now, wait a second! Wait a second. Just a goddamn second here. This story doesn't hold water. *(to* EDDIE, *who stays seated)* You're not gonna' let her off the hook with that one are ya'? That's the dumbest version I ever heard in my whole life. She never blew her brains out. Nobody ever told me that. Where the hell did that come from? *(to* EDDIE, *who remains seated)* Stand up!

Get on yer feet now goddammit! I wanna' hear the male side a' this thing. You gotta' represent me now. Speak on my behalf. There's no one to speak for me now! Stand up!

(EDDIE *stand slowly. Stares at* THE OLD MAN.)

THE OLD MAN: Now tell her. Tell her the way it happened. We've got a pact. Don't forget that.

EDDIE: *(calmly to* THE OLD MAN*)* It was your shotgun. Same one we used to duck-hunt with. Browning. She never fired a gun before in her life. That was her first time.

THE OLD MAN: Nobody told me any a' that. I was left completely in the dark.

EDDIE: You were gone.

THE OLD MAN: Somebody could've found me! Somebody could've hunted me down. I wasn't that impossible to find.

EDDIE: You were gone.

THE OLD MAN: That's right, I was gone! I was gone. You're right. But I wasn't disconnected. There was nothing cut off in me. Everything went on just the same as though I'd never left. *(to* MAY*)* But *your* mother—your mother wouldn't give it up, would she?

(THE OLD MAN *moves toward* MAY *and speaks directly to her.* MAY *keeps her eyes on* EDDIE, *who very slowly turns toward her in the course of* THE OLD MAN'S *speech. Once their eyes meet they never leave each other's gaze.*)

THE OLD MAN: *(to* MAY*)* She drew me to her. She went out of her way to draw me in. She was a force. I told her I'd never come across for her. I told her that right from the very start. But she opened up to me. She wouldn't listen. She kept opening up her heart to me. How could I turn her down when she loved me like that? How could I turn away from her? We were completely whole.

(EDDIE *and* MAY *just stand there staring at each other.* THE OLD MAN *moves back to* EDDIE. *Speaks to him directly.*)

THE OLD MAN: *(to* EDDIE*)* What're you doin'? Speak to her. Bring her around to our side. You gotta' make her see this thing in a clear light.

(*Very slowly* EDDIE *and* MAY *move toward each other.*)

THE OLD MAN: *(to* EDDIE*)* Stay away from her! What the hell are you doin'? Keep away from her! You two can't come together! You gotta' hold up my end a' this deal. I got nobody now! Nobody! You can't betray me! You gotta' represent me now! You're my son!

(EDDIE *and* MAY *come together center stage. They embrace. They kiss each other tenderly. Headlights suddenly arc across stage again from up right, cutting across the stage through window, then disappearing off left. Sound*

of loud collision, shattering glass, an explosion. Bright orange and blue light of a gasoline fire suddenly illuminates upstage window. Then sounds of horses screaming wildly, hooves galloping on pavement, fading, then total silence. Light of gas fire continues now to end of play. EDDIE *and* MAY *never stop holding each other through all this. Long pause. No one moves. Then* MARTIN *stands and moves upstage to window, peers out through Venetian blinds. Pause.*)

MARTIN: *(upstage at window, looking out into flames)* Is that your truck with the horse trailer out there?

EDDIE: *(stays with* MAY*)* Yeah.

MARTIN: It's on fire.

EDDIE: Yeah.

MARTIN: All the horses are loose.

EDDIE: *(steps back away from* MAY*)* Yeah, I figured.

MAY: Eddie—

EDDIE: *(to* MAY*)* I'm just gonna' go out and take a look. I gotta' at least take a look, don't I?

MAY: What difference does it make?

EDDIE: Well, I can't just let her get away with that. What am I supposed to do? *(moves toward stage-left door)* I'll just be a second.

MAY: Eddie—

EDDIE: I'm only gonna' be a second. I'll just take a look at it and I'll come right back. Okay?

(EDDIE *exits stage-left door.* MAY *stares at door, stays where she is.* MARTIN *stays upstage.* MARTIN *turns slowly from window upstage and looks at* MAY. *Pause.* MAY *moves to bed, pulls suitcase out from underneath, throws it on bed and opens it. She goes into bathroom and comes out with clothes. She packs the clothes in suitcase.* MARTIN *watches her for a while, then moves slowly downstage to her as she continues.*)

MARTIN: May—

(MAY *goes back into bathroom and comes back out with more clothes. She packs them.*)

MARTIN: Do you need some help or anything? I got a car. I could drive you somewhere if you want. *(pause.* MAY *just keeps packing her clothes)* Are you going to go with him?

(*She stops. Straightens up. Stares at* MARTIN. *Pause.*)

MAY: He's gone.

MARTIN: He said he'd be back in a second.

MAY: *(pause)* He's gone.

(MAY *exits with suitcase out stage-left door. She leaves the door open behind her.* MARTIN *just stands there staring at open door for a while.* THE OLD MAN *looks stage left at his rocking chair, then a little above it, in blank space. Pause.* THE OLD MAN *starts moving slowly back to platform.*)

THE OLD MAN: *(pointing into space, stage left)* Ya' see that picture over there? Ya' see that? Ya' know who that is? That's the woman of my dreams. That's who that is. And she's mine. She's all mine. Forever.

(He reaches rocking chair, sits, but keeps staring at imaginary picture. He begins to rock very slowly in the chair. After THE OLD MAN *sits in rocker, Merle Haggard's "I'm the One Who Loves You" starts playing as lights begin a very slow fade.* MARTIN *moves slowly upstage to window and stops. He stares out with his back to audience. The fire glows through window as stage lights fade.* THE OLD MAN *keeps rocking slowly. Stage lights keep fading slowly to black. Fire glows for a while in the dark, then cuts to black. Song continues in dark and swells in volume.)*

Figure 1. May (Kathy Baker) clings desperately to Eddie (Ed Harris)
in the opening moments of *Fool for Love*, in the Magic Theater of San
Francisco's Production presented at the Circle Repertory Company,
1983. (Photograph: Gerry Goodstein.)

Figure 2. Eddie (Ed Harris) starts to dismantle his shotgun while May (Kathy Baker) watches him closely, in the Magic Theater of San Francisco's Production of *Fool for Love* presented at the Circle Repertory Company, 1983. (Photograph: Gerry Goodstein.)

Figure 3. May (Kathy Baker) tries to explain to Martin (Dennis Ludlow) that "Everything's OK" after Martin has tackled Eddie (Ed Harris) to the floor in the Magic Theater of San Francisco's Production of *Fool for Love* presented at the Circle Repertory Company, 1983. (Photograph: Gerry Goodstein.)

Staging of *Fool for Love*

REVIEW OF THE CIRCLE REPERTORY
COMPANY PRODUCTION, 1983,
BY FRANK RICH

No one knows better than Sam Shepard that the true American West is gone forever, but there may be no writer alive more gifted at reinventing it out of pure literary air. Like so many Shepard plays, "Fool for Love," at the Circle Repertory Company, is a western for our time. We watch a pair of figurative gunslingers fight to the finish—not with bullets, but with piercing words that give ballast to the weight of a nation's buried dreams.

As theater, "Fool for Love" could be called an indoor rodeo. The setting is a present-day motel room on the edge of the Mojave Desert, where, for 90 minutes, May (Kathy Baker) and Eddie (Ed Harris) constantly batter one another against the walls. May and Eddie have been lovers for 15 years; they may even, like the fratricidal antagonists of "True West," be siblings. But May has had it: she'd now like nothing more than to "buffalo" Eddie by stabbing him in the middle of a passionate kiss.

Eddie is some sort of rancher, complete with saddle, rifle and lasso. Yet there's no more range—Marlboro men ride only on television—and he lives in a tin trailer. The motel room is May's most recent home. With its soiled green walls and a window facing black nothingness, it looks like a jail cell; its doors slam shut with a fierce metallic clang. When Eddie uses his rope, all he can snare is a bedpost. When the two lovers want to escape, they don't mount horses for a fast getaway—they merely run to the parking lot and back.

But if the West is now reduced to this—a blank empty room with an unmade bed—Mr. Shepard fills that space with reveries as big as all outdoors. When the play's fighting lets up, we hear monologues resembling crackling campfires tales. The characters—who also include May's new suitor (Dennis Ludlow) and a ghostly "old man" (Will Marchetti) sipping Jim Beam in a rocking chair—try to find who they are and where they are. Though the West has become but a figment of the movies, Eddie contends that "there's not a movie in this town that can match the story I can tell."

Laced with the floating images of cattle herds, old cars and even a spectral Spencer Tracy looming in the dark, these hallucinatory stories chart the Shepard vision. His characters are "disconnected"; they fear being "erased"; they hope to be "completely whole." In "Fool for Love," each story gives us a different "version" of who May, Eddie and the old man are, and the stories rarely mesh in terms of facts. Yet they do cohere as an expression of the author's consciousness: as Shepard's people race verbally through the debris of the West, they search for the identities and familial roots that have disappeared with the landscape of legend.

Not finding what they seek, they use their dreams as weapons, to wipe each other out. The old man, a ghostly figure who may be May and Eddie's father, tells the couple that they could be "anybody's children"—"I don't recognize myself in either of you and never did." Eddie and May respond in kind, even as they obliterate their own shared past. "You got me confused with someone else," says May to her lover, vowing never again to be suckered into one of his "little fantasies." What remains of Eddie's fantastical West is ultimately destroyed, too: his few horses burn in the play's apocalyptic finale.

Mr. Shepard's conceits are arresting and funny. Eddie, in explaining his particular erotic fixation, tells May that her neck keeps "coming up for some reason." The old man contends he is married to Barbara Mandrell and announces, without much fear of contradiction, that the singer's picture is hanging on an empty wall. There is a strange poignancy to May's suitor, a gentle maintenance man too lost even to dream of a self. Like a much talked-about "countess" of Eddie's supposed acquaintance, this sweet gentleman caller, intentionally or not, provides "Fool for Love" with an odd, unlikely echo of Tennessee Williams.

The production at the Circle Rep allows New York audiences to see the play in its native staging. "Fool for Love" has been transported here from Mr. Shepard's home base, the Magic Theater of San Francisco, complete with the original cast under the author's direction. The actors are all excellent: With utter directness, they create their own elusive yet robust world—feisty, muscular, sexually charged—and we either enter it or not.

"Fool for Love" isn't the fullest Shepard creation one ever hopes to encounter, but, at this point in this writer's prolific 20-year career, he almost demands we see his plays as a continuum: they bleed together. In the mode of his recent work, this play has a title and beat that's more redolent of country music than rock; the theatrical terms are somewhat more realistic than outright mythic (though reality is always in the eye of the beholder). The knockabout physical humor sometimes becomes excessive both in the writing and the playing; there are also, as usual, some duller riffs that invite us to drift away.

It could be argued, perhaps, that both the glory and failing of Mr. Shepard's art is its extraordinary afterlife: His works often play more feverishly in the mind after they're over than they do while they're before us in the theater. But that's the way he is, and who would or could change him? Like the visionary pioneers who once ruled the open geography of the West, Mr. Shepard rules his vast imaginative frontier by making his own, ironclad laws.

MARSHA NORMAN

1947–

Like Caryl Churchill and Wendy Wasserstein, Marsha Norman is among the most outstanding of the many women who have energized contemporary theater with plays that embody and explore female experience. Indeed, her best-known plays, *Getting Out* (1977) and *'night, Mother* (1983), focus on the psychic crises of women whose lives have been vexed by a complex array of disturbing and thwarting personal relationships, particularly their relationships with their mothers. In works such as these, Norman expresses her commitment "to a full, rich, and self-controlled life for the women on this planet." Her concern with the self-control of women is evidently rooted at least in part in her childhood experience of growing up in a highly repressive home, dominated by the moral strictures of her mother, who did not allow her to watch television, did not permit her to play with the neighborhood children because they were not "good enough," and did not let her "say anything that was in the least angry or that had any conflict in it at all."

Born and raised in a middle-class neighborhood in Louisville, Kentucky, Norman sought to escape the loneliness and solitude of her childhood through reading, through playing with an imaginary friend, and through writing stories. After graduating from high school, she attended Agnes Scott College in Decatur, Georgia, a liberal arts college for women, where she majored in philosophy and received her B.A. degree in 1969. Having returned to Louisville after graduation, she married one of her former English teachers (whom she divorced in 1974), studied for an M.A., which she received in 1971, and then went to work at the Kentucky Central State Hospital, as a teacher of disturbed adolescents. In her work at the hospital, she found herself confronted by "children who never talked at all," by others "who would just as soon stab you in the back as talk to you," but most of all by "violent kids," one of whom was so vicious that the memory of the terror she aroused in Norman provided the seminal idea for Norman's first play, *Getting Out*, which focuses on the psychic life of a recently rehabilitated woman parolee.

But Norman's work at the hospital school did not immediately lead her into playwriting. From 1973 to 1976, she worked at a school for gifted children, teaching filmmaking and developing a curriculum in the arts and humanities. It was during this period, evidently influenced by her creatively talented students, that she began to try her own hand at writing—mostly pieces for the local newspapers, but also a children's musical and scripts for a children's television program. During this time, she also first met Jon Jory, artistic director of the Actors Theatre of Louisville, one of several regional American theaters that has been particularly influential in the development of new plays and playwrights. Though she went to Jory seeking his advice about an arts program she was then developing to stimulate the interest of young people in the performing arts, he instead encouraged her to think about writing a play herself, in particular, a docu-drama about busing, which had recently hit Louisville and thus was a prominent local issue. But the subject of busing interested her less than Jory's subsequent suggestion that she think of writing a play about "a painful subject"— a suggestion that led her to think about the violent thirteen-year-old girl who had terrified her several years earlier at the hospital school.

Stimulated by that memory, Norman decided to write a play that would in some way incorporate a convulsively disturbed and disturbing young adolescent woman. But Norman was not content to focus just on someone like the violent young prisoner she had known, for in *Getting Out* she portrays two sides of a woman who has just been released from prison and is trying to make a new life for herself. In order to dramatize two sides of a single person, Norman created two distinctly different but clearly interrelated characters: Arlene Holsclaw, the protagonist, who, having served eight years in prison for robbery, kidnapping, and manslaughter, is shown during her first day out of prison, trying to fix up her apartment and in the process trying to deal with her past; and Arlie, the embodiment of her younger, vicious self, who suddenly appears at moments when Arlene's memory calls her into being, or when Arlene is cruelly reminded of her past by visits she receives from her former pimp, her former prison guard, and her mother. In working out the complex psychic drama of Arlene/ Arlie, Norman drew not only on her memory of the vicious adolescent she had encountered in the hospital school, but also on extensive interviews with fifteen women prisoners who told her at length "exactly what it was like to be in prison and exactly what it was like to be out." She also drew on her own personal experience of feeling emotionally imprisoned, as she made clear in her forthright acknowledgment that "that person locked up was me" and that "the writing of *Getting Out* for me was my own opening of the door."

Though it was her first professionally staged play, *Getting Out* was produced not only at the Actors Theatre of Louisville in 1977, but also at the Mark Taper Forum in Los Angeles in 1978, and at the Phoenix Theater in Manhattan in 1978, where critics and audiences responded so enthusiastically that it was revived in 1979 for an eight-month run at the Theatre de Lys. *Getting Out* brought Norman several awards for the best new play by a new American playwright, and it evidently stimulated her to devote herself entirely to playwriting. During 1978 and 1979, she continued to work with the Actors Theatre of Louisville, though she moved to New York City at the end of 1978 with her new husband. As a playwright-in-residence during 1978, she completed a highly successful pair of one-acts: *The Laundromat*, which depicts the encounter of a widow and a woman involved in a failed marriage; and *The Pool Hall*, which portrays the owner of the hall in conversation with the son of a notorious pool shark. In these short naturalistic pieces, as in the less successful *Circus Valentine* (1979), which portrays the attempt of a woman aerialist to save a failing family circus, Norman continued to focus on the painful experience of "folks you wouldn't even notice in life."

Her next major success in dramatizing the lives of such people came with the Pulitzer Prize–winning *'night, Mother*, which was first staged in January 1983 at the American Repertory Theater in Cambridge before its Broadway opening in March 1983. In this spare and relentlessly worked-out study of a woman's decision to commit suicide, Norman creates a challengingly different kind of protagonist from the Arlene of *Getting Out*, for Jessie Cates, heroine of *'night,*

Mother, is by no means passive or emotionally imprisoned. In contrast to Arlene, she is vocally and actively concerned with regaining a significant measure of self-control in her life, so much so that she is willing to put an end to it, since she cannot imagine a tolerable future, afflicted as she is by the painful circumstances of her past. Given Jessie's clear-cut and reiterated announcement of her intention to commit suicide, the energy of *'night Mother* inevitably arises not out of whether (or when, or even how) she will go through with her decision, but rather out of how she attempts to make sense of such a momentous decision both for herself and for her mother.

Making sense of Jessie's decision is the work of the play for both characters and audience, and Norman deliberately chooses to emphasize the realistic world of the characters so as to contrast the abnormality of Jessie's decision, at first, with the setting in which it takes place. Her stage directions stress the "ordinary" quality of the house, and insist that "under no circumstances should the set and its dressing make a judgment about the intelligence or taste of Jessie and Mama. It should simply indicate that they are very specific real people who happen to live in a particular part of the country." Thus the kitchen so realistically presented in Heidi Landesman's set for the New York production at the John Golden Theater (see Figure 1) and the many details of stage properties create a world which seems familiar and "real" to the audience. At the same time, Jessie's list-making and deliberate handling of all the props, from the gun which she carefully cleans (see Figure 2) to the seemingly endless supply of candy for her mother, represents her attempt to control this world from which she feels alienated and which she can finally control only by "getting out" of it. The laughter which the play evokes in performance similarly functions as both protective and horrifying; the audience may laugh at familiar mother-daughter routines as well as at telling comments about the absent family members, and yet recoil from the laughter because it is inappropriate to the subject and situation.

Norman's combination of the ordinary and the extraordinary, of laughter and horror, has provoked equally contradictory reactions in critics, as suggested by the two reviews of the New York production reprinted following the text. Some reviewers, such as Douglas Watt, found the basic situation of the play to be "alien, pat, and unlikely," while others, such as Frank Rich, found themselves gradually drawn into Jessie's "inexorable logic." A further complication of the play is that it addresses not just the question of suicide, but the larger questions concerning a woman's identity in a world dominated by men. Though no men appear in the play, Jessie and Mama do, after all, talk constantly about Jessie's dead father, her brother, her husband, and her delinquent son. And shortly after the pistol shot, Mama seeks the counsel not of another woman, but of a man—"Loretta, let me talk to Dawson, honey." Norman's vision of the prison in which women find themselves, and put themselves, is unsparing. Readers and audiences will have to decide if it is also hopeless.

'NIGHT, MOTHER

BY MARSHA NORMAN

CHARACTERS

JESSIE CATES, *in her late thirties or early forties, is pale and vaguely unsteady physically. It is only in the last year that* JESSIE *has gained control of her mind and body, and tonight she is determined to hold on to that control. She wears pants and a long black sweater with deep pockets, which contain scraps of paper, and there may be a pencil behind her ear or a pen clipped to one of the pockets of the sweater.*

As a rule, JESSIE *doesn't feel much like talking. Other people have rarely found her quirky sense of humor amusing. She has a peaceful energy on this night, a sense of purpose, but is clearly aware of the time passing moment by moment. Oddly enough,* JESSIE *has never been as communicative or as enjoyable as she is on this evening, but we must know she has not always been this way. There is a familiarity between these two women that comes from having lived together for a long time. There is a shorthand to the talk and a sense of routine comfort in the way they relate to each other physically. Naturally, there are also routine aggravations.*

THELMA CATES, *"MAMA," is* JESSIE's *mother, in her late fifties or early sixties. She has begun to feel her age and so takes it easy when she can, or when it serves her purpose to let someone help her. But she speaks quickly and enjoys talking. She believes that things* are *what she says they are. Her sturdiness is more a mental quality than a physical one, finally. She is chatty and nosy, and this* is *her house.*

SCENE

The play takes place in a relatively new house built way out on a country road, with a living room and connecting kitchen, and a center hall that leads off to the bedrooms. A pull cord in the hall ceiling releases a ladder which leads to the attic. One of these bedrooms opens directly onto the hall, and its entry should be visible to everyone in the audience. It should be, in fact, the focal point of the entire set, and the lighting should make it disappear completely at times and draw the entire set into it at others. It is a point of both threat and promise. It is an ordinary door that opens onto absolute nothingness. That door is the point of all the action, and the utmost care should be given to its design and construction.

The living room is cluttered with magazines and needle-work catalogues, ashtrays and candy dishes. Examples of MAMA's *needlework are everywhere—pillows, afghans, and quilts, doilies and rugs, and they are quite nice examples. The house is more comfortable than messy, but there is quite a lot to keep in place here. It is more personal than charming. It is not quaint. Under no circumstances should the set and its dressing make a judgment about the intelligence or taste of* JESSIE *and* MAMA. *It should simply indicate that they are very specific real people who happen to live in a particular part of the country. Heavy accents, which would further distance the audience from* JESSIE *and* MAMA, *are also wrong.*

The time is the present, with the action beginning about 8:15. Clocks onstage in the kitchen and on a table in the living room should run throughout the performance and be visible to the audience.

MAMA *stretches to reach the cupcakes in a cabinet in the kitchen. She can't see them, but she can feel around for them, and she's eager to have one, so she's working pretty hard at it. This may be the most serious exercise* MAMA *ever gets. She finds a cupcake, the coconut-covered, raspberry-and-marshmallow-filled kind known as a snowball, but sees that there's one missing from the package. She calls to* JESSIE, *who is apparently somewhere else in the house.*

MAMA: (*Unwrapping the cupcake*) Jessie, it's the last snow-ball, sugar. Put it on the list, O.K.? And we're out of Hershey bars, and where's that peanut brittle? I think maybe Dawson's been in it again. I ought to put a big mirror on the refrigerator door. That'll keep him out of my treats, won't it? You hear me, honey? (*Then more to herself.*) I hate it when the coconut falls off. Why does the coconut fall off?

(JESSIE *enters from her bedroom, carrying a stack of newspapers.*)

JESSIE: We got any old towels?

MAMA: There you are!

JESSIE: (*Holding a towel that was on the stack of newspapers*) Towels you don't want anymore. (*Picking up* MAMA's *snowball wrapper.*) How about this swimming towel Loretta gave us? Beach towel, that's the name of it. You want it? (MAMA *shakes her head no.*)

MAMA: What have you been doing in there?

JESSIE: And a big piece of plastic like a rubber sheet or something. Garbage bags would do if there's enough.

MAMA: Don't go making a big mess, Jessie. It's eight o'clock already.

JESSIE: Maybe an old blanket or towels we got in a soap box sometime?

MAMA: I said don't make a mess. You hair is black enough, hon.

JESSIE: (*Continuing to search the kitchen cabinets, finding two or three more towels to add to her stack*) It's not for my hair, Mama. What about some old pillows anywhere, or a foam cushion out of a yard chair would be real good.

MAMA: You haven't forgot what night it is, have you? (*Holding up her fingernails.*) They're all chipped, see? I've been waiting all week, Jess. It's Saturday night, sugar.

JESSIE: I know. I got it on the schedule.

MAMA: (*Crossing to the living room*) You want me to wash 'em now or are you making your mess first? (*Looking at the snowball.*) We're out of these. Did I say that already?

JESSIE: There's more coming tomorrow. I ordered you a whole case.

MAMA: (*Checking the TV Guide*) A whole case will go stale, Jessie.

JESSIE: They can go in the freezer till you're ready for them. Where's Daddy's gun?

MAMA: In the attic.

JESSIE: Where in the attic? I looked your whole nap and couldn't find it anywhere.

MAMA: One of his shoeboxes, I think.

JESSIE: Full of shoes. I looked already.

MAMA: Well, you didn't look good enough, then. There's that box from the ones he wore to the hospital. When he died, they told me I could have them back, but I never did like those shoes.

JESSIE: (*Pulling them out of her pocket*) I found the bullets. They were in an old milk can.

MAMA: (*As* JESSIE *starts for the hall*) Dawson took the shotgun, didn't he? Hand me that basket, hon.

JESSIE: (*Getting the basket for her*) Dawson better not've taken that pistol.

MAMA: (*Stopping her again*) Now my glasses, please. (JESSIE *returns to get the glasses.*) I told him to take those rubber boots, too, but he said they were for fishing. I told him to take up fishing.

(JESSIE *reaches for the cleaning spray and cleans* MAMA's *glasses for her*)

JESSIE: He's just too lazy to climb up there, Mama. Or maybe he's just being smart. That floor's not very steady.

MAMA: (*Getting out a piece of knitting*) It's not a floor at all, hon, it's a board now and then. Measure this for me. I need six inches.

JESSIE: (*As she measures*) Dawson could probably use some of those clothes up there. Somebody should have them. You ought to call the Salvation Army before the whole thing falls in on you. Six inches exactly.

MAMA: It's plenty safe! As long as you don't go up there.

JESSIE: (*Turning to go again*) I'm careful.

MAMA: What do you want the gun for, Jess?

JESSIE: (*Not returning this time. Opening the ladder in the hall.*) Protection. (*She steadies the ladder as* MAMA *talks.*)

MAMA: You take the TV way too serious, hon. I've never seen a criminal in my life. This is way too far to come for what's out here to steal. Never seen a one.

JESSIE: (*Taking her first step up*) Except for Ricky.

MAMA: Ricky is mixed up. That's not a crime.

JESSIE: Get your hands washed. I'll be right back. And get 'em real dry. You dry your hands till I get back or it's no go, all right?

MAMA: I thought Dawson told you not to go up those stairs.

JESSIE: (*Going up*) He did.

MAMA: I don't like the idea of a gun, Jess.

JESSIE: (*Calling down from the attic*) Which shoebox, do you remember?

MAMA: Black.

JESSIE: The box was black?

MAMA: The shoes were black.

JESSIE: That doesn't help much, Mother.

MAMA: I'm not trying to help, sugar. (*No answer.*) We don't have anything anybody'd want, Jessie. I mean, I don't even want what we got, Jessie.

JESSIE: Neither do I. Wash your hands. (MAMA *gets up and crosses to stand under the ladder.*)

MAMA: You come down from there before you have a fit. I can't come up and get you, you know.

JESSIE: I know.

MAMA: We'll just hand it over to them when they come, how's that? Whatever they want, the criminals.

JESSIE: That's a good idea, Mama.

MAMA: Ricky will grow out of this and be a real fine boy, Jess. But I have to tell you, I wouldn't want Ricky to know we had a gun in the house.

JESSIE: Here it is. I found it.

MAMA: It's just something Ricky's going through. Maybe he's in with some bad people. He just needs some time, sugar. He'll get back in school or get a job or one day you'll get a call and he'll say he's sorry for all the trouble he's caused and invite you out for supper someplace dress-up.

JESSIE: (*Coming back down the steps*) Don't worry. It's not for him, it's for me.

MAMA: I didn't think you would shoot your own boy, Jessie. I know you've felt like it, well, we've all felt like shooting somebody, but we don't do it. I just don't think we need . . .

JESSIE: (*Interrupting*) Your hands aren't washed. Do you want a manicure or not?

MAMA: Yes, I do, but . . .

JESSIE: (*Crossing to the chair*) Then wash your hands and don't talk to me any more about Ricky. Those two rings he took were the last valuable things *I* had, so now he's started in on other people, door to door. I hope they put him away sometime. I'd turn him in myself if I knew where he was.

MAMA: You don't mean that.

JESSIE: Every word. Wash your hands and that's the last time I'm telling you.

(JESSIE *sits down with the gun and starts cleaning it, pushing the cylinder out, checking to see that the chambers and barrel are empty, then putting some oil on a small patch of cloth and pushing it through the barrel with the push rod that was in the box.* MAMA *goes to the kitchen and washes her hands, as instructed, trying not to show her concern about the gun.*)

MAMA: I shoulda got you to bring down that milk can. Agnes Fletcher sold hers to somebody with a flea market for forty dollars apiece.

JESSIE: I'll go back and get it in a minute. There's a wagon wheel up there, too. There's even a churn. I'll get it all if you want.

MAMA: (*Coming over, now, taking over now*) What are you doing?

JESSIE: The barrel has to be clean, Mama. Old powder, dust gets in it . . .

MAMA: What for?

JESSIE: I told you.

MAMA: (*Reaching for the gun*) And I told you, we don't get criminals out here.

JESSIE: (*Quickly pulling it to her*) And I told you . . . (*Then trying to be calm.*) The gun is for me.

MAMA: Well, you can have it if you want. When I die, you'll get it all, anyway.

JESSIE: I'm going to kill myself, Mama.

MAMA: (*Returning to the sofa*) Very funny. Very funny.

JESSIE: I am.

MAMA: You are not! Don't even say such a thing, Jessie.

JESSIE: How would you know if I didn't say it? You want it to be a surprise? You're lying there in your bed or maybe you're just brushing your teeth and you hear this . . . noise down the hall?

MAMA: Kill yourself.

JESSIE: Shoot myself. In a couple of hours.

MAMA: It must be time for your medicine.

JESSIE: Took it already.

MAMA: What's the matter with you?

JESSIE: Not a thing. Feel fine.

MAMA: You feel fine. You're just going to kill yourself.

JESSIE: Waited until I felt good enough, in fact.

MAMA: Don't make jokes, Jessie. I'm too old for jokes.

JESSIE: It's not a joke, Mama.

(MAMA *watches for a moment in silence.*)

MAMA: That gun's no good, you know. He broke it right before he died. He dropped it in the mud one day.

JESSIE: Seems O.K. (*She spins the chamber, cocks the pistol, and pulls the trigger. The gun is not yet loaded, so all we hear is the click, but it will definitely work. It's also obvious that* JESSIE *knows her way around a gun.* MAMA *cannot speak.*) I had Cecil's all ready in there, just in case I couldn't find this one, but I'd rather use Daddy's.

MAMA: Those bullets are at least fifteen years old.

JESSIE: (*Pulling out another box*) These are from last week.

MAMA: Where did you get those?

JESSIE: Feed store Dawson told me about.

MAMA: Dawson!

JESSIE: I told him I was worried about prowlers. He said he thought it was a good idea. He told me what kind to ask for.

MAMA: If he had any idea . . .

JESSIE: He took it as a compliment. He thought I might be taking an interest in things. He got through telling me all about the bullets and then he said we ought to talk like this more often.

MAMA: And where was I while this was going on?

JESSIE: On the phone with Agnes. About the milk can, I guess. Anyway, I asked Dawson if he thought they'd send me some bullets and he said he'd just call for me, because he knew they'd send them if he told them to. And he was absolutely right. Here they are.

MAMA: How could he do that?

JESSIE: Just trying to help, Mama.

MAMA: And then I told you where the gun was.

JESSIE: (*Smiling, enjoying this joke*) See? Everybody's doing what they can.

MAMA: You told me it was for protection!

JESSIE: It *is*! I'm still doing your nails, though. Want to try that new Chinaberry color?

MAMA: Well, I'm calling Dawson right now. We'll just see what he has to say about this little stunt.

JESSIE: Dawson doesn't have any more to do with this.

MAMA: He's your brother.

JESSIE: And that's all.

MAMA: (Stands up, moves toward the phone) Dawson will put a stop to this. Yes he will. He'll take the gun away.

JESSIE: If you call him, I'll just have to do it before he gets here. Soon as you hang up the phone, I'll just walk in the bedroom and lock the door. Dawson will get here just in time to help you clean up. Go ahead, call him. Then call the police. Then call the funeral home. Then call Loretta and see if *she'll* do your nails.

MAMA: You will not! This is crazy talk, Jessie!

(MAMA *goes directly to the telephone and starts to dial, but* JESSIE *is fast, coming up behind her and taking the receiver out of her hand, putting it back down.*)

JESSIE: (Firm and quiet) I said no. This is private. Dawson is not invited.

MAMA: Just me.

JESSIE: I don't want anybody else over here. Just you and me. If Dawson comes over, it'll make me feel stupid for not doing it ten years ago.

MAMA: I think we better call the doctor. Or how about the ambulance. You like that one driver, I know. What's his name, Timmy? Get you somebody to talk to.

JESSIE: (Going back to her chair) I'm through talking, Mama. You're it. No more.

MAMA: We're just going to sit around like every other night in the world and then you're going to kill yourself? (JESSIE *doesn't answer.*) You'll miss. (Again there is no response.) You'll just wind up a vegetable. How would you like that? Shoot your ear off? You know what the doctor said about getting excited. You'll cock the pistol and have a fit.

JESSIE: I think I can kill myself, Mama.

MAMA: You're not going to kill yourself, Jessie. You're not even upset! (JESSIE *smiles, or laughs quietly, and* MAMA *tries a different approach.*) People don't really kill themselves, Jessie. No, mam, doesn't make sense, unless you're retarded or deranged, and you're as normal as they come, Jessie, for the most part. We're all *afraid* to die.

JESSIE: I'm not, Mama. I'm cold all the time, anyway.

MAMA: That's ridiculous.

JESSIE: It's exactly what I want. It's dark and quiet.

MAMA: So is the back yard, Jessie! Close your eyes. Stuff cotton in your ears. Take a nap! It's quiet in your room. I'll leave the TV off all night.

JESSIE: So quiet I don't know it's quiet. So nobody can get me.

MAMA: You don't know what dead is like. It might not be quiet at all. What if it's like an alarm clock and you can't wake up so you can't shut it off. Ever.

JESSIE: Dead is everybody and everything I ever knew, gone. Dead is dead quiet.

MAMA: It's a sin. You'll go to hell.

JESSIE: Uh-huh.

MAMA: You will!

JESSIE: Jesus was a suicide, if you ask me.

MAMA: You'll go to hell just for saying that, Jessie!

JESSIE: (With genuine surprise) I didn't know I thought that.

MAMA: Jessie!

(JESSIE *doesn't answer. She puts the now-loaded gun back in the box and crosses to the kitchen. But* MAMA *is afraid she's headed for the bedroom.*)

MAMA: (In a panic) You can't use my towels! They're my towels. I've had them for a long time. I like my towels.

JESSIE: I asked you if you wanted that swimming towel and you said you didn't.

MAMA: And you can't use your father's gun, either. It's mine now, too. And you can't do it in my house.

JESSIE: Oh, come on.

MAMA: No. You can't do it. I won't let you. The house is in my name.

JESSIE: I have to go in the bedroom and lock the door behind me so they won't arrest you for killing me. They'll probably test your hands for gunpowder, anyway, but you'll pass.

MAMA: Not in my house!

JESSIE: If I'd known you were going to act like this, I wouldn't have told you.

MAMA: How am I supposed to act? Tell you to go ahead? O.K. by me, sugar? Might try it myself. What took you so long?

JESSIE: There's just no point in fighting me over it, that's all. Want some coffee?

MAMA: Your birthday's coming up, Jessie. Don't you want to know what we got you?

JESSIE: You got me dusting powder, Loretta got me a new housecoat, pink probably, and Dawson got me new slippers, too small, but they go with the robe, he'll say. (MAMA *cannot speak.*) Right? (Apparently JESSIE *is right.*) Be back in a minute.

(JESSIE *takes the gun box, puts it on top of the stack of towels and garbage bags, and takes them into her bedroom.* MAMA, *alone for a moment, goes to the phone, picks up the receiver, looks toward the bedroom, starts to dial, and then replaces the receiver in its cradle as* JESSIE *walks back into the room.* JESSIE *wonders, silently. They have lived together for so long there is very rarely any reason for one to ask what the other was about to do.*)

MAMA: I started to, but I didn't. I didn't call him.

JESSIE: Good. Thank you.

MAMA: (Starting over, a new approach) What's this all about, Jessie?

JESSIE: About?

(JESSIE *now begins the next task she had "on the sched-ule," which is refilling all the candy jars, taking the empty papers out of the boxes of chocolates, etc.* MAMA *generally snitches when* JESSIE *does this. Not tonight, though. Nevertheless,* JESSIE *offers.*)

MAMA: What did I do?

JESSIE: Nothing. Want a caramel?

MAMA: (*Ignoring the candy*) You're mad at me.

JESSIE: Not a bit. I am worried about you, but I'm going to do what I can before I go. We're not just going to sit around tonight. I made a list of things.

MAMA: What things?

JESSIE: How the washer works. Things like that.

MAMA: I know how the washer works. You put the clothes in. You put the soap in. You turn it on. You wait.

JESSIE: You do something else. You don't just wait.

MAMA: Whatever else you find to do, you're still mainly waiting. The waiting's the worst part of it. The waiting's what you pay somebody else to do, if you can.

JESSIE: (*Nodding*) O.K. Where do we keep the soap?

MAMA: I could find it.

JESSIE: See?

MAMA: If you're mad about doing the wash, we can get Loretta to do it.

JESSIE: Oh now, that might be worth staying to see.

MAMA: She'd never in her life, would she?

JESSIE: Nope.

MAMA: What's the matter with her?

JESSIE: She thinks she's better than we are. She's not.

MAMA: Maybe if she didn't wear that yellow all the time.

JESSIE: The washer repair number is on a little card taped to the side of the machine.

MAMA: Loretta doesn't ever have to come over here again. Dawson can just leave her at home when he comes. And we don't ever have to see Dawson either if he bothers you. Does he bother you?

JESSIE: Sure he does. Be sure you clean out the lint tray every time you use the dryer. But don't ever put your house shoes in, it'll melt the soles.

MAMA: What does Dawson do, that bothers you?

JESSIE: He just calls me Jess like he knows who he's talking to. He's always wondering what I do all day. I mean, I wonder that myself, but it's my day, so it's mine to wonder about, not his.

MAMA: Family is just accident, Jessie. It's nothing per-sonal, hon. They don't mean to get on your nerves. They don't even mean to be your family, they just are.

JESSIE: They know too much.

MAMA: About what?

JESSIE: They know things about you, and they learned it before you had a chance to say whether you wanted them to know it or not. They were there

when it happened and it don't belong to them, it belongs to you, only they got it. Like my mail-order bra got delivered to their house.

MAMA: By accident!

JESSIE: All the same . . . they opened it. They saw the little rosebuds on it. (*Offering her another candy.*) Chewy mint?

MAMA: (*Shaking her head no*) What do they know about you? I'll tell them never to talk about it again. Is it Ricky or Cecil or your fits or your hair is falling out or you drink too much coffee or you never go out of the house or what?

JESSIE: I just don't like their talk. The account at the grocery is in Dawson's name when you call. The number's on a whole list of numbers on the back cover of the phone book.

MAMA: Well! Now we're getting somewhere. They're none of them ever setting foot in this house again.

JESSIE: It's not them, Mother. I wouldn't kill myself just to get away from them.

MAMA: You leave the room when they come over, any-way.

JESSIE: I stay as long as I can. Besides, it's you they come to see.

MAMA: That's because I stay in the room when they come.

JESSIE: It's not them.

MAMA: Then what is it?

JESSIE: (*Checking the list on her note pad*) The grocery won't deliver on Saturday anymore. And if you want your order the same day, you have to call before ten. And they won't deliver less than fifteen dollars' worth. What I do is tell them what we need and tell them to add on cigarettes until it gets to fifteen dollars.

MAMA: It's Ricky. You're trying to get through to him.

JESSIE: If I thought I could do that, I would stay.

MAMA: Make him sorry he hurt you, then. That's it, isn't it?

JESSIE: He's hurt me, I've hurt him. We're about even.

MAMA: You'll be telling him killing is O.K. with you, you know. Want him to start killing next? Nothing wrong with it. Mom did it.

JESSIE: Only a matter of time, anyway, Mama. When the call comes, you let Dawson handle it.

MAMA: Honey, nothing says those calls are always going to be some new trouble he's into. You could get one that he's got a job, that he's getting married, or how about he's joined the army, wouldn't that be nice?

JESSIE: If you call the Sweet Tooth before you call the grocery, that Susie will take your fudge next door to the grocery and it'll all come out together. Be sure you talk to Susie, though. She won't let them put it in the bottom of a sack like that one time, remember?

MAMA: Ricky could come over, you know. What if he calls us?

JESSIE: It's not Ricky, Mama.

MAMA: Or anybody could call us, Jessie.

JESSIE: Not on Saturday night, Mama.

MAMA: Then what is it? Are you sick? If your gums are swelling again, we can get you to the dentist in the morning.

JESSIE: No. Can you order your medicine or do you want Dawson to? I've got a note to him. I'll add that to it if you want.

MAMA: Your eyes don't look right. I thought so yesterday.

JESSIE: That was just the ragweed. I'm not sick.

MAMA: Epilepsy is sick, Jessie.

JESSIE: It won't kill me. (*A pause.*) If it would, I wouldn't have to.

MAMA: You don't *have* to.

JESSIE: No, I don't. That's what I like about it.

MAMA: Well, I won't let you!

JESSIE: It's not up to you.

MAMA: Jessie!

JESSIE: I want to hang a big sign around my neck, like Daddy's on the barn. GONE FISHING.

MAMA: You don't like it here.

JESSIE: (*Smiling*) Exactly.

MAMA: I meant here in my house.

JESSIE: I know you did.

MAMA: You never should have moved back in here with me. If you'd kept your little house or found another place when Cecil left you, you'd have made some new friends at least. Had a life to lead. Had your own things around you. Give Ricky a place to come see you. You never should've come here.

JESSIE: Maybe.

MAMA: But I didn't force you, did I?

JESSIE: If it was a mistake, we made it together. You took me in. I appreciate that.

MAMA: You didn't have any business being by yourself right then, but I can see how you might want a place of your own. A grown woman should . . .

JESSIE: Mama . . . I'm just not having a very good time and I don't have any reason to think it'll get anything but worse. I'm tired. I'm hurt. I'm sad. I feel used.

MAMA: Tired of what?

JESSIE: It all.

MAMA: What does that mean?

JESSIE: I can't say it any better.

MAMA: Well, you'll have to say it better because I'm not letting you alone till you do. What were those other things? Hurt . . . (*Before* JESSIE *can answer.*) You had this all ready to say to me, didn't you? Did you write this down? How long have you been thinking about this?

JESSIE: Off and on, ten years. On all the time, since Christmas.

MAMA: What happened at Christmas?

JESSIE: Nothing.

MAMA: So why Christmas?

JESSIE: That's it. On the nose.

(*A pause.* MAMA *knows exactly what* JESSIE *means. She was there, too, after all.*)

JESSIE: (*Putting the candy sacks away*) See where all this is? Red hots up front, sour balls and horehound mixed together in this one sack. New packages of toffee and licorice right in back there.

MAMA: Go back to your list. You're hurt by what?

JESSIE: (MAMA *knows perfectly well*) Mama . . .

MAMA: O.K. Sad about what? There's nothing real sad going on right now. If it was after your divorce or something, that would make sense.

JESSIE: (*Looking at her list, then opening the drawer*) Now, this drawer has everything in it that there's no better place for. Extension cords, batteries for the radio, extra lighters, sandpaper, masking tape, Elmer's glue, thumbtacks, that kind of stuff. The mousetraps are under the sink, but you call Dawson if you've got one and let him do it.

MAMA: Sad about what?

JESSIE: The way things are.

MAMA: Not good enough. What things?

JESSIE: Oh, everything from you and me to Red China.

MAMA: I think we can leave the Chinese out of this.

JESSIE: (*Crosses back into the living room*) There's extra light bulbs in a box in the hall closet. And we've got a couple of packages of fuses in the fuse box. There's candles and matches in the top of the broom closet, but if the lights go out, just call Dawson and sit tight. But don't open the refrigerator door. Things will stay cool in there as long as you keep the door shut.

MAMA: I asked you a question.

JESSIE: I read the paper. I don't like how things are. And they're not any better out there than they are in here.

MAMA: If you're doing this because of the newspapers, I can sure fix that!

JESSIE: There's just more of it on TV.

MAMA: (*Kicking the television set*) Take it out, then!

JESSIE: You wouldn't do that.

MAMA: Watch me.

JESSIE: What would you do all day?

MAMA: (*Desperately*) Sing. (JESSIE *laughs.*) I would, too. You want to watch? I'll sing till morning to keep you alive, Jessie, please!

JESSIE: No. (*Then affectionately.*) It's a funny idea, though. What do you sing?

MAMA: (*Has no idea how to answer this*) We've got a good life here!

JESSIE: (*Going back into the kitchen*) I called this morning and canceled the papers, except for Sunday, for your puzzles; you'll still get that one.

MAMA: Let's get another dog, Jessie! You liked a big dog, now, didn't you? That King dog, didn't you?

JESSIE: (*Washing her hands*) I did like that King dog, yes.

MAMA: I'm so dumb. He's the one run under the tractor.

JESSIE: That makes him dumb, not you.

MAMA: For bringing it up.

JESSIE: It's O.K. Handi-Wipes and sponges under the sink.

MAMA: We could get a new dog and keep him in the house. Dogs are cheap!

JESSIE: (*Getting big pill jars out of the cabinet*) No.

MAMA: Something for you to take care of.

JESSIE: I've had you, Mama.

MAMA: (*Frantically starting to fill pill bottles*) You do too much for me. I can fill pill bottles all day, Jessie, and change the shelf paper and wash the floor when I get through. You just watch me. You don't have to do another thing in this house if you don't want to. You don't have to take care of me, Jessie.

JESSIE: I know that. You've just been letting me do it so I'll have something to do, haven't you?

MAMA: (*Realizing this was a mistake*) I don't do it as well as you. I just meant if it tires you out or makes you feel used . . .

JESSIE: Mama, I know you used to ride the bus. Riding the bus and it's hot and bumpy and crowded and too noisy and more than anything in the world you want to get off and the only reason in the world you don't get off is it's still fifty blocks from where you're going? Well, I can get off right now if I want to, because even if I ride fifty more years and get off then, it's the same place when I step down to it. Whenever I feel like it, I can get off. As soon as I've had enough, it's my stop. I've had enough.

MAMA: You're feeling sorry for yourself!

JESSIE: The plumber's helper is under the sink, too.

MAMA: You're not having a good time! Whoever promised you a good time? Do you think I've had a good time?

JESSIE: I think you're pretty happy, yeah. You have things you like to do.

MAMA: Like what?

JESSIE: Like crochet.

MAMA: I'll teach you to crochet.

JESSIE: I can't do any of that nice work, Mama.

MAMA: Good time don't come looking for you, Jessie. You could work some puzzles or put in a garden or go to the store. Let's call a taxi and go to the A&P!

JESSIE: I shopped you up for about two weeks already. You're not going to need toilet paper till Thanksgiving.

MAMA: (*Interrupting*) You're acting like some little brat, Jessie. You're mad and everybody's boring and you don't have anything to do and you don't like me and you don't like going out and you don't like staying in and you never talk on the phone and you don't watch TV and you're miserable and it's your own sweet fault.

JESSIE: And it's time I did something about it.

MAMA: Not something like killing yourself. Something like . . . buying us all new dishes! I'd like that. Or maybe the doctor would let you get a driver's license now, or I know what let's do right this minute, let's rearrange the furniture.

JESSIE: I'll do that. If you want. I always thought if the TV was somewhere else, you wouldn't get such a glare on it during the day. I'll do whatever you want before I go.

MAMA: (*Badly frightened by those words*) You could get a job!

JESSIE: I took that telephone sales job and I didn't even make enough money to pay the phone bill, and I tried to work at the gift shop at the hospital and they said I made people real uncomfortable smiling at them the way I did.

MAMA: You could keep books. You kept your dad's books.

JESSIE: But nobody ever checked them.

MAMA: When he died, they checked them.

JESSIE: And that's when they took the books away from me.

MAMA: That's because without him there wasn't any business, Jessie!

JESSIE: (*Putting the pill bottles away*) You know I couldn't work. I can't do anything. I've never been around people my whole life except when I went to the hospital. I could have a seizure any time. What good would a job do? The kind of job I could get would make me feel worse.

MAMA: Jessie!

JESSIE: It's true!

MAMA: It's what you think is true!

JESSIE: (*Struck by the clarity of that*) That's right. It's what I think is true.

MAMA: (*Hysterically*) But I can't do anything about that!

JESSIE: (*Quietly*) No. You can't. (MAMA *slumps, if not physically, at least emotionally.*) And I can't do anything either, about my life, to change it, make it better, make me feel better about it. Like it better, make it work. But I can stop it. Shut it down, turn it off like the radio when there's nothing on I want to listen to. It's all I really have that belongs to me and I'm going to say what happens to it. And it's going to stop. And I'm going to stop it. So. Let's just have a good time.

MAMA: Have a good time.

JESSIE: We can't go on fussing all night. I mean, I could ask you things I always wanted to know and you could make me some hot chocolate. The old way.

MAMA: (*In despair*) It takes cocoa, Jessie.

JESSIE: (*Gets it out of the cabinet*) I bought cocoa, Mama. And I'd like to have a caramel apple and do your nails.

MAMA: You didn't eat a bite of supper.

JESSIE: Does that mean I can't have a caramel apple?

MAMA: Of course not. I mean . . . (*Smiling a little.*) Of course you can have a caramel apple.

JESSIE: I thought I could.

MAMA: I make the best caramel apples in the world.

JESSIE: I know you do.

MAMA: Or used to. And you don't get cocoa like mine anywhere anymore.

JESSIE: It takes time, I know, but . . .

MAMA: The salt is the trick.

JESSIE: Trouble and everything.

MAMA: (*Backing away toward the stove*) It's no trouble. What trouble? You put it in the pan and stir it up. All right. Fine. Caramel apples. Cocoa. O.K.

(JESSIE *walks to the counter to retrieve her cigarettes as* MAMA *looks for the right pan. There are brief near-smiles, and maybe* MAMA *clears her throat. We have a truce, for the moment. A genuine but nevertheless uneasy one.* JESSIE, *who has been in constant motion since the beginning, now seems content to sit.*)

(MAMA *starts looking for a pan to make the cocoa, getting out all the pans in the cabinets in the process. It looks like she's making a mess on purpose so* JESSIE *will have to put them all away again.* MAMA *is buying time, or trying to, and entertaining.*)

JESSIE: You talk to Agnes today?

MAMA: She's calling me from a pay phone this week. God only knows why. She has a perfectly good Trimline at home.

JESSIE: (*Laughing*) Well, how is she?

MAMA: How is she every day, Jessie? Nuts.

JESSIE: Is she really crazy or just silly?

MAMA: No, she's really crazy. She was probably using the pay phone because she had another little fire problem at home.

JESSIE: Mother . . .

MAMA: I'm serious! Agnes Fletcher's burned down every house she ever lived in. Eight fires, and she's due for a new one any day now.

JESSIE: (*Laughing*) No!

MAMA: Wouldn't surprise me a bit.

JESSIE: (*Laughing*) Why didn't you tell me this before? Why isn't she locked up somewhere?

MAMA: 'Cause nobody ever got hurt, I guess. Agnes woke everybody up to watch the fires as soon as she set 'em. One time she set out porch chairs and served lemonade.

JESSIE: (*Shaking her head*) Real lemonade?

MAMA: The houses they lived in, you knew they were going to fall down anyway, so why wait for it, is all I could ever make out about it. Agnes likes a feeling of accomplishment.

JESSIE: Good for her.

MAMA: (*Finding the pan she wants*) Why are you asking about Agnes? One cup or two?

JESSIE: One. She's your friend. No marshmallows.

MAMA: (*Getting the milk, etc.*) You have to have marshmallows. That's the old way, Jess. Two or three? Three is better.

JESSIE: Three, then. Her whole house burns up? Her clothes and pillows and everything? I'm not sure I believe this.

MAMA: When she was a girl, Jess, not now. Long time ago. But she's still got it in her, I'm sure of it.

JESSIE: She wouldn't burn her house down now. Where would she go? She can't get Buster to build her a new one, he's dead. How could she burn it up?

MAMA: Be exciting, though, if she did. You never know.

JESSIE: You do too know, Mama. She wouldn't do it.

MAMA: (*Forced to admit, but reluctant*) I guess not.

JESSIE: What else? Why does she wear all those whistles around her neck?

MAMA: Why does she have a house full of birds?

JESSIE: I didn't know she had a house full of birds!

MAMA: Well, she does. And she says they just follow her home. Well, I know for a fact she's still paying on the last parrot she bought. You gotta keep your life filled up, she says. She says a lot of stupid things. (JESSIE *laughs,* MAMA *continues, convinced she's getting somewhere.*) It's all that okra she eats. You can't just willy-nilly eat okra two meals a day and expect to get away with it. Made her crazy.

JESSIE: She really eats okra twice a day? Where does she get it in the winter?

MAMA: Well, she eats it a lot. Maybe not two meals, but . . .

JESSIE: More than the average person.

MAMA: (*Beginning to get irritated*) I don't know how much okra the average person eats.

JESSIE: Do you know how much okra Agnes eats?

MAMA: No.

JESSIE: How many birds does she have?

MAMA: Two.

JESSIE: Then what are the whistles for?

MAMA: They're not real whistles. Just little plastic ones on a necklace she won playing Bingo, and I only told you about it because I thought I might get a laugh out of you for once even if it wasn't the truth, Jessie. Things don't have to be true to talk about 'em, you know.

JESSIE: Why won't she come over here?

(MAMA *is suddenly quiet, but the cocoa and milk are in the pan now, so she lights the stove and starts stirring.*)

MAMA: Well now, what a good idea. We should've had more cocoa. Cocoa is perfect.

JESSIE: Except you don't like milk.

MAMA: (*Another attempt, but not as energetic*) I hate milk. Coats your throat as bad as okra. Something just downright disgusting about it.

JESSIE: It's because of me, isn't it?

MAMA: No, Jess.

JESSIE: Yes, Mama.

MAMA: O.K. Yes, then, but she's crazy. She's as crazy as they come. She's a lunatic.

JESSIE: What is it exactly? Did I say something, sometime? Or did she see me have a fit and's afraid I might have another one if she came over, or what?

MAMA: I guess.

JESSIE: You guess what? What's she ever said? She must've given you some reason.

MAMA: Your hands are cold.

JESSIE: What difference does that make?

MAMA: "Like a corpse," she says, "and I'm gonna be one soon enough as it is."

JESSIE: That's crazy.

MAMA: That's Agnes. "Jessie's shook the hand of death and I can't take the chance it's catching, Thelma, so I ain't comin' over, and you can understand or not, but I ain't comin'. I'll come up the driveway, but that's as far as I go."

JESSIE: (*Laughing, relieved*) I thought she didn't like me! She's scared of me! How about that! Scared of me.

MAMA: I could make her come over here, Jessie. I could call her up right now and she could bring the birds and come visit. I didn't know you ever thought about her at all. I'll tell her she just has to come and she'll come, all right. She owes me one.

JESSIE: No, that's all right. I just wondered about it. When I'm in the hospital, does she come over here?

MAMA: Her kitchen is just a tiny thing. When she comes over here, she feels like . . . (*Toning it down a little.*) Well, we all like a change of scene, don't we?

JESSIE: (*Playing along*) Sure we do. Plus there's no birds diving around.

MAMA: I hate those birds. She says I don't understand them. What's there to understand about birds?

JESSIE: Why Agnes likes them, for one thing. Why they stay with her when they could be outside with the other birds. What their singing means. How they fly. What they think Agnes is.

MAMA: Why do you have to know so much about things, Jessie? There's just not that much *to* things that I could ever see.

JESSIE: That you could ever *tell*, you mean. You didn't have to lie to me about Agnes.

MAMA: I didn't lie. You never asked before!

JESSIE: You lied about setting fire to all those houses and about how many birds she has and how much okra she eats and why she won't come over here. If I have to keep dragging the truth out of you, this is going to take all night.

MAMA: That's fine with me. I'm not a bit sleepy.

JESSIE: Mama . . .

MAMA: All right. Ask me whatever you want. Here.

(*They come to an awkward stop, as the cocoa is ready and* MAMA *pours it into the cups* JESSIE *has set on the table.*)

JESSIE: (*As* MAMA *takes her first sip*) Did you love Daddy?

MAMA: No.

JESSIE: (*Pleased that* MAMA *understands the rules better now*) I didn't think so. Were you really fifteen when you married him?

MAMA: The way he told it? I'm sitting in the mud, he comes along, drags me in the kitchen, "She's been there ever since"?

JESSIE: Yes.

MAMA: No. It was a big fat lie, the whole thing. He just thought it was funnier that way. God, this milk in here.

JESSIE: The cocoa helps.

MAMA: (*Pleased that they agree on this, at least*) Not enough, though, does it? You can still taste it, can't you?

JESSIE: Yeah, it's pretty bad. I thought it was my memory that was bad, but it's not. It's the milk, all right.

MAMA: It's a real waste of chocolate. You don't have to finish it.

JESSIE: (*Putting her cup down*) Thanks, though.

MAMA: I should've known not to make it. I knew you wouldn't like it. You never did like it.

JESSIE: You didn't ever love him, or he did something and you stopped loving him, or what?

MAMA: He felt sorry for me. He wanted a plain country woman and that's what he married, and then he held it against me the rest of my life like I was supposed to change and surprise him somehow. Like I remember this one day he was standing on the porch and I told him to get a shirt on and he went in and got one and then he said, real peaceful, but to the point, "You're right, Thelma. If God had meant for people to go around without any clothes on, they'd have been born that way."

JESSIE: (*Sees* MAMA'S *hurt*) He didn't mean anything by that, Mama.

MAMA: He never said a word he didn't have to, Jessie. That was probably all he'd said to me all day, Jessie. So if he said it, there was something to it, but I never did figure that one out. What did that mean?

JESSIE: I don't know. I liked him better than you did, but I didn't know him any better.

MAMA: How could I love him, Jessie. I didn't have a thing he wanted. (JESSIE *doesn't answer.*) He got his share, though. You loved him enough for both of us. You followed him around like some . . . Jessie, all the man ever did was farm and sit . . . and try to think of somebody to sell the farm to.

JESSIE: Or make me a boyfriend out of pipe cleaners and sit back and smile like the stick man was about to dance and wasn't I going to get a kick out of that. Or sit up with a sick cow all night and leave me a chain of sleepy stick elephants on my bed in the morning.

MAMA: Or just sit.

JESSIE: I liked him sitting. Big old faded blue man in the chair. Quiet.

MAMA: Agnes gets more talk out of her birds than I got from the two of you. He could've had that GONE FISHING sign around his neck in that chair. I saw him stare off at the water. I saw him look at the weather rolling in. I got where I could practically see the boat myself. But you, you knew what he was thinking about and you're going to tell me.

JESSIE: I don't know, Mama! His life, I guess. His corn. His boots. Us. Things. You know.

MAMA: No, I don't know, Jessie! You had those quiet little conversations after supper every night. What were you whispering about?

JESSIE: We weren't whispering, you were just across the room.

MAMA: What did you talk about?

JESSIE: We talked about why black socks are warmer than blue socks. Is that something to go tell Mother? You were just jealous because I'd rather talk to him than wash the dishes with you.

MAMA: I was jealous because you'd rather talk to him than anything! (JESSIE *reaches across the table for the small clock and starts to wind it.*) If I had died instead of him, he wouldn't have taken you in like I did.

JESSIE: I wouldn't have expected him to.

MAMA: Then what would you have done?

JESSIE: Come visit.

MAMA: Oh, I see. He died and left you stuck with me and you're mad about it.

JESSIE: (*Getting up from the table*) Not anymore. He didn't mean to. I didn't have to come here. We've been through this.

MAMA: He felt sorry for you, too, Jessie, don't kid yourself about that. He said you were a runt and he said it from the day you were born and he said you didn't have a chance.

JESSIE: (*Getting the canister of sugar and starting to refill the sugar bowl*) I know he loved me.

MAMA: What if he did? It didn't change anything.

JESSIE: It didn't have to. I miss him.

MAMA: He never really went fishing, you know. Never once. His tackle box was full of chewing tobacco and all he ever did was drive out to the lake and sit in his car. Dawson told me. And Bennie at the bait shop, he told Dawson. They all laughed about it. And he'd come back from fishing and all he'd have to show for it was . . . a whole pipe-cleaner *family*— chickens, pigs, a dog with a bad leg—it was creepy strange. It made me sick to look at them and I hid his pipe cleaners a couple of times but he always had more somewhere.

JESSIE: I thought it might be better for you after he died. You'd get interested in things. Breathe better. Change somehow.

MAMA: Into what? The Queen? A clerk in a shoe store? Why should I? Because he said to? Because you said to? (JESSIE *shakes her head.*) Well I wasn't here for his entertainment and I'm not here for yours either, Jessie. I don't know what I'm here for, but then I don't think about it. (*Realizing what all this means.*) But I bet you wouldn't be killing yourself if he were still alive. That's a fine thing to figure out, isn't it?

JESSIE: (*Filling the honey jar now*) That's not true.

MAMA: Oh no? Then what were you asking about him for? Why did you want to know if I loved him?

JESSIE: I didn't think you did, that's all.

MAMA: Fine then. You were right. Do you feel better now?

JESSIE: (*Cleaning the honey jar carefully*) It feels good to be right about it.

MAMA: It didn't matter whether I loved him. It didn't matter to me and it didn't matter to him. And it didn't mean we didn't get along. It wasn't important. We didn't talk about it. (*Sweeping the pots off the cabinet.*) Take all these pots out to the porch!

JESSIE: What for?

MAMA: Just leave me this one pan. (*She jerks the silverware drawer open.*) Get me one knife, one fork, one big spoon, and the can opener, and put them out where I can get them. (*Starts throwing knives and forks in one of the pans.*)

JESSIE: Don't do that! I just straightened that drawer!

MAMA: (*Throwing the pan in the sink*) And throw out all the plates and cups. I'll use paper. Loretta can have what she wants and Dawson can sell the rest.

JESSIE: (*Calmly*) What are you doing?

MAMA: I'm not going to cook. I never liked it, anyway. I like candy. Wrapped in plastic or coming in sacks. And tuna. I like tuna. I'll eat tuna, thank you.

JESSIE: (*Taking the pan out of the sink*) What if you want to make apple butter? You can't make apple butter in that little pan. What if you leave carrots on cooking and burn up that pan?

MAMA: I don't like carrots.

JESSIE: What if the strawberries are good this year and you want to go picking with Agnes.

MAMA: I'll tell her to bring a pan. You said you would do whatever I wanted! I don't want a bunch of pans cluttering up my cabinets I can't get down to, anyway. Throw them out. Every last one.

JESSIE: (*Gathering up the pots*) I'm putting them all back in. I'm not taking them to the porch. If you want them, they'll be here. You'll bend down and get them, like you got the one for the cocoa. And if somebody else comes over here to cook, they'll have something to cook in, and that's the end of it!

MAMA: Who's going to come cook here?

JESSIE: Agnes.

MAMA: In my pots. Not on your life.

JESSIE: There's no reason why the two of you couldn't just live here together. Be cheaper for both of you and somebody to talk to. And if the birds bothered you, well, one day when Agnes is out getting her hair done, you could take them all for a walk!

MAMA: (*As* JESSIE *straightens the silverware*) So that's why you're pestering me about Agnes. You think you can rest easy if you get me a new babysitter? Well, I don't want to live with Agnes. I barely want to talk with Agnes. She's just around. We go back, that's all. I'm not letting Agnes near this place. You don't get off as easy as that, child.

JESSIE: O.K., then. It's just something to think about.

MAMA: I don't like things to think about. I like things to go on.

JESSIE: (*Closing the silverware drawer*) I want to know what Daddy said to you the night he died. You came storming out of his room and said I could wait it out with him if I wanted to, but you were going to watch *Gunsmoke*. What did he say to you?

MAMA: He didn't have *anything* to say to me, Jessie. That's why I left. He didn't say a thing. It was his last chance not to talk to me and he took full advantage of it.

JESSIE: (*After a moment*) I'm sorry you didn't love him. Sorry for you, I mean. He seemed like a nice man.

MAMA: (*As* JESSIE *walks to the refrigerator*) Ready for your apple now?

JESSIE: Soon as I'm through here, Mama.

MAMA: You won't like the apple, either. It'll be just like the cocoa. You never liked eating at all, did you? Any of it! What have you been living on all these years, toothpaste?

JESSIE: (*As she starts to clean out the refrigerator*) Now, you know the milkman comes on Wednesdays and Saturdays, and he leaves the order blank in an egg box, and you give the bills to Dawson once a month.

MAMA: Do they still make that orangeade?

JESSIE: It's not orangeade, it's just orange.

MAMA: I'm going to get some. I thought they stopped making it. You just stopped ordering it.

JESSIE: You should drink milk.

MAMA: Not anymore, I'm not. That hot chocolate was the last. Hooray.

JESSIE: (*Getting the garbage can from under the sink*) I told them to keep delivering a quart a week no matter what you said. I told them you'd run out of Cokes and you'd have to drink it. I told them I knew you wouldn't pour it on the ground . . .

MAMA: (*Finishing her sentence*) And you told them you weren't going to be ordering anymore?

JESSIE: I told them I was taking a little holiday and to look after you.

MAMA: And they didn't think something was funny about that? You who doesn't go to the front steps? You, who only sees the driveway looking down from a stretcher passed out cold?

JESSIE: (*Enjoying this, but not laughing*) They said it was about time, but why didn't I take you with me? And I said I didn't think you'd want to go, and they said, "Yeah, everybody's got their own idea of vacation."

MAMA: I guess you think that's funny.

JESSIE: (*Pulling jars out of the refrigerator*) You know there never was any reason to call the ambulance for me. All they ever did for me in the emergency room was let me wake up. I could've done that here. Now, I'll just call them out and you say yes or no. I know you like pickles. Ketchup?

MAMA: Keep it.

JESSIE: We've had this since last Fourth of July.

MAMA: Keep the ketchup. Keep it all.

JESSIE: Are you going to drink ketchup from the bottle or what? How can you want your food and not want your pots to cook it in? This stuff will all spoil in here, Mother.

MAMA: Nothing I ever did was good enough for you and I want to know why.

JESSIE: That's not true.

MAMA: And I want to know why you've lived here this long feeling the way you do.

JESSIE: You have no earthly idea how I feel.

MAMA: Well, how could I? You're real far back there, Jessie.

JESSIE: Back where?

MAMA: What's it like over there, where you are? Do people always say the right thing or get whatever they want, or what?

JESSIE: What are you talking about?

MAMA: Why do you read the newspaper? Why don't you wear that sweater I made for you? Do you remember how I used to look, or am I just any old woman now? When you have a fit, do you see stars or what? How did you fall off the horse, really? Why did Cecil leave you? Where did you put my old glasses?

JESSIE: (*Stunned by* MAMA's *intensity*) They're in the bottom drawer of your dresser in an old Milk of Magnesia box. Cecil left me because he made me choose between him and smoking.

MAMA: Jessie, I know he wasn't that dumb.

JESSIE: I never understood why he hated it so much when it's so good. Smoking is the only thing I know that's always just what you think it's going to be. Just like it was the last time, right there when you want it and real quiet.

MAMA: Your fits made him sick and you know it.

JESSIE: Say seizures, not fits. Seizures.

MAMA: It's the same thing. A seizure in the hospital is a fit at home.

JESSIE: They didn't bother him at all. Except he did feel responsible for it. It *was* his idea to go horseback riding that day. It was his idea I could do *anything* if I just made up my mind to. I fell off the horse because I didn't know how to hold on. Cecil left for pretty much the same reason.

MAMA: He had a girl, Jessie. I walked right in on them in the toolshed.

JESSIE: (*After a moment*) O.K. That's fair. (*Lighting another cigarette.*) Was she very pretty?

MAMA: She was Agnes's girl, Carlene. Judge for yourself.

JESSIE: (*As she walks to the living room*) I guess you and Agnes had a good talk about that, huh?

MAMA: I never thought he was good enough for you. They moved here from Tennessee, you know.

JESSIE: What are you talking about? You liked him better than I did. You flirted him out here to build your porch or I'd never even met him at all. You thought maybe he'd help you out around the place, come in and get some coffee and talk to you. God knows what you thought. All that curly hair.

MAMA: He's the best carpenter I ever saw. That little house of yours will still be standing at the end of the world, Jessie.

JESSIE: You didn't need a porch, Mama.

MAMA: All right! I wanted you to have a husband.

JESSIE: And I couldn't get one on my own, of course.

MAMA: How were you going to get a husband never opening your mouth to a living soul?

JESSIE: So I was quiet about it, so what?

MAMA: So I should have let you just sit here? Sit like your daddy? Sit here?

JESSIE: Maybe.

MAMA: Well, I didn't think so.

JESSIE: Well, what did you know?

MAMA: I never said I knew much. How was I supposed to learn anything living out here? I didn't know enough to do half the things I did in my life. Things happen. You do what you can about them and you see what happens next. I married you off to the wrong man, I admit that. So I took you in when he left. I'm sorry.

JESSIE: He wasn't the wrong man.

MAMA: He didn't love you, Jessie, or he wouldn't have left.

JESSIE: He wasn't the wrong man, Mama. I loved Cecil so much. And I tried to get more exercise and I tried to stay awake. I tried to learn to ride a horse. And I tried to stay outside with him, but he always knew I was trying, so it didn't work.

MAMA: He was a selfish man. He told me once he hated to see people move into his houses after he built them. He knew they'd mess them up.

JESSIE: I loved that bridge he built over the creek in back of the house. It didn't have to be anything special, a couple of boards would have been just fine, but he used that yellow pine and rubbed it so smooth . . .

MAMA: He had responsibilities here. He had a wife and son here and he failed you.

JESSIE: Or that baby bed he built for Ricky. I told him he didn't have to spend so much time on it, but he said it had to last, and the thing ended up weighing two hundred pounds and I couldn't move it. I said, "How long does a baby bed have to last, anyway?" But maybe he thought if it was strong enough, it might keep Ricky a baby.

MAMA: Ricky is too much like Cecil.

JESSIE: He is not. Ricky is as much like me as it's possible for any human to be. We even wear the same size pants. These are his, I think.

MAMA: That's just the same size. That's not you're the same person.

JESSIE: I see it on his face. I hear it when he talks. We look out at the world and we see the same thing: Not Fair. And the only difference between us is Ricky's out there trying to get even. And he knows not to trust anybody and he got it straight from me. And he knows not to try to get work, and guess where he got that. He walks around like there's loose boards in the floor, and you know who laid that floor, I did.

MAMA: Ricky isn't through yet. You don't know how he'll turn out!

JESSIE: (Going back to the kitchen) Yes I do and so did Cecil. Ricky is the two of us together for all time in too small a space. And we're tearing each other apart, like always, inside that boy, and if you don't see it, then you're just blind.

MAMA: Give him time, Jess.

JESSIE: Oh, he'll have plenty of that. Five years for forgery, ten years for armed assault . . .

MAMA: (Furious) Stop that! (Then pleading.) Jessie, Cecil might be ready to try it again, honey, that happens sometimes. Go downtown. Find him. Talk to him. He didn't know what he had in you. Maybe he sees things different now, but you're not going to know that till you go see him. Or call him up! Right now! He might be home.

JESSIE: And say what? Nothing's changed, Cecil, I'd just like to look at you, if you don't mind? No. He loved me, Mama. He just didn't know how things fall down around me like they do. I think he did the right thing. He gave himself another chance, that's all. But I did beg him to take me with him. I did tell him I would leave Ricky and you and everything I loved out here if only he would take me with him, but he couldn't and I understood that. (Pause.) I wrote that note I showed you. I wrote it. Not Cecil. I said "I'm sorry, Jessie, I can't fix it all for you." I said I'd always love me, not Cecil. But that's how he felt.

MAMA: Then he should've taken you with him!

JESSIE: (Picking up the garbage bag she has filled) Mama, you don't pack your garbage when you move.

MAMA: You will not call yourself garbage, Jessie.

JESSIE: (Taking the bag to the big garbage can near the back door) Just a way of saying it, that's all. (Opening the can, putting the garbage in, then securing the lid.) Well, a little more than that. I was trying to say it's all right that Cecil left. It was . . . a relief in a way. I never was what he wanted to see, so it was better when he wasn't looking at me all the time.

MAMA: I'll make your apple now.

JESSIE: No thanks. You get the manicure stuff and I'll be right there.

(JESSIE *ties up the big garbage bag in the can and replaces the small garbage bag under the sink, all the time trying desperately to regain her calm.* MAMA *watches, from a distance, her hand reaching unconsciously for the phone. Then she has a better idea. Or rather she thinks of the only other thing left and is willing to try it. Maybe she is even convinced it will work.)*

MAMA: Jessie, I think your daddy had little . . .

JESSIE: (*Interrupting her*) Garbage night is Tuesday. Put it out as late as you can. The Davis's dogs get in it if you don't. (*Replacing the garbage bag in the can under the sink.*) And keep ordering the heavy black bags. It doesn't pay to buy the cheap ones. And I've got all the ties here with the hammers and all. Take them out of the box as soon as you open a new one and put them in this drawer. They'll get lost if you don't, and rubber bands or something else won't work.

MAMA: I think your daddy had fits, too. I think he sat in his chair and had little fits. I read this a long time ago in a magazine, how little fits go, just little black-outs where maybe their eyes don't even close and people just call them "thinking spells."

JESSIE: (*Getting the slipcover out of the laundry basket*) I don't think you want this manicure we've been looking forward to. I washed this cover for the sofa, but it'll take both of us to get it back on.

MAMA: I watched his eyes. I know that's what it was. The magazine said some people don't even know they've had one.

JESSIE: Daddy would've known if he'd had fits, Mama.

MAMA: The lady in this story had kept track of hers and she'd had eighty thousand of them in the last eleven years.

JESSIE: Next time you wash this cover, it'll dry better if you put it on wet.

MAMA: Jessie, listen to what I'm telling you. This lady had anywhere between five and five hundred fits a day and they lasted maybe fifteen seconds apiece, so that out of her life, she'd only lost about two weeks altogether, and she had a full-time secretary job and an IQ of 120.

JESSIE: (*Amused by* MAMA'*s approach*) You want to talk about fits, is that it?

MAMA: Yes. I do. I want to say . . .

JESSIE: (*Interrupting*) Most of the time I wouldn't even know I'd had one, except I wake up with different clothes on, feeling like I've been run over. Sometimes I feel my head start to turn around or hear myself scream. And sometimes there *is* this dizzy stupid feeling a little before it, but if the TV's on, well, it's easy to miss.

(*As* JESSIE *and* MAMA *replace the slipcover on the sofa and the afghan on the chair, the physical struggle somehow mirrors the emotional one in the conversation.*)

MAMA: I can tell when you're about to have one. Your eyes get this big! But, Jessie, you haven't . . .

JESSIE: (*Taking charge of this*) What do they look like? The seizures.

MAMA: (*Reluctant*) Different each time, Jess.

JESSIE: O.K. Pick one, then. A good one. I think I want to know now.

MAMA: There's not much to tell. You just . . . crumple, in a heap, like a puppet and somebody cut the strings all at once, or like the firing squad in some Mexican movie, you just slide down the wall, you know. You don't know what happens? How can you not know what happens?

JESSIE: I'm busy.

MAMA: That's not funny.

JESSIE: I'm not laughing. My head turns around and I fall down and then what?

MAMA: Well, your chest squeezes in and out, and you sound like you're gagging, sucking air in and out like you can't breathe.

JESSIE: Do it for me. Make the sound for me.

MAMA: I will not. It's awful-sounding.

JESSIE: Yeah. It felt like it might be. What's next?

MAMA: Your mouth bites down and I have to get your tongue out of the way fast, so you don't bite yourself.

JESSIE: Or you. I bite you, too, don't I?

MAMA: You got me once real good. I had to get a teta-nus! But I know what to watch for now. And then you turn blue and the jerks start up. Like I'm standing there poking you with a cattle prod or you're sticking your finger in a light socket as fast as you can . . .

JESSIE: Foaming like a mad dog the whole time.

MAMA: It's bubbling, Jess, not foam like the washer overflowed, for God's sake; it's bubbling like a baby spitting up. I go get a wet washcloth, that's all. And then the jerks slow down and you wet yourself and it's over. Two minutes tops.

JESSIE: How do I get to the bed?

MAMA: How do you think?

JESSIE: I'm too heavy for you now. How do you do it?

MAMA: I call Dawson. But I get you cleaned up before he gets here and I make him leave before you wake up.

JESSIE: You could just leave me on the floor.

MAMA: I want you to wake up someplace nice, O.K.? (*Then making a real effort.*) But, Jessie, and this is the reason I even brought this up! You haven't had a seizure for a solid year. A whole year, do you realize that?

JESSIE: Yeah, the phenobarb's about right now, I guess.

MAMA: You bet it is. You might never have another one, ever! You might be through with it for all time!

JESSIE: Could be.

MAMA: You are. I know you are!

JESSIE: I sure am feeling good. I really am. The double vision's gone and my gums aren't swelling. No rashes or anything. I'm feeling as good as I ever felt in my life. I'm even feeling like worrying or getting mad and I'm not afraid it will start a fit if I do, I just go ahead.

MAMA: Of course you do! You can even scream at me, if you want to. I can take it. You don't have to act like you're just visiting here, Jessie. This is your house, too.

JESSIE: The best part is, my memory's back.

MAMA: Your memory's always been good. When couldn't you remember things? You're always reminding me what . . .

JESSIE: Because I've made lists for everything. But now I remember what things mean on my lists. I see "dish towels," and I used to wonder whether I was supposed to wash them, buy them, or look for them because I wouldn't remember where I put them after I washed them, but now I know it means wrap them up, they're a present for Loretta's birthday.

MAMA: (*Finished with the sofa now*) You used to go looking for your lists, too, I've noticed that. You always know where they are now! (*Then suddenly worried.*) Loretta's birthday isn't coming up, is it?

JESSIE: I made a list of all the birthdays for you. I even put yours on it. (*A small smile.*) So you can call Loretta and remind her.

MAMA: Let's take Loretta to Howard Johnson's and have those fried clams. I *know* you love that clam roll.

JESSIE: (*Slight pause*) I won't be here, Mama.

MAMA: What have we just been talking about? You'll be here. You're well, Jessie. You're starting all over. You said it yourself. You're remembering things and . . .

JESSIE: I won't be here. If I'd ever had a year like this, to think straight and all, before now, I'd be gone already.

MAMA: (*Not pleading, commanding*) No, Jessie.

JESSIE: (*Folding the rest of the laundry*) Yes, Mama. Once I started remembering, I could see what it all added up to.

MAMA: The fits are over!

JESSIE: It's not the fits, Mama.

MAMA: Then it's me for giving them to you, but I didn't do it!

JESSIE: It's not the fits! You said it yourself, the medicine takes care of the fits.

MAMA: (*Interrupting*) Your daddy gave you those fits, Jessie. He passed it down to you like your green eyes and your straight hair. It's not my fault!

JESSIE: So what if he had little fits? It's not inherited. I fell off the horse. It was an accident.

MAMA: The horse wasn't the first time, Jessie. You had a fit when you were five years old.

JESSIE: I did not.

MAMA: You did! You were eating a popsicle and down you went. He gave it to you. It's *his* fault, not mine.

JESSIE: Well, you took your time telling me.

MAMA: How do you tell that to a five-year-old?

JESSIE: What did the doctor say?

MAMA: He said kids have them all the time. He said there wasn't anything to do but wait for another one.

JESSIE: But I didn't have another one.

(*Now there is a real silence.*)

JESSIE: You mean to tell me I had fits all the time as a kid and you just told me I fell down or something and it wasn't till I had the fit when Cecil was looking that anybody bothered to find out what was the matter with me?

MAMA: It wasn't *all the time*, Jessie. And they changed when you started to school. More like your daddy's. Oh, that was some swell time, sitting here with the two of you turning off and on like light bulbs some nights.

JESSIE: How many fits did I have?

MAMA: You never hurt yourself. I never let you out of my sight. I caught you every time.

JESSIE: But you didn't tell anybody.

MAMA: It was none of their business.

JESSIE: You were ashamed.

MAMA: I didn't want anybody to know. Least of all you.

JESSIE: Least of all me. Oh, right. That was mine to know, Mama, not yours. Did Daddy know?

MAMA: He thought you were . . . you fell down a lot. That's what he thought. You were careless. Or maybe he thought I beat you. I don't know what he thought. He didn't think about it.

JESSIE: Because you didn't tell him!

MAMA: If I told him about you, I'd have to tell him about him!

JESSIE: I don't like this. I don't like this one bit.

MAMA: I didn't think you'd like it. That's why I didn't tell you.

JESSIE: If I'd known I was an epileptic, Mama, I wouldn't have ridden any horses.

MAMA: Make you feel like a freak, is that what I should have done?

JESSIE: Just get the manicure tray and sit down!

MAMA: (*Throwing it to the floor*) I don't want a manicure!

JESSIE: Doesn't look like you do, no.

MAMA: Maybe I did drop you, you don't know.

JESSIE: If you say you didn't, you didn't.

MAMA: (*Beginning to break down*) Maybe I fed you the wrong thing. Maybe you had a fever sometime and I didn't know it soon enough. Maybe it's a punishment.

JESSIE: For what?

MAMA: I don't know. Because of how I felt about your father. Because I didn't want any more children. Because I smoked too much or didn't eat right when I was carrying you. It has to be something I did.

JESSIE: It does not. It's just a sickness, not a curse. Epilepsy doesn't mean anything. It just is.

MAMA: I'm not talking about the fits here, Jessie! I'm talking about this killing yourself. It has to be me that's the matter here. You wouldn't be doing this if it wasn't. I didn't tell you things or I married you off to the wrong man or I took you in and let your life get away from you or all of it put together. I don't know what I did, but I did it, I know. This is all my fault, Jessie, but I don't know what to do about it now!

JESSIE: *(Exasperated at having to say this again)* It doesn't have anything to do with you!

MAMA: Everything you do has to do with me, Jessie. You can't do *anything,* wash your face or cut your finger, without doing it to me. That's right! You might as well kill me as you, Jessie, it's the same thing. This has to do with me, Jessie.

JESSIE: Then what if it does! What if it has everything to do with you! What if you are all I have and you're not enough? What if I could take all the rest of it if only I didn't have you here? What if the only way I can get away from you for good is to kill myself? What if it is? I can *still* do it!

MAMA: *(In desperate tears)* Don't leave me, Jessie! *(JESSIE stands for a moment, then turns for the bedroom.)* No! *(She grabs JESSIE's arm.)*

JESSIE: *(Carefully taking her arm away)* I have a box of things I want people to have. I'm just going to go get it for you. You . . . just rest a minute.

(JESSIE is gone. MAMA heads for the telephone, but she can't even pick up the receiver this time and, instead, stoops to clean up the bottles that have spilled out of the manicure tray.)

(JESSIE returns, carrying a box that groceries were delivered in. It probably says Hershey Kisses or Starkist Tuna. MAMA is still down on the floor cleaning up, hoping that maybe if she just makes it look nice enough, JESSIE will stay.)

MAMA: Jessie, how can I live here without you? I need you! You're supposed to tell me to stand up straight and say how nice I look in my pink dress, and drink my milk. You're supposed to go around and lock up so I know we're safe for the night, and when I wake up, you're supposed to be out there making the coffee and watching me get older every day, and you're supposed to help me die when the time comes. I can't do that by myself, Jessie. I'm not like you, Jessie. I hate the quiet and I don't want to die and I don't want you to go, Jessie. How can I . . . *(Has to stop a moment.)* How can I get up every day knowing you had to kill yourself to make it stop hurting and I was here all the time and I never even saw it. And then you gave me this chance to make it better, convince you to stay alive, and I couldn't do it. How can I live with myself after this, Jessie?

JESSIE: I only told you so I could explain it, so you wouldn't blame yourself, so you wouldn't feel bad. There wasn't anything you could say to change my mind. I didn't want you to save me. I just wanted you to know.

MAMA: Stay with me just a little longer. Just a few more years. I don't have that many more to go, Jessie. And as soon as I'm dead, you can do whatever you want. Maybe with me gone, you'll have all the quiet you want, right here in the house. And maybe one day you'll put in some begonias up the walk and get just the right rain for them all summer. And Ricky will be married by then and he'll bring your grandbabies over and you can sneak them a piece of candy when their daddy's not looking and then be real glad when they've gone home and left you to your quiet again.

JESSIE: Don't you see, Mama, everything I do winds up like this. How could I think you would understand? How could I think you would want a manicure? We could hold hands for an hour and then I could go shoot myself? I'm sorry about tonight, Mama, but it's exactly why I'm doing it.

MAMA: If you've got the guts to kill yourself, Jessie, you've got the guts to stay alive.

JESSIE: I know that. So it's really just a matter of where I'd rather be.

MAMA: Look, maybe I can't think of what you should do, but that doesn't mean there isn't something that would help. *You* find it. *You* think of it. You can keep trying. You can get brave and try some more. You don't have to give up!

JESSIE: I'm *not* giving up! This *is* the other thing I'm trying. And I'm sure there are some other things that might work, but *might* work isn't good enough anymore. I need something that *will* work. *This* will work. That's why I picked it.

MAMA: But something might happen. Something that could change everything. Who knows what it might be, but it might be worth waiting for! *(JESSIE doesn't respond.)* Try it for two more weeks. We could have more talks like tonight.

JESSIE: No, Mama.

MAMA: I'll pay more attention to you. Tell the truth when you ask me. Let you have your say.

JESSIE: No, Mama! We wouldn't have more talks like tonight, because it's this next part that's made this last part so good, Mama. No, Mama. *This* is how I have my say. This is how I say what I thought about it *all* and I say no. To Dawson and Loretta and the Red Chinese and epilepsy and Ricky and Cecil and you. And me. And hope. I say no! *(Then going to MAMA on the sofa.)* Just let me go easy, Mama.

MAMA: How can I let you go?

JESSIE: You can because you have to. It's what you've always done.

MAMA: You are my child!

JESSIE: I am what became of your child. *(MAMA cannot answer.)* I found an old baby picture of me. And it was somebody else, not me. It was somebody pink and fat who never heard of sick or lonely, somebody who cried and got fed, and reached up and got held and kicked but didn't hurt anybody, and slept whenever she wanted to, just by closing her eyes. Somebody who mainly just laid there and laughed at the colors waving around over her head and chewed on a polka-dot whale and woke up knowing some new trick nearly every day, and rolled over and drooled on the sheet and felt your hand pulling my quilt back up over me. That's who I started out and this is who is left. (*There is no self-pity here.*) That's what this is about. It's somebody I lost, all right, it's my own self. Who I never was. Or who I tried to be and never got there. Somebody I waited for who never came. And never will. So, see, it doesn't much matter what else happens in the world or in this house, even. I'm what was worth waiting for and I didn't make it. Me . . . who might have made a difference to me . . . I'm not going to show up, so there's no reason to stay, except to keep you company, and that's . . . not reason enough because I'm not . . . very good company. (*Pause.*) Am I.

MAMA: (*Knowing she must tell the truth*) No. And neither am I.

JESSIE: I had this strange little thought, well, maybe it's not so strange. Anyway, after Christmas, after I decided to do this, I would wonder, sometimes, what might keep me here, what might be worth staying for, and you know what it was? It was maybe if there was something I really liked, like maybe if I really liked rice pudding or cornflakes for breakfast or something, that might be enough.

MAMA: Rice pudding is good.

JESSIE: Not to me.

MAMA: And you're not afraid?

JESSIE: Afraid of what?

MAMA: I'm afraid of it, for me, I mean. When my time comes. I know it's coming, but . . .

JESSIE: You don't know when. Like in a scary movie.

MAMA: Yeah, sneaking up on me like some killer on the loose, hiding out in the back yard just waiting for me to have my hands full someday and how am I supposed to protect myself anyhow when I don't know what he looks like and I don't know how he sounds coming up behind me like that or if it will hurt or take very long or what I don't get done before it happens.

JESSIE: You've got plenty of time left.

MAMA: I forget what for, right now.

JESSIE: For whatever happens, I don't know. For the rest of your life. For Agnes burning down one more house or Dawson losing his hair or . . .

MAMA: (*Quickly*) Jessie, I can't just sit here and say O.K., kill yourself if you want to.

JESSIE: Sure you can. You just did. Say it again.

MAMA: (*Really startled*) Jessie! (*Quiet horror.*) How dare you! (*Furious.*) How dare you! You think you can just leave whenever you want, like you're watching television here? No, you can't, Jessie. You make me feel like a fool for being alive, child, and you are so wrong! I like it here, and I will stay here until they make me go, until they drag me screaming and I mean screeching into my grave, and you're real smart to get away before then because, I mean, honey, you've never heard noise like that in your life. (JESSIE *turns away.*) Who am I talking to? You're gone already, aren't you? I'm looking right through you! I can't stop you because you're already gone! I guess you think they'll all have to talk about you now! I guess you think this will really confuse them. Oh yes, ever since Christmas you've been laughing to yourself and thinking, "Boy, are they all in for a surprise." Well, nobody's going to be a bit surprised, sweetheart. This is just like you. Do it the hard way, that's my girl, all right. (JESSIE *gets up and goes into the kitchen, but* MAMA *follows her.*) You know who they're going to feel sorry for? Me! How about that! Not you, me! They're going to be *ashamed* of you. Yes. *Ashamed!* If somebody asks Dawson about it, he'll change the subject as fast as he can. He'll talk about how much he has to pay to park his car these days.

JESSIE: Leave me alone.

MAMA: It's the truth!

JESSIE: I should've just left you a note!

MAMA: (*Screaming*) Yes! (*Then suddenly understanding what she has said, nearly paralyzed by the thought of it, she turns slowly to face* JESSIE, *nearly whispering.*) No. No. I . . . might not have thought of all the things you've said.

JESSIE: It's O.K., Mama.

(MAMA *is nearly unconscious from the emotional devastation of these last few moments. She sits down at the kitchen table, hurt and angry and desperately afraid. But she looks almost numb. She is so far beyond what is known as pain that she is virtually unreachable and* JESSIE *knows this, and talks quietly, watching for signs of recovery.*)

JESSIE: (*Washes her hands in the sink*) I remember you liked that preacher who did Daddy's, so if you want to ask him to do the service, that's O.K. with me.

MAMA: (*Not an answer, just a word*) What.

JESSIE: (*Putting on hand lotion as she talks*) And pick some songs you like or let Agnes pick, she'll know exactly which ones. Oh, and I had your dress cleaned that you wore to Daddy's. You looked real good in that.

MAMA: I don't remember, hon.

JESSIE: And it won't be so bad once your friends start coming to the funeral home. You'll probably see people you haven't seen for years, but I thought about what you should say to get you over that nervous part when they first come in.

MAMA: (*Simply repeating*) Come in.

JESSIE: Take them up to see their flowers, they'd like that. And when they say, "I'm so sorry, Thelma," you just say, "I appreciate your coming, Connie." And then ask how their garden was this summer or what they're doing for Thanksgiving or how their children . . .

MAMA: I don't think I should ask about their children. I'll talk about what they have on, that's always good. And I'll have some crochet work with me.

JESSIE: And Agnes will be there, so you might not have to talk at all.

MAMA: Maybe if Connie Richards does come, I can get her to tell me where she gets that Irish yarn, she calls it. I know it doesn't come from Ireland. I think it just comes with a green wrapper.

JESSIE: And be sure to invite enough people home afterward so you get enough food to feed them all and have some left for you. But don't let anybody take anything home, especially Loretta.

MAMA: Loretta will get all the food set up, honey. It's only fair to let her have some macaroni or something.

JESSIE: No, Mama. You have to be more selfish from now on. (*Sitting at the table with* MAMA.) Now, somebody's bound to ask you why I did it and you just say you don't know. That you loved me and you know I loved you and we just sat around tonight like every other night of our lives, and then I came over and kissed you and said, "'night, Mother," and you heard me close my bedroom door and the next thing you heard was the shot. And whatever reasons I had, well, you guess I just took them with me.

MAMA: (*Quietly*) It was something personal.

JESSIE: Good. That's good, Mama.

MAMA: That's what I'll say, then.

JESSIE: Personal. Yeah.

MAMA: Is that what I tell Dawson and Loretta, too? We sat around, you kissed me, "'night, Mother"? They'll want to know more, Jessie. They won't believe it.

JESSIE: Well, then, tell them what we did. I filled up the candy jars. I cleaned out the refrigerator. We made some hot chocolate and put the cover back on the sofa. You had no idea. All right? I really think it's better that way. If they know we talked about it, they really won't understand how you let me go.

MAMA: I guess not.

JESSIE: It's private. Tonight is private, yours and mine, and I don't want anybody else to have any of it.

MAMA: O.K., then.

JESSIE: (*Standing behind* MAMA *now, holding her shoulders*) Now, when you hear the shot, I don't want you to come in. First of all, you won't be able to get in by yourself, but I don't want you trying. Call Dawson, then call the police, and then call Agnes. And then you'll need something to do till somebody gets here, so wash the hot-chocolate pan. You wash that pan till you hear the doorbell ring and I don't care if it's an hour, you keep washing that pan.

MAMA: I'll make my calls and then I'll just sit. I won't need something to do. What will the police say?

JESSIE: They'll do that gunpowder test, I guess, and ask you what happened, and by that time, the ambulance will be here and they'll come in and get me and you know how that goes. You stay out here with Dawson and Loretta. You keep Dawson out here. I want the police in the room first, not Dawson, O.K.?

MAMA: What if Dawson and Loretta want me to go home with them?

JESSIE: (*Returning to the living room*) That's up to you.

MAMA: I think I'll stay here. All they've got is Sanka.

JESSIE: Maybe Agnes could come stay with you for a few days.

MAMA: (*Standing up, looking into the living room*) I'd rather be by myself, I think. (*Walking toward the box* JESSIE *brought in earlier.*) You want me to give people those things?

JESSIE: (*They sit down on the sofa,* JESSIE *holding the box on her lap*) I want Loretta to have my little calculator. Dawson bought it for himself, you know, but then he saw one he liked better and he couldn't bring both of them home with Loretta counting every penny the way she does, so he gave the first one to me. Be funny for her to have it now, don't you think? And all my house slippers are in a sack for her in my closet. Tell her I know they'll fit and I've never worn any of them, and make sure Dawson hears you tell her that. I'm glad he loves Loretta so much, but I wish he knew not everybody has her size feet.

MAMA: (*Taking the calculator*) O.K.

JESSIE: (*Reaching into the box again*) This letter is for Dawson, but it's mostly about you, so read it if you want. There's a list of presents for you for at least twenty more Christmases and birthdays, so if you want anything special you better add it to this list before you give it to him. Or if you want to be surprised, just don't read that page. This Christmas, you're getting mostly stuff for the house, like a new rug in your bathroom and needlework, but next Christmas, you're really going to cost him next Christmas. I think you'll like it a lot and you'd never think of it.

MAMA: And you think he'll go for it?

JESSIE: I think he'll feel like a real jerk if he doesn't. Me telling him to, like this and all. Now, this number's where you call Cecil. I called it last week and he answered, so I know he still lives there.

MAMA: What do you want me to tell him?

JESSIE: Tell him we talked about him and I only had good things to say about him, but mainly tell him to find Ricky and tell him what I did, and tell Ricky you have something for him, out here, from me, and to come get it. (*Pulls a sack out of the box.*)

MAMA: (*The sack feels empty*) What is it?

JESSIE: (*Taking it off*) My watch. (*Putting it in the sack and taking a ribbon out of the sack to tie around the top of it.*)

MAMA: He'll sell it!

JESSIE: That's the idea. I appreciate him not stealing it already. I'd like to buy him a good meal.

MAMA: He'll buy dope with it!

JESSIE: Well, then, I hope he gets some good dope with it, Mama. And the rest of this is for you. (*Handing* MAMA *the box now.* MAMA *picks up the things and looks at them.*)

MAMA: (*Surprised and pleased*) When did you do all this? During my naps, I guess.

JESSIE: I guess. I tried to be quiet about it. (*As* MAMA *is puzzled by the presents.*) Those are just little presents. For whenever you need one. They're not bought presents, just things I thought you might like to look at, pictures or things you think you've lost. Things you didn't know you had, even. You'll see.

MAMA: I'm not sure I want them. They'll make me think of you.

JESSIE: No they won't. They're just things, like a free tube of toothpaste I found hanging on the door one day.

MAMA: Oh. All right, then.

JESSIE: Well, maybe there's one present in there somewhere. It's Granny's ring she gave me and I thought you might like to have it, but I didn't think you'd wear it if I gave it to you right now.

MAMA: (*Taking the box to a table nearby*) No. Probably not. (*Turning back to face her.*) I'm ready for my manicure, I guess. Want me to wash my hands again?

JESSIE: (*Standing up*) It's time for me to go, Mama.

MAMA: (*Starting for her*) No, Jessie, you've got all night!

JESSIE: (*As* MAMA *grabs her*) No, Mama.

MAMA: It's not even ten o'clock.

JESSIE: (*Very calm*) Let me go, Mama.

MAMA: I can't. You can't go. You can't do this. You didn't say it would be so soon, Jessie. I'm scared. I love you.

JESSIE: (*Takes her hands away*) Let go of me, Mama. I've said everything I had to say.

MAMA: (*Standing still a minute*) You said you wanted to do my nails.

JESSIE: (*Taking a small step backward*) I can't. It's too late.

MAMA: It's not too late!

JESSIE: I don't want you to wake Dawson and Loretta when you call. I want them to still be up and dressed so they can get right over.

MAMA: (*As* JESSIE *backs up,* MAMA *moves in on her, but carefully*) They wake up fast, Jessie, if they have to. They don't matter here, Jessie. You do. I do. We're not through yet. We've got a lot of things to take care of here. I don't know where my prescriptions are and you didn't tell me what to tell Dr. Davis when he calls or how much you want me to tell Ricky or who I call to rake the leaves or . . .

JESSIE: Don't try and stop me, Mama, you can't do it.

MAMA: (*Grabbing her again, this time hard*) I can too! I'll stand in front of this hall and you can't get past me. (*They struggle.*) You'll have to knock me down to get away from me, Jessie. I'm not about to let you . . .

(MAMA *struggles with* JESSIE *at the door and in the struggle* JESSIE *gets away from her and—*)

JESSIE: (*Almost a whisper*) 'night, Mother. (*She vanishes into her bedroom and we hear the door lock just as* MAMA *gets to it.*)

MAMA: (*Screams*) Jessie! (*Pounding on the door.*) Jessie, you let me in there. Don't you do this, Jessie. I'm not going to stop screaming until you open this door, Jessie. Jessie! Jessie! What if I don't do any of the things you told me to do! I'll tell Cecil what a miserable man he was to make you feel the way he did and I'll give Ricky's watch to Dawson if I feel like it and the only way you can make sure I do what you want is you come out here and make me, Jessie! (*Pounding again.*) Jessie! Stop this! I didn't know! I was here with you all the time. How could I know you were so alone?

(*And* MAMA *stops for a moment, breathless and frantic, putting her ear to the door, and when she doesn't hear anything, she stands up straight again and screams once more.*)

Jessie! Please!

(*And we hear the shot, and it sounds like an answer, it sounds like No.*)

(MAMA *collapses against the door, tears streaming down her face, but not screaming anymore. In shock now.*)

Jessie, Jessie, child . . . Forgive me. (*Pause.*) I thought you were mine.

(*And she leaves the door and makes her way through the living room, around the furniture, as though she didn't know where it was, not knowing what to do. Finally, she goes to the stove in the kitchen and picks up the hot-chocolate pan and carries it with her to the telephone and holds on to it while she dials the number. She looks down at the pan, holding it tight like her life depended on it. She hears Loretta answer.*)

MAMA: Loretta, let me talk to Dawson, honey.

Figure 1. Mama (Anne Pitoniak) shares her memories of Daddy with Jessie (Kathy Bates) in the John Golden Theater production of *'night, Mother,* directed by Tom Moore, 1983. (Photograph: Richard M. Feldman.)

Figure 2. Jessie (Kathy Bates) examines Daddy's gun, while Mama (Anne Pitoniak) tries to convince her that it's broken, in the John Golden Theater production of *'night, Mother,* directed by Tom Moore, 1983. (Photograph: Richard M. Feldman.)

Staging of 'night, Mother

**REVIEW OF THE JOHN GOLDEN THEATER
PRODUCTION, 1983, BY DOUGLAS WATT**

Marsha Norman doesn't fool around. In 'night, Mother, which came to the Golden last night, the author of the schizophrenic *Getting Out* of a few seasons back offers a clinical study of a suicide—of the last 85 minutes (the play's exact length) in the life of a hopeless young woman. It's a spellbinding idea, and one held in tight control by the playwright's spare, effective dialogue; but it is less involving than one might expect, even with that final offstage gunshot.

There are several reasons for this, not the least of them the fact that the act of suicide is, in its most profound sense, as mysterious as life itself. But then, there is the troublesome situation Norman has posed.

Jessie Cates lives with her mother, Thelma, in the latter's "relatively new house, built way out on a country road," someplace in the South, judging from speech patterns and the author's Louisville background. At the very start, Jessie asks where her late father's gun has been kept, then retrieves it from a shoebox in the storage space above the ceiling, starts cleaning and oiling it and, pushing bullets into the chambers, announces her intention of killing herself this very evening.

But not until she's polished her mother's fingernails (she never gets around to this, though), given instructions about milk and other deliveries, specified people to phone, bagged the garbage and relined the pail, attended to countless other details with cool efficiency, tidied up in general and resisted any attempt on Thelma's part to dissuade her from taking her life.

The way Jessie feels about it is that her life and her disposal of it is the one thing she has complete control over. The lonely and, until now, uncommunicative child of a loveless marriage (a married brother lives nearby), she has been divorced by her husband and has given up on a son who is already a common thief and who, she is certain, will end up in prison as a result of the coming together in him of the worst aspects of herself and her former husband.

That's not all, though. Jessie, as she learns now for the first time, has been subject to epileptic fits since childhood, manifestations that have been explained away by her mother as dizzy spells or "seizures." What with one thing and another, Jessie has decided that wherever her life might end (she compares it to riding on a bus and either getting off at will or continuing to a known and undesirable destination), it will never improve, so why not make a decisive move and end it right here instead of going on sinking deeper and deeper within herself in these tacky surroundings while looking after a mother who apparently is capable of caring for herself and, worse, listening to her endlessly foolish chatter.

So the evening is spent in watching the homely preparations made for the inevitable act and listening to the mundane, often joking, conversation. Norman's intent, somewhat akin to Hitchcock's frequent juxtaposition, is to build horror—though with much more deadly intensity than the film maker sought—within the familiar, commonplace, everyday world.

The troubling aspect of the play is that Jessie is not a truly tragic figure. Her self-containment as she busily sets things to order about the house suggests one dedicated to her awful purpose, true, but also suggests a congenitally deranged woman. And Thelma's actual acceptance of the situation, having at last given up arguing against it, has a surreal air about it, as strange in its way as Jessie's early announcement of her purpose and subsequent behavior, including a break to share cocoa with her mother. The final cap-pistol report from behind a bedroom door is as weak as the play's premise. The mother's faltering steps to the kitchen area following the gunshot and her near-blind dialing of the phone to call the brother is the evening's most real moment.

Kathy Bates holds our interest as the plump, tight-lipped, bustling Jessie, who breaks down briefly just once or twice, and Anne Pitoniak is a lanky flibberti-gibbet of a vacant mother whose speech, sometimes a bit hard to understand, should have been cleared up by the director, Tom Moore, who otherwise has done a serviceable job. Heidi Landesman's set is, indeed, neat, new-looking and impersonal enough to drive any occupant to suicide sooner or later, given that secret urge to begin with.

Norman's writing is diamond-sharp and expressive, under the circumstances. It's just the circumstances that struck me as alien, pat, and unlikely.

"We've got a good life here," says Thelma Cates to her daughter, Jessie, in Marsha Norman's new play, *'night, Mother.* Many would agree. Thelma, who is a widow, and Jessie, who is divorced, live together in a spick-and-span house on a country road somewhere in the New South. There are no money problems. Nights are spent in such relaxed pursuits as crocheting and watching television.

But on the particular, ordinary Saturday night that we meet Thelma (Anne Pitoniak) and Jessie (Kathy Bates), we learn that the good life may not be so good after all. As the daughter prepares to perform her weekly ritual of giving her mother a manicure, she says calmly, almost as a throwaway line, "I'm going to kill myself, Mama." And, over the next 90 minutes, Mama—and the rest of us—must face the fact that Jessie is not kidding.

'night, Mother, which has traveled to Broadway's John Golden Theater from Harvard's American Repertory Theater, is a shattering evening, but it looks like simplicity itself. A totally realistic play, set in real time counted by onstage clocks, it shows us what happens after Jessie makes her announcement. What happens, unsurprisingly, is that the first skeptical and then terrified mother tries to cajole and talk her child out of suicide. "People don't really kill themselves," argues Thelma, "unless they're retarded or deranged."

But Jessie isn't deranged—she's never felt better in her life—and that's why *'night, Mother* is more complex than it looks, more harrowing than even its plot suggests. Miss Norman's play is simple only in the way that an Edward Hopper painting is simple. As she perfectly captures the intimate details of two individual, ordinary women, this playwright locates the emptiness that fills too many ordinary homes on too many faceless streets in the vast country we live in now.

Why does Jessie want to kill herself? There are many conceivable motives. She's a fat, lumpy, anonymous-looking woman in her thirties who spends her days indoors, eating junk food. Her son is a hoodlum. Her last job, working at a gift shop in a hospital, didn't work out. She misses her dead father, as well as the husband who left her. She suffers from epilepsy, though it's now been brought under control by medication.

As the play progresses, her mother enumerates all these disappointments, desperately offering to solve any of them she can. But Jessie will have none of it. She instead wants to use her last hours to help her mother get the house in order and to sit around chatting "like every other night of our lives." The daughter insists that they make cocoa, re-cover the couch and clean out the refrigerator.

Jessie is at peace about her decision because she has decided that nothing can change it. "It doesn't really matter what else happens in the world or in this house," she says, for the real problem is "nobody out there, but my own self." In Jessie's opinion, that self—her interior life—is something that she "lost" and that will "never show up." It is also the only "real" possession she has, and she claims the right to "stop it, shut it down, turn it off."

Although it is likely to kindle many debates about the subject, *'night, Mother* is not a message play about the choice to commit suicide. It's about contemporary life and what gives it—or fails to give it—value. We first get a sense of the Cates's existence before *'night, Mother* begins. Heidi Landesman's disturbing set, in view as we enter the theater, is an all-American living room and kitchen, right out of a television sitcom: homey, appointed with the right appliances, conventionally tasteful. But, when James F. Ingalls's cruelly bright lighting comes up, we see the house is colorless and dead—a pair of antiseptic model rooms, framed like a department-store window.

Miss Norman's dialogue maps the rest of the vacuum. When Thelma at first mistakes Jessie's preoccupation with guns for a fear of burglars, she says, "We don't have anything people would want." And we come to see that neither mother nor daughter do. Their lives are built on neighborhood gossip, ritualized familial obligations and housekeeping. Before tonight—when a gun is literally to their heads—they've never expressed their real feelings to one another or to anybody else. The more loneliness that is exposed the more we realize that the most horrifying aspect of *'night, Mother* is not Jessie's decision to end her life but her mother's gradual awakening—and ours—to the inexorable logic of that decision.

The play would never work, never make that logic real, if Miss Norman for a second condescended to her characters by painting them as fools—or if she stuck in authorial speeches that commented on or judged their predicament. As she previously demonstrated in *Getting Out,* Miss Norman is far too honest a writer to fall into those traps.

Jessie and Thelma are not caricatured as stupid yokels. They are not without wit. When the mother begs the daughter to stay around "for a few more years" until her own death, she uses every argument that the smartest member of the audience might muster. Jessie, meanwhile, knocks those arguments down with brutal, eloquent force.

The strongest argument, of course, is the blood tie. Miss Norman draws the mother-daughter relationship painfully, with all the guilt and anger and twisted passion it can contain. During the course of the play, Thelma and Jessie ask each other every question they've ever wanted to ask—from "Why did your husband leave you?" to "Why did you never wear the sweater I made you?" As they do, the women often switch roles, to the excruciating point at which Thelma becomes a tantrum-throwing infant, lashing out at Jessie any way she can.

At more tender times, we see the love between these women, but we also see that it's not enough to make a difference to Jessie, who has no self-love. "You are my child!" cries the mother, in a primal plea. "No," says the daughter. "I am what became of your child."

Under the brilliant, unerring choreographic hand of the director Tom Moore—who follows the playwright by refusing to gild or theatricalize any moment—the superb actresses, both veterans of Louisville's Actors Theater, circle each other in a grueling dance of death that ebbs and flows so naturally that every violent transition catches us by surprise. There are pockets of hu-mor—the mother even gets a laugh describing her daughter's youthful epileptic fits—and there is warmth.

But there is also the sight of Miss Pitoniak's Thelma, a gabby "plain country woman," turning white and dumb with fear as she realizes that the daughter through whom she's lived by proxy is beyond her reach—"already gone," even though still alive. And there is the moment when the otherwise deliberate Miss Bates turns away from her whimpering mother to wail defiantly, "I say *no* to hope."

Does *'night, Mother* say no to hope? It's easy to feel that way after reeling from this play's crushing blow. But there *can* be hope if there is understanding, and it is Marsha Norman's profound achievement that she brings both understanding and dignity to forgotten and tragic American lives.

AUGUST WILSON

1945–

Though he has been preceded in the American theater by several well-known black playwrights and plays—Langston Hughes (*Don't You Want to Be Free*, 1936), Theodore Ward (*Our Lan'*, 1941), Lorraine Hansberry (*A Raisin in the Sun*, (1959), Imamu Amiri Baraka (*Dutchman*, 1963), and Charles Fuller (*A Soldier's Story*, 1981)—August Wilson is unquestionably the most ambitious and likely to be the most widely produced and highly regarded black dramatist of the twentieth century. His ambitiousness may be seen in his intention to write a cycle of ten plays about the experience of African Americans, one for each decade of the twentieth century, each one focused on a distinctively different but emblematic set of characters and situations. The likelihood of his achieving that ambition is quite strong, given the fact that, since 1980, he has written six of the ten projected plays in the cycle. The quality of his accomplishments thus far may be judged from the fact that four of the most recent plays in the cycle have been widely produced and enthusiastically received: *Ma Rainey's Black Bottom* (1984), *Fences* (1985), and *Joe Turner's Come and Gone* (1986), all of which have won the prestigious New York Drama Critics Circle Award, and *The Piano Lesson* (1989), which, like *Fences*, won the Pulitzer Prize.

Wilson's probing drama of African-American experience is deeply rooted in his own quite complex personal experience of growing up in the Hill district of Pittsburgh, a black slum community, where he was raised in a two-room coldwater flat by his mother, after she had been abandoned by the white man who fathered all of her six children. Although he bears the name of his natural father, who died in 1965, Wilson knew him only from occasional visits and remembers him largely as a hard-drinking German baker who turned up intermittently with a bag of rolls in his hand. And though he acquired a stepfather, David Bedford, during his early adolescent years, Wilson found himself at odds with Bedford when, at the age of fifteen, he decided to quit his high school football team and drop out of school. Wilson's decision to quit school, as it turns out, was provoked largely by the racial harassment he suffered after his family moved into the heavily white community of Hazlewood, Pennsylvania.

Out of school, Wilson continued his education in the local library, where he discovered and read his way through a small section of some thirty "Negro" books by such eminent writers as Ralph Ellison, Langston Hughes, and Richard Wright—a discovery that he remembers as having been especially significant for him. "Those books were a comfort. Just the idea black people would write books. I wanted my book up there, too." From that point on, Wilson evidently read voraciously in the fiction, poetry, and drama of black and white writers alike, and then began to try his own hand at fiction and poetry writing. Looking back on that time, he recalls himself as having been heavily influenced by the theatricality of Dylan Thomas's verse, by the "psychic shorthand" of John Berryman's poetry, and by the jazzy street style of Baraka's poetry and plays.

But Wilson primarily describes himself as having been influenced by the extraordinary diversity of African-American culture—by the street talk and the street violence that he witnessed growing up in the black ghetto of Pittsburgh, by the Black Power movement that he became involved in during the late 1960s and early 1970s, and by the blues, which he regards as "a book of literature" that contains the "blacks' cultural response to the world" and which "influences everything I do." The Black Power movement initially attracted Wilson to the theater, for it led him to see drama as a powerful means to "politicize the community and raise consciousness." Indeed, during the 1960s, he co-founded a black activist theater in Pittsburgh, the Black Horizon on the Hill, which staged his earliest plays.

Paradoxically, however, Wilson did not really develop his unique talents as a dramatist of black experience until he moved away from the familiar world of his roots in Pittsburgh to the strikingly different community of St. Paul, Minnesota. There he became involved with the Playwrights Center of Minneapolis, and there, too, he began to remember in vivid detail the language and experience of the black ghetto, as well as to see the rich dramatic potentialities in the experience of that world. Thus during the late 1970s and early 1980s, Wilson began to write plays that aimed at a realistic evocation of African-American life as he had come to know it through his past experience in Pittsburgh. In *Jitney* (1982), for example, he focused attention on the lives that intersect in a Pittsburgh gypsy-cab station.

A similarly high degree of concentration is evident in his three best-known plays. *Ma Rainey's Black Bottom* is set in a Chicago recording studio in 1927; *Fences* in the front yard of a two-story brick house in Pittsburgh in 1957; and *Joe Turner's Come and Gone* in a Pittsburgh rooming house in 1911. Such highly localized settings enable Wilson to develop in each case an intensely focused human situation. *Ma Rainey's Black Bottom* relentlessly explores the tensions within an African-American musical group as well as between the musicians and the white men who manage and own the musical business. *Fences* documents the discord within a single family, in particular between Troy Maxson, the fifty-three-year-old protagonist; his wife Rose, whose love he betrays during the course of the play; and their son Cory, whose desire for fatherly affection Troy cannot fulfill. *Joe Turner's Come and Gone* follows the internal conflicts of black freedman Herald Loomis as he searches for his wife, who, during the period of her husband's enslavement by white bounty hunter Joe Turner, had fled to the North.

Ultimately such particularized situations enable Wilson to dramatize some of the most distinctive, significant, and complex aspects of African-American experience within the context of an authentically human predicament. The significance of *Fences*, for example, grows in part from Wilson's skillful manipulation of the myth of baseball as the all-American game and the game through which the color barrier was broken in professional sports—although too late for the play's protagonist, Troy Maxson, who thinks constantly of his batting record in the Negro leagues. For Troy, baseball provides a rich source of metaphors with which to express the frustrating conditions of his world, a world where "you born with two strikes on you before you come to the plate," and where Death is "the fastball in the outside corner." Thus, within the framework of family conflict, Wilson explores what it meant to be an African American in the 1950s.

Ma Rainey's Black Bottom is equally concerned with social issues, but draws its central image from the world of popular music, in particular from "singing the blues." Through its focus on this distinctive aspect of African-American culture, the play bears witness to the white exploitation of black performers in the racist world of Sturdyvant's recording studio. Ma Rainey (see Figure 1), the African-American singer known as "the Mother of the Blues" (1886–1939), never forgets that her manager is "always talking about sticking together," always treating her solicitously in public, but "the only time he had me in his house was to sing for some of his friends." The play's tension, however, is not just between white and black people but between blacks as well, a tension that is epitomized by the difference between the old-fashioned "jug-band music" favored by Ma as opposed to the newer "jazz" on which Levee hopes to make his name. Much of the first act, for example, concerns which version of Ma's signature song the band will play—Levee's, with an instrumental introduction, or Ma's, with a spoken one. But the real issue that fuels this conflict is what kind of identity and thus what kind of power is possible for an African-American person in the America of the 1920s.

Reviewers of the New York production (which originated at the Yale Repertory Theatre) recognized Wilson's broadly cultural concerns but disagreed about whether the political and social issues overwhelmed the dramatic experience. Some felt that nothing happens in the play until the final scene, whereas others, such as Frank Rich, whose review is reprinted following the text, perceived the play to be following a musical strategy in which the emphasis is placed on the "backup men" rather than on the lead singer. Each of the four African-American musicians (see Figure 2) does get a chance to solo, to have his say, in the true jazz tradition, and each of these extended speeches reveals the character of its speaker. While all of the speakers reflect an intense personal awareness of white oppression, no one is as angry or restless or ambitious as Levee, the brilliant trumpet player. So it is that each of the two acts in the play culminates in a scene focusing on the destructive (and self-destructive) rage of Levee. And while Levee's anger dominates the climax of *Ma Rainey*, the ending of *Fences* (produced the following year but dealing with a historical period thirty years later) is marked by another trumpet player, the war-wounded and mentally impaired Gabriel, blowing on a soundless trumpet and then dancing "a slow strange dance, eerie and life giving." Such strikingly different endings suggest the range of Wilson's vision, which embraces both the painfulness and the possibilities of twentieth-century African-American experience.

MA RAINEY'S BLACK BOTTOM

BY AUGUST WILSON

CHARACTERS

STURDYVANT, *studio owner*
IRVIN, *Ma Rainey's manager*
CUTLER, *guitar and trombone player*
TOLEDO, *piano player*
SLOW DRAG, *bass player*

LEVEE, *trumpet player*
MA RAINEY, *blues singer*
POLICEMAN
DUSSIE MAE, *Ma Rainey's companion*
SYLVESTER, *Ma Rainey's nephew*

They tore the railroad down
so the Sunshine Special can't run
I'm going away baby
build me a railroad of my own

　　　—Blind Lemon Jefferson

THE SETTING

There are two playing areas: what is called the "band room," and the recording studio. The band room is at stage left and is in the basement of the building. It is entered through a door up left. There are benches and chairs scattered about, a piano, a row of lockers, and miscellaneous paraphernalia stacked in a corner and long since forgotten. A mirror hangs on a wall with various posters.

The studio is upstairs at stage right, and resembles a recording studio of the late 1920s. The entrance is from a hall on the right wall. A small control booth is at the rear and its access is gained by means of a spiral staircase. Against one wall there is a line of chairs, and a horn through which the control room communicates with the performers. A door in the rear wall allows access to the band room.

THE PLAY

It is early March in Chicago, 1927. There is a bit of a chill in the air. Winter has broken but the wind coming off the lake does not carry the promise of spring. The people of the city are bundled and brisk in their defense against such misfortunes as the weather, and the business of the city proceeds largely undisturbed.

Chicago in 1927 is a rough city, a bruising city, a city of millionaires and derelicts, gangsters and roughhouse dandies, whores and Irish grandmothers who move through its streets fingering long black rosaries. Somewhere a man is wrestling with the taste of a woman in his cheek. Somewhere a dog is barking. Somewhere the moon has fallen through a window and broken into thirty pieces of silver.

It is one o'clock in the afternoon. Secretaries are returning from their lunch, the noon Mass at St. Anthony's is over, and the priest is mumbling over his vestments while the altar boys practice their Latin. The procession of cattle cars through the stockyards continues unabated. The busboys in Mac's Place are cleaning away the last of the corned beef and cabbage, and on the city's Southside, sleepy-eyed negroes move lazily toward their small cold-water flats and rented rooms to await the onslaught of night, which will find them crowded in the bars and juke joints both dazed and dazzling in their rapport with life. It is with these negroes that our concern lies most heavily: their values, their attitudes, and particularly their music.

It is hard to define this music. Suffice it to say that it is music that breathes and touches. That connects. That is in itself a way of being, separate and distinct from any other. This music is called blues. Whether this music came from Alabama or Mississippi or other parts of the South doesn't matter anymore. The men and women who make this music have learned it from the narrow crooked streets of East St. Louis, or the streets of the city's Southside, and the Alabama or Mississippi roots have been strangled by the northern manners and customs of free men of definite and sincere worth, men for whom this music often lies at the forefront of their conscience and concerns. Thus they are laid open to be consumed by it; its warmth and redress, its braggadocio and roughly poignant comments, its vision and prayer, which would instruct and allow them to reconnect, to reassemble and gird up for the next battle in which they would be both victim and the ten thousand slain.

ACT 1

The lights come up in the studio. IRVIN enters, carrying a microphone. He is a tall, fleshy man who prides himself on his knowledge of blacks and his ability to deal with them. He hooks up the microphone, blows into it, taps it, etc. He crosses over to the piano, opens it, and fingers a few keys. STURDYVANT is visible in the control booth. Preoccupied *with money, he is insensitive to black performers and prefers to deal with them at arm's length. He puts on a pair of earphones.*

STURDYVANT: *(Over speaker)* Irv . . . let's crack that mike, huh? Let's do a check on it.

IRVIN: *(Crosses to mike, speaks into it)* Testing . . . one . . . two . . . three . . .

(There is a loud feedback. STURDYVANT *fiddles with the dials.)*

Testing . . . one . . . two . . . three . . . testing. How's that, Mel?

*(*STURDYVANT *doesn't respond.)*

Testing . . . one . . . two . . .

STURDYVANT: *(Taking off earphones)* Okay . . . that checks. We got a good reading. *(Pause.)* You got that list, Irv?

IRVIN: Yeah . . . yeah, I got it. Don't worry about nothing.

STURDYVANT: Listen, Irv . . . you keep her in line, okay? I'm holding you responsible for her . . . If she starts any of her . . .

IRVIN: Mel, what's with the goddamn horn? You wanna talk to me . . . okay! I can't talk to you over the goddamn horn . . . Christ!

STURDYVANT: I'm not putting up with any shenanigans. You hear, Irv?

*(*IRVIN *crosses over to the piano and mindlessly runs his fingers over the keys.)*

I'm just not gonna stand for it. I want you to keep her in line. Irv?

*(*STURDYVANT *enters from the control booth.)*

Listen, Irv . . . you're her manager . . . she's your responsibility . . .

IRVIN: Okay, okay, Mel . . . let me handle it.

STURDYVANT: She's your responsibility. I'm not putting up with any Royal Highness . . . Queen of the Blues bullshit!

IRVIN: Mother of the Blues, Mel. Mother of the Blues.

STURDYVANT: I don't care what she calls herself. I'm not putting up with it. I just want to get her in here . . . record those songs on that list . . . and get her out. Just like clockwork, huh?

IRVIN: Like clockwork, Mel. You just stay out of the way and let me handle it.

STURDYVANT: Yeah . . . yeah . . . you handled it last time. Remember? She marches in here like she owns the damn place . . . doesn't like the songs we picked out . . . says her throat is sore . . . doesn't want to do more than one take . . .

IRVIN: Okay . . . okay . . . I was here! I know all about it.

STURDYVANT: Complains about the building being cold

. . . and then . . . trips over the mike wire and threatens to sue me. That's taking care of it?

IRVIN: I've got it all worked out this time. I talked with her last night. Her throat is fine . . . We went over the songs together . . . I got everything straight, Mel.

STURDYVANT: Irv, that horn player . . . the one who gave me those songs . . . is he gonna be here today? Good. I want to hear more of that sound. Times are changing. This is a tricky business now. We've got to jazz it up . . . put in something different. You know, something wild . . . with a lot of rhythm. *(Pause.)* You know what we put out last time, Irv? We put out garbage last time. It was garbage. I don't even know why I bother with this anymore.

IRVIN: You did all right last time, Mel. Not as good as you did before, but you did all right.

STURDYVANT: You know how many records we sold in New York? You wanna see the sheet? And you know what's in New York, Irv? Harlem. Harlem's in New York, Irv.

IRVIN: Okay, so they didn't sell in New York. But look at Memphis . . . Birmingham . . . Atlanta. Christ, you made a bundle.

STURDYVANT: It's not the money, Irv. You know I couldn't sleep last night? This business is bad for my nerves. My wife is after me to slow down and take a vacation. Two more years and I'm gonna get out . . . get into something respectable. Textiles. That's a respectable business. You know what you could do with a shipload of textiles from Ireland?

(A buzzer is heard offstage.)

IRVIN: Why don't you go upstairs and let me handle it, Mel?

STURDYVANT: Remember . . . you're responsible for her.

*(*STURDYVANT *exits to the control booth.* IRVIN *crosses to get the door.* CUTLER, SLOW DRAG, *and* TOLEDO *enter.* CUTLER *is in his mid-fifties, as are most of the others. He plays guitar and trombone and is the leader of the group, possibly because he is the most sensible. His playing is solid and almost totally unembellished. His understanding of his music is limited to the chord he is playing at the time he is playing it. He has all the qualities of a loner except the introspection.* SLOW DRAG, *the bass player, is perhaps the one most bored by life. He resembles* CUTLER, *but lacks* CUTLER's *energy. He is deceptively intelligent, though, as his name implies, he appears to be slow. He is a rather large man with a wicked smile. Innate African rhythms underlie everything he plays, and he plays with an ease that is at times startling.* TOLEDO *is the piano player. In control of his instrument, he understands and recognizes that its limitations are an extension of himself. He is the only one in the group who can read. He is self-taught but misunderstands and misapplies his knowledge, though he is quick to penetrate to the core of a situation and his insights are thought-provoking. All*

of the men are dressed in a style of clothing befitting the members of a successful band of the era.)

IRVIN: How you boys doing, Cutler? Come on in. (*Pause.*) Where's Ma? Is she with you?

CUTLER: I don't know, Mr. Irvin. She told us to be here at one o'clock. That's all I know.

IRVIN: Where's . . . huh . . . the horn player? Is he coming with Ma?

CUTLER: Levee's supposed to be here same as we is. I reckon he'll be here in a minute. I can't rightly say.

IRVIN: Well, come on . . . I'll show you to the band room, let you get set up and rehearsed. You boys hungry? I'll call over to the deli and get some sandwiches. Get you fed and ready to make some music. Cutler . . . here's the list of songs we're gonna record.

STURDYVANT: (*Over speaker*) Irvin, what's happening? Where's Ma?

IRVIN: Everything under control, Mel. I got it under control.

STURDYVANT: Where's Ma? How come she isn't with the band?

IRVIN: She'll be here in a minute, Mel. Let me get these fellows down to the band room, huh?

(*They exit the studio. The lights go down in the studio and up in the band room.* IRVIN *opens the door and allows them to pass as they enter.*)

You boys go ahead and rehearse. I'll let you know when Ma comes.

(IRVIN *exits.* CUTLER *hands* TOLEDO *the list of songs.*)

CUTLER: What we got here, Toledo?

TOLEDO: (*Reading*) We got . . . "Prove It on Me" . . . "Hear Me Talking to You" . . . "Ma Rainey's Black Bottom" . . . and "Moonshine Blues."

CUTLER: Where Mr. Irvin go? Them ain't the songs Ma told me.

SLOW DRAG: I wouldn't worry about it if I were you, Cutler. They'll get it straightened out. Ma will get it straightened out.

CUTLER: I just don't want no trouble about these songs, that's all. Ma ain't told me them songs. She told me something else.

SLOW DRAG: What she tell you?

CUTLER: This "Moonshine Blues" wasn't in it. That's one of Bessie's songs.

TOLEDO: Slow Drag's right . . . I wouldn't worry about it. Let them straighten it up.

CUTLER: Levee know what time he supposed to be here?

SLOW DRAG: Levee gone out to spend your four dollars. He left the hotel this morning talking about he was gonna go buy some shoes. Say it's the first time he ever beat you shooting craps.

CUTLER: Do he know what time he supposed to be here? That's what I wanna know. I ain't thinking about no four dollars.

SLOW DRAG: Levee sure was thinking about it. That four dollars liked to burn a hole in his pocket.

CUTLER: Well, he's supposed to be here at one o'clock. That's what time Ma said. That nigger get out in the streets with that four dollars and ain't no telling when he's liable to show. You ought to have seen him at the club last night, Toledo. Trying to talk to some gal Ma had with her.

TOLEDO: You ain't got to tell me. I know how Levee do.

(*Buzzer is heard offstage.*)

SLOW DRAG: Levee tried to talk to that gal and got his feelings hurt. She didn't want no part of him. She told Levee he'd have to turn his money green before he could talk with her.

CUTLER: She out for what she can get. Anybody could see that.

SLOW DRAG: That's why Levee run out to buy some shoes. He's looking to make an impression on that gal.

CUTLER: What the hell she gonna do with his shoes? She can't do nothing with the nigger's shoes.

(SLOW DRAG *takes out a pint bottle and drinks.*)

TOLEDO: Let me hit that, Slow Drag.

SLOW DRAG: (*Handing him the bottle*) This some of that good Chicago bourbon!

(*The door opens and* LEVEE *enters, carrying a shoe box. In his early thirties,* LEVEE *is younger than the other men. His flamboyance is sometimes subtle and sneaks up on you. His temper is rakish and bright. He lacks fuel for himself and is somewhat of a buffoon. But it is an intelligent buffoonery, clearly calculated to shift control of the situation to where he can grasp it. He plays trumpet. His voice is strident and totally dependent on his manipulation of breath. He plays wrong notes frequently. He often gets his skill and talent confused with each other.*)

CUTLER: Levee . . . where Mr. Irvin go?

LEVEE: Hell, I don't know. I ain't none of his keeper.

SLOW DRAG: What you got there, Levee?

LEVEE: Look here, Cutler . . . I got me some shoes!

CUTLER: Nigger, I ain't studying you.

(LEVEE *takes the shoes out of the box and starts to put them on.*)

TOLEDO: How much you pay for something like that, Levee?

LEVEE: Eleven dollars. Four dollars of it belong to Cutler.

SLOW DRAG: Levee say if it wasn't for Cutler . . . he wouldn't have no new shoes.

CUTLER: I ain't thinking about Levee or his shoes. Come on . . . let's get ready to rehearse.

SLOW DRAG: I'm with you on that score, Cutler. I wanna get out of here. I don't want to be around here all night. When it comes time to go up there and record them songs . . . I just wanna go up there and do it. Last time it took us all day and half the night.

TOLEDO: Ain't but four songs on the list. Last time we recorded six songs.

SLOW DRAG: It felt like it was sixteen!

LEVEE: (*Finishes with his shoes*) Yeah! Now I'm ready! I can play some good music now!

(*He goes to put up his old shoes and looks around the room.*)

Damn! They done changed things around. Don't never leave well enough alone.

TOLEDO: Everything changing all the time. Even the air you breathing change. You got, monoxide, hydrogen . . . changing all the time. Skin changing . . . different molecules and everything.

LEVEE: Nigger, what is you talking about? I'm talking about the room. I ain't talking about no skin and air. I'm talking about something I can see! Last time the band room was upstairs. This time it's downstairs. Next time it be over there. I'm talking about what I can see. I ain't talking about no molecules or nothing.

TOLEDO: Hell, I know what you talking about. I just said everything changin'. I know what you talking about, but you don't know what I'm talking about.

LEVEE: That door! Nigger, you see that door? That's what I'm talking about. That door wasn't there before.

CUTLER: Levee, you wouldn't know your right from your left. This is where they used to keep the recording horns and things . . . and damn if that door wasn't there. How in hell else you gonna get in here? Now, if you talking about they done switched rooms, you right. But don't go telling me that damn door wasn't there!

SLOW DRAG: Damn the door and let's get set up. I wanna get out of here.

LEVEE: Toledo started all that about the door. I'm just saying that things change.

TOLEDO: What the hell you think I was saying? Things change. The air and everything. Now you gonna say you was saying it. You gonna fit two propositions on the same track . . . run them into each other, and because they crash, you gonna say it's the same train.

LEVEE: Now this nigger talking about trains! We done went from the air to the skin to the door . . . and now trains. Toledo, I'd just like to be inside your head for five minutes. Just to see how you think. You done got more shit piled up and mixed up in there than the devil got sinners. You been reading too many goddamn books.

TOLEDO: What you care about how much I read? I'm gonna ignore you 'cause you ignorant.

(LEVEE *takes off his coat and hangs it in the locker.*)

SLOW DRAG: Come on, let's rehearse the music.

LEVEE: You ain't gotta rehearse that . . . ain't nothing but old jug-band music. They need one of them jug bands for this.

SLOW DRAG: Don't make me no difference. Long as we get paid.

LEVEE: That ain't what I'm talking about, nigger. I'm talking about art!

SLOW DRAG: What's drawing got to do with it?

LEVEE: Where you get this nigger from, Cutler? He sound like one of them Alabama niggers.

CUTLER: Slow Drag's all right. It's you talking all that weird shit about art. Just play the piece, nigger. You wanna be one of them . . . what you call . . . virtuoso or something, you in the wrong place. You ain't no Buddy Bolden or King Oliver . . . you just an old trumpet player come a dime a dozen. Talking about art.

LEVEE: What is you? I don't see your name in lights.

CUTLER: I just play the piece. Whatever they want. I don't go talking about art and criticizing other people's music.

LEVEE: I ain't like you, Cutler. I got talent! Me and this horn . . . we's tight. If my daddy knowed I was gonna turn out like this, he would've named me Gabriel. I'm gonna get me a band and make me some records. I done give Mr. Sturdyvant some of my songs I wrote and he say he's gonna let me record them when I get my band together. (*Takes some papers out of his pocket.*) I just gotta finish the last part of this song. And Mr. Sturdyvant want me to write another part to this song.

SLOW DRAG: How you learn to write music, Levee?

LEVEE: I just picked it up . . . like you pick up anything. Miss Eula used to play the piano . . . she learned me a lot. I knows how to play *real* music . . . not this old jug-band shit. I got style!

TOLEDO: Everybody got style. Style ain't nothing but keeping the same idea from beginning to end. Everybody got it.

LEVEE: But everybody can't play like I do. Everybody can't have their own band.

CUTLER: Well, until you get your own band where you can play what you want, you just play the piece and stop complaining. I told you when you came on here, this ain't none of them hot bands. This is an accompaniment band. You play Ma's music when you here.

LEVEE: I got sense enough to know that. Hell, I can look at you all and see what kind of band it is. I can look at Toledo and see what kind of band it is.

TOLEDO: Toledo ain't said nothing to you now. Don't let Toledo get started. You can't even spell music, much less play it.

LEVEE: What you talking about? I can spell music. I got a dollar say I can spell it! Put your dollar up. Where your dollar?

(TOLEDO *waves him away.*)

Now come on. Put your dollar up. Talking about I can't spell music.

(LEVEE *peels a dollar off his roll and slams it down on the bench beside* TOLEDO.)

TOLEDO: All right, I'm gonna show you. Cutler. Slow Drag. You hear this? The nigger betting me a dollar he can spell music. I don't want no shit now!

(TOLEDO *lays a dollar down beside* LEVEE'*s.*)

All right. Go ahead. Spell it.

LEVEE: It's a bet then. Talking about I can't spell music.

TOLEDO: Go ahead, then. Spell it. Music. Spell it.

LEVEE: I can spell it, nigger! M-U-S-I-K. There!

(*He reaches for the money.*)

TOLEDO: Naw! Naw! Leave that money alone! You ain't spelled it.

LEVEE: What you mean I ain't spelled it? I said M-U-S-I-K!

TOLEDO: That ain't how you spell it! That ain't how you spell it! It's M-U-S-I-C! C, nigger. Not K! C! M-U-S-I-C!

LEVEE: What you mean, C? Who say it's C?

TOLEDO: Cutler. Slow Drag. Tell this fool.

(*They look at each other and then away.*)

Well, I'll be a monkey's uncle!

(TOLEDO *picks up the money and hands* LEVEE *his dollar back.*)

Here's your dollar back, Levee. I done won it, you understand. I done won the dollar. But if don't nobody know but me, how am I gonna prove it to you?

LEVEE: You just mad 'cause I spelled it.

TOLEDO: Spelled what! M-U-S-I-K don't spell nothing. I just wish there was some way I could show you the right and wrong of it. How you gonna know something if the other fellow don't know if you're right or not? Now I can't even be sure that I'm spelling it right.

LEVEE: That's what I'm talking about. You don't know it. Talking about C. You ought to give me that dollar I won from you.

TOLEDO: All right. All right. I'm gonna show you how ridiculous you sound. You know the Lord's Prayer?

LEVEE: Why? You wanna bet a dollar on that?

TOLEDO: Just answer the question. Do you know the Lord's Prayer or don't you?

LEVEE: Yeah, I know it. What of it?

TOLEDO: Cutler?

CUTLER: What you Cutlering me for? I ain't got nothing to do with it.

TOLEDO: I just want to show the man how ridiculous he is.

CUTLER: Both of you all sound like damn fools. Arguing about something silly. Yeah, I know the Lord's Prayer. My daddy was a deacon in the church. Come asking me if I know the Lord's Prayer. Yeah, I know it.

TOLEDO: Slow Drag?

SLOW DRAG: Yeah.

TOLEDO: All right. Now I'm gonna tell you a story to show just how ridiculous he sound. There was these two fellows, see. So, the one of them go up to this church and commence to taking up the church learning. The other fellow see him out on the road and he say, "I done heard you taking up the church learning," say, "Is you learning anything up there?" The other one say, "Yeah, I done take up the church learning and I's learning all kinds of things about the Bible and what it say and all. Why you be asking?" The other one say, "Well, do you know the Lord's Prayer?" And he say, "Why, sure I know the Lord's Prayer, I'm taking up learning at the church ain't I? I know the Lord's Prayer backwards and forewards." And the other fellow says, "I bet you five dollars you don't know the Lord's Prayer, 'cause I don't think you knows it. I think you be going up to the church 'cause the Widow Jenkins be going up there and you just wanna be sitting in the same room with her when she cross them big, fine, pretty legs she got." And the other one say, "Well, I'm gonna prove you wrong and I'm gonna bet you that five dollars." So he say, "Well, go on and say it then." So he commenced to saying the Lord's Prayer. He say, "Now I lay me down to sleep, I pray the Lord my soul to keep." The other one say, "Here's your five dollars. I didn't think you knew it."

(*They all laugh.*)

Now, that's just how ridiculous Levee sound. Only 'cause I knowed how to spell music, I still got my dollar.

LEVEE: That don't prove nothing. What's that supposed to prove?

(TOLEDO *takes a newspaper out of his back pocket and begins to read.*)

TOLEDO: I'm through with it.

SLOW DRAG: Is you all gonna rehearse this music or ain't you?

(CUTLER *takes out some papers and starts to roll a reefer.*)

LEVEE: How many times you done played them songs? What you gotta rehearse for?

SLOW DRAG: This a recording session. I wanna get it right the first time and get on out of here.

CUTLER: Slow Drag's right. Let's go on and rehearse and get it over with.

LEVEE: You all go and rehearse, then. I got to finish this song for Mr. Sturdyvant.

CUTLER: Come on, Levee . . . I don't want no shit now.

You rehearse like everybody else. You in the band like everybody else. Mr. Sturdyvant just gonna have to wait. You got to do that on your own time. This is the band's time.

LEVEE: Well, what is you doing? You sitting there rolling a reefer talking about let's rehearse. Toledo reading a newspaper. Hell, I'm ready if you wanna rehearse. I just say there ain't no point in it. Ma ain't here. What's the point in it?

CUTLER: Nigger, why you gotta complain all the time?

TOLEDO: Levee would complain if a gal ain't laid across his bed just right.

CUTLER: That's what I know. That's why I try to tell him just play the music and forget about it. It ain't no big thing.

TOLEDO: Levee ain't got an eye for that. He wants to tie on to some abstract component and sit down on the elemental.

LEVEE: This is get-on-Levee time, huh? Levee ain't said nothing except this some old jug-band music.

TOLEDO: Under the right circumstances you'd play anything. If you know music, then you play it. Straight on or off to the side. Ain't nothing abstract about it.

LEVEE: Toledo, you sound like you got a mouth full of marbles. You the only cracker-talking nigger I know.

TOLEDO: You ought to have learned yourself to read . . . then you'd understand the basic understanding of everything.

SLOW DRAG: Both of you all gonna drive me crazy with that philosophy bullshit. Cutler, give me a reefer.

CUTLER: Ain't you got some reefer? Where's your reefer? Why you all the time asking me?

SLOW DRAG: Cutler, how long I done known you? How long we been together? Twenty-two years. We been doing this together for twenty-two years. All up and down the back roads, the side roads, the front roads . . . We done played the juke joints, the whorehouses, the barn dances, and city sit-downs . . . I done lied for you and lied with you . . . We done laughed together, fought together, slept in the same bed together, done sucked on the same titty . . . and now you don't wanna give me no reefer.

CUTLER: You see this nigger trying to talk me out of my reefer, Toledo? Running all that about how long he done knowed me and how we done sucked on the same titty. Nigger, you *still* ain't getting none of my reefer!

TOLEDO: That's African.

SLOW DRAG: What? What you talking about? What's African?

LEVEE: I know he ain't talking about me. You don't see me running around in no jungle with no bone between my nose.

TOLEDO: Levee, you worse than ignorant. You ignorant without a premise. (*Pauses.*) Now, what I was saying is what Slow Drag was doing is African. That's what you call an African conceptualization. That's when you name the gods or call on the ancestors to achieve whatever your desires are.

SLOW DRAG: Nigger, I ain't no African! I ain't doing no African nothing!

TOLEDO: Naming all those things you and Cutler done together is like trying to solicit some reefer based on a bond of kinship. That's African. An ancestral retention. Only you forgot the name of the gods.

SLOW DRAG: I ain't forgot nothing, I was telling the nigger how cheap he is. Don't come talking that African nonsense to me.

TOLEDO: You just like Levee. No eye for taking an abstract and fixing it to a specific. There's so much that goes on around you and you can't even see it.

CUTLER: Wait a minute . . . wait a minute. Toledo, now when this nigger . . . when an African do all them things you say and name all the gods and whatnot . . . then what happens?

TOLEDO: Depends on if the gods is sympathetic with his cause for which he is calling them with the right names. Then his success comes with the right proportion of his naming. That's the way that go.

CUTLER: (*Taking out a reefer*) Here, Slow Drag. Here's a reefer. You done talked yourself up on that one.

SLOW DRAG: Thank you. You ought to have done that in the first place and saved me all the aggravation.

CUTLER: What I wants to know is . . . what's the same titty we done sucked on. That's what I want to know.

SLOW DRAG: Oh, I just threw that in there to make it sound good.

(*They all laugh.*)

CUTLER: Nigger, you ain't right.

SLOW DRAG: I knows it.

CUTLER: Well, come on . . . let's get it rehearsed. Time's wasting.

(*The musicians pick up their instruments.*)

Let's do it. "Ma Rainey's Black Bottom." One . . . two . . . You know what to do.

(*They begin to play.* LEVEE *is playing something different. He stops.*)

LEVEE: Naw! Naw! We ain't doing it that way.

(TOLEDO *stops playing, then* SLOW DRAG.)

We doing my version. It say so right there on that piece of paper you got. Ask Toledo. That's what Mr. Irvin told me . . . say it's on the list he gave you.

CUTLER: Let me worry about what's on the list and what ain't on the list. How you gonna tell me what's on the list?

LEVEE: 'Cause I know what Mr. Irvin told me! Ask Toledo!

CUTLER: Let me worry about what's on the list. You just play the song I say.

LEVEE: What kind of sense it make to rehearse the

wrong version of the song? That's what I wanna know. Why you wanna rehearse that version.

SLOW DRAG: You supposed to rehearse what you gonna play. That's the way they taught me. Now, *whatever* version we gonna play . . . let's go on and rehearse it.

LEVEE: That's what I'm trying to tell the man.

CUTLER: You trying to tell me what we is and ain't gonna play. And that ain't none of your business. Your business is to play what I say.

LEVEE: Oh, I see now. You done got jealous cause Mr. Irvin using my version. You done got jealous cause I proved I know something about music.

CUTLER: What the hell . . . nigger, you talk like a fool! What the hell I got to be jealous of you about? The day I get jealous of you I may as well lay down and die.

TOLEDO: Levee started all that 'cause he too lazy to rehearse. (*To* LEVEE.) You ought to just go on and play the song . . . What difference does it make?

LEVEE: Where's the paper? Look at the paper! Get the paper and look at it! See what it say. Gonna tell me I'm too lazy to rehearse.

CUTLER: We ain't talking about the paper. We talking about you understanding where you fit in when you around here. You just play what I say.

LEVEE: Look . . . I don't care what you play! All right? It don't matter to me. Mr. Irvin gonna straighten it up! I don't care what you play.

CUTLER: Thank you. (*Pauses.*) Let's play this "Hear Me Talking to You" till we find out what's happening with the "Black Bottom." Slow Drag, you sing Ma's part. (*Pauses.*) "Hear Me Talking to You." Let's do it. One . . . Two . . . You know what to do.

(*They play.*)

SLOW DRAG: (*Singing*)

> *Rambling man makes no change in me*
> *I'm gonna ramble back to my used-to-be*
> *Ah, you hear me talking to you*
> *I don't bite my tongue*
> *You wants to be my man*
> *You got to fetch it with you when you come.*
>
> *Eve and Adam in the garden taking a chance*
> *Adam didn't take time to get his pants*
> *Ah, you hear me talking to you*
> *I don't bite my tongue*
> *You wants to be my man*
> *You got to fetch it with you when you come.*
>
> *Our old cat swallowed a ball of yarn*
> *When the kittens were born they had sweaters on*
> *Ah, you hear me talking to you*
> *I don't bite my tongue*
> *You wants to be my man*
> *You got to fetch it with you when you come.*

(IRVIN *enters. The musicians stop playing.*)

IRVIN: Any of you boys know what's keeping Ma?

CUTLER: Can't say, Mr. Irvin. She'll be along directly, I reckon. I talked to her this morning, she say she'll be here in time to rehearse.

IRVIN: Well, you boys go ahead.

(*He starts to exit.*)

CUTLER: Mr. Irvin, about these songs . . . Levee say . . .

IRVIN: Whatever's on the list, Cutler. You got that list I gave you?

CUTLER: Yessir, I got it right here.

IRVIN: Whatever's on there. Whatever that says.

CUTLER: I'm asking about this "Black Bottom" piece . . . Levee say . . .

IRVIN: Oh, it's on the list. "Ma Rainey's Black Bottom" on the list.

CUTLER: I know it's on the list. I wanna know what version. We got two versions of that song.

IRVIN: Oh. Levee's arrangement. We're using Levee's arrangement.

CUTLER: Ok. I got that straight. Now, this "Moonshine Blues" . . .

IRVIN: We'll work it out with Ma, Cutler. Just rehearse whatever's on the list and use Levee's arrangement on that "Black Bottom" piece.

(*He exits.*)

LEVEE: See, I told you! It don't mean nothing when I say it. You got to wait for Mr. Irvin to say it. Well, I told you the way it is.

CUTLER: Levee, the sooner you understand it ain't what you say, or what Mr. Irvin say . . . it's what Ma say that counts.

SLOW DRAG: Don't nobody say when it come to Ma. She's gonna do what she wants to do. Ma says what happens with her.

LEVEE: Hell, the man's the one putting out the record! He's gonna put out what he wanna put out!

SLOW DRAG: He's gonna put out what Ma want him to put out.

LEVEE: You heard what the man told you . . . "Ma Rainey's Black Bottom," Levee's arrangement. There you go! That's what he told you.

SLOW DRAG: What you gonna do, Cutler?

CUTLER: Ma ain't told me what version. Let's go on and play it Levee's way.

TOLEDO: See, now . . . I'll tell you something. As long as the colored man look to white folks to put the crown on what he say . . . as long as he looks to white folks for approval . . . then he ain't never gonna find out who he is and what he's about. He's just gonna be about what white folks want him to be about. That's one sure thing.

LEVEE: I'm just trying to show Cutler where he's wrong.

CUTLER: Cutler don't need you to show him nothing.

SLOW DRAG: (*Irritated*) Come on, let's get this shit rehearsed! You all can bicker afterward!

CUTLER: Levee's confused about who the boss is. He don't know Ma's the boss.

LEVEE: Ma's the boss on the road! We at a recording session. Mr. Sturdyvant and Mr. Irvin say what's gonna be here! We's in Chicago, we ain't in Memphis! I don't know why you all wanna pick me about it, shit! I'm with Slow Drag . . . Let's go on and get it rehearsed.

CUTLER: All right. All right. I know how to solve this. "Ma Rainey's Black Bottom." Levee's version. Let's do it. Come on.

TOLEDO: How that first part go again, Levee?

LEVEE: It go like this. (*He plays.*) That's to get the people's attention to the song. That's when you and Slow Drag come in with the rhythm part. Me and Cutler play on the breaks. (*Becoming animated.*) Now we gonna dance it . . . but we ain't gonna countrify it. This ain't no barn dance. We gonna play it like . . .

CUTLER: The man ask you how the first part go. He don't wanna hear all that. Just tell him how the piece go.

TOLEDO: I got it. I got it. Let's go. I know how to do it.

CUTLER: "Ma Rainey's Black Bottom." One . . . two . . . You know what to do.

(*They begin to play.* LEVEE *stops.*)

LEVEE: You all got to keep up now. You playing in the wrong time. Ma come in over the top. She got to find her own way in.

CUTLER: Nigger, will you let us play this song? When you get your own band . . . then you tell them that nonsense. We know how to play the piece. I was playing music before you was born. Gonna tell me how to play . . . All right. Let's try it again.

SLOW DRAG: Cutler, wait till I fix this. This string started to unravel. (*Playfully.*) And you know I want to play Levee's music right.

LEVEE: If you was any kind of musician, you'd take care of your instrument. Keep it in tip-top order. If you was any kind of musician, I'd let you be in my band.

SLOW DRAG: Shhheeeeet!

(*He crosses to get his string and steps on* LEVEE's *shoes.*)

LEVEE: Damn, Slow Drag! Watch them big-ass shoes you got.

SLOW DRAG: Boy, ain't nobody done nothing to you.

LEVEE: You done stepped on my shoes.

SLOW DRAG: Move them the hell out the way, then. You was in my way . . . I wasn't in your way.

(CUTLER *lights up another reefer.* SLOW DRAG *rummages around in his belongings for a string.* LEVEE *takes out a rag and begins to shine his shoes.*)

You can shine these when you get done, Levee.

CUTLER: If I had them shoes Levee got, I could buy me a whole suit of clothes.

LEVEE: What kind of difference it make what kind of shoes I got? Ain't nothing wrong with having nice shoes. I ain't said nothing about your shoes. Why you wanna talk about me and my Florsheims?

CUTLER: Any man who takes a whole week's pay and puts it on some shoes—you understand what I mean, what you walk around on the ground with—is a fool! And I don't mind telling you.

LEVEE: (*Irritated*) What difference it make to you, Cutler?

SLOW DRAG: The man ain't said nothing about your shoes. Ain't nothing wrong with having nice shoes. Look at Toledo.

TOLEDO: What about Toledo?

SLOW DRAG: I said ain't nothing wrong with having nice shoes.

LEVEE: Nigger got them clodhoppers! Old brogans! He ain't nothing but a sharecropper.

TOLEDO: You can make all the fun you want. It don't mean nothing. I'm satisfied with them and that's what counts.

LEVEE: Nigger, why don't you get some decent shoes? Got nerve to put on a suit and tie with them farming boots.

CUTLER: What you just tell me? It don't make no difference about the man's shoes. That's what you told me.

LEVEE: Aw, hell, I don't care what the nigger wear. I'll be honest with you. I don't care if he went barefoot. (SLOW DRAG *has put his string on the bass and is tuning it.*) Play something for me, Slow Drag. (SLOW DRAG *plays.*) A man got to have some shoes to dance like this! You can't dance like this with them clodhoppers Toledo got.

(LEVEE *sings.*)

Hello Central give me Doctor Jazz
He's got just what I need I'll say he has
When the world goes wrong and I have got the blues
He's the man who makes me get on my dancing shoes.

TOLEDO: That's the trouble with colored folks . . . always wanna have a good time. Good times done got more niggers killed than God got ways to count. What the hell having a good time mean? That's what I wanna know.

LEVEE: Hell, nigger . . . it don't need explaining. Ain't you never had no good time before?

TOLEDO: The more niggers get killed having a good time, the more good times niggers wanna have.

(SLOW DRAG *stops playing.*)

There's more to life than having a good time. If there ain't, then this is a piss-poor life we're having . . . if that's all there is to be got out of it.

SLOW DRAG: Toledo, just 'cause you like to read them books and study and whatnot . . . that's your good time. People get other things they likes to do to have a good time. Ain't no need you picking them about it.

CUTLER: Niggers been having a good time before you was born, and they gonna keep having a good time after you gone.

TOLEDO: Yeah, but what else they gonna do? Ain't nobody talking about making the lot of the colored man better for him here in America.

LEVEE: Now you gonna be Booker T. Washington.

TOLEDO: Everybody worried about having a good time. Ain't nobody thinking about what kind of world they gonna leave their youngens. "Just give me the good time, that's all I want." It just makes me sick.

SLOW DRAG: Well, the colored man's gonna be all right. He got through slavery, and he'll get through whatever else the white man put on him. I ain't worried about that. Good times is what makes life worth living. Now, you take the white man . . . The white man don't know how to have a good time. That's why he's troubled all the time. He don't know how to have a good time. He don't know how to laugh at life.

LEVEE: That's what the problem is with Toledo . . . reading all them books and things. He done got to the point where he forgot how to laugh and have a good time. Just like the white man.

TOLEDO: I know how to have a good time as well as the next man. I said, there's got to be more to life than having a good time. I said the colored man ought to be doing more than just trying to have a good time all the time.

LEVEE: Well, what is you doing, nigger? Talking all them highfalutin ideas about making a better world for the colored man. What is you doing to make it better? You playing the music and looking for your next piece of pussy same as we is. What is you doing? That's what I wanna know. Tell him, Cutler.

CUTLER: You all leave Cutler out of this. Cutler ain't got nothing to do with it.

TOLEDO: Levee, you just about the most ignorant nigger I know. Sometimes I wonder why I ever bother to try and talk with you.

LEVEE: Well, what is you doing? Talking that shit to me about I'm ignorant! What is you doing? You just a whole lot of mouth. A great big windbag. Thinking you smarter than everybody else. What is you doing, huh?

TOLEDO: It ain't just me, fool! It's everybody! What you think . . . I'm gonna solve the colored man's problems by myself? I said, we. You understand that? We. That's every living colored man in the world got to do his share. Got to do his part. I ain't talking about what I'm gonna do . . . or what you or Cutler or Slow Drag or anybody else. I'm talking about all of us together. What all of us gonna do. That's what I'm talking about, nigger!

LEVEE: Well, why didn't you say that, then?

CUTLER: Toledo, I don't know why you waste your time on this fool.

TOLEDO: That's what I'm trying to figure out.

LEVEE: Now there go Cutler with his shit. Calling me a fool. You wasn't even in the conversation. Now you gonna take sides and call me a fool.

CUTLER: Hell, I was listening to the man. I got sense enough to know what he was saying. I could tell it straight back to you.

LEVEE: Well, you go on with it. But I'll tell you this . . . I ain't gonna be too many more of your fools. I'll tell you that. Now you put that in your pipe and smoke it.

CUTLER: Boy, ain't nobody studying you. Telling me what to put in my pipe. Who's you to tell me what to do?

LEVEE: All right, I ain't nobody. Don't pay me no mind. I ain't nobody.

TOLEDO: Levee, you ain't nothing but the devil.

LEVEE: There you go! That's who I am. I'm the devil. I ain't nothing but the devil.

CUTLER: I can see that. That's something you know about. You know all about the devil.

LEVEE: I ain't saying what I know. I know plenty. What you know about the devil? Telling me what I know. What you know?

SLOW DRAG: I know a man sold his soul to the devil.

LEVEE: There you go! That's the only thing I ask about the devil . . . to see him coming so I can sell him this one I got. 'Cause if there's a god up there, he done went to sleep.

SLOW DRAG: Sold his soul to the devil himself. Name of Eliza Cotter. Lived in Tuscaloosa County, Alabama. The devil came by and he done upped and sold him his soul.

CUTLER: How you know the man done sold his soul to the devil, nigger? You talking that old-woman foolishness.

SLOW DRAG: Everybody know. It wasn't no secret. He went around working for the devil and everybody knowed it. Carried him a bag . . . one of them carpetbags. Folks say he carried the devil's papers and whatnot where he put your fingerprint on the paper with blood.

LEVEE: Where he at now? That's what I want to know. He can put my whole handprint if he want to!

CUTLER: That's the damnedest thing I ever heard! Folks kill me with that talk.

TOLEDO: Oh, that's real enough, all right. Some folks go arm in arm with the devil, shoulder to shoulder, and talk to him all the time. That's real, ain't nothing wrong in believing that.

SLOW DRAG: That's what I'm saying. Eliza Cotter is one of them. All right. The man living up in an old shack on Ben Foster's place, shoeing mules and horses, making them charms and things in secret. He done hooked up with the devil, showed up one day all fancied out with just the finest clothes you ever seen on a colored man . . . dressed just like one of them crackers . . . and carrying this bag with them papers and things. All right. Had a pocketful of money, just living the life of a rich man. Ain't done no more work or nothing. Just had him a string of women he run around with and throw his money away on. Bought him a big fine house . . . Well, it wasn't all that big, but it did have one of them white picket fences around it. Used to hire a man once a week just to paint that fence. Messed around there and one of the fellows of them gals he was messing with got fixed on him wrong and Eliza killed him. And he laughed about it. Sheriff come and arrest him, and then let him go. And he went around in that town laughing about killing this fellow. Trial come up, and the judge cut him loose. He must have been in converse with the devil too . . . 'cause he cut him loose and give him a bottle of whiskey! Folks ask what done happened to make him change, and he'd tell them straight out he done sold his soul to the devil and ask them if they wanted to sell theirs 'cause he could arrange it for them. Preacher see him coming, used to cross on the other side of the road. He'd just stand there and laugh at the preacher and call him a fool to his face.

CUTLER: Well, whatever happened to this fellow? What come of him? A man who, as you say, done sold his soul to the devil is bound to come to a bad end.

TOLEDO: I don't know about that. The devil's strong. The devil ain't no pushover.

SLOW DRAG: Oh, the devil had him under his wing, all right. Took good care of him. He ain't wanted for nothing.

CUTLER: What happened to him? That's what I want to know.

SLOW DRAG: Last I heard, he headed north with that bag of his, handing out hundred-dollar bills on the spot to whoever wanted to sign on with the devil. That's what I hear tell of him.

CUTLER: That's a bunch of fool talk. I don't know how you fix your mouth to tell that story. I don't believe that.

SLOW DRAG: I ain't asking you to believe it. I'm just telling you the facts of it.

LEVEE: I sure wish I knew where he went. He wouldn't have to convince me long. Hell, I'd even help him sign people up.

CUTLER: Nigger, God's gonna strike you down with that blasphemy you talking.

LEVEE: Oh, shit! God don't mean nothing to me. Let him strike me! Here I am, standing right here. What you talking about he's gonna strike me? Here I am! Let him strike me! I ain't scared of him. Talking that stuff to me.

CUTLER: All right. You gonna be sorry. You gonna fix yourself to have bad luck. Ain't nothing gonna work for you.

(Buzzer sounds offstage.)

LEVEE: Bad luck? What I care about some bad luck? You talking simple. I ain't knowed nothing but bad luck all my life. Couldn't get no worse. What the hell I care about some bad luck? Hell, I eat it everyday for breakfast! You dumber than I thought you was . . . talking about bad luck.

CUTLER: All right, nigger, you'll see! Can't tell a fool nothing. You'll see!

IRVIN: (IRVIN *enters the studio, checks his watch, and calls down the stairs*) Cutler . . . you boys' sandwiches are up here . . . Cutler?

CUTLER: Yessir, Mr. Irvin . . . be right there.

TOLEDO: I'll walk up there and get them.

(TOLEDO exits. The lights go down in the band room and up in the studio. IRVIN *paces back and forth in an agitated manner.* STURDYVANT *enters.)*

STURDYVANT: Irv, what's happening? Is she here yet? Was that her?

IRVIN: It's the sandwiches, Mel. I told you . . . I'll let you know when she comes, huh?

STURDYVANT: What's keeping her? Do you know what time it is? Have you looked at the clock? You told me she'd be here. You told me you'd take care of it.

IRVIN: Mel, for Chrissakes! What do you want from me? What do you want me to do?

STURDYVANT: Look what time it is, Irv. You told me she'd be here.

IRVIN: She'll be here, okay? I don't know what's keeping her. You know they're always late, Mel.

STURDYVANT: You should have went by the hotel and made sure she was on time. You should have taken care of this. That's what you told me, huh? "I'll take care of it."

IRVIN: Okay! Okay! I didn't go by the hotel! What do you want me to do? She'll be here, okay? The band's here . . . she'll be here.

STURDYVANT: Okay, Irv. I'll take your word. But if she doesn't come . . . if she doesn't come . . .

*(STURDYVANT *exits to the control booth as* TOLEDO *enters.)*

TOLEDO: Mr. Irvin . . . I come up to get the sandwiches.

IRVIN: Say . . . uh . . . look . . . one o'clock, right? She said one o'clock.

TOLEDO: That's what time she told us. Say be here at one o'clock.

IRVIN: Do you know what's keeping her? Do you know why she ain't here?

TOLEDO: I can't say, Mr. Irvin. Told us one o'clock.

(The buzzer sounds. IRVIN *goes to the door. There is a flurry of commotion as* MA RAINEY *enters, followed closely by the* POLICEMAN, DUSSIE MAE, *and* SYLVESTER. MA RAINEY *is a short, heavy woman. She is dressed in a full-length fur coat with matching hat, an emerald-green dress, and several strands of pearls of varying lengths. Her hair is secured by a headband that matches her dress. Her manner is simple and direct, and she carries herself in a royal fashion.* DUSSIE MAE *is a young, dark-skinned woman whose greatest asset is the sensual energy which seems to flow from her. She is dressed in a fur jacket and a tight-fitting canary-yellow dress.* SYLVESTER *is an Arkansas country boy, the size of a fullback. He wears a new suit and coat, in which he is obviously uncomfortable. Most of the time, he stutters when he speaks.)*

MA RAINEY: Irvin . . . you better tell this man who I am! You better get him straight!

IRVIN: Ma, do you know what time it is? Do you have any idea? We've been waiting . . .

DUSSIE MAE: *(To* SYLVESTER) If you was watching where you was going . . .

SYLVESTER: I was watching . . . What you mean?

IRVIN: *(Notices* POLICEMAN) What's going on here? Officer, what's the matter?

MA RAINEY: Tell the man who he's messing with!

POLICEMAN: Do you know this lady?

MA RAINEY: Just tell the man who I am! That's all you gotta do.

POLICEMAN: Lady, will you let me talk, huh?

MA RAINEY: Tell the man who I am!

IRVIN: Wait a minute . . . wait a minute! Let me handle it. Ma, will you let me handle it?

MA RAINEY: Tell him who he's messing with!

IRVIN: Okay! Okay! Give me a chance! Officer, this is one of our recording artists . . . Ma Rainey.

MA RAINEY: Madame Rainey! Get it straight! Madame Rainey! Talking about taking me to jail!

IRVIN: Look, Ma . . . give me a chance, okay? Here . . . sit down. I'll take care of it. Officer, what's the problem?

DUSSIE MAE: *(To* SYLVESTER) It's all your fault.

SYLVESTER: I ain't done nothing . . . Ask Ma.

POLICEMAN: Well . . . when I walked up on the incident . . .

DUSSIE MAE: Sylvester wrecked Ma's car.

SYLVESTER: I d-d-did not! The m-m-man ran into me!

POLICEMAN: *(To* IRVIN) Look, buddy . . . if you want it in a nutshell, we got her charged with assault and battery.

MA RAINEY: Assault and what for what!

DUSSIE MAE: See . . . we was trying to get a cab . . . and so Ma . . .

MA RAINEY: Wait a minute! I'll tell you if you wanna know what happened. *(She points to* SYLVESTER) Now, that's Sylvester. That's my nephew. He was driving my car . . .

POLICEMAN: Lady, we don't know whose car he was driving.

MA RAINEY: That's my car!

DUSSIE MAE and SYLVESTER: That's Ma's car!

MA RAINEY: What you mean you don't know whose car it is? I bought and paid for that car.

POLICEMAN: That's what you say, lady . . . We still gotta check. *(To* IRVIN.) They hit a car on Market Street. The guy said the kid ran a stoplight.

SYLVESTER: What you mean? The man c-c-come around the corner and hit m-m-me!

POLICEMAN: While I was calling a paddy wagon to haul them to the station, they try to hop into a parked cab. The cabbie said he was waiting on a fare . . .

MA RAINEY: The man was just sitting there. Wasn't waiting for nobody. I don't know why he wanna tell that lie.

POLICEMAN: Look, lady . . . will you let me tell the story?

MA RAINEY: Go ahead and tell it then. But tell it right!

POLICEMAN: Like I say . . . she tries to get in this cab. The cabbie's waiting on a fare. She starts creating a disturbance. The cabbie gets out to try and explain the situation to her . . . and she knocks him down.

DUSSIE MAE: She ain't hit him! He just fell!

SYLVESTER: He just s-s-s-slipped!

POLICEMAN: He claims she knocked him down. We got her charged with assault and battery.

MA RAINEY: If that don't beat all to hell. I ain't touched the man! The man was trying to reach around me to keep his car door closed. I opened the door and it hit him and he fell down. I ain't touched the man!

IRVIN: Okay. Okay . . . I got it straight now, Ma. You didn't touch him. All right? Officer, can I see you for a minute?

DUSSIE MAE: Ma was just trying to open the door.

SYLVESTER: He j-j-just got in t-t-the way!

MA RAINEY: Said he wasn't gonna haul no colored folks . . . if you want to know the truth of it.

IRVIN: Okay, Ma . . . I got it straight now. Officer?

*(*IRVIN *pulls the* POLICEMAN *off to the side.)*

MA RAINEY: *(Noticing* TOLEDO) Toledo, Cutler and everybody here?

TOLEDO: Yeah, they down in the band room. What happened to your car?

STURDYVANT: *(Entering)* Irv, what's the problem? What's going on? Officer . . .

IRVIN: Mel, let me take care of it. I can handle it.

STURDYVANT: What's happening? What the hell's going on?

IRVIN: Let me handle it, Mel, huh?

*(*STURDYVANT *crosses over to* MA RAINEY.)*

STURDYVANT: What's going on, Ma. What'd you do?

MA RAINEY: Sturdyvant, get on away from me! That's the last thing I need . . . to go through some of your shit!

IRVIN: Mel, I'll take care of it. I'll explain it all to you. Let me handle it, huh?

(STURDYVANT *reluctantly returns to the control booth.*)

POLICEMAN: Look, buddy, like I say . . . we got her charged with assault and battery . . . and the kid with threatening the cabbie.

SYLVESTER: I ain't done n-n-nothing!

MA RAINEY: You leave the boy out of it. He ain't done nothing. What's he supposed to have done?

POLICEMAN: He threatened the cabbie, lady! You just can't go around threatening people.

SYLVESTER: I ain't done nothing to him! He's the one talking about he g-g-gonna get a b-b-baseball bat on me! I just told him what I'd do with it. But I ain't done nothing 'cause he didn't get the b-b-bat!

IRVIN: (*Pulling the* POLICEMAN *aside*) Officer . . . look here . . .

POLICEMAN: We was on our way down to the precinct . . . but I figured I'd do you a favor and bring her by here. I mean, if she's as important as she says she is . . .

IRVIN: (*Slides a bill from his pocket*) Look, Officer . . . I'm Madame Rainey's manager . . . It's good to meet you. (*He shakes the* POLICEMAN's *hand and passes him the bill.*) As soon as we're finished with the recording session, I'll personally stop by the precinct house and straighten up this misunderstanding.

POLICEMAN: Well . . . I guess that's all right. As long as someone is responsible for them.

(*He pockets the bill and winks at* IRVIN.)

No need to come down . . . I'll take care of it myself. Of course, we wouldn't want nothing like this to happen again.

IRVIN: Don't worry, Officer . . . I'll take care of everything. Thanks for your help.

(IRVIN *escorts the* POLICEMAN *to the door and returns. He crosses over to* MA RAINEY.)

Here, Ma . . . let me take your coat. (*To* SYLVESTER.) I don't believe I know you.

MA RAINEY: That's my nephew, Sylvester.

IRVIN: I'm very pleased to meet you. Here . . . you can give me your coat.

MA RAINEY: That there is Dussie Mae.

IRVIN: Hello . . .

(DUSSIE MAE *hands* IRVIN *her coat.*)

Listen, Ma, just sit there and relax. The boys are in the band room rehearsing. You just sit and relax a minute.

MA RAINEY: I ain't for no sitting. I ain't never heard of such. Talking about taking me to jail. Irvin, call down there and see about my car.

IRVIN: Okay, Ma . . . I'll take care of it. You just relax.

(IRVIN *exits with the coats.*)

MA RAINEY: Why you all keep it so cold in here? Sturdyvant try and pinch every penny he can. You all wanna make some records, you better put some heat on in here or give me back my coat.

IRVIN: (*Entering*) We got the heat turned up, Ma. It's warming up. It'll be warm in a minute.

DUSSIE MAE: (*Whispering to* MA RAINEY) Where's the bathroom?

MA RAINEY: It's in the back. Down the hall next to Sturdyvant's office. Come on, I'll show you where it is. Irvin, call down there and see about my car. I want my car fixed today.

IRVIN: I'll take care of everything, Ma.

(*He notices* TOLEDO.)

Say . . . uh . . . uh . . .

TOLEDO: Toledo.

IRVIN: Yeah . . . Toledo. I got the sandwiches, you can take down to the rest of the boys. We'll be ready to go in a minute. Give you boys a chance to eat and then we'll be ready to go.

(IRVIN *and* TOLEDO *exit. The lights go down in the studio and come up in the band room.*)

LEVEE: Slow Drag, you ever been to New Orleans?

SLOW DRAG: What's in New Orleans that I want?

LEVEE: How you call yourself a musician and ain't never been to New Orleans.

SLOW DRAG: You ever been to Fat Back, Arkansas? (*Pauses.*) All right, then. Ain't never been nothing in New Orleans that I couldn't get in Fat Back.

LEVEE: That's why you backwards. You just an old country boy talking about Fat Back, Arkansas, and New Orleans in the same breath.

CUTLER: I been to New Orleans. What about it?

LEVEE: You ever been to Lula White's?

CUTLER: Lula White's? I ain't never heard of it.

LEVEE: Man, they got some gals in there just won't wait! I seen a man get killed in there once. Got drunk and grabbed one of the gals wrong . . . I don't know what the matter of it was. But he grabbed her and she stuck a knife in him all the way up to the hilt. He ain't even fell. He just stood there and choked on his own blood. I was just asking Slow Drag 'cause I was gonna take him to Lula White's when we get down to New Orleans and show him a good time. Introduce him to one of them gals I know down there.

CUTLER: Slow Drag don't need you to find him no pussy. He can take care of his own self. Fact is . . . you better watch your gal when Slow Drag's around. They don't call him Slow Drag for nothing. (*He laughs.*) Tell him how you got your name Slow Drag.

SLOW DRAG: I ain't thinking about Levee.

CUTLER: Slow Drag break a woman's back when he dance. They had this contest one time in this little town called Bolingbroke about a hundred miles outside of Macon. We was playing for this dance and they was giving twenty dollars to the best slow draggers. Slow Drag looked over the competition, got down off the bandstand, grabbed hold of one of them gals, and stuck to her like a fly to jelly. Like wood to glue. Man had that gal whooping and hollering so . . . everybody stopped to watch. This fellow come in . . . this gal's fellow . . . and pulled a knife a foot long on Slow Drag. 'Member that, Slow Drag?

SLOW DRAG: Boy that mama was hot! The front of her dress was wet as a dishrag!

LEVEE: So what happened? What the man do?

CUTLER: Slow Drag ain't missed a stroke. The gal, she just look at her man with that sweet dizzy look in her eye. She ain't about to stop! Folks was clearing out, ducking and hiding under tables, figuring there's gonna be a fight. Slow Drag just looked over the gal's shoulder at the man and said, "Mister, if you'd quit hollering and wait a minute . . . you'll see I'm doing you a favor. I'm helping this gal win ten dollars so she can buy you a gold watch." The man just stood there and looked at him, all the while stroking that knife. Told Slow Drag, say, "All right, then, nigger. You just better make damn sure you win." That's when folks started calling him Slow Drag. The women got to hanging around him so bad after that, them fellows in that town ran us out of there.

(TOLEDO *enters, carrying a small cardboard box with the* sandwiches.)

LEVEE: Yeah . . . well, them gals in Lula White's will put a harness on his ass.

TOLEDO: Ma's up there. Some kind of commotion with the police.

CUTLER: Police? What the police up there for?

TOLEDO: I couldn't get it straight. Something about her car. They gone now . . . she's all right. Mr. Irvin sent some sandwiches.

(LEVEE *springs across the room.*)

LEVEE: Yeah, all right. What we got here?

(*He takes two sandwiches out of the box.*)

TOLEDO: What you doing grabbing two? There ain't but five in there . . . How you figure you get two?

LEVEE: 'Cause I grabbed them first. There's enough for everybody . . . What you talking about? It ain't like I'm taking food out of nobody's mouth.

CUTLER: That's all right. He can have mine too. I don't want none.

(LEVEE *starts toward the box to get another sandwich.*)

TOLEDO: Nigger, you better get out of here. Slow Drag, you want this?

SLOW DRAG: Naw, you can have it.

TOLEDO: With Levee around, you don't have to worry about no leftovers. I can see that.

LEVEE: What's the matter with you? Ain't you eating two sandwiches? Then why you wanna talk about me? Talking about there won't be no leftovers with Levee around. Look at your own self before you look at me.

TOLEDO: That's what you is. That's what we all is. A leftover from history. You see now, I'll show you.

LEVEE: Aw, shit . . . I done got the nigger started now.

TOLEDO: Now, I'm gonna show you how this goes . . . where you just a leftover from history. Everybody come from different places in Africa, right? Come from different tribes and things. Soonawhile they began to make one big stew. You had the carrots, the peas, and potatoes and whatnot over here. And over there you had the meat, the nuts, the okra, corn . . . and then you mix it up and let it cook right through to get the flavors flowing together . . . then you got one thing. You got a stew.

Now you take and eat the stew. You take and make your history with that stew. All right. Now it's over. Your history's over and you done ate the stew. But you look around and you see some carrots over here, some potatoes over there. That stew's still there. You done made your history and it's still there. You can't eat it all. So what you got? You got some leftovers. That's what it is. You got leftovers and you can't do nothing with it. You already making you another history . . . cooking you another meal, and you don't need them leftovers no more. What to do?

See, we's the leftovers. The colored man is the leftovers. Now, what's the colored man gonna do with himself? That's what we waiting to find out. But first we gotta know we the leftovers. Now, who knows that? You find me a nigger that knows that and I'll turn any whichaway you want me to. I'll bend over for you. You ain't gonna find that. And that's what the problem is. The problem ain't with the white man. The white man knows you just a leftover. 'Cause he the one who done the eating and he know what he done ate. But we don't know that we been took and made history out of. Done went and filled the white man's belly and now he's full and tired and wants you to get out the way and let him be by himself. Now, I know what I'm talking about. And if you wanna find out, you just ask Mr. Irvin what he had for supper yesterday. And if he's an honest white man . . . which is asking for a whole heap of a lot . . . he'll tell you he done ate your black ass and if you please I'm full up with you . . . so go on and get off the plate and let me eat something else.

SLOW DRAG: What that mean? What's eating got to do with how the white man treat you? He don't treat you no different according to what he ate.

TOLEDO: I ain't said it had nothing to do with how he treat you.

CUTLER: The man's trying to tell you something, fool!

SLOW DRAG: What he trying to tell me? Ain't you here. Why you say he was trying to tell *me* something? Wasn't he trying to tell you too?

LEVEE: He was trying all right. He was trying a whole heap. I'll say that for him. But trying ain't worth a damn. I got lost right there trying to figure out who puts nuts in their stew.

SLOW DRAG: I knowed that before. My grandpappy used to put nuts in his stew. He and my grandmama both. That ain't nothing new.

TOLEDO: They put nuts in their stew all over Africa. But the stew they eat, and the stew your grandpappy made, and all the stew that you and me eat, and the stew Mr. Irvin eats . . . ain't in no way the same stew. That's the way that go. I'm through with it. That's the last you know me to ever try and explain something to you.

CUTLER: (*After a pause*) Well, time's getting along . . . Come on, let's finish rehearsing.

LEVEE: (*Stretching out on a bench*) I don't feel like rehearsing. I ain't nothing but a leftover. You go and rehearse with Toledo . . . He's gonna teach you how to make a stew.

SLOW DRAG: Cutler, what you gonna do? I don't want to be around here all day.

LEVEE: I know my part. You all go on and rehearse your part. You all need some rehearsal.

CUTLER: Come on, Levee, get up off your ass and rehearse the songs.

LEVEE: I already know them songs . . . What I wanna rehearse them for?

SLOW DRAG: You in the band, ain't you? You supposed to rehearse when the band rehearse.

TOLEDO: Levee think he the king of the barnyard. He thinks he's the only rooster know how to crow.

LEVEE: All right! All right! Come on, I'm gonna show you I know them songs. Come on, let's rehearse. I bet you the first one mess be Toledo. Come on . . . I wanna see if he know how to crow.

CUTLER: "Ma Rainey's Black Bottom," Levee's version. Let's do it.

(*They begin to rehearse. The lights go down in the band room and up in the studio.* MA RAINEY *sits and takes off her shoe, rubs her feet.* DUSSIE MAE *wanders about looking at the studio.* SYLVESTER *is over by the piano.*)

MA RAINEY: (*Singing to herself*)

> *Oh, Lord, these dogs of mine*
> *They sure do worry me all the time*
> *The reason why I don't know*
> *Lord, I beg to be excused*
> *I can't wear me no sharp-toed shoes.*
> *I went for a walk*
> *I stopped to talk*
> *Oh, how my corns did bark.*

DUSSIE MAE: It feels kinda spooky in here. I ain't never been in no recording studio before. Where's the band at?

MA RAINEY: They off somewhere rehearsing. I don't know where Irvin went to. All this hurry up and he goes off back there with Sturdyvant. I know he better come on 'cause Ma ain't gonna be waiting. Come here . . . let me see that dress.

(DUSSIE MAE *crosses over.* MA RAINEY *tugs at the dress around the waist, appraising the fit.*)

That dress looks nice. I'm gonna take you tomorrow and get you some more things before I take you down to Memphis. They got clothes up here you can't get in Memphis. I want you to look nice for me. If you gonna travel with the show you got to look nice.

DUSSIE MAE: I need me some more shoes. These hurt my feet.

MA RAINEY: You get you some shoes that fit your feet. Don't you be messing around with no shoes that pinch your feet. Ma know something about bad feet. Hand me my slippers out my bag over yonder.

(DUSSIE MAE *brings the slippers.*)

DUSSIE MAE: I just want to get a pair of them yellow ones. About a half-size bigger.

MA RAINEY: We'll get you whatever you need. Sylvester, too . . . I'm gonna get him some more clothes. Sylvester, tuck your clothes in. Straighten them up and look nice. Look like a gentleman.

DUSSIE MAE: Look at Sylvester with that hat on.

MA RAINEY: Sylvester, take your hat off inside. Act like your mama taught you something. I know she taught you better than that.

(SYLVESTER *bangs on the piano.*)

Come on over here and leave that piano alone.

SYLVESTER: I ain't d-d-doing nothing to the p-p-piano. I'm just l-l-looking at it.

MA RAINEY: Well. Come on over here and sit down. As soon as Mr. Irvin comes back, I'll have him take you down and introduce you to the band.

(SYLVESTER *comes over.*)

He's gonna take you down there and introduce you in a minute . . . have Cutler show you how your part go. And when you get your money, you gonna send some of it home to your mama. Let her know you doing all right. Make her feel good to know you doing all right in the world.

(DUSSIE MAE *wanders about the studio and opens the door leading to the band room. The strains of* LEVEE's *version of "Ma Rainey's Black Bottom" can be heard.* IRVIN *enters.*)

IRVIN: Ma, I called down to the garage and checked on your car. It's just a scratch. They'll have it ready for you this afternoon. They're gonna send it over with one of their fellows.

MA RAINEY: They better have my car fixed right too. I ain't going for that. Brand-new car . . . they better fix it like new.

IRVIN: It was just a scratch on the fender, Ma . . . They'll take care of it . . . don't worry . . . they'll have it like new.

MA RAINEY: Irvin, what is that I hear? What is that the band's rehearsing? I know they ain't rehearsing Levee's "Black Bottom." I know I ain't hearing that?

IRVIN: Ma, listen . . . that's what I wanted to talk to you about. Levee's version of that song . . . it's got a nice arrangement . . . a nice horn intro . . . It really picks it up . . .

MA RAINEY: I ain't studying Levee nothing. I know what he done to that song and I don't like to sing it that way. I'm doing it the old way. That's why I brought my nephew to do the voice intro.

IRVIN: Ma, that's what the people want now. They want something they can dance to. Times are changing. Levee's arrangement gives the people what they want. It gets them excited . . . makes them forget about their troubles.

MA RAINEY: I don't care what you say, Irvin. Levee ain't messing up my song. If he got what the people want, let him take it somewhere else. I'm singing Ma Rainey's song. I ain't singing Levee's song. Now that's all there is to it. Carry my nephew on down there and introduce him to the band. I promised my sister I'd look out for him and he's gonna do the voice intro on the song my way.

IRVIN: Ma, we just figured that . . .

MA RAINEY: Who's this "we"? What you mean "we"? I ain't studying Levee nothing. Come talking this "we" stuff. Who's "we"?

IRVIN: Me and Sturdyvant. We decided that it would . . .

MA RAINEY: You decided, huh? I'm just a bump on the log. I'm gonna go which ever way the river drift. Is that it? You and Sturdyvant decided.

IRVIN: Ma, it was just that we thought it would be better.

MA RAINEY: I ain't got good sense. I don't know nothing about music. I don't know what's a good song and what ain't. You know more about my fans than I do.

IRVIN: It's not that, Ma. It would just be easier to do. It's more what the people want.

MA RAINEY: I'm gonna tell you something, Irvin . . . and you go on up there and tell Sturdyvant. What you all say don't count with me. You understand? Ma listens to her heart. Ma listens to the voice inside her. That's what counts with Ma. Now, you carry my nephew on down there . . . tell Cutler he's gonna do the voice intro on that "Black Bottom" song and that Levee ain't messing up my song with none of his music shit. Now, if that don't set right with you

and Sturdyvant . . . then I can carry my black bottom on back down South to my tour, 'cause I don't like it up here no ways.

IRVIN: Okay, Ma . . . I don't care. I just thought . . .

MA RAINEY: Damn what you thought! What you look like telling me how to sing my song? This Levee and Sturdyvant nonsense . . . I ain't going for it! Sylvester, go on down there and introduce yourself. I'm through playing with Irvin.

SYLVESTER: Which way you go? Where they at?

MA RAINEY: Here . . . I'll carry you down there myself.

DUSSIE MAE: Can I go? I wanna see the band.

MA RAINEY: You stay your behind up here. Ain't no cause in you being down there. Come on, Sylvester.

IRVIN: Okay, Ma. Have it your way. We'll be ready to go in fifteen minutes.

MA RAINEY: We'll be ready to go when Madame says we're ready. That's the way it goes around here.

(MA RAINEY and SYLVESTER exit. The lights go down in the studio and up in the band room. MA RAINEY enters with SYLVESTER.)

Cutler, this here is my nephew Sylvester. He's gonna do that voice intro on the "Black Bottom" song using the old version.

LEVEE: What you talking about? Mr. Irvin says he's using my version. What you talking about?

MA RAINEY: Levee, I ain't studying you or Mr. Irvin. Cutler, get him straightened out on how to do his part. I ain't thinking about Levee. These folks done messed with the wrong person this day. Sylvester, Cutler gonna teach you your part. You go ahead and get it straight. Don't worry about what nobody else say.

(MA RAINEY exits.)

CUTLER: Well, come on in, boy. I'm Cutler. You got Slow Drag . . . Levee . . . and that's Toledo over there. Sylvester, huh?

SYLVESTER: Sylvester Brown.

LEVEE: I done wrote a version of that song what picks it up and sets it down in the people's lap! Now she come talking this! You don't need that old circus bullshit! I know what I'm talking about. You gonna mess up the song Cutler and you know it.

CUTLER: I ain't gonna mess up nothing. Ma say . . .

LEVEE: I don't care what Ma say! I'm talking about what the intro gonna do to the song. The peoples in the North ain't gonna buy all that tent-show nonsense. They wanna hear some music!

CUTLER: Nigger, I done told you time and again . . . you just in the band. You plays the piece . . . whatever they want! Ma says what to play! Not you! You ain't here to be doing no creating. Your job is to play whatever Ma says!

LEVEE: I might not play nothing! I might quit!

CUTLER: Nigger, don't nobody care if you quit. Whose heart you gonna break?

TOLEDO: Levee ain't gonna quit. He got to make some money to keep him in shoe polish.

LEVEE: I done told you all . . . you all don't know me. You don't know what I'll do.

CUTLER: I don't think nobody too much give a damn! Sylvester, here's the way your part go. The band plays the intro . . . I'll tell you where to come in. The band plays the intro and then you say, "All right, boys, you done seen the rest . . . Now I'm gonna show you the best. Ma Rainey's gonna show you her black bottom." You got that? (SYLVESTER *nods.*) Let me hear you say it one time.

SYLVESTER: "All right, boys, you done s-s-seen the rest n-n-now I'm gonna show you the best. M-m-m-m-m-m-ma Rainey's gonna s-s-show you her black b-b-bottom."

LEVEE: What kind of . . . All right, Cutler! Let me see you fix that! You straighten that out! You hear that shit, Slow Drag? How in the hell the boy gonna do the part and he can't even talk!

SYLVESTER: W-w-w-who's you to tell me what to do, nigger! This ain't your band! Ma tell me to d-d-d-do it and I'm gonna do it. You can go to hell, n-n-n-nigger!

LEVEE: B-b-b-boy, ain't nobody studying you. You go on and fix that one, Cutler. You fix that one and I'll . . . I'll shine your shoes for you. You go on and fix that one!

TOLEDO: You say you Ma's nephew, huh?

SYLVESTER: Yeah. So w-w-what that mean?

TOLEDO: Oh, I ain't meant nothing . . . I was just asking.

SLOW DRAG: Well, come on and let's rehearse so the boy can get it right.

LEVEE: I ain't rehearsing nothing! You just wait till I get my band. I'm gonna record that song and show you how it supposed to go!

CUTLER: We can do it without Levee. Let him sit on over there. Sylvester, you remember your part?

SYLVESTER: I remember it pretty g-g-good.

CUTLER: Well, come on, let's do it, then.

(*The band begins to play.* LEVEE *sits and pouts.* STURDYVANT *enters the band room.*)

STURDYVANT: Good . . . you boys are rehearsing, I see.

LEVEE: (*Jumping up.*) Yessir! We rehearsing. We know them songs real good.

STURDYVANT: Good! Say, Levee, did you finish that song?

LEVEE: Yessir, Mr. Sturdyvant. I got it right here. I wrote that other part just like you say. It go like:

You can shake it, you can break it
You can dance at any hall
You can slide across the floor
You'll never have to stall

My jelly, my roll,
Sweet Mama, don't you let it fall.

Then I put that part in there for the people to dance, like you say, for them to forget about their troubles.

STURDYVANT: Good! Good! I'll just take this. I wanna see you about your songs as soon as I get the chance.

LEVEE: Yessir! As soon as you get the chance, Mr. Sturdyvant.

(STURDYVANT *exits.*)

CUTLER: You hear, Levee? You hear this nigger? "Yes-suh, we's rehearsing, boss."

SLOW DRAG: I heard him. Seen him too. Shuffling them feet.

TOLEDO: Aw, Levee can't help it none. He's like all of us. Spooked up with the white man.

LEVEE: I'm spooked up with him, all right. You let one of them crackers fix on me wrong. I'll show you how spooked up I am with him.

TOLEDO: That's the trouble of it. You wouldn't know if he was fixed on you wrong or not. You so spooked up by him you ain't had the time to study him.

LEVEE: I studies the white man. I got him studied good. The first time one fixes on me wrong, I'm gonna let him know just how much I studied. Come telling me I'm spooked up with the white man. You let one of them mess with me, I'll show you how spooked up I am.

CUTLER: You talking out your hat. The man come in here, call you a boy, tell you to get up off your ass and rehearse, and you ain't had nothing to say to him, except "Yessir!"

LEVEE: I can say "yessir" to whoever I please. What you got to do with it? I know how to handle white folks. I been handling them for thirty-two years, and now you gonna tell me how to do it. Just 'cause I say "yessir" don't mean I'm spooked up with him. I know what I'm doing. Let me handle him my way.

CUTLER: Well, go on and handle it, then.

LEVEE: Toledo, you always messing with somebody! Always agitating somebody with that old philosophy bullshit you be talking. You stay out of my way about what I do and say. I'm my own person. Just let me alone.

TOLEDO: You right, Levee. I apologize. It ain't none of my business that you spooked up by the white man.

LEVEE: All right! See! That's the shit I'm talking about. You all back up and leave Levee alone.

SLOW DRAG: Aw, Levee, we was all just having fun. Toledo ain't said nothing about you he ain't said about me. You just taking it all wrong.

TOLEDO: I ain't meant nothing by it Levee. (*Pauses.*) Cutler, you ready to rehearse?

LEVEE: Levee got to be Levee! And he don't need nobody messing with him about the white man—cause you don't know nothing about me. You don't know Levee. You don't know nothing about what kind of blood I got! What kind of heart I got beating here! (*He pounds his chest.*) I was eight years old when I watched a gang of white mens come into my daddy's house and have to do with my mama any way they wanted. (*Pauses.*) We was living in Jefferson County, about eighty miles outside of Natchez. My daddy's name was Memphis . . . Memphis Lee Green . . . had him near fifty acres of good farming land. I'm talking about good land! Grow anything you want! He done gone off of shares and bought this land from Mr. Hallie's widow woman after he done passed on. Folks called him an uppity nigger 'cause he done saved and borrowed to where he could buy this land and be independent. (*Pauses.*) It was coming on planting time and my daddy went into Natchez to get him some seed and fertilizer. Called me, say, "Levee you the man of the house now. Take care of your mama while I'm gone." I wasn't but a little boy, eight years old. (*Pauses.*) My mama was frying up some chicken when them mens come in that house. Must have been eight or nine of them. She standing there frying that chicken and them mens come and took hold of her just like you take hold of a mule and make him do what you want. (*Pauses.*) There was my mama with a gang of white mens. She tried to fight them off, but I could see where it wasn't gonna do her any good, I didn't know what they were doing to her . . . but I figured whatever it was they may as well do to me too. My daddy had a knife that he kept around there for hunting and working and whatnot. I knew where he kept it and I went and got it.

I'm gonna show you how spooked up I was by the white man. I tried my damndest to cut one of them's throat! I hit him on the shoulder with it. He reached back and grabbed hold of that knife and whacked me across the chest with it.

(LEVEE *raises his shirt to show a long ugly scar.*)

That's what made them stop. They was scared I was gonna bleed to death. My mama wrapped a sheet around me and carried me two miles down to the Furlow place and they drove me up to Doc Albans. He was waiting on a calf to be born, and say he ain't had time to see me. They carried me up to Miss Etta, the midwife, and she fixed me up.

My daddy came back and acted like he done accepted the facts of what happened. But he got the names of them mens from mama. He found out who they was and then we announced we was moving out of that county. Said good-bye to everybody . . . all the neighbors. My daddy went and smiled in the face of one of them crackers who had been with my mama. Smiled in his face and sold him our land. We moved over with relations in

Caldwell. He got us settled in and then he took off one day. I ain't never seen him since. He sneaked back, hiding up in the woods, laying to get them eight or nine men. (*Pauses.*) He got four of them before they got him. They tracked him down in the woods. Caught up with him and hung him and set him afire. (*Pauses.*) My daddy wasn't spooked up by the white man. Nosir! And that taught me how to handle them. I seen my daddy go up and grin in this cracker's face . . . smile in his face and sell him his land. All the while he's planning how he's gonna get him and what he's gonna do to him. That taught me how to handle them. So you all just back up and leave Levee alone about the white man. I can smile and say yessir to whoever I please. I got time coming to me. You all just leave Levee alone about the white man.

(*There is a long pause.* SLOW DRAG *begins playing on the bass and sings.*)

SLOW DRAG: (*Singing*)

If I had my way
If I had my way
If I had my way
I would tear this old building down.

ACT 2

(*The lights come up in the studio. The musicians are setting up their instruments.* MA RAINEY *walks about shoeless, singing softly to herself.* LEVEE *stands near* DUSSIE MAE, *who hikes up her dress and crosses her leg.* CUTLER *speaks to* IRVIN *off to the side.*)

CUTLER: Mr. Irvin, I don't know what you gonna do. I ain't got nothing to do with it, but the boy can't do the part. He stutters. He can't get it right. He stutters right through it every time.
IRVIN: Christ! Okay. We'll . . . Shit! We'll just do it like we planned. We'll do Levee's version. I'll handle it, Cutler. Come on, let's go. I'll think of something.

(*He exits to the control booth.*)

MA RAINEY: (*Calling* CUTLER *over*) Levee's got his eyes in the wrong place. You better school him, Cutler.
CUTLER: Come on, Levee . . . let's get ready to play! Get your mind on your work!
IRVIN: (*Over speaker*) Okay, boys, we're gonna do "Moonshine Blues" first. "Moonshine Blues," Ma.
MA RAINEY: I ain't doing no "Moonshine" nothing. I'm doing the "Black Bottom" first. Come on, Sylvester. (*To* IRVIN.) Where's Sylvester's mike? You need a mike for Sylvester. Irvin . . . get him a mike.
IRVIN: Uh . . . Ma, the boys say he can't do it. We'll have to do Levee's version.

MA RAINEY: What you mean he can't do it? Who say he can't do it? What boys say he can't do it?

IRVIN: The band, Ma . . . the boys in the band.

MA RAINEY: What band? The band work for me! I say what goes! Cutler, what's he talking about? Levee, this some of your shit?

IRVIN: He stutters, Ma. They say he stutters.

MA RAINEY: I don't care if he do. I promised the boy he could do the part . . . and he's gonna do it! That's all there is to it. He don't stutter all the time. Get a microphone down here for him.

IRVIN: Ma, we don't have time. We can't . . .

MA RAINEY: If you wanna make a record, you gonna find time. I ain't playing with you, Irvin. I can walk out of here and go back to my tour. I got plenty fans. I don't need to go through all of this. Just go and get the boy a microphone.

(IRVIN and STURDYVANT consult in the booth, IRVIN exits.)

STURDYVANT: All right, Ma . . . we'll get him a microphone. But if he messes up . . . He's only getting one chance . . . The cost . . .

MA RAINEY: Damn the cost. You always talking about the cost. I make more money for this outfit than anybody else you got put together. If he messes up he'll just do it till he gets it right. Levee, I know you had something to do with this. You better watch yourself.

LEVEE: It was Cutler!

SYLVESTER: It was you! You the only one m-m-mad about it.

LEVEE: The boy stutter. He can't do the part. Everybody see that. I don't know why you want the boy to do the part no ways.

MA RAINEY: Well, can or can't . . . he's gonna do it! You ain't got nothing to do with it!

LEVEE: I don't care what you do! He can sing the whole goddamned song for all I care!

MA RAINEY: Well, all right. Thank you.

(IRVIN enters with a microphone and hooks it up. He exits to the control booth.)

MA RAINEY: Come on, Sylvester. You just stand here and hold your hands like I told you. Just remember the words and say them . . . That's all there is to it. Don't worry about messing up. If you mess up, we'll do it again. Now, let me hear you say it. Play for him, Cutler.

CUTLER: One . . . two . . . you know what to do.

(The band begins to play and SYLVESTER curls his fingers and clasps his hands together in front of his chest, pulling in opposite directions as he says his lines.)

SYLVESTER: "All right, boys, you d-d-done s-s-seen the best . . .

(LEVEE stops playing.)

Now I'm g-g-g-gonna show you the rest . . . Ma R-r-rainey's gonna show you her b-b-b-black b-b-b-bottom."

(The rest of the band stops playing.)

MA RAINEY: That's all right. That's real good. You take your time, you'll get it right.

STURDYVANT: *(Over speaker)* Listen, Ma . . . now, when you come in, don't wait so long to come in. Don't take so long on the intro, huh?

MA RAINEY: Sturdyvant, don't you go trying to tell me how to sing. You just take care of that up there and let me take care of this down here. Where's my Coke?

IRVIN: Okay, Ma. We're all set up to go up here. "Ma Rainey's Black Bottom," boys.

MA RAINEY: Where's my Coke? I need a Coke. You ain't got no Coke down here? Where's my Coke?

IRVIN: What's the matter, Ma? What's . . .

MA RAINEY: Where's my Coke? I need a Coca-Cola.

IRVIN: Uh . . . Ma, look, I forgot the Coke, huh? Let's do it without it, huh? Just this one song. What say, boys?

MA RAINEY: Damn what the band say! You know I don't sing nothing without my Coca-Cola!

STURDYVANT: We don't have any, Ma. There's no Coca-Cola here. We're all set up and we'll just go ahead and . . .

MA RAINEY: You supposed to have Coca-Cola. Irvin knew that. I ain't singing nothing without my Coca-Cola!

(She walks away from the mike, singing to herself. STURDYVANT enters from the control booth.)

STURDYVANT: Now, just a minute here, Ma. You come in an hour late . . . we're way behind schedule as it is . . . the band is set up and ready to go . . . I'm burning my lights . . . I've turned up the heat . . . We're ready to make a record and what? You decide you want a Coca-Cola?

MA RAINEY: Sturdyvant, get out of my face.

(IRVIN enters.)

Irvin . . . I told you keep him away from me.

IRVIN: Mel, I'll handle it.

STURDYVANT: I'm tired of her nonsense, Irv. I'm not gonna put up with this!

IRVIN: Let me handle it, Mel. I know how to handle her. (IRVIN to MA RAINEY.) Look, Ma . . . I'll call down to the deli and get you a Coke. But let's get started, huh? Sylvester's standing there ready to go . . . the band's set up . . . let's do this one song, huh?

MA RAINEY: If you too cheap to buy me a Coke, I'll buy my own. Slow Drag! Sylvester, go with Slow Drag and get me a Coca-Cola.

(SLOW DRAG *comes over.*)

Slow Drag, walk down to that store on the corner and get me three bottles of Coca-Cola. Get out my face, Irvin. You all just wait until I get my Coke. It ain't gonna kill you.

IRVIN: Okay, Ma. Get your Coke, for Chrissakes! Get your coke!

(IRVIN *and* STURDYVANT *exit into the hallway followed by* SLOW DRAG *and* SYLVESTER. TOLEDO, CUTLER *and* LEVEE *head for the band room.*)

MA RAINEY: Cutler, come here a minute. I want to talk to you.

(CUTLER *crosses over somewhat reluctantly.*)

What's all this about "the boys in the band say"? I tells you what to do. I says what the matter is with the band. I say who can and can't do what.

CUTLER: We just say 'cause the boy stutter . . .

MA RAINEY: I know he stutters. Don't you think I know he stutters. This is what's gonna help him.

CUTLER: Well, how can he do the part if he stutters? You want him to stutter through it? We just thought it be easier to go on and let Levee do it like we planned.

MA RAINEY: I don't care if he stutters or not! He's doing the part and I don't wanna hear any more of this shit about what the band says. And I want you to find somebody to replace Levee when we get to Memphis. Levee ain't nothing but trouble.

CUTLER: Levee's all right. He plays good music when he puts his mind to it. He knows how to write music too.

MA RAINEY: I don't care what he know. He ain't nothing but bad news. Find somebody else. I know it was his idea about who to say who can do what.

(DUSSIE MAE *wanders over to where they are sitting.*)

Dussie Mae, go sit your behind down somewhere and quit flaunting yourself around.

DUSSIE MAE: I ain't doing nothing.

MA RAINEY: Well, just go on somewhere and stay out of the way.

CUTLER: I been meaning to ask you, Ma . . . about these songs. This "Moonshine Blues" . . . that's one of them songs Bessie Smith sang, I believes.

MA RAINEY: Bessie what? Ain't nobody thinking about Bessie. I taught Bessie. She ain't doing nothing but imitating me. What I care about Bessie? I don't care if she sell a million records. She got her people and I got mine. I don't care what nobody else do. Ma was the *first* and don't you forget it!

CUTLER: Ain't nobody said nothing about that. I just said that's the same song she sang.

MA RAINEY: I been doing this a long time. Ever since I was a little girl. I don't care what nobody else do.

That's what gets me so mad with Irvin. White folks try to be put out with you all the time. Too cheap to buy me a Coca-Cola. I lets them know it, though. Ma don't stand for no shit. Wanna take my voice and trap it in them fancy boxes with all them buttons and dials . . . and then too cheap to buy me a Coca-Cola. And it don't cost but a nickle a bottle.

CUTLER: I knows what you mean about that.

MA RAINEY: They don't care nothing about me. All they want is my voice. Well, I done learned that, and they gonna treat me like I want to be treated no matter how much it hurt them. They back there now calling me all kinds of names . . . calling me everything but a child of god. But they can't do nothing else. They ain't got what they wanted yet. As soon as they get my voice down on them recording machines, then it's just like if I'd be some whore and they roll over and put their pants on. Ain't got no use for me then. I know what I'm talking about. You watch. Irvin right there with the rest of them. He don't care nothing about me either. He's been my manager for six years, always talking about sticking together, and the only time he had me in his house was to sing for some of his friends.

CUTLER: I know how they do.

MA RAINEY: If you colored and can make them some money, then you all right with them. Otherwise, you just a dog in the alley. I done made this company more money from my records than all the other recording artists they got put together. And they wanna balk about how much this session is costing them.

CUTLER: I don't see where it's costing them all what they say.

MA RAINEY: It ain't! I don't pay that kind of talk no mind.

(*The lights go down on the studio and come up on the band room.* TOLEDO *sits reading a newspaper.* LEVEE *sings and hums his song.*)

LEVEE: (*Singing*)

> *You can shake it, you can break it*
> *You can dance at any hall*
> *You can slide across the floor*
> *You'll never have to stall*
> *My jelly, my roll,*
> *Sweet Mama, don't you let it fall.*

Wait till Sturdyvant hear me play that! I'm talking about some real music, Toledo! I'm talking about *real* music!

(*The door opens and* DUSSIE MAE *enters.*)

Hey, mama! Come on in.

DUSSIE MAE: Oh, hi! I just wanted to see what it looks like down here.

LEVEE: Well, come on in . . . I don't bite.

DUSSIE MAE: I didn't know you could really write music. I thought you was just jiving me at the club last night.

LEVEE: Naw, baby . . . I knows how to write music. I done give Mr. Sturdyvant some of my songs and he says he's gonna let me record them. Ask Toledo. I'm gonna have my own band! Toledo, ain't I give Mr. Sturdyvant some of my songs I wrote?

TOLEDO: Don't get Toledo mixed up in nothing.

(He exits.)

DUSSIE MAE: You gonna get your own band sure enough?

LEVEE: That's right! Levee Green and his Footstompers.

DUSSIE MAE: That's real nice.

LEVEE: That's what I was trying to tell you last night. A man what's gonna get his own band need to have a woman like you.

DUSSIE MAE: A woman like me wants somebody to bring it and put it in my hand. I don't need nobody wanna get something for nothing and leave me standing in my door.

LEVEE: That ain't Levee's style, sugar. I got more style than that. I knows how to treat a woman. Buy her presents and things . . . treat her like she wants to be treated.

DUSSIE MAE: That's what they all say . . . till it come time to be buying the presents.

LEVEE: When we get down to Memphis, I'm gonna show you what I'm talking about. I'm gonna take you out and show you a good time. Show you Levee knows how to treat a woman.

DUSSIE MAE: When you getting your own band?

LEVEE: *(Moves closer to slip his arm around her)* Soon as Mr. Sturdyvant say. I done got my fellows already picked out. Getting me some good fellows know how to play real sweet music.

DUSSIE MAE: *(Moves away)* Go on now, I don't go for all that pawing and stuff. When you get your own band, maybe we can see about this stuff you talking.

LEVEE: *(Moving toward her)* I just wanna show you I know what the women like. They don't call me Sweet Lemonade for nothing.

(LEVEE takes her in his arms and attempts to kiss her.)

DUSSIE MAE: Stop it now. Somebody's gonna come in here.

LEVEE: Naw they ain't. Look here, sugar . . . what I wanna know is . . . can I introduce my red rooster to your brown hen?

DUSSIE MAE: You get your band, then we'll see if that rooster know how to crow.

(He grinds up against her and feels her buttocks.)

LEVEE: Now I know why my grandpappy sat on the back porch with his straight razor when grandma hung out the wash.

DUSSIE MAE: Nigger, you crazy!

LEVEE: I bet you sound like the midnight train from Alabama when it crosses the Mason-Dixon line.

DUSSIE MAE: How's you get so crazy?

LEVEE: It's women like you . . . drives me that way.

(He moves to kiss her as the lights go down in the band room and up in the studio. MA RAINEY *sits with* CUTLER *and* TOLEDO.*)*

MA RAINEY: It sure done got quiet in here. I never could stand no silence. I always got to have some music going on in my head somewhere. It keeps things balanced. Music will do that. It fills things up. The more music you got in the world, the fuller it is.

CUTLER: I can agree with that. I got to have my music too.

MA RAINEY: White folks don't understand about the blues. They hear it come out, but they don't know how it got there. They don't understand that's life's way of talking. You don't sing to feel better. You sing 'cause that's a way of understanding life.

CUTLER: That's right. You get that understanding and you done got a grip on life to where you can hold your head up and go on to see what else life got to offer.

MA RAINEY: The blues help you get out of bed in the morning. You get up knowing you ain't alone. There's something else in the world. Something's been added by that song. This be an empty world without the blues. I take that emptiness and try to fill it up with something.

TOLEDO: You fill it up with something the people can't be without, Ma. That's why they call you the Mother of the Blues. You fill up that emptiness in a way ain't nobody ever thought of doing before. And now they can't be without it.

MA RAINEY: I ain't started the blues way of singing. The blues always been here.

CUTLER: In the church sometimes you find that way of singing. They got blues in the church.

MA RAINEY: They say I started it . . . but I didn't. I just helped it out. Filled up that empty space a little bit. That's all. But if they wanna call me the Mother of the Blues, that's all right with me. It don't hurt none.

(SLOW DRAG and SYLVESTER enter with the Cokes.)

It sure took you long enough. That store ain't but on the corner.

SLOW DRAG: That one was closed. We had to find another one.

MA RAINEY: Sylvester, go and find Mr. Irvin and tell him we ready to go.

(SYLVESTER *exits. The lights in the band room come up while the lights in the studio stay on.* LEVEE *and* DUSSIE MAE *are kissing.* SLOW DRAG *enters. They break their embrace.* DUSSIE MAE *straightens up her clothes.*)

SLOW DRAG: Cold out. I just wanted to warm up with a little sip.

(*He goes to his locker, takes out his bottle and drinks.*)

Ma got her Coke, Levee. We about ready to start.

(SLOW DRAG *exits.* LEVEE *attempts to kiss* DUSSIE MAE *again.*)

DUSSIE MAE: No . . . Come on! ·I got to go. You gonna get me in trouble.

(*She pulls away and exits up the stairs.* LEVEE *watches after her.*)

LEVEE: Good God! Happy birthday to the lady with the cakes!

(*The lights go down in the band room and come up in the studio.* MA RAINEY *drinks her Coke.* LEVEE *enters from the band room. The musicians take their places.* SYLVESTER *stands by his mike.* IRVIN *and* STURDYVANT *look on from the control booth.*)

IRVIN: We're all set up here, Ma. We're all set to go. You ready down there?

MA RAINEY: Sylvester you just remember your part and say it. That's all there is to it. (*To* IRVIN.) Yeah, we ready.

IRVIN: Okay, boys. "Ma Rainey's Black Bottom." Take one.

CUTLER: One . . . two . . . You know what to do.

(*The band plays.*)

SYLVESTER: All right boys, you d-d-done s-s-seen the rest . . .

IRVIN: Hold it!

(*The band stops.* STURDYVANT *changes the recording disk and nods to* IRVIN.)

Okay. Take two.

CUTLER: One . . . two . . . You know what to do.

(*The band plays.*)

SYLVESTER: All right, boys, you done seen the rest . . . now I'm gonna show you the best. Ma Rainey's g-g-g-gonna s-s-show you her b-b-black bottom.

IRVIN: Hold it! Hold it!

(*The band stops.* STURDYVANT *changes the recording disk.*)

Okay. Take three. Ma, let's do it without the intro, huh? No voice intro . . . you just come in singing.

MA RAINEY: Irvin, I done told you . . . the boy's gonna do the part. He don't stutter all the time. Just give

him a chance. Sylvester, hold your hands like I told you and just relax. Just relax and concentrate.

IRVIN: All right. Take three.

CUTLER: One . . . two . . . You know what to do.

(*The band plays.*)

SYLVESTER: All right, boys, you done seen the rest . . . now, I'm gonna show you the best. Ma Rainey's gonna show you her black bottom.

MA RAINEY: (*Singing*)

Way down south in Alabamy
I got a friend they call dancing Sammy
Who's crazy about all the latest dances
Black Bottom stomping, two babies prancing

The other night at a swell affair
As soon as the boys found out that I was there
They said, come on, Ma, let's go to the cabaret.
When I got there, you ought to hear them say,

I want to see the dance you call the black bottom
I want to learn that dance
I want to see the dance you call your big black bottom
It'll put you in a trance.

All the boys in the neighborhood
They say your black bottom is really good
Come on and show me your black bottom
I want to learn that dance

I want to see the dance you call the black bottom
I want to learn that dance
Come on and show the dance you call your big black bottom
It puts you in a trance.

Early last morning about the break of day
Grandpa told my grandma, I heard him say,
Get up and show your old man your black bottom
I want to learn that dance.

(*Instrumental break.*)

I done showed you all my black bottom
You ought to learn that dance.

IRVIN: Okay, that's good, Ma. That sounded great! Good job, boys!

MA RAINEY: (*To* SYLVESTER) See! I told you. I knew you could do it. You just have to put your mind to it. Didn't he do good, Cutler? Sound real good. I told him he could do it.

CUTLER: He sure did. He did better than I thought he was gonna do.

IRVIN: (*Entering to remove* SYLVESTER's *mike*) Okay, boys

... Ma ... let's do "Moonshine Blues" next, huh? "Moonshine Blues," boys.

STURDYVANT: (*Over speaker*) Irv! Something's wrong down there. We don't have it right.

IRVIN: What? What's the matter Mel ...

STURDYVANT: We don't have it right. Something happened. We don't have the goddamn song recorded!

IRVIN: What's the matter? Mel, what happened? You sure you don't have nothing?

STURDYVANT: Check that mike, huh, Irv. It's the kid's mike. Something's wrong with the mike. We've got everything all screwed up here.

IRVIN: Christ almighty! Ma, we got to do it again. We don't have it. We didn't record the song.

MA RAINEY: What you mean you didn't record it? What was you and Sturdyvant doing up there?

IRVIN: (*Following the mike wire*) Here ... Levee must have kicked the plug out.

LEVEE: I ain't done nothing. I ain't kicked nothing!

SLOW DRAG: If Levee had his mind on what he's doing ...

MA RAINEY: Levee, if it ain't one thing, it's another. You better straighten yourself up!

LEVEE: Hell ... it ain't my fault. I ain't done nothing!

STURDYVANT: What's the matter with that mike, Irv? What's the problem?

IRVIN: It's the cord, Mel. The cord's all chewed up. We need another cord.

MA RAINEY: This is the most disorganized ... Irvin, I'm going home! Come on. Come on, Dussie.

(MA RAINEY *walks past* STURDYVANT *as he enters from the control booth. She exits offstage to get her coat.*)

STURDYVANT: (*To* IRVIN) Where's she going?

IRVIN: She said she's going home.

STURDYVANT: Irvin, you get her! If she walks out of here ...

(MA RAINEY *enters carrying her and* DUSSIE MAE's *coat.*)

MA RAINEY: Come on, Sylvester.

IRVIN: (*Helping her with her coat*) Ma ... Ma ... listen. Fifteen minutes! All I ask is fifteen minutes!

MA RAINEY: Come on, Sylvester, get your coat.

STURDYVANT: Ma, if you walk out of this studio ...

IRVIN: Fifteen minutes, Ma!

STURDYVANT: You'll be through ... washed up! If you walk out on me ...

IRVIN: Mel, for Chrissakes, shut up and let me handle it!

(*He goes after* MA RAINEY, *who has started for the door.*)

Ma, listen. These records are gonna be hits! They're gonna sell like crazy! Hell, even Sylvester will be a star. Fifteen minutes. That's all I'm asking! Fifteen minutes.

MA RAINEY: (*Crosses to a chair and sits with her coat on*) Fifteen minutes! You hear me, Irvin? Fifteen min-utes ... and then I'm gonna take my black bottom on back down to Georgia. Fifteen minutes. Then Madame Rainey is leaving!

IRVIN: (*Kisses her*) All right, Ma ... fifteen minutes. I promise. (*To the band.*) You boys go ahead and take a break. Fifteen minutes and we'll be ready to go.

CUTLER: Slow Drag, you got any of that bourbon left?

SLOW DRAG: Yeah, there's some down there.

CUTLER: I could use a little nip.

(CUTLER *and* SLOW DRAG *exit to the band room, followed by* LEVEE *and* TOLEDO. *The lights go down in the studio and up in the band room.*)

SLOW DRAG: Don't make me no difference if she leave or not. I was kinda hoping she would leave.

CUTLER: I'm like Mr. Irvin ... After all this time we done put in here, it's best to go ahead and get something out of it.

TOLEDO: Ma gonna do what she wanna do, that's for sure. If I was Mr. Irvin, I'd best go on and get them cords and things hooked up right. And I wouldn't take no longer than fifteen minutes doing it.

CUTLER: If Levee had his mind on his work, we wouldn't be in this fix. We'd be up there finishing up. Now we got to go back and see if that boy get that part right. Ain't no telling if he ever get that right again in his life.

LEVEE: Hey, Levee ain't done nothing!

SLOW DRAG: Levee up there got one eye on the gal and the other on his trumpet.

CUTLER: Nigger, don't you know that's Ma's gal?

LEVEE: I don't care whose gal it is. I ain't done nothing to her. I just talk to her like I talk to anybody else.

CUTLER: Well, that being Ma's gal, and that being that boy's gal, is one and two different things. The boy is liable to kill you ... but you' ass gonna be out there scraping the concrete looking for a job if you messing with Ma's gal.

LEVEE: How am I messing with her? I ain't done nothing to the gal. I just asked her her name. Now, if you telling me I can't do that, then Ma will just have to go to hell.

CUTLER: All I can do is warn you.

SLOW DRAG: Let him hang himself, Cutler. Let him string his neck out.

LEVEE: I ain't done nothing to the gal! You all talk like I done went and done something to her. Leave me go with my business.

CUTLER: I'm through with it. Try and talk to a fool ...

TOLEDO: Some mens got it worse than others ... this foolishness I'm talking about. Some mens is excited to be fools. That excitement is something else. I know about it. I done experienced it. It makes you feel good to be a fool. But it don't last long. It's over in a minute. Then you got to tend with the consequences. You got to tend with what comes after.

That's when you wish you had learned something about it.

LEVEE: That's the best sense you made all day. Talking about being a fool. That's the only sensible thing you said today. Admitting you was a fool.

TOLEDO: I admits it, all right. Ain't nothing wrong with it. I done been a little bit of everything.

LEVEE: Now you're talking. You's as big a fool as they make.

TOLEDO: Gonna be a bit more things before I'm finished with it. Gonna be foolish again. But I ain't never been the same fool twice. I might be a different kind of fool, but I ain't gonna be the same fool twice. That's where we parts ways.

SLOW DRAG: Toledo, you done been a fool about a woman?

TOLEDO: Sure. Sure I have. Same as everybody.

SLOW DRAG: Hell, I ain't never seen you mess with no woman. I thought them books was your woman.

TOLEDO: Sure I messed with them. Done messed with a whole heap of them. And gonna mess with some more. But I ain't gonna be no fool about them. What you think? I done come in the world full-grown, with my head in a book? I done been young. Married. Got kids. I done been around and I done loved women to where you shake in your shoes just at the sight of them. Feel it all up and down your spine.

SLOW DRAG: I didn't know you was married.

TOLEDO: Sure. Legally. I been married legally. Got the papers and all. I done been through life. Made my marks. Followed some signs on the road. Ignored some others. I done been all through it. I touched and been touched by it. But I ain't never been the same fool twice. That's what I can say.

LEVEE: But you been a fool. That's what counts. Talking about I'm a fool for asking the gal her name and here you is one yourself.

TOLEDO: Now, I married a woman. A good woman. To this day I can't say she wasn't a good woman. I can't say nothing bad about her. I married that woman with all the good graces and intentions of being hooked up and bound to her for the rest of my life. I was looking for her to put me in my grave. But, you see . . . it ain't all the time what you' intentions and wishes are. She went out and joined the church. All right. There ain't nothing wrong with that. A good Christian woman going to church and wanna do right by her god. There ain't nothing wrong with that. But she got up there, got to seeing them good Christian mens and wondering why I ain't like that. Soon she figure she got a heathen on her hands. She figured she couldn't live like that. The church was more important than I was. So she left. Packed up one day and moved out. To this day I ain't never said another word to her. Come home one day and my house was empty! And I sat down

and figured out that I was a fool not to see that she needed something that I wasn't giving her. Else she wouldn't have been up there at the church in the first place. I ain't blaming her. I just said it wasn't gonna happen to me again. So, yeah, Toledo been a fool about a woman. That's part of making life.

CUTLER: Well, yeah, I been a fool too. Everybody done been a fool once or twice. But, you see, Toledo, what you call a fool and what I call a fool is two different things. I can't see where you was being a fool for that. You ain't done nothing foolish. You can't help what happened, and I wouldn't call you a fool for it. A fool is responsible for what happens to him. A fool cause it to happen. Like Levee . . . if he keeps messing with Ma's gal and his feet be out there scraping the ground. That's a fool.

LEVEE: Ain't nothing gonna happen to Levee. Levee ain't gonna let nothing happen to him. Now, I'm gonna say it again. I asked the gal her name. That's all I done. And if that's being a fool, then you looking at the biggest fool in the world . . . 'cause I sure as hell asked her.

SLOW DRAG: You just better not let Ma see you ask her. That's what the man's trying to tell you.

LEVEE: I don't need nobody to tell me nothing.

CUTLER: Well, Toledo, all I gots to say is that from the looks of it . . . from your story . . . I don't think life did you fair.

TOLEDO: Oh, life is fair. It's just in the taking what it gives you.

LEVEE: Life ain't shit. You can put it in a paper bag and carry it around with you. It ain't got no balls. Now, death . . . death got some style! Death will kick your ass and make you wish you never been born! That's how bad death is! But you can rule over life. Life ain't nothing.

TOLEDO: Cutler, how's your brother doing?

CUTLER: Who, Nevada? Oh, he's doing all right. Staying in St. Louis. Got a bunch of kids, last I heard.

TOLEDO: Me and him was all right with each other. Done a lot of farming together down in Plattsville.

CUTLER: Yeah, I know you all was tight. He in St. Louis now. Running an elevator, last I hear about it.

SLOW DRAG: That's better than stepping in muleshit.

TOLEDO: Oh, I don't know now. I liked farming. Get out there in the sun . . . smell that dirt. Be out there by yourself . . . nice and peaceful. Yeah, farming was all right by me. Sometimes I think I'd like to get me a little old place . . . but I done got too old to be following behind one of them balky mules now.

LEVEE: Nigger talking about life is fair. And ain't got a pot to piss in.

TOLEDO: See, now, I'm gonna tell you something. A nigger gonna be dissatisfied no matter what. Give a nigger some bread and butter . . . and he'll cry 'cause he ain't got no jelly. Give him some jelly, and he'll cry 'cause he ain't got no knife to put it on with. If there's one thing I done learned in this life, it's that you can't satisfy a nigger no matter what you do. A nigger's gonna make his own dissatisfaction.

LEVEE: Niggers got a right to be dissatisfied. Is you gonna be satisfied with a bone somebody done throwed you when you see them eating the whole hog?

TOLEDO: You lucky they let you be an entertainer. They ain't got to accept your way of entertaining. You lucky and don't even know it. You's entertaining and the rest of the people is hauling wood. That's the only kind of job for the colored man.

SLOW DRAG: Ain't nothing wrong with hauling wood. I done hauled plenty wood. My daddy used to haul wood. Ain't nothing wrong with that. That's honest work.

LEVEE: That ain't what I'm talking about. I ain't talking about hauling no wood. I'm talking about being satisfied with a bone somebody done throwed you. That's what's the matter with you all. You satisfied sitting in one place. You got to move on down the road from where you sitting . . . and all the time you got to keep an eye out for that devil who's looking to buy up souls. And hope you get lucky and find him!

CUTLER: I done told you about that blasphemy. Talking about selling your soul to the devil.

TOLEDO: We done the same thing, Cutler. There ain't no difference. We done sold Africa for the price of tomatoes. We done sold ourselves to the white man in order to be like him. Look at the way you dressed . . . That ain't African. That's the white man. We trying to be just like him. We done sold who we are in order to become someone else. We's imitation white men.

CUTLER: What else we gonna be, living over here?

LEVEE: I'm Levee. Just me. I ain't no imitation nothing!

SLOW DRAG: You can't change who you are by how you dress. That's what I got to say.

TOLEDO: It ain't all how you dress. It's how you act, how you see the world. It's how you follow life.

LEVEE: It don't matter what you talking about. I ain't no imitation white man. And I don't want to be no white man. As soon as I get my band together and make them records like Mr. Sturdyvant done told me I can make, I'm gonna be like Ma and tell the white man just what he can do. Ma tell Mr. Irvin she gonna leave . . . and Mr. Irvin get down on his knees and beg her to stay! That's the way I'm gonna be! Make the white man respect me!

CUTLER: The white man don't care nothing about Ma. The colored folks made Ma a star. White folks don't care nothing about who she is . . . what kind of music she make.

SLOW DRAG: That's the truth about that. You let her go down to one of them white-folks hotels and see how big she is.

CUTLER: Hell, she ain't got to do that. She can't even get a cab up here in the North. I'm gonna tell you something. Reverend Gates . . . you know Reverend Gates? . . . Slow Drag know who I'm talking about. Reverend Gates . . . now I'm gonna show you how this go where the white man don't care a thing about who you is. Reverend Gates was coming from Tallahassee to Atlanta, going to see his sister, who was sick at that time with the consumption. The train come up through Thomasville, then past Moultrie, and stopped in this little town called Sigsbee . . .

LEVEE: You can stop telling that right there! That train don't stop in Sigsbee. I know what train you talking about. That train got four stops before it reach Macon to go on to Atlanta. One in Thomasville, one in Moultrie, one in Cordele . . . and it stop in Centerville.

CUTLER: Nigger, I know what I'm talking about. You gonna tell me where the train stop?

LEVEE: Hell, yeah, if you talking about it stop in Sigsbee. I'm gonna tell you the truth.

CUTLER: I'm taking about *this* train! I don't know what train you been riding. I'm talking about *this* train!

LEVEE: Ain't but one train. Ain't but one train come out of Tallahassee heading north to Atlanta, and it don't stop at Sigsbee. Tell him, Toledo . . . that train don't stop at Sigsbee. The only train that stops at Sigsbee is the Yazoo Delta, and you have to transfer at Moultrie to get it!

CUTLER: Well, hell, maybe that what he done! I don't know. I'm just telling you the man got off the train at Sigsbee . . .

LEVEE: All right . . . you telling it. Tell it your way. Just make up anything.

SLOW DRAG: Levee, leave the man alone and let him finish.

CUTLER: I ain't paying Levee no never mind.

LEVEE: Go on and tell it your way.

CUTLER: Anyway . . . Reverend Gates got off this train in Sigsbee. The train done stopped there and he figured he'd get off and check the schedule to be sure he arrive in time for somebody to pick him up. All right. While he's there checking the schedule, it come upon him that he had to go to the bathroom. Now, they ain't had no colored rest rooms at the station. The only colored rest room is an outhouse they got sitting way back two hundred yards or so from the station. All right. He in the outhouse and the train go off and leave him there. He don't know nothing about this town. Ain't never been there before—in fact, ain't never even heard of it before.

LEVEE: I heard of it! I know just where it's at . . . and he ain't got off no train coming out of Tallahassee in Sigsbee!

CUTLER: The man standing there, trying to figure out what he's gonna do . . . where this train done left him in this strange town. It started getting dark. He see where the sun's getting low in the sky and he's trying to figure out what he's gonna do, when he noticed a couple of white fellows standing across the street from this station. Just standing there, watching him. And then two or three more come up and joined the other one. He look around, ain't seen no colored folks nowhere. He didn't know what was getting in these here fellows' minds, so he commence to walking. He ain't knowed where he was going. He just walking down the railroad tracks when he hear them call him. "Hey, nigger!" See, just like that. "Hey, nigger!" He kept on walking. They called him some more and he just keep walking. Just going down the tracks. And then he heard a gunshot where somebody done fired a gun in the air. He stopped then, you know.

TOLEDO: You don't even have to tell me no more. I know the facts of it. I done heard the same story a hundred times. It happened to me too. Same thing.

CUTLER: Naw, I'm gonna show you how the white folks don't care nothing about who or what you is. They crowded around him. These gang of mens made a circle around him. Now, he's standing there, you understand . . . got his cross around his neck like them preachers wear. Had his little Bible with him what he carry all the time. So they crowd on around him and one of them ask who he is. He told them he was Reverend Gates and that he was going to see his sister who was sick and the train left without him. And they said, "Yeah, nigger . . . but can you dance?" He looked at them and commenced to dancing. One of them reached up and tore his cross off his neck. Said he was committing a heresy by dancing with a cross and Bible. Took his Bible and tore it up and had him dancing till they got tired of watching him.

SLOW DRAG: White folks ain't never had no respect for the colored minister.

CUTLER: That's the only way he got out of there alive . . . was to dance. Ain't even had no respect for a man of God! Wanna make him into a clown. Reverend Gates sat right in my house and told me that story from his own mouth. So . . . the white folks don't care nothing about Ma Rainey. She's just another nigger who they can use to make some money.

LEVEE: What I wants to know is . . . if he's a man of God, then where the hell was God when all of this was going on? Why wasn't God looking out for him. Why didn't God strike down them crackers with some of this lightning you talk about to me?

CUTLER: Levee, you gonna burn in hell.

LEVEE: What I care about burning in hell? You talk like a fool . . . burning in hell. Why didn't God strike some of them crackers down? Tell me that! That's

the question! Don't come telling me this burning-in-hell shit! He a man of God . . . why didn't God strike some of them crackers down? I'll tell you why! I'll tell you the truth! It's sitting out there as plain as day! 'Cause he a white man's God. That's why! God ain't never listened to no nigger's prayers. God take a nigger's prayers and throw them in the garbage. God don't pay niggers no mind. In fact . . . God hate niggers! Hate them with all the fury in his heart. Jesus don't love you, nigger! Jesus hate your black ass! Come talking that shit to me. Talking about burning in hell! God can kiss my ass.

(CUTLER *can stand no more. He jumps up and punches* LEVEE *in the mouth. The force of the blow knocks* LEVEE *down and* CUTLER *jumps on him.*)

CUTLER: You worthless . . . That's my God! That's my God! That's my God! You wanna blaspheme my God!

(TOLEDO *and* SLOW DRAG *grab* CUTLER *and try to pull him off* LEVEE.)

SLOW DRAG: Come on, Cutler . . . let it go! It don't mean nothing!

(CUTLER *has* LEVEE *down on the floor and pounds on him with a fury.*)

CUTLER: Wanna blaspheme my God! You worthless . . . talking about my God!

(TOLEDO *and* SLOW DRAG *succeed in pulling* CUTLER *off* LEVEE, *who is bleeding at the nose and mouth.*)

LEVEE: Naw, let him go! Let him go!

(*He pulls out a knife.*)

That's your God, huh? That's your God, huh? Is that right? Your God, huh? All right. I'm gonna give your God a chance. I'm gonna give your God a chance. I'm gonna give him a chance to save your black ass.

(LEVEE *circles* CUTLER *with the knife.* CUTLER *picks up a chair to protect himself.*)

TOLEDO: Come on, Levee . . . put the knife up!

LEVEE: Stay out of this, Toledo!

TOLEDO: That ain't no way to solve nothing.

(LEVEE *alternately swipes at* CUTLER *during the following.*)

LEVEE: I'm calling Cutler's God! I'm talking to Cutler's God! You hear me? Cutler's God! I'm calling Cutler's God. Come on and save this nigger! Strike me down before I cut his throat!

SLOW DRAG: Watch him, Cutler! Put that knife up, Levee!

LEVEE: (*To* CUTLER) I'm calling your God! I'm gonna

give him a chance to save you! I'm calling your God! We gonna find out whose God he is!

CUTLER: You gonna burn in hell, nigger!

LEVEE: Cutler's God! Come on and save this nigger! Come on and save him like you did my mama! Save him like you did my mama! I heard her when she called you! I heard her when she said, "Lord, have mercy! Jesus, help me! Please, God, have mercy on me, Lord Jesus, help me!" And did you turn your back? Did you turn your back, motherfucker? Did you turn your back?

(LEVEE *becomes so caught up in his dialogue with God that he forgets about* CUTLER *and begins to stab upward in the air, trying to reach God.*)

Come on! Come on and turn your back on me! Turn your back on me! Come on! Where is you? Come on and turn your back on me! Turn your back on me, motherfucker! I'll cut your heart out! Come on, turn your back on me! Come on! What's the matter? Where is you? Come on and turn your back on me! Come on, what you scared of? Turn your back on me! Come on! Coward, motherfucker!

(LEVEE *folds his knife and stands triumphantly.*)

Your God ain't shit, Cutler.

(*The lights fade to black.*)

MA RAINEY: (*Singing*)

Ah, you hear me talking to you
I don't bite my tongue
You wants to be my man
You got to fetch it with you when you come.

(*Lights come up in the studio. The last bars of the last song of the session are dying out.*)

IRVIN: (*Over speaker*) Good! Wonderful! We have that, boys. Good session. That's great, Ma. We've got ourselves some winners.

TOLEDO: Well, I'm glad that's over.

MA RAINEY: Slow Drag, where you learn to play the bass at? You had it singing! I heard you! Had that bass jumping all over the place.

SLOW DRAG: I was following Toledo. Nigger got them long fingers striding all over the piano. I was trying to keep up with him.

TOLEDO: That's what you supposed to do, ain't it? Play the music. Ain't nothing abstract about it.

MA RAINEY: Cutler, you hear Slow Drag on that bass? He make it do what he want it to do! Spank it just like you spank a baby.

CUTLER: Don't be telling him that. Nigger's head get so big his hat won't fit him.

SLOW DRAG: If Cutler tune that guitar up, we would really have something!

CUTLER: You wouldn't know what a tuned-up guitar sounded like if you heard one.

TOLEDO: Cutler was talking. I heard him moaning. He was all up in it.

MA RAINEY: Levee . . . what is that you doing? Why you playing all them notes? You play ten notes for every one you supposed to play. It don't call for that.

LEVEE: You supposed to improvise on the theme. That's what I was doing.

MA RAINEY: You supposed to play the song the way I sing it. The way everybody else play it. You ain't supposed to go off by yourself and play what you want.

LEVEE: I was playing the song. I was playing it the way I felt it.

MA RAINEY: I couldn't keep up with what was going on. I'm trying to sing the song and you up there messing up my ear. That's what you was doing. Call yourself playing music.

LEVEE: Hey . . . I know what I'm doing. I know what I'm doing, all right. I know how to play music. You all back up and leave me alone about my music.

CUTLER: I done told you . . . it ain't about *your* music. It's about *Ma's* music.

MA RAINEY: That's all right, Cutler. I done told you what to do.

LEVEE: I don't care what you do. You supposed to improvise on the theme. Not play note for note the same thing over and over again.

MA RAINEY: You just better watch yourself. You hear me?

LEVEE: What I care what you or Cutler do? Come telling me to watch myself. What's that supposed to mean?

MA RAINEY: All right . . . you gonna find out what it means.

LEVEE: Go ahead and fire me. I don't care. I'm gonna get my own band anyway.

MA RAINEY: You keep messing with me.

LEVEE: Ain't nobody studying you. You ain't gonna do nothing to me. Ain't nobody gonna do nothing to Levee.

MA RAINEY: All right, nigger . . . you fired!

LEVEE: You think I care about being fired? I don't care nothing about that. You doing me a favor.

MA RAINEY: Cutler, Levee's out! He don't play in my band no more.

LEVEE: I'm fired . . . Good! Best thing that ever happened to me. I don't need this shit!

(LEVEE *exits to the band room.* IRVIN *enters from the control booth.*)

MA RAINEY: Cutler, I'll see you back at the hotel.

IRVIN: Okay, boys . . . you can pack up. I'll get your money for you.

CUTLER: That's cash money, Mr. Irvin. I don't want no check.

IRVIN: I'll see what I can do. I can't promise you nothing.

CUTLER: As long as it ain't no check. I ain't got no use for a check.

IRVIN: I'll see what I can do, Cutler.

(CUTLER, TOLEDO, *and* SLOW DRAG *exit to the band room.*)

Oh, Ma, listen . . . I talked to Sturdyvant, and he said . . . Now, I tried to talk him out of it . . . He said the best he can do is to take your twenty-five dollars of your money and give it to Sylvester.

MA RAINEY: Take what and do what? If I wanted the boy to have twenty-five dollars of my money, I'd give it to him. He supposed to get his own money. He supposed to get paid like everybody else.

IRVIN: Ma, I talked to him . . . He said . . .

MA RAINEY: Go talk to him again! Tell him if he don't pay that boy, he'll never make another record of mine again. Tell him that. You supposed to be my manager. All this talk about sticking together. Start sticking! Go on up there and get that boy his money!

IRVIN: Okay, Ma . . . I'll talk to him again. I'll see what I can do.

MA RAINEY: Ain't no see about it! You bring that boy's money back here!

(IRVIN *exits. The lights stay on in the studio and come up in the band room. The men have their instruments packed and sit waiting for* IRVIN *to come and pay them.* SLOW DRAG *has a pack of cards.*)

SLOW DRAG: Come on, Levee, let me show you a card trick.

LEVEE: I don't want to see no card trick. What you wanna show me for? Why you wanna bother me with that?

SLOW DRAG: I was just trying to be nice.

LEVEE: I don't need you to be nice to me. What I need you to be nice to me for? I ain't gonna be nice to you. I ain't even gonna let you be in my band no more.

SLOW DRAG: Toledo, let me show you a card trick.

CUTLER: I just hope Mr. Irvin don't bring no check down here. What the hell I'm gonna do with a check?

SLOW DRAG: All right now . . . pick a card. Any card . . . go on . . . take any of them. I'm gonna show you something.

TOLEDO: I agrees with you, Cutler. I don't want no check either.

CUTLER: It don't make no sense to give a nigger a check.

SLOW DRAG: Okay, now. Remember your card. Remember which one you got. Now . . . put it back in the deck. Anywhere you want. I'm gonna show you something.

(TOLEDO *puts the card in the deck.*)

You remember your card? All right. Now I'm gonna shuffle the deck. Now . . . I'm gonna show you what card you picked. Don't say nothing now. I'm gonna tell you what card you picked.

CUTLER: Slow Drag, that trick is as old as my mama.

SLOW DRAG: Naw, naw . . . wait a minute! I'm gonna show him his card . . . There it go! The six of diamonds. Ain't that your card? Ain't that it?

TOLEDO: Yeah, that's it . . . the six of diamonds.

SLOW DRAG: Told you! Told you I'd show him what it was!

(*The lights fade in the band room and come up full on the studio.* STURDYVANT *enters with* IRVIN.)

STURDYVANT: Ma, is there something wrong? Is there a problem?

MA RAINEY: Sturdyvant, I want you to pay that boy his money.

STURDYVANT: Sure, Ma. I got it right here. Two hundred for you and twenty-five for the kid, right?

(STURDYVANT *hands the money to* IRVIN, *who hands it to* MA RAINEY *and* SYLVESTER.)

Irvin misunderstood me. It was all a mistake. Irv made a mistake.

MA RAINEY: A mistake, huh?

IRVIN: Sure, Ma. I made a mistake. He's paid, right? I straightened it out.

MA RAINEY: The only mistake was when you found out I hadn't signed the release forms. That was the mistake. Come on, Sylvester.

(*She starts to exit.*)

STURDYVANT: Hey, Ma . . . come on, sign the forms, huh?

IRVIN: Ma . . . come on now.

MA RAINEY: Get your coat, Sylvester. Irvin, where's my car?

IRVIN: It's right out front, Ma. Here . . . I got the keys right here. Come on, sign the forms, huh?

MA RAINEY: Irvin, give me my car keys!

IRVIN: Sure, Ma . . . just sign the forms, huh?

(*He gives her the keys, expecting a trade-off.*)

MA RAINEY: Send them to my address and I'll get around to them.

IRVIN: Come on, Ma . . . I took care of everything, right? I straightened everything out.

MA RAINEY: Give me the pen, Irvin.

(*She signs the forms.*)

You tell Sturdyvant . . . one more mistake like that and I can make my records someplace else.

(*She turns to exit.*)

Sylvester, straighten up your clothes. Come on, Dussie Mae.

(She exits, followed by DUSSIE MAE *and* SYLVESTER. *The lights go down in the studio and come up on the band room.)*

CUTLER: I know what's keeping him so long. He up there writing out checks. You watch. I ain't gonna stand for it. He ain't gonna bring me no check down here. If he do, he's gonna take it right back upstairs and get some cash.

TOLEDO: Don't get yourself all worked up about it. Wait and see. Think positive.

CUTLER: I am thinking positive. He positively gonna give me some cash. Man give me a check last time . . . you remember . . . we went all over Chicago trying to get it cashed. See a nigger with a check, the first thing they think is he done stole it someplace.

LEVEE: I ain't had no trouble cashing mine.

CUTLER: I don't visit no whorehouses.

LEVEE: You don't know about my business. So don't start nothing. I'm tired of you as it is. I ain't but two seconds off your ass no way.

TOLEDO: Don't you all start nothing now.

CUTLER: What the hell I care what you tired of. I wasn't even talking to you. I was talking to this man right here.

*(*IRVIN *and* STURDYVANT *enter.)*

IRVIN: Okay boys. Mr. Sturdyvant has your pay.

CUTLER: As long as it's cash money, Mr. Sturdyvant. 'Cause I have too much trouble trying to cash a check.

STURDYVANT: Oh, yes . . . I'm aware of that. Mr. Irvin told me you boys prefer cash, and that's what I have for you.

(He starts handing out the money.)

That was a good session you boys put in . . . That's twenty-five for you. Yessir, you boys really know your business and we are going to . . . Twenty-five for you . . . We are going to get you back in here real soon . . . twenty-five . . . and have another session so you can make some more money . . . and twenty-five for you. Okay, thank you, boys. You can get your things together and Mr. Irvin will make sure you find your way out.

IRVIN: I'll be out front when you get your things together, Cutler.

*(*IRVIN *exits.* STURDYVANT *starts to follow.)*

LEVEE: Mr. Sturdyvant, sir. About them songs I give you? . . .

STURDYVANT: Oh, yes, . . . uh . . . Levee. About them songs you gave me. I've thought about it and I just don't think the people will buy them. They're not the type of songs we're looking for.

LEVEE: Mr. Sturdyvant, sir . . . I done got my band picked out and they's real good fellows. They knows how to play real good. I know if the peoples hear the music, they'll buy it.

STURDYVANT: Well, Levee, I'll be fair with you . . . but they're just not the right songs.

LEVEE: Mr. Sturdyvant, you got to understand about that music. That music is what the people is looking for. They's tired of jug-band music. They wants something that excites them. Something with some fire to it.

STURDYVANT: Okay, Levee. I'll tell you what I'll do. I'll give you five dollars a piece for them. Now that's the best I can do.

LEVEE: I don't want no five dollars, Mr. Sturdyvant. I wants to record them songs, like you say.

STURDYVANT: Well, Levee, like I say . . . they just aren't the kind of songs we're looking for.

LEVEE: Mr. Sturdyvant, you asked me to write them songs. Now, why didn't you tell me that before when I first give them to you? You told me you was gonna let me record them. What's the difference between then and now?

STURDYVANT: Well, look . . . I'll pay you for your trouble . . .

LEVEE: What's the difference, Mr. Sturdyvant? That's what I wanna know.

STURDYVANT: I had my fellows play your songs, and when I heard then, they just didn't sound like the kind of songs I'm looking for right now.

LEVEE: You got to hear *me* play them, Mr. Sturdyvant! You ain't heard *me* play them. That's what's gonna make them sound right.

STURDYVANT: Well, Levee, I don't doubt that really. It's just that . . . well, I don't thnk they'd sell like Ma's records. But I'll take them off your hands for you.

LEVEE: The people's tired of jug-band music, Mr. Sturdyvant. They wants something that's gonna excite them! They wants something with some fire! I don't know what fellows you had playing them songs . . . but if I could play them! I'd set them down in the people's lap! Now you told me I could record them songs!

STURDYVANT: Well, there's nothing I can do about that. Like I say, it's five dollars a piece. That's what I'll give you. I'm doing you a favor. Now, if you write any more, I'll help you out and take them off your hands. The price is five dollars apiece. Just like now.

(He attempts to hand LEVEE *the money, finally shoves it in* LEVEE's *coat pocket and is gone in a flash.* LEVEE *follows him to the door and it slams in his face. He takes the money from his pocket, balls it up and throws it on the floor. The other musicians silently gather up their belongings.* TOLEDO *walks past* LEVEE *and steps on his shoe.)*

LEVEE: Hey! Watch it . . . Shit Toledo! You stepped on my shoe!

TOLEDO: Excuse me there, Levee.

LEVEE: Look at that! Look at that! Nigger, you stepped on my shoe. What you do that for?

TOLEDO: I said I'm sorry.

LEVEE: Nigger gonna step on my goddamn shoe! You done fucked up my shoe! Look at that! Look at what you done to my shoe, nigger! I ain't stepped on your shoe! What you wanna step on my shoe for?

CUTLER: The man said he's sorry.

LEVEE: Sorry! How the hell he gonna be sorry after he gone ruint my shoe? Come talking about sorry!

(Turns his attention back to TOLEDO.*)*

Nigger, you stepped on my shoe! You know that!

*(*LEVEE *snatches his shoe off his foot and holds it up for* TOLEDO *to see.)*

See what you done done?

TOLEDO: What you want me to do about it? It's done now. I said excuse me.

LEVEE: Wanna go and fuck up my shoe like that. I ain't done nothing to your shoe. Look at this!

*(*TOLEDO *turns and continues to gather up his things.* LEVEE *spins him around by his shoulder.)*

LEVEE: Naw . . . naw . . . look what you done!

(He shoves the shoe in TOLEDO's *face.)*

Look at that! That's my shoe! Look at that! You did it! You did it! You fucked up my shoe! You stepped on my shoe with them raggedy-ass clodhoppers!

TOLEDO: Nigger, ain't nobody studying you and your shoe! I said excuse me. If you can't accept that, then the hell with it. What you want me to do?

*(*LEVEE *is in a near rage, breathing hard. He is trying to get a grip on himself, as even he senses, or perhaps only he senses, he is about to lose control. He looks around, uncertain of what to do.* TOLEDO *has gone back to packing, as have* CUTLER *and* SLOW DRAG. *They purposefully avoid looking at* LEVEE *in hopes he'll calm down if he doesn't have an audience. All the weight in the world suddenly falls on* LEVEE *and he rushes at* TOLEDO *with his knife in his hand.)*

LEVEE: Nigger, you stepped on my shoe!

(He plunges the knife into TOLEDO's *back up to the hilt.* TOLEDO *lets out a sound of surprise and agony.* CUTLER *and* SLOW DRAG *freeze.* TOLEDO *falls backward with* LEVEE, *his hand still on the knife, holding him up.* LEVEE *is suddenly faced with the realization of what he has done. He shoves* TOLEDO *forward and takes a step back.* TOLEDO *slumps to the floor.)*

He . . . he stepped on my shoe. He did. Honest, Cutler, he stepped on my shoe. What he do that for? Toledo, what you do that for? Cutler, help me. He stepped on my shoe, Cutler.

(He turns his attention to TOLEDO.*)*

Toledo! Toledo, get up.

(He crosses to TOLEDO *and tries to pick him up.)*

It's okay, Toledo. Come on . . . I'll help you. Come on, stand up now. Levee'll help you.

*(*TOLEDO *is limp and heavy and awkward. He slumps back to the floor.* LEVEE *gets mad at him.)*

Don't look at me like that! Toledo! Nigger, don't look at me like that! I'm warning you, nigger! Close your eyes! Don't you look at me like that! (*He turns to* CUTLER) Tell him to close his eyes. Cutler. Tell him don't look at me like that.

CUTLER: Slow Drag, get Mr. Irvin down here.

(The sound of a trumpet is heard, LEVEE's *trumpet, a muted trumpet struggling for the highest of possibilities and blowing pain and warning.)*
(Black out.)

Figure 1. Irvin (Lou Criscuolo) cringingly tries to placate Ma Rainey (Theresa Merrit), while Toledo (Robert Judd), Cutler (Joe Seneca, *partly hidden*), and Sturdyvant (Richard M. Davidson) listen to Ma's complaints in the Yale Repertory Theatre production of *Ma Rainey's Black Bottom*, directed by Lloyd Richards, 1984. (Photograph: William B. Carter.)

Figure 2. Levee (Charles S. Dutton) dances and sings a jazz tune—
"Hello Central give me Doctor Jazz"—accompanied by Slow Drag (Leon-
ard Jackson), while Toledo (Robert Judd) tries to convince Cutler (Joe
Seneca) that "Good times got more niggers killed than God got ways to
count" in the Yale Repertory Theatre production of *Ma Rainey's Black
Bottom,* directed by Lloyd Richards, 1984. (Photograph: William B.
Carter.)

Staging of *Ma Rainey's Black Bottom*

**REVIEW OF THE YALE REPERTORY THEATRE
PRODUCTION, 1984, BY FRANK RICH**

Late in Act I of *Ma Rainey's Black Bottom*, a somber, aging band trombonist (Joe Seneca) tilts his head heavenward to sing the blues. The setting is a dilapidated Chicago recording studio of 1927, and the song sounds as old as time. "If I had my way," goes the lyric, "I would tear this old building down."

Once the play has ended, that lyric has almost become a prophecy. In *Ma Rainey's Black Bottom*, the writer August Wilson sends the entire history of black America crashing down upon our heads. This play is a searing inside account of what white racism does to its victims— and it floats on the same authentic artistry as the blues music it celebrates. Harrowing as *Ma Rainey's* can be, it is also funny, salty, carnal and lyrical. Like his real-life heroine, the legendary singer Gertrude (Ma) Rainey, Mr. Wilson articulates a legacy of unspeakable agony and rage in a spellbinding voice.

The play is Mr. Wilson's first to arrive in New York, and it reached here, via the Yale Repertory Theatre, under the sensitive hand of the man who was born to direct it, Lloyd Richards. On Broadway, Mr. Richards has honed *Ma Rainey's* to its finest form. What's more, the director brings us an exciting young actor—Charles S. Dutton—along with his extraordinary dramatist. One wonders if the electricity at the Cort is the same that audiences felt when Mr. Richards, Lorraine Hansberry and Sidney Poitier stormed into Broadway with *A Raisin in the Sun* a quarter-century ago.

As *Ma Rainey's* shares its director and Chicago setting with *Raisin*, so it builds on Hansberry's themes: Mr. Wilson's characters want to make it in white America. And, to a degree, they have. Ma Rainey (1886–1939) was among the first black singers to get a recording contract—albeit with a white company's "race" division. Mr. Wilson gives us Ma (Theresa Merritt) at the height of her fame. A mountain of glitter and feathers, she has become a despotic, temperamental star, complete with a retinue of flunkies, a fancy car and a kept young lesbian lover.

The evening's framework is a Paramount-label recording session that actually happened, but whose details and supporting players have been invented by the author. As the action swings between the studio and the band's warm-up room—designed by Charles Henry McClennahan as if they might be the festering last-chance saloon of *The Iceman Cometh*—Ma and her four accompanying musicians overcome various mishaps to record "Ma Rainey's Black Bottom" and other songs. During the delays, the band members smoke reefers, joke around and reminisce about past gigs on a well-traveled road stretching through whorehouses and church socials from New Orleans to Fat Back, Ark.

The musicians' speeches are like improvised band solos—variously fizzy, haunting and mournful. We hear how the bassist Slow Drag (Leonard Jackson) got his nickname at a dance contest, but also about how a black preacher was tortured by being forced to "dance" by a white vigilante's gun. Gradually, we come to know these men, from their elusive pipe dreams to their hidden scars, but so deftly are the verbal riffs orchestrated that we don't immediately notice the incendiary drama boiling underneath.

That drama is ignited by a conflict between Ma and her young trumpeter Levee, played by Mr. Dutton. An ambitious sport eager to form his own jazz band, Levee mocks his employer's old "jugband music" and champions the new dance music that has just begun to usurp the blues among black audiences in the urban North. Already Levee has challenged Ma by writing a swinging version of "Ma Rainey's Black Bottom" that he expects the record company to use in place of the singer's traditional arrangement.

Yet even as the battle is joined between emblematic representatives of two generations of black music, we're thrust into a more profound war about identity. The African nationalist among the musicians, the pianist Toledo (Robert Judd), argues that, "We done sold ourselves to the white man in order to be like him." We soon realize that, while Ma's music is from the heart, her life has become a sad, ludicrous "imitation" of white stardom. Levee's music is soulful, too, but his ideal of success is having his "name in lights"; his pride is invested in the new shoes on which he's blown a week's pay.

Ma, at least, senses the limits of her success. Though she acts as if she owns the studio, she can't hail a cab in the white city beyond. She knows that her clout with the record company begins and ends with her viability as a commercial product: "When I've finished recording," she says, "it's just like I'd been some whore, and they roll over and put their pants on." Levee, by contrast, has yet to learn that a black man can't name his own terms if he's going to sell his music to a white world. As he plots his future career, he deceives himself into believing that a shoeshine and Uncle Tom smile will win white backers for his schemes.

Inevitably, the promised door of opportunity slams, quite literally, in Levee's face, and the sound has a violent ring that reverberates through the decades. Levee must confront not just the collapse of his hopes but the destruction of his dignity. Having played the white man's game and lost to its rigged rules, he is left with less than nothing: Even as he fails to sell himself to whites, Levee has sold out his own sense of self-worth.

Mr. Dutton's delineation of this tragic downfall is red-hot. A burly actor a year out of Yale, he is at first as jazzy as his music. With his boisterous wisecracks and jumpy sprinter's stance, he seems ready to leap into the stratosphere envisioned in his fantasies of glory. But once he crash lands, the poison of self-hatred ravages his massive body and distorts his thundering voice. No longer able to channel his anger into his music, he directs it to God, crying out that a black man's prayers are doomed to be tossed "into the garbage." As Mr. Dutton careens about with unchecked, ever escalating turbulence, he transforms an anonymous Chicago bandroom into a burial ground for a race's aspirations.

Mr. Dutton's fellow band members are a miraculous double-threat ensemble: They play their instruments nearly as convincingly as they spin their juicy monologues. Aleta Mitchell and Lou Criscuolo, as Ma's gum-chewing lover and harried white manager, are just right, and so is Scott Davenport-Richards, as Ma's erstwhile Little Lord Fauntleroy of a young nephew. It's one of the evening's more grotesquely amusing gags that Ma imperiously insists on having the boy, a chronic stutterer, recite a spoken introduction on her record.

Miss Merritt is Ma Rainey incarnate. A singing actress of both wit and power, she finds bitter humor in the character's distorted sense of self: When she barks her outrageous demands to her lackeys, we see a show business monster who's come a long way from her roots. Yet the roots can still be unearthed. In a rare reflective moment, she explains why she sings the blues. "You don't sing to feel better," Miss Merritt says tenderly. "You sing because that's a way of understanding life."

The lines might also apply to the play's author. Mr. Wilson can't mend the broken lives he unravels in *Ma Rainey's Black Bottom*. But, like his heroine, he makes their suffering into art that forces us to understand and won't allow us to forget.

VÁCLAV HAVEL

1936–

Václav Havel's life and writing have been so profoundly influenced by political events that it is almost impossible to see his plays as other than political statements. He has been highly visible on the international scene, first as president of Czechoslovakia in 1989 after the "Velvet Revolution" that freed that country from Communist domination, and now as president of the newly created Czech Republic. This position must have seemed unthinkable when the Communists ruled, from 1968 to 1988, and Havel was so frequently imprisoned for opposing the government that he gained international recognition for his defiance of the repression. Even his early days reflect the pressure of political conditions. When the Communist government nationalized business in 1948, Havel's father lost all his investments and property, and Havel, in turn, was unable to go to university but worked in a chemical laboratory by day and attended school at night. After compulsory military service, he began writing critical essays, worked as a stagehand, and became involved in the Czechoslovakian theater.

Havel's affiliation with the avant-garde group the Theater on the Balustrade gave him the opportunity during the early- to mid-1960s to direct plays, to work as a dramaturg (literary adviser), and ultimately to write for the theater. His time with this group coincided, happily, with the political thaw in Czechoslovakia between 1962 and 1968, so Havel's first major works, *The Garden Party* (1963) and *The Memorandum* (1965), were not suppressed and achieved both critical and popular success. But just as the political climate allowed Havel to flourish and even to travel to the United States—where he saw *The Memorandum* performed and honored as the best Off-Broadway foreign play of 1967–68—so the repression that followed the Soviet invasion of Czechoslovakia in August 1968 led to the reconfiscation of Havel's passport and a total ban on both publication and production of his work. After 1969 none of his works was professionally performed in Czechoslovakia until shortly before the 1989 democratic uprising, and even an amateur production of his adaptation of John Gay's *The Beggar's Opera* in 1975 led to a police raid, interrogation of the actors, and threats of reprisal against the audience. Havel himself went to prison in 1977 after signing and speaking publicly for Charter 77, a document asking the government to respect its own human rights laws. After serving four months, he was released and joined VONS (the Czech acronym for the Committee for the Defense of the Unjustly Persecuted); this led to further arrests, trials, and imprisonments, including a sentence of four and a half years.

Given the absurd existence that was forced on him by the political conditions in communist Czechoslovakia, it is not surprising that Havel's plays owe much to the tradition of contemporary absurdist theater. Both *The Garden Party* and *The Memorandum,* for example, deal with the problematic nature of language and authority and with the way in which language may ultimately be used to serve an irrational and tyrannical bureaucracy. The Rumanian playwright, Eugène Ionesco, one of the central figures in mid-century absurdist drama, had vividly expressed such concerns in *The Lesson* (1951), where a professor first intellectually overpowers a student by jabbering about the similarity of all languages and then rapes her, and in *The Chairs* (1952), where two elderly people arrange chairs for a whole room of invisible guests, all of whom are waiting for "the message," which is finally delivered by an orator who turns out to be unable to speak. In a similar spirit, Havel's *The Memorandum* envisions a nameless and seemingly purposeless bureaucracy where a new language, Ptydepe, is introduced, with words formed "by the least probable combination of letters." Such a language is cumbersome (the longest word in the language is "wombat" and has 319 letters), but because of its unintelligibility, it is perfectly suited for manipulation by ambitious and power-hungry bureaucrats. At the end of the play, when Ptydepe is finally rejected, a new language, Chorukor, is about to take over, a language in which words now resemble each other as much as possible. Even Gross, the protagonist, who had lost all his power when Ptydepe came in, rejoins the ladder of authority and succumbs to the new language with the rationalization that he must try "to salvage the last remains of Man's humanity." The structure of *The Memorandum*, twelve scenes, moving in a regular pattern between three settings, underlines the circularity of the play and the irony of the ending.

Repetition is, for Havel, as it was for Ionesco, a major theatrical device and mode of thematic expression, reinforcing his view of a world in which change is illusory. In *Largo Desolato* (1984, first performed in 1986 in a translation by Tom Stoppard), a play which alludes indirectly to Havel's own difficulties with the government, specific lines and actions recur almost obsessively. For example, the central character, Professor Nettles, is first shown staring at his front door, looking through the peephole, and then listening to hear if anyone is approaching. These actions are repeated three times at the beginning of the first scene and—with variations such as taking pills and washing his face—four times in the fifth scene. This sense of paranoia is completely understandable when one remembers the number of times that Havel was arrested. So, too, the outburst from Nettles, "It was wonderful when nobody was interested in me—when nobody expected anything from me, nobody urging me to do anything—" takes on extra resonance in the light of Havel's public image as a writer banned, attacked, and imprisoned by the government. And just as *The Memorandum* ends with the protagonist joining up with the forces he has been fighting for most of the play, so *Largo Desolato* ends with Nettles refusing to sign a statement saying that he is someone else and discovering, anticlimactically, that the authorities are no longer interested in his signature, that he has, through his own isolation, already lost the identity he has been trying to preserve.

The ironic endings of these plays anticipate the central dilemma of *Temptation* (1986), a play which grows out of both the Faust legend and Havel's realization that he had been used by the government he had resisted so strenuously. While imprisoned because of his support for Charter 77, Havel had written a request asking for release, couched in terms which he later realized were "dangerously close—by chance as it were—to what the authorities wanted to hear." He was indeed released, and on that day extracts from his letter appeared in the press, implying that he had gained his freedom in exchange for toning down his support for Charter 77. His later actions and subsequent arrests made clear that he had not wavered in his support for human rights, nor recanted (like

Galileo), but the political and personal crisis provoked by this incident led Havel to the rueful comment that "truth lies not only in what is said, but also in who says it, and to whom, why, how, and under what circumstances it is expressed." That comment, which appears in letters Havel wrote to his wife, Olga, from prison, and which he has repeated often in interviews, turns up in *Temptation* in the mouth of Fistula, who is, as his name implies, a Mephistophilis figure. In a series of conversations Fistula and Dr. Foustka probe each other's identities, behavior, and beliefs while raising for the audience, as Bernard Shaw might have done, questions of intellectual honesty, morality, and politics. Just as Shaw gives the most resonant lines in *Major Barbara* to Andrew Undershaft, whom he associates with both Machiavelli and the devil, so Havel sees his imprisoned self in Dr. Foustka, who believes he can cheat the devil, and his more enlightened self in Fistula who points out, "If the devil exists, then above all he exists within our own selves."

While *Temptation* raises serious moral and political questions, it is also, as Michael Billington's review makes clear, an exuberant and comic play in the absurdist tradition of *The Memorandum*. For example, the work of the scientific Institute, where much of the action takes place, seems to consist primarily of wearing white coats, drinking coffee, and sitting at staff meetings; no research activity is ever discussed or dramatized in the play. The Institute's meaninglessness and the total dependency of the characters on the power of the bureaucracy is even more noticeable on stage because of the dramatically silent character of Petrushka. Although she is present whenever the Deputy Director speaks, always holding his hand, no one ever explains who she is or why she is there (see Figure 1). The Director himself, who is, like the Deputy Director and the Secret Messenger, nameless, is both authoritative and comic, whether hinting at his desire for a personal relationship with Foustka (see Figure 2) or being interrupted by the Secret Messenger every time he starts to speak. Both text and performance emphasize Fistula's smelly feet (see Figure 3), creating both the sense that one could dismiss this unprepossessing, scruffy man, and yet reminding the audience of his demonic origin. Thus the play in performance shows the absurd world in which Foustka finds himself and against which he hopes to triumph. The ending, with its "crazy orgiastic masked ball or witches' sabbath," and finally smoke-filled stage and theater, implies how unlikely, either for a Faust-figure or a modern playwright, any kind of triumph might be.

TEMPTATION

BY VÁCLAV HAVEL / TRANSLATED BY MARIE WINN

CHARACTERS

DR. HENRY FOUSTKA, *scientist*
FISTULA, *a retired cripple*
DIRECTOR
VILMA, *a scientist*
DEPUTY DIRECTOR
MARKETA, *a secretary*
DR. LIBUSHE LORENCOVA, *a scientist*
DR. VILEM KOTRLY, *a scientist*
DR. ALOIS NEUWIRTH, *a scientist*
MRS. HOUBOVA, FOUSTKA'S *landlady*
DANCER
PETRUSHKA
SECRET MESSENGER
LOVER (*male*)
LOVER (*female*)

SCENES

The Institute
Foustka's apartment

The garden of the Institute
Vilma's apartment
The Institute

Intermission

Foustka's apartment
The Institute
Vilma's apartment
Foustka's apartment
The garden of the Institute

NOTE: *Before the curtain rises, during the pauses between scenes, and during the intermission, a particular piece of rock music of the "cosmic" or "astral" type may be heard. It is important that the pauses between scenes be as short as possible; consequently, the scene changes—in spite of various scenic requirements due to the alternating stage settings—should be carried out as swiftly as possible.*

SCENE 1

(*One of the rooms of the scientific Institute where* FOUSTKA *is employed. It is something between a business office, a doctor's office, a library, a club room, and a lobby. There are three doors, one at the rear, one at the front left, one at the front right. At the right rear is a bench, a small table, and two chairs; against the rear wall is a bookcase, a narrow couch covered with oilcloth, and a white cabinet with glass windows containing various exhibits, such as embryos, models of human organs, cult objects of primitive tribes, etc. At the left is a desk with a typewriter and various papers on it, behind it is an office chair, and against the wall is a file cabinet; in the middle of the room hangs a large chandelier. There might be some additional equipment around, such as a sun lamp, a sink, or an exercise apparatus against the wall (specifically, a rypstol, a Swedish ladderlike gymnastic apparatus). The furnishings of the room are not an indication of any specific areas of interest or even of any particular personality but correspond, rather, to the indeterminate mission of the entire Institute. The combination of objects of various sorts and of various designs emphasizes the timeless anonymity of a space in which things have been brought together more by chance than for any definite purpose. As the curtain rises,* LORENCOVA, KOTRLY, *and* NEUWIRTH *are onstage.* LORENCOVA, *wearing a white doctor's coat, is seated at the desk, with a mirror propped up against the typewriter, where she is powdering her nose.* KOTRLY, *wearing a white coat, is sprawled out on the bench reading a newspaper.* NEUWIRTH, *dressed in everyday clothing, is standing in the rear by the bookcase, his back to the audience, looking at a book. There is a short pause.*)

LORENCOVA: (*Calling*) Marketa . . .
MARKETA: (*Wearing an office smock, enters through the door at left*) Yes, Doctor?
LORENCOVA: Would you please make me a cup of coffee?
MARKETA: Certainly.
KOTRLY: (*Without glancing up*) One for me too, please.
NEUWIRTH: (*Without turning around*) And me.
MARKETA: Will that be three, then?
LORENCOVA: Right.

(MARKETA *exits through the left door. A short pause, after which* FOUSTKA *enters quickly through the rear door, a bit out of breath. He is wearing black trousers and a black sweater and carries a briefcase.*)

FOUSTKA: Hi.
KOTRLY: (*Putting aside the newspaper*) Hello, Henry.
NEUWIRTH: (*Puts aside the book and turns around*) Hi.

(LORENCOVA *tucks the compact away in the pocket of her jacket and crosses the stage to the bench where* KOTRLY *is sitting, obviously making way at the desk for* FOUSTKA. *He sets his briefcase on it and hastily takes out some papers. The others watch him with interest.*)

FOUSTKA: Were they here yet?

KOTRLY: Not yet.

LORENCOVA: What's with Vilma?

FOUSTKA: She just ran across the street for some oranges.

(MARKETA *enters through the left door with three cups of coffee on a small tray. She puts two down on the table in front of* LORENCOVA *and* KOTRLY, *the third she hands to* NEUWIRTH, *who is standing in the rear, leaning against the bookcase.*)

LORENCOVA: Thank you.

FOUSTKA: Marketa . . .

MARKETA: (*Stops*) Yes, Doctor?

FOUSTKA: I'm sorry, but could you possibly make one more cup for me?

MARKETA: Certainly.

FOUSTKA: Thanks a lot.

(MARKETA *exits through the left door.* LORENCOVA, KOTRLY, *and* NEUWIRTH *stir their coffees, at the same time watching* FOUSTKA, *who has seated himself at the desk and is straightening out various papers and files. Finally* KOTRLY *interrupts the rather long and somewhat tense silence.*)

KOTRLY: (*To* FOUSTKA) So, what?

FOUSTKA: What, what?

KOTRLY: How's it going?

FOUSTKA: How's what going?

(LORENCOVA, KOTRLY, *and* NEUWIRTH *exchange glances and smile. A short pause.*)

LORENCOVA: Why, your private studies.

FOUSTKA: I don't know what studies you're talking about.

(LORENCOVA, KOTRLY, *and* NEUWIRTH *exchange glances and smile. A short pause.*)

NEUWIRTH: Come on, Henry, even the birds and bees in the trees are buzzing about it!

FOUSTKA: I'm not interested in what the birds and bees in the trees are buzzing about, and I have no other scholarly pursuits besides those directly concerned with my work at our Institute.

KOTRLY: You don't trust us, do you? I don't blame you. In certain situations caution is definitely in order.

NEUWIRTH: Especially if a person is playing both ends against the middle.

FOUSTKA: (*Quickly looks over at* NEUWIRTH) What do you mean by that?

(NEUWIRTH *moves his outstretched finger meaningfully around the room, pointing finally to the door at right, by which he means to indicate the powers that run the Institute, after which he points up and down, by which he means to indicate the power of heaven and hell.*)

You've all got overactive imaginations! Is the office party on tonight?

LORENCOVA: Of course.

(*The* DEPUTY DIRECTOR, *in everyday clothes, and* PETRUSHKA, *in a white coat, enter through the right door. They are holding hands, and will continue to hold hands during the entire play.*

This means that PETRUSHKA, *who doesn't speak a word during the entire play, usually follows the* DEPUTY DIRECTOR. *He, however, doesn't pay her any special attention, creating the impression, therefore, that he is dragging her around with him as some sort of prop or mascot.* LORENCOVA, KOTRLY, *and* FOUSTKA *stand up.*)

KOTRLY: Good morning, Sir.

DEPUTY: Hello there, my friends! And please sit down. You know that neither I nor the director like to stand on ceremony here.

(LORENCOVA, KOTRLY, *and* FOUSTKA *sit down again. A short pause.*)

So what's new. Did you all get a good night's sleep? Do you have any problems? I don't see Vilma here.

FOUSTKA: She called to say that her bus broke down. But apparently she managed to get a taxi and ought to be here very soon.

(*Short pause.*)

DEPUTY: Well, are you looking forward to the party? I hope you're all coming.

KOTRLY: I'm definitely coming.

LORENCOVA: We're all coming.

DEPUTY: Wonderful! I personally consider our office parties to be a marvelous thing—mainly for their collectively psycho-therapeutic effect. Just think how quickly and easily those interpersonal problems that crop up among us from time to time are resolved in that informal atmosphere! And that's entirely due to the fact that as individuals we loosen up there somehow, while as a community we somehow tighten up. Isn't that the truth?

KOTRLY: That's precisely the way I feel about it.

DEPUTY: Apart from the fact that it would be an outright sin not to use such a beautiful garden at least once in a while! (*Pause.*) I came a little early on purpose . . .

NEUWIRTH: Did something happen?

DEPUTY: The director will tell you himself. Let me just ask you to be sensible, to try to understand him, and to try not to make his already rather difficult situation even more difficult unnecessarily. After all, we know we can't knock down walls with our heads, can we—why, then, should we complicate life for others and for our own selves! I think we can be glad we have the kind of director we have, so that by helping him we'll actually be helping our own selves. We should all bear in mind that essentially he's working for a good cause, that even he is not his own master, and that therefore we have no other alternative than to exercise at least that minimal amount of self-control necessary to make sure that neither he, our Institute, nor, consequently, any of us has any unnecessary problems. Actually there's nothing unusual about any of this. After all, a certain amount of inner discipline is required of everyone everywhere in today's world! I believe that you understand what I'm saying and that you won't expect me to tell you more than I can and have already told you. We're adults, after all, aren't we?

KOTRLY: Yes.

DEPUTY: So there you are! Have you received the soap allotment yet?

FOUSTKA: I'm going to distribute it today.

DEPUTY: Splendid!

(*The* DIRECTOR, *wearing a white coat, enters through the right door.* LORENCOVA, KOTRLY, *and* FOUSTKA *stand up immediately.*)

KOTRLY: Good morning, Sir.

DIRECTOR: Hello there, my friends! And please sit down. You know that I don't like to stand on ceremony here!

DEPUTY: That's precisely what I was telling our colleagues here just a second ago, Sir!

(LORENCOVA, KOTRLY, *and* FOUSTKA *sit down again. The* DIRECTOR *looks intently at those present for a while, then steps up to* FOUSTKA *and holds out his hand.* FOUSTKA, *surprised, rises.*)

DIRECTOR: (*To* FOUSTKA) Did you get a good night's sleep?

FOUSTKA: Yes, thank you.

DIRECTOR: Do you have any problems?

FOUSTKA: Not really . . .

(*The* DIRECTOR *presses* FOUSTKA's *elbow in a friendly way and turns to the others.* FOUSTKA *sits down again.*)

DIRECTOR: Where's Vilma?

DEPUTY: She called to say that her bus broke down. But apparently she managed to get a taxi and ought to be here very soon.

(MARKETA *enters through the left door with a cup of coffee. She hands it to* FOUSTKA.)

FOUSTKA: Thank you.

MARKETA: Don't mention it. (*Exits through the left door.*)

DIRECTOR: Well, are you looking forward to our party?

KOTRLY: Very much, Sir.

DEPUTY: Friends, I have some very good news for you on that subject: our director has promised to drop in for a moment tonight.

LORENCOVA: Just for a moment?

DIRECTOR: That will depend on the circumstances. (*To* FOUSTKA) I hope you're coming.

FOUSTKA: Of course, Sir.

DIRECTOR: Look, colleagues, there's no sense in my dragging this out unnecessarily—we've all got enough work of our own. So, to get to the point: as you probably know by now, there have been an increasing number of complaints lately that our Institute is not fulfilling its mission in a way that responds to the present situation . . .

NEUWIRTH: What situation?

DIRECTOR: Let's not beat around the bush, my friend! Aren't you forgetting that we're supposed to be the first to hear about certain things and also the first to react to them? Isn't that what we're paid for! But that's not the problem. We're simply beginning to feel more and more pressure to start taking the offensive, meaning that through our widely publicized, popularized, pedagogical, cultural, scholarly, and individually therapeutic scientific work we must finally start confronting—

DEPUTY: In the spirit of scientific inquiry, of course . . .

DIRECTOR: Doesn't that go without saying?

DEPUTY: Excuse me, Sir, but there does exist, unfortunately, a certain science that is not based on the spirit of scientific inquiry.

DIRECTOR: That, in my opinion, is not a science! Where was I?

KOTRLY: You were saying that somehow we're supposed to finally start confronting . . .

DIRECTOR: Certain rather isolated but nonetheless alarming manifestations of those irrational attitudes cropping up primarily among a particular segment of the younger generation, and originating in an incorrect . . .

(*The* SECRET MESSENGER *enters through the right door, steps up to the* DIRECTOR, *and whispers at length into his ear. The* DIRECTOR *nods his head gravely as he whispers. After a long while the* MESSENGER *concludes. The* DIRECTOR *nods one more time. The* MESSENGER *exits through the right door. A short pause.*)

Where was I?

KOTRLY: You were saying that those irrational attitudes we're supposed to confront originate in an incorrect . . .

DIRECTOR: Understanding of the systemic complexity of natural phenomena and the historical dynamic of civilizational processes out of which certain incomplete aspects are extracted, only to be interpreted either in the spirit of pseudoscientific theory . . .

DEPUTY: We know for a fact that a number of illegal typescripts by C. G. Jung are circulating among the youth . . .

DIRECTOR: . . . or in the spirit of an entire spectrum of mystical prejudices, superstitions, obscure doctrines, and practices disseminated by certain charlatans, psychopaths, and intelligent people . . .

(VILMA, *out of breath, rushes in through the rear door, holding a bag of oranges.*)

VILMA: Please excuse me, Sir—I'm so sorry—but can you imagine that the bus I was riding—

DIRECTOR: I know about it, sit down . . .

(VILMA *sits on the oilcloth-covered couch, waves at* FOUSTKA, *and tries to communicate something to him via gestures and mime.*)

Look, colleagues, there's no sense in my dragging this out unnecessarily—we've all got enough work of our own. I've acquainted you with the basic facts of the situation, and our consequent duties, so now everything depends entirely on you. I would only like to ask you to be sensible, to try to understand me, and to try not to make my already rather difficult situation even more difficult unnecessarily. It's all for a good cause, after all! Aren't we living in a modern day and age, for heaven's sake?

KOTRLY: We are.

DIRECTOR: So there you are! Have you received the soap allotment yet?

FOUSTKA: I'm going to distribute it today.

(*The* DIRECTOR *steps up to* FOUSTKA; FOUSTKA *stands up. The* DIRECTOR *places his hand on his shoulder and gravely looks at him for a short while.*)

DIRECTOR: (*Gently*) I'm counting on you, Henry.

FOUSTKA: For the soap?

DIRECTOR: The soap and everything else!

(*The curtain falls.*)

SCENE 2

(FOUSTKA's *apartment. It is a smallish bachelor quarters with one door at the right rear. The walls are covered with bookshelves, which are filled with a great quantity of books. At the left is a window, in front of which is a desk covered with many papers and more books. Behind it is a chair. At the right is a low sofa. Beside it is a large globe. A star chart is hanging somewhere on the bookshelves. As the curtain rises,* FOUSTKA, *in a dressing gown, is kneeling in the middle of the room with four burning candles on the floor around him. He holds a fifth one in his left hand and a piece of chalk in his right hand, with which he draws a circle around himself and the four candles. A large old volume lies opened on the floor beside him. The room is dimly lit. When* FOUSTKA *completes his circle he glances at the book and studies something in it for a while. Then he shakes his head and mumbles something. At that moment someone knocks at the door.* FOUSTKA *is startled and jumps to his feet.*)

FOUSTKA: (*Calling out*) Just a minute!

(FOUSTKA *quickly turns on the light, blows out the candles, hastily puts them away somewhere behind his desk, puts away the volume, looks around, then with his foot tries to erase the chalk circle he had drawn on the floor.*)

(Calling) Who is it?

HOUBOVA: (*Offstage*) It's me, Professor.

FOUSTKA: (*Calling*) Come in, Mrs. Houbova.

HOUBOVA: (*Entering*) Boy, it's really smoky in here. You ought to air the place out.

FOUSTKA: I will, right away. Did something happen?

HOUBOVA: You have a visitor.

FOUSTKA: Me? Who?

HOUBOVA: I don't know. He didn't introduce himself.

FOUSTKA: So it's someone you don't know.

HOUBOVA: He hasn't been here before—at least I've never seen him.

FOUSTKA: What does he look like?

HOUBOVA: Well—how can I put it—a little seedy—and mainly, well . . .

FOUSTKA: What?

HOUBOVA: It's embarrassing . . .

FOUSTKA: Just say it, Mrs. Houbova!

HOUBOVA: Well, he simply . . . smells . . .

FOUSTKA: Really? But how?

HOUBOVA: It's hard to describe . . . sort of like Limburger cheese . . .

FOUSTKA: My word! Well, never mind, show him in.

(HOUBOVA *exits, leaving the door ajar.*)

HOUBOVA: (*Offstage*) This way, please.

(FISTULA *enters. He is a smallish person, almost a dwarf, limping, and giving off a distinctly unsavory impression. He holds a paper bag containing his slippers.* HOUBOVA *casts a final glance after him, shrugs at* FOUSTKA, *and exits, closing the door behind her.* FISTULA *is grinning stupidly.* FOUSTKA *looks at him with surprise. A pause.*)

FOUSTKA: Good evening.

FISTULA: Greetings. (*Pause. Looks around him with interest.*) What a cozy place you have here, just as I'd imagined it. Good books—a rare globe—everything somehow as it ought to be—the balances don't lie.

FOUSTKA: I don't know what balances you're talking about. But first of all I don't even know who I'm speaking to . . .

FISTULA: All in good time. May I sit down?

FOUSTKA: Please.

(FISTULA *sits on the couch. Takes off his shoes, removes the slippers from the paper bag, puts them on, puts the shoes into the bag, and then places it on the sofa beside him. A pause.*)

FISTULA: I assume that I don't have to ask you not to mention my visit to anyone, for your sake as well as mine.

FOUSTKA: Why shouldn't I mention it?

FISTULA: You'll see why soon enough. My name is Fistula. Where I'm employed is of no importance, and in any event I don't even have a permanent position, nor do I need to have one, since I'm a cripple with a pension. (*Grins stupidly as if he has made a joke.*)

FOUSTKA: I'd guess that you work in a safety-match factory.

FISTULA: (*Chuckles, then suddenly grows serious*) That comes from a certain unidentified fungus of the foot. It makes me quite miserable and I do what I can for it, even though there's not much I can do.

(FOUSTKA *sits on the corner of the desk and looks at* FISTULA. *In his look we sense a mixture of curiosity, mistrust, and revulsion. A longer pause.*)

Aren't you going to ask me what I want or why I've come?

FOUSTKA: I'm ever hopeful that you'll tell me that yourself.

FISTULA: That, of course, would be quite possible, but I had a particular reason for not doing it until now.

FOUSTKA: What was it?

FISTULA: I was interested to see whether you'd figure it out for yourself.

FOUSTKA: (*Irately*) How could I figure it out when I've never seen you before in my life! In any case, I have neither the time nor the inclination to play guessing games with you. Unlike you, I happen to have a job and I'm leaving in a few minutes . . .

FISTULA: For the office party, right? But you've got heaps of time for that!

FOUSTKA: How do you know that I'm going to the office party?

FISTULA: And before my arrival you weren't exactly behaving like someone in a hurry either . . .

FOUSTKA: You don't know a thing about what I was doing before your arrival.

FISTULA: I beg your pardon, but I certainly know better than you do what I know and what I don't know, and how I know what I know!

(FISTULA *grins stupidly. A longer pause. Then* FOUSTKA *stands up, crosses to the other side of his desk, and turns gravely to* FISTULA.)

FOUSTKA: Look, Mister . . .

FISTULA: Fistula.

FOUSTKA: Look, Mister Fistula, I'm asking you plainly and simply, in all seriousness, and I'm expecting a plain and simple, serious answer from you: What do you want?

(*A short pause.*)

FISTULA: Does the name Marbuel say anything to you? Or Loradiel? Or Lafiel?

(FOUSTKA *gives a start, quickly regains his control, gives a long shocked look at* FISTULA.)

FOUSTKA: (*Exclaiming*) Out!

FISTULA: Excuse me?

FOUSTKA: I said: Out!

FISTULA: What do you mean—out?

FOUSTKA: Leave my apartment immediately and never set foot in it again!

(FISTULA *rubs his hands contentedly.*)

Did you hear me?

FISTULA: I heard you clearly and I'm delighted by this reaction of yours because it absolutely confirms that I've come to the right place.

FOUSTKA: What do you mean?

FISTULA: Your fright, don't you see, makes it perfectly clear that you're fully aware of the importance of my contacts, which you wouldn't be if you hadn't been interested in the aforementioned powers earlier.

FOUSTKA: Those names don't mean a thing to me, I haven't the faintest idea of what you're talking about; moreover, the suddenness of my demand that you leave merely reflected the suddenness with which I became fed up with you. My disgust coming at the same time that you pronounced those names was a complete coincidence! And now, having given you this explanation, I can only repeat what I said before, but this time without any fear that you might mistake my meaning: Leave my apartment immediately and never set foot in it again!

FISTULA: Your first request for me to leave—that I'll naturally grant, though probably not quite immediately. Your second request I will not grant, for which you will be very grateful to me later on.

FOUSTKA: You missed my meaning. Those weren't two independent requests, in fact they weren't requests at all. It was a demand—a single and indivisible one at that!

FISTULA: I'll make a note of it. But I'd also like to point something out: the haste with which you slipped in an additional motivation for your demand, together with the interesting fact that even though you claimed to be fed up with me, you considered it important enough to slip in this additional motivation even at the risk of delaying my longed-for departure—that haste together with that interesting fact are proof to me of one single thing: that your original fear of me as a middleman for certain contacts has now been superseded by a fear of me as a potential informer. Let me assure you, however, that I was counting on this phase as well. In fact had it not set in I would have felt quite uneasy. I would have considered it peculiar and would have wondered myself whether in fact *you* weren't an informer yourself. But now let me get down to business. There's obviously no way I can prove to you that I'm not an informer; even if I were to conjure up Ariel himself at this moment it still wouldn't eliminate the possibility of my being an informer. Therefore, you have only three choices. First, to consider me an informer and to continue to insist on my immediate departure. Second, not to consider me an informer and to trust me. Third, not to make up your mind for the time being as to whether I'm an informer or not, but to adopt a waiting attitude, meaning on the one hand not to kick me out immediately and on the other hand not to say anything in front of me that might eventually be used against you if I actually *were* an informer. I'd like to recommend the third alternative.

(FOUSTKA *paces the room deep in thought; finally he sits down at his desk and looks over at* FISTULA.)

FOUSTKA: Very well, I'll accept that, but I'd like to point out that there's obviously no need for me to control or restrict my speech in any way because there's absolutely nothing I could possibly think, much less say, that might possibly be used against me.

FISTULA: (*Exclaiming*) Marvelous! (*Claps his hands with pleasure.*) You delight me! If I were an informer I'd have to admit that you avoided the first trap beautifully! Your declaration is clear evidence of your absolutely solid caution, intelligence, and quick wit, qualities that I eagerly welcome, since they give me hope that I'll be able to depend on you and that we'll be able to work together well.

(*Pause.*)

FOUSTKA: Listen, Mister . . .

FISTULA: Fistula.

FOUSTKA: Listen, Mister Fistula, I'd like to tell you two things. First of all, your talk is a bit redundant for my taste. You really ought to get to the point of what brought you here more quickly. You've said virtually nothing, even though I asked you ages ago for a serious, direct, and concise answer to the question of what you actually want. And secondly, it surprises me greatly to hear that we're supposed to be working together on something. That requires two people, after all . . .

FISTULA: Your answer had eighty-six words. Considering its semantic value that isn't exactly a small number, and if I were you I wouldn't reproach anybody too severely for redundancy.

FOUSTKA: Bullshit is infectious, as we know.

FISTULA: I hope that as time goes by you'll adopt some of my more important skills as well.

FOUSTKA: You actually want to teach me something?

FISTULA: Not only to teach . . .

FOUSTKA: What else, for God's sake?

FISTULA: (*Crying out*) Leave him out of this!

FOUSTKA: Well, what else are you planning to do with me?

FISTULA: (*Smiling*) To initiate you . . .

(FOUSTKA *stands up abruptly and bangs his fist on the table.*)

FOUSTKA: (*Shouting*) That's enough! I'm a scientist with a scientific outlook on life, holding down a responsible job at one of our foremost scientific establishments! If anyone were to speak in my presence in a way that's obviously intended to spread superstition, I'd be forced to proceed in accordance with my scientific conscience!

(*For a moment* FISTULA *stares stupidly at* FOUSTKA, *then he suddenly begins to laugh wildly and dance around the room. Just as suddenly he falls silent, comes to a stop, stoops to the ground, and with his finger slowly traces the circle that* FOUSTKA *had drawn there earlier, after which he jumps up and begins to laugh wildly again. Then he goes over to the desk, seizes one of the hidden candlesticks, waves it in the air and, still laughing, places it on the desk.* FOUSTKA *watches him, goggle-eyed. Then suddenly,* FISTULA *becomes serious again, returns to the couch, and sits down.*)

FISTULA: (*Matter-of-factly*) I know your views well, Doctor Foustka. I know how much you love your work at the Institute, and I apologize for my foolish joke. Anyhow, it's high time for me to cut out all this preliminary joking around. As your director emphasized again this morning, one of your Institute's tasks is to fight against certain manifestations of irrational mysticism that keep cropping up here and there as a sort of obscurely preserved residue of the prescientific thinking of primitive tribes and the Dark Ages of history. As a scientist you know perfectly well that the more thoroughly you're armed with knowledge about what you're supposed to be fighting against, that much more effective your fight will be. You have at your disposal quite a decent collection of occult literature—almost all the basics are here, from Agrippa and Nostradamus to Eliphas Levy and Papus—nevertheless, theory isn't everything, and I can't believe that you've never felt the need to acquaint yourself with the practice of black magic directly. I come to you as a sorcerer with several hundred successful magical and theurgical evocations under his belt who is ready and willing to acquaint you with certain aspects of this practice in order to give you a base for your scientific studies. And in case you're asking yourself why in the world a sorcerer should want to join a battle against witchcraft, I can even give you a convincing reply to that: I seem to be in a tricky situation in which I might come to a bad end without cover of some sort. I am therefore offering you my own self for study, and I ask nothing in return besides your vouching for me, if the need arises, that I turned myself over to the disposition of science, and that therefore it would be unfair to hold me responsible for the propagation of something which, in reality, I was helping to fight against.

(FISTULA *looks gravely at* FOUSTKA; FOUSTKA *reflects.*)

FOUSTKA: *(Quietly)* I have a suggestion.

FISTULA: I'm listening.

FOUSTKA: To expedite our communications I'm going to pretend that I'm not endowed with a scientific outlook and that I'm interested in certain things purely out of curiosity.

FISTULA: I accept your suggestion!

(FISTULA *steps up to* FOUSTKA *and offers him his hand;* FOUSTKA *hesitates a moment, then gives his hand to* FISTULA, *who clasps it.* FOUSTKA *instantly pulls his hand away in alarm.*)

FOUSTKA: *(Crying out)* Ow! *(Gasps with pain, rubs his hand and waves it in the air.)* Man, your temperature must be fifty below zero.

FISTULA: *(Laughing)* Not quite.

(FOUSTKA *finally recovers and resumes his seat at his desk.* FISTULA *also sits down, folds his hands in his lap, and stares with theatrically doglike resignation at* FOUSTKA. *A long pause.*)

FOUSTKA: So?

(A long pause.)

What's going on?

(A long pause.)

What's wrong with you. Have you lost your tongue all of a sudden?

FISTULA: I'm waiting.

FOUSTKA: For what?

FISTULA: For your command.

FOUSTKA: I don't understand: What command?

FISTULA: What better way for me to acquaint you with my work than for you to assign me certain tasks whose fulfillment you can verify for yourself and whose fulfillment matters to you for some reason?

FOUSTKA: Aha, I see. And what kind of tasks—roughly—should they be?

FISTULA: That's for you to say!

FOUSTKA: All right—but still and all—it's hard to think of anything under the circumstances . . .

FISTULA: Don't worry, I'll help you out. I think I have an idea for an innocent little beginning of sorts. If I'm not mistaken, there's a certain young lady you admire.

FOUSTKA: I don't know what you're talking about.

FISTULA: Doctor Foustka, after everything we've said here, you really must admit that I might occasionally know somebody's little secret.

FOUSTKA: If you're talking about the secretary of our Institute, I'm not denying that she's a pretty girl, but that doesn't necessarily mean . . .

FISTULA: What if tonight at the office party—quite unexpectedly and of course quite briefly—she were to fall in love with you? How about that?

(FOUSTKA *paces nervously for a short while, and then turns abruptly to* FISTULA.)

FOUSTKA: Please leave!

FISTULA: Me? Why?

FOUSTKA: I repeat—go away!

FISTULA: Are you beginning that again? I thought we'd reached an agreement.

FOUSTKA: You've insulted me.

FISTULA: How? In what way?

FOUSTKA: I'm not so badly off as to need magic for help in my love life! I'm neither a weakling incapable of manfully facing the facts when he doesn't manage to win by his own efforts, nor a cad who would carry out experiments on innocent and completely unsuspecting young girls for his own sensual pleasure. Do you take me for some sort of Bluebeard or what, Fistula?

FISTULA: Which of us knows what we really are! But that's not the issue now. If my well-intentioned, innocent, and quite spur-of-the-moment little idea touched a raw nerve for some reason, I naturally apologize and withdraw it!

FOUSTKA: And I didn't even mention my main objection: I'm involved in a serious relationship, and I'm faithful to my girl friend.

FISTULA: Just as faithful as she is to you?

FOUSTKA: *(Startled)* What do you mean by that?

FISTULA: Forget it.

FOUSTKA: Wait a minute, I'm not going to let you get away with making dirty insinuations like that! I'm not interested in gossip, and I don't like impudence!

FISTULA: I'm sorry I said anything. If you've decided to be blind, that's your business.

(FISTULA *removes his shoes from the paper bag and slowly begins to change footgear.* FOUSTKA *watches him uneasily. A pause.*)

FOUSTKA: You're leaving? *(Pause.)* I guess I blew up a little.

(*Pause.* FISTULA *has changed into his shoes, places his slippers in the bag, stands up, and slowly walks towards the door.*)

So what's going to happen?

FISTULA: *(Stops and turns around)* With what?

FOUSTKA: Well, with our agreement.

FISTULA: What about it?

FOUSTKA: Is it on?

FISTULA: That depends entirely on you. *(He grins.)*

(The curtain falls.)

SCENE 3

(The garden of the Institute. It is night, and the garden is illuminated by Chinese lanterns strung along wires attached to trees. In the middle of the stage is a small bower. Beyond it in the background is a space serving as a dance floor. In the front at the left is a garden bench; at the right is an outdoor table with a variety of bottles and glasses on it. All around are trees and bushes; these, together with the darkness, make it hard to see the dancing in the background as well as the various movements of figures in the garden. Only the action in the foreground is always clearly visible. As the curtain rises, the music grows softer and its character changes; faintly audible as if from a great distance are strains of popular dance music that will continue for the entire scene. The male and female LOVERS are in the bower; they will remain there for the entire scene, gently embracing, caressing each other, kissing, and whispering into each other's ears, oblivious to the various goings-on around them. The DEPUTY with PETRUSHKA, and KOTRLY with LORENCOVA, are dancing as couples on the dance floor, while VILMA and the DIRECTOR are also there, each swaying separately to the music. FOUSTKA is standing at the table, pouring drinks into two glasses. MARKETA is sitting on the bench. Everyone is wearing evening clothes; the women wear long gowns. As the scene begins, FOUSTKA is explaining something to MARKETA, who is listening intently. As he is speaking FOUSTKA finishes pouring the drinks and slowly crosses over with them towards MARKETA.)

FOUSTKA: We must realize that out of an infinity of possible speeds, the expanding universe chose precisely the one that would allow the universe itself to come into being as we know it, that is, having sufficient time and other requirements needed for the formation of solid bodies so that life would be able to begin on them—at least on one of them! Isn't that a remarkable coincidence!

MARKETA: That's really amazing!

(FOUSTKA comes up to MARKETA, hands her a glass, sits down beside her, and both take a drink.)

FOUSTKA: So there you are, and if you probe a bit further you'll discover that you owe your very existence to so unbelievable a multitude of similarly unbelievable coincidences that it exceeds the bounds of all probability. All those things can't exist just for themselves, can they? Don't they conceal some deeper design of existence, of the world, and of nature willing you to be you, and me to be me, willing life, simply, to exist, and at its very height, as we understand it for now, the human soul, capable of fathoming it all! Or could it be, perhaps, that the cosmos directly intended that one fine day it would see itself thus through our eyes and ask itself thus through our lips the very questions we're asking ourselves here and now?

MARKETA: Yes, yes, that's exactly the way I see it!

(VILMA, who has in the interim left the dance floor, now appears at the table and pours herself a drink.)

VILMA: Are you enjoying yourselves?

FOUSTKA: Marketa and I are doing a bit of philosophizing.

VILMA: Well, I seem to be in the way here. *(VILMA disappears with her glass, and after a while she can again be seen dancing alone in the background. A pause.)*

FOUSTKA: And here's another thing. Modern biology has known for a long time that while the laws of survival and mutations and the like explain all sorts of things, they don't begin to explain the main thing: why does life actually exist in the first place, and above all why does it exist in that infinitely bright-colored multiplicity of its often quite self-serving manifestations, which almost seem to be here only because existence wants to demonstrate its own power through them? But to demonstrate to whom? To itself? Have you ever wondered about that?

MARKETA: To tell you the truth, no, not in this way . . . but from now on I'll probably think about it all the time. You know how to say things so nicely.

(NEUWIRTH emerges from somewhere at the right. He steps up to the bench and bows to MARKETA.)

NEUWIRTH: May I have the honor?

MARKETA: *(In confusion)* Yes . . . of course.

(She throws FOUSTKA a pleading, unhappy glance, and then rises.)

FOUSTKA: You'll come back again, won't you?

MARKETA: Of course! Everything was so very interesting.

(NEUWIRTH offers his arm to MARKETA and disappears with her. After a while they can be seen in the background dancing. FOUSTKA sips his drink, deep in thought. Shortly thereafter the DIRECTOR, who has in the interim left the dance floor, emerges from behind a bush at left, just in back of the bench.)

DIRECTOR: A pleasant evening, isn't it?

(FOUSTKA is a bit startled, and then quickly stands up.)

FOUSTKA: Yes. We're in luck with the weather.

DIRECTOR: Please sit down. May I join you for a moment?

FOUSTKA: Of course.

(They both sit down on the bench. An awkward pause. Then the DIRECTOR casually takes Foustka's hand and peers into his eyes.)

DIRECTOR: Henry . . .

FOUSTKA: Yes?

DIRECTOR: What do you actually think of me?

FOUSTKA: I? Well . . . how shall I say it . . . I think that everyone in our Institute is glad that you're the one in charge . . .

DIRECTOR: You don't understand. I'm interested in what you yourself think of me—as a person—or, to be more precise, what you feel about me . . .

FOUSTKA: I respect you . . .

DIRECTOR: Is that all?

FOUSTKA: Well . . . how shall I say it . . . it's hard to . . . well, it's . . .

(At that moment the DEPUTY, with PETRUSHKA, who have in the interim left the dance floor, appear at the right, holding hands. When the DIRECTOR sees them he drops FOUSTKA's hand. FOUSTKA is obviously relieved.)

DEPUTY: Here you are, Sir! We've been looking high and low for you.

DIRECTOR: Did something happen?

(Making the most of the situation, FOUSTKA quietly stands up and quickly disappears.)

DEPUTY: Nothing in particular. It's only that Petrushka here has a request to make of you, but she's just a little bashful about coming out with it . . .

DIRECTOR: What request?

DEPUTY: Whether she couldn't have a dance with you.

DIRECTOR: I don't know how to lead, and I'd only step all over her skirt. Really, there are so many better dancers here . . .

DEPUTY: In that case would you at least accept our invitation to come to the pool where our colleague Kotrly has constructed an adorable underwater light show.

(The DIRECTOR peevishly gets to his feet and goes off somewhere to the right with the DEPUTY and PETRUSHKA. Just then KOTRLY and LORENCOVA, who have in the interim left the dance floor, appear at the left. They go to the table.)

KOTRLY: Have you seen my underwater light show yet?

LORENCOVA: You're doing it stupidly, Willy.

KOTRLY: What am I doing stupidly?

(They go up to the table and KOTRLY pours out two drinks and hands one to LORENCOVA. They sip their drinks.)

LORENCOVA: You're being such an ass-kisser that even those two idiots will get sick of you. You'll end up a total joke and everybody will turn against you.

KOTRLY: Maybe I'm doing it stupidly, but it's still a lot better than pretending not to be interested, and all the while telling them everything!

LORENCOVA: Are you referring to Neuwirth?

KOTRLY: Who, for instance, was the first to begin talking about Foustka's interest in black magic? If they get wind of it, it'll be Neuwirth's doing!

LORENCOVA: But we all gossiped about it! You're being unfair to him and your only excuse is that you're jealous . . .

KOTRLY: It's just like you to stick up for him!

LORENCOVA: Are you beginning that again?

KOTRLY: Libby, give me your word of honor that you never had a thing with him!

LORENCOVA: Word of honor! Come on, let's dance!

(KOTRLY and LORENCOVA put down their glasses on the table and exit somewhere off to the right. After a while they can be seen in the background, dancing. Meanwhile NEUWIRTH and MARKETA enter from the left. MARKETA sits down on the bench. NEUWIRTH hangs around nearby. FOUSTKA emerges from the bushes directly behind the bench and sits down next to MARKETA. An awkward pause.)

NEUWIRTH: Oh dear, I seem to be in the way here.

(NEUWIRTH vanishes. After a while he can be seen in the background, dancing with LORENCOVA; he has evidently cut in on KOTRLY. Meanwhile the DEPUTY and PETRUSHKA have appeared on the dance floor as well, dancing together, as well as the DIRECTOR, dancing alone again. A short pause.)

MARKETA: Tell me more! Every word you say opens my eyes. I don't understand how I could have been so blind, so superficial . . .

FOUSTKA: I'll begin, if you don't mind, by taking a new tack. Has it ever occurred to you that we wouldn't be able to understand even the simplest moral action that doesn't serve some practical purpose? In fact, it would have to seem quite absurd to us if we didn't recognize that hidden somewhere in its deepest depths is the presumption of something higher, some sort of absolute, omniscient, and infinitely fair judge or moral authority through which and within which all our activities are somehow mysteriously appraised and validated and by means of which each one of us is constantly in touch with eternity?

MARKETA: Yes, yes, that's exactly how I've felt about it all my life! I just wasn't able to see it, let alone say it so beautifully.

FOUSTKA: So there you are! What's even more tragic is that modern man has repressed everything that might allow him somehow to transcend himself, and he ridicules the very idea that something about him might even exist and that his life and the world might have a higher meaning of some sort! He has crowned himself as the highest authority, so he can then observe with horror how the world is going to the dogs under that authority!

MARKETA: How clear and simple it is! I admire the way you're able to think about everything so . . . so, well, in your own way somehow, differently from the way most people usually talk about it, and how deeply you feel all those things! I don't think I'll ever forget this evening! I have a feeling that I'm becoming a new person every minute I'm with you. Please forgive me for saying it so openly, but it's as if something were radiating from inside of you that—I don't understand how I could have walked by you so indifferently before—it's simply that I've never felt anything like this before . . .

(KOTRLY *emerges from somewhere at the right, goes up to the bench, and bows to* MARKETA.)

KOTRLY: May I have the honor?

MARKETA: I'm sorry, but I . . .

KOTRLY: Come on, Marketa, we haven't had a single dance together!

(MARKETA *looks unhappily at* FOUSTKA, *who just shrugs his shoulders helplessly;* MARKETA *stands up.*)

MARKETA: *(To* FOUSTKA) You'll wait here, won't you?

FOUSTKA: Of course I'll wait.

(KOTRLY *offers an arm to* MARKETA *and disappears with her. After a while they may be seen in the background, dancing.* FOUSTKA *sips his drink, deep in thought. After a short while the* DIRECTOR, *who has in the interim left the dance floor, emerges from behind a bush directly in back of the bench.*)

DIRECTOR: Alone again?

(FOUSTKA *is a bit startled, then quickly stands up.*)

Sit down, Henry.

(FOUSTKA *sits again. The* DIRECTOR *sits down beside him. A short pause.*)

Do you smell that wonderful fragrance? Acacias . . . nasturtiums . . .

FOUSTKA: I don't know very much about fragrances.

(*An awkward pause. Then the* DIRECTOR *again casually takes Foustka's hand and gazes closely into his eyes.*)

DIRECTOR: Henry . . .

FOUSTKA: Yes?

DIRECTOR: Would you like to be my deputy?

FOUSTKA: Me?

DIRECTOR: I could arrange it.

FOUSTKA: But you already have a deputy.

DIRECTOR: If you only knew what a pain in the ass he gives me!

(*Just then the* SECRET MESSENGER *enters, goes up to the* DIRECTOR, *leans over, and whispers at length into his ear. The* DIRECTOR *gravely nods his head. After a longer time the* MESSENGER *concludes. The* DIRECTOR *nods one more time. The* MESSENGER *exits to the right. The* DI-RECTOR, *who had not dropped* FOUSTKA's *hand during the whispering, turns again to* FOUSTKA *and gazes closely into his eyes for a longer time.*)

Henry.

FOUSTKA: Yes?

DIRECTOR: Wouldn't you like to stop over at my place for a little while after the party? Or if you don't want to stay to the end, we could both slip away without anyone noticing. I've got some homemade

cherry liqueur. I could show you my collection of miniatures, we could chat in peace and quiet, and if we happened to go on too long and you didn't feel like going home that late, you could easily spend the night at my place! You know that I live all alone, and what's more, it's only a hop and a skip from our Institute, so you'd have it that much easier in the morning—what do you say?

FOUSTKA: I'm very honored by your invitation, Sir, but I'm afraid I've already promised that I'd go to . . .

DIRECTOR: To Vilma's?

(FOUSTKA *nods. The* DIRECTOR *gazes closely into his eyes for another moment, then, all at once, drops his hand briskly, stands up abruptly, crosses over to the table, pours himself a drink, and quickly drains it.* FOUSTKA *remains seated on the bench, embarrassed. Then the* DEPUTY, *with* PETRUSHKA, *who have in the interim left the dance floor, emerge from the left, holding hands.*)

DEPUTY: Here you are! We've been looking all over . . .

DIRECTOR: Did something happen?

DEPUTY: Nothing in particular. Me and Petrushka here, we just wanted to ask you if you had any plans after the party. We'd consider it quite an honor if you'd accept our invitation to come over for a little night-cap before bedtime. You could even spend the night at our house—if you wanted to, of course . . .

DIRECTOR: I'm tired and I have to go home. Goodbye.

(*The* DIRECTOR *exits quickly to the right. The* DEPUTY *looks after him in confusion, then, somewhat crestfallen, disappears with* PETRUSHKA *to the left. After a while they may be seen in the background, dancing. Just then* NEU-WIRTH *and* LORENCOVA, *who have in the interim left the dance floor, appear near the table at the right.*)

NEUWIRTH: I've seen a lot of things in my day, but an educated person sucking up to his idiot bosses with ridiculous stunts like those light bulbs in the pool—that really takes the cake! (*He pours two drinks, hands one to* LORENCOVA; *they both sip.*)

LORENCOVA: Sucking up with the light bulbs is still a lot better than pretending not to be interested and all the while telling them everything!

NEUWIRTH: It's just like you to stick up for him!

LORENCOVA: Are you beginning that again?

NEUWIRTH: Libby, give me your word of honor that you never had a thing with him!

LORENCOVA: Word of honor! Come on, let's dance!

(NEUWIRTH *and* LORENCOVA *put their glasses down on the table and exit somewhere to the left. After a while they can be seen in the background, dancing. Meanwhile* KOTRLY *and* MARKETA *enter from the right.* MARKETA *sits down on the bench next to* FOUSTKA. KOTRLY *hangs around nearby. An awkward pause.*)

KOTRLY: Oh dear, I seem to be in the way here.

(KOTRLY *vanishes. After a while he can be seen in the background, dancing with* LORENCOVA. *He has evidently cut in on* NEUWIRTH.)

FOUSTKA: When a person casts God from his heart, he opens a door for the devil. When you think about the increasingly stupid willfulness of the powerful and the increasingly stupid submission of the powerless, and the awful destruction committed in today's world in the name of science—and after all we *are* its somewhat grotesque standard-bearers—isn't all that truly the work of the devil? We know that the devil is a master of disguises, and what more ingenious disguise could one imagine than the one offered him by the godlessness of modern times? Why, he must find the most promising base of operations in those very places where people have stopped believing in him! Please forgive me for speaking so openly, Marketa, but I can't keep it stifled inside me any longer! And who else can I confide in besides you?

(MARKETA *throws her glass into the bushes and grasps* FOUSTKA's *hand emotionally.*)

MARKETA: (*Exclaiming*) I love you!

FOUSTKA: No!

MARKETA: Yes, I'll love you forever!

FOUSTKA: Oh, you poor creature! I'd be your ruin!

MARKETA: I'd rather be ruined with you and live the truth than be without you and live a lie!

(MARKETA *embraces* FOUSTKA *and begins to kiss him passionately. Just then* VILMA, *who has in the interim left the dance floor, appears at the table. For a moment she observes the embracing couple.*)

VILMA: (*Icily*) Are you enjoying yourselves?

(FOUSTKA *and* MARKETA *immediately pull apart and look at* VILMA *in a state of shock.*)

(*The curtain falls.*)

SCENE 4

(VILMA's *apartment. It is a cozy boudoir, furnished with antiques. There is a door at the rear. At the left is a large bed with a canopy. At the right are two small armchairs, a large Venetian mirror, and a vanity table with a large collection of perfumes on it. Scattered about the room are various female odds and ends and trinkets. The only thing folded neatly is* FOUSTKA's *evening outfit next to the bed. The colors are all feminine, predominantly pink and purple. As the curtain rises,* FOUSTKA *is sitting in his undershorts at the edge of the bed, and* VILMA, *in a lacy slip, is sitting at the vanity table combing her hair, facing the mirror with her back to* FOUSTKA. *A short pause.*)

FOUSTKA: When was he here last?

VILMA: Who?

FOUSTKA: Stop asking stupid questions!

VILMA: You mean that dancer? About a week ago.

FOUSTKA: Did you let him in?

VILMA: He just brought me some violets. I told him I had no time, that I was hurrying to meet you.

FOUSTKA: I asked you whether you let him in.

VILMA: I don't remember anymore . . . maybe he came in for a moment.

FOUSTKA: So you kissed him!

VILMA: I kissed him on the cheek to thank him for the violets, that's all.

FOUSTKA: Vilma, don't treat me like a fool, for goodness sake! I just bet you could buy him off with a mere kiss on the cheek once you let him in! Surely he tried to dance with you at the very least.

VILMA: Henry, drop it, for goodness sake! Can't you talk about anything more interesting?

FOUSTKA: Did he try or not?

VILMA: All right, he did, if you really must know! But I won't tell you another thing! I simply refuse to keep talking to you on this level, because it's embarrassing, undignified, insulting, and ridiculous! You know very well that I love you, and that no dancer could possibly be a threat to you, so stop tormenting yourself with this endless cross-examination! I don't keep pumping you for details either—and I'd have far more reason to do so!

FOUSTKA: So you refuse to tell? Well in that case everything is quite clear.

VILMA: But I've told you a hundred times that I don't go out of my way to see him, I don't care for him, I don't dance with him, so what else am I supposed to do, damn it!

FOUSTKA: He hangs around you, he flatters you, he wants to dance with you all the time—and you enjoy it! If you didn't enjoy it, you'd have gotten rid of him long ago.

VILMA: I won't deny that I enjoy it—any woman would enjoy it. His persistence is touching, and so is the very fact that he never gives up, even though he knows perfectly well that he doesn't have a chance. Would you, for instance, be capable of driving here at night from God knows where for no other reason than to bring me some violets, even though you knew the situation was hopeless?

FOUSTKA: He's persistent because you deliberately dash his hopes in a way that keeps them alive and you deliberately reject him in a way that makes him long for you more and more! If you really slammed the door on his hopes he'd never show up here again. But you wouldn't do that, because it amuses you to play cat and mouse with him. You're a whore!

VILMA: You've decided to insult me?

FOUSTKA: How long did you dance together?

VILMA: Enough, Henry, you're beginning to be disgusting! I've always known that you're eccentric, but I really never suspected that you're capable of being this nasty! What's suddenly brought on this pathological jealousy of yours? This insensitivity, tactlessness, maliciousness, vengefulness? At least if you had any objective reason for it . . .

FOUSTKA: So you're planning to keep whoring around?

VILMA: You have no right to talk to me like that! You kept pawing at that girl all evening, everybody's embarrassed, I wander around like an idiot—people feel sorry for me all over the place—and now you have the nerve to reproach me! Me! You do as you damn well please, I just have to suffer in silence, and finally you make a scene here on account of some crazy dancer! Do you see how absurd it is? Do you realize how terribly unfair it is? Do you have the faintest idea of how selfish and cruel you are?

FOUSTKA: In the first place, I was certainly not pawing anyone and I'd like you to please refrain from using words like that, especially when you're referring to pure creatures like Marketa. In the second place, we're not discussing me, but you, so kindly stop changing the subject. Sometimes I get a feeling that there's some monstrous plan hidden behind all this. First, you'll resurrect feelings within me that I'd assumed were dead long ago, and then once you've deprived me thus of my well-known objectivity, you'll begin to tighten a web of deceit around my heart, lightly at first, but then ever more painfully, an especially treacherous one because it is composed of a multitude of delicate threads of dancerly pseudoinnocence! But I won't let myself be tortured on this rack any longer! I'll do something either to myself—or to him—or to you—or to all of us!

(VILMA *puts down her comb, begins to clap her hands, and walks toward's* FOUSTKA *with a smile.* FOUSTKA *also begins to smile, stands up, and walks towards* VILMA.)

VILMA: You keep getting better and better!

FOUSTKA: You weren't bad yourself.

(FOUSTKA *and* VILMA *gently embrace, kiss, and then slowly get into bed together. They settle down together comfortably, lean back against the pillows, and cover their legs with a blanket.* FOUSTKA *lights a cigarette for himself and for* VILMA. VILMA *finally ends a long pause by speaking.*)

VILMA: Henry.

FOUSTKA: Hmm . . .

VILMA: Isn't it beginning to get on your nerves just a bit?

FOUSTKA: What?

VILMA: You know, that I keep making you play these games.

FOUSTKA: It did bother me for quite a long time.

VILMA: And now?

FOUSTKA: Now just the opposite—it's beginning to scare me.

VILMA: To scare you? Why?

FOUSTKA: I have a feeling that I'm beginning to get into it too much.

VILMA: (*Exclaiming*) Henry! Don't tell me you're really beginning to get jealous! Now that's fantastic! Never in my wildest dreams did I hope it would succeed like this! I had become resigned to the idea that you'd never feel any jealousy other than the make-believe kind.

FOUSTKA: I'm sorry, but I can't share your delight.

VILMA: I don't understand what you're afraid of!

FOUSTKA: My own self!

VILMA: Come on!

FOUSTKA: Don't underestimate it, Vilma. Something's happening to me. I suddenly feel capable of doing all sorts of things that have always been alien to me. It's as if something dark inside of me were suddenly beginning to flow out of its hiding place and into the open.

VILMA: What an alarmist you are! You're beginning to feel a little healthy jealousy and that throws you into a complete panic! There's nothing wrong with you. Maybe you're just a little upset because your situation at the Institute came to a head this evening with that unfortunate incident with the director. That's obviously on your mind, and it's working away at your unconscious, looking for some way out, even though you won't admit it. That's why you're beginning to see bogeymen all over the place.

FOUSTKA: If only it were that simple.

(*Pause.*)

VILMA: Do you think he'll destroy you?

FOUSTKA: He'll certainly try. The question is whether he has enough power to do it.

VILMA: But he's got all the power he wants—all the power there is, actually—at least as far as we're concerned.

FOUSTKA: There are other kinds of power besides the kind he dispenses.

(VILMA, *horrified, jumps up and kneels on the pillow opposite* FOUSTKA.)

VILMA: Do you mean that seriously?

FOUSTKA: Hmm . . .

VILMA: Now you're scaring me! Promise me you won't dabble in that sort of thing!

FOUSTKA: And what if I won't promise?

VILMA: The minute you mentioned that cripple I knew there'd be hell to pay! He's addled your brains! You'd actually go so far as to get involved with him?

FOUSTKA: Why not?

VILMA: This is horrible!

FOUSTKA: At least you see that I wasn't just kidding around before.

(*Just then the doorbell rings.* VILMA *cries out in horror and quickly huddles up under the blankets.* FOUSTKA *smiles, calmly gets out of bed, and dressed just as he is— that is, in his undershorts—goes to the door and quickly opens it. There stands the* DANCER *holding a bunch of violets behind his back.*)

DANCER: Good evening. Is Vilma home?

FOUSTKA: Why?

DANCER: (*Points to the flowers*) I just wanted to give her a little something.

FOUSTKA: (*Calling to the bed*) Vilma, you have a visitor.

(VILMA *climbs out of bed, is a bit confused, can't quickly find anything to cover up with, and therefore goes to the door dressed only in her slip.* FOUSTKA *steps to the side, but does not go away.*)

VILMA: (*To the dancer, with embarrassment*) Is that you?

DANCER: I'm sorry to disturb you at this hour—we were on tour—I just wanted to give you—here.

(*The* DANCER *hands* VILMA *the violets,* VILMA *takes them and sniffs them.*)

VILMA: Thank you.

DANCER: Well, I'll be going again. I apologize again for disturbing you.

VILMA: Bye-bye.

(*The* DANCER *exits.* VILMA *closes the door, smiles uncertainly at* FOUSTKA, *puts down the violets somewhere, steps up to him, embraces him, and gently kisses his forehead, lips, and cheek.* FOUSTKA *stands motionless and looks coldly in front of him.*)

I love you.

(FOUSTKA *doesn't move a hair.* VILMA *continues to kiss him. Then, suddenly,* FOUSTKA *slaps her brutally in the face.* VILMA *falls to the ground.* FOUSTKA *kicks her.*)

(*The curtain falls.*)

SCENE 5

(*The same room at the Institute as in Scene 1. As the curtain rises, nobody is onstage, but very soon* VILMA *and* FOUSTKA *enter through the rear door.* FOUSTKA *is wearing the same evening clothes he wore at the party the previous day.* VILMA *is wearing a white coat. She has a black eye. They both seem happy.*)

VILMA: We can't be the first!

FOUSTKA: Have you noticed that you come to work on time only when I stay over at your place?

VILMA: You're exaggerating.

(FOUSTKA *sits down at the desk and begins to sort out some papers.* VILMA *sits down on the oilcloth couch.*)

(*Calling*) Marketa.

(MARKETA, *wearing an office smock, enters through the left door. When she sees* FOUSTKA *she stops abruptly and lowers her eyes.*)

Would you please make us two cups of coffee? A bit stronger, if possible.

MARKETA: Yes, of course.

(MARKETA *goes a bit nervously towards the left door, stealthily glancing over at* FOUSTKA, *who looks up from his papers and smiles at her jovially.*)

FOUSTKA: Well, did you get a good night's sleep?

MARKETA: (*Stuttering*) Thank you—yes—actually no. There were so many thoughts racing through my head. (MARKETA, *in some confusion, exits through the left door.*)

VILMA: I think you turned that poor little thing's head last night.

FOUSTKA: Oh, she'll get over it.

(*Pause.*)

VILMA: Henry.

FOUSTKA: Yes, darling?

VILMA: It hasn't been that good in a long time, has it?

FOUSTKA: Hmm . . .

(LORENCOVA *in a dress,* KOTRLY *also in civilian clothes, and* NEUWIRTH *in a white coat enter through the rear door.*)

KOTRLY: You're here already?

VILMA: Hard to believe, isn't it?

(LORENCOVA *and* KOTRLY *sit down at their places on the bench;* NEUWIRTH *leans against the bookcase.*)

LORENCOVA: (*Looks at Vilma's face*) My God, what's that?

VILMA: Oh you know, deathless passion.

(MARKETA *enters through the left door with two cups of coffee on a tray. She hands one to* VILMA, *and sets down the other with somewhat trembling hands in front of* FOUSTKA.)

FOUSTKA: Thanks.

LORENCOVA: Some for us too, Marketa.

MARKETA: Yes, Doctor Lorencova.

(MARKETA *exits quickly through the left door. The* DEPUTY, *in a white coat, and* PETRUSHKA, *in a dress, enter through the right door. They are holding hands. Everyone stands.*)

KOTRLY: Good morning, Sir.

DEPUTY: Hello there, my friends! I see we've got perfect attendance here today—that's fantastic—today of all days I would have least expected it. (*Everyone sits down again.)* I think that yesterday was a real success. You all deserve thanks for that. But I must express special appreciation to our colleague Kotrly here for his underwater light effects.

KOTRLY: Please don't mention it.

DEPUTY: Well, my friends, there's no point in beating around the bush any longer.

NEUWIRTH: Did something happen?

DEPUTY: The director will tell you himself. At this time I just want to implore you all to understand that certain things have to be the way they are, to meet us halfway as we meet you halfway, and, mainly, to keep a cool head, a glowing heart, and clean hands at this crucial point in time. In short, there are times when people either come through with flying colors, and then they have nothing to fear, or they don't come through, and then they have only themselves to blame for the unnecessary troubles they create as a result. But you're educated people, after all—I don't have to spell it all out for you. Who'll volunteer for garden cleanup?

KOTRLY: I might as well, after all I have to go there anyhow to terminate the light bulbs.

DEPUTY: Splendid!

(The DIRECTOR, in civilian clothes, enters through the right door. Everyone stands again.)

KOTRLY: Good morning, Sir.

DIRECTOR: Hello there, my friends! I see we've got perfect attendance here today—that's fantastic—today of all days I would have least expected it and today of all days it's especially important.

DEPUTY: That's precisely what I was telling our colleagues just a second ago, Sir.

(Everyone sits again. The DIRECTOR looks intently at those present for a moment and then steps up to KOTRLY and shakes his hand. KOTRLY stands up, surprised.)

DIRECTOR: Did you get a good night's sleep?

KOTRLY: Yes, thank you.

DIRECTOR: Do you have any problems?

KOTRLY: Not really.

(The DIRECTOR presses KOTRLY's elbow in a friendly way and turns again to the others. KOTRLY sits again.)

DIRECTOR: There's no point in beating around the bush, friends . . .

NEUWIRTH: Did something happen?

DIRECTOR: As we know, our Institute is a kind of lighthouse of truthful knowledge. I'd even go so far as to say it's something of a faithful watchdog over the scientific core of science itself—it's something like the avant-garde of progress. Therefore one might simplify it thus: We think it today, they'll live it tomorrow!

DEPUTY: I've already reminded our colleagues, Sir, of the responsibility that our mission involves.

DIRECTOR: But here's why I'm saying all this: a serious thing has happened . . .

(Just then the SECRET MESSENGER enters through the right door, steps up to the DIRECTOR, and whispers at length into his ear. The DIRECTOR gravely nods his head. After a long while the MESSENGER concludes. The DIRECTOR nods one more time and continues speaking. The MESSENGER exits through the right door.)

But here's why I'm saying all this: a serious thing has happened . . .

(Just then MARKETA enters through the left door carrying a tray with three cups of coffee on it. She places two on the table in front of LORENCOVA and KOTRLY and hands the third to NEUWIRTH. Then she heads back towards the left door.)

But here's why I'm saying all this: a serious thing has happened . . .

(MARKETA stops in her tracks, glances at the DIRECTOR and at FOUSTKA, then she quietly goes up to the left door and eavesdrops.)

NEUWIRTH: Did something happen?

DEPUTY: *(To NEUWIRTH)* Please stop interrupting the director! Didn't you hear him say that he's about to tell you . . .

DIRECTOR: A serious thing has happened: a virus has lodged itself where one would have least expected it, yet in the very place it can do the worst damage—that is, in the very center of antiviral battle—indeed, if I'm to stick with this metaphor, right in the central antibiotic warehouse!

(Everyone looks at each other anxiously. VILMA and FOUSTKA exchange a glance that reveals they know there's trouble ahead. FOUSTKA nervously gropes for a cigarette and lights up.)

KOTRLY: Are you saying, Sir, that right here, among us, there's someone . . .

DIRECTOR: Yes, with deep sorrow, bitterness, and shame I must say precisely that. We have a scientific worker here at this Institute—let me emphasize the word *scientific*—who has long and of course secretly, which only confirms his two-faced nature, been involved with various so-called occult disciplines, from astrology through alchemy all the way to black magic and theurgy, in order to probe those murky waters for a would-be hidden wealth of an allegedly higher—that is prescientific—kind of learning.

KOTRLY: You mean he believes in spirits?

DIRECTOR: Not only that, but he is actually attempting to move from theory to practice! We have ascertained that he has established contact—

LORENCOVA: With spirits?

DEPUTY: He'd have a bit of trouble doing that, wouldn't he, Sir?

DIRECTOR: That's enough! Please don't joke about things that leave a black mark on the work of our Institute, things that are a direct assault on its reputation and therefore a low blow to us all, and especially to me as the one responsible for all of its scientific credibility. It is a grave and sad matter, my friends, and it's up to all of us to come to grips with it honorably! Where was I?

DEPUTY: You were discussing those contacts . . .

DIRECTOR: Ah yes. Well, then, we have learned that not long ago he established direct contact with a certain element from that no-man's-land of pseudoscience, common criminality, and moral turpitude, who is suspect not only because he spreads superstition and deludes the credulous by means of various tricks, but who actually dabbles in Satanism, black magic, and other such poisonous practices. That's the fact of the matter, and now I'd like to open this up for discussion. Does anyone have any questions?

(An oppressive pause.)

KOTRLY: *(Quietly)* Might I ask the name of this colleague?

DIRECTOR: *(To the DEPUTY)* Say it!

DEPUTY: I can hardly utter the words, but name him I must. We're talking about Doctor Foustka, here.

(An oppressive pause.)

DIRECTOR: Who else wishes to speak?

MARKETA: *(Timidly)* I do.

FOUSTKA: *(Quietly to MARKETA)* Please, I beg of you, stay out of this!

DIRECTOR: This concerns us all. Even the secretary here deserves a chance to speak her mind.

MARKETA: Please excuse me, Sir. I'm not a scientist and I don't know how to express myself too well, but that simply can't be true! Doctor Foustka is a wise and honorable man—I know he is—he worries about questions that we really all should be worrying about—he thinks for himself—he tries to get to the bottom of the deepest questions—the source of morality—of universal order—and all those other things—and those contacts you mentioned—I simply don't believe it! Surely these are all wicked lies spread by bad people who want to harm him.

(A deathly silence falls over the room. FOUSTKA is obviously in despair over MARKETA's outburst. After a while the DIRECTOR turns matter-of-factly to the DEPUTY.)

DIRECTOR: *(To the DEPUTY)* As soon as we're finished, please arrange for her immediate dismissal! Now of all times our Institute truly can't allow itself the luxury of employing a secretary who accuses the administration of lying!

DEPUTY: I'll take care of it, Sir.

DIRECTOR: *(To MARKETA)* You may go get your things together.

FOUSTKA: *(In a muffled voice to MARKETA)* You've gone mad—to ruin your life so foolishly like this—why, you won't get a job anywhere!

MARKETA: I want to suffer with you!

FOUSTKA: Excuse me, Sir, but wouldn't it be more sensible to have her hospitalized? It's perfectly obvious that she doesn't know what she's saying.

DIRECTOR: Psychiatry, Doctor Foustka, is not a garbage dump for girls you've used and thrown away.

MARKETA: Henry, are you renouncing me? And everything you told me last night, are you renouncing that too?

FOUSTKA: *(Speaking furiously through clenched teeth)* For God's sake, keep quiet!

(MARKETA bursts into tears and runs out the left door. An awkward pause.)

VILMA: *(Quietly to FOUSTKA)* If she does something rash it'll be your fault!

FOUSTKA: *(Quietly to VILMA)* And then you'll be satisfied, won't you?

VILMA: *(Quietly)* Don't start that again.

FOUSTKA: I'm the one who started? Right?

DIRECTOR: Stop that! I'll ask at a higher level whether one of the local housing projects couldn't take her on as a cleaning lady.

LORENCOVA: I think that would be a very fortunate, humane, and sensible solution.

DIRECTOR: *(To FOUSTKA)* Do you want to take advantage of your right to respond to the charges against you?

(FOUSTKA stands up slowly and leans against the desk as if it were a speaker's podium.)

FOUSTKA: Gentlemen, colleagues! I have complete faith in the objectivity and conscientiousness with which my case will be considered and I presume that at the right moment I will be given the opportunity to make an extensive explanation, and that certain circumstances with which I will acquaint you on that occasion will help prove my complete innocence. For the time being, therefore, I will confine myself to expressing the hope that the proceedings in this case—in keeping with our scientific approach to reality and our scientific morality—will be impartially and fully directed towards one goal alone: to discover the truth. This will further not only my own interests nor only the interests of science as such which this Institute is entrusted to guard and cultivate, but the interests of each of you as well. A different course of action, you see, might easily make my case merely the first link of a long chain of injustices the end of which I hardly dare contemplate. Thank you for your attention!

(FOUSTKA sits down. An awkward pause. Everyone is slightly uneasy, albeit each for different reasons.)

DIRECTOR: We're living in a modern day and age, and

nobody here has any intention of staging any kind of witch-hunt. That would merely resurrect the same ancient ignorance and fanaticism against which we are battling, but in a new guise. Let the manner in which our colleague Foustka's case is resolved become an inspirational model of a truly scientific approach to the facts! The truth must prevail, come what may!

(*A short pause.*)

Who volunteered for garden clean-up?

KOTRLY: I did, Sir.

(*The* DIRECTOR *steps up to* KOTRLY. KOTRLY *stands up; the* DIRECTOR *places a hand on his shoulder and looks gravely into his eyes for a while.*)

DIRECTOR: (*Tenderly*) I'm glad you took the job, Vilem. I'll come to help you.

(MARKETA *enters through the left door, wearing a dress and carrying a small suitcase in her hand. Her face is tear-stained; she crosses the room as if sleepwalking and leaves through the rear door. Just as she closes it behind her, the chandelier crashes to the floor. It doesn't hit anyone but shatters into pieces on the floor.*)

(*The curtain falls.*)

SCENE 6

(FOUSTKA'S *apartment again. As the curtain rises,* FISTULA *is alone on stage. He is sitting at the desk, going through the papers lying on it. He is wearing slippers, and the paper bag with his shoes in it is lying on the desk among the papers. After a while* FOUSTKA *enters, still in evening clothes. When he spots* FISTULA *he gives a start and cries out.*)

FOUSTKA: What are you doing here?

FISTULA: I'm waiting for you.

FOUSTKA: How did you get in?

FISTULA: Not through the chimney, if that's what you're wondering. Through the door, which Mrs. Houbova kindly opened for me before she went out shopping, because I explained to her how urgently you needed to speak to me and how hard it would be for me to wait for you outside, what with my lame foot.

FOUSTKA: So you tricked her—how like you!

FISTULA: You don't believe that I'm a cripple?

FOUSTKA: My having to urgently speak to you is an out-and-out lie. Quite the contrary, after everything that happened I'd hoped I'd never see you again.

FISTULA: Quite the contrary, it's precisely *because* of what happened that our meeting has become many times more urgent.

FOUSTKA: And how dare you go through my papers!

FISTULA: Well, I had to do something to while away the time, didn't I?

FOUSTKA: And what about those shoes?

FISTULA: You make such a fuss about everything! (FISTULA *begins to grin stupidly, then he takes his bag, goes to the sofa, sits down, and places the bag beside him.*) Won't you sit down?

(FOUSTKA, *irritated, crosses to his desk, sits, and glares at* FISTULA.)

So what do you say to our success?

FOUSTKA: What success?

FISTULA: I never expected it to work so easily and so quickly. You're truly a gifted student.

FOUSTKA: I don't know what you're talking about!

FISTULA: You know perfectly well! We had agreed to do an innocent little experiment first, hadn't we? And that turned out to surpass our fondest expectations, don't you agree?

FOUSTKA: If you're referring to the fact that that unfortunate child developed a bit of a crush on me, then I'd like to say just two things. First, there was no magic involved, especially not yours; the only reason it happened was because it was the first time—

FISTULA: By pure chance—

FOUSTKA: That I actually had an opportunity to have a real talk with that young woman and because I happened to be—

FISTULA: By pure chance—

FOUSTKA: In pretty good form last night, so that my thoughts charmed her. Well, and as things seem to work with young girls, soon her interest was transferred—

FISTULA: By pure chance—

FOUSTKA: From what was being explained to the one who was explaining. I don't see anything about it that goes beyond the bounds of the ordinary. Second of all, seeing what happened to that poor child as a result of our conversation, my conscience is filled with heavy reproaches that it happened at all, even though I certainly never knew, and had no way of knowing, that our talk would have such consequences . . .

(FISTULA *begins to chortle and merrily slaps his thigh.*)

What's so funny about that?

FISTULA: (*Becomes serious*) My dear Doctor Foustka! Everybody knows that you don't believe in pure chance or coincidence. Don't you wonder how it happened that a person like you who could hardly stutter a request for a cup of coffee from that young woman until that moment suddenly found himself endowed with such impressive eloquence combined with the courage to express thoughts that are more than dangerous to express on the premises of your Institute? And doesn't it surprise you that it happened at just the very moment we had dreamed up our little idea? Honestly, aren't you a bit amazed at how your thoughts suddenly broke down that young woman's defenses—as if someone had waved a magic wand and allowed her to fall madly and indelibly in love in no time at all.

FOUSTKA: We all have moments in our lives when we seem to outdo ourselves.

FISTULA: That's just what I'm talking about!

FOUSTKA: I don't understand what you mean.

FISTULA: You didn't really expect Jeviel, the spirit of love, to arrive at your office party dressed in evening clothes all ready to fix everything up for you as if he were some sort of matchmaker? How else do you imagine he could do it than by means of your own self? He simply incorporated himself into you! Or rather, he simply awakened and liberated certain things that had always been dormant inside of you! Or to be even more precise, it was actually you yourself who decided to drop the reins restraining certain of your inner powers, and you yourself, therefore, who filled in for him, so to speak, or who fulfilled his intentions and thus won the day in his image, bearing his name!

FOUSTKA: There you are!

FISTULA: Of course a person isn't a static system of some sort—why you as a scientist must know that better than I. If a little seed is to sprout it must first be planted by someone.

FOUSTKA: If it's true that you and your . . .

FISTULA: Jeviel.

FOUSTKA: If you and your Jeviel are really responsible for planting this unfortunate seed, then I curse you from the bottom of my heart! You're a devil and I don't want to have anything to do with you.

FISTULA: You're missing the point again! If the devil exists, then above all he exists within our own selves!

FOUSTKA: Then you, needless to say, must be his favorite residence!

FISTULA: You overestimate my value at least as much as you overestimated your own just a second ago. Think of it this way: I'm only a catalyst who helps his fellow creatures awaken or accelerate things that have long existed within themselves even without his help. My help, you see, merely enables them to discover their own courage to experience and enjoy something thrilling in life and consequently to become more fulfilled themselves! We only live once; why then should we spend those precious few decades that have been allotted to us stifling under the cover of some sort of philistine scruples? Do you know why you called me a devil? In order to shift your own responsibility—purely out of fear of your own scruples and of that thing within you that breaks them down—to a place outside of your own ego, in this case onto me, and by means of this "transference" as you scientists call it, or "projec-

tion," to ease your conscience! You hoped to fool your own scruples by using this kind of maneuver, and by assigning me that insulting name you hoped you'd actually even please them. But think of it this way, Doctor Foustka: I—a certain cripple, Fistula—wouldn't be able to move you an inch if you hadn't secretly dreamed about moving in that direction yourself long ago! Our little experiment had no other purpose than to clarify these little trivialities for you.

FOUSTKA: And what about your assurance that it was innocent? That was a dirty trick!

FISTULA: Wrong again! You're still only deceiving your own self! After all, you could have talked to the girl about the beauties of the scientific worldview and the worldwide significance of your Institute and she would have avoided any danger. But even after you did it the other way, you didn't have to abandon her so selfishly when things began to seem hopeless! But that's not the point now. There's one thing I've got to hand you, with my deepest compliments, especially since you're a beginner: your disguise—that classic tool of Jeviel's—in the pious habit of an ecstatic seeker after that one (*points his finger skyward*) as the true source of meaning of all creation and of all moral imperatives—that was truly brilliant! Congratulations!

FOUSTKA: (*Angrily*) What disguise? I was only saying what I believed!

FISTULA: My dear friend . . .

FOUSTKA: I'm not your friend!

FISTULA: My dear Sir, the truth isn't merely what we believe, after all, but also why and to whom and under what circumstances we say it!

(FOUSTKA *stares vacantly at* FISTULA *for a moment, then sadly nods his head, paces back and forth across the room a few times, and sits down again. After a while he begins to speak.*)

FOUSTKA: (*Quietly*) It's not altogether clear to me how they did it, but they sniffed out my contacts with you somehow, for which I'll most likely be fired from the Institute, punished as an example, publicly disgraced, and probably deprived of my livelihood and everything else. But certainly all this is merely superficial and immaterial, at least as far as I'm personally concerned. I see the true significance of what is in store for me as something else. It will be a deserved punishment for the unforgivable irresponsibility with which I behaved; for losing my moral vigilance and giving in to temptation, while under the poisonous influence of unjustified, malicious, and totally self-centered jealousy. I was trying to kill two birds with one stone and, in this way, hoping to win over one person and at the same time to wound another. I was truly blinded by something diabolical within me, and therefore I'm grateful to you for enabling me to have this experience, no matter how or why you did it. You simultaneously awakened both that temptation and that mean-spirited jealousy in me, and thus you made it possible for me to come to understand my own self better, especially my darkest sides. But that's not all. Your explanation has helped illuminate the true source of my doubt, which really does lie nowhere else but in my own self. Therefore I have no regrets about our meeting, if one can use that word to describe the way you forced yourself on me. It was an important lesson, and your dark designs have helped me discover a new inner light. I'm telling you this because it's my hope that we'll never see each other again, since I'm hoping that you'll leave this place immediately.

(A long pause. FISTULA *slowly takes his shoes out of the bag, looks at them thoughtfully for a while, sniffs them, then finally places them on the ground in front of him and turns with a smile to* FOUSTKA.*)*

FISTULA: Each of us is master of his own fate! I really wanted to mention something else, but now I'm not sure whether it wouldn't be better to wait for a time when you'll be in more of a—please pardon the expression—hot spot and, therefore, more receptive.

FOUSTKA: What did you want to mention?

FISTULA: I know that mechanism of thought rotation which you just demonstrated as well as I know these shoes of mine! We sorcerers call it the Smichovsky Compensation Syndrome.

FOUSTKA: What's that?

FISTULA: When a novice first manages to break through the armor of his old defenses and opens himself up to the immense horizons of his hidden potential, after a little while something like a hangover sets in and he sinks into an almost masochistic state of self-accusation and self-punishment. Psychologically this emotional reaction is quite understandable: in an effort to mollify his betrayed scruples, almost as an afterthought, the novice mentally transforms the action through which he betrayed them into some sort of purifying lesson which he had to learn in order to become better. He makes of it, in short, a sort of small dance floor on which to perform ritual celebrations of his principles. It usually doesn't last long, and when he comes to his senses he recognizes what we, of course, knew from the start, but what we couldn't really explain to him: that is, the grotesque discrepancy between the dubious values in whose name he called down the most frightful punishment on himself, and the fundamental, existential significance of the experience that he is trying to atone for by means of this punishment.

*(*FOUSTKA *jumps up and angrily smashes the table.)*

FOUSTKA: That's it—now I've really had enough! If you think that all your high-flown oratory can get me tangled up in some new pseudoadventure, you're very much mistaken!

FISTULA: It's you who are very much mistaken if you think you aren't already tangled up . . .

FOUSTKA: *(Crying out)* Get out!

FISTULA: I'd just like to warn you that when you get back in touch with reality and suddenly feel the need for a consultation, I won't necessarily be available. But that's your business, after all . . .

FOUSTKA: Please—go away! I want to be alone with my Smichovsky Compensation Syndrome!

*(*FISTULA *slowly takes his shoes in his hands, all the while shaking his head in disbelief. Then, suddenly, he slams the shoes down on the floor, jumps up, and begins to wildly smack himself on the forehead.)*

FISTULA: I can hardly believe it! Because he dared to philosophize for a few minutes with another woman, his mistress throws a fit and denounces him for associating with a sorcerer.

FOUSTKA: What? That's a dirty lie!

FISTULA: And for that he'd be willing to give up his earnings, his scientific future, and maybe everything he owns without a fight! I've seen a lot of things, but this is a first! Smichovsky himself would have had his mind blown by this one!

FOUSTKA: I don't believe she'd stoop that low! After all those golden hours of sheer happiness we've had together!

FISTULA: Ah, what do you know about a woman's heart? Maybe the very memory of those hours provides the key to what she did! *(*FISTULA *calms down, sits down, slowly takes off his slippers, sniffs them, then carefully puts them away in his bag and begins to put on his shoes. A long pause.)*

FOUSTKA: *(Quietly)* And what, in your opinion, could I still do?

FISTULA: Let's not get into that.

FOUSTKA: Come on, tell me.

FISTULA: As you've probably realized, I don't give concrete advice and I don't make arrangements for anybody. At most I occasionally inspire . . . *(His shoes on, he grabs his bag with the slippers and heads for the door.)*

FOUSTKA: *(Screaming out)* Say it straight out, damn it!

*(*FISTULA *stops, stands completely still for a moment, and then turns to* FOUSTKA.*)*

FISTULA: It would be enough if you mobilized, in the name of a good cause, at least one thousandth of the cunning that your director mobilizes from morning till night in the name of a bad one!

(FISTULA *begins to grin stupidly.* FOUSTKA *stares at him with amazement.*)

(*The curtain falls.*)

SCENE 7

(*The same room of the Institute in which Scenes 1 and 5 take place. Instead of the chandelier, a light bulb is suspended from an electrical wire. As the curtain rises,* LORENCOVA, KOTRLY, *and* NEUWIRTH *are onstage.* LORENCOVA, *wearing a white coat, is sitting at the desk, a compact propped up against the typewriter, powdering her nose.* KOTRLY, *wearing a white coat, is sprawled out on the bench, reading the newspaper.* NEUWIRTH, *in civilian clothes, is standing at the rear by the bookcase, his back to the audience, examining a book. A short pause.*)

LORENCOVA: What are we going to do about the coffee?
KOTRLY: (*Without looking up*) Why don't you make it?
LORENCOVA: Why don't you?

(FOUSTKA, *wearing a black sweater and black pants, quickly enters through the rear door, a briefcase in his hand, slightly out of breath.*)

FOUSTKA: Hi.
NEUWIRTH: (*Without turning around*) Hi.

(*No one reacts to* FOUSTKA's *entrance; all continue doing what they were doing before.* FOUSTKA *sets his briefcase down on the desk and begins to take out various papers.*)

FOUSTKA: Were they here yet?
NEUWIRTH: (*Without turning around*) Not yet.

(*When* FOUSTKA *sees that* LORENCOVA *is not going to free the desk for him he crosses over to the bench where* KOTRLY *is sitting and sits down next to him. A pause.*)

LORENCOVA: Poor Marketa.

(FOUSTKA *looks up.*)

KOTRLY: (*Without looking up*) What's with her?
LORENCOVA: She tried to slit her wrists.

(FOUSTKA *stands up, shaken.*)

KOTRLY: (*Without turning around*) So it's true after all?
NEUWIRTH: (*Without turning around*) They say she's in the psychiatric ward.
LORENCOVA: Poor thing.

(FOUSTKA *sits down again. The* DEPUTY, *in everyday clothes, and* PETRUSHKA, *in a white coat, enter through the right door, holding hands.* LORENCOVA *shoves the compact into her coat pocket.* KOTRLY *folds his newspaper.* NEUWIRTH *puts aside the book and turns around.* LORENCOVA, KOTRLY, *and* FOUSTKA *stand up.*)

KOTRLY: Good morning, Sir.
DEPUTY: Hello there, my friends! And please sit down.

(LORENCOVA, KOTRLY, *and* FOUSTKA *sit down again. A short pause.*)

I don't see Vilma here.
FOUSTKA: She's at the dentist.

(*Short pause.*)

DEPUTY: As you well know, the task we're facing today is not an easy one. Nobody here—as our director said so nicely—has any intention of staging a witch-hunt. The truth must prevail, come what may. But for that very reason we must remind ourselves that looking for the truth means looking for the whole, unadulterated truth. That is to say that the truth isn't only something that can be demonstrated in one way or another, it is also the purpose for which the demonstrated thing is used or for which it may be misused, and who boasts about it and why, and in what context it finds itself. As scientists we know well that by tearing a certain fact out of its context we can not only completely shift or change its meaning, but we can stand it right on its head and thus make a lie out of the truth or vice versa. In short, then, we shouldn't allow the living background of the acts with which we are going to concern ourselves to disappear from our field of vision, nor the conclusions which we will draw about them. I hope I don't have to elaborate any further—we aren't little children, damn it! Or are we?
KOTRLY: We aren't.
DEPUTY: So there you are! Who's feeding the carrier pigeons today?
NEUWIRTH: I am.
DEPUTY: Splendid!

(*The* DIRECTOR, *wearing a white coat, enters through the right door.* LORENCOVA, KOTRLY, *and* FOUSTKA *rise immediately.*)

KOTRLY: Hi.
DIRECTOR: Hello there, my friends! And please sit down.

(LORENCOVA, KOTRLY, *and* FOUSTKA *sit down. A short pause.*)

I don't see Vilma.
DEPUTY: I didn't see her either when I came. She's apparently at the dentist.

(*The* DIRECTOR *approaches* KOTRLY *and holds out his hand.* KOTRLY *rises.*)

DIRECTOR: (*To* KOTRLY) Did you get a good night's sleep?
KOTRLY: Very good, thank you.

(*The* DIRECTOR *presses* KOTRLY's *elbow in a friendly manner and turns to the others.* KOTRLY *sits down.*)

DIRECTOR: As you well know, the task we're facing today is not an easy one.

DEPUTY: That's precisely what I was telling our colleagues just a second ago, Sir!

DIRECTOR: We all know the issue, so we can skip the preliminaries . . .

(VILMA, *out of breath, and carrying a large paper box in her hand, rushes in through the rear door.*)

VILMA: Please excuse me, Sir, I'm very sorry . . . I had an appointment at the dentist this morning, and can you imagine, I—

DIRECTOR: I know about it, sit down.

(VILMA *sits on the oilcloth couch, places the box at her feet, communicates something through gestures to* FOUSTKA, *and then shows that she is crossing her fingers for him.* LORENCOVA *leans over to her.*)

LORENCOVA: (*Quietly*) What's this?

VILMA: (*Quietly*) A toaster from the repair shop.

LORENCOVA: (*Quietly*) I thought it was a new hat.

VILMA: (*Quietly*) No.

DIRECTOR: Where was I?

KOTRLY: You were saying that we can skip the preliminaries . . .

DIRECTOR: Ah yes. So we can skip the preliminaries and get right to the subject. Doctor Foustka, if you would kindly . . .

(*The* DIRECTOR *motions to* FOUSTKA *to come to the front.* FOUSTKA *rises, crosses to the middle of the room, and stands in the place where the* DIRECTOR *has indicated.*)

There, that's good. Shall we begin?

FOUSTKA: Certainly.

DIRECTOR: Well, then, could you tell us, my friend, whether it's true that for some time now . . .

(*At that moment the* SECRET MESSENGER *enters through the right door, steps up to the* DIRECTOR, *and whispers something at length in his ear. The* DIRECTOR *gravely nods his head. After a longer while the* SECRET MESSENGER *concludes. The* DIRECTOR *nods his head one last time. The* SECRET MESSENGER *exits through the right door.*)

Where was I?

KOTRLY: You were asking him whether it's true that for some time now . . .

DIRECTOR: Ah yes. Well, then, could you tell us, Sir, whether it's true that for some time now you've been engaged in the study of what's known as occult literature?

FOUSTKA: It's true.

DIRECTOR: For how long?

FOUSTKA: I don't know exactly . . .

DIRECTOR: A round number will do. A half a year? A year?

FOUSTKA: Something like that.

DIRECTOR: How many such books, in your estimation, did you read in that period?

FOUSTKA: I didn't count them.

DIRECTOR: A round number will do. Five? Thirty? Fifty?

FOUSTKA: Maybe fifty.

DIRECTOR: To whom did you lend them out?

FOUSTKA: No one.

DIRECTOR: Now, now, Sir, you aren't going to tell us that nobody borrowed such desirable and rare books from you, books impossible to come by these days! Your friends obviously had to see them at your place.

FOUSTKA: I don't invite friends over to my place, and I never lend books.

DIRECTOR: Very well, then. And now please concentrate—this is an important question: what led you to these studies? Why, actually, did you begin a systematic investigation of these things?

FOUSTKA: I'd been uneasy for a long time about our young people's mounting interest in everything that has anything to do with the so-called supernatural. As a result of this uneasiness of mine I gradually decided to write a brochure in which I would try to demonstrate, by means of mysticism itself, how incongruous that conglomeration of twisted fragments from various cultural circles is, and how strikingly inconsistent these various idealistic and mystical theories of the past are with contemporary scientific knowledge. At the same time I especially chose mysticism as the subject for my critical attention rather than any other because of the uncritical interest it is enjoying today. My project, of course, required—

DIRECTOR: (*Interrupting*) None of us doubted, Sir, that you would answer that question precisely as you did. But in the meanwhile, none of us knows how you intend to explain the shocking fact that you allegedly practiced black magic yourself.

FOUSTKA: I didn't really practice it much; mostly I just spread the word that I did.

DIRECTOR: Why?

FOUSTKA: Because that was the only way to build trust among people as mistrustful as today's sorcerers are.

DIRECTOR: So you craved their trust? Interesting, interesting! How far did you get in achieving it?

FOUSTKA: So far I've been only modestly successful, my success taking the form of a certain source who visited me two times, about whom you have been informed.

DIRECTOR: Did that source tell you why it sought you out?

FOUSTKA: Apparently it knew about my interest in the practice of black magic and was willing to initiate me into it.

DIRECTOR: Did you agree to that?

FOUSTKA: Not expressly, but at the same time I didn't expressly refuse. We're in a state of so-called mutual discussion.

DIRECTOR: What does it want in return?

FOUSTKA: For me to testify that it put itself at the disposal of science, if the need arises.

DEPUTY: Do you hear that, Sir! What a cunning bunch they are!

DIRECTOR: It seems to me, Foustka, that it's high time to ask our pivotal question: how do you explain the fact that on the one hand you claim to have a scientific viewpoint, and consequently must know that black magic is sheer charlatanism, while on the other hand you're trying to gain the trust of sorcerers, and when one of them actually seeks you out, not only do you *not* kick him out and laugh in his face, but on the contrary, you make plans to collaborate with him, and indeed, even to cover up for him? You'll surely find it hard to explain these murky contacts and activities by invoking scientific-critical interests.

FOUSTKA: It may seem foolish to you, but I simply felt from the very first that my efforts to help those seduced by charlatans and my intentions to fight effectively against such seducers must not be confined to mere theoretical-propagandistic work. I was and am to this day convinced that it wouldn't be honest to keep my hands entirely clear of living reality in an effort to keep them clean, as it were, and to lull my conscience with illusions about God knows what great practical results coming out of my theoretical struggle. I simply felt that if you start something you're obliged to finish it, and that it is my civic duty to put my theoretical knowledge in the service of the practical struggle, which means concretely searching for the hotbed of those activities, and then uncovering and convicting the perpetrators. Why, we're constantly boasting about our battle against fakery, mysticism, and superstition, but if we had to point a finger at even a single disseminator of these poisons, we couldn't do it! But not just us—it's almost unbelievable how little success anybody has had in infiltrating those areas, and thanks to that, how little is known about them! Small wonder, then, that they're spreading so rampantly. That's why I decided to win the confidence of those circles, infiltrate them, and there, in the field, to gather evidence of their guilt! Which of course I couldn't do without pretending to have at least partial belief in their spirits, initiations, evocations, magical spells, incubi, and succubi and all that other rubbish. I'd probably even be forced to swear oaths of silence or provide eventual cover-ups. In short, I decided to enlist as an inconspicuous and possibly solitary soldier in this silent war, as one might call it, because I arrived at the conclusion that my expertise put me under a direct obligation to do so. We're dealing, you see, with a sphere in which, unfortunately, a so-called broad perspective is still considered valuable, if not an actual prerequisite for any participation in its life.

(A long pause. Everyone present is stunned, each looks in confusion at the others, then finally all looks come to center on the DIRECTOR.)

DIRECTOR: So that you actually . . . I see . . . I see . . . *(Pause.)* Well, in fact, it wouldn't be such a bad thing if our Institute could pull off a truly concrete victory like that! Our colleague Foustka is right about one thing, brochures have never won wars.

DEPUTY: *(To FOUSTKA)* You would therefore be willing, if I understand you correctly, to provide us with notes about each of your encounters, whether with that source of yours or with any others.

FOUSTKA: Of course! That's exactly why I'm doing it!

DEPUTY: That wouldn't be such a bad thing, as our director has already pointed out. But just one thing isn't clear to me: why did we have to hear about your praiseworthy initiative only now, after certain unfair—as it turns out—accusations have been leveled against you? Why didn't you yourself keep us informed right from the start about your decision and your first steps?

FOUSTKA: I see now that it was a mistake. But I looked at it in a completely different way. As a researcher who is inexperienced in hands-on fieldwork, I unconsciously compared my role to the situation of an independent scientific worker, who doesn't keep a running account of each of his professional moves either. I thought that it would be sufficient—just as it is in theoretical work—to write a report about my work only at the point where there is really something to report about, that is, when I actually had something concretely relevant and useful in hand. It absolutely never crossed my mind that some chance information about my activities from someone uninformed about their purpose might in some way shake the confidence that I had hitherto enjoyed here.

DIRECTOR: You really can't be surprised at that, Foustka. Your decision, however noble-minded, is unfortunately so unusual, and, truth to tell, so totally unexpected from you of all people, that logically our first conclusions were more likely to be on the negative side.

DEPUTY: You really can't be surprised at that, Dr. Foustka.

DIRECTOR: Never mind—let's come to some sort of conclusion, then. You've convinced me that this was all a sheer misunderstanding, and I'm glad that everything was cleared up so quickly. Needless to say, I think highly of your brave decision and I can assure you that this work of yours will be prized all the more for it, especially once you get in the habit of keeping thorough records of it and simultaneously keeping us informed. Does anyone have anything further to add? *(An awkward pause.)* Nobody does? In that case, the time has come for a small surprise:

tomorrow's get-together at the Institute garden will
   be a costume party!

LORENCOVA: Bravo!

KOTRLY: A great idea!

DEPUTY: Oh, yes! I like it a lot too.

LORENCOVA: And what theme will it have?

DIRECTOR: Isn't it obvious? A witches' sabbath!

(A wave of commotion runs through the room.)

A gathering of devils, witches, sorcerers, and magi-
   cians. Classy, what? Originally I only saw it as an
   attempt to liven up the office party tradition with a
   certain parodistic element. It seemed to me that if
   at night we made fun of the very thing we have to
   fight against so seriously and soberly during the
   day, we could—in the spirit of modern group-cos-
   tume therapy—enhance our relationship to our
   own work. Simply by treating the problem with
   frivolity for a few moments we would emphasize its
   permanent unfrivolity, by making light of it we
   would emphasize its gravity, by stepping away from
   it we would get closer to it. Now, however, thanks
   to a timely coincidence, I think we can see it in yet
   another way: as a playful tribute to the work of our
   colleague Foustka here, who not only needs to find
   a disguise, in the metaphorical sense of the word,
   but also may face the unenviable task of finding a
   literal disguise soon—on that occasion when he decides to infiltrate some actual black mass or other!
   (Polite laughter.) Ah well, let's all look at it—at least
   in part—as a sort of jolly little ending to the serious
   transaction we just concluded! Who's feeding the
   carrier pigeons today?

NEUWIRTH: I am.

DIRECTOR: Splendid! *(To* KOTRLY*)* Vilem, don't forget!

(The curtain falls.)

SCENE 8

*(*VILMA's *apartment again. As the curtain rises,*
FOUSTKA, *wearing undershorts, is sitting on the bed, and*
VILMA, *wearing a slip, is combing her hair at the mirror—
the situation is the same as at the beginning of Scene 4.)*

FOUSTKA: I just bet you could buy him off with a mere
   kiss on the cheek, once he was in the house! Surely
   he tried to dance with you at the very least!

VILMA: Henry, drop it, for goodness sake! I don't keep
   pumping you for details either—and I'd have far
   more reason to do so!

(A short pause. Then FOUSTKA *gets up and begins to
walk back and forth, deep in thought.* VILMA *stops combing her hair and looks at him in surprise.)*

What's wrong?

FOUSTKA: What should be wrong?

VILMA: You began so well.

FOUSTKA: Somehow I'm not in the mood for it today.

VILMA: Does it arouse you too much?

FOUSTKA: It's not that.

VILMA: So what happened?

FOUSTKA: You know very well.

VILMA: I don't!

FOUSTKA: You really don't know? And who denounced
   me to the director about the sorcerer coming to see
   me, you don't know that either?

*(*VILMA *freezes, then throws down the comb, jumps up
excitedly, and looks at* FOUSTKA *with astonishment.)*

VILMA: For God's sake, Henry, you don't think that—

FOUSTKA: Nobody else at the Institute knew about it!

VILMA: Are you crazy? Why would I do it, for goodness
   sake? If you're going to insult me with the thought
   that I could denounce anybody at all to that imbecile, how can you imagine that I'd go and denounce
   you? Why, that would be as bad as denouncing my
   own self! You know how much I want you to be
   happy, and how I'm constantly worrying about you!
   How could I possibly want to destroy you all of a
   sudden? And my own self at the same time—our
   relationship—our life together—our make-believe
   jealousy games—our love—so marvelously confirmed by those flashes of true jealousy that you've
   begun to show in recent days, our memories of all
   those golden hours of sheer happiness we've had
   together—why, it would be pure madness!

FOUSTKA: What if it were precisely the memory of those
   golden hours that provided the key to such an act?
   What do I know about a woman's heart? Maybe you
   wanted to get even with me over Marketa—or
   maybe it was just fear of that cripple and an effort
   to save me from what you thought were his clutches
   in this way.

*(*VILMA *runs to the bed, throws herself face down on the
pillows, and begins to sob desperately.* FOUSTKA *doesn't
know what to do. He looks at* VILMA *helplessly for a
while, then sits down beside her cautiously and begins to
stroke her hair.)*

Come on, Vilma.

(Pause. VILMA *sobs.)*

I didn't mean it that way.

(Pause. VILMA *sobs.)*

I was just kidding.

(Pause. VILMA *sobs.)*

I just wanted to try a new game.

(Pause. VILMA *suddenly sits up briskly, dries her eyes with
a handkerchief, and snuffles her nose to clear it. When
she feels herself sufficiently calm and strong she speaks
coldly.)*

VILMA: Go away!

(FOUSTKA *tries to stroke her; she pushes him away and cries out.*)

Don't touch me—just go!

FOUSTKA: Vilma! I didn't say anything all that terrible! How many times did you want me to tell you far more terrible things!

VILMA: That was different. Are you even aware of what you just did? Why, you actually accused me of being a stool pigeon. I'm asking you to get dressed, to leave, and never to try to repair what you just destroyed so brutally!

FOUSTKA: Are you serious?

VILMA: At least we'll have it over with. It would have happened sooner or later in any case!

FOUSTKA: Because of that dancer?

VILMA: No.

FOUSTKA: Why, then?

VILMA: I'm beginning to lose my respect for you.

FOUSTKA: This is the first I've heard of it.

VILMA: It doesn't take long to happen, you know. I actually realized it only today, when I saw the way you saved your neck at the Institute. Offering the director to inform for him, and so shamelessly, in front of everybody! And now, to top it all off, you, a voluntary and self-declared stool pigeon, dare to accuse me, innocent and devoted me, of informing—and what's more, of informing on you! Do you see how absurd it is? What's happened to you? What's gotten into you? Are you actually the same person anymore? Maybe you really *are* possessed by some devil! That fellow addled your brains. God knows what stuff he told you. God knows what spell he cast on you.

(FOUSTKA *gets up and begins to walk back and forth across the room in agitation.*)

FOUSTKA: For your information he doesn't cast spells, he only helps people understand their own selves better and face all the bad things dormant inside them! Furthermore, about my being a stool pigeon, as you put it, not only was that the only way I could save myself, it was also the only way I could help him as well! If they believe that I'm controlling him, they'll leave him alone. And the third thing, my suspecting that they found out about him from you—I simply couldn't hide it from you. What would that have done to our relationship! You might have said something unintentionally—in front of someone you trusted by mistake—or somebody could have accidentally overheard you . . .

VILMA: I never said anything intentionally or not, and what bothers me about your suspicions is not your speaking up about them, or even that you spoke up so crudely, which you're now belatedly trying to make up for, but that they occurred to you at all! If you're capable of thinking something like that

about me for even a split second, then there's really no point in our staying together.

(*Pause.* FOUSTKA *sits down dejectedly in the armchair and stares dully into space.*)

FOUSTKA: I was a fool to say anything to you. I always spoil everything so stupidly. What am I going to do without you? I can't stand myself.

VILMA: And now you're even feeling sorry for yourself!

FOUSTKA: Do you remember what we said to each other that time under the elms at the riverbank?

VILMA: Don't drag those elms into this, it won't do you any good. You've hurt me too much to talk your way out of it by manipulating our memories of the past. And besides, I asked you to do something . . .

FOUSTKA: You mean that I should leave?

VILMA: Exactly!

FOUSTKA: You're expecting the dancer, aren't you?

VILMA: I'm not expecting anyone, I simply want to be alone!

(*A short pause. Then* FOUSTKA *suddenly jumps up, runs over to* VILMA, *knocks her down roughly on the bed, and grabs her wildly by the neck.*)

FOUSTKA: (*In a dark voice*) You're lying, you whore!

VILMA: (*Crying out in terror*) Help!

(FOUSTKA *begins to strangle* VILMA. *Just then the door-bell rings.* FOUSTKA *drops* VILMA *immediately, jumps away from her in confusion, stands there for a moment helplessly, then slowly heads for the armchair and lowers himself into it heavily.* VILMA *stands up, quickly straightens herself up a bit, goes to the door, and opens it. There stands the* DANCER, *holding a bunch of violets behind his back.*)

DANCER: Excuse me for disturbing you so late, I only wanted to bring you these. (*The* DANCER *hands* VILMA *the violets.*)

VILMA: Thanks! Come in, please, and stay a while . . .

(*The* DANCER *looks at* VILMA *in surprise, and then at* FOUSTKA *collapsed in the armchair staring absently into space. An awkward pause.*)

He's not feeling well, you see—I'm a little worried.

DANCER: Some sort of heart trouble?

VILMA: Probably.

DANCER: So in the meanwhile we could dance a little bit, what do you say? Maybe it would distract him.

(*The curtain falls.*)

SCENE 9

(FOUSTKA'S *apartment again. As the curtain rises,* FOUSTKA *is alone onstage. Dressed in a dressing gown, he is pacing back and forth, deep in thought. After a long while someone knocks at the door.* FOUSTKA *stops in his tracks, hesitates for a moment, and then calls.*)

FOUSTKA: Who is it?

HOUBOVA: *(Offstage)* It's me, Doctor Foustka.

FOUSTKA: *(Calling)* Come in, Mrs. Houbova.

HOUBOVA: *(Entering)* You've got a visitor.

FOUSTKA: I do? Who?

HOUBOVA: Well, it's him again . . . you know . . . the one that . . .

FOUSTKA: That smells?

HOUBOVA: Yes.

FOUSTKA: Show him in.

(A short pause; HOUBOVA stands uncertainly.)

What's the matter?

HOUBOVA: Doctor Foustka . . .

FOUSTKA: Did something happen?

HOUBOVA: I'm just a stupid woman. I know it's not my place to give you advice about anything.

FOUSTKA: What's on your mind?

HOUBOVA: I'm sorry, but if I were in your place I wouldn't trust that fellow! I can't really explain it—I don't even know what business he has with you—I just have a sort of strange feeling about him.

FOUSTKA: Last time you let him in yourself!

HOUBOVA: Because I was scared of him.

FOUSTKA: I'll admit he looks disreputable, but basically he's harmless. Or, to be more precise, he's too insignificant to do any serious damage.

HOUBOVA: Do you have to associate with people like him? You?

FOUSTKA: Mrs. Houbova, I'm a grown-up and I know what I'm doing, after all!

HOUBOVA: But I'm so worried about you! Don't you see, I remember you as a three-year-old. I don't have children of my own . . .

FOUSTKA: Of course, that's fine, I'm really grateful for your concern. I understand and I appreciate it, but I think that in this case it's really unnecessary. Show him in and don't worry about it anymore.

(HOUBOVA exits, leaving the door ajar.)

HOUBOVA: *(Offstage)* This way, Mister.

(FISTULA enters, carrying his bag in his hand. HOUBOVA takes one last look after him into the room, shakes her head anxiously, and closes the door. FISTULA, grinning stupidly, rushes directly to the sofa, sits down, takes off his shoes, takes his slippers out of the bag and puts them on, puts the shoes into the bag, which he then places on the sofa beside him. He looks up at FOUSTKA and begins to grin.)

FISTULA: So, what?

FOUSTKA: What, what?

FISTULA: I'm waiting for you to begin your usual song and dance.

FOUSTKA: What song and dance?

FISTULA: That I should leave immediately and so on.

(FOUSTKA walks around the room, deep in thought, then sits at his desk.)

FOUSTKA: Listen! In the first place, I've come to understand that it's impossible simply to get rid of you and therefore it makes no sense to waste time trying to do something that's doomed to failure in advance. In the second place, without making too much of your inspirational influence, as you call it, I've come to the conclusion that time spent with you doesn't have to be a complete waste after all. If I have to be a subject for you, why, then, shouldn't you be a subject for me in turn? Or isn't that how your original proposal went: that you offer me an inside look at your practices, for which I, in exchange, guarantee you a certain cover? I've decided to accept your proposal.

FISTULA: I knew you'd work yourself up to it, which was one of the reasons for my persistence. I'm glad that my persistence is finally rewarded. But not to be too humble about it, again: I don't attribute your decision to my persistence alone, but also to the obvious accomplishments our collaboration has achieved . . .

FOUSTKA: What accomplishments are you referring to now?

FISTULA: Not only that you kept your job at the Institute, but that you actually even improved your position there. Meanwhile, it gives me great joy to state that in this particular case you even managed to avoid Smichovsky's Compensatory Syndrome, which is a sign of real progress.

FOUSTKA: If you're trying to suggest that I lost all my moral values and gave in to whatever it is that you're trying to awaken inside of me, then you are very much mistaken. I'm still the same person. I'm just cooler and more in control as a result of my recent experiences, which allows me to know at all times just how far and in which direction—however new it might be for me—I am able to go, without the risk of letting myself in for something that I might bitterly regret later on.

(FISTULA grows slightly uneasy, fidgets a bit, looks around.)

What's the matter with you?

FISTULA: Oh nothing, nothing.

FOUSTKA: You look like you're afraid, which is a condition I don't recognize in you and which would especially surprise me after the explicit promise of cover I just gave you.

(FISTULA takes off his slippers and rubs the soles of his feet with both hands, sighing all the while.)

Does it hurt?

FISTULA: It's nothing, it'll go away. *(After a while he puts on his slippers again. Then he suddenly begins to cackle.)*

FOUSTKA: What's so funny now?

FISTULA: May I be completely frank?

FOUSTKA: Suit yourself.

FISTULA: You are!

FOUSTKA: What? You find me funny? What nerve!

(FISTULA *grows serious and stares at the ground. After a while he suddenly glances up at* FOUSTKA.)

FISTULA: Look here, Doctor Foustka. The fact that you saved your neck by means of a little dirty work is quite all right. Why, Hajaha and I—

FOUSTKA: Who?

FISTULA: Hajaha, the spirit of politics—we were pointing you in that very direction! What's not quite all right is that in the process you forgot the rules of the game!

FOUSTKA: What rules? What game? What the devil are you talking about?

FISTULA: Don't you suppose that our work together has rules of its own too? Break down your own scruples as much as you want—as you know, I always welcome that sort of thing on principle. But to double-cross the very one who is leading you along this thrilling and, I might even say, revolutionary path—that, you really shouldn't do! Even a revolution has its laws! Last time you called me a devil. Imagine for a moment that I really were one! How do you suppose I'd react to your amateurish attempt to deceive me?

FOUSTKA: But I'm not trying to deceive you.

FISTULA: Look, without actually making any explicit promises, we certainly reached a sort of unspoken agreement not to talk about our work together with anyone, much less make reports on it to hostile and threatening authorities. One might even go so far as to say that we had begun—naturally with some caution—to trust each other. If you failed to understand the inner meaning of our agreement and you decided to thumb your nose at it, that was your first serious mistake. You've done enough reading, after all, to know that there are certain limits—even in my sphere—that you can't overstep; in fact, precisely here, with so much at stake, the commandment against overstepping them is especially severe. Don't you understand that if we're capable of playing around with the whole world, it is only and entirely because we depend on contacts that we're absolutely forbidden to play around with? To deceive a liar is fine, to deceive a truth teller is still allowable, but to deceive the very instrument that gives us the strength to deceive and that allows us in advance to deceive with impunity—that, you truly cannot expect to get away with! That one (*points skyward*) overwhelms Man with a multitude of unkeepable commandments, and therefore there's nothing left for him but to forgive occasionally. The others, on the other hand, liberate Man from all those unkeepable commandments, and therefore, understandably, they are totally rid of

the need, opportunity, and, finally, even the capacity to forgive. But even if that weren't so, they wouldn't be able to forgive the betrayal of the very agreement releasing all that boundless freedom. Why, such forgiveness would make their entire world collapse! But really, might not the obligation to be faithful to the authority which gives us that sort of freedom actually be the only guarantee of freedom from all obligation? Do you see what I mean?

(FOUSTKA, *who has been growing increasingly nervous during* FISTULA's *speech, stands up and begins to pace about the room. A long pause.* FISTULA *watches him carefully. Then* FOUSTKA *suddenly comes to a stop at his desk, leans against it as if against a speaker's podium, and turns to* FISTULA.)

FOUSTKA: I see what you mean perfectly well, but I'm afraid you don't see what *I* mean!

FISTULA: Is that so?

FOUSTKA: You can look at the promise you're obviously referring to as an attempt to betray you only because you don't know why I made it and was able to make it with a clear conscience!

FISTULA: You made it in order to save your neck.

FOUSTKA: Of course, but what good would it be if the price were betrayal! I'm not that stupid! The only reason that I was able to make the promise was because I was determined right from the start not only *not* to keep it, but at the same time to cleverly use the position it gained for me—naturally in close consultation with you—for our purposes and to our advantage. In other words, to gain control over their information, while flooding them with our own disinformation; to erase the real tracks, while keeping them busy with false ones; to use their own organization to rescue those of us who are threatened, while drowning those who threaten us. And with all this, to serve our cause by being our own man hidden in the heart of the enemy, indeed, in the very heart of the enemy's division specifically designed to fight against us! I'm surprised and disappointed that you didn't understand and appreciate my plan immediately.

(FOUSTKA *sits.* FISTULA *leaps up and begins to cackle and jump around the room wildly. Then he suddenly stops and quite matter-of-factly turns to* FOUSTKA.)

FISTULA: Even if you just invented this conceit, I'll still accept it, if only to give you one last chance. Actually it *is* possible to forgive, and to give people a chance to make amends, even in our realm. If I claimed the opposite a little while ago, it was only to scare you into coming out with precisely the sort of unambiguous offer as the one you just made, thereby allowing you to save yourself at the very edge of the abyss. But obviously, and luckily for you, I'm really not the devil. He would never have let you get away with the betrayal that I just let you get away with, never!

(FOUSTKA *is visibly relieved, can't hide it, goes to* FISTULA *and embraces him.* FISTULA *jumps aside, his teeth begin to chatter, and he begins to quickly rub his arms.*)

Man, you must be a hundred below zero!

FOUSTKA: (*Laughing*) Not quite.

(*The curtain falls.*)

SCENE 10

(*The Institute garden once again. Except that the bench is now on the right and the table with drinks now on the left, everything is exactly the same as it was in Scene 3, including the lighting. As the curtain rises, the music becomes quiet and changes in style just as at the beginning of Scene 3. This time, too, it will provide a background for the entire scene unless otherwise indicated. The two* LOVERS *and* FOUSTKA *are onstage. The* LOVERS *dance together in the background, where they will continue to dance without interruption for almost the entire scene, leaving their bower empty for now.* FOUSTKA *is sitting on the bench, deep in thought. All three are wearing costumes that suit the "magic" theme of the party.* FOUSTKA *is wearing the traditional theatrical costume for Faust. All characters appearing in this scene are dressed or in some cases painted in this same spirit. Some of the best-known and most common motifs traditionally used in the theater for "hellish" or "witchlike" themes should make an appearance in this scene; for instance, the colors red and black should predominate, as well as a profusion of pendants and amulets of various sorts, wildly tangled women's wigs, devils' tails, hoofs, and chains, etc. A long pause. Then, from the right,* LORENCOVA *emerges with a broom under her arm. She crosses the stage towards the table, where she pours herself a drink. Pause.*)

FOUSTKA: Do you happen to know if the director is here yet?

LORENCOVA: No I don't.

(*Pause.* LORENCOVA *finishes her drink, puts the glass down, and vanishes to the left. After a while she can be seen in the background, dancing alone with her broom. Pause. Then the* DEPUTY *enters from the left.*)

DEPUTY: Have you seen Petrushka?

FOUSTKA: She hasn't been here.

(*The* DEPUTY *shakes his head uncomprehendingly and vanishes to the right. After a while he may be seen in the background, swaying alone to the dance music.* FOUSTKA *gets up and goes to the table, where he pours himself a drink. The* DIRECTOR *and* KOTRLY, *holding hands, enter from the right. Unless otherwise noted, they will be holding hands for the whole scene. The* DIRECTOR, *in a particularly conspicuous devil costume, has horns on his head. The* DIRECTOR *and* KOTRLY *pay no attention to*

FOUSTKA *and stop in the middle of the stage.* FOUSTKA, *at the table, watches them.*)

DIRECTOR: (*To* KOTRLY) Where will you actually put it? Around here?

KOTRLY: I thought I'd put it in the bower.

DIRECTOR: All right. That would be better for safety reasons too.

KOTRLY: I'll light it in the gardener's shed, then I'll secretly bring it here—it takes a few minutes to warm up. I'll set it down in the bower, and a little while later you'll see . . .

(*The* DIRECTOR *and* KOTRLY *head towards the left.*)

FOUSTKA: Excuse me, Sir . . .

(*The* DIRECTOR *and* KOTRLY *stop.*)

DIRECTOR: Yes, Foustka?

FOUSTKA: I wonder if you have a minute or two?

DIRECTOR: I'm sorry, Foustka, but certainly not now.

(*The* DIRECTOR *and* KOTRLY *disappear to the left. After a while they may be seen in the background, dancing together.* FOUSTKA, *holding his glass, crosses back to the bench, deep in thought, and sits down. The music grows noticeably louder, some well-known tango may be heard, for instance, "Tango Milonga."* VILMA *and the* DANCER *rush onstage from the left and begin to do some complicated tango figures together. These are choreographed mainly by the* DANCER, *obviously a professional, who continues to glide about the stage elaborately and skillfully with* VILMA. FOUSTKA *stares at them in astonishment. After a while the tango comes to a climax and* VILMA *and the* DANCER *do a closing figure. The music grows softer and changes its character. Out of breath but happy,* VILMA *and the* DANCER *are holding hands and smiling at each other.*)

FOUSTKA: Are you enjoying yourselves?

VILMA: As you can see.

(*The* DEPUTY, *who has in the interim left the dance floor, enters from the left.*)

DEPUTY: Have you seen Petrushka?

VILMA: She hasn't been here.

(*The* DEPUTY *shakes his head impatiently and vanishes to the right. After a while he may be seen in the background, swaying alone to the dance music.* VILMA *seizes the* DANCER *by the hand and leads him away. They both disappear to the left. After a while they may be seen in the background, dancing.* FOUSTKA *stands up, crosses to the table, and pours himself a drink. The* DIRECTOR *and* KOTRLY, *who have in the interim disappeared from the dance floor, enter from the right, holding hands. They pay no attention to* FOUSTKA *but stop in the middle of the stage.* FOUSTKA, *at the table, watches them.*)

KOTRLY: (*To the* DIRECTOR) How will I know when it's the right time for it?

DIRECTOR: You'll figure it out somehow, or else I'll give you a signal. I'm worried about something else.

KOTRLY: What?

DIRECTOR: Can you really guarantee that nothing will go wrong?

KOTRLY: What should go wrong?

DIRECTOR: Well, somebody might suffocate—or something might catch fire . . .

KOTRLY: Don't worry.

(The DIRECTOR and KOTRLY head towards the left.)

FOUSTKA: Excuse me, Sir . . .

DIRECTOR: Yes, Foustka?

FOUSTKA: I realize that you have a lot of other things on your mind just now, but I won't keep you long, and I'm certain that the thing I want to talk to you about will interest you.

DIRECTOR: I'm sorry, but now it's really impossible . . .

(Just then the SECRET MESSENGER enters from the right, goes up to the DIRECTOR, leans over, and whispers in his ear at length. The DIRECTOR nods his head. While the MESSENGER is whispering, LORENCOVA, who has in the interim left the dance floor, enters from the right holding her broom in her hand. She remains standing near the bench and gazes at the MESSENGER. After a long while the MESSENGER concludes. The DIRECTOR nods one last time, at which point he disappears to the left with KOTRLY. After a while they may be seen in the background, dancing together. The MESSENGER heads towards the right, just opposite LORENCOVA. She is smiling at him. He stops directly in front of her. For a moment both of them stare at each other intently, then the MESSENGER, without taking his eyes off her, takes her broom from her hand, places it on the ground meaningfully, and commences to embrace LORENCOVA. She embraces him in return. For a moment they gaze meltingly into each other's eyes, then they begin to kiss. When they move apart after a while, they disappear together to the right, arms around each other's waists. After a while they may be seen in the background, dancing. FOUSTKA, glass in hand and deep in thought, crosses the stage to the bench and sits down. Suddenly, he becomes attentive and listens. Offstage a girl's voice may be heard, singing the melody of the music that is just playing, Ophelia's song from Hamlet.)

MARKETA: *(Singing offstage)*

And will 'a not come again?
And will 'a not come again?
No, no, he is dead,
Go to thy death bed,

(MARKETA emerges at left. She is barefoot, her hair is loose and flowing; on her head is a wreath made of wild flowers. She is wearing a white nightgown with the word "psychiatry" stamped at the bottom in large letters. She approaches FOUSTKA slowly, singing. He rises, aghast.)

He never will come again.
His beard was as white as snow
All flaxen was his poll
He is gone, he is gone,
And we cast away moan.
God 'a' mercy on his soul!

FOUSTKA: *(Crying out)* Marketa!

MARKETA: Oh where is that handsome Prince of Denmark?

(FOUSTKA, horrified, walks backward in front of MARKETA, she walks behind him, they slowly circle the stage.)

FOUSTKA: What are you doing here, for God's sake? Did you run away?

MARKETA: Tell him, please, when you see him, that all those things can't exist just for themselves, but that they must conceal some deeper design of existence, of the world, and of nature willing you . . .

FOUSTKA: Marketa, don't you recognize me? It's Henry . . .

MARKETA: Or could it be, perhaps, that the cosmos directly intended that one fine day it would see itself thus through our eyes and ask itself thus through our lips the very questions we're asking ourselves here and now?

FOUSTKA: You ought to go back—they'll help you—everything will be all right again—you'll see . . .

MARKETA: *(Singing)*

How should I your true love know
From another one?
By his cockle hat and staff,
And his sandal shoon.

(MARKETA vanishes to the right. Offstage the sound of her singing can still be heard, gradually fading away. FOUSTKA, upset, crosses over to the table, quickly pours himself a drink, downs it in one gulp, and pours himself another. The DIRECTOR and KOTRLY, who have in the interim left the dance floor, appear at the right, holding hands. They pay no attention to FOUSTKA but are absorbed in their conversation.)

DIRECTOR: Surely he tried to dance with you at the very least . . .

KOTRLY: Please stop it! Can't you talk about anything more interesting?

DIRECTOR: Did he try or not?

KOTRLY: All right, he did, if you really must know, then he did! But I won't tell you another thing.

(The DIRECTOR and KOTRLY slowly cross the stage and head for the exit at left.)

FOUSTKA: Excuse me, Sir . . .

(The DIRECTOR and KOTRLY stop.)

DIRECTOR: What do you want, Foustka?

(*Just then a cry of pain is heard from behind the bench.*)

NEUWIRTH: (*Offstage*) Ow!

(*The* DIRECTOR, KOTRLY, *and* FOUSTKA *look towards the bench with surprise. Out of the bushes emerges* NEUWIRTH, *holding his ear, obviously wounded. He is groaning.*)

KOTRLY: What in the world happened to you, Louie?
NEUWIRTH: Oh, nothing.
DIRECTOR: Is something the matter with your ear?

(NEUWIRTH *nods.*)

KOTRLY: Did something bite you?

(NEUWIRTH *nods, and with his head indicates the bushes from which he had just emerged and out of which now emerges an embarrassed* PETRUSHKA. *She is nervously straightening her hair and her costume. The* DIRECTOR *and* KOTRLY *grin and exchange knowing looks.* NEUWIRTH, *groaning and holding his ear, drags himself off to the right and disappears.* PETRUSHKA *timidly crosses the stage to the table and with shaking hands pours herself a small drink, which she swiftly drinks. The* DIRECTOR *and* KOTRLY *try to leave.*)

FOUSTKA: Excuse me, Sir . . .
DIRECTOR: What do you want, Foustka?

(*Just then the* DEPUTY *enters from the left. At first he doesn't see* PETRUSHKA, *who is hidden by* FOUSTKA.)

DEPUTY: Have you seen Petrushka?

(PETRUSHKA *goes up to the* DEPUTY, *smiles at him, and takes his hand; from this moment on they will hold hands as before.*)

Where were you, sweetie pie?

(PETRUSHKA *whispers something to the* DEPUTY, *he listens carefully, finally he nods in satisfaction. The* DIRECTOR *and* KOTRLY *try to leave.*)

FOUSTKA: Excuse me, Sir . . .
DIRECTOR: What do you want, Foustka?
FOUSTKA: I realize that you have a lot of other things on your mind right now, but on the other hand . . . having learned my lesson by what happened before . . . I wouldn't want to neglect anything . . . You see, I have some new findings . . . I've even written them down on a piece of paper . . .

(FOUSTKA *begins to search, obviously looking for the paper. The* DIRECTOR *and the* DEPUTY *exchange knowing glances and then take a few steps forward, the one leading* KOTRLY *by the hand, the other,* PETRUSHKA, *and move to the center of the stage, where all four automatically form a sort of semicircle around* FOUSTKA. *A short pause.*)

DIRECTOR: Don't bother.

(FOUSTKA *looks at the* DIRECTOR *in surprise, then looks around at the others. A short, suspenseful pause.*)

FOUSTKA: I thought I . . .

(*Again, a suspenseful pause, which is finally interrupted by the* DIRECTOR.)

DIRECTOR: (*Sharply*) I'm not interested in what you thought, I'm not interested in your piece of paper, I'm not interested in you. The comedy, my dear Sir, is ended!
FOUSTKA: I don't understand—what comedy?
DIRECTOR: You greatly overestimated yourself and you greatly underestimated us, taking us for bigger idiots than we are.
DEPUTY: You still don't understand?
FOUSTKA: No.
DIRECTOR: Very well, then, I'll give it to you straight. We knew all along what you thought of us, we knew you were merely pretending to be loyal while hiding your real interests and ideas from us. But in spite of that we decided to give you a last chance. And so while seeming to believe that cock-and-bull story about your intention to work for us out in the field, we were curious to see how you would behave after having had your lesson and your supposed narrow escape, wondering whether you might not come to your senses after all. But instead, you took the hand we offered you and spat on it in a despicable way, thus definitively sealing your own fate.
FOUSTKA: That's not true!
DIRECTOR: You know perfectly well that it is!
FOUSTKA: Then prove it!
DIRECTOR: (*To the* DEPUTY) Shall we oblige him?
DEPUTY: I'm in favor of it.

(*The* DIRECTOR *sharply whistles on his fingers. From the bower, where he had apparently been hidden for the entire scene,* FISTULA *leaps out.* FOUSTKA *is alarmed to see him.* FISTULA *quickly limps over to the* DIRECTOR.)

FISTULA: Did you call, Boss?
DIRECTOR: What did he tell you when you were at his house yesterday?
FISTULA: That he would pretend to be working as an informer for you, but in reality he, together with those you are fighting against, would use all their power to damage your information service. He literally said that he would be our—meaning their—man hidden in the heart of the enemy . . .
FOUSTKA: (*Screaming*) He's lying!
DIRECTOR: What did you say? Would you repeat that?
FOUSTKA: I said he's lying.
DIRECTOR: Man, you really have some nerve! How dare you accuse my close and faithful friend of many years and one of our best external agents of lying! Fistula never lies to us!

DEPUTY: That's precisely what I wanted to say, Sir! Fistula never lies to us!

(LORENCOVA *and the* SECRET MESSENGER *appear from the left, while at the same time the* LOVERS *appear from the right, all of whom have, in the interim, left the dance floor. Both pairs are holding hands. They join the others in such a way that the semicircle in the center of which* FOUSTKA *is standing unobtrusively widens at both sides in order to incorporate them.*)

FOUSTKA: So Fistula was an informer after all, and you planted him on me to test me! What an imbecile I was not to throw him out right away! Vilma, I apologize to you for my absurd suspicions that made me lose you! Mrs. Houbova, I apologize to you—of course you knew the truth right away.

DIRECTOR: Who's he talking to?

FISTULA: His landlady, Boss.

DIRECTOR: Naturally you're not the only person in the world I'm interested in. I test everybody—you'd be surprised how long it sometimes takes, compared to your trivial case—for me to get at the truth, in one way or another!

FOUSTKA: (*To* FISTULA) So I fell for your line after all!

FISTULA: I beg your pardon, Doctor Foustka. (*To the* DIRECTOR) Is he still a doctor?

DIRECTOR: Who gives a shit?

FISTULA: I beg your pardon, Doctor Foustka, but there you go again, oversimplifying! Didn't I make it clear all along, by dropping hints and even spelling it out, that you had a number of alternatives, and that you alone were the master of your fate! You weren't a victim of my line, but of your own; or rather, of your pride, which made you think that you'd be able to play both ends against the middle and still get away with it! Or have you forgotten how carefully I explained to you that if a person doesn't want to come to a bad end, he must respect some form of authority, it almost doesn't matter which, and that even a revolution has its own laws? I don't see how I could have made things more obvious than that! My conscience is clear, I did what I could. Why, I couldn't have fulfilled my mission more correctly! The fact that you didn't understand anything, well, I'm afraid that's your tough luck.

DIRECTOR: Fistula is right, as ever. You cannot serve two masters at once and deceive them both at the same time! You cannot take from everyone and give nothing in return! You simply must take a side!

DEPUTY: That's precisely what I just wanted to say, Sir! You simply must take a side!

(*The music grows noticeably louder. The tango that played earlier is heard again. At the same moment* VILMA *runs onstage from the left and the* DANCER *from the right, having in the interim left the dance floor. They run through the group of people to the center of the stage,* *where they fall into each other's arms and commence to do another complicated tango figure, during which the* DANCER *does a "dip" almost to the ground with* VILMA. *The music suddenly grows quiet, and* VILMA *and the* DANCER, *holding hands just as all the other couples in the room are doing, quietly join the semicircle.*)

FOUSTKA: It's paradoxical, but now that I've definitively lost and my knowledge serves no purpose to me, I'm finally beginning to understand it all! Fistula is right: I was an arrogant madman who thought he could exploit the devil without signing away his soul to him! But as everyone knows, one can't deceive the devil!

(NEUWIRTH, *with a large bandage on his ear, enters from the right, just as* MARKETA *runs in from the left. When she sees* NEUWIRTH *she calls out to him.*)

MARKETA: Papa!

(MARKETA *runs up to* NEUWIRTH *and seizes his hand. He is a little embarrassed. And even they reluctantly become part of the semicircle.*)

FISTULA: Wait a minute, now! Hold it! I never said that there is such a thing as a devil, not even while I was engaged in that provocation.

FOUSTKA: But I'm saying it! And he's actually here among us!

FISTULA: Are you referring to me?

FOUSTKA: You're just a subordinate little fiend!

DIRECTOR: I know your opinions, Foustka, and therefore I understand this metaphor of yours as well. Through me, you want to accuse modern science of being the true source of all evil. Isn't that right?

FOUSTKA: No, it isn't! Through you, I want to accuse the pride of that intolerant, all-powerful, and self-serving power that uses the sciences merely as a handy weapon for shooting down anything that threatens it, that is, anything that doesn't derive its authority from this power or that is related to an authority deriving its powers elsewhere.

DIRECTOR: That's the legacy you wish to leave this world, Foustka?

FOUSTKA: Yes!

DIRECTOR: I find it a little banal. In countries without censorship every halfway clever little hack journalist churns out stuff like that these days! But a legacy is a legacy, so in spite of what you think of me, I'll give you an example of how tolerant I am by overlooking my reservations and applauding your last testament!

(*The* DIRECTOR *begins to clap lightly, and all the others gradually join in. At the same time the music grows louder—it is hard, wild, and aggressive rock music, a variation of the music heard before the performance and during the pauses. The clapping soon becomes rhythmic, in time with the music, which grows ever louder, slowly becoming almost deafening. Everyone onstage, with the exception of* FOUSTKA, *gradually begins to move suggestively in time with the music. At first, while clapping, they begin to wriggle gently, swaying and shaking to the music. Then this movement slowly changes into dancing. At first they each dance alone, then in couples, and finally all together. The dance is ever wilder, until it becomes a crazy, orgiastic masked ball or witches' sabbath.* FOUSTKA *does not participate but wanders around in confusion, weaving in and out among the dancers, who variously bump into him, so that he completely loses his sense of direction and is unable to escape, though he would clearly like to.* KOTRLY, *who slipped away from the witches' sabbath earlier, now returns, carrying a bowl with flames playing at the surface. He twists in and out among the dancers with it, trying to get to the bower, where he finally succeeds in putting the bowl down. However, on the way there he also manages to ignite* FOUSTKA's *cape, so that a new chaotic element is added to the witches' sabbath in the person of the burning* FOUSTKA, *who now, completely panicked, races around the stage. Shortly thereafter everyone is surrounded by a thick cloud of smoke streaming in from the bower where* KOTRLY *has placed his bowl. The music blasts away. Nothing can be seen onstage. Smoke penetrates the audience. Then the music suddenly stops, the house lights go on, the smoke fades, and it becomes evident that at some point during all this the curtain has fallen. After a very brief silence, music comes on again, now at a bearable level of loudness—the most banal commercial music possible. If the smoke—or the play itself—hasn't caused the audience to flee, and if there are still a few left in the audience who might even want to applaud, let the first to take a bow and thank the audience be a fireman in full uniform with a helmet on his head and a fire extinguisher in his hand.)*

Figure 1. The Director of the Institute (Paul Webster) solemnly addresses his staff—Dr. Foustka (John Shrapnel, *back to camera*), Dr. Neuwirth (Trevor Martin), Vilma (Julie Legrand), Dr. Lorencova (Susan Colverd), and, in back, Petrushka (Shirley King) holding hands with the Deputy Director (Barrie Rutter)—in the Royal Shakespeare Company production of *Temptation,* directed by Roger Michell, 1987. (Photograph: Joe Cocks Studio.)

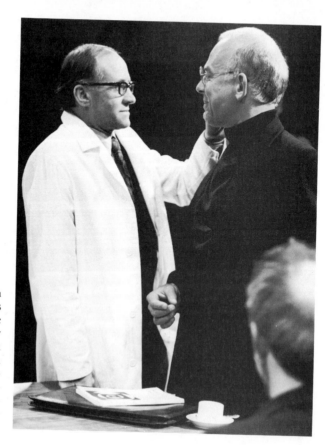

Figure 2. Dr. Foustka (John Shrapnel) smiles nervously as the Director of the Institute (Paul Webster) solicitously tugs his ear and asks "Did you get a good night's sleep?" in the Royal Shakespeare Company production of *Temptation,* directed by Roger Michell, 1987. (Photograph: Joe Cocks Studio.)

Figure 3. Dr. Foustka (John Shrapnel) looks skeptically at the scruffy Fistula (David Bradley) in the Royal Shakespeare Company production of *Temptation*, directed by Roger Michell, 1987. (Photograph: Joe Cocks Studio.)

Staging of *Temptation*

REVIEW OF THE ROYAL SHAKESPEARE COMPANY PRODUCTION, 1987, BY MICHAEL BILLINGTON

Václav Havel's *Largo Desolato*, seen in Bristol last October, gained much of its resonance from our knowledge of the author's personal plight as a reluctant dissident figurehead in present-day Czechoslovakia. But Havel's *Temptation*, now getting its British premiere at Stratford's Other Place, strikes me as a more complex and intriguing work: an absurdist comedy that combines a replay of the Faust legend, anti-bureaucratic satire and a passionate comment on the relativity of truth in any repressive regime.

It is an intoxicatingly theatrical piece that uses each of its ten scenes to take its argument a stage further. Its hero, Dr. Foustka, works for an anonymous scientific Institute but privately engages in hermetic practices from astrology to black magic.

Drawing chalk circles on the floor, he conjures up an evil-smelling, diabolical agent (or possibly agent provocateur) in the shape of Fistula. The Institute prides itself on fighting heretical mysticism. The temptation put before Foustka is to acquaint himself with contemporary magical practice; and the result takes him on a parodic Faustian journey that ends up in a chaotic, smoke-filled, fancy-dress *Walpurgisnacht** in the Institute garden.

"Truth," Fistula says at one point, "is not merely what we are thinking but also why, to whom, and under what circumstances"; and that seems to me the intellectual core of this highly entertaining play. To his skeptical colleagues at the Institute, Foustka is engaged in an undercover exploration of the irrational: to Fistula he is a genuine seeker after knowledge. With his mistress, Vilma, he indulges in erotic bedroom games of pathological jealousy: with the Institute secretary Maggie (the Faustian Marguerita) he becomes a blazing-eyed proponent of an absolute, omniscient, infinitely just moral authority.

---

*Walpurgisnacht (Walpurgis Night): The feast day for St. Walpurga (A.D. 779) falls on May Day; the night before is known as *Walpurgisnacht*, a night when witches are believed to ride to an appointed rendezvous.

Havel's point is not merely the familiar one that we change selves depending on who we are with. He is saying that in any unjust, dictatorial society truth itself becomes, of necessity, a shifting, permanently changing concept.

What makes the play work, however, is the boldness with which Havel fleshes out the idea. The Institute itself is satirically seen as a place of endless power-jockeying where promotion may depend on fixing underwater lights for the office garden party or granting sexual favors to the Director: the climactic Witches Sabbath, with red smoke issuing from parti-colored snakes and hooved devils dancing together, also demonstrates the power vested in authority however deranged it may be. And Foustka's tormented bedroom scenes with Vilma show the thin dividing line between jealousy as a sexual stimulus and maniacal idée fixe.

At times (as when Maggie turns into a distraught waif singing Ophelia's mad songs) one feels Havel is over-egging the pudding. But the piece (in George Theiner's translation) is both symmetrically structured and frantically inventive in its application of the Faust story. And Roger Michell's production succeeds in creating a world existing at a tangent to reality even down to the use of intricate dance patterns to cover the multiple scene changes.

John Shrapnel carries the strenuous burden of the evening as Foustka and cleverly makes him seem equally plausible whether he is vindicating his researches to his colleagues, proclaiming a moral universe to Maggie or shyly resisting the Director's sexual advances. There is good support from David Bradley as the seedy, scrofulous, black-bereted Fistula clutching a carrier-bag, from Julie Legrand as the quixotically changeable mistress, and from Paul Webster as the Institute Director who is one moment a dangerous power-figure and the next an ardent wooer offering to show Foustka his miniatures.

But all the performances reinforce Havel's central point that, in certain societies, truth is determined less by dogmatic certainty than by appropriate context.

DAVID HENRY HWANG

1957–

"Study your face and you will see—the shape of your face is the shape of faces back many generations—across an ocean, in another soil. You must become one with your family before you can hope to live away from it." In these haunting lines from David Henry Hwang's third play, a native Chinese character speaking to his Chinese-American great-nephew defines one of the central problems of identity that have perenially vexed immigrants and children of immigrants— the problem of how to honor one's ethnic heritage while at the same time making a new life in a new land. Hwang (pronounced "Wong"), a first-generation Chinese-American, has explored such problems in a series of plays, each offering a slightly different perspective on the central question of constructing and maintaining one's identity, culminating in the award-winning *M. Butterfly* (1988). Hwang's parents were both born in China, his father emigrating to Los Angeles in the late 1940s to study business at the University of Southern California, his mother arriving in 1952 to study music. His father worked first as an accountant and then went into business for himself, eventually founding the first federally chartered Asian-American bank in the United States. Such notable business success led to almost complete assimilation for the children, all born in America; they studied Chinese for a while but then were withdrawn from those classes. Hwang took violin lessons, participated in debate competition at his private school, and entered Stanford University with plans to study law.

While at Stanford, Hwang became interested in writing plays, despite minimal theatrical experience, and switched his major to English. He saw Sam Shepard's new plays as they were produced at the San Francisco Magic Theater, spent the summer of 1977 working odd jobs in a theater, and in 1978, signed up for a playwriting workshop run by Sam Shepard. As a result, he drafted his first play, *FOB*, which was then produced by his Stanford dormitory as part of a campus festival of student-written plays. He also sent *FOB* to the 1979 Playwrights' Conference at the O'Neill Theater Center in Waterford, Connecticut, where it became one of the twelve selected for development. A year later, in June 1980, Joseph Papp produced *FOB* at the New York Shakespeare Festival Public Theater, thus beginning an association that would last for three years, during which Hwang saw five plays produced in New York.

FOB (the initials stand for "Fresh Off the Boat" in Hwang's play, as well as for "Free on Board" in standard shipping terminology) embodies many of the issues that dominate Hwang's writing. Most centrally, the play dramatizes the question of how Chinese-Americans cope with their various "faces." Each of the play's three characters represents a different stage in the process of cultural mixing and therefore a different balance of the dual heritage: Steve, the FOB, son of a wealthy Hong Kong souvenir manufacturer, has just arrived in Los Angeles; Grace, a first-generation Chinese-American, works in a Chinese restaurant; and Dale, Grace's cousin, a second-generation American of Chinese descent, calls himself an ABC ("American Born Chinese") and despises all FOBs. Yet Hwang asks the audience to see that Dale's verbal attack on Steve is part of his desperate attempt to assimilate—"To not be a Chinese, a yellow, a slant, a gook." Faced with a heritage he cannot escape, in a world he wishes to join, Dale mocks Steve's accent, dumps a bottle of hot sauce all over Steve's food, and competes with Steve for Grace's attention. But in addition to the rivalry over Grace, which is depicted primarily in realistic confrontations, Hwang also presents a symbolic conflict between Grace and Steve staged as a ritual battle. Grace takes on the persona of Fa Mu Lan, the Chinese woman warrior, while Steve assumes the persona of Gwan Gung, the god of fighters and writers. Grace follows her victory over Steve with a peace-offering of Chinese food, the same food Steve asked for at the play's beginning, and then, in a swift return to the play's more realistic mode, invites Steve out for an evening of dancing.

While *FOB* ends with a staged battle, Hwang's second play, *The Dance and the Railroad* (1981), is concerned with performance as a way of accepting one's heritage. Set in 1867, on a mountaintop near the transcontinental railroad, the play presents just two characters: Lone, a dancer from the Chinese Opera, working as a railroad builder, and Ma, who has been in the country for four weeks and is also working on the railroad. By juxtaposing the highly disciplined and ritualistic world of Chinese opera with the unlikely setting of the American West, Hwang underscores Lone's intense commitment to his Chinese heritage. Ma, at first a naïve newcomer (another FOB), gradually wins Lone's respect, and in the play's final scene the two men stage their own "opera," with Ma as the hero.

Though Hwang's third play, *Family Devotions* (1981) also explores issues of Chinese and American identity, it draws much more directly on details from Hwang's own life: a prosperous Southern California setting, a Chinese-American banker, his violinist son, and elderly relations who, like Hwang's own family, are "born-again Christians." The vivid portrayal of the opulent California lifestyle, complete with sunroom, barbecue grill, and tennis courts, is replete with satiric detail, including an opening scene in which characters find the barbecue grill smoking and toss a series of burnt chickens all over the tennis court. As in his earlier plays, Hwang creates confrontations between figures who differ in their affiliation to their shared past. Di-Gou, a resident of the People's Republic of China, has come to California to bring his older sisters back to China. By exposing an unpleasant truth about their aunt See-Goh-Poh, who has become a legend through her status as a Christian missionary, Di-Gou tries to pull his sisters back to their common Chinese heritage, but the shock kills them. Perhaps there is hope only for the younger generation since, at the play's end, Chester, the violinist about to leave for Boston, stands in the same spotlight that singled out his great-uncle Di-Gou at the play's beginning. And, just as Di-Gou argued that "the shape of your face is the shape of faces back many generations," so Hwang's final stage direction reads "the shape of Chester's face begins to change."

Hwang's plays not only probe his own life as a Chinese-American but celebrate his rediscovery of the traditions of Oriental theater. While creating *The Dance and the Railroad*, Hwang drew on the extensive background in traditional Chinese dance and theater of his actors, John Lone (who appeared as Steve in the New York production of *FOB*) and Tzi Ma; so crucial was their special training that he named the characters for these actors. Likewise, in *The Sound of a Voice*, a one-act play about "a warrior who goes into the woods to kill a witch and winds up falling in love with her," Hwang originally imagined the Woman as an *onnagata* role, that is, to be played, as in Kabuki theater, by a man who specializes in playing women's roles. Although eventually an actress played the Woman, Hwang's intention creates double meanings throughout the text; the warrior's first line is "You are very kind to take me in" while near the end of the play the Woman demonstrates her ability to handle a sword and then apologizes by saying, "My skills—they're so—inappropriate. I look like a man."

So when Hwang heard what one might call a real-life *onnagata* story, involving a French diplomat and a performer from the Peking Opera, he found a situation that poignantly embodied many of his long-standing preoccupations with identity. In the Afterword to *M. Butterfly* (reprinted following the play), Hwang wonders "What did Bouriscot [the diplomat] think he was getting in this Chinese actress?" And his answer is "He probably thought he had found Madame Butterfly," or, as Hwang explains "the submissive Oriental number." In deconstructing the story that Puccini's opera has made world famous—the story of the ill-fated romance between Pinkerton, an American naval officer, and Butterfly, a young Japanese woman whom Pinkerton buys as a wife, impregnates, and then deserts—Hwang investigates yet again the question "What is the relationship between the Oriental and the Westerner?" But instead of working from the point of view of the Asian-American, who feels split between two worlds, Hwang suggests that the image of the Oriental is actually a deeply held cultural construction that reveals Western desires and fears. Gallimard (the renamed Bouriscot) falls in love with Song Liling as Butterfly—their first meeting comes after a performance of Butterfly's death scene—and tells his story to the audience in a desperate wish to rewrite the story, "always searching for a new ending . . . where she returns at last to my arms."

The unique theatricality of the play and its constant juxtaposing of "performance" and "reality" in the story of Gallimard were stunningly realized on stage in the original production directed by John Dexter. Eiko Ishioka's design surrounded the black rectangular central acting area with a curved ramp, swirling across and around the stage (see Figure 1). Clive Barnes, writing in the *New York Post*, called it "a runway equally fit for an Oriental queen or even Hollywood's Rita Hayworth," and indeed to many viewers, the ramp recalled the Japanese *hanamichi* (a long entrance platform in Kabuki theater) as well as the more Western version often used by strippers. The ornate costumes associated with Oriental theater and with Western opera (see Figure 2) made Song Liling a striking figure. In fact, even when not performing Butterfly, Song's attire seems to recall the suave elegance of Anna May Wong, a Chinese-American actress familiar to thousands of Americans through her appearance in Hollywood films (see Figure 3). By emphasizing the appealing exoticism of Song Liling's world, Hwang, Dexter, and Ishioka put the audience in the position of the protagonist, Gallimard. The gorgeous costumes, the choreographed movement, the music (both Oriental and Western) all work to seduce the audience so that Gallimard's surprising betrayal is ultimately ours as well.

M. BUTTERFLY

BY DAVID HENRY HWANG

CHARACTERS

RENE GALLIMARD
SONG LILING
MARC/MAN #2/CONSUL SHARPLESS
RENEE/WOMAN AT PARTY/GIRL IN MAGAZINE
COMRADE CHIN/SUZUKI/SHU FANG
HELGA
M. TOULON/MAN #1/JUDGE
KUROGO [dancers/stagehands]

PLAYWRIGHT'S NOTES

A former French diplomat and a Chinese opera singer have been sentenced to six years in jail for spying for China after a two-day trial that traced a story of clandestine love and mistaken sexual identity. . . . Mr. Bouriscot was accused of passing information to China after he fell in love with Mr. Shi, whom he believed for twenty years to be a woman.

—*The New York Times*, May 11, 1986

This play was suggested by international newspaper accounts of a recent espionage trial. For purposes of dramatization, names have been changed, characters created, and incidents devised or altered, and this play does not purport to be a factual record of real events or real people.

*I could escape this feeling
With my China girl . . .*

—David Bowie & Iggy Pop

SETTING

The action of the play takes place in a Paris prison in the present, and in recall, during the decade 1960 to 1970 in Beijing, and from 1966 to the present in Paris.

ACT 1 / SCENE 1

(M. GALLIMARD's *prison cell. Paris. Present.*)
(*Lights fade up to reveal* RENE GALLIMARD, *65, in a prison cell. He wears a comfortable bathrobe, and looks old and tired. The sparsely furnished cell contains a wooden crate upon which sits a hot plate with a kettle, and a portable tape recorder.* GALLIMARD *sits on the crate staring at the recorder, a sad smile on his face.*

Upstage SONG, *who appears as a beautiful woman in traditional Chinese garb, dances a traditional piece from the Peking Opera, surrounded by the percussive clatter of Chinese music.*

Then, slowly, lights and sound cross-fade; the Chinese opera music dissolves into a Western opera, the "Love Duet" from Puccini's Madame Butterfly. SONG *continues dancing, now to the Western accompaniment. Though her movements are the same, the difference in music now gives them a balletic quality.*

GALLIMARD *rises, and turns upstage towards the figure of* SONG, *who dances without acknowledging him.*)

GALLIMARD: Butterfly, Butterfly . . .

(*He forces himself to turn away, as the image of* SONG *fades out, and talks to us.*)

GALLIMARD: The limits of my cell are as such: four-and-a-half meters by five. There's one window against the far wall; a door, very strong, to protect me from autograph hounds. I'm responsible for the tape recorder, the hot plate, and this charming coffee table.

When I want to eat, I'm marched off to the dining room—hot, steaming slop appears on my plate. When I want to sleep, the light bulb turns itself off—the work of fairies. It's an enchanted space I occupy. The French—we know how to run a prison.

But, to be honest, I'm not treated like an ordinary prisoner. Why? Because I'm a celebrity. You see, I make people laugh.

I never dreamed this day would arrive. I've never been considered witty or clever. In fact, as a young boy, in an informal poll among my grammar school classmates, I was voted "least likely to be invited to a party." It's a title I managed to hold on to for many years. Despite some stiff competition.

But now, how the tables turn! Look at me: the life of every social function in Paris. Paris? Why be modest? My fame has spread to Amsterdam, London, New York. Listen to them! In the world's smartest parlors. I'm the one who lifts their spirits!

(*With a flourish,* GALLIMARD *directs our attention to another part of the stage.*)

ACT 1 / SCENE 2

(*A party. Present.*)
(*Lights go up on a chic-looking parlor, where a well-*

dressed trio, two men and one woman, make conversation. GALLIMARD *also remains lit; he observes them from his cell.*)

WOMAN: And what of Gallimard?

MAN 1: Gallimard?

MAN 2: Gallimard!

GALLIMARD (*To us*): You see? They're all determined to say my name, as if it were some new dance.

WOMAN: He still claims not to believe the truth.

MAN 1: What? Still? Even since the trial?

WOMAN: Yes. Isn't it mad?

MAN 2 (*Laughing*): He says . . . it was dark . . . and she was very modest!

(*The trio break into laughter.*)

MAN 1: So—what? He never touched her with his hands?

MAN 2: Perhaps he did, and simply misidentified the equipment. A compelling case for sex education in the schools.

WOMAN: To protect the National Security—the Church can't argue with that.

MAN 1: That's impossible! How could he not know?

MAN 2: Simple ignorance.

MAN 1: For twenty years?

MAN 2: Time flies when you're being stupid.

WOMAN: Well, I thought the French were ladies' men.

MAN 2: It seems Monsieur Gallimard was overly anxious to live up to his national reputation.

WOMAN: Well, he's not very good-looking.

MAN 1: No, he's not.

MAN 2: Certainly not.

WOMAN: Actually, I feel sorry for him.

MAN 2: A toast! To Monsieur Gallimard!

WOMAN: Yes! To Gallimard!

MAN 1: To Gallimard!

MAN 2: Vive la différence!

(*They toast, laughing. Lights down on them.*)

ACT 1 / SCENE 3

(M. GALLIMARD'*s cell.*)

GALLIMARD (*Smiling*): You see? They toast me. I've become patron saint of the socially inept. Can they really be so foolish? Men like that—they should be scratching at my door, begging to learn my secrets! For I, Rene Gallimard, you see, I have known, and been loved by . . . the Perfect Woman.

Alone in this cell, I sit night after night, watching our story play through my head, always searching for a new ending, one which redeems my honor, where she returns at last to my arms. And I imagine you—my ideal audience—who come to understand and even, perhaps just a little, to envy me.

(*He turns on his tape recorder. Over the house speakers, we hear the opening phrases of* Madame Butterfly.)

GALLIMARD: In order for you to understand what I did and why, I must introduce you to my favorite opera: *Madame Butterfly.* By Giacomo Puccini. First produced at La Scala, Milan, in 1904, it is now beloved throughout the Western world.

(*As* GALLIMARD *describes the opera, the tape segues in and out to sections he may be describing.*)

GALLIMARD: And why not? Its heroine, Cio-Cio-San, also known as Butterfly, is a feminine ideal, beautiful and brave. And its hero, the man for whom she gives up everything, is—(*He pulls out a naval officer's cap from under his crate, pops it on his head, and struts about*)—not very good-looking, not too bright, and pretty much a wimp: Benjamin Franklin Pinkerton of the U.S. Navy. As the curtain rises, he's just closed on two great bargains: one on a house, the other on a woman—call it a package deal.

Pinkerton purchased the rights to Butterfly for one hundred yen—in modern currency, equivalent to about . . . sixty-six cents. So, he's feeling pretty pleased with himself as Sharpless, the American consul, arrives to witness the marriage.

(MARC, *wearing an official cap to designate* SHARPLESS, *enters and plays the character.*)

SHARPLESS/MARC: Pinkerton!

PINKERTON/GALLIMARD: Sharpless! How's it hangin'? It's a great day, just great. Between my house, my wife, and the rickshaw ride in from town, I've saved nineteen cents just this morning.

SHARPLESS: Wonderful. I can see the inscription on your tombstone already: "I saved a dollar, here I lie." (*He looks around*) Nice house.

PINKERTON: It's artistic. Artistic, don't you think? Like the way the shoji screens slide open to reveal the wet bar and disco mirror ball? Classy, huh? Great for impressing the chicks.

SHARPLESS: "Chicks"? Pinkerton, you're going to be a married man!

PINKERTON: Well, sort of.

SHARPLESS: What do you mean?

PINKERTON: This country—Sharpless, it is okay. You got all these geisha girls running around—

SHARPLESS: I know! I live here!

PINKERTON: Then, you know the marriage laws, right? I split for one month, it's annulled!

SHARPLESS: Leave it to you to read the fine print. Who's the lucky girl?

PINKERTON: Cio-Cio-San. Her friends call her Butterfly. Sharpless, she eats out of my hand!

SHARPLESS: She's probably very hungry.

PINKERTON: Not like American girls. It's true what they say about Oriental girls. They want to be treated bad!

SHARPLESS: Oh, please!

PINKERTON: It's true!

SHARPLESS: Are you serious about this girl?

PINKERTON: I'm marrying her, aren't I?

SHARPLESS: Yes—with generous trade-in terms.

PINKERTON: When I leave, she'll know what it's like to have loved a real man. And I'll even buy her a few nylons.

SHARPLESS: You aren't planning to take her with you?

PINKERTON: Huh? Where?

SHARPLESS: Home!

PINKERTON: You mean, America? Are you crazy? Can you see her trying to buy rice in St. Louis?

SHARPLESS: So, you're not serious.

(Pause.)

PINKERTON/GALLIMARD (As PINKERTON): Consul, I am a sailor in port. (As GALLIMARD) They then proceed to sing the famous duet, "The Whole World Over."

(The duet plays on the speakers. GALLIMARD, as PINKERTON, lip-syncs his lines from the opera.)

GALLIMARD: To give a rough translation: "The whole world over, the Yankee travels, casting his anchor wherever he wants. Life's not worth living unless he can win the hearts of the fairest maidens, then hotfoot it off the premises ASAP." (He turns towards MARC) In the preceding scene, I played Pinkerton, the womanizing cad, and my friend Marc from school . . . (MARC bows grandly for our benefit) played Sharpless, the sensitive soul of reason. In life, however, our positions were usually—no, always—reversed.

ACT 1 / SCENE 4

(Ecole Nationale. Aix-en-Provence. 1947.)

GALLIMARD: No, Marc, I think I'd rather stay home.

MARC: Are you crazy?! We are going to Dad's condo in Marseilles! You know what happened last time?

GALLIMARD: Of course I do.

MARC: Of course you don't! You never know. . . . They stripped, Rene!

GALLIMARD: Who stripped?

MARC: The girls!

GALLIMARD: Girls? Who said anything about girls?

MARC: Rene, we're a buncha university guys goin' up to the woods. What are we gonna do—talk philosophy?

GALLIMARD: What girls? Where do you get them?

MARC: Who cares? The point is, they come. On trucks. Packed in like sardines. The back flips open, babes hop out, we're ready to roll.

GALLIMARD: You mean, they just—?

MARC: Before you know it, every last one of them— they're stripped and splashing around my pool. There's no moon out, they can't see what's going on, their boobs are flapping, right? You close your eyes, reach out—it's grab bag, get it? Doesn't matter whose ass is between whose legs, whose teeth are

sinking into who. You're just in there, going at it, eyes closed, on and on for as long as you can stand. (Pause) Some fun, huh?

GALLIMARD: What happens in the morning?

MARC: In the morning, you're ready to talk some philosophy. (Beat) So how 'bout it?

GALLIMARD: Marc, I can't . . . I'm afraid they'll say no— the girls. So I never ask.

MARC: You don't have to ask! That's the beauty—don't you see? They don't have to say yes. It's perfect for a guy like you, really.

GALLIMARD: You go ahead . . . I may come later.

MARC: Hey, Rene—it doesn't matter that you're clumsy and got zits—they're not looking!

GALLIMARD: Thank you very much.

MARC: Wimp.

(MARC walks over to the other side of the stage, and starts waving and smiling at women in the audience.)

GALLIMARD (To us): We now return to my version of Madame Butterfly and the events leading to my recent conviction for treason.

(GALLIMARD notices MARC making lewd gestures.)

GALLIMARD: Marc, what are you doing?

MARC: Huh? (Sotto voce) Rene, there're a lotta great babes out there. They're probably lookin' at me and thinking, "What a dangerous guy."

GALLIMARD: Yes—how could they help but be impressed by your cool sophistication?

(GALLIMARD pops the SHARPLESS cap on MARC's head, and points him offstage. MARC exits, leering.)

ACT 1 / SCENE 5

(M. GALLIMARD's cell.)

GALLIMARD: Next, Butterfly makes her entrance. We learn her age—fifteen . . . but very mature for her years.

(Lights come up on the area where we saw SONG dancing at the top of the play. She appears there again, now dressed as Madame Butterfly, moving to the "Love Duet." GALLIMARD turns upstage slightly to watch, transfixed.)

GALLIMARD: But as she glides past him, beautiful, laughing softly behind her fan, don't we who are men sigh with hope? We, who are not handsome, nor brave, nor powerful, yet somehow believe, like Pinkerton, that we deserve a Butterfly. She arrives with all her possessions in the folds of her sleeves, lays them all out, for her man to do with as he pleases. Even her life itself—she bows her head as she whispers that she's not even worth the hundred yen he paid for her. He's already given too much, when we know he's really had to give nothing at all.

(Music and lights on SONG *out.* GALLIMARD *sits at his crate.)*

GALLIMARD: In real life, women who put their total worth at less than sixty-six cents are quite hard to find. The closest we come is in the pages of these magazines. *(He reaches into his crate, pulls out a stack of girlie magazines, and begins flipping through them)* Quite a necessity in prison. For three or four dollars, you get seven or eight women.

I first discovered these magazines at my uncle's house. One day, as a boy of twelve. The first time I saw them in his closet . . . all lined up—my body shook. Not with lust—no, with power. Here were women—a shelfful—who would do exactly as I wanted.

(The "Love Duet" creeps in over the speakers. Special comes up, revealing, not SONG *this time, but a pinup girl in a sexy negligee, her back to us.* GALLIMARD *turns upstage and looks at her.)*

GIRL: I know you're watching me.

GALLIMARD: My throat . . . it's dry.

GIRL: I leave my blinds open every night before I go to bed.

GALLIMARD: I can't move.

GIRL: I leave my blinds open and the lights on.

GALLIMARD: I'm shaking. My skin is hot, but my penis is soft. Why?

GIRL: I stand in front of the window.

GALLIMARD: What is she going to do?

GIRL: I toss my hair, and I let my lips part . . . barely.

GALLIMARD: I shouldn't be seeing this. It's so dirty. I'm so bad.

GIRL: Then, slowly, I lift off my nightdress.

GALLIMARD: Oh, god. I can't believe it. I can't—

GIRL: I toss it to the ground.

GALLIMARD: Now, she's going to walk away. She's going to—

GIRL: I stand there, in the light, displaying myself.

GALLIMARD: No. She's—why is she naked?

GIRL: To you.

GALLIMARD: In front of a window? This is wrong. No—

GIRL: Without shame.

GALLIMARD: No, she must . . . like it.

GIRL: I like it.

GALLIMARD: She . . . she wants me to see.

GIRL: I want you to see.

GALLIMARD: I can't believe it! She's getting excited!

GIRL: I can't see you. You can do whatever you want.

GALLIMARD: I can't do a thing. Why?

GIRL: What would you like me to do . . . next?

(Lights go down on her. Music off. Silence, as GALLIMARD *puts away his magazines. Then he resumes talking to us.)*

GALLIMARD: Act Two begins with Butterfly staring at the ocean. Pinkerton's been called back to the U.S., and he's given his wife a detailed schedule of his plans. In the column marked "return date," he's written "when the robins nest." This failed to ignite her suspicions. Now, three years have passed without a peep from him. Which brings a response from her faithful servant, Suzuki.

*(*COMRADE CHIN *enters, playing* SUZUKI.*)*

SUZUKI: Girl, he's a loser. What'd he ever give you? Nineteen cents and those ugly Day-Glo stockings? Look, it's finished! Kaput! Done! And you should be glad! I mean, the guy was a woofer! He tried before, you know—before he met you, he went down to geisha central and plunked down his spare change in front of the usual candidates—everyone else gagged! These are hungry prostitutes, and they were not interested, get the picture? Now, stop slathering when an American ship sails in, and let's make some bucks—I mean, yen! We are broke!

Now, what about Yamadori? Hey, hey—don't look away—the man is a prince—figuratively, and, what's even better, literally. He's rich, he's handsome, he says he'll die if you don't marry him—and he's even willing to overlook the little fact that you've been deflowered all over the place by a foreign devil. What do you mean, "But he's Japanese?" You're Japanese! You think you've been touched by the whitey god? He was a sailor with dirty hands!

*(*SUZUKI *stalks offstage.)*

GALLIMARD: She's also visited by Consul Sharpless, sent by Pinkerton on a minor errand.

*(*MARC *enters, as* SHARPLESS.*)*

SHARPLESS: I hate this job.

GALLIMARD: This Pinkerton—he doesn't show up personally to tell his wife he's abandoning her. No, he sends a government diplomat . . . at taxpayer's expense.

SHARPLESS: Butterfly? Butterfly? I have some bad—I'm going to be ill. Butterfly, I came to tell you—

GALLIMARD: Butterfly says she knows he'll return and if he doesn't she'll kill herself rather than go back to her own people. *(Beat)* This causes a lull in the conversation.

SHARPLESS: Let's put it this way . . .

GALLIMARD: Butterfly runs into the next room, and returns holding—

(Sound cue: a baby crying. SHARPLESS, *"seeing" this, backs away.)*

SHARPLESS: Well, good. Happy to see things going so well. I suppose I'll be going now. Ta ta. Ciao. *(He turns away. Sound cue out)* I hate this job. *(He exits)*

GALLIMARD: At that moment, Butterfly spots in the harbor an American ship—the *Abramo Lincoln!*

(*Music cue: "The Flower Duet."* SONG, *still dressed as Butterfly, changes into a wedding kimono, moving to the music.*)

GALLIMARD: This is the moment that redeems her years of waiting. With Suzuki's help, they cover the room with flowers—

(CHIN, *as* SUZUKI, *trudges onstage and drops a lone flower without much enthusiasm.*)

GALLIMARD: —and she changes into her wedding dress to prepare for Pinkerton's arrival.

(SUZUKI *helps Butterfly change.* HELGA *enters, and helps* GALLIMARD *change into a tuxedo.*)

GALLIMARD: I married a woman older than myself— Helga.
HELGA: My father was ambassador to Australia. I grew up among criminals and kangaroos.
GALLIMARD: Hearing that brought me to the altar—

(HELGA *exits.*)

GALLIMARD: —where I took a vow renouncing love. No fantasy woman would ever want me, so, yes, I would settle for a quick leap up the career ladder. Passion, I banish, and in its place—practicality!
  But my vows had long since lost their charm by the time we arrived in China. The sad truth is that all men want a beautiful woman, and the uglier the man, the greater the want.

(SUZUKI *makes final adjustments of Butterfly's costume, as does* GALLIMARD *of his tuxedo.*)

GALLIMARD: I married late, at age thirty-one. I was faithful to my marriage for eight years. Until the day when, as a junior-level diplomat in puritanical Peking, in a parlor at the German ambassador's house, during the "Reign of a Hundred Flowers," I first saw her . . . singing the death scene from *Madame Butterfly.*

(SUZUKI *runs offstage.*)

ACT 1 / SCENE 6

(*German ambassador's house. Beijing. 1960.*)
(*The upstage special area now becomes a stage. Several chairs face upstage, representing seating for some twenty guests in the parlor. A few "diplomats"*—RENEE, MARC, TOULON—*in formal dress enter and take seats.*
  GALLIMARD *also sits down, but turns towards us and continues to talk. Orchestral accompaniment on the tape is now replaced by a simple piano.* SONG *picks up the death scene from the point where Butterfly uncovers the hara-kiri knife.*)

GALLIMARD: The ending is pitiful. Pinkerton, in an act of great courage, stays home and sends his Amer-

ican wife to pick up Butterfly's child. The truth, long deferred, has come up to her door.

(SONG, *playing Butterfly, sings the lines from the opera in her own voice—which, though not classical, should be decent.*)

SONG: "Con onor muore/ chi non puo serbar/ vita con onore."
GALLIMARD (*Simultaneously*): "Death with honor/ Is better than life/ Life with dishonor."

(*The stage is illuminated; we are now completely within an elegant diplomat's residence.* SONG *proceeds to play out an abbreviated death scene. Everyone in the room applauds.* SONG, *shyly, takes her bows. Others in the room rush to congratulate her.* GALLIMARD *remains with us.*)

GALLIMARD: They say in opera the voice is everything. That's probably why I'd never before enjoyed opera. Here . . . here was a Butterfly with little or no voice—but she had the grace, the delicacy . . . I believed this girl. I believed her suffering. I wanted to take her in my arms—so delicate, even I could protect her, take her home, pamper her until she smiled.

(*Over the course of the preceding speech,* SONG *has broken from the upstage crowd and moved directly upstage of* GALLIMARD.)

SONG: Excuse me. Monsieur . . . ?

(GALLIMARD *turns upstage, shocked.*)

GALLIMARD: Oh! Gallimard. Mademoiselle . . . ? A beautiful . . .
SONG: Song Liling.
GALLIMARD: A beautiful performance.
SONG: Oh, please.
GALLIMARD: I usually—
SONG: You make me blush. I'm no opera singer at all.
GALLIMARD: I usually don't like *Butterfly.*
SONG: I can't blame you in the least.
GALLIMARD: I mean, the story—
SONG: Ridiculous.
GALLIMARD: I like the story, but . . . what?
SONG: Oh, you like it?
GALLIMARD: I . . . what I mean is, I've always seen it played by huge women in so much bad makeup.
SONG: Bad makeup is not unique to the West.
GALLIMARD: But, who can believe them?
SONG: And you believe me?
GALLIMARD: Absolutely. You were utterly convincing. It's the first time—
SONG: Convincing? As a Japanese woman? The Japanese used hundreds of our people for medical experiments during the war, you know. But I gather such an irony is lost on you.
GALLIMARD: No! I was about to say, it's the first time I've seen the beauty of the story.
SONG: Really?

GALLIMARD: Of her death. It's a . . . a pure sacrifice. He's unworthy, but what can she do? She loves him . . . so much. It's a very beautiful story.

SONG: Well, yes, to a Westerner.

GALLIMARD: Excuse me?

SONG: It's one of your favorite fantasies, isn't it? The submissive Oriental woman and the cruel white man.

GALLIMARD: Well, I didn't quite mean . . .

SONG: Consider it this way: what would you say if a blonde homecoming queen fell in love with a short Japanese businessman? He treats her cruelly, then goes home for three years, during which time she prays to his picture and turns down marriage from a young Kennedy. Then, when she learns he has remarried, she kills herself. Now, I believe you would consider this girl to be a deranged idiot, correct? But because it's an Oriental who kills herself for a Westerner—ah!—you find it beautiful.

(Silence.)

GALLIMARD: Yes . . . well . . . I see your point . . .

SONG: I will never do Butterfly again, Monsieur Gallimard. If you wish to see some real theatre come to the Peking Opera sometime. Expand your mind.

(SONG walks offstage.)

GALLIMARD *(To us)*: So much for protecting her in my big Western arms.

ACT 1 / SCENE 7

(M. GALLIMARD's apartment. Beijing. 1960.)
(GALLIMARD changes from his tux into a casual suit. HELGA enters.)

GALLIMARD: The Chinese are an incredibly arrogant people.

HELGA: They warned us about that in Paris, remember?

GALLIMARD: Even Parisians consider them arrogant. That's a switch.

HELGA: What is it that Madame Su says? "We are a very old civilization." I never know if she's talking about her country or herself.

GALLIMARD: I walk around here, all I hear every day, everywhere is how *old* this culture is. The fact that "old" may be synonymous with "senile" doesn't occur to them.

HELGA: You're not going to change them. "East is east, west is west, and . . ." whatever that guy said.

GALLIMARD: It's just that—silly. I met . . . at Ambassador Koening's tonight—you should've been there.

HELGA: Koening? Oh god, no. Did he enchant you all again with the history of Bavaria?

GALLIMARD: No. I met, I suppose, the Chinese equivalent of a diva. She's a singer in the Chinese opera.

HELGA: They have an opera, too? Do they sing in Chinese? Or maybe—in Italian?

GALLIMARD: Tonight, she did sing in Italian.

HELGA: How'd she manage that?

GALLIMARD: She must've been educated in the West before the Revolution. Her French is very good also. Anyway, she sang the death scene from *Madame Butterfly*.

HELGA: *Madame Butterfly!* Then I should have come. *(She begins humming, floating around the room as if dragging long kimono sleeves)* Did she have a nice costume? I think it's a classic piece of music.

GALLIMARD: That's what *I* thought, too. Don't let her hear you say that.

HELGA: What's wrong?

GALLIMARD: Evidently the Chinese hate it.

HELGA: She hated it, but she performed it anyway? Is she perverse?

GALLIMARD: They hate it because the white man gets the girl. Sour grapes if you ask me.

HELGA: Politics again? Why can't they just hear it as a piece of beautiful music? So, what's in their opera?

GALLIMARD: I don't know. But, whatever it is, I'm sure it must be *old*.

(HELGA exits.)

ACT 1 / SCENE 8

(Chinese opera house and the streets of Beijing. 1960.)
(The sound of gongs clanging fills the stage.)

GALLIMARD: My wife's innocent question kept ringing in my ears. I asked around, but no one knew anything about the Chinese opera. It took four weeks, but my curiosity overcame my cowardice. This Chinese diva—this unwilling Butterfly—what did she do to make her so proud?

　　The room was hot, and full of smoke. Wrinkled faces, old women, teeth missing—a man with a growth on his neck, like a human toad. All smiling, pipes falling from their mouths, cracking nuts between their teeth, a live chicken pecking at my foot—all looking, screaming, gawking . . . at her.

(The upstage area is suddenly hit with a harsh white light. It has become the stage for the Chinese opera performance. Two dancers enter, along with SONG. GALLIMARD stands apart, watching. SONG glides gracefully amidst the two dancers. Drums suddenly slam to a halt. SONG strikes a pose, looking straight at GALLIMARD. Dancers exit. Light change. Pause, then SONG walks right off the stage and straight up to GALLIMARD.)

SONG: Yes. You. White man. I'm looking straight at you.

GALLIMARD: Me?

SONG: You see any other white men? It was too easy to spot you. How often does a man in my audience come in a tie?

(SONG starts to remove her costume. Underneath, she wears simple baggy clothes. They are now backstage. The show is over.)

SONG: So, you are an adventurous imperialist?

GALLIMARD: I . . . thought it would further my education.

SONG: It took you four weeks. Why?

GALLIMARD: I've been busy.

SONG: Well, education has always been undervalued in the West, hasn't it?

GALLIMARD (*Laughing*): I don't think that's true.

SONG: No, you wouldn't. You're a Westerner. How can you objectively judge your own values?

GALLIMARD: I think it's possible to achieve some distance.

SONG: Do you? (*Pause*) It stinks in here. Let's go.

GALLIMARD: These are the smells of your loyal fans.

SONG: I love them for being my fans, I hate the smell .they leave behind. I too can distance myself from my people. (*She looks around, then whispers in his ear*) "Art for the masses" is a shitty excuse to keep artists poor. (*She pops a cigarette in her mouth*) Be a gentleman, will you? And light my cigarette.

(GALLIMARD *fumbles for a match.*)

GALLIMARD: I don't . . . smoke.

SONG (*Lighting her own*): Your loss. Had you lit my cigarette, I might have blown a puff of smoke right between your eyes. Come.

(*They start to walk about the stage. It is a summer night on the Beijing streets. Sounds of the city play on the house speakers.*)

SONG: How I wish there were even a tiny cafe to sit in. With cappuccinos, and men in tuxedos and bad expatriate jazz.

GALLIMARD: If my history serves me correctly, you weren't even allowed into the clubs in Shanghai before the Revolution.

SONG: Your history serves you poorly, Monsieur Gallimard. True, there were signs reading "No dogs and Chinamen." But a woman, especially a delicate Oriental woman—we always go where we please. Could you imagine it otherwise? Clubs in China filled with pasty, big-thighed white women, while thousands of slender lotus blossoms wait just outside the door? Never. The clubs would be empty. (*Beat*) We have always held a certain fascination for you Caucasian men, have we not?

GALLIMARD: But . . . that fascination is imperialist, or so you tell me.

SONG: Do you believe everything I tell you? Yes. It is always imperialist. But sometimes . . . sometimes, it is also mutual. Oh—this is my flat.

GALLIMARD: I didn't even—

SONG: Thank you. Come another time and we will further expand your mind.

(SONG *exits.* GALLIMARD *continues roaming the streets as he speaks to us.*)

GALLIMARD: What was that? What did she mean, "Sometimes . . . it is mutual"? Women do not flirt with me. And I normally can't talk to them. But tonight, I held up my end of the conversation.

ACT 1 / SCENE 9

(GALLIMARD'*s bedroom. Beijing. 1960.*)
(HELGA *enters.*)

HELGA: You didn't tell me you'd be home late.

GALLIMARD: I didn't intend to. Something came up.

HELGA: Oh? Like what?

GALLIMARD: I went to the . . . to the Dutch ambassador's home.

HELGA: Again?

GALLIMARD: There was a reception for a visiting scholar. He's writing a six-volume treatise on the Chinese revolution. We all gathered that meant he'd have to live here long enough to actually write six volumes, and we all expressed our deepest sympathies.

HELGA: Well, I had a good night too. I went with the ladies to a martial arts demonstration. Some of those men—when they break those thick boards— (*She mimes fanning herself*) whoo-whoo!

(HELGA *exits. Lights dim.*)

GALLIMARD: I lied to my wife. Why? I've never had any reason to lie before. But what reason did I have tonight? I didn't do anything wrong. That night, I had a dream. Other people, I've been told, have dreams where angels appear. Or dragons, or Sophia Loren in a towel. In my dream, Marc from school appeared.

(MARC *enters, in a nightshirt and cap.*)

MARC: Rene! You met a girl!

(GALLIMARD *and* MARC *stumble down the Beijing streets. Night sounds over the speakers.*)

GALLIMARD: It's not that amazing, thank you.

MARC: No! It's so monumental, I heard about it halfway around the world in my sleep!

GALLIMARD: I've met girls before, you know.

MARC: Name one. I've come across time and space to congratulate you. (*He hands* GALLIMARD *a bottle of wine*)

GALLIMARD: Marc, this is expensive.

MARC: On those rare occasions when you become a formless spirit, why not steal the best?

(MARC *pops open the bottle, begins to share it with* GALLIMARD.)

GALLIMARD: You embarrass me. She . . . there's no reason to think she likes me.

MARC: "Sometimes, it is mutual"?

GALLIMARD: Oh.

MARC: "Mutual"? "Mutual"? What does that mean?

GALLIMARD: You heard?

MARC: It means the money is in the bank, you only have to write the check!

GALLIMARD: I am a married man!

MARC: And an excellent one too. I cheated after . . . six months. Then again and again, until now—three hundred girls in twelve years.

GALLIMARD: I don't think we should hold that up as a model.

MARC: Of course not! My life—it is disgusting! Phooey! Phooey! But, you—you are the model husband.

GALLIMARD: Anyway, it's impossible. I'm a foreigner.

MARC: Ah, yes. She cannot love you, it is taboo, but something deep inside her heart . . . she cannot help herself . . . she must surrender to you. It is her destiny.

GALLIMARD: How do you imagine all this?

MARC: The same way you do. It's an old story. It's in our blood. They fear us, Rene. Their women fear us. And their men—their men hate us. And, you know something? They are all correct.

(They spot a light in a window.)

MARC: There! There, Rene!

GALLIMARD: It's her window.

MARC: Late at night—it burns. The light—it burns for you.

GALLIMARD: I won't look. It's not respectful.

MARC: We don't have to be respectful. We're foreign devils.

(Enter SONG, in a sheer robe. The "One Fine Day"° aria creeps in over the speakers. With her back to us, SONG mimes attending to her toilette. Her robe comes loose, revealing her white shoulders.)

MARC: All your life you've waited for a beautiful girl who would lay down for you. All your life you've smiled like a saint when it's happened to every other man you know. And you see them in magazines and you see them in movies. And you wonder, what's wrong with me? Will anyone beautiful ever want me? As the years pass, your hair thins and you struggle to hold onto even your hopes. Stop struggling, Rene. The wait is over. *(He exits)*

GALLIMARD: Marc? Marc?

(At that moment, SONG, her back still towards us, drops her robe. A second of her naked back, then a sound cue: a phone ringing, very loud. Blackout, followed in the next beat by a special up on the bedroom area, where a

---

"One Fine Day," the opera's most famous aria, "Un bel di" ("One Fine Day"), in which Madame Butterfly rapturously describes the imagined return of Pinkerton.

phone now sits. GALLIMARD stumbles across the stage and picks up the phone. Sound cue out. Over the course of his conversation, area lights fill in the vicinity of his bed. It is the following morning.)

GALLIMARD: Yes? Hello?

SONG *(Offstage)*: Is it very early?

GALLIMARD: Why, yes.

SONG *(Offstage)*: How early?

GALLIMARD: It's . . . it's 5:30. Why are you—?

SONG *(Offstage)*: But it's light outside. Already.

GALLIMARD: It is. The sun must be in confusion today.

(Over the course of SONG's next speech, her upstage special comes up again. She sits in a chair, legs crossed, in a robe, telephone to her ear.)

SONG: I waited until I saw the sun. That was as much discipline as I could manage for one night. Do you forgive me?

GALLIMARD: Of course . . . for what?

SONG: Then I'll ask you quickly. Are you really interested in the opera?

GALLIMARD: Why, yes. Yes I am.

SONG: Then come again next Thursday. I am playing *The Drunken Beauty*. May I count on you?

GALLIMARD: Yes. You may.

SONG: Perfect. Well, I must be getting to bed. I'm exhausted. It's been a very long night for me.

(SONG hangs up; special on her goes off. GALLIMARD begins to dress for work.)

ACT 1 / SCENE 10

(SONG LILING's apartment. Beijing. 1960.)

GALLIMARD: I returned to the opera that next week, and the week after that . . . she keeps our meetings so short—perhaps fifteen, twenty minutes at most. So I am left each week with a thirst which is intensified. In this way, fifteen weeks have gone by. I am starting to doubt the words of my friend Marc. But no, not really. In my heart, I know she has . . . an interest in me. I suspect this is her way. She is outwardly bold and outspoken, yet her heart is shy and afraid. It is the Oriental in her at war with her Western education.

SONG *(Offstage)*: I will be out in an instant. Ask the servant for anything you want.

GALLIMARD: Tonight, I have finally been invited to enter her apartment. Though the idea is almost beyond belief, I believe she is afraid of me.

(GALLIMARD looks around the room. He picks up a picture in a frame, studies it. Without his noticing, SONG enters, dressed elegantly in a black gown from the twen-

ties. She stands in the doorway looking like Anna May Wong.°)

SONG: That is my father.

GALLIMARD (*Surprised*): Mademoiselle Song . . .

(She glides up to him, snatches away the picture.)

SONG: It is very good that he did not live to see the Revolution. They would, no doubt, have made him kneel on broken glass. Not that he didn't deserve such a punishment. But he is my father. I would've hated to see it happen.

GALLIMARD: I'm very honored that you've allowed me to visit your home.

(SONG curtseys.)

SONG: Thank you. Oh! Haven't you been poured any tea?

GALLIMARD: I'm really not—

SONG (*To her offstage servant*): Shu-Fang! Cha! Kwai-lah! (*To* GALLIMARD) I'm sorry. You want everything to be perfect—

GALLIMARD: Please.

SONG: —and before the evening even begins—

GALLIMARD: I'm really not thirsty.

SONG: —it's ruined.

GALLIMARD (*Sharply*): Mademoiselle Song!

(SONG sits down.)

SONG: I'm sorry.

GALLIMARD: What are you apologizing for now?

(Pause; SONG starts to giggle.)

SONG: I don't know!

(GALLIMARD laughs.)

GALLIMARD: Exactly my point.

SONG: Oh, I am silly. Lightheaded. I promise not to apologize for anything else tonight, do you hear me?

GALLIMARD: That's a good girl.

(SHU-FANG, a servant girl, comes out with a tea tray and starts to pour.)

SONG (*To* SHU-FANG): No! I'll pour myself for the gentleman!

(SHU-FANG, staring at GALLIMARD, exits.)

SONG: No, I . . . I don't even know why I invited you up.

GALLIMARD: Well, I'm glad you did.

(SONG looks around the room.)

SONG: There is an element of danger to your presence.

GALLIMARD: Oh?

SONG: You must know.

GALLIMARD: It doesn't concern me. We both know why I'm here.

SONG: It doesn't concern me either. No . . . well perhaps . . .

GALLIMARD: What?

SONG: Perhaps I am slightly afraid of scandal.

GALLIMARD: What are we doing?

SONG: I'm entertaining you. In my parlor.

GALLIMARD: In France, that would hardly—

SONG: France. France is a country living in the modern era. Perhaps even ahead of it. China is a nation whose soul is firmly rooted two thousand years in the past. What I do, even pouring the tea for you now . . . it has . . . implications. The walls and windows say so. Even my own heart, strapped inside this Western dress . . . even it says things—things I don't care to hear.

(SONG hands GALLIMARD a cup of tea. GALLIMARD puts his hand over both the teacup and SONG's hand.)

GALLIMARD: This is a beautiful dress.

SONG: Don't.

GALLIMARD: What?

SONG: I don't even know if it looks right on me.

GALLIMARD: Believe me—

SONG: You are from France. You see so many beautiful women.

GALLIMARD: France? Since when are the European women—?

SONG: Oh! What am I trying to do, anyway?!

(SONG runs to the door, composes herself, then turns towards GALLIMARD.)

SONG: Monsieur Gallimard, perhaps you should go.

GALLIMARD: But . . . why?

SONG: There's something wrong about this.

GALLIMARD: I don't see what.

SONG: I feel . . . I am not myself.

GALLIMARD: No. You're nervous.

SONG: Please. Hard as I try to be modern, to speak like a man, to hold a Western woman's strong face up to my own . . . in the end, I fail. A small, frightened heart beats too quickly and gives me away. Monsieur Gallimard, I'm a Chinese girl. I've never . . . never invited a man up to my flat before. The forwardness of my actions makes my skin burn.

GALLIMARD: What are you afraid of? Certainly not me, I hope.

SONG: I'm a modest girl.

GALLIMARD: I know. And very beautiful. (*He touches her hair*)

SONG: Please—go now. The next time you see me, I shall again be myself.

GALLIMARD: I like you the way you are right now.

SONG: You are a cad.

Anna May Wong (1907–1961), Chinese-American actress, stereotyped as the "Oriental enchantress."

GALLIMARD: What do you expect? I'm a foreign devil.

(GALLIMARD *walks downstage.* SONG *exits.*)

GALLIMARD (*To us*): Did you hear the way she talked about Western women? Much differently than the first night. She does—she feels inferior to them—and to me.

ACT 1 / SCENE 11

(*The French embassy. Beijing. 1960.*)
(GALLIMARD *moves towards a desk.*)

GALLIMARD: I determined to try an experiment. In *Madame Butterfly*, Cio-Cio-San fears that the Western man who catches a butterfly will pierce its heart with a needle, then leave it to perish. I began to wonder: had I, too, caught a butterfly who would writhe on a needle?

(MARC *enters, dressed as a bureaucrat, holding a stack of papers. As* GALLIMARD *speaks,* MARC *hands papers to him. He peruses, then signs, stamps, or rejects them.*)

GALLIMARD: Over the next five weeks, I worked like a dynamo. I stopped going to the opera, I didn't phone or write her. I knew this little flower was waiting for me to call, and, as I wickedly refused to do so, I felt for the first time that rush of power—the absolute power of a man.

(MARC *continues acting as the bureaucrat, but he now speaks as himself.*)

MARC: Rene! It's me!

GALLIMARD: Marc—I hear your voice everywhere now. Even in the midst of work.

MARC: That's because I'm watching you—all the time.

GALLIMARD: You were always the most popular guy in school.

MARC: Well, there's no guarantee of failure in life like happiness in high school. Somehow I knew I'd end up in the suburbs working for Renault and you'd be in the Orient picking exotic women off the trees. And they say there's no justice.

GALLIMARD: That's why you were my friend?

MARC: I gave you a little of my life, so that now you can give me some of yours. (*Pause*) Remember Isabelle?

GALLIMARD: Of course I remember! She was my first experience.

MARC: We all wanted to ball her. But she only wanted me.

GALLIMARD: I had her.

MARC: Right. You balled her.

GALLIMARD: You were the only one who ever believed me.

MARC: Well, there's a good reason for that. (*Beat*) C'mon. You must've guessed.

GALLIMARD: You told me to wait in the bushes by the cafeteria that night. The next thing I knew, she was on me. Dress up in the air.

MARC: She never wore underwear.

GALLIMARD: My arms were pinned to the dirt.

MARC: She loved the superior position. A girl ahead of her time.

GALLIMARD: I looked up, and there was this woman . . . bouncing up and down on my loins.

MARC: Screaming, right?

GALLIMARD: Screaming, and breaking off the branches all around me, and pounding my butt up and down into the dirt.

MARC: Huffing and puffing like a locomotive.

GALLIMARD: And in the middle of all this, the leaves were getting into my mouth, my legs were losing circulation, I thought, "God. So this is *it?*"

MARC: You thought that?

GALLIMARD: Well, I was worried about my legs falling off.

MARC: You didn't have a good time?

GALLIMARD: No, that's not what I—I had a great time!

MARC: You're sure?

GALLIMARD: Yeah. Really.

MARC: 'Cuz I wanted you to have a good time.

GALLIMARD: I did.

(*Pause.*)

MARC: Shit. (*Pause*) When all is said and done, she was kind of a lousy lay, wasn't she? I mean, there was a lot of energy there, but you never knew what she was doing with it. Like when she yelled "I'm coming!"—hell, it was so loud, you wanted to go, "Look, it's not that big a deal."

GALLIMARD: I got scared. I thought she meant someone was actually coming. (*Pause*) But, Marc?

MARC: What?

GALLIMARD: Thanks.

MARC: Oh, don't mention it.

GALLIMARD: It was my first experience.

MARC: Yeah. You got her.

GALLIMARD: I got her.

MARC: Wait! Look at that letter again!

(GALLIMARD *picks up one of the papers he's been stamping, and rereads it.*)

GALLIMARD (*To us*): After six weeks, they began to arrive. The letters.

(*Upstage special on* SONG, *as Madame Butterfly. The scene is underscored by the "Love Duet."*)

SONG: Did we fight? I do not know. Is the opera no longer of interest to you? Please come—my audiences miss the white devil in their midst.

(GALLIMARD *looks up from the letter, towards us.*)

GALLIMARD (*To us*): A concession, but much too dignified. (*Beat; he discards the letter*) I skipped the opera again that week to complete a position paper on trade.

(The bureaucrat hands him another letter.)

SONG: Six weeks have passed since last we met. Is this your practice—to leave friends in the lurch? Sometimes I hate you, sometimes I hate myself, but always I miss you.

GALLIMARD *(To us)*: Better, but I don't like the way she calls me "friend." When a woman calls a man her "friend," she's calling him a eunuch or a homosexual. *(Beat; he discards the letter)* I was absent from the opera for the seventh week, feeling a sudden urge to clean out my files.

(Bureaucrat hands him another letter.)

SONG: Your rudeness is beyond belief. I don't deserve this cruelty. Don't bother to call. I'll have you turned away at the door.

GALLIMARD *(To us)*: I didn't. *(He discards the letter; bureaucrat hands him another)* And then finally, the letter that concluded my experiment.

SONG: I am out of words. I can hide behind dignity no longer. What do you want? I have already given you my shame.

(GALLIMARD gives the letter back to MARC, slowly. Special on SONG fades out.)

GALLIMARD *(To us)*: Reading it, I became suddenly ashamed. Yes, my experiment had been a success. She was turning on my needle. But the victory seemed hollow.

MARC: Hollow?! Are you crazy?

GALLIMARD: Nothing, Marc. Please go away.

MARC *(Exiting, with papers)*: Haven't I taught you anything?

GALLIMARD: "I have already given you my shame." I had to attend a reception that evening. On the way, I felt sick. If there is a God, surely he would punish me now. I had finally gained power over a beautiful woman, only to abuse it cruelly. There must be justice in the world. I had the strange feeling that the ax would fall this very evening.

ACT 1 / SCENE 12

(AMBASSADOR TOULON's residence. Beijing. 1960.)
(Sound cue: party noises. Light change. We are now in a spacious residence. TOULON, the French ambassador, enters and taps GALLIMARD on the shoulder.)

TOULON: Gallimard? Can I have a word? Over here.

GALLIMARD *(To us)*: Manuel Toulon. French ambassador to China. He likes to think of us all as his children. Rather like God.

TOULON: Look, Gallimard, there's not much to say. I've liked you. From the day you walked in. You were no leader, but you were tidy and efficient.

GALLIMARD: Thank you, sir.

TOULON: Don't jump the gun. Okay, our needs in China are changing. It's embarrassing that we lost Indo-china. Someone just wasn't on the ball there. I don't mean you personally, of course.

GALLIMARD: Thank you, sir.

TOULON: We're going to be doing a lot more information-gathering in the future. The nature of our work here is changing. Some people are just going to have to go. It's nothing personal.

GALLIMARD: Oh.

TOULON: Want to know a secret? Vice-Consul LeBon is being transferred.

GALLIMARD *(To us)*: My immediate superior!

TOULON: And most of his department.

GALLIMARD *(To us)*: Just as I feared! God has seen my evil heart—

TOULON: But not you.

GALLIMARD *(To us)*: —and he's taking her away just as . . . *(To TOULON)* Excuse me, sir?

TOULON: Scare you? I think I did. Cheer up, Gallimard. I want you to replace LeBon as vice-consul.

GALLIMARD: You—? Yes, well, thank you, sir.

TOULON: Anytime.

GALLIMARD: I . . . accept with great humility.

TOULON: Humility won't be part of the job. You're going to coordinate the revamped intelligence division. Want to know a secret? A year ago, you would've been out. But the past few months, I don't know how it happened, you've become this new aggressive confident . . . thing. And they also tell me you get along with the Chinese. So I think you're a lucky man, Gallimard. Congratulations.

(They shake hands. TOULON exits. Party noises out. GALLIMARD stumbles across a darkened stage.)

GALLIMARD: Vice-consul? Impossible! As I stumbled out of the party, I saw it written across the sky: There is no God. Or, no—say that there is a God. But that God . . . understands. Of course! God who creates Eve to serve Adam, who blesses Solomon with his harem but ties Jezebel to a burning bed— that God is a man. And he understands! At age thirty-nine, I was suddenly initiated into the way of the world.

ACT 1 / SCENE 13

(SONG LILING's apartment. Beijing. 1960.)
(SONG enters, in a sheer dressing gown.)

SONG: Are you crazy?

GALLIMARD: Mademoiselle Song—

SONG: To come here—at this hour? After . . . after eight weeks?

GALLIMARD: It's the most amazing—

SONG: You bang on my door? Scare my servants, scandalize the neighbors?

GALLIMARD: I've been promoted. To vice-consul.

(Pause.)

SONG: And what is that supposed to mean to me?

GALLIMARD: Are you my Butterfly?

SONG: What are you saying?

GALLIMARD: I've come tonight for an answer: are you my Butterfly?

SONG: Don't you know already?

GALLIMARD: I want you to say it.

SONG: I don't want to say it.

GALLIMARD: So, that is your answer?

SONG: You know how I feel about—

GALLIMARD: I do remember one thing.

SONG: What?

GALLIMARD: In the letter I received today.

SONG: Don't.

GALLIMARD: "I have already given you my shame."

SONG: It's enough that I even wrote it.

GALLIMARD: Well, then—

SONG: I shouldn't have it splashed across my face.

GALLIMARD: —if that's all true—

SONG: Stop!

GALLIMARD: Then what is one more short answer?

SONG: I don't want to!

GALLIMARD: Are you my Butterfly? (Silence; he crosses the room and begins to touch her hair) I want from you honesty. There should be nothing false between us. No false pride.

(Pause.)

SONG: Yes, I am. I am your Butterfly.

GALLIMARD: Then let me be honest with you. It is because of you that I was promoted tonight. You have changed my life forever. My little Butterfly, there should be no more secrets: I love you.

(He starts to kiss her roughly. She resists slightly.)

SONG: No . . . no . . . gently . . . please, I've never . . .

GALLIMARD: No?

SONG: I've tried to appear experienced, but . . . the truth is . . . no.

GALLIMARD: Are you cold?

SONG: Yes. Cold.

GALLIMARD: Then we will go very, very slowly.

(He starts to caress her; her gown begins to open.)

SONG: No . . . let me . . . keep my clothes . . .

GALLIMARD: But . . .

SONG: Please . . . it all frightens me. I'm a modest Chinese girl.

GALLIMARD: My poor little treasure.

SONG: I am your treasure. Though inexperienced, I am not . . . ignorant. They teach us things, our mothers, about pleasing a man.

GALLIMARD: Yes?

SONG: I'll do my best to make you happy. Turn off the lights.

(GALLIMARD gets up and heads for a lamp. SONG, propped up on one elbow, tosses her hair back and smiles.)

SONG: Monsieur Gallimard?

GALLIMARD: Yes, Butterfly?

SONG: "Vieni, vieni!"°

GALLIMARD: "Come, darling."

SONG: "Ah! Dolce notte!"

GALLIMARD: "Beautiful night."

SONG: "Tutto estatico d'amor ride il ciel!"

GALLIMARD: "All ecstatic with love, the heavens are filled with laughter."

(He turns off the lamp. Blackout.)

ACT 2 / SCENE 1

(M. GALLIMARD's cell. Paris. Present.)
(Lights up on GALLIMARD. He sits in his cell, reading from a leaflet.)

GALLIMARD: This, from a contemporary critic's commentary on Madame Butterfly: "Pinkerton suffers from . . . being an obnoxious bounder whom every man in the audience itches to kick." Bully for us men in the audience! Then, in the same note: "Butterfly is the most irresistibly appealing of Puccini's 'Little Women.' Watching the succession of her humiliations is like watching a child under torture." (He tosses the pamphlet over his shoulder) I suggest that, while we men may all want to kick Pinkerton, very few of us would pass up the opportunity to be Pinkerton.

(GALLIMARD moves out of his cell.)

ACT 2 / SCENE 2

(GALLIMARD and Butterfly's flat. Beijing. 1960.)
(We are in a simple but well-decorated parlor. GALLIMARD moves to sit on a sofa, while SONG, dressed in a chong sam, enters and curls up at his feet.)

GALLIMARD (To us): We secured a flat on the outskirts of Peking. Butterfly, as I was calling her now, decorated our "home" with Western furniture and Chinese antiques. And there, on a few stolen afternoons or evenings each week, Butterfly commenced her education.

SONG: The Chinese men—they keep us down.

GALLIMARD: Even in the "New Society"?

SONG: In the "New Society," we are all kept ignorant equally. That's one of the exciting things about loving a Western man. I know you are not threatened by a woman's education.

"Vieni, vieni," the words are from the love duet at the end of Madame Butterfly's first act.

GALLIMARD: I'm no saint, Butterfly.

SONG: But you come from a progressive society.

GALLIMARD: We're not always reminding each other how "old" we are, if that's what you mean.

SONG: Exactly. We Chinese—once, I suppose, it is true, we ruled the world. But so what? How much more exciting to be part of the society ruling the world today. Tell me—what's happening in Vietnam?

GALLIMARD: Oh, Butterfly—you want me to bring my work home?

SONG: I want to know what you know. To be impressed by my man. It's not the particulars so much as the fact that you're making decisions which change the shape of the world.

GALLIMARD: Not the world. At best, a small corner.

(TOULON *enters, and sits at a desk upstage.*)

ACT 2 / SCENE 3

(*French embassy. Beijing. 1961.*)
(GALLIMARD *moves downstage, to* TOULON's *desk.* SONG *remains upstage, watching.*)

TOULON: And a more troublesome corner is hard to imagine.

GALLIMARD: So, the Americans plan to begin bombing?

TOULON: This is very secret, Gallimard: yes. The Americans don't have an embassy here. They're asking us to be their eyes and ears. Say Jack Kennedy signed an order to bomb North Vietnam, Laos. How would the Chinese react?

GALLIMARD: I think the Chinese will squawk—

TOULON: Uh-huh.

GALLIMARD: —but, in their hearts, they don't even like Ho Chi Minh.

(*Pause.*)

TOULON: What a bunch of jerks. Vietnam was *our* colony. Not only didn't the Americans help us fight to keep them, but now, seven years later, they've come back to grab the territory for themselves. It's very irritating.

GALLIMARD: With all due respect, sir, why should the Americans have won our war for us back in '54 if we didn't have the will to win it ourselves?

TOULON: You're kidding, aren't you?

(*Pause.*)

GALLIMARD: The Orientals simply want to be associated with whoever shows the most strength and power. You live with the Chinese, sir. Do you think they like Communism?

TOULON: I live in China. Not with the Chinese.

GALLIMARD: Well, I—

TOULON: *You* live with the Chinese.

GALLIMARD: Excuse me?

TOULON: I can't keep a secret.

GALLIMARD: What are you saying?

TOULON: Only that I'm not immune to gossip. So, you're keeping a native mistress? Don't answer. It's none of my business. (*Pause*) I'm sure she must be gorgeous.

GALLIMARD: Well . . .

TOULON: I'm impressed. You have the stamina to go out into the streets and hunt one down. Some of us have to be content with the wives of the expatriate community.

GALLIMARD: I do feel . . . fortunate.

TOULON: So, Gallimard, you've got the inside knowledge—what *do* the Chinese think?

GALLIMARD: Deep down, they miss the old days. You know, cappuccinos, men in tuxedos—

TOULON: So what do we tell the Americans about Vietnam?

GALLIMARD: Tell them there's a natural affinity between the West and the Orient.

TOULON: And that you speak from experience?

GALLIMARD: The Orientals are people too. They want the good things we can give them. If the Americans demonstrate the will to win, the Vietnamese will welcome them into a mutually beneficial union.

TOULON: I don't see how the Vietnamese can stand up to American firepower.

GALLIMARD: Orientals will always submit to a greater force.

TOULON: I'll note your opinions in my report. The Americans always love to hear how "welcome" they'll be. (*He starts to exit*)

GALLIMARD: Sir?

TOULON: Mmmm?

GALLIMARD: This . . . rumor you've heard.

TOULON: Uh-huh?

GALLIMARD: How . . . widespread do you think it is?

TOULON: It's only widespread within this embassy. Where nobody talks because everybody is guilty. We were worried about you, Gallimard. We thought you were the only one here without a secret. Now you go and find a lotus blossom . . . and top us all. (*He exits*)

GALLIMARD (*To us*): Toulon knows! And he approves! I was learning the benefits of being a man. We form our own clubs, sit behind thick doors, smoke—and celebrate the fact that we're still boys. (*He starts to move downstage, towards* SONG) So, over the—

(*Suddenly* COMRADE CHIN *enters.* GALLIMARD *backs away.*)

GALLIMARD (*To* SONG): No! Why does she have to come in?

SONG: Rene, be sensible. How can they understand the story without her? Now, don't embarrass yourself.

(GALLIMARD *moves down center.*)

GALLIMARD (*To us*): Now, you will see why my story is

so amusing to so many people. Why they snicker at parties in disbelief. Please—try to understand it from my point of view. We are all prisoners of our time and place. *(He exits)*

ACT 2 / SCENE 4

(GALLIMARD and Butterfly's flat. Beijing. 1961.)

SONG *(To us)*: 1961. The flat Monsieur Gallimard rented for us. An evening after he has gone.

CHIN: Okay, see if you can find out when the Americans plan to start bombing Vietnam. If you can find out what cities, even better.

SONG: I'll do my best, but I don't want to arouse his suspicions.

CHIN: Yeah, sure, of course. So, what else?

SONG: The Americans will increase troops in Vietnam to 170,000 soldiers with 120,000 militia and 11,000 American advisors.

CHIN *(Writing)*: Wait, wait. 120,000 militia and—

SONG: —11,000 American—

CHIN: —American advisors. *(Beat)* How do you remember so much?

SONG: I'm an actor.

CHIN: Yeah. *(Beat)* Is that how come you dress like that?

SONG: Like what, Miss Chin?

CHIN: Like that dress! You're wearing a dress. And every time I come here, you're wearing a dress. Is that because you're an actor? Or what?

SONG: It's a . . . disguise, Miss Chin.

CHIN: Actors, I think they're all weirdos. My mother tells me actors are like gamblers or prostitutes or—

SONG: It helps me in my assignment.

(Pause.)

CHIN: You're not gathering information in any way that violates Communist Party principles, are you?

SONG: Why would I do that?

CHIN: Just checking. Remember: when working for the Great Proletarian State, you represent our Chairman Mao in every position you take.

SONG: I'll try to imagine the Chairman taking my positions.

CHIN: We all think of him this way. Good-bye, comrade. *(She starts to exit)* Comrade?

SONG: Yes?

CHIN: Don't forget: there is no homosexuality in China!

SONG: Yes, I've heard.

CHIN: Just checking. *(She exits)*

SONG *(To us)*: What passes for a woman in modern China.

(GALLIMARD sticks his head out from the wings.)

GALLIMARD: Is she gone?

SONG: Yes, Rene. Please continue in your own fashion.

ACT 2 / SCENE 5

(Beijing. 1961–63.)

(GALLIMARD moves to the couch where SONG still sits. He lies down in her lap, and she strokes his forehead.)

GALLIMARD *(To us)*: And so, over the years 1961, '62, '63, we settled into our routine, Butterfly and I. She would always have prepared a light snack and then, ever so delicately, and only if I agreed, she would start to pleasure me. With her hands, her mouth . . . too many ways to explain, and too sad, given my present situation. But mostly we would talk. About my life. Perhaps there is nothing more rare than to find a woman who passionately listens.

(SONG remains upstage, listening, as HELGA enters and plays a scene downstage with GALLIMARD.)

HELGA: Rene, I visited Dr. Bolleart this morning.

GALLIMARD: Why? Are you ill?

HELGA: No, no. You see, I wanted to ask him . . . that question we've been discussing.

GALLIMARD: And I told you, it's only a matter of time. Why did you bring a doctor into this? We just have to keep trying—like a crapshoot, actually.

HELGA: I went, I'm sorry. But listen: he says there's nothing wrong with me.

GALLIMARD: You see? Now, will you stop—?

HELGA: Rene, he says he'd like you to go in and take some tests.

GALLIMARD: Why? So he can find there's nothing wrong with both of us?

HELGA: Rene, I don't ask for much. One trip! One visit! And then, whatever you want to do about it—you decide.

GALLIMARD: You're assuming he'll find something defective!

HELGA: No! Of course not! Whatever he finds—if he finds nothing, we decide what to do about nothing! But go!

GALLIMARD: If he finds nothing, we keep trying. Just like we do now.

HELGA: But at least we'll know! *(Pause)* I'm sorry. *(She starts to exit)*

GALLIMARD: Do you really want me to see Dr. Bolleart?

HELGA: Only if you want a child, Rene. We have to face the fact that time is running out. Only if you want a child. *(She exits)*

GALLIMARD *(To SONG)*: I'm a modern man, Butterfly. And yet, I don't want to go. It's the same old voodoo. I feel like God himself is laughing at me if I can't produce a child.

SONG: You men of the West—you're obsessed by your odd desire for equality. Your wife can't give you a child, and *you're* going to the doctor?

GALLIMARD: Well, you see, she's already gone.

SONG: And because this incompetent can't find the defect, you now have to subject yourself to him? It's unnatural.

GALLIMARD: Well, what is the "natural" solution?

SONG: In Imperial China, when a man found that one wife was inadequate, he turned to another—to give him his son.

GALLIMARD: What do you—? I can't . . . marry you, yet.

SONG: Please. I'm not asking you to be my husband. But I am already your wife.

GALLIMARD: Do you want to . . . have my child?

SONG: I thought you'd never ask.

GALLIMARD: But, your career . . . your—

SONG: Phooey on my career! That's your Western mind, twisting itself into strange shapes again. Of course I love my career. But what would I love most of all? To feel something inside me—day and night—something I know is yours. *(Pause)* Promise me . . . you won't go to this doctor. Who is this Western quack to set himself as judge over the man I love? I know who is a man, and who is not. *(She exits)*

GALLIMARD *(To us)*: Dr. Bolleart? Of course I didn't go. What man would?

ACT 2 / SCENE 6

(Beijing. 1963.)

(Party noises over the house speakers. RENEE enters, wearing a revealing gown.)

GALLIMARD: 1963. A party at the Austrian embassy. None of us could remember the Austrian ambassador's name, which seemed somehow appropriate. *(To RENEE)* So, I tell the Americans, Diem must go. The U.S. wants to be respected by the Vietnamese, and yet they're propping up this nobody seminarian as her president. A man whose claim to fame is his sister-in-law imposing fanatic "moral order" campaigns? Oriental women—when they're good, they're very good, but when they're bad, they're Christians.

RENEE: Yeah.

GALLIMARD: And what do you do?

RENEE: I'm a student. My father exports a lot of useless stuff to the Third World.

GALLIMARD: How useless?

RENEE: You know. Squirt guns, confectioner's sugar, hula hoops . . .

GALLIMARD: I'm sure they appreciate the sugar.

RENEE: I'm here for two years to study Chinese.

GALLIMARD: Two years?

RENEE: That's what everybody says.

GALLIMARD: When did you arrive?

RENEE: Three weeks ago.

GALLIMARD: And?

RENEE: I like it. It's primitive, but . . . well, this is the place to learn Chinese, so here I am.

GALLIMARD: Why Chinese?

RENEE: I think it'll be important someday.

GALLIMARD: You do?

RENEE: Don't ask me when, but . . . that's what I think.

GALLIMARD: Well, I agree with you. One hundred percent. That's very farsighted.

RENEE: Yeah. Well of course, my father thinks I'm a complete weirdo.

GALLIMARD: He'll thank you someday.

RENEE: Like when the Chinese start buying hula hoops?

GALLIMARD: There're a billion bellies out there.

RENEE: And if they end up taking over the world—well, then I'll be lucky to know Chinese too, right?

(Pause.)

GALLIMARD: At this point, I don't see how the Chinese can possibly take—

RENEE: You know what I *don't* like about China?

GALLIMARD: Excuse me? No—what?

RENEE: Nothing to do at night.

GALLIMARD: You come to parties at embassies like everyone else.

RENEE: Yeah, but they get out at ten. And then what?

GALLIMARD: I'm afraid the Chinese idea of a dance hall is a dirt floor and a man with a flute.

RENEE: Are you married?

GALLIMARD: Yes. Why?

RENEE: You wanna . . . fool around?

(Pause.)

GALLIMARD: Sure.

RENEE: I'll wait for you outside. What's your name?

GALLIMARD: Gallimard. Rene.

RENEE: Weird. I'm Renee too. *(She exits)*

GALLIMARD *(To us)*: And so, I embarked on my first extra-marital affair. Renee was picture perfect. With a body like those girls in the magazines. If I put a tissue paper over my eyes, I wouldn't have been able to tell the difference. And it was exciting to be with someone who wasn't afraid to be seen completely naked. But is it possible for a woman to be *too* uninhibited, *too* willing, so as to seem almost too . . . masculine?

(Chuck Berry blares from the house speakers, then comes down in volume as RENEE enters, toweling her hair.)

RENEE: You have a nice weenie.

GALLIMARD: What?

RENEE: Penis. You have a nice penis.

GALLIMARD: Oh. Well, thank you. That's very . . .

RENEE: What—can't take a compliment?

GALLIMARD: No, it's very . . . reassuring.

RENEE: But most girls don't come out and say it, huh?

GALLIMARD: And also . . . what did you call it?

RENEE: Oh. Most girls don't call it a "weenie," huh?

GALLIMARD: It sounds very—

RENEE: Small, I know.

GALLIMARD: I was going to say, "young."

RENEE: Yeah. Young, small, same thing. Most guys are

pretty, uh, sensitive about that. Like, you know, I had a boyfriend back home in Denmark. I got mad at him once and called him a little weeniehead. He got so mad! He said at least I should call him a great big weeniehead.

GALLIMARD: I suppose I just say "penis."

RENEE: Yeah. That's pretty clinical. There's "cock," but that sounds like a chicken. And "prick" is painful, and "dick" is like you're talking about someone who's not in the room.

GALLIMARD: Yes. It's a . . . bigger problem than I imagined.

RENEE: I—I think maybe it's because I really don't know what to do with them—that's why I call them "weenies."

GALLIMARD: Well, you did quite well with . . . mine.

RENEE: Thanks, but I mean, really *do* with them. Like, okay, have you ever looked at one? I mean, really?

GALLIMARD: No, I suppose when it's part of you, you sort of take it for granted.

RENEE: I guess. But, like, it just hangs there. This little . . . flap of flesh. And there's so much fuss that we make about it. Like, I think the reason we fight wars is because we wear clothes. Because no one knows—between the men, I mean—who has the bigger . . . weenie. So, if I'm a guy with a small one, I'm going to build a really big building or take over a really big piece of land or write a really long book so the other men don't know, right? But, see, it never really works, that's the problem. I mean, you conquer the country, or whatever, but you're still wearing clothes, so there's no way to prove absolutely whose is bigger or smaller. And that's what we call a civilized society. The whole world run by a bunch of men with pricks the size of pins. *(She exits)*

GALLIMARD *(To us)*: This was simply not acceptable.

(A high-pitched chime rings through the air. SONG, dressed as Butterfly, appears in the upstage special. She is obviously distressed. Her body swoons as she attempts to clip the stems of flowers she's arranging in a vase.)

GALLIMARD: But I kept up our affair, wildly, for several months. Why? I believe because of Butterfly. She knew the secret I was trying to hide. But, unlike a Western woman, she didn't confront me, threaten, even pout. I remembered the words of Puccini's *Butterfly:*

SONG: "Noi siamo gente avvezza/ alle piccole cose/ umili e silenziose."

GALLIMARD: "I come from a people/ Who are accustomed to little/ Humble and silent." I saw Pinkerton and Butterfly, and what she would say if he were unfaithful . . . nothing. She would cry, alone, into those wildly soft sleeves, once full of possessions, now empty to collect her tears. It was her tears and her silence that excited me, every time I visited Renee.

TOULON *(Offstage)*: Gallimard!

(TOULON enters. GALLIMARD turns towards him. During the next section, SONG, up center, begins to dance with the flowers. It is a drunken dance, where she breaks small pieces off the stems.)

TOULON: They're killing him.

GALLIMARD: Who? I'm sorry? What?

TOULON: Bother you to come over at this late hour?

GALLIMARD: No . . . of course not.

TOULON: Not after you hear my secret. Champagne?

GALLIMARD: Um . . . thank you.

TOULON: You're surprised. There's something that you've wanted, Gallimard. No, not a promotion. Next time. Something in the world. You're not aware of this, but there's an informal gossip circle among intelligence agents. And some of ours heard from some of the Americans—

GALLIMARD: Yes?

TOULON: That the U.S. will allow the Vietnamese generals to stage a coup . . . and assassinate President Diem.

(The chime rings again. TOULON freezes. GALLIMARD turns upstage and looks at Butterfly, who slowly and deliberately clips a flower off its stem. GALLIMARD turns back towards TOULON.)

GALLIMARD: I think . . . that's a very wise move!

(TOULON unfreezes.)

TOULON: It's what you've been advocating. A toast?

GALLIMARD: Sure. I consider this a vindication.

TOULON: Not exactly. "To the test. Let's hope you pass."

(They drink. The chime rings again. TOULON freezes. GALLIMARD turns upstage, and SONG clips another flower.)

GALLIMARD *(To TOULON)*: The test?

TOULON *(Unfreezing)*: It's a test of everything you've been saying. I personally think the generals probably will stop the Communists. And you'll be a hero. But if anything goes wrong, then your opinions won't be worth a pig's ear. I'm sure that won't happen. But sometimes it's easier when they don't listen to you.

GALLIMARD: They're your opinions too, aren't they?

TOULON: Personally, yes.

GALLIMARD: So we agree.

TOULON: But my opinions aren't on that report. Yours are. Cheers.

(TOULON turns away from GALLIMARD and raises his glass. At that instant SONG picks up the vase and hurls it to the ground. It shatters. SONG sinks down amidst the shards of the vase, in a calm, childlike trance. She sings softly, as if reciting a child's nursery rhyme.)

SONG *(Repeat as necessary)*: "The whole world over, the white man travels, setting anchor, wherever he likes. Life's not worth living, unless he finds, the finest maidens, of every land . . ."

(GALLIMARD *turns downstage towards us.* SONG *continues singing.*)

GALLIMARD: I shook as I left his house. That coward! That worm! To put the burden for his decisions on my shoulders!

I started for Renee's. But no, that was all I needed. A schoolgirl who would question the role of the penis in modern society. What I wanted was revenge. A vessel to contain my humiliation. Though I hadn't seen her in several weeks, I headed for Butterfly's.

(GALLIMARD *enters* SONG's *apartment.*)

SONG: Oh! Rene . . . I was dreaming!

GALLIMARD: You've been drinking?

SONG: If I can't sleep, then yes, I drink. But then, it gives me these dreams which—Rene, it's been almost three weeks since you visited me last.

GALLIMARD: I know. There's been a lot going on in the world.

SONG: Fortunately I am drunk. So I can speak freely. It's not the world, it's you and me. And an old problem. Even the softest skin becomes like leather to a man who's touched it too often. I confess I don't know how to stop it. I don't know how to become another woman.

GALLIMARD: I have a request.

SONG: Is this a solution? Or are you ready to give up the flat?

GALLIMARD: It may be a solution. But I'm sure you won't like it.

SONG: Oh well, that's very important. "Like it?" Do you think I "like" lying here alone, waiting, always waiting for your return? Please—don't worry about what I may not "like."

GALLIMARD: I want to see you . . . naked.

(Silence.)

SONG: I thought you understood my modesty. So you want me to—what—strip? Like a big cowboy girl? Shiny pasties on my breasts? Shall I fling my kimono over my head and yell "ya-hoo" in the process? I thought you respected my shame!

GALLIMARD: I believe you gave me your shame many years ago.

SONG: Yes—and it is just like a white devil to use it against me. I can't believe it. I thought myself so repulsed by the passive Oriental and the cruel white man. Now I see—we are always most revolted by the things hidden within us.

GALLIMARD: I just mean—

SONG: Yes?

GALLIMARD: —that it will remove the only barrier left between us.

SONG: No, Rene. Don't couch your request in sweet words. Be yourself—a cad—and know that my love is enough, that I submit—submit to the worst you can give me. (*Pause*) Well, come. Strip me. Whatever happens, know that you have willed it. Our love, in your hands. I'm helpless before my man.

(GALLIMARD *starts to cross the room.*)

GALLIMARD: Did I not undress her because I knew, somewhere deep down, what I would find? Perhaps. Happiness is so rare that our mind can turn somersaults to protect it.

At the time, I only knew that I was seeing Pinkerton stalking towards his Butterfly, ready to reward her love with his lecherous hands. The image sickened me, pulled me to my knees, so I was crawling towards her like a worm. By the time I reached her, Pinkerton . . . had vanished from my heart. To be replaced by something new, something unnatural, that flew in the face of all I'd learned in the world—something very close to love.

(*He grabs her around the waist; she strokes his hair.*)

GALLIMARD: Butterfly, forgive me.

SONG: Rene . . .

GALLIMARD: For everything. From the start.

SONG: I'm . . .

GALLIMARD: I want to—

SONG: I'm pregnant. (*Beat*) I'm pregnant. (*Beat*) I'm pregnant.

(*Beat.*)

GALLIMARD: I want to marry you!

ACT 2 / SCENE 7

(GALLIMARD *and Butterfly's flat. Beijing. 1963.*)
(*Downstage,* SONG *paces as* COMRADE CHIN *reads from her notepad. Upstage,* GALLIMARD *is still kneeling. He remains on his knees throughout the scene, watching it.*)

SONG: I need a baby.

CHIN (*From pad*): He's been spotted going to a dorm.

SONG: I need a baby.

CHIN: At the Foreign Language Institute.

SONG: I need a baby.

CHIN: The room of a Danish girl . . . What do you mean, you need a baby?!

SONG: Tell Comrade Kang—last night, the entire mission, it could've ended.

CHIN: What do you mean?

SONG: Tell Kang—he told me to strip.

CHIN: *Strip?!*

SONG: Write!

CHIN: I tell you, I don't understand nothing about this case anymore. Nothing.

SONG: He told me to strip, and I took a chance. Oh, we Chinese, we know how to gamble.

CHIN (*Writing*): ". . . told him to strip."

SONG: My palms were wet, I had to make a split-second decision.

CHIN: Hey! Can you slow down?!

(*Pause.*)

SONG: You write faster, I'm the artist here. Suddenly, it hit me—"All he wants is for her to submit. Once a woman submits, a man is always ready to become 'generous.'"

CHIN: You're just gonna end up with rough notes.

SONG: And it worked! He gave in! Now, if I can just present him with a baby. A Chinese baby with blond hair—he'll be mine for life!

CHIN: Kang will never agree! The trading of babies has to be a counterrevolutionary act!

SONG: Sometimes, a counterrevolutionary act is necessary to counter a counterrevolutionary act.

(*Pause.*)

CHIN: Wait.

SONG: I need one . . . in seven months. Make sure it's a boy.

CHIN: This doesn't sound like something the Chairman would do. Maybe you'd better talk to Comrade Kang yourself.

SONG: Good. I will.

(CHIN *gets up to leave.*)

SONG: Miss Chin? Why, in the Peking Opera, are women's roles played by men?

CHIN: I don't know. Maybe, a reactionary remnant of male—

SONG: No. (*Beat*) Because only a man knows how a woman is supposed to act.

(CHIN *exits.* SONG *turns upstage, towards* GALLIMARD.)

GALLIMARD (*Calling after* CHIN): Good riddance! (*To* SONG) I could forget all that betrayal in an instant, you know. If you'd just come back and become Butterfly again.

SONG: Fat chance. You're here in prison, rotting in a cell. And I'm on a plane, winging my way back to China. Your President pardoned me of our treason, you know.

GALLIMARD: Yes, I read about that.

SONG: Must make you feel . . . lower than shit.

GALLIMARD: But don't you, even a little bit, wish you were here with me?

SONG: I'm an artist, Rene. You were my greatest . . . acting challenge. (*She laughs*) It doesn't matter how rotten I answer, does it? You still adore me. That's why I love you, Rene. (*She points to us*) So—you were telling your audience about the night I announced I was pregnant.

(GALLIMARD *puts his arms around* SONG's *waist. He and* SONG *are in the positions they were in at the end of Scene 6.*)

ACT 2 / SCENE 8

(*Same.*)

GALLIMARD: I'll divorce my wife. We'll live together here, and then later in France.

SONG: I feel so . . . ashamed.

GALLIMARD: Why?

SONG: I had begun to lose faith. And now, you shame me with your generosity.

GALLIMARD: Generosity? No, I'm proposing for very selfish reasons.

SONG: Your apologies only make me feel more ashamed. My outburst a moment ago!

GALLIMARD: Your outburst? What about my request?!

SONG: You've been very patient dealing with my . . . eccentricities. A Western man, used to women freer with their bodies—

GALLIMARD: It was sick! Don't make excuses for me.

SONG: I have to. You don't seem willing to make them for yourself.

(*Pause.*)

GALLIMARD: You're crazy.

SONG: I'm happy. Which often looks like crazy.

GALLIMARD: Then make me crazy. Marry me.

(*Pause.*)

SONG: No.

GALLIMARD: What?

SONG: Do I sound silly, a slave, if I say I'm not worthy?

GALLIMARD: Yes. In fact you do. No one has loved me like you.

SONG: Thank you. And no one ever will. I'll see to that.

GALLIMARD: So what is the problem?

SONG: Rene, we Chinese are realists. We understand rice, gold, and guns. You are a diplomat. Your career is skyrocketing. Now, what would happen if you divorced your wife to marry a Communist Chinese actress?

GALLIMARD: That's not being realistic. That's defeating yourself before you begin.

SONG: We conserve our strength for the battles we can win.

GALLIMARD: That sounds like a fortune cookie!

SONG: Where do you think fortune cookies come from!

GALLIMARD: I don't care.

SONG: You do. So do I. And we should. That is why I say I'm not worthy. I'm worthy to love and even to be loved by you. But I am not worthy to end the career of one of the West's most promising diplomats.

GALLIMARD: It's not that great a career! I made it sound like more than it is!

SONG: Modesty will get you nowhere. Flatter yourself, and you flatter me. I'm flattered to decline your offer. *(She exits)*

GALLIMARD *(To us)*: Butterfly and I argued all night. And, in the end, I left, knowing I would never be her husband. She went away for several months—to the countryside, like a small animal. Until the night I received her call.

(A baby's cry from offstage. SONG *enters, carrying a child.)*

SONG: He looks like you.

GALLIMARD: Oh! *(Beat; he approaches the baby)* Well, babies are never very attractive at birth.

SONG: Stop!

GALLIMARD: I'm sure he'll grow more beautiful with age. More like his mother.

SONG: "Chi vide mai/ a bimbo del Giappon . . ."

GALLIMARD: "What baby, I wonder, was ever born in Japan"—or China, for that matter—

SONG: ". . . occhi azzurrini?"

GALLIMARD: "With azure eyes"—they're actually sort of brown, wouldn't you say?

SONG: "E il labbro."

GALLIMARD: "And such lips!" *(He kisses* SONG*)* And such lips.

SONG: "E i ricciolini d'oro schietto?"

GALLIMARD: "And such a head of golden"—if slightly patchy—"curls?"

SONG: I'm going to call him "Peepee."

GALLIMARD: Darling, could you repeat that because I'm sure a rickshaw just flew by overhead.

SONG: You heard me.

GALLIMARD: "Song Peepee"? May I suggest Michael, or Stephan, or Adolph?

SONG: You may, but I won't listen.

GALLIMARD: You can't be serious. Can you imagine the time this child will have in school?

SONG: In the West, yes.

GALLIMARD: It's worse than naming him Ping Pong or Long Dong or—

SONG: But he's never going to live in the West, is he?

(Pause.)

GALLIMARD: That wasn't my choice.

SONG: It is mine. And this is my promise to you: I will raise him, he will be our child, but he will never burden you outside of China.

GALLIMARD: Why do you make these promises? I want to be burdened! I want a scandal to cover the papers!

SONG *(To us)*: Prophetic.

GALLIMARD: I'm serious.

SONG: So am I. His name is as I registered it. And he will never live in the West.

*(*SONG *exits with the child.)*

GALLIMARD *(To us)*: Is it possible that her stubbornness only made me want her more. That drawing back at the moment of my capitulation was the most brilliant strategy she could have chosen. It is possible. But it is also possible that by this point she could have said, could have done . . . anything, and I would have adored her still.

ACT 2 / SCENE 9

(Beijing. 1966.)
(A driving rhythm of Chinese percussion fills the stage.)

GALLIMARD: And then, China began to change. Mao became very old, and his cult became very strong. And, like many old men, he entered his second childhood. So he handed over the reins of state to those with minds like his own. And children ruled the Middle Kingdom with complete caprice. The doctrine of the Cultural Revolution implied continuous anarchy. Contact between Chinese and foreigners became impossible. Our flat was confiscated. Her fame and my money now counted against us.

(Two dancers in Mao suits and red-starred caps enter, and begin crudely mimicking revolutionary violence, in an agitprop fashion.)

GALLIMARD: And somehow the American war went wrong too. Four hundred thousand dollars were being spent for every Viet Cong killed; so General Westmoreland's remark that the Oriental does not value life the way Americans do was oddly accurate. Why weren't the Vietnamese people giving in? Why were they content instead to die and die and die again?

*(*TOULON *enters.)*

TOULON: Congratulations, Gallimard.

GALLIMARD: Excuse me, sir?

TOULON: Not a promotion. That was last time. You're going home.

GALLIMARD: What?

TOULON: Don't say I didn't warn you.

GALLIMARD: I'm being transferred . . . because I was wrong about the American war?

TOULON: Of course not. We don't care about the Americans. We care about your mind. The quality of your analysis. In general, everything you've predicted here in the Orient . . . just hasn't happened.

GALLIMARD: I think that's premature.

TOULON: Don't force me to be blunt. Okay, you said China was ready to open to Western trade. The only thing they're trading out there are Western heads. And, yes, you said the Americans would succeed in Indochina. You were kidding, right?

GALLIMARD: I think the end is in sight.

TOULON: Don't be pathetic. And don't take this personally. You were wrong. It's not your fault.

GALLIMARD: But I'm going home.

TOULON: Right. Could I have the number of your mistress? (Beat) Joke! Joke! Eat a croissant for me.

(TOULON exits. SONG, wearing a Mao suit, is dragged in from the wings as part of the upstage dance. They "beat" her, then lampoon the acrobatics of the Chinese opera, as she is made to kneel onstage.)

GALLIMARD (Simultaneously): I don't care to recall how Butterfly and I said our hurried farewell. Perhaps it was better to end our affair before it killed her.

(GALLIMARD exits. COMRADE CHIN walks across the stage with a banner reading: "The Actor Renounces His Decadent Profession!" She reaches the kneeling SONG. Percussion stops with a thud. Dancers strike poses.)

CHIN: Actor-oppressor, for years you have lived above the common people and looked down on their labor. While the farmer ate millet—

SONG: I ate pastries from France and sweetmeats from silver trays.

CHIN: And how did you come to live in such an exalted position?

SONG: I was a plaything for the imperialists!

CHIN: What did you do?

SONG: I shamed China by allowing myself to be corrupted by a foreigner . . .

CHIN: What does this mean? The People demand a full confession!

SONG: I engaged in the lowest perversions with China's enemies!

CHIN: What perversions? Be more clear!

SONG: I let him put it up my ass!

(Dancers look over, disgusted.)

CHIN: Aaaa-ya! How can you use such sickening language?!

SONG: My language . . . is only as foul as the crimes I committed . . .

CHIN: Yeah. That's better. So—what do you want to do now?

SONG: I want to serve the people.

(Percussion starts up, with Chinese strings.)

CHIN: What?

SONG: I want to serve the people!

(Dancers regain their revolutionary smiles, and begin a dance of victory.)

CHIN: What?!

SONG: I want to serve the people!!

(Dancers unveil a banner: "The Actor Is Rehabilitated!" SONG remains kneeling before CHIN, as the dancers bounce around them, then exit. Music out.)

ACT 2 / SCENE 10

(A commune. Hunan Province. 1970.)

CHIN: How you planning to do that?

SONG: I've already worked four years in the fields of Hunan, Comrade Chin.

CHIN: So? Farmers work all their lives. Let me see your hands.

(SONG holds them out for her inspection.)

CHIN: Goddamn! Still so smooth! How long does it take to turn you actors into good anythings? Hunh. You've just spent too many years in luxury to be any good to the Revolution.

SONG: I served the Revolution.

CHIN: Serve the Revolution? Bullshit! You wore dresses! Don't tell me—I was there. I saw you! You and your white vice-consul! Stuck up there in your flat, living off the People's Treasury! Yeah, I knew what was going on! You two . . . homos! Homos! Homos! (Pause; she composes herself) Ah! Well . . . you will serve the people, all right. But not with the Revolution's money. This time, you use your own money.

SONG: I have no money.

CHIN: Shut up! And you won't stink up China anymore with your pervert stuff. You'll pollute the place where pollution begins—the West.

SONG: What do you mean?

CHIN: Shut up! You're going to France. Without a cent in your pocket. You find your consul's house, you make him pay your expenses—

SONG: No.

CHIN: And you give us weekly reports! Useful information!

SONG: That's crazy. It's been four years.

CHIN: Either that, or back to rehabilitation center!

SONG: Comrade Chin, he's not going to support me! Not in France! He's a white man! I was just his plaything—

CHIN: Oh yuck! Again with the sickening language? Where's my stick?

SONG: You don't understand the mind of a man.

(Pause.)

CHIN: Oh no? No I don't? Then how come I'm married, huh? How come I got a man? Five, six years ago, you always tell me those kind of things, I felt very bad. But not now! Because what does the Chairman say? He tells us I'm now the smart one, you're now the nincompoop! You're the blockhead, the harebrain, the nitwit! You think you're so smart? You understand "The Mind of a Man"? Good! Then you go to France and be a pervert for Chairman Mao!

(CHIN and SONG exit in opposite directions.)

ACT 2 / SCENE 11

(Paris. 1968–70.)
(GALLIMARD enters.)

GALLIMARD: And what was waiting for me back in Paris? Well, better Chinese food than I'd eaten in China. Friends and relatives. A little accounting, regular schedule, keeping track of traffic violations in the suburbs. . . . And the indignity of students shouting the slogans of Chairman Mao at me—in French.

HELGA: Rene? Rene? *(She enters, soaking wet)* I've had a . . . a problem. *(She sneezes)*

GALLIMARD: You're wet.

HELGA: Yes, I . . . coming back from the grocer's. A group of students, waving red flags, they—

(GALLIMARD fetches a towel.)

HELGA: — they ran by, I was caught up along with them. Before I knew what was happening—

(GALLIMARD gives her the towel.)

HELGA: Thank you. The police started firing water cannons at us. I tried to shout, to tell them I was the wife of a diplomat, but—you know how it is . . . *(Pause)* Needless to say, I lost the groceries. Rene, what's happening to France?

GALLIMARD: What's—? Well, nothing, really.

HELGA: Nothing?! The storefronts are in flames, there's glass in the streets, buildings are toppling—and I'm wet!

GALLIMARD: Nothing! . . . that I care to think about.

HELGA: And is that why you stay in this room?

GALLIMARD: Yes, in fact.

HELGA: With the incense burning? You know something? I hate incense. It smells so sickly sweet.

GALLIMARD: Well, I hate the French. Who just smell—period!

HELGA: And the Chinese were better?

GALLIMARD: Please—don't start.

HELGA: When we left, this exact same thing, the riots—

GALLIMARD: No, no . . .

HELGA: Students screaming slogans, smashing down doors—

GALLIMARD: Helga—

HELGA: It was all going on in China, too. Don't you remember?!

GALLIMARD: Helga! Please! *(Pause)* You have never understood China, have you? You walk in here with these ridiculous ideas, that the West is falling apart, that China was spitting in our faces. You come in, dripping of the streets, and you leave water all over my floor. *(He grabs HELGA's towel, begins mopping up the floor)*

HELGA: But it's the truth!

GALLIMARD: Helga, I want a divorce.

(Pause; GALLIMARD continues mopping the floor.)

HELGA: I take it back. China is . . . beautiful. Incense, I like incense.

GALLIMARD: I've had a mistress.

HELGA: So?

GALLIMARD: For eight years.

HELGA: I knew you would. I knew you would the day I married you. And now what? You want to marry her?

GALLIMARD: I can't. She's in China.

HELGA: I see. You want to leave. For someone who's not here, is that right?

GALLIMARD: That's right.

HELGA: You can't live with her, but still you don't want to live with me.

GALLIMARD: That's right.

(Pause.)

HELGA: Shit. How terrible that I can figure that out. *(Pause)* I never thought I'd say it. But, in China, I was happy. I knew, in my own way, I knew that you were not everything you pretended to be. But the pretense—going on your arm to the embassy ball, visiting your office and the guards saying, "Good morning, good morning, Madame Gallimard"—the pretense . . . was very good indeed. *(Pause)* I hope everyone is mean to you for the rest of your life. *(She exits)*

GALLIMARD *(To us)*: Prophetic.

(MARC enters with two drinks.)

GALLIMARD *(To MARC)*: In China, I was different from all other men.

MARC: Sure. You were white. Here's your drink.

GALLIMARD: I felt . . . touched.

MARC: In the head? Rene, I don't want to hear about the Oriental love goddess. Okay? One night—can we just drink and throw up without a lot of conversation?

GALLIMARD: You still don't believe me, do you?

MARC: Sure I do. She was the most beautiful, et cetera, et cetera, blasé blasé.

(Pause.)

GALLIMARD: My life in the West has been such a disappointment.

MARC: Life in the West is like that. You'll get used to it. Look, you're driving me away. I'm leaving. Happy, now? *(He exits, then returns)* Look, I have a date tomorrow night. You wanna come? I can fix you up with—

GALLIMARD: Of course. I would love to come.

(Pause.)

MARC: Uh—on second thought, no. You'd better get ahold of yourself first.

(He exits; GALLIMARD nurses his drink.)

GALLIMARD (*To us*): This is the ultimate cruelty, isn't it? That I can talk and talk and to anyone listening, it's only air—too rich a diet to be swallowed by a mundane world. Why can't anyone understand? That in China, I once loved, and was loved by, very simply, the Perfect Woman.

(SONG *enters, dressed as Butterfly in wedding dress.*)

GALLIMARD (*To* SONG): Not again. My imagination is hell. Am I asleep this time? Or did I drink too much?

SONG: Rene?

GALLIMARD: God, it's too painful! That you speak?

SONG: What are you talking about? Rene—touch me.

GALLIMARD: Why?

SONG: I'm real. Take my hand.

GALLIMARD: Why? So you can disappear again and leave me clutching at the air? For the entertainment of my neighbors who—?

(SONG *touches* GALLIMARD.)

SONG: Rene?

(GALLIMARD *takes* SONG's *hand. Silence.*)

GALLIMARD: Butterfly? I never doubted you'd return.

SONG: You hadn't . . . forgotten—?

GALLIMARD: Yes, actually, I've forgotten everything. My mind, you see—there wasn't enough room in this hard head—not for the world *and* for you. No, there was only room for one. (*Beat*) Come, look. See? Your bed has been waiting, with the Klimt poster you like, and—see? The xiang lu [incense burner] you gave me?

SONG: I . . . I don't know what to say.

GALLIMARD: There's nothing to say. Not at the end of a long trip. Can I make you some tea?

SONG: But where's your wife?

GALLIMARD: She's by my side. She's by my side at last.

(GALLIMARD *reaches to embrace* SONG. SONG *sidesteps, dodging him.*)

GALLIMARD: Why?!

SONG (*To us*): So I did return to Rene in Paris. Where I found—

GALLIMARD: Why do you run away? Can't we show them how we embraced that evening?

SONG: Please. I'm talking.

GALLIMARD: You have to do what I say! I'm conjuring you up in *my* mind!

SONG: Rene, I've never done what you've said. Why should it be any different in your mind? Now split—the story moves on, and I must change.

GALLIMARD: I welcomed you into my home! I didn't have to, you know! I could've left you penniless on the streets of Paris! But I took you in!

SONG: Thank you.

GALLIMARD: So . . . please . . . don't change.

SONG: You know I have to. You know I will. And anyway, what difference does it make? No matter what your eyes tell you, you can't ignore the truth. You already know too much.

(GALLIMARD *exits.* SONG *turns to us.*)

SONG: The change I'm going to make requires about five minutes. So I thought you might want to take this opportunity to stretch your legs, enjoy a drink, or listen to the musicians. I'll be here, when you return, right where you left me.

(SONG *goes to a mirror in front of which is a wash basin of water. She starts to remove her makeup as stagelights go to half and houselights come up.*)

ACT 3 / SCENE 1

(*A courthouse in Paris. 1986.*)

(*As he promised,* SONG *has completed the bulk of his transformation, onstage by the time the houselights go down and the stagelights come up full. He removes his wig and kimono, leaving them on the floor. Underneath, he wears a well-cut suit.*)

SONG: So I'd done my job better than I had a right to expect. Well, give him some credit, too. He's right—I was in a fix when I arrived in Paris. I walked from the airport into town, then I located, by blind groping, the Chinatown district. Let me make one thing clear: whatever else may be said about the Chinese, they are stingy! I slept in doorways three days until I could find a tailor who would make me this kimono on credit. As it turns out, maybe I didn't even need it. Maybe he would've been happy to see me in a simple shift and mascara. But . . . better safe than sorry.

That was 1970, when I arrived in Paris. For the next fifteen years, yes, I lived a very comfy life. Some relief, believe me, after four years on a fucking commune in Nowheresville, China. Rene supported the boy and me, and I did some demonstrations around the country as part of my "cultural exchange" cover. And then there was the spying.

(SONG *moves upstage, to a chair.* TOULON *enters as a judge, wearing the appropriate wig and robes. He sits near* SONG. *It's 1986, and* SONG *is testifying in a courtroom.*)

SONG: Not much at first. Rene had lost all his high-level contacts. Comrade Chin wasn't very interested in parking-ticket statistics. But finally, at my urging, Rene got a job as a courier, handling sensitive documents. He'd photograph them for me, and I'd pass them on to the Chinese embassy.

JUDGE: Did he understand the extent of his activity?

SONG: He didn't ask. He knew that I needed those documents, and that was enough.

JUDGE: But he must've known he was passing classified information.

SONG: I can't say.

JUDGE: He never asked what you were going to do with them?

SONG: Nope.

(Pause.)

JUDGE: There is one thing that the court—indeed, that all of France—would like to know.

SONG: Fire away.

JUDGE: Did Monsieur Gallimard know you were a man?

SONG: Well, he never saw me completely naked. Ever.

JUDGE: But surely, he must've . . . how can I put this?

SONG: Put it however you like. I'm not shy. He must've felt around?

JUDGE: Mmmmm.

SONG: Not really. I did all the work. He just laid back. Of course we did enjoy more . . . complete union, and I suppose he *might* have wondered why I was always on my stomach, but. . . . But what you're thinking is, "Of course a wrist must've brushed . . . a hand hit . . . over twenty years!" Yeah. Well, Your Honor, it was my job to make him think I was a woman. And chew on this: it wasn't all that hard. See, my mother was a prostitute along the Bundt before the Revolution. And, uh, I think it's fair to say she learned a few things about Western men. So I borrowed her knowledge. In service to my country.

JUDGE: Would you care to enlighten the court with this secret knowledge? I'm sure we're all very curious.

SONG: I'm sure you are. *(Pause)* Okay, Rule One is: Men always believe what they want to hear. So a girl can tell the most obnoxious lies and the guys will believe them every time—"This is my first time"—"That's the biggest I've ever seen"—or *both,* which, if you really think about it, is not possible in a single lifetime. You've maybe heard those phrases a few times in your own life, yes, Your Honor?

JUDGE: It's not my life, Monsieur Song, which is on trial today.

SONG: Okay, okay, just trying to lighten up the proceedings. Tough room.

JUDGE: Go on.

SONG: Rule Two: As soon as a Western man comes into contact with the East—he's already confused. The West has sort of an international rape mentality towards the East. Do you know rape mentality?

JUDGE: Give us your definition, please.

SONG: Basically, "Her mouth says no, but her eyes say yes."

The West thinks of itself as masculine—big guns, big industry, big money—so the East is feminine—weak, delicate, poor . . . but good at art, and full of inscrutable wisdom—the feminine mystique.

Her mouth says no, but her eyes say yes. The West believes the East, deep down, *wants* to be dominated—because a woman can't think for herself.

JUDGE: What does this have to do with my question?

SONG: You expect Oriental countries to submit to your guns, and you expect Oriental women to be submissive to your men. That's why you say they make the best wives.

JUDGE: But why would that make it possible for you to fool Monsieur Gallimard? Please—get to the point.

SONG: One, because when he finally met his fantasy woman, he wanted more than anything to believe that she was, in fact, a woman. And second, I am an Oriental. And being an Oriental, I could never be completely a man.

(Pause.)

JUDGE: Your armchair political theory is tenuous, Monsieur Song.

SONG: You think so? That's why you'll lose in all your dealings with the East.

JUDGE: Just answer my question: did he know you were a man?

(Pause.)

SONG: You know, Your Honor, I never asked.

ACT 3 / SCENE 2

(Same.)

(Music from the "Death Scene" from Butterfly *blares over the house speakers. It is the loudest thing we've heard in this play.*

GALLIMARD *enters, crawling towards* SONG's *wig and kimono.)*

GALLIMARD: Butterfly? Butterfly?

(SONG remains a man, in the witness box, delivering a testimony we do not hear.)

GALLIMARD *(To us):* In my moment of greatest shame, here, in this courtroom—with that . . . person up there, telling the world. . . . What strikes me especially is how shallow he is, how glib and obsequious . . . completely . . . without substance! The type that prowls around discos with a gold medallion stinking of garlic. So little like my Butterfly.

Yet even in this moment my mind remains agile, flip-flopping like a man on a trampoline. Even now, my picture dissolves, and I see that . . . witness . . . talking to me.

(SONG suddenly stands straight up in his witness box, and looks at GALLIMARD.)

SONG: Yes. You. White man.

(SONG steps out of the witness box, and moves downstage towards GALLIMARD. *Light change.)*

GALLIMARD *(To* SONG): Who? Me?

SONG: Do you see any other white men?

GALLIMARD: Yes. There're white men all around. This is a French courtroom.

SONG: So you are an adventurous imperialist. Tell me, why did it take you so long? To come back to this place?

GALLIMARD: What place?

SONG: This theatre in China. Where we met many years ago.

GALLIMARD (*To us*): And once again, against my will, I am transported.

(*Chinese opera music comes up on the speakers.* SONG *begins to do opera moves, as he did the night they met.*)

SONG: Do you remember? The night you gave your heart?

GALLIMARD: It was a long time ago.

SONG: Not long enough. A night that turned your world upside down.

GALLIMARD: Perhaps.

SONG: Oh, be honest with me. What's another bit of flattery when you've already given me twenty years' worth? It's a wonder my head hasn't swollen to the size of China.

GALLIMARD: Who's to say it hasn't?

SONG: Who's to say? And what's the shame? In pride? You think I could've pulled this off if I wasn't already full of pride when we met? No, not just pride. Arrogance. It takes arrogance, really—to believe you can will, with your eyes and your lips, the destiny of another. (*He dances*) C'mon. Admit it. You still want me. Even in slacks and a button-down collar.

GALLIMARD: I don't see what the point of—

SONG: You don't? Well maybe, Rene, just maybe—I want you.

GALLIMARD: You do?

SONG: Then again, maybe I'm just playing with you. How can you tell? (*Reprising his feminine character, he sidles up to* GALLIMARD) "How I wish there were even a small cafe to sit in. With men in tuxedos, and cappuccinos, and bad expatriate jazz." Now you want to kiss me, don't you?

GALLIMARD (*Pulling away*): What makes you—?

SONG: —so sure? See? I take the words from your mouth. Then I wait for you to come and retrieve them. (*He reclines on the floor*)

GALLIMARD: Why?! Why do you treat me so cruelly?

SONG: Perhaps I *was* treating you cruelly. But now—I'm being nice. Come here, my little one.

GALLIMARD: I'm not your little one!

SONG: My mistake. It's I who am *your* little one, right?

GALLIMARD: Yes, I—

SONG: So come get your little one. If you like. I may even let you strip me.

GALLIMARD: I mean, you were! Before . . . but not like this!

SONG: I was? Then perhaps I still am. If you look hard enough. (*He starts to remove his clothes*)

GALLIMARD: What—what are you doing?

SONG: Helping you to see through my act.

GALLIMARD: Stop that! I don't want to! I don't—

SONG: Oh, but you asked me to strip, remember?

GALLIMARD: What? That was years ago! And I took it back!

SONG: No. You postponed it. Postponed the inevitable. Today, the inevitable has come calling.

(*From the speakers, cacophony:* Butterfly *mixed in with Chinese gongs.*)

GALLIMARD: No! Stop! I don't want to see!

SONG: Then look away.

GALLIMARD: You're only in my mind! All this is in my mind! I order you! To stop!

SONG: To what? To strip? That's just what I'm—

GALLIMARD: No! Stop! I want you—!

SONG: You want me?

GALLIMARD: To stop!

SONG: You know something, Rene? Your mouth says no, but your eyes say yes. Turn them away. I dare you.

GALLIMARD: I don't have to! Every night, you say you're going to strip, but then I beg you and you stop!

SONG: I guess tonight is different.

GALLIMARD: Why? Why should that be?

SONG: Maybe I've become frustrated. Maybe I'm saying "Look at me, you fool!" Or maybe I'm just feeling . . . sexy. (*He is down to his briefs*)

GALLIMARD: Please. This is unnecessary. I know what you are.

SONG: You do? What am I?

GALLIMARD: A—a man.

SONG: You don't really believe that.

GALLIMARD: Yes I do! I knew all the time somewhere that my happiness was temporary, my love a deception. But my mind kept the knowledge at bay. To make the wait bearable.

SONG: Monsieur Gallimard—the wait is over.

(SONG *drops his briefs. He is naked. Sound cue out. Slowly, we and* SONG *come to the realization that what we had thought to be* GALLIMARD's *sobbing is actually his laughter.*)

GALLIMARD: Oh god! What an idiot! Of course!

SONG: Rene—what?

GALLIMARD: Look at you! You're a man! (*He bursts into laughter again*)

SONG: I fail to see what's so funny!

GALLIMARD: "You fail to see—!" I mean, you never did have much of a sense of humor, did you? I just think it's ridiculously funny that I've wasted so much time on just a man!

SONG: Wait. I'm not "just a man."

GALLIMARD: No? Isn't that what you've been trying to convince me of?

SONG: Yes, but what I mean—

GALLIMARD: And now, I finally believe you, and you tell me it's not true? I think you must have some kind of identity problem.

SONG: Will you listen to me?

GALLIMARD: Why?! I've been listening to you for twenty years. Don't I deserve a vacation?

SONG: I'm not just any man!

GALLIMARD: Then, what exactly are you?

SONG: Rene, how can you ask—? Okay, what about this?

(*He picks up Butterfly's robes, starts to dance around. No music.*)

GALLIMARD: Yes, that's very nice. I have to admit.

(SONG *holds out his arm to* GALLIMARD.)

SONG: It's the same skin you've worshiped for years. Touch it.

GALLIMARD: Yes, it does feel the same.

SONG: Now—close your eyes.

(SONG *covers* GALLIMARD's *eyes with one hand. With the other,* SONG *draws* GALLIMARD's *hand up to his face.* GALLIMARD, *like a blind man, lets his hands run over* SONG's *face.*)

GALLIMARD: This skin, I remember. The curve of her face, the softness of her cheek, her hair against the back of my hand . . .

SONG: I'm your Butterfly. Under the robes, beneath everything, it was always me. Now, open your eyes and admit it—you adore me. (*He removes his hand from* GALLIMARD's *eyes*)

GALLIMARD: You, who knew every inch of my desires—how could you, of all people, have made such a mistake?

SONG: What?

GALLIMARD: You showed me your true self. When all I loved was the lie. A perfect lie, which you let fall to the ground—and now, it's old and soiled.

SONG: So—you never really loved me? Only when I was playing a part?

GALLIMARD: I'm a man who loved a woman created by a man. Everything else—simply falls short.

(*Pause.*)

SONG: What am I supposed to do now?

GALLIMARD: You were a fine spy, Monsieur Song, with an even finer accomplice. But now I believe you should go. Get out of my life!

SONG: Go where? Rene, you can't live without me. Not after twenty years.

GALLIMARD: I certainly can't live with you—not after twenty years of betrayal.

SONG: Don't be stubborn! Where will you go?

GALLIMARD: I have a date . . . with my Butterfly.

SONG: So, throw away your pride. And come . . .

GALLIMARD: Get away from me! Tonight, I've finally learned to tell fantasy from reality. And, knowing the difference, I choose fantasy.

SONG: I'm your fantasy!

GALLIMARD: You? You're as real as hamburger. Now get out! I have a date with my Butterfly and I don't want your body polluting the room! (*He tosses* SONG's *suit at him*) Look at these—you dress like a pimp.

SONG: Hey! These are Armani slacks and—! (*He puts on his briefs and slacks*) Let's just say . . . I'm disappointed in you, Rene. In the crush of your adoration, I thought you'd become something more. More like . . . a woman.

But no. Men. You're like the rest of them. It's all in the way we dress, and make up our faces, and bat our eyelashes. You really have so little imagination!

GALLIMARD: You, Monsieur Song? Accuse me of too little imagination? You, if anyone, should know—I am pure imagination. And in imagination I will remain. Now get out!

(GALLIMARD *bodily removes* SONG *from the stage, taking his kimono.*)

SONG: Rene! I'll never put on those robes again! You'll be sorry!

GALLIMARD (*To* SONG): I'm already sorry! (*Looking at the kimono in his hands*) Exactly as sorry . . . as a Butterfly.

ACT 3 / SCENE 3

(M. GALLIMARD's *prison cell. Paris. Present.*)

GALLIMARD: I've played out the events of my life night after night, always searching for a new ending to my story, one where I leave this cell and return forever to my Butterfly's arms.

Tonight I realize my search is over. That I've looked all along in the wrong place. And now, to you, I will prove that my love was not in vain—by returning to the world of fantasy where I first met her.

(*He picks up the kimono; dancers enter.*)

GALLIMARD: There is a vision of the Orient that I have. Of slender women in chong sams and kimonos who die for the love of unworthy foreign devils. Who are born and raised to be the perfect women. Who take whatever punishment we give them, and bounce back, strengthened by love, unconditionally. It is a vision that has become my life.

(*Dancers bring the wash basin to him and help him make up his face.*)

GALLIMARD: In public, I have continued to deny that Song Liling is a man. This brings me headlines, and is a source of great embarrassment to my French colleagues, who can now be sent into a coughing fit by the mere mention of Chinese food. But alone, in my cell, I have long since faced the truth.

And the truth demands a sacrifice. For mistakes made over the course of a lifetime. My mistakes were simple and absolute—the man I loved was a cad, a bounder. He deserved nothing but a kick in the behind, and instead I gave him . . . all my love.

Yes—love. Why not admit it all? That was my undoing, wasn't it? Love warped my judgment, blinded my eyes, rearranged the very lines on my face . . . until I could look in the mirror and see nothing but . . . a woman.

(Dancers help him put on the Butterfly wig.)

GALLIMARD: I have a vision. Of the Orient. That, deep within its almond eyes, there are still women. Women willing to sacrifice themselves for the love of a man. Even a man whose love is completely without worth.

(Dancers assist GALLIMARD in donning the kimono. They hand him a knife.)

GALLIMARD: Death with honor is better than life . . . life with dishonor. *(He sets himself center stage, in a seppuku position)* The love of a Butterfly can withstand many things—unfaithfulness, loss, even abandonment. But how can it face the one sin that implies all others? The devastating knowledge that, underneath it all, the object of her love was nothing more, nothing less than . . . a man. *(He sets the tip of the knife against his body)* It is 19——. And I have found her at last. In a prison on the outskirts of Paris. My name is Rene Gallimard—also known as Madame Butterfly.

(GALLIMARD turns upstage and plunges the knife into his body, as music from the "Love Duet" blares over the speakers. He collapses into the arms of the dancers, who lay him reverently on the floor. The image holds for several beats. Then a tight special up on SONG, who stands as a man, staring at the dead GALLIMARD. He smokes a cigarette; the smoke filters up through the lights. Two words leave his lips.)

SONG: Butterfly? Butterfly?

(Smoke rises as lights fade slowly to black.)

AFTERWORD

It all started in May of 1986, over casual dinner conversation. A friend asked, had I heard about the French diplomat who'd fallen in love with a Chinese actress, who subsequently turned out to be not only a spy, but a man? I later found a two-paragraph story in *The New York Times*. The diplomat, Bernard Bouriscot, attempting to account for the fact that he had never seen his "girlfriend" naked, was quoted as saying, "I thought she was very modest. I thought it was a Chinese custom."

Now, I am aware that this is *not* a Chinese custom, that Asian women are no more shy with their lovers than are women of the West. I am also aware, however, that Bouriscot's assumption was consistent with a certain stereotyped view of Asians as bowing, blushing flowers. I therefore concluded that the diplomat must have fallen in love, not with a person, but with a fantasy stereotype. I also inferred that, to the extent the Chinese spy encouraged these misperceptions, he must have played up to and exploited this image of the Oriental woman as demure and submissive. (In general, by the way, we prefer the term "Asian" to "Oriental," in the same way "Black" is superior to "Negro." I use the term "Oriental" specifically to denote an exotic or imperialistic view of the East.)

I suspected there was a play here. I purposely refrained from further research, for I was not interested in writing docudrama. Frankly, I didn't want the "truth" to interfere with my own speculations. I told Stuart Ostrow, a producer with whom I'd worked before, that I envisioned the story as a musical. I remember going so far as to speculate that it could be some "great *Madame Butterfly*–like tragedy." Stuart was very intrigued, and encouraged me with some early funding.

Before I can begin writing, I must "break the back of the story," and find some angle which compels me to set pen to paper. I was driving down Santa Monica Boulevard one afternoon, and asked myself, "What did Bouriscot think he was getting in this Chinese actress?" The answer came to me clearly: "He probably thought he had found Madame Butterfly."

The idea of doing a deconstructivist *Madame Butterfly* immediately appealed to me. This, despite the fact that I didn't even know the plot of the opera! I knew Butterfly only as a cultural stereotype; speaking of an Asian woman, we would sometimes say, "She's pulling a Butterfly," which meant playing the submissive Oriental number. Yet, I felt convinced that the libretto would include yet another lotus blossom pining away for a cruel Caucasian man, and dying for her love. Such a story has become too much of a cliché not to be included in the archetypal East-West romance that started it all. Sure enough, when I purchased the record, I discovered it contained a wealth of sexist and racist clichés, reaffirming my faith in Western culture.

Very soon after, I came up with the basic "arc" of my play: the Frenchman fantasizes that he is Pinkerton and his lover is Butterfly. By the end of the piece, he realizes that it is he who has been Butterfly, in that the Frenchman has been duped by love; the Chinese spy, who exploited that love, is therefore the real Pinkerton. I wrote a proposal to Stuart Ostrow, who found it very exciting. (On the night of the Tony Awards, Stuart produced my original two-page treatment, and we were gratified to see that it was, indeed, the play I eventually wrote.)

I wrote a play, rather than a musical, because, having "broken the back" of the story, I wanted to start immediately and not be hampered by the lengthy process of collaboration. I would like to think, however, that the play has retained many of its musical roots. So *Monsieur Butterfly* was completed in six weeks between September and mid-October, 1986. My wife, Ophelia, thought *Monsieur Butterfly* too obvious a title, and suggested I abbreviate it in the French fashion. Hence, *M. Butterfly*, far more mysterious and ambiguous, was the result.

I sent the play to Stuart Ostrow as a courtesy, assuming he would not be interested in producing what had become a straight play. Instead, he flew out to Los Angeles immediately for script conferences. Coming from a background in the not-for-profit theater, I suggested that we develop the work at a regional institution. Stuart, nothing if not bold, argued for bringing it directly to Broadway.

It was also Stuart who suggested John Dexter to direct. I had known Dexter's work only by its formidable reputation. Stuart sent the script to John, who called back the next day, saying it was the best play he'd read in twenty years. Naturally, this predisposed me to like him a great deal. We met in December in New York. Not long after, we persuaded Eiko Ishioka to design our sets and costumes. I had admired her work from afar ever since, as a college student, I had seen her poster for *Apocalypse Now* in Japan. By January, 1987, Stuart had optioned *M. Butterfly*, Dexter was signed to direct, and the normally sloth-like pace of commercial theater had been given a considerable prod.

On January 4, 1988, we commenced rehearsals. I was very pleased that John Lithgow had agreed to play the French diplomat, whom I named Rene Gallimard. Throughout his tenure with us, Lithgow was every inch the center of our company, intelligent and professional, passionate and generous. B. D. Wong was forced to endure a five-month audition period before we selected him to play Song Liling. Watching B. D.'s growth was one of the joys of the rehearsal process, as he constantly attained higher levels of performance. It became clear that we had been fortunate enough to put together a company with not only great talent, but also wonderful camaraderie.

As for Dexter, I have never worked with a director more respectful of text and bold in the uses of theatricality. On the first day of rehearsal, the actors were given movement and speech drills. Then Dexter asked that everyone not required at rehearsal leave the room. A week later, we returned for an amazingly thorough run-through. It was not until that day that I first heard my play read, a note I direct at many regional theaters who "develop" a script to death.

We opened in Washington, D.C., at the National Theatre, where *West Side Story* and *Amadeus* had premiered. On the morning after opening night, most of the reviews were glowing, except for *The Washington Post*. Throughout our run in Washington, Stuart never pressured us to make the play more "commercial" in reaction to that review. We all simply concluded that the gentleman was possibly insecure about his own sexual orientation and therefore found the play threatening. And we continued our work.

Once we opened in New York, the play found a life of its own. I suppose the most gratifying thing for me is that we had never compromised to be more "Broadway"; we simply did the work we thought best. That our endeavor should be rewarded to the degree it has is one of those all-too-rare instances when one's own perception and that of the world are in agreement.

Many people have subsequently asked me about the "ideas" behind the play. From our first preview in Washington, I have been pleased that people leaving the theater were talking not only about the sexual, but also the political, issues raised by the work.

From my point of view, the "impossible" story of a Frenchman duped by a Chinese man masquerading as a woman always seemed perfectly explicable; given the degree of misunderstanding between men and women and also between East and West, it seemed inevitable that a mistake of this magnitude would one day take place.

Gay friends have told me of a derogatory term used in their community: "Rice Queen"—a gay Caucasian man primarily attracted to Asians. In these relationships, the Asian virtually always plays the role of the "woman"; the Rice Queen, culturally and sexually, is the "man." This pattern of relationships had become so codified that, until recently, it was considered unnatural for gay Asians to date one another. Such men would be taunted with a phrase which implied they were lesbians.

Similarly, heterosexual Asians have long been aware of "Yellow Fever"—Caucasian men with a fetish for exotic Oriental women. I have often heard it said that "Oriental women make the best wives." (Rarely is this heard from the mouths of Asian men, incidentally.) This mythology is exploited by the Oriental mail-order bride trade which has flourished over the past decade. American men can now send away for catalogues of "obedient, domesticated" Asian women looking for husbands. Anyone who believes such stereotypes are a thing of the past need look no further than Manhattan cable television, which advertises call girls from "the exotic east, where men are king; obedient girls, trained in the art of pleasure."

In these appeals, we see issues of racism and sexism intersect. The catalogues and TV spots appeal to a strain in men which desires to reject Western women for what they have become—independent, assertive, self-possessed—in favor of a more reactionary model—the pre-feminist, domesticated geisha girl.

That the Oriental woman is penultimately feminine does not of course imply that she is always "good." For every Madonna there is a whore; for every lotus blossom there is also a dragon lady. In popular culture, "good" Asian women are those who serve the White protagonist in his battle against her own people, often sleeping with him in the process. Stallone's *Rambo II*, Cimino's *Year of the Dragon*, Clavell's *Shogun*, Van Lustbader's *The Ninja* are all familiar examples.

Now our considerations of race and sex intersect the issue of imperialism. For this formula—good natives serve Whites, bad natives rebel—is consistent with the mentality of colonialism. Because they are submissive and obedient, good natives of both sexes necessarily take on "feminine" characteristics in a colonialist world. Gunga Din's unfailing devotion to his British master, for instance, is not so far removed from Butterfly's slavish faith in Pinkerton.

It is reasonable to assume that influences and attitudes so pervasively displayed in popular culture might also influence our policymakers as they consider the world. The neo-Colonialist notion that good elements of a native society, like a good woman, desire submission to the masculine West speaks precisely to the heart of our foreign policy blunders in Asia and elsewhere.

For instance, Frances Fitzgerald wrote in *Fire in the Lake*, "The idea that the United States could not master the problems of a country as small and underdeveloped as Vietnam did not occur to Johnson as a possibility." Here, as in so many other cases, by dehumanizing the enemy, we dehumanize ourselves. We become the Rice Queens of *realpolitik*.

M. Butterfly has sometimes been regarded as an anti-American play, a diatribe against the stereotyping of the East by the West, of women by men. Quite to the contrary, I consider it a plea to all sides to cut through our respective layers of cultural and sexual misperception, to deal with one another truthfully for our mutual good, from the common and equal ground we share as human beings.

For the myths of the East, the myths of the West, the myths of men, and the myths of women—these have so saturated our consciousness that truthful contact between nations and lovers can only be the result of heroic effort. Those who prefer to bypass the work involved will remain in a world of surfaces, misperceptions running rampant. This is, to me, the convenient world in which the French diplomat and the Chinese spy lived. This is why, after twenty years, he had learned nothing at all about his lover, not even the truth of his sex.

D. H. H.

New York City
September, 1988

Figure 1. At the opening of the play, Gallimard (John Lithgow) sits in his prison cell while Song Liling (B. D. Wong) poses above. The swirling ramp was designed by Eiko Ishioka for the 1988 production of *M. Butterfly* directed by John Dexter. (Photograph: Martha Swope.)

Figure 2. Song Liling (B. D. Wong) as Butterfly in the 1988 production of *M. Butterfly* directed by John Dexter. (Photograph: Martha Swope.)

Figure 3. Gallimard (John Lithgow) and Song Liling (B. D. Wong) in her Beijing apartment in the 1988 production of *M. Butterfly* directed by John Dexter. (Photograph: Martha Swope.)

Staging of *M. Butterfly*

REVIEW OF THE NEW YORK PRODUCTION, 1988, BY FRANK RICH

It didn't require genius for David Henry Hwang to see that there were the makings of a compelling play in the 1986 newspaper story that prompted him to write "M. Butterfly." Here was the incredible true-life tale of a career French foreign service officer brought to ruin—conviction for espionage—by a bizarre 20-year affair with a Beijing Opera diva. Not only had the French diplomat failed to recognize that his lover was a spy; he'd also failed to figure out that "she" was a he in drag. "It was dark, and she was very modest," says Gallimard (John Lithgow), Mr. Hwang's fictionalized protagonist, by half-joking way of explanation. When we meet him in the prison cell where he reviews his life, Gallimard has become, according to his own understatement, "the patron saint of the socially inept."

But if this story is a corker, what is it about, exactly? That's where Mr. Hwang's imagination, one of the most striking to emerge in the American theater in this decade, comes in, and his answer has nothing to do with journalism. This playwright, the author of "The Dance and the Railroad" and "Family Devotions," does not tease us with obvious questions such as is she or isn't she?, or does he know or doesn't he? Mr. Hwang isn't overly concerned with how the opera singer, named Song Liling (B. D. Wong), pulled his hocus-pocus in the boudoir, and he refuses to explain away Gallimard by making him a closeted, self-denying homosexual. An inversion of Puccini's "Madama Butterfly," "M. Butterfly" is also the inverse of most American plays. Instead of reducing the world to an easily digested cluster of sexual or familial relationships, Mr. Hwang cracks open a liaison to reveal a sweeping, universal meditation on two of the most heated conflicts—men versus women, East versus West—of this or any other time.

As a piece of playwriting that manages to encompass phenomena as diverse as the origins of the Vietnam War and the socio-economic code embedded in Giorgio Armani fashions, "M. Butterfly" is so singular that one hates to report that a visitor to the Eugene O'Neill Theater must overcome a number of obstacles to savor it. Because of some crucial and avoidable lapses—a winning yet emotionally bland performance from Mr. Lithgow and inept acting in some supporting roles—the experience of seeing the play isn't nearly as exciting as thinking about it after the curtain has gone down. The production only rises to full power in its final act, when the evening's triumphant performance, Mr. Wong's mesmerizing account of the transvestite diva, hits its own tragic high notes. Until then, one must settle for being grateful that a play of this ambition has made it to Broadway, and that the director, John Dexter, has

realized as much of Mr. Hwang's far-ranging theatricality as he has.

As usual, Mr. Hwang demands a lot from directors, actors and theatergoers. A 30-year-old Chinese-American writer from Los Angeles, he has always blended Oriental and Western theater in his work, and "M. Butterfly" does so on an epic scale beyond his previous plays, let alone such similarly minded Western hybrids as "Pacific Overtures" or "Nixon in China." While ostensibly constructed as a series of Peter Shafferesque flashbacks narrated by Gallimard from prison, the play is as intricate as an infinity of Chinese boxes. Even as we follow the narrative of the lovers' affair, it is being refracted through both overt and disguised burlesque deconstructions of "Madama Butterfly." As Puccini's music collides throughout with a percussive Eastern score by Lucia Hwong, so Western storytelling and sassy humor intermingle with flourishes of martial-arts ritual, Chinese opera (Cultural Revolution Maoist agitprop included) and Kabuki. Now and then, the entire mix is turned inside out, Genet and Pirandello style, to remind us that fantasy isn't always distinguishable from reality and that actors are not to be confused with their roles.

The play's form—whether the clashing and blending of Western and Eastern cultures or of male and female characters—is wedded to its content. It's Mr. Hwang's starting-off point that a cultural icon like "Madama Butterfly" bequeaths the sexist and racist roles that burden Western men: Gallimard believes he can become "a real man" only if he can exercise power over a beautiful and submissive woman, which is why he's so ripe to be duped by Song Liling's impersonation of a shrinking butterfly. Mr. Hwang broadens his message by making Gallimard an architect of the Western foreign policy in Vietnam. The diplomat disastrously reasons that a manly display of American might can bring the Viet Cong to submission as easily as he or Puccini's Pinkerton can overpower a Madama Butterfly.

Lest that ideological leap seem too didactic, the playwright shuffles the deck still more, suggesting that the roles played by Gallimard and Song Liling run so deep that they cross the boundaries of nations, cultures, revolutions and sexual orientations. That Gallimard was fated to love "a woman created by a man" proves to be figuratively as well as literally true: we see that the male culture that inspired his "perfect woman" is so entrenched that the attitudes of "Madama Butterfly" survive in his cherished present-day porno magazines. Nor is the third world, in Mr. Hwang's view, immune from adopting the roles it condemns in foreign devils. We're sarcastically told that men continue to play women in

Chinese opera because "only a man knows how a woman is supposed to act." When Song Liling reassumes his male "true self," he still must play a submissive Butterfly to Gallimard—whatever his or Gallimard's actual sexual persuasions—unless he chooses to play the role of aggressor to a Butterfly of his own.

Mr. Hwang's play is not without its repetitions and its overly explicit bouts of thesis mongering. When the playwright stops trusting his own instinct for the mysterious, the staging often helps out. Using Eiko Ishioka's towering, blood-red Oriental variant on the abstract sets Mr. Dexter has employed in "Equus" and the Metropolitan Opera "Dialogues of the Carmelites," the director stirs together Mr. Hwang's dramatic modes and settings until one floats to a purely theatrical imaginative space suspended in time and place. That same disorienting quality can be found in Mr. Wong's Song Liling—a performance that, like John Lone's in the early Hwang plays, finds even more surprises in the straddling of cultures than in the blurring of genders.

But Mr. Dexter's erratic handling of actors, also apparent in his Broadway "Glass Menagerie" revival, inflicts a serious toll. John Getz and Rose Gregorio, as Gallimard's oldest pal and wife, are wildly off-key, wrecking the intended high-style comedy of the all-Western scenes. Mr. Lithgow, onstage virtually throughout, projects intelligence and wit, and his unflagging energy drives and helps unify the evening. Yet this engaging, ironic Gallimard never seems completely consumed by passion, whether the eroticism of imperialism or of the flesh, and the performance seems to deepen more in pitch than despair from beginning to end. Though "M. Butterfly" presents us with a visionary work that bridges the history and culture of two worlds, the production stops crushingly short of finding the gripping human drama that merges Mr. Hwang's story with his brilliant play of ideas.

TIMBERLAKE WERTENBAKER

1946–

When Timberlake Wertenbaker told a *New York Times* interviewer in 1990, "The whole thing about being a writer is that you can have a floating identity," she spoke out of her own experience as a person of several nationalities and cultures. Born in America, raised in the Basque country in France, and now living in London, Wertenbaker was bilingual from an early age. Though her elementary and secondary education took place in France, she returned to America for college and in 1966 graduated from St. John's College in Annapolis, Maryland, best-known for its "Great Books" curriculum. After working as a writer for Time-Life Books in New York, she taught French for a year in Greece, a year marking her debut as a playwright, which began with pieces for schoolchildren to perform. When Wertenbaker moved to London in the 1970s, she found both her home and her career, starting with adaptations and translations, as well as her own plays for London fringe theaters and provincial theaters. By 1984, she had become "writer-in-residence" at the government-supported Royal Court Theatre, and it was their production of *The Grace of Mary Traverse* (1985) that attracted widespread critical attention, leading to further commissions from the Royal Court and new ones with the Royal Shakespeare Company.

The Grace of Mary Traverse focuses on a fictional woman in a real historical setting, as had several of Wertenbaker's earlier plays such as *New Anatomies* (1981), which presents a young woman at the turn of the century traveling through Europe and Algeria, and *Home Leave* (1982), which deals with women factory workers at the end of World War II. Mary Traverse, a merchant's daughter in late eighteenth-century London, is first seen practicing polite conversation with an imaginary nobleman, represented by an empty chair. Her rejection of such limited opportunities and her insistence on knowing "the world as it is" take her on a journey that leads to sexual initiation, gambling, prostitution, pregnancy, and even participation in the Gordon Riots of 1780, when an anti-Catholic petition triggered days of mob violence. Wertenbaker thus offers what might be called a female version of "The Rake's Progress," the famous series of engravings (1735) by William Hogarth. But while Hogarth's Tom Rakewell ends up in the insane asylum, Mary's last appearance is in a garden, with her daughter and father and companion, Sophie, still hoping for understanding.

The search for knowledge about oneself and the world is central to Wertenbaker's plays, and particularly in her two works based on Greek mythology. In *The Love of the Nightingale* (1988), Wertenbaker vividly and evocatively dramatizes the haunting story of Philomele, the Athenian princess transformed into a nightingale after being raped by her royal brother-in-law. As in Ovid's *Metamorphoses*, the well-known Roman version of the myth, Tereus, king of Thrace, marries Procne, sister of Philomele; then after pretending that Procne is dead, he rapes Philomele and cuts out her tongue to prevent her from revealing his crime. Before the rape, Wertenbaker presents Philomele as being a naive young woman, asking Procne questions about sex or proclaiming as she watches a play about Phaedra that "love is a god and you cannot control him." After the rape, Wertenbaker stresses Philomele's outspoken anger. By giving Philomele a voice that Tereus must silence, Wertenbaker dramatically emphasizes what the myth implies: the power of a woman's speech and the power of the victim.

In 1991, Wertenbaker again turned to Greek drama, not only translating Sophocles' three Theban plays, *Oedipus, Oedipus at Colonus,* and *Antigone,* but also writing another work of her own based on Greek myth, namely, *Three Birds Alighting on a Field.* But in this case, rather than literally dramatizing the story of a mythic Greek character, Wertenbaker constructs a plot paralleling a contemporary painter named Stephen Ryle, whose work is out of fashion, with the situation of a mythic Greek warrior, Philoctetes, whose infected wound was so disgusting to his Greek comrades that he suddenly found himself out of favor, only to be sought out by them when they once again needed his skill. The parallels between Philoctetes and Stephen Ryle raise challenging questions about the value of art, as well as about the motives behind the creation of art and the acquisition of art. In probing these issues, Wertenbaker focuses not only on the painter Ryle, but also on Biddy, a wealthy nonentity who turns to the art world in an effort to save her second marriage. When her husband threatens her, "I can't afford a wife who does nothing," she starts looking at paintings, hoping that art collecting will make her interesting and slowly comes to discover herself. By the end of the play, Stephen Ryle is painting Biddy, now fully visible: "When I started this painting, there were three birds and you were a vanishing figure, but you've taken over the canvas." Biddy's change attests to the creative power of the artistic process, a power even more strikingly affirmed in Wertenbaker's best-known play, *Our Country's Good* (1988), winner of the Laurence Olivier Play of the Year Award.

While most of Wertenbaker's other plays focus on the transformation of a single individual, *Our Country's Good* is about the collaborative work that forms the center of all theatrical experience. The play itself is, in fact, the result of multiple collaborations, beginning with the choice by Max Stafford-Clark, director of the Royal Court Theatre, to stage *The Recruiting Officer,* George Farquhar's 1706 social comedy about two young women and the men who pursue them through comic misunderstandings to a happy ending. Farquhar's play subsequently inspired Thomas Keneally's novel, *The Playmaker* (1987), which deals with the first performance of Farquhar's play in Australia, staged by convicts on June 4, 1789. Given the fascinating story of that unlikely production, Stafford-Clark asked Wertenbaker to adapt the novel into a play, thus giving his acting company the exciting challenge of presenting a "classic" and a new play together. Wertenbaker, Stafford-Clark, and ten actors began their collaboration with a two-week workshop. After reading a detailed account of the penal colony in Australia as well as source material about the poverty-stricken world of eighteenth-century London from which the convicts came, each actor had to present one of the real people to the rest of the group. The actors also researched acting styles of the period, a session that provided the details for Sideway's attempts at "establishing melancholy" in "The First Rehearsal."

After the two-week workshop, Wertenbaker began drafting the play, but inevitably ideas from the rehearsals of *The Recruiting Officer* also found their way into *Our Country's Good*. Wertenbaker's use of *The Recruiting Officer* constantly draws parallels between Farquhar's characters and the convicts playing them, sometimes quite ironic as in the casting of Liz Morden the thief as the wealthy Melinda, sometimes direct as in the developing love affair between Mary Brenham and Lt. Ralph Clark, who take the parts of Silvia and Captain Plume, the central couple in Farquhar's play. She also makes unexpected use of Farquhar's lines, as in "The Second Rehearsal" when officers opposed to the rehearsals cruelly mock the convicts; at this point, lines from a scene between two lovers suddenly become disturbingly relevant to the context, as Sideway declares that "I shall meet with less cruelty among the most barbarous nations than I have found at home."

Just as *Our Country's Good* interweaves Restoration comedy with the grim details of convict life in the late eighteenth century, so the original production of the play blended nonrealistic and realistic modes of presentation. The play, for example, includes twenty-two characters, but these were performed by just ten actors, with everyone playing at least two roles (except for David Haig as Ralph Clark). This doubling of parts meant that women played men's roles, a theatrical convention that echoes the disguise motif in *The Recruiting Officer* when Silvia dresses herself up as a new recruit in order to pursue Captain Plume. Though the women donned wigs and jackets, they kept their skirts on as well (see Figure 1), so the audience was always aware of their role-playing. The doubling also invites the audience to look for parallels and differences: the generous-spirited Governor Philip (see Figure 1) is also the most intelligent of the convicts, John Wisehammer (see Figure 4); the acerbic Major Ross (see Figure 1) is also the convict, Ketch Freeman, ostracized by the other convicts because he has accepted the job of hangman (see Figure 3). The nonrealistic production style extended also to the setting. Thus when Harry Brewer takes Duckling rowing, he creates the boat with four crates and two oars (see Figure 2). Such interplay between the deliberate theatricality of the presentation and the often painful reality of the human relationships serves to heighten Wertenbaker's central concern with the collaborative spirit that is fundamental to the success both of theater and of society. So it is that the theatrical process, fragile and illusionary as it is, may nonetheless help to create a humane existence amid inhuman circumstances.

OUR COUNTRY'S GOOD

BY TIMBERLAKE WERTENBAKER/BASED ON THE NOVEL *THE PLAYMAKER* BY THOMAS KENEALLY

CHARACTERS

CAPTAIN ARTHUR PHILLIP, RN (*Governor-in-Chief of New South Wales*)
MAJOR ROBBIE ROSS, RM
CAPTAIN DAVID COLLINS, RM (*Advocate General*)
CAPTAIN WATKIN TENCH, RM
CAPTAIN JEMMY CAMPBELL, RM
REVEREND JOHNSON
LIEUTENANT GEORGE JOHNSTON, RM
LIEUTENANT WILL DAWES, RM
SECOND LIEUTENANT RALPH CLARK, RM
SECOND LIEUTENANT WILLIAM FADDY, RM
MIDSHIPMAN HARRY BREWER, RN (*Provost Marshal*)
AN ABORIGINAL AUSTRALIAN
JOHN ARSCOTT
BLACK CAESAR
KETCH FREEMAN
ROBERT SIDEWAY
JOHN WISEHAMMER
MARY BRENHAM
DABBY BRYANT
LIZ MORDEN
DUCKLING SMITH
MEG LONG

[Though there are twenty-two roles, the original production used only ten actors. The doubling works as follows:
PHILLIP/WISEHAMMER
ROSS/FREEMAN
COLLINS/SIDEWAY
TENCH/ABORIGINE/CAESAR
CAMPBELL/BREWER/ARSCOTT
REV. JOHNSON/MARY/MEG
JOHNSTON/DUCKLING

DAWES/LIZ
FADDY/DABBY
RALPH]

The play takes place in Sydney, Australia in 1788/9

ACT 1

ACT 2

ACT 1 / SCENE 1 The Voyage Out

(*The hold of a convict ship bound for Australia, 1787. The convicts huddle together in the semi-darkness. On deck, the convict* ROBERT SIDEWAY *is being flogged.* SECOND LIEUTENANT RALPH CLARK *counts the lashes in a barely audible, slow and monotonous voice.*)

RALPH CLARK: Forty-four, forty-five, forty-six, forty-seven, forty-eight, forty-nine, fifty.

(SIDEWAY *is untied and dumped with the rest of the convicts. He collapses. No one moves. A short silence.*)

JOHN WISEHAMMER: At night? The sea cracks against the ship. Fear whispers, screams, falls silent, hushed. Spewed from our country, forgotten, bound to the dark edge of the earth, at night what is there to do but seek English cunt, warm, moist, soft, oh the comfort, the comfort of the lick, the thrust into the nooks, the crannies of the crooks of England. Alone, frightened, nameless in this stinking hole of hell, take me, take me inside you, whoever you are. Take me, my comfort and we'll remember England together.

JOHN ARSCOTT: Hunger. Funny. Doesn't start in the

stomach, but in the mind. A picture flits in and out of a corner. Something you've eaten long ago. Roast beef with salt and grated horseradish.

MARY: I don't know why I did it. Love, I suppose.

ACT 1 / SCENE 2 A lone Aboriginal Australian describes the arrival of the First Convict Fleet in Botany Bay on January 20, 1788

THE ABORIGINE: A giant canoe drifts onto the sea, clouds billowing from upright oars. This is a dream which has lost its way. Best to leave it alone.

ACT 1 / SCENE 3 Punishment

(Sydney Cove. GOVERNOR ARTHUR PHILLIP, JUDGE DAVID COLLINS, CAPTAIN WATKIN TENCH, MIDSHIP-MAN HARRY BREWER. *The men are shooting birds.)*

PHILLIP: Was it necessary to cross fifteen thousand miles of ocean to erect another Tyburn?°

TENCH: I should think it would make the convicts feel at home.

COLLINS: This land is under English law. The court found them guilty and sentenced them accordingly. There: a bald-eyed corella.

PHILLIP: But hanging?

COLLINS: Only the three who were found guilty of stealing from the colony's stores. And that, over there on the Eucalyptus, is a flock of 'cacatua galerita'—the sulphur-crested cockatoo. You have been made Governor-in-Chief of a paradise of birds, Arthur.

PHILLIP: And I hope not of a human hell, Davey. Don't shoot yet, Watkin, let's observe them. Could we not be more humane?

TENCH: Justice and humaneness have never gone hand in hand. The law is not a sentimental comedy.

PHILLIP: I am not suggesting they go without punishment. It is the spectacle of hanging I object to. The convicts will feel nothing has changed and will go back to their old ways.

TENCH: The convicts never left their old ways, Governor, nor do they intend to.

PHILLIP: Three months is not long enough to decide that. You're speaking too loud, Watkin.

COLLINS: I commend your endeavour to oppose the baneful influence of vice with the harmonising acts of civilisation, Governor, but I suspect your edifice will collapse without the mortar of fear.

PHILLIP: Have these men lost all fear of being flogged?

COLLINS: John Arscott has already been sentenced to 150 lashes for assault.

TENCH: The shoulder-blades are exposed at about 100 lashes and I would say that somewhere between 250 and 500 lashes you are probably condemning a man to death anyway.

COLLINS: With the disadvantage that the death is slow, unobserved and cannot serve as a sharp example.

PHILLIP: Harry?

HARRY: The convicts laugh at hangings, Sir. They watch them all the time.

TENCH: It's their favourite form of entertainment, I should say.

PHILLIP: Perhaps because they've never been offered anything else.

TENCH: Perhaps we should build an opera house for the convicts.

PHILLIP: We learned to love such things because they were offered to us when we were children or young men. Surely no one is born naturally cultured? I'll have the gun now.

COLLINS: We don't even have any books here, apart from the odd play and a few Bibles. And most of the convicts can't read, so let us return to the matter in hand, which is the punishment of the convicts, not their education.

PHILLIP: Who are the condemned men, Harry?

HARRY: Thomas Barrett, age 17. Transported seven years for stealing one ewe sheep.

PHILLIP: Seventeen!

TENCH: It does seem to prove that the criminal tendency is innate.

PHILLIP: It proves nothing.

HARRY: James Freeman, age 25, Irish, transported fourteen years for assault on a sailor at Shadwell Dock.

COLLINS: I'm surprised he wasn't hanged in England.

HARRY: Handy Baker, marine and the thieves' ringleader.

COLLINS: He pleaded that it was wrong to put the convicts and the marines on the same rations and that he could not work on so little food. He almost swayed us.

TENCH: I do think that was an unfortunate decision. My men are in a ferment of discontent.

COLLINS: Our Governor-in-Chief would say it is justice, Tench, and so it is. It is also justice to hang these men.

TENCH: The sooner the better, I believe. There is much excitement in the colony about the hangings. It's their theatre, Governor, you cannot change that.

PHILLIP: I would prefer them to see real plays: fine language, sentiment.

TENCH: No doubt Garrick° would relish the prospect of eight months at sea for the pleasure of entertaining a group of criminals and the odd savage.

Tyburn, place of public executions in London.

Garrick, David Garrick (1717–1779), noted Shakespearean actor and manager of Drury Lane Theatre.

PHILLIP: I never liked Garrick, I always preferred Macklin.°

COLLINS: I'm a Kemble° man myself. We will need a hangman.

PHILLIP: Harry, you will have to organise the hanging and eventually find someone who agrees to fill that hideous office.

(PHILLIP *shoots*.)

COLLINS: Shot.

TENCH: Shot.

HARRY: Shot, Sir.

COLLINS: It is my belief the hangings should take place tomorrow. The quick execution of justice for the good of the colony, Governor.

PHILLIP: The good of the colony? Oh, look! We've frightened a kankaroo.

(*They look.*)

ALL: Ah!

HARRY: There is also Dorothy Handland, 82, who stole a biscuit from Robert Sideway.

PHILLIP: Surely we don't have to hang an 82-year-old woman?

COLLINS: That will be unnecessary. She hanged herself this morning.

ACT 1 / SCENE 4 The Loneliness of Men

(RALPH CLARK's *tent. It is late at night.* RALPH *stands, composing and speaking his diary.*)

RALPH: Dreamt, my beloved Alicia, that I was walking with you and that you was in your riding-habit—oh my dear woman when shall I be able to hear from you—

All the officers dined with the Governor—I never heard of any one single person having so great a power vested in him as Captain Phillip has by his commission as Governor-in-Chief of New South Wales—dined on a cold collation but the Mutton which had been killed yesterday morning was full of maggots—nothing will keep 24 hours in this dismal country I find—

Went out shooting after breakfast—I only shot one cockatoo—they are the most beautiful birds—

Major Ross ordered one of the Corporals to flog with a rope Elizabeth Morden for being impertinent to Captain Campbell—the Corporal did not play with her but laid it home which I was very glad to see—she has long been fishing for it—

Macklin, Charles Macklin (1699–1797), noted Shakespearean actor. *Kemble,* name of a major theatrical family. John Philip Kemble (1757–1823) was, like Garrick, an actor-manager.

On Sunday as usual, kissed your dear beloved image a thousand times—was very much frightened by the lightning as it broke very near my tent—several of the convicts have run away.

(*He goes to his table and writes in his journal.*)

If I'm not made 1st Lieutenant soon . . .

(HARRY BREWER *has come in.*)

RALPH: Harry—

HARRY: I saw the light in your tent—

RALPH: I was writing my journal.

(*Silence.*)

Is there any trouble?

HARRY: No. (*Pause.*) I just came.

Talk, you know. If I wrote a journal about my life it would fill volumes. Volumes. My travels with the Captain—His Excellency now, no less, Governor-in-Chief, power to raise armies, build cities—I still call him plain Captain Phillip. He likes it from me. The war in America and before that, Ralph, my life in London. That would fill a volume on its own. Not what you would call a good life.

(*Pause.*)

Sometimes I look at the convicts and I think, one of those could be you, Harry Brewer, if you hadn't joined the navy when you did. The officers may look down on me now, but what if they found out that I used to be an embezzler?

RALPH: Harry, you should keep these things to yourself.

HARRY: You're right, Ralph.

(*Pause.*)

I think the Captain suspects, but he's a good man and he looks for different things in a man—

RALPH: Like what?

HARRY: Hard to say. He likes to see something unusual. Ralph, I saw Handy Baker last night.

RALPH: You hanged him a month ago, Harry.

HARRY: He had a rope—Ralph, he's come back.

RALPH: It was a dream. Sometimes I think my dreams are real—But they're not.

HARRY: We used to hear you on the ship, Ralph, calling for your Betsey Alicia.

RALPH: Don't speak her name on this iniquitous shore!

HARRY: Duckling's gone silent on me again. I know it's because of Handy Baker. I saw him as well as I see you. Duckling wants me, he said, even if you've hanged me. At least your poker's danced its last shindy, I said. At least it's young and straight, he said, she likes that. I went for him but he was gone. But he's going to come back, I know it. I didn't want to hang him, Ralph, I didn't.

RALPH: He did steal that food from the stores.

(*Pause.*)

I voted with the rest of the court those men should be hanged, I didn't know His Excellency would be against it.

HARRY: Duckling says she never feels anything. How do I know she didn't feel something when she was with him? She thinks I hanged him to get rid of him, but I didn't, Ralph.

(Pause.)

Do you know I saved her life? She was sentenced to be hanged at Newgate° for stealing two candlesticks but I got her name put on the transport lists. But when I remind her of that she says she wouldn't have cared. Eighteen years old, and she didn't care if she was turned off.

(Pause.)

These women are sold before they're ten. The Captain says we should treat them with kindness.

RALPH: How can you treat such women with kindness? Why does he think that?

HARRY: Not all the officers find them disgusting, Ralph—haven't you ever been tempted?

RALPH: Never! (Pause.) His Excellency never seems to notice me.

(Pause.)

He finds time for Davey Collins, Lieutenant Dawes.

HARRY: That's because Captain Collins is going to write about the customs of the Indians here—and Lieutenant Dawes is recording the stars.

RALPH: I could write about the Indians.

HARRY: He did suggest to Captain Tench that we do something to educate the convicts, put on a play or something, but Captain Tench just laughed. He doesn't like Captain Tench.

RALPH: A play? Who would act in a play?

HARRY: The convicts of course. He is thinking of talking to Lieutenant Johnston, but I think Lieutenant Johnston wants to study the plants.

RALPH: I read *The Tragedy of Lady Jane Grey*° on the ship. It is such a moving and uplifting play. But how could a whore play Lady Jane?

HARRY: Some of those women are good women, Ralph, I believe my Duckling is good. It's not her fault— if only she would look at me, once, react. Who wants to fuck a corpse!

(Silence.)

I'm sorry. I didn't mean to shock you, Ralph, I have shocked you, haven't I? I'll go.

RALPH: Is His Excellency serious about putting on a play?

HARRY: When the Captain decides something, Ralph.

RALPH: If I went to him—no. It would be better if you did, Harry, you could tell His Excellency how much I like the theatre.

HARRY: I didn't know that Ralph, I'll tell him.

RALPH: Duckling could be in it, if you wanted.

HARRY: I wouldn't want her to be looked at by all the men.

RALPH: If His Excellency doesn't like *Lady Jane* we could find something else.

(Pause.)

A comedy perhaps . . .

HARRY: I'll speak to him, Ralph. I like you.

(Pause.)

It's good to talk . . .

(Pause.)

You don't think I killed him then?

RALPH: Who?

HARRY: Handy Baker.

RALPH: No, Harry. You did not kill Handy Baker.

HARRY: Thank you, Ralph.

RALPH: Harry, you won't forget to talk to His Excellency about the play?

ACT 1 / SCENE 5 An Audition

(RALPH CLARK, MEG LONG. MEG LONG *is very old and very smelly. She hovers over* RALPH.)

MEG: We heard you was looking for some women, Lieutenant. Here I am.

RALPH: I've asked to see some women to play certain parts in a play.

MEG: I can play, Lieutenant, I can play with any part you like. There ain't nothing puts Meg off. That's how I got my name: Shitty Meg.

RALPH: The play has four particular parts for young women.

MEG: You don't want a young woman for your peculiar, Lieutenant, they don't know nothing. Shut your eyes and I'll play you as tight as a virgin.

RALPH: You don't understand, Long. Here's the play. It's called *The Recruiting Officer*.

MEG: Oh, I can do that too.

RALPH: What?

MEG: Recruiting. Anybody you like. (She whispers.) You want women: you ask Meg. Who do you want?

RALPH: I want to try some out.

MEG: Good idea, Lieutenant, good idea. Ha! Ha! Ha!

RALPH: Now if you don't mind—

(MEG *doesn't move.*)

Long!

Newgate, England's main prison, dating from the twelfth century. **The Tragedy of Lady Jane Grey,** performed in 1715, written by Nicholas Rowe.

MEG (*frightened but still holding her ground*): We thought you was a madge cull.

RALPH: What?

MEG: You know, a fluter, a mollie. (*Impatiently.*) A prissy cove, a girl! You having no she-lag on the ship. Nor here, neither. On the ship maybe you was seasick. But all these months here. And now we hear how you want a lot of women, all at once. Well, I'm glad to hear that, Lieutenant, I am. You let me know when you want Meg, old Shitty Meg.

(*She goes off quickly and* ROBERT SIDEWAY *comes straight on.*)

SIDEWAY: Ah, Mr Clark.

(*He does a flourish.*)

I am calling you Mr Clark as one calls Mr Garrick Mr Garrick, we have not had the pleasure of meeting before.

RALPH: I've seen you on the ship.

SIDEWAY: Different circumstances, Mr Clark, best forgotten. I was once a gentleman. My fortune has turned. The wheel . . . You are doing a play, I hear, ah, Drury Lane,° Mr. Garrick, the lovely Peg Woffington.° (*Conspiratorially.*) He was so cruel to her. She was so pale—

RALPH: You say you were a gentleman, Sideway?

SIDEWAY: Top of my profession, Mr Clark, pickpocket, born and bred in Bermondsey. Do you know London, Sir, don't you miss it? In these my darkest hours, I remember my happy days in that great city. London Bridge at dawn—hand on cold iron for good luck. Down Cheapside with the market traders—never refuse a mince pie. Into St Paul's churchyard—I do love a good church—and begin work in Bond Street. There, I've spotted her, rich, plump, not of the best class, stands in front of the shop, plucking up courage, I pluck her. Time for coffee until five o'clock and the pinnacle, the glory of the day: Drury Lane. The coaches, the actors scuttling, the gentlemen watching, the ladies tittering, the perfumes, the clothes, the handkerchiefs.

(*He hands* RALPH *the handkerchief he has just stolen from him.*)

Here, Mr Clark, you see the skill. Ah, Mr Clark, I beg you, I entreat you, to let me perform on your stage, to let me feel once again the thrill of a play about to begin. Ah, I see ladies approaching: our future Woffingtons, Siddons.°

Drury Lane, major London theater, dating from the seventeenth century; the present building, designed by Christopher Wren, opened in 1674 and is still in use today. **Peg Woffington** (1714–1740), a leading actress both in Dublin and in London. **Sarah Siddons** (1755–1831), renowned Shakespearean actress, sister of John Philip Kemble.

(DABBY BRYANT *comes on, with a shrinking* MARY BRENHAM *in tow.* SIDEWAY *bows.*)

Ladies.
    I shall await your word of command, Mr Clark, I shall be in the wings.

(SIDEWAY *scuttles off.*)

DABBY: You asked to see Mary Brenham, Lieutenant. Here she is.

RALPH: Yes—the Governor has asked me to put on a play. (*To* MARY.) You know what a play is?

DABBY: I've seen lots of plays, Lieutenant, so has Mary.

RALPH: Have you, Brenham?

MARY (*inaudibly.*): Yes.

RALPH: Can you remember which plays you've seen?

MARY (*inaudibly.*): No.

DABBY: I can't remember what they were called, but I always knew when they were going to end badly. I knew right from the beginning. How does this one end, Lieutenant?

RALPH: It ends happily. It's called *The Recruiting Officer.*

DABBY: Mary wants to be in your play, Lieutenant, and so do I.

RALPH: Do you think you have a talent for acting, Brenham?

DABBY: Of course she does, and so do I. I want to play Mary's friend.

RALPH: Do you know *The Recruiting Officer,* Bryant?

DABBY: No, but in all those plays, there's always a friend. That's because a girl has to talk to someone and she talks to her friend. So I'll be Mary's friend.

RALPH: Silvia—that's the part I want to try Brenham for—doesn't have a friend. She has a cousin. But they don't like each other.

DABBY: Oh. Mary doesn't always like me.

RALPH: The Reverend Johnson told me you can read and write, Brenham?

DABBY: She went to school until she was ten. She used to read to us on the ship. We loved it. It put us to sleep.

RALPH: Shall we try reading some of the play?

(RALPH *hands her the book.* MARY *reads silently, moving her lips.*)

I meant read it aloud. As you did on the ship. I'll help you, I'll read Justice Balance. That's your father.

DABBY: Doesn't she have a sweetheart?

RALPH: Yes, but this scene is with her father.

DABBY: What's the name of her lover?

RALPH: Captain Plume.

DABBY: A Captain! Mary!

RALPH: Start here, Brenham.

(MARY *begins to read.*)

MARY: 'Whilst there is life there is hope, Sir.'

DABBY: Oh, I like that, Lieutenant. This is a good play, I can tell.

RALPH: Shht. She hasn't finished. Start again, Brenham, that's good.

MARY: 'Whilst there is life there is hope, Sir; perhaps my brother may recover.'

RALPH: That's excellent, Brenham, very fluent. You could read a little louder. Now I'll read.
'We have but little reason to expect it. Poor Owen! But the decree is just; I was pleased with the death of my father, because he left me an estate, and now I'm punished with the loss of an heir to inherit mine.'

(Pause. He laughs a little.)

This is a comedy. They don't really mean it. It's to make people laugh. 'The death of your brother makes you sole heiress to my estate, which you know is about twelve hundred pounds a year.'

DABBY: Twelve hundred pounds! It must be a comedy.

MARY: 'My desire of being punctual in my obedience requires that you would be plain in your commands, Sir.'

DABBY: Well said, Mary, well said.

RALPH: I think that's enough. You read very well, Brenham. Would you also be able to copy the play? We have only two copies.

DABBY: Course she will. Where do I come in, Lieutenant? The cousin.

RALPH: Can you read, Bryant?

DABBY: Not those marks in the books, Lieutenant, but I can read other things. I read dreams very well, Lieutenant. Very well.

RALPH: I don't think you're right for Melinda. I'm thinking of someone else. And if you can't read . . .

DABBY: Mary will read me the lines, Lieutenant.

RALPH: There's Rose . . .

DABBY: Rose. I like the name. I'll be Rose. Who is she?

RALPH: She's a country girl . . .

DABBY: I grew up in Devon, Lieutenant. I'm perfect for Rose. What does she do?

RALPH: She—well, it's complicated. She falls in love with Silvia.

(MARY begins to giggle but tries to hold it back.)

But it's because she thinks Silvia's a man. And she—they—she sleeps with her. Rose. With Silvia. Euh. Silvia too. With Rose. But nothing happens.

DABBY: It doesn't? Nothing?

(DABBY burst out laughing.)

RALPH: Because Silvia is pretending to be a man, but of course she can't—

DABBY: Play the flute? Ha! She's not the only one around here. I'll do Rose.

RALPH: I would like to hear you.

DABBY: I don't know my lines yet, Lieutenant. When I know my lines, you can hear me do them. Come on, Mary—

RALPH: I didn't say you could—I'm not certain you're the right—Bryant, I'm not certain I want you in the play.

DABBY: Yes you do, Lieutenant. Mary will read me the lines and I, Lieutenant, will read you your dreams.

(There's a guffaw. It's LIZ MORDEN.*)*

RALPH: Ah. Here's your cousin.

(There is a silence. MARY *shrinks away.* DABBY *and* LIZ *stare at each other, each holding her ground, each ready to pounce.)*

Melinda. Silvia's cousin.

DABBY: You can't have her in the play, Lieutenant.

RALPH: Why not?

DABBY: You don't have to be able to read the future to know that Liz Morden is going to be hanged.

*(*LIZ *looks briefly at* DABBY, *as if to strike, then changes her mind.)*

LIZ: I understand you want me in your play, Lieutenant. Is that it?

(She snatches the book from RALPH *and strides off.)*

I'll look at it and let you know.

ACT 1 / SCENE 6 The Authorities Discuss the Merits of the Theatre

(GOVERNOR ARTHUR PHILLIP, MAJOR ROBBIE ROSS, JUDGE DAVID COLLINS, CAPTAIN WATKIN TENCH, CAPTAIN JEMMY CAMPBELL, REVEREND JOHNSON, LIEUTENANT GEORGE JOHNSTON, LIEUTENANT WILL DAWES, SECOND LIEUTENANT RALPH CLARK, SECOND LIEUTENANT WILLIAM FADDY.
It is late at night, the men have been drinking, tempers are high. They interrupt each other, overlap, make jokes under and over the conversation but all engage in it with the passion for discourse and thought of eighteenth-century men.)

ROSS: A play! A f—

REVD. JOHNSON: Mmhm.

ROSS: A frippery frittering play!

CAMPBELL: Aheeh, aeh, here?

RALPH *(timidly)*: To celebrate the King's birthday, on June the 4th.

ROSS: If a frigating ship doesn't appear soon, we'll all be struck with stricturing starvation—and you—you—a play!

COLLINS: Not putting on the play won't bring us a supply ship, Robbie.

ROSS: And you say you want those contumelious convicts to act in this play. The convicts!

CAMPBELL: Eh, kev, weh, discipline's bad. Very bad.

RALPH: The play has several parts for women. We have no other women here.

COLLINS: Your wife excepted, Reverend.

REVD. JOHNSON: My wife abhors anything of that nature. After all, actresses are not famed for their morals.

COLLINS: Neither are our women convicts.

REVD. JOHNSON: How can they be when some of our officers set them up as mistresses.

(*He looks pointedly at* LIEUTENANT GEORGE JOHNSTON.)

ROSS: Filthy, thieving, lying whores and now we have to watch them flout their flitty wares on the stage!

PHILLIP: No one will be forced to watch the play.

DAWES: I believe there's a partial lunar eclipse that night. I shall have to watch that. The sky of this southern hemisphere is full of wonders. Have you looked at the constellations?

(*Short pause.*)

ROSS: Constellations. Plays! This is a convict colony, the prisoners are here to be punished and we're here to make sure they get punished. Constellations! Jemmy? Constellations!

(*He turns to* JEMMY CAMPBELL *for support.*)

CAMPBELL: Tss, weh, marines, marines: war, phoo, discipline. Eh? Service—His Majesty.

PHILLIP: We are indeed here to supervise the convicts who are already being punished by their long exile. Surely they can also be reformed?

TENCH: We are talking about criminals, often hardened criminals. They have a habit of vice and crime. Many criminals seem to have been born that way. It is in their nature.

PHILLIP: Rousseau would say that we have made them that way, Watkin: 'Man is born free, and everywhere he is in chains.'

REVD. JOHNSON: But Rousseau was a Frenchman.

ROSS: A Frenchman! What can you expect? We're going to listen to a foraging Frenchman now—

COLLINS: He was Swiss actually.

CAMPBELL: Eeh, eyeh, good soldiers, the Swiss.

PHILLIP: Surely you believe man can be redeemed, Reverend?

REV. JOHNSON: By the grace of God and a belief in the true church, yes. But Christ never proposed putting on plays to his disciples. However, he didn't forbid it either. It must depend on the play.

JOHNSTON: He did propose treating sinners, especially women who have sinned, with compassion. Most of the convict women have committed small crimes, a tiny theft—

COLLINS: We know about your compassion, not to say passion, for the women convicts, George.

TENCH: A crime is a crime. You commit a crime or you don't. If you commit a crime, you are a criminal.

Surely that is logical? It's like the savages here. A savage is a savage because he behaves in a savage manner. To expect anything else is foolish. They can't even build a proper canoe.

PHILLIP: They can be educated.

COLLINS: Actually, they seem happy enough as they are. They do not want to build canoes or houses, nor do they suffer from greed and ambition.

FADDY (*looking at* RALPH): Unlike some.

TENCH: Which can't be said of our convicts. But really, I don't see what this has to do with a play. It is at most a passable diversion, an entertainment to wile away the hours of the idle.

CAMPBELL: Ttts, weh, heh, the convicts, bone idle.

DAWES: We're wiling away precious hours now. Put the play on, don't put it on, it won't change the shape of the universe.

RALPH: But it could change the nature of our little society.

FADDY: Second Lieutenant Clark change society!

PHILLIP: William!

TENCH: My dear Ralph, a bunch of convicts making fools of themselves, mouthing words written no doubt by some London ass, will hardly change our society.

RALPH: George Farquhar was not an ass! And he was from Ireland.

ROSS: An Irishman! I have to sit there and listen to an Irishman!

CAMPBELL: Tss, tt. Irish. Wilde.° Wilde.

REVD. JOHNSON: The play doesn't propagate Catholic doctrine, does it, Ralph?

RALPH: He was also an officer.

FADDY: Crawling for promotion.

RALPH: Of the Grenadiers.

ROSS: Never liked the Grenadiers myself.

CAMPBELL: Ouah, pheuee, grenades, pho. Throw and run. Eh. Backs.

RALPH: The play is called *The Recruiting Officer*.

COLLINS: I saw it in London I believe. Yes. Very funny if I remember. Sergeant Kite. The devious ways he used to serve his Captain . . .

FADDY: Your part, Ralph.

COLLINS: William, if you can't contribute anything useful to the discussion, keep quiet!

(*Silence.*)

REVD. JOHNSON: What is the plot, Ralph?

RALPH: It's about this recruiting officer and his friend, and they are in love with these two young ladies from Shrewsbury and after some difficulties, they marry them.

Wilde, may be the eighteenth-century actor William Wilde, but quite possibly an anachronistic pun on the great Irish comic playwright, Oscar Wilde (1854–1900).

REVD. JOHNSON: It sanctions Holy Matrimony then?

RALPH: Yes, yes, it does.

REVD. JOHNSON: That wouldn't do the convicts any harm. I'm having such trouble getting them to marry instead of this sordid cohabitation they're so used to.

ROSS: Marriage, plays, why not a ball for the convicts!

CAMPBELL: Euuh. Boxing.

PHILLIP: Some of these men will have finished their sentence in a few years. They will become members of society again, and help create a new society in this colony. Should we not encourage them now to think in a free and responsible manner?

TENCH: I don't see how a comedy about two lovers will do that, Arthur.

PHILLIP: The theatre is an expression of civilisation. We belong to a great country which has spawned great playwrights: Shakespeare, Marlowe, Jonson, and even in our own time, Sheridan. The convicts will be speaking a refined, literate language and expressing sentiments of a delicacy they are not used to. It will remind them that there is more to life than crime, punishment. And we, this colony of a few hundred will be watching this together, for a few hours we will no longer be despised prisoners and hated gaolers. We will laugh, we may be moved, we may even think a little. Can you suggest something else that will provide such an evening, Watkin?

DAWES: Mapping the stars gives me more enjoyment, personally.

TENCH: I'm not sure it's a good idea having the convicts laugh at officers, Arthur.

CAMPBELL: No. Pheeoh, insubordination, heh, ehh, no discipline.

ROSS: You want this vice-ridden vermin to enjoy themselves?

COLLINS: They would only laugh at Sergeant Kite.

RALPH: Captain Plume is a most attractive, noble fellow.

REVD. JOHNSON: He's not loose, is he Ralph? I hear many of these plays are about rakes and encourage loose morals in women. They do get married? Before, that is, before. And for the right reasons.

RALPH: They marry for love and to secure wealth.

REVD. JOHNSON: That's all right.

TENCH: I would simply say that if you want to build a civilisation there are more important things than a play. If you want to teach the convicts something, teach them to farm, to build houses, teach them a sense of respect for property, teach them thrift so they don't eat a week's rations in one night, but above all, teach them how to work, not how to sit around laughing at a comedy.

PHILLIP: The Greeks believed that it was a citizen's duty to watch a play. It was a kind of work in that it required attention, judgement, patience, all social virtues.

TENCH: And the Greeks were conquered by the more practical Romans, Arthur.

COLLINS: Indeed, the Romans built their bridges, but they also spent many centuries wishing they were Greeks. And they, after all, were conquered by barbarians, or by their own corrupt and small spirits.

TENCH: Are you saying Rome would not have fallen if the theatre had been better?

RALPH (very loud): Why not? (Everyone looks at him and he continues, fast and nervously.) In my own small way, in just a few hours, I have seen something change. I asked some of the convict women to read me some lines, these women who behave often no better than animals. And it seemed to me, as one or two—I'm not saying all of them, not at all—but one or two, saying those well-balanced lines of Mr Farquhar, they seemed to acquire a dignity, they seemed— they seemed to lose some of their corruption. There was one, Mary Brenham, she read so well, perhaps this play will keep her from selling herself to the first marine who offers her bread—

FADDY (under his breath): She'll sell herself to him, instead.

ROSS: So that's the way the wind blows—

CAMPBELL: Hooh. A tempest. Hooh.

RALPH (over them): I speak about her, but in a small way this could affect all the convicts and even ourselves, we could forget our worries about the supplies, the hangings and the floggings, and think of ourselves at the theatre, in London with our wives and children, that is, we could, euh—

PHILLIP: Transcend—

RALPH: Transcend the darker, euh—transcend the—

JOHNSTON: Brutal—

RALPH: The brutality—remember our better nature and remember—

COLLINS: England.

RALPH: England.

(A moment.)

ROSS: Where did the wee Lieutenant learn to speak?

FADDY: He must have had one of his dreams.

TENCH (over them): You are making claims that cannot be substantiated, Ralph. It's two hours, possibly of amusement, possibly of boredom, and we will lose the labour of the convicts during the time they are learning the play. It's a waste, an unnecessary waste.

REVD. JOHNSON: I'm still concerned about the content.

TENCH: The content of a play is irrelevant.

ROSS: Even if it teaches insubordination, disobedience, revolution?

COLLINS: Since we have agreed it can do no harm, since it might, possibly, do some good, since the only person violently opposed to it is Major Ross for reasons he has not made quite clear, I suggest we allow Ralph to rehearse his play. Does anyone disagree?

ROSS: I—I—

COLLINS: We have taken your disagreement into account, Robbie.

CAMPBELL: Ah, eeh, I—I—*(He stops.)*

COLLINS: Thank you, Captain Campbell. Dawes? Dawes, do come back to earth and honour us with your attention for a moment.

DAWES: What? No? Why not? As long as I don't have to watch it.

COLLINS: Johnston?

JOHNSTON: I'm for it.

COLLINS: Faddy?

FADDY: I'm against it.

COLLINS: Could you tell us why?

FADDY: I don't trust the director.

COLLINS: Tench?

TENCH: Waste of time.

COLLINS: The Reverend, our moral guide, has no objections.

REVD. JOHNSON: Of course I haven't read it.

TENCH: Davey, this is not an objective summing up, this is typical of your high-handed manner—

COLLINS *(angrily)*: I don't think you're the one to accuse others of a high-handed manner, Watkin.

PHILLIP: Gentlemen, please.

COLLINS: Your Excellency, I believe, is for the play and I myself am convinced it will prove a most interesting experiment. So let us conclude with our good wishes to Ralph for a successful production.

ROSS: I will not accept this. You willy-wally wobbly words, Greeks, Romans, experiment, to get your own way. You don't take anything seriously, but I know this play—this play—order will become disorder. The theatre leads to threatening theory and you, Governor, you have His Majesty's commission to build castles, cities, raise armies, administer a military colony, not fandangle about with a lewdy play! I am going to write to the Admiralty about this. *(He goes.)*

PHILLIP: You're out of turn, Robbie.

CAMPBELL: Aah—eeh—a. Confusion. *(He goes.)*

DAWES: Why is Robbie so upset? So much fuss over a play.

JOHNSTON: Major Ross will never forgive you, Ralph.

COLLINS: I have summed up the feelings of the assembled company, Arthur, but the last word must be yours.

PHILLIP: The last word will be the play, gentlemen.

ACT 1 / SCENE 7 Harry and Duckling Go Rowing

(HARRY BREWER, DUCKLING SMITH. HARRY *is rowing,* DUCKLING *is sulking.)*

HARRY: It's almost beginning to look like a town. Look, Duckling, there's the Captain's house. I can see him in his garden.

(HARRY *waves.* DUCKLING *doesn't turn around.)*

Sydney. He could have found a better name. Mobsbury. Lagtown.° Duckling Cove, eh?

(HARRY *laughs.* DUCKLING *remains morose.)*

The Captain said it had to be named after the Home Secretary. The courthouse looks impressive all in brick. There's Lieutenant Dawes' observatory. Why don't you look, Duckling?

(DUCKLING *glances, then turns back.)*

The trees look more friendly from here. Did you know the Eucalyptus tree can't be found anywhere else in the world? Captain Collins told me that. Isn't that interesting? Lieutenant Clark says the three orange trees on his island are doing well. It's the turnips he's worried about, he thinks they're being stolen and he's too busy with his play to go and have a look. Would you like to see the orange trees, Duckling?

(DUCKLING *glowers.)*

I thought you'd enjoy rowing to Ralph's island. I thought it would remind you of rowing on the Thames. Look how blue the water is. Duckling. Say something. Duckling!

DUCKLING: If I was rowing on the Thames, I'd be free.

HARRY: This isn't Newgate, Duckling.

DUCKLING: I wish it was.

HARRY: Duckling!

DUCKLING: At least the gaoler of Newgate left you alone and you could talk to people.

HARRY: I let you talk to the women.

DUCKLING *(with contempt)*: Esther Abrahams, Mary Brenham!

HARRY: They're good women.

DUCKLING: I don't have anything to say to those women, Harry. My friends are in the women's camp—

HARRY: It's not the women you're after in the women's camp, it's the marines who come looking for buttock, I know you, who do you have your eye on now, who, a soldier? Another marine, a Corporal? Who, Duckling, who?

(Pause.)

You've found someone already haven't you? Where do you go, on the beach? In my tent, like with Handy Baker, eh? Where, under the trees?

DUCKLING: You know I hate trees, don't be so filthy.

HARRY: Filthy, you're filthy, you filthy whore.

Mobsbury, Lagtown, names reflecting the actual inhabitants, i.e., a mob of people, or criminals ("lags").

(Pause.)

I'm sorry, Duckling, please. Why can't you?—can't you just be with me? Don't be angry. I'll do anything for you, you know that. What do you want, Duckling?

DUCKLING: I don't want to be watched all the time. I wake up in the middle of the night and you're watching me. What do you think I'm going to do in my sleep, Harry? Watching, watching, watching. JUST STOP WATCHING ME.

HARRY: You want to leave me. All right, go and live in the women's camp, sell yourself to a convict for a biscuit. Leave if you want to. You're filthy, filthy, opening your legs to the first marine—

DUCKLING: Why are you so angry with your Duckling, Harry? Don't you like it when I open my legs wide to you? Cross them over you—the way you like? What will you do when your little Duckling isn't there anymore to touch you with her soft fingertips, Harry, where you like it? First the left nipple and then the right. Your Duckling doesn't want to leave you, Harry.

HARRY: Duckling . . .

DUCKLING: I need freedom sometimes, Harry.

HARRY: You have to earn your freedom with good behaviour.

DUCKLING: Why didn't you let them hang me and take my corpse with you, Harry? You could have kept that in chains. I wish I was dead. At least when you're dead, you're free.

(Silence.)

HARRY: You know Lieutenant Clark's play?

(DUCKLING is silent.)

Do you want to be in it?

(DUCKLING laughs.)

Dabby Bryant is in it too and Liz Morden. Do you want to be in it? You'd rehearse in the evenings with Lieutenant Clark.

DUCKLING: And he can watch over me instead of you.

HARRY: I'm trying to make you happy, Duckling, if you don't want to—

DUCKLING: I'll be in the play.

(Pause.)

How is Lieutenant Clark going to manage Liz Morden?

HARRY: The Captain wanted her to be in it.

DUCKLING: On the ship we used to see who could make Lieutenant Clark blush first. It didn't take long, haha.

HARRY: Duckling, you won't try anything with Lieutenant Clark, will you?

DUCKLING: With that Mollie? No.

HARRY: You're talking to me again. Will you kiss your Harry?

(They kiss.)

I'll come and watch the rehearsals.

ACT 1 / SCENE 8 The Women Learn Their Lines

(DABBY BRYANT is sitting on the ground muttering to herself with concentration. She could be counting. MARY BRENHAM comes on.)

MARY: Are you remembering your lines, Dabby?

DABBY: What lines? No. I was remembering Devon. I was on my way back to Bigbury Bay.

MARY: You promised Lieutenant Clark you'd learn your lines.

DABBY: I want to go back. I want to see a wall of stone. I want to hear the Atlantic breaking into the estuary. I can bring a boat into any harbour, in any weather. I can do it as well as the Governor.

MARY: Dabby, what about your lines?

DABBY: I'm not spending the rest of my life in this flat, brittle burnt-out country. Oh, give me some English rain.

MARY: It rains here.

DABBY: It's not the same. I could recognize English rain anywhere. And Devon rain, Mary, Devon rain is the softest in England. As soft as your breasts, as soft as Lieutenant Clark's dimpled cheeks.

MARY: Dabby, don't!

DABBY: You're wasting time, girl, he's ripe for the plucking. You can always tell with men, they begin to walk sideways. And if you don't—

MARY: Don't start. I listened to you once before.

DABBY: What would you have done without that lanky sailor drooling over you?

MARY: I would have been less of a whore.

DABBY: Listen, my darling, you're only a virgin once. You can't go to a man and say, I'm a virgin except for this one lover I had. After that, it doesn't matter how many men go through you.

MARY: I'll never wash the sin away.

DABBY: If God didn't want women to be whores he shouldn't have created men who pay for their bodies. While you were with your little sailor there were women in that stinking pit of a hold who had three men on them at once, men with the pox, men with the flux, men biting like dogs.

MARY: But if you don't agree to it, then you're not a whore, you're a martyr.

DABBY: You have to be a virgin to be a martyr, Mary, and you didn't come on that ship a virgin. 'A. H. I love thee to the heart', ha, tattooed way up there—

(DABBY begins to lift MARY's skirt to reveal a tattoo high up on the inner thigh. MARY leaps away.)

MARY: That was different. That was love.

DABBY: The second difficulty with being a martyr is that you have to be dead to qualify. Well, you didn't die, thanks to me, you had three pounds of beef a week instead of two, two extra ounces of cheese.

MARY: Which you were happy to eat!

DABBY: We women have to look after each other. Let's learn the lines.

MARY: You sold me that first day so you and your husband could eat!

DABBY: Do you want me to learn these lines or not?

MARY: How can I play Silvia? She's brave and strong. She couldn't have done what I've done.

DABBY: She didn't spend eight months and one week on a convict ship. Anyway, you can pretend you're her.

MARY: No. I have to be her.

DABBY: Why?

MARY: Because that's acting.

DABBY: No way I'm being Rose, she's an idiot.

MARY: It's not such a big part, it doesn't matter so much.

DABBY: You didn't tell me that before.

MARY: I hadn't read it carefully. Come on, let's do the scene between Silvia and Rose. *(She reads.)* 'I have rested but indifferently, and I believe my bedfellow was as little pleased; poor Rose! Here she comes'—

DABBY: I could have done something for Rose. Ha! I should play Silvia.

MARY: 'Good morrow, my dear, how d'ye this morning?' Now you say: 'Just as I was last night, neither better nor worse for you.'

(LIZ MORDEN comes on.)

LIZ: You can't do the play without me. I'm in it! Where's the Lieutenant?

DABBY: She's teaching me some lines.

LIZ: Why aren't you teaching me the lines?

MARY: We're not doing your scenes.

LIZ: Well do them.

DABBY: You can read. You can read your own lines.

LIZ: I don't want to learn them on my own.

(LIZ thrusts DABBY away and sits by MARY.)

I'm waiting.

DABBY: What are you waiting for, Liz Morden, a blind man to buy your wares?

MARY *(quickly)*: We'll do the first scene between Melinda and Silvia, all right?

LIZ: Yea. The first scene.

(MARY gives LIZ the book.)

MARY: You start.

(LIZ looks at the book.)

You start. 'Welcome to town, cousin Silvia'—

LIZ: 'Welcome to town, cousin Silvia'—

MARY: Go on—'I envied you'—

LIZ: 'I envied you'—You read it first.

MARY: Why?

LIZ: I want to hear how you do it.

MARY: Why?

LIZ: Cause then I can do it different.

MARY: 'I envied you your retreat in the country; for Shrewsbury, methinks, and all your heads of shires'—

DABBY: Why don't you read it? You can't read!

LIZ: What?

(She lunges at DABBY.)

MARY: I'll teach you the lines.

DABBY: Are you her friend now, is that it? Mary the holy innocent and thieving bitch—

(LIZ and DABBY seize each other. KETCH FREEMAN appears.)

KETCH *(with nervous affability)*: Good morning, ladies. And why aren't you at work instead of at each other's throats?

(LIZ and DABBY turn on him.)

LIZ: I wouldn't talk of throats if I was you, Mr Hangman Ketch Freeman.

DABBY: Crap merchant.

LIZ: Crapping cull. Switcher.

MARY: Roper.

KETCH: I was only asking what you were doing, you know, friendly like.

LIZ: Stick to your ropes, my little galler, don't bother the actresses.

KETCH: Actresses? You're doing a play?

LIZ: Better than dancing the Paddington frisk in your arms—noser!

KETCH: I'll nose on you, Liz, if you're not careful.

LIZ: I'd take a leap in the dark sooner than turn off my own kind. Now take your whirligigs out of our sight, we have lines to learn.

(KETCH slinks away as LIZ and DABBY spit him off.)

DABBY *(after him)*: Don't hang too many people, Ketch, we need an audience!

MARY: 'Welcome to town, cousin Silvia.' It says you salute.

LIZ *(giving a military salute)*: 'Welcome to town, cousin—Silvia.'

ACT 1 / SCENE 9 Ralph Clark Tries to Kiss His Dear Wife's Picture

(RALPH's tent. Candlelight. RALPH paces.)

RALPH: Dreamt my beloved Betsey that I was with you and that I thought I was going to be arrested.

(He looks at his watch.)

I hope to God that there is nothing the matter with you my tender Alicia or that of our dear boy—

(He looks at his watch.)

My darling tender wife I am reading Proverbs waiting till midnight, the Sabbath, that I might kiss your picture as usual.

(He takes his Bible and kneels. Looks at his watch.)

The Patrols caught three seamen and a boy in the women's camp.

(He reads.)

'Let thy fountain be blessed: and rejoice with the wife of thy youth.'
    Good God what a scene of whoredom is going on there in the women's camp.

(He looks at his watch. Gets up. Paces.)

Very hot this night.
    Captain Shea killed today one of the kankaroos— it is the most curious animal I ever saw.

(He looks at his watch.)

Almost midnight, my Betsey, the Lord's day—

(He reads.)

'And behold, there met him a woman with the attire of an harlot, and subtle of heart.
So she caught him, and kissed him with an impudent face.'
    Felt ill with the toothache my dear wife my God what pain.

(Reads.)

'So she caught him and kissed him with an impudent face . . .'
    I have perfumed my bed with myrrh, aloes, cinnamon—
    Sarah McCormick was flogged today for calling the doctor a c—midnight—
    This being Sunday took your picture out of its prison and kissed it—God bless you my sweet woman.

(He now proceeds to do so. That is, he goes down on his knees and brings the picture to himself. KETCH FREEMAN *comes into the tent.* RALPH *jumps.)*

KETCH: Forgive me, Sir, please forgive me, I didn't want to disturb your prayers. I say fifty Hail Mary's myself every night, and 200 on the days when—I'll wait outside, Sir.
RALPH: What do you want?
KETCH: I'll wait quietly, Sir, don't mind me.
RALPH: Why aren't you in the camp at this hour?
KETCH: I should be, God forgive me, I should be. But I'm not. I'm here. I have to have a word with you, Sir.

RALPH: Get back to the camp immediately, I'll see you in the morning, Ketch.
KETCH: Don't call me that, Sir, I beg you, don't call me by that name, that's what I came to see you about, Sir.
RALPH: I was about to go to sleep.
KETCH: I understand, Sir, and your soul in peace, I won't take up your time, Sir, I'll be brief.

(Pause.)

RALPH: Well?
KETCH: Don't you want to finish your prayers? I can be very quiet. I used to watch my mother, may her poor soul rest in peace, I used to watch her say her prayers, every night.
RALPH: Get on with it!
KETCH: When I say my prayers I have a terrible doubt. How can I be sure God is forgiving me? What if he will forgive me, but hasn't forgiven me yet? That's why I don't want to die, Sir. That's why I can't die. Not until I am sure. Are you sure?
RALPH: I'm not a convict: I don't sin.
KETCH: To be sure. Forgive me, Sir. But if we're in God's power, then surely he makes us sin. I was given a guardian angel when I was born, like all good Catholics, why didn't my guardian angel look after me better? But I think he must've stayed in Ireland. I think the devil tempted my mother to London and both our guardian angels stayed behind. Have you ever been to Ireland, Sir? It's a beautiful country. If I'd been an angel I wouldn't have left it either. And when we came within six fields of Westminster, the devils took over. But it's God's judgement I'm frightened of. And the women's. They're so hard. Why is that?
RALPH: Why have you come here?
KETCH: I'm coming to that, Sir.
RALPH: Hurry up, then.
KETCH: I'm speaking as fast as I can, Sir—
RALPH: Ketch—
KETCH: James, Sir, James, Daniel, Patrick, after my three uncles. Good men they were too, didn't go to London. If my mother hadn't brought us to London, may God give peace to her soul and breathe pity into the hearts of hard women—because the docks are in London and if I hadn't worked on the docks, on that day, May 23rd, 1785, do you remember it, Sir? Shadwell Dock. If only we hadn't left, then I wouldn't have been there, then nothing would have happened, I wouldn't have become a coal heaver on Shadwell Dock and been there on the 23rd of May when we refused to unload because they were paying us so badly, Sir. I wasn't even near the sailor who got killed. He shouldn't have done the unloading, that was wrong of the sailors, but I didn't kill him, maybe one blow, not to look stupid, you know, just to show I was with the lads, even if I wasn't, but I didn't kill him. And they caught five

at random, Sir, and I was among the five, and they found the cudgel, that's all, and when they said to me later you can hang or you can give the names, what was I to do, what would you have done, Sir?

RALPH: I wouldn't have been in that situation, Freeman.

KETCH: To be sure, forgive me, Sir. I only told on the ones I saw, I didn't tell anything that wasn't true, death is a horrible thing, that poor sailor.

RALPH: Freeman, I'm going to go to bed now—

KETCH: I understand, Sir, I understand. And when it happened again, here! And I had hopes of making a good life here. It's because I'm so friendly, see, so I go along, and then I'm the one who gets caught. That theft, I didn't do it, I was just there, keeping a look out, just to help some friends, you know. But when they say to you, hang or be hanged, what do you do? Someone has to do it. I try to do it well. God had mercy on the whore, the thief, the lame, surely he'll forgive the hang—it's the women—they're without mercy—not like you and me, Sir, men. What I wanted to say, Sir, is that I heard them talking about the play.

(*Pause.*)

Some players came into our village once. They were loved like the angels, Lieutenant, like the angels. And the way the women watched them—the light of a spring dawn in their eyes.
        Lieutenant—
        I want to be an actor.

ACT 1 / SCENE 10 John Wisehammer and Mary Brenham Exchange Words

(MARY *is copying* The Recruiting Officer *in the afternoon light.* JOHN WISEHAMMER *is carrying bricks and piling them to one side. He begins to hover over her.*)

MARY: 'I would rather counsel than command; I don't propose this with the authority of a parent, but as the advice of your friend'—

WISEHAMMER: Friend. That's a good word. Short, but full of promise.

MARY: 'That you would take the coach this moment and go into the country.'

WISEHAMMER: Country can mean opposite things. It renews you with trees and grass, you go rest in the country, or it crushes you with power: you die for your country, your country doesn't want you, you're thrown out of your country.

(*Pause.*)

I like words.

(*Pause.*)

My father cleared the houses of the dead to sell the old clothes to the poor houses by the Thames. He found a dictionary—Johnson's dictionary°—it was as big as a Bible. It went from A to L. I started with the A's. Abecedarian: someone who teaches the alphabet or rudiments of literature. Abject: a man without hope.

MARY: What does indulgent mean?

WISEHAMMER: How is it used?

MARY (*reads*): 'You have been so careful, so indulgent to me'—

WISEHAMMER: It means ready to overlook faults.

(*Pause.*)

You have to be careful with words that begin with 'in.' It can turn everything upside down. Injustice. Most of that word is taken up with justice, but the 'in' twists it inside out and makes it the ugliest word in the English language.

MARY: Guilty is an uglier word.

WISEHAMMER: Innocent ought to be a beautiful word, but it isn't, it's full of sorrow. Anguish.

(MARY *goes back to her copying.*)

MARY: I don't have much time. We start this in a few days.

(WISEHAMMER *looks over her shoulder.*)

I have the biggest part.

WISEHAMMER: You have a beautiful hand.

MARY: There is so much to copy. So many words.

WISEHAMMER: I can write.

MARY: Why don't you tell Lieutenant Clark? He's doing it.

WISEHAMMER: No . . . no . . . I'm—

MARY: Afraid?

WISEHAMMER: Diffident.

MARY: I'll tell him. Well, I won't. My friend Dabby will. She's—

WISEHAMMER: Bold.

(*Pause.*)

Shy is not a bad word, it's soft.

MARY: But shame is a hard one.

WISEHAMMER: Words with two L's are the worst. Lonely, loveless.

MARY: Love is a good word.

WISEHAMMER: That's because it only has one L. I like words with one L: Luck. Latitudinarian.

(MARY *laughs.*)

Laughter.

Johnson's dictionary, Samuel Johnson single-handedly compiled the first major English dictionary, published in 1755.

ACT 1 / SCENE 11 The First Rehearsal

(RALPH CLARK, ROBERT SIDEWAY, JOHN WISEHAM-
MER, MARY BRENHAM, LIZ MORDEN, DABBY BRYANT,
DUCKLING SMITH, KETCH FREEMAN.)

RALPH: Good afternoon, ladies and gentlemen—

DABBY: We're ladies now. Wait till I tell my husband
I've become a lady.

MARY: Sshht.

RALPH: It is with pleasure that I welcome you—

SIDEWAY: Our pleasure, Mr Clark, our pleasure.

RALPH: We have many days of hard work ahead of us.

LIZ: Work! I'm not working. I thought we was acting.

RALPH: Now, let me introduce the company—

DABBY: We've all met before, Lieutenant, you could say
we know each other, you could say we'd know each
other in the dark.

SIDEWAY: It's a theatrical custom, the company is formally introduced to each other, Mrs Bryant.

DABBY: Mrs Bryant? Who's Mrs Bryant?

SIDEWAY: It's the theatrical form of address, Madam.
You may call me Mr Sideway.

RALPH: If I may proceed—

KETCH: Shhh! You're interrupting the director.

DABBY: So we are, Mr Hangman.

(The women all hiss and spit at KETCH.)

RALPH: The ladies first: Mary Brenham who is to play
Silvia. Liz Morden who is to play Melinda. Duckling
Smith who is to play Lucy, Melinda's maid.

DUCKLING: I'm not playing Liz Morden's maid.

RALPH: Why not?

DUCKLING: I live with an officer. He wouldn't like it.

DABBY: Just because she lives chained up in that old toss
pot's garden.

DUCKLING: Don't you dare talk of my Harry—

RALPH: You're not playing Morden's maid, Smith,
you're playing Melinda's. And Dabby Bryant, who
is to play Rose, a country girl.

DABBY: From Devon.

DUCKLING (to DABBY): Screw jaws!

DABBY (to DUCKLING): Salt bitch!

RALPH: That's the ladies. Now, Captain Plume will be
played by Henry Kable.

(He looks around.)

Who seems to be late. That's odd. I saw him an
hour ago and he said he was going to your hut to
learn some lines, Wisehammer?

(WISEHAMMER is silent.)

Sergeant Kite is to be played by John Arscott, who
did send a message to say he would be kept at work
an extra hour.

DABBY: An hour! You won't see him in an hour!

LIZ (under her breath): You're not the only one with new
wrinkles in your arse, Dabby Bryant.

RALPH: Mr Worthy will be played by Mr Sideway.

(SIDEWAY takes a vast bow.)

SIDEWAY: I'm here.

RALPH: Justice Balance by James Freeman.

DUCKLING: No way I'm doing a play with a hangman.
The words would stick in my throat.

(More hisses and spitting. KETCH shrinks.)

RALPH: You don't have any scenes with him, Smith.
Now if I could finish the introductions. Captain
Brazen is to be played by John Wisehammer.
The small parts are still to be cast. Now. We can't
do the first scene until John Arscott appears.

DABBY: There won't be a first scene.

RALPH: Bryant, will you be quiet please! The second
scene. Wisehammer, you could read Plume.

(WISEHAMMER comes forward eagerly.)

No, I'll read Plume myself. So, Act One, Scene Two,
Captain Plume and Mr Worthy.

SIDEWAY: That's me. I'm at your command.

RALPH: The rest of you can watch and wait for your
scenes. Perhaps we should begin by reading it.

SIDEWAY: No need, Mr Clark. I know it.

RALPH: Ah, I'm afraid I shall have to read Captain
Plume.

SIDEWAY: I know that part too. Would you like me to
do both?

RALPH: I think it's better if I do it. Shall we begin? Kite,
that's John Arscott, has just left—

DABBY: Running.

RALPH: Bryant! I'll read the line before Worthy's entrance: 'None at present. 'Tis indeed the picture of
Worthy, but the life's departed.' Sideway? Where's
he gone?

(SIDEWAY has scuttled off. He shouts from the wings.)

SIDEWAY: I'm preparing my entrance, Mr Clark, I won't
be a minute. Could you read the line again, slowly?

RALPH: 'Tis indeed the picture of Worthy, but the life's
departed. What, arms-a-cross, Worthy!'

(SIDEWAY comes on, walking sideways, arms held up in
a grandiose eighteenth-century theatrical pose. He suddenly stops.)

SIDEWAY: Ah, yes, I forgot. Arms-a-cross. I shall have
to start again.

(He goes off again and shouts.)

Could you read the line again louder please?

RALPH: 'What, arms-a-cross, Worthy!'

(SIDEWAY rushes on.)

SIDEWAY: My wiper! Someone's buzzed my wiper!°
There's a wipe drawer in this crew, Mr Clark.

Someone's buzzed my wiper, someone's stolen my handkerchief.

RALPH: What's the matter?

SIDEWAY: There's a pickpocket in the company.

DABBY: Talk of the pot calling the kettle black.

(SIDEWAY *stalks around the company threateningly.*)

SIDEWAY: My handkerchief. Who prigged° my handkerchief?

RALPH: I'm sure it will turn up, Sideway, let's go on.

SIDEWAY: I can't do my entrance without my handkerchief. (*Furious.*) I've been practising it all night. If I get my mittens on the rum diver I'll—

(*He lunges at* LIZ, *who fights back viciously. They jump apart, each taking threatening poses and* RALPH *intervenes with speed.*)

RALPH: Let's assume Worthy has already entered, Sideway. Now, I say: 'What arms-a-cross, Worthy! Methinks you should hold 'em open when a friend's so near. I must expel this melancholy spirit.'

(SIDEWAY *has dropped to his knees and is sobbing in a pose of total sorrow.*)

What are you doing down there, Sideway?

SIDEWAY: I'm being melancholy. I saw Mr Garrick being melancholy once. That is what he did. Hamlet it was.

(*He stretches his arms to the ground and begins to repeat.*)

'Oh that this too, too solid flesh would melt. Oh that this too too solid flesh would melt. Oh that this too too—'

RALPH: This is a comedy. It is perhaps a little lighter. Try simply to stand normally and look melancholy. I'll say the line again. (SIDEWAY *is still sobbing.*) The audience won't hear Captain Plume's lines if your sobs are so loud, Sideway.

SIDEWAY: I'm still establishing my melancholy.

RALPH: A comedy needs to move quite fast. In fact, I think we'll cut that line and the two verses that follow and go straight to Worthy greeting Plume.

WISEHAMMER: I like the word melancholy.

SIDEWAY: A greeting. Yes. A greeting looks like this.

(*He extends his arms high and wide.*)

'Plume!' Now I'll change to say the next words. 'My dear Captain', that's affection isn't it? If I put my hands on my heart, like this. Now, 'Welcome'. I'm not quite sure how to do 'Welcome'.

RALPH: I think if you just say the line.

SIDEWAY: Quite. Now.

(*He feels* RALPH.)

RALPH: Sideway! What are you doing?

SIDEWAY: I'm checking that you're safe and sound returned. That's what the line says: 'Safe and sound returned.'

RALPH: You don't need to touch him. You can see that!

SIDEWAY: Yes, yes. I'll check his different parts with my eyes. Now, I'll put it all together, 'Plume! My dear Captain, welcome. Safe and sound returned!'

(*He does this with appropriate gestures.*)

RALPH: Sideway—it's a very good attempt. It's very theatrical. But you could try to be a little more—euh—natural.

SIDEWAY: Natural! On the stage! But Mr Clark!

RALPH: People must—euh—believe you. Garrick after all is admired for his naturalness.

SIDEWAY: Of course. I thought I was being Garrick—but never mind. Natural. Quite. You're the director, Mr Clark.

RALPH: Perhaps you could look at me while you're saying the lines.

SIDEWAY: But the audience won't see my face.

RALPH: The lines are said to Captain Plume. Let's move on. Plume says: 'I 'scaped safe from Germany', shall we say—America? It will make it more contemporary—

WISEHAMMER: You can't change the words of the playwright.

RALPH: Mm, well, 'and sound, I hope, from London: you see I have—'

(BLACK CAESAR *rushes on.*)

RALPH: Caesar, we're rehearsing—would you—

CAESAR: I see that well, Monsieur Lieutenant. I see it is a piece of theatre, I have seen many pieces of theatre in my beautiful island of Madagascar so I have decided to play in your piece of theatre.

RALPH: There's no part for you.

CAESAR: There is always a part for Caesar.

SIDEWAY: All the parts have been taken.

CAESAR: I will play his servant.

(*He stands next to* SIDEWAY.)

RALPH: Farquhar hasn't written a servant for Worthy.

DUCKLING: He can have my part. I want to play something else.

CAESAR: There is always a black servant in a play, Monsieur Lieutenant. And Caesar is that servant. So, now I stand here just behind him and I will be his servant.

RALPH: There are no lines for it, Caesar.

CAESAR: I speak in French. That makes him a more high up gentleman if he has a French servant, and that is good. Now he gets the lady with the black servant. Very chic.

RALPH: I'll think about it. Actually, I would like to rehearse the ladies now. They have been waiting patiently and we don't have much time left. Freeman, would you go and see what's happened to Arscott. Sideway, we'll come back to this scene another time,

---

prigged, stole.

but that was very good, very good. A little, a little euh, but very good.

(SIDEWAY *bows out, followed by* CAESAR.)

Now we will rehearse the first scene between Melinda and Silvia. Morden and Brenham, if you would come and stand here. Now the scene is set in Melinda's apartments. Silvia is already there. So, if you stand here, Morden. Brenham, you stand facing her.

LIZ (*very, very fast*): 'Welcome to town cousin Silvia I envied you your retreat in the country for Shrewsbury methinks and all your heads of shires are the most irregular places for living—'

RALPH: Euh, Morden—

LIZ: Wait, I haven't finished yet. 'Here we have smoke noise scandal affectation and pretension in short everything to give the spleen and nothing to divert it when the air is intolerable—'

RALPH: Morden, you know the lines very well.

LIZ: Thank you, Lieutenant Clark.

RALPH: But you might want to try and act them.

(*Pause.*)

Let's look at the scene.

(LIZ *looks.*)

You're a rich lady. You're at home. Now a rich lady would stand in a certain way. Try to stand like a rich lady. Try to look at Silvia with a certain assurance.

LIZ: Assurance.

WISEHAMMER: Confidence.

RALPH: Like this. You've seen rich ladies, haven't you?

LIZ: I robbed a few.

RALPH: How did they behave?

LIZ: They screamed.

RALPH: I mean before you—euh—robbed them.

LIZ: I don't know. I was watching their purses.

RALPH: Have you ever seen a lady in her own house?

LIZ: I used to climb into the big houses when I was a girl, and just stand there, looking. I didn't take anything. I just stood. Like this.

RALPH: But if it was your own house, you would think it was normal to live like that.

WISEHAMMER: It's not normal. It's not normal when others have nothing.

RALPH: When acting, you have to imagine things. You have to imagine you're someone different. So, now, think of a rich lady and imagine you're her.

(LIZ *begins to masticate.*)

What are you doing?

LIZ: If I was rich I'd eat myself sick.

DABBY: Me too, potatoes.

(*The convicts speak quickly and over each other.*)

SIDEWAY: Roast beef and Yorkshire pudding.

CAESAR: Hearts of palm.

WISEHAMMER: Four fried eggs, six fried eggs, eight fried eggs.

LIZ: Eels, oysters—

RALPH: Could we get on with the scene, please? Brenham, it's your turn to speak.

MARY: 'Oh, Madam, I have heard the town commended for its air.'

LIZ: 'But you don't consider Silvia how long I have lived in't!'

RALPH (*to* LIZ): I believe you would look at her.

LIZ: She didn't look at me.

RALPH: Didn't she? She will now.

LIZ: 'For I can assure you that to a lady the least nice in her constitution no air can be good above half a year change of air I take to be the most agreeable of any variety in life.'

MARY: 'But prithee, my dear Melinda, don't put on such an air to me.'

RALPH: Excellent, Brenham. You could be a little more sharp on the 'don't.'

MARY: 'Don't.' (MARY *now tries a few gestures.*) 'Your education and mine were just the same, and I remember the time when we never troubled our heads about air, but when the sharp air from the Welsh mountains made our noses drop in a cold morning at the boarding-school.'

RALPH: Good! Good! Morden?

LIZ: 'Our education cousin was the same but our temperaments had nothing alike.'

RALPH: That's a little better, Morden, but you needn't be quite so angry with her. Now go on Brenham.

LIZ: I haven't finished my speech!

RALPH: You're right, Morden, please excuse me.

LIZ (*embarrassed*): No, no, there's no need for that, Lieutenant. I only meant—I don't have to.

RALPH: Please do.

LIZ: 'You have the constitution of a horse.'

RALPH: Much better, Morden. But you must always remember you're a lady. What can we do to help you? Lucy.

DABBY: That's you, Duckling.

RALPH: See that little piece of wood over there? Take it to Melinda. That will be your fan.

DUCKLING: I'm not fetching nothing for Liz.

RALPH: She's not Morden, she's Melinda, your mistress. You're her servant, Lucy. In fact, you should be in this scene. Now take her that fan.

DUCKLING (*gives the wood to* LIZ): Here.

LIZ: Thank you, Lucy, I do much appreciate your effort.

RALPH: No, you would nod your head.

WISEHAMMER: Don't add any words to the play.

RALPH: Now, Lucy, stand behind Morden.

DUCKLING: What do I say?

RALPH: Nothing.

DUCKLING: How will they know I'm here? Why does she get all the lines? Why can't I have some of hers?

RALPH: Brenham, it's your speech.

MARY: 'So far as to be troubled with neither spleen, colic, nor vapours—'

(The convicts slink away and sink down, trying to make themselves invisible as MAJOR ROSS, followed by CAPTAIN CAMPBELL, come on.)

'I need no salt for my stomach, no—'

(She sees the officers herself and folds in with the rest of the convicts.)

RALPH: Major Ross, Captain Campbell, I'm rehearsing.

ROSS: Rehearsing! Rehearsing!

CAMPBELL: Tssaach. Rehearsing.

ROSS: Lieutenant Clark is rehearsing. Lieutenant Clark asked us to give the prisoners two hours so he could rehearse, but what has he done with them? What?

CAMPBELL: Eeeh. Other things, eh.

ROSS: Where are the prisoners Kable and Arscott, Lieutenant?

CAMPBELL: Eh?

RALPH: They seem to be late.

ROSS: While you were rehearsing, Arscott and Kable slipped into the woods with three others, so five men have run away and it's all because of your damned play and your so-called thespists. And not only have your thespists run away, they've stolen food from the stores for their renegade escapade, that's what your play has done.

RALPH: I don't see what the play—

ROSS: I said it from the beginning. The play will bring down calamity on this colony.

RALPH: I don't see—

ROSS: The devil, Lieutenant, always comes through the mind, here, worms its way, idleness and words.

RALPH: Major Ross, I can't agree—

ROSS: Listen to me, my lad, you're a Second Lieutenant and you don't agree or disagree with Major Ross.

CAMPBELL: No discipline, tcchhha.

(ROSS looks over the convicts.)

ROSS: Caesar! He started going with them and came back.

RALPH: That's all right, he's not in the play.

CAESAR: Yes I am, please Lieutenant, I am a servant.

ROSS: John Wisehammer!

WISEHAMMER: I had nothing to do with it!

ROSS: You're Jewish aren't you? You're guilty. Kable was last seen near Wisehammer's hut. Liz Morden! She was observed next to the colony's stores late last night in the company of Kable who was supposed to be repairing the door. *(To LIZ.)* Liz Morden, you will be tried for stealing from the stores. You know the punishment? Death by hanging. *(Pause.)* And now you may continue to rehearse, Lieutenant.

(ROSS goes. CAMPBELL lingers, looking at the book.)

CAMPBELL: Ouusstta. *The Recruiting Officer.* Good title. Arara. But a play, tss, a play.

(He goes. RALPH and the convicts are left in the shambles of their rehearsal. A silence.)

ACT 2 / SCENE 1 Visiting Hours

(LIZ, WISEHAMMER, ARSCOTT, CAESAR all in chains. ARSCOTT is bent over, facing away.)

LIZ: °Luck? Don't know the word. Shifts its bob when I comes near. Born under a ha'penny planet I was. Dad's a nibbler,° don't want to get crapped.° Mum leaves. Five brothers, I'm the only titter.° I takes in washing. Then. My own father. Lady's walking down the street, he takes her wiper. She screams, he's shoulder-clapped,° says, it's not me, Sir, it's Lizzie, look, she took it. I'm stripped, beaten in the street, everyone watching. That night, I take my dad's cudgel and try to kill him, I prig all his clothes and go to my older brother. He don't want me. Liz, he says, why trine for a make, when you can wap for a winne?° I'm no dimber mort,° I says. Don't ask you to be a swell mollisher,° Sister, men want Miss Laycock, don't look at your mug.° So I begin to sell my mother of saints. I thinks I'm in luck when I meet the swell cove.° He's a bobcull:° sports a different wiper every day of the week. He says to me, it's not enough to sell your mossie face,° Lizzie, it don't bring no shiners° no more. Shows me how to spice° the swells. So. Swell has me up the wall, flashes a pocket watch, I lifts it. But one time, I stir my stumps° too slow, the swell squeaks beef,° the snoozie° hears, I'm nibbed.° It's up the ladder to rest,° I thinks when I goes up before the fortune teller,° but no, the judge's a bobcull, I nap° the King's pardon and it's seven years across the herring pond.° Jesus Christ the hunger on the ship, sailors won't touch me: no rantum scantum,° no food. But here, the Governor says, new life. You could nob° it here, Lizzie, I thinks, bobcull Gov, this niffynaffy° play, not too much work, good crew of rufflers,° Kable, Arscott, but no, Ross don't like my

Liz's speech is full of eighteenth-century slang, some of it particularly associated with criminals. **nibbler,** petty thief. **crapped,** hung. **titter,** girl. **shoulder-clapped,** arrested. **trine . . . winne,** Why steal for a half-penny when you can have sex and make a penny? **dimber mort,** pretty girl. **swell mollisher,** fashionable woman. **mug,** face. **cove,** fellow. **bobcull,** good fellow. **mossie face,** female genitals. **shiners,** money, especially guineas. **spice,** rob. **stumps,** legs. **squeaks beef,** yells "thief." **snoozie,** night-constable. **nibbed,** caught. **It's up the ladder to rest,** to be hanged. **fortune teller,** judge. **nap,** take. **across the herring pond,** to be transported (across the sea). **rantum scantum,** sex. **nob,** make money. **niffynaffy,** fussy. **crew of rufflers,** group of vagabonds.

mug, I'm nibbed again and now it's up the ladder to rest for good. Well. Lizzie Morden's life. And you, Wisehammer, how did you get here?

WISEHAMMER: Betrayal. Barbarous falsehood. Intimidation. Injustice.

LIZ: Speak in English, Wisehammer.

WISEHAMMER: I am innocent. I didn't do it and I'll keep saying I didn't.

LIZ: It doesn't matter what you say. If they say you're a thief, you're a thief.

WISEHAMMER: I am not a thief. I'll go back to England to the snuff shop of Rickett and Loads and say, see, I'm back, I'm innocent.

LIZ: They won't listen.

WISEHAMMER: You can't live if you think that way.

(Pause.)

I'm sorry. Seven years and I'll go back.

LIZ: What do you want to go back to England for? You're not English.

WISEHAMMER: I was born in England. I'm English. What do I have to do to make people believe I'm English?

LIZ: You have to think English. I hate England. But I think English. And him, Arscott, he's not said anything since they brought him in but he's thinking English, I can tell.

CAESAR: I don't want to think English. If I think English I will die. I want to go back to Madagascar and think Malagasy. I want to die in Madagascar and join my ancestors.

LIZ: It doesn't matter where you die when you're dead.

CAESAR: If I die here, I will have no spirit. I want to go home. I will escape again.

ARSCOTT: There's no escape!

CAESAR: This time I lost my courage, but next time I ask my ancestors and they will help me escape.

ARSCOTT *(shouts)*: There's no escape!

LIZ: See. That's English. You know things.

CAESAR: My ancestors will know the way.

ARSCOTT: There's no escape I tell you.

(Pause.)

You go in circles out there, that's all you do. You go out there and you walk and walk and you don't reach China. You come back on your steps if the savages don't get you first. Even a compass doesn't work in this foreign upside-down desert. Here. You can read. Why didn't it work? What does it say?

(He hands WISEHAMMER *a carefully folded, wrinkled piece of paper.)*

WISEHAMMER: It says north.

ARSCOTT: Why didn't it work then? It was supposed to take us north to China, why did I end up going in circles?

WISEHAMMER: Because it's not a compass.

ARSCOTT: I gave my only shilling to a sailor for it. He said it was a compass.

WISEHAMMER: It's a piece of paper with north written on it. He lied. He deceived you, he betrayed you.

*(*SIDEWAY, MARY *and* DUCKLING *come on.)*

SIDEWAY: Madam, gentlemen, fellow players, we have come to visit, to commiserate, to offer our humble services.

LIZ: Get out!

MARY: Liz, we've come to rehearse the play.

WISEHAMMER: Rehearse the play?

DUCKLING: The Lieutenant has gone to talk to the Governor. Harry said we could come see you.

MARY: The Lieutenant has asked me to stand in his place so we don't lose time. We'll start with the first scene between Melinda and Brazen.

WISEHAMMER: How can I play Captain Brazen in chains?

MARY: This is the theatre. We will believe you.

ARSCOTT: Where does Kite come in?

SIDEWAY *(bowing to* LIZ*)*: Madam, I have brought you your fan. *(He hands her the 'fan', which she takes.)*

ACT 2 / SCENE 2 His Excellency Exhorts Ralph

*(*PHILLIP, RALPH.*)*

PHILLIP: I hear you want to stop the play, Lieutenant.

RALPH: Half of my cast is in chains, Sir.

PHILLIP: That is a difficulty, but it can be overcome. Is that your only reason, Lieutenant?

RALPH: So many people seem against it, Sir.

PHILLIP: Are you afraid?

RALPH: No, Sir, but I do not wish to displease my superior officers.

PHILLIP: If you break conventions, it's inevitable you make enemies, Lieutenant. This play irritates them.

RALPH: Yes and I—

PHILLIP: Socrates irritated the state of Athens and was put to death for it.

RALPH: Sir—

PHILLIP: Would you have a world without Socrates?

RALPH: Sir, I—

PHILLIP: In the Meno, one of Plato's great dialogues, have you read it, Lieutenant, Socrates demonstrates that a slave boy can learn the principles of geometry as well as a gentleman.

RALPH: Ah—

PHILLIP: In other words, he shows that human beings have an intelligence which has nothing to do with the circumstances into which they are born.

RALPH: Sir—

PHILLIP: Sit down, Lieutenant. It is a matter of reminding the slave of what he knows, of his own intelligence. And by intelligence you may read goodness, talent, the innate qualities of human beings.

RALPH: I see—Sir.

PHILLIP: When he treats the slave boy as a rational human being, the boy becomes one, he loses his fear, and he becomes a competent mathematician. A little more encouragement and he might become an extraordinary mathematician. Who knows? You must see your actors in that light.

RALPH: I can see some of them, Sir, but there are others . . . John Arscott—

PHILLIP: He has been given 200 lashes for trying to escape. It will take time for him to see himself as a human being again.

RALPH: Liz Morden—

PHILLIP: Liz Morden—*(He pauses.)* I had a reason for asking you to cast her as Melinda. Morden is one of the most difficult women in the colony.

RALPH: She is indeed, Sir.

PHILLIP: Lower than a slave, full of loathing, foul mouthed, desperate.

RALPH: Exactly, Sir. And violent.

PHILLIP: Quite. To be made an example of.

RALPH: By hanging?

PHILLIP: No, Lieutenant, by redemption.

RALPH: The Reverend says he's given up on her, Sir.

PHILLIP: The Reverend's an ass, Lieutenant. I am speaking of redeeming her humanity.

RALPH: I am afraid there may not be much there, Sir.

PHILLIP: How do we know what humanity lies hidden under the rags and filth of a mangled life? I have seen soldiers given up for dead, limbs torn, heads cut open, come back to life. If we treat her as a corpse, of course she will die. Try a little kindness, Lieutenant.

RALPH: But will she be hanged, Sir?

PHILLIP: I don't want a woman to be hanged. You will have to help, Ralph.

RALPH: Sir!

PHILLIP: I had retired from His Majesty's Service, Ralph. I was farming. I don't know why they asked me to rule over this colony of wretched souls, but I will fulfil my responsibility. No one will stop me.

RALPH: No, Sir, but I don't see—

PHILLIP: What is a statesman's responsibility? To ensure the rule of law. But the citizens must be taught to obey that law of their own will. I want to rule over responsible human beings, not tyrannise over a group of animals. I want there to be a contract between us, not a whip on my side, terror and hatred on theirs. And you must help me, Ralph.

RALPH: Yes, Sir. The play—

PHILLIP: Won't change much, but it is the diagram in the sand that may remind—just remind the slave boy—Do you understand?

RALPH: I think so.

PHILLIP: We may fail. I may have a mutiny on my hands. They are trying to convince the Admiralty that I am mad.

RALPH: Sir!

PHILLIP: And they will threaten you. You don't want to be a Second Lieutenant all your life.

RALPH: No, Sir!

PHILLIP: I cannot go over the head of Major Ross in the matter of promotion.

RALPH: I see.

PHILLIP: But we have embarked, Ralph, we must stay afloat. There is a more serious threat and it may capsize us all. If a ship does not come within three months, the supplies will be exhausted. In a month, I will cut the rations again. *(Pause.)* Harry is not well. Can you do something? Good luck with the play, Lieutenant. Oh, and Ralph—

RALPH: Sir—

PHILLIP: Unexpected situations are often matched by unexpected virtues in people, are they not?

RALPH: I believe they are, Sir.

PHILLIP: A play is a world in itself, a tiny colony we could almost say.

(Pause.)

And you are in charge of it. That is a great responsibility.

RALPH: I will lay down my life if I have to, Sir.

PHILLIP: I don't think it will come to that, Lieutenant. You need only do your best.

RALPH: Yes, Sir, I will, Sir.

PHILLIP: Excellent.

RALPH: It's a wonderful play, Sir. I wasn't sure at first, as you know, but now—

PHILLIP: Good, Good. I shall look forward to seeing it. I'm sure it will be a success.

RALPH: Thank you, Sir. Thank you.

ACT 2 / SCENE 3 Harry Brewer Sees the Dead

(HARRY BREWER's tent. HARRY sits, drinking rum, speaking in the different voices of his tormenting ghosts and answering in his own.)

HARRY: Duckling! Duckling! 'She's on the beach, Harry, waiting for her young Handy Baker.' Go away, Handy, go away! 'The dead never go away, Harry. You thought you'd be the only one to dance the buttock ball with your trull,° but no one owns a whore's cunt, Harry, you rent.' I didn't hang you. 'You wanted me dead.' I didn't. 'You wanted me hanged.' All right, I wanted you hanged. Go away! *(Pause.)* 'Death is horrible, Mr Brewer, it's dark, there's nothing.' Thomas Barrett! You were hanged because you stole from the stores. 'I was seventeen, Mr Brewer.' You lived a very wicked life. 'I didn't.' That's what you said that morning, 'I have led a very wicked life.' 'I had to say something, Mr Brewer, and make sense of dying. I'd heard the Reverend say we were all wicked, but it was horrible, my body hanging, my tongue sticking out.' You

---

trull, harlot.

shouldn't have stolen that food! 'I wanted to live, go back to England, I'd only be twenty-four. I hadn't done it much, not like you.' Duckling! 'I wish I wasn't dead, Mr Brewer I had plans. I was going to have my farm, drink with friends and feel the strong legs of a girl around me—' You shouldn't have stolen. 'Didn't you ever steal?' No! Yes. But that was different. Duckling! 'Why should you be alive after what you've done?' Duckling! Duckling!

(DUCKLING *rushes on.*)

DUCKLING: What's the matter, Harry?
HARRY: I'm seeing them.
DUCKLING: Who?
HARRY: All of them. The dead. Help me.
DUCKLING: I heard your screams from the beach. You're having another bad dream.
HARRY: No. I see them.

(*Pause.*)

Let me come inside you.
DUCKLING: Now?
HARRY: Please.
DUCKLING: Will you forget your nightmares?
HARRY: Yes.
DUCKLING: Come then.
HARRY: Duckling . . .

(*She lies down and lifts her skirts. He begins to go down over her and stops.*)

What were you doing on the beach? You were with him, he told me, you were with Handy Baker.

ACT 2 / SCENE 4 The Aborigine Muses on the Nature of Dreams

THE ABORIGINE: Some dreams lose their way and wander over the earth, lost. But this is a dream no one wants. It has stayed. How can we befriend this crowded, hungry and disturbed dream?

ACT 2 / SCENE 5 The Second Rehearsal

(RALPH CLARK, MARY BRENHAM *and* ROBERT SIDEWAY *are waiting.* MAJOR ROSS *and* CAPTAIN CAMPBELL *bring the three prisoners* CAESAR, WISEHAMMER *and* LIZ MORDEN. *They are still in chains.* ROSS *shoves them forward.*)

ROSS: Here is some of your caterwauling cast, Lieutenant.
CAMPBELL: The Governor, chhht, said, release, tssst. Prisoners.
ROSS: Unchain Wisehammer and the savage, Captain Campbell. (*Points to* LIZ.) She stays in chains. She's being tried tomorrow, we don't want her sloping off.

RALPH: I can't rehearse with one of my players in chains, Major.
CAMPBELL: Eeh. Difficult. Mmmm.
ROSS: We'll tell the Governor you didn't need her and take her back to prison.
RALPH: No. We shall manage. Sideway, go over the scene you rehearsed in prison with Melinda, Please.
CAESAR: I'm in that scene too, Lieutenant.
RALPH: No you're not.
LIZ and SIDEWAY: Yes he is, Lieutenant.
SIDEWAY: He's my servant.

(RALPH *nods and* LIZ, SIDEWAY *and* CAESAR *move to the side and stand together, ready to rehearse, but waiting.*)

RALPH: The rest of us will go from Silvia's entrance as Wilful. Where's Arscott?
ROSS: We haven't finished with Arscott yet, Lieutenant.
CAMPBELL: Punishment, eeeh, for escape. Fainted. Fifty-three lashes left. Heeeh.
ROSS (*pointing to* CAESAR): Caesar's next. After Morden's trial.

(CAESAR *cringes.*)

RALPH: Brenham, are you ready? Wisehammer? I'll play Captain Plume.
ROSS: The wee Lieutenant wants to be in the play too. He wants to be promoted to convict. We'll have you in the chain gang soon, Mr Clark, haha. (*A pause.* ROSS *and* CAMPBELL *stand watching. The* CONVICTS *are frozen.*)
RALPH: Major, we will rehearse now.

(*Pause. No one moves.*)

We wish to rehearse.
ROSS: No one's stopping you, Lieutenant.

(*Silence.*)

RALPH: Major, rehearsals need to take place in the utmost euh—privacy, secrecy you might say. The actors are not yet ready to be seen by the public.
ROSS: Not ready to be seen?
RALPH: Major, there is a modesty attached to the process of creation which must be respected.
ROSS: Modesty? Modesty! Sideway, come here.
RALPH: Major. Sideway—stay—
ROSS: Lieutenant, I would not try to countermand the orders of a superior officer.
CAMPBELL: Obedience. Ehh, first euh, rule.
ROSS: Sideway.

(SIDEWAY *comes up to* ROSS.)

Take your shirt off.

(SIDEWAY *obeys.* ROSS *turns him and shows his scarred back to the company.*)

One hundred lashes on the Sirius for answering an officer. Remember, Sideway? Three hundred lashes for trying to strike the same officer.

I have seen the white of this animal's bones, his wretched blood and reeky convict urine have spilled on my boots and he's feeling modest? Are you feeling modest, Sideway?

(*He shoves* SIDEWAY *aside.*)

Modesty.
Bryant. Here.

(DABBY *comes forward.*)

On all fours.

(DABBY *goes down on all fours.*)

Now wag your tail and bark, and I'll throw you a biscuit. What? You've forgotten? Isn't that how you begged for your food on the ship? Wag your tail, Bryant, bark! We'll wait.
Brenham.

(MARY *comes forward.*)

Where's your tattoo, Brenham? Show us. I can't see it. Show us.

(MARY *tries to obey, lifting her skirt a little.*)

If you can't manage, I'll help you. (MARY *lifts her skirt a little higher.*) I can't see it.

(*But* SIDEWAY *turns to* LIZ *and starts acting, boldly, across the room, across everyone.*)

SIDEWAY: 'What pleasures I may receive abroad are indeed uncertain; but this I am sure of, I shall meet with less cruelty among the most barbarous nations than I have found at home.'

LIZ: 'Come, Sir, you and I have been jangling a great while; I fancy if we made up our accounts, we should the sooner come to an agreement.'

SIDEWAY: 'Sure, Madam, you won't dispute your being in my debt—my fears, sighs, vows, promises, assiduities, anxieties, jealousies, have run on for a whole year, without any payment.'

CAMPBELL: Mmhem, good, that. Sighs, vows, promises, hehem, mmm. Anxieties.

ROSS: Captain Campbell, start Arscott's punishment.

(CAMPBELL *goes.*)

LIZ: 'A year! Oh Mr Worthy, what you owe to me is not to be paid under a seven years' servitude. How did you use me the year before—'

(*The shouts of* ARSCOTT *are heard.*)

'How did you use me the year before—'

(*She loses her lines.* SIDEWAY *tries to prompt her.*)

SIDEWAY: 'When taking advantage—'

LIZ: 'When taking the advantage of my innocence and necessity—'

(*But she stops and drops down, defeated. Silence, except for the beating and* ARSCOTT's *cries.*)

ACT 2 / SCENE 6 The Science of Hanging

(HARRY, KETCH FREEMAN, LIZ, *sitting, staring straight ahead of her.*)

KETCH: I don't want to do this.
HARRY: Get on with it, Freeman.
KETCH (*to* LIZ): I have to measure you.

(*Pause.*)

I'm sorry.

(LIZ *doesn't move.*)

You'll have to stand, Liz.

(LIZ *doesn't move.*)

Please.

(*Pause.*)

I won't hurt you. I mean, now. And if I have the measurements right, I can make it quick. Very quick. Please.

(LIZ *doesn't move.*)

She doesn't want to get up, Mr Brewer. I could come back later.

HARRY: Hurry up.

KETCH: I can't. I can't measure her unless she gets up. I have to measure her to judge the drop. If the rope's too short, it won't hang her and if the rope is too long, it could pull her head off. It's very difficult, Mr Brewer, I've always done my best.

(*Pause.*)

But I've never hung a woman.

HARRY (*in* TOM BARRETT's *voice*): 'You've hung a boy.' (*To* KETCH.) You've hung a boy.

KETCH: That was a terrible mess, Mr Brewer, don't you remember. It took twenty minutes and even then he wasn't dead. Remember how he danced and everyone laughed. I don't want to repeat something like that, Mr Brewer, not now. Someone had to get hold of his legs to weigh him down and then—

HARRY: Measure her, Freeman!

KETCH: Yes, Sir. Could you tell her to get up. She'll listen to you.

HARRY (*shouts*): Get up, you bitch.

(LIZ *doesn't move.*)

Get up!

(*He seizes her and makes her stand.*)

Now measure her!

KETCH (*measuring the neck, etc., of* LIZ): The Lieutenant is talking to the Governor again, Liz, maybe he'll change his mind. At least he might wait until we've done the play.

(*Pause.*)

I don't want to do this.
   I know, you're thinking in my place you wouldn't. But somebody will do it, if I don't, and I'll be gentle. I won't hurt you.

(LIZ *doesn't move, doesn't look at him.*)

It's wrong, Mr Brewer. It's wrong.

HARRY (*in* TOM BARRETT's *voice*): 'It's wrong. Death is horrible.' (*In his own voice to* KETCH.) There's no food left in the colony and she steals it and gives it to Kable to run away.

KETCH: That's true, Liz, you shouldn't have stolen that food. Especially when the Lieutenant trusted us. That was wrong, Liz. Actors can't behave like normal people, not even like normal criminals. Still, I'm sorry. I'll do my best.

HARRY: 'I had plans.' (*To* KETCH.) Are you finished?

KETCH: Yes, yes. I have all the measurements I need. No, one more. I need to lift her. You don't mind, do you, Liz?

(*He lifts her.*)

She's so light. I'll have to use a very long rope. The fig tree would be better, it's higher. When will they build me some gallows, Mr Brewer? Nobody will laugh at you, Liz, you won't be shamed, I'll make sure of that.

HARRY: 'You could hang yourself.' Come on, Freeman. Let's go.

KETCH: Goodbye, Liz. You were a very good Melinda. No one will be as good as you.

(*They begin to go.*)

LIZ: Mr Brewer.

HARRY: 'You wanted me dead.' I didn't. You shouldn't've stolen that food!

KETCH: Speak to her, please, Mr Brewer.

HARRY: What?

LIZ: Tell Lieutenant Clark I didn't steal the food. Tell him—afterwards. I want him to know.

HARRY: Why didn't you say that before? Why are you lying now?

LIZ: Tell the Lieutenant.

HARRY: 'Another victim of yours, another body. I was so frightened, so alone.'

KETCH: Mr Brewer.

HARRY: 'It's dark. There's nothing.' Get away, get away!

LIZ: Please tell the Lieutenant.

HARRY: 'First fear, then a pain at the back of the neck. Then nothing.' I can't see. It's dark. It's dark.

(HARRY *screams and falls.*)

ACT 2 / SCENE 7 The Meaning of Plays

THE ABORIGINE: Ghosts in a multitude have spilled from the dream. Who are they? A swarm of ancestors comes through unmended cracks in the sky. But why? What do they need? If we can satisfy them, they will go back. How can we satisfy them?

(MARY, RALPH, DABBY, WISEHAMMER, ARSCOTT. MARY *and* RALPH *are rehearsing. The others are watching.*)

RALPH: 'For I swear, Madam, by the honour of my profession, that whatever dangers I went upon, it was with the hope of making myself more worthy of your esteem, and if I ever had thoughts of preserving my life, 'twas for the pleasure of dying at your feet.'

MARY: 'Well, well, you shall die at my feet, or where you will; but you know, Sir, there is a certain will and testament to be made beforehand.'
   I don't understand why Silvia has asked Plume to make a will.

DABBY: It's a proof of his love, he wants to provide for her.

MARY: A will is a proof of love?

WISEHAMMER: No. She's using will in another sense. He must show his willingness to marry her. Dying is used in another sense, too.

RALPH: He gives her his will to indicate that he intends to take care of her.

DABBY: That's right, Lieutenant, marriage is nothing, but will you look after her?

WISEHAMMER: Plume is too ambitious to marry Silvia.

MARY: If I had been Silvia, I would have trusted Plume.

DABBY: When dealing with men, always have a contract.

MARY: Love is a contract.

DABBY: Love is the barter of perishable goods. A man's word for a woman's body.

WISEHAMMER: Dabby is right. If a man loves a woman, he should marry her.

RALPH: Sometimes he can't.

WISEHAMMER: Then she should look for someone who can.

DABBY: A woman should look after her own interests, that's all.

MARY: Her interest is to love.

DABBY: A girl will love the first man who knows how to open her legs. She's called a whore and ends up here. I could write scenes, Lieutenant, women with real lives, not these Shrewsbury prudes.

WISEHAMMER: I've written something. The prologue of this play won't make any sense to the convicts: 'In ancient times, when Helen's fatal charms' and so on. I've written another one. Will you look at it, Lieutenant?

(RALPH *does so and* WISEHAMMER *takes* MARY *aside.*)

You mustn't trust the wrong people, Mary. We could make a new life together, here. I would marry you, Mary, think about it, you would live with me, in a house. He'll have to put you in a hut at the bottom of his garden and call you his servant in public, that is, his whore. Don't do it, Mary.

DABBY: Lieutenant, are we rehearsing or not? Arscott and I have been waiting for hours.

RALPH: It seems interesting, I'll read it more carefully later.

WISEHAMMER: You don't like it.

RALPH: I do like it. Perhaps it needs a little more work. It's not Farquhar.

WISEHAMMER: It would mean more to the convicts.

RALPH: We'll talk about it another time.

WISEHAMMER: Do you think it should be longer?

RALPH: I'll think about it.

WISEHAMMER: Shorter? Do you like the last two lines? Mary helped me with them.

RALPH: Ah.

WISEHAMMER: The first lines took us days, didn't they, Mary?

RALPH: We'll rehearse Silvia's entrance as Jack Wilful. You're in the scene, Wisehammer. We'll come to your scenes in a minute, Bryant. Now, Brenham, remember what I showed you yesterday about walking like a gentleman? I've ordered breeches to be made for you, you can practise in them tomorrow.

MARY: I'll tuck my skirt in. (*She does so and takes a masculine pose.*) 'Save ye, save ye, gentlemen.'

WISEHAMMER: 'My dear, I'm yours.'

(*He kisses her.*)

RALPH (*angrily*): It doesn't say Silvia is kissed in the stage directions!

WISEHAMMER: Plume kisses her later and there's the line about men kissing in the army. I thought Brazen would kiss her immediately.

RALPH: It's completely wrong.

WISEHAMMER: It's right for the character of Brazen.

RALPH: No it isn't. I'm the director, Wisehammer.

WISEHAMMER: Yes, but I have to play the part. They're equal in this scene. They're both Captains and in the end fight for her. Who's playing Plume in our performance?

RALPH: I will have to, as Kable hasn't come back. It's your line.

WISEHAMMER: Will I be given a sword?

RALPH: I doubt it. Let's move on to Kite's entrance, Arscott has been waiting too long.

ARSCOTT (*delighted, launches straight in*): 'Sir, if you please—'

RALPH: Excellent, Arscott, but we should just give you our last lines so you'll know when to come in. Wisehammer.

WISEHAMMER: 'The fellow dare not fight.'

RALPH: That's when you come in.

ARSCOTT: 'Sir, if you please—'

DABBY: What about me? I haven't done anything either. You always rehearse the scenes with Silvia.

RALPH: Let's rehearse the scene where Rose comes on with her brother Bullock. It's a better scene for you Arscott. Do you know it?

ARSCOTT: Yes.

RALPH: Good. Wisehammer, you'll have to play the part of Bullock.

WISEHAMMER: What? Play two parts?

RALPH: Major Ross won't let any more prisoners off work. Some of you will have to play several parts.

WISEHAMMER: It'll confuse the audience. They'll think Brazen is Bullock and Bullock Brazen.

RALPH: Nonsense, if the audience is paying attention, they'll know that Bullock is a country boy and Brazen a Captain.

WISEHAMMER: What if they aren't paying attention?

RALPH: People who can't pay attention should not go to the theatre.

MARY: If you act well, they will have to pay attention.

WISEHAMMER: It will ruin my entrance as Captain Brazen.

RALPH: We have no choice and we must turn this necessity into an advantage. You will play two very different characters and display the full range of your abilities.

WISEHAMMER: Our audience won't be that discerning.

RALPH: Their imagination will be challenged and trained. Let's start the scene. Bryant?

DABBY: I think *The Recruiting Officer* is a silly play. I want to be in a play that has more interesting people in it.

MARY: I like playing Silvia. She's bold, she breaks rules out of love for her Captain and she's not ashamed.

DABBY: She hasn't been born poor, she hasn't had to survive, and her father's a Justice of the Peace. I want to play myself.

ARSCOTT: I don't want to play myself. When I say Kite's lines I forget everything else. I forget the judge said I'm going to have to spend the rest of my natural life in this place getting beaten and working like a slave. I can forget that out there it's trees and burnt grass, spiders that kill you in four hours and snakes. I don't have to think about what happened to Kable, I don't have to remember the things I've done, when I speak Kite's lines I don't hate any more. I'm Kite. I'm in Shrewsbury. Can we get on with the scene, Lieutenant, and stop talking?

DABBY: I want to see a play that shows life as we know it.

WISEHAMMER: A play should make you understand something new. If it tells you what you already know, you leave it as ignorant as you went in.

DABBY: Why can't we do a play about now?

WISEHAMMER: It doesn't matter when a play is set. It's better if it's set in the past, it's clearer. It's easier to understand Plume and Brazen than some of the officers we know here.

RALPH: Arscott, would you start the scene?

ARSCOTT: 'Captain, Sir, look yonder, a-coming this way, 'tis the prettiest, cleanest, little tit.'

RALPH: Now Worthy—He's in this scene. Where's Sideway?

MARY: He's so upset about Liz he won't rehearse.

RALPH: I am going to talk to the Governor, but he has to rehearse. We must do the play, whatever happens. We've been rehearsing for five months! Let's go on. 'Here she comes, and what is that great country fellow with her?'

ARSCOTT: 'I can't tell, Sir.'

WISEHAMMER: I'm not a great country fellow.

RALPH: Act it, Wisehammer.

DABBY: 'Buy chickens, young and tender, young and tender chickens.' This is a very stupid line and I'm not saying it.

RALPH: It's written by the playwright and you have to say it. 'Here, you chickens!'

DABBY: 'Who calls?'

RALPH: Bryant, you're playing a pretty country wench who wants to entice the Captain. You have to say these lines with charm and euh—blushes.

DABBY: I don't blush.

RALPH: I can't do this scene without Sideway. Let's do another scene.

(Pause.)

Arscott, let's work on your big speeches, I haven't heard them yet. I still need Sideway. This is irresponsible, he wanted the part. Somebody go and get Sideway.

(No one moves.)

ARSCOTT: I'll do the first speech anyway, Sir. 'Yes, Sir, I understand my business, I will say it; you must know, Sir, I was born a gypsy, and bred among that crew till I was ten years old, there I learned canting and lying;—'

DABBY: That's about me!

ARSCOTT: 'I was bought from my mother Cleopatra by a certain nobleman, for three guineas, who liking my beauty made me his page—'

DABBY: That's my story. Why do I have to play a silly milkmaid? Why can't I play Kite?

MARY: You can't play a man, Dabby.

DABBY: You're playing a man: Jack Wilful.

MARY: Yes, but in the play, I know I'm a woman, whereas if you played Kite, you would have to think you were a man.

DABBY: If Wisehammer can think he's a big country lad, I can think I'm a man. People will use their imagination and people with no imagination shouldn't go to the theatre.

RALPH: Bryant, you're muddling everything.

DABBY: No. I see things very clearly and I'm making you see clearly, Lieutenant. I want to play Kite.

ARSCOTT: You can't play Kite! I'm playing Kite! You can't steal my part!

RALPH: You may have to play Melinda.

DABBY: All she does is marry Sideway, that's not interesting.

(DABBY stomps off. KETCH comes on.)

KETCH: I'm sorry I'm late, Lieutenant, but I know all my lines.

RALPH: We'll rehearse the first scene between Justice Balance and Silvia. Brenham.

(ARSCOTT stomps off.)

MARY: 'Whilst there is life there is hope, Sir; perhaps my brother may recover.'

KETCH: 'We have but little reason to expect it—'

MARY: I can't. Not with him. Not with Liz—I can't.

(She runs off.)

RALPH: One has to transcend personal feelings in the theatre.

(WISEHAMMER runs after MARY.)

(To KETCH.) We're not making much progress today, let's end this rehearsal.

(He goes. KETCH is left alone, bewildered.)

ACT 2 / SCENE 8 Duckling Makes Vows

(Night. HARRY, ill. DUCKLING.)

DUCKLING: If you live, I will never again punish you with my silence. If you live, I will never again turn away from you. If you live, I will never again imagine another man when you make love to me. If you live, I will never tell you I want to leave you. If you live, I will speak to you. If you live, I will be tender with you. If you live, I will look after you. If you live, I will stay with you. If you live, I will be wet and open to your touch. If you live, I will answer all your questions. If you live, I will look at you. If you live, I will love you.

(Pause.)

If you die, I will never forgive you.

(She leans over him. Listens. Touches. HARRY is dead.)

I hate you.
No. I love you.

(She crouches into a foetal position, cries out.)

How could you do this?

ACT 2 / SCENE 9 A Love Scene

(The beach. Night. MARY, *then* RALPH.*)*

MARY *(to herself)*: 'Captain Plume, I despise your listing-money;° if I do serve, 'tis purely for love—of that wench I mean. For you must know,' etc—

'So you only want an opportunity for accomplishing your designs upon her?'

'Well, Sir, I'm satisfied as to the point in debate; but now let me beg you to lay aside your recruiting airs, put on the man of honour, and tell me plainly what usage I must expect when I'm under your command.'

(She tries that again, with a stronger and lower voice. RALPH *comes on, sees her. She sees him, but continues.)*

'And something tells me, that if you do discharge me 'twill be the greatest punishment you can inflict; for were we this moment to go upon the greatest dangers in your profession, they would be less terrible to me than to stay behind you. And now your hand—this lists me—and now you are my Captain.'

RALPH *(as plume)*: 'Your friend.' *(Kisses her.)* "Sdeath! There's something in this fellow that charms me.'

MARY: 'One favour I must beg—this affair will make some noise—'

RALPH: Silvia—

(He kisses her again.)

MARY: 'I must therefore take care to be impressed by the Act of Parliament—'

RALPH: 'What you please as to that. Will you lodge at my quarters in the meantime? You shall have part of my bed.' Silvia. Mary.

MARY: Am I doing it well? It's difficult to play a man. It's not the walk, it's the way you hold your head. A man doesn't bow his head so much and never at an angle. I must face you without lowering my head. Let's try it again.

RALPH: 'What you please as to that.—Will you lodge at my quarters in the meantime? You shall have part of my bed.' Mary!

(She holds her head straight. Pause.)

Will you?

(Pause.)

MARY: Yes.

(They kiss.)

RALPH: Don't lower your head. Silvia wouldn't.

(She begins to undress, from the top.)

I've never looked at the body of a woman before.

MARY: Your wife?

---

listing-money, money given to a new recruit.

RALPH: It wasn't right to look at her.
Let me see you.

MARY: Yes.
Let me see you.

RALPH: Yes.

(He begins to undress himself.)

ACT 2 / SCENE 10 The Question of Liz

*(*RALPH, ROSS, PHILLIP, COLLINS, CAMPBELL.*)*

COLLINS: She refused to defend herself at the trial. She didn't say a word. This was taken as an admission of guilt and she was condemned to be hanged. The evidence against her, however, is flimsy.

ROSS: She was seen with Kable next to the food stores. That is a fingering fact.

COLLINS: She was seen by a drunken soldier in the dark. He admitted he was drunk and that he saw her at a distance. He knew Kable was supposed to be repairing the door and she's known to be friends with Kable and Arscott. She won't speak, she won't say where she was. That is our difficulty.

ROSS: She won't speak because she's guilty.

PHILLIP: Silence has many causes, Robbie.

RALPH: She won't speak, Your Excellency, because of the convict code of honour. She doesn't want to beg for her life.

ROSS: Convict code of honour. This pluming play has muddled the muffy Lieutenant's mind.

COLLINS: My only fear, Your Excellency, is that she may have refused to speak because she no longer believes in the process of justice. If that is so, the courts here will become travesties. I do not want that.

PHILLIP: But if she won't speak, there is nothing more we can do. You cannot get at the truth through silence.

RALPH: She spoke to Harry Brewer.

PHILLIP: But Harry never regained consciousness before he died.

RALPH: James Freeman was there and told me what she said.

PHILLIP: Wasn't this used in the trial?

COLLINS: Freeman's evidence wasn't very clear and as Liz Morden wouldn't confirm what he said, it was dismissed.

ROSS: You can't take the word of a crooked crawling hangman.

PHILLIP: Why won't she speak?

ROSS: Because she's guilty.

PHILLIP: Robbie, we may be about to hang the first woman in this colony. I do not want to hang the first innocent woman.

RALPH: We must get at the truth.

ROSS: Truth! We have 800 thieves, perjurers, forgers, murderers, liars, escapers, rapists, whores, coiners in this scrub-ridden, dust-driven, thunder-bolted, savage-run, cretinous colony. My marines who are trained to fight are turned into gouly gaolers, fed less than the prisoners—

PHILLIP: The rations, Major, are the same for all, prisoners and soldiers.

ROSS: They have a right to more so that makes them have less. Not a ship shifting into sight, the prisoners running away, stealing, drinking and the wee ductile Lieutenant talks about the truth.

PHILLIP: Truth is indeed a luxury, but its absence brings about the most abject poverty in a civilisation. That is the paradox.

ROSS: This is a profligate prison for us all, it's a hellish hole we soldiers have been hauled to because they blame us for losing the war in America. This is a hateful, hary-scary, topsy-turvy outpost, this is not a civilisation. I hate this possumy place.

COLLINS: Perhaps we could return to the question of Liz Morden. (*Calls.*) Captain Campbell.

(CAMPBELL *brings in* LIZ MORDEN.)

Morden, if you don't speak, we will have to hang you; if you can defend yourself, His Excellency can overrule the court. We would not then risk a miscarriage of justice. But you must speak. Did you steal that food with the escaped prisoner Kable?

(*A long silence.*)

RALPH: She—

COLLINS: It is the accused who must answer.

PHILLIP: Liz Morden. You must speak the truth.

COLLINS: We will listen to you.

(*Pause.*)

RALPH: Morden. No one will despise you for telling the truth.

PHILLIP: That is not so, Lieutenant. Tell the truth and accept the contempt. That is the history of great men. Liz, you may be despised, but you will have shown courage.

RALPH: If that soldier has lied—

ROSS: There, there, he's accusing my soldiers of lying. It's that play, it makes fun of officers, it shows an officer lying and cheating. It shows a corrupt justice as well, Collins—

CAMPBELL: Good scene that, very funny, hah, scchhh.

COLLINS: Et tu, Campbell?°

CAMPBELL: What? Meant only. Hahah. If he be so good at gunning he shall have enough—he may be of use against the French, for he shoots flying, hahaha. Good, and then there's this Constable ha—

ROSS: Campbell!

Et tu, Campbell? allusion to Julius Caesar's line as he realized that his friend Brutus was about to stab him, *Et tu, Brute,* "And you also, Brutus?"

PHILLIP: The play seems to be having miraculous effects already. Don't you want to be in it, Liz?

RALPH: Morden, you must speak.

COLLINS: For the good of the colony.

PHILLIP: And of the play.

(*A long silence.*)

LIZ: I didn't steal the food.

COLLINS: Were you there when Kable stole it?

LIZ: No. I was there before.

ROSS: And you knew he was going to steal it?

LIZ: Yes.

ROSS: Guilty. She didn't report it.

COLLINS: Failure to inform is not a hangable offence.

ROSS: Conspiracy.

COLLINS: We may need a retrial.

PHILLIP: Why wouldn't you say any of this before?

ROSS: Because she didn't have time to invent a lie.

COLLINS: Major, you are demeaning the process of law.

PHILLIP: Why, Liz?

LIZ: Because it wouldn't have mattered.

PHILLIP: Speaking the truth?

LIZ: Speaking.

ROSS: You are taking the word of a convict against the word of a soldier—

COLLINS: A soldier who was drunk and uncertain of what he saw.

ROSS: A soldier is a soldier and has a right to respect. You will have revolt on your hands, Governor.

PHILLIP: I'm sure I will, but let us see the play first. Liz, I hope you are good in your part.

RALPH: She will be, Your Excellency, I promise that.

LIZ: Your Excellency, I will endeavour to speak Mr Farquhar's lines with the elegance and clarity their own worth commands.

ACT 2 / SCENE 11 Backstage

(*Night.* THE ABORIGINE.)

THE ABORIGINE: Look: oozing pustules on my skin, heat on my forehead. Perhaps we have been wrong all this time and this is not a dream at all.

(*The* ACTORS *come on. They begin to change and make up.* THE ABORIGINE *drifts off.*)

MARY: Are the savages coming to see the play as well?

KETCH: They come around the camp because they're dying: smallpox.

MARY: Oh.

SIDEWAY: I hope they won't upset the audience.

MARY: Everyone is here. All the officers too.

LIZ (*to* DUCKLING): Dabby could take your part.

DUCKLING: No. I will do it. I will remember the lines.

MARY: I've brought you an orange from Lieutenant Clark's island. They've thrown her out of Harry Brewer's tent.

WISEHAMMER: Why? He wouldn't have wanted that.

DUCKLING: Major Ross said a whore was a whore and I was to go into the women's camp. They've taken all of Harry's things.

(She bursts into tears.)

MARY: I'll talk to the Lieutenant.

LIZ: Let's go over your lines. And if you forget them, touch my foot and I'll whisper them to you.

SIDEWAY *(who has been practising on his own)*: We haven't rehearsed the bow. Garrick used to take his this way: you look up to the circle, to the sides, down, make sure everyone thinks you're looking at them. Get in a line.

(They do so.)

ARSCOTT: I'll be in the middle. I'm the tallest.

MARY: No, Arscott. (MARY *places herself in the middle.*)

SIDEWAY: Dabby, you should be next to Mary.

DABBY: I won't take the bow.

SIDEWAY: It's not the biggest part, Dabby, but you'll be noticed.

DABBY: I don't want to be noticed.

SIDEWAY: Let's get this right. If we don't all do the same thing, it will look a mess.

(They try. DABBY *is suddenly transfixed.)*

DABBY: Hurray, hurray, hurray.

SIDEWAY: No, they will be shouting bravo, but we're not in a line yet.

DABBY: I wasn't looking at the bow, I saw the whole play, and we all knew our lines, and Mary, you looked so beautiful, and after that, I saw Devon and they were shouting bravo, bravo Dabby, hurray, you've escaped, you've sailed thousands and thousands of miles on the open sea and you've come back to your Devon, bravo Dabby, bravo.

MARY: When are you doing this, Dabby?

DABBY: Tonight.

MARY: You can't.

DABBY: I'll be in the play till the end, then in the confusion, when it's over, we can slip away. The tide is up, the night will be dark, everything's ready.

MARY: The Lieutenant will be blamed, I won't let you.

DABBY: If you say anything to the Lieutenant, I'll refuse to act in the play.

ARSCOTT: When I say my lines, I think of nothing else. Why can't you do the same?

DABBY: Because it's only for one night. I want to grow old in Devon.

MARY: They'll never let us do another play, I'm telling the Lieutenant.

ALL: No, you're not.

DABBY: Please, I want to go back to Devon.

WISEHAMMER: I don't want to go back to England now. It's too small and they don't like Jews. Here, no one has more of a right than anyone else to call you a foreigner. I want to become the first famous writer.

MARY: You can't become a famous writer until you're dead.

WISEHAMMER: You can if you're the only one.

SIDEWAY: I'm going to start a theatre company. Who wants to be in it?

WISEHAMMER: I will write you a play about justice.

SIDEWAY: Only comedies, my boy, only comedies.

WISEHAMMER: What about a comedy about unrequited love?

LIZ: I'll be in your company, Mr Sideway.

KETCH: And so will I. I'll play all the parts that have dignity and gravity.

SIDEWAY: I'll hold auditions tomorrow.

DABBY: Tomorrow.

DUCKLING: Tomorrow.

MARY: Tomorrow.

LIZ: Tomorrow.

(A long silence. [Un ange passe.°])

MARY: Where are my shoes?

(RALPH comes in.)

RALPH: Arscott, remember to address the soldiers when you talk of recruiting. Look at them: you are speaking to them. And don't forget, all of you, to leave a space for people to laugh.

ARSCOTT: I'll kill anyone who laughs at me.

RALPH: They're not laughing at you, they're laughing at Farquhar's lines. You must expect them to laugh.

ARSCOTT: That's all right, but if I see Major Ross or any other officer laughing at me, I'll kill them.

MARY: No more violence. By the way, Arscott, when you carry me off the stage as Jack Wilful, could you be a little more gentle? I don't think he'd be so rough with a young gentleman.

RALPH: Where's Caesar?

KETCH: I saw him walking towards the beach earlier. I thought he was practising his lines.

ARSCOTT: Caesar!

(He goes out.)

WISEHAMMER *(to* LIZ*)*: When I say 'Do you love fishing, Madam?', do you say something then?—

RALPH *(goes over to* DUCKLING*)*: I am so sorry, Duckling. Harry was my friend.

DUCKLING: I loved him. But now he'll never know that. I thought that if he knew he would become cruel.

RALPH: Are you certain you don't want Dabby to take your part?

DUCKLING: No! I will do it. I want to do it.

(Pause.)

He liked to hear me say my lines.

Un ange passe, "An angel passes," proverbial for a moment when everyone suddenly falls silent.

RALPH: He will be watching from somewhere. (*He goes to* MARY.) How beautiful you look.

MARY: I dreamt I had a necklace of pearls and three children.

RALPH: If we have a boy we will call him Harry.

MARY: And if we have a girl?

RALPH: She will be called Betsey Alicia.

(ARSCOTT *comes in with* CAESAR *drunk and dishevelled.*)

ARSCOTT: Lying on the beach, dead drunk.

CAESAR (*to* RALPH, *pleading*): I can't. All those people. My ancestors are angry, they do not want me to be laughed at by all those people.

RALPH: You wanted to be in this play and you will be in this play—

KETCH: I'm nervous too, but I've overcome it. You have to be brave to be an actor.

CAESAR: My ancestors will kill me.

(*He swoons.* ARSCOTT *hits him.*)

ARSCOTT: You're going to ruin my first scene.

CAESAR: Please, Lieutenant, save me.

RALPH: Caesar, if I were back home, I wouldn't be in this play either. My ancestors wouldn't be very pleased to see me here—But our ancestors are thousands of miles away.

CAESAR: I cannot be a disgrace to Madagascar.

ARSCOTT: You will be more of a disgrace if you don't come out with me on that stage. NOW.

MARY: Think of us as your family.

SIDEWAY (*to* RALPH): What do you think of this bow?

RALPH: Caesar, I am your Lieutenant and I command you to go on that stage. If you don't, you will be tried and hanged for treason.

KETCH: And I'll tie the rope in such a way you'll dangle there for hours full of piss and shit.

RALPH: What will your ancestors think of that, Caesar?

(CAESAR *cries but pulls himself together.*)

KETCH (*to* LIZ): I couldn't have hanged you.

LIZ: No?

RALPH: Dabby, have you got your chickens?

DABBY: My chickens? Yes. Here.

RALPH: Are you all right?

DABBY: Yes. (*Pause.*) I was dreaming.

RALPH: Of your future success?

DABBY: Yes. Of my future success.

RALPH: And so is everyone here, I hope. Now, Arscott.

ARSCOTT: Yes, Sir!

RALPH: Calm.

ARSCOTT: I have been used to danger, Sir.

SIDEWAY: Here.

LIZ: What's that?

SIDEWAY: Salt. For good luck.

RALPH: Where did you get that from?

SIDEWAY: I have been saving it from my rations. I have saved enough for each of us to have some.

(*They all take a little salt.*)

WISEHAMMER: Lieutenant?

RALPH: Yes, Wisehammer.

WISEHAMMER: There's—there's—

MARY: There's his prologue.

RALPH: The prologue. I forgot.

(*Pause.*)

Let me hear it again.

WISEHAMMER:

> *From distant climes o'er wide-spread seas we come,*
> *Though not with much éclat or beat of drum,*
> *True patriots all; for be it understood,*
> *We left our country for our country's good;*
> *No private views disgraced our generous zeal,*
> *What urg'd our travels was our country's weal,*
> *And none will doubt but that our emigration*
> *Has prov'd most useful to the British nation.*

(*Silence.*)

RALPH: When Major Ross hears that, he'll have an apoplectic fit.

MARY: I think it's very good.

DABBY: So do I. And true.

SIDEWAY: But not theatrical.

RALPH: It is very good, Wisehammer, it's very well written, but it's too—too political. It will be considered provocative.

WISEHAMMER: You don't want me to say it.

RALPH: Not tonight. We have many people against us.

WISEHAMMER: I could tone it down. I could omit 'We left our country for our country's good.'

DABBY: That's the best line.

RALPH: It would be wrong to cut it.

WISEHAMMER: I worked so hard on it.

LIZ: It rhymes.

SIDEWAY: We'll use it in the Sideway Theatre.

RALPH: You will get much praise as Brazen, Wisehammer.

WISEHAMMER: It isn't the same as writing.

RALPH: The theatre is like a small republic, it requires private sacrifices for the good of the whole. That is something you should agree with, Wisehammer.

(*Pause.*)

And now, my actors, I want to say what a pleasure it has been to work with you. You are on your own tonight and you must do your utmost to provide the large audience out there with a pleasurable, intelligible and memorable evening.

LIZ: We will do our best, Mr Clark.

MARY: I love this!

RALPH: Arscott.

ARSCOTT (*to* CAESAR): You walk three steps ahead of me. If you stumble once, you know what will happen to you later? Move!

RALPH: You're on.

(ARSCOTT *is about to go on, then remembers.*)

ARSCOTT: Halberd! Halberd!

(*He is handed his halberd and goes upstage and off, preceded by* CAESAR *beating the drum. Backstage, the remaining actors listen with trepidation to* KITE's *first speech.*)

ARSCOTT: 'If any gentlemen soldiers, or others, have a mind to serve Her Majesty, and pull down the French King; if any prentices have severe masters, any children have undutiful parents; if any servants have too little wages or any husband too much wife; let them repair to the noble Sergeant Kite, at the Sign of the Raven, in this good town of Shrewsbury, and they shall receive present relief and entertainment' . . .

(*And to the triumphant music of Beethoven's* Fifth Symphony *and the sound of applause and laughter from the First Fleet audience, the first Australian performance of* The Recruiting Officer *begins.*)

Figure 1. Major Robbie Ross (Mark Lambert, *far right*) argues against letting the convicts produce a play. Listening to him are, *left to right*, Reverend Johnson (Lesley Sharp, *seated*), Lieutenant Ralph Clark (David Haig), Governor Arthur Philip (Ron Cook, *seated*), and Captain David Collins (Nick Dunning) in the 1988 Royal Court Theatre production of *Our Country's Good*, directed by Max Stafford-Clark. (Photograph: Donald Cooper / Photostage.)

Figure 2. Harry Brewer (Jim Broadbent) tries to get Duckling Smith (Alphonsia Emmanuel) to listen to him as he takes her rowing in the 1988 Royal Court Theatre production of *Our Country's Good*, directed by Max Stafford-Clark. (Photograph: Donald Cooper / Photostage.)

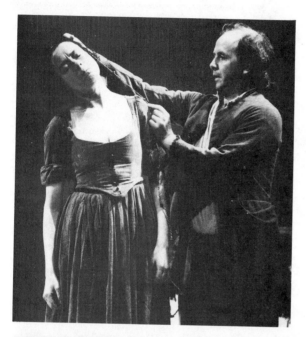

Figure 3. Ketch Freeman (Mark Lambert) stolidly measures Liz Morden (Linda Bassett) for hanging in the 1988 Royal Court Theatre production of *Our Country's Good,* directed by Max Stafford-Clark. (Photograph: Donald Cooper / Photostage.)

Figure 4. Wisehammer (Ron Cook, *left*) and Ralph Clark (David Haig, *right*) argue about whether or not Brazen, the character Wisehammer plays, should kiss Silvia, the character played by Mary Brenham (Lesley Sharp, *center*) in the 1988 Royal Court Theatre production of *Our Country's Good,* directed by Max Stafford-Clark. (Photograph: Donald Cooper / Photostage.)

Staging of *Our Country's Good*

**REVIEW OF THE ROYAL COURT THEATRE
PRODUCTION, 1988, BY MICHAEL BILLINGTON**

I am normally wary of plays based on novels. But Timberlake Wertenbaker's *Our Country's Good* at the Royal Court is a triumph. It takes off from Thomas Keneally's novel *The Playmaker* without being tied to it by a dogged literalism. At the same time, it comes across as a moving and affirmative tribute to the transforming power of drama itself.

Like the book it starts from a single extraordinary fact: that in 1789 a young marine lieutenant, Ralph Clark, gave the Australian penal colonies their first taste of drama with a production of *The Recruiting Officer* cast from assorted felons, pickpockets and burglars. Clark's project is vehemently opposed by a couple of superior officers who see it as an incitement to mutiny. It also takes place against a background of vindictive punishment with the actress playing Melinda being threatened with hanging for stealing food. But the insane excitement of playmaking takes over and the production miraculously occurs; and Clark himself, who has stayed obstinately faithful to his wife back home, falls in love with the clothes thief playing Silvia and forms a second marriage.

What Ms. Wertenbaker has done is to seize on one strand in the book and make it the heart and centre of her play: the notion that drama releases something in the psyche and rescues these hapless convicts from an internal cycle of crime and punishment. The idea is articulated by the Governor-General, a benign classicist who harks back to the Greek concept of drama as a means of instilling the social virtues. But Ms. Wertenbaker doesn't merely talk about this. She demonstrates it theatrically, not least in one superb scene where the woman convict who is about to be hanged breaks her self-incriminating vow of silence and sweeps out saying she hopes to speak Mr. Farquhar's lines "with the elegance and clarity their own worth commands." In context, it is as powerful as similar moments of self-realisation in *Pygmalian* and *Roots*.

In highlighting one of Keneally's themes, Ms. Wertenbaker inevitably plays down others: I was sorry to see go the process by which the Governor-General treats a captured Aborigine as a social experiment while himself being regarded by the native with horrified awe. Ms. Wertenbaker also softens the original by omitting Clark's tormented nightmares and allowing him to play Plume to his beloved Silvia.

But, against that, she constantly reminds us that Farquhar's comedy is being rehearsed against a background of floggings, beatings and threatened starvation. She also brings out clearly one of the book's points which is that both officers and convicts are locked in the same "profligate prison" as they try to create a workable colony in a remote corner of New South Wales.

It makes for a wonderful evening's theatre: a Brechtian parable with an optimistic conclusion. By using the same cast currently playing *The Recruiting Officer*, Max Stafford-Clark's stirring production shows what could be achieved if the Royal Court could afford a permanent ensemble. David Haig brings to Ralph Clark the same kind of nervous decency he does to Captain Plume: in particular, he has the touching Boy-Scout earnestness of a man trying to redeem people through drama and draw what the Governor-General calls "a diagram in the sand."

Lesley Sharp as the quondam thief cast as Silvia burgeons beautifully and makes her final cry of "I love this" (putting on plays) heart-warming and funny. There is also some notable doubling: from Jim Broadbent as both a haunted midshipman and a jovially repressive Scottish captain and from Ron Cook as the enlightened Governor-General and a Jewish snuff-stealer who discovers through acting the joy of writing.

But what makes this play work is its very assumption that drama has the capacity to change lives and liberate imaginations: in these crass times it is heartening to find someone standing up for theatre's antique spiritual power.

Appendix: Film and Video Productions of Plays in *Modern and Contemporary Drama*

NOTE: ADDRESSES, TELEPHONE, AND FAX NUMBERS FOR DISTRIBUTORS FOLLOW THIS LIST OF FILM AND VIDEO PRODUCTIONS.

Baraka, *Dutchman*
55 min., B/W, 1967.
With Shirley Knight, Al Freeman, Jr.
Directed by Anthony Harvey.

Brecht, *Life of Galileo*
155 min., color, 1973.
16 mm film.
With Topol, Colin Blakely, Margaret Leighton, and
    John Gielgud.
Directed by Joseph Losey.
Distributed by Films, Inc.

Büchner, *Woyzeck*
82 min., 1978.
VHS, 3/4U.
German with English subtitles.
Directed by Werner Herzog.
With Klaus Kinski, Eva Mattes, and Wolfgang
    Reichmann.
Distributed by New Yorker Video.

Büchner, *Woyzeck*
60 min., 1978.
VHS, Beta, 3/4U.
Hosted by José Ferrer.
Distributed by Films, Inc.

Chekhov, *The Cherry Orchard*
44 min., 1968.
VHS, Beta, 3/4U.
Selected scenes.
Distributed by Britannica Films.

Fugard, *"Master Harold"* . . .
90 min., 1984.
VHS, Beta.
With Matthew Broderick.
Directed by Michael Lindsay-Hogg.
Distributed by Lorimar Home Video, Warner
    Home Video Inc.

Ibsen, *A Doll's House*
89 min., B/W, 1959.
VHS, Beta.
With Julie Harris, Christopher Plummer, Jason
    Robards, Jr., Hume Cronyn, and Eileen
    Heckart.
Distributed by MGM/United Artists Home Video.

Ibsen, *A Doll's House*
63 min., 1968.
VHS, Beta, 3/4U.
Distributed by Encyclopedia Britannica Films.

Ibsen, *A Doll's House*
85 min., color, 1973.
VHS, Beta, Laser.
With Claire Bloom, Anthony Hopkins, Ralph
    Richardson, Denholm Elliott, Anna Massey,
    and Edith Evans.
Directed by Patrick Garland.
Distributed by Films, Inc.

Ibsen, *A Doll's House*
98 min., color, 1973.
VHS, Beta.
With Jane Fonda and Trevor Howard.
Directed by Joseph Losey.
Distributed by Starmaker Entertainment, Inc.,
    Prism Entertainment.

Ibsen, *A Doll's House*
39 min., 1977.
VHS, Beta, 3/4U.
With Claire Bloom.
Selected scenes.
Distributed by AIMS Media.

Lorca, *The House of Bernarda Alba*
1987.
Directed by Nuria Espert and Stuart Burge.
Holms Productions/Channel Four/WNET-13
    (British US).
Not presently available for rental.

Miller, *Death of a Salesman*
115 min., B/W, 1951.
16 mm film.
With Frederick March and Mildred Dunnock in
    their Broadway premiere roles.
Distributed by rental agencies throughout the
    United States.

Miller, *Death of a Salesman*
135 min., color, 1985.
VHS, Beta, 16 mm film.
With Dustin Hoffman, Kate Reid, John Malkovich,
    and Charles Durning.

Directed by Volker Schlondorff.
Produced by Dustin Hoffman and Arthur Miller.
Distributed by Lorimar Home Video.

Norman, 'night, Mother
97 min., color, 1986.
VHS, Beta, Laser.
With Sissy Spacek and Anne Bancroft.
Directed by Tom Moore.
Distributed by MCA Home Video.

O'Casey, *Juno and the Paycock*
96 min., B/W, 1930.
VHS.
With Sara Allgood, Edward Chapman and John
  Longden.
Directed by Alfred Hitchcock.
Distributed by Nostalgia Family Video, Valencia
  Entertainment Corporation, Hollywood Home
  Theatre.

O'Casey, *Juno and the Paycock*
85 min., B/W, 1930.
16 mm film.
With Sara Allgood.
Directed by Alfred Hitchcock.
Distributed by Classic Films Museum.

Pinter, *The Homecoming*
111 min., color, 1973.
16 mm film.
With Cyril Cusack, Ian Holm, and Vivien
  Merchant.
Directed by Peter Hall.
An American Film Theatre Production.
Distributed by various rental agencies in the United
  States.

Pirandello, *Six Characters in Search of an Author*
60 min., 1978.
VHS, Beta, 3/4U.
Hosted by José Ferrer and Ossie Davis.
Distributed by Films, Inc.

Pirandello, *Six Characters in Search of an Author*
52 min., color.
VHS, Beta, 3/4U, 16 mm film.
Large section of the play, but not the entire work.
Distributed by Films for the Humanities.

Shaw, *Major Barbara*
135 min., B/W, 1941.
VHS, Beta, 3/4U.

With Wendy Hiller, Rex Harrison, Robert Morley,
  Sybil Thorndike, Emlyn Williams, and
  Deborah Kerr.
Directed by Gabriel Pascal.
Distributed by Learning Corporation of America.

Shepard, *Fool for Love*
108 min., 1986.
VHS, Beta.
With Sam Shepard, Kim Basinger, Randy Quaid,
  and Harry Dean Stanton.
Directed by Robert Altman.
Distributed by Grapevine Video, Facets
  Multimedia, Inc.

Strindberg, *Miss Julie*
90 min., B/W, 1950.
VHS, Beta.
Swedish.
With Anita Bjork, Ulf Palme, and Anders
  Henrickson.
Directed by Alf Sjöberg.
Distributed by Sultan Entertainment.

Strindberg, *Miss Julie*
60 min., 1978.
VHS, Beta, 3/4U.
With Patrick Stewart and Lisa Harrow.
Distributed by Films, Inc.

Stoppard, *Professional Foul*
1977.
With Peter Barkworth.
Directed by Michael Lindsay-Hogg.
BBC-2.
Not presently available for rental.

Williams, *Cat on a Hot Tin Roof*
108 min., color, 1958.
VHS, Beta, Laser.
With Elizabeth Taylor, Paul Newman, Burl Ives,
  and Jack Carson.
Directed by Richard Brooks.
Distributed by MGM/United Artists Home Video.

Williams, *Cat on a Hot Tin Roof*
1984.
VHS, Beta, Laser, 16 mm film.
With Jessica Lange, Tommy Lee Jones, and Rip
  Torn.
Distributed by Live Home Video.

DIRECTORY OF FILM AND VIDEO DISTRIBUTORS

AIMS Media
9710 De Soto Ave.
Chatsworth, CA 91311-9734
tele: (818) 773-4300
toll-free: (800) 367-2467
fax: (818) 341-6700

Britannica Films
310 S. Michigan Ave.
Chicago, IL 60604
tele: (312) 347-7956
fax: (312) 347-7996

Classic Films Museum
6 Union Square
Dover-Foxcroft, ME 04426
tele: (207) 564-8371

Encyclopedia Britannica Educational Corporation
310 S. Michigan Ave.
Chicago, IL 60604
tele: (312) 347-7900
toll-free: (800) 554-9862
fax: (312) 347-7903

Films for the Humanities
P.O. Box 2053
Princeton, NJ 08543
tele: (609) 452-1128
toll-free: (800) 257-5126

Films, Inc.
c/o Public Media, Inc.
5547 N. Ravenwood Ave.
Chicago, IL 60640
tele: (312) 898-2600
toll-free: (800) 323-4222
fax: (312) 878-8648

Facets Multimedia, Inc.
1517 W. Fullerton Ave.
Chicago, IL 60614
tele: (312) 281-9075

Grapevine Video
P.O. Box 46161
Phoenix, AZ 85063
tele: (602) 245-0210

Hollywood Home Theatre
1540 N. Highland Ave.
Suite 110
Hollywood, CA 90028
tele: (213) 466-0127

Learning Corporation of America
4640 Lankashim Blvd.
Suite 600
North Hollywood, CA 91602
tele: (818) 769-0400
toll-free: (800) 228-2122
fax: (818) 509-7887

Live Home Video
15400 Sherman Way
P.O. Box 10124
Van Nuys, CA 91406
tele: (818) 908-0303

Lorimar Home Video
4000 Warner Blvd., #19
Burbank, CA 91522
tele: (818) 954-6266
toll-free: (800) 626-9000
fax: (818) 954-6540

MCA Home Video
70 Universal City Plaza
Universal City, CA 91608
tele: (818) 777-4300
fax: (818) 777-6419

MGM/United Artists Home Video
10000 W. Washington Blvd.
Culver City, CA 90232
tele: (310) 280-6212
toll-free: (800) 443-5500, ext 792

New Yorker Video
16 W. 61st St.
New York, NY 10023
tele: (212) 247-6100
toll-free: (800) 447-0196
fax: (212) 307-7855

Nostalgia Family Video
P.O. Box 606
Baker City, OR 97814
tele: (503) 523-9034

Prism Entertainment
1888 Century Park East
Suite 1000
Los Angeles, CA 90067
tele: (213) 277-3270
fax: (213) 203-8036

Starmaker Entertainment, Inc.
151 Industrial Way, E.
Eatontown, NJ 07724
tele: (908) 389-1020
toll-free: (800) 233-3738
fax: (908) 389-1021

Sultan Entertainment
335 N. Maple Drive
Suite 351
Beverly Hills, CA 90210-3899
tele: (310) 385-6000

Valencia Entertainment Corporation
28231 Ave Crocker
Suite 120
Valencia, CA 91355
tele: (805) 257-6054
toll-free: (800) 323-2601
fax: (805) 949-3400

Warner Home Video Inc.
4000 Warner Blvd.
Burbank, CA 91522
tele: (818) 954-6000

CREDITS (continued from p. ii)